AN ENCYCLOPEDIC DICTIONARY OF CONFLICT AND CONFLICT RESOLUTION, 1945–1996

AN ENCYCLOPEDIC DICTIONARY OF CONFLICT AND CONFLICT RESOLUTION, 1945–1996

JOHN E. JESSUP

GREENWOOD PRESS
Westport, Connecticut • London

Library of Congress Cataloging-in-Publication Data

Jessup, John E.
   An encyclopedic dictionary of conflict and conflict resolution,
1945–1996 / John E. Jessup.
      p.   cm.
   Includes bibliographical references and index.
   ISBN 0–313–28112–2 (alk. paper)
      1. Military history, Modern—20th century—Dictionaries.
   2. Conflict management—History—20th century—Dictionaries.
   3. Political violence—History—20th century—Dictionaries.
   I. Title.
   D842.J47   1998
   903—dc21   97–40852

British Library Cataloguing in Publication Data is available.

Library of Congress Catalog Card Number: 97–40852
ISBN: 0–313–28112–2

First published in 1998

Greenwood Press, 88 Post Road West, Westport, CT 06881
An imprint of Greenwood Publishing Group, Inc.

Printed in the United States of America

The paper used in this book complies with the
Permanent Paper Standard issued by the National
Information Standards Organization (Z39.48–1984).

10 9 8 7 6 5 4 3 2 1

For Jean

CONTENTS

INTRODUCTION

"An event has happened, upon which it is difficult to speak, and impossible to be silent."

Edmund Burke, 1789

This book deals with conflict and violence in their manifest forms and with the manner in which humanity has come to resolve those matters that afflict the human condition. How these terms are used here requires some explanation, as it is by understanding their meanings that one can recognize the significance of the acts performed.

Conflict generally deals with the result of a real or imagined antagonism between two sides, or among several, that may result in violence. Violence does not necessarily attend conflict, but it is often true that savage acts are the end result of confrontation. Religion, territory, presumed and anticipated rights, conquest and, above all, attainment of power are the most easily recognized of the antagonisms that beset humanity. War, invasion, subversion, assassination, massacre and genocide are but a few of the forms of violence that attend such antagonisms.

The forms of the attendant violence vary based on the culture, the means at hand, and the perceived insult caused by the initial disagreement between the opponents or among the several antagonists. One of the more interesting aspects of this paradigm is that the majority of violent conflicts are started not by soldiers but, rather, by politicians who order soldiers to create the acts of violence. In most cases the military becomes the instrument of the politicians' inability to find others means of gaining power. Although this is not always the case, conflict occurs often enough in this fashion to prove Frederick the Great's adage, "If my soldiers were to begin to think, not one would remain in the ranks."

Another aspect of this issue may be seen in those incidents in which the military creates the conflict through usurpation of power, most often in the form of the coup or the seizure of power. This is most often done to sustain a status quo, not so much for the soldier as for the generals. Much of the violence of the last 50 years has taken this form. The terrible apparition of ethnic warfare, one form of which took the cloak of a Nazi "master race" in World War II, finds its way in the modern world. The plight of Rwanda leaves little doubt about ethnic hatred still finding an outlet. However, of all the violence, conflict over religion, which seems the most absurd, is the major cause of the violence observed since 1945. The Middle East and Northern Ireland make this point very clearly, both in the main events that have transpired and in the secondary form of terrorism that has grown out of these arenas.

Terrorism, another form of violence, has existed from antiquity. In the last 50 years, however it has flourished and has become the preferred tool of many groups bent on imposing their will on others. An act of terrorism is only successful if that act receives publicity. Senator John Glenn summed it up when he said "International publicity was the mother's milk of terrorism" (*U.S. News and World Report*, 8 July 1983). The people's eagerness for information has proven to be the lynchpin that keeps the terrorist in business and has fostered an atmosphere in which no one is safe when a terrorist group seeks ever more spectacular acts of violence to insure their place on the evening news.

The one satisfying aspect of this study is the glimmer of hope raised by people of good will who have sought and continue to seek resolution of conflict, not only to end violence but also to allow humanity to move forward along its course. There have been some serious blunders in the process, but the United Nations appears to be learning how to keep or make peace. There are still "outlaw" nations, there are still racial and ethnic hatreds and there are still princes of darkness who rule with the corruption of absolute power. They follow a shorter path to oblivion than do those who seek a just future for humanity.

PREFACE

In 1989, Greenwood Press published *The Chronology of Conflict and Resolution: 1945-1985*. That work chronicled the various manifestations of violence that humanity tends to habitually impose upon itself and the efforts that have been made to resolve those issues. When that book was written, few of us would have regarded what has happened in the intervening years as being possible, even less as probable. Terrorist bombings such as that of the New York Trade Center, the invasion of Kuwait and, most of all, the collapse of the Soviet Union and the destruction of communist hegemony in Eastern Europe are all indicative of the continuing tableau of violence and resolution that has affected almost everyone on earth in one way or another. The only constant is the threat of violence in the weaving of the tapestry of history.

This work is devoted to an encyclopedic review of the period 1945–1996, including some background information on events leading to the post–1945 period. Much of the material covered in the *Chronology* is represented here in a different format, one in which the particular person, event or place is delineated as the point of focus rather than as a player at a particular point in time. This enables a much more detailed exposition of the background of the people, incidents and locales that have affected our lives over the last five decades—a time when we all should have been luxuriating in the glow of having defeated the enemy in one of the most horrendous conflicts ever fought, World War II.

Preparing a book of this type is not without its perils, however, not the least of which is the time involved in the research necessary to draw together the facts and to ascertain a coherent vernacular with which to present them. The realization that not everything known about a person, event or place could be included made for some hard choices. I must conclude, therefore, that not everyone will be satisfied with what is contained in this work, especially the people who have lived through these tribulations, large and small, who will be incensed because the name of a fallen patriot was overlooked, or because the outcome reported was not as remembered. I must thank Michael J. Varhola for his excellent work in preparing the index and for his help in finalizing the manuscript. Although I had his splendid assistance and some help from others in collecting data from the multitude of sources utilized, I am alone responsible for errors of fact or omission in this work.

SOME NOTES ON USING THIS WORK

As with any comparable study of such encompassing events, choices had to be made. First of all, the mechanics of the number of pages that can be profitably bound into a volume or volumes constrained how much detail could be put into the individual entries. A second point was which of the items in the *Chronology* were sufficiently important to warrant entries in this work. Cities and towns included in the *Chronology* were generally referenced to the country in this work, even where they are not specifically mentioned in the country article. A few exceptions were made. In almost all cases, place names were referenced to the inclusive article that, in general terms, describes what occurred at that place. In some cases, such a cross-reference pointing to a country will lead only to that country's overall place in history, not to the specific location

Similarly, the names of individuals were divided into those who had a direct relationship to the events, those who were players in the course of the events and those whose role was tertiary to the events. Members of this last category were generally dropped and do not appear in this work, except as mentioned in the article on the event. Cross-referencing has been accomplished by the use of "quod vide" (qv) as appropriate and through the use of "(*See* ...)" references, which direct the reader to other articles. If the specific locale is the site of an important event, such as a battle or a terrorist incident, it probably has been included. Group names such as types of aircraft, naval craft, missiles and other weapons, troop unit designations or satellite systems have also been relegated to oblivion, except where an individual weapons platform or piece of equipment performed a specific act in a specific role in an event. In general, locales, especially countries, and a number of people who became major players are examined from their origins to allow the reader the sense of the process that brought them into the present.

Where alternate spellings of names and places were readily available, they are shown, after the Westernized versions used as the primary spelling. Also, as the Anglicization of many foreign words fails to follow a single pattern or design, alternate spellings are also shown.

Last, a conscious decision was made early on to absorb the space that should have been given over to entries about the United States and the now-defunct Soviet Union. The last 50 years have been to an almost total entent a manifestation of the superpower confrontation that began in 1945 and is only now, years after the Bolshevik demise, beginning to show signs of abatement. Therefore, no entries appear for these two giants, yet one cannot turn a page in this book without reference to one or the other.

BIBLIOGRAPHICAL NOTE

A number of basic sources were used to distill the material presented in this work. The backbone of the book was the nearly eleven thousand entries in my *Chronology of Conflict and Resolution: 1945-1985*, which was published by Greenwood Press in 1989. Several of the standard encyclopedias were referred to for verification of information, and this process was speeded up by using CD-Rom versions of several of the better selections. *Facts on File* was used extensively in preparing biographical information, as were a number of the more standardized biographical reference works. The details on terrorist groups and activities flowed from my personal collection of data on a subject upon which I dwelt heavily for nearly three decades. A variety of atlases were also used extensively in preparing the sketches on each country involved and in adapting a standardized method of locating the countries and places.

One of the better sources of information on the nations of the world is found in the *Area Handbook Series* prepared by American University and published by the Department of Army in the DA Pamphlet 550 series. Although a number of the individual volumes are somewhat out of date, they are still very useful. Much useful information was also found in the *Acta*, the *Reviews*, and the *Bibliographies* published by the *Commission Internationale d'Histoire Militaire* in Brussels. There are many good sources on material on the United States and the Soviet Union. The specific area of interest will determine the selection in these two areas.

To ease the reader's burden in further researching a particular subject, in many, but not all cases, I have given *"Reading"* suggestions at the end of an entry. These books represent only some of the sources of particular information on the subject and are all relatively recent vintage which should improve chances of finding them in a larger library or bookstore. This is at least a place to start, several are indeed themselves bibliographies, and all are in English. I must add that not all of these suggested readings agreed with any conclusions I may have reached in the writing of each article. Some are diametrically opposed to my view of the events, some of panegyrics to people I deem evil, some are propaganda. It is up to the readers to choose in their own quests for truth.

A

Aba. *See* Nigeria.

Abadan. *See* Iran.

Abbas, (Mahmoud) Abul. An Arab terrorist leader of the Palestine Liberation Front (PLF), a splinter group of the Palestine Liberation Organization (PLO) (qv), Abbas is believed to have masterminded the hijacking of the *SS Achille Lauro*, an Italian cruise ship in the Mediterranean, on 7 October 1985. During the seizure, Leon Klinghoffer, a wheelchair-bound American, was murdered. Abbas was sent by Yasser Arafat (qv) to act as his negotiator in a meeting requested by Italy's socialist prime minister, Bettino Craxi (qv). When this was discovered, the United States demanded Abbas's arrest, as he was a known terrorist. Instead, Abbas was allowed to leave Italy and return to Egypt because, as Craxi said, he was under Egyptian protection and was carrying an Iraqi diplomatic passport. Abbas was known to be a member of the PLO executive committee.

Abbas, Ferhat. (b. 24 October 1899, Taber, near Djidjelli, Constantine Department, Algeria—d. 24 December 1985, Algiers) Born the son of an Arab official, Abbas was educated in the French style at Philippville and Algiers University. He served two years in the French army before becoming a pharmacist in Setif. He entered state service as a member of the consular service in Constantine, and in 1931 he became active in the early Algerian movements against French overlordship of his country. In World War II, however, he voluntarily served in the French army, only to return to his pro-Algeria work at war's end. He was involved in the presentation of the Algerian Manifesto to the Allies in February 1943 and was instrumental in the 1946 plan that would have given Algeria autonomy in a French federation. That plan was rejected. When the Algerian uprising began in 1954, he cautioned against violence, but he was forced to flee to Cairo to avoid arrest by the French and the retribution of the more-agitated Algerians. In 1956 he joined the National Liberation Front (FLN) and in 1958 formed the Algerian provisional government in exile in Cairo and was appointed prime minister of the group. He resigned in 1961, and in 1962 he was elected president of the Algerian parliament. In 1965, he opposed Achmed Ben-Bella's rule of the country and was arrested and confined to his home. He was subsequently released in 1965.

Abboud, Ibrahim. (b. 26 October 1900, Mohamammed-Gol, Sudan) After attending the Gordon Memorial College and the Military Academy in Khartoum, Abboud was first commissioned in the Egyptian army in 1918 and then in the Sudanese Defense Force (SDF) in 1925. During World War II Abboud served in Eritrea and Ethiopia with the SDF and with the British Eighth Army in North Africa. By 1949, he was commander of the SDF; by 1954, he was assistant commander in chief. When Sudan gained its independence in 1956, Abboud was appointed commander in chief. When Abdullah Khalil was overthrown in an army-led coup on 16 November 1958, Abboud became the new head of government. Opposition to the rule of Abboud and his Supreme Council of Twelve soon rose within the army, but he was quick to suppress it. Although some economic stability was achieved, Abboud's political problems remained, especially the southern problem centered around non-Moslem, non-Arabic factions opposed to military rule led by Moslem Arabs. By 1963, a full-scale civil war had begun in which the northern-dominated government fought against a southern guerrilla movement. The unrest spread into the north after Abboud's attempts to gain popular support. The government banned political debate at Khartoum University in 1964 which caused a general strike. Rather than suppress the opposition, Abboud dissolved the government on 26 October 1964. He resigned on 15 November 1964, and retired to private life.

Abdallah, Ahmed. (b. ?—d. Moroni, Comoros, 26 November 1989) Ousted as president of Comoros by coup in 1975, Abdallah was restored to power by another coup on 13 May 1978 and took Mohammed Ahmed as co-president. In 1981, his government was accused of human rights violations by the International Federation for the Rights of Man and by Amnesty International. In 1983, he declared amnesty to all those serving less than ten years for political and criminal offenses. Also in 1983, Abdallah cracked down on the Democratic Front opposition and arrested 40 of its more prominent members. An attempted palace coup against Abdallah was thwarted in March 1985 while he was on a private visit to France. Three rebels were killed in the attempt, and scores were arrested in its aftermath. That November, 18 rebels were sentenced to life in prison, while 47 others were given lesser sentences. Thereafter, a major shakeup of the cabinet took place. In 1989, Abdallah engineered a change in the constitution that allowed his accepting a third six-year term as president. Rioting followed, which was linked to South African-financed mercenary troops, including the Presidential Guard, billeted on Comoros soil. On the night of 26–27 November 1989 President Abdallah was shot to death under circumstances that leave doubt as to the assassin's identity or purpose, although an attempted coup cannot be ruled out.

Abdullah, Emir Seif al-Islam. *See* Yemen.

Abdullah ibn Husain. (b. 1882, Mecca—d. 20 July 1951, Jerusalem) Born the second son of Sharif Husain (who became king of the Hejaz), Abdullah was educated in Turkey and subsequently became a member of the Ottoman parliament for Mecca. He was very active in the Arab uprising against the Turks during World War I and, in 1920, led an Arab army into Transjordan, where he was declared emir by Great Britain in March 1921. While he ruled his people with great care, and with British support, his political ambitions to extend the Hashemite rule to Syria and Iraq led to serious confrontations with the Wahhabi rulers of Saudi Arabia. In World War II, Abdullah sent his Arab Legion to support British forces operating in Syria and Iraq. He was rewarded for his service in 1946 by Great Britain, which granted his country full independence. Transjordan was renamed Jordan, and Abdullah was proclaimed its king. In 1947, he accepted the UN plan to partition Palestine, the only Arab leader to do so. He did, however, send his British-led Arab Legion into Palestine, where they fought the Jews and captured the city of Jerusalem. In 1950, he annexed all Jordanian-held Palestinian lands for Jordan. Although this removed these lands from immediate Israeli control, the action infuriated most of the surrounding Arab states, which had expected the territories to be established as a separate Arab Palestinian state. The onset of the flood of Palestinian refugees from Israeli-occupied Palestine led to shifts in the political scene in Jordan and to Abdullah's murder by a young Palestinian supporter of the former Grand Mufti of Jerusalem (qv) in the Aqsa mosque.

Abdullah, Sheikh Mohammed. (b. 5 December 1905, Srinagar, Kashmir—d. 8 September 1982, Srinagar, Kashmir) Known as the "The Lion of Kashmir," Abdullah was the leader of the Kashmir (later the National) Muslim Conference. He was an early fighter against British and, later, Indian rule in Kashmir. His activities brought him into conflict with the law, and he spent many years in jail or under detention, the first such incident occurring in 1931. He was appointed prime minister of Kashmir in 1948. When India became independent he strongly supported Jawaharlal Nehru, but was considered by many to be merely ensuring his own place in the succession to the Indian presidency. Abdullah was dismissed in 1953 and again imprisoned. During the next 11 years he refused to pledge his loyalty to India and spent most of the time in prison or under house arrest. In 1964 he was ordered released by Nehru when he agreed to discuss the Kashmir problem with Indian officials. The subsequent talks appeared to be working, and Abdullah was sent on a fruitless diplomatic mission to Pakistan. He was rearrested by the Indians and not released until 1968. Following his release, he worked with the Plebiscite Party in an attempt to gain Kashmiri autonomy, but his party was defeated by the Congress Party in the 1972 elections. In 1975 he was appointed the chief minister of Jammu and Kashmir and finally convinced Indian Prime Minister Indira Gandhi (qv) to allow a truncated form of autonomy for Kashmir. Charges of corruption led to a loss popular support but, to his death, he was still much admired.

Abeche (Abecher, Abechr). *See* Chad.

Abel, Rudolf. (b. 1903 (?) d.15 November 1971, USSR) Little is known of one of the most famous spies of the modern age. His real name has never been revealed. Abel was probably first trained in espionage in the Soviet Union in 1927. After spending nine years in the United States and living under at least five other aliases, he was arrested for espionage after microfilm hidden in a coin was discovered by an alert cleaning establishment employee in clothing Abel left to be cleaned. Abel was subsequently tried as an enemy agent and sentenced to 30 years hard labor. The nature of the material he was accused of passing to his Soviet handlers was never disclosed. Abel was exchanged for Francis Gary Powers (qv), the U-2 pilot, in 1962.

Aberdare Forest. *See* Kenya.

Aboukir (Abukir) Bay. *See* Egypt.

Abu Aweigila (Abu Ageila), Sinai. *See* Israel.

Abu Dhabi. *See* United Arab Emirates.

Abu Musa. *See* Sharjah. *Abu Musa* is also the name used by a faction of the Palestine Liberation Organization (PLO) (qv). The name was taken from the leader of the group, Abu Musa (aka Mohammed Said Musa Maragha), one of the PLO leaders who did not rally to the standard of Yasser Arafat (qv) following the 8 December 1987 Palestinian uprising *(intifadeh),* which was brought about when an Israeli army truck killed four Palestinians. *Reading:* Andrew Gowers and Tony Walker, *Behind the Myth: Yasser Arafat and the Palestinian Revolution* (1992).

Abu Nidal. Often called *Fatah,* The Revolutionary Council, the name Abu Nidal uses when it attacks Israeli targets, Abu Nidal has used a number of pseudonyms as a means of protecting its identity. It has also been called the Abu Nidal Group. The term Abu Nidal comes from the war name of its leader, Sabri al-Banna (aka Amim al-Sirr). A major group within the Palestine Liberation Organization, Abu Nidal was formed in 1956. Originally, the group operated as Black June. Later it assumed the name Arab Revolutionary Army when it attacked targets in the Persian Gulf area (1980s). The Abu Nidal group also calls itself Black September when it operates against Jordanian and Palestinian targets and uses Revolutionary Organization of Socialist Muslims (ROSM) when it attacks British targets. The group did not become active until it rose in opposition to Yasser Arafat (qv) and his policy of negotiation as a means of settling Palestinian questions. Abu Nidal is believed to have been based in Libya. The PLO usually refuses to acknowledge complicity in any Abu Nidal activities.When it operated as the Black June Organization (BJO), which received support from both Iraq and Syria, its principal targets were Israelis, but it also attacked enemies of its patrons as well as moderate Palestinians and others who espoused diplomacy as a means toward a Middle East settlement. The BJO was linked to the assassination of the first secretary of the Kuwaiti embassy in Madrid because of Kuwait's lack of support for Palestinian interests in Lebanon. In June 1982, the BJO was responsible for the failed attempt to assassinate the Israeli ambassador in Great Britain. On 23 September 1983, a Omani Gulf Air jetliner blew up in flight, killing all 111 on board. Under another of its cover name, Arab Revolutionary Brigades, the group took credit for the incident, claiming it was in retaliation for the repression of the PLO in the United Arab Emirates. In March 1985, Abu Nidal kidnapped a British newsman in Lebanon. Abu Nidal was also suspected of bombing the British Airways office in Madrid on 1 July 1985, killing one Spanish woman and injuring at least 27 others. It was also accused of throwing a hand grenade into the Jordanian airlines office minutes later. On 11 July, Abu Nidal claimed credit for attacking two crowded outdoor cafes in Kuwait, killing eight and injuring 89 more. The group, operating as Black September, threw two hand grenades into the lobby of a Greek hotel in Glyfada injuring 19 Britons. On 25 September 1985, Abu Nidal (operating as ROSM) blew up the British Airways office in Rome and attacked the Cafe de Paris 100 yards from the American Embassy. The cafe was frequented by American and British tourists in that city, 38 of whom were injured. In November 1985, Abu Nidal (acting as the Arab Revolutionary Brigades), apparently working with another terrorist organization known as Egyptian Revolution (qv), hijacked an Egyptair jetliner to Malta, killing two Israeli women passengers and wounding three Americans, one of whom subsequently died. In December, Abu Nidal terrorists killed 20 persons and injured 120 more in machine gun and grenade attacks at the Rome and Vienna international airport El Al (Israeli) ticket counters. Within hours of the 14 April 1986 raid by American jets on Libya, Abu Nidal retaliated by shooting and seriously wounding William J. Calkins, a U.S. embassy official in Khartoum, Sudan. By the end of 1985, at least 21 members of Abu Nidal were in prisons in Austria, France, Greece, Italy, Malta, Portugal, Spain and Great Britain. During the the 1980s, Abu Nidal suffered two major set-backs. The first came in 1982, when the Israeli invasion of Lebanon caused a total military defeat of *Fatah* and caused its forced evacuation of that country; the second came when the Israeli aerial bombing of its headquarters in Tunisia led to a drastic reduction of its personnel in Tunisia. Now, *Fatah* forces are scattered among Algeria, Iraq, Sudan and Yemen, and some are still in Lebanon. Most of the PLO's intelligence and security officers at posts around the world are *Fatah* members. In January 1992, two key *Fatah* figures, Abu Iyad, the chief of PLO intelligence, and Hayil Abd al-Hamid, the *Fatah* security chief, were assassinated. This has greatly weakened, but has not destroyed, the organization. *Reading:* Patrick Seale, *Abu Nidal: A Gun For Hire* (1992); Yossi Melman, *The Master Terrorist: A True Story Behind Abu Nidal* (1986).

Abu Rudeis. *See* Egypt.

Accelerated Model Plan. *See* Vietnam.

Accelerated Pacification Campaign (APC). *See* Vietnam.

Accord of Nkomati. On 16 March 1984, the governments of the Republic of South Africa and Mozambique signed a non-aggression pact, the Accord of Nkomati, in which each side promised to cease giving aid and comfort to rebels operating within their adjacent territories. The agreement was made at a site near the Nkomati river in Mozambique after talks that began in January to halt the establishment of guerrilla bases in either country. The pact had a primary effect on the African National Congress (ANC) (qv) guerrilla campaign against South Africa and the Mozambique National Resistance (MNR) campaign against the Mozambique government. The agreement was condemned by both resistance groups and by a number of African leaders in other countries.

Accra. *See* Ghana.

Achakzai, Abdus Samad Khan. The leader of the National Awami Party (NAP) who was murdered in Baluchistan, Pakistan (qv), in December 1973. Serious rioting broke out after the assassination.

Acheampong, Ignatius Kutu. (b. 23 September 1931, Kumasi, Gold Coast—d. 16 June 1979, Accra, Ghana) A teacher, Acheampong lectured for a time at a commercial college before attending the British officer training school at Aldershot, England. He later attended the U.S. Army Command and General Staff College, Fort Leavenworth, Kansas. After Kwame Nkrumah's (qv) overthrow in 1966, Acheampong served two years as chairman of the junta's administrative council in the western region. He was promoted to lieutenant colonel in 1971 and promoted himself to lieutenant general in 1976. On 13 January 1972, he led a military revolt that seized power from the civilian government of Kofi Busia (qv). Acheampong attempted to establish a "union government" composed of both military and civilian leaders, but the plan foundered in internal political squabbling. He was overthrown on 5 July 1978 by another military coup, led by Lieutenant General Fred W. K. Akuffo (qv). When Akuffo was ousted by Lieutenant Jerry Rawlings (qv), Acheampong was taken into custody and held under house arrest, then executed by a firing squad. Ten days later, Akuffo met the same fate.

Action Directe **(AD).** A left-wing terrorist organization operating in France and Belgium since 1979. It is believed to be an outgrowth of earlier anarchistic groups operating in France that occasionally resorted to violence, but never showed the sophistication seen in the newer group. The organization had, until 1984, traditionally attacked French government targets. In 1984, however, the group opened a campaign against NATO and Western defense targets, including the Atlantic Institute for International Affairs (12 July 1984), and the European Space Agency (2 August). AD is often found allied with the German Red Army Faction (qv) and the Belgian Communist Combatant Cells (CCC) (qv); there were also allegations of much wider alignments. An attempt to bomb the Western European Union (22 August 1984) failed when the bomb's detonator did not work. At least two other bombings were attributed to the AD that year. Almost all of the AD leadership was captured by French police in February 1987, whereafter the group became less active. *Reading:* Michael Y. Dartnell, *Action Directe: Ultra-Left Terrorism in France, 1979–1987* (1995).

Acyl, Abmat (Ahmat). *See* Chad.

Adan, Abraham. *See* Israel.

Adana. *See* Turkey.

Addis Ababa. *See* Ethiopia.

Aden. *See* Yemen.

Adenauer, Konrad. *See* Germany.

Adoula, Cyrille. (b.13 September 1921, Leopoldville, Belgian Congo—d. 24 May 1978, Lausanne, Switzerland) Adoula helped found the *Movement Nationale Congolais* in 1958 and served as a senator and as minister of the interior when the Congo received its independence from Belgium in 1960. He then served as prime minister, from 1961 until 1964, during which time he faced a number of mounting crises, including the abortive secession of Kantanga Province, which was suppressed by Congo and UN forces. He was replaced by the leader of the Kantangan movement, Moise Tshombe (qv), in July 1964. Adoula became ambassador to Belgium and then to the United States and served as foreign minister until his retirement in 1970.

Adrisi, Mustafa. In 1979, Ugandan vice president Adrisi was criticized by Idi Amin (qv) for ordering the resignations of corrupt prison officials in Uganda. Adrisi, who was also the defense minister, had been earlier seriously injured in an auto accident and had been flown to Egypt for treatment. In the melee following the crash, Adrisi's bodyguards opened fire on the crowd and killed 12 people. When Idi Amin was ousted from power, Adrisi was captured by Tanzanian forces on 25 April 1979. On June 8, he, along with about 100,000 others, was thought to have fled across Uganda's northern border into Sudan after the Sudanese government announced there would be no extradition.

Aduldet, Phumiphon (Rama IX) (Bhumibol Adulyadej). (b. 5 December 1927, Cambridge, Massachusetts) King Ananda Mahidol (Rama VIII) (qv) of Siam (Thailand) was assassinated on 9 June 1946. His brother, Phumiphon Aduldet (Rama IX), took the throne that same day; but because he was a minor, a regency was established until 5 May 1950, when Aduldet achieved his majority. In the interim, he was educated in European schools and did not return to Thailand until November 1951. Although his country has had more than its share of uprisings and government overthrows, he still ruled in 1995.

Afabet. *See* Ethiopia.

Afars. *See* Djibouti.

Afghanistan (*Da Afghanestan Jamhawriyat*). A landlocked, mountainous, inhospitable country, the Republic of Afghanistan is located in south-central Asia and is bordered by Pakistan on the east and south, by Iran on the west, and by Kazakhstan on the north. The capital city is Kabul. Variously known as Ariana and Bactria in ancient times and Khorasam as in the Middle Ages, Afghanistan lies astride a number of major migration and trade routes in use since antiquity and was a part of the Persian Empire when it was captured by Alexander the Great. The Arabs conquered it, introducing Islam to its populace, in the eighth century A.D. The country was later conquered by Ghenghis Khan in the twelfth century and by Tamerlane in the fourteenth century and was a part of the Mongol Empire from the sixteenth century until 1747, when a revolt brought about a period of independence. Afghanistan served as buffer between the British Raj and Imperial Russia during the late eighteenth and nineteenth centuries, during which time the legendary struggles in the Khyber Pass took place. The country achieved complete independence in 1919 and was proclamed a republic in 1973. A military coup in 1978 led to an internal struggle that finally compelled a Soviet invasion in December 1979 and an ensuing civil war that lasted until a UN-mediated agreement brought semblance of peace and the beginning of a Soviet withdrawal in 1989. The civil war continued, however, even though an early collapse of the government was expected at any moment. In preparation for such an eventuality the *mujahideen* maintained a government-in-exile in Pakistan. A military coup attempt failed in March 1990. When the Najibullah government was finally overthrown in 1992, a rebel coalition set up a new government, but the ancient rivalries between the tribes inhibited any real progress toward peace. Islamic fundamentalism also appeared to be gaining the upper hand in the country. *See also* Amin, Hafizullah. *Reading:* John E. Jessup, "Low-Intensity Warfare: Afghanistan, The Soviet Decision to Intervene," *ACTA of the Commission International d'Histoire Militaire (CIHM)*, vol. 2, no. 14, (1989), pp. 728–749; John E. Jessup, "National Insurgency: Soviet Military Operations in Afghanistan, 1979–1989," *ACTA of CIHM*, No. 20, (1995), pp. 421–432; Roland Michaud & Sabrina Michaud, *Afghanistan* (1990).

African National Congress (ANC). The African National Congress was a black resistance movement that favored majority rule in a number of countries in Africa. The forms of resistance employed often included violence and terrorist activity. The ANC is the oldest insurgent group in Africa. The group was outlawed by the South African government in 1960, following a period of nonviolent resistance. In 1975, the ANC was active in Rhodesia. In June of that year fighting broke out in Salisbury between rival factions of the organization. The ANC successfully attacked a major oil refinery and a synthetic petroleum facility in South Africa. The following year, in celebration of the fifth anniversary of the Republic of South Africa, the ANC carried out a series of attacks. In retaliation South African forces attacked ANC bases in Lesotho (qv). The South African Air Force headquarters in Pretoria was attacked in 1983; 18 were killed and over 200 injured in that incident. In 1985, the ANC attempted the bombing of the Johannesburg Army Medical Center. The timing of the attack missed the opportunity to inflict heavy casualties. Most of the terrorism carried out by the ANC was aimed at government targets; in 1983, possibly without the authority of the ANC high command, ANC members exploded a car bomb outside the headquarters of the South African defense forces, killing 18 and injuring 217 others, most civilian passers-by. In 1984 over three dozen bombings of government offices, transportation lines, electrical power transformers and other infrastructural facilities were attributed to the ANC. In 1985, a swing toward more indiscriminate attacks on civilians may be noted. This was an attempt to create further unrest and to shake white confidence. A daylight bombing in the port city of Durban on 3 April 1984, for instance, killed five whites, including children. The ANC status as an outlawed group was changed in 1990 as South Africa reacted to increased external pressure and to white political unrest. Nelson Mandela (qv) was one of the leaders of the ANC. *Reading:* Stephen M. Davis , *Aparthied's Rebels: Inside South Africa* (1987); Morgan Norval, *Inside the ANC: The Evolution of a Terrorist Organization* (1991); Morgan Norval, *Politics by Other Means: The ANC's War on South Africa* (1993); Peter Walshe, *The Rise of Nationalism in South Africa: The African National Congress, 1912–1952* (1971).

African Party for the Independence of Guinea and Cape Verde (PAIGC). An African resistance movement that began operations about 1962 in Portuguese Guinea. In 1973, the group's Moscow-supported leader, Amilcar Cabral (qv) was assassinated in front of his house in Conakry, Guinea. In April 1973, the PAIGC was credited with having shot down a Portuguese Fiat G-91 aircraft with a Soviet-built SA-7 (Grail) shoulder-fired, surface to air missile. In September of that same year, the PAIGC declared the independence of Guinea-Bissau (qv) from Portugal, stating it controlled three-quarters of the country. The new state was immediately recognized by a number of African states and by Yugoslavia. The Organization of African Unity (OAU) (qv) furnished nearly a quarter-million dollars to aid in the transition. Portugal dismissed the entire procedure but eventually granted the country its independence on 10 September 1974.

Agana. *See* Guam.

"Agent Orange." A strong herbicidal mixture containing the chemical 2,4,5-T that was used massively as a defoliant in the American war in Southeast Asia. The defoliation program was called "Ranch Hand," and the defoliant was spread by large, low-flying aircraft that blanketed large areas in one pass. The "Orange" designation signified the color markings on the barrels used to transport the chemical. The effect of Agent Orange on humans has been the subject of numerous government and private studies in the United States following medical complaints suffered by servicemen stationed near where it was used in Vietnam. *Reading:* Michael Goug, *Dioxin, Agent Orange: The Facts* (1986).

Agra. *See* India.

Aguyi-Ironsi, Johnson. On 16 January 1966, a violent military coup took place in Nigeria (qv). Prime Minister Abubakar Tafawa Balewa (qv) was killed in the fighting. Then, a struggle began among the military for control of the country. General Johnson Aguyi-Ironsi emerged the victor and set about establishing a provisional government. On 29 July 1966, a second coup took place in which Aguyi-Johnson was killed by opposition Muslim Hausa tribesmen. Colonel Yakubu Gowon (qv) then took power.

al-Ahadub, Abdul Aziz. On 11 March 1976, Brigadier General Abdul Aziz al-Ahadub, the military commander of Beirut, Lebanon, declared a state of emergency and demanded the government resign, following two days of heavy fighting among warring factions within the city. President Suleiman Franjieh (qv) refused to resign, and the fighting continued. *See* Lebanon.

Ahermoumou Training Center. The scene of an incident on 10–11 July 1971, when a small party of disgruntled generals coerced a group of recruits to attack the guests at a royal birthday party at the nearby seaside resort of Skhirat, Morocco. A number of dignitaries, including three Moroccan generals and the Belgian ambassador were killed in the melee. Four generals and a number of junior officers were executed in the aftermath of the incident. *See* Morocco.

Ahidjo (Alhaji), Ahmadou. (b. Garoua, Cameroon, 24 August 1924—d. Dakar, Senegal, 30 November 1989) After graduation from high school in 1942, Ahidjo worked as a radio operator from 1942 to 1946. He was elected in 1947 to a regional assembly, where he served two terms before being elected as the assembly president. In 1957 he was appointed prime minister of Cameroon and in 1958 formed the *Union Camerounaise* political party. He is credited with attempting the unification of French Cameroon (north) and British Cameroon (south) when the Cameroons were declared independent in 1960. After being proclaimed President of the Republic of Cameroon in 1960, he won four successive elections, returning him to office until 1982, when he stepped aside because of poor health. He was succeeded by Paul Biha, his former prime minister, as president. Ahidjo held an intransigent nationalistic position concerning normalization of relations with his nation's former rulers, especially the French. Even so, he could not placate certain powerful groups who opposed his policies. By 1974, accords had been reached with France. In subsequent actions, Ahidjo joined the Zairian-controlled Central and East African OCAM. The headquarters of OCAM was then moved from Yaounde, Cameroon, to Bangui, in the Central African Republic. Ahidjo was later accused (August 1983) of plotting the overthrow of Biha, after a period when relations between the two deteriorated. Ahidjo left the country and lived in exile in France and Senegal. When Ahidjo attempted a return to power in 1983, Biha had him tried by a military tribunal (1984) for treason and sentenced to death in absentia.

Ahmadiya (Amadiye). *See* Israel.

Ahmed (Ahmad), Imam Seif el-Islam (Ahmad, Imam). (d.18 September 1962) The Imam was put in power in Yemen by a palace revolt on 2 February 1948. Beginning in 1954, he actively opposed the British plan for a confederation of South Arabia and led his country into a campaign of raiding and subversion against the British that lasted for years. He survived a coup attempt led by Emir Seif al-Islam Abdullah (qv) on 2–5 April 1955. In 1956, he signed the Jidda Pact, which joined his country in an alliance with Egypt and Saudi Arabia, and in 1958 joined the United Arab Republic in a federation known as the United Arab States (dissolved 1961). He died 1962 and was succeeded by his son, Mohammed al-Badr. *See* Yemen.

Ahmed, Khandakar Mushtaque. (b. 1918, Daudkandi, Comilla District, East Bengal) Ahmed received his early education at Khidipur Academy in Calcutta. He received his law degree from Dacca University and became active in the independence movement seeking to free India from British domination. He was imprisoned in 1946. When released he joined with Sheikh Mujibur in the Bengali revitalization movement that followed the independence of Pakistan and then in the establishment of the Awami League Party (1949). While acting as the first secretary of the party in Tangail he was arrested and detained by Pakistani officials, but in 1954 he was elected a member of the East Pakistani Legislative Assembly. While in office, he was again arrested for making anti-Pakistani speeches. Upon his release he became a leader of the United Front, a parliamentary party working against the Pakistani government in East Bengal. He was arrested again in 1958 upon the imposition of martial law in the region. In 1964, when the last of the restrictions were lifted, Ahmed helped reorganize the Awami League and, in 1970, was elected a member of the National Assembly. In 1971, he helped in the difficult negotiations between Mujibur and Pakistani president Agha Yahya Khan (qv). When Mujibur was arrested, Ahmed took over the leadership of the league and became foreign minister in the provisional government set up in Mukibnagar in mid-1971. When East Bengal received its independence six months later as Bangladesh, Ahmed began to criticize Mujibur's pro-Soviet and pro-Indian tendancies. This forced his removal as foreign minister, and he took up an adversarial role until he was installed as president following a coup against the Mujibur regime in August 1975. Ahmed remained in office less than 90 days; he resigned after a confrontation with the military following the execution of a number of senior officials of the former Mujibur government.

Ahmed, Manzur (Mohammed Abdul Mazoor). Ahmed was the leader of a failed military coup against the government of of his friend, President Ziaur Rahman (qv) of Bangladesh, on 30 May 1981. Rahman was killed in his sleep in the port city of Chittagong; many others were also slain in the attempted coup. Major General Manzur Ahmed and 11 other conspirators were subsequently executed when order was restored.

Ahmed, Mohammed. Served as co-president of the Comoro Islands with Ahmed Abdallah (qv) following the ouster of Ali Soilih (qv) on 13 May 1978. Ahmed, who had been living in exile in France, returned to the Comoros on 21 May.

Ahmedabad (Ahmadabad). *See* India.

Ahomadegbe, Justin Timotin. *See* Benin.

Ahwaz. *See* Iran.

Ai-hui. *See* China.

Ait Ba Amrane Tribe. A Berber tribe found in southern Morocco that followed the Malikite rite of the Sunni Muslim religion. In November 1957, a major revolt led by the Ait Ba Amrane was put down with much bloodshed by army troops.The incident took place in the Spanish Infi enclave at the southern terminus of the Anti-Atlas mountains.

Aix-les-Bains. *See* France.

Akali-Dal. A Sikh religious sect found in the Punjab region of northern India. The group originated in the post-World War I era during the violence over control of the temples *(gurudwara)*. The radical Akalis were determined it should be their organization rather than the hereditary Hindu *Mahants* who had control of the holy places. Unrest continued for years; 30,000 Akalis were detained, for example, by British authorities between 1922 and 1925. In 1925, the "Temples Act" was promulgated, which established a committee to control the temples *(Shiromani Gurdwara Prabandhak)* (SGPC) and clearly identified the Sikhs as a part of the *Khalsa*, those baptised into the Hindu religion. The Sikhs had avoided this Hindu custom, and the passage of the new law profoundly affected their future relations with the Hindus. At the same time, the Akali-Dal had become the dominant Sikh political organization. The World War II period was one of relative peace in the Punjab, with the Sikhs carrying out the typical role of being soldiers of the king. The division of Punjab between India and Pakistan (qv), which came after the independence of India, led to a Sikh demand for an independent Punjab. When this was refused by the central Indian government, Sikh agitation and terrorism grew as a mass movement of non-Sikhs out of Punjab created a vacuum that was filled by immigrant Sikhs entering what most hoped would be an independent homeland. Fighting broke out between Hindus and Sikhs in October 1978. Throughout the period, the Akali-Dal led the struggle for an independent homeland. In 1982, the Akali Dal turned down Indian Prime Minister Indira Gandhi's (qv) plan for allocation of the waters of two rivers between the Punjab and several surrounding states, seeing the move as a Hindu trick to hasten the absorption of the Sikhs into the more central Hindu faith. The Akali Dal also demanded the city of Amritsar be declared "holy" and championed the passage of a law that would have allowed Sikhs to carry daggers on commercial airliners. Of greater importance, however, was their campaign for independence. In 1973, the Akali Dal passed a resolution *(Anandpur Sahib)* that demanded a separate constitution and declared Punjab an independent state. When the central Indian government balked, the Akali Dal instructed its members to defy authority *(morcha)*. Over 25,000 arrests resulted, and the Dal almost disrupted the Asian Games (19 November 1982) being held in Delhi. In 1983, the agitiation led to several terrorist attacks, and the government's retaliation resulted in a large number of deaths and injuries. In the following year, on 31 May 1984, Jarnail Singh Bhindranwale (qv), a Dal leader and activist, took refuge in the Golden Temple in Amritsar and announced that he and his followers were amply supplied with food, weapons and supplies. This brought an immediate reaction from Indian security forces, who attacked the temple. Several hundred Sikhs, including Jarnail, were killed in the ensuing battle on 6 June 1984. In 1985, Sant Harchand Singh Longowal (qv), president of the Akali-Dal, was assassinated, soon after he had gained an agreement with the central government that would have ended three years of fighting. His killers were Sikh extremists bent on a continuation of the struggle. The Indian government, led by Rajiv Gandhi (qv), adhered to the agreement; and elections were held for the Sikh parliament (*Lok Sabha*). By 1988, however, terrorism continued, although there were signs the government was gaining control. Terrorism continued into the 1990s; in 1990, for example, Sikh terrorists kidnapped the Romanian charge d'affaires. He was released unharmed after nearly two months in captivity. In a more grisly incident, Sikh terrorists boarded a train in Punjab on 26 December 1991 and murdered 49 Hindus. Meanwhile The Akali-Dal maintained, albeit more lightly, pressure for independence. *Reading:* Mohinder Singh, *The Akali Struggle: A Retrospective* (1988); Man Singh Deora, *Akali Agitation to Operation Bluestar* (1992*).

Akuffo, Fred W. K. (b. 21 March 1937, Akropong, Gold Coast—d. 26 June 1979, Accra, Ghana) For a short time the strong man in Ghana, Akuffo was a professional soldier who graduated from Britain's Royal Military Academy, Sandhurst, England. He was trained as an airborne officer and commanded the Ghanaan airborne brigade. He also served with the UN peacekeeping force in the Congo and attended the Indian National War College in 1973. In 1975 he was appointed to the ruling Supreme Military Council of Ghana; in 1976, he was named head of the Ghanaan defense staff. He became Ghana's leader when he ousted Ignatius Acheampong (qv) in a 1978 coup. Akuffo was in turn ousted by Flight Lieutenant Jerry Rawlings on 2 July 1978 and was subsequently executed.

Al-Ahram. *See* Egypt.

Al Aqsa Mosque. *See* Israel.

Al-Arish. *See* Israel.

Albania (*Shqipëria*). A largely mountainous Balkan country, the Republic of Albania is bordered on the east by Macedonia, on the southeast by Greece, on the southwest and west by the Adriatic, and on the north and northeast by Yugoslavia (Serbia) The capital city is Tirana. First inhabited by Illyrians, since 1000 B.C. and a part of the Roman Empire after 168 B.C., the region was placed under Byzantine control after 395 A.D. It managed to maintain its lingual and cultural integrity through the succeeding centuries until the death of Skanderbeg, its great leader, and the subsequent submission to the Ottoman Empire in the fifteenth century. Albania declared its independence in 1912 after four centuries of Ottoman-Turkish domination. After a period of Allied trusteeship following World War I, Albania became a constitutional monarchy in 1920. King Zog I ruled from 1925 until 1939, when the country was invaded by Italy. After World War II, communist partisan forces took control of the government, and the country became a Soviet puppet state. When the Soviet Union was de-Stalinized in 1960, Albania severed its relations with Moscow and drifted toward affiliation, including a military alliance, with Communist China. Albania was the first state to declare itself atheist and to abolish all public forms of religious worship, in 1967. After 1978, however, China cut most of its extensive aid programs to Albania after Tirana criticized Peking's policies after the death of Mao Tse-tung. Large-scale purges of senior officials followed as the government of Envor Hoxha (qv) consolidated its power. Hoxha died on 11 April 1985, after 40 years in power. Religious freedom and freedom of movement was restored to Albania in 1990. This set in motion a mass immigration out of Albania to nearby Italy and Greece. Multiparty elections were held for the first time in 1992, with noncommunists winning three-quarters of the seats. Meanwhile, the economy of Albania continued to flounder. Because of the economic conditions, Ramiz Alia (qv), Hoxha's successor, was forced to look to the West for help. Even so, the 1995 elections rid the government of its last vestiges of communism and ended Alia's term in office. *Reading:* Raymond Zickel, ed., *Albania: A Country Study* (Area Handbook, DA Pam 550–98) (1994); Miranda Vickers, *Albanians: A Modern History* (1995).

Albertville. *See* Zaire.

Al-Burkan ("Volcano"). Al-Burkan was an exile Libyan group that was one of two organizations (the other was the Shi'ite Moslem group Musa Sadr Brigade) that took credit for the 11 September 1984 wounding of a Libyan Embassy employee in Madrid by two gunmen carrying Lebanese passports. Al-Burkan claimed credit through an anonymous phone call placed in London.

al-Dali (*Dhala*). *See* Yemen.

Al Darmhour. *See* Lebanon.

Aldergrove Airport. *See* Northern Ireland.

Aldershot Military Base. *See* Great Britain.

Aleppo. *See* Syria.

Alexandria (*Al Iskandariyah*). *See* Egypt.

al-Fatah. *See* Abu Nidal.

Alfonsin, Raul. (b. 13 May 1926, Chascomus, Buenos Aires Province, Argentina) Born the son of a shopkeeper, Alfonsin attended the Military Academy for five years and then studied law, graduating in 1950 from the University of Buenos Aires Law School. He practiced law in his home district and became associated with the Radical Party (*Union Civica Radical*) that fought Peronism. He was elected to the Chascomas Town Council at 24 and then was elected to the National Congress. In 1965, he became president of the provincial Radical Party; he formed a left-of-center faction of the party in 1972, because of the conciliatory manner in which Ricardo Balbin, the party leader, treated the Peronists. Alphonsin's faction, known as "Renovation and Change," became the center of party activity after Balbin's death in 1982, and all wings of the party supported his campaign to end corruption and restore civil liberties when the Peronist junta announced that free elections would be held in Argentina in 1983. He was elected president of Argentina in October and sworn into a six-year term in office on 10 December 1983. Alfonsin moved immediately to send nine junta members, including former leader Leopoldo Galtieri (qv), to trial for their activities in government. He then moved to abrogate an amnesty law that had protected a group of seven left-wing terrorists and directed that they be tried by a civilian court. As a result, a number of high-ranking officials and former officials were sentenced to long imprisonment. Alfonsin remained in office until 1989, when he was replaced by a democratically elected successor.

Algeciras. *See* Spain.

Algeria. More properly known as the "Democratic and Popular Republic of Algeria" (*al-Jumhuriya al-Jazairiya ad-Dimuqratiya ash-Shabiya*), the capital is Algiers. This African country is bordered by the Mediterranean Sea on the north, by Tunisia on the northeast, by Libya on the southeast, by Niger on the south, by Mali on the south and southwest and by Mauritanea, Western Sahara and

Morocco on the northwest and is the second largest nation on the continent after Sudan. The country was originally inhabited by Berbers, then by Phoenicians, Romans and Vandals. It was conquered by the Arabs in the seventh century and was invaded and occupied by the Ottoman Turks from 1519 until 1830, when France invaded and took the country. In more recent times, French occupation and colonization failed to bring Algerian nationalism to heel, Algeria was given its independence in 1962, following a long period of bitter terrorist activity and guerrilla warfare. Achmed Ben Bella (qv) became the nation's first president in 1963. Among his first acts was the nationalization of all abandoned colonial enterprises. He also announced, at the same time, his support for nationalist movements around the world. The subsequent conflict with Morocco and a faltering economy, coupled with Ben Bella's increasingly dictatorial method of rule, led to a bloodless coup in 1965 that ousted Ben Bella and brought Houari Boumedienne (qv) to power. Thereafter, Algeria became a Third World state, which undertook support of Polisario operations leading to the establishment of Western Sahara as a nation. Boumedienne also nationalized all French oil interests in Algeria. These plus natural gas concessions, put Algeria on an economic road to recovery and helped Boumedienne get reelected in 1984 and 1988. By February 1989, Algeria had pulled away from its commitment to socialism. Multiparty elections were held in June 1990, for the first time since 1962, which evoked violence from those factions favoring an Islamic fundamentalist state. The government reacted by declaring a state of siege, which lasted from June until September 1991. The president, Chadi Benjedid, was forced to resign on 11 January 1992, at which point the army seized control of the country. After cancelling the upcoming runoff elections, the ruling junta outlawed the fundamentalist Islamic Salvation Front (FIS). An appointed government was installed (1994), but there was no immediate return to constitutional government as unrest continued. Numbers of moderate Algerians were assassinated by the fundamentalists, and foreigners were threatened if they did not immediately leave the country. The crisis continued into 1995, with casualties from the fighting that began in 1992 numbering about 40,000 killed. *Reading:* Helen Chapin Metz, *Algeria: A Country Study (Area Handbook Series)* (1995); Martha Hutchinson, *Revolutionary Terrrorism: The FLN in Algeria, 1954–1962* (1978).

Ali Jawat. On 25 September 1957, Iraq's prime minister, Ali Jawat, attended a conference in Damascus, Syria, aimed at strengthening Arab unity during his brief premiership. Others at the meeting included King Saud of Saudi Arabia and representatives of Syria and Egypt. Iraq's part in the United Arab Republic and any role that Ali Jawat might have played ended on 14 July 1958, however, when Brigadier Abdul Karim Kassem (qv) seized power in Iraq.

Ali, Kamal Hassan. *See* Egypt.

Ali-Agca, Mehmet. A 23-year-old right-wing Turkish terrorist, possibly in the pay of Bulgaria, Mehmet Ali-Agca attempted the assassination of Pope John Paul II during a ceremony in Saint Peter's Square in Rome on 13 May 1981. The Pope was severely wounded when Ali-Agca shot him as he rode through a crowd in the Vatican city square. The suspect was apprehended at the scene. It was later ascertained that Ali-Agca had escaped from a Turkish prison in November 1979, where he was being held for the murder of a left-wing newpaper editor in Istanbul. Ali-Agca had been tried in absentia and was under death sentence for that crime when he shot the Pope and wounded two female tourist bystanders. He was subsequently tried in an Italian court under the terms of a treaty between the Vatican and Italy. During the trial it was claimed that Ali-Agca was part of an international conspiracy. It was also disclosed that he was a member of a right-wing Turkish terrorist organization known as the "Grey Wolves." At his trial evidence was presented that his attempt on the Pope's life was ordered by the Bulgarian secret police. That testimony was largely discredited, however, and charges against Bulgarian officials were dropped. Mehmet Ali-Agca was sentenced to life imprisonment. Upon his recovery, the Pope forgave his would-be assassin for his sins.

Alia, Ramiz. (b. 18 October 1925, Shkoder, Albania) The son of poor Muslim parents, Alia took part in the patriotic youth movement organized by King Zog I. During World War II he was a member of the communist-led National Liberation Movement (NLM), where he became allied with Enver Hoxha. Alia was sent to Moscow after the war for ideological training, and in 1948 he joined the newly organized Albanian Party of Labor that had risen from the ashes of the NLM. That same year he was appointed to the party's Central Committee. Two years later (1950), Alia was elected to the People's Assembly and by 1961 was a full member of the Albanian Politburo and a member of the party secretariat. In 1981, upon the suicide of the premier, Mehmet Shehu, Hoxha made Alia chairman of the Presidium of the People's Assembly. His frequent public appearances with Hoxha gave convincing testimony to the theory that Hoxha had chosen Alia as the future party leader. Gaining more and more authority as Hoxha's health failed after 1984, Alia was confirmed as first secretary of the Albanian Party of Labor. Alia gave the eulogy at Hoxha's funeral, leaving no doubt that he had assumed the reigns of power in Albania. Following the collapse of communism in Eastern Europe, Albania set off on a program of democratization that nearly brought the country to a complete collapse. Following the emergence of several noncommunist parties, the remaining communists in government were ousted following a general strike that ended Alia's rule on 22 February 1995.

Allende Gossens, Salvador. (b. 26 July 1908, Santiago, Chile—d. 11 September 1973, Santiago) Allende was educated in both law and medicine but soon took up politics as his vocation. Allende was the first avowed Marxist ever elected president in a freely held election when he gained that office on 9 November 1970 in Chile. Although an individual of considerable personal wealth, Allende became a Marxist early in his career; by the mid-1930s, had become the leader of the country's Socialist Party, which followed the Maoist party line. His 1970 election, his third try for the presidency, came as a result of the runoff among three candidates in which he gained the support of the Christian Democrats in the Chilean Congress. Winning 153 of 200 votes, Allende's victory was as much a surprise to him as it was to his opponents. In 1972, a trucker's strike created a major crisis for Allende when it blossomed into a general strike affecting the entire nation. Allende was reelected in 1973, however, when his Unidad Party took 44 percent of the vote. A wave of antigovernment terrorism followed that culminated in the assassinations of one of Allende's aides and a number of other senior government officials. A major military revolt in September 1973 led to Allende's demise when the presidential palace was stormed and he was killed ostensibly in the crossfire. *Reading:* Edward Boorstein, *Allende's Chile: An Inside View* (1977); Nathaniel Davis, *The Last Two Years of Salvador Allende* (1985); Edy Kaufman, *Crisis in Allende's Chile: New Perspectives* (1988).

Alley, Alphonse. Lieutenant Colonel Alphonse Alley, along with a small group of officers, attempted to overthrow the government of the West African nation of Dahomey on 12 July 1969. Alley was a former head of state of that country. Forces loyal to President Emile Derlin Zinsou (qv) thwarted the attempt and arrested the group and submitted them to an undetermined fate. Zinsou was overthrown in December.

All-India Sikh Student Federation. *See* India.

Allon, Yigil. (b. 10 October 1918, Kfar Tabor, Palestine—d. 29 February 1980, Afula, Israel) A soldier who fought with the British against the Vichy French in Lebanon and Syria, Allon joined the Palmach after the war and, in defiance of British restrictions, helped smuggle Jews into Palestine until Israel received its independence in 1948. In the ensuing months, Allon, a commander in the Palmach, drew the ire of David Ben-Gurion by refusing to turn the Palmach over to the Zionist Haggadah, which was emerging as the foundation of the embryonic Israeli Army. When that issue was settled, Allon rose quickly through the ranks and participated in the campaign against Egypt, in which he was instrumental in the capture of Gamal Abdel Nasser (qv), then a junior officer, but destined to become the Egyptian strongman who would lead his people against Israel. In 1955, Allon entered politics, running for the Knesset as the representative of *Ahdut Ha Avoda*. He served in the cabinets of Ben-Gurion, Levi Eshkol and Golda Meir. He was being groomed to become the head of the Labor Party when he died unexpectedly in February 1980.

Alta Verapaz. *See* Guatemala.

Alvarez Armelino, Gregorio Conrado. (b. 26 November 1925, Montevideo, Uruguay) Born into a military family, Alvarez entered the Uruguayan military academy in 1940. Twenty-two years later he was appointed the head of the mounted police in Montevideo; in 1971 he was promoted to general, at which time he became the Commander of the Combined Armed Forces Command (*Esmaco*), which had the primary mission of counterterrorist activities against the Tupamaros (qv). He gained additional prestige and power through the skillful use of captured information against corruption within the government of President Juan Bordaberry. By 1973, Alvarez appeared near the pinnacle of power as the permanent secretary of the National Security Council (*Cosena*). It was the *Cosena* that issued an ultimatum to Bordaberry and assumed veto power over the government's operations. By 1977, however, Alvarev was passed over for promotion from command of the 4th Military Region to the 1st Military Region and appeared to be losing his influence. This trend was reversed in 1978, when he was appointed commander in chief of the army. One year later, after he had retired, he was replaced by his arch-rival, Lieutenant General Luis Queirolo. Once again, he appeared to be losing power even though many of his supporters in the military were promoted. In early 1981, he apparently masterminded a plan that uncovered massive corruption among his opponents and led to their ouster. Largely on the basis of this incident, Lieutenant General Alvarez was elected president, succeeding Aparicio Mendez in that office on 1 September 1981. During his tenure, he moved to restore democratic government and legalized opposition parties. When one of the exiled opposition leaders, Wilson Ferreira Aldunate, returned to Uruguay, however, he was immediately arrested (June 1984). In the November 1984 elections, the Colorado Party candidate won; and on 1 March 1985 Alvarez stepped down, to be replaced by Julio Maria Sanguinetti Cairolo.

Al Wadeiah. *See* Saudi Arabia.

Amagh. *See* Northern Ireland (Ulster).

Amanzimatoti, Natal. *See* South Africa.

Amazon. *See* Brazil.

Amchitka Island. Amchitka is one of the larger islands in the Rat Islands, the western-most group in the Aleutians chain that separates the Pacific Ocean from the Bering Sea. The island stands to the west of the important Amchitka Passage, which links the two bodies of water. On 6 November 1971, the United States conducted an underground test of a five-megaton (5 MT) hydrogen (Spartan warhead) bomb on Amchitka as a part of the Anti-Ballistic Missile (ABM) test series. Canada and Japan, as well as a number of conservation groups. protested against the test but failed to stop it.

Amer, Abdal Hakim. On 15 September 1967, Field Marshal Abdal Hakim Amer, the minister of war and commander in chief of the armed forces of Egypt, committed suicide following his arrest on charges stemming from the Arab defeat in the 1967 Arab-Israeli War.

American Board Mission. On 23 April 1976, a bomb exploded at the entrance to the American Language and Trade Institute, a private girls' school operated by the American Board Mission and the Young Mens' Christian Association (YMCA) in Istanbul, Turkey. There was little damage and no injuries. This was the first instance of an attack on a nonmilitary American target in Turkey. At the same time as the attack on the school, another bomb exploded at the Iran Airlines office in Istanbul, which was probably tied to the expected visit of the Reza Pahlavi (qv), Shah of Iran, to the Turkish seaside resort city of Izmir.

American Communist Party (ACP). The ACP was founded in 1919 from left-wing elements of the Socialist Party. The party operated in secret during its early years. In 1920, as a result of what was called the "Red Scare," 2,000 American communists were arrested, with many of the noncitizens in the group being deported. In 1921, Moscow ordered the development of an open and legal party in the United States. The Worker's Party of America emerged from this order, but the Communist Party remained underground until 1923, when Moscow ordered it disbanded. The Workers' Party continued to operate as a legal party but was segmented by bickering. In 1929, Moscow again stepped in and restored discipline. At the point the Communist Party of the United States of America (CPUSA) was organized as a branch of the Communist International with Earl Browder as its secretary general. He would serve in that post until 1945. In the 1936 elections, the ACP entered a slate of candidates, including Earl Browder for president; none was successful. The Voorhis Act of 1940 forced the party to limit much of its revolutionary activity; it reformed into a political association in 1944. During World War II, the party attempted to work within the system to assist the war effort, especially insofar as support for the Soviet Union was concerned. In 1944, the CPUSA changed its name to the Communist Political Association. After the war, Moscow ordered a reassertion of revolutionary zeal and a dissassociation from the traditional political system in the United States. When Browder refused, he was roundly denounced both here and abroad for failing to follow Moscow's orders and was expelled from the party. The American group's name was then changed back to CPUSA (July 1945). On 14 October 1949, eleven party leaders were convicted under the 1940 Smith Act, which made it a criminal act to advocate the violent overthrow of the government. Subsequent Supreme Court decisions helped clarify the terms of the Smith Act and gave some relief to American communists. The death of Stalin (qv) in 1953 and the exposé of his excessive use of power marked a further decline in membership. Thereafter, avowed commuinists found it more and more difficult to hold public office and were excluded from many jobs, such as teaching. The ACP was outlawed in the United States by an Executive Order signed on 24 August 1954. Even so, the ACP continued to exist and to hold its congresses. It did, however, cease to run candidates for public office. In 1959, Eugene Dennis was elected national secretary, William Z. Foster became chairman emeritus and Gus Hall became secretary general. During this time the party undertook a lengthy court battle to set aside the regulations of the Subversive Activities Control Act of 1950, which required all ACP members to be registered with the government. In 1961, the Supreme Court stated the that the Subversive Activities Control Act was a regulation but not a prohibition and therefore could not be used to punish communists. In 1964 the court ruled that party members could not be denied passports simply because they were communists. A 1965 ruling declared the registration requirement of the Subversive Activities Contol Act to be unconstitutional. In 1966, the party reassumed its open role and held another congress. In 1984, Gus Hall won over

35,000 votes in his bid for the presidency of the United States. Since then, there have been no serious threats of communists gaining political office at the national or state levels. When the Soviet Union collapsed in 1991, the CPUSA membership plummeted. *Reading:* Philip J. Jaffe. *The Rise and Fall of American Communism* (1975); F. X. Sutton, *Ideology and Social Structure* (1990).

American Language and Trade Institute. *See* American Mission Board.

American University in Beirut. *See* Lebanon and *Islamic Jihad.*

Ames, Aldrich. On 21 February 1994, Aldrich Ames and his wife, Maria del Rosario Casas Ames, were arrested by the Federal Bureau of Investigation and charged with espionage. They were arraigned the following day and specifically charged with selling classified information to the Soviet Union and its successor state, Russia. While there have been several crucially important cases of spying brought against Americans, many of whom held highly sensitive posts in the U.S. government, few were as damaging as the case against Ames. Ames, up until the day of his arrest, had been a high-ranking desk officer in the East European and Soviet counterintelligence unit of the CIA, a position in which he had knowledge of almost all U.S. intelligence agents and operations being carried out in that region. At least ten Soviet citizens, allegedly in the CIA's employ, were executed based on information provided by Ames to his Soviet handlers. Ames and his wife were paid an estimated $2.5 million by the other side for their treason. On 28 April 1994, following a plea bargain, Ames pleaded guilty to spying and to tax evasion in the federal district court for Washington, DC, in return for a life sentence and his cooperation in the ongoing investigation. Because she had a five-year-old child, Maria del Rosario also received a lenient sentence (63 months) after pleading guilty. Although Ames described his exposure of at least 55 U.S. agents in the Soviet Union and Russia and at least 100 CIA operations, the full extent of his crimes is yet to be disclosed. Also under investigation is how a top American intelligence officer could live in such a lavish style without arousing suspicion among his counterparts. The CIA took a considerable amount of criticism for the fact that none of Ames's superiors received more than a slap on the wrist for alleged dereliction of duty. The pressure finally forced the resignation of CIA director (DCI) R. James Woolsey, Jr., on 28 December 1994.

Amgala. *See* Morocco.

Amin, Hafizullah. (b. 1 August 1929, Paghman, Afghanistan—d. 27 December 1979, Kabul) Amin was a graduate of Columbia University in the United States. After returning to Afghanistan he joined the *Wikh-i-Zalmayan* ("awakened youth") movement, which sought to reform the country. In 1963, he joined the *Khalq* ("banner" or "flag") party, a leftist organization. On 27 April 1978, Amin, who had become the leader of Khalq, engineered a coup that toppled the government of Sardar Mohammed Daud Khan (qv). Daud Khan had himself become ruler by overthrowing the government of his cousin and half-brother, King Mohammed Zahir Khan (qv). When the new government was formed, Nur

Mohammed Taraki (qv), another Khalq leader, was named president of the Revolutionary Council and premier while Amin was relegated to the post of deputy premier and foreign secretary. On 27 March 1979, Amin was elevated to the premiership. One month later, Soviet Army general A. A. Yepishev, the chief of the Main Political Directorate of the Soviet Ministry of Defense, visited Kabul along with six or seven other Soviet general officers. The purpose of the visit was never disclosed, but it was assumed to be a fact-finding mission similar to the one Yepishev paid to Czechoslovakia before the Soviet invasion of that country in 1968. Throughout the remainder of the spring and early summer of 1979, the repressive acts of the Taraki government continued to grow and intensify. More than 20,000 political opponents are known to have perished during that period. Under the direction of Hafizullah Amin, the campaign of repression took on the appearance of a completely dispassionate massacre of all elements opposed to the government with Amin exhibiting a totally uncontrolled desire for personal power. In August 1979, the Soviet Defense Minister and Commander in Chief of Soviet Ground Forces, Army General I. G. Pavlovsky, who had commanded the Soviet invasion of Czechoslovakia, arrived in Kabul. His visit to Kabul lasted two months. On 14–15 September 1979, Soviet agents, apparently operating with the full knowledge of the Soviet ambassador in Kabul, A. Puzanov, attempted the assassination of Amin and failed. The following day, Amin, using loyal troops, attacked Taraki and killed him. Amin emerged as the undisputed leader of the Khalq and of the Afghan government. This is exactly what the Soviets had not wanted; Amin was uncontrollable and was deemed a threat to Soviet security. The world was not informed of Amin's takeover until 9 October. The reason for the delay is not clearly understood, but it made little difference, as by that date, 22 of the 28 provinces in Afghanistan were already in rebel hands. During the period, Amin threw the Soviet ambassador out of the country and complained loudly about Soviet interference in Afghan internal affairs. He also approached Pakistani strongman Mohammed Zia-ul-Haq (qv) and other non aligned or Western-oriented countries for support. In Moscow, the apparent loss of influence in Afghanistan was cause for the Soviets to raise the level of threat posed by Amin and to order his removal. On 28 November, MVD Lieutenant General Victor Patutin, an officer in the Soviet state security forces arrived in Kabul, ostensibly to discuss police and internal security matters with Amin. After a number of unsuccessful attempts to place KGB agents in the Afghan secret police and to allow Soviet forces access to Afghanistan, an attempt was made on Amin by the Soviets, with Patutin most likely being the triggerman. Amin was wounded but survived the attack, but his nephew was killed in a separate attack on the state security (KAM) headquarters. There is little doubt that Soviet Spetsnaz (Special Forces) troops were used in the operation. On 27 December 1979, after Moscow had made the decision to intervene in Afghanistan, Radio Kabul, probably already under Soviet control, announced that Amin had been deposed and that he was, in fact, a agent of the American CIA. The facts surrounding Amin's death are shrouded in some mystery, but it is known that General Patutin was killed in the fight at Darulaman Palace and that President Amin's personal guard was wiped out almost to a man. Amin and his family were thereafter summarily executed by their Soviet captors. The upshot of the affair was the Soviet intervention into Afghanistan. *See* Afghanistan.

Amin Dada, Idi Oumee. (b. 1925, Koboko, Uganda) A member of the Kakwa tribe in East Africa, born to devout Muslim parents, Amin joined the British Colonial Army before World War II and served in Burma with the King's African Rifles. He remained in the army after the war and fought in Kenya against the Mau Mau rebel uprising. For ten years Amin was heavyweight boxing champion of Uganda and was an avid rugby football player. He rose through the ranks in the army, achieving the highest enlisted grade of sergeant major and was commissioned an officer in 1961, one year before Uganda achieved its independence (1962). He subsequently left the British army and within four years was appointed commander of the Uganda army. His long-time association with President Milton Obote (qv), during which time he helped foil at least two coup attempts and a number of army mutinies and personal assassination attempts, began to sour when Obote decided on changes in the army (1969). These disagreements turned to open hostility and led to Obote's decision to remove Amin as army commander. Thereupon, Amin staged a successful coup in January 1971 and seized the rule of Uganda for himself. Amin accused the Israelis of attempting to subvert his regime in March 1972 and refused to renew the military aid pact he had with them. Then, on 4 August 1972, he ordered all noncitizens of Asian descent out of Uganda within 90 days. Foreign journalists began to be arrested in September, after reports that the rebel "People's Army" forces supported by Tanzanian regulars had invaded Uganda (17 September). The action, later confirmed, was inconclusive, and Ugandan forces were able to drive out the invaders. On 7 July 1973, Amin had 112 Peace Corps volunteers detained on charges of being mercenaries. They were released unharmed two days later. In a bizarre incident on 29 October 1973, Amin ordered the U.S. Marine security guards at the U.S. embassy in Kampala removed on charges they were carrying out subversive activities. In March 1974, after the body of the former defense minister (Lieutenant Colonel Michael Ondoga) whom Amin had dismissed in February was found in the Nile, Amin successfully faced an army revolt led by Brigadier Charles Arube and troops of the rival Lugbara tribe. Arube and a large number of the rebels were killed in the ensuing suppression of the uprising. Amin was then faced with opposition centered around Wanume Kibedi and two other former members of the administration, who had all fled the country. In spite of Amin's threats against their persons and against their relatives still in Uganda, Kibedi spoke out denouncing Amin for the killing of more than 90,000 since he seized power. He was specifically accused of murdering the former Chief Justice, Benedicto Kiwanuka. Amin appointed a commission to investigate the allegations and was, as might have been expected, cleared of all charges. At the same time, an indictment was rendered against

Milton Obote for having engineered the entire incident. In a subsequent action, the International Commission of Jurists accused Amin and his government of carrying out a reign of terror in Uganda. Amin retaliated by reducing the staff of the British High Commission from 50 to five persons and threatened further action if all foreign allegations against him were not stopped immediately. The British government reacted by ordering large numbers of Ugandans out of the country. Amin then urged a military campaign against Rhodesia and offered seven battalions of troops to lead the attack. In March 1974 he accused Tanzania and Zambia of plotting an invasion of Uganda to restore Obote to power. Although Tanzania disclaimed the invasion plan, Amin put his country on alert and began rounding up alleged Tanzanian "spies." By August 1974, that incident was settled, but the economic woes of the country deepened. On 24 March 1974, an abortive military uprising took place that was not put down by loyal troops until after six hours of bitter fighting. Two days later, Amin began the systematic execution of all officers involved. Amin moved reinforcement to the Tanzanian border on 1 August, after accusing Tanzania of spying. Uganda did withdraw its claim to disputed territory along the common border with Kenya in February 1976, possibly to reduce the number of directions from which threats to the Amin regime could emanate. An attempt on Amin's life failed on 10 June 1976, just 14 days before he had himself proclaimed "president-for-life." In early July 1976, Uganda became the focal point of the Palestinian hijacking of an Air France airliner out of Athens; it was flown to Entebbe Airfield near Kampala. On 3–4 July 1976, Israeli commandos flying from Israel carried out a superbly planned and executed raid that led to the release of a number of Jewish passengers and others being held at the airfield. Later evaluation of the incident shows without doubt that Idi Amin was directly involved in the affair. Heavy Ugandan military equipment losses were also incurred by the already debt-ridden Ugandan government. This manifested itself on 8 July, when Kenya ordered the Ugandans to pay, in Kenyan currency, for all Ugandan goods and passengers transiting Kenya because of the debts already owed. Amin then began a bloodbath (11 July) against Kenyans residing in Uganda; those who could fled back to Kenya. On 16 July, Kenyan truck drivers and railway personnel refused to cross into Uganda. Then, on 25 July 1976, Kenya cut off the flow of oil to Uganda, and Idi Amin threatened war. On 30 July, however, Amin agreed to negotiate the problem. Persistent rumors came out of Uganda in February 1977 that Amin had had three opposition leaders, one of them the Anglican archbishop of Uganda, murdered by his secret police, the infamous State Research Unit. In September 1978, Amin banned most Christian church activities, claiming they were subversive. On 12 October 1978, Ugandan radio claimed Tanzanian forces had invaded Uganda. Tanzania replied that the reports were "complete lies." On 27 October 1978, in fact, Amin had invaded Tanzania, annexing about 700 square miles of territory in the Kagera Salient (1 November). Then, on 4 November, Amin announced he was withdrawing his forces, but foreign intelligence reported that the fighting was continuing.

Tanzanian casualties at this point were estimated at about 10,000 killed or wounded. The Tanzanians quickly regrouped and carried the invasion back into Uganda (27 November). On 25 February 1979, Uganda admitted its forces were facing disaster and asked friendly countries for immediate assistance. The only friend that responded was Libya, and Libyan troops began arriving early in March. Even so, Tanzanian troops had pushed into Entebbe on 26 March and had captured Kampala on 11 April 1979. On 13 April 1979, Idi Amin fled Uganda, thereby ridding the country of his cruel and vicious rule. Amin fled first to Iraq, then to Libya, and finally to Saudi Arabia. Even after his departure, however, troops loyal to Amin carried out a number of atrocities while dressed as Tanzanians in an attempt to provoke a pro-Amin uprising against the invaders. On 15 May 1979, Libya paid Tanzania $40 million for the return of Libyan prisoners of war taken during the fighting in Uganda. By 4 June the fighting was over, and the country was under total Tanzanian and Ugandan rebel control. On 5 August, the provisional government of President Godfrey L. Binaisa (qv) offered a substantial reward for the capture and return of Idi Amin. Sometime later, using a false passport, Amin apparently attempted reentry into Uganda from Zaire. When the plot was uncovered, Uganda demanded Amin's extradition back to Ugandan control. Zaire refused, but sent Amin back to his reluctant host in Saudi Arabia. *See* Uganda. *Reading:* David Martin, *General Amin* (1975); Martin Jamison, comp., *Idi Amin and Uganda: An Annotated Bibliography,* African Special Bibliography Series, No. 17 (1992).

Amman. *See* Jordan.

Amnesty International. A well-known and influential organization that investigates case of human right violations and which seeks the release of political prisoners or, at least, their humane treatment.

Ampil. *See* Kampuchea (Cambodia).

Amritsar. *See* India.

Amsterdam. *See* Netherlands.

Ananda (Rama VIII). (b. 1925—d. 9 June 1946) In March 1935, upon the abdication of King Prajadhipok, King Ananda Mahidol (Rama VIII) was enthroned as King of Siam. He was a ten-year-old student in a Swiss school at that time, and a regency was established to rule in his place until he came of age. On 9 June 1946, Ananda was found shot to death under circumstances that appeared to have been the work of an assassin. As the heir to the throne, his brother Phumiphon Aduldet (Bhumibol Adulyadej) (qv), was a minor, a regency was set up with Pridi Phanomyong (qv) remaining the power behind the throne.

Andhra Pradesh. *See* India.

Andom, Aman Michael. (b. 1924, Eritrea—d. 24 November 1974, Ethiopia) Andom fought with Eritrean guerrilla forces against the Italians during their occupation of Ethiopia. After World War II he entered the regular military service and fought with Ethiopian forces as a part of the United Nations Command in Korea. He later became commandant of the military college at Harer. In settling a border dispute with Somalia, he became known as the

"Desert Lion," but his subsequent demands for political reform caused him to fall into disfavor. Selassie had him removed from command and given an ineffectual government assignment. Instead of diminishing his stature, however, the demotion enhanced Andom's power, and after the officers' revolt against the emperor (1974) (*see* Ethiopia), he was installed as the army chief of staff and promoted to lieutenant general. He was later appointed defense minister. Within months, however, Andom's personal policies put him again in disfavor, this time with the ruling junta, which had him removed from office, arrested and summarily executed.

Andreotti, Giulio. (b. 14 January 1919, Rome, Italy) Androtti was educated in law at the University of Rome, where he was president of the Catholic student union. He was elected to the general assembly in June 1946 and served as undersecretary to Premier Alcide De Gasperi, a post he held until 1953. Andreotti held various ministerial posts in succeeding governments until he was asked to form a new government in 1972. It lasted only four months, when a government crisis led to his forming a new government. He was able to form the third of his cabinets in 1976, when the communists boycotted the vote. At age 70, Andreotti again became prime minister on 23 July 1989 and remained in that post until 24 April 1992, when the government resigned in the face of mounting charges of corruption. In September 1995, Andreotti was put on trial in Palermo as the protector of the Sicilian Mafia. Additional charges were leveled against him in November of that year.

Andriamahazo, Gilles. On 11 February 1975, President (Colonel) Richard Ratsimandrava (qv) was assassinated in the capital city of Tananarive, Malagasy Republic. The military junta then appointed General Gilles Andriamahazo head of state. He remained in power only until 15 June 1975, when the military junta appointed Commander Didier Ratsiraka head of state in his place.

Andropov, Yuri Vladimirovich. (b. 15 June 1914, Nagutskaya, Stavropol Region, Russia—d. 9 February 1984, Moscow, USSR) The son of a railroad worker of Armenian decent, Andropov joined the Komsomol (Young Communist League) in 1933 at age 16 and graduated from the Inland Waterway Transport College in Rybinsk in 1936. Before and after college he worked as a Volga boatman. In 1939, he joined the CPSU, and in 1940 he was appointed first secretary of the Komsomol in the Karelo-Finnish Autonomous Republic. In 1947, he was the second secretary of the Communist Party in Karelia. In 1953, Nikita Khrushchev brought him to Moscow and the following year appointed him ambassador to Hungary. In Hungary, in 1956, he assisted in the suppression of the Hungarian Uprising, and aided in establishing János Kádár (qv) as the Hungarian leader in the aftermath. After his return to Moscow in 1957, he became the head of the Communist Party department that supervised the party apparatus in other countries. He was appointed head of the Committee of State Security (KGB) by Leonid Brezhnev in May 1967 and one month later was made a candidate member of the Politburo. (It would later become clear that Brezhnev had not supported Andropov as his successor and had instead favored Konstantin

Chernenko [qv].) Andropov was appointed a full member of the Politburo in April 1973. He relinquished his KGB post after being reelected Secretary of the Central Committee a few days later on 24 May 1982. When Brezhnev died on 10 November 1982, Andropov was "unanimously" elected General Secretary by the Central Committee (12 November), probably with the support of the military in the person of Marshal Dmitry Ustinov, the defense minister. The change in government was extremely swift and harmonious. Considered a liberal by foreign observers, Andropov took as his main emphasis fighting against corruption within the Soviet government and striving for division among the Western allies. In May 1983, Andropov was confirmed as the chairman of the State Defense Council, a move indicating his consolidation of power over the Chernenko faction. In June, he was elected chairman (president) of the Presidium of the Supreme Soviet. He was last seen in public on 18 August 1983. Worldwide discussion of his health came to the fore when he became the first Soviet leader ever to miss the November 5 ceremony celebrating the Great October Revolution. In his place, Marshal Ustinov made the principal address on that occasion. Andropov's death from multiple internal ailments, including diabetes and intestinal nephritis, was reported in February 1984. Andropov's rule as Soviet leader is best remembered as including the time a Soviet fighter plane shot down an unarmed Boeing 747 (KAL-007) near the Kamchatka Peninsula, killing the 269 passengers and crew on board. The decision to shoot down the aircraft was a military one, and Andropov was apparently not notified until after the incident had taken place. *Reading:* Zhores Medvedev, *Andropov* (1983); Martin Ebob, *The Andropov File: The Life and Ideas of Yuri V. Andropov, General Secretary of the Communist Party of the Soviet Union* (1983).

Anduradhapura. *See* Sri Lanka.

Angkor Wat. *See* Cambodia (Kampuchea).

Anglo-Egyptian 1936 Treaty. On 23 September 1945, the Egyptian government demanded an end to British occupation through a modification of the 1936 Anglo-Egyptian Treaty. The 20-year treaty had been signed in London on 26 August 1936, following a crisis in the Egyptian government and at the time of the ascendency of King Farouk I (qv) to the throne. By its terms, Britain was to provide protection to Egypt in time of war and to gradually reduce its military presence as Egypt became able to defend itself. There were no significant provisions in the treaty that dealt with the Anglo-Egyptian Sudan, although Egypt, in the 23 September demand, also called for the Egyptian annexation of that region. By 1947, the question of the dispute between Britain and Egypt over the treaty's terms was taken up by the United Nations (5 August), but no decision was reached. On 6 August 1951, the Egyptian foreign minister announced that Egypt had abrogated of the treaty. A period of anti-British, antiforeign unrest began culminating in the seizure of power on 22–23 July 1952 by Lieutenant Colonel Gamal Abdel-Nasser (qv).

Anglo-Iranian Oil Company (AIOC). The AIOC was known earlier as the Anglo-Persian Oil Company, Limited, and was later renamed the British Petroleum Company. The AIOC did much of the detailed oil exploration carried out in Iran. The company was incorporated on 14 April 1909, to operate a major oilfield located at Chiah Surkh, 135 miles from Abadan Island. On 30 April 1951, the Iranian government nationalized the holdings of the AIOC, and by October oil production had ceased. Iran eventually broke diplomatic relations with Great Britain over the oil issue. Production did not begin again until August 1954, under the auspices of the National Iranian Oil Company.

Anglo-Malaysian Defense Agreement. A military treaty between Great Britain and Malaysia, the agreement was reaffirmed on 13 February 1969 at a time of increasing conflict between the Malay and Chinese communities in Malaysia.

Anglo-South African Naval Defense Agreement. In 1957, in return for a 20-year guarantee of the continued use of its naval facilities at Simonstown on the Cape of Good Hope, the British government turned the base there over to South Africa. A British naval base since 1814 it was the headquarters of the Royal Navy's South Atlantic Squadron. A new treaty signed on 27 January 1967 reapportioned responsibilities for the Cape of Good Hope sea route around the southern tip of Africa. The new treaty also relocated the headquarters of the British commander in chief, South Atlantic, out of Simonstown as a part of the ongoing shifting of defense responsibilities to the new Republic of South Africa (qv). On 16 July 1975, the agreement officially ended, and all naval cooperation with the British was withdrawn by the South Africans.

Angola. With its capital at the port city of Luanda, Angola is located on the southwestern coast of Africa and is bordered on the north and northeast by Zaire, on the southeast by Zambia, on the south by Namibia, and on the west by the Atlantic Ocean. By 1500 A.D. Bantu tribes had occupied most of the region of present-day Angola. By 1583, with the help of more northerly African tribes, the Portuguese had entered the region and established a slave trade. The country was known as Portuguese West Africa until it was granted its independence in 1975 following a long period (from 1961) of guerrilla warfare waged by three groups favoring independence. Thereafter, the three groups fought a protracted civil war for control of the country. Finally, with much Cuban military help, the Soviet-backed Popular Movement for the Liberation of Angola (MPLA) won the country. This led to a civil war that involved U. S. (1985) and South African support for the National Union for Total Independence of Angola (UNITA). A Cuban withdrawal was finally achieved on 25 May 1991, and peace for the country became something of a reality on 31 May 1991. Outbreaks of fighting continued, however, especially after UNITA repudiated the results of the September 1992 presidential elections. The first U.S. recognition of Angola was given on 19 May 1993, but the fighting lasted until 1994, by which time UNITA held most of the countryside. During this period several hundred thousand Angolans died of starvation and other causes related to the continued warfare. Peace was achieved on 20 November 1994, when UNITA signed a new peace agreement with the government in Lusaka, Zambia. Soon afterwards, 7,000 UN peacekeepers began arriving in Angola to supervise the transition. Over 1.2 million people had been displaced by the fighting. Even though the peace held into 1995, no one could guarantee that it would continue. *Reading:* W. Martin James, *A Political History of the Civil War in Angola, 1974–1990,* East South Relations Series (1991); Herbert Ekwe-Ekwe, *Conflict and Intervention in Africa: Nigeria, Angola, Zaire* (1990); David Birmingham, *Frontline Nationalism in Angola and Mozambique* (1993); David Deutschmann, ed., *Changing the History of Africa: Angola and Namibia* (1991).

Anguilla. *See* St. Kitts and Nevis.

An Hoa. *See* Vietnam.

Ankara. *See* Turkey.

Ankrah, Joseph A. The nation of Ghana suffered severe socio-economic troubles under dictatorial President Kwame Nkrumah (qv),. On 24 February 1966, Nkrumah was out of the country when a military coup led by Lieutenant General Joseph A. Ankrah deposed him. A National Liberation Council was established with Ankrah as chairman of its executive council. Ankrah remained in that post until 1 April 1969, when he resigned and was replaced by Brigadier Akwasi A. Afrifa. Ankrah's resignation was prompted by revelations concerning his improper use of government funds in his own bid for the presidency in the forthcoming promised general elections. His departure signalled a further loss of stabilty in the precarious political situation in Ghana, as he had been considered above reproach by most citizens. *See* Ghana.

An Loc (Hon Quan). *See* Vietnam.

Anti-Fascist Patriotic Front. On 22 August 1975, a U.S. Marine security guard on duty at the American consulate in Valencia, Spain, was shot and wounded by gunmen in a passing automobile. The Anti-Fascist Patriotic Front claimed credit for the attack. The day of the attack in Valencia, the Spanish cabinet approved a tough new antiterrorist law that provided military summary courts for captured terrorists. As a consequence, 11 terrorists, including members of the Patriotic

Anti-Fascist People's Freedom League (AFPFL). Front, were sentenced to death between 29 August and 20 September. On 19 July 1947, the AFPFL was the majority party in Burma. On that day, U Aung San (qv), the party's leader, and a number of his senior colleagues were assassinated in Rangoon by members of the opposition party headed by U Saw (qv). All of the participants in the assassination were captured, tried and executed by 8 May 1948. *See* Burma.

Antonescu, Ion. (b. 15 June 1882, Pitesti, Romania—d. 1 June 1946, Fort Jilava) Formerly the Romanian Army chief of staff, Antonescu was appointed prime minister by King Carol II on 5 September 1940. In this capacity he formed a dictatorship of unlimited power within his country while becoming a puppet of Adolf Hitler. Antonescu led Romania into World War II as a Nazi ally and carried out a program of extermination against the Jews, gypsies and other minority groups. He was deposed in the Romanian uprising in August 1944 (which led to a communist takeover) and executed for war crimes by the Romanians in 1946. *See* Romania. *Reading:* Larry L. Watts, *Romanian Cassandra: Ian Antonescu and the Struggle for Reform, 1916–1941* East European Mongraphs, No. 358. (1993).

Anyanya (Anya-Nya) Tribesmen. On 16 February 1972, representatives of the government of Sudan and the South Sudan Liberation Movement (SSLM) met in Addis Ababa, Ethiopia, to settle a war that had raged for 16 years. The struggle was generally centered around the issue of central government Muslim domination of the largely non-Muslim three provinces in the south of the country. The military wing of the SSLM was the Anyanya tribe. Following the peace agreement on 28 February, a general amnesty was declared (16 March), and some 6,000 members of the Anyanya were integrated into a military force to police the new autonomous area. The final agreement was ratified on 27 March 1972.

ANZUK. An abbreviation used to designate Australia, New Zealand, and the United Kingdom is ANZUK.

ANZUS Pact. A treaty between Australia, New Zealand and the United States signed on 1 September 1951 was the first formalization of relations between Australia and the United States, and was established, in part, to allay Australian concerns over the concessions given Japan as a part of the peace agreement following World War II. At about the same time as the signing of the ANZUS Pact, the three nations formed the Pacific Council (4 August 1952). *See also* South East Asia Treaty Organization.

Apartheid. The official policy of racial segregation carried out against the black population by the government of the Republic of South Africa so as to promote white supremacy was called apartheid. *See* South Africa. *Reading:* Robert Price, *The Apartheid State in Crisis: Political Transformations in South Africa, 1975–1990* (1992); Philip Bonner et al. eds., *Apartheid's Genesis 1935–1962* (1994).

Ap Bac. *See* Vietnam.

Ap Bia Mountain (Hill 937). *See* Vietnam.

April 6 Liberation Movement. On 22 August 1980, a Filipino terrorist organization calling itself the "April 6 Liberation Movement" claimed credit for a series of bombings of public buildings and businesses in Manila. In staking its claim to credit for the bombings, the group condemned the regime of Ferdinand E. Marcos (qv). The group's name came from demonstrations that took place on that date against the Marcos regime in 1978. Between the 22 August attacks and 19 October 1980, at least 30 bombs were detonated, one of them (12 September) killing an American woman. Another narrowly missed killing Marcos on 19 October. By November, at least 60 people had been arrested in connection with the bombings.

April 19 Movement (M-19). In one of the most spectacular terrorist attacks ever recorded, members of the April 19 Movement (M19) shot their way into the Dominican Republic Embassy in Bogota, Colombia, on 27 February 1980. The attack was timed to coincide with an official diplomatic reception. The terrorists took 57 hostages, including 13 ambassadors (Austria, Brazil, Costa Rica, Egypt, Guatemala, Haiti, Israel, Mexico, Switzerland,United States, Uruguay, Venezuela and the host Dominican Republic). The Uruguayan ambassador, Fernando Gomez, later escaped, in retaliation for which the Uruguayan Embassy was attacked by a different group from M-19 on 15 April in a vain attempt at capturing the then acting ambassador Raul Lira. The terrorists in the Dominican embassy demanded the release of 311 prisoners, a payment of $50 million, and safe passage out the country. Negotiations were protracted. The terrorists constantly scaled down their demands and released most of their hostages over the next 60 days and finally settled for safe passage to Cuba and a $2.5 million privately paid ransom. On 29 May 1980, after the original group had left the country, a police and special army unit ambush caught an M-19 team attempting to recover the ransom money. Two of the terrorists were killed and seven captured. On 6 November 1985, the well-armed M-19 group carried out another spectacular operation when it captured the Palace of Justice building in Bogota, taking a large number of hostages. President Belisario Betancur Cuartes refused to negotiate with the terrorists; and on 8 November, Colombian army troops stormed the building, freeing 38 of the hostages but killing at least 100 others, including the president of the Supreme Court, Alfonso Reyes Echandia, and eleven other justices, court employees and visitors and all of the terrorists. The defeat helped demoralize the M-19 group for the moment; but later in 1985, M-19, together with elements of the Ecuadoran leftist group known as *Alfaro Vive, Carajo (AVC)* and possibly some other terrorist organizations, banded together to form a regional insurgent force known as the "America Battalion." This group engaged the Colombian army on several occasions before the end of the year.

Aptidon, Hassan Gouled. On 12 June 1981, Aptidon, an Issa Somali, was reelected president of Djibouti. That same year, he ordered the arrest of two former premiers upon their return to Djibouti (7 September), after they had formed a new opposition party in Paris. By 1983, Aptidon's position was relatively secure, and in the 1987 elections he was reelected president in a one-candidate race. There was a coup attempt against him on 8–9 January 1991, which resulted in the arrest of a number of the conspirators. Violence around the country rose in December of that year. Aptidon remained president of Djibouti in 1995. *See* Djibouti.

Apurimac District. *See* Peru.

Aqaba (*Al Aqabah*). *See* Jordan.

Aquino, Benigno ("Ninoy") Simeon, Jr. (b. 27 November 1932, Tarlac Province, Philippines—d. 21 August 1983, Manila, Philippines) Benigno Aquino's murder at the hands of an assassin has been directly associated with the regime of President Ferdinand E. Marcos (qv). Aquino's death was the act that helped topple the Filipino dictator. In earlier years, from 1965 on Aquino had become a respected senator who became the leader of the opposition to the Marcos regime. After completing school, Aquino had worked for a short time as a journalist before beginning a career in politics. He was elected mayor of Concepcion in 1954 and, at the age of 22, was the youngest mayor in all of the Philippines. In 1959, he was elected provincial vice governor, and in 1961 he succeeded to the governorship of Tarlac Province. Again, he was the youngest official in the capacity in the Philippines. He was reelected to that office in 1963 and married Corazon Cojuangco, the daughter of a wealthy landowner. Aquino became the secretary general of the Liberal Party in 1966, the year following Marcos' departure from the party and subsequent election as president as the Nationalist Party candidate. Aquino gained national attention as an orator and the only liberal candidate elected to the Senate in 1967. Seen as a potential presidential candidate in 1973 after his victory Aquino was arrested by Marcos after the dictator declared martial law in September 1972. He was sentenced to death on charges of murder and subversion and spent eight years in prison before Marcos allowed him to travel to the U.S. for open-heart surgery in 1980. He remained in self-imposed exile in the U.S. until 1983, when news of Marcos' failing health convinced him it was time to return to the Philippines. He was assassinated upon his arrival in Manila. The assassin was allegedly shot down immediately by Filipino security police. *See* Philippines and Ver, Fabian.

Arab Communist Organization. On 14 August 1974, a homemade bomb exploded during the night near the entrance to the U.S. Pavilion at the Damascus International Fair in Syria. A pavilion guard and a Syrian policeman were injured in the blast. The next day, the Arab Communist Organization claimed credit for the attack. On 10 October 1974, a bomb killed a Syrian office boy and a cleaning woman working in the offices of the National Cash Register Company in Damascus. The two-story building housing the company was severely damaged, and most of its contents were destroyed. On 11 October, the NCR offices in Aleppo were also bombed. The Arab Communist Organization again claimed credit for the incidents. These attacks came on the eve of a visit by U.S. Secretary of State Henry Kissinger to Damascus.

Arab Confederation. In November 1970, Syria announced it was joining the United Arab Republic, Sudan and Libya in forming a new Arab confederation. This announcement signalled the end of a struggle for power in Syria and put to rest rumors that the government of Hafez al-Assad (qv) might be favorably disposed toward Israel and the West.

Arab Defense Council. A group of 18 Arab nations who, on 27–31 January 1973, met in Cairo to map out a common strategy against Israel comprised the Arab Defense Council. The resultant military and political plan included a Jordanian promise to reopen its operational front against Israel, and all participants bowed to the Palestine Liberation Organization's (qv) demand for renewed and intensified fighting against the Jewish state. The result of this agreement was the Arab-Israeli (Yom Kippur) War of 1973.

Arab Eastern Command. On 17 March 1969, King Hussein (Husain) (qv) of Jordan announced the formation of an Arab Eastern Command comprising the military forces of Iraq, Jordan and Syria, those Arab nations lying to the east of Israel.

Arab Federation. The formation of the Arab Federation was announced on 14 February 1958 by King Hussein of Jordan (qv). Jordan and Iraq were merged under Iraq's King Faisal II (qv). On 14 July 1958, a military coup, led by General Abdul Karim el-Kassem (qv), seized power in Iraq and killed King Faisal II. Iraq was then proclaimed a republic. Hussein declared himself the leader of the Arab Federation and requested military aid from the U.S. and Turkey. Instead, British airborne forces from the "Red Devil" Brigade were committed to the defense of Jordan. The next day (15 July 1958), more than 8,000 U.S. marine and army forces landed in Lebanon to assist in the defense of that country. On 19 July, Iraq announced it had sided with the United Arab Republic (qv).

Arab-Israeli Wars. *See* Israel, Syria and Egypt.

Arab League. The Arab League was formed when seven nations (Egypt, Iraq, Lebanon, Syria, Saudi Arabia, Transjordan, and Yemen) signed the pact in Cairo, Egypt, on 22 March 1945. The general purpose of the loose confederation was the political and economic stability of the Arab world. A central council was to handle the affairs of the group with each member state having one vote. A secretariat was established in Cairo and 'Abd-al-Rahman 'Azzam, an Egyptian, was appointed its first secretary general. The League did not really succeed at first because of divided interests and the differing agendas among its members. The League did grow, however, as Arab nations gained their independence. Libya joined in 1953, followed by Sudan (1956), Morocco and Tunisia (1958), Kuwait (1961), Algeria (1962) and the People's Republic of South Yemen (1968). Interpretations of the number of members have varied as the United Arab Republic (Egypt and Syria) are listed as one country on some documents, as two on others. The League's intervention in the 1948 Israeli War of Independence and the subsequent year-long war it fought against the Israelis illustrated the obvious differences among the Arab states, who were either unwilling or ill-prepared to devote resources to a common cause. From that point on, the differences among the members became more obvious than the common Arab heritage. Some common problems, such as that of Palestine, did bring some unity, but there was little else in which the states could find common cause. In 1950, the League did establish a collective security agreement, but the subsequent rift between Egypt and the other Arab states neutralized the strength of the pact, except during the Suez Crisis of 1956. In 1959, the League did declare the procommunist government in Iraq to be a threat to regional peace, even though a number of members boycotted the meeting (4 April). In July 1960, the government in Tehran recognized Israel, and the League imposed an economic boycott on Iranian goods. In 1961, another opportunity for Arab common cause arose in the dispute between Tunisia and France. The League failed to show any resolve, however, because of internal frictions such as Iraq's stated claim to Kuwait and its objection to Kuwait's admittance to membership in the League. As a consequence, the Arab League raised a force to protect Kuwait against Iraq, rather than facing France in a display of Arab unity over the

Tunisian question. It did vote money to supply weapons to Algerian rebels fighting the French in that same year. In subsequent years, the principal focus of the League became the Israeli question. Whether it was the diversion of Jordan river to deny its waters to the Israelis (1964) or the establishment of a Joint Arab Command (1964), the only focus the League could sustain was against Israel. When civil war broke out in Yemen in 1962, the League proved helpless to stop it or to prevent its members (Saudi Arabia and Egypt) from becoming individually involved. Numerous summit conferences were called, but after 1969, these meetings were postponed more often than held. By the end of 1967, Arab leaders around the world were openly critical of the League for its lack of effective leadership during the 1967 Arab-Israeli War. In areas of lesser importance, such as Arab studies in the humanities and some of its economic planning, the League was more effective. In August 1969, a meeting of the League's foreign ministers ended in the calling of a *jihad* (holy war) against Israel. That same year, the League accused the United States of blocking peace efforts in the Middle East. In 1971, the Jordanian prime minister, Wasfi Tal (qv), was assassinated by Black September terrorists while attending an Arab League conference in Cairo (28 November). In 1972, the League was able to conclude a cease-fire between the two Yemens. In 1974, the Arab League once again backed the attack on Israel by financing the PLO and Lebanon in their military operations against the Israelis.The Arab League refused support to Somalia in September 1977 in its fight against Ethiopia. On 2 July 1978, the League voted to boycott South Yemen and its newly established pro-Marxist government. In November of that year, the League voted $3.5 billion to support efforts against the Egypt-Israeli peace treaty.The League then offered Egypt $50 billion in aid if it broke off the peace talks. Egypt's president Sadat (qv) refused. When Egypt did sign the peace accord with Israel, 19 of the 22 Arab League nations broke diplomatic relations with Cairo. Only Somalia, Oman and Sudan retained their embassies in Egypt. In 1982, following proposals put forth by the United States, the League offered a Saudi-sponsored Middle East peace plan, which called for the establishment of a Palestinian state. The Israelis rejected this plan, and the conflict in the Middle East continued. In 1985, the League split over which side to support in the Iran-Iraq War. Several of the members boycotted the emergency session held in Casablanca to discuss the situation. In the early 1990s the Arab League exhibited the same disunity of purpose, especially regarding its position on the Iraq invasion of Kuwait and the subsequent coalition effort against Baghdad. *Reading:* Robert W. MacDonald, *League of Arab States: A Study in the Dynamics of Regional Organization* (1965); Tawfig Hasou, *Struggle for the Arab World: Egypt's Nasser and the Arab League* (1986); Istvan S. Pogany, *The Arab League and Peacekeeping in Lebanon* (1988)

Arab League Peacekeeping Force. In November 1976, following a period of civil war between Muslim and Christian factions in Lebanon, the Arab League dispatched multinational military forces to restore order in the complex web of

Lebanese life. On 10 November, Syrian troops occupied Beirut and most of southern Lebanon. This put the Israelis on alert, and they began reinforcing their northern border garrisons. On 1 December 1976, the commander of the peacekeeping forces ordered both Muslim and Christian Lebanese militias to turn in their weapons. Neither side paid too much attention to the order. Then, on 13 December, Lebanon ordered the PLO regular forces to leave the country by the end of the month. The peacekeeping forces ordered all heavy-caliber weapons not in the hands of the Lebanese army to be turned in. One week later, the Arab forces began a series of raids to force compliance. Strict curbs were also imposed on PLO political and military activities (13 February). On 26 October 1978 the League extended its mandate and ordered the peacekeeping force to remain in Lebanon another six months. In 1993, some elements of the Arab League force were still in Lebanon ostensibly to maintain order. *Reading:* Istvan S. Pogany, *The Arab League and Peacekeeping in Lebanon* (1988).

Arab Legion. The evacuation of the Turks from Arabic lands led to the establishment of the Kingdom of Transjordan under the British mandate in 1921. The British established an elite military unit manned with Bedouin soldiers and British officers; the unit was called the Arab Legion. In 1939, command of the unit was given to John Bagot Glubb (qv), who would become known as Glubb Pasha. When the British mandate expired in 1948, the Legion fought as a part of the Arab forces against the Israelis in their bid for an independent homeland. The Arab campaign was relatively successful; and a large segment of Palestine, including Bethlehem, Hebron and part of Jerusalem, were in Arab hands when the Jordan-Israeli armistice was signed on 3 April 1949. The Legion was disbanded on 26 May 1956 as a part of a general house-cleaning of British advisers and military support by the new king of Jordan, Hussein (Husain) (qv).

Arab Liberation Army (ALA). A confederation of volunteers from all over the Arab world the Arab Liberation Army launched its first attack against the Jewish settlement of Kafr Szold in British controlled Palestine on 10 January 1948. The attack came out of Syria and was commanded by an Iraqi, General Ismail Safwat. On 15 May, after the end of the British mandate, ALA forces moved through Gvulot and Beersheeba (*Be'er Sheva'*) (taken 20 May) and into Hebron (21 May). Palestinian Arabs gave the invading ALA considerable support. By 7 June, much of the region north of the Sea of Galilee was in ALA/Lebanese hands. These forces were dislodged, however, in October, when an Israeli counteroffensive effectively drove the ALA out of what was then Israeli territory.

Arab Liberation Front for Eritrea. A terrorist organization calling itself the Arab Liberation Front for Eritrea blew up an Ethiopian airliner at Frankfurt Airport in West Germany on 11 March 1969. On 18 June, they blew up a second Ethiopian airliner at Karachi Airport in Pakistan.

Arab Liberation Movement. *See* Syria.

Arab National Youth for the Liberation of Palestine States. A TWA jet bound from Tel Aviv, Israel, to New York City crashed into the Ionian Sea off the Greek coast on 8 September 1974. There were no survivors among the 88 persons on board, 17 of whom were Americans. The Arab National Youth for the Liberation of Palestine issued a press release in Beirut saying that a member of their group exploded a charge he was carrying strapped to his waist, causing his own death and the destruction of the aircraft and its occupants. On 11 January 1975, the U.S. National Transportation Safety Board released its report of the investigation of fragments brought up from the sea bed. Their conclusion was that the aircraft was destroyed by a high-explosive charge.

ben Arafa, Moulay (Mulay) Mohammed. Since 1927, Mohammed V (Sidi Mohammed ben Yusuf) (qv) had sat on the throne of Morocco. On 14 August 1954, he was deposed in a French-engineered coup; but he was replaced, over French objections, by the elderly prince Moulay Mohammed ben Arafa (qv). Two days later, a Berber uprising deposed the new sultan. With a week, he was back on the throne although remaining relatively quiescent, Moulay Mohammed played an important role in the subsequent independence of Morocco.

Arafat, Yasser (Yasir) (aka Abu Ammar "The Builder"). (b. 17 February 1929, Jerusalem) Born Muhammed Abed Ar'rouf al-Qudwah al-Husayni, he was one of seven children in a family of well-to-do merchants and landowners in the Ramallah (or possibly Jenin) district north of Jerusalem. His mother was a relative of the fiercely anti-Zionist Grand Mufti of Jerusalem, Amin al-Husayni. His family fled Palestine in 1948, when the state of Israel was proclaimed, and moved to Jordan and Lebanon. Arafat went to school in Gaza and was later graduated as a civil engineer from Cairo University. While studying in Cairo he joined the Muslim Brotherhood and the Union of Palestinian Students. He served as president of the latter group from 1952 until 1956. He served in the Egyptian Army as an engineer during the Suez campaign of 1956. After his military service, Arafat moved first to Beirut (1959), where he joined a consortium, and then moved to join the firm of Emile Bustani in Kuwait, where he opened a building contracting firm. He remained in the construction business until the early 1960s, when he became the cofounder, along with Salah Khalaf and Khaled al-Wazir (aka Abu Ayad or Abu Jihad) of *al-Fatah* (qv) (1965), one of the military components of the Palestine Liberation Organization (PLO). He became the chairman of the PLO in 1969 and, two years later, commander in chief of the Palestinian Revolutionary Forces. His power eroded somewhat in June-September 1970 as a result of clashes between the *al-Fatah* guerrillas and the Jordanian army for which he was criticized by his own followers and by the extremist Popular Front for the Liberation of Palestine (PFLP) and its leader, George Habash. Although Arafat had been forced into the open defiance of King Hussein's (Husain) (qv) rule, he later had to fight with his own deputies, who wanted to make peace with the Jordanian leader. By 1983, Arafat's long-term, undisputed leadership of the PLO was on the wane. His forces (about 5,000) had been trapped by the Palestine Liberation Army and Syrian forces in the Tripoli area of Lebanon, and he was forced to evacuate the city in December. Thereafter, Arafat began the rounds of the Arab capitals in hopes of restoring some of his lost authority. In 1989, he was successful in getting himself elected the president of the State of Palestine, even though in doing so he became the head of a nonexistent nation. He was also elected chairman of the Central Committee of *al-Fatah*, the largest faction of the PLO. In November 1991, Arafat is reported to have secretly married his aide, 28-year-old Suha Tawil, a Palestinian Christian. In late 1991, Arafat was able to reach an accommodation with Syrian president Hafez al-Assad (qv), which settled a long-standing dispute between the two leaders. On 7 April 1992, his Soviet-built aircraft crashed in the Libyan desert; Arafat survived the crash. In 1993, he formally recognized the existence of Israel and participated in the negotiations that led to an Israeli-PLO accord that laid out a five-year plan to return control of part of the West Bank and the Gaza Strip to Palestinian control. Arafat and Israeli prime minister Yitzak Rabin were awarded the Nobel peace prize for this achievement in 1994. In 1996, Arafat became the president of the Palestine Authority, the governing body for the Gaza Strip and the West Bank. *Reading:* Andrew Gowers & Tony Walker. *Behind the Myth: Yasser Arafat and the Palestinian Revolution* (1992; Shaul Mishal, *The PLO under Arafat: Between Gun and Olive Branch,* (1986).

Aramburu, Pedro Eugenio. (b. 21 May 1903, Rio Cuarto, Cordoba Province, Argentina—d. June/July 1970, Timote, Buenos Aires Province, Argentina) An army officer, Aramburu joined three other senior officers in 1950 in deposing Juan Peron as president. He thereafter served as provisional president of Argentina from 1955 (13 November) until 1958. During his tenure, he reinstituted the constitution of 1853 and set a date of 1958 for a democratic election. Aramburu also barred himself and his government from contesting any of the offices in that election. In 1963, however, Aramburo ran for the presidency, but he was defeated. He was kidnapped by Peronista terrorists on 29 May 1970 and was executed on 1 June for "crimes against the people" during his tenure as president. His body was found six weeks later (16 July).

Aranyaprathet. *See* Thailand.

Arbenz Guzman, Jacobo. (b. 14 September 1913, Quezaltenango, Guatemala—d. 27 January 1971, Mexico City) Until 1944, when he appeared as a member of the ruling military junta that overthrew the government, Arbenz Guzman was an obscure army officer. When the new president, Juan Jose Arevalo, took office in March 1945, he appointed Arbenz minister of defense. In 1951 he was himself elected president and served in that office until 1954, when he was ousted by a right-wing military coup that objected to his leftist tendencies. On a number of occasions Arbenz, known as the "Red Colonel," crossed swords with the U.S. and, on at least one occasion, expropriated American-owned property in Guatemala. He died in exile in Mexico City.

Arévalo, Juan José. Arévalo was inaugurated president of Guatemala in March 1945 after the ouster (20 October 1944) of General Federico Ponce Vaides, who had just proclaimed his intention to retain the power he had taken in June, when Jorge Ubico was forced to resign. During his tenure, Arévalo was able to shift power away from the military and toward organized labor. This led to an upsurge in communist activity that eventually placed Jacabo Arbenz Guzman (qv) in power (March 1951).

Argentina. Argentina is a country in South America bordered on the north by Bolivia and Paraguay, on the east by Brazil, Uruguay and the Atlantic Ocean, on the south by the Drake Passage, and on the west by Chile. The capital is Buenos Aires. Originally inhabited by nonnomadic Indians, it was discovered by Juan Diaz de Solis in 1515 and was a Spanish colony from 1620 until 1816, when it declared its independence. There followed a long period of violence before a strong central government could be established. During this time heavy immigration took place, with large numbers of Germans, Italians, and Spaniards settling the land. Since the 1920s, the country has been rocked by a series of military uprisings, and coups were the primary method of government reform between 1930 and 1946. One such coup (1943) propelled Juan Peron (qv) to power. While there was some land reform during the Peronista regime, there was even greater suppression of human rights. The country soon became mired in debt, and in 1955 Peron was ousted and exiled. A series of military and civilian governments succeeded each other until 1973, when Peron returned to Argentina and was reelected president. Upon his death ten months later, his second wife, Isabel Peron (qv), who had been elected vice president, succeeded him. Isabel was ousted by a military coup in 1976. Insurgency then gripped the country, and thousands were killed or injured in widespread fighting; human rights abuses abounded. This phase of Argentine history ended in December 1985, when, after five months of trial, a number of junta leaders were found guilty of various charges stemming from abuse of office. The list of those convicted included two former presidents of Argentina, Jorge Videla (qv) and General Roberto Eduardo Viola (qv). In April 1982, Argentina invaded the British-held Falkland Islands (qv), claiming sovereignty over the group. In the disastrous war that followed, Great Britain carried out a humiliating and thorough defeat of the Argentine armed forces and reasserted authority over the Falklands. Argentine president Leopoldo Galtieri (qv) was forced to resign in June as a result. A period of democratic rule followed the elections of 1983, when Raul Alfonsin's (qv) Radical Civic Union Party (RCUP) gained an absolute majority in the congress. Alfonsin's crackdown on the perpetrators of past human rights crimes and the Falklands debacle led to military uprisings in 1986, but the vast majority of Argentinians approved of his actions. By 1989, however, inflation was at 6,000 percent, and looting and rioting was reported in many of the larger cities; the government was forced to establish a 30-day state of siege, which was followed by harsh new economic regulations. The RCUP lost the 1989 elections as a result of the continued economic problems, and the Peronistas regained control of the country. However, discontent among the military remained a major problem, and as one means of abating the unrest, the new president pardoned many of the military convicted of human rights violations. This action was heavily criticized in Argentina and around the world, but did curry some favor from the military. The Argentines came to terms with

Great Britain over the Falklands and reestablished diplomatic ties in October 1989. As the economy began to recover, a constitutional amendment was approved (1994) that would allow a president to serve two terms. This was accomplished to allow Carlos Saul Menem, a Peronista, to remain in office and to prevent Alfonsin's return. *Reading:* Eduardo Crawley, *A House Divided: Argentina, 1880–1980* (1984); Donald C. Hodges, *Argentina's "Dirty War": An Intellectual Biography,* (1991).

Argentinian Treaty with Chile. *See* Beagle Channel Incident.

Argov, Shlomo. On 3 June 1982, the Israeli ambassador in London, Shlomo Argov, was shot and critically wounded by a member of Abu Nidal's Black June (*al Ashifa*) terrorist group. The attack took place as Argov left a diplomatic reception at a London hotel. This incident led to the Israeli invasion of Lebanon three days later, allegedly to destroy the PLO infrastructure.

Arias Espinosa, Ricardo. In the elections held in Panama on 11 May 1952, José Remón easily won over his opponent, Roberto Francisco Chiari (qv). He was assassinated, however, on 2 January 1955. His successor, José Ramón Guizado, was in office only a few days when he was dismissed by the National Assembly for his part in the Remón assassination. Ricardo Arias Espinosa presided over the caretaker government until he was replaced by the duly elected Ernesto de la Guardia, Jr., on 1 October 1956.

Arias Madrid, Arnulfo. (b. 15 August 1901, Penonome, Colombia—d. 10 August 1988, Miami, Florida) Although interested in politics from the 1920s, Arias Madrid was educated in the United States at the University of Chicago and Harvard Medical School. He was the younger brother of Harmodio Aris Madrid, who was president of Panama in 1932. Arnulfo served as the Panamanian ambassador to France and England in the 1930s and won his first term as president of Panama in 1940. After less than a year in office he was deposed by a military junta even though he had established a social security system and had given the vote to women. His ouster came after he abrogated the constitution and extended his term in office to six years. He was reelected president in 1948 inplebiscite marred by fraud and scandal. The vote was thrown out by the courts, but Arias remained in office until the election was finally recognized eighteen months later. In 1951, Arias was again deposed for again attempting to revoke the constitution. He ran again for president in 1964 in another controversy-ridden election. In 1968 he was elected president but served only 11 days before the military once again reacted and Arias was out of a job. He ran again in 1984, this time losing to General Omar Torrijos, in an election openly marked with fraud. Arias then moved to the U.S. where he carried on an opposition campaign against Torrijos and his successor, Manuel Noriega (qv).

Arif, Abdul Rahman. On 5 September 1965, Brigadier Abdul Razzaq Arif, a follower of Egypt's Gamal Abdul Nasser (qv), was appointed prime minister of Iraq to replace General Taher Yahya, who had resigned. Twelve days later, on 17 September, the prime minister attempted a coup against President Abdul Salam Arif, who was visiting Casablanca. The coup was defeated by the president's elder brother, Abdul Rahman Arif, who was army chief of staff. When Abdul Razzaq Arif was killed in an airplane crash near Basra, on 13 April 1966, Abdul Rahman Arif assumed the presidency. His tenure was highlighted by his attempts to settle the long-standing struggle with the Kurds. He was forced to remove himself from office by a Baathist-led revolt (17 July 1968) and was replaced by Major General Ahmed Hassan al-Bakr (qv).

Armed Forces for National Liberation (FALN). A Puerto Rican terrorist organization, the FALN advocated independence for Puerto Rico. On 4 April 1980, 11 members of the group were arrested in Evanston, Illinois, and charged with violation of a number of state and federal laws, including 28 bombings. All 11 were subsequently convicted.

Armenian Revolutionary Army (ARA). A rightist separatist terrorist group responsible for a series of attacks in Western Europe. On 20 June 1984, for instance, the ARA claimed responsibility for a car bombing that killed the Turkish Labor Attache in Vienna. A number of others were injured in the blast. On 12 March 1985, the Turkish embassy in Ottawa was seized by three ARA members. One embassy guard was killed. The terrorists surrendered after holding the building for four hours. The Turkish ambassador, Coskum Kirca, escaped by jumping out of an upper story window. He was injured in the fall, but survived.

Armenian Secret Army for the Liberation of Armenia (ASALA). A leftist separatist terrorist group that, before 1984, was quite active in the European area, ASALA began its operations before 1975. Between 1975 and 1983, it claimed credit for or was blamed for attacks on Turkish diplomats in 16 different countries. In 1981, ASALA carried out more international attacks than any other terrorist organization. Its primary targets were Turkish diplomats and diplomatic facilities. ASALA also operated under a number of cover names. Using the name "Orly Organization," for example, ASALA attacked French interests after the arrest of one of their members (November 1981), who attempted to enter France with a false passport through Orly Airport. In 1981, ASALA carried out 40 attacks in 11 countries. While most of these attacks were against Swiss and French targets, the most serious were against Turkish diplomats. On 24 September 1981, for instance, the Turkish Embassy in Paris was seized by ASALA terrorists claiming to be the "Armenian Suicide Commando Yeghia Kechichian, Van Operation." A number of Turkish diplomats were assassinated by ASALA in Switzerland, Denmark and France. In the last incident, the Turkish ambassador and his chauffeur were killed while driving to their embassy in Paris from a luncheon at the Austrian embassy, by two gunmen using submachineguns. On 16 June 1983, ASALA terrorists bombed a bazaar in Istanbul, Turkey, killing two and injuring 23 others. Also in 1983, ASALA attacked Orly Airport (15 July) outside Paris with a bomb that killed five and injured 50 more. The bomb was hidden in baggage deposited at the Turkish Airlines check-in counter. On 27 July 1983, five ASALA members shot their way into the Turkish embassy in Lisbon, Portugal, where they then blew up the building and themselves. One terrorist was shot to death before the explosion and four were killed, along with a police officer and a civilian, in the blast. During the mid-1980s the group apparently suffered serious internal division over the indiscriminate use of violence. *Reading:* Anat Kurz & Ariel Merari, *ASALA: Irrational Terror or Political Tool* (1985).

Armenian Suicide Commando Yeghia Kechichian, Van Operation. This little-known terrorist group, claiming to be a faction of ASALA, stormed the Turkish embassy in Paris on 24 September 1981. A Turkish security guard was killed, and two terrorists were wounded in the attack. They demanded the immediate release of all Armenian prisoners in Turkish jails plus five Turkish revolutionaries and five Kurds. After 15 hours, the terrorists released their hostages and surrendered. *See* Armemian Secret Army for the Liberation of Armenia (ASALA).

Army of National Liberation (ALN). *See* Algeria.

Arosemena Monroy, Carlos Julio. In August 1947, Arosemena headed one of the several provisional governments that ruled Ecuador after the ouster of José María Velasco Ibarra (qv). In 1961, Arosemena was serving as vice president when Velasco Ibarra, who had returned from exile and won his fourth term as president, resigned in the face of growing economic unrest in the country. Arosemena became the president at that time. His tenure was a turbulent one. On 11–12 July 1963, the armed forces carried out a military coup that removed Arosemena from office. The ruling junta immediately set about removing the communist influences in government that Arosemena had tolerated.

Arosemena, Domingo. On 10 May 1951, Domingo Arosemena became the president of Panama, following the impeachment of Arnulfo Arias (qv). Arosemena had been serving as vice president when the move against Arias took place. Arosemena did not run in the 1952 elections. His term in office was a short one.

Arosemena, Florencio. Florencio Arosemena was president of Panama, when he died in office on 25 August 1949. His death led to a power struggle that was influenced by protracted negotiations over U.S. basing rights in Panama. Arnulfo Arias (qv) succeeded to the presidency later that same year.

Arregui Izaguirre, Jose Ignacio. A suspected member of the military wing of *Euzkadi ta Azkatasuna* (ETA), the outlawed Basque terrorist organization, Arregui was arrested on 4 February 1981, in connection with the murder of a Spanish Civil Guard (federal police) officer. He was allegedly tortured and died in a prison hospital on 16 February. Two days of rioting accompanied a general strike in Spain that followed announcement of his death. His death resulted in the resignations of a number of top-ranking police officials in a government attempt to defuse a situation that the ETA hoped to turn into a military coup against the government of Adolfo Suárez González. González was replaced as premier on 28 February 1981.

Arron, Henck. *See* Chin A Sen.

Arroyo (Araya?), Arturo. Captain Arturo Arroyo was the naval aide to President Salvador Allende Gossens (qv) in Chile. He was assassinated on 27 July 1973.

His death may have been part of the plan that led to the 11 September 1973 military takeover of Chile that ended the pro-Marxist Allende government.

Ascension Island. A volcanic island in the South Atlantic, Ascansion has been a British dependency since 1922, when it was placed under the control of St. Helena 700 miles to the southeast. Ascension played a crucial role as a base of operations for Great Britain during the Falklands War. In more peaceful times it serves as a major U.K./U.S. communications station.

Ascuncion. *See* Paraguay.

Asencio, Diego C. *See* April 19 Movement (M-19).

A Shau Valley. *See* Viet Nam.

Ashdod. *See* Israel.

Asluj. *See* Israel.

Asmara. *See* Ethiopia.

al-Assad, Hafez (aka Abu Suleiman). (b. 6 October 1930, Qardaha, Lataki Province, Syria) President of Syria. One of the Arab world's most adept survivors and a member of the Alawi sect, Assad joined the Baath Party (qv) in 1946 and graduated from the Syrian Military Academy at Homs in 1955 as a commissioned air force pilot. He spent 1958-1961 in Egypt as an exchange officer during the period of the United Arab Republic (qv). In March 1965, he was appointed commander-in-chief of the Air Force and became minister of defense following the overthrow of the Amin Hafez government in which he took part in February 1966. He was instrumental in thwarting a counter-coup in September 1966 and became military leader of the Baath Party in 1967, following the disastrous war with Israel. Assad seized power on 18 November 1970 after major disputes within the party over Syrian intervention in Jordan. Most of his opponents were arrested during this period. In 1971, he entered into an Arab union with Egypt and Libya and was elected president of Syria by universal suffrage. He supported Anwar Sadat's (qv) ill-fated campaign against Israel in 1973 (Yom Kippur War) in which they were soundly defeated. In 1974, Assad, although agreeing to a U.S.-proposed disengagement with Israel, maintained a belligerent attitude that included demands to other Arab states to be prepared to continue war against the Jews. He also continued a war of attrition against Israeli forces in the Golan. At stake were Syria's claim to reoccupy all territory seized by Israel since 1967 and the return of some 170,000 displaced persons to the occupied territories. Assad was somewhat successful in these endeavors, and an agreement was signed on 29 May 1974, which only partially settled the dispute between the two countries. The Syrian, sought and received substantial moral and material support from the Soviet Union during this period. Assad invited U.S. president Richard Nixon to Damascus, where U.S.-Syrian diplomatic relations were normalized (15 June 1974) for the first time since 1967. Assad was also able to reestablish diplomatic relations with West Germany (7 August 1974). After 1976 he faced considerable opposition from the Sunni Muslims and from the left following the Syrian intervention in Lebanon. He was, nonetheless, reelected president in 1978. In 1979, he attempted a union with Iraq, but a coup attempt in Iraq that seemingly involved Syria foiled the plan. In 1980, Assad signed a 20-year friendship and cooperation treaty with the Soviet Union. That same year saw a widening rift between Syria and Iraq after Assad sided with Tehran in the Iran-Iraq War. In 1981 there were few signs of improvement, especially in the economy, as Syria continued its military presence in Lebanon and defiant stand toward Israel. In the mid-1980s, Assad suffered ill health, and there was some question about his ability to hold on to power. In 1991, however, Assad sided with the international coalition against Iraq, and Syrian troops took part in the Desert Storm operation, although they engaged in little fighting. By 1993, Assad had not budged from his position on the Arab boycott of Israel, but he did not interpose any conditions on the plans for limited self-rule for the Palestinians in the Gaza Strip and West Bank enclaves. Preparation for talks between Assad and high ranking-Israeli officials came to light in 1994, but there were few hopes for success in the near future, and the situation actually worsened in 1995. The death of Assad's eldest son, in an automobile accident in 1993 left a question as to the selection of Assad's probable successor. *Reading:* Patrick Seale, *Asad of Syria: The Struggle for the Middle East* (1989); Charles Patterson, *Hafiz Al Asad of Syria* (1991).

Assam. *See* India.

Association of Southeast Asian Nations. Known as ASEAN, the organization was formed in 1967 as an economic partnership among Brunei, Indonesia, Malaysia, the Philippines, Singapore and Thailand.

al-Atasi, Hashim. (b. 1875, Homs, Syria - d. 1960) Having served his apprenticeship in the Ottoman administration, following World War I Atasi rose to some prominence in the short-lived government of Amir Faisal before becoming a leader in the nationalist movement opposed to French rule in his country. In 1936, he led the Syrian delegation that hammered out the Franco-Syrian Treaty, which promised Syrian independence. Atasi was elected president of Syria that same year. When the treaty was broken in 1939, Atasi resigned the presidency. Following a military coup in 1949, Atasi was named first prime minister and then president. In late 1949, Syria was moving toward union with Iraq when Adib Shishakli (qv) seized power. Although Atasi remained in office, his power was held at the whim of Shishakli, and he finally resigned in 1951. When Shishakli was overthrown in 1954, Atasi returned to the presidency, served until the 1955 elections and then retired. He died at age 85.

Athens. *See* Greece.

Atlas Mountains. *See* Morocco, Algeria and Tunisia.

Atlit. *See* Israel.

al-Attassi, Nureddin. When Hafez al-Assad seized power on 18 November 1970, he unseated the chairman of the Presidency Council and prime minister of Syria, Nureddin al-Attassi. Assad had placed al-Attassi under house arrest on 13 November following the failure of the Baath Party congress to reconcile the differences between the competing factions.

Attlee, Clement R., 1st Earl. *See* Great Britain. *Reading:* Kenneth Harris, *Attlee* (1995); Nick Tiratsoo, ed., *The Attlee Years* (1991).

Attopeu (Attapu) (Muang Mai). *See* Laos.

Auckland Harbor. *See* New Zealand.

Audran, Rene. A French Defense Ministry official in charge of international arms sales, General Rene Audran was assassinated by an unkown assailant outside his home on 25 January 1985. An anonymous phone caller claimed credit for the attack in the name of a group known as Commando Elizabeth Van Dyck of *Action Directe* (qv).

Auka. *See* Honduras.

Aures. *See* Algeria.

Auriol, Vincent. (b. 27 August 1884, Reval, Haute-Garonne, France—d. 1 January 1966, Paris) Auriol began his career before World War I as a journalist and lawyer in Toulouse. He was elected a deputy in April 1914 and became secretary general of the Socialist Party in 1919. He served as minister of finance in the Blum government (June 1936–June 1937) and was one of 80 deputies who voted against Petain's petition for full power in July 1940. For this, he was arrested in September. After his release in April 1941, he first went into hiding and then escaped to England in 1943. He served as a member of the French Consultative Assembly in Algiers and, after returning to Paris, became minister of state in the de Gaulle government (September 1945). In 1946 he served as president of both the first and second Constituent Assemblies and was elected president of the Republic on 16 June 1947. He refused to run for reelection in 1954 and resigned from the Socialist Party in 1958. Athough he held a seat in the Constitutional Council of the Fifth Republic (from 1959), he refused to serve after July 1960 because of political differences with that body. He died in Paris at age 82 in 1966.

Austin, Hudson. On 19–20 October 1983, General Austin Hudson led the Revolutionary Military Council in assuming control of the former British colony of Grenada. This action followed the 13 October overthrow of the government of prime minister Maurice Bishop (qv). Austin, along with co-conspirator Bernard Coard (qv), was captured during the U.S.-led operations in Grenada (qv) and was subsequently sentenced to death (4 December 1986) for the murders of Maurice Bishop and others. *See* Grenada.

Australia. The smallest, most isolated, and least densely populated of the continents, Australia lies between the Pacific and Indian oceans in the southern hemisphere. The capital city is Canberra, and approximately 50 percent of the continent is desert and dry scrub. The Aborigines first migrated into the region about 40,000 years ago. Originally discovered by European (Dutch) explorers in 1606, it was claimed for Great Britain in 1770, following the exploration of the east coast by Captain James Cook. The first foreign inhabitants of any number were members, boths prisoners and guards, of the penal colony at Botany Bay (1788). Captain William Bligh of *HMS Bounty* fame was one of the colony's early governors. By 1830, the entire continent was under British control. Immigration of free settlers began that year. The Aborigines were indiscriminately slaughtered or driven off as the white settlers acquired more and more land. The Commonwealth of Australia came into being on 1 January 1901. Of singular importance to Australia was its participation in the Great War of 1914–1918, in which 330,000 Australian (and New Zealand) (ANZAC) volunteers fought a major segment of Britain's war and suffered one of the highest casualty rates of any participant of either side. The landing at Gallipoli, 25 April 1915, is celebrated as Anzac Day and as the day Australia came of age. Australia took decades to recover from the manpower losses during the war, a situation that was worsened by the 1929 depression. Australia, following Britain's lead, supported the appeasement that led to World War II. When the war began (1939) Australia sent its small army to Europe. When Japan entered the war, Australia was nearly defenseless until the United States was able to provide forces for its security. Douglas MacArthur's headquarters was in Australia until the liberation of the Philippines. The Labor government helped strengthen ties with the U.S. through such treaties as the ANZUS Pact (qv). Australia also became a charter member of the United Nations in 1945. At that point, Australia became a sentimental relative of Great Britain but began to steer its own course, involving itself in Asian and Pacific affairs. Australians fought in Korea and in Vietnam as a result. In 1973, racial discrimination was dropped as an immigration tool; almost 300,000, half of whom were British, had immigrated into Australia at that point since 1945. There was a severe recession in 1990–1993, from which the country recovered in quick order. The Labor Party has held power in Australia since 1983, and plans have been announced to declare Australia a republic in 2001. *Reading:* John Rikard, *Australia: A Cultural History* (1997); William Livingston & William Roger Louis, eds., *Australia, New Zealand and the Pacific Islands Since the First World War* (1979).

Austria. Austria is a landlocked republic in west central Europe and is bordered on the north by the Czech Republic, on the northeast by Slovakia, on the east by Hungary, on the south by Slovenia, Italy and Switzerland, and on west by Liechtenstein and Switzerland. Roman legions conquered the country from the Celts in 15 B.C. Austria was incorporated into the Carolingian (Charlemagne) empire on 788. By the fourteenth century, the House of Hapsburg had gained control of the empire, and over the next few centuries it came to dominate vast regions of Europe with populations of Germans, Hungarians and Slavs. Its capital, Vienna, was the seat of government of the Austro-Hungarian Empire, which was dismembered as a result of World War I. The assassination of the Archduke Franz Ferdinand in Sarajevo brought about that war and led to the empire's destruction. The small republic of Austria was annexed (*Anschluss*) by Nazi Germany in 1938. After World War II, it was occupied by the Allies, including Soviet troops, until 1955, when it was declared independent. The country has maintained a neutral position since that time but has had its share of problems. In July 1977, 19 Bosnian rebels, who had been assembled in Austria, crossed into Yugoslavia and, in a running gun-battle, killed 13 members of the

Yugoslav security forces. Palestinian terrorists hijacked the Moscow-Vienna train (28 September 1973) and took Jewish hostages, demanding that Austria close its Schonau Jewish transit point and restrict Jewish emigration. The government acceded to that request the next day. On 4 October, the government repudiated this decision in the face of a public outcry. On 21 December 1975, Palestinian terrorists attacked an OPEC meeting being held in Vienna, taking 60 hostages. The next day the government allowed the terrorists to fly out of the country with ten of their hostages. The hostages were released in Algiers, but the Algerian government refused the Austrian request for the extradition of the terrorists. A Lebanese terrorist team hijacked the Vienna-to-Paris Air France flight on 27 August 1983; poor airport security at Vienna was blamed for the success of the incident. The passengers were eventually released in Tehran. On 20 June 1984, the Turkish labor attache was killed by a car bomb in Vienna. The Portuguese Revolutionary Armed Action Group (qv) group claimed credit in the attack. The former Libyan ambassador to Austria was severely injured in an assassination attempt near his home in Vienna on 28 February 1985. In 1980, this man had broken with Libyan strongman Muammar Qadaffi (qv). In 1988, an international tribunal decided that Austria's president, Kurt Waldheim (qv), had known of Nazi atrocities committed in Greece and Yugoslavia during World War II, and had later concealed this knowledge, especially during his time at the United Nations. After 1993, Austria suffered an increase in violence, especially against minorities. Some bombings have been attributed to neo-Nazi groups. These attacks have caused widespead popular protests against the perpetrators. Austria joined the European Union on 1 January 1995. *Reading:* Barbara Jelavich, *Modern Austria: Empire and Republic, 1815–1986* (1987).

Avendano, Guillermo Flores. On 24 October 1957 a three-man military junta took charge of the government of Guatemala amid charges that the elections held on 20 October had been rigged. Three days later, on 27 October, Guillermo Flores Avendano was appointed provisional president. He was eventually replaced by Ydígoras Fuentes (qv), who was declared president by the assembly on 2 March 1958.

Awadallah, Abibakr. Awadallah, a former chief justice, became prime minister of Sudan following the 25 May 1969 overthrow of the government of Mohammed Ahmed Mahgoub (qv) by a left-wing military coup led by Colonel Mohammed Gaafar al-Nimeiry (qv), who assumed the presidency. Awadallah, who was known for his radical leanings, headed a cabinet that included three members of the Sudanese communist party. In October 1969, Awadallah was removed from office by Nimeiry, who took over the role of prime minister, while Awadallah was relegated to the duties of minister of foreign affairs and of justice.

Awali River. *See* Lebanon.

Ayacucho District. *See* Peru.

Ayub Khan, Mohammed. (b. 14 May 1907, British India—d. 20 April 1974, Islamabad, Pakistan) Born in Rihana, Northwest Frontier Province, in what is today Pakistan, Ayub Khan attended Aligarh Muslim University in India and then the Royal Military Academy, Sandhurst. In 1928, Ayub Khan was commissioned into the Indian army, where he rose through the officer ranks to command a battalion in Burma in World War II. In 1951, after Pakistan gained its independence, he became the commander in chief of the newly formed Pakistani army and, three years later, minister of defense. In October 1958, following a period of internal unrest, President Iskander Mirza (qv) annulled the constitution and was forced into exile in England. Ayub Khan declared martial law and took control of the country. He established a new representative form of local government and was subsequently confirmed as the nation's new president. He was reelected president in 1965, even though the economic and social conditions in Pakistan had failed to respond favorably to his programs. Continued student rioting and general unrest during 1968 and 1969 led Ayub Khan to retire from public life on 26 March 1969. *Reading:* Lawrence Ziring, *The Ayub Khan Era: Politics in Pakistan, 1958–1969* (1971).

Azhari, Gholam Reza. General Gholan Reza Azhari, the armed forces chief of staff, became prime minister of Iran on 6 November 1978, following Jaafar Sarif-Emami's resignation (5 November) in the wake of major anti-Shah demonstrations in Tehran. Azhari assumed his new duties at the head of a military government installed by Shah Reza Pahlavi (qv) in hopes of stemming the rising dissension in the country. A number of Iranians were arrested during Azhari's first few days in office. Azhari resigned office on 1 January 1979, in the final days of the Shah's attempt to retain control through the imposition of military rule. Azhari was replaced on 4 January by Shahpour Bakhtiar (qv).

Aziz, Faisal ibn Musad ibn Abdul. On 25 March 1975, Prince Faisal ibn Musad ibn Abdul Aziz assassinated his uncle, King Faisal (qv) of Saudi Arabia. The 27-year-old Aziz was said to be mentally unbalanced, but a medical tribunal declared him sane, and he was publicly beheaded in Riyadh on 18 June 1975.

Aziz, Khalid ibn Abdul (Khalid 'ibn Abd al-'Aziz Al Saud). (b. 1913, Riyadh— d. 13 June 1982, Ta'if, Saudi Arabia) Khalid, the fourth son of Ibn Saud, became king of Saudi Arabia upon the assassination of his half-brother Faisal (qv) on 25 March 1975. He served in several government posts from the 1930s, but illness in the 1970s seemed to preclude his ever being king. He was confirmed, however, and did serve after Faisal's death. Much of the administrative power, he gave to his half-brother Faud, who would succeed him. He had been nominated crown prince in 1965. He died quietly at age 69.

Aziz, Saud ibn Abdel (King Saud ibn 'Abd al-'Aziz). Saud was proclaimed king of Saudi Arabia on 9 November 1953 upon the death of his father, Ibn Saud. Saud's brother Faisal (qv) became the heir apparent. He also became Saud's chief rival for power. Saud was the protector of the old Muslim ways; Faisal was the Westernizer. In March 1958, after a protracted struggle for power, Saud transferred all executive functions to Faisal. In December 1960, Faisal was forced to resign, and Saud transferred the prime ministership for a time into his own hands. Faisal was restored in 1962 and, on 2 November 1964, helped depose his brother and took the throne.

Azurdia, Enrique Peralta. On 31 March 1963, Enrique Peralta Azurdia, the defense minister of Guatemala, led an armed coup that ousted President Ydigoras Fuentes (qv). Fuentes was overthrown because he had allowed former president Juan Jose Arévalo to reenter the country, adding to the possibility that more political trouble would begin in the country. Azurdia became provisional president and cancelled the scheduled November elections. A new election was scheduled in March 1966, at which time the military regime was defeated and stepped down.

B

Baabda. *See Lebanon.*

Baader, Andreas. (b. 1943?, Munich, Germany—d. 18 October 1977, Stuttgart, West Germany) The son of middle-class parents, Baader began his career as an anarchist and terrorist by participating in student protests in West Germany in the 1960s. In 1968 he was arrested and jailed for setting a series of fires in Frankfurt department stores. He formed, with Ulrike Meinhof, the Red Army Faction (*Rote Armee Fraktion*) (qv), better known as the Baader-Meinhof Gang (qv), ostensibly to carry out urban guerrilla warfare against German materialism and the United States military presence in Europe. In fact, the Baader-Meinhof Gang concentrated on bank robbery for personal gain as much as to carry forward the espoused cause. Arrested and imprisoned, Baader was broken out of jail by his gang and set out upon a series of political assassinations and terrorist attacks. He was again captured in 1977 and sentenced to life imprisonment. In an attempt to free him, Palestinian terrorists hijacked a Lufthansa airliner enroute from Germany to Majorca. After the hijacking failed at Mogadishu, Somalia, and all the hijackers were killed or captured, Baader and two fellow gang members were found dead in their prison cells, supposedly having committed suicide upon finding out the hijacking to gain their release had failed.. *See* Red Army Faction and Baader-Meinhof Gang.

Baader-Meinhof Gang. Also known as the Red Army Faction (qv), this West German terrorist gang was led by Andreas Baader (qv) and Ulrike Meinhof, both of whom died in prison. Although supposedly committed to the overthrow of the capitalist system, many of their acts of terrorism, such as bank robberies, were better characterized as criminal, with the intent to receive money for personal use. With the death of the two leaders the gang has become a minor threat. *See* Red Army Factions. *Reading:* Joanna Wright, *Terrorist Propaganda: The Red Army Faction and the Provisional IRA, 1968–86* (1991); Stefan Aust, *The Baader-Meinhof Group: The Inside Story of a Phenomenon* (1987).

Baalabakk (Baalbek). *See* Lebanon.

Baath (Ba'th, Ba'ath) Party (*Hizb al-Ba'th al-'Arabi al-Ishtiraki*). Founded in
Damascus, Syria, in 1943 by Michel 'Alfaq and Salah ad-Din al-Bitar, the Baath
Party drew up its constitution in 1947 and entered a coalition with the Syrian
Socialist Party in 1953. Out of the merger, the Arab Socialist Baath Party came
into being. On 8 March 1963, after having dissolved Parliament (20 September
1952), the government of Syria was overthrown by a pro-Egyptian group
supported by the Baath Party. A new, largely Baath Party–pro–Nasser
government was installed on 9 March. The Baathist–pro–Nasser coalition broke
up on 8 May with pro–Nasser rioting breaking out in Damascus. After several
attempts to form a new government, the Baathists remained in power on 10 July.
A pro–Nasser coup was staged on 18 July, but it failed. Factionalism among the
Baathists continued into 1970, dye largely to differences between the nationalist
and progressive elements over the manner in which the highly centralized and
authoritarian nature of the Party should be controlled. After it had lost power in
Iraq in 1963, there was a Baathist-led revolt in that country on 17 July 1968.
President Abdel Rahman Arif (qv) was compelled to resign. Major General
Ahmed Hassan al-Bakr (qv), a Baathist, thereupon assumed the presidency of
Iraq. In Syria, on 28 February 1969, the defense minister, Lieutenant General
Hafez al-Assad (qv) seized power on behalf of the nationalist faction, ousting
President al-Attassi (qv) and, at the same time, removing General Salah Jadid
as the head of the Baath Party. On 17 February 1973, 17 Iraqi army officers
were executed after being convicted of participating in a coup attempt against
the Baathist government. Specific differences between the Syrian and Iraqi form
of Baathism have prevented any unification of the two countries, in part because
each of the two parties entered into various coalitions that were at the time
inimical to the other country. These coalitions were required because of varying
levels of threat posed by the chief opponents in the two nations; the Muslim
Brotherhood in Syria, and the Kurdish and Shi'ite groups in Iraq. The reality of
the differences between the two nation Baathist groups appeared in 1990, when
20,000 Syrian troops joined the coalition forces arrayed against Iraq following
the invasion of Kuwait. *See* Syria and Iraq. *Reading*: David Roberts, *The Ba'th
and the Creation of Modern Syria* (1987).

Babangida, Ibrahim. (B. 17 August 1941, Niger Province, Nigeria) Babangida
began his career as a military cadet in Nigeria and was commissioned in 1963
following training at Kaduna and at the Indian Military Academy. Upon
Completing additional military training in the United Kingdom, he was assigned
as an instructor at the Nigerian Defense Academy. He was then sent to the
United States, where he attended the U.S. Army Command and General Staff
College; he was promoted to major general upon his return to Nigeria. In 1975,
he became a member of Murtala Mohammed's Supreme Military Council. He
participated in the bloodless overthrow (1983) of the government of Alhaji
Shehu Shagari (qv) that installed Major General Mohammad Buhari (qv) as the
new president. Then, in 1985, Babangida led another bloodless coup and
installed himself as president. His first act was to clear out most of Buhari's

cabinet ministers in order to establish an "open government." Babingida moved to end military rule in September 1990 by reorganizing the armed forces and began the process of reducing the military strength by one-half. Islamic fundamentalists created violence in January 1992, with more than 260 being arrested following rioting that took ten lives in Katsina province. Ethnic violence, which began in October 1991, took more than 100 lives in March 1992 alone. At the same time, election irregularities caused the cancellation of the first round of presidential balloting. On 4 January 1993, a transitional council was inaugurated that was to to exist until a democratically elected government was installed in August. Babangida continued to hold the real power, however, until the elections in June 1993. Suddenly, when it became obvious that the "wrong" candidate had been elected, the referendum was annulled. A period of violence followed. Then, a new election was scheduled for July, but before it could be held, Babangida announced that an interim government would take office on 27 August. That day, Babangida stepped down and turned the control of Nigeria over to a group of steadfast followers. On 17 November 1993, the government was seized by the military, ending Babangida's authority. *See* Nigeria.

Babu (Bubu), Abdul Rahman Muhammad. Babu, the leader of the left-wing Tanzanian Umma (The Masses) Party, was arrested on 14 April 1972 following the assassination of Sheikh Abeid Amani Karume (qv) on 7 April. Babu had been minister of defense in the Karume government. Several members of the army group that carried out the assassination who were killed in the attempt were linked to the Umma Party, which had merged with Karume's Afro-Shirazi Party in 1964. Babu, along with 80 others, was tried in May 1974 amid much protest against Karume's rule in Zanzibar. Of those tried, 54 were found guilty 34 of them being sentenced to death. Eighteen of those found guilty, including 14 of those sentenced to death, were held in Tanzania and their extradition to Zanzibar was refused. Babu died in 1996.

Ba Cut. *See* Vietnam.

Badakhshan Province. *See* Afghanistan.

al-Badr, Mohammed, Saif al-Islam. *See* Yemen.

Baffin Bay. First discovered by William Baffin while searching for the Northwest Passage (1615–1616), Baffin Bay is a large body of water lying between Greenland on the east and Baffin Island on the west. This remote, usually ice-covered region of the sea was the scene of the crash, in 1968, of a U.S. B-52 bomber carrying four hydrogen bombs. Although there was no nuclear detonation, the political fallout from the crash caused the government in Denmark, the possessor of Greenland, to fall.

Bagaza, Jean-Baptiste. (b. 1946, Rotovu, Bururi Province, Burundi) In his youth, Bagaza attended military schools in Belgium and then served as the assistant to the chief of the Burundian armed forces. In November 1976, he led a bloodless coup against the government of Michel Micambero (qv) and was appointed president by the Supreme Revolutionary Council. Bagaza abolished the post of prime minister in 1984 and was elected head of state and government. He was, in turn, overthrown in 1987 by Major Pierre Buyoya (qv).

Baghdad. *See* Iraq.

Baghdad Pact. First called the Turko-Iraqi Pact, the Baghdad Pact is a 24 February 1955 mutual security treaty signed initially by Great Britain (5 April 1955), Iran (12 October 1954), Iraq (24 February 1955), Pakistan (23 September 1954) and Turkey (5 February 1955) as a means of insuring Middle East peace. Iraq removed itself from the treaty on 24 March 1959. Egypt and Saudi Arabia rejected the treaty on 11 June 1955, but agreed to cooperate on defense matters and to place their military forces under a joint unified command. The treaty headquarters was moved to Ankara, Turkey, about this same time, and the organization was renamed CENTO for Central Treaty Organization (19 August 1959) . The United States did not sign the treaty, but it became an indirect member in 1959 when it signed bilateral agreements with all the Middle Eastern participants. On 6 June 1968, Pakistan announce that it would gradually withdraw from CENTO and from the Southeast Asia Treaty Organization (SEATO); it finally withdrew from CENTO on 12 March 1979. Turkey withdrew on 15 March 1979. CENTO ceased to exist on 28 September 1979. *Reading:* Elie Podeh, *The Quest for Hegemony in the Arab World: The Struggle over the Baghdad Pact,* Social, Economic, and Political Studies of the Middle East, no. 52 (1995).

Bagram Airport. *See* Afghanistan.

Bahadur, Sir Osman Ali Khan. On 7 September 1948, after the persistent refusal of the state of Hyderabad (qv), located in the center of the Indian subcontinent, to join the Dominion of India, Prime Minister Pandit Nehru threatened military action. Two days later (9 September), Sir Osman Ali Khan Bahadur, the Moslem Nizam of Hyderabad, appealed to the United States for assistance. On 13 September Indian forces invaded the province. A week later, Hyderabad was pacified and, on 26 January 1950, made a part of the Indian Union.

Bahonor (Bahonar), Mohammad Javad. (b. 1933, Kerman, Iran—d. 30 August 1931, Teheran, Iran) Imprisoned during the reign of the Shah Reza Pahlavi (qv), Bahonor became one of those who drafted the new constitution after the Shah's fall in 1979. In March 1981, Bahonor was appointed minister of education and took up the unfinished work of Mohammad Ali Raja'i in "purifying" the universities in Iran of Western "Satanic" influences. He became the leader of the Islamic Republican Party in June 1981, after the assassination of Ayatollah Mohammad Hossein Beheshti (qv). After the fall of Abohassan Bani-Sadr's (qv) government in June and the election of Mohammad Ali Raja'i as president, Bohonor became prime minister. Bahonor and Raja'i were killed by an assassin's bomb, which detonated in Bahonor's office.

Bahrain (Bahrein). A small group of Arab-controlled islands forming an archipelago that lies in the Gulf of Bahrain, that empties into the Persian Gulf off the coast of eastern Saudi Arabia are known as Bahrain. The capital city is Manama. Known in antiquity, in more recent times Bahrain was a British protectorate, from 1820 until independence was declared in August 1971. The first oil-producing nation in the region (since 1932), Bahrain established a strong entrepreneurial position in the Middle East even though its petroleum supply had been dwindling. A U.S. naval facility at Jufair (from 1971) was ordered removed after the U.S. supported Israel in the 1973 Arab-Israeli War. The government was able to blunt an Iranian-inspired coup attempt in 1981. Over this period, Bahrain established a political and defensive relationship with Saudi Arabia and allowed coalition forces the use of its seaport and air bases during the Persian Gulf War of 1991. *Reading:* Hamad bin Isa al Khalifah, *First Light: Modern Bahrain and Its Heritage* (1995); Fred H. Lawson, *Bahrain: The Modernization of Autocracy* (1989).

Baie d'Along (Ha Long Bay) Agreement. On 5 June 1948, the State of Vietnam was established by the Baie d'Along Agreement signed by Emperor Bao Dai (qv), French commissioner Emile Bollaert, and General Nyugen Van Xuan. Bao Dai was named head of state of the new member of the French Union. Earlier, in February 1946, the Sino–French Treaty released Nationalist China from its occupation duties in northern Indochina. In March of that year, the Viet Minh (qv) negotiated with the French for a referendum that would have proclaimed the Democratic Republic of Vietnam, most likely under Viet Minh control, which would have been a free state within the French Union and the Indochinese federation (Vietnam, Cambodia, Laos). During the negotiations fighting broke out between the French and the Viet Minh, which culminated in a seven year war (1947–1954). During that period, France negotiated separate treaties with each of the three Indochinese states. Baie d'Along was thought to have settled the Vietnamese question, but events would prove otherwise.

Bakhtiar, Shahpour (Shahpur). (b. 1914, Tehran, Iran—d. 6 August 1991, Suresnes, France) Educated in Paris, France, Bakhtiar became a member of the opposition to the rule of Shah Mohammad Reza Pahlavi (qv). In 1951, he joined the National Front government of Doctor Mossadeq and served as deputy minister until 1953. Imprisoned several times for his anti-Shah activities, he rose to the deputy leadership of the National Front in 1979. That same year (January-February) he served as prime minister and chairman of the Regency Council, only to resign upon the return of the Ayatollah Khomeini (qv). In exile in Paris, he became the leader of the National Movement of Iranian Resistance. After two unsuccessful assassination attempts against his life, Bakhtiar was finally stabbed to death in his home by unknown assailants on 6 August 1991.

Bakkar Mosque. *See* Lebanon.

al-Bakr, Ahmed (Ahmad) Hassan. (b. 1914, Takrit, Mesopotamia—d. 4 October 1982, Baghdad, Iraq) After studying to be a teacher, Bakr joined the army in 1938, only to retire three years later because of his involvement in the Rashid Ali affair. He returned to active duty just before the July 1958 uprising led by General Abdul Karim al-Kassem (qv), which overthrew the Iraqi monarchy. Bakr became a member of the Baath Party after he became disillusioned with the new regime. In February 1963, because of the part he played in another coup that toppled the Kassem government, Bakr was named vice president. In November of that same year, however, a counter-coup, led by Field Marshal Abd as-Salam Arif, forced the Baath government out of power. Bakr again went into retirement, where he remained until 1965 when, in September, Arif was killed in a plane crash. After the seizure of power by Arif's brother, Abdul Rahman Arif (qv), Bakr began plotting and, in 1968, overthrew Arif and took power himself. A bloody purge followed, which was especially hard on the communists, whom he had only recently embraced as allies. He did negotiate with the Kurds in the north of the country and made a temporary peace with them until he was able to gain a rapproachment with the Shah of Iran, which led to the defeat of the Kurdish rebellion. By 1976, in failing health, Bakr had ceded most of his power to his cousin Saddam Hussein, although he remained the presidental figurehead until 1979. Bakr died of natural causes in 1982.

Bakroush (Bakkush), Abdul Hamid. On 17 November 1984, the Egyptian government announced it had foiled a Libyan attempt to assassinate the former Libyan prime minister, Abdul Hamid Bakroush, an anti-Qaddafi (qv) Libyan living in Egypt. The Egyptians arrested four Libyans, whom they forced to send false information to the Libyan Embassy in Malta to the effect that they had been successful in their mission. The elaborate ruse worked, as the Libyan government formally announced that one of its suicide teams had liquidated another one of the "enemies of the revolution."

Balaguer y Ricardo, Joaquin Vidella. (b. 1 September 1907, Villa Bisono, Dominican Republic) Balaguer taught law at the University of Santo Domingo from 1938 until his appointment as ambassador to Colombia and Mexico in the 1940s. Thereafter, he entered politics, serving in the government of the dictator Rafael Trujillo. When Trujillo was assassinated in 1961, Balaguer fled to the United States (1962) where he remained in exile until 1965, when he returned as the leader of the Christian Social Reform Party (PRSC) to win the nation's presidency (1966). He served three terms (1970, 1974) as president and left office. The subsequent economic failures of the DominicanRevolutionary Party (PRD) leadership brought Balaguer and the PRSC back to power in 1986. He was reelected in 1990, and in 1995 he narrowly won his seventh term as president in 1995 amid charges of flagrant election fraud.

Balewa, Sir Abubakar Tafawa. (b. 1912, Bauchi, Northern Nigeria—d. January 1966, Ifo, Nigeria) Educated in Great Britain, Balewa entered politics in 1947 as a Northern People's Congress member of the Nigerian Federal Assembly. He became minister of works in 1952, and of transportation in 1953. He was elected prime minister in 1957 and was knighted by the British crown when Nigeria received its independence in 1960. During a military uprising in 1966, Balewa was assassinated. *See* Nigeria.

Bali. *See* Indonesia.

Balkan Alliance. A treaty that was signed in 1953-1954, the Balkan Alliance allied Greece, Turkey and Yugoslavia against the threat of attack by or through Bulgaria. By the terms of the treaty, an attack on any member of the entente would be considered an attack on all three. This treaty is a restatement of a similar agreement reached in 1934 that included all of the 1953 signatories and Romania against an attack by another Balkan nation.

Balkans. *See* individual countries. *Reading*: John E. Jessup, *Balkan Military History: A Bibliography* (1986).

Ballivan, Hugo. On 16 May 1951, a military junta led by General Hugo Ballivan forced the resignation of Bolivian president Mamerto Urriolagoita (qv) Ballivan then assumed power as the head of a three-man military junta. On 11 April 1952, the junta was in turn ousted after a three-day revolt led by the National Revolutionary Movement (MNR) (qv).

Baluchistan. *See* Pakistan.

Baluza. *See* Israel.

Balzano Province. *See* Italy.

Banda, Hastings Kazumu (b. 1905, Nyasaland) Educated first in philosophy (c. 1920) in South Africa, Banda also worked as a clerk at the Witwatersrand gold mines. Banda then studied history and political science at the universities of Indiana and Chicago before entering medicine at Meharry Medical College at Nashville, Tennessee, He then moved to Edinburgh, Scotland, where he graduated as a physician in 1941. After practicing medicine in England until 1955, he returned to his native soil circuitously via Ghana, arriving in Nyasaland (later Malawi) in 1958 to take up the struggle against the ruling Central African Federation, a cause he had espoused in England. After taking up the leadership of the Malawi African Congress Party, he was arrested and jailed in 1959. In 1961, he became minister of natural resources and in 1963, he became prime minister. He was elected president of the new independent Republic of Malawi in 1966 and president for life in 1971. His one-man rule was not without opposition, but he always managed to steer a foreign policy course that has left his country relatively untouched by much of the turmoil in Africa. However, an economic crisis developed in the late 1970s that created a greater differentiation among the social stratas in Malawi. This situation was worsened by Banda's open support of Renamo, the Mozambican insurgency movement, and the stream of Mozambican refugees which flowed into the country. By the early 1990s the situation in Malawi had reached a point where Banda was forced to acknowledge a multiparty political system. The ailing Banda was turned out of office in 1994 and was arrested in January 1995 on charges of having murdered three of his cabinet minister in 1983. The trial against Banda finally began without his attendance as his age (90) and failing health demanded his absence.

Bandar Abbas. *See* Iran.

Bandaranaike, Sirimavo Ratwatte Dias. (b. 17 April 1916, Ratnapura, Ceylon) Born the daughter of aristocratic Buddhist parents involved in the government of a district in Ceylon, Bandaranaike's early education was, however, received in Roman Catholic convents. She was married in 1940 to Solomon West Ridgeway Dias Bandaranaike, who was prime minister in 1956 and was assassinated by a Buddhist monk in September 1959. She entered politics as a leader of a radical party associated with communist and Trotskyite groups. Madame Bandaranaike served as prime minister of Sri Lanka from 1960 to1965 and from 1970 to1977. She was the first woman in the world to ever hold that office. During her first term, she nationalized most British and American petroleum works, the private schools in her country, and part of the rubber industry. A number of her popular social reforms were abrogated by her successor, Dudley Senanayake (1965-1970). When she again became prime minister, she reintroduced much of her earlier social program. Although she was active in the Columbo conference (1962) aimed at solving the Sino-Indian border dispute, Madame Bandaranaike steered her country toward alignment with the Soviet bloc, all the while claiming she was leading her country toward independence and social freedom. In July 1977, however, her party lost most of its popular support, and her government was turned out. The Sri Lankan parliament subsequently stripped her of her rights and barred her from reentering politics (1980). Most of her rights were returned when she received a presidential pardon in 1986.

Bandar Khomeini. *See* Iran.

Bandung Conference. A 1955 conference held in Bandung, Java, of 29 African and Asian nations opposed to colonialism.

Bangkok. *See* Thailand.

Bangladesh. The state of Bangladesh came into being in 1971, following a civil war that brought about the separation of East and West Pakistan and the independence of the new state, which is virtually surrounded by India except on the south, where it rests upon the Bay of Bengal, and at the southeastern corner of its border, which touches Burma. Bangladesh has been the scene of a number of coup attempts since its independence. One took place in 1982–1983, culminating in a series of moves by which General Hossein Ershad (qv) became president. He remained in office through period of internal turmoil until December 1990, when he was finally forced to step down. In February 1991, a new government was installed with Begum Khaleda Zia ur-Rahman as prime minister. In 1972, a treaty of friendship and mutual defense was signed with India. The abject poverty of the country, however, has caused periods of strained relations with its giant neighbor as throngs of its citizens have attempted to emigrate out of the country. Bangladesh contiues to be one of the most heavily populated and economically distressed countries in the world with violent anti-government protests taking place in 1994–1995. *See* Pakistan. *Reading:* B. L. C. Johnson, *Bangladesh* (2nd ed.) (1982); Subrata Chowdhury, *The Genesis of Bangladesh* (1972).

Bangui. *See* Central African Republic.

Bangura, John. On 18 April 1968, a group of noncommissioned officers overthrewthe Sierra Leone government of Andrew Juxton-Smith (qv) in what became known as the "Sergeant's Revolt." In his place, Colonel John Bangura, an officer in exile, was installed as prime minister. His tenure was marked by violence, which resulted in a state of emergency being declared in November

1968 that lasted until March 1969. He was replaced in 1969 by Siaka Stevens (qv).

Banias (Baniyas). *See* Syria.

Bani-Sadr, Abohassan. (b. 22 March 1933, Hamadan, Adadan, Iran) Born the son of Ayatollah Sayed Nasrollah Bani-Sadr, Abohassan was educated in Paris at the Sorbonne and at the University of Tehran, where he studied theology and economics. He was a supporter of Prime Minister Mossadeq (qv) (1951-1953) and soon became a member of the anti-Shah underground movement (1953). He was imprisoned during the rioting in 1963 that followed the Shah's land reforms. Bani-Sadr went into exile (1963) in France, where he taught at the Sorbonne. He became associated with and an ardent follower of the Ayatollah Ruhollah Khomeini and returned to Iran after the overthrow of the Shah in 1979. A member of Khomeini's Revolutionary Council and a member of the Supervisory Board of the Central Bank of Iran (1979-1981), he was appointed minister of economic and financial affairs in 1979. While retaining that post, he was appointed acting foreign minister in November 1979. Although he was dismissed from that post, he served as president of Iran from 1980 to1981. During that period, he twice escaped death in helicopter crashes. On 21 June 1981, Bani-Sadr was replaced as president; he had again fled to France before he could be arrested. In France, he formed, along with Massoud Rajavi, the National Council of Resistance against the Khomeini regime. He was made the leader of the Mujaheddin Kalq and leader of the Democratic Party of Kurdistan. He subsequently associated himself with numerous other resistance groups.

Ban Me Thuot (Lac Giao). *See* Vietnam.

Banzer-Suarez, Hugo. (b. 10 May 1926, Santa Cruz Province, Bolivia) Banzer was educated in Bolivian and U.S. military schools. He became president of Bolivia in August 1971, after participating in an antileftist military coup that overthrew the government of General Juan Jose Torres Gonzales (qv). More than 100 were killed in fighting that took place as the army rallied to the new authority. One of Banzer's first acts in office was to reestablish close ties with the United States, ties that had deteriorated during the two preceding administrations. In 1977, after six years in office, Banzer set the date for elections, 9 July 1978, to select his replacement, as he stated he would not run again. Force had to be used in that same year to surpress popular unrest in the country. In July 1978, Juan Pereda Asbún (qv) was elected, but voting irregularities were discovered; Pereda did not take office until 21 July, when a coup forced Banzer to resign. Pereda lasted only to 24 November. Banzer, in the meantime, indicated he would run again in the next election. He ran in the 1979 election, but he did not win a majority. Another candidate, Walter Guevara Arze, was chosen, according to Bolivian law, by the Congress of Deputies and the Senate.

Bao Dai. (b. 1913, Hue, Indochina) Born the son of Emperor Khai Dai, Bao Dai ruled as emperor of Annam from 1932 until 1945. With the reinstitution of French control after World War II, he renounced his hereditary title and went into luxurious exile abroad. In 1949, he returned to Saigon as the chief of state within the French Union. He was ousted from power in 1955, before the Republic of Vietnam was declared, and returned to his luxurious exile in France.

Barcelona. *See* Spain.

Barikot. *See* Afghanistan.

Bar-Lev, Haim. (b. 1924, Austria) General Bar-Lev was educated at the Mikhev Agricultural School in Palestine and at Columbia University in New York, where he studied in the School of Economics and Administration (1961). In 1942 in Palestine, he joined the Israeli Palmach, a quasimilitary militia dedicated to the Israeli cause. From 1942 until 1947 he commanded successively larger military formations, including the Eighth Regiment of the Nevev Brigade, and a training base for non-command-line Palmach officers. In 1948, he was sequentially the operations officer for Israeli forces and the commander of armored forces. From 1949 until 1952, he served as an instructor and as the commander of the Battalion Commanders School, and from 1952 until 1953 as the chief of staff of the Northern Command. He then became the commander of the Givati Brigade (1954-1955); and the director of the General Headquarters' Training Division (1956). During the Sinai Campaign he fought as the commander of an armored brigade and as the commander, armored forces (1957-1961). For the next three years he toured Western European and U.S. military installations, attended Columbia University and visited U.S. military bases in the Philippines, Japan, Thailand and the Republic of Vietnam. In 1964 he was appointed chief of operations and in 1967 deputy chief of staff of the Israeli Defense Forces. In 1968 he became chief of staff. In 1972 he was appointed minister of commerce and industry until 1977, when he was elected to the Knesset (Senate). He became the secretary general of the Labor Party in 1978 and minister of police affairs after September 1984.

Bar-Lev Line. Named for Haim Bar-Lev (qv), the Bar-Lev Line was an Israeli military position established on the east bank of the Suez Canal in 1973.

Barrientos y Ortuna, Rene. (b. 30 May 1919, Tunary, Cochabamba, Bolivia—d. 27 April 1969, near Tocopaya, Bolivia) Serving as the chief of the Bolivian air forces from the 1950s, Barrientos led the coup that ousted the government of Victor Pas Estenssoro (qv). He then served as co-president with General Alfredo Ovando Candia (qv) until 1964, when he became sole president of his country. His death came when the helicopter in which he was flying crashed into a high-tension wire, killing all on board.

Baruch, Bernard M(annes). (b. 19 August 1870, Camden, South Carolina—d. 20 June 1965, New York City) Known as the "advisor of presidents," Bernard Baruch began his career as an office boy after his graduation from the City College of New York (CCNY) in 1889. He worked for a time for a linen company and then went to Wall Street, where over the years he amassed a considerable fortune in the market. His philanthropic work made him a popular figure, and in 1916 he was appointed to the advisory council on national defense. He later became the director of the War Industries Board. After that time, Baruch's counsel was sought by succeeding presidents until after World War II.

Even though he was a close friend of Franklin Roosevelt and often advised him, FDR did not appoint Baruch to any other public office after he refused to become the war mobilization director. He served instead as special advisor to the Director of Economic Stabilization, James F. Byrnes. He went along as Byrnes' advisor when Byrnes took the job at War Mobilization that had been originally offered to him. He had been one of FDR's original "brain trust" although he was often at odds with the president over domestic policies in the "New Deal." Another of his close friends was Winston Churchill, with whom he maintained a lively correspondence before, during and after the war. The Baruch Plan came into being when he was appointed the US delegate to the United Nations Atomic Energy Commission by Harry Truman (qv). Baruch set forth a program for international control of atomic energy under the UN. The Soviets vetoed the plan. Baruch died at age 95, after having served every president from Woodrow Wilson to John F. Kennedy.

al-Barzani, Mullah Mustafa. (b. 1902 (?), Sulaymaniyah, Kirkuk Province, Iraq —d. 2 March 1979, Washington, DC) Born the son of a Mesopotamian landlord, Barzani became leader of the Kurdish freedom movement upon the death of his brother, Sheikh Ahmed (late 1930s). For more than four decades, this movement had attempted the formation of an independent state of Kurdistan that would have incorporated over 12 million Kurds living in Iraq, Iran, Turkey and the USSR. In 1945, he became the leader of the Kurdish Democratic Party (KDP). After an internal struggle against Qazi Mohammed, Barzani emerged as president of the short-lived, Soviet-supported a Kurdish Republic of Mahabad (January, 1946) in northern Iran. The withdrawal of Soviet forces brought about the immediate demise of the Kurdish state and its reoccupation by Iran. At that point, Barzani fled to the Soviet Union (Azerbaijan), where he remained until 1958. The Iraqi revolution led by Abd al-Karim Kassem (qv) allowed Barzani's return to Iraq, but he was not allowed outside the limits of Baghdad. He rejected a 1960 plan that would have established a Kurdish homeland in northern Iraq. Thereafter, Barzani led a decade-long armed insurgency against Iraqi authority that lasted until a cease-fire was arranged with Iraqi President Ahmed Hassan al-Bakr (qv) on 11 March 1970. In 1974, Barzani repudiated another Iraqi offer of Kurdish autonomy and ordered his forces to again take up the fight against the central government. With Iranian support, Barzani's forces gained an initial advantage until Iraq renounced its territorial demands against Iran in March 1975. With that issue settled, Iran withdrew its aid. When the Kurds were overrun by Iraq, Barzani was into exile, first in Tehran, and then in the U.S., where he was granted asylum. Ill since 1974, Barzani died of a heart attack while undergoing lung cancer therapy in Washington, DC. *Reading:* Edgar O'Ballance, *The Kurdish Struggle, 1920–94* (1996).

Basque Anti-Capitalist Autonomous Commandos. On 22 April 1983, a group calling itself the Basque Anticapitalist Autonomous Commandos blew up a Michelin Tire warehouse in the Basque region of Spain. This incident, and the Basque Fatherland (qv) incident were part of the Basque separatist campaign.

Basque Fatherland. On 29 June 1985, terrorist gunmen assassinated Vice Admiral Fausto Escrigas Estrada, the Spanish director general of defense policy, in Madrid. The Basque Fatherland group and another group known as the Liberty-Military Wing both claimed responsibility for the attack. On 9 September 1985, both groups again claimed responsibility when a car bomb detonated in Madrid, injuring 18 members of the Spanish Civil Guard. An American was also at the scene and died of his injuries. There was evidence that the two groups were in fact one and the same.

Basra (Al Basrah). *See* Iraq.

Basutoland. *See* Lesotho.

Batangan Peninsula. *See* Vietnam.

Batavia. *See* Jakarta.

Batholomew, Reginald. The United States ambassador in Lebanon in 1983–1984, Bartholomew was among those injured when a terrorist suicide attack seriously damaged the U.S. Embassy Annex in East Beirut on 20 September 1984. At least 3,000 pounds of explosive carried in a lorry were detonated at the US Embassy compound gate. The Islamic Jihad claimed credit fot the attack, which killed 14 people (two Americans) and injured 70 more, including Batholomew and 19 other Americans.

Batista (y Zaldivar), Fulgencio. (b. 16 January 1901, Banes, Oriente Province, d. 6 August 1973, Guadalmina, Spain) Born the son of a laborer, Bastista took part in the army-led overthrow of President Machado on 4 September 1933. During the coup preparations he promoted was from sergeant major to colonel and remained close to the power center until his own election as president in 1940. As he could not succeed himself, he left office in 1944. When his chosen successor failed to win the election, he went into voluntary exile in Florida and remained there until 1948, when he returned to Cuba. Shortly before the 1952 elections he led the coup against President Prio and seized power for himself. His dictatorship remained in power until it was overthrown by Fidel Castro on 1 January 1959. He fled into exile in the Dominican Republic and later settled on Portuguese Madeira and finally in Spain, where he died in 1973. *Reading:* Jay Mallin, *Fulgencio Batista: Ousted Cuban Dictator* (1974).

Battle of Ahmadiya. *See* Israel.

Battle of Hwai Hai. *See* China.

Battle of Quang Tri City. *See* Vietnam.

Battle of Rafid. *See* Israel.

Battle of Taejon. *See* Korea.

Battle of the Chinese Farm. *See* Israel.

Ba Tu (Three Selves). On 15 November 1969, President Nguyen Van Thieu (qv) of the Republic of Vietnam repudiated the American term "Vietnamization" and directed that henceforth the program designed to turn the war over to the South Vietnamese would be called "Ba Tu." *See* Vietnamization.

Bavaria. *See* Germany.

Bayhan. *See* Yemen.

Bay of Pigs (*Bahia de los Cochinos*). A bay on the southern coast of Cuba that was the site of the disasterous anti-Castro invasion of 17 April 1961, where a force of 1,500 U.S.-trained Cuban freedom fighters was destroyed because the U.S. failed to próvide the promised aerial and naval gunfire support necessary to complete the operation. *Reading*: Trumbull Higgins, *The Perfect Failure: Kennedy, Eisenhower, and the CIA at the Bay of Pigs* (1989); S.L.A. Marshall, *JFK Plus BOP (Bay of Pigs; The Inside Story of the Bay of Pigs)* (1992); Luis Aguilar, *Operation Zapata: the Ultrasensitive Report and Testimony of the Board of Inquiry on the Bay of Pigs* (1981).

Bay of Tonkin. *See* Vietnam.

Beagle Channel. The Beagle Channel is part of the waterway system in the Tierra del Fuego archipelago separated from the southernmost tip of the South American mainland by the Straits of Magellan. The east-west-oriented Beagle Channel is part of the boundary settlement agreed upon in 1881 by Chile and Argentina and separates the main island of Terra del Fuego from the two smaller islands of Hoste and Navarino to the south. The Beagle Islands (Lennox, Nueva and Picton) became the focus of the Beagle Channel incident when they were awarded to Chile by an arbitration court of the International Court of Justice in May 1977, which redefined the 1881 agreement. Argentina immediately stated it did not accept the decision and would use the nine months the court had authorized to determine its position in the case. Argentina's objections to the decision and Chile's insistence on adherence to it were both based on strong indications of large off-shore oil deposits, plus the obvious wealth in fishing and minerals, in the region. There were numerous claims and counterclaims by both sides concerning incursions into what each claimed as sovereign territory. On 25 January 1978, Argentina officially rejected the arbitration decision. A new 1800-day period for negotiation was established in February and ended in November without success. By December 1978, war appeared imminent as both sides moved military ground and naval forces into the region. On 23 December, however, both sides accepted the intervention of the Vatican. Pope John Paul II (qv) designated Antonio Cardinal Samorè as his representative in the issue. These decisions were reinforced by a joint declaration issued on 8 January 1979 that the two sides would use military force to settle the matter and that each accepted papal intervention. There followed a long period of tension as the Pope's representative carefully worked out a settlement. A treaty designed to bind both sides to settle the Beagle Channel dispute by peaceful means was initialed at the Vatican on 28 January 1984. The formal treaty that gave the Beagle Islands to Chile was signed at the Vatican on 29 November 1984.

Beaumont Castle. A twelfth century Crusader fortress (keep) located in Arnun in southern Lebanon, Beaumont Castle was used in 1980 by Palestinian guerrillas and was first attacked by Israeli forces on 25 August 1980. On a later operation in Lebanon, Israeli forces captured the fortification on 7 June 1982.

Bechuanaland. *See* Botswana.

Beddawi. *See* Lebanon.

Beersheeba (Be'er Sheva). *See* Israel.

Begin, Menachem. (b. 1913, Brest-Litovsk, East Prussia—d. 8 March 1992, Israel) After studying law at the University of Warsaw, Begin became active in the Zionist movement and became the leader of the Betar Zionist group in Poland in 1935. When the Nazis invaded Poland in 1939, Begin fled to Lithuania, only to be arrested by Soviet authorities. After being held for two years, Begin was freed in 1941 and immediately joined the Free Polish Army. He was sent to Palestine in 1942 and released from the army in 1943. He then joined the Israeli terrorist organization Irgun Zvai Leumi, where he soon was credited with a number of terrorist acts including the bombing of the King George Hotel in Jerusalem. In 1948 he founded the right-wing Herut Freedom Movement and served three successive terms as a member of the Knesset (Senate). In 1973, Begin helped weld together and lead three right-wing political groups to form the Likud Front, which succeeding in ousting the Israel Labor Party in 1977. Begin formed a new government and became prime minister. He was reelected to that post in 1981. Although known as a hard-liner in dealing with Arab questions, he sought a relaxation of regional tensions through a series of conferences (Jerusalem in 1977, Camp David in1978). In 1978, Begin and Egyptian president Anwar Sadat (qv) were awarded the Nobel Peace Prize. Begin retired from political life in 1983. Thereafter, he generally refused to be interviewed about his public life. He suffered a heart attack and died in retirement in Israel on 8 March 1992. *Reading:* Harry Zvi Hurwitz & Patrick R. Denker, eds., *Begin: A Portrait* (1994).

Beheshti, Ayatollah Mohammad Hossein. (b. 1929, Isfahan, Iran—d. 28 June 1981, Tehran, Iran) A long-time member of the religiously oriented Islamic Republican Party (IRP), Beheshti was appointed by the Ayatollah Ruhollah Khomeini as a member of the ruling Islamic Revolutionary Council on 3 February 1979 and later became its first secretary. When the Majlis (Parliament) was inaugurated on 28 May 1980, Beheshti became the leader of the IRP. During the hostage crisis with the U.S., Beheshti is reputed to have been a key figure and one of the architects of the plan. He was also instrumental in the ouster of President Abolhassan Bani-Sadr in 1981. He and 71 others were killed in a bomb explosion at a party meeting in Tehran on 28 June 1981.

Beihl, Eugen. On 1 December 1970, Beihl, the West German Honorary Consul in San Sabastian, Spain, was kidnapped by Basque terrorists of the *Euzkadi to Azkatasuna* (ETA) (qv). For his release, the ETA demanded the release of 16 ETA members who were to be tried by a military court on 3 December. The Basques were tried on schedule, but the sentences were withheld as the Spanish government worked for Beihl's release. He was released unharmed on 24 December. The sentences were then announced (six to be executed; nine given long terms in prison; one, a woman acquitted. The death sentences were then commuted to 30-year jail sentences.

Beilen. *See* Netherlands.

Beira-Mutare Pipeline. This petroleum pipeline runs between the port city of Beira in Mozambique and Mutare in Zimbabwe, a distance of approximately 150 miles. Antigovernment guerrillas blew up the pipeline on 5 January 1983, even though it and an adjacent railroad were protected by thousands of troops from Mozambique and Zimbabwe.

Beirset Military Airfield. *See* Belgium.

Beirut (Beyrouth, Bayrut). The capital and chief port city of Lebanon, Beirut once considered one of the most beautiful cities in the world, is located on St. George's Bay on the north side of a point of land jutting into the eastern Mediterranean Sea. Beirut was founded by the Phoenicians and was known from the early fifteenth century, B.C. It was an important port in Greek and Roman times. Beirut was captured by the Arabs in 635 A.D. and was the locale of many battles during the Crusades. Later captured by the Ottoman Turks, it was ruled, in the Turkish custom, by native Druse, a people practicing Islam with Christian overtones, but who paid homage to the Sublime Porte. The original plan of the city almost totally disappeared with modernization during the nineteenth century. During World War I, the port fell into disrepair, and the town in 1918 was variously held by British, Arab and French forces. Under French mandate Beirut became the capital city of Lebanon in 1920 . During World War II, control of the city fell to the Free French and the British. In the years between 1920 and 1958, Beirut became the trade and financial center of the Middle East. Foreign capital and culture abounded and the American University, founded in 1966, became one of the leading educational institutions in the Middle East. In 1958, however, factional strife began that was primarily focused on conflict between Christian and Muslim elements in the city. In the process, the city was divided between Christian East Beirut, where several groups held various quarters, including the Phalangist group whose command post was in the Holiday Inn, and the western part of the city held by a multitude of Muslim factions. The Syrians intervened in 1976 and virtually occupied the city, bringing a new set of problems to the Christian enclave. In addition, Palestinian Muslim refugees escaping from Israel flocked to Lebanon. Until even more fighting between Israeli and factional forces further destroyed the country and the city, Beirut was looked upon by many as the headquarters of the PLO. In 1982, Israeli military pressure forced the PLO to evacuate the city. The following year, serious fighting once again broke out and has continued at various levels ever since, although the 1990s seems to be a quiet period thus far. In 1973 (19 October), for instance, five Arab terrorists seized the Bank of America and held 40 hostages, demanding $10 million dollars to support the Arab war against Israel. Lebanese army troops and police stormed the building, killing two terrorists and one of the hostages. In the 1980s, Beirut became the locus of numerous terrorist kidnappings, mostly with the approval of Iranian Shi'ite leaders and of major terrorist bombing attacks, the most notable of which was the attack on the American Embassy and the French airborne battalion's barracks in October 1983, in which almost 300 military personnel assigned to peacekeeping forces billeted at the two locations were killed by Muslim Arab fanatics . Allied peacekeeping forces had been introduced into Lebanon under a UN mandate (1982).One of their primary mission was to insure that the International Airport, subjected to relentless shelling by Druze artillery, remained open. The carnage and destruction wreaked in Beirut by the years of warfare, according to most authorities, will take decades to correct once a true peace is finally restored. *Reading:* Michael Jansen, *The Battle of Beirut: Why Israel Invaded Lebanon* (1983); Anthony McDermott & Skell Skjelsbaek, eds., *The Multinational Force in Beirut, 1982–1984* (1991); Selim Nassib, *Beirut: Frontline Story* (1983).

Beit Shean. *See* Israel.

Beja. *See* Portugal.

Bekaa (Beqaa) Valley. *See* Lebanon.

Belaúnde Terry, Fernando. (b. 7 October 1912, Lima, Peru) Born into a diplomatic and political family, Belaúnde Terry entered politics and was serving in the Chamber of Deputies, when the government his father headed was overthrown on 29 October 1948. In 1956, he founded the Popular Action Party and began his own campaign for the nation's leadership. He was elected president in 1963. Belaúnde Terry was still the president of Peru when his government was deposed on 3 October 1968, in a bloodless military coup led by the army's chief of staff, Major General Juan Velasco Alvarado (qv). On 18 May 1980 Belaúnde returned from exile and won the first presidential election held in Peru since 1968. On 28 July 1985, he turned over the presidency to Alan Garcia Perez in the first orderly transfer of power in 40 years.

Belenko, Victor Ivanovich. On 6 September 1976, Soviet Air Force lieutenant Victor I. Belenko flew his Soviet-built MiG-25 fighter aircraft out of Soviet airspace and landed without incident at Hakodate civil airport on the northern island of Hokkaido, Japan. Asking for political asylum, Belenko was allowed to enter the United States on 9 September under an order signed by President Gerald Ford. Belenko's aircraft was minutely disassembled by American and Japanese intelligence experts and was eventually returned to the Soviet Union in crates with each part neatly packed and labeled.

Belfast. *See* Northern Ireland.

Belgian Congo. *See* Zaire, Democratic Republic of Congo, Congo-Kinshasa and Congo (Brazzaville).

Belgium. A country in northern Europe, Belgium occupies a strategically important location with the North Sea to the west, France to the south, The Netherlands to the north and Germany and Luxembourg to the east. The capital city is Brussels. Belgium began as a Roman province (Gallia Belgica) and was populated by tribes of predominantly Celtic origin. Belgium was later a part of Charlemagne's empire. It was then subjected first to Spain, then to Austria, France and, finally, The Netherlands, to whom Belgium remained tied until 1830, when a rebellion overthrew William of Orange. On 20 January 1831, Belgium became independent, but not free of conflict. In 1853, for instance, after the coup d'etat that put Napoleon III on the throne of France, the liberal press of Belgium carried on a relentless campaign against the French neighbor. The reaction from Paris forced Belgium to undertake the fortification of some of its more strategically important regions. Trouble with France continued, and Napoleon III's attempt at the annexation of the Duchy of Luxembourg in 1863 further exacerbated the situation, even though the French plan failed. When the Franco-Prussian War of 1870 broke out, Belgium mobilized and prepared to fight any invader, determined as it was to maintain its neutrality. France's defeat in that war and the subsequent ascendancy of Germany forced Belgium to expend hugh amounts to further strengthen the defenses of its frontiers. This situation continued until the outbreak of World War I, when Belgium, still desiring neutrality, found itself in the path of the German plan for the conquest of France (Schlieffen Plan). On 2 August, German forces crossed into Luxembourg. Two days later, Belgium itself was invaded. The Imperial German army treated the Belgians poorly; many died or were deported to labor camps. The government was forced to flee to France. The aftermath of the armisticebrought changes in Belgium's status that allowed a defensive alliance with France. In 1922, the Belgium–Luxembourg Economic Union was formed. This would be surplanted after World War II by the Benelux countries (Belgium, the Netherlands and Luxembourg) becoming three of the first six signatories on the European Economic Community (EEC) (1958). On 10 May 1940, after repeated assurances that Hitler would honor Belgian sovereignty, Nazi forces crossed the border. Britain and France honored their commitments and moved troops into the beleaguered country. The following 18 days of heavy fighting saw overwhelming German forces smash the Allied and Belgian defenders and set the stage for the Allied withdrawal over the beaches at Dunkerque (Dunkirk). Belgium remained occupied by the Nazis for four years, with the king interned at Stuyvenberg Castle at Laeken. Resistance to the occupation was prevalent throughout the country. The liberation of Belgium began on 3 September 1944, when Allied ground forces entered the country and were supported by an underground army of mixed quality. After the war, Belgium suffered through a period of communist activity aimed at turning the government away from the West. When this failed, Belgium emerged as a strong member of the Benelux Union, the United Nations, and NATO. Belgium still had to suffer from the dissolution of its relatively small but important overseas empire, principally the Belgian Congo, and from the devisive problem of dual language. In 1967, following France's withdrawal from the alliance, NATO headquarters moved to Mons, outside of Brussels. Some tensions have affected Belgium, primarily that of the language division between the Flemish- and Walloon-speaking populations. This led to some violence and massive strikes, but the issue was settled peacefully in 1962–1963 by an act of Parliament which designated specific boundaries between the two language areas. This led to further adjustments that created a federal state that appeared to satisfy most of the citizenry. King Baudoun, one of the chief architects of the language *rapprochement*, died on 31 July 1993. The accession of Albert to the throne promised the continuation of better than average peaceful conditions within Belgium. *Reading*: Robert Pateman, *Belgium* (Cultures of the World) (1966); Marina Boudart et al, *Modern Belgium* (1990); Donald Cowie, *Belgium: The Land and the People* (1977).

Belgrade (Beograd). *See* Yugoslavia.

Belgrano. *See* Falkland Islands.

Belize. Formerly British Honduras, Belize is a small country on the southern edge of the Yucatan Peninsula. Belize is bordered on the north by Mexico and on the west and south by Guatemala; to the east is the Gulf of Honduras and the northern Caribbean. The capital city is Belmopan; the principal port is Belize City. It was first occupied by English hardwood loggers in the seventeenth century and became a British Colony in 1884. In 1964, it became a self-governing member of the Commonwealth and changed its name to Belize in 1973. In 1975, British airborne forces were deployed to Belize when Guatemala threatened to annex the country. In subsequent years. Other countries also provided forces to insure the territorial integrity of the tiny country. Belize achieved full independence within the Commonwealth in 1981. Guatemala has refused to recognize the country, and British troops have remained there since its independence to insure its sovereignty. Belize is a member of the United Nations and the Organization of American States. *Reading*: Peggy Wright & Brian E. Coutts, *Belize* (World Bibliography Series, vol. 21) (1993); Tim L. Miller, *Guyana and Belize: Country Studies*. (DA Area Handbook) (1993).

Bem Square. *See* Hungary.

Ben Bella, Achmed. (b. 1918, Maghnia, Algeria) After service in the French army in World War II, Ben Bella organized an extremist Algerian group to defy French rule in his country in 1947. Between 1948–1950, he helped found the *Organization Speciale* (OS) and led an armed revolt against the French. He robbed a post office in 1950 to keep the OS operating, but was arrested and jailed for the crime. He escaped from prison in 1952. Ben Bella was again arrested in 1956 and charged with, among other things, gun-running. This time, he spent six years in jail. When released, he expounded his ideology of traditionalist Muslim fundamentalism mixed with socialism. In 1962, when Algeria received its independence from France, he became its first prime minister. He was elected president of the new-independent state in 1963, but was overthrown in an army-led coup (*see* Boumedienne) in 1965 and was held in isolation for 14 years. In 1979, he was "released" into house arrest until 30 October 1980, when he was sent into exile. He was allowed to return to Algeria in September 1990, under a general amnesty. *See* Algeria.

Benelux Nations. Also known as the Low Countries and consisting of Belgium, the Netherlands and Luxembourg, Benelux is an economic union that was first initialed on 5 September 1944. The agreement was later modified by the Hague Protocol of 14 March 1947 and went into full effect in 1948. The concept of the Benelux agreement was not altered by an earlier economic agreement between

Belgium and Luxembourg that was signed in 1921. The Benelux agreement is considered a forerunner of the much more encompassing European Economic Community (EEC) plan formed in 1958. Before the three countries joined the EEC, their ministers had established the Benelux Economic Union in 1960.

Benes, Edward .(Edvard). (b.28 May 1884, Kozlany, NW Bohemia—d. 3 September 1948, Sezimovo, Czechoslovakia) Born the tenth child of a farmer, Benes was well educated, having studied law and other social sciences in Prague, Paris and Dijon (1908). Doctor Benes became a lecturer at the Prague Commercial Academy (1909) and, later (1913), a professor of sociology at the University of Prague. When World War I began, he went first to to Paris and then to Switzerland, where he worked with Thomas G. Masaryk, the great Czech nationalist, against the Austrian overlordship of his country. When Masaryk went to London, Benes returned to Paris with Milan Stefanik, the Slovakian nationalist leader. In 1916, when the Czechoslovak National Council was formed, Benes was appointed its secretary general. Near the end of World War I and with the emergence of the new Czechoslovak state (14 October 1918), this group became the first government. From 1918 until 1935 Benes served as foreign minister to the new Czechoslovak state. In 1919, Benes led the Czechoslovak delegation to the Paris peace conference. He also served two years as premier (1921-1922) and led the Czech delegation at the League of Nations. In 1935 he succeeded Masaryk as president of the republic but resigned the office in 1938. In 1941 he assumed the title of president with the government in exile in London following the Nazi occupation of his country. In 1945 he returned to Czechoslovakia via the Soviet Union and was reelected its president in 1946. He again resigned his post following the communist takeover of the country. He died of a broken heart in 1948, following the murder of his lifelong friend, Jan Masaryk, by the Soviets. *Reading:* Igor Lukes, *Czechoslovakia Between Stalin and Hitler: The Diplomacy of Edvard Benes in the 1930s* (1996).

Bengal. *See* India (West Bengal) and Bangladesh (East Bengal).

Ben-Gal, Avigdor. Ben-Gal was the Israeli general who, on 14 April 1980, along with General Emmanuel Erskine, the UN peacekeeping force commander in Lebanon, demanded the immediate withdrawal of the Irish Battalion assigned to the United Nations forces. Hard evidence had been collected that the Irish were aiding Palestinian terrorists.

Bengazi (Benghazi). *See* Libya.

Ben Het Ranger Camp. *See* Vietnam.

Benia. *See* Nigeria.

Benin. Formerly the West African republic of Dahomey, the country became the People's Republic of Benin in 1975, one year after a Marxist takeover of power in that country. As the West African Republic of Dahomey, the nation had gained its independence from France in 1960. In earlier times, the Kingdom of Abomey had gained ascendancy by defeating neighboring tribes. In the late nineteenth century, the region came under French influence and was incorporated into French West Africa in 1904. A series of coups followed the 1960 independence, the last one occurring in 1972, when Colonel Ahmed Kerekou seized power. Two years later, he declared his country a socialist state with a "Marxist-Leninist" ideology. On 16 January 1977, a force of mercenaries, ostensibly trained in Morocco, was airlanded at Cotonou Airport with the mission of overthrowing the Kerekou government. The mercenaries were probably in the pay of ousted president Emile Zinsou (qv) and others. Troops from a number of neighboring states were used to restore order. In 1989, Kerekou declared that socialism was no longer the acceptable doctrine. Two years later, in 1991, Kerekou was defeated by Nicephore Sogio in the first popular election in Benin in 30 years. An army coup against Sogio failed in June 1992. This attempt followed by one month a strike by government workers demanding better pay and other benefits. In July 1992, a mutiny broke out that was tied to the June coup attempt. The mutiny was quelled without bloodshed. An odd clash took place in April 1993, when violence broke out between Muslims and voodoo worshipers following a February voodoo arts conference. Two deaths were reported from the fighting. In 1994, Sogio overrode the National Assembly budget and imposed his own plan, but his plan was declared unconstitutional. The Supreme Court also overturned election results in 13 districts following the March 1995 elections.New elections had to be held to settle the issue. In April 1995, Benin sent troops into Rwanda following a UN call for peacekeeping forces. *Reading:* Chris Allen et al., *Benin/the Congo/Burkina Faso: Economy, Politics and Society.* Marxist Regimes Series (1989); D. Ronen, *Dahomey: Between Tradition and Modernity* (1975).

Ben Slimane. *See* Morocco.

Benti, Teferi. Brigadier General Teferi Benti, the chief of state and chairman of the Provisional Military Administration of Ethiopia, was shot and killed when a gunfight broke out during a meeting of the ruling junta at Mengistu on 3 February 1977. At least six others at the meeting were also killed. Benti had been elected chairman of the revolutionary council on 28 November 1974.

Benyahia, Mohammad Seddik. (b. 1934, Djidjolli, Algeria—d. 4 May 1982, Iran-Iraq border) Benyahia studied law at the University of Algiers where he became the president of the Union of Algerian Muslim Students. He also became an early member of the *Front de Liberation Nationale* (FLN), which opposed French rule in his country. He represented the FLN in Indonesia in 1956 and in London during the Algerian fight for independence. In 1962, he was instrumental in hammering out the Evian Agreement that granted independence to Algeria. He was also involved in the drafting of the FLN's "Tripoli Charter," which established a socialist form of government in the country. He was Algeria's special envoy to Moscow and served in a number of ministries (information, education and finance) before service as foreign minister from 1979 until his death, when his plane was shot down by Iranian antiaircraft during the Iran-Iraq War. Benyahia had helped in gaining the release of the American hostages seized at the U.S. Embassy in Tehran on 4 November 1979.

Berbera. *See* Somalia.

Berembau, Jorge. Jorge Berembau, an Argentian industrialist, was kidnapped and held for ransom by Tupamaro (qv) terrorists in Montevideo, Uruguay, on 14 July 1971. He was released unharmed on 26 November, after an exorbitant ransom was paid.

Beria, Lavrenti Pavlovich. (b. 1899, Mercheuli, Georgia—d. December 1953, Moscow) Born a peasant, Beria began his career as a Bolshevik organizer at a college in Baku in 1917. From 1921 to 1931, he was a member of the secret police (OGPU) in the Caucasus, and he became first secretary of the Georgian Communist Party in 1931. A close friend of Josef Stalin, he was appointer minister of internal affairs of the Soviet Union in 1938, a duty that earned him a reputation as a sinister, ruthless plotter and organizer of forced labor and mass murderer. During World War II he served directly under Stalin as the vice-chairman of the State Defense Council and was given the mostly honorary title of Marshal of the Soviet Union in 1945. Upon Stalin's death in 1953, Beria attempted to seize power but was tharted by his opponents. He was arrested by Marshal Georgi Zhukov, found guilty of treason and executed. *Reading:* Amy Knight, *Beria: Stalin's Lieutenant* (1996); Jean Farrow, tr., *The Beria Affair: The Secret Transcripts of the Meetings Signalling the End of Stalinism* (1992).

Berkeley. *See* "People's Park."

Berlin. *See* El Salvador.

Berlin. *See* Germany.

Bermudez, Francisco Morales. (b. 11 December 1932, Leon, Nicaragua—d.16 February 1991, Managua, Nicaragua) Born into a poor family, Bermudez joined the Nicaraguan army and rose through the ranks to become a colonel during the dictatorship of Anastasio Somoza Debayle (qv). When the Sandinista-led insurrection overthrew Somoza in 1979, Bermudez was serving as the Nicaraguan military attache in Washington, DC. He was able to organize, with substantial U.S. support, a 20,000-man "Contra" force to work against the Marxist Sandinista government. Bermudez became a symbol among the peasantry of the fight against the repressive Sandinista regime and gained wide popular support. In 1990, when the Sandinistas were defeated in 1990 by the National Opposition Union, the Contra movement, many of whom were in Honduras, signalled their willingness to surrender their arms. Bermudez, who maintained a residence in Maimi, Florida, returned to Nicaragua to negotiate an agreement with the new government that would have returned all rights to the Contras. On 16 February 1991, he was assassinated in the parking lot of his hotel. Government officials and Contra leaders both accused the other side of paying professional assassins to kill Bermudez.

Bernadotte, Count Folke. (b. 1895, Stockholm, Sweden - d. 1948, Jerusalem, Palestine) Born the nephew of Sweden's King Gustavus V, Bernadotte was a diplomat who served humanity as a peace negotiator during both world wars. He was the United Nations-appointed negotiator in the Palestine situation and had just presented a partition proposal when he was assassinated by Israeli terrorists.

Berri, Nabih. (b. about 1938, Sierra Leone) Born the son of a Lebanese overseas merchant, Berri returned to Lebanon as a youth and entered Lebanese University in Beirut. After graduation in 1963 he journeyed to Paris to continue his education. He then practiced law in Beirut and aided in the founding of the Amal party within the Shi'ite Islamic movement in 1974. Formerly married to an American, he visited the United States on a number of occasions to visit his children. Berri took over the leadership of Amal after its founder, Imam Musa al-Sadr (qv) disappeared on a visit to Libya in 1978. He was active in the affairs of Amal and worked to change it from an obscure party to an active pro-PLO politicomilitary organization that opposed the partition of Lebanon. He was instrumental in gaining the release of American and French hostages held in Lebanon in 1984 and participated in talks aimed at an early Israeli withdrawal from Lebanon in 1985. Many Shi'ites opposed those talks, and Berri's Amal forces clashed with Christian and other Moslem forces both Sunni and Shi'ite, in Lebanon and with Israeli occupation forces. Although a moderate, Berri was scarred by Amal excesses, but he was still able to maintain a high level of regard among Western associates. In 1989, Berri and Druse leader Walid Jumblatt demanded an enlargement of the National Assembly and a reorganization of the Lebanese army. He remained active, although with a somewhat lower profile, into 1995.

Betancourt, Romulo. (b. 22 February 1908, Guatire, Miranda, Venezuela—d. 28 September 1981, New York City) As a student at the University of Caracas, Betancourt led demonstrations against the dictatorship of Juan Vincente Gomez. For these activities, he was imprisoned and then sent into exile in Costa Rica. There, he joined the Communist Party and secretly returned to Venezuela (1936), where he lived in hiding for the next two years. He was subsequently captured by the authorities, who once again expelled him from the country (1938). In 1941 he was allowed to return to Venezuela and once there founded the *Accion Democratica,* a left-wing but anticommunist political organization. During these years, Betancourt adopted the mantle of a left-wing anticommunist and, in 1945, seized power in a bloody coup d'ctat aimed at the regime of General Medina Angarita. Once installed as president, Betancourt implemented a vigorous democratic and economic reform campaign, but was turned out of office in 1948. His successor's fall to another coup forced Betacourt into a ten-year exile in the U.S., Cuba, Costa Rica and Puerto Rico. While in exile, Betancourt continued to lead the now-outlawed *Accion Democratica* party. When, in 1959, General Marcos Perez Jimenez was thrown out of office, he returned to Venezuela. Later in that year, Betancourt and his party won a stunning victory and served as the elected president from 1959 to1964. He again pressed his reform programs. Upon leaving office in 1964, the impoverished Betancourt moved to Switzerland, where he resided for eight years. In 1972 he returned to Venezuela to continue his struggle for democracy. He died in New York City on 28 September 1982. Venezuela mourned his loss.

Betancur Cuartes, Belisario. (b. 1923, Amaga District, Colombia) Born in extreme poverty, Betancur was able to finish the University of Medellin where he studied architecture and law. Working as a journalist, he became interested in politics. In 1950 he was appointed to the Constituent Assembly as a conservative opponent of President Gustavo Rojas Pinilla (qv). After Rojas Pinilla was forced to resign in May 1957, Betancur was arrested and imprisoned by the ruling military junta. After his release he served in a number of government posts, as ambassador to Spain and as a law professor. He was elected president of Colombia on 30 May 1982. Betancur served as president until 6 August 1986, when he was replaced by a duly-elected successor, Virgilio Barco Vargas.

Bethlehem (Bet Lehem) City and University. *See* Israel.

Betong. *See* Thailand.

Bhindranwale, Sant Jarnail Singh. (b. 1946, Rode Punjab, India—d. 6 June 1984, Amritsar, Punjab, India) Born the son of a farmer and Punjabi Sikh leader, Jarnail trained from the age of five at the orthodox Damdani Taksal Sikh missionary school. There, he became a priest or holy man (*Sant*), and by 1971 he had become the school's chief priest. When his long-time friend and mentor, Sant Kartar Sikh Bhindranwale, died in 1977, he assumed the name of Bhindranwale. He was befriended and encouraged by Sanjay Gandhi, the son of Indira Gandhi, who wished to divide the Sikh Akali Dal movement. To that end, throughout the later 1970s, Jarnail campaigned against the Nirankari Sikhs, calling them heretical. In 1980 he led an armed attack against a group of Nirankaris and became a fugitive after police charged him with murder in the deaths of a number of those attacked in this incident and several others. In 1981 Jarnail called for the establishment of an autonomous Punjab state, to be called Khalistan. This caused a series of bloody Hindu-Sikh confrontations during the early 1980s that brought the central government into the picture. He was arrested by the police, but released in September 1981. On 31 May 1984, Jarnail announced he had taken refuge in the so-called Golden Temple in Amritsar and that he and his followers were amply supplied with food, weapons and supplies. This brought an immediate reaction from Indian security forces who mounted an operation called "Blue Star." Several hundred Sikhs, including Jarnail, were killed in the ensuing battle on 6 June 1984.

Bhiwandi, Bombay. *See* India.

Bhutan (*Druk Yul*). A small, very isolated state lying in the eastern Himalayan mountains between Tibet, and India, Bhutan is an ancient country known more in tradition than in fact. Bhutan is known to have been settled by Tibetans who had driven out opposing Indian tribesmen. From then until the recent past, the country was maintained in a near-primitive and isolated state as a means of protecting it against outsiders. The wheel was not known in Bhutan until twentieth century. Bhutan came under Tibetan rule in the sixteenth century and fell under British influence in the nineteenth. A monarchy was established as a British protectorate in in 1907-1910. The country became independent in 1949 and has since been closely related to Indian affairs. The capital city is Thimpu

(*Tashi-chho Dzang*). The country maintains its old ways, even in the education of its children, who are blocked from exposure to Western ideas. *Reading:* Robert Z. Apte, *Three Kingdoms on the Roof of the World: Bhutan, Nepal, and Ladakh* (1990); Ramesh Dogra, *Bhutan* (World Bibliographical Series, vol. 116) (1991).

Bhutto, Zulfikar Ali. (b. 5 January 1928, Larkana, Sind Province, India—d. 4 April 1979, Rawalpindi, Pakistan) Born the son of a wealthy Sindi aristocrat and landowner, Bhutto received his education at the University of California and at the University of Oxford, England. He became a barrister in London (Middle Temple) and taught international law at Southampton University from 1952 to 1953 before returning to Pakistan to continue teaching. Upon his return, he joined the Muslim League. In 1958 he was appointed minister of commerce in the government of Iskanda Mirza. He continued to serve in that post under the new president, Field Marshal Muhammad Ayub Khan (qv) until he was appointed foreign minister and served from 1963 until 1966. He founded the Pakistan People's Party in 1967 and was jailed on several occasions between 1968 and 1969, for party activities.. After Ayub Khan was deposed by a military coup led by General Yahya Khan (qv). Pakistan suffered a military defeat in a brief war with India and the defection of Bangladesh. Yahya Khan was then forced to hand over power to Bhutto (December, 1971), who served as president, introduced a new Islamic-oriented constitution and, in addition, became prime minister (1973). Although he retained the martial law statute of his predecessor, he did manage a successful reform program that improved life in his country. He was accused of election-rigging by right-wing Islamic factions in the opposition, in his resounding victory in the 1977 election. An army-led coup headed by Lieutenant General Agha Muhammad Zia-al-Haq (qv) ousted him from power. Bhutto was then charged with corruption and conspiring to murder. He was sentenced to death on 18 March 1978, and despite worldwide protest, he refused to ask for clemency after the national supreme court upheld his sentence. Bhutto was executed by hanging on 4 April 1979. *Reading:* Stanley Wolpert, *Zulfi Bhutto of Pakistan: His Life and Times* (1993); Shahid Javed Burki, *Pakistan under Bhutto* (1980)

Biafra. *See* Nigeria.

Bidault, Georges Augustin. (b. 5 October 1899, Moulins, Allier, France—d. 26 January 1983, Cambo-les Bains, France) Educated in Paris, Bidault became a professor of history and editor of the Catholic newspaper *L'Aube.* He saw military service in World War I. In service again during World War II, he was captured by the Germans. After France fell to the Germans, many French prisoners were released, among them Bidault, who returned to Paris, where he joined the resistance (*Movement Republicaine Populaire*). In 1943 he became the president of the National Council of the Resistance. He served as prime minister in 1946 and again from 1949 to1950. He was foreign minister in 1944, 1947, and 1953-1954. When he was again named prime minister in 1958, he voiced opposition to DeGaulle's handling of the Algerian crisis and was charged with plotting against the state. He went into exile in 1962 and did not return to France until 1968. He lived out the remainder of his life a virtual recluse.

Bien Hoa. *See* Vietnam.

Bignone, Reynaldo Benito Antonio. (b. 21 January 1928, Moron, Argentina) Bignone spent his youth as a cadet in the Argentine Military Academy. On 1 July 1982, following Leopoldo Galtieri's resignation from the presidency (17 June), Major General Bignone was installed by the junta as the head of state. This move caused two members of the junta (Air Force and Navy) to resign, but the junta repaired itself on 10 September and continued to function. Bignone loosened some of political restraints in Argentina and announced general elections. But Bignone's party became embroiled in internal disputes over who was to be their candidate and lost the election to the Radical Civic Union candidate, Raul Alfonsin (qv). Bignone then slipped quietly into obscurity.

Big Powers. *See* Four Powers.

Bihar. *See* India.

Bikini Atoll. An atoll in the Ralik group of the western Marshall Islands, Bikini is part of the commonwealth of the United States as a part of the Trust Territory of the Pacific. From 1948 until 1958, the atoll served as an open air test site for weapons that were part of the American arsenal. The first test, in July 1946, was called "Crossroads" and was an aircraft-delivered 20-kiloton nuclear weapon employed against an array of naval targets including aged battleships, aircraft carriers and submarines. Live animals were also used in the test. A second test in the series called for the detonation of a weapon placed underwater. In a later test, in 1954, serious radiation levels were observed over an area of about 240 miles downwind and 40 miles wide. This accident required the evacuation of U.S. test personnel and the inhabitants living on the nearby islands of Rongelap and Utirik. Three years passed before they could return to their homes. Fishermen aboard a Japanese trawler that was 85 miles from ground zero at the time of the detonation were not discovered until March 1954, when they were found to be contaminated and had to be hospitalized, one dying of radiation poisoning. In 1956, hydrogen weapons were also air-dropped over Bikini.

Biko, Steven Bantu. (b. 18 December 1946, King William's Town, Cape Province —d. 12 September 1977, Pretoria) A medical student at Natal University, Biko became interested in politics and was one of the founders (1969) of the South African Students Organization (also known as the "Black Consciousness Movement"), in which he served as the group's first president. In 1972 he was made an honorary president of the Black People's Convention. He was also the founder and leader of the Black Consciousness Movement. Because of his political activities he was served with a banning order in 1973, which severely restricted his activities. He was at the same time expelled from the University of Natal. In 1975, the banning order was further expanded, and he was arrested on several occasions and subjected to police interrogations. He was most likely beaten to death and, thus, murdered by South African police. His death drew worldwide protest and made Biko a hero-martyr of the antiapartheid movement.

Binaisa, Godfrey Lukwongwa. (b. 30 May 1920, Kampala, Uganda) Born a
Bagandan tribesman, Binaisha attended preparatory school in Uganda. After
attending King's College in Budo, Uganda, and Makerere University in
Kampala, Binaisa subsequently studied law at King's College, the University of
London, graduating in 1955. He was called to the bar at Lincoln's Inn, London,
and was in private practice from 1956 until 1962. During this time he became
interested in politics. In October 1959 in Uganda he founded the Uganda
League, which joined other native organizations opposed to the British
protectorship of their homeland. In April 1962 he was appointed attorney
general in the government of Premier Milton Obote. In October 1962, Uganda
was granted its independence by Great Britain. Binaisa took part in the Obote
campaign against the king of the Baganda tribe, who vainly sought the country's
leadership (1962-1966). In 1967, however, Binaisa broke with Obote over the
premier's use of authoritarian tactics and returned to the private practice of law.
In 1968 he became te president of the Uganda Law Society and the chairman of
the Law Development Center. In 1970 he was appointed a member of the
Uganda Judicial Service Commission and in 1972 was named chairman of the
Commonwealth Lawyers' Conference. Although opposed to Obote's rule,
Binaisa did not favor Idi Amin's coup in 1971 and was forced into exile, where
he set up a law practice in New York. While there he actively campaigned
against Amin's rule. After Amin's overthrow in April of 1979, Yusufu Lule was
appointed president in his place. Lule failed to achieve the needed democratic
realignment, and Binaisa was asked to return and assume the leadership of the
country. He served as president for one year and then first as Uganda's minister
of foreign affairs and then as its defense minister. He was appointed chancellor
of Makerere University in late 1979. From 1980 until January 1981, he was
under house arrest. He left Uganda in January 1981 and moved back to England.
See Uganda.

Binh Dinh Province. *See* Vietnam.

Binh Duong Province. *See* Vietnam.

Binh Gia. *See* Vietnam.

Binh Long Province. *See* Vietnam.

Binh Thuan Province. *See* Vietnam.

Binh Xuyen District. *See* Vietnam.

Bir Gifgafa. *See* Sinai.

Birgunj. *See* Nepal.

Bir Hama. *See* Sinai.

Bir Hassnah (Bir Hassaneh). *See* Sinai.

Birmingham. *See* Great Britain.

Bir Rud. *See* Sinai.

Bir Zeit University. *See* Israel.

Bishop, Maurice. (b. 29 May 1944, Grenada—d. 19 October 1983, St. George's,
Grenada) Bishop received his early education at St. George's Roman Catholic
School and the Catholic Presentation College on the island. He worked for the

civil service before going to England to enter the University of London (Gray's Inn). He took the bar in 1969. He returned to Grenada, where he became involved in the "New Jewel" Movement, which stressed Joint Endeavors for Welfare Education and Liberation. Bishop's socialist tendencies became apparent during this time. On 18 November 1973, Bishop and a group of his followers were set upon by members of the rival Mongoose Gang in full view of the police. The New Jewel group was then thrown in jail and left without medical attention. Bishop was so badly beaten that he had to seek care in Barbados. Two months later, Bishop's father, Rupert, was murdered while trying to defend a group of women and children who were being attacked by police and Mongoose Gang members. Bishop, by this time a Marxist, then swore to rid Granada of Gairy and his followers. On 13 March 1979, a coalition of opposition groups moved against the premiership of Sir Eric Gairy, who was deposed in a coup. Bishop was appointed prime minister and promised to return his country to democracy, a promise not kept when the press was suppressed, elections cancelled and political opposition limited. Although the Soviets furnished considerable aid, including Cuban advisors, Bishop attempted a rapproachment with the United States. Bishop was overthrown in a coup apparently engineered by Bernard Coard (qv), his deputy prime minister, but actually led by Hudson Austin. (Coard subsequently disappeared.) Bishop's supporters were successful in breaking him out of his army-imposed house arrest, but a subsequent demonstration in front of the military compound at St. Rupert led to Bishop's recapture and his subsequent execution, along with his cabinet ministers, inside the compound. *See* Grenada.

Bista, Kirti Nidhi. (b. 1927) Bista received his education at Tri-Chanda College, Katmandu, Nepal, and Lucknow University. He was appointed to the ministry of education in 1961 and became minister in 1962 to 1964. He was then transferred to the ministry of foreign affairs after which he became vice-chairman of the council of ministers and minister of foreign affairs and economic planning. from 1966 until 1967. After holding a series of increasingly important governmental positions he was appointed Permanent Representative to the United Nations from 1968 to 1969. He was then appointed prime minister, where he served during the withdrawal of Indian troops. He continued periodically as prime minister until 30 May 1979. On that date he was replaced by a 28-member Council of Ministers. After serious rioting that year, the Nepalese king announced (24 May) a referendum to determine the future political course of the country. The referendum was held on 2 May 1980; at the general election held in May 1981, Bista, until that time a member of the *panchayat* (national council), was not on the ballot.

Bitar, Salal al-Din. (b. 1912, Damascus, Syria—d. 21 July 1980, Paris) Founder of the Baath Party, Bitar served as premier of Syria on four occasions and was finally ousted in 1966 because of his ultra conservative policies. Bitar had served earlier as minister of state in the Egyptian-Syrian alliance called the United Arab Republic. In exile after his 1966 expulsion, Bitar served for ten years as editor of the *Arab Renaissance* (*Al Ahaa a-Arabi*) in Paris and used that journal to critcize the course of the Baath Party. He was murdered outside his Paris office in what has been called an assassination ordered by Hafez al-Assad.

Bitat, Rabah. On 27 December 1978, Algeria's president, Houari Boumedienne (qv) died in his sleep. Rabah Bitat, the speaker of the National Assembly, replaced him as interim president. On 31 December 1979, Chadri Bendjedid was nominated as the sole candidate for president. He was confirmed in an election held 7 February. Bitat then returned to the National Assembly.

Biya, Paul. (b. 13 February 1933, Muomeka'a, Sangmelima District, Cameroon) Born a Roman Catholic, Biya first attended the mission school at Ndem and the seminaries at Edea and Akono. His secondary education came at the Lycee Leclerc in Yaounde. His initial intention was to become a Catholic priest. Instead, he attended University of Paris where he studied law and political science, including study at the "colonial school" (*Institut des Hautes Etudes d'Outre Mer*). From 1962 he held a number of increasingly important governmental posts in Cameroon until President Ahidjo (qv) appointed him prime minister in 1975. Biya became president of Cameroon in 1982. Among his first acts as president was to abolish the position of prime minister and to appoint his own cabinet. There was an attempt to overthrow Biya in 1984 by followers of Ahidjo. Led by Colonel Ibrahim Saleh (qv), commander of the Palace Republican Guard, the attempt failed after two days of intense fighting. Biya won a resounding reelection in 1988. It was soon evident that, while Biya favored reform, he also savored the power he held. Unrest was evident in 1990, and at least six died in demonstrations. He was forced to accede to demands for a multiparty political system and for a wide-scale amnesty for political prisoners. The process of constitutional reform that Biya had also promised began in 1992 but was suspended in 1995. However, Biya remained in the presidency.

Bizerte (Bizerta). *See* Tunisia.

Black Panther Movement. The Black Panther Party originated in Alabama as an outgrowth of the civil rights movement of the 1960s, under the leadership of Huey P. Newton, Bobby G. Seale and Eldridge Cleaver, the organization's chief propagandist. The Black Panthers espoused a black nationalist credo that at first was aimed at community action as a self-defense mechanism for black people, but it soon turned into an aggressive mode of conduct in which confrontation with the police became a standard tactic of resistance. The murder of Dr. Martin Luther King, Jr. (qv), swung the group farther to the revolutionary left. The first major incident involving the Black Panthers occurred in May 1967, when a group of them invaded the California state legislature to protest a recently approved gun-control law. After the killing of an Oakland, California, police officer, Newton was tried and convicted for the murder. The conviction was subsequently overturned on appeal. Twenty-one Black Panther members were charged on 2 April 1969, with planning to bomb five New York stores. Also, in 1969, two Black Panther leaders were killed by Chicago police in an incident that may have been an orchestrated set-up. On 31 July 1972, five Black Panther members hijacked a Delta Airlines jet over Florida and demanded a ransom of $1 million and a flight to Algeria for the release of their hostages. The hostages were released in Miami, and the five were flown to Algeria. Most of the hijackers were arrested in Paris, however, in 1976, where they went on trial for the hijacking. Newton was again charged with murder following a street brawl but fled to Cuba before he could be tried. Seale was charged with the torture and murder of a suspected police informer in the Black Panther ranks but was found not guilty. Cleaver fled the country to avoid imprisonment for a parole violation. Several members of the Black Panthers were known to have moved into more terrorist-oriented organizations. At the same time, the Black Panthers themselves appear to have sobered and began to follow more legal means of resistance to what was seen as white oppression. In 1981, however, two Black Panther members were implicated in a Brink's robbery. Seale nearly won the mayoral race in Oakland in 1973. Cleaver returned to the United States to become a Christian missionary. In 1980, Newton received a doctorate in California.

Black September. Also known as the Popular Front for the Liberation of Palestine (PFLP), this Palestinian terrorist group is a radical element of the PLO, that has been in existence since before the 1970s. One of the first important terrorist operations of Black September took place on 28 November 1971, when four gunmen assassinated Jordanian prime minister Wasfi al-Tal (qv), while he was attending an Arab League (qv) meeting in Cairo. At that time, the group was identified as a faction of *al-Fatah* (Abu Nidal) (qv), rather than a separate organization. This group was also identified as being responsible for the 15 December assassination attempt on the life of the Jordanian ambassador in London and the 16 September attempt on the Jordanian ambassador in Geneva. Black September's most active year was 1972; on 9 May, Black September terrorists hijacked a Belgian Sabena airliner and held it at Israel's Lod International Airport. The terrorists demanded the Israelis release a large number of Arab terrorists being held in Israeli prisons. Instead, Israeli commandos stormed the aircraft, killing two of the four hijackers. One passenger was also killed. On 30 May, another attack was staged at Lod Airport in which 28 died and scores were wounded. Responsibility for the attack was never fixed in the open literature, but a safe assumption would lay the blame on Black September. Certainly one of the most daring terrorist escapades was the 5 September 1972 attack on the Israeli Olympic team during the games being held in Munich. In an early morning raid, a Black September terrorist squad scaled a wall in the Olympic Village and forced their way into the Israeli men's domitory. Two Israelis, who resisted, were killed immediately; nine others were taken hostage. West German security forces surrounded the builing while the horrified world watched the unfolding events on the "Wide World of Sports" television program.The terrorists demanded the release of about 200 Arabs held in Israeli jails. At ten in the evening on 5 September, although no deal had been struck, the terrorists were convinced they had won and took their blindfolded hostages on busses to waiting helicopters, which in turn carried the group to Fürstenfeldbruck airbase. There, while two of the terrorists inspected the Boeing 727 that was to carry them to safety in the Middle East, a poorly executed West German rescue operation began. One of the terrorists then threw a hand grenade into the hostage helicopter, killing all nine of the Jewish hostages. One German policeman was also killed, along with five of the Arabs involved in the attack. Three others were captured, but were later released in a bizarre episode that began with the Black September hijacking of a Lufthansa airliner going to Frankfurt from Damascus on 29 October. The West German government allowed the three Munich terrorists to leave the country in return for the lives of the hostages on the aircraft. The three killers and the Arab team that took the aircraft were given a hero's welcome in Tripoli. Libya. In another 1972 incident, four Black September terrorists seized the Israeli embassy in Bangkok, Thailand, on 28–29 December. Nineteen hours later all of the hostages were released unharmed and the terrorists given safe passage to Egypt. In 1973, eight Black September terrorists captured the Saudi Arabian embassy in Khartoum, Sudan, during a reception on 1 March 1973. The terrorists demanded the release of prisoners held in three countries, including Sirhan Sirhan, Bobby Kennedy's killer (held in the U.S.), and the Baader-Meinhof Gang (held in West Germany). They also demanded 60 Palestinians held by Jordan and all Arab women imprisoned in Israel. The relatively inept terrorists allowed many of the diplomats to escape, but apparently murdered(2 March) the newly appointed U.S. ambassador, Cleo Noel, Jr. (qv), and the outgoing U.S. charge d'affairs, Guy Eid (qv). The Belgian charge d'affairs was also murdered. On 4 March the terrorists were flown to Egypt, where President Anwar Sadat (qv) apparently turned them over to the PLO. Another embassy was seized by Black September in 1975, this time the Egyptian embassy in Madrid (15 September). Four armed gunmen demanded Egypt renounce the Sinai Agreement (qv) or they would kill all the hostages. After being assured the Egyptians would comply, the four fled to Algeria, using the Algerian and Iraqi ambassadors as their shields. The Algerians immediately released the terrorists. Whether the group that emerged in the 1980s was the same organization that used the name in the 1970s is open to question. Some analysts say it is a new group that has assumed the old name as a cover and for its publicity value. This may be partially explained by the fact that, in March 1978, a radical splinter group of the PFLP was dealt a major setback with the death from natural causes of Wadi Haddad, a noted planner and organizer of transnational terrorist operations. (Haddad died of cancer in an East German hospital.) A series of bloody attacks followed at Paris's Orly airfield and on a London street in an effort to prove that the group was still active. But, in fact, the PFLP's international terrorist operations were sharply curtailed following Haddad's death. Seemingly, no one could be found to replace his organizational skills. In 1979, Carlos, the Venezuelan-born terrorist, surfaced for the first time since the 1975 raid on the OPEC summit, to tell the press he would be returning to prominence. That event never occurred. The death of Haddad did nothing, however, to heal the rift with the main body of the PFLP headed by George Habash (qv). Many of the attacks blamed on the PFLP were in fact perpetrated by the Haddad faction; it may be that the PFLP never split and that Habash used this technique to distance himself from the fanatical Haddad. In January 1979, the reputed planner of Black September's attack on the Israeli atheletes at the Munich Olympics, Ali Hassan Salameh, was assassinated in Beirut. This loss affected not only the PFLP but also *al Fatah*. Regardless of these factors, the PFLP has received support from many parts. In 1980, for instance, there were persistent rumors that the PFLP's chief supporter was Libya's Colonel Qaddafi (qv). This support included financing PFLP terrorist operations, weapons procurement and supply, the use of training camps in Libya, although the PFLP is known to maintain its major training facilities in South Yemen, and the use of Libyan diplomatic facilities abroad as support bases for terrorist operations. Syria has also been a principal supporter of PFLP activities. The chief targets of the PFLP had been, up to that time, the Israelis and their principal venue has been Lebanon. During the latter part of 1980, the PFLP was relatively inactive because of the incapacitation of its leader, George Habbash, who was recovering from surgery. In December 1984, however, a Jordanian diplomat was murdered in Bucharest, Romania. A Palestinian student was arrested for the crime, and Black September claimed credit, as it had a month earlier in Athens when a similar attack was made on another Jordanian official. On 29 December 1985, two Black September gunmen assassinated Fahd Kawasmeh, a high PLO official, in Jordan. In 1987, the PFLP was known to be based in Damascus, Syria. That year, on 25 November, a PFLP terrorist, using a hang-glider, attacked an Israeli outpost in northern Galilee. This unique attack left six Israeli soldiers dead and produced a severe reaction by the Israelis against Palestinians living in Gaza and the West Bank. A radical splinter group of the PFLP known as the "General Command" (GC) was credited with the December 1988 bombing of PanAm Flight 103 over Lockabee, Scotland. The GC is headed by Ahmed Jabril and was, at the time of the PanAm incident, most likely in the employ of the Iranian government. PanAm 103 was carrying 270 people when it blew up. *Reading:* Christopher Dobson, *Black September: Its Short Violent History* (1974).

Blagoveshchensk. *See* USSR.

Blaize, Herbert A. (b. 26 February 1918, Carriacou—d. 19 December 1989) Educated at Grenada Boy's Secondary School, he entered government civil service in 1937 in the Treasury Department. In 1944, he moved to Aruba, where he taught English at an oil refinery. He returned to Grenada in 1952, and in 1953 he founded the centrist Grenada National Party (GNP) to oppose the Grenada United Labor Party of Eric Gairy. He became prime minister, following Gairy's removal by the British government on charges of corruption, after holding a series of ministerial posts and remained in that position until independence in 1974. He then led the official opposition until 1979, when he was forced into hiding following the left-wing coup led by Maurice Bishop. In 1983, after the U.S. invasion of Grenada, Blaize returned and aided in the reconstruction of his country. He won the general election in 1984 and served until his death from cancer in 1989. Although his ailment prevented him from carrying out all of his duties he rebuffed all moves, even from his own party, to have him step down before he died.

Bluff Cove. *See* Falklands Islands.

B'nai B'rith Headquarters. One of three buildings seized in Washington, DC on 9 March 1977, by terrorists belonging to the Hanafi Muslim sect, an American group embracing Islam. The Islamic Center and the District (of Columbia) Building were also taken in the bizarre incident. One person was killed, and a number were injured in the takeover.

Bogota. *See* Colombia.

Boipatong. *See* South Africa.

Bokassa, Jean Bedel. (born as Eddine Ahmed Bokassa) (b. 1921, Bobangui, French Equatorial Africa) After receiving a Christian missionary education, Bokassa joined the French army in 1939. During his military service, he fought in Indochina, rose to the rank of captain in the French colonial forces, and was decorated with the Legion of Honor and the Croix de Guerre. Bokassa continued to serve until the independence of the Central African Republic in 1963. At that time he was appointed the commander in chief of the new nation's armed forces with the rank of colonel. On 1 January 1966, Bokassa led the coup that overthrew the government of President David Dacko (qv). In a series of steps aimed at insuring his own personal power, Bokassa annulled the constitution and had himself declared president-for-life. On 4 December 1977 he was crowned Emperor Bokassa I in a lavish Napoleon-like ceremony that nearly bankrupted his impoverished nation. From 1977 to 1979, a record of murder of men, women, and children was laid at his feet. In 1979, he was ousted from power and fled the country. He returned in 1988, however, and stood trial for his crimes. He was found guilty and sentenced to be executed. His death sentence was later commuted and he was released in 1993. *Reading:* Brian Titley, *Dark Age: The Political Odyssey of Emperor Bokassa* (1997).

Bolivia. A landlocked country in west-central South America that is bordered on the northwest by Peru, on the north and east by Brazil, on the southeast by Paraguay, on the south by Argentina, and on the southwest by Chile, the Republic of Bolivia has its administrative capital at La Paz and its judicial capital at Sucre. The country is named for Simon Bolivar, who helped win its independence from Spain in 1825. The region had been originally conquered by the Incas in the thirteenth century A.D. and was then taken by the Spaniards in 1530. Unlucky in war, Bolivia lost its Pacific ocean coastline to Chile after a war that lasted from 1879 to 1884. As a result of the Chaco War (1935), Bolivia was deprived of resource- rich land and an Atlantic outlet by Brazil (rubber) and Paraguay (oil). From 1952 through 1981 a series of coups and coup attempts punctuated the economic chaos and political instability in the country. In July 1982, a military junta took control of the country and remained in power until October of that year to allow the democratically elected Congress time to reorganize and take control of the country. Bolivia is a center of the illegal drug trade, and because of U.S. pressure on the Bolivian government to reduce coca growing and trafficking, there have been serious clashes between segments of the population and the police. In October 1982, Hernan Siles Zuazo became president after returning from exile. He was immediately faced with a crop failure that led to rioting. General strikes also impacted on his first year in office. At year's end, a discovered conspiracy between drug traffickers and high-ranking military officers led to a sweeping purge of the armed forces. The year 1983 saw the mass resignation of the Cabinet following two days of a communist-inspired general strike. On 30 June 1984, Siles was kidnapped during an attempted government overthrow led by mid-ranking army and police personnel, many of whom had known ties to the drug dealers. The president was released after ten days. Once again, on 8 October 1984, the Cabinet resigned. Siles left office under heavy pressure and the threat of a coup d'etat on 6 August 1985. Former president (1952–1956)Victor Paz Estenssoro replaced him in that office. Following the imposition of stringent economic reform programs, the country's economy continued to deteriorate for a time, but soon showed some improvement. Even so, unrest increased and the drug trade flourished. During this period, a program against the drug dealers began in which U.S. forces were involved in raids on processing factories and crop destruction. In 1989, Jaime Paz Zamora became president following a peaceful election, and the war against the drug dealers continued. In 1993, Paz Zamora stepped down and Gonzalo Sanchez de Lozada Bustimente became president, Among his early moves was the privatization of a number of major companies in Bolivia, which led to another round of protests. At about this same time, the U.S. was accused by some of accusing Paz Zamora of complicity in the drug trade. In mid-1994, unrest arose again, primarily instigated by farmers, especially after the U.S.-directed destruction of many acres of farmland devoted to growing coca, the basis of cocaine. A state of emergency was declared. *Reading:* James Dunkerley, *Rebellion in the Veins: Political Struggle in Bolivia, (1952–1982)* (1984); James M. Malloy & Eduardo Gamarra, *Revolution and Reaction: Bolivia 1964–1972* (1987).

Bologna. *See* Italy.

Boloven (Bolovon) Plateau. *See* Laos.

Bombay. *See* India.

Bongo, Albert-Bernard (Omar). (b. 30 December 1935, Lewai, Franceville, French Equatorial Africa) Bongo served in the French air force from 1958 to1960. After joining the civil service in 1960, Bongo rose steadily in the government until 1967, when he became president at age 32 upon the death of the ailing Leon M'ba. In 1968, Bongo created a one-party state around the Gabonese Democratic Party. In 1973, he converted to Islam and assumed the name Omar. In 1977 he was elected chairman of the Organization of African

Unity (OAU). His astute leadership, especially in the area of economic development, has turned Gabon into one of the most self-reliant black African states. Bongo was reelected to a third term as president in 1986. Bongo's tenure was relatively unmarked by turmoil until January 1990, when university students rioted against the under supported education system. After five students were killed by the police (February), Bongo was forced to bow to pressure and institute a multiparty political system in Gabon (accomplished in May). Bongo then had to face rioting from other corners and the assassination of one of the opposition leaders. Forty parties participated in the March 1991 elections, with Bongo's party winning handily. He was still faced, however, with political turmoil and more student demonstrations. French troops were used to protect foreign nationals. Bongo was again returned to power in 1993 following an election that was marred by charges of disorganization and fraud. He needed most of 1994 to reassert his authority. Bongo is believed to have ordered several opposition leaders detained by refusing them travel documents to visit France. French-Gabonese relations were strained at the time because of devaluation of French currency. By 1995, Bongo had mended most of his fences and continued making concessions favorable to Gabon's future.

Bong Sai Pa. *See* Vietnam.

Bong Son Pass. *See* Vietnam.

Bonn. *See* Germany.

Bonn Agreement. Following lengthy negotiations, the internal independence of West Germany was guaranteed by the three Western Allies, the U.S., Britain and France. The agreement was signed on 26 May 1952 and was immediately followed by a curtailment of east-west communications by the Soviet-supported East Germans, who sought to derail the terms of the agreement.

Bophuthatswana. *See* Republic of South Africa.

Bordaberry Arocena, Juan Maria. (b. 17 June 1928, Montevideo, Uruguay) Born the son of wealthy landowners in Uruguay, Bordaberry began an education in law at Montevideo University, but he gave it up at the time of his father's death. He sought and won his first political office in 1962 when he was elected to the Senate as a Blanco Party candidate. In 1965, however, he broke with the party to support a single-president form of government to supplant the collegial system endorsed by the Blancos. He joined the Colorado government as minister of agriculture and was in that capacity when he was nominated for president in 1971. In a strange election based on a plebiscite that refused the Jose Pacheco Areco government the opportunity to succeed itself, Bordaberry won the presidency. Winning by only 10,000 votes, Bordaberry had campaigned on a fear of communism. Within two years, the economic and social chaos in Uruguay led to a bloodless military coup (February 1973) that stripped Bordaberry of much of his authority but left him in office. In June 1973, Bordaberry abolished parliamentary government, placing the real control of the country in a Security Council (Council of State) composed of senior military officers and hand-picked civilians. He was also required to accept a list of 19 demands that further increased the authority of the military. In July, on his orders, military forces occupied the capital. He was removed from office on 12 June 1976 in a bloodless military coup. Bordaberry then became a rancher.

Borneo. The third largest island in the world, located in the Malay Archipelago, Borneo lies north of Java and southwest of the Philippines and is presently composed of the states of Kalimantan, which is part of Indonesia and is approximately 70 percent of the Borneo landmass, and Sabah (North Borneo), Sarawak, now a part of Malaysia, and the Sultanate of Brunei. Borneo is known in both Chinese and Arab annals and somewhat less known in early Indian contacts. Western knowledge of Borneo begins with traveler's reports in the fourteenth century A.D., but Ptolemy mentions the island in 160 A.D. Portugal explored the island in 1511. Trade was monopolized by Spain and Portugal into the seventeenth century, when the English and Dutch moved in to reduce piracy in the region. In 1787, the Dutch East India company established itself in Brunei, which controlled much of the island at the time. The British occupied the Dutch possessions during the Napoleonic Wars, but the Dutch claims were reasserted after 1816 and put to treaty in 1826, with the Dutch receiving East Borneo by cession. The British hegemony over West Borneo (1872) and British North Borneo (1882) was finally settled late in the nineteenth century. The Japanese invaded and occupied Borneo in 1941–1942. In 1944, Allied forces began a bombing campaign to limit Japanese use of the island's enormous strategic reserves. Australian forces began the liberation of Borneo in 1945. In 1946, Sarawak and British North Borneo became crown colonies. In Dutch Borneo a nationalist uprising began that eventually involved both Dutch and British regular forces. The Dutch eventually transferred control of their holdings to Indonesia (27 December 1949), with amalgamation into the republic in August 1950. Indonesian-controlled raids against British North Borneo and Sarawak continued until 1966 when the issue was settled by treaty. Communist infiltration also took place during this time. A major confrontation between Indonesia and the newly formed Malaysia Federation involved Borneo for a time; but by 1967 British forces were being withdrawn from Sabah and Sarawak, while only one battalion was left in support of the British-protected Sultan of Brunei Darussalam. Brunei became a sovereign state within the Commonwealth on 1 January 1984. The Sultan of Brunei was later linked to the Iran-Contra scandal as having donated $10 million to the contras, money that was subsequently "misplaced." *Reading:* Peter Dennis & Jeffrey Grey, *Emergency and Confrontation: Australian Military Operation in Malaya and Borneo 1950–1966* (1996); E. D. Smith, *Malaya and Borneo (Counter-Insurgency Operations: 1)* (1986).

Bosch, Juan D. (b. 30 June 1909, La Vega, Dominican Republic) Bosch was forced into exile in 1937 because of his opposition to the regime of Rafael Trujillo (qv). In 1939 he founded the left-wing Dominican Revolution Party (PRD) and, through the PRD, won the first democratic election in the Dominican Republic in December 1962. He found monumental problems facing his office after his inauguration in February 1963. In addition, Bosch found himself caught between the United States, which opposed any leftist government in the Caribbean, and most of the power groups in the country and the church. Because of these pressures, Bosch was overthrown on 25 September 1963. He went into exile in Puerto Rico and was not allowed to return to the Dominican Republic until September 1965. He again ran for the presidency, but his attempt lacked the drive necessary to win, and he was defeated by Joaquin Balaguer (qv). In February 1973, following rumors of an rebel invasion along the south coast, made more convincing by an armed clash between government troops and rebels, the government ordered the arrest of a number of opposition leaders, including Bosch. Bosch denied any knowledge of the rebels and was not detained. In 1973, Bosch resigned from the PRD, which rejoined the mainstream political system, and formed a new party, the Party of Dominican Liberation (PLD). Bosch mounted several more campaigns but lost each time to what he said was vote fraud.

Bosnia. More often seen along with its neighbor as Bosnia-Herzogovina, it is one of the six states that, until recently, comprised the Federal People's Republic of Yugoslavia, which was established in 1946. Sarajevo is Bosnia's capital. Originally settled by Illyrian tribesmen (c. 1000 B.C.) before Roman times, the region was occupied by the Romans following a major war with the Illyrians and Macedonians; the Romans incorporated it into the province of Illyricum (168 A.D.). It was overrun by the Huns and Visigoths during the third through the fifth centuries. The following onset of Slavic movement through the region left a much more lasting impression; by the end of the seventh century the region was ethnicized into a Slavic land. Serbian incursions followed in the seventh century, followed by Hungarian incursions in the twelfth century. In the fourteenth century, the Turks invaded Bosnia (1386). The Bosnians defeated the Turks at Bileca but were in turn defeated as they attempted to aid the Serbian allies at Kosovo (1389). Bosnia became a Turkish province in 1463 after the defeat of King Stephen Tomasevic. The neighboring principality of Herzogovina fell to the Turks in 1482. Bosnia was a Ottoman outpost through the sixteenth and seventeenth centuries. After the 1878 Congress of Berlin, Bosnia-Herzogovina was ceded to Austria-Hungary without the approval of the people. It took an Austrian army of 200,000 to pacify the country. On 28 June 1914, the Archduke Ferdinand and his wife were assassinated in Sarajevo, touching off World War I. Not until the collapse of the Austro-Hungarian Empire at the end of that war did Bosnia have a momentary glimpse of freedom: on 26 October 1918, Bosnia entered into a union with its neighbors to form Yugoslavia. In World War II, the Bosnian region was ravaged by the Nazi puppet state of Croatia, another of the Yugoslav states. The disintegration of Yugoslavia in the 1990s led to bitter ethnic and religious fighting in Bosnia–Herzogovina. Croatia left the federation in 1991. and Bosnia–Herzogovina gained its independence shortly afterwards. The Bosnian Serbs refused the arrangement, demanding instead to remain a part of

Yugoslavia (Serbia). A Bosnian Serb attempt was made in 1992 to divide the country along ethnic lines, but this plan also failed. A civil war then began with Bosnian Serbs pitted against Bosnian Muslims and Croats. This type of struggle led to a campaign of "ethnic cleansing" in which the dominant force in each area began the forced ejection or massacre of the other groups. Serbian Bosnian forces began the bombardment of Sarajevo immediately after the U.S. and the European Community (EC) recognized Bosnian independence on 7 April. A number of other cities in the predominantly Muslim areas of Bosnia were attacked by Yugoslavian (Serbian) and Bosnian Serb forces with a heavy toll among the civilian Bosnian Muslim population. Atrocities matched the worst in recorded history and caused untold grief and irreparable damage to the people and the country. By the end of 1994 at least 200,000 were dead and more than two million homeless. By 1995, a UN peacekeeping forced had failed because of the UN's inability to make decisions without debate. NATO forces were deployed to Bosnia in 1995 to keep the peace. A fragile peace agreement was reached in December 1995. The presence of NATO forces who were strong enough and willing to fight has helped maintain at least a semblance of order although the Serbs still refuse full cooperation. *Reading*: Noel Malcolm, *Bosnia: A Short History* (1996); Sherry Ricchiardi, *Bosnia: The Struggle for Peace* (1996); Robert J. Donia & John V. A. Fine, *Bosnia and Herzogovina: A Tradition Betrayed* (1995); Edgar O'Ballance, *Civil War in Bosnia, 1992-94* (1995); Norman Cigar, *Genocide in Bosnia: The Policy of Ethnic cleansing* (1995); Paul F. Diehl, *International Peacekeeping: With a New Epilogue on Somalia, Bosnia and Cambodia* (1995).

Botha, (P)ieter (W)illiam. (B. 12 January 1916, Paul Roux, Orange Free State) Born the son of a farmer, Botha was studying law when he came to the attention of D. F. Malan (qv), the leader of the Purified National Party (PNP). Botha was appointed organizing secretary of the party for Cape Province in 1936. During World War II, when the PNP reunited with the old National Party (NP), Botha's reputation as an organizer grew. In 1946 he became the first secretary of the *Nasionale Jeugbund*, the NP's youth group. In 1948 he was appointed chief secretary of the group for the Cape. When the 1948 election swept Malan into power as prime minister, Botha entered the Parliament as the member for George. (He has subsequently become its longest-serving member.) He became a cabinet minister in the Verwoerd government in 1961 and served as minister of community development and of colored affairs. In 1965 he became minister of defense where he labored to build a military force to defend the white minority against the total onslaught of Black Africa, although he had attempted to introduce legislation that would have granted more rights to blacks. He succeeded B. J. Vorster as prime minister in 1978 and won reelection in 1981. In 1984, Botha became the first executive state president under the new South African constitution, which, although granting some rights to biracial and Asians, left the vast black population without direct influence in the tricameral parliament. In February 1989, Botha suffered a stroke, which forced him to give up the leadership of the National Party; and in August 1989, he was forced out of the presidency by his party successor, F. W. De Clerk.

Botswana. Formerly known as Bechuanaland, the British protectorate of Botswana is located in the central region of southern Africa and is bordered on the west and north by Namibia, on the northeast by Zimbabwe and on east and the south by the Republic of South Africa. Botswana embraces the Okovango Delta, the Makarikari Salt Plain and the Kalahari Desert. The present capital is Gaborone. It was originally settled by Sotho Bantu people, who were followed by the Tswana (hence, its present name) and was first explored by Westerners in 1801. In 1813, the London Missionary Society established a mission on the Kudumane River. Zulu raiders harassed the country until they were driven out by the "Great Trek" of the Boers to the north after 1835. This brought Bechuanaland into conflict with the Boers and led to long period of border incidents. Further disputes arose when gold was discovered in the disputed regions in 1867. By 1881, the southern area was in a state of chaos after the British refused to insert a military force to protect the gold fields and the population. Finally, in 1885, a British force under Sir Charles Warren asserted a peace over the area. In 1935 and afterwards, London thwarted a number of South African attempts to annex the region. On 30 June 1966, the Republic of Botswana was born as a part of the British Commonwealth, and has played an active role in the movement toward self-government and independence in Africa. Botswana has also had its share of involvement in guerrilla activities throughout southern Africa, especially dissident activities against Rhodesia (Zimbabwe) in the late 1970s and in support of African National Congress forces operating against the Republic of South Africa's white supremacy rule. Thousands of refugees flooded into Botswana to avoid the fighting. Rhodesian troops entered Botswana in February 1978 and massacred a number of civilians. In 1980, Botswana was instrumental in the creation of the South African Development Coordination Conference (SADCC) which helped organize the economies of nine southern African countries. South Africa and Namibia are not members. During the six-year period 1984–1990, Botswana was caught up in the struggle in South Africa. South African forces twice entered Botswana (1985–1986) and killed a number of people. Upon the independence of South West Africa (Namibia) in 1990, peace fell upon Botswana and has remained since that time. *Reading:* Anthony Sillery, *Bechuanaland Protectorate* (1983); Richard Vengroff, *Botswana: Rural Development in the Shadow of Apartheid* (1977); Richard Dale, *Botswana's Search for Autonomy in Southern Africa (Contributions in Political Science, No. 358)* (1995); John A. Wiseman, *Botswana (World Bibliographical Series, Vol. 150)* (1992).

Boumedienne, Houari (Mohammed Ben Brahim Boukharrouba). (b. 23 August 1927, Clauzel, Algeria—d. 27 December 1978, Algiers, Algeria) Born the son of a peasant farmer, Boumedienne was educated first in religion at the Islamic Institute in Constantine, Algeria, and then at al-Azhar University in Cairo, Egypt. In 1954, after the start of hostilities with France, Boumedienne began his military studies and, one year later, joined the anti-French Algerian Nationalist Movement as a guerrilla leader in western Algeria. By 1958, he was chief of operations in the western sector, and in 1960 he was appointed chief of staff of the Algerian liberation army. When Algeria was granted its independence by France, Boumedienne became its first defense minister (1962–1965) after leading his troops into Algiers in a show of power. While vice president of his country, he led the military coup that overthrew the government of Achmed Ben Bella (qv) in June 1965 and ruled Algeria until his death from a rare blood disease in 1979. Boumedienne had been ill for some time before his death and had been receiving treatment in Moscow.

Bourges-Mannoury (Maunoury), Maurice. The Radical Party premier of France in 1957 who was forced to deal with the Algerian situation. Bourges-Mannoury was elected to office in June 1957 and replaced in November of that same year. He departure was caused by the so-called Algiers Lobby. *See* France.

Bourguiba, Habib ibn Ali. (b. 1903, Monastir, Tunisia) Bourguiba studied law in Paris and in 1934 became a member of the radical Tunisian National Party. He spent three terms in French prisons over the next 20 years. Compared to others, however, Bourguiba was considered a moderate Arab, and the French government of Pierre Mendes-France accepted him as Tunisia's first prime minister in 1956. He became president of Tunisia in 1957. By 1962, Bourguiba had been able to remove the last vestiges of French colonial power from his country and thereafter established close economic ties with Paris. In 1975, Bourguiba was declared president-for-life. In 1983 and 1984 he was able to withstand threats to his government posed by Islamic fundamentalists. Although remaining in power, his authority had become significantly eroded. On 7 November1987, at age 84 and considered to be senile, he was constitutionally deposed by his prime minister, General Zine al-Abidine Ben Ali. *See* Tunisia. *Reading:* Norma Selim, *Habib Bourguiba, Islam, and the Creation of Tunisia* (1984).

Bouterse, Daysi. The leader of a coup in Suriname that overthrew the government of President Johan Ferrier (qv) in August 1980, Sergeant Major Bouterse had also taken part in the February 1980 coup that removed Prime Minister Henck Arron (qv). Bouterse was a part of the National Military Council (NMC), made up primarily of noncommissioned officers. Bouterse then led the August coup in which Ferrier was dismissed and two other NMC members arrested. Bouterse then placed the former prime minister, Hendrick R. Chin A Sen (qv) in the presidency. By 1981, cracks began to appear in the facade of normalcy between the NMC and the Chin A Sen government, especially in how to deal with foreign affairs and the economy. As the situation became more unstable, Chin A Sen and his government resigned on 4 February 1982. Nearly a year of turmoil followed until, on 9 December 1982, Bouterse became head of state. Bouterse's first act was to carry out a bloody purge of his political opponents; a UN Human Rights Committee reported in 1985 that at least 15 opposition leaders had been murdered. A civilian cabinet was appointed (26 February 1983) in an attempt to head off the cessation of aid from the U.S. and the Netherlands. Shortly after that, Bouterse sent all of the Cuban advisors home, fearing a repeat of the US invasion of Grenada in his country. In 1985, Bouterse promised a new constitution and a democratically elected government before April 1987. On 25 February 1986, the state of emergency was lifted and Bouterse once again promised a return to civilian rule by April 1987. Still, the economy continued to decline as rebel activity increased. Bouterse was accused of attempting to use drug money to reinvigorate the economy following the arrest of one of the NMC's leaders in a drug bust in Miami, Florida. The promised elections were held in November 1987, and the Bouterse regime was overwhelmingly defeated. However, the new constitution was so constructed as to leave ultimate power with the military. At the same time, Bouterse's tightening of links with Libya raised concern among Surinam's neighbors. The installation of a civilian government in January 1988 actually did little to impede Bouterse's power, but at the moment, the key issue was the reinstallation of foreign aid. Bouterse, who was now commander of the army, rejected the government's truce with the rebels (21 July 1989), a rejection that was seconded by a number of other groups in Surinam. Bouterse had his troops attack Ronnie Brunswijk, the leader of the principal opposition rebel force, on 26 March 1990. Brunswijk was captured and several of his delegation were killed, even through his party had been given safe-conduct by the government to attend a meeting. One reason for the assault was Bouterse's fear that Brunswijk was about to produce evidence about his involvement in the cocaine trade.On 23 December 1990, Bouterse resigned his army post. The next day, his second-in-command led a bloodless coup that installed a new government; Bouterse was quickly returned to his military duties as head of the armed forces. After the May 1991 elections, Bouterse was replaced as the head of the military and the new commander ordered a number of Bouterse's followers removed from the armed forces (April 1993). Information later surfaced (10 January 1995) that Bouterse had received bribes during his tenure from Dutch trading companies for favored treatment. A number of officials had already been dismissed on these charges. Nevertheless, Bouterse announced that he would seek the presidency in 1996. *See* Surinam.

Boyog. *See* Philippines.

Branco, Humberto de Alencar Castelo. A Brazilian general appointed president on 11 April 1964, to serve out the term of João Goulart (qv), who was overthrown in a military coup on 1 April 1964, Branco was inaugurated on 15 April. The Brazilian Congress then extended his term to 15 March 1967. On 27 October 1965, General Branco abolished all political parties and gave military tribunals broad authority over the Brazilian populace. Before leaving office, Branco promulgated Institutional Act Number 3, which provided for indirect election of the new president. Those in opposition refused to participate, and the Congress elected Branco's successor, General Artur da Costa e Silva. Branco left office in December 1966.

Brandt, Willy. (b. 18 December 1913, Lubeck, Germany—d. 9 October 1992) Born an illegitimate child and named Herbert Ernst Karl Frahm, Brandt was educated in Lubeck and worked as a ship broker until he was forced to flee the Nazis by going to Norway in 1933. He assumed the name "Willy Brandt" after his arrival in Oslo, where he worked as a newspaperman and as the secretary of a charity organization. He was also active in German resistance movements against Hitler. He moved to Sweden when Norway fell to the German invasion. In Sweden he obtained Norwegian citizenship and spent the remainder of the war working as a journalist and in support of the Norwegian underground. At the end of the war, Brandt went to Berlin to become the Norwegian press attache. In 1947 he regained his German citizenship, and 1950 he became the chiefeditor of the *Berliner Stadtblatt*, at the same time taking an active role in the Social Democratic Party (SDP) movement in Germany. He became president of the Berlin Chamber of Deputies in 1955 and mayor of West Berlin in 1957. He was elected deputy chairman of the SDP in 1962 and its chairman in 1964. Brandt served in the federal parliament (*Bundestag*) from 1949 until 1987, served as the president of of the *Deutscher Stadetag* 1958–1963 and as minister of foreign affairs and federal vice chancellor 1966–1969. He was the SDP candidate for the chancellorship of Germany in 1961 and 1965 and served as Chancellor of Germany from 1969 until 1974. The revelation that one of his top aides was an East German spy forced Brandt to resign the chancellorship in 1974. Brandt continued as chairman of the SDP until 1987, when he resigned. He was elected president of the Socialist International in 1976 and was a member of the European Parliament 1979–1983. Brandt won the Nobel Prize for Peace in 1971for his *Ostpolitik* and was also the recipient of numerous other awards and prizes. He died in 1992.

Bratislava. *See* Czechoslovakia.

Brazil. A country in South America that covers nearly one-half of the continent, Brazil is the fifth largest nation in the world. The capital city is Brasilia. The country was discovered by a Portuguese explorer in 1500 and was colonized by the Portuguese into the nineteenth century. Slavery was not abolished in Brazil until 1888. The Kingdom of Brazil came into being when the King of Portugal fled his country before the advancing army of Napoleon and went to Brazil. There, he ruled as Dom Joao VI. When Portugal was restored after Napoleon's defeat, Dom Joao's son proclaimed Brazil independent in 1822. In 1889, the emperor was deposed and the nation declared a republic, called the United States of Brazil. From 1930, the country was a military dictatorship under Getulio Vargas (qv), but popular unrest ended the regime on 25 October 1945. During World War II, Brazilian troops fought alongside other Allied troops in the Italian campaign. After September 1946, only "democratic" parties were allowed, and the Communist Party was outlawed in May 1947. On 3 October 1950, former dictator Vargas was elected president. He was forced to resign on 8 August 1954 in the face of rising unrest and violence and allegedly committed suicide on 24 August. A military junta took control of the country on 11 November

1955 to prevent the establishment of another dictatorship that would have prevented the inauguration of the duly-elected president, Juscelino Kubitschek (qv). Another government was forced to resign on 25 August 1961, when Janio Quadros had been in office less than seven months, when the military moved to prevent a civil war that was brewing in the country. There was a military revolt in in September 1963 that was crushed by loyal troops. The government of President Joao Goulart (qv) was overthrown in a military coup (1 April 1964). U.S. naval units assembled to prevent a communist takeover, but the military junta began an anticommunist purge in the government and the U.S. forces were withdrawn. Also, in 1964, the capital moved from Rio de Janeiro to the newly built city of Brasilia located over 500 miles inland on the Central Plateau. On 6 May 1965, Brazilian troops were added to the list of forces assembled as a part of the Inter-American Peacekeeping Forces. On 27 October 1965, the government abolished all political parties in Brazil and gave sweeping authority to military tribunals. Brazil refused to sign the Nuclear Non-Proliferation Treaty in July 1968. On 13 December 1968, President Artur Costa e Silva (qv) seized absolute power. This led to an increase in rebel activity, to which the government reacted in August 1969 with a military campaign in the Atlantic coastal region. Costa e Silva suffered a stroke on 31 August 1969 and was replaced by a junta that took control of the country. On 6 December 1969, the junta invoked a strict censorship law to prevent disclosure of human rights violations against Brazilian Indians and political prisoners. Insurgency increased during this period, with a number of kidnappings of foreign dignitaries. Following the issuance of a U.S. Department of State report on human rights violations in Brazil, the government cancelled a 25-year U.S. military aid program and refused to accept a $50 million military sales order (March 1977). The Brazilians followed this up by abrogating four military treaties with the U.S. on on 21 September. In April 1983, serious rioting broke out in Sao Paulo over the issue of unemployment. This was followed in July by a major strike among oil and metal workers protesting the government's austerity program. Almost 200,000 marched in Sao Paulo on 25 January 1984 demanding greater democracy in Brazil. In a repudiation of military control, the indirect elections held in 1985 placed Tancredo de Almeida Neves in the presidency. He died before taking office, however, and the new stability was demonstrated by the vice-president-elect assuming the presidency without incident. Political parties were again legalized in Brazil, including a land grant program for peasants and a provision to allow 16-year-olds to vote. All censorship was banned. While a free direct election was authorized for November 1989, the 1990s became a new period of unrest caused principally by voter apathy. Corruption and other scandals led to impeachment proceedings that ended with the resignation of Fernando Collor de Mello as president. By 1995, there was little in the way of positive internal results in politics or the economy for Brazil, which also stands in the vortex of the controversy over the destruction of the great Amazon rain forest and the impact on present and future weather conditions. *Reading:* An excellent bibliographical source in Solena V. Bryant, *Brazil* (1985).

Brazzaville. *See* Congo.

Breton Liberation Front. Named for the area of its origin in Brittany, on the French coast, the Breton Revolutionary Army, the military wing of the Breton Liberation Front, was the terrorist organization that claimed credit for the bombing of the seventeenth century Palace of Versailles outside Paris on 26 June 1978. The south wing of the palace was severely damaged in the explosion.

Brezhnev, Leonid Ilyich. (B. 19 December 1906, Dneprodzerzhinsk, Kamenkoye, Ukraine—d. 10 November 1982, Moscow, USSR) Brezhnev's early training was as an agricultural surveyor working in Belorussia and the Urals. After belonging to the *Komsomol* (Young Communist League) from 1923, Brezhnev joined the Communist Party in 1931 and performed his obligatory military service in the tank corps in the 1930s. Thereafter, he joined the party as an *apparatchik* and became the deputy chairman of the regional committee for Dneprodzerzhinsk. In 1938, he was appointed part propaganda chief at Dnepropetovsk. When World War II began, Brezhnev was called back into the army and saw service as a political commissar with the Southern Army Group, eventually attaining the rank of major general. During his service he became acquainted with Nikita Khushchev: after the war, he assisted Khrushchev, who was then first secretary of the party in the Ukraine. In 1950, Brezhnev was sent to Moldavia to establish party control in that province. In 1952, his work in Moldavia came to the attention of Josef Stalin, and he was elected to the Central Committee of the Communist Party of the Soviet Union (CPSU) and was a candidate member of the Politburo and a member of its secretariat. He lost the latter two seats after the death of Stalin, but after Khrushchev assumed the mantle of power, Brezhnev was sent to Kazakhstan where he supervised the "Virgin Lands" experiment. By 1957 he had been reinstalled in the Politburo and made a full member of that body. In May 1960 be was elected chairman of the Presidium of the Supreme Soviet and held that post until June 1964, when he led the plot that overthrew Khrushchev. Brezhnev was elected First Secretary of the CPSU in 1966 and took over the reigns of power in the Soviet Union. After the Warsaw Pact invasion of Czechoslovakia in 1968, he enunciated his so-called Brezhnev Doctrine, which called for Soviet intervention in any case where the essential interests of other socialist countries were at stake. In his dealings with the West, Brezhnev pushed for detente and a normalization of relations with West Germany. In 1972 and 1973, he and President Nixon exchanged visits in Washington and Moscow. In May 1977 Brezhnev became the first person in Soviet history to hold both the title of president of the Prsidium and first secretary at the same time. Brezhnev lost enthusiasm for detente, however, in 1979, when the U.S. Senate refused to ratify the SALT II agreement that had been hammered out in Vienna with President Carter. Probably as a result, Soviet forces entered Afghanistan in December of that year. On 7 November 1982, just three days before his death, Brezhnev warned the world that any "potential aggressor" would feel the power of immediate Soviet retaliation. *Reading:* Stuart A. Kallin, *The Brezhnev Era* (1992); Alexander Dallin, ed., *The Khrushchev and Brezhnev Years* (1992).

British Guiana. *See* Guyana.

Brown, H. "Rap" (Hubert Gerold Brown). (b. 4 October 1943) Brown became the leader of the Student Nonviolent Coordinating Committee in 1967. An advocate of revolution and violence, he was indicted in a Maryland federal court for riot and arson and was eventually convicted of federal firearms violations. While awaiting an appeal (1970), he went into hiding, but he was again arrested in 1971 for his part in a New York City robbery. He was sentenced to prison for 5-15 years. While serving he converted to Islam and assumed the name Jamil Abdullah al-Amin. He was paroled in 1976 after the federal firearms charges were dropped. Brown became involved in the leadership of a mosque in Atlanta, Georgia, and opened a community grocery store in 1988. He was arrested on 8 August 1995 on firearms charges in connection with the shooting of William Miles. On 17 August, Miles recanted his charge that it had been Brown who shot him, claiming the police and federal agents had forced him to implicate Brown.

Brunei. *See* Borneo.

Brussels. *See* Belgium.

Brussels Treaty. Signed on 17 March 1948, the treaty was a 50-year mutual assistance alliance that bound Belgium, France, Great Britain, Luxembourg and The Netherlands to a common defense. These nations later merged their treaty forces into NATO on 20 December 1950.

Bucharest. *See* Romania.

Bucher, Giovanni Enrico. The Swiss ambassador to Brazil, Bucher was kidnapped in Rio de Janeiro on 7 December 1970 by terrorists of the National Liberation Alliance (also identified as the Popular Revolutionary Vanguard). A Brazilian security guard assigned to protect Ambassador Bucher was killed in the incident. He was released unharmed on 16 January 1971, after the Brazilian government released 70 prisoners, who were flown to Santiago, Chile, and released on 14 January.

Buckley, William. Buckley was the CIA Chief of Station at the U.S. Embassy in Beirut, Lebanon, on 16 March 1984, when he was kidnapped in West Beirut by members of the Islamic Jihad. He was later killed by the terrorists.

Budapest. *See* Hungary.

Buenos Aires. *See* Argentina.

Buganda Province. *See* Uganda.

Buhari, Mohammad. (b. 17 December 1942, Daura, Katsina Province of Kaduna State, Nigeria) Buhari received his early education at the Katsina Secondary School and later trained as an officer cadet at the Nigerian Military Training School and at the Mons Officers' Cadet School at Aldershot, England. Buhari entered (1962) and was commissioned into the Nigerian army in 1963. By 1975, he had risen through the ranks and, as a lieutenant colonel, helped engineer the coup that ousted General Yakubu Gowon (qv), the head of the military government that had ruled Nigeria since 1966. Buhari then served as military governor of the North Eastern State at Maiduguri. He served briefly as military governor of Borno State before being appointed federal commissioner for petroleum resources. In 1977, his office was amalgamated with the Nigerian National Oil Corporation, and Buhari became its chairman. In a simultaneous move, General Olusegun Obasanjo (qv), the head of the ruling junta since the assassination of Brigadier Murtala Mohammed (qv), appointed Buhari the military secretary for the army at the junta's supreme military headquarters (1978). In 1979–1980, Buhari gave up the oil post and returned to full duty as the commanding general, 4th Division and, later, the commander of the 1st Mechanized Division at Jos in the Plateau State. He remained at that post until December 1983, when the army once again seized power in Nigeria and ousted the four month old elected civilian government of Shehu Shigari. Major General Mohammed Buhari was appointed head of state of the new government as well as chairman of the military council and commander in chief of the armed forces. In 1985, he was ousted from power and placed under house arrest, where he remained until 1988.

Bukoba. *See* Tanzania.

Bulawayo. *See* Zimbabwe.

Bulganin, Nikolai Aleksandrovich. (b.11 June 1895, Nizhni-Novgorod—d. 24 February 1975, Moscow) A lifelong communist, Bulganin served in the Soviet Secret Police (Cheka) from 1918 until 1922. He was mayor of Moscow from 1933 until 1937 and became a full member of the Central Committee of the Communist Party in 1939. During the World War II, Bulganin served on several military councils and was appointed a marshal at the end of the war. He became deputy commissar of defense in 1944 and minister of defense in 1946, when he succeeded Josef Stalin in that office. After Stalin's death in 1953, Bulganin became vice premier in the Malenkov government and became premier when Malenkov resigned in 1955. From 1955 until March 1958, Bulganin served as Nikita Khrushchev's alter ego in what became known as the "B and K" duo, but Khrushchev held the real power. In March 1958, Khrushchev deprived Bulganin of his position and, by August, Bulganin had all but disappeared from the scene. He was given a minor post as chairman of an obscure economic council. In 1961, he was forced out of his seat on the Central Committee. He died in 1975.

Bulgaria. An ancient country of the Balkans, Bulgaria has a northern boundary formed by the Danube river and Romania. To the east is the Black Sea. The former Yugoslavia, especially Serbia and Yugoslav Macedonia, are on the west, and Greek Macedonia is on the south. The capital city is Sofia. The region was first settled by the Slavs in the sixth century A.D. and by the Turkish Bulgars in the seventh century. The country was Christianized by the ninth century, and in 1396 it was invaded by the Ottoman Turks, who occupied the lands into the nineteenth century. Bulgaria became an independent kingdom in 1908, following the revolt of 1876 that became a part of the subsequent Russo-Turkish War of 1877-1878. Bulgaria profitted by the First Balkan War when it expanded into

Macedonia but was forced to give up its Adriatic coastline as a result of its being on the losing side in World War I. Bulgaria once again joined the Axis in World War II but withdrew in 1944. Much as in other Balkan countries, communist "baggage train" governments were installed in the wake of the Soviet advance into the region. In 1946, Bulgaria became a People's Republic. In 1947, the country's leading political group, the Agrarian Party, was dissolved by the communists. In the same year, an Allied peace agreement was signed (21 February), and the Soviet occupation forces were withdrawn (15 December). Also in that year, Bulgaria, along with Albania and Yugoslavia, began an active campaign to support the overthrow of the legimate government in Greece. Following the collapse of the Soviet government in the 1989, Bulgaria became a free country once again. The Communist Party's leadership and the 35-year dictator of Bulgaria, Todor Zhikov, was ousted (10 November) and jailed (January 1990) on charges of abuse of power and corruption. He was tried and convicted in September 1992 and sentenced to seven years. The Communist Party had its dominant-party status revoked in January 1990. Bulgaria faced severe economic problems during this period of democratization. *Reading:* R.J.Crampton, *The Short History of Bulgaria* (1987); Richard J. Crampton, *Bulgaria (World Bibliographical Series, No. 107)* (1990).

Bunche, Ralph Johnson. (b. 7 August 1904, Detroit—d. 11 October 1971, New York) Born the grandson of a slave, Bunche was educated at Harvard, the University of Capetown, and the London School of Economics. In 1928 he became an assistant professor of political science at Howard University in Washington, D.C. During World War II he advised the Allies on African strategic policy; he also was instrumental in drafting the UN Charter, especially those parts dealing with trusteeship territories. In 1947 he became the head of the trusteeship department at the UN and remained in that capacity until 1948, when he became UN mediator in Palestine, succeeding Count Folke Bernadotte, who had been assassinated. After arranging a cease-fire he was awarded the Nobel Prize for Peace in 1950. From 1954 until 1957 he served as undersecretary of the UN until his death in 1971. During these latter years he was instrumental in helping solve the Suez Crisis, the troubles in the Congo, and the Indo-Pakistani War. President John F. Kennedy awarded Dr. Bunche the Medal of Freedom in 1963. *Reading:* Brian Urquhart, *Ralph Bunche: An American Life* (1993); Benjamin Rivlin, ed., *Ralph Bunche: The Man and His Times* (1990).

Bunker, Ellsworth. (b. 11 May 1894, Yonkers, NY—d. 27 September 1984, Brattleboro, VT) Born the son of an importer, Bunker worked in the family sugar business for 35 years before entering public life. A Yale graduate, he became a career diplomat in 1951 and served under seven presidents. He was appointed ambassador to Argentina by President Harry S.Truman (qv) (1951) and U.S. representative in Italy in 1952. He then served as the president of the American Red Cross (1953–1956). In 1956, he was appointed ambassador to India and Nepal. He remained at that post until 1961, when he was reassigned to Washington. In 1962, he mediated the West New Guinea conflict between The Netherlands and Indonesia, and in 1964 he became the U.S. representative at the Organization of American States (OAS). In that office, he helped bring an end to the fighting in the Dominican Republic that had persisted since the assassination of Rafael Trujillo (qv) in 1961. This established him as a troubleshooter for the State Department and earned him the reputation of being unflappable. President Lyndon Johnson appointed him in 1967 ambassador to the Republic of Vietnam, where he attempted to use his negotiating skills in dealing with the government of President Nguyen Van Thieu (qv). In this role he was criticized by many who saw him as too conciliatory to the communist Hanoi regime. He left Vietnam in 1973, having witnessed the "Vietnamization" of the country and the withdrawal of American forces. He then took up the task of negotiating the Panama Canal treaties. He retired to his farm in Vermont in 1978 and died there on 27 September 1984.

Bu Prang. *See* Vietnam.

Buraimi Oasis. *See* Muscat and Oman and Saudi Arabia.

Burbano, Poveda. On 11 January 1976, Vice Admiral Poveda Burbano led a bloodless coup that took over the government of Ecuador after the resignation of President Guillermo Rodriguez Lara (qv). A three-man junta ruled until 10 August 1979, when Jaime Roldós Aguilera (qv) peacefully assumed the presidency.

Burj al-Brajneh Camp. *See* Lebanon.

Burkina Faso (Upper Volta). A landlocked country in Western Africa, Burkina Faso is surrounded on the west and northwest by Mali, on the northeast by Niger, on the southeast by Benin and Togo, on the south by Ghana and on the southwest by Ivory Coast. The capital city is Ouagadougou. The region was first inhabited by man in prehistoric times, but there is more reliable evidence that it was occupied by Mossi tribesmen in the fourteenth century A.D. The region was explored by Westerners only in the late nineteenth century. In 1896, France established its hegemony by defeating the tribesmen of the Wobogo and Gourounsi regions. In 1897, the lands of the Lobi and Bobo tribes were annexed, but the natives were not completely subdued until 1903. In 1898, an Anglo-French convention stabilized the borders of Upper Volta. It was first set up as part of French Sudan but became a separate French colony in 1919. The region was partitioned among French Sudan, Ivory Coast and Niger in 1932. In 1947, Upper Volta became an overseas territory within the French Union, becoming semiautonomous in 1957. The nation became independent on 5 August 1960 under a pro-French government. On 3 January 1966, a military coup overthrew the government and established a military dictatorship that has succeeeded itself through attrition or additional coups such as the ones on 8 February 1974, 25 November 1980 and 7 November 1982 or the frustrated coup attempt in May 1983 that forced the removal of the Libyan charge d'affairs for his part in the conspiracy. Captain Thomas Sankara (qv), a former premier, carried out a successful coup in August 1983. On 4 August 1984, the name of the country was officially changed to Burkina Faso. Another coup overthrew Sankara in October 1987. As a result, Sankara was executed, and a new government under Captain Blaise Compaore was established. Compaore won the presidential election in 1991, in which only 28 percent of the electorate voted. After much debate, a National Reconciliation Forum was arranged in February 1992 to attempt to end the situation. By 1993, the economic situation had improved, but the austerity program put in effect was protested by students and union workers. In 1995, a two-day strike by university students in the capital followed the deaths of two students during a demonstration on 9 May. Although censorship had been eased, a cabinet minister was sentenced to six months for "insulting" the president in print. *Reading*: Chris Allen et al., *Benin/the Congo/Burkina Faso: Economy, Politics and Society*. Marxist Regimes Series (1989).

Burma (Myanmar). An ancient country in southeastern Asia, Burma was mentioned by Ptolemy in 140 A.D. Those people who became the Burmese arrived from Tibet before the ninth century. Early Indian influences helped shape the country, but it remained largely untouched by outside factors except Buddhism. Internecine struggles continued in the region until the late thirteenth century, when the Mongol emperor Kublai Khan invaded and subjugated the country until the sixteenth century. Great Britain won control of Burma after fighting three wars there between 1824 and 1844. Britain ruled the country as a part of India until 1937, when it became self-governing. Burma gained its independence as a republic (outside the Commonwealth) on 4 January 1948. In March of that year a communist-inspired insurgency began. In 1949, rebel Karen tribesmen with communist support declared a separate state of Toungoo. This enclave was retaken by government forces in March 1950. Communist rebel activity continued in the countryside until 1974. Burma entered into a ten-year nonaggression pact with Communist China in 1960. From 1962 until 1988, the Ne Win (qv) government followed a program of socialization that drove Indians from the civil service and isolated the country from foreign influence. In Rangoon, North Korean terrorists killed a number of South Korean diplomats in October 1983. This led to a rupture of relations with North Korea. In 1987, the United Nations granted Burma the status of least developed country. For a while civil war seemed imminent. When Ne Win resigned, a civilian government tried to correct the situation, but the government was quickly overthrown by Ne Win supporters. The country changed its name to Myanmar (Myanma) in 1989. The first free elections in 60 years took place in May 1990. *Reading*: Bertil Lintner, *Burma in Revolt: Opium and Insurgency since 1948* (1994); Alan Clements & Leslie Kean, *Burma's Revolution of the Spirit: The Struggle for Democratic Freedom and Dignity* (1994); Patricia M. Herbert. *Burma* (World Bibliographical Series, Vol. 132) (1991).

Burnham, (Linden) Forbes (Sampson). (b. 20 February 1923, Kitty, Guyana—d.6 August 1985, Georgetown, Guyana) After studying law in London, Burnham returned to Guyana and became the co-founder of the Marxist-Leninist People's

Progressive Party (PPP) in 1949. In 1955 he broke away from the PPP and helped form the more moderate People's National Congress. He was appointed prime minister of Guyana in 1964 and presided over the country's gaining its independence in 1966. In 1970, Burnham declared Guyana a "Cooperative Socialist Republic." He subsequently won two terms (1968, 1973) as president, although there was a widespread belief that the elections had been rigged. In 1980, under a new constitution, he was appointed executive president and filled that office until his death in 1985 following throat surgery.

Burundi. A republic in east equatorial Africa, Burundi is bordered on the east and south by Tanzania, on the southwest by Lake Tanganyika in the Rift Valley, on the west by the People's Republic of Congo and on the north by Rwanda. The capital city is Bujumbura. The country was first occupied by pygmy tribesmen of the Twa. These natives were subsequently displaced by Bantu tribes, who were in turn defeated by the Watusi (Tutsi), who invaded out of Ethiopia and who founded the kingdoms of Ruanda and Urundi. The country fell under German control in 1890 and under Belgian control during World War I (1916). Belgium accepted a League of Nations' trusteeship of the country in 1924. In 1925, it was linked to the Belgian Congo in an administrative union. This trusteeship was reasserted by the United Nations in 1946. In 1961, Ruanda declared itself an independent republic following a coup d'etat. In 1962, both states rejected a UN proposal to federate, and both attained their separate independence. A major rebellion took place in 1972–1973 among tribesmen of the Hutu against the ruling Watusi. The death toll ended in the hundreds of thousands. Attempts at reconciliation continue, but it is proving a hard struggle because of the abject poverty of the region and the density of the population. A plan was developed in January 1978 to end the chronic problem of food shortages by 1982. Also, in 1978, Lieutenant Colonel Jean-Baptise Bagaza (qv) took power as head of state following the elimination of the office of prime minister. One of his first acts was to expel more than 50 clergy who were charged with inciting riot among the Hutu and against the ruling Tutsi. Although Burundi remained one of the poorest nations on earth, Bagaza's policies appeared to be working during the next few years; but in 1987 he was overthrown on 9 September in a bloodless coup by Major Pierre Buyoya. Earlier that year, a severe strain was placed on Burundi when Tanzania expelled several thousand illegal Burundian settlers. The nation also witnessed an escalation of the ongoing struggle the country was having with the Roman Catholic Church. Severe restrictions were placed on all church activities and led to a breakdown of relations with Belgium, the erstwhile colonial ruler of Burundi. Buyoya was able to report some improvement in the struggle for human rights during his first year as president. This was all lost, however, when new fighting broke out between the Hutu and Tutsi in which about 10,000 (some reports say 5,000) Hutus were massacred (August 1988). Some 40,000 Hutus fled the country. By 1989, there were some hopes for improvement after Hutus were given a majority of portfolios in the government. This encouraged many Hutus to join the army, which had been a Tutsi domain. A Charter of National Unity signed in 1991 further codified the attempts to curb tribal violence. However, in November 1991, nearly 300 died when rebels carried out a series of coordinated attacks in the northwestern provinces. This led to another mass exodus of refugees into Rwanda and Zaire. By January 1992 the death toll had risen to over 500, with between 10,000 and 50,000 refugees. In March 1992 a Tutsi coup led by those opposed to Hutus in the cabinet failed. In the June 1993 multiparty elections were held for the first time. The Hutu majority placed Melchior Ndadaye, a Hutu, in the presidency. This greatly upset the Tutsi who mounted a coup on 21 October 1993 in which Ndadaye was killed and the prime minister, Sylvie Kinigi, a Tutsi woman, was forced to take refuge in the French embassy. Tribal violence ensued in which thousands of Hutu were killed and their villages destroyed. Over 750,000 fled the country. A provisional president, Cyrien Ntaryamira, took over the country pending a new election, which was held on 13 January 1994. Ntaryamira and the Rwanan president Juvenal Habyarimans, were killed in a plane crash in April. At that time it was revealed that Burundi army units had participated in the 1993 coup and that about 50,000 Hutus had been killed. Sylvestre Ntibantunganya was inaugurated president in October, although he held the office from April. New violence broke out in April 1994 following Ntaryamira's death. Many thousands more were killed. By year's end the country was in chaos and was taking on the appearance of Rwanda, with its own intertribal warfare. By 1995, many Tutsi had withdrawn from government. Throughout the year, the killing continued as the country descended further into a state of anarchy. The Organization of African Unity (OAU) and the UN then began belated discussions over the need for the insertion of a peacekeeping force. *Reading:* David Ross, *The Burundi Ethnic Massacres, 1988* (1992); Morna Daniels, *Burundi (World Bibliographical Series, No 145)* (1992); Rene Lemarchand, *Burundi; Ethnocide as Discourse and Practice (Woodrow Wilson Center Press Series)* (1993).

Busia, Kofi Abrefa. (b. 11 July 1913, Ashanti, Gold Coast—d. 28 August 1978, Oxford, England) Busia was educated in England at Oxford and the University of London and began his career as a scholar and teacher. In 1943 he became the assistant district commissioner for Ashanti. In 1946 he returned to Oxford to complete his doctorate, and in 1947 he returned to Gold Coast to undertake a social survey for the government. In 1951 he entered the legislature and led the opposition to Kwame Nkrumah. In 1957, as head of the National Unity Party, Busia fought the policies of the ruling Ghana National Assembly. He was forced into exile in The Netherlands and Britain, where he remained until 1966, when a military coup overthrew the government.He was called to serve but declined until the situastion in Ghana stabilized. He returned to Ghana in 1967, to head the ruling junta's advisory committee and served as prime minister from September 1969 until January 1972.

Busser, Carlos. *See* Falkland Islands.

Bustamante y Rivera, Jose Luis. (b. 15 January 1894, Arequipa, Peru—d. 11 January 1989, Lima, Peru) Bustamante was educated in law at the universities of Arequipa and Cuzco and served as a professor of civil law at the University of Arequipa from 1931 to 1934. He was elected president of Peru in 1945 and served until his government fell in 1948 to a coup d'etat in 1948 that was led by Manuel Odria, his minister of interior. He returned to teaching law and became dean of the law school at the University of Lima. In the interim he served as his nation's ambassador to Uruguay and Bolivia. In 1961 Bustamante was appointed a judge of the International Court of Justice at the Hague, and in 1967 he became its president. He served in that capacity until 1970. In 1977 he mediated the dispute between El Salvador and Honduras, which eventually (1980) led to a peace accord. In his tenure as Peru's president he instituted the 200-mile off-shore sovereignty law, which became a standard among many nations.

Butterworth. *See* Malaysia.

Buyoya, Pierre. (b. 1949?) Little is known of the man who became president of Burundi on 3 September 1987, after the bloodless ouster of the nation's chief of state, Colonel Jean-Baptiste Bagaza (qv) and his Uprona Party, while Bagaza was attending a meeting of the heads of French-speaking states in Quebec. Buyoya was thought to be about 38 years old and a member of the Tutsi tribe. An army officer, he was trained in Belgium and studied in France and in West Germany and was pro-Western in his thinking. He was able to improve human rights and lifted many of the repressive measures imposed on his people after taking office, but this was reversed by renewed Tutsi-Hutu confrontations in which at least 5,000 Hutus were massacred. To offset this slaughter, Buyoya appointed a Hutu prime minister (19 October 1988). This act plus the appointment of addition Hutu ministers led to the 1989 return of about 40,000 Hutus to Burundi, and a number of Hutus joined the almost exclusively Tutsi army. In February 1991 Buyoya signed the Charter of National Unity as another step in halting the intertribal fighting that had plagued Burundi. A rebel problem in 1992 led to another mass exodus of Hutus. Buyoya, on a visit to France at the time, returned to find his political equilibrium at risk. This was in part demonstrated by an unsuccessful coup attempt by soldiers loyal to former president Bagaza (4 March 1992) and several hard-line Tutsi former officials. Buyoya announced democratic elections in April 1993, which went to the opposition candidate Melchior Ndadaye, a Hutu. Ndadaye took office on 2 June, but he was killed in Tutsi coup attempt on 21 October. Thousands died in the ensuing rioting. In the meantime, Buyoya simply faded into the background.

Bydgoszcz. *See* Poland.

C

Cabelleros, Jorge Lucas. The Christian Democratic Party's (PDC) presidential candidate in Guatemala in 1970 was Cabelleros. An attempt on his life during the campaign failed, although an anticommunist editor was killed in another attack (January). A state of seige was declared in Guatemala as a result of the two incidents. In the election, Cabelleros received only 22 percent of the vote and was not elected.

Cabora Bassa Dam. *See* Mozambique.

Cabral, Amilcar. (b. 1926, Cape Verde Islands—d. 20 January 1973, Conakry, Republic of Guinea) After studying agronomy at Lisbon, Cabral returned to Portuguese Guinea in 1952. At that time he became a member of the colonial civil service. Two years later, in 1954, he resigned, convinced that colonial rule was oppressing the nation. After moving to Angola he became involved in the Popular Movement for the Liberation of Angola (MPLA). Seeing the usefulness of such groups he returned to Portuguese Guinea and, with his brother, Luis de Almeida Cabral (qv), he formed the *Partido Africano de Independencia da Guinea e Capo Verde* (PAIGC) in 1956. In 1963, he became active in the leadership of PAIGC guerrilla operations against the Portuguese authorities. Cabral was an avowed Marxist who stressed the importance of the political education of the people and their participation in the revolution. He did not live to see the fruits of his labors as he was assassinated in front of his home 20 months before Guinea-Bissau gained its independence, alleged by discontented members of his own group. *Reading:* Patrick Chabal, *Amilcar Cabral: Revolutionary Leadership and People's War* (1983).

Cabral, Luis de Almeida. (b.1931, Bissau) Co-founder, with his brother Amilcar (qv), of the *Partido Africano de Independencia da Guinae e Capo Verde* (PAIGC) in 1956, Cabral served until 1970 as a member of its political bureau and central committee. During the Portuguese-sponsored invasion of Conakry in November 1970, Cabral fled to Senegal. Cabral was secretary general of the National Union of Workers of Guinea-Bissau in 1961 and a member of the PAIGC Council of War from 1965 to 1980. He concurrently served in a number of other positions, including that of president of the State Council (chief of state) until 14 November 1980, when his government was overthrown by forces loyal to Premier Joao Bernado Vieira (qv). Cabral was arrested but subsequently released on 1 January 1982. He then went into exile in Cuba.

Cadieux, Leo. *See* Canada.

Caetano, Marcello. (b. 17 August 1906, Lisbon—d. 26 October 1980, Rio de Janiero) Trained in the law, Caetano taught at the University of Lisbon from 1933 until 1940. During this period he joined the Portuguese dictator Antonio de Oliveira Salazar's (qv), National Union Party. In 1940, Caetano became the director of the national youth movement. He thereafter assumed more and more responsible government positions until, in 1955, he was appointed minister to the president. Although there were periods of dissension, Caetano embraced Salazar's ultraconservative policies, and upon Salazar's retirement (due to illness), he became premier. His principal objective lay in maintaining Portugal's overseas empire in Africa. He was, however, less capable than Salazar in carrying out the types of suppressive actions necessary to thwart African nationalist movements. This coupled with severe economic problems at home that were largely exacerbated by the drain caused by the fighting in Africa led to his downfall. Premier Caetano was overthrown along with President Americo Tomas (qv) by a military coup on 25 April 1974 that put General Antonio de Spinola (qv) in power. Caetano left Portugal and assumed an easy exile in Brazil, where he became the director of the Institute of Comparative Law in Rio de Janeiro. He died in Brazil on 26 October 1980.

Café Filho, Joao. On 24 August 1954, Vice President Joao Café Filho was installed as president of Brazil following the resignation and suicide of Getulio Vargas (qv) amid widespread violence and disorder.Café spent much of his time dealing with the military presence in his cabinet and with preparations for the elections scheduled for 3 October 1955. When Juscelino Kubitschek (qv) won the election in a close three-way race, apparently with communist support, rumors spread the Café was planning some action to prevent his inauguration. On 8 November 1955, Café suffered a mild heart attack and transferred power to his constitutional successor, Speaker Carlos Luz of the Chamber of Deputies. When Luz indicated he would take additional steps to prevent Kubitschek's inauguration, military forces loyal to Kubitschek staged a coup on 11 November that put power in Kubitschek's hands.

Cairo (Al Qahirah). *See* Egypt.

Cajal y Lopez, Maximo. On 31 January 1980, the Spanish ambassador, Maximo Cajal y Lopez, and a number of others were taken hostage when the embassy in Guatemala City, Guatemala, was seized by a group of 39 Quiche Indians who claimed to be members of a leftist organization. When the police stormed the building, it burned to the ground in a fire probably caused by a gasoline bomb carried by one of the terrorists. Thirty-eight terrorists and all of the hostages except the ambassador were killed in the police action. The ambassador was later kidnapped from the hospital bed in which he was recuperating and was murdered (1 February).

Calderon, Guido Vildoso. Calderon was chief of staff of the Bolivian army at the time of the political crisis of July 1982, when President Celso Torrelio Villa's government was accused of complicity in the drug trade and of exporting paramilitary forces. Upon Torrelio's resignation (19 July), a military junta took power. The junta was possibly linked to the *Nueva Razón de Patria*, a secret league of military officers suspected of ties with the drug lords, and on 21 July it appointed Calderon as head of state. On 12 August, Calderon announced sweeping changes in the election laws that set off nationwide strikes that paralyzed Bolivia. As a result, the election changes were abrogated and the Congress was recalled to confirm the election of 1980, which had given Hernan Siles Zuazo the presidency. The army had, up to this time, denied him access to the chair, but now, in light of the growing paralysis gripping the nation, the Calderon and the army junta resigned, and Siles Zuazo was installed as president on 10 October.

Cali. *See* Colombia.

Calley, William Laws, Jr. (b. 1943) A U.S. army second lieutenant leading a platoon in Company "C," 1st Battalion, 20th Infantry of the 23rd (Americal) Division in Vietnam, Calley led a patrol into the village of My Lai (qv), Quang Ngai Province, on 16 March 1968. The platoon then raped, sodomized and murdered about 122 men, women, and children in what became known as the the largest massacre ever perpetrated by soldiers of the United States. Calley was returned to the United States and was given a general courts martial (ordered by the Department of the Army on 12 November 1969, following a long investigation) for his crimes amid a public outcry that he was a scapegoat for the equally horrendous crimes of his superiors, who were thought to have ordered the massacre in retaliation for enemy Viet Cong activities in the area and an even more heinous cover-up of the crime. After a long and difficult trial in which he claimed he was only obeying orders in committing the massacre, Calley was found guilty (29 March 1971), reduced in rank to private, dishonorably discharged and sentenced to 20 years at hard labor. Calley served only a few months of his sentence and was then quietly released into obscurity. *Reading:* Gerald Kurland, *My Lai Massacre* (1973); William Laws Calley, *Body Count: Lieutenant Calley's Story, as told to John Sack* (1975); William R. Peers & Joseph Goldstein, *The My Lai Massacre and Its Cover-Up: Beyond the Reach of the Law?: The Peer's Report* (1976).; Mary T. McCarthy, *Medina* (1972); Seymour Hirsch, *Cover-Up: The Army's Secret Investigation of the Massacre at My Lai* (1973).

Caluco. *See* El Salvador.

Cambodia. Known for a while as Kampuchea, Cambodia was the site of the Khmer Empire that flourished from 500 until 1450 A.D. and that stemmed from Fu-nan, a first century Khmer kingdom that grew out of a mixture of native and Indian blood. Thai incursions in the fifteenth century brought about the decline of the Khmer Empire, especially after they captured the capital city of Phnom Penh in c. 1434. It became a Thai satrap and remained as such until the eighteenth century. In 1840, a national uprising prevented Cambodia's annexation by

Vietnam. Cambodia became a part of French Indochina in 1863 by forcing Prince Norodom I to submit to French protection in the face of Siamese (Thai) objections. Siam was given two western Khmer provinces to assuage its sensibilities. These provinces were returned to Cambodian control in 1907. In 1941, Imperial Japanese Army troops occupied the country and gave the two provinces back to Thailand as a gift of good faith. The two provinces, Battambang and Siem Reap, were returned to Cambodian control in 1946 at the end of World War II. In the subsequent decade, Cambodia was a part of the battleground as France struggled to maintain its Indochinese empire against nationalist and Viet Minh communist insurgencies. The latter shifted later on into the Khmer Rouge communist uprising. The United States signed the Pentalateral Agreement with France, Cambodia, Laos and Vietnam in December 1950, which authorized indirect U.S. military assistance in Indochina. The French withdrew from Cambodia in 1953-1956, and the corrupt and weak government of Prince Norodom Sihanouk (qv) failed to established security in the countryside. For this, Sihanouk blamed the United States and South Vietnam and refused any further U.S. military or economic aid, breaking relations with the U.S. in 1965. Relations with the U.S. were restored in 1969, but Prince Sihanouk was removed from power in 1970 by the pro-U.S. government headed by Lon Nol. As a first act, Lon Nol ordered the 40,000 North Vietnamese troops in Cambodia to leave. Another early act was to abolish the monarchy. Sihanouk fled to Communist China and established a government in exile. By 1971, further North Vietnamese incursions had cut deeply into the border areas of Cambodia, and had directly aided the communist insurrection. Khmer Rouge sappers destroyed almost every plane in the Cambodian air force in one daring raid on the airport at Phnom Penh. That same year Cambodia's name was changed to the Khmer Republic. The U.S. closed its embassy in Phnom Pehn in April 1975 because of the deteriorating situation. A week later, on 17 April, the government surrendered to the Khmer Rouge, under the leadership of Pol Pot. There began a reign of terror hardly equalled in the history of the world; over three million people died (out of an estimated population of 21 million) through starvation or murder at the hands of the communists. During the Pol Pot reign of terror the country's name was changed to Democratic Kampuchea. On 25 April 1975, Sihanouk was named the head of the Khmer Rouge government. On 12 May, a Cambodian gunboat seized a U.S. flag merchant freighter in international waters, which prompted a poorly executed U.S. military response in which 15 U.S. servicemen were killed and 50 were wounded. The year also witnessed a number of clashes between Cambodian and communist Vietnamese forces. In 1978-1979, Vietnamese troops entered Cambodia and quickly attained superiority over the Khmer Rouge supported by the Kampuchean (Cambodian) National United Front. Thereafter, a virtual occupation of Cambodia continued, with communist Vietnamese forces maintaining a semblance of order; however, the Khmer Rouge still controlled about 20 percent of the countryside. In 1983, Vietnamese operations to clear rebels in the western parts of the country led to serious border clashes with Thai troops. Under heavy pressure from the United

States, Hanoi announced it would begin withdrawing its troops in 1989. UN-sponsored elections were held in May 1993, but the Khmer Rouge boycotted the process. The new constitution (21 September), which reestablished the monarchy, did little to settle the Khmer Rouge objections and sporadic fighting continued. In 1991, Norodom Sihanouk was elected president of Cambodia's Supreme National Council. In September 1993, following a UN-sponsored election (May 1993), Sihanouk was proclaimed king. Sihanouk's first full year (1994) on the throne was spent largely receiving treatment for cancer in China. Had he been at home, he would have faced considerable upheaval within Cambodia's government, including a failed coup attempt led by his half-brother. *Reading:* Karl D. Jackson, *Cambodia 1975–1978: Rendezvous with Death* (1992); Martin Wright, ed., *Cambodia: A Matter of Survival* (1989); Nelles Verlag, *Cambodia, Laos* (1994); Judy Mayotte, *Disposable People? The Plight of Refugees* (1993); Robert Kaplan, *The Ends of the Earth: From Togo to Turkmenistan, from Iran to Cambodia; A Journey to the Frontiers of Anarchy* (1997); David P. Chandler, *A History of Cambodia* (1992); David P. Chandler, *The Land and People of Cambodia* (1991); James Mayal, ed., *The New Interventionism, 1991–1994: United Nations Experience in Cambodia, Former Yugoslavia, and Somalia* (1996); Janet E. Heininger, *Peacekeeping in Transition: The United Nations in Cambodia* (1994); David P. Chandler, *The Tragedy of Cambodian History: Politics, War, and Revolution Since 1945* (1993); K. Conboy & K. Bowra, *War in Cambodia 1970–75* (1991); E. Willard Miller, *The 3rd World: Vietnam, Laos, and Cambodia, A Bibliography* (1989);

Cameroon. The Federal Republic of Cameroon is located in west central Africa and is bordered on the north and northwest by Nigeria, on northeast by Chad, on the east by the Central African Republic, the south by Congo, Gabon and Equatorial Guinea, and on the west by the Atlantic Ocean. Its shoreline is on the Gulf of Biafra in the Gulf of Guinea. The capital city is Yaounde. The Portuguese first explored the region in the fifteenth century. The Dutch followed the Portuguese and were in turn followed by the British, who, in the main, attempted to suppress the active slave trade that was carried out there. By 1849, the English had established an active relationship with the local chieftains of the Bights of Benin and Biafra. In 1868, German influence began to assert itself. By 1884, a treaty had been signed between the Germans and the Duala chiefs to set up a German protectorate in one part of the land while a French protectorate was established in the lands of the Malimba. In World War I, a British and French expedition chased out the Germans and, in the aftermath of the war, the western region became British Cameroon, while French Cameroun consolidated the protectorate already held by France. In 1940, French Cameroun joined the Free French, and in 1946 Cameroun was made an associated territory within the French Constitution of 1946 by the United Nations. By 1956, widespread anticolonial unrest spread across the land. On 1 October 1961, British (West) Cameroon and French (East) Cameroun were united as the Federal Republic of Cameroon. The following year, a communist inspired insurrection began that lasted until 1971. From time to time there have been civil and military uprisings in Cameroon, such as the attempted coup in April 1984 in which the Palace Republican Guard was foiled in its attempt to seize the government. France was accused of complicity in the affair (1985), but there was little in the way of fallout from the accusation. Over 20,000 people were killed or injured in a volcanic explosion in August 1986. In that same year, Paul Biya began taking action to lessen the human rights violations against his country. He then began work (1988) to lower the inflation rate through austerity brought on in part by a decline in oil production. In this process, the IMF and World Bank helped Cameroon draft its 1989–1990 budget. In 1990 Biya faced the dilemma of democratizing Cameroon at the cost of losing power. Part of this was brought on by an increasing number of demonstrations, protests and rioting. In one instance, six demonstrators were killed when police opened fire (1990). As a result, Biya was forced to remove his rejection of multiparty politics and to grant the populace a number of basic freedoms and rights. His attempt at democratization fell short, however, when in 1991 he refused to hold elections that would have changed the political alignment of the government. This led to a wave of strikes and violent protests. By year's end, the military controlled at least seven provinces, and the government temporarily suspended all of the newly formed political parties. At the same time, border clashes with Nigeria continued. Multiparty elections in 1992 kept Biya in power and in control of the parliament, although by only a slim margin. However, 1992 also witnessed suppression of several rival newspapers and other forms of media. The trouble along the Nigerian border erupted into open warfare in January 1994, when roughly a battalion of Nigerian soldiers occupied two islands in Cameroon territory. Attempts to settle the matter through negotiation were hampered by political problems within Nigeria and Cameroon, where factional fighting claimed the lives of eight members of the ruling party. The factional political squabbles continued in Cameroon into 1995, and Biya still held power. *Reading:* Tambi Eyondetah, *A History of Cameroon* (1974); Philip Burnham, *The Politics of Cultural Difference in Northern Cameroon* (1996); Mark Delancey & Virginia Delancey, *Bibliography of Cameroon* (1975).

Camp David. The official retreat of the president of the United States, Camp David is a government facility located in the Appalachian Mountains of central Maryland. Camp David is frequently used for private conversations between other heads of state and the president and for secluded meetings of the president and his advisors. In September 1978, President Jimmy Carter met there with Israel's Menachim Begin (qv) and Egypt's Anwar Sadat (qv) and forged a peace treaty that became known as the *Camp David Accords*. Many Arab nations reacted violently to Egypt's signing of the accords; Jordan and Saudi Arabia announced (24 September) that they would not be bound by the treaty. Even the Israeli government gave only a qualified approval to Begin's work in forging the agreement. Indeed, the treaty was never ratified by either side. *Reading:* William B. Quandt, *Camp David: Peacemaking and Politics* (1986);William B. Quandt, ed., *The Middle East: Ten Years After Camp David* (1988).

Campos, Roger Vergara. Lieutenant Colonel Campos was the director of intelligence of the Chilean army during the regime of Major General Augusto Pinochet Ugarte (qv). Campos was assassinated on 16 July 1980. The four assassins, members of the Revolutionary Left Movement, escaped. Campos' driver was also killed in the attack.

Cam Ranh Bay. *See* Vietnam.

Canada. The northernmost country on the North American continent, Canada is recorded as having been founded by Jacques Cartier in 1534, although others probably saw and visited the country's eastern seaboard in much earlier times. Quebec City was established in 1608 as the first French settlement. Canada was declared the colony of New France in 1663. An English settlement was begun in Nova Scotia in 1717; the end of the French and Indian War (1754-1763), an extension of the Seven Years War (1756-1763), gave Canada to Great Britain. Under the Quebec Act of 1774, inhabitants of that region were allowed to retain the French language and customs. Many Royalist Americans fled to Canada during the American Revolution. The Canadian Pacific coast was explored by Siir Alexander Mackenzie in 1793. After the War of 1812, in which much military activity was concentrated along the American-Canadian border, the upper and lower portions of the country were consolidated into one British colony called "Canada." The British North American Act of 1 July 1867 confederated all of Canada into a British Dominion. Canada was declared a self-governing dominion in 1931 and severed its last legislative tie with Great Britain in 1982. Subsequent legislative activities, such as the Meech Lake Agreement of 1987, which granted certain rights to Quebec, met with severe criticism in other regions of the country and exacerbated already tense relations between Quebec and the rest of the country. This in turn gave rise to the rise of a Free Quebec movement that resulted in both legislative and terrorist activities aimed at Quebec's separation from Canada. Neither of these activities achieved the desired results, however, and Quebec remains a part of Canada. The periods of rioting were serious, however, as were the terrorist attacks, especially in the decade of the 1970s. In its external relations, Canada has had periods of anti-American feeling over the decades, yet the border between Canada and the United States is the longest unprotected demarcation in the world, and cooperation in security matters has always been high. In February 1965, for instance, a combined FBI, New York City Police, Royal Canadian Mounted Police team broke up an extremist plot to blow up the Statue of Liberty. Similarly, in 1980, the Canadian embassy in Tehran gave sanctuary to six Americans who would otherwise have become hostages of the Iranian fanatics who seized the U.S. embassy in that city. The Canadians eventually got the Americans out of Iran with doctored Canadian papers. Canada's relations with Great Britain also have been strained on occasion, yet in World War II, Canada joined in the British war effort, but as an independent dominion. After the war, Canada joined the United Nations, fought in Korea, and has furnished Canadian military forces to a number of UN peace-keeping operations. In 1958, Canada joined the U.S. in establishing the North American Air Defense Command

(NORAD) to protect the continent from Soviet air attack. Later that same year, Canada and the U.S. also formed a Committee on Joint Defense. Canada again stiffened toward the United States in 1963, when Washington openly criticized the Canadians for lack of progress in bring their military forces into the nuclear age. The tiff was short lived, however, and the two countries agreed upon nuclear arms cooperation. In 1979, the Canadian Coast Guard seized eight American fishing vessels supposedly operating within Canada's self-imposed 200-mile fishing limit. In 1969, Canada began withdrawing its forces from Europe and from NATO control. The following year, 1970, Canada recognized Communist China in the face of heavy opposition, especially from the U.S. By 1978, however, Canada had adopted and announced a nonnuclear policy in many of its military operations. In 1985, the government announced it would not join the U.S. in the Strategic Defense Initiative (SDI) program. Although there were bitter discussions over trade tariffs were going on at the time (1986), Canada signed an agreement with the United States extending the North American Aerospace Command charter for another five years. A cabinet shakeup in 1987 was caused in part by a brewing scandal involving a minister involved in land speculation. A new comprehensive free-trade agreement was reached with the U.S. in 1987 (ratified in 1988, in effect 1 January 1989). In March 1987, Canada had closed its ports to French fishing vessels in a dispute over fishing quotas that were unacceptable to Newfoundland. On 15 December 1988, the Canadian Supreme Court declared that Quebec could not make French the province's official language. The provincial premier announced that Quebec would fundamentally ignore the high court decision. In May 1988, Canada sent a team of observers to oversee the Soviet withdrawal from Afghanistan, and in August it sent a detachment of 500 troops into Iraq to observe the Iranian border following the Iran–Iraq War. Later that year, a Nobel Prize was awarded to Canada for its UN peacekeeping participation. Canada also expelled eight Soviet diplomats on spy charges in 1988. The French fishing issue had escalated over the last few years and was finally settled when both parties agreed to an international commission to oversee fishing in the disputed waters. The dispute was finally settled in 1992. After holding out for 32 years, Canada joined the Organization of American States (OAS) in 1989. The language issue in Quebec continued to grow in 1990, with the provincial premier announcing he would no longer participate in first ministers' meetings. There was an armed confrontation between Mohawk Indians and Quebec's provincial police when the Mohawks attempted to block encroachment onto tribal lands (July 1990). One police officer was killed in the initial engagement. More Indians joined the uprising and blocked crucial roads, which interfered with traffic flow. Canadian army units were then sent in, and after sporadic negotiations but no shooting, an agreement was reached and the matter settled. A group of Indians were taken into custody and charged with a variety of crimes including riot and possession of illegal weapons. This culminated a year-long series of incidents involving this same Mohawk clan (St. Regis-Akwesasne). Canada supported the UN stand during the Kuwait crisis, and several Canadian naval vessels joined the coalition forces arrayed before Iraq, if only as observers. Germany-based Canadian fighters soon joined the force. In 1991, Canada began reducing its troop strength in Europe. Also in 1991, Canada joined in the North American Free Trade Agreement (NAFTA) talks. The year 1992 saw the defeat of a new constitution for Canada. In essence this was a victory for French-speaking Quebec and the *Parti Quebecois,* whose aim was independence. Canada sent a battalion of peacekeepers to Croatia and Bosnia as a part of the enlarged UN commitment to secure that region's peace in March 1992. Nine hundred other forces were sent into Somalia in 1993, although, in this latter role, several Canadian soldiers were charged with torture and brutality in the deaths of four Somalis. Canada, in an attempt to establish some distance from U.S. foreign policy, resumed aid to Cuba in 1994. Canada did, however, participate in the later phase of the Haiti intervention by sending some troops and Royal Mounted Police to the country. Throughout the period, Canada maintained contingents in UN peacekeeping operations in Bosnia and Rwanda. On 9 March 1995, a Canadian patrol boat intercepted a Spanish fishing trawler carrying on what was considered illegal fishing. The boat was ordered into port. The European Union stepped in and demanded the release of the boat and its crew. Spain then sent warships into the area off Newfoundland to protect its fishermen. The matter was settled quickly, and stricter international rules for fishing were imposed. Another fishing dispute, this time over size of Pacific salmon catches by Canada and the U.S., had been brewing for two years with no resolution. International mediators ordered a large reduction, which satisfied different people in different ways. *Reading:* Alvin Finkel & Margaret Conrad, *History of the Canadian Peoples, Vol. 2: 1867 to the Present* (1993); Tracey Arial, *I Volunteered: The Story of Canadia Vietnam Veterans* (1997); Norman Hillmer & J. L. Granatstein, *For Better or Worse: Canada and the United States to the 1990s* (1994); George Woodcock, *The Century That Made Us: Canada, 1814–1914* (1989); David B. Dewitt & David Leyton-Brown, *Canada's International Security Policy (1995).*

Can Tho. *See* Vietnam.

Canton (*Quangzhou*). *See* China.

Cao Dai. Cao Daism is a militant religious sect found in Southeast Asia. The Cao Dai combine elements of the Buddhist, Catholic, Confusian and Taoist faiths within a disciplined organizational structure. The religion was founded at the beginning of the twentieth century by Phy Ngo Can Chieu, a one-time administrative delegate of Phu-Quoc, a holy missionary involved in spiritualism. Doctor Sun Yat Sen, the founder of modern China, was a Cao Daist, as was Victor Hugo, the French poet. The holiest place in the Cao Dai religion is in Tay Ninh Province at the foot of Black Virgin Mountain (*Nui Ba Den*). In 1954, more than 1.5 million Vietnamese adhered to the religion, most of them located in and around Tay Ninh northwest of Saigon. The religion has its own clergy and a pope. The religion grew out of French repression of nationalist parties in the 1930s. The Cao Dai boasted a membership of one million in 1939. Followers of the Cao Dai religion believe in a form of spiritualism that includes communication with the departed. In one phase of their worship, Cao Dais practice marriage of a living partner with a ghost or dead one. The Cao Dai maintained a private army until the early 1960s, which fought against any encroachment, including that of the central government, into Tay Ninh province. *Reading:* Jayne S. Werner, *Peasant Politics and Religious Sectarianism: Peasant and Priest in the Cao Dia in Vietnam* (1981).

Cape of Good Hope. *See* South Africa.

Cape Province. *See* South Africa.

Cape Town. *See* South Africa.

Cape Verde Islands. *See* Principe.

Caqueta District. *See* Colombia.

Caracas. See Venezuela.

Caraccioli, Hector. Leader of a three-man military junta, Caraccioli staged a bloodless military coup that forced the resignation of Honduran president Julio Lozano Dias (qv) on 21 October 1956. Caraccioli's administration was benevolent, and his country prospered under his short rule. In September 1957, a constitutional assembly was elected. A new president, Ramón Villeda Morales (qv), was elected and seated on 21 December 1957.

Carington, Peter Alexander Rupert, Lord, Sixth Baron of Carrington. (Ireland) (Note difference in spelling of family name and title.) *See* Falkland Islands.

Carltonville, Transvaal. *See* South Africa.

Carmichael, Stokley. (b.1941) Born in Trinidad, Carmichael graduated from the Bronx (New York) High School of Science in 1960 and received a baccalaureate from Howard University in Washington, DC, in 1964. He became politically active while at Howard,and took part in the "Freedom Rides" of the Congress of Racial Equality. Upon his graduation he became a field organizer of the Student Nonviolent Coordinating Committee (SNCC) in Mississippi. He later directed SNCC's civil rights activities in the rural south. In August 1967, Carmichael publicly called for all Blacks to arm themselves to carry on a revolution against white America. At that time he was admitted to membership in the Black Panthers' militant movement. He resigned, however, in 1969, because of the group's dogmatic program and because of its dealings with white organizations. In 1969 he moved to Guinea, where he changed his name to Kwame Toure and took up the cause of the Pan-African movement. He later returned to the United States, but remained aloof from further civil rights activities.

Carrillo, Santiago. (b. 1915) Carrillo joined the Communist Party in 1936 when the Popular Front won the Spanish elections. He became the head of security for Madrid and was subsequently accused of engineering the massacre of prisoners at Paracuellos (November 1936). He travelled to Latin America following the communist defeat in the Spanish civil war, and he later lived in Paris. In July1974 he helped found the *Junta Democrática Española*, an organization of a number of parties opposed to the Franco (qv) regime. In March 1977, Carrillo participated in the founding of *Coordinación Democrática*, which brought together the opposition parties and the regional governments, especially those of the Basque and Catalan regions, in Spain. As the Spanish Communist Party

(PCE) secretary general, in June 1977 Carrillo precipitated a period of tension between the party and Moscow when he told the Soviets to stay out of Spanish internal party affairs, after the publication of an article in the the the Soviet *New Times* weekly journal criticizing him and his party. That same year he was shunned at a meeting in Moscow celebrating the 60th anniversary of the Boshevik Revolution. Later he visited the United States and lectured on European communism at Harvard and Yale.

Cartagena (Carthagena). *See* Colombia.

Carter, James Earl (Jimmy). (b. 1924, Plains, Georgia) Carter, the 39th president of the United States, graduated from the U.S. Naval Academy in 1946 and served as a naval officer until 1953. He then took over the family's peanut business in Georgia. He was elected governor of Georgia in 1970 and served four years in that capacity. In 1976, he was nominated for the Democratic candidacy for president over several much more prominent candidates. Carter won the election by a narrow margin, unseating President Gerald Ford (qv). Carter's tenure was marked by few notable achievements other than the Camp David Accords (qv) in 1978. That same year he presided over the Panama Treaty that was not so favorably received by the American public. The seizure of the U.S. embassy in Tehran in 1979, followed by Carter's indecisive leadership in the crisis, led to his loss in his reelection bid against Ronald Reagan (qv) in 1980. Since leaving office, he has often acted as an informal ambassador for peace around the world.

Casablanca (*Dar-al-Beida*). *See* Morocco.

"Casablanca States." *See* Charter of Casablanca.

Casteau, Belgium. *See* NATO.

Castillo Armas, Carlos. The president of Guatemala, Carlos Castillo Armas, was assassinated on 26 July 1957. Armas had been placed in office by a military junta in June 1954 following the bloodless ouster of Arbenz Guzmán (qv). Castillo Armas had been attempting to unravel the communist influence in his country when he was killed.

Castrejon Diez, Dr. Jaime. On 19 November 1971, the rector of the State University at Guerrero, Mexico, Dr. Jaime Castrejon Diez, was kidnapped by terrorists. A ransom of $500,000 was paid for his release. In addition, nine political prisoners were released from Mexican jails and sent to Cuba. Castrejon was released unharmed on 1 December.

Castro, Fidel. (b. 13 August 1926, Birán, Oriente Province, Cuba) Born the son of a wealthy sugar planter, Castro studied law in Cuba and established a practic in Havana. In 1953, along with his brother, Raul, he was arrested after an unsuccessful uprising against the Batista (qv) regime. Castro was sentenced to 15 years in prison, but was released after only one year. He immediately fled to the United States and then to Mexico. In both countries, he helped organize anti-Batista groups. He returned to Cuba secretly in 1956 with a small band of revolutionary guerrillas. He was at once betrayed and was almost captured in the government ambush. He fled again, this time into the Sierra Maestra mountains. From there he waged a relentless insurgent campaign against Batista that culminated in Batista fleeing the country on 1 January 1959. Castro entered Havana (3 January) and assumed the role of prime minister. In February, he announced that his was a Marxist-Leninist government. His reform programs, following mass executions and transportation of all who stood in opposition to his regime, failed to achieve any of their goals. His regime withstood the ill-conceived and poorly executed Bay of Pigs affair (April 1961), in which a vascillating American government first condoned, then shunned, a Cuban-emigre invasion attempt to recapture their country. The upshot of all of this was Castro's selling out to the Soviet Union in return for financial support for his failing economy. In 1962, the Soviets, with or without Castro's support, began introducing offensive missiles into Cuba. The U.S. reaction triggered the "Cuban Missile Crisis" (qv), which almost led to war between the U.S. and the USSR. After the Russians were forced to back down and remove their missiles, Castro still retained much of his popular support and has remained in power to this day. In December 1993, Castro's daughter, calling her father a tyrant, defected to the U. S. *Reading:* Sebastian Balfour, *Castro* (1990); Robert E. Quick, *Fidel Castro* (1993); Judith Bentley, *Fidel Castro of Cuba* (1991).

Catanzaro. *See* Italy.

Ceaucescu, Nicolae. (b. 26 January 1918, Scornicesti, Romania—d.25 December 1989, environs of Bucharest) Ceaucescu was born of peasant stock in the foothills of the Carpathian Mountains and was educated at the Academy of Economic Studies in Bucharest, Romania. He joined the Communist Party Union of Communist Youth at age 15 and was twice imprisoned for his party activities against the fascist Antonescu regime. In 1945, Ceaucescu was appointed secretary of the party's Bucharest branch. In 1954, he joined the Central Committee Secretariat, and he was elected to the Politburo in 1955. He became general secretary of the Romanian Communist Party in 1965 and was named president of the State Council in 1967. Ceaucescu was elected president of Romania in 1974. He was "reelected" in 1980 and 1985, by which time he held the country in a strict nationalist communist dictatorship. On several occasions, he openly criticized the Soviet Union, emphasizing national sovereignty and independence as the basis of Romanian foreign policy. Practicing his own form of nepotism, he appointed his wife, Elena, and other members of his family to high positions in the state and in the party. Few of his programs for his people worked, and Romanian economic conditions bordered on chaotic. If not always so, Ceaucescu's conduct became bizarre in the 1980s; his repression of Hungarian and Gypsy minorities and of all opposition in Romania became more strident. Finally, in November 1989, Nicolae Ceaucescu and his regime were overthrown, after the army refused to carry out his orders to disperse a crowd in Timisoara with gunfire. Ceaucescu fled, but he and his wife were captured on 17 December. The two were executed on 25 December 1989, in a move designed by the new government to prevent "any going back." *Reading:* Edward Behr, *Kiss the Hand You Cannot Bite: The Rise and Fall of the Ceaucescus* (1991); Ion M. Pacepa, *Red Horizons: Chronicles of a Communist* (1987).

Celebes (Sulawesi). *See* Indonesia.

Central African Republic. A small landlocked county in central Africa, the Central African Republic is bordered on the east by Sudan, on the north by Chad, on the west by Niger, Nigeria and Cameroon and on the south by Congo and Zaire. The capital is Bangui, located on the Oubangui River along its southern border with Zaire. The region is populated largely by members of the Bantu tribe. The Central African Republic was known previously as *Ubangui Shari*, and from 1894 until 1960, it was one of the four provinces of French Equatorial Africa. In 1960, it became independent and quickly became the center of Chinese influence in central Africa. In 1965, however, relations with communist China were severed after Jean-Bedel Bokassa seized power. In December 1976, Bokassa had himself proclaimed emperor and changed the country's name to Central African Empire. Bokassa was overthrown in a French-supported coup in September 1979 and replaced by his cousin, David Dacko (qv). At that time, the country was renamed Central African Republic. In 1981, Dacko was ousted, amid a growing political and economic crisis, and replaced by General Andre Kolingba (qv) and a military-controlled government. The military government lasted until 1985, when Kolingba replaced it with a 25-member cabinet. In 1987, Kolingba was reelected to a six-year term, and although legislative elections were held in 1987, he retained effective control of all aspects a the government. In 1988, Kolingba commuted the death sentence against the former emperor (*see* Bokassa) to life imprisonment. Relations with France remained quiet but strained, even though Paris thanked Kolingba for his assistance in the Chad crisis. Diplomatic relations were broken with Sudan in 1989 because of that country's refusal to allow Kolingba to fly over its space as he attempted to visit Israel. The Central African Republic had been involved in rebel incidents along the Sudanese border for several years. (Relations were restored in mid-1990.) At the same time, Kolingba was beset by economic problems caused by a swollen bureaucracy. This led to increased unrest in 1991, which was heralded by increased demands for a mult party system. Strikes occurred in August, which forced Kolingba to grant amnesty to political opposition prisoners and to legalize three of the opposition parties. Still, Kolingba resisted moves toward democracy, which culminated in the August 1992 killing of one of the opposition. Two days later, on 3 August, a strike in the capital effectively closed down the government. As a result, Kolingba announced presidential and legislative elections for February 1993. Kolingba was subsequently defeated and left office on 27 September 1993, after attempting to invalidate the election, an action that brought a swift reaction from France. Just before his departure Kolingba suspended the sentences of numerous prisoners, including Bokassa. Strikes continued after the inaugeration, because most civil servants had not been paid in months. Opposition continued to build in 1995 after the government issued a number of decrees that gave the impression of reinstalling a police state. On 18 April 1996, an army mutiny broke out as soldiers demanded back pay. By May this had turned into a full-scale insurrection. French troops had to be called in to restore order. At year's end, trouble still prevailed. *Reading:* John Allan,

Central African Republic, (1977); Pierre Kalck, *Central African Republic (World Bibliographic Series)* (1993).

Central American Liberation Front. A rightest organization formed in El Salvador around 1980. The Central American Liberation Front first made an appearance of any note when the leftist February 28 Popular League seized the Spanish Embassy in San Salvador on 5 February 1980. The Central American Liberation Front threatened to burn Spain's embassy down if the leftist rebels did not leave immediately. The leftists left the embassy after their demands were met on 18 February. The Central American Liberation Front was one of dozens of small rightest and leftist groups that established themselves and then disappeared either because of police action or through amalgamation into other organizations.

Central Coastal Region. *See* Vietnam.

Central Highlands. *See* Vietnam.

Central High School, Little Rock, Arkansas. The site of the 1957 confrontation between the governor of Arkansas, Orval Faubus (qv), and the U.S. government was Central High School. On 3 September 1957, Faubus ordered units of the Arkansas National Guard to surround the school and prevent its forced integration school by refusing admission to black students. To end the stand-off that ensued, President Dwight Eisenhower ordered federal troops (101st Airborne Division) into Little Rock to prevent insurrection. The Arkansas National Guard was federalized, thereby effectively taken out of the control of Governor Faubus, and ordered to remain in its assembly areas (armories). Order was quickly restored by the federal troops, although there followed a long period of federal presence near the school.

Central Treaty Organization (CENTO). *See* Baghdad Pact.

Cernik, Oldrich. (b. 27 October 1921, Ostrava, Czechoslovakia) Cernik worked in the Vitkovice Iron Works as a machine fitter from 1937 to 1949. He was secretary of the District Committee of the Czech Communist Party from 1949 to1954, chairman of the Ostrava Regional Committee from 1954 to 1956, and secretary of the Czech Communist Party from 1956 to 1960. Thereafter, he held a number of governmental posts until 1963, when he became deputy prime minister and chairman of the State Planning Committee. From 1963 to 1968, he was prime minister and, after 1968, prime minister of the federal government of the Czechoslovak Socialist Republic. In October 1968, he allowed 70,000 Soviet troops to be stationed in Czechoslovakia, and in January 1969 he announced that his country would pay a larger share of the Warsaw Pact costs. From 1969 to 1970, he was a member of the party's Central Committee and held numerous posts in the Czech government. In 1970, he left office to be replaced by Lubomir Strougal (qv). *See* Czechoslovakia.

Cerron Grande. *See* El Salvador.

Ceuta (*Sebta*). One of five Spanish enclaves on the Mediterranean coast of Morocco, Ceuta is a Spanish military station and free port. The enclave is on the southern side of the Straits of Gibralta. Gibralta is 14 miles to the north. The area has been occupied since Cathaginian times and was called Septum Frates during the

Roman period. Later, it was held by the Vandals, Goths and Byzantines. Into more modern times it was a major trading center in ivory, brass, gold and slaves. The Portuguese captured the place in 1415. The Spanish took it in 1580 and won clear title to the region by the terms of the Treaty of Lisbon (1588). The Moors often beseiged Ceuta; one such investment beginning in 1674 lasting 26 years. The British occupied the area in 1810 to forestall Napoleonic moves in the region, which was returned to Spain after the fall of Bonaparte. Ceuta was the jumping-off point for Francisco Franco's national movement in 1936. Since early times, Ceuta has been a target of Berber and Moorish movements to rid the Mediterranean littoral of foreign influences. In February 1975, the Moroccan government laid claim to the two enclaves, and Spain sent warships to reinforce their rights of sovereignty. Maintaining control, Spain granted Ceuta limited autonomy in 1995.

Ceylon. *See* Sri Lanka.

Chaco Province (*El Chaco*). *See* Argentina.

Chad. A landlocked country in north central Africa, Chad is bounded on the north by Libya, on the west by Niger, Nigeria and Cameroon, on the south by the Central African Republic, and on the east by Sudan. The capital is N'Djamena. The northern half of Chad lies within the Sahara Desert. The region has been inhabited since Neolithic times; the land was under constant migration by various nomadic and Arabic groups. The Sao tribesmen are counted among the first inhabitants. Chad passed through a period of small kingdoms of various Saharan Berber tribesmen, the most notable of which was the sixteenth-century kingdom of Kanem-Bornu, which controlled one of the important trade routes northward to Tripoli on the Mediterranean coast. In the seventeenth century, the kingdom of Ouaddai emerged out of the Islamization of the region and held sway over the land, setting up in the process a highly successful slave business at the expense of its neighbors to the south. Internicene feuding and incessant wars left the numerous kingdoms open to outside attack, and by 1893, most of the region of Chad had fallen to Rabah Zubayr, a Sudanese adventurer. In 1900, Rabah was overthrown by the French-supported Kanembu during the later stages of the partitioning of Africa by the European powers. In 1910, Chad was assimilated as one of the four regions of French Equatorial Africa. After World War II, it was granted status as an overseas possession of France. In 1958, Chad became an autonomous republic in the French Community and was granted its complete independence on 11 August 1960. Chad joined the Union of Central African States in February 1968. A major Arab uprising began in the Tibesti region in 1968. After heavy fighting, the uprising was finally quelled, with French military assistance, by 1971. After a Libyan-inspired coup failed, Chad broke diplomatic relations with that country. In retaliation, Libya recognized the rebel government in Chad as the nation's true leaders. Chad's president, N'Garta Tombalbaye, was murdered by a group of rampaging soldiers on 13 April 1975. A military council was then formed to run the country. Another coup attempt, this one led by a group of Nomad Guards, took place in April 1977. This one failed, however, and caused France to increase aid to Chad in order to lessen Libyan influence.

In January 1978 a cease-fire was arranged with the National Liberation Front (Frolinat), and the government once again broke diplomatic relations with Libya which had been supporting the rebels. Later in the year, the government demanded that all Libyan forces leave Chad territory. Within a year, however, fresh fighting had erupted (12 February 1979) between the Christian forces (ANT) of President Felix Malloum (qv) and those loyal (FAN or Armed Forces of the North) to the Muslim Premier, Hissen Habre (qv). As the fighting spread through the countryside, remnants of the Frolinat forces joined in. When four French civilians were killed, the French government reacted by greatly strengthening its garrison in Chad and by sending direct advisory assistance to Chad's (ANT) military forces. As the fighting continued, Malloum took refuge in the French garrison, and the chief of the National Police took power. Fighting ended with a cease-fire on 19 February 1979, but began again in early March. This time, other African nations stepped in to force a cease-fire among the 11 feuding factions in Chad (KanoAgreement, 16 March 1979). In response to a Frolinat demand, France agreed to withdraw its forces from Chad. Malloum and Habre were forced to resign in favor of Premier Goukouni Oueddei (qv). On 22 August 1979, an agreement was reached that ended nearly 16 years of civil war in Chad. In March 1980, fighting broke out again between rival factions loyal to Habre (ANT) and Oueddei. In the first weeks of fighting nearly 1,500 were killed in battle for control of the capital. Muammar al-Qaddafi sent Libyan troops to support Oueddei in November 1980. By the end of the year, Libyan forces were 35 miles from N'Djamena. On 16 December, at the request of Oueddei, Libyan forces took the capital, destroying much of the city in the process. Before the end of the year, Oueddei ordered all French forces out of the country and virtually surrendered Chad to Libya. On 6 January 1981, Quaddafi declared a union between Libya and Chad. France then cut off military sales to Libya (March 1981). In June, the OAU ordered a peacekeeping force into Chad, and by November, Libyan forces had begun a withdrawal. On 11 February 1982, the OAU warned Oueddei it would withdraw its forces if the president did not reach an internal accord with the warring factions in Chad. In June, however, Habre's force captured N'Djamena, and Habre established his own provisional government. On 22 June, Oueddei fled the country and went into exile in Algeria. This did not end the matter, however, as the two rival governments continued contention for control. On March 1983, Chad asked the United Nations for support in stopping continuing Libyan border incidents. Other African nations then began sending troops into Chad to help thwart the Libyan-backed rebels. Then, on 6 August, Chad asked France for military assistance. In response, France began sending ground and air combat forces into Chad as Libyan-backed and -supported rebel forces opened an offensive campaign in the north. By September, both France and Libya began withdrawing their forces. Subsequent peace talks, this time held in Congo, again failed as the the warring factions battled over who represented the government. At the same time, Libya dragged its feet in removing its forces, and France indicated it would not assist Chad in forcing a Libyan removal. In 1987, Chad military forces drove the last of the Libyan forces out of the strongholds in the north. The Libyans abandoned almost $1 billion in military stores when they withdrew. An unsuccessful coup led by Brahim Mahamot Into, the interior minister, and several army officers took place in April 1989. One officer was killed and Itno was captured. The other officer, Idriss Deby, escaped and opened a new rebel campaign against the government. By late 1990, Habre was forced to flee Chad. Deby then set up a new government, suspended the constitution and denied receiving assistance from Libya, although evidence to the contrary was abundant. Some of the other opposition groups joined Deby in 1991, but at least some did not. An army mutiny took place in September, and another abortive coup occurred in October. Then, in December, Chadian troops were engaged in a so-called invasion near Lake Chad. In September 1991, Chad signed a security agreement with Libya. France reinforced its garrison in Chad in January 1992 as the rebel forces around Lake Chad made some impressive gains. Another coup attempt against Deby took place in February 1992 in which French residents were allegedly involved. There was another coup attempt in June, which also failed. On 15 January 1993, a national reconciliation opened, but it was suspended four days later. Habre supporters attempted another coup, but it too failed. In October yet another coup attempt failed. During the year, the national conference reformed and elected a trade-unionist as its chairman. By that point nearly 70 opposition groups existed, at least one of which was still fighting near Lake Chad. Government troops began a massacre of natives in southern Chad in March 1993, forcing some 15,000 to seek refuge in the Central African Republic. Fighting against rebel forces continued through 1994. In 1995, the situation remained much the same, with opposition candidates willing to stand against Deby beginning to line up. When the elections were held in June 1996, the initial resolve among the opposition quickly faded as Deby won the run-off. By the end of the year there were some signs that the situation in Chad was levelling off. *Reading:* Mario Azavedo, ed., *Cameroon and Chad in Historical and Contemporary Perspective* (1989); Sam C. Nolutshungu, *Limits of Anarchy: Intervention and State Formation in Chad* (1996); Virginia McLean, *Conflict in Chad* (1981); John L. Wright, *Libya, Chad and the Central Sahara* (1989); Michael P. Kelley, *A State of Disarray: Conditions of Chad's Survival* (1986).

Chalatenango. *See* El Salvador.

Challe, Maurice Prosper Felix. (b. 2 September 1905, Pontet, Vaucluse, France—d. 18 January 1979, Paris) Challe graduated from the French Military Academy at St. Cyr and was serving as a major on the French general staff when World War II began. Remaining in France, he joined the Resistance in November 1942 and stayed with that organization until France was liberated. He then returned to the French army and took part in the attack on Germany. In 1949, Challe was promoted to genral officer rank and given command of the French air force in Morocco. In 1949, he was appointed chief of the air staff. In 1951, he was appointed commandant of the *École Supérieure de Guerre Aérienne*; in 1955 he was made chief of staff of the air force. Challe was sent to Algeria as commander of French forces fighting the Algerian rebels, immediately after Charles DeGaulle (qv) assumed power in France (1 June 1958). When DeGualle announced his policy of allowing the Algerians to choose their own destiny, a series of revolts broke out in which French inhabitants in Algeria rebelled against the policy. Challe, along with several other generals, led the second of these revolts (22 April 1961). On 26 April 1961, after four days of fighting loyal troops, Challe surrendered, was returned to France and was put on trial. He was convicted and sentenced to 15 years imprisonment. DeGaulle pardoned him after he had served five and one-half years (1966).

Chaloryu, Sa-ngad. When a military coup in Thailand overthrew the civilian government of Prime Minister Seni Pramoj (qv) on 6 October 1976, following days of violence in the country, the military junta, calling itself the Administration Reform Council, placed Admiral Sa-ngad Chaloryu, the defense minister, at the head of government. He was replaced on 8 October by Thanin Kraivichien. *See* Thailand.

Chamorro Cardenal, Pedro Joaquin. Editor of the anti-Somoza newspaper *La Prensa*, Chamorro was assassinated on 10 January 1978. The murder sparked major rioting in the Nicaragua's capital city of Managua. A general strike followed on 23 January that paralyzed the country. Anastasio Somoza Debayle (qv), the dictator head of the nation, rejected demands that he resign as a result of the incident. *See* Nicaragua.

Chamoun, Camille. (b. 3 April 1900, Dayr-al-Qamar, Ash Shuf, Lebanon—d. 7 August 1987, Beirut) Chamoun was educated in French Catholic schools in Lebanon. He was accepted to the bar in 1924 and was elected to the Lebanese Parliament in 1934. Chamoun held several other government posts between 1934 and 1944. In 1945, while serving as Lebanese ambassador in London (1944–1947), he took part in the founding of the United Nations as the Lebanese representative. Chamoun was elected president in 1952 following the resignation of Bishara Khouri (qv). In 1958, Chamoun, a Maronite Christian, was forced to ask for U.S. assistance when an armed insurrection. which had begun in 1957 erupted among several Muslim groups. He left office in 1958 and began working with his National Liberal Party to maintain a delicate political balance of power in his country following the breakout of a United Arab Republic-inspired uprising. When the civil war began in 1975, Chamoun sided with the Christian cause and established a Maronite stronghold at Juniyah. After 1980, when Lebanon began degenerating into a lawless state, Chamoun continued his efforts toward reestablishing a viable government and opposing the Syrian presence in Lebanon. During these years he survived at least five assassination attempts.After Syria invaded Lebanon, he retired from public office, but he returned to fill a number of ministerial tasks in 1984–1985.

Chandernagore. One of a group of French enclaves on the Indian subcontinent in West Bengal. In May 1956, France relinquished control of all of them to the Indian government.

Chang Ch'un-ch'iao. A member of the "Gang of Four," Chang, the former mayor of Shanghai, along with Chiang Ch'ing (qv), Mao's widow, was sentenced to death in the 1981 treason trials held in Peking. The sentences against both were suspended for two years to allow time for atonement and confession of treason. The other two defendants received lesser sentences.

Ch'angch'un. *See* China.

Chang Doc Province. *See* Vietnam.

Char Bahar. *See* Iran.

Charikar. *See* Afghanistan.

Charter of Casablanca. On 7 January 1961, Ghana (qv), Guinea (qv), Mali (qv), Morocco (qv) and the United Arab Republic (UAR) (qv) formed an organization of African states based upon a NATO formula. This became the Charter of Casablanca and indirectly led to the establishment of the Organization of African Unity (OAU) (qv).

"Charter 77" Human-Rights Movement. A group of Czechoslovakian dissidents who opposed the communist regime in that country. Charter 77 issued a manifesto on 7 January 1977 bearing the signatures of 300 prominent Czech citizens. The document assailed human rights violations and demanded the government carry out the laws of the land pertaining to human, political and social rights. By September 1977, the movement had issued 13 documents dealing with a number of legal issues. By midyear, more than 700 citizens were regularly signing these manifestos. The government's reactions to these attacks were mixed; on 14–17 January, for instance, 16 dissidents were arrested as a result of the first manifesto. The government eventually arrested a large number of people on unspecified charges and launched a countermanifesto campaign. One of the signators of the manifesto was Vaclav Pavel, a dramatist, who would become president of Czechoslovakia after the fall of the communist world. Pavel spent four months in prison for signing the manifesto. World reaction to the Charter 77 movement did much to undermine the communist regime in Czechoslovakia. *Reading:* Janusz Bugajski, *Czechoslovakia, Charter 77's Decade of Dissent* (1987).

Chau Doc Province. *See* Vietnam.

Chaves, Frederico. (b. 1881—d. 24 April 1978, Asunción, Paraguay) A lifelong member of the Colorado Party, Chavez served as foreign minister and as Paraguay's ambassador in France and Spain. He was elected president in 1949 as a Democratic Wing candidate. Facing ever-growing opposition from the Conservative Wing, Chavez began taking what were considered oppressive actions to maintain his office. On 3 May 1954, an Army-led revolt ousted Chavez from office and placed strongman Alfredo Stroessner (qv) in power.

Chechens (Chechnya). People of the Chechen-Ingush Autonomous Soviet Soviet Republic who inhabit the territory north of the Greater Caucasus mountain range. The Chechens—Cossacks by nature—occupied a region that resisted Imperial Russian encroachment until 1859, when the Cossack leader Shamil was captured and the area north of the Terek River subjugated. In 1936, Chechen was joined to the Ingush region to form the Chechen-Ingush ASSR. During World War II, the name was changed to Grozny Oblast (after the area's principal city), as a part of the on-going Russification process. By the end of the war, the Chechen and Ingush people, along with the Balkars, Kalmycks, and Karachais (qqv) had been branded as traitors by Stalin because of real and imagined comfort given to the German invaders. In January 1957, the Chechens and the others were rehabilitated in an official decree that was a part of the overall de-Stalinization program. The Chechen-Ingush ASSR was reestablished at that time, but their boundaries were shifted somewhat. After the fall of the Soviet Union, the Checheno-Ingushetia oblast became a part of the Russian Federation. The situation remained relatively stable until 1991, when secessionist sentiments arose. In August a Chechen politician, former Soviet air force General Dzhozkhar Dudayev, led a successful coup against the communist-controlled oblast government. By October, a Chechen state was established with Dudayev as president. A unilateral independence declaration was promulgated in November. In 1992, two republics, Chechnya and Ingushetia were declared. The ultranationalistic, Russia-hating policies of the Chechnya government soon created severe economic problems for the tiny republic. Dudayev then dissolved (1993) the parliament. This created internal problems that spawned an insurgent group that was supported by Russia. The civil war that ensued proved unable to topple the government, and on 11 December 1994 Russian troops invaded the republic. Resistance was stronger than expected, however, and Russian assaults on the capital at Grozny were repelled after fierce fighting that partially destroyed the city. By March 1995, a numerically superior Russian force of almost 40,000 troops took Grozny but did not conquer the fighting spirit of the Chechens. Casualty figures were placed at 100,000 during the main force operations. On April 1996, the 52-year-old Dudayev was killed by Russian fire. A cease-fire was signed in August, but Chechnya remained, at least for the time being, independent.

Cheng Heng. A Cambodian National Assembly chairman, Cheng Heng assumed powers as head of state following the ouster of Prince Norodom Sihanouk (qv) on 18 March 1970. He resigned office on 10 March 1972 and turned the government over to Lon Nol (qv).

Chen-pao (Damanski) Island. *See* Manchuria.

Cherbourg Harbor. *See* France.

Cheribon Agreement. Although called the Cheribon Agreement, the pact that settled the fighting that had erupted between Indonesian rebels and Dutch and British forces in October 1945, was signed at the resort village of Linggadyati, about 15 miles south of the Javanese port city of Cheribon. The truce agreement came after troops of the Indonesian People's Army attacked the Allied occupation force. The Dutch had earlier offered (12 October 1945) autonomy to the Netherlands East Indies within the Kingdom of the Netherlands, but fighting began (19 October), followed by a rejection of the offer from the Indonesian Republican Party (6 November 1945). The Dutch and British forces were successfully pushing the rebels out of key territories when the negotiated settlement was achieved (13 November 1946). Indonesia (qv) was recognized as a sovereign state. By May 1947, however, the terms of the Cheribon Agreement were proving unworkable, and a period of tension began between the Dutch and Indonesian governments. Among the other countervailing problems, Western Java nationalists proclaimed their independence on 4 May 1947. A joint Dutch-Indonesian military campaign against dissident, primarily communist, elements on Java who were disrupting the agreement was organized at Indonesian suggestion during a time when the new government was in a state of chaos. Although the British withdrew their forces (November 1947), the Dutch stayed in the game, and fighting continued sporadically until 1949, when an new agreement transferred sovereignty to the United States of Indonesia. *See* Indonesia.

Chernenko, Konstantin Ustinovich. (b. 24 September 1911, Bolshaya Tes, Krasnoyarsk, Siberia—d. 10 March 1985, Moscow) Born the son of peasant farmers, Chernenko worked on a farm in his youth. Chernenko began his ideological life when he joined the Young Communist League (Komsomol) in 1926. He joined the Communist Party in 1931 and held several local posts in Krasnoyarsk from 1933. He was regional secretary when the Great Patriotic War began. In 1948 Chernenko was assigned the post of chief of propaganda in Moldavia; there he became an associate of Leonid Brezhnev (qv). He moved to Moscow in 1956 and became a chief aide to Brezhnev upon his elevation to the position of chairman of the Presidium of the Supreme Soviet (1960). Chernenko became a member of the Communist Party Central Committee in 1971 and of the Politburo in 1978. After the death of Mihail Suslov in 1982, he became the chief ideologist in the party. Chernenko challenged Yuri Andropov (qv) for Party leadership in the November 1982 power struggle and became the secretary general following Andropov's death in 1984. Chernenko died of emphysema in Moscow that same year. He was replaced by Mikail Gorbachev (qv).

Chiang Ch'ing. *See* Jiang Qing.

Chiang Ching-kuo. (b. 18 March 1910, Fenghua, Chekiang Province—d. 13 January 1988, Taipei, Taiwan) Son of Premier Chiang Kai-shek (qv), Chiang Ching-kuo was born of his father's first marriage. In 1925 he went to Moscow to finish his education after a career of radical student activity in Shanghai and Peking. While in Moscow he became a member of the Communist Party and followed the Trotsky school of the ideology. He also married a Soviet citizen while working on a collective farm in the USSR. In 1937 he returned to China, where he renounced his Soviet ties and took up his father's anticommunist campaign. He held numerous posts in the government during the Sino-Japanese War, especially in the secret police. In post-World War II China he worked unsuccessfully to improve economic conditions. After the fall of mainland China to the communists, Chiang moved to Taiwan with the Nationalist government and continued his government activities. He was named to the KMT Standing Committee. He was appointed deputy premier and chaired a number of planning commissions. He was appointed minister of national defense in 1965 and held the post until 1969. An attempt on his life was made in 1970 in New York City. In 1972, the ailing Chiang Kai-shek named his son premier. Upon the death of Chiang Kai-shek in 1975, Chiang Ching-kuo was became the chairman of the Kuomintang (KMT) and was elected president in 1978. He was reelected in

1984. In 1986, Chiang announced sweeping changes for the future of Nationalist China. There would be no more military rule and the martial law imposed years earlier was to be lifted. He also lifted the ban on opposition parties. For the first time, contested elections were held in December 1986. He died in office in 1988.

Chiang Kai-shek. (b. 31 October 1887, Fenghwa, Chekiang Province, China—d. 4 April 1975, Taipei, Taiwan) Chiang Kai-shek received his military training in Tokyo (1907–1911), where he became a follower of Sun Yat-sen. He fought in the 1911 Chinese Revolution, which overthrew the Manchu (Ch'ing) government. After the war he was first sent on a mission to the Soviet Union and then appointed commandant of the Whampoa Military Academy, which trained Kuomintang (KMT) officers following the Russian model. In 1926, he took command of the field army sent to reunify China, a task he accomplished by 1928. During this time he became a fervent anticommunist and worked against communist infiltration of the KMT. In this period he divorced his first wife and married (December 1927) his second, Soong Mei-ling (known later to the world as Madame Chiang Kai-shek and the sister-in-law of Sun Yat-sen). In 1928, he became the president of the republic, having already moved the capital to Nanking, and fought against several opposition groups who still held regions of the country. Upon his leaving office in 1931, he had not completed the task, and several opposition groups retained sufficient power to pose a threat to the future. In 1939, Chiang's first wife, whom he had already divorced, was killed in a Japanese bombing raid. From 1935 to 1941, Chiang was the head of the executive body ruling China, and from 1941 to 1945, he commanded the united Chinese forces at war with Imperial Japan. During the war years, Chiang allowed a number of corrupt officials to erode the KMT power base and the coalition with the communist forces opposing Japan began to disintegrate. Following the end of World War II, the communists began a campaign to overthrow Chiang and the KMT government. This campaign climaxed in 1948 with the collapse of the KMT and the rout of Chinese Nationalist forces to Taiwan. There Chiang set up the seat of government of the Chinese Nationalists under the protection of the United States. He was in his sixth term as president when he died there on 4 April 1975. *Reading:* Sven Anders, *Chiang Kai-Shek, Marshal of China* (1975); Ch'en Chieh Ju & Lloyd E. Eastman, eds., *Chiang Kai-Shek's Secret Past: The Memoir of His Second Wife* (1994).

Chiari, Roberto F. As President of Panama, Chiari demanded the US revise the Panama Canal treaty and turn the canal over to the Panamanian government (1 October 1961). On 10 January 1964, Chiari broke diplomatic relations with the United States and repudiated the canal treaty. Chiari was replaced by Arnulfo Arias (qv) in 1968.

Chichigalpa. *See* Nicaragua.

Chichontepec Volcano. *See* El Salvador.

Chi Lang Training Center. *See* Vietnam.

Chile. A country located on the western coast of South America, Chile is bounded on the north by Peru, Bolivia on the northeast, Argentina on the east, the Drake Passage (which connects the Atlantic and Pacific Oceans) on the south, and the Pacific Ocean on the west. The capital city is Santiago. The Spaniards conquered the Inca nation in northern Chile in the mid-sixteenthth century. The southern Araucanian indians in the south were not subdued until the mid-nineteenth century. Chile gained its indendence from Spain in 1810–1818 under the leadership of Jose de San Martin and Bernardo O'Higgins and fought victorious wars against Bolivia and Peru in 1836–1839 and 1879–1884. The Communist Party was founded in Chile in 1921. In 1924, however, a military junta seized power in the country under the leadership Carlos Ibáñez del Campo. A new constitution was written in 1925 that gave far-reaching power to the president. Ibáñez remained in power until 1931, when he resigned and left Chile. The country's ensuing period of turmoil lasted through subsequent administrations and juntas. From 1938 until 1952, Chile was run by Radical Party presidents. During World War II, Chile's position was ambivalent with elements wavering between support of the Axis powers and those placing reliance in the Catholic Church. Relations with the Axis powers were not broken until 1943. In 1947, Chile broke diplomatic relations with the Soviet Union and Czechoslovakia because of communist-inspired rioting in the country. In September 1948, the Communist Party was outlawed in Chile; the party was restored, however, in 1958. Growing economic unrest in the country forced the Chilean Congress to give the president sweeping dictatorial powers in April 1957. In April 1962, Bolivia severed its relations with Chile over disputed navigational rights on the Lauca River. Bolivia would eventually leave the OAS 17 June 1963 over that organization's handling of the dispute. In 1969 elements of the army mutinied, requiring a declaration of martial law. This state of emergency remained in effect through 1970, when a Marxist, Dr. Salvador Allende Gossens (qv) was elected president. The new government's inability to deal with the continuing decline, which was exacerbated by poorly planned socialist economic programs and the activities of some of the government's police organizations, led to further chaos. Also in 1970, despite an OAS embargo, Chile sold $11 million in foodstuffs to Cuba. In 1973, a second coup attempt of the year proved successful, and a military junta seized power (11 September 1973), Allende supposedly committing suicide during the takeover. General strikes followed, and rioting spread through the countryside. The junta leader, Major General Augusto Pinochet Ugarte began a campaign of terror aimed at erasing "Marxism" in the country. Over 6,000 citizens were arrested in the first few days of the crackdown in Santiago alone. In March 1974, Great Britain halted its arms supply program with Chile, partially in response to the human rights violations rampant under the Pinochet government. Later that same year, Mexico severed its diplomatic ties with Santiago. In 1975, however, Bolivia restored its mission in Santiago after 12 years of inactivity. By the 1976, the reign of terror had reached such a pitch that the Organization of American States (OAS) raised formal charges against Chile. On 21 September 1976,

Pinochet agents assassinated former leftist Chilean cabinet minister Orlando Letelier in Washington, DC. After a long investigation, the United States demanded the extradition of Chilean secret police officials to stand trial in the U.S. When Pinochet refused, Washington imposed severe sanctions. On 11 March 1978, Pinochet ended the four and one-half years of martial law that had been imposed by his Marxist predecessor, and in June he consented to a United Nations investigation of the human rights violations charges. Still later that year, Pinochet announced his plans to remain in office until 1985, when a civil-military government could assume power. In 1979, martial law was reintroduced. In September 1982 Chile and Argentina signed an agreement extending their 1972 non-aggression pact and reiterating acceptance of the terms of the Vatican-mediated Beagle Channel pact (qv). The era of the 1980s witnessed a continuation of the Pinochet regime and an extension of the repression of the Chilean people. In July 1985, a car bomb detonated outside the American consulate in Santiago. A leftist group claimed responsibility and blamed the US for supporting the Pinochet regime. In a plebiscite held on 5 October 1988, the electorate rejected a proposal that Pinochet continue his rule until 1997 to allow for completion of his campaign to rid the country of subversive Marxist elements. Pinochet then ordered a presidential election, apparently accepting the will of the people. In December 1989, the people removed Pinochet from office and, in a series of subsequent events, elected Patricio Aylwin Azocar president. Interestingly, Pinochet was installed as army commander for an eight-year term until 1998. *Reading:* Gabriel Smirnow, *The Revolution Disarmed: Chile, 1970–1973* (1981); Mark Falcoff, *Modern Chile, 1970–1989: A Critical History* (1989); Samuel Valenzuela & Arturo Valenzuela, eds., *Military Rule in Chile: Dictatorship and Oppositions* (1986); Simon Collier & William F. Sater, *A History of Chile, 1808–1994* (1996); Leslie Bethell, *Chile Since Independence* (1993).

China. A country in Asia slightly larger than the United States, China is bordered on the north by Mongolia, on the northeast by Siberia (Russia), on the northwest by Kazachstan and by North Korea, on the east by the yellow and East China Seas, on the southeast by North Vietnam, on the south by Burma and Bhutan, on the southwest and west by India, and on the west by Afghanistan. The capital city is Beijing (Peking). Historically, an old and cultured land, China has undergone a long series of dynastic rules dating from the millennium before Christ, although archaeologists have demonstrated much earlier habitation. China has been a country of dynastic and interdynastic wars from its infancy and was ruled by foreigners from 1271 to 1368 A.D., when Mongols seized the country (Yuan Dynasty), and by the Manchus of the Chi'ng Dynasty, who ruled from 1644 to 1911. The nineteenth century was a time of great social and political change in China, as it was the time of foreign exploitation. The Portuguese reached China in much earlier times and began the external pressure, but the 1800s was the period of British, Japanese and Russian establishment of spheres of influence in which both political and economic control rested with the outsiders. Britain introduced opium to China during this period. In 1895, following a war with

Japan, China was forced to cede Korea, Formosa (Taiwan) and other islands to the Japanese. In 1912 the Wuchang Uprising brought a reassertion of Chinese leadership to the country when Dr. Sun Yat Sen and the Koumintang (KMT) party wrested control from from the Manchus. In 1931, Japan seized Manchuria and established a puppet government under the leadership of the last of the Manchu line. Japan invaded China in 1937 and fought a protracted war that spilled over into the World War II period. China fought on the Allied side during the World War II under the leadership of Chiang Kai-shek (qv) with the sometimes assistance of the large Chinese communist movement headed by Mao Tse-tung (Mao Zedung) (qv). Almost immediately after the end of the war, an open civil war erupted that eventually witnessed the forced withdrawal of the Nationalist Chinese to Taiwan (1949) (qv) and the establishment of the communist People's Republic of China. This new state, commonly called Communist China came into being as a result of the civil war that erupted among the Koumintang, the communists, and other factions scattered over the post-World War II Chinese mainland. By the end of 1949, the communists had conquered most of China; the Chinese Nationalists (Koumintang) had evacuated the mainland and moved their much-diminished base of operations to Taiwan (Formosa). On 21 September 1949, the communists proclaimed the People's Republic in Peking (Beijing). On 1 January 1950, Peking announced it intended to intervene both politically and militarily in the affairs of Tibet (qv). On 16 January 1950, the Peking government recognized the communist government in Hanoi, Vietnam (qv); on 15 February, it signed a treaty of "friendship, alliance, and mutual assistance" with the Soviet Union. Many western nations, including the United States, withheld recognition of the new communist state. In October 1950, Mao Tse-tung (Mao Zedung) (qv), the Chinese communist leader, warned the U.S. that China would retaliate, if the United Nations forces fighting in Korea (qv) crossed the 38th parallel. On 1 November 1950, the first so-called Chinese volunteers were detected in Korea in contact with UN forces. By the beginning of 1951, the communist Chinese had fundamentally taken over the war in Korea. Internally, the 1950s were a time of ideological cleansing. By Chinese accounts, 800,000 people were executed (Mao Tse-tung,1957). Most outside sources claim the number was much higher. In 1958, the Great Leap Forward movement began a move aimed at communizing every aspect of Chinese life. By the end of the decade the plan had been largely abandoned because of popular resistance and the economic chaos it engendered. In the 1960s, the great friendship between China and the USSR began to show signs of deterioration. Major border incidents along the common border punctuated clashes over ideology and the rightful leadership of the world communist movement. Soviet aid, especially military aid, was cut off, while the Chinese mounted a massive anti-Soviet propaganda campaign, aided by new friends, such as Albania. China claimed it led the world in maintaining the Marxist tradition. In June of 1961, China's Chou En-lai (Zhou Enlai) (qv) met with North Vietnam's Premier Pham Van Dong to assail U.S. aggression in South Vietnam. The build-up of Chinese communist forces along the coast facing

Taiwan (1962) prompted the U.S. president to warn Peking that any attack on the islands of Quemoy and Matsu (qv) would force a US response. Also, in 1962, India asked the United States for military assistance to stem the Chinese aggression along its northeastern border. In 1965, the Great Proletarian Cultural Revolution began, which aimed at the destruction of bureacracy and pragmatism. The relocation of millions of young Chinese began, accompanied by a literal bloodbath of those accused of treason against the communist state. During the purge, millions were summarily executed, especially petty officials, teachers, scientists, and the elderly being among the main targets. When the purge had run its course, the country was again in a state of economic and social chaos. Many of those purged who had not been executed were returned to office to get the industrial and educational systems back into operation. In 1972, U.S. president Richard M. Nixon (qv) made a much heralded official visit to China following an invitation from Zhou Enlai. One diplomatic outcome of the trip was the beginning of a period of normalization of relations between the two countries, which was first manifested by the exchange of liaison offices in May–June 1973. This was followed by U.S. recognition of the People's Republic of China, on 15 December 1978, as the sole legitimate representative of the Chinese people and by the subsequent establishment of full diplomatic relations on 1 January 1979. Also, in the 1970s, China's relations with Vietnam deteriorated. After the Vietnamese invasion of Cambodia, Peking accused Vietnam of persecuting ethnic Chinese and, in 1978, invaded four border provinces in northern Vietnam. After a period of heavy fighting, the Chinese withdrew. Following the deaths of Mao Tse-tung and Chou En-lai (Zhou Enlai) (qv) in 1976, Mao's wife, Chiang Ch'ing (Jiang Quing) (qv) and three others were purged and eventually put on trial. The purge and trial of the "Gang of Four" (qv) (1981) exemplified the continuing reassessment of the policies of Mao Tse-tung. The 1980s witnessed a relaxation of some of the economic programs that had been strangling the country. By the end of the decade, however, the old-line party leaders had failed to reform the social and economic programs far enough, and a massive demonstration by more than 100,000 Chinese took place in Beijing, beginning on 4 May 1989. The demonstration continued into the period of the visit of Mikail Gorbachev (qv) to Beijing on 15–18 May. By that time the demonstrations had grown to more than a million people in Beijing with similar activities in at least 20 other cities. On 20 May, the government declared martial law, but the demonstrations continued. On 3–4 June 1989, Chinese troops were ordered into Beijing, where a great confrontation took place in Tiananmen Square before the Great Hall of the People. In the ensuing fighting more than 5,000 were killed, and many more thousands injured; hundreds of students and workers were arrested. In subsequent trials, many were condemned. To the outside world, the government's violent reaction did much to tarnish the diplomatic successes that Beijing had enjoyed. Ongoing signs of dissatisfaction were highlighted in June 1993, by the apparent attempts by thousands of young Chinese to flee the country to the United States to avoid a sterilization program being adopted in

China to help curb a very high birth rate. *See also* Taiwan. *Reading:* John King Fairbank, *China: A New History* (1994); Milton W. Meyer, *China: A Concise History* (1994); Jian Chen, *China's Road to the Korean War:. The Making of the Sino–American Confrontation* (1994);Donald Shanor & Constance Shanor, *China Today: How Population Control, Human Rights, Government Repression, Hong Kong, and Democratic Reform Affect Life in China and Will Shape the World* (1995); Daniel Norman & Dan N. Jacobs, *Borodin, Stalin's Man in China* (1981).

Chin A Sen, Hendrick Rudolf. (b. 18 January 1934, Albina, Marowijne, Dutch Guiana) A practicing physican, Chin A Sen was trained at the medical school in Paramiribo and at the University of Utrecht, the Netherlands. He set up a medical practice in internal diseases at Nieuw Nickerie Hospital in 1969 and, in 1970, joined the staff of St. Vincentius Hospital in Paramiribo. He extended his medical studies at Nanjing University, China, in 1979. From March to November 1980, he was appointed prime minister and minister of general and foreign affairs after a military coup ousted the government of Henck Arron. In November, Chin A Sen became president of Suriname when another coup, this time led by Sergeant Major Daysi Bouterse (qv) overthrew President Johan Ferrier. He survived a coup attempt led by Sergeant Major Willem Hawker (qv) in 1981. Following a bloody coup attempt in December 1982 by the Movement for the Liberation of Suriname, Chin A Sen resigned and went into exile in the Netherlands. He returned to Suriname in 1987.

Chinchow. *See* China.

Chipatima, Sant. Leader of a military coup attempt that failed to overthrow the Thai government of Prime Minister Prem Tinsulanoud (qv), Sant Chipatima had been deputy commander of the army when a corruption scandal shook the Thai government to its foundations. On 1 April 1981, Sant Chitapima's followers occupied a number of government buidings after Prem Tinsulanoud attempted to change the retirement law so as to remain commander in chief of the army after age 60. Several thousand loyal troops moved into Bangkok and restored order. Sant Chipatima and 11 other military officers were dismissed, and Sant Chipatime fled to Burma.

Chipyong. *See* Korea.

Chittagong. *See* Bangladesh.

Choiseul Sound. *See* Falklands Islands.

Chongpyong Reservoir. *See* Korea.

Chorwon. *See* Korea.

Chosin Reservoir. *See* Korea.

Christian Democratic Party (PDC). *See* Guatemala.

Christian National Liberal Party (NPL). *See* Lebanon.

Christmas Island. An coral atoll in the Gilbert group just north of the Equator, Christmas Island was the 1957 site of a series of successful hydrogen bomb tests by the British. The atoll was also used for a series of US nuclear tests in 1962. In 1979, the atoll became part of the newly independent Republic of Kiribati.

Chtaura. *See* Lebanon.

Chuguchak (T'ach'eng). *See* China.

Chukaku-Ha **(Nucleus Faction).** This radical leftist terrorist group was organized in 1963 and has about 200 hard-core members. It has been termed the most powerful faction of Japan's 23 New Left factions and has a philosophy of mass struggle. Operations in the group are closely guarded and not much is publicly known about its inner workings. In 1986–1988, there were some indications that the group might be changing its orientation to include human as opposed to facility and building targets. Several people were killed or injured by direct attack in September 1986. The first attack was in June 1979 against Haneda Airport. The group claimed credit for the 1 January 1985 rocket attack on the U.S. consulate in Kobe, Japan. On 29 November of that same year, the group claimed credit for cutting the Japanese Nation Railway system communications in 16 places and fire-bombing a railway station. These acts disrupted railway operations and stranded more than 11 million travellers. In January 1988, the group attacked Tokyo's Narita Airport.

Chu Lai. *See* Vietnam.

Chun Doo Hwan. (b. 18 January 1931, Nae Chon Ri, Korea) One of nine children of a farmer, Chun attended the technical high school in Taegu, graduating in 1951. Chun then entered the Republic of Korea Military Academy at the height of the Korean War. After four years of study (his was the first class to get the four-year curriculum) Chun entered the army as an infantry officer. In 1958, he married Lee Soon Ja, the daughter of the chief of staff at the military academy. In 1959, he joined the Korean Special Forces and was trained in the United States. His military star rose quickly: command of the White Horse Division in Vietnam, command of the Capital Garrison in Seoul, command of the First Airborne Special Forces Group and, later, the First Division. In 1979, he took command of the Defense Security Command as a lieutenant general. Following the October 1979 assassination of President Pak Chung Hee (qv) and the subsequent government crisis, Chun, who had been in charge of the investigation of Pak's murder, carried out a military coup that put a group of younger army officers in control of the army and, hence, the government. President Choi Kyu Hah remained in office, but his was a ceremonial position. The real power lay in Chun's hands as the chairman of a military junta. On 22 August 1980, Chun retired from the army. Five days later, he was formally elected president of the Republic of Korea. His subsequent policies were stern but conciliatory, and South Korea took on an air of stability. Chun lifted the martial law edict that had been declared upon Pak's death (January 1981) and released opponents from bans that prohibited political activity (March 1983). On 9 October 1983, however, while on a state visit to Burma, Chun narrowly missed an assassination attempt engineered by North Korea. In all, 21 of Chun's top aides were killed in the bomb explosion. The Republic of Korea's army went on alert; and Burma broke diplomatic relations with North Korea (4 November) when two North Korean "commandos" were captured and confessed to the assassination attempt.

Chung Huh. Serving as South Korean foreign minister, Chung Huh succeeded Syngman Rhee (qv) as provisional president of a caretaker government, when Rhee was forced to resign on 17 April 1960. Chung Huh was replaced by Yun Po Sun (qv) on 12 August 1960.

Cierna nad Tisou. *See* Czechoslovakia.

Ciudad Trujillo (Santo Domingo). *See* Dominican Republic.

Clark Amendment. On 27 January 1976, the U.S. Congress passed legislation thatcut off further aid to the two pro-Western Angolan factions fighting the Soviet and Cuban-supported government there. The congressional vote was partially in response to the introduction of South African troops into the fighting in support of the FNLA and UNITA forces and rejected President Ford's request for aid to offset that supplied by the communist bloc.. The action of the U.S. Congress assured the Cuban-backed MPLA of a victory. The fighting in Angola continued, however, and, as the situation clarified, the US Senate voted on 11 June 1985 to repeal the Clark Amendment. As a result, the Angolan government broke off normalization talks with the United States. *See* Angola.

Clementis, Vladimir. (b. 1902, Tesovec, Slovakia—d. 3 December 1952, Prague) Clementis studied at Prague University and became a member of the Communist Party. In 1935, he was elected to parliament on the communist ticket. After World War II, in 1945, he became vice-minister of foreign affairs in the first Czech government. In 1948, he was one of the chief organizers of the 1948 coup. He then became foreign minister, but he was forced to resign in 1950, when he was accused of deviationism. Following the 1952 purge, he was convicted of treason and hanged.

Coard, Bernard. Coard was the deputy prime minister of Grenada in October 1983 and led the group of dissidents that arrested Prime Minister Maurice Bishop (qv) on 13 October. Bishop was murderd on 19 October. Coard was subsequently apprehended (29 October) after US military forces landed on 25 October. Coard, nine other members of the New Jewel Movement (NJM) party, and nine others (a total of 19) were placed on trial for the murders of Bishop and seven others in October 1984. After numerous delays and postponements the trial concluded on 4 December 1986. Coard's was among 14 death sentences passed down for the murders. Three other defendants were found guilty of manslaughter, and one was acquitted. *See* Grenada.

Coco (Segoria) River. *See* Honduras.

Cod War. In circumstances similar to some 1958 events, a new series of Icelandic-British confrontations took place 1972–1976. Both sets of incidents have been whimsically called the "Cod Wars." In the latter series of incidents, however, armed confrontation became a part of events. On 14 July 1972, a new coalition of leftist parties within the Icelandic government put into law an extension of Iceland's territorial fishing waters from 12 to 50 miles. The new claim was put into effect on 1 September. Immediately upon the passage of the legislation, Great Britain (and West Germany) formally protested and took the case to the International Court of Justice. The court ruled in favor of Great Britain in an interim order handed down on 17 August. Iceland rejected the decision and sent warships out to the new fishing line to drive off British fishing trawlers, which had regularly fished the area for years. Iceland reached agreements with several of the smaller fishing nations, but not with Britain. Confrontation between Icelandic and British ships inside the exclusion zone became commonplace as talks between the two nations collapsed in November 1972. On 26 May 1973, an Icelandic gunboat fired on a British trawler fishing inside the 50-mile limit. Then, on 7 June 1973, an incident occurred between a British warship and an Icelandic Coast Guard cutter in which each claimed to have been rammed by the other. Both sides lodged formal protests. This incident was followed by another on 28 June, when an Icelandic patrol boat fired on a West German trawler. On 13 August, an Icelandic gunboat pursued another British trawler for 100 miles into undeniably international waters. On 10 September, another collision occurred between a British frigate and an Icelandic cutter. The next day (11 September), Iceland threatened to break diplomatic relations with Great Britain if the British kept ramming their gunboats. On 13 November 1973, Iceland and Great Britain reached an interim agreement to halt the escalating "Cod War." On 19 July 1974, however, the Icelandic gunboat *Thor* attacked and captured a British fishing vessel, the *C. S. Forester*, for allegedly fishing inside the exclusion zone. On 25 July, the World Court handed down a ruling in matter which blamed Iceland for having broken international law. Iceland once again denied the court's jurisdiction. In late November 1975, matters took a turn for the worse when a second round of talks between Great Britain and Iceland broke down and a report was received that an Icelandic gunboat deliberately cut a British trawler's net lines. London ordered warships into the area with orders to protect the trawlers that were operating in international waters. By 7 December, at least three British frigates were on patrol in the area. In retaliation, Iceland once again threatened to break relations with Great Britain and to reevaluate its position in NATO. In an attempt to make NATO force British compliance with the fishing restrictions, the Icelandic government began a campaign of blocking the entrances to outlying radar and communications sites operating in support of the vital NATO base at Keflavik. This tactic was not universally accepted by all Icelanders, however, and soon disappeared. In the face of increasing British naval activity in what Iceland claimed as its sovereign waters, Iceland broke off diplomatic relations with Great Britain on 19 February 1976. Great Britain announced a settlement to the dispute on 30 May 1976, following negotiations held in Oslo, Norway. The British ordered their warships out of the disputed waters. Diplomatic relations were reestablished on 1 June. This was not the first instance of a "Cod War." A similar incident occurred in 1958 when Iceland extended its limits to 12 miles on 1 September 1958, following the results of a congress in Geneva to discuss the problem of territorial limits earlier that year. In response to the Icelandic move the British sent warships into the area to accompany their fishing fleet. That dispute was not settled until 27 February 1961.

Coimbra da Luz, Carlos. The presidency of Carlos Coimbra da Luz of Brazil was overthrown by a military junta led by Lieutenant General H. B. D. Teixeira (qv). The ouster came about when it was discovered (11 November 1955) that Coimbra planned to prevent the assumption of the presidency by his duly-elected successor Juscelino Kubitschek (qv). Kubitschek was sworn in on schedule on 31 January 1956.

Collins-Ely Agreements. *See* Indochina.

Colom Argueta, Manuel. On 25 March 1979, unidentified right-wing gunmen assassinated Manuel Colom Argueta, the former mayor of Guatemala City and the leader of the Opposition United Front of the Revolutionary Party of Guatemala. In retaliation for this and other right-wing killings, the left assassinated General David Cancinos Barrios, the army chief of staff.

Colombia. A country in northwest South America, Colombia forms the link between South and Central America. The capital city is Bogota. The original European settlers were Spaniards who completed the conquest of the territory by 1550. The land had been inhabited for centuries by various Indian cultures (primary Chibcha tribes), most likely because of its location at the terminus of the natural land bridge from the north. A Spanish colonial government ran Colombia until 1740, when the land was made a part of the viceroyalty of New Granada. Simon Bolivar liberated Colombia from Spanish rule in 1819. The new republic lasted until 1830, when internal frictions brought about a realignment of borders and a breakup of the New Granada complex. Subsequently, Colombia stood alone, as did Venezuela and Ecuador. The Republic of Colombia was proclaimed in 1886, but not before periods of civil war (1840–1842, 1855–1857) wracked the land. In 1899, another civil war broke out that led to the region of Panama revolting (1903) against Colombian rule and, with the assistance of the United States, gaining its independence and the Panama Canal. By that point in time, Colombia had suffered 27 civil wars. In more modern times, Colombia has continued to suffer from internal dissention, dictators, abridgement of human rights, death squads, palace coups, rioting, long periods of martial law, hostage taking, airplane hijackings, government corruption and involvement in the drug trade. In 1948, for example, the assassination of a left-wing liberal leader led to widespread rioting that disrupted a meeting of the Pan-American Council and caused over 1,400 deaths. Colombia became a charter member of the Organization of American States in 1951. Colombian troops fought with distinction with the United Nations Command during the Korean War. In 1972, however, insurgency had grown to a point where rebel bands were openly attacking towns. In 1975, a U.S. Consul was kidnapped and murdered in Cordoba; in 1980, the U.S. ambassador was held hostage as terrorists demanded the release of political prisoners. In 1982, two U.S. Drug Enforcement Administration agents were shot and left for dead in a botched assassination attempt. US corporations were singled out for attack in 1976, when bombings were perpetrated against a number of offices in Bogota. In the mid 1980s, the violence centered on terrorism against government officials who would not bend to the will of the drug lords who virtually ran the country. Some order was restored in 1984, when two leftist guerrilla organizations signed a truce with the government. By 1985, the government was attempting to resolve the drug problem, but the power of the drug lords remained great. That same year saw a renewal of attacks on American corporations in that country. In November 1985, the Supreme Court of Colombia in Bogota was seized by terrorists, and the ensuing battle with police led to the deaths of about 100, including several jurists. In December of that year, another U.S. firm was attacked, with the resultant death of one American. The resultant analysis of the incident proved the power of the terrorists and the inability of the government to protect its citizens. Similarly, the power of the drug lords was becoming even more evident. Antiguerrilla government activity also created major problems. The 1990 elections were dominated by the drug lords, whose activities against tougher drug laws cost the lives of three presidential candidates and hundreds of other citizens. Even so, the election put Cesar Gaviria Trujillo, a strong advocate of antidrug legislation, in the presidency. One of the results of his anti-drug campaign was the attempted recapture and subsequent death of Pablo Escobar, the escaped head of the Medellin drug cartel on 2 December 1993, after a running battle with police and army units. This led to an almost immediate step-up of activity by the rival Cali drug lords, who supplied about 80 percent of the drugs smuggled into the U.S. The drug lords did offer to quit all illegal activities if they were, in effect, pardoned, but nothing came of what was depicted by authorities as a publicity stunt. At the same time, counterguerrilla activities continued with over 1,200 rebels having been killed in the preceding six months. Trujillo left office in August 1994 and was replaced by Ernesto Samper Pizano. The elections were not without incident, as many acts of violence took place during the campaign. Violence also occurred when a Colombian soccer player accidentally scored at his own end of the field in the World Cup. Angered fans murdered him upon his return to Colombia. The most important fact that came out of this period was the realization that the Medellin drug cartel was not finished, as it promised death to all politicians supported by the rival Cali group. By 1995, however, Cali controlled about 70 percent of the drug traffic. In a renewed antidrug campaign (1995), Colombian forces were successful in neutralizing number of Cali drug lords. The drug war was by no means over, but the battlefield was changing. *Reading:* Javier Giraldo, *Colombia: The Genocidal Democracy* (1996); Herbert Braun, *Our Guerrillas, Our Sidewalks: A Journey into the Violence of Colombia* (1994); Ana Carrigan, *The Palace of Justice: A Colombian Tragedy* (1993); Harvey Cline, *Colombia: Democracy under Assault* (1995).

Colombo. *See* Sri Lanka (Ceylon).

Colombo Plan. The plan was named after the city of Colombo, Ceylon (Sri Lanka), where representatives of Australia, Ceylon, Great Britain, India, New Zealand and Pakistan met in June 1951 to work out the details of a technical assistance and financing plan for the countries of south and southeast Asia. The United States and other nations, such as Indonesia (1952) and Thailand (1954), joined the plan later. The group meets annually, but a standing committee performs the daily functions. Each project is arranged bilaterally with the government concerned or with the International Bank for Reconstruction and Development.

SS Columbia Eagle. On 14 March 1970, the US cargo ship, *SS Columbia Eagle*, loaded with ammunition bound for Thailand, was highjacked by two crewmen who forced the ship into Cambodian waters. The Cambodian government held the ship until 29 March before allowing its release. The ship did not clear Cambodian waters until 8 April 1970.

Columbia University. *See* United States.

Comite National de Liberation. *See* Zaire.

Commando Andreas Baader, Red Army Faction. *See* Red Army Faction.

Commando Elizabeth Van Dyck of Action Direct. *See Action Directe*.

Commando George Jackson. A German terrorist group named after George Jackson, a member of the American Black Panther group, thought by U.S. intelligence services to be a terrorist organization, who was killed during an attempted prison break from San Quentin in August 1971. Jackson was known as one of the three black convicts calling themselves the Soledad Brothers. Jackson's name was used by a German Red Army Faction (RAF) (qv) as the reason for killing a U.S. airman stationed at Weisbaden Air Force Base in West Germany on 7 August 1985. The RAF then used the dead serviceman's identification card to gain access to Rhein-Main Air Base where they detonated (8 August) a car bomb killing, two more US servicemen and injuring 20 others.

Commando Patrick O'Hara. A group named after Patrick O'Hara, a member of the Irish National Liberation Army (INLA), who died of starvation while on a hunger strike in British prison in 1981. O'Hara's name was used as a reason for a Red Army Faction (RAF) (qv) terrorist attack on 1 February 1985, in which two RAF members forced their way into the home of West German industrialist Ernst Zimmermann, tortured him and then mortally shot him in the head.

Communist Combatant Cells (*Cellules Communistes Combattante*)(CCC). A relatively new left-wing terrorist organization, the CCC announced its arrival in 1984, by carrying out a series of attacks on the Belgian offices of Litton Data Systems, a German truck company known as MAN and the Honeywell-Europe facilities in Brussels. The organization has its headquarters in Brussels; the suspected leader was Pierre Carette. The attacks began on 2 October 1984 and were claimed to have been made against organizations associated with NATO "imperialists." The CCC also attacked a number of Belgian political party offices on the same pretext. On 26 November, two bombs detonated near an antenna tower at Bierset Military Airfield near Liege. This attack was allegedly carried out, the CCC claimed, because NATO aircraft were stationed there. On 11 December, six bombs damaged the NATO emergency pipelines around Belgium. Then, on 15 January 1985, a car bomb was exploded in front of the U.S. NATO Support Activity building near Brussels. One American serviceman was injured. Although no one claimed credit for the attack, the CCC was blamed. The group caused its first fatalities in May 1985, when two Belgian firemen were killed trying to disarm one of its unexploded bombs. Because of the bad publicity the group received upon the deaths of the firemen, they issued a communique blaming the police for being slow in responding to the report of the bomb threat and by bombing the gendarmarie administrative headquarters in Brussels. Several of the CCC leadership were captured in December 1985, and the group's safehouse network was uncovered.

Communist New People's Army (NPA). *See* The Philippines.

Communist Party of Indonesia (PKI). *See* Indonesia.

Comodoro Rivadivia Air Force Base. *See* Argentina.

Comoros. Properly known as the Federal Islamic Republic of the Comoros (*Jumhuriyat al-Qumur al-Ittihadiy al-Islamiyah)*, the Comoros are a group of volcanic islands lying at the north end of the Mozambique Channel that separates the east African mainland from the island of Madagascar (Malagasy Republic). There are four islands in the group: Mayotte, Grande Comoroe (*Njazidja*) Island, Anjouan (*Nzwani*) and Moheli (*Mwali*). The capital is Moroni on Grande Comore. The islands were first charted in 1527 but were apparently not visited until 1591. The principal inhabitants of the island were Arabs controlled by various sultans. The French took possession of Mayotte in 1841. By 1886, the sultans of the other islands had requested French protection. After 1914, the Comoros were put under the control of the French colonial government on Madagascar. In 1925, France granted the islands an independent administration. In 1947, the Comoros became a territory of France. In 1958, the islands voted to retain their overseas territory status and, in 1960, were granted autonomy. The islands voted for complete independence in 1974. In 1975 the French National Assembly moved to allow each island to choose its own path. In a July 1975 referendum, all of the Comoros Islands, except Mayotte, which remained a French possession, voted for independence from France. French troops began withdrawing that same year, except for a small garrison on Mayotte. On 3 August 1975 a pro-French coup overthrew the leftist government of Ahmed Abdullah. Ahmed was returned to power in 1978, however, when another coup led by French mercenaries seized power. Abdullah was reelected in 1984 without opposition. After surviving three coup attempts, he was assassinated on 26 November 1989, following another coup attempt. This brought a French reaction, which included naval units operating in Comoran waters and a French manhunt for Paul Denard, the mercenary leader of the royal guard. Upon the restablishment of order the interim president, Said Mohammed Djohar, asked for French troops to remain in Comoros for the present. Djohar was elected in his own right in subsequent elections, but was ousted by a coup (September 1995) led by French mercenaries. This brought an immediate French reaction, in which French troops were landed on Grande Comore and forced the surrender of the rebels. Djohar was again restored to power. After some political manuevering in late 1995 to early 1996, the 80-year-old Djohar was given a ceremonial post and a younger man elected to the presidency. *Reading:* Malyn Newitt, *The Comoro Islands: Struggle against Dependency in the Indian Ocean* (1984).

Conakry. *See* Guinea.

Concepcion. *See* Chile.

Conciliation Commission for Palestine. *See* United Nations.

Confederation of Reformist Workers' Union (DISK). *See* Turkey.

Congo. *See* Zaire.

Congo-Brazzaville. *See* Republic of Congo.

Congo-Katanga. *See* Zaire.

Congo-Kinshasa. *See* Zaire.

Congolese National Liberation Front (FNLC). *See* Zaire.

Congress of Europe. The first meeting of the Congress of Europe took place in The Hague, Netherlands, on 7 May 1948 to discuss plans for a European Union. The work of attempting a European Union continued into 1993 with some success. *Reading:* Neill Nugent, *The Government and Politics of the European Union* (1994); Louise B. Van Tartwijk-Novey, *The European House of Cards: Towards a United States of Europe?* (1995).

Constantine. *See* Algeria.

Constantine II. (b. 1940) Born the son of Paul II, King of Greece, Constantine was groomed for the crown from birth. In 1964, he acceded to the throne and soon after married Princess Anne-Marie of Denmark. Constantine was forced to flee Greece during the right-wing "Colonels' Coup" in April 1967. When an attempt to retake power failed, Constantine went into exile in Rome (December 1967). Constantine was formally deposed in June 1973, and the monarchy was abolished on 8 December 1974 by a popular referendum, which voted 2:1 for a republican form of government.

Contadora Nations (Contadora Group). A group of South and Central American member nations, the Contadora Group formed in January 1983, at the invitation of Panamanian president, Ricardo de la Espriella (qv). The Contadora Group's original membership included Columbia, Mexico, Panama and Venezuela and was organized to monitor the peace of the region and to assist in negotiating peaceful settlements to disputes. In 1984, the group drafted a peace treaty for the region based on a mutual reduction of arms and foreign advisors, including those from the United States. In October 1984, the UN approved the plan. Nicaragua accepted the proposition, but that acceptance was challenged by the United States and others unless sufficient safeguards could be established to insure Nicaraguan compliance. A second draft of the treaty was presented to the unsettled nations of Central America, including El Salvador, Honduras, Guatemala and Nicaragua and to the United Nations in 1985. The group also stated that, unless the treaty was ratified, the Contadora Group would end its role as peace negotiators. Later in 1985, a Contadora support group was established that included Argentina, Brazil, Peru and Uruguay. In January 1986, the Contadora nations signed the Caraballeda Declaration, which promised a continuation of the search for peace through diplomacy. At Esquilulas, Guatemala, in May 1987, the Contadora peace plan was presented to the members of the Central American Common Market (CACM). Although the treaty was not signed, an agreement was reached to set up a Central American Parliament. Also, in 1987, Cuba endorsed the Coontadora program. In 1988, the secretary general of the United Nations visited the capitals of the Contadora

Group nations as a show of support for their program. In the end, however, the Contadora peace plan failed to materialize. *Reading:* Roberto Alvarez & Bruce Bagley, *Contadora and the Central American Peace Process: Selected Documents* (1985); Bruce Bagley, *ed., Contadora and the Diplomacy of Peace in Central America: The United States, Central America and Contadora* (1987).

Conte, Lansana. (b. 1934?, Coyah, Guinea) Conte was born a member of the Susu tribe and was raised a Muslim. He attended military school in Buigerville, Ivory Coast, and the military college in Senegal. In 1955, Conte joined the French army. By 1964 he serving in the Guinean army as a captain. In 1970, he took part in the defense of the capital city of Conakry during the unsuccessful invasion of Guinea from Portuguese Guinea (Guinea–Bissau). He fought with the Portuguese Guineans as a colonel, commanding the Boke Region in West Guinea in 1973 during their bid for independence. He was sent to the Soviet Union in 1974 for technical studies at Minsk and, in 1975, he was appointed deputy chief of land forces in Guinea. He led a bloodless coup and was named president of Guinea on 5 April 1984 by the military junta that seized power (3 April 1984) following the death of Sekou Toure (qv). Conte then established the Military Committee for National Recovery (*Comite militaire de redressement nationale* (CMRN) to run the country. In 1985, an attempt to overthrow his government was suppressed by troops loyal to the regime. Conte's rule was marked by his attempts to restore human rights gaurantees for his people.

Con Thien District. *See* Vietnam.

Contreras Sepulveda, Manuel. On 15 May 1979, the U.S. ordered its ambassador home from Chile after the Chilean government refused to extradite three secret police officials, including the head of the Chilean Secret Police (DINA), General Manuel Contreras Sepulveda, who had been indicted for the planning and implementation of the assassination of Orlando Letelier (qv) in Washington, DC, in 1976.

Contra Rebels. *See* Nicaragua.

Convention on the Prevention and Punishment of Genocide. Adopted by the United Nations on 9-10 December 1948. The treaty was ratified by the Soviet Union on 3 May 1954 with one reservation.

Coquilhatville. *See* Independent Congo Republic.

Cordoba. *See* Argentina.

Cordoba. *See* Colombia.

Corfu (*Coccyra, Kerkira, Kerkyra*). A Greek Island in the Ionian Sea, Corfu is the main island of a small group lying off the west coast of Greece at Epirus (*Ipeiros*). The northern part of the island faces Albania. Corfu is separated from the mainland by the Corfu Channel which, is quite narrow in the northern, Albanian, area. The capital city is called *Kerkira* in Greek. Corfu's history dates to antiquity, when it was called Corcyra or Coccyra. After the breakup of the Venetian Kingdon, Corfu was given to France (Treaty of Campo Formio, 1797). A joint Russian-Turkish force then took it in 1799. After Tilsit, Corfu again became a part of the French Empire, only to be lost to the British in 1815. In

1864, Corfu, along with the other Ionian Islands, was ceded to Greece. Italy bombarded the island in 1923 following the assassination of Italian members of a League of Nations team negotiating a cease-fire in the Greek-Albania border dispute. The town and the island were again bombarded and occupied between 1941 and 1945 by Italian and German forces. It also became a focal point in the civil war that raged in Greece after the end of World War II. On 22 October 1946, the "Corfu Channel Incident" took place, in which two British destroyers were damaged by Albanian mines while transitting the strait. Other attacks also took place in which both mines and shore artillery fire were used by the Albanians. On 9 April 1949, Albania was found guilty of causing the damage and ordered to pay reparations to the British by the International Court of Justice. In 1958, a joint Albanian-Greek task force began the task of sweeping the mines from the channel. The Albanian government certified the channel was clear on 30 July 1958.

Corinto. *See* Nicaragua.

Corps Tactical Zones. *See* Vietnam.

Corsica. *See* France.

Costa Mendez, Nicanor. On 30 April 1982, Argentine foreign minister Nicanor Costa Mendez stated that the issue of sovereignty over the Falkland Islands was "non-negotiable." *See* Falklands Islands.

Costa e Silva, Artur. In Brazil, a coup took place on 13 December 1968, in which President Artur de Costa e Silva seized absolute power. Congress and all other legislative bodies in the country were ordered closed, and the constitution suspended. On 31 August 1969, the 66-year-old Costa e Silva suffered a stroke, and his incapacitation led to control being taken by the ministers of the three branches of the armed forces. On 6 October 1969, the interim government installed a career army officer, General Garrastazu Medici, to rule in Costa e Silva's name. On 25 October 1969, Garrastazu was elected president by the recently returned Congress, and he was installed on 30 October. *See* Brazil.

Costa Rica. A republic in Central America bordered on the north by Nicaragua and on the south by Panama. The country's west coast is on the Pacific Ocean while its east coast faces the Atlantic. The capital city is San Jose. The first Europeans to visit Costa Rica were the Spaniards under Christopher Columbus (1502). There they found the lands inhabited by Guaymi Indians, who possessed one of the main items Columbus sought, gold. A settlement was established (originally called Nueva Cartago), but was soon abandoned after attacks by the natives. The country was pacified by 1540 and remained in Spanish thrall until 1815, when Costa Rica followed Mexico in declaring its independence from Spain. Thereafter, Costa Rica joined Mexico in a loose alliance and, in 1824, joined the Central American Federation. When the federation collapsed in 1838, Costa Rica went along its own path. By the mid-1850s, foreign demand for coffee had put Costa Rica on the road to economic independence. In 1855, Costa Rican forces aided Nicaragua in defeating William Walker and his invasion force. Border disputes with Nicaragua were settled by treaty in 1896. A dispute over rights on the San Juan River led to a 1916 decision of the Central American

Court of Justice that declared Nicaragua had violated the treaty. Nicaragua and her partner, the United States, which had already settled an award on Costa Rica, balked at paying reparations, and the matter ended with the only visible result being the damage done to the reputation of the Central American Court, which ceased to exist soon after. Costa Rica's southern border disputes with Panama were not settled until 1941. During World War I, Costa Rica declared war on Germany, but Woodrow Wilson succeeded in preventing Costa Rican troops from joining the fight because Costa Rica was headed by a dictator, Federico Tinoco. Internal problems and the threat of American intervention caused Tinoco to resign and flee in 1919. On 8 December 1941, hours before the American Congress met to declare war, Costa Rica declared war on Japan. The country was swept by a communist-instigated revolution in 1948, but a duly-elected president was seated and a new constitution adopted and the Commuinist Party outlawed. There was a failed coup attempt against the government of Jose Figueres (qv) in 1949. Still in power in 1955, Figueres accused Nicaragua of complicity in a number of rebel attacks in Costa Rica, but the issue was settled amicably in 1956. This problem flared up again in 1960; in November Costa Rican troops attacked Nicaraguan guerrillas as the assembled for another cross-border raid. In 1965, Costa Rica participated in the establishment of the Inter-American Peacekeeping Force, which included U.S. troops. Events remained relatively peaceful in Costa Rica until 1978, when Nicaraguan forces crossed the border ostensibly in pursuit of "insurgents." Venezuelan fighters using Costa Rican bases attacked Nicaraguan invasion forces. Costa Rica then broke off diplomatic relations with Nicaragua and referred the dispute to the OAS (22 November 1978). The fighting continued, however, into 1979, and sporadically thereafter until 1985. In 1986, Oscar Arias Sanchez succeeded Luis Alberto Monge Alvarez as president. Arias faced manifold problems, not the least of which was a staggering foreign debt and illegal drug trafficking through his country into North America. His efforts in these and other Pan-American endeavors won him the Nobel peace prize in 1987. Ineligible for reelection in 1990, Arias was succeeded by Rafael Angel Calderon Fournier, an opposition leader, as president. *Reading:* John Patrick Bell, *Crisis in Costa Rica: The 1948 Revolution* (1971); Martha Honey, *Hostile Acts: U.S. Policy in Costa Rica in the 1980s* (1994); Charles L. Stansifer, *comp., Costa Rica* (World Bibliography Series) (1991).

Cotonou Airport. *See* Benin.

Coty, Rene. *See* France.

Council for Mutual Economic Assistance (Comecon). Founded in 1949, this trade association of communist states included the Soviet Union, the Soviet eastern bloc, Mongolia and North Vietnam. Comecon coordinated the economics of the Soviet-bloc countries. The council ceased to exist with the breakup of the communist bloc in 1991.

Council of Europe. Originally an organization of ten-member nations formed in London on 5 May 1949, the Council soon grew to 16 members with a headquarters at Strasbourg, France. Among its initial members were Belgium,

Great Britain, Denmark, France, Ireland, Italy, Luxembourg, the Netherlands, Norway and Sweden. Greece, Turkey and Iceland joined later. The Federal Republic of Germany (West Germany) was admitted in 1950 as the 16th member. The Saar was admitted as an observer. The council was set up with two operating bodies, the Committee of Ministers and the Consultative Assembly, as a representative organization to promote common action, although it had no means of enforcing its results. The council was forbidden by its charter from discussing military affairs and spent its time in the sociocultural arena, where it achieved some success, at least in the ability of often hostile European governments to work together. On 3 November 1950, the council signed the Convention for the Protection of Human Rights and Fundamental Freedoms. In 1969, Greece withdrew from the council in advance of its being ousted because of human rights violations. In 1970, the council condemned Greece, even though no longer a member, for those civil-rights violations. In 1983, Turkey was suspended until democracy was restored in that country. In 1992, the council's Committee for the Prevention of Torture and Inhuman or Degrading Punishment issued a report condemning conditions in three British prisons. *Reading:* Neill Nugent, *The Government and Politics of the European Union* (1994); Louise B. Van Tartwijk-Novey, *The European House of Cards: Toward a United States of Europe?* (1995).

Coutinho, Antonio Alba Rosa. (b. 14 February 1926, Lisbon) Coutinho was born the son of well-to-do parents and was educated at the Portuguese Naval Academy and at Lisbon University. He also studied at the Scripps Institute of Oceanography in the U.S.. In 1947, he was commissioned into the Portuguese navy and served aboard ship until 1954. In 1958 he headed a hydrographic mission to Angola and was imprisoned in Zaire in 1961. From 1964 until 1972, he headed dredging operations in Mozambique, and in 1973 he took command of a Portuguese frigate. He became a member of the Portuguese Armed Forces Movement in 1974 and, in 1975 joined the military junta that took power in September 1974. In 1975, Coutinho served on the Supreme Revolutionary Council. In addition, from 1974, he served as president of the Angolan government junta and as High Commissioner of Angola from 1974 until 1975, when he was dismissed following an attempted coup against the government of President Francisco de Costa Gomes. In January 1977, he was accused, and subsequently acquitted (July), of human rights violations. He was forced to resign as naval chief of staff in August 1977, but was reinstated in January 1978. He voluntarily retired in December 1982.

Crabtree, Kenneth. A U.S. army lieutenant colonel killed in a bomb blast in Oshahti, in northern South West Africa (Namibia), on 15 April 1984, Crabtree, along with U.S. diplomat Dennis Keough (qv), was in the area to observe the withdrawal of South African troops from Angola. The South West African People's Organization (SWAPO) was blamed for the murders, but the group denied the charges.

Cracow (Krakow). *See* Poland.

Craxi (Crazi), Bettino (Benedetto). (b. 24 February 1934, Milan) Born the son of
a Sicilian lawyer, Craxi was active in the Socialist Youth Movement and joined
the Central Committee of the Italian Socialist Party in 1957. He was a member
of the party's National Executive in 1965. He was a deputy secretary from 1970
until 1976, when he became general secretary. Craxi became the first Socialist
prime minister of Italy in August 1983. In 1984, he confirmed Maltese neutrality
by reaffirming Italy's protection of the island. After forming a new government
in 1986, Craxi resigned in 1987. In 1993, he was charged with several counts
of political corruption. While denying the charges, he was forced to resign the
party leadership and went into exile in Tunisia. By 1994, after a exhaustive
investigation by the Italian government, Craxi was tried in absentia and found
guilty of the charges.

Crete. *See* Greece.

Croatia (*Hravatska*). The second largest of the republics that, until recently, formed
Yugoslavia, Croatia lies in the northwest of the old country and is bordered by
another Yugoslav state, Slovenia, to the northwest, by Hungary on the northeast,
by the states of Vojvodina and Serbia on the east, and by Bosnia-Herzogovina
(qv) on the south. Croatia surrounds Bosnia on its north and west borders.
Croatia's western border is on the Adriatic Sea. The ancestors of Croatia's
present inhabitants, the Slavic Croats, migrated into the region in the
sixth-seventh centuries A.D. from the Danube valley. Earlier they had inhabited
a region of the Ukraine known as White Croatia. Upon arriving on the Adriatic,
the Croats defeated the Roman garrison Salona (614) and began settling in the
provinces of Pannonia and Dalmatia. There they fought and defeated the Avars,
began building an independent state and embraced Christianity before the end
of the century. From the beginning, the common language among the Christian
Croats, Serbs and the Moslem (later) Bosnians was Serbo-Croatian (*Hrvatska*).
Language variations developed because of cultural and geographic
differentiations. In the ninth century, Pannonian Croatia became a part of the
Frankish Empire. By 820, however, the Croats had thrown off the Frankish yoke
and, along with Dalmatia, formed an independent duchy. With Byzantiums help,
Croatia established and defended itself against Bulgarian and Venetian
incursions into the eleventh century, when Croatia broke with Byzantium. A
period of religious civil war followed until 1091, when the Hungarians took
Pannonia and the Byzantines reasserted control over Dalmatia. At the beginning
of the twelfth century, Croatia became associated with the Austro-Hungarian
Empire and remained in that realm until the end of the World War I (1918),
when the Kingdom of the Serbs, Croats and Slovenes was formed. This later
became Yugoslavia (1 December 1918) and remained so under Serbian
dominance until 1941. In 1929, the Croatian terrorist organization Ustasha came
into existence. In that same year, with the reorganization of Yugoslavia, Croatia
and Slavonia were combined to form the county of Savska. In 1934, Ustashan
terrorists assassinated the Serbian king of Yugoslavia. This act deepened the
growing hatred between Serbs and Croats. Civil strife followed between the two
national groups. In 1939 Savska county was united with Primorje county to

form the county of Croatia. The hatred still existed and was further exacerbated on 10 April 1941, when Croatia proclaimed its independence from the already dismembered and occupied (by Nazis) Yugoslavia. Four days later, on 15 April 1941, both Nazi Germany and Fascist Italy recognized the new Croatian state; the head of Ustasha was named its leader, and he ruled with a sadistic hand. The end of World War II saw the end of the repressive government of the "independent" Croatia and its amalgamation into the communist-dominated reassemblage of Yugoslavia under the leadership of Tito (qv), a half-Slovene, half-Croat who ruled with an even more sadistic hand. In 1946 Croatia was granted the status of constituent republic by the Yugoslav central government in Belgrade. In 1989, the communist world collapsed, but Croatia was held in the grip of a neo-Fascist leadership who, among other things, terrorized the Serbian population of the country. In turn, the Serbian Communist Party, led by Slobodan Milosevic, began its own reign of terror against the Muslim Bosnians and all Croats in general. In effect, the civil war that had existed before the Nazi invasion was back in place after a 45-year hiatus of relative peace, there were dissident incidents in 1971 and 1972, under a communist dictatorship. On 25 June 1991, Croatia declared its unilateral independence from Yugoslavia. The long-smoldering ethnic hatred between the Croats and the Serbs flared once again, and the fighting continued into 1993. Croatia and the U.S. signed a military cooperation pact in November 1994, which came about as a result of US brokering of a truce (30 March 1994) in the conflict with the Croatian Serbs. However, the subsequent peace terms were shattered when Croatian Serbs attacked the Bosnian town of Bihac. This brought a strong Croatian reaction and the dispatch of Croatian troops into northern Bosnia to reinforce that country's defenses against the Serbs. Croatian successes marked 1995. Much of rebel-held Croatian territory was recaptured by government forces. As a result, UN forces were reduced, but the situation still remained precarious, and fighting continued. *Reading:* Marcus Tanner, *Croatia: A Thousand-Year Dream* (1997); Simon Vladovich, *Croatia: The Making of a Nation* (1995); John Prcela & Stanko Gulescu, eds., *Operation Slaughterhouse* (1995).

Cross, James R. A British diplomat stationed in Canada in 1970, Cross was kidnapped by French-Canadian terrorists on 5 October. He was subsequently released unharmed on 3 December after his captors were allowed to fly to Cuba.

Crowley, Donald J. A U.S. air force officer serving as air attache to the U.S. embassy in the Dominican Republic, Crowley was kidnapped on 24 March 1970 by terrorists, who demanded and got the release of 20 political prisoners held by the Dominican government (26 March) in exchange for his life.

Cruz-Uclés, Ramon Ernesto. (b. 4 January 1903, San Juan de Flores, Francisco Morazán department, Honduras—d. 6 August 1985, Honduras) Cruz studied law and social science at the Central University of Honduras and, after a long career before the bar and as a magistrate, was appointed to the Honduran Supreme Court in 1949. Concurrently, he served on the faculty of the Central University. In 1958 he was appointed to serve as the Honduran representative in the Nicaraguan border dispute before the International Court of Justice, The

Hague. In 1963 Cruz was nominated as the National Party's candidate for the presidency, but the elections were thwarted when a military coup led by Colonel Osvaldo Arellano Lopez (qv) overthrew the incumbent Morales government. Cruz was subsequently elected president in March 1971, but he was himself deposed by another military coup that reinstalled Arellano Lopez on 4 December 1972.

Cuba. The Republic of Cuba rests on an island located 90 miles southeast of the lower tip of Florida. The island was discovered by Christopher Columbus in 1492 and was named after the Cubanacan Indian tribes found residing there. From its earliest European settlement, Cuba remained essentially under Spanish domination as a sugar-producing colony until 1898, when U.S. forces and Cuban insurgents, led by Jose Marti, freed the country. Thereafter, the United States assumed a dominant role in Cuban life until 1959, when Fidel Castro (qv) assumed power. Under 1903 and 1934 agreements, the US leases Guantanamo Bay (qv) in southeastern Cuba as a military base. In 1952, Fulgencio Batista (qv) seized power and established a dictatorship. In 1954, a rigged election continued Batista in power. From 1956, a Castro-led uprising developed enormous strength and eventually toppled the Batista regime on 1 January 1959. Castro then announced his Marxist philosophy and began a bloodbath that effectively removed most opposition to his own dictatorship. Three-quarters of a million people fled Cuba, mostly to the United States, to avoid the Castro-driven economic and social chaos that followed. In 1961, an abortive invasion of Cuban rebels was defeated by Castro in the Bay of Pigs incident (qv), primarily because of internal U.S. political decisions of the Kennedy administration. Most U.S. property in Cuba was seized by the government and, in retaliation, the U.S. imposed a strict embargo (1962) on the island nation. Cuba's sole source of support became the Soviet Union, while its chief export became terrorism and revolution throughout South and Central America. In 1960, Nikita Khrushchev (qv) warned the U.S. that the USSR would fight to protect Cuba from an American invasion. In 1961 (3 January) the United States broke diplomatic relations with Cuba; later that year (1 May), Castro proclaimed Cuba a "Socialist Republic" and declared himself a "Marxist-Leninist" (2 December). In the fall of 1962, after the OAS expelled Cuba (14 February), U.S. intelligence sources identified the placement of Soviet intermediate-range nuclear weapons on Cuban soil. In the ensuing weeks, the Khrushchev government in the USSR was forced to back down in the face of a U.S. ultimatum and threat of war. Although Castro was fundamentally ignored throughout the incident and lost some prestige as a result, he nonetheless remained in power. In 1965, the Castro government allowed an emigation of those wishing to leave Cuba for the U.S. Almost 250,000 accepted the offer and fled their homeland for a chance at freedom in the United States. Between 1975 and 1978, Cuban forces were engaged in the Angolan Civil War (qv). In 1983, the U.S. invaded Grenada (qv) as a result of the extension of Cuban power to that island. In the 1990s, signs of Cuban economic problems began manifesting themselves after the demise of the Soviet Union and the end of aid. Castro remained in power, however, and showed few signs of letting go the reins of his dictatorship. *Reading:* Earle Rice, *The Cuban Revolution* (1995).

Cuscatlan Bridge. *See* El Salvador.

Cypriot National Front. *See* Cyprus.

Cyprus. The third largest island in the Mediterannean Sea, Cyprus lies 60 miles east of Syria and 45 miles south of Turkey. The capital is Nicosia. The island has been populated since Neolithic times. Cyprus was conquered by Egypt in the second millenium B.C. Later Achaean and Mycenaean cultural characteristics have been noted. Assyrian domination began after 709 B.C. followed by Phoenician and Egyptian periods. In the first century B.C., Rome annexed the island. Byzantium became the dominant factor after 365 A.D. and remained so until 1571, when the island fell to the Ottoman Turks. In 1878, the Ottoman sultan gave Cyprus to Great Britain in return for a British promise of support if Imperial Russia attacked the eastern provinces. The British annexed Cyprus in November 1914. In 1915, Britain offered the island to Greece, if Greece entered the fighting (World War I) against the Bulgarian invasion of Serbia. Greece refused, and the offer was withdrawn. The Treaty of Lausanne (1924) formalized the British annexation and was recognized by Turkey but not by Greece. In 1925, Cyprus became a British crown colony. During World War II, Cypriot units fought with the British forces; the island itself withstood a series of enemy air raids, but otherwise weathered the war with little or no threat. Greek agitation for *enosis* (union), which had surfaced in 1931, became intense in 1955. The largely Greek Cypriot population favored union with Greece, but the Turkish Cypriot population (roughly 18 percent) did not. Violence erupted as a result, lasting into 1956. At that point, a conference of British, Turkish, Greek and Cypriot leaders settled on a plan to establish Cyprus as an independent republic, with guarantees for the Turkish minority. Archbishop Makarios (qv), the former leader of the union movement, was elected president of the new republic which formally received its independence on 16 August 1960. Continued fighting between Greek and Turkish Cypriots forced the dispatch of the UN Peacekeeping Force to Cyprus in 1964. This force was to remain on Cyprus as sporadic outbreaks continued. Makarios was reelected president in 1968 and again in 1973. On 15 July 1974, Greek National Guard units seized the government; Makarios fled the country. Five days later (20 July) Turkish forces invaded the island, and war with Greece seemed imminent. Conflict was averted, however, and a cease-fire put into effect on 22 July. After the collapse of a peace conference, fighting erupted (14 August) with Turkish forces seizing control of the northeastern half of the island by 16 August. On 19 August 1974, the U.S. ambassador and a U.S. embassy employee were assassinated by Greek Cypriots. The presence of the UN force had no influence on the fighting or its severity. At that point (December), Makarios returned to Cyprus and resumed his presidency until his death in 1977. On 8 July 1975, the Turkish Cypriot population voted overwhelmingly to establish a separate Turkish Cypriot republic. After the election of a Turkish government, a mass eviction of Greek Cypriots began out of Turkish territory. At the same time, an equally large immigration from the Turkish mainland began. Throughout this latter period, Cyprus has been the scene of serious terrorist activity, especially that carried out by the PLO. By 1995, the Cypriot situation had quieted, but had not disappeared. The feeling was growing that only reunification of the two regions would resolve the issue, but there was little movement in that direction. *Reading:* Norma Salem, *Cyprus: A Regional Conflict and Its Resolution* (1992); Thomas Streissguth, *Cyprus: Divided Island* (1997); Zaim M. Necatigil, *The Cyprus Question and the Turkish Position in International Law* (1993).

Czechoslovakia. A country in Central Europe, Czechoslovakia is bounded on the north by Poland, on the east by the Ukraine, on the southeast by Hungary, on the southwest by Austria and on the east by Germany. Czechoslovakia was formed in 1918 out of the former Austro-Hungarian territories of Bohemia, Moravia and parts of Silesia. In the ninth century, AD, Greater Moravia was made up of Bohemia, Moravia and Slovakia. Slovakia was later overrun by the Magyars, while Bohemia and Moravia were absorbed into the Holy Roman Empire. Later, these two principalities became part of Austria-Hungary. Jan Masaryk and other formed a provisional government during World War I that was eventually proclaimed the Republic of Czechoslovakia. The country grew and prospered in the interwar period, led by such men as Tomas Masaryk and Eduard Benes (qv). Ruthenia was added to the republic in 1920. In 1938, Nazi Germany was ceded the area known as the Sudetenland, a largely German-speaking region in western Czechoslovakia, at the Munich Conference. The Czech government had little or no say in the West's, primarily England's and France's, appeasement of Hitler. On 15 March 1939, Hitler unilaterally dissolved Czechoslovakia, giving Bohemia and Moravia protectorate status while allowing Slovakia to declare its independence. Soviet troops entered Prague, the nation's capital, in 1944 in the final months of World War II in Europe. Thereafter, the country fell into the Soviet thrall. In 1968, Alexander Dubcek (qv) embarked on a liberal program often called the "Prague Spring." This ended within months when Soviet and other Warsaw Pact (Bulgaria, East Germany, Hungary and Poland) forces invaded the country, reestablishing strict communist control. In 1989, with the breakup of the Soviet hegemony, a new noncommunist-led cabinet was installed (10 December). Free elections were held in 1990, and the country began a return to democracy. In July 1990, Slovakia declared its independence. On 23 July, by mutual consent the Czech Republic and Slovakia became independent states with an effective date of 1 January 1993. *Reading:* Jaroslav Krejci & Pavel MacHonin, *Czechoslovakia, 1918–92: A Laboratory for Social Change* (1996); Jiri Musil, ed., *The End of Czechoslovakia* (1995); Mark Sommer, *Living in Freedom: The Exhilaration and Anguish of Prague's Second Spring* (1992); Carol Skalnik Leff, *National Conflict in Czechoslovakia: The Making and Remaking of a State, 1918–1987* (1988); Jiri Valenta, *Soviet Intervention in Czechoslovakia, 1968: Anatomy of a Decision* (1991); Condoleezza Rice, *The Soviet Union and the Czechoslovak Army, 1948-1983: Uncertain Allegiance* (1984); Jaroslav Krejci, *Czechoslovakia at the Crossroads of European History* (1991); H. Gordon Skilling, ed., *Czechoslovakia,*

1918–1988: Seventy Years from Independence (1991); Andrew C. Janos, *Czechoslovakia and Yugoslavia: Ethnic Conflict and the Dissolution of Multinational States* (1997).

Czech Republic. *See* Czechoslovakia. *Reading:* Carol Skalnik Leff, *The Czech and Slovak Republics: Nation versus State* (1996).

D

Dacca (Dhaka). *See* Bangladesh.

Dacko, David. (b. 24 March 1930, Bouchia, Lobaye District, Ubangi-Shari, French Equatorial Africa) A member of the powerful Mbaka tribe, Dacko was trained from youth to be a teacher. In 1951 he became a primary school teacher in Bangui. By 1955 he was headmaster of Kouanga school when he met Barthélémy Boganda. This encounter set Dacko on his political career; he was elected to the territorial assembly in 1957, at which time Boganda, now the head of government, appointed him to be minister of agriculture in the first Oubangui-Shari government council. In December 1958, after Oubangi-Shari had become the Central African Republic, Boganda appointed Dacko minister of internal affairs. When Boganda disappeared in an airplane crash on 19 March 1959, Dacko moved quickly to establish himself as the only successor to the chair of state. He brushed aside Abel Goumba, the vice president, and had himself elected head of government. At the same time, Dacko assumed the leadership of the *Mouvement d'Evolution Sociale de l'Afrique Noire* (MESAN) one of the two major political parties in the country. The other party, *Mouvement pour l'Evolution Democratique de l'Afrique Centrale* (MEDAC), was headed by Goumba, now Dacko's sworn enemy. When full independence was achieved on 13 August 1960, Dacko began his move to rid himself of his opposition. In November 1962, he abolished MEDAC and all other political parties in the country except his own MESAN party. Goumba and a number of other rival leaders were arrested. Goumba eventually moved into exile, but for the Central African Republic there was now only one party, MESAN, and one leader, Dacko. Dacko's victory was short-lived, however, as Jean Bedel Bokassa (qv) overthrew him on 31 December 1965. At first, Dacko was placed in a Bangui prison, but he was eventually allowed to return to his village. In 1976, Bokassa appointed Dacko his personal counselor. On 21 September 1979, with the aid of French airborne troops, Dacko ousted Bokassa, whose excesses by that time had created an atmosphere favorable to his removal. Bokassa was on a state visit to Libya when the coup took place. With the aid of French bayonets, Dacko simply proclaimed himself president. By 27 September 1979, a new government had been formed. Unrest began to develop, however, and, by March 1981,

Dacko was forced to declare a state of emergency and ask for French military assistance in an attempt to restore order; in August martial law was declared. On 2 September 1981, General Andre Kolingba, the army chief of staff, took the government in a relatively bloodless coup. A military government was established, and the constitution was suspended.

el-Dahab, 'Abd ar-Rahman Sower (Siwar). On 27 March 1985, Sudanese President Gaafar Nimeiry (qv) began a private visit to the United States. On 6 April, an army-led coup headed by Defense Minister 'abd ar-Rahman Sower el-Dahab, carried out a bloodless coup. el-Dahab became the nation's new leader (prime minister). In April 1985, the first free democratic elections were held in the Sudan. Sadiq al-Mahdi of the Umma Party won the election and became prime minister. After 6 May 1986, el-Dahab became chairman of the supreme council, which ruled the country. El-Dahab stepped down during 1987.

Dahomey. *See* Benin.

Dakar. *See* Senegal.

Dak Pek. *See* Vietnam.

Dak Seang. *See* Vietnam

Dak To. *See* Vietnam.

Dalai Lama. The title of the leader of the Tibetan Buddhist order of *Dge-'dungrub-pa is Dalai Lama.* The sect was formed in 1391, and the first leader served from that date to 1474. Successive leaders are considered reincarnations of the abbot of the Tashilhumpo monastery. The fourteenth Dalai Lama *(Bstan-'dzin-rgya-mtsho)* was born in 1935 in China's Ch'ing Hai (Tsinghai) Province of Tibetan parents. He was enthroned in 1940 at Potala. His absolute rule was disrupted following the Chinese Communist invasion of his country on 7 October 1950. He fled into exile on on 31 March 1959 with 100,000 followers, as the Tibetan people revolted against the Chinese Communists after they had dissolved the government and replaced the Dalai Lama with a puppet, the Panchen Lama. Thereafter, the Dalai Lama resided in Dharamsala in northwest India. In 1989, the Dalai Lama was awarded the Nobel peace prize for his nonviolent campaign to end the Chinese communist domination of his country. *Reading:* Christopher Gibb, *The Dalai Lama: The Exiled Leader of the People of Tibet and Tireless Worker for World Peace* (1990); Dalai Lama, *Freedom in Exile: The Autobiography of the Dalai Lama* (1991).

Dalat. *See* Vietnam.

Damao. *See* Portuguese India (Damao).

Damascus (*Dimashq ash Sham*). *See* Syria.

Damietta (*Dumyat*). *See* Egypt.

Damur. *See* Lebanon.

Danang. *See* Vietnam.

Dan-Banyas. *See* Israel.

Danube Conference. On 30 July 1948, a Danube Conference was convened in Belgrade, Yugoslavia. This was a post-World War II convocation of the European Commission of the Danube, a body established in 1856 by the terms of the Treaty of Paris, which ended the Crimean War and further extended the Eastern Question. The commission's headquarters was originally located in the Romanian city of Galati and was composed of eight member nations. The original role of the commission was the control of the Danubian delta below the Romanian city of Braila. By the term of the Treaty of Bucharest (May 1918), the commission was reduced by the Central Powers to member states that lived on the Danube or European countries bordering the Black Sea. In June 1919, the Treaty of Versailles redefined the role of the European commission as being as stated in the 1856 accord. Only Great Britain, France, Italy and Romania were authorized membership on the European Commission of the Danube. The treaty also designated the establishment of a new international commission to control the river above Braila to the German city of Ulm, the up-river limit of navigability. This new body was to be composed of two representatives each of the German riparian states (bordering states such as Bavaria), one from each other riparian state, and one representative of all member states of the European Commission of the Danube. From 1921, when the Danube Statute was signed in Paris (23 July), until 1939, the nonriparian members of the commission were Great Britain, France and Italy. From the beginning of World War II (1939–1940), Nazi Germany controlled the Danube. In 1946, the meeting of the Allied Council of Foreign Ministers meeting in New York announced that, as soon as peace treaties were acknowledged with Bulgaria, Hungary and Romania, a new Danube convention would be established. The three peace treaties were signed on 10 February 1947 in Paris. The non-riparian members of the old commission attempted to reestablish "free and open" navigation on the Danube when the commission met for the first time in Belgrade, Yugoslavia on 30 July 1948. The Soviet delegate, who appeared based on their having become a riparian state, along with the communist-controlled riparian delegates, moved to replace the 1921 convention with a new one that formed a commission around a single delegate from each Danubian state. Germany, still a conquered territory, had no vote. The effect of this action was the 2 August 1948 nullification of the 1921 accord and the establishment of a Soviet-controlled commission that gave the USSR control of the Danube. The action was approved in final form on 11 November 1949 over strong Allied objections. The headquarters was moved to Budapest (1953). In 1955, Austria was able to restore some of its assets, which had been confiscated. In the ensuing decades up to the 1990s the Danube has been relatively free of political intrigue. The end of the Soviet bloc has further diminished the role of politics over economics in the use of the Danube region. *Reading:* Spirodon G. Focas, *The Lower Danube River: In the Southeastern Europe Political and Economic Complex from Antiquity to the Conference of Belgrade of 1948* (1987).

Danubian Csepel Island. *See* Hungary.

Daoud, Abu. (b. 1937, Selwa, Jordan) Muhammad Daoud Auda (a.k.a. Abu Daoud) was born in a village near Jerusalem, on the Jordanian West Bank. He worked for some time as a teacher in Jordan and Saudi Arabia before serving in the Kuwaiti Ministry of Justice. During these years he was an avowed communist but later joined the Palestine Liberation Organization's (PLO) (qv) *al-Fatah* group. He is thought to have headed the *al-Fatah* intelligence group during this period. In 1972, he was thought to have masterminded the murder of the Israeli athletes at the Munich Olympics. He was captured in Amman, Jordan, in February 1973 and sentenced to death for committing acts of sabotage. In March, his release was sought by a group of terrorists holding hostages in the Saudi Embassy in Khartoum (qv). Jordan's King Hussein commuted his sentence to life imprisonment some time later, but Daoud was instead released in the general amnesty for all Palestinian terrorists jailed in Jordan in September 1973. In January 1977, Daoud travelled to Paris on an Iraqi passport to attend the funeral of the assassinated Mahmoud Saleh. He was arrested in by French security forces on 7 January 1977, under an Interpol warrant issued in connection with Daoud's part in the 1972 Munich murders of 11 Israeli Olympic Team members and on suspicion of being a member of the Palestine Revolutionary Council. Eleven days later, he was released by a French judge even though both West Germany and Israel had requested his extradition. Daoud immediately flew to Algiers amid the cheers of much of the Arab world. East German records indicated that Daoud had lived in that country on and off after 1978. In 1981, Daoud was shot and seriously wounded in a hotel in Warsaw, Poland, but he recovered. On 18 October 1995, Daoud admitted he had taken part in the 1972 Munich Olympics massacre.

Darbandikhan. *See* Iraq.

Dar-es-Salaam. *See* Tanzania.

Darlac Province. *See* Vietnam.

Darul Islam. A fanatical Muslim organization that operated in Java in the early 1950s. At one time (March 1951), the Indonesian government sent 25,000 troops against this organization and a group of associated communist and outlaw bands conducting terrorist activities in Java. *Reading:* Karl D. Jackson, *Traditional Authority, Islam, and Rebellion: A Study of Indonesian Political Behavior* (1980); Cornelius Van Dijk, *Rebellion under the Banner of Islam: The Darul Islam in Indonesia* (1982).

Darwin. *See* Argentina.

Dass, Arjun. A leading member of the Indian parliament, Dass was assassinated by Sikh terrorists on 4 September 1985, during a reign of murders and bombings.

Daud Khan, Sadar Mohammed. (b. 18 July 1909, Kabul, Afghanistan—d. 27 April 1978, Kabul) Born a member of the century-old Barakzai clan (royal dynastic order established in 1826), Daud was educated at Habibia College in Afghanistan and in Paris. In 1932, he was appointed governor-general of Kandahar Province by his uncle King Mohammad Nadir Khan. The following year, Nadir Khan was assassinated. In 1939, Daud took command of an army corps stationed in Kabul and, from 1946, he was minister of defense, except for a stint as ambassador to France. In 1953, he became prime minister; his principal activities were establishing friendly relations with the USSR. In March 1973, his cousin and half-brother, King Mohammed Zahir Khan, forced Daud's resignation and arranged legislation that would have banned all members of the royal family from holding public office. In July 1973, Daud deposed Zahir Khan and subsequently had himself elected president. Daud's programs stressed political liberalization, constitutionalism, and nonalignment. These programs were opposed by a number of leftist organizations, especially *Khalq*, whose leader Nur Mohammed Taraki (qv) was defeated in his own bid for president after the death of Zahir Khan. Another faction of *Khalq*, *Parcham*, headed by Babrak Karmal (qv), continued to support Daud until he found he no longer needed the group, at which point (mid-1975) he dispensed with its services. *Parcham* reunited with *Khalq* and formed the new People's Democratic Party of Afghanistan. In April 1978, Daud was deposed in a bloody military coup led by Hafizullah Amin (qv). In the fighting, Daud along with many members of his family and associates, was killed. Nur Mohammed Taraki was named president of a revolutionary council to replace him. *See* Afghanistan.

Davao City. *See* Philippines.

Davies, Rodger Paul. (b. 7 May 1921, Berkeley, California—d. 19 August 1974, Nicosia, Cyprus) A career diplomat, Davies was deputy assistant secretary of state for Near East and South Asian Affairs when he was posted to Cyprus (1974) as U.S. ambassador. Shortly after Davies took up his duties in Nicosia, Archbishop Makarios's government was ousted. In the ensuing melee, Ambassador Davies and a Foreign Service officer on the embassy staff were assassinated by a Greek Cypriot. A number of arrests, trials and convictions ensued, but none of those found guilty in the plot were ever punished.

Dawalibi, Maarouf. A pro-Soviet Syrian premier, Dawalibi was placed in office on 28 November 1951 and ousted by a coup on 29 November 1951.

Dawa Party. A terrorist organization also known as the Islamic Dawa Party, operating in Kuwait, the Dawa Party was involved in the bombing of a motorcade carrying the emir of Kuwait on 25 May 1985. Six people were killed and 12 injured in the blast. The Emir escaped with minor injuries. The Islamic Jihad claimed responsibility for the attack in the name of the Iranian-backed Dawa Party. The attack was carried out because of Kuwait's refusal to release Shi'ite terrorists it had imprisoned. The Dawa Party was also linked to attacks on Iraq aimed at killing Saddam Hussein and establishing an Islamic fundamentalist republic in the country. *See also* Hizballah.

Dawson Field. During the period 6–9 September 1970, three airliners were hijacked. Over three hundred passengers were taken hostage in these incidents. All three aircraft were flown into Dawson Field in Jordan, where Popular Front for the Liberation of Palestine (PFLP) terrorists threatened to blow up the U.S., British and Swiss planes and their passengers if the three governments did not arrange the release of Palestinian "commandos" held in European and Israeli prisons. When most of the PFLP demands were met on 30 September, the hostages were released, but the three aircraft were blown up and destroyed.

Dayan, Moshe. (b. 20 May 1915, Degania, Alef, Palestine—d. 16 October 1981, Tel
Aviv, Israel) Dayan began his life as a farmer in the Nahalal cooperative near
his kibbutz (village). During this period he joined the Haganah, a secret and
militant Jewish organization. In 1937, however, he served in the British forces
under Captain Ord Wingate (later a hero of World War II in Burma) in a
counterguerrilla command against Arab infiltrators. He was arrested in 1939 by
the British authorities for his Haganah activities and was imprisoned for two
years (of a ten-year sentence). In 1941 he joined the Australian army, where he
led a Jewish-manned detachment against the Vichy-controlled government in
Syria. He was seriously wounded and lost his left eye as a result. In 1948, during
the Israeli war for independence, he commanded the Jerusalem sector, during
which time his diplomatic talents allowed him to achieve an armistice with the
Jordanians. He served as chief of the Israeli general staff from 1953 until his
military retirement in 1958. His leadership was a crucial factor in the success of
the Sinai campaign in 1956. In 1959, he was elected to the Knesset and
appointed minister of agriculture. He resigned the ministry over differences with
the Labor (*Mapai*) Party government. He then joined David Ben-Gurion in
forming the *Rafi* Party. During the Arab-Israeli Six-Day War of 1967, Dayan
served as minister of defense and was the chief architect of victory in that
conflict. He again served as minister of defense between 1969 and 1974. When
the Arab-Israeli War of October 1973 (Yom Kippur War) began, he was blamed
for Israeli unpreparedness and, upon the departure of Golda Meir (qv) as prime
minister (1974), Dayan was dropped from the cabinet. He was appointed foreign
minister by Menachem Begin (qv) in 1977 and served until his resignation in
1979. During his tenure, Dayan played a major role in the establishment of the
Camp David Accords. In 1981, Dayan formed the *Telem* Party whose main
platform stressed disengagement from the occupied territories. He died before
his plans could be fully implemented. *Reading:* Moshe Dayan, *Moshe Dayan:
Story of My Life* (1992); Robert Slater, *Warrior Statesman: The Life of Moshe
Dayan* (1991).

Dean, William F. *See* Korea.

Declaration of Arusha. *See* Kenya and Somalia.

Declaration of Ayacucho. Named for a city in the Occidental Andes in Peru, the
Declaration of Ayacucho was an agreement among the Andean nations of South
America (Argentina, Bolivia, Chile, Colombia, Ecuador, Peru and Venezuela),
all members of the Latin American Free Trade Association (LAFTA), to limit
the importation of military equipment into the region. The formal signing of the
agreement took place in Lima on 9 December 1974. Brazil was not included in
the agreement. Chile, Ecuador and Peru, all of whom did sign, would make
subsequent large-scale purchases of weapons.

Declaration of Independence, Rhodesia. *See* Zimbabwe.

Declaration of San Jose. At a meeting of the Organization of American States held
in San Jose, Costa Rica, on 20–28 August 1959, the Western Hemisphere
Foreign Ministers issued a declaration condemning Sino-Soviet attempts to
import communism into the hemisphere. A second Declaration of San Jose was

signed on 19 March 1963, in which the United States pledged American economic aid for the region to help thwart communist infiltration into Latin America. Six Latin American states also signed that declaration.

Declaration of Santiago. In a declaration signed in Santiago, Chile, on 18 August 1959, 21 member states of the Organization of American States (OAS) condemned dictatorships and other nations who try to overthrow them.

Declaration of Washington. President Dwight D. Eisenhower and British Prime Minister Anthony Eden reaffirmed a common policy on the Middle East in the Declaration of Washington signed on 1 February 1956.

Defense Sports Group. On 26 September 1980, at the height of the *Oktoberfest* in Munich, a bomb went off at the entrance to one of the pavilions at the fairgrounds, killing 12 and injuring at least 200. Had the explosive device not gone off prematurely while it was being positioned, hundreds might have been killed. The terrorist who was killed while placing the bomb belonged to the outlawed right-wing extremist group known as the Defense Sports Group.

Degania. *See* Israel.

de Gaulle, Charles. (b. 22 November 1890, Lille, France—d. 9 November 1970, Colombey-lex-Deux-Eglises, France) De Gaulle was born the son of a professor of philosophy and literature and was educated in the classics. In 1909, he entered the École Spéciale Militaire of Saint-Cyr. Graduating as a second lieutenant, he joined the 33rd Infantry Regiment (1913), where he came under the influence of its commanding officer, Philippe Petain. In World War I, de Gaulle was wounded three times and was taken prisoner during the 1916 battle of Verdun. While a prisoner, he made five attempts to escape. After the war he joined his old regiment and fought in the Polish campaign of 1920 against the Bolsheviks. During this period he served under Maxime Weygand. In 1921 he joined the faculty of Saint-Cyr and then attended the École Supérieure de Guerre (1924). He joined the staff of Marshal Petain and later, in 1927, joined the army of occupation in the Rhineland. From 1929 until 1931 de Gaulle served in Lebanon. Degaulle's writings made him somewhat unpopular as he stressed mechanized warfare and a professional army as opposed to the French policy of conscription and reliance on the Maginot Line or static warfare. When World War II began, de Gaulle commanded a tank brigade, and in 1940 he was given command of the 4th Armored Division, making him the youngest brigadier general in the French army. He was appointed undersecretary of state for war on 6 June 1940 and twice travelled to England for meetings with Winston Churchill (qv). When Petain surrendered France to the Nazis, de Gaulle fled to England and announced himself as the head of the Free French movement. Because of his broadcasts urging the French people to resist the Nazis, he was sentenced to death in absentia on 7 July 1940. For the Allied leaders, Roosevelt, Eisenhower and Churchill, de Gaulle was an irksome and often troublesome proponent of French interests. Churchill was quoted as saying, "We all have our crosses to bear and ours is the Cross of Lorraine." Before the Normandy invasion, Eisenhower had to threaten de Gaulle with detention, if the French leader did not cooperate with the plan for calling on Frenchmen to support the landings. When

France was liberated (10 September 1944), de Gaulle formed a provisional government. He resigned, however, on 20 January 1946 and formed a new right-wing party, the *Rassemblement du Peuple Français*. When this party failed, de Gaulle retired to the countryside and wrote his memoirs. In 1958, he was called back to form a new government and deal with the crisis in Algeria (qv). On 21 December 1958 he was elected president of the Fifth Republic. He was successful in closing the Algerian episode and in leading France back to a position of international stature. In 1966, he withdrew France from NATO over the objections of many senior advisors. He was reelected president in December 1965. Rising above internal social unrest, he was again reelected in 1968. In 1969, after his reform proposals were rejected by the Senate, de Gaulle resigned and retired once again to write his memoirs. At age 80, Charles DeGaulle died in November 1970. *Reading:* Hans Schmitt, *European Union from Hitler to DeGaulle* (1979); Simon Serfaty, *France, DeGaulle and Europe: The Policy of the Fourth and Fifth Republics Toward the Continent* (1968).

Degodia Tribesmen. A Kenya-based native tribe, the Degodia inhabit the area near the border with Somalia. On 2 March 1984, several high-ranking Kenyan government officials accused the military of carrying out a campaign of extermination against the Degodia tribe, aimed at breaking the link between the Degodias and the Somali guerrilla forces operating along the border. As many as 5,000 Degodias were thought to have been tortured and massacred in the incident.

Dehloran. *See* Iran.

Deir el-Kamar. *See* Lebanon.

Delgado Chalbaud, Carlos. Colonel Carlos Delgado Chalbaud led a junta, including Marcos Perez Jimenez (qv), that overthrew the government of Romulo Gallegos in Venezuela on 24 November 1948. On 13 November 1950, he was assassinated under mysterious circumstances. Marcos Perez Jimenez took control of the junta at that time and installed Suarez Flammerich (qv) as president.

Delgado, Humberto da Silva. A Portuguese lieutenant general, Humberto da Silva Delgado was a 1958 candidate for election to the presidency. On 22 January 1958, a group of hijackers seized the Portuguese liner *SS Santa Maria* with over six hundred passengers on board in Delgado's name. American and British warships joined the search for the ship in the Atlantic Ocean. The ship landed in Recife, Brazil on 2 February. No one was injured in the adventure.

Delouvrier, Paul. The French representative to Algeria who replaced General Raoul Salan (qv) on 12 December 1958, Salan was relieved by President Charles de Gaulle (qv) and given the assignment of inspector general of the French armed forces.

Demicheli, Alberto. On 12 June 1976, Uruguay's president, Juan Maria Bordaberry (qv), was removed from office in a bloodless military coup. Alberto Demicheli was appointed interim president and served until 1 September, when a new president was elected.

Demilitarized Zone (DMZ), Korea. A supposedly neutral area between the front lines of the opposing sides on the Korean peninsula. The line separating North and South Korea before the war was the 38th parallel. This boundary disappeared during the course of the Korean War (1950–1953). The cease-fire line of 27 November 1951 is the general trace of the DMZ as it was established when the war ended in 1953 and as it is known to date. Since the end of the war there have been numerous incidents in which one side accused the other of violating the truce agreement by penetrating the DMZ. On 20 June 1959, for instance, the United Nations Command accused the North Koreans of building fortifications in the DMZ. On 2 November 1966, six American and one South Korea soldier were killed in a skirmish with North Koreans on the DMZ. Similar firefights have taken place periodically, such as the one between U.S. and North Korean forces on 11 March 1969. The situation became so intense that the Department of Defense authorized combat pay for personnel stationed on the DMZ and the issuance of the Combat Infantryman's Badge to appropriate infantryman engaged in that near-war situation. In the 1970s, the UN Command began finding elaborate tunnels dug beneath the DMZ from the North Korean side. At least one tunnel was large enough for two trucks to run side-by-side. The first tunnel was discovered in 1974. The third tunnel, discovered in October 1978, was so large that 30,000 troops could pass through it every hour. When President Carter (qv) noted a sizeable build-up of North Korean military strength along the DMZ in February 1979, he ordered a halt to the ongoing withdrawal of American forces for that theater. Another period of build-up of North Korean military strength near the DMZ occurred in 1984. On 23 November 1984, a Soviet defector who fled into the DMZ to reach South Korea precipitated a firefight in which one South Korean and three North Korea soldiers were killed. The incident halted ongoing talks between the two sides at Panmunjom (qv).

Demilitarized Zone, Vietnam. On 8 May 1954, a 19-member international conference that had convened in Geneva (*See*Geneva and Vietnam) took up the issue of Indochina, one day after the French lost Dien Bien Phu (qv). This conference concluded in the Geneva Accords, which among other things led to a cease-fire, the termination of French rule in Indochina, and the partition of the country of Vietnam (Cambodia and Laos were made separately independent) along the 17th parallel. The provisional boundary between North and South Vietnam was to last only until free elections could be held throughout the country and was in actuality south of the 17th parallel, running along the Ben Hai River to Bo Ho Su and then due west to the Laotian border. One aspect of the partition was the establishment of a demilitarized zone three miles (5 km) deep on each side of the partition line. Both sides violated the no-military zone and, on occasion, heavy fighting took place in the strip during the Vietnam War.

Demirel, Suleyman. (b. 6 October1924, Isparta [Islâmköy], Turkey) Trained in Istanbul as a construction engineer, Demirel traveled twice to the United States before being appointed director of the Turkish state hydrological service (1955). He was, therefore, one of the most important aides to Premier Adnan Menderes (qv), whose principal development project was the institution of a water power electrical and irrigation system in Turkey. After Menderes was ousted by a military coup in May 1960, Demirel left the government and opened a successful construction business. In 1964, Demirel became the leader of his party, which followed the Menderes line; and in 1965, he became the leader of the majority Justice Party in the Turkish government and was named prime minister. He held this post for six years, until another military coup ousted his government on 12 March 1971. In 1973, after the martial law edict was lifted, Demirel was left behind as the rival Republican People's Party of Bulent Ecevit (qv) took power. After Ecevit's success in the Turkish invasion of Cyprus in 1974, Demirel attempted to consolidate his position with new elections. When his plan failed, Demirel was able to rally right-wing support around his Justice Party as the Nationalist Front. His authority was not complete, however, as Ecevit was able to gain significant power in the elections of 1975. Demirel also moved his policies toward Moscow after the United States exhibited its displeasure over the Turkish intervention in Cyprus. This period of Demirel's rule was marked with violence and terrorism. He was defeated again in June 1977, but he returned to power in July 1977 and served his sixth term as prime minister from November 1979 until 12 September 1980, when a military coup again ousted his government. He returned as prime minister in November 1991 and resigned his post in May 1993 after his election to the presidency of Turkey.

Democratic Front for the Liberation of Palestine. A Syrian-supported terrorist splinter element of the Palestine Liberation Organization (PLO) (qv). On 4 February 1980, the Democratic Front for the Liberation of Palestine claimed credit for a bomb explosion in the Tel Aviv, Israel, suburb of Rehovot. On 17 July 1981, Israeli jets attacked the organization's headquarters in a crowded area of Beirut, Lebanon (qv), killing over 350 civilians and injuring 1,000 more.

Democratic Party Convention, 1968. The scene of the 29 August 1968 intervention of 5,000 Illinois National Guardsmen to reinforce 12,000 Chicago police attempting to restore order after rioting followed a massive demonstration opposing the nomination of Hubert Humphrey as the Democratic candidate for president of the United States.

Democratic Republic of Congo. *See* Zaire.

Democratic Republic of Germany. *See* East Germany.

Democratic Union of Timor (DUT). On 10 August 1975, a group known as the DUT led a coup that seized control of the island of Timor in the Malay Archipelago. Timor was in the process of gaining its independence from Portugal at the time of the coup. The island had been promised a referendum on independence in July 1975. After the coup, DUT found itself confronted by its chief rival for power, the Revolutionary Front for the Independence of East Timor (Fretilin), and a civil war erupted. In December, Indonesia stepped in after Portugal admitted it had lost control of the situation. Indonesian troops invaded the island, ending DUT's struggle and absorbing Timor into the Indonesian state. *See also* Indonesia and Timor.

Denard, Robert ("Bob"). (b. 20 January 1929, France) Denard was a member of the French navy and served in Indochina from 1949 to 1954. Denard then appeared in Morocco, most likely as a member of the French secret service. There he aided in a French campaign of support for Moulay ibn Arafa (qv) against Morocco's king Mohammed V (qv). In 1960, Denard appeared in the Belgian Congo, which had just received its independence. There he joined the forces of the Katangan separatist leader, Moise Tshombe (qv) and helped train the notorious "*Gendamerie.*" Denard then made his way to Yemen, where he served Saudi Arabia's King Faisal against the royalist movement there. He then returned to the Congo and again served Tshombe against Joseph Mobutu (qv). While there he participated in a mercenary revolt, fighting at Kisangani in command of a French-speaking mercenary commando unit. After being wounded he was flown to Rhodesia for treatment. When recovered, he went to Angola and then returned to France. In 1968, Denard turned up in Biafra as a soldier in the forces of Odumegwo Ojukwu (qv). In 1975, he helped install Ali Soilih (qv) to power in the Comoros Islands. In January 1977, Denard was accused of participating in a failed coup attempt ordered by Emile Derlin Zinsou (qv). In May 1978, Denard led a mercenary force in the successful overthrow of Ali Soilih (qv) in the Comoros Islands and possibly participated in his subsequent murder. Denard was appointed chief of staff of the Comoran army but was forced to resign because of international pressure on Said Moustapha Mahdjou (qv), the man he put in power. Denard subsequently left the Comoros. Over the years, Denard was known by several aliases: Maurin, Colonel Bourgeaud and Colonel Said Moustapha Mahdjou. *See* Comoros.

Denfield, Louis E. On 27 October 1949, the U.S. Secretary of Defense, Louis Johnson (qv), relieved the Chief of Naval Operations, Admiral Louis Denfield, for his part in the "Revolt of the Admirals" (qv). Denfield's aggressiveness in the squabble over the supercarrier versus the B-36 bomber, in other words, the fight for funds between the navy and the air force brought about his relief.

Deng Xiaoping. (b.4 February 1904, Szechwan Province, China—d.19 February 1997, Peking) Born the son of wealthy landowners, Deng was sent to Paris in 1920 to complete his studies. While there he met Zhou Enlai (Chou En-Lai) (qv). Upon his return to China in 1926, Deng became involved in the Communist activities, took part in the Long March (1934–1935) and was involved in the final defeat of Chiang Kai-shek (qv) on the Chinese mainland. Upon the proclamation of the People's Republic of China (1949), Deng became vice premier and general secretary of the party. He was purged during the Cultural Revolution, but returned to the power structure in early 1976, apparently having been coopted to succeed his old friend Zhou Enlai, who died in January. Within four months, however, the "Gang of Four" (qv) had successfully blocked Deng's accession, a situation that lasted until the Gang of Four were themselves ousted from power. Deng was then restored to power and began the implementation of his long program for bring China into the modern world. By 1981, as vice chairman of the Chinese Communist Party, Deng was clearly the most powerful leader in the country, powerful enough to upset the plan laid down by Mao Zedung (Mao Tse-tung) (qv) to have Hua Guofeng (Hua Kuo-feng) named his successor. Deng was also successful in carrying forth a program of downgrading the Mao mystique in order to implement his own modernization programs. Deng remained in power until 1987, when he began relinquishing some of his party and politburo functions. He resigned as chairman of the powerful Military Commission in November 1989. Even so, he still retained ultimate control of China. In April–June 1989, Deng supported the military suppression of the democratic movement that culminated in the massacre in Tiananmen Square. He became less and less visible, making few public appearances, until his death, but through his last years he remained adamantly opposed to any form of democratic reform in China. By 1996, the 92-year-old Deng had grown frail, and he was seen only on very special occasions. His role in affairs of state had diminished, and most of his duties were taken over by others. He died a year later in 1997.

Denktash, Rauf. (b. 27 January 1924, Ktima, Cyprus) Denktash was the youngest son of a judge and was took his early education in the public schools of Cyprus. From 1941 until 1943, heheld positions as an interpreter, court clerk, and teacher. In 1943, he was sent to England to study law at Lincoln Inn. Graduating in 1947, he returned to Cyprus and practiced law for one year before being appointed to the Consultative Assembly established by the British crown to hear the case for the Cypriot petition for independence. In 1949 he became an assistant crown counsel; in 1954, the crown counsel; and in 1956, solicitor general of Cyprus. One year later, he resigned to become the chairman of the Federation of Turkish Associations in Cyprus. From 1959, Denktash played a leading role in presenting the Turkish Cyriot side in the negotiations between the Greek and Turkish governments over Cypriot independence. He led the Turkish delegation involved in the military arrangements and, later, the Turkish deputation on the commission drafting the new Cyriot nation's constitution. Denktash became president of the Turkish Communal Chamber in 1960. Thereafter, in 1964, he attended the London conference and the United Nations Security Council sessions on Cyprus. On his return to Cyprus, however, he was refused reentry on the direct orders of Archbishop Makarios; he resided in Turkey until 1967. He attempted to secretly enter Cyprus but was captured by Greek Cypriot police. After 13 days of captivity, public pressure had mounted to such a point that the Greek Cypriot government was forced to release him; but, in doing so, they deported him back to Turkey. On 13 April 1968, Denktash was allowed to return to Cyprus. In June 1968, he became the spokesman for the Turkish side in intercommunal talks as president of the Turkish Communal Chamber. On 13 February 1975, Dentash proclaimed the independence of Turkish Cyprus and claimed 40 percent of the Cypriot countryside as its domain, the Turkish Federated State of Cyprus (*see* Cyprus). The Turks again proclaimed their independence in November 1983. In 1995, Dentash remained as president of the Turkish Region of North Cyprus, having weathered a number of political crises on the small, separated island of Cyprus.

Denmark. A kingdom (constitutional monarchy) located in northern Europe on a peninsula (Jutland) that separates the North Sea on the east from the Baltic Sea on the west. Denmark has Germany as its southern neighbor; it is separated from Sweden and Norway on the north and northeast by the strategically important Skagerrak and Kattegat water passages. The capital is Copenhagen (qv). Denmark also has sovereignty over Greenland (qv) and the Faeroe Islands and, until 1941, Iceland (qv). The origins of Denmark are found in antiquity. The tribes of the region were united and converted to Christianity by a Viking, Harold Bluetooth, in the tenth century. The Danes also controlled the English islands for a period after 1013. From 1397 (Treaty of Kalmar), Sweden (qv) and Norway (qv) also paid homage to Denmark. Sweden became powerful enough to break away in 1523 and, in 1814, to occupy Norway. During World War I, Denmark maintained its neutrality, albeit with difficulty. After the war, Denmark helped draft the covenant for the League of Nations. In August 1939, Nazi Germany stated it would respect Danish neutrality. On 9 April 1940, German forces swept into Denmark following the presentation of a note from the German foreign ministry that the move was solely to protect Denmark against a British occupation. Resistance to the occupation was slow in developing, primarily because the king, who remained in Copenhagen, contrary to the policy of fleeing followed by many other European monarchs at the time, ordered the people to maintain law and order. On 4 May 1945, the German garrison capitulated, and British forces began moving into Denmark. Breaking its long-standing tradition of neutrality, Denmark joined NATO in April 1949. In April 1950, the Danish parliament officially recognized the *fait accompli* and dissolved the union with Iceland, which had proclaimed its independence in 1944, even though separated by the Allied occupation of Iceland and the German occupation of Denmark in 1940–1941. In 1951, Denmark signed a mutual defense pact with the U.S. for the defense of Greenland. In 1968, however, the crash of a U.S. nuclear-armed B-52 bomber in Baffin Bay, caused the defeat of the government in the Danish elections. In 1983, Denmark, along with other countries in Europe, witnessed massive protests against the deployment of U.S. nuclear missiles on the continent. On 10 May 1983, the Danish parliament approved a bill to stop payment to the NATO fund in order to stop the deployment. In 1984, Denmark joined other Scandinavian countries in discussions aimed at declaring their region a "Nuclear Free Zone." A series of terrorist bomb attacks were carried in Copenhagen on 22 July 1985 by the Islamic Jihad in retaliation for Israeli attacks on PLO camps in Jordan. In 1992, Danish voters rejected the EC Treaty on European union. Danish forces have been quick to respond to UN calls for emergency forces. *Reading:* W. Glyn Jones, *Denmark: A Modern History* (1986); Palle Lauring, *A History of Denmark* (1986).

Deno, Francisco Caamano. On 19 December 1965, an attempt was made on the life of Francisco Caamano Deno, a reputed rebel leader in the Dominican Republic. Although the attempt failed, renewed fighting broke out between government forces and communist-inspired rebel forces in and around Santo Domingo.

Desai, Shri Mooraji Ranchhodji. (b. 29 February 1896, Bulsar District, Gurjurat State, India) After being educated in Bombay, Desai entered the civil service in 1918 and served quietly until 1930, when he resigned and joined Mahatma Gandhi's (qv) Civil Disobedience Movement. Desai became the secretary of the Gurjarat Provincial Congress Committee from 1931 until 1937 and again in the 1939–1946 period. He was appointed minister of revenue and home affairs in the Bombay provincial cabinet in 1946. Premier Nehru (qv) appointed him to the Indian central government post of minister of commerce (later foreign minister) in 1956. Desai was appointed deputy prime minister in 1967. In 1969, Desai resigned over differences in fiscal policies. In the ensuing split in the Congress Party, Desai became the leader of the Opposition Congress. He held seats in the Parliament through several elections. When Indira Gandhi was made prime minister, she had Desai imprisoned during one of the states of emergency that has plagued India. Once again freed two months before the new elections in March 1977, Desai led the Janata Party campaign that unseated Indira Gandhi. Made prime minister, Desai served two years and then resigned (1979).

Deseret. Named by the Mormons after the state they proposed to build in 1849, Deseret, Utah, was the site of the Fort Douglas biological warfare testing facility in 1971. The site was eventually dismantled as the United States destroyed all of its BW weapons.

Deversoir Military Base. *See* Egypt.

Dhahran (Az Zahran). *See* Saudi Arabia.

Dhaka. *See* Dacca.

Dhekelia. *See* Cyprus.

Dhofar. *See* Oman.

Dias Gomide, Aloysío. In late July 1970, Dias, a Brazilian diplomat in Uruguay ,was one of three foreign officials (the other two were the Americans Dan Mitrione (qv) and Claude Fly) kidnapped by Tupamaro terrorists. Dias was held for seven months before his released was arranged on 21 February 1971. A ransom of about one-half million US dollars was paid to the kidnappers.

Diefenbaker, John George. (b. 18 September 1895, Grey County, Canada—d. 16 August 1979, Ottawa) Diefenbaker practiced law in Saskatchewan until 1940, when he was elected to the Canadian House of Commons. In 1956 he was made elected leader of the Progressive Conservative Party. The following year, he became Canada's first conservatiove prime minister in over two decades. He served in that office until 1963, during which time he further separated Canadian from U.S. interests; among other things, he refused to arm the Canadian army assigned to NATO with nuclear weapons. He did agree to a Joint Defense Agreement with the United States in July 1958. He lost his office in the 1967, partially because of Canada's nuclear policies. Diefenbaker returned to the House of Commons, however, and was serving his thirteenth term in office when he died.

Diego Suarez Naval Base. *See* Malagasy (Madagascar).

Dien Bien Phu. A village in northeast Vietnam that was the scene of a heroic, but futile French defense against massed Viet Minh forces commanded by General

Giap. The siege began on 20 November 1953; on occasion, as on 14 March 1954, the Viet Minh threw as many as 10,000 men against the small French fortification. At that time (20 March), the French commander, General Paul Ely, told the United States that American combat troops would be required, if the situation were to be saved. The bastion fell to the communists on 7 May 1954. The town has subsequently been renamed Dien Bien. *See* Indochina and Vietnam.

Dier Yassin, Palestine. *See* Israel.

Dikko, Alhaji Umaru. (b. 31 December 1936, Wamba, Kaduna State, Nigeria) Born in a small village near Zaria in northern Nigeria, Dikko spent his adolescence in London. In Great Britain he worked for the British Broadcasting System's Hausa Bureau. He was back in Nigeria when the government of Yakubu Gowon (qv) was overthrown on 29 July 1975. Dikko was arrested and charged with corruption. Although found guilty of an often capital crime, Dikko reappeared in 1979 after civil rule was restored. He was appointed minister of transportation and became a confidant of President Alhaji Shehu Shagari. Although never a candidate for public office himself, Dikko masterminded Shagari's successful reelection bid in 1983. Rumors persist that Dikko was reappointed minister of transport only because of Shagari's gratitude; Dikko had made many enemies in and out of Nigerian political affairs. When Shagari was deposed 31 December 1983, Dikko fled to England after the Buhari (qv) government accused him of gross corruption in office. On 5 July 1984, British authorities foiled a Nigerian attempt to kidnap Dikko and two other men and smuggle them out of the country in packing crates. A Nigerian and two Israelis were subsequently arrested (11 July) by the British police in connection with the incident. On 13 July, the Nigerian High Commissioner and two diplomats were expelled from Great Britain. This set off a round of counterexpulsions of British diplomats in Nigeria.

Dili. *See* Timor.

Dimka, Bukar S. On 13 February 1976, Lieutenant Colonel Bukar S. Dimka led an abortive coup attempt against the government of Nigeria's president, Murtala Mohammed (qv). Mohammed was killed in the fighting. On 11 March 1976, 30 conspirators, including Mohammed's defense minister, were executed. Dimka and seven others were executed on 15 March. At the same time, the Nigerian government demanded the extradition of Yakubu Gowon (qv) from Great Britain to be tried for his complicity in the plot. Mohammed had deposed Gowon in July 1975. The British refused, and relations between the two countries became strained.

Dinh Tuong Province. *See* Vietnam.

Din Sol Peninsula. *See* Vietnam.

Diori, Hamani. On 15 April 1974, the government of Niger's president Hamani Diori was overthrown by a relatively bloodless military coup led by Lieutenant Colonel Seyni Kountie (Kountche) (qv). Diori had ruled Niger since its independence in 1960.

Dire Dawe. *See* Ethiopia.

District (of Columbia) Building (US). *See* Washington, DC, and B'nai B'rith.

Diu. A former Portuguese possession in India, the enclave of Diu is located on an island at the southern end of the Kathiawar peninsula. The Portuguese had held the island since 1535, and it was subject to the Portuguese governor of Goa (qv). The Indian government occupied the area in December 1961. See *also* Damao and Gao.

Dizful. *See* Iran.

Djakarta. *See* Jakarta.

Djibouti (Jibuti). Formerly the capital city and chief port of French Somaliland, Djibouti is now an independent republic formed on 27 June 1977. French occupation of the region began in 1862 and continued expanding into the 1900s, when the town they had developed as Djibouti became the capital of French Somaliland (1892). The seaport grew dramatically during World War II. In 1949, Djibouti became a free port. In 1967, French Somaliland became the French Territory of Afars and Issas. In 1976 there were a series of military clashes between the Afars, who are ethnically tied to the Ethiopians, and the Issas, who favored the Somalis. In 1977, the French withdrew, leaving an impoverished but independent land that still required extensive French support; a military alliance is part of that support. Also, on 20 September 1977, Djibouti was given full membership in the United Nations. Afar–Issa ethnic rivalry continued, but was not the only problem facing the country. The problem of the city of Djibouti itself created major class, ethnic and other demographic inconsistencies that had to be faced. Ethiopian and Somali refugees compounded these problems and, although the UN offered some assistance, the continued instability in Somalia, for example, did little to alleviate the Djiboutan issue. This led to human rights violations by government forces trying to maintain control. Ethnic clashes continued to occur on a regular basis; these were quite often the result of one group or the other favoring a particular side in the ongoing struggle in Somalia. On 26 March 1990, Somali forces created a border incident as they attempted to destroy rebel forces in what was deemed Djiboutan territory. During the Gulf Crisis of 1990–1991, Djibouti, usually a supporter of Iraq, was forced to support France, which has been its chief benefactor and protector. On 8–9 January 1991, a coup attempt failed and led to a series of arrests. Throughout that year, a number of disturbances led to the deaths of a number of innocent by-standers in a Djibouti slum. Ethnic warfare broke out in late 1991 and continued into 1992. In February 1992, French troops were introduced into the streets of Djibouti to restore and keep order. A cease-fire was arranged in late February 1992. Yet, fighting continued sporadically into 1993, with hundreds more dead or injured. Bickering occurred between factions of the rebel movement in March 1994. That same year, more people died in Djibouti city when Afar homes were leveled for "security" reasons. Also in 1994, France signed a new assistant pact with Djibouti. The internal situation remained tense through 1995 and into 1996. Reading: Robert St. Veran, *Djibouti: Pawn of the Horn of Africa* (1981); Charles W. Koburger, *Naval Strategy East of Suez: The Role of Djibouti* (1992); Colin Darch, *A Soviet View* *of Africa: An Annotated Bibliography on Ethiopia, Somalia and Djibouti* (1980).

Dodd, Francis T. On 7 April 1952, a well-orchestrated revolt began among the communist prisoners of war held in the United Nations prison compound on Koje Island off the southern tip of the Korean peninsula. The camp commander, US Brigadier General Francis T. Dodd, foolishly allowed himself to be captured by the inmates, who used him for propaganda as Dodd's successor, Brigadier General Charles E. Colson, bartered for his freedom by acknowledging alleged abuses, which did not in fact exist, of communist POWs.

Dodecanese (*Dhodhekanisos*) Islands. *See* Greece.

Doe, Samuel Kanyon. (b. 6 May 1951(?), Tuzon, Liberia—d. 9 or 10 September 1990, Monrovia, Liberia) Doe, a member of the Krahn tribe, joined the army following completion of the eleventh grade. Doe continued his education in night school and trained as a signalman in the army. He also trained with U.S. Special Forces in Liberia. In April 1980, as a master sergeant, he led a a small band of Krahn soldiers in a military revolt that overthrew the government of President William R. Tolbert, Jr.(qv), killing Tolbert and 30 others at the executive mansion in the process. Doe became the head of state and, as a first order of business, ordered the executions of 13 other ex-government leaders. A total of 27 prominent Liberians and their family members were thus eliminated. In 1981, Doe became the target of a failed coup attempt which was crushed with much violence. Doe lifted the ban on political activity in 1984, a ban he had imposed in 1980. In 1984, he narrowly averted an assassination attempt which had been engineered by the deputy commander of the palace guard, Colonel Flanzamaton (qv). Flanzamaton was subsequently tried and executed. In 1985, Doe accused Sierra Leone of complicity in another failed coup attempt against his regime. He won a close reelection in 1985 amid charges that it was rigged. One month later, he smashed another coup attempt. In 1989, he fought against two rival tribal chieftains who sought to unseat him. In September 1990, he was forced to fortify the executive mansion, where he fought against another coup attempt. Doe was wounded in both legs during the ensuing fight. Taken into custody, he was apparently tortured to death on 10 September.

Dokan Dam. *See* Iraq.

Dome of the Rock. *See* Jerusalem and Israel.

Dominican Republic. Christopher Columbus discovered Hispaniola in the West Indies in 1492. The island lies to the east southeast of Cuba and is approximately 700 miles southeast of Florida. The native Arawak and Carib Indians found there by Columbus were the original inhabitants. The city of Santo Domingo, now the Dominican Republic's capital, was founded in 1496 and is the oldest inhabited New World settlement. The colony was called Santo Domingo for the next 300 years. In 1697, Spain ceded the western third of the island (Haiti) to France. Santo Domingo was ceded to France in 1795, but was later recovered by Spain. Haiti (qv) occupied Santo Domingo in 1801, but Spain returned intermittently until 1821. In those two decades, several native republics rose and fell, often with French or British military assistance. Haiti continued its oppressive rule of the country until an uprising led by Juan Pablo Duarte freed the country. On 27 February 1844, the Dominican Republic was declared independent. During the following decades the U.S., Great Britain and France protected the country from Haitian invasion. In 1861, the government of the Dominican Republic engineered a new cession to Spain, but this proved unpopular and an insurgency began that the Spanish army could not control. In 1865, at the end of the American Civil War, Spain, fearing a confrontation with the United States, withdrew from the island. A move was then made to request U.S. annexation of the country, but the U.S. Congress thwarted the move. Great disorder followed until 1882, when the Heureaux government imposed a harsh and despotic control of the country. This brought about a period of relative quiet that lasted until Heureaux died in 1899. Another period of disorder followed until 1905, when the U.S., as the result of arbitration, undertook the collection of customs and the settlement of foreign claims against the government in Santo Domingo. The next decade witnessed a series of coups and other destabilizing activities that continued until November 1916, when U.S. Marines occupied the country and installed a U.S. military government that lasted until 1924. During that period, the Marines trained a new army; but, in 1930, when it was needed, the military failed to respond to protect the government against an uprising that eventually placed General Rafael Leonidas Trujillo Molina (qv) in power. A hurricane destroyed Santo Domingo in September of the year. Trujuillo ruled for the next 31 years. In 1935, the border dispute with Haiti was settled, but two years later, the two countries were again on the verge of war when the massacre of several thousand Haitians living in the Dominican Republic was reported. In 1941, the Dominican Republic declared war on Germany and Japan immediately following the US declaration. The government was able to expel a Cuban-sponsored invasion in 1959, but it was condemned by the OAS that same year for its aggression against Venezuela. It was again condemned by the OAS for its part in the assassination of Venezuela's president, Romulo Betancourt (qv), in 1960; OAS sanctions were placed against the country. The Trujillo government's corruption and its oppressive tactics against any opposing factions coontinued to bring much criticism until Trujillo's assassination in 1961. Trujillo followers thereafter fled the country. Juan Bosch (qv) was elected president in 1962, but was ousted by a military coup in September 1963. A period of serious unrest followed, and 400 U.S. Marines landed, ostensibly to protect US interests in the country. There was strong criticism of the U.S. action within the western hemisphere and some from abroad. The U.S. force was greatly increased in the succeeding period and was supported by forces from other OAS countries. A truce was arranged among the feuding factions and Hector Garcia-Godoy (qv) was elected president (September 1965). Communist-inspired unrest erupted into civil war until the inter-American force took offensive action to occupy the rebel-held portions of the city. On 3 June 1966, Joaquin Balaguer (qv) was elected president and the inter-American force withdrew. Another OAS peacekeeping force was dispatched to the country in May 1968. Again, in February 1973, the unfounded threat of an invasion from abroad provoked the government into arresting a number of opposition leaders, including Juan Bosch. In 1978, the government announced an amnesty that affected several hundred political prisoners in custody. In 1982, President Guzman Fernandez (qv) committed suicide. Although the country was relatively free of major disturbance after that, the economic situation continued to plague the government. Guzman's successor, Salvador Jorge Blanco, served until 1986 and managed to keep order and relative tranquility in the land. An economic decline and the imposition of an austerity program produced rioting and strikes, however, that brought Joaquin Balaguer, now aged and nearly blind, back to the presidency. Blanco was then convicted of corruption. Balaguer won reelection in 1990, but civil disorder accompanied the victory, even though at a much lesser scale. Real trouble broke out in 1992 during the 500th anniversary of Columbus's landing, in which police killed the leader of the human rights movement. Although ten policemen were arrested in the incident, a new political uprising followed in which a number of high-ranking members of the Dominican Liberation Party resigned. Revelations that members of the Balaguer government were involved in drug trafficking also upset the political balance. Fraud was charged in the 1994 elections, but Balaguer won his seventh term as president. New elections were held in 1996, and Balaguer lost his office after being barred from running for reelection. *Reading:* Bruce Palmer, *Intervention in the Caribbean: The Dominican Crisis of 1965* (1990); Piero Gleijeses, *The Dominican Crisis: The 1965 Constitutional Revolt and American Intervention* (1978); John E. Fagg, *Cuba, Haiti and the Dominican Republic* (1965); Rayford W. Logan, *Haiti and the Dominican Republic* (1968).

Dong Ha, SVN. *See* Vietnam.

Dong Hoi, SVN. *See* Vietnam.

Dong Tam, SVN. *See* Vietnam.

Dong Xoai, SVN. *See* Vietnam.

Douglas Settlement. *See* Falkland Islands.

Dow Chemical Plant. The Dow Chemical Company plant at Lavrion, located 40 miles from Athens, Greece, was blown up on 22 February 1974. A terrorist group calling itself the People's Resistance Army took credit for the attack. Four bombs exploded, causing considerable damage. Two Greek demolitions experts were killed while trying to disarm a fifth bomb that was found at the scene.

Dozier, James Lee. (b. 10 April 1931, Arcadia, Florida) After graduation from the United States Military Academy, West Point in 1956, Dozier served in a number of assignments in the U.S. Army. In December 1981, as a brigadier general, he was assigned to the North Atlantic Treaty Organization (NATO) as a senior logistics officer and was stationed at Verona, Italy, at the Southern Command headquarters. In 17 December, he was kidnapped from his home by a group of Red Brigades (qv) terrorists and held captive 42 days before rescue by the Italian special police unit known as the "Leatherheads" on 28 January 1982. The story of Dozier's kidnapping and detention provided much copy for the newspapers, but some inconsistencies in the accounting of the affair did not do Dozier much good militarily, especially after his release. He did manage to keep his captors off balance with false information as he was being held in an apartment in Padua, but the rumor that he had classified documents in his possession at home before his capture, a practice frowned on by the military, did not help his case. The affair did bring on a massive hunt for Red Brigades members; a large number were captured and given stiff sentences. Antonio Savasta, one of the ringleaders in the kidnapping, received only a 15-year sentence at his March 1982 hearing. That sentence was handed down after he turned state's evidence against at least 50 other Red Brigades members.

Drenthe Province. *See* Netherlands.

Duarte, Jose Napoleon. (b. 23 November 1925, San Salvador—d. 23 February 1990, San Salvador) A 1948 graduate of Notre Dame University in Indiana, Duarte became a civil engineer in his native country. He held that position until 1964, when he was elected mayor of San Salvador. He then set about organizing the Christian Democrat Party. In 1972, he was elected president, but was thrown out of the country by the ruling military. Duarte spent the next seven years in Venezuela, in virtual exile. He was brought back to El Salvador as a member of a five-man junta and was named president of El Salvador on 13 December 1980, the first civilian leader of the country in over 40 years. At the time, a civil war raged in his country, and the intensity and the casualties of the fighting were increasing daily. Although Duarte visited the U.S., and received assurances of support from President Reagan and although numerous international organizations and France and Mexico attempted to step in and bring peace, the situation continued to deteriorate. Duarte would not recognize the Frente Farabundo Marti para la Liberacion Nacional as a national opposition party and counted on the elections of 1982–1983 to stabilize the country. Upon his reelection in May 1984, however, this situation grew worse. Duarte imposed rigid restrictions on the nation's military and the federal police organizations, placing them under a newly established ministry. In October 1984, Duarte offered to meet with the rebel leaders. The offer was accepted, and the first talks were held in La Palma, in Chalatenango Province on 15 October 1984. The result of the meeting was an agreement to form a joint commission to end the five-year-old war. But Duarte could end neither the fighting nor the activities of death squads operating within his government. He was diagnosed as having cancer in 1988, but he served out his term of office before his death in 1990.

Duarte Duran, Ines Guadalupe. On 10 September 1985, terrorists belonging to the Pedro Pablo Castillo Front kidnapped Salvadoran president Jose Napoleon Duarte's (qv) eldest daughter, Ines Guadalupe Duarte Duran and a female companion in a bloody shootout outside her university in San Salvador. One security guard was killed and another was mortally wounded. The two women were held for nearly two months and were released (24 October) only after the government freed 22 political prisoners and 100 wounded rebel prisoners.

Dubai. *See* United Arab Emirates.

Dubcek, Alexander. (b. 27 November 1921, Uhrovec Czechoslovakia—d. 7 November 1992, Prague) Dubcek received his early education in the Soviet Union and returned to Czechoslovakia with his family in 1938. Dubcek's father was a hard-core communist. In Czechoslovakia Dubcek became a member of the outlawed communist party in Slovakia. During the German occupation he worked with the Czech underground. He continued his party activity after the war, and in 1962 he became a full member of the Presidium of the Central Committee. On 5 January 1968, the communist party chief in Czechoslovakia, Antonin Novotny (qv), a Stalinist, was removed from power. He was replaced by Dubcek, a progressive. Dubcek almost immediately became troublesome to the Soviet Union and other bloc nations by demanding a revision of the Warsaw Pact (qv) to prevent its use for political purposes (15 July 1968). At the same time, Czechoslovakia underwent a change of attitude toward its own citizens and to the world at large. This period became known as the "Prague Spring." A major rift appeared between Prague and Moscow, which was settled in the usual Soviet way, by force. On 20–21 August 1968, more than 200,000 Warsaw Pact troops invaded Czechoslovakia. Dubcek was arrested, hauled off to Moscow and forced to make major concessions, including approval of the invasion. He was then allowed to return to Prague. Eventually 650,000 troops were involved in the occupation. Under the threat of this force, the Czech leadership for required to abrogate a series of reforms instituted by Dubcek and to return to the old Soviet style of leadership. Many senior Czech officials were forced to step down by the Soviets. Dubcek himself was forced to resign as first secretary in 17 April 1969. He did, however, retain his seat in the Presidium. He served as ambassador to Turkey in 1970 and as a forestry official from 1970 until 1988. Dubcek, who had been kept under close surveillance by the Czech secret police (STB), complained loudly through the Western press in October 1974, for which he was roundly criticized by the premier, Gustav Husak. Although the situation eventually quieted in Czechoslovakia, there was a resurgence of popular protest in 1974–1975. When Czechoslovakia threw off its communist yoke in 1989, Dubcek returned to prominence and held the largely symbolic office of chairman of the Federal Assembly. He died of natural causes on 7 November 1992, at the age of 71.

Dublin (*Baile Atha Cliath*). *See* Ireland.

Dubs, Adolph. (b. 4 August 1920, Chicago—d. 14 February 1979, Kabul, Afghanistan) A career diplomat, Dubs graduated from Georgetown University in Washington, DC, and entered the Foreign Service. In 1950, he was the first U.S. diplomat assigned to the newly revived West Germany. He then served in Liberia, Canada, the USSR, and Yugoslavia. After a tour of duty in the US, Dubs returned to the USSR (1961) as minister counselor and served briefly as acting chief of the mission (1972–1974). In 1975, he was assistant deputy secretary of state for Eastern and South Asian affairs. In 1978, Dubs was killed in the cross-fire when Afghan police stormed the hotel where he was being held in a Soviet-engineered kidnapping by four right-wing Muslim terrorists. Dubs had been riding in his official car when the terrorists took him. The terrorists, opponents of the repressive Afghan government, demanded the release of three of their compatriots taken prisoner by the government. After the botched police raid and Dubs's subsequent death, U.S. officials were shown four bodies the authorities claimed were the terrorists. Witnesses to the police raid said one terrorist had been killed and two wounded. There was no way of ascertaining whether the four bodies belonged to the assailants.

Dulles, John Foster. (b. 25 February 1888, Washington, DC—d. 24 May 1959) John Foster Dulles attended Princeton University and George Washington University law school; he then studied at the Sorbonne. In 1911, he entered and international law firm and, by 1927, he was its head. After World War I, Dulles served as the U.S. legal counsel at the Versailles conference and was appointed to the Reparations Commission by Woodrow Wilson. During World War II, Dulles was instrumental in the founding of the United Nations helping both at Dumbarton Oaks in the preparation of its charter and as a senior advisor at inaugural session at San Francisco. In 1949, he served briefly in the U.S. Senate, filling out an unexpired term. In 1950, as an advisor to the Department of State, Dulles helped conclude the peace treaty with Japan. In 1953, he was appointed secretary of state in the Eisenhower administration. During his tenure he coined the phrase "agonizing reappraisal," when he stated what the U.S. would have to effect, if the French continued wavering on the issue of European defense. In all, he actively pursued a course of strenuously opposing communism and the Soviet cause. This led to the coinage of a second new word, "brinkmanship," as reflective of his style of diplomacy, whereby, as he was often criticized for doing, he led the nation to the brink of war. More astute politicians and statesmen credit his policies with strengthening the West at one of the most crucial and difficult periods of the Cold War. Seriously ill with cancer, John Foster Dulles resigned his office on 15 April 1959. He died on 24 May 1959. His brother, Allen Welsh Dulles (b. 1893—d. 1969), followed a somewhat similar life of public service and was Director of Central Intelligence from 1953 until 1961.

Dundalk. *See* Ireland.

Dunn, Gardner, On 28 November 1979, South African ambassador Gardner Dunn was kidnapped by leftist terrorists of the Popular Liberation Front in El Salvador. The terrorist demanded $20 million in ransom and the publication of a manifesto denouncing the Salvadoran government in return for his release. When the terms were not met, the terrorists murdered Dunn on 10 October 1980.

Durand Line Agreement. In 1893, the border between Afghanistan and British India was stipulated in the Durand Line Agreement. When the British withdrew from India on 14 August 1947, Pakistan acquired self-government as a largely Islamic state within India, and with dominion status in the British Commonwealth. In 1949, a year of border clashes occurred as Pakistan and Afghanistan both moved to readjust their positions.

Durban. *See* Republic of South Africa.

D'Urso, Giovanni. On 12 December 1980, Red Brigade (qv) terrorists kidnapped the director general (chief judge) of Italy's Ministry of Justice, Giovanni D'Urso. This was but one of a series of major kidnappings of prominent Italians during 1980. As ransom for D'Urso, the terrorists demanded the closing of the maximum security prison on the island of Asinara. D'Urso was released on 15 January 1981 in Rome.

Dutch East Indies. Until 1949, the Dutch East Indies were a territory of the Kingdom of the Netherlands. From December 1949 the island group, lying south of the Indochinese peninsula between the Indian and Pacific Oceans has been known as the Republic of Indonesia (qv). The group consists of the larger island of Sumatra, Java, Celebes, the Moluccas, the Lesser Sunda Islands, and Dutch Borneo. Other islands in the general group (Misool, Salawati, Waigeo) remained under Dutch control until 1962, when they were conceded to Indonesia and renamed Irian Barat. Some islands in the Lesser Sundas (eastern Timor) remained under Portuguese control. In 1922, the Netherlands Indies were granted equal status as a territory by the Dutch. The entire region was under Japanese control during World War II. The end of the war witnessed the beginning of strong nationalist resistance to outside rule, which lasted until independence. *See also* Cheribon Agreement and Indonesia.

Dutch West New Guinea. *See* Indonesia.

Dutra, Enrico (Eurico) Gaspar. (b. 18 May 1885, Cuiaba, Mato Grosso, Brazil—d. 11 June 1974, Rio de Janeiro) Dutra was commissioned into the Brazilian army in 1910 as a cavalry officer. He served in successive and colorless assignments for the next 20 years until 1930, when Getulio Vargas (qv) overthrew the government. Although not involved in the politics of the moment, Dutra rose to prominence during the anti-Vargas Sao Paulo rebellion in 1932. By 1935, he was commander of the Brazilian army troops who put down a communist uprising in Rio de Janeiro. In 1936 Dutra was appointed minister of war and held that post until 1945. In 1937 he helped establish the Getulio Vargas dictatorship, and in 1944 he organized the Brazilian army expeditionary force that fought alongside the Allied forces in the Italian campaign. Selected to stand for the office of president in 1945, Dutra was able to disarm Vargas in a coup d'etat, when Vargas attempted to block the election. Dutra was elected president of Brazil on 2 December 1945. His otherwise lackluster administration marked the resurgence of democracy in Brazil after decades of dictatorship. He served in office until 1950, until the Brazilian electorate repudiated him and replaced him with Getulio Vargas (21 January 1951).

Dutschke, Rudi. (b. 7 March 1940, Schonefeld, Germany—d. 24 December 1979, Arhus, Denmark) Born the son of a postal worker, Dutschke was educated in the Evangelical Christian tradition in the Eastern Zone of Germany. He escaped into West Berlin just before construction of the Berlin Wall (qv) (1961) to avoid service in the East German armed forces, where he knew he would be exposed to relentless Marxist indoctrination. He helped found and became the leader of the Socialist Students League in West Berlin, and in 1966, after the coalition of the Social Democrats and the Christian Democrats in Bonn, he formed the Extra-Parliamentary Opposition Party. He narrowly escaped assassination in April 1968, when, after his return from a visit to Prague, he was shot in the head. This incident fermented wide-scale rioting throughout Western Europe. Dutschke obtained a doctorate in philosophy from West Berlin's Free University and continued postdoctoral studies in Italy and in Great Britain. At Cambridge, however, he was expelled in 1971 for subversive activities. He soon became interested in the environment and moved into the "Green" Party activities. While lecturing in Denmark, he suffered a seizure, probably associated with his head wound, and died by drowning in his bathtub on 24 December 1979.

Duvalier, Francois "Papa Doc." (b. 14 April 1907, Port-au-Prince—d. 21 April 1971, Port-au-Prince) One of the most vicious dictators of all time, Duvalier was educated as a physician (1934) at the University of Haiti's medical college. In the following years, working under a U.S. grant, Duvalier travelled throughout the rural sections of Haiti treating cases of yaws, a bacterial disease of the subtropics. Although treatment was rudimentary in the pre-penicillin period, Duvalier's reputation as a physician earned him the nickname "Papa Doc" and a large following among the largely illiterate peasantry of Haiti. In 1948, Duvalier was appointed secretary of labor in the government of Paul Magloire (qv). A coup in 1950 ousted the Magloire regime and thus postponed Duvalier's entry into the political arena. After a series of intervening coups, Duvalier was elected president on 22 September 1957 on the points of the army's bayonets. He immediately established himself as a ruthless leader by rounding up all those he considered troublemakers. Within months he had total control of Haiti, which was maintained under the watchful eyes of the Tontons Macoutes, a private army of thugs and bullies Duvalier used to keep himself in power. In one instance, within a month of Duvalier's assuming office, an American citizen was beaten to death by the police. In 1960, he ordered martial law throughout the tiny nation to thwart rioting at the University of Haiti. In 1963, the police violated diplomatic immunity by breaking into the embassy of the Dominican Republic in Port-au-Prince looking for "troublemakers." He appointed himself president-for-life and had the Haitian constitution rewritten to ensure the succession of his son, Jean-Claude, to the same office. Duvalier died of a terminal illness on 21 April 1971.

Duvalier, Jean-Claude "Baby Doc." (b. 3 July 1951, Port-au-Prince, Haiti) After having received his education in the Roman Catholic schools of Port-au-Prince, Jean-Claude Duvalier was beginning the study of law when his father, Francois Duvalier (qv) became ill. At age 21 and with no experience, Jean-Claude found himself president-for-life of Haiti, following in the footsteps of his father, one of the most savage dictators in history. Jean-Claude soon discovered, or had it told to him, that he was a leader in name only and that the real power lay in the hands of his mother, Simone Ovide Duvalier, and five or six other family members or close associates who controlled all of the organs of power in Haiti. Among young Duvalier's inheritances was the *Tontons Macoutes*, a secret police organization of extraordinary viciousness. With a symbol of the Duvalier mystique ensconced in the National Palace, it appeared to be business as usual in Haiti; but, after a time, the economic and social conditions in the country persuaded many in the government that changes in the system were required to exploit foreign investment. Among the initial moves was the supposed suppression of the secret police and other cosmetic endeavors meant for external consumption. By 1980, however, the still-repressive nature of the government was demonstrated in the arrest of more than 200 Haitians on charges of criticizing "Baby Doc." By 1985, the criticism had turned to open rebellion as thousands of Haitians took to the streets demanding the removal of the Duvalier regime. In early 1986, Duvalier and his family fled the country.

Duvalier, Marie Denise Dominique. Sister to Jean-Claude Duvalier (qv), and his personal secretary after his installation as president of Haiti, Marie Denise was forced to flee the country when it was discovered she was involved in a plot to overthrow her brother's government in August 1973.

E

East African High Commission. In December 1945, Great Britain announced the formation of the East African High Commission came about as a result of the necessity for closer supervision and collaboration among the British-held African territories after World War II. The commission's role was the establishment of common communications and technical services to be shared by the territories. The organization was based in Nairobi and was made up of the governors of the British East African territories of Kenya, Tanganyika (Tanzania) and Uganda. The governor of Kenya served as the chairman. The group also had oversight of the Royal East African Navy, transportation, postal services and the railroads in the region. A Central Legislative Assembly met to legislate the decisions of the commission. An East African Court of Appeals was established in 1951 and sat in Nairobi. By 1963, all three of the territories had gained their independence, and the need for the commission ended. It was replaced by the East African Common Services Organization (EACSO), which held its charter from the East African Common Services Authority (EACSA), composed of the heads of the three states.

East Berlin. See Berlin and East Germany.

"Easter Offensive." *See* Vietnam.

East Falkland (Soledad) Island. *See* Falklands Islands.

East Germany. The Democratic Republic of Germany (DDR) came into existence on 7 October 1949, when the Soviet Union, which was occupying that part of conquered Germany, proclaimed the event. On 6 June 1950, East Germany and Poland, both under Soviet domination, signed a treaty establishing the Oder-Neisse Line (qv) as the common border. On the same day that West Germany (qv) received its internal independence (Bonn Agreement, 26 May 1952), East Germany began a Soviet-inspired campaign of pressure through the curtailment of east-west communications. The Soviet Control Commission that held governance in East Germany was abolished on 28 May 1953, and replaced with a Soviet high commissioner. Also, in June 1953, East Germany relaxed its rules against demonstrations. East German workers immediately took to the streets demanding a general strike and shouting antigovernment slogans (16 June). The next day, martial law was declared, and Soviet armored units were sent into East

German government lifted all restrictions on travel between east and west as a means of placating the demonstrators. A mass exodus began that drained the country of its most talented workers. In November 1953, many East Germans were overjoyed when loved ones who had been Soviet prisoners of war since 1945 or earlier were released. On 25 May 1954, the East German government announced its full sovereignty, although none of the larger Western powers acknowledged its existence. In November, the Soviet Union reaffirmed its conferral of sovereignty and gave East Germany sole authority over civilian traffic between Berlin and the West. The Soviet Union continued to garrison a large force in the newly "sovereign" state for security reasons and to fulfill the terms of the Four-Power Potsdam Agreement (qv). At the same time, the Soviets began rearming the East Germany army (seven divisions), and a heavily militarized police force poised on the East-West Berlin border. When West Germany joined the European defense community, East Germany announced a prohibited zone along the 600-mile common border with West Germany. Telephone communications were also cut between East and West Berlin. Throughout the period there was a mass exodus of East Germans seeking freedom in the West. The Soviet yoke forced the East Germans into an economic system that brought chaos to the country. In the early 1960s, the East Germans did two things: In 1961 they cut the principal escape route for those seeking the freedom of the West by building a wall to separate East from West Berlin (15–17 August 1961), and they instituted a "New Economic System," which introduced a modest level of improvement through capitalistic profit-making by industry and workers' bonuses. A treaty of friendship with the USSR on 12 June 1964 fell considerably short of the separate peace treaty the Soviet Union had promised. In February 1965, East German president Walter Ulbricht (qv) was invited to Egypt as the guest of Gamal Nasser (qv). This caused West Germany to cut off all economic aid to Cairo. Also in 1965, when the East Germans closed the autobahn between Berlin and the West, an American convoy challenged the blockage by driving through the East German zone without incident (8 April). During the Czech Uprising of 1968, East German forces participated in the Warsaw Pact intervention (21–22 August 1968) that ended the period known as the "Prague Spring" (qv). On 9 February 1969, East Germany announced that the West German Federal Assembly would not be allowed to cross East German territory to hold their presidential elections in Berlin. The elections were held without incident. The East Germans would also protest periodically and interfere with the flow of traffic between West Germany and Berlin, as in 21–28 January 1970, but would do little more to prevent the Berlin meetings of a committee of the West German *Bundestag*. By 1972, East Germany held the highest standard of living among the Warsaw Pact nations. Also, in December 1972, a treaty was signed between East and West Germany that effectively recognized East German sovereignty. In the late 1970s, the East German economy had slowed because of a lack of natural resources and a dwindling labor pool. Many East Germans still found ways to escape to the West. When the Soviet Union began its program of *glasnost*, East Germany resisted any relaxation of party discipline. In October 1989, mass demonstrations began that demanded political reform. President Erich Honecker (qv), in office since 1976, was forced to resign (18 October 1989). On 4 November, East Germany began opening its borders, first with Czechoslovakia, then the West and to allow free passage of refugees. The infamous "Berlin Wall" began to fall on 4 November 1989. On 23 August 1990, the East German Parliament approved a measure calling for reunification with West Germany. This plan went into effect on 3 October 1990. *See also* Germany and West Germany. *Reading:* David Childs & Richard Popplewell, *The Stati: The East German Intelligence and Security Service* (1996); Klaus Harpprecht & Starles Wheeler, *East German Rising, Seventeenth June 1953* (1979); Martin McCauley, *The German Democratic Republic since 1945* (1984); Mary Fulbrook, *Anatomy of a Dictatorship: Inside the GDR, 1949–1989* (1995).

East Ghor Canal. *See* Jordan.

East Pakistan. *See* Bangladesh and Pakistan.

Ecuador. The land that is today the Republic of Ecuador was part of the northern Incan empire when it was captured by the Spaniards in 1633. The natives of the region were aboriginal and belonged to the complex Andean cultural group. The country is called Ecuador because it lies on the equator. It is bounded on the north by Colombia and on the east and south by Peru. The boundary between Colombia and Ecuador is the Putumayo River, a tributary of the Amazon. To the west lies the Pacific Ocean. The capital city is Quito, which is situated in the Cordillera Central mountains. Spain held the land until it was defeated in 1822 by Colombian and Peruvian forces. Ecuador was then absorbed into the Great Colombia Republic. On 24 May 1830 after the Battle of Pichincha, which was fought by forces under Antonio Jose de Sucre, a lieutenant of Simon Bolívar, Ecuador declared its independence from Spain and, in September 1830, from the Great Colombia Republic. The next thirty years were marked by internal struggles and wars with neighbors which ended with the rule of Gabriel Garcia Moreno (1861–1865, 1860–1875). That was a time of steady growth. In 1875, Mareno was assassinated while running for reelection. Another period of troubles followed. During the years 1894 and 1895, civil war tore the country even further apart. In the early 1900s, a succession of good leaders helped reunite the country, but in 1912 Eloy Alfaro was killed by a mob as he sought to return to the presidency. Serious economic and social turmoil continued into the 1940s, when Ecuador was invaded by Peru. Before it was over, Peru had annexed a large section of Oriente province. Finally, in 1944, a military coup took the government and placed José María Velasco Ibarra (qv) in power. In 1946 he abrogated the constitution, which alienated the socialists and communists who had endorsed the radical constitution. World War II did not directly affect Ecuador, but the immediate postwar period further crippled the economy. Civil unrest began, and in August 1947, Velasco Ibarra was ousted by the military. Free elections were held in 1948 that placed Galo Plaza in the presidency. In 1951, fighting began between Ecuador and Peru over access to the Amazon River. Plaza finished his term in 1952, when Velasco Ibarra was returned to office. He was replaced in 1956 and immediately went into exile. He returned in 1960 and was again elected president. In November 1961, he resigned in the face of growing popular unrest and was replaced by the vice president, Carlos Julio Arosemena Monroy (qv). He was removed from office by the military in July 1963 by a military junta that promised a strong anticommunist government, especially against Cuba. By 1966, after the military junta was forced from office, a new constitution was prepared. But, since 1968, when anti-American rioting broke out protesting the visit of Governor Nelson Rockefeller (qv) of New York, the country has been in the hands of a procession of civilian and military dictators. In June 1969, the Ecuadorian navy captured two American and three Japanese fishing boats they claimed were fishing within 200 miles of their coast. Then, on 3 July 1969, the U.S. lifted a ban on credits for arms sales to Ecuador that had been imposed in December 1968. On 22 June 1970, President Velasco Ibarra assumed dictatorial powers in the face of major rioting in the universities at Quito and Guayaquil. On 18 January 1971, the U.S. cut off all aid to Ecuador because of its continuing policy of seizing American fishing boats inside Ecuador's self-proclaimed 200-mile limit. On 27 January, Ecuador filed a formal protest with the Organization of American States (OAS) protesting continued U.S. violation of the 200-mile limit. On 1 February, the government ordered the withdrawal of the U.S. military mission in Ecuador because of the deadlocked negotiations over fishing rights. The government of Velasco Ibarra was overthrown by a military coup on 15 February 1972; General Guillermo Rodriguez Lara took his place. On 20 January 1973, another American fishing trawler was seized in international waters off the Galapagos Islands. Peru also stepped up its campaign against American fishing craft inside their 200-mile limit. President Lara was able to crush a right-wing coup attempt led by General Raul Gonzales Alvear (qv) on 1 September 1975. Many were killed or injured in the fighting. Lara was, however, removed from office in a bloodless coup led by Vice Admiral Poveda Burbano (qv) on 11 January 1976. In February 1977, the United States blocked the sale of Israeli fighter-bombers to Ecuador, claiming the sale would destabilize the region. On 15 January 1981, another American fishing trawler was seized. As a result, the U.S. Congress blocked the sale of the destroyer *USS Southerland* to the Quito government. At the same time, Ecuadorian troops invaded Peru (28 January 1975) in what became a yearly ritual of border incursions. Ecuador declared a state of emergency because of the fighting. In March the two sides agreed to withdraw their troops from the contested border areas. On 24 May 1981, President Jaime Roldos Aguilera (qv), his wife and his defense minister were killed in an air crash in the Andes. In March 1987, a major earthquake left an estimated 20,000 homeless and severely damaged the country's main pipeline. Because of this latter problem, Ecuador was forced to suspend payments on its estimated $8.2 billion foreign debt. In 1988, orderly elections were held, although the country's economic condition continued to deteriorate. In 1989, the government joined in the war on drugs. In November 1992, Ecuador withdrew from the oil cartel, OPEC, for economic reasons, citing the annual dues to OPEC of $1.5 million, without an equitable return to the small producers. Of singular importance in Latin America, Ecuador began training its military personnel in human rights and regional security issues in 1993 in a UN and OAS-approved program. In 1994, the land reform program went into effect. Violent protests broke out among Indians who saw the plan as a degradation of their cultural heritage. A state of emergency was declared on 20 June; army troops were dispatched to restore order. This situation was excerbated in 1995, when a border war erupted with Peru over disputed territory. Ecuadorian reservists were called up. As the fighting continued, the four guarantors (Rio Protocol of 1942) proposed a truce, but it was largely ignored. Although peace was restored (February 1995), the effect on the economy was devastating. Amid charges of corruption, Ecuador entered 1996. Economic problems continued to spawn resentment among the populace. *Reading:* Government Printing Office. *Ecuador: A Country Study, 3rd ed.* (1993); E. Willard Miller, *The 3rd World–Chile, Bolivia, Peru, Ecuador: A Bibliography (Public Administration Series)* (1990).

Eden, (Robert) Anthony (1st Earl of Avon). (b. 12 June 1897, Windlestone, England—d. 14 January 1977, Alvediston, England) Eden was educated at Eton and at Christ Church, Oxford. He served as foreign secretary under Neville Chamberlain in 1938, but resigned in protest of the Munich Agreement, which he saw as an approval of Nazi aggression. Eden reentered public life at the beginning of World War II as dominions secretary under Chamberlain and later, served under Winston Churchill in 1940, again as foreign secretary. He served with distinction in that post, working on the wartime alliance on the issue of the French war in Indochina in the early 1950s and on the establishment of NATO. During those same years, Eden became progressively more ill; several operations failed to correct the problem. Nonetheless, in 1952, Eden married the niece of Churchill and , in April 1955, succeeded him in the post of prime minister. He became a Knight of the Garter in 1954. His service as prime minister was marred by the Egyptian seizure and nationalization of the Suez Canal, which led to an Anglo-French-supported Israeli invasion of Egypt, in which Eden was accused of ignoring the United Nations and risking World War III. With the alienation of the U.S. and most of the dominions, Eden was forced to resign in January 1957, claiming "ill health." He spent the next decade writing and publishing his memoirs. Eden was made Earl of Avon in 1961. *Reading:* Alan Lawrence & Peter Dodd, *Anthony Eden, 1897–1977: A Bibliography* (1995).

Effiong, Philip. Brigadier Philip Effiong assumed the leadership of the Biafran (qv) movement in Nigeria when C. Odumegu Ojukwu fled to Ivory Coast. When the strategically important town of Owerri fell to the Nigerians in January 1970, Effiong capitulated, bringing to an end two and one-half years of civil war in which more than two million people died.

Egan, John P. On 26 February 1975, 12 terrorists belonging to an organization known as the Montoneros Group abducted US Honorary Consul Agent John P. Egan from his home in Cordoba, Argentina. The kidnappers demanded the release of four Montoneros members imprisoned in Argentina. When the Argentine government refused to negotiate for his release, Egan was murdered (28 February?). His body, draped with a Montoneros flag, was left by the side of a road outside Cordoba.

Egypt. The Arab Republic of Egypt began its history in the fifth millenium B.C. A unified kingdom arose around 3200 B.C. that at its zenith encompassed parts of Syria on the west and Nubia in the south. In the first millennium BC invaders came, and by 341 B.C. the last Egyptian dynasty fell to the Persians. A parade of conquers followed including Alexander and the Greeks, Romans, Byzantines, and Arabs. The last brought with them Islam and a form of the Arabic language, ancient Egyptian being preserved only in Coptic litanies. Mamluk Caucasians ruled Egypt from 1260 until 1517, when the Ottoman Turks seized control. The British entered Egypt in 1882 and established control over the administration of the country even though the Ottoman Empire still claimed Egypt's allegiance until 1914. Thereafter, the British established a protectorate in Egypt that lasted until 1922. By 1936, Egypt had achieved much autonomy, although the British maintained control over numerous bases and the Suez Canal and held, with the Egyptians, condominium over Sudan (qv). World War I witnessed considerable military activity in Egypt, and heavy fighting took place there in World War II. In 1948, when Israel gained its independence, Egypt joined the Arab war against the new state and was defeated. In 1951, Egypt abrogated the 1936 treaty with Great Britain (Sudan became independent in 1956.) In 1952, King Farouk (qv) was forced to abdicate (23 July) when the Society of Free Officers, led by Major General Mohammed Naguib (qv), carried out a coup. A republic was proclaimed, with Naguib named its first president and premier (18 June 1953). In a second coup (1954), Lieutenant Colonel Gamal Abdel Nasser (qv) overthrew Naguib and became premier. Nasser was elected president in 1956. After a series of terrorist raids into Israeli territory, Israel invaded Egypt's Sinai on 29 October 1956. When Egypt rejected an Anglo-French cease-fire demand, the two countries attacked Egypt with airpower and on 5–6 November landed forces. Egypt was forced to accept a UN-mandated cease-fire on 7 November 1956. A UN emergency force was inserted to guard the Israeli-Egyptian border and remained in position until 19 May 1967, when Nasser demanded its withdrawal. Egyptian forces entered Gaza and and the Sharm el Sheikh region, closing the Strait of Tiran to Israeli shipping. War again broke out between Israel and Egypt on 5 June 1967 and ended only after the Gaza and the Sinai had been captured. Israel then controlled the east bank of the Suez Canal (qv). The fighting ended when another UN-mandated cease-fire went into effect on 10 June. From 1968 to 1970 fighting continued along the border and in the air over the Suez and the Sinai. The fighting ended on 7 August 1970, but peace negotiations failed to settle the issue. Upon Nasser's death in 1970, Vice President Anwar Sadat (qv) became president. On 6 October 1973, Egyptian forces, along with those of Syria and other Arab states, invaded Israel. Before the fighting ended Israeli forces had recovered from the initial surprise attack and had crossed the Suez into Egyptian territory, threatening the city of Suez. A

UN cease-fire went into effect on 24 October 1973. Under the terms of a disengagement agreement signed on 18 January 1974, Israel withdrew from the west bank of the Suez and Egyptian troops were allowed to occupy positions along the Canal's east bank. In November 1977, Sadat paid a surprise visit to Jerusalem and opened a dialogue leading to a peace treaty signed in Washington on 26 March 1979 (Camp David Accords). Embassies were exchanged at that time. Tension increased in Egypt as Islamic fundamentalists, who had started a campaign in 1981 to gain control of the government, took to the streets and rioted. A wide-spread government crackdown followed that culminated in the assassination of Anwar Sadat by Muslim fanatics at an Army parade on 6 October 1981. Muhammed Hosni Mubarek (qv) became president. Israel returned the Sinai to Egyptian control in April 1982. During the war against Iraq in 1991, Egypt supported the UN both diplomatically and militarily. Mubarek remained in power in 1993 although a wave of political violence, especially against foreigners, continued to grow and expand into 1994, coming mostly from Islamic militants. Severe repression of fundamentalist groups appeared to have little effect. In February 1994, a wave of bank bombings further exacerbated an already dangerous situation. Over 800 died during the period of unrest. At the same time, however, Egypt played an important role in securing the signing of the Israeli-Palestinian Agreement (1995). Violence continued into 1995, and captured documents verified that the end purpose was the overthrow of the Egyptian government. Still, in 1996, Murbarek held fast in not allowing for the democratization of his country. Terrorism continued and escalated. *Reading:* Emma W. Loveridge, *Egypt (Country Fact Files)* (1997); Selma Botman, *Egypt from Independence to Revolution, 1919–1952* (1991); John Waterbury, *The Egypt of Nasser and Sadat: The Political Economy of Two Regimes* (1983); Cole C. Kingseed, *Eisenhower and the Suez Crisis of 1956* (1995).

Egyptian Revolution. On 20 August 1985, the Israeli administrative attache in Cairo was assassinated by gunmen in a passing automobile. His wife and secretary were injured in the attack. The Egyptian Revolution, a previously unknown organization, took credit for the murder.

Eichmann, Adolf. (b. 19 March 1906, Solingen, Rhineland—d. 31 March 1962, Israel) Eichman, a Protestant, was raised in Linz, Austria, by a harsh stepmother. After received poor grades in school, he became a travelling salesman for the Vacuum Oil Company. In 1932, he joined the Austrian National Socialist Party. He later moved to Germany, where he joined the *Schutzstaffel* (SS) and was assigned to the concentration camp at Dachau. There he was enlisted in the *SS Totenkopf Verbande* (Death's-Head Formations) that guarded the camps. In 1934, as a corporal, he joined the *Sicherheitsdienst* (SD), the Security Service under Reinhard Heydrich. His interest in Jews and Jewish affairs led him to the Jewish Section of the *Gestapo* and to the Reich Security Office, where he attained the rank of lieutenant colonel in the SS. After the 1938 *Anschluss* he took charge of the Office of Jewish Emigration in Vienna. Over 100,000 Austrian Jews were emigrated under his supervision; they were required to leave most of their possessions and wealth behind. Sometime later, Heydrich informed

Eichmann of the "Final Solution," and he was put in charge of the mass deportation of Jews to extermination camps (January 1942). His motives, he would say later, were purely political and not anti-Semitic. In March 1944, he was assigned to Budapest to organize the removal of Hungarian Jews to Auschwitz. In August 1944, he was recalled to Germany. He had already amassed a personal fortune that was carefully hidden from his superiors. Much of the money came from selling Jews their lives. In April 1945, after saying goodbye to Himmler, he fled to the south, where he was captured by the Americans. Unrecognized, he escaped and secured false papers, in the name of Otto Henniger, and moved himself and his family to the Middle East and eventually, to Argentina. He was probably aided in his escape by "Odessa" (*Organisation der Ehemaligen SS-Angehörigen*), a secret SS escape group that operated after 1947 to help former SS personnel flee Germany. In 1960, Israeli agents captured Eichmann in Argentina and secretly moved him to Israel, where he was put on trial for war crimes. In Israel, Eichmann confessed all before being put on public trial on 11 April 1961. On 15 December 1961, having been found guilty, he was sentenced to death and was executed by hanging on 31 May 1962.

Eid, Guy. On 1 March 1973, eight members of the Black September Organization (qv) invaded the Saudi Arabian embassy in Khartoum, Sudan, and took several hostages, including the Belgian charge d'affaires, Guy Eid. The new U.S. ambassador Cleo Noel (qv) and the outgoing deputy chief of the U.S, mission, George Moore, and the Saudi ambassador were also taken, while many of the diplomats at the reception were able to escape. The terrorists demanded the release of 60 Palestinians held in Jordan, all the Arab women held in Israel, Sirhan Sirhan (qv), the assassin of Robert Kennedy (qv), and imprisoned members of the Baader-Meinhof Gang (qv) in Germany. When negotiations failed, the terrorists murdered Eid, Noel and Moore. The terrorist surrendered on 3 March and were, after some delay, tried and sentenced to life terms. The sentences were reduced to seven years by Sudanese President Numaryi, who then deported them to Egypt. In Egypt, President Anwar Sadat (qv) released the prisoners to the Palestinian Liberation Organization (PLO).

Eilat (Elat, Elath). *See* Israel and Gulf of Aqaba.

Eisenhower, Dwight David. (b. 14 October 1890, Denison, Texas—d. 28 March 1969, Washington, DC) Eisenhower was born the third of seven sons of a railroad worker. The family returned to Abilene, Kansas, in 1891. In 1911, young Eisenhower entered the US Military Academy at West Point, where he graduated number three in his class (1915). During World War I he served as the commander of a tank training center and was a pioneer in the use of armor in combat. He married Mamie Doud in 1916 and had two sons, Dwight (b. 1917—d. 1921, scarlet fever) and John (b. 1922). Eisenhower was promoted to the rank of major at the end of the war. He served in Panama from 1922 until 1924. He graduated first in his class at the U.S. Army Command and General Staff College in 1926, and at the Army War College in 1928. He then toured Europe for a year, revising a guidebook to the World War I battlefields.

Eisenhower was then posted to Washington, where he helped prepare an industrial mobilization plan and was instrumental in the founding of the Army Industrial College. From 1933 to 1935, he served in the office of then Army Chief of Staff Douglas MacArthur (qv). In September 1935, he accompanied MacArthur to the Philippines when the latter was appointed commissioner there. Eisenhower returned to the U.S. in 1939 after the outbreak of war in Europe. In 1941, he was chief of staff of the U.S. Third Army and was promoted to brigadier general after coming to the attention of Army Chief of Staff George C. Marshall (qv). In December 1941, after Pearl Harbor, he was ordered to Washington to take over the Army's War Plans Division (WPD). On 25 June 1942 he became commander of the European Theater of Operations (ETO). In late 1942, he commanded the Allied invasion of North Africa. He remained in command of the forces in the Mediterranean until November 1943, when he returned to London to take command of the preparationsfor the invasion of the continent of Europe (6 June 1944). In December 1944, he was promoted to the five-star rank of general of the army. He commanded the western Allied occupation forces briefly after the war before returning to Washington to become chief of staff. Eisenhower retired in 1948 and became president of Columbia University. In January 1948, after being approached by both parties, he stated he had no intention of running for public office. Eisenhower's tenure at Columbia was not marked by great success. Indeed, he became known as a conservative and lost much of his liberal support. In December 1950, President Harry Truman (qv) appointed him supreme commander allied forces, Europe, the military arm of NATO. In 1952, he returned to the United States and ran for the presidency after a bitter Republican convention fight and overwhelmed his Democratic opponent Adlai Stevenson. He was inaugurated the 34th president of the United States on 20 January 1953 and, true to his promise, brought the war in Korea to a close (July 1953). During his first term, Eisenhower suffered a heart attack (24 September 1955) and spent additional time in the hospital recuperating from surgery (June 1956, from ileitis). He easily won a second term in 1956, again defeating Adlai Stevenson. His administrations were marked by his bringing peace in Korea, his establishment of the International Atomic Energy Commission, his establishment of alliances, such as the South East Asia Treaty Organization (SEATO) (qv), his attempt at disarmament - destroyed by Nikita Khruschev (qv)—his prevention of U.S. military involvement in Indochina in 1954 and the downswing in his overall popularity because of the Soviet success in the launching of *Sputnik* in 1957. In September 1957, Eisenhower moved quickly to prevent the use of the Arkansas National Guard to obstruct integration. Also on 7 March 1957, the Eisenhower Doctrine was approved by Congress. This doctrine authorized the president to use armed force to protect any Middle Eastern country requesting aid against aggression by any communist nation. The doctrine also called for aiding any Middle Eastern state in developing its economic potential. Eisenhower left office on 3 January 1961 and retired to his farm at Gettysburg, Pennsylvania, where he wrote several best-selling books. He died at age 79 at Walter Reed Army Medical Center.

Ejercito de Liberacion Nacional (ELN). Members of the leftist Bolivian terrorist organization ELN assassinated a former Bolivian secret police official, Roberto Quitanilla, in Hamburg, Germany, on 1 April 1971. The group also took credit for the bombing of several U.S. firms in Medellin, Columbia, on 7 February 1985, although this attack may have been carried out by the Che Guevara faction of Colombia's ELN, another terrorist organization.

Ejercito Revolucionario del Pueblo (ERP). On 23 May 1971, the British honorary consul in Rosario, Argentina, was kidnapped by terrorists representing the left-wing ERP (People's Revolution Party). He was released unharmed when a ransom of $100,000 was paid. The director of the Fiat plant, Doctor Oberdan Sallustro, was not so lucky, however, when he was kidnapped by the same group on 21 March 1972. His body was discovered in a Buenos Aires suburb on 10 April. On 18 May 1974, the Argentine government mounted a military campaign in Tucuman Province to rid the country of the ERP.

El Aiun. *See* Morocco.

El Arish. *See* Israel.

Elat (Eilat, Elath). *See* Israel.

Elbrick, C. Burke. On 4 September 1969, the U.S. ambassador to Brazil, C. Burke Elbrick, was kidnapped on the street in Rio de Janiero. His kidnappers were members of a revolutionary terrorist group known MR8. They demanded the release of 15 political prisoners for Elbrick's safe release. He was released unharmed on 7 September, after the ransom terms were met.

Elefis. *See* Greece.

Elizabethville, Independent Congo Republic. *See* Congo.

El Paisnal. *See* El Salvador.

El Paraiso. *See* Colombia.

El Paraiso. *See* El Salvador.

Elrom, Ephraim. On 17 May 1971, terrorist members of the Turkish People's Liberation Party kidnapped Ephraim Elrom, the Israeli consul general in Istanbul. The kidnappers demanded the release of political prisoners as his ransom. On 23 May, his body was discovered in an Istanbul apartment less than a quarter-mile from the Israeli consulate.

El Salto. *See* El Salvador.

El Salvador. Shaped in a rectangle, El Salvador is bordered on the west by Guatemala, on the north and east by Honduras, and on the south by the Pacific Ocean. Its southeast corner is separated from Nicaragua by the Gulf of Fonseca. El Salvador is one of the smallest and poorest countries in Central America. The Spaniards first entered the country in 1524 and found a dense native Indian population. None of the early native tribes has been accurately identified, but they are known to have had an advanced civilization. At first, El Salvador was a province of Guatemala. Guatemala proclaimed its independence from Spain in September 1821, but it was not until 30 January 1841 that El Salvador was independent, and then only provisionally so until 1856. For most of the next century, the country had conservative governments—and a series of short wars with Guatemala and Honduras. In one of the later scraps with Honduras, fought over the presence of more than a quarter-million Salvadoran workers in Honduras, 2,000 were killed. Clashes continued into 1970 and 1974, but an agreement was reached on 11 August 1976 whereby each side withdrew its troops from the common border. In 1979, amid increasing unrest in El Salvador, President Carlos Humberto Romero (qv) imposed a state of siege (24 May). On 17 October 1979, Romero was forced out of office by a military coup. The junta could not, however, quell the civil war that continued as 10,000 leftist insurgents, supported from Nicaragua and Cuba, wreaked havoc within the country. By the 1980s, the insurgents controlled more than 25 percent of the country, despite massive US aid to the government and extreme measures carried out by or in the name of the government. Right-wing death squads killed over one thousand suspected leftists in 1983 alone. Assassinations occurred on an almost daily basis. In May 1984, José Napoleón Duarte (qv) won election to the presidency with 54 percent of the vote. The civil war continued, however, and by the end of 1991 more than 75,000 had died as a consequence. On 16 January 1992, a formal peace agreement was signed by the government and the leaders of the rebellion. A UN observer team was installed to insure that both sides abided by the terms of the treaty. The UN published a scathing report (March 1993) on the atrocities committed by government troops back to 1981, suggesting trials and punishment for the guilty parties. Instead, the Legislative Assembly granted amnesty to all those involved. When the UN secretary-general denounced the action, El Salvador accused the body of meddling in internal affairs. To this the US responded by announcing it would withhold aid until the guilty were brought to justice. By the end of the year, some officers had been forced to resign, but the number was small compared to the magnitude of the crime. The 1994 elections were marred by murder and other violence that was coupled with accusations by opposition parties that El Salvador had reneged on the peace agreement. Fraud was claimed in the election, but the ruling Arena Party reclaimed the government. In 1995, gang violence overwhelmed the police. Troops were brought in to support the effort against what were sometimes thought to be gangs of Americans. Death squads also reappeared. Some progress was made toward restoring order, but at a high price in lives. The country did not improve in 1996, and the political structure of the Arena Party coalition began to come apart at the seams. *Reading:* Americas Watch, *El Salvador's Decade of Terror: Human Rights since the Assassination of Archbishop Romero* (1993); Tommie Sue Montgomery, *Revolution in El Salvador: From Civil Strife to Civil Peace* (1995).

Ely, Paul. General Paul Ely was the French commander in Indochina who, in February 1954, directly notified the President of the United States that, unless U.S. military forces intervened immediately in Indochina, the cause was lost.

Elysse Agreement. The Elysse Agreement was signed on 8 March 1949 in the form of letters exchanged between the Emperor of Annam, Bao Dai (qv), and Vincent Auriol (qv), the president France. The agreement established a new framework for French-Vietnamese relations. By the agreement's terms France recognized Vietnamese independence while retaining the right to maintain troops in Vietnam. The agreement was later broadened in June to include Cambodia and Laos.

England. *See* Great Britain.

Eniwetok (Enewetak) Island. An island in the Marshall Islands group located on a line approximately halfway between Honolulu and the southern end of the Philippean Islands. Eniwetok was taken from the Japanese in February 1944 and utilized until the end of World War II as a naval base. The island was then.used as a U.S. nuclear weapons test site beginning in 1952 until 1956. During this period the natives were evacuated to other islands. After an extensive decontamination of the island, the native population was allowed to return to Eniwetok. Within a year, however, they were again relocated because of severe contamination of the soil. The island in now a part of the Republic of the Marshall Islands.

Enrile, Juan Ponce. Enrile was the minister of defense in the Philippines in 1972. An attempt was made on his life on 23 September. The attack was unsuccessful but, when coupled with other acts of violence, led President Ferdinand Marcos (qv) to declare martial law and to arrest a number of his critics to protect his regime against a "communist rebellion."

Entebbe. *See* Uganda.

Entebbe Airport. On 27 June 1976, pro-Palestinian terrorists hijacked an Air France jetliner as it took off from Athens Airport in Greece. The aircraft was bound for Tel Aviv when it was taken, and there were 103 passengers, 80 of whom were Israelis, plus the crew on board. The hijackers ordered the crew to fly the plane to Entebbe Airport in Uganda, where the passengers and crew were held hostage against the release of 53 prisoners being held in five countries. As soon as the situation was understood in Israel a rescue mission was planned. On the night of 3–4 July 1976, 100 to 200 Israeli commandos, led by Brigadier General Dan Shomron (qv), attacked the Entebbe Airport in a daring operation that freed most of the hostages. In addition, seven of the 10 hijackers were killed, along with about 20–30 Ugandan soldiers. One Israeli officer was killed, and an elderly Israeli woman hostage, who was confined in a Ugandan hospital at the time, was murdered in revenge for the raid. Idi Amin (qv) was convinced of Kenyan complicity in the rescue mission and threatened war over the incident.

Enugu. *See* Biafra.

EOKA. The *Ethniki Organosis Kypriokou Agonos* (National Organization of Cyriot Struggle) (EOKA) was a Greek Cypriot terrorist organization that began operations around 1955. Its primary goal was to drive the British out of Cyprus (qv). During its existence, EOKA enjoyed wide support among the Greek Cyriot population. Its principal targets were British servicemen and installations. EOKA operations required the British to reinforce their garrison on Cyprus. EOKA-B was a reinstitution of the older organization and was formed in 1971 with the goal of bringing union (*enosis*) with Greece. General George Grivas (qv), the EOKA leader, died in 1974. With his death and the independence of Cyprus, the organization was adrift until it disbanded on 10 February 1978.

Equatorial Guinea. More properly the Republic of Equatorial Africa, and formerly known as Spanish Guinea, Equatorial Guinea is located on the west coast of Africa and is bordered on the north by Cameroon and on the east and south by Gabon. To the west is the Gulf of Guinea, more specifically, the Bight of Biafra and the Atlantic Ocean. Equatorial Guinea lies astride the Equator, and the large island of Bioko (Fernando Po),off the Cameroon coast is part of its territory. The mainland province is called Rio Muni. Fernando Po was discovered in 1472 and was originally called Formosa. Although the Portuguese held the original rights in Africa (Treaty of Tordesillas, 1494), they granted Spain the rights to Fernando Po and another island, Annobón, as well as the rights tp a section of the mainland coast between the Ogooué and Niger rivers. This gave Spain access to the slave market in this area. The Spanish withdrew from Fernando Po in 1781 because of the spread of yellow fever. In 1827, they granted the British basing rights at two locations on the island. The island was then used as a repository for freed slaves, some from as far away as Jamaica. The British left the island in 1843. In 1844, the Spanish reoccupied the island and began exploration of the mainland. From 1879, the island was used as a penal colony for Cubans. After the Spanish American War, Spanish Guinea became the last major overseas possession of Spain. Not until 1939 did the mainland province of Rio Muni receive any real attention. In 1959, the colony was reorganized into two provinces. In 1963, limited autonomy was granted, and the two provinces assumed the name of Equatorial Guinea. Independence was granted on 12 October 1968. Immediately trouble began between the the island province of Fernando Po and the more backward Rio Muni, part of it fostered by the Spanish. On 28 February 1969, the government asked the United Nations for a peacekeeping force to help thwart the aggression. On 5 March 1969, a coup attempt against President Francisco Macias Nguma (qv) was unsuccessful. A number of senior officials were executed as a result, and Nguma assumed dictatorial powers. In April, the Spanish withdrew the last of their personnel from the country. In 1972, Masie (Marcius) Nguema Biyogo (qv), a mainlander, became president for life. Before he was ousted by a military coup on 3 August 1979, he carried out a reign of terror and bankrupted his country. Masie was subsequently tried and executed. Lieutenant Colonel Teodoro Obiang Nguema Mbasogo (qv), a relative of the deposed president, took over the reigns of government. Nguema remained in power in 1992 amid widespead unrest throughout the country. There were widespread arrests of opposition party members even though a multi-party democracy had been earlier promised. The UN reiterated its condemnation of the country for its human rights record in 1993. Among other things, the U.S. ambassador received a death threat, which was traced back to the government. A legislative election held in late 1993 was roundly criticized by foreign observers. Spain broke diplomatic relations with Equatorial Guinea after its consul general had been expelled for adding his voice to the condemnation and withdrew the last of its troops from the country. Outside pressure forced the government to back down on its threats to try one of the opposition leaders for treason in 1995. Still, the arrests and repression continued. Presidential elections held in 1996 kept the regime of Obiang Nguema Mbasogo in power. Charges of blatant voter fraud were widespread. *Reading:* Randall Fegley, *Equatorial Guinea: An African Tragedy* (1989); Max Liniger-Goumaz & John Wood, *Small Is Not Always Beautiful: The Story of Equatorial Guinea* (1989); Randall Fegley, *Equatorial Guinea (World Bibliographical Series, Vol. 136)* (1992).

Erbil. *See* Iraq.

Erim, Nihat. On 17 April 1972, Prime Minister Nihat Erim of Turkey resigned. His government had been in power since 11 December 1971. His decision to resign was based on his inability to get sufficient authority to deal with the worsening crisis in Turkey. An interim government headed by the minister of defense, Ferit Melen (qv), replaced Erim, but Melen was not confirmed until 22 May, after much political maneuvering and grumblings from the military.

Eritrea. The history of Eritrea may be said to begin when Semitic tribes from Sheba (Saba) migrated into the region about 1000 B.C. and established the Kingdom of Aksum. By the fourth century A.D. the kingdom had expanded over the Ethiopian plateau and the Ethiopian province of Tigré. Before its decline in the sixth century Aksum controlled all the lands to Egypt and Yemen. In the tenth century, the Kingdom of Etiopia had expanded into the area and held sway over Eritrea as the region became known. By the sixteenth century, Ottoman Turks controlled the Red Sea coastline. In the eighteenth century, the history of Eritrea became intertwined with that of Tigré. In 1820 the Egyptians invaded Sudan and penetrated into the region, at the same time the Turks were expanding their claims over the land. In 1882, Italy assumed control of part of the Red Sea area from an Italian company which had purchased rights there (1869). Italian troops pushed aside the Egyptians and Turks in 1885. By 1890, Eritrea was an Italian colony. In 1935, it was used as the base for the Italian invasion of Ethiopia. In 1941, British and Ethiopian forces defeated the Italians at Keren, and Eritrea became a major Allied base during World War II. On 10 February 1947, Italy was stripped of its African possessions (Libya, Italian Somaliland and Eritrea). On 11 September 1952, the government of Ethiopia formally accepted the transfer of Eritrea from Great Britain and made it a part of Ethiopia. Eritrea became the northernmost province of Ethiopia. It is located adjacent to the Red Sea on the east and borders Sudan on the north. The capital city is Asmara. The Eritrean National Assembly voted union with Ethiopia on 14 November 1962. A long period of unrest began as procommunist and other elements fought the union. As insurgent activity increased, the Ethiopian government declared a state of emergency in the Eritrean province on 16 December 1970. Major Eritrean insurgent groups, such as the Eritrean Liberation Front (ELF) and the Eritrean People's Liberation Front (EPLF) began to coordinate their activities against the Ethiopian government. In February 1975, another state of emergency was declared in the wake of heavy fighting in which at least 1,200 were killed in Asmara. By May of 1976, Ethiopia was calling up reservists along the Eritrean border as the war deepened. Then, in June 1976, the Ethiopian government halted its operations against the Eritrean secessionists and disbanded its mostly

Christian peasant army along the border. A new offensive was launched against Eritrea on 15 May 1978, however, as Ethiopia moved to restore its control over the province and offered amnesty to the rebel forces (7 June). On 29 June, the Eritrean rebel forces offered unconditional talks with Ethiopia to end the 17 years of fighting that had ensued. The fighting continued, however, and by January 1979 the rebels had made significant advances in consolidating their hold over key regions in Eritrea. The conflict continued into 1989, when former U.S. president Jimmy Carter arranged peace talks between the two sides in Atlanta, Georgia. The fighting went on, however. EPLF forces captured the important town of Masawa, one of Ethiopia's two port cities, in 1990. At that point it became clear that Ethiopia was losing the battle against Eritrean independence. In 1991, the Marxist government in Addis Ababa collapsed under the pressure of insurgent movements in Eritrea and other regions of Ethiopia. In Eritrea, an interim government was established, but plans to declare independence were delayed for two years, until 23–25 April 1993. In the meantime, sporadic fighting continued, but the EPLF was primarily engaged in a major reconstruction program to rebuild a country devasted by 30 years of war. The newly independent country established a transitional government, which was recognized by Ethiopia and other countries. Eritrea's bitterness toward the UN and OAU was evident at an OAU meeting in June 1993, as the reason why Ethiopia had held Eritrea so long. Eritrea broke diplomatic relations with Sudan (December 1944) after government forces had killed a group of Islamic fundamentalists attempting to infiltrate the country. In 1995, Eritrea took the lead in opposing the military regime in Sudan and began arming Sudanese opposition groups. Because of this and other reasons, 1996 witnessed a decline in its foreign relations. The Sudanese situation continued to deteriorate, armed conflict broke out with Yemen over control of the Hanish Islands in the Red Sea and Djibouti also accused Eritrea of firing on its territory *See also* Ethiopia. *Reading:* Dan Connell, *Against All Odds: A Chronicle of the Eritrean Revolution* (1993); Robert MacHida, *Eritrea: A Struggle for Independence* (1987).

Eritrean Liberation Front (ELF). In 1971, the Eritrean Liberation Front (ELF) took over the leadership of the struggle for independence of the Ethiopian province of Eritrea. The insurgency associated with the struggle had begun in 1964. In March 1978, the ELF joined forces with the Eritrean People's Liberation Front, another of the several groups working against the central Ethiopian government in Addis Ababa. *See* Eritrea and Ethiopia.

Eritrean People's Liberation Front (EPLF). The Eritrean People's Liberation Front (EPLF) was one of several groups engaged in an insurgency against the central Ethiopian government in Addis Ababa. In March 1978, the EPLF joined together with the Eritrean Liberation Front (ELF) to coordinate their efforts. In January 1979, the two groups formed a joint political organization to help settle the civil war that was raging. In January 1980, the EPLF claimed it had killed, wounded or captured over 5,000 government troops in a battle at the Mehimet army base. *See also* Eritrea and Ethiopia.

Ershad, Mohammad Hossain. On 24 March 1982, Lieutenant General Ershad led a coup that overthrew the government of President Abdus Sattar in Bangladesh. Ershad then abrogated the constitution and imposed martial law. On 11 December 1983, he proclaimed himself president and extended martial law until the elections promised in 1985. In March 1985, he withdrew the planned parliamentary and presidential elections scheduled for April. Parliamentary elections were held in 1986, but Ershad remained in power until 6 December 1990, when rising unrest forced his resignation.

Erskine, Emmanuel. The commander of UN peacekeeping forces in Lebanon in 1980, General Erskine demanded the withdrawal of the Irish Battalion under his command for allegedly aiding the Palestine Liberation Front against the Israelis.

Escrigea Estrada, Fausto. Vice Admiral Escrigea Estrada, the Director General of Defense Policy of Spain, was assassinated in Madrid on 29 July 1985. Both the Basque Fatherland (qv) and Liberty-Military Wing claimed credit for the murder.

Espriella, Ricardo de la. On 13 February 1984, Ricardo de la Espriella left office as the president of Panama. Espriella was thought by many to be a person capable of saving the country from the Noriega (qv) dictatorship, which gripped the country. However, 1984 was an election year, and Espriella was ineligible to run for reelection. In the face of growing political unrest in the country and pressure from Noriega, he resigned and turned the presidency over to the vice president, Jorge Illueca, who held the post until Ardito Barletta was elected (6 May) and inaugurated (11 October).

Esteli. *See* Nicaragua.

Estima. *See* Portugal.

Estime, Dumarsais. On 11 January 1946, a military coup led by Colonel Paul Magloire (qv) overthrew the government of President Elie Lescot (qv) of Haiti. Dumarais Estime became the new head of state. The military junta formally elected him president on 16 August. Colonel Magliore again led a coup that ousted Estime, on 10 May 1950. *See* Haiti.

Ethiopia. Ethiopia is located on the Red Sea in the Horn of Africa. It is bordered on the north by Eritrea and on the west by Sudan. To the south lie Kenya and Somalia. Djibouti forms an enclave in the northeast. The capital is Addis Ababa. Ethiopia predates Christianity and has been a feudal monarchy since the earliest times. The nation claims its ancestry from the joining of Solomon and Sheba and has expanded southward over the last two millennia, with the greatest expansion during the reign of Menelik II (1889–1913). During the last two decades of the nineteenth century, Italian colonial influence expanded into the country, overcoming Egyptian and Turkish resistance. In 1896, however, the Italian army was defeated at the Battle of Aduwa, and although some arrangements were made that seemingly gave Ethiopia over to Italy, it remained one of the few African countries to resist colonialism. The Italians carried out a second campaign against Ethiopia in 1935, this time successfully. With Menelik's death in 1913, Lij Yasu became emperor (1913–1916). The outbreak of World War I led the emperor to favor the Muslim side (Turkey) and the Central Powers. In

1916, Lij Yasu was dethroned and replaced by the Empress Zauditu with Ras Tafari, better known by his Christian name of Haile Selassie (qv), as heir-apparent. In 1930, Zauditu died and Haile Selassie became emperor. Selassie was forced to flee when his country was invaded by Italy, but he returned in triumph after the British liberated Ethiopia during World War II. Ethiopian troops fought as part of the UN force in Korea in the 1950s. Selassie ruled until 1974, when a Marxist military coup overthrew his rule. The leader of the Provisional Military Admistration Council (PMAC), Mengitsu Haile Mariam, became head of state. During Haile Selassie's reign famine, government corruption and social unrest plagued the country. Separatist movements began in many sections, with the most active in Eritrea (qv), Tigre (Tigrai), and Western Somalia. After the military takeover in 1974, Ethiopia shifted away from the United States and Western Europe and embraced the Soviet Union and the Eastern Bloc. By the end of 1978 most secessionist-held territory was in the hands of government forces supported by Soviet and Cuban troops. About 500 political prisoners were released in September 1981, some of whom had been in custody since 1974. The government also set up people's courts (1981) to deal with "corruption" and joined Libya and Yemen (Aden) in condemning the United States for its activities in the Indian Ocean. In 1987, Ethiopia approved a new constitution that proclaimed the People's Democratic Republic of Ethiopia, and a civilian, communist-oriented government was installed. By 1984, the hitherto fragmented guerrilla war against the Mengitsu regime was changing into one in which the rebels were joining forces to better fight their war. Ethiopia was accused of supporting Sudanese rebels, a charge that strained relations with the Sudanese government. On 5 September 1987, PMAC was dissolved and Mengitsu became president. An attempted military coup took place in May 1989, which resulted in the executions of 30 high-ranking military officers and the arrests of numerous others accused of being part of the plot. By year's end, the war against the rebels had assumed a higher level of activity, and the rebels held larger areas of Ethiopia and Eritrea by year's end. Prosecution of the war wrecked the Ethiopian economy. At the same time, the Soviet Union, suffering its own troubles at home, backed away from much of its support of the Mengitsu regime. This forced Ethiopia to move toward a mixed market economy. Mengitsu was faced with growing unrest at home that finally forced him to flee to Zimbabwe on 21 May 1991. The major rebel groups quickly moved in and after some internal conflict put a new government in place. Numerous acts of sabotage were reported in Addis Ababa during this period as Mengitsu sympathizers took to the streets to disrupt the return of order. This exacerbated the conditions caused by the famine that was plaguing that part of Africa at the time. Another problem was caused by the pending independence of Eritrea and the very large refugee population in Ethiopia. There were reports that local groups fired on Sudanese refugees to force them back across the border. By 1993 violence was widespread, but it was quickly dispersed by government forces. Another aspect of the situation was the government's continued deferral in bringing Mengitsu followers to justice for human rights crimes and atrocities committed during that regime, possibly because atrocities had also been committed by those now in power. A Constituent Assembly was elected in June 1994, which followed a doctrine of ethnic federalism with the concept of self-determination for each group within the country. A new constitution was adopted in December 1994, but the deferral of atrocity trials continued into 1995. In 1996 a Federal Democratic Republic of Ethiopia was proclaimed. *Reading:* Patrick Gilkes, *Conflict in Somalia and Ethiopia* (1994); Kinfe Abraham, *Ethiopia: From Bullets to the Ballot Box: The Bumpy Road to Democracy and the Political Economy of Transition* (1995); Harold G. Marcus, *A History of Ethiopia* (1995); Albert Sbacchi, *Legacy of Bitterness: Ethiopia and Fascist Italy, 1935–1941* (1997); Edmund Keller, *Revolutionary Ethiopia: From Empire to People's Republic* (1991).

Et-Kap (El Kap). *See* Sinai.

Et Tur (El Tur). *See* Sinai.

Etzion. *See* Israel.

European Army Plan. The European Army Plan was to be the military arm of the European Defense Community (EDC) (qv). The concept had the backing of the U.S. and Great Britain and was of sufficient importance to warrant discussions between the two Allied heads of state, Winston Churchill (qv) and Harry Truman (qv) (5 January 1952). For Churchill and Truman the European Army constituted a means of strengthening NATO without a concomitant commitment of Allied manpower. The reluctance of various EDC members, especially France, to commit themselves resulted in the U.S. Secretary of State's warning NATO to get the European Army Plan moving or the United States would have to make an "agonizing reappraisal" of its policy on defending Europe. The French eventually scuttled the EDC and with it the plan for a European army.

European Atomic Community (EURATOM). More properly called the European Atomic Energy Community, Euratom was established at the same time as the European Economic Community (EEC) (qv) by the 1957 Treaty of Rome. Its purpose was to form a common market for the development of nuclear power for peaceful purposes in Europe.

European Common Market. The nationalistic excesses of preWorld War II Europe were nowhere better illustrated than in the almost total destruction of the economy during the war. Post-World War II Europe verged on an irreversible destabilization of the social and political order, if new forms of economic and political cooperation could not be found. This was not a new notion; it had been postulated in the nineteenth century. However, now it was a crucial ingredient in the recovery of Europe, even if it ran counter to the lifelong competition among those who would have to cooperate. In 1950, Paul-Henri Spaak of Belgium and Robert Schuman and Jean Monnet of France guided the establishment of the first of three organizations that would become the European Community (EC). An independent agency was established by the those nations willing to delegate authority over their coal and steel industries. The "Six," as Belgium, France, West Germany, Italy, Luxembourg and The Netherlands were known, agreed. The Schuman Plan, as it became known, was codified in the

1951 Treaty of Paris, which activated the European Coal and Steel Community (ECSE) on 25 July 1952. The success of the ECSE prompted the Six to move forward on a broader front, one aimed at still greater political unity, by the creation of two more organizations (1957, Treaty of Rome), the European Economic Community (EEC), commonly called the Common Market, and Euratom (qv). The Common Market was established as an organization designed to remove trade barriers among member nations and went into operation on 1 January 1958. By the end of 1959, a 10 percent internal tariff reduction had been achieved. All of this was not without drama, however, as France's Charles DeGaulle (qv) stated his categorical opposition to British admission into the EEC (14 January 1963). At the same time he rejected French participation in a NATO multilateral nuclear force. On 1 July 1967, the European Community (EC) was born when the ECSE, EEC and Euratom merged. Denmark, the United Kingdom and Ireland became members in 1973; Greece in 1981; and Spain and Portugal in 1986. Turkey's bid for membership, which began in 1987, was rejected in 1989. Under the EEC, all internal tariffs were abandoned in 1968 with the establishment of the Customs Union. The transitional phase of the EEC ended on 31 December 1969, when full economic union was achieved among the members. In later years, the EEC was able to show its power, as on 6 April 1982, when it ordered an embargo on Argentina after the Argentine invasion of the Falkland Islands (qv). In 1993, plans moved forward for a complete union of Europe, with free trade and free movement of capital (1999) and people as the next step (Treaty of Maastricht) Once again, however, problems exist that are focused on national rather than pan-European needs. *Reading:* Steve Terrell, *The 90's; Decade of the Apocalypse: The European Common Market – The End Has Begun* (1994); Wolfgang H. Reinicke, *Building a New Europe: The Challenge of System Transformation and Systemic Reform* (1993).

European Convention for the Repression of Terrorism. On 27 January 1977, 17 ministers of the Council of Europe signed a European Convention for the Repression of Terrorism at Strasbourg. Ireland and Malta refused to sign the agreement: France refused to ratify it. Norway, Italy and Portugal stated reservations about the convention. The principal difficulties lay in the definition of what constituted political crime and the establishment of a procedure for handling individual appeals to the European Commission on Human Rights. These objections were leveled at the convention's procedures for the speedy extradition and prosecution of terrorists. The convention was ratified in 1977 when the third signator's national assembly approved it. Most counterterrorist specialists considered the primary benefit of the convention tp be the growing international awareness of terrorism, but felt individual national legal technicalities would prevail. In October 1978, the EEC (qv) justice ministers announced a supplemental agreement among the nine EEC members that solved some of the technical legal problems in the convention. The Nine also agreed to study a French proposal that would establish a "judicial zone" over Europe that would obviate national legal technicalities. Also in the fall of 1978, European ministers met in Vienna to establish a method of exchanging terrorist information and toward unifying counterterrorist training programs. As the convention's value began to be felt and regional cooperation took on demonstrable applications, a meeting was held in May 1979 that tied the police departments of 17 major European cities together in the antiterrorist war. By December 1979, more resolution had been found to the technical legal difficulties when the EEC signed additional articles that clarified the convention. In December 1980, 15 NATO foreign ministers adopted a Declaration on Terrorism that vigorously condemned terrorist acts as particularly odious regardless of their cause or objectives. That same month, Spain introduced a stiff resolution at the Conference on Security and Cooperation in Europe, held in Madrid, that condemned terrorism. To date, however, most professionals see little concrete evidence of growing cooperation above the working level from the proclamations.

European Defense Community (EDC). The first talk of a European Defense Community came about as a result of President Truman's choice of General Dwight Eisenhower (qv) to be the Supreme Allied Commander, Europe (SACEUR), in December 1950. The subsequent debate in Congress over Truman's pledge to reinforce Europe against the Soviet threat allowed four more U.S. divisions to be deployed into the Western Shield (February 1951). Great Britain then followed the U.S. example and reinforced its forces on the continent. France, however, proved more reluctant to commit itself , although it did half-heartedly approve the rearming of Germany, but only as part of a European defensive structure, the EDC, which was an outgrowth of the European Coal and Steel Community (ECSC) nations' desire for a European Army (qv) that would maintain liaison with the British and eventually be integrated into NATO. On 27 May 1952, a series of documents were signed in Paris that created a unified EDC composed of the Netherlands, Belgium, Luxembourg, France, and West Germany. The signatories also initialled a treaty with Great Britain that promised British aid if any of the five EDC members were attacked. The U.S. and the United Kingdom also signed a treaty with France, guaranteeing its security. Lastly, NATO guaranteed the security of West Germany. On 16 April 1954, the U.S. assured the EDC that U.S. forces would remain in Europe as long as the Soviet threat existed. By July 1954, every EDC nation but France had ratified the agreement. To help the French make up their minds, the U.S. Senate voted unanimously (30 July) to authorize restoration of West German sovereignty, if France failed to ratify the EDC. On 30 August 1954, the French Assembly rejected the 1952 EDC plan, thereby jeopardizing the plan to revitalize Europe and rearm West Germany. Meeting in London on 3 October, nine nations, without France's participation, agreed upon a formula that would economically and militarily integrate West Germany into the Western Alliance and NATO, rather than into the EDC. This action effectively blocked France's veto of West German participation in the EDC. The EDC succumbed, in essence, to French obstinacy and was replaced by NATO and the 1955 Western European Union (WEU) (qv) concept.

European Defense Plan. *See* North Atlantic Treaty Organization (NATO).

European Economic Community (EEC). *See* European Common Market.

"Europeanized Europe." A phrase used by Charles DeGaulle (qv) in 1966 to describe a Europe free of American and Soviet influence. To emphasize his point, DeGaulle withdrew France from the integrated NATO command on 11 March 1966 and ordered NATO's headquarters removed from French soil by 1 April.

European Recovery Plan (Program). At a 17-nation Western European meeting held in Paris 12–15 July 1947, a committee was established to chart a European Recovery Program (ERP). The Soviet Union, along with its bloc nations, refused to attend the meeting. In a subsequent meeting held in Paris on 16 April 1948, the nations involved in the program established their permanent apparatus for economic cooperation. The basic idea behind the ERP was the Marshall Plan, suggested by U.S. Secretary of State George C. Marshall (qv) in a speech at Harvard on 5 June 1947. The group established to operate the ERP was the Paris-based Organization for European Economic Cooperation (OEEC). While this framework was being set up, the U.S. Congress appropriated interim funds to help the recovery. On 3 April 1948, the Economic Cooperation Act (Foreign Assistance Act, passed 31 March 1948) was signed into law. The first appropriation under this act was for $5.6 billion for the first 15 months of operation. The plan called for about $17 billion in aid over a four-year period. On 1 June 1948, Germany was admitted to the ERP. On 4 August 1949, however, the U.S. Senate refused to extend the Marshall Plan to Spain, because of Franco's (qv) rule in that country. The Marshall Plan expired on 31 December 1951.

Eustis, Ralph W. Commander Ralph W. Eustis was the commander of the U.S. Coast Guard cutter *Vigilant* on station off Martha's Vineyard, Massachusetts, on 23 November 1970, when a Lithuanian seaman attempted to defect by jumping off a passing Soviet freighter onto *Vigilant's* deck. After much fumbling, the commandant of the First Coast Guard District ordered Eustis to return the seaman to Soviet control, which he did. When the White House was advised of the incident, an irate President Richard M. Nixon (qv) charged the First District commandant, his chief of staff, and Eustis with dereliction of duty. Eustis was relieved of command but remained in service. The other two, more senior, officers were reprimanded, but were allowed to retire (21 December). It was later ascertained that the Lithuanian seaman was imprisoned in the Soviet Union but was eventually freed and allowed to immigrate.

Euzkadi za Azkarasuna **(ETA).** A Marxist-Leninist-oriented group of Basque terrorists the ETA achieved sufficient notoriety to be reported in 1979 by assassinating several important Spanish military officials. These attacks by factions of the ETA (Basque Fatherland and Liberty Movement) led to repressive governmental measures that the Basques hoped would bring popular support for an independent Basque homeland. The ETA also attacked French targets in Spain in hopes of disrupting Franco-Spanish cooperation against the Basques. Numerous bombings were carried out on one weekend in 1979 that focused on air and rail terminals and killed five people (113 injured). Spanish rightists (GAL), despairing of firm government action, adopted vigilante tactics and carried out raids against prominent Basque leaders in France. In 1980, ETA attacks continued with the assassination of dozens of Spanish police and military officers. By 1981, ETA had defined itself into two groups, ETA-PM and ETA-M. Early in January of that year the Spanish government granted greater autonomy for the Basque region in an attempt to decrease tension, but it did not stop the terrorists. During the next few months there were numerous attacks credited to the ETA. In January, for instance, ETA terrorists fired antitank weapons into two government buildings in two Basque cities, kidnapped a prominent citizen in Bilbao and kidnapped and murdered the chief nuclear engineer at the Lemoniz power plant in northern Spain. On 20 February, ETA kidnappers abducted the honorary counsels in Spain from Austria, El Salvador and Uruguay. Three days later, the ETA-PM faction announced its intention to abandon terrorism. Shortly thereafter ETA-M, the military wing of ETA, increased its level of terrorist activity, bombing government facilities, attacking police patrols and assassinating prominent members of the Spanish government. Attacks of this sort continued over the next few years. In 1985, ETA-M was Spain's most serious terrorist threat. Spanish and French counterterrorist operations were relatively successful, and GAL continued its extermination campaign against suspected ETA members, yet the ETA-M carried out a series of bombings against tourist targets in the spring and summer, but with limited results. The group also continued its attacks against Spanish police targets. During September - November 1985, there was a cessation of activity as Basque leaders met with Madrid to discuss autonomy. By 1992, the ETA threat continued. As Spain prepared to host the Olympics, mass roundups of suspected ETA members were ordered in Spain and France. Security at the Olympic venues was very heavy and the games proceeded without serious incident.

Eva Peron Commando. An Argentinan terrorist organization, the relatively unknown Eva Peron Commando group broke four prisoners out of a Buenos Aires jail on 26 June 1971.

Evran, Kenan. General Kenan Evran, the Turkish Armed Forces chief of staff, overthrew the government of Ihsan Sabri Caglayangil on 12 September 1980 in a bloodless coup. Evran then dissolved the parliament and abrogated the constitution. On 27 October, Evran became the chief of state under the powers established on the that date that transferred authority from the parliament to the National Security Council. A new constitution was prepared in 1982, and Evran was appointed president of Turkey. Evran remained in office until 9 November 1989, upon the expiration of his term of office. He was replaced by Turgut Ozal, the former prime minister, who was elected president on 31 October 1989.

Eward-Biggs, Christopher T. E. On 21 July 1976, the new British ambassador to the Republic of Ireland, Christopher T. E. Eward-Biggs was killed by an IRA bomb placed under his car at his residence in Dublin Mountains. Several other embassy personnel were killed (one a woman, Judith Cook) and two others injured in the explosion.

Eyadema, Etienne (Gnassingbe). On 13 January 1967, a military coup d'etat led by Lieutenant Colonel Etienne Eyadema overthrew the government of Togo. Eyadema promoted himself to general and took the presidency. In 1969, he announced that normal political activities would soon resume; he later reversed his positon and continued the ban on all political movements. In 1977, Eyadema civilianized his cabinet. When Togo approved a new constitution in December 1979, Eyadema was reelected president in a single-list election that brought out 99 percent of the voters. Eyadema remained in power in 1996.

F

Fabião, Carlos. On 25 November 1975, a state of emergency was declared in Lisbon Military District of Portugal following days of violent demonstrations against the provisional government. The provisional government had been formed by the Armed Forces Movement (AFM) when the fourth coalition government fell on 17 July. On 21 November, the rioting had forced the AFM provisional government to suspend operations. By 24 November, fighting had broken out between government forces and communist rebels in and around Lisbon. The next day President Francisco da Costa Gomes declared the state of emergency. When order had been restored on 27 November, the president dismissed a number of senior left-wing military officers, including the Army chief of staff, General Carlos Fabião, and Admiral Antonio Rosa Coutinho. Coutinho's ouster sparked new rioting in which left-wing rebels captured four air force bases in northern and central Portugal. Order was quickly restored (28 November).

Fadlallah, Muhammad Husayn. The spiritual leader of Hizbullah (qv), a Lebanese religious (Sh'ia) terrorist organization, Muhammad Husayn Fadlallah, was assassinated on 8 March 1985, when a bomb planted in his automobile detonated in front of his house in south Beirut. Eighty people were killed in the blast, and another 250 injured. An estimated 250 kilograms of explosive were used in the bomb. No one claimed credit for the attack.

Fahd ibn 'Abd al-'Aziz al-Saud. (b. 1922, Riyadh) On 13 June 1982, King Khalid ibn Abd-Aziz (qv) of Saudi Arabia died. Crown Prince Fahd, Khalid's half-brother, immediately succeeded him to the throne and became prime minister at the same time. Fahd was born the first son of Ibn Saud (qv) and his second wife, Hassa Sudairi. Fahd was proclaimed crown prince when Khalid took the throne upon the murder of King Faisal (qv) (1975). Fahd's reign was marked by the modernization of Saudi Arabian life, including new airports. Fahd also attempted a Middle East solution, but without much success. Fahd led his country through the Gulf crisis in 1991, when his country was the base for the Desert Storm operation.

Fahmy, Mahmoud Abdel Rahman. Rear Admiral Mahmoud Abdel Rahman Fahmy, Egypt's naval commander, resigned on 28 October 1972 to protest President Anwar Sadat's (qv) attempt at reconciliation with the Soviet Union. Two days earlier, Fahmy's army counterpart, General Muhammed Sadek (qv) resigned for the same reason.

Faisal ibn abd al-Aziz. (b. 1905, Riyadh, Saudi Arabia—d. 25 March 1975, Riyadh) Faisal was born the fourth son of King 'Abd-al-'Aziz ibn Saud (qv), and was named Viceroy of Hejaz (Hijaz) (and Mecca) (1927). In 1953, Faisal was named Saudi Arabia's first prime minister. When Ibn Saud died (1953), Saud II, his first son, was proclaimed king. Faisal was then named crown prince and commander in chief. He retained the position of prime minister. On 28 February 1964, Faisal was given royal powers, and on 2 November 1964, when Saud II was deposed because of his fiscal mismanagement, Faisal was proclaimed king. An assassination plot against him was foiled in June 1969. In August of that year he called for an Islamic summit to discuss the protection of the Holy Places. In 1970, his diplomacy ended the civil war that had raged in North Yemen. He then set about establishing close economic ties with the United States, which would have given Saudi Arabia industrial information it needed. He stipulated, however, that the U.S. had to curtail its support of Zionism in the Middle East (30 August 1973). When the U.S. failed to respond, Faisal threatened to cut off oil shipments. He carried out this threat in October 1973 with dire results for the US economy and as a prelude to the planned attack on Israel (qv). He was also instrumental in bringing about cooperation between Egypt and Jordan that was vital to the attack plan against Israel. The cooperation with the U.S. he desired was forthcoming, but on 25 March 1975, Faisal was murdered by his nephew, Prince Faisal ibn Musad ibn Abdul Aziz. Khalid ibn Abd Aziz (qv), Faisal's brother. was proclaimed king.

King Faisal II of Iraq. (b. 1935—d. 14 July 1958) Faisal was an 18-year-old student at England's Harrow when he was ordered home to become king on 2 May 1953. He was not an impressive individual: He was small of stature, quiet and an asthma sufferer. He was, however, a generally popular ruler, even though some of his decisions did not square with the populace or the parliament. He worked toward improving the national economy through the exploitation of Iraq's immense petroleum deposits as a means of defusing the resentment of those who were disenfranchised by the abolition of political parties in 1952. Nuri Pasha became prime minister, and chief adviser to Faisal in mid-1954. Once again political parties were banned—even Nuri Pasha's own party was abolished. The press was suppressed, and a strict anticommunist policy imposed. Both Faisal and Nuri Pasha were pro-Western. In 1955, a defensive alliance was concluded with Turkey, the opening round in the establishment of the Baghdad Pact (qv). There was little question that the principal orientation of the pact was to counter any Soviet moves into the region. The pact was, however, generally rebuked by many of the anti-Nuri factions within Iraq and by the followers of the Egyptian, procommunist persuasion. Iraqi–Egyptian relations deteriorated rapidly. Yet, when Britain, France and Israel attacked Suez in October–November 1956, Iraq was one of the first Arab states to break relations with France and came very close to doing the same thing with its chief benefactor, Great Britain. Anti-Western rioting broke out in Iraq, which was followed by a declaration of martial law. Iraq also temporarily removed itself from the Baghdad Pact. Faisal was also able to overcome the devastating financial losses when Syria blew up the pumping stations owned by the Iraq Petroleum Company. Following this episode, there was a shifting of Iraqi relations: Those with Saudi Arabia improved; those with Syria worsened; those with Jordan improved. In fact, as a counter to the formation of the United Arab League by Egypt and Syria in February 1958, Iraq and Jordan united their countries as the Arab (Hashemite) Federation (Union), with King Faisal as the overall ruler. A new constitution was drafted, and Nuri Pasha appointed was prime minister. During the 1957–1958 period, Faisal also announced his betrothal to a Turkish–Egyptian princess, but the union was never consummated. On 14 July 1958, a bloody military revolt led by Brigadier Abdul Karim Kassem (qv) overthrew the government and killed Faisal, the royal family and Nuri Pasha in a gory display of winner's bravado. Kassem was appointed prime minister under a revolutionary council, and a republic was declared. Jordan was dismayed and Egypt applauded.

Faisans, Georges. On 25 July 1985, rioting broke out in Point-a-Pitre, on the French Caribbean island of Guadaloupe. The demonstrators were seeking the release of the leader of the separatist *Mouvment Populaire pour le Guadaloupe Independente*, Georges Faisans. Faisans was imprisoned in France, but he was released on 29 July pending an appeal. The violence in Pointe-a-Pitre subsided, but the political situation that caused it in the first place continued.

Faizabad. *See* Afghanistan.

Fakih, Mahmoud. As a part of ongoing negotiations for an Israeli troop withdrawal from Lebanon, the Israelis released Mahmoud Fakih from custody and returned him to Beirut on 17 November 1984. Fakih was a leading Lebanese Shi'ite activist who became a bargaining chip in the UN-sponsored Lebanese–Israeli talks aimed at securing the Israeli northern border from further guerrilla attacks.

Falkland Islands. The Falkland Islands, also called *Islas Malvinas,* are located 250 miles east of southern Argentina in the South Atlantic Ocean. The two principal islands, East Falkland and West Falkland, are separated by Falkland Sound, a 25-mile-wide strait running northeast to southwest. The islands were discovered in 1592 by the English explorer John Davys. In 1594, Sir Richard Hawkins, another English navigator, sailed the islands' northern waters. They were named in 1690 after Lord Falkland (Lucius Carey), who was at the time treasurer of the English navy. A French settlement was established on East Falkland in 1794. In 1795, the islands were claimed for Great Britain by Captain John Byron. In 1766, the French withdrew under Spanish pressure, and the Spaniards forcibly ejected the English in 1770. War between Spain and Great Britain was only narrowly averted. The British reestablished a settlement at Port Egmont in 1771; it was withdrawn in 1774. In 1829, the Republic of Buenos Aires, which claimed all Spanish territory in the region, established a presence in the islands that existed until 1831, when the Buenos Aires resident governor seized three American sealing ships. The arrival of the frigate *USS Lexington* and the subsequent destructive bombardment of the settlement led to an American declaration that the islands were without "governance." In 1833, Great Britain reclaimed the Falklands and placed them under Royal Navy control. In 1841 a civil administration was established at Port Louis and remained in existence until modern times. In both world wars the Falklands were the scene of much military and naval activity. In the post-World War II years both Argentina and Chile made substantial claims, some of them reiterations of long-standing desires for control of the Falklands proper and other islands and territories including the British Antarctic Territory and a number of important islands including South Georgia Island and the South Orkney and South Shetland island groups (all of which were a part of the Falklands until 3 March 1962, when the government changed the alignment). Great Britain sought arbitration of the claims before the International Court of Justice, but the court refused to hear the case because Argentina and Chile refused to accept the court's competency to adjudicate the matter. All three countries relied on the 1959 Antarctic Agreement, which spelled out the peaceful use of the continent to avoid conflict. On 1 July 1971, Great Britain and Argentina announced they would settle their dispute by negotiation. But, on 5 February 1976, an Argentine destroyer fired on a British research vessel in what Argentina claimed were its Antarctic shelf waters. Through 1977–1978, negotiations were attempted, but the parties failed to reach a settlement. On 3 March 1982, the Argentine government reasserted its claim to the *Islas Malvinas*, stating (1 March) that "other means" would be sought to settle the dispute, if it could not be settled through diplomacy. On 29 March, Argentina began mobilizing its forces. Three days later, at 9 A.M. (0900 local) on 1 April 1982, 70 Argentine marines of the *Buzo Tactico*, the Argentine equivalent of Britain's elite Special Boat Squadron, landed on 2 April on what had been designated by the alerted British as "Purple Beach." The force moved to capture the Royal Marine barracks at Moody Point and the Government House. At the Government House the Royal Marines refused to surrender, and the Argentines opened fire; the other Argentine unit found the marine barracks empty. During this period, U.S. president Ronald Reagan (qv) called Argentine president Leopoldo Galtieri (qv) to ask him to halt the invasion. Galtieri rebuffed Reagan, which moved the United States firmly onto the side of the British. In the Falklands, another Argentine force of ten frogmen had been put ashore near Pembroke Light at Port Stanley. Then, about 600 Argentine marines in amphibious vehicles from a landing ship entered York Harbor. A naval squadron consisting of an obsolete aircraft carrier and several destroyers provided additional cover for the landing force. The British Royal Marines, armed only with small arms, held out for three hours, until Governor Rex Hunt (qv) ordered them to lay down their arms and surrender. Argentine casualties have never been accurately stated. The British casualties in this first phase of the war were zero. Argentina claimed its invasion was provoked by continuing British evasions and delays in turning over control of the *Malvinas* (2 April).

The same day, London severed diplomatic relations with Buenos Aires, and the UN Security Council issued Resolution 502 calling for an immediate cessation of hostilities (3 April). British prime minister Margaret Thatcher (qv) informed Parliament that a strong military force was being dispatched to recover control of the Falklands (3 April). Some fighting was reported on 3 April, when an Argentine force landed at Grytviken on South Georgia Island. The British garrison there (23 Royal Marines) shot down several Argentine aircraft, severely damaged an Argentine warship, killed 15 Argentine marines, and wounded 20 others before surrendering. One British Marine was wounded. Also on 3 April, the Argentines released 86 British marines and civilians captured in the Falklands in Montevideo, Uruguay. On 5 April, a British naval task force, with the carrier *HMS Hermes* as flagship, sailed from England, after Queen Elizabeth II approved (4 April) the requisition of a fleet of merchant ships. "Operation Corporate" had began. That same day, news and intelligence reports indicated that the Argentine marine forces that had carried out the invasion had been withdrawn and replaced with army conscripts, some with less than two months' service. On 6 April the European Economic Community (EEC) voted an embargo against Argentina. Also on 6 April, Chile alerted its military forces and reinforced its southern garrisons in response to the situation. Peru sent its Mirage fighters to support the Argentines, but none of them got into combat. The Soviet Union offered direct military assistance to Argentina, but Buenos Aires was smart enough to hold off the USSR, making the public statement that it would not accept aid "until the last possible moment." On 7 April, Great Britain declared a 200-mile exclusion area around the Falklands and warned that any Argentinian vessels found inside that area after 11 April would be considered hostile. Also on that day, Chile, anticipating Argentine action in the Beagle Channel (qv), ordered additional naval units into that area. On 9 April, Argentina announced the appointment of a military governor in the *Malvinas*. Martial law was declared in the Falklands, and severe penalties for violations of the new regulations were announced. By 14 April, intelligence sources reported at least 10,000 Argentine troops in the islands. On 15 April, Argentine naval units began deploying out of their home ports, but they stayed in shallow water away from the exclusion zone to prevent attack by British submarines. At the same time, two Soviet electronic warfare ships arrived at the naval port of Ushusia on the Argentine mainland. On 21 April, British Harrier VTOL fighters intercepted and turned back an Argentine Air Force Boeing 707 as it attempted to reconnoiter the British task force steaming toward the Falklands. Between 21 and 23 April, Special Boat Squadron (SBS) commandos reconnoitered South Georgia Island preparatory to an assault landing by the 42d Royal Marine Commando (RMC). Two British helicopters were lost in a blizzard that swept the island with 70-knot winds. In London, the government extended the exclusion zone to include all ships and aircraft threatening its forces. Late in the afternoon of 26 April, 100 men of Company M, 42 RMC, landed and recaptured the island. In all, 156 Argentine military personnel and 39 Argentine civilians were captured. There were no casualties on either side. On 27 April, Special Air

Service (SAS) and SBS reconnaisance teams were put ashore on East Falkland and West Falkland. On 30 April, London further extended the exclusion area to include all aircraft. That same day, Washington announced its support of Great Britain in the Falkland crisis. The U.S. suspended military exports to Argentina and offered the British the use of American facilities on Ascension Island (qv). The U.S., using its giant C-5A transports, also flew ammunition and other logistics missions for the British. Flying from Ascension, a lone British Vulcan bomber attacked the Port Stanley Airport on 1 May. The aircraft refueled three times enroute to the target and returned safely after the mission. Port Stanley airport and Goose Green were also attacked by carrier based Harriers, and Goose Green was later attacked by rocket-firing helicopters. Also on 1 May, British land operations on East Falkland and West Falkland began when SAS and SBS teams were put ashore. At the same time, Buenos Aires was calling up 80,000 reservists for active duty. On 2 May, three Argentine naval squadrons set out to attack the British fleet. The Argentinian cruiser *General Belgrano* (ex-*USS Phoenix* CL-46) in company with two destroyers, was attacked and sunk by the British nuclear-powered submarine *HMS Conqueror* after it received specific orders from London to launch the attack. Of the ship's company of 1,024 officers and men, 368 were lost. On 4 May, six Argentine aircraft attacked the British radar picket ship *HMS Sheffield* on its station 70 miles northeast of Port Stanley. The ship was hit by one French-built AM-39 *Exocet* air-to-ground missile. The ship burned to the hull and suffered personnel losses of 20 killed and 30 wounded. While rescue operations were underway, *HMS Yarmouth* sank an unidentified submarine lurking near the burning ship. While the air and naval war continued, Argentina began to feel the weight of world opinion and to tote up its losses in men and treasure. On 9 May, Buenos Aires issued a new statement couched in more conciliatory terms, saying that the Falklands were no longer a nonnegotiable issue and, negotiations were a strong possibility. For the British, however, the gauntlet was still on the ground and nothing short of a military victory would suffice. It was going to be, however, a victory with a high price tag. Although the British had been successful in sinking an Argentine intelligence gathering ship (AGI) (25 crewmen rescued) and had been shelling the airport at Port Stanley to deny its use to incoming aircraft, the war was far from over. On 10 May additional British warships joined the growing force surrounding the Falklands group. It now became clear why South Georgia Island had been taken early in the campaign; it became the staging area for Operation Corporate. On 21 May, the British ground assault began when 2,500 Royal Marines and airborne personnel of the Red Devil Brigade landed on East Falkland Island. These forces were heavily reinforced later that same day. In a counterstrike, 70 Argentine aircraft sank *HMS Ardent* and damaged four other ships of the landing force. At least 20 Argentine aircraft were destroyed in that action. By 22 May more than 5,000 British personnel were on the ground on East Falkland Island. In general, Argentine air strikes suffered heavy losses throughout the campaign. On 28 May, at Goose Green, the Argentinians put up the white flag of surrender; but when a lieutenant and two enlisted men of the

Second Parachute Regiment moved forward to discuss terms, the Argentine positions opened fire, killing all three. After that there was no quarter given in the battle. As a result of that most controversial act of the war, Argentine losses at Goose Green were 234 killed, 120 wounded, 1,400 captured and masses of equipment captured or destroyed. On 31 May, the British Fifth Brigade was landed at Port San Carlos. The landing phase was now complete, and Major General Jeremy Moore took command of the operation. On 2 June, the final preparations were begun for the attack on Port Stanley; but two days later, the shelling was still going on as the British continued their interminable preparations. On 5 June it was reported that Israel was supplying Argentina with large amounts of aviation materiel, including Skyhawk aircraft. On 8 May, the Liberian tanker *SS Hercules*, 480 nautical miles north of the Falklands, was attacked by an Argentine C-130 that had been converted into a bomber. The tanker was damaged and had to change course for the nearest safe port. On 9 June, intelligences sources stated that not only Israel, but also Iraq and Libya were supplying aircraft and Exocet missiles to Argentina. By 14 June, Port Stanley was completely surrounded by British forces. Repeated radio broadcasts to the Argentine governor were finally answered, and a surrender was arranged. By the 15th, most Argentine troops had surrendered. In all, 11,200 were taken prisoner. Between 700 and 1,000 had been killed. British losses totalled 255, including Falkland civilians caught in the crossfire. All Argentinian prisoners were repatriated by the last week in June. On 17 June Argentine president Galtieri and most of those responsible for the war were thrown out of office by an irate populace. The war for the Falklands was over. In 1989, Argentina and Great Britain held a series of discussions over Argentine fishing rights near the Falklands and about the renewal of diplomatic relations. The question of sovereignty over the Falklands was put off indefinitely. The people of the Falklands rejected all pro-Argentine candidates for the eight-seat legislature and elected an all pro-British slate that same year. *Reading:* Sunday Times of London, *War in the Falklands: The Full Story* (1982); Nicholas Van Der Bijl, *Argentine Forces in the Falklands* (1993); Louise Richardson, *When Allies Differ: Anglo-American Relations During the Suez and Falklands Crises* (1996); Barry Gough, *The Falkland Islands/Malvinas: The Contest for Empire in the South Atlantic* (1993); Eugene L. Rasor, *The Falklands/Malvinas Campaign: A Bibliography* (1991).

Faluja. *See* Israel.

Fanfani, Amantori (Amantore). (b. 1908, near Arezzo, Italy) Italian political leader, university professor, and historian. Fanfani was premier of Italy for 11 days in 1954. He served again as premier in 1958–1959 and 1960–1963. In 1965 he was appointed foreign minister. That same year he became the president of the United Nations General Assembly. On 28 December, he announced his resignation as the foreign minister of Italy. The resignation was brought about because of his handling of a North Vietnamese peace feeler. In 1966, he was again named premier and served until 1968. He was elected president of the Italian senate in 1968 and remained in that post until 1972. He was then elected a life senator. Fanfani, a Christain Democrat politican, at age 74 again became premier of Italy on 30 November 1982. He resigned on 29 April 1983 in a dispute with the Socialist Party over the direction in which the Italian government was moving. He again served as premier from 18 to 28 April 1987, but actually remaind in that office until 29 July, when his successor was sworn in.

Farabundo Marti National Liberation Front (FMNL). More correctly *Frente Farabundo Marti para la Liberacion Nacional,* the FMNL is a terrorist organization in El Salvador, the military wing of the leftist *Frente Democrático Revolucionario.* In December 1980, the FMNL announced a renewed offensive against the junta ruling El Salvador. On 10 January 1981, it opened its campaign. By 12 January, two days later, it claimed to be fighting in 50 towns and to hold four of them, including the important city of Santa Ana in the northern part of the country. Although not confirming the reports, the government did impose a nationwide curfew at that same time. On 23 February of that year, U.S. Secretary of State Alexander Haig (qv) accused Nicaragua of supplying arms to the FMNL. The prolonged internal conflict that ensued in El Salvador took many forms and was accompanied by terrorists acts by both the left- and right-wing factions opposed to the ruling junta. On 23 May 1983, for instance, in the fourth year of the civil war, FMNL gunmen shot and killed Lieutenant Commander Albert A. Schaufelberger, III, the deputy commander of the US Military Advisory Group in El Salvador, as he sat in his car on a university campus. In subsequent communiques, the FMNL threatened the lives of other Americans, especially military personnel, in the country. In fact, Schaufelberger was assassinated by a dissident element of the FMNL, the Clara Elizabeth Ramirez Front (CERF), which was a part of the FMNL's Central American Revolutionary Worker's Party. By 1983, the FMNL had become the central focus of opposition to the government, with most left-wing insurgent groups under its banner. By then, there was little doubt that Nicaragua and Cuba were supplying it with arms and ideology. The FMNL could field thousands of armed combatants On 30 December, the FMNL felt strong enough to attack and capture the army garrison at El Paraiso in Chalatenango Province, just 40 miles north of the capital city, San Salvador. Over 100 members of the garrison were killed, and the guerrillas were able to hold the garrison for six hours before withdrawing. In addition to operations against the Salvadoran army, FMNL engaged in kidnappings, sabotage, and other terrorist actions. "Metropolitan" units engaged in terrorist activities in the cities. In the spring of 1984, for instance, the Mardoqueo Cruz Urban Commando Group, a part of the FMNL's Central American Revolutionary Worker's Party (PRTC), began terrorist operations in the San Salvador area, mainly against transportation and communications facilities. Also, in 1984, CERF operatives murdered at least two Salvadoran employees of the U.S. Embassy and in November raked the US Embassy with machine-gun fire. On 15 October 1984, President José Duarte (qv) and the FMNL met at La Palma to settle the differences between the right and left. By 30 November 1984, little had been accomplished, and by the end of the year nearly 52,000 were dead in El Salvador in the five-year civil war even though the numbers killed in 1984 alone were down from previous years. In 1985, the FMNL increased its urban campaign and upgraded its metropolitan front groups in an apparent change of tactics brought about by recent military setbacks in the field. On 19 June 1985, the Mardoqueo Cruz Urban Commando Group gunned down 13 people, including four off-duty U.S. Marines and two U.S. businessmen in a cafe in the Zona Rosa district of San Salvador. A message delivered to a foreign news agency claimed that the attack was a part of an operation that it called "Yankee Aggressor." The message went on to warn, "Another Vietnam awaits you." On 10 September 1985, Inez Duarte Duran, the president's daughter, and a companion were kidnapped on a San Salvadoran university campus during a scuffle that left one security guard dead and another mortally wounded. The girl was held for nearly two months before being released in an exchange for two dozen captured FMNL guerrillas. In this case, it was the Pedro Pablo Castillo Command cell that carried out the kidnapping. Subsequent heavy losses among the various urban guerrilla cells as a result of more efficient security operations diminished the severity of attacks thereafter, but the guerrilla campaign continued until the two sides signed a formal peace treaty on 16 January 1992.

Farouk (Faruk) I. (b. 11 February 1920, Cairo—d. 18 March 1965, Rome) Born the son of King Fuad I, Farouk was educated in Egypt and England. He succeeded to his father's throne in May 1936 at age 16. During his minority the country was governed by a council of regents. Farouk assumed full power on 29 July 1937. In 1938, he was married to the daughter of an Egyptian judge (Farida), but that marriage was dissolved in 1948 after the birth of three daughters. In 1951, he married Narriman, the daughter of another Egyptian, who bore him a son. As king of Egypt, Farouk displayed his father's hatred for the dominant Wafd Party, especially its leader, Mustafa al-Nahas Pasha. Also on the king's hate list was Sir Miles Lampson, the British ambassador in Cairo. Farouk did, however, maintain friendly relations with a number of members of Axis power delegations in his country. This led to a British ultimatum to Farouk (4 February 1942), which was delivered by Lampson at the head of a substantial force of British troops. The ultimatum required Farouk to bring the Wafd into the government immediately or abdicate. There being few alternatives, Farouk called for Nahas Pasha to form a new government. In October 1944, Farouk had gathered enough strength to dismiss the Wafd, but his power was tenuous at best and was further diminished by the disastrous Palestine campaign in 1948, in which many of Farouk's advisors were implicated in corruption surrounding suspicious arms purchases that led to the Egyptian military failure in the campaign. On 23 July 1952, Farouk and his government were overthrown in a military coup led by General Mohammed Naguib Bey (qv). On 26 July, Farouk was obliged to abdicate and leave the country. He thereafter lived on the Italian Riviera in regal splendor until his death in 1965.

Fatah. *See* Abu Nidal.

Fatherland Front. On 18 November 1945, the Bulgarian Communist Party, using the sobriquet "Fatherland Front," won a single-list election that was completely dominated, supervised and controlled by the Soviet military occupying forces. The communists retained power until 1989, when the Soviet bloc began to self-destruct.

Faubus, Orval. (b. 7 January 1919, Greasy Creek, Arkansas - d. 14 December 1994, Conway, Arkansas) In 1954, Orval Faubus, a publisher by profession, became governor of Arkansas. In 1957, his administration ran afoul of the federal government over the integration issue. Although school integration had begun in Arkansas without incident in at least six towns with small black populations, when it came time for the fall opening of Little Rock's Central High School in September 1957, trouble began. On 3 September, Faubus ordered 270 men of the Arkansas National Guard out to maintain order around the school. In effect, the order was to bar nine black students from entering the high school, which ran against federal guidelines dealing with desegregation. On 22 September, a federal judge issued an order calling for the removal of the troops. In Little Rock, Faubus withdrew the National Guardsmen, but segregationist mobs created a tense situation around the school. Police had to be used to protect the black children. On 24 September, at a meeting in the White House, President Dwight D. Eisenhower (qv) instructed the Army Chief of Staff Maxwell Taylor (qv) to take the necessary steps to restore order and enforce federal court orders. The 101st Airborne Division was alerted for deployment into Little Rock. Over 1,100 federal troops were sent into Little Rock. At the same time, the Arkansas National Guard was federalized (i.e., put under federal orders and not the orders of the governor) and ordered to remain in its assembly areas. Although Faubus defied federal authority in that instance, he won the 1958 Democratic nomination for a third term as governor for a large majority. When Arkansas' request for a 30-month extension of the desegregation law was turned down by the U.S. Supreme Court, Faubus ordered a special session of the state legislature to ask for a series of segregation bills, the most serious of which was to close all the high schools in Little Rock. All of the plans ran into trouble in the federal courts, and by 1959 the schools were reopened with at least token integration. In 1960, Faubus ran for president on the National States Rights ticket and lost to John F. Kennedy, running a dismal third behind Richard Nixon, and ahead of Socialist Labor candidate Eric Hass. Faubus continued in the governor's office, however, until 1968, winning an unprecedented sixth term in 1966. *Reading:* Roy Reed, *Faubus: The Life and Times of an American Prodigal* (?).

Faure, Edgar Jean. (b. 18 August 1908, Béziers—d. 30 March 1988, Paris) Born the son of a military doctor, Faure studied law and Russian and worked as a barrister in Paris until 1942, when he escaped to Algiers to join the Free French. There he served as director of legislative affairs. In 1946 he was appointed to the International Military Tribunal at Nürnberg. Later in 1946, he was elected a deputy in the National Assembly. He served as premier for six weeks in 1952. On 5 February 1955, Pierre Mendès-France (qv) was removed from office as premier of France by the National Assembly, which balked at his policies toward North Africa, especially Tunisia. His former minister of finance, Edgar Faure, succeeded him on 23 February and, by 22 April, was successful in the Franco–Tunisian negotiation. On 21 August, Faure met with Moroccan leaders at Aix-les Bains in hopes of putting an end to the widespread strife in that French colony. Faure engineered a number of steps that led to the Assmbly's acceptance (29 August) of his peace plan for North Africa. On 29 November 1955, however, the Faure government was ousted from office by the Assembly. The following day, as his last act, Faure dissolved that body in hopes that elections would establish one with more coherent goals. With the advent of Charles DeGaulle (qv), Faure was effectively excluded from the government, although he remained in the National Assembly. Later, however, while Faure taught law at Dijon University, he was given several important missions abroad, among which he negotiated the normalization of relations with China. In 1966, Faure was appointed minister of agriculture. Following the student rebellion in May–June 1968, he was appointed minister of education. While his educational reforms were effective, they were not accepted by President Georges Pompidou, who took office after DeGaulle resigned in 1969. Faure was again forced from office (June), but he remained in the National Assembly until 1978. In July 1972, Faure reappeared on the political scene in the government of Pierre Messmer, where he served as minister of state for labor and social affairs. In that office, his primary role was getting the nation ready for the anticipated general election of 1973. During this period, Faure began to emerge as a possible presidential candidate for 1976. In 1978 he was elected to the Académie Française. Faure was appointed the French representative at the European Parliament (1979–1981). He refused an appointment in the government of François Mitterand (qv) and went into semiretirement, where he continued to write history and, under the pseudonym of Edgar Sanday, detective stories.

Fawzi, Mahmoud. (b. 19 September 1900, Cairo—d. 12 June 1981, Cairo) Mahmoud Fawzi was educated in Egypt, Great Britain, and the United States. Trained as a lawyer, he took his doctorate at the University of Rome. He joined the diplomatic service and, by 1941, was the consul general in Jerusalem. After three years in that post, he returned to Egypt where, in 1947, he was appointed the head of the Egyptian delegation to the United Nations. In 1952, he became the Egyptian ambassador in London. After the 1952 revolution in Egypt, Fawzi was appointed foreign minister first of Egypt and, after the union with Syria, of the United Arab Republic (qv). At the time of the death of Gamal Abdul Nasser (qv) on 28 September 1970, Fawzi still served in that post. On 20 October, the new president, Anwar Sadat (qv), appointed the 70-year-old Fawzi as prime minister. (Nasser had held both the presidency and the premiership at the time of his death.) When Sadat secured his base of power by removing a large number of ministers and senior officials (May 1971), Fawzi was asked to remain and head the new cabinet. On 17 January 1972, as Egypt prepared for war against Israel, Fawzi was replaced by Aziz Sidky as prime minister and given the post of vice-president, which he held until his retirement at age 74, in 1974. He died quietly in 1981.

Faya Largeau. *See* Chad.

February 28 Popular League. *See* Farabundo Marti National Liberation Front.

Federal Party. *See* Sri Lanka.

Federal Republic of Cameroon. *See* Cameroon.

Federal Republic of Germany. *See* West Germany.

Federation of Arab Republics. On 17 April 1971, Egypt, Libya and Syria agreed to form a Federation of Arab Republics. On 4 October, Egypt's Anwar Sadat (qv) was chosen to be the new federation's first president. The agreement was initialed in Benghazi, and the new constitution was signed by the heads of each state following a three-day meeting in Damascus. Heavy majorities favored the federation in subsequent referenda. One purpose of the federation was to end Syria's isolation in the Arab World after Syria gave its adherence to the Declaration of Tripoli (27 November 1970).

Federation of Revolutionary Youth. On 17 March 1970, a number of anti-American protests that ostensibly proclaimed "independence week," held at several universities throughout Turkey, erupted into violence. The leftist Federation of Revolutionary Youth supported by militant workers from the Confederation of Reformist Workers' Unions (DISK) were at the forefront of the demonstrations. The protests culminated in a clash in Istanbul between police and DISK members that left several people dead (15–16 June). Martial law was declared and stayed in effect until 16 September.

Federation of South Arabia. In 1963 the Aden Protectorate, which had been in existence since 1937, was renamed the Protectorate of South Arabia under the protection of Great Britain. The area was later to be called the People's Republic of Southern Yemen (qv). In July 1964, the British government announced that the federation formed by six of the chieftains in 1958, in hopes of offsetting the effects of Egyptian and communist incursions, had grown as other chieftains joined and would become independent in 1968. In the intervening years, considerable violence occurred, primarily with Egyptian backing. In April 1967 a UN commission arrived in Aden but left almost immediately, claiming its work had been impeded by the British. The British then announced that freedom was to granted on 9 January 1968 and that Britain would supply financial and military aid to the new state. Before that date, however, two rival nationalist factions, the Front for the Liberation of Occupied South Yemen (FLOSY) and the National Liberation Front (NLF), opened hostilities over who was to take power when the British withdrew. The British-trained South Arabian Army sided with the NLF. The People's Republic of Southern Yemen was the result. *See also* Southern Yemen.

Ferreira Aldunate, Wilson. (b. 28 January 1918, Nico Perez, Uruguay—d. 15 March 1988, Montevideo) On 16 June 1984, an Argentinian ferry in which Ferreira was riding crossed into Uruguayan waters, The boat was stopped by Uruguayan officials, who arrested Ferreira, along with 100 of his followers from the opposition liberal Blanco Party. The group was on their way to a rally in Montevideo. Ferreira had been in exile in Argentina (also in Spain and Britain) since 1973, when the military regime of Juan María Bordaberry (qv) had dissolved the Uruguayan legislature. On at least one occasion, the Bordaberry regime had tried to kidnap Ferreira in Argentina as he continued his campaign against the human rights abuses in his homeland. Ferreira had served 34 years in the Uruguayan legislature and had run for president against Bordaberry in the 1971 election, narrowly losing in what was said to be a rigged vote that propelled Bordaberry into the presidency in 1972. After his 1984 arrest, Ferreira was jailed for a time but was released after the election that removed Bordaberry from power. He returned to the leadership of the Blanco Party and was preparing for the 1989 presidential election when he died of apparently natural causes at age 70.

Ferrier, Johan *See* Chin A Sen.

Fez (Fès, Fas). *See* Morocco.

15 May Arab Organization. On 11 August 1982, a bomb exploded aboard a Pan Am flight bound from Tokyo's Narita Airport for Honolulu. The plane was 140 miles from Oahu when the device detonated. One passenger was killed in the explosion, and 14 others were injured. The aircraft landed safely at Honolulu. The 15 May Arab Organization was suspected of planting the bomb. This terrorist organization was a rejectionist Palestinian group, supported by Iraq, which conducted its attacks mainly against Israeli targets and operates, as does Abu Nidal (qv), outside the control of the PLO. The group claimed responsibility for the bombing of an Israeli-owned restaurant in West Berlin in January 1982, in which one person was killed and 24 injured.

Figueres Ferrer, José. (b. 25 September 1906, San Ramón—d. 8 June 1990, San Jose, Costa Rica) Figueres studied economics and engineering in the United States. In his early life he became an enemy of all Latin American dictators and donated both time and money to the "Caribbean Legion," which fought dictatorships. In 1948, a pro-communist faction attempted to block the installation of Costa Rica's newly elected president, Otilio Ulate. José Figueres, a landowner and a socialist, led the fight against Ulate's enemies in what turned into a civil war. His total force was 700 men was backed by the Costa Rican army against the communist insurgents. On 8 May 1948, Figueres's military junta announced the the National Union Party (known more properly as the National Liberation Party) had won the struggle. That same day the Communist Party was outlawed in Costa Rica. Ulate was given the government, and a new constitution was approved in 1949. The military junta soon lost trust in the Ulate government, and by 1953 Figueres had been elected president. Figueres left office in 1958, when he was replaced by Mario Echandi Jiménez. Known affectionately as Don Pepe, Figueres remained a political power behind the scenes for many years and was elected president of Costa Rica again in 1970. Figueres remained in office until 8 May 1974. He died in 1990 at age 84.

Fiji. An island nation in the southwestern Pacific made up of more than 300 islands forming an archipelago that covers 7,055 square miles of ocean, Fiji lies about 500 miles southwest of Samoa. The larger islands in the group are of volcanic origin and are mountainous. The smaller islands are coral atolls. The two primary islands are Viti Levu, with the capital city of Suva, and Vanua Levu.

These comprise about 90 percent of the land mass of the island group. The islands were discovered in 1643 by Abel Jansen Tasman, a Dutch navigator. Captain James Cook visited the islands in 1774. Captain William Bligh found the islands after being set adrift in a small boat during the mutiny on the *Bounty* 1789 and returned to explored the islands in 1792. Christian missionaries came to the islands in 1830 and brought the natives away from cannabalism. The king of Fiji was christianized in 1854. Fiji was a crown colony after it was ceded to Great Britain by the Fijians (1874) at a time of political crisis caused by European interference. In the late nineteenth century, the British imported Indian laborers to work the Fijian sugar fields. Today (1993) about half of all Fijians are of Indian descent. Fiji gained its independence on 10 October 1970. In May 1987, a military coup led by Lieutenant Colonel Sitiveni Rabuka overthrew the government. Because of internal squabbling, Rabuka led another coup in September and, in October, declared Fiji a republic. Civilian government was reinstated in December 1987, with Rabuka becoming prime minister on 2 June 1992. On 15 December 1993, President Ratu Sir Penaia Ganilau died while visiting Washington and was replaced by Ratu Sir Kamisese Mara. Fiji continued on its course without undue violence into 1996, but it still faced the multi-ethnic (European, Indian and Fijian) problem of constituency that had plagued it since its independence. *Reading:* Stephanie Lawson, *Tradition versus Democracy in the South Pacific: Fiji, Tonga and Western Samoa* (1996); Brij V. Lal, *Broken Waves: A History of the Fiji Islands in the Twentieth Century* (1992).

Finland. A country located in northern Europe, Finland is bordered on the east by Russia, on the north by Norway, on the west by Sweden, although separated in part by the Gulf of Bothnia, and on the south by the Baltic Sea and the Gulf of Finland. The early Finns probably migrated from the Ural mountains in what is today central Russia. (c. 100 A.D.). The country came under Swedish control in 1154 and remained so until until 1809, when Finland became an independent duchy under the protection of Imperial Russia. This period of Russian servitude set the character of the Finnish people and developed a strong independent spirit. On 6 December 1917, Finland declared its independence, and in 1919 it became a republic. On 30 November 1939, the Soviet Union invaded Finland. Although the Finns fought bravely and extracted a heavy toll from the USSR, they were forced to yield to superior numbers and had to give up 16,200 square miles of territory, including the isthmus of Karelia, Viipuri, and Lake Ladoga. During World War II, Finland sided with the Germans and suffered accordingly, losing even more territory as a result and seeing many of its wartime leaders imprisoned as war criminals. In 1948, Finland signed a treaty of mutual assistance with the USSR. In 1949, communist-instigated strikes and violence were put down by the government in response to a strong anticommunist public reaction. However, in 1954, the government was forced to resign because of spiralling inflation. As a gesture of good will, the Soviet Union returned the territory of Porkkala (signed 19 September 1955, completed 26 January 1956), which had been ceded to the USSR as a naval base. At the same time, the

Soviets released Finnish prisoners of war who had been held since World War II. In December of 1958, the Finnish government admitted that its chief foreign policy goal was maintaining good relations with the USSR. In October 1961, Moscow declared the threat of aggression posed by West Germany to be so great that it demanded consultation based on the Finno-Soviet Mutual Defense Treaty signed in 1948. In October 1968, Finland sided with the West against the Soviet Union in demanding an immediate withdrawal of Soviet troops from Czechoslovakia. Yet, in July 1970, Finland extended its treaty of friendship with the USSR to 1990. In 1983, the treaty was again given a 20-year extension. On 2 November 1970, Helsinki became the site of the first SALT talks. With the dissolution of the Soviet Union and its satellites, Finland has been suffering severe economic setbacks. In May 1992, Finland asked to join the European Community, but the country's tenuous economic situation forestalled a decision. The country was also shaken that year by reports that its president from 1956 to 1981, Urho Kekkonen, had been a pawn of the USSR. Similarly, Finland hesitated regarding membership in NATO because of its long border with the Soviet Union. During 1994, Finland's economic situation worsened, but in 1994 it joined the European Union (formal joining, 1995) and began to see some recovery. *Reading:* Risto E. J. Penttilla, *Finland's Search for Security Through Defence, 1944–1989* (1991); Fred Singleton, *A Short History of Finland* (1990); Anatole Mazour, *Finland Between East and West* (1976).

"Fishhook." *See* "Cambodian Invasion" in Vietnam.

Fitzroy. *See* Falkland Islands.

Fiumicino Airport. On 17 December 1973, five Palestinian terrorists opened fire in the customs area at Fiumicino Airport, Rome, killing a number of people. They then seized a number of hostages and threw hand grenades into a Pan Am 707 as it was being readied for a flight to Beirut. A number of passengers were killed, including 14 American employees of ARAMCO. Next, with their hostages, the terrorists hijacked a Lufthansa airliner to Athens, where they demanded the release of a group of PLO terrorists being held by Greek authorities. They then flew to Kuwait and surrendered. On 2 March 1974, the terrorists were flown to Egypt, where they were to be tried by the PLO. Upon their arrival, however, the Egyptian authorities refused to release them and jailed them until 22 November, when they were flown to Tunis as a part of a ransom agreement in exchange for hostages aboard a hijacked British Airways jet. After the exchange, the terrorists were flown to Libya, where they were released. Fiumicino Airport was the scene of another incident on 27 December 1985, when Abu Nidal terrorists armed with Soviet-made AK-47 rifles and hand grenades attacked the Israeli El Al ticket counter, killing five Americans and 10 other persons, and wounding 15 Americans and nearly 60 others. Airport security personnel killed three terrorists and captured another.

Flammerich, Suarez. On 27 November 1950, the ruling military junta in Venezuela appointed Suarez Flammerich president. This action occurred 14 days after the assassination of Lieutenant Carlos Delgado Chalbaud, the leader of the counterrevolution, who had led the November 1948 coup, and the rise of a new strongman, Major Marcos Pérez Jiménez. The new president's role was purely ceremonial.

Flanzamaton, Moses. On 1 April 1985, President Samuel K. Doe of Liberia narrowly escaped being assassinated in a plot led by Lieutenant Colonel Moses Flanzamaton, the deputy commander of the Palace Guard. Flanzamaton was tried, convicted and executed on 7 April.

Florence (*Firenze*). *See* Italy.

Flores Larin, Hector. Hector Flores Larin, a leader of the Salvadoran National Conciliation Party, was assassinated by an unknown gunman on March 14, 1984. *See* El Salvador.

Fontainebleau Conference. On 6 June 1946, the two-month-old Franco–Vietnamese negotiations held at the Fontainebleau Palace, in France, reached an impasse and were halted.The breakup of this conference, which was to reconcile the differences between the French and Vietnamese positions on the future of Indochina, led directly to the beginning of the war in Southeast Asia. *See* Indochina and Vietnam.

Ford, Gerald R(udolph). (b. 14 July 1913, Omaha) The 38th president of the United States, Ford did his undergraduate studies at the University of Michigan and received his law degree at Yale. He served in the U.S. navy in World War II, and was elected to Congress after the war. In 1965, he was elected Republican minority leader of the House and held that office until October 1963, when he was nominated to be the Republican Party's choice as vice president. Eight month's later, facing certain impeachment over the Watergate Affair, Richard M. Nixon (qv) resigned the presidency and Ford was sworn in (9 August 1974). Initially high, his public appeal plummeted when he pardoned Nixon (8 September) for crimes committed in office. He did, however, continue the policy of his five predecessors by telling the Vietnamese people that the United States would not abandon them. On 16 September, Ford signed a conditional amnesty for deserters and draft dodgers from the Vietnamese conflict. In November, he met Leonid Brezhnev in Vladivostok and signed an accord limiting nuclear weapons, and on 22 January 1975, he signed a protocol banning the manufacture, storage, or use of biological weapons. By July, Ford was at odds with the House over his desire to restore the sale of arms to Turkey and was handed a resounding defeat when Congress refused to reinstate the program. (Ironically, Ford had earlier vetoed a House bill to restore arms shipments.) The House also refused to approve a bill for arms for pro-Western factions in Angola, even though there was irrefutable evidence that the USSR was supplying the other side with massive amounts of weaponry. Two attempts were made on Ford during his short time in office. Gerald Ford left the White House on 20 January 1977 after being defeated by Jimmy Carter (qv).

Formosa. *See* Argentina.

Formosa. *See* Taiwan.

Forrestal, James Vincent. (b. 15 February 1892, Beacon, New York—d. 22 May 1949, Bethesda, Maryland) Forrestal was educated at Dartmouth College and at Princeton, where he graduated in 1915. He served as a naval aviator in World

War I. After the war he joined a New York investment brokerage and became its president in 1938. He became the administrative assistant of Franklin Roosevelt in June 1940 and, in August, was appointed undersecretary of the navy. He was appointed secretary of the navy upon the death of Frank Knox in May 1944. On 6 July 1947, Forresthal was appointed the first secretary of defense under the new National Security Act of 1947, which aimed at unification of the military services. On 28 March 1949, an exhausted Forrestal resigned. He entered Bethesda Naval Hospital suffering acute, severe depression, and on 22 May ended his life by jumping to his death from a hospital window. Navy medical personnel said his type of depression was seen only in those who had served in combat.

Fort Caobang. *See* Indochina.

Four Powers. A term originally used in the Four Power Pact of 13 December 1921, which was one of the seven treaties that emerged from the Conference on Limitation of Armaments held in Washington from 12 November 1921, to 6 February 1922. This treaty replaced the Anglo–Japanese alliance of 1902, which had expired in 1921. In the latter part of World War II, the term "Four Powers" achieved currency, along with such other terms as "Big Four," although it often denoted different groupings of the Allied nations. In general, the term usually denoted the United States, Great Britain, the Soviet Union and a fourth nation, usually either France or China. In 1945, General Douglas MacArthur (qv) planned to set up a Four Powers board in occupied Japan to deal with such major problems as health in the occupied territories. In the European theater, France replaced China as the fourth power on the Allied Control Council (ACC) set up by General Eisenhower (qv) to administer Germany. A Four Powers conference opened in London on 25 November 1947. Although the conference lasted until 16 December, it once again failed to agree upon a solution to the question of the future of East Germany. On 20 March 1948, the Soviets walked out of the ACC after accusing the Western powers of undermining the Four Powers administration of Germany. However, on 10 March 1952, the USSR called for a summit to discuss the issues of German reunification and rearmament. The Western Allies suggested (17 August 1953) a Four Power meeting to be held in London on 31 August to settle the terms of the Austrian peace treaty. This suggestion came about one day (16 August) after the USSR proposed a Four Powers meeting, to be held within six months, with a preliminary meeting between East and West German representatives to set up a program for reunification. The "Big Four" foreign ministers' conference that was held in Berlin was hopelessly deadlocked and adjourned on 18 February 1954. A new conference was scheduled to be held in Geneva to discuss Far Eastern affairs, with Communist China scheduled to be invited to attend. The Soviets then requested a meeting (6 October 1954) to discuss the reunification and neutralization of Germany. The issue of the Austrian peace treaty was settled at Vienna on 15 May 1955. At the Geneva summit held 18–23 July 1955, US President Eisenhower proposed a Soviet–American exchange of military information and aerial inspections as a means of controlling the nuclear arms race. Other topics discussed at the meeting included the perennial issues of German reunification and European security. Then, on 27 November 1958, Nikita Khrushchev demanded that the Four Powers occupation of Berlin be ended immediately. In September 1960, the Western Allies called upon the Four Powers Agreements on Berlin, when the USSR announced that traffic to and from Berlin would require East German documentation. By 26 October 1961, the East German harassment led to a military confrontation on the East–West Berlin border, which was settled by diplomatic means, proving the validity of the agreements. In effect, Western diplomats crossed back and forth across the border to test the force of the agreements and the resolve of the Soviets. This was considered an extremely serious breach of the agreements by the West. In the aftermath of that incident, the Western Allies pointed out that, when the Soviets walked out of the Allied Kommandantura, the Four Powers agency responsible for Berlin, on 16 April 1948, an action that led to the Berlin Blockade (qv), it in no way altered the terms of the agreements. In the late 1960s, the ongoing Middle East crisis became a topic of Four Powers discussion. Another working conference on disarmament, which had lasted 39 months, was closed without success in January 1962. This series of meetings did, however, lay much of the groundwork for later Strategic Arms Limitations Treaty talks (SALT) (qv). Also, by the end of the 1960s, it was becoming apparent that the "Big Four" no longer held the clout that they had immediately after World War II. Israel, for example, on 30 March 1969 rejected all peace proposals, including those put forward by the Big Four, that were contrary to the nation's best interests. Complete polarity was being achieved between East and West at about this point; and only two powers, the U.S. and the USSR, that really mattered, even though smaller nations such as France clung to the old beliefs in equality of impact in decision making. Thereafter, the term "Big Four" or "Four Powers" tended to relate to the two superpowers. Thus, when the U.S. urged the "Big Four" to slow the shipment of arms to the Middle East in February 1970, the suggestion was actually pointed at the Soviet Union. One of the last vestiges of Four Powers diplomacy occurred in 1971, when the U.S., USSR, U.K. and France regularized the status of Berlin (23 August), in what became the framework for West German Chancellor Willy Brandt's (qv) *Ostpolitik* (1972). In February 1974, when East Germany once again began interfering with vehicular traffic between the West and Berlin, the Four Powers Agreements were called upon to halt the practice. Another use of the term "Four Power" may be seen in the establishment of a Four Powers Joint Military Commission, which attempted to achieve a cease-fire between South Vietnamese and communist forces on 17 February 1973. *Reading:* Hua Qingzhao, *From Yalta to Panmunjom: Truman's Diplomacy and the Four Powers, 1945–1953* (1993).

Fox Bay. *See* Falkland Islands.

France. In ancient times, France was known as Gaul and was inhabited by Celtic tribes. In 58–51 B.C., Julius Caesar conquered the country, and a Roman rule was imposed that lasted 500 years. Later, France emerged as a part of the

Carolingian Empire. After Charlemagne's death, France emerged as one of the successor kingdoms. The monarchy remained until the French Revolution (1789–1793) overthrew the crown with great bloodshed. The First Republic that followed was quickly overtaken by the First Empire (1804–1815) under Napoleon. From 1814 until 1870, a succession of monarchies and republics alternated in the rule of France and established many of the characteristics of France as it is seen today. In 1871, the Third Republic was formed. It commenced in the shadow of the disastrous Franco-Prussian War and witnessed severe losses in wealth and manpower in the World War I, when it became the main arena of the conflict. By the terms of the Treaty of Versailles, France recovered the territories of Alsace and Lorraine, which the Germans had taken in 1871. In 1940, Germany again invaded France, creating a situation in which the French were required to submit to a humiliating armistice and subjugation to the Nazi yoke through a puppet government in Vichy. A provisional Free French government was formed in London under Charles de Gaulle (qv), which lasted until 1946 and the beginning of the Fourth Republic. France was required to give up its possessions in Indochina (qv) in 1954, and then those in Morocco and Algeria in 1956. France lost most of its remaining African possessions by 1962. In 1958, a government crisis returned deGaulle to the premiership. A new constitution signalled the beginning of the Fifth Republic. De Gaulle's tenure witnessed a resurgence in the French economy and a reinstitution of French independence in its foreign affairs. In 1966, France withdrew its forces from NATO but remained in the political committees of that organization. France did continue its occupation of Germany, where 60,000 French troops were stationed. In May 1968, nationwide rioting and strikes broke out that forced the government to make wide-ranging concessions. A new election won a landslide victory for de Gaulle, but in April 1969 he resigned after losing a nationwide referendum on constitutional reform. In 1981 François Mitterand, a socialist, was elected president, and the government began nationalizing a number of industries and the nation's banking system. Five years later, a privatization program commenced in which a number of state-owned companies were sold. Mitterand was elected to a second seven-year term in 1988. On 10 July 1985, French agents sank the Greenpeace flagship, *Rainbow Warrior* (qv), in Auckland harbor, New Zealand, which created a major diplomatic incident. Mitterand remained in office in 1993 after a difficult period of adjustment to new pressures for a unified European state. The year 1994 was relatively peaceful for France, except for its role in attempting to halt the disintegration of Rwanda (*see* Rwanda). France withdrew its troops stationed in Rwanda and evacuated all French nationals in the first half of the year, but it put a new peacekeeping force in country in late June. These and all other Frence troops were withdrawn in August, having been replaced by African peacekeepers. France also expelled (31 August) 20 of 26 Islamic leaders arrested following the assassination of five French citizens in Algiers on 3 August. In reprisal, Islamic terrorists hijacked an Air France airbus on 24 December, killing three passengers before being killed by a French antiterrorist team in Marseilles. Also in 1994, some French proposals were made to withdraw French troops from the UN peacekeeping force in Bosnia, but the move never eventuated. France did withdraw from Bosnia in 1995, when NATO took over the peacekeeping mission. At the same time, France drew worldwide scorn when it announced (5 September) it would resume nuclear testing at Mururoa (qv). Algerian terrorists also carried out a series of attacks in France in 1995 as a part of the three-year-old Algerian civil war. *Reading:* Pierre Goubert, *The Course of French History* (1991); Joseph De Maistre, *Considerations on France* (1994).

Franco Bahamonde, Francisco. (b. 6 December 1892, Galicia, Spain—d. 20 November 1975) Franco graduated from Spain's Infantry Academy in Toledo in 1907. He twice served in Morocco, the second time (beginning in 1920) as deputy commander of the Spanish Foreign Legion and, in 1923, as its commander. In 1925, he helped crush the Rif uprising and was promoted to rigadier general the following year. In 1927 Franco became commandant of the Spanish Military Academy at Saragossa. When the Spanish republic was proclaimed in 1931, he was transferred to the Balearic Islands. After helping quell the miner's revolt in 1934, Franco was appointed chief of staff. In 1936, however, he was sent into oblivion as governor of the Canary Islands by the new Popular Front president. During this period Franco became involved in the secret *Unión Militar Española* and took part in the plot to seize the government in July 1936. When the organization's leader was killed in a airplane crash, Franco was chosen head of state and supreme commander. The various factions in Spain fell into two general categories, the conservative group, called Falangists, and the republican or Loyalist group. The Falangist group, led by Franco, won the Civil War that ensued and followed up with 36 years of authoritarian rule, during which Franco managed to avoid involvement in World War II, although he had taken considerable aid from Hitler and Mussolini. In December 1946, the UN moved to condemn Franco and imposed a diplomatic and economic boycott on Spain. This only tended to strengthen Franco's hand at home, and in 1950 the UN lifted its sanctions. Earlier, on 31 March 1947, Franco declared Spain a monarchy, choosing Don Juan Carlos (qv) as king with himself as regent. In 1953, Franco granted military basing rights to the U.S. in return for military and economic aid. In 1969, Juan Carlos was invested before the Cortes. Six years later, in 1975, Francisco Franco died at the age of 83.

Franco, Rafael. On 17 February 1936, the Febrerist party, led by Colonel Rafael Franco, seized power in Paraguay. In 1939, José Félix Estigarribia was elected president but was killed in an airplane crash. General Higinio Morínigo took power and, in effect, abrogated the country's new constitution, with his Colorado party establishing an oppresive dictatorship. After a general strike in 1944 brought severe reprisals, plans were laid to rid the country of its dictator. In March 1947, Franco and his Febreristas, joined by Liberales and a part of the army, rose in revolt and attempted to seize the government. Although they held several centers of the country for a while, the rebels were forced to disband (August), and the revolt ended with no change in the regime. Franco ceased to be a factor in Paraguayan affairs.

Franco-German Treaty. Signed 27 October 1956, the Franco-German Treaty returned the important coal-producing Saar region to German control. The League of Nations had taken control of the region after World War I and administered it until 1935. Germany agitated for its return in what became known as the Saar Plebiscite. The area was occupied by Allied forces in May 1945 and then placed under French military government in July 1945. The frontier was revised in June 1947, increasing the size of the Saarland from 737 square miles to 991 square miles. In December 1947, a constitution went into effect that provided for a representative government and economic union with France. This status was confirmed by parliamentary elections in 1952, and Saar independence within the Western European Union was proposed in Paris in May 1955. The people, however, rejected this plan and treaty was signed with reunification with Germany taking place in January 1957.

Franjieh, Suleiman Kabalan. (b. 14 June 1910, Zgharta, Lebanon—d. 23 July 1992, Beirut) Franjieh was born the son of a well-to-do Maronite Christian farmer-businessman and was educated in Lebanon. In 1930, he entered the family business. In 1957, he was implicated in the murders of several rival clan members and fled to Syria. He did not enter politics until 1960, when he ran for his brother's seat in the parliament. He won the election and was subsequently appointed minister of trade and economics. Although a man of the highest reputation, he was a surprise candidate for the presidency in 1970. Franjieh became president of Lebanon on 17 September (sworn in 23 September) 1970. Among his first acts was to appoint a cabinet of authorities and experts and to shy away from political opportunists. He also immediately asserted authority over Palestinian guerrillas who roamed the countryside at will. In June 1972, for instance, Franjieh ordered all Palestinian commando forces in southern Lebanon to suspend operations against Israel and to move their bases away from the Lebanese-Israeli border. President Franjieh was able to restore a relative sense of order in his country, but the divisiveness of the situation could not be overcome. On 11 March 1976, the military commander of Beirut, faced by a near mutiny among his troops, declared a state of emergency and asked for the government's resignation. Franjieh refused and barricaded himself in the Presidential Palace at Baabda. Leftist troops prepared to assault the town but were stopped by the Syrians. General fighting then broke out in and around Beirut (13–14 March). On 25 March, Franjieh fled for the Christian Lebanese positions near Juniyah when the palace came under artillery bombardment. On 10 April Parliament met and voted to change the constitution to enable new elections. Franjieh was forced to sign the order on 24 April. On 8 May, Elias Sarkis (qv) was elected president, but Franjieh then refused to step down. Not until 28 September was Sarkis sworn in. In 1978, Christian Phalangist gunmen murdered Franjieh's son, daughter-in-law, and grandchild in an act of revenge against the elder Franjieh.

Frankfurt (Frankfurt am Main). *See* Germany.

Frankfurt Airport. *See* Germany.

Freedom Fighters. *See* Hungary.

Free Islamic Republic. On 26 January 1980, the Afghan rebel leader Zia Khan Nassry was interviewed in Islamabad, Pakistan. In the interview, the rebel leader claimed his forces controlled the Afghan provinces of Ghazni, Logar and Paktia in the eastern part of the country. He also claimed that the Free Islamic Republic was the rightful government of Afghanistan.

Free Yemen Republic. *See* North Yemen.

Frei Montalva, Eduardo. On 3 November 1970, Chile's president, Eduardo Frei Montalva, stepped aside and turned the office over to the newly elected president, socialist Salvador Allende Gossens. Earlier in that year (27 June), Frei was required to declare a six-month state of emergency in Santiago province because of the unrest and killings that were dominating the region.

French Action Directe. *See Action Directe.*

French-Indochinese War. *See* Vietnam and Indochina.

French Sudan. *See* Mali.

French West Africa (*Afrique Occidentale Française*) (*AOF*). Until 1959, French West Africa constituted a federation of eight territories divided into two groups. The first group was composed of Mauritania, Niger, Senegal, French Sudan and Upper Volta. The second group was made up of Dahomey, Guinea and Ivory Coast. French West Africa was constituted in 1895. During World War II, the region remained under the control of Vichy until November 1942, when the French authorities there joined the Free French government in Algiers. In 1946, the colonies became territories of the French Republic. In 1958, seven of them became autonomous states in the French Community; with Guinea accepting its immediate independence. French West Africa was dissolved as an entity on 21 January 1959. In 1960, the remaining seven states declared their independence. (For more information, *see* the individual nations.) *Reading:* Anthony Kirk-Greene & Daniel Bach, eds., *State and Society in Francophone Africa since Independence* (1995);Gloria D. Westfall, *French Colonial Africa: A Guide to Official Sources* (1992); John F. Clark & David E. Gardinier, eds., *Political Reform in Francophone Africa* (1997).

***Frente de Liberatacao de Mocambique* (FRELIMO).** The Mozambique Liberation Front was a political and military organization formed by exiles from the Portuguese colony of Mozambique in neighboring Tanzania in 1962. The formation of the organization led to a 12-year rebellion against the colony in which FRELIMO was the primary participant. The movement was originally led by Eduardo Chivambo Mondlane (qv), who was able to get assistance from both the East and the West in building a force of several thousand guerrilla fighters. This force initiated its operations in 1962 in northern Mozambique. Mondland was assassinated in Dar-es-Salaam on 3 February 1969 and was replaced by Samora Machel (qv). Marchel was able to expand FRELIMO's area of operations into central Mozambique. By the mid-1960s, Portugal had to deploy over 70,000 troops in Mozambique to help thwart the rebellion. On 10 February 1972, in one of their most daring operations, FRELIMO rebels attacked a Portuguese outpost near the strategically important Cabora Bassa Dam. In November of that year, they opened new offensives in Manica Sofala and Tete provinces, further expanding the fighting. On 1 July 1973, FRELIMO forces attacked the major military communications center at Estima, which controlled the Cabora Bassa Dam, using Soviet-made 122 mm rockets. Sweden announced it would triple its support of FRELIMO on 24 March 1974. An army coup overthrew the government in Portugal on 25 April 1974; Mozambique won its independence a year later (25 June 1975) after an agreement had been signed (7 September 1974) between the Portuguese and FRELIMO in Zambia. Although a provisional government was set up to rule in the interim, Portuguese authorities in Mozambique had already released hundreds of FRELIMO prisoners (1 May 1974). Machel established a FRELIMO government in the country. The new government was forced to crush a military revolt by rebellious soldiers and police on 18 December 1975. FRELIMO was subsequently restructured into a Marxist-Leninist party that tried to revive the chaotic economy. The Marxist-Leninist tactics employed to that end failed and raised the specter of a new dissident group, RENAMO (Mozambican National Resistance [MNR]) (*see* Mozambique), a white Rhodesian-sponsored, later South African-sponsored group that challenged FRELIMO in 1976. By the 1980s, the economy and everyday life in Mozambique were at a standstill because of RENAMO activity and a severe drought. In 1989, the Marxist-Leninist philosophy was dropped by the government, and a new constitution adopted, which went into effect on 30 November 1990. By this point the MNR had killed at least 100,000 and had made nearly two million refugees. On 4 October 1992, a peace accord was signed to end the civil war, and free multiparty elections were held in October 1994. FRELIMO retained control of the country.

Fromme, Lynette "Squeaky." On 5 September 1975, Lynette "Squeaky" Fromme made an attempt on the life of US President Gerald Ford (qv) in Sacramento, California. Fromme had been a member of the Manson family, a cult held together by Charles Manson. In the attack, Fromme pointed a loaded gun at the president from a distance of two feet. She was disarmed by a Secret Service agent before firing a shot and was quickly subdued. Ford was hurriedly taken into the state capitol, where he gave an address on violent crime.

Frondizi, Arturo. (b. 1908, Paso de los Libres, Corrientes, Argentina) Frondizi, a member of the House of Delegates, was sworn in as president of Argentina on 1 May 1958, after winning a landslide election as the Intransigent Radical Party's candidate. His first year in office was marked by a policy of peace and democracy, punctuated with the establishment of trade with communist countries and political unrest at home. His economic programs, especially those aimed at austerity, have been blamed for much of the trouble that emanated from both left and right. In legislative elections in March 1960, his party suffered a crushing defeat. On 28 March 1962, he was ousted from office by a military coup led by General Raúl Poggi. Frondizi was placed under arrest.

Front de Libération Nationale **(FLN).** When the French Assembly refused to listen to a proposal for Algerian independence in 1947 and instead passed legislation binding Algeria to France, the groundwork was laid for a popular uprising among the Algerian people. On 31 October–1 November 1954, the Algerian uprising began after long and careful preparation. The leaders of the revolt took the name FLN and focused their early attacks on isolated police stations. FLN operations also took a political course in which the group worked through several channels, especially out of Cairo, to gain recognition for a free Algeria. On 20 August 1955, the uprising took on more ominous tones following the massacre of Frenchmen near Philippeville (Skikda) and the subsequent executions of a large number of Muslims in the stadium in that city. By 1957, the French had deployed crack airborne troops in Algeria to suppress the widespread terrorism that gripped the country. French overtures toward making an accommodation with the FLN in May 1958 led to French demonstrations in Algiers and to a major political crisis in France. The latter led to Charles DeGaulle's (qv) assumption of power. In October 1958, discussions began with the FLN, the outcome of which was the announcement that Algerians would be given the right to choose their future once order had been restored. This led to another major insurrection among the French in Algeria in January 1960, which quickly collapsed under the pressure of the French army, some 500,000 of whom were deployed in that country. Unrest continued, however, and as no decision could be reached, led to a second French uprising, this time including French military personnel, who protested the notion of a free Algeria. When DeGaulle assumed extraordinary powers on 25–26 April, the revolt collapsed. In March 1962, a cease-fire was arranged and secret negotiations were begun. Independence came to Algeria on 5 July 1962. Almost one million French left the country at that time. The FLN was absorbed into the new government.

Front for the Liberation of Lebanon from Aliens (FLLA). This little-known terrorist organization took credit for a botched car bombing in Sidon, Lebanon, on 17 September 1981. In the incident, a car bomb had been placed outside the PLO command post in Sidon in anticipation of a meeting between PLO officials and leftist Lebanese leaders. The bomb exploded prematurely before any of the dignitaries had arrived. At least 20 people were killed, however, and another 100 injured in the blast.

Front for the Liberation of Lebanon from Foreigners (FLLF). On 28 January 1983, an explosion leveled the security headquarters of the PLO in the Bekaa Valley of Lebanon. The headquarters was within the Syrian-controlled area of the Bekaa. The Front for the Liberation of Lebanon from Foreigners took credit for the attack. The FLLF attacked again on 5 February 1983, when the Palestine Research Center, the site of a PLO office, was the target of a car bombing that killed 10 and injured 40 more. On 7 August, the FLLF claimed credit for a vehicle bomb attack on a crowded market in the Syrian-controlled town of Baalabakk that killed 33 people and injured 133.

Front for the Liberation of South Yemen (FLOSY). On 26 September 1972, South Yemen rebels belonging to FLOSY supported by members of the South Arab League and tribesmen from North Yemen (San'a) attacked al-Dali (Dhala) on the North Yemen-South Yemen border. FLOSY had been banned in the Marxist People's Democratic Republic of Yemen (South Yemen) (PDRY). The September attack led to a general border war between the PDRY and the Yemen

Arab Republic (North Yemen). By November an Arab League mediation council was able to end the fighting (13 October) and to reach a union agreement between the two Yemens (28 November).

Fuad II. Upon the abdication of Farouk I as King of Egypt on 23 July 1952, his infant son, Ahmed Fuad II, became king, with a regency council to rule the country. On 10 February, Mohammed Naguib assumed "supreme powers" and on 18 June 1952, Egypt was declared a republic. Fuad's rule was over.

Fuchs, Klaus Emil Julian (b. 29 December 1911, Rüsselsheim, Germany—d. 28 January 1988, East Germany) On 1 March 1950, German-born Klaus Fuchs, a respected English physicist, who had worked for a time with the American nuclear program at Los Alamos, was found guilty of spying for the Soviet Union. He was specifically charged with transferring nuclear information. Fuchs' arrest came about as a result of the defection of Igor Gouzenko, an official at the Soviet embassy in Ottawa, Canada, on September 1945. British intelligence was able to uncover Fuchs and Alan Nunn, another traitor working for Soviet intelligence within the British nuclear research program, from statements made by Gouzenko. Their revelations may have given the Soviet Union the hydrogen bomb. At the same time that Fuchs was caught, Harry Gold, an American associate, and David and Ruth Greenglass and Julius and Ethel Rosenberg were uncovered as Soviet spies. Fuchs served nine years before being released in 1959. *Reading:* Norman Moss, *Klaus Fuchs: The Man Who Stole the Atom Bomb* (1987); Robert C. Williams, *Klaus Fuchs, Atom Spy* (1988).

Fuentes, Ydigoras. On 2 March 1958, following nine months of political unrest, Ydigoras Fuentes was sworn in as president of Guatemala. On 31 March 1963, the Fuentes government was overthrown by a right-wing coup led by Defense Minister Colonel Enrique Peralta Azurdia. Fuentes' National Democratic Reconciliation Party rule was ended because of his policies, which some saw as leading to a return of communist influence in Guatemala.

***Fuerzas Revolucionarias Armadas Populare* (FRAP).** On 4 May 1973, the U.S. consul in Guadalajara, Mexico, Terence Leahardy, was kidnapped by members of a little-known organization calling itself *Fuerzas Revolucionarias Armadas Populare.* The terrorists demanded a ransom of one million pesos ($80,000), which when paid, on 7 May, secured the release of Leahardy unharmed.

Fujairah. One of the seven kingdoms comprising the United Arab Emirates (qv). In June 1972, tribal warfare broke out over disputed land between Fujairah and Shahjah (qv). About 20 people were killed in the fighting. The dispute was settled by a concilation commission set up by the year-old UAE.

Fukien Province. *See* China.

G

Gabes. *See* Tunisia.

Gabon. The nation of Gabon straddles the Equator on the west coast of Africa. It is bordered by Cameroon and Equatorial Guinea on the north, Congo on the south and east and the Atlantic Ocean on the west. The original inhabitants were people of the Myéné language group. Gabon was first explored by Portuguese traders in the fifteenth century. The slave trade, although abolished in 1815, flourished until 1880, with indigenous natives collecting slaves from other inland tribes and transporting them down the several rivers to ports where they were collected by Dutch, English, French, Portuguese and other slave traders. In 1886 Gabon was incorporated into the colony of French Congo; in 1910 it became a territory of French Equatorial Africa. In World War II, Gabon was occupied by Free French forces and, in 1946, the country was made an overseas territory of France. On 28 November 1958 Gabon became independent within the French Community, and it gained its complete independence as the Gabon Republic on 17 August 1960. On 17–18 February 1964, the government of President Leon Mba was overthrown, but it was restored to power on 19 February following the arrival of French troops flown in to suppress the insurrection. In May 1968, Gabon was among the first African states to recognize the rebellious state of Biafra (qv). Since that time, Gabon prosperity has managed to overcome most obstacles in spite of the country's one-party political system. One of Gabon's greatest contributions to history is the fact that it was the home for many years of the great medical missionary and humanitarian Albert Schweitzer, who maintained his hospital in Lambarn. A multiparty political system was introduced in 1990, and a new constitution was enacted in 1991. However, student strikes and rioting in January 1990 underlined the problem of the lack of fundamental tools of education. After five students were gunned down by police, rioting spread throughout the tiny country. As the rioting spread and escalated, French troops began the evacuation of foreign nationals (May). When the teachers joined the students on strike, it took until September to get the country's schools open. One teacher was killed in a continuation of the clashes with police in March 1992. Violence continued until after the first multiparty elections which were held in December 1993. Omar Bongo was returned to office in what international observers called a fraudulent election. Bongo spent most of 1994 in a state of siege, trying to recoup his power. Many of his political opponents he had under virtual house arrest. By 1995, the political situation had settled somewhat, but the country faced severe economic problems, especially those surrounding the price of food. *Reading:* James F. Barnes, *Gabon: Beyond the Colonial Legacy* (1992).

Gaborone. *See* Botswana.

Gairy, Sir Eric. (b. 18 February 1922, Grenada) Gairy received his education at private schools and served as a school teacher in the late 1930s. He later worked for a Dutch oil refinery on the island of Aruba and there became interested in the the labor movement. After his return to Grenada in 1951 he worked as a labor organizer. That same year, he was elected to Grenada's legislative council. In 1956, he became minister of trade and production. From 1953, Gairy's United Labor Party won almost every election held on the island. In 1961, Gairy became chief minister and minister of finance; he became premier in 1962. On 7 February 1974, Gairy became prime minister of the fully independent government of Grenada. With independence, Grenada was faced with increased violence, strikes and political unrest, all of which seemed to revolve around Gairy and his methods of operation. On an island inhabited by 105,000, Gairy was considered a dictator by a diverse group, including leftists, wealthy landowners and intellectuals, who accused him of ruling through his secret police organization (Mongoose Squad). Many Grenadans fled the country, and tourism fell off dramatically. Gairy's highhanded tactics continued into 1975; new laws were passed to suppress opposition, and the New Jewel Party headquarters were ransacked by Gairy's thugs. Similar looting continued into 1976. Gairy's party was returned to office in the general elections, but with a significantly reduced majority. Regardless of these and other allegations, Gairy was knighted in 1977 by the British Crown. On 13 March 1979, while Gairy was away on a trip, Maurice Bishop (qv) and the New Jewel Party carried out a successful coup that overthrew the Gairy government. The new government immediately established close links with Cuba, but other governments, including the United States, also recognized the new leftist regime in Grenada. Cuba supplied weapons and advisors to help prepare to repel a Gairy-led mercenary invasion of the island. Gairy had apparently secreted large sums of money out of the country in anticipation of just such an eventuality.

Galapagos Islands. *See* Ecuador.

Galilee. *See* Israel, Syria and Jordan.

Galtieri, Leopoldo Fortunato. (b. 1926) Born the son of Italian immigrants to Argentina, Galtieri's entire life centered around the army. Early in 1981, he was appointed commander of the army. One of his first acts was to close the Argentine–Chilean border (29 April 1981) after Chilean police arrested two Argentine army officers on spy charges (25 April). On 11 December 1981, after serving less than one year in office, President Roberto Eduardo Viola was removed from office by a three-man military junta. On 22 December, Lieutenant General Leopoldo Galtieri, one of the junta members, was sworn in as

Argentina's new president. At the same time, he retained the position of army commander. On 2 April 1982, Galtieri and the other junta members made the fateful decision to invade the Falkland Islands (qv). Galtieri's apparent reasoning was twofold: to settle a 150-year-old dispute over ownership of the islands and, and possibly more significant, as a diversion of attention from the ever-worsening economic and political situation at home. Following the disastrous defeat by the British in June 1982, Galtieri resigned as commander of the army (17 June) and was replaced by an interim president the next day. In December 1985, Galtieri and three others were acquitted of charges of murder and human rights violations; nine more were given life or long-term sentences. Galtieri and two of those acquitted were still held on charges stemming from the Falklands fiasco, however, and were tried and convicted of gross incompetence. All three were deprived of their rank and given jail sentences; Galtieri received 12 years (1986).

Galvão, Henrique Malta. On 22 January 1961, a group of anti-Salazar (qv) rebels, led by former Portuguese naval captain Henrique Malta Galvão, hijacked the Portuguese liner *SS Santa Maria* in the Caribbean Sea in the name of Lieutenant General Humberto da Silva Delgado, a former (1958) presidential candidate. There were over 600 passengers on board at the time. The hijacking was apparently part of larger plan for uprisings in Angola (qv) and other Portuguese colonies. None of the other plans were executed, however, and the Salazar government requested assistance in retaking the ship. American and British warships joined the search for the ship in the Atlantic Ocean. The ship landed in Recife, Brazil, on 2 February 1961. No one was injured in the adventure. The hijackers were all given asylum.

Gambia, The. The Republic of The Gambia is an African nation smaller than the state of Connecticut. It is composed of two narrow strips of land on each side of the lower Gambia river where the river enters the Atlantic at the western tip of Africa. The capital city is Bangul. The Gambia is surrounded on three sides by Senegal (qv). The area became the first British colony on the continent in 1598. The Gambia became independent as a dominion of the British Empire on 18 February 1965 and joined the British Commonwealth as a republic in 1970. One of the few functioning democracies in Africa, the country suffered a severe famine in 1977–1978. On 4 December 1980, The Gambia broke diplomatic relations with Libya because of its invasion of Chad. On 30–31 July 1981, an attempted coup led by socialist elements under the leadership of Kukli Samba (qv) took place against the government of Sir Dawda Kairaba Jawara (qv) while he was on a visit to London. Jawara asked and received help from the Senegalese who sent troops into the country (1 August). Order was restored, but not without significant bloodshed. During the fighting the rebels took 135 hostages. On 4–5 August, the Senegalese rescue force crushed the rebel resistance and freed the hostages. On 14 November 1981, the Gambian government announced it had formed a loose federation with Senegal, to be known as Senegambia (qv). The federation came into being on 1 February 1982.

The confederation was dissolved, however, on 30 September 1989, following the unannounced August withdrawal of Senegalese troops that had been in The Gambia since 1981. The governmment then announced that the confederation had not worked and there was no benefit in its continuation. In 1990, The Gambia joined in peacekeeping operations in Liberia. A treaty of friendship and cooperation was signed with Senegal on 8 January 1991 that renewed relations between the two countries, strained since the dissolution of the federation in 1989. When civil war broke out in Senegal in 1992, Gabon became the haven for refugees fleeing the fighting. On 7 April 1993, The Gambia undertook the unusual step of abolishing the death sentence. This was in line with its announced policy of preserving human rights. At about the same time, opposition party leaders who had fled the country following the 1981 coup attempt were allowed to return. Amid these signs of democratization, a military coup overthrew the government on 22 July 1994. The president, Sir Dawda Jawara, and his family sought sanctuary on an American naval vessel and subsequently sought asylum in Senegal. The coup was caused by military pay disputes. Lieutenant Yahya Jammeh took control of the country and, as a first act, suspended all political activity. There was a new coup attempt to restore civilian government in January 1995. Its failure led to the arrest of two officers of the ruling junta and the subsequent dismissal and arrest of other senior officials. By October a number of citizens had been arrested for advocating civilian rule. Elections promised for 1996 failed to materialize as promised, but when they did take place, the elections were so contrived that Jammeh easily won election as president. *See also* Senegal. *Reading:* Michael Tomkinson, *Gambia* (1995); Philip Koslow, *Senegambia: Land of the Lion* (1996); David P. Gamble, *The Gambia (World Bibiographical Series, No. 91)* (1988).

Gamil Airport, Sinai. *See* Israel.

Gandhi, Indira. (b. 19 November 1917, Allahabad—d. 31 October 1984, Delhi) Born the only child of Kamala and Jawaharlal Nehru (qv) (later prime minister), Indira Gandhi joined the Indian independence movement at age 12, being active in the so-called Monkey Army made up of children who ran errands in the nonviolent resistance against the British Raj. She received a sporadic education in India and Switzerland, studied art and dancing at the Indian university at Santiniketan in 1934 and later attended Oxford in England. In March 1942, she married Feroze Gandhi, a man she had met during her studies in England. In that same year, she and her husband were arrested in India for speaking out against the British in the "Quit India" campaign. After Indian independence in 1947, Gandhi toured the refugee camps to aid the victims of the Hindu–Muslim religious war. She also accompanied Jawaharlal Nehru on his visits around the world, and on his election campaigns at home. During the 18-year marriage the couple had two sons, Rajiv (qv) and Sanjay. Feroze Gandhi died in 1960. In 1959, Indira Gandhi became the president of the Indian National Congress (INC), the majority political party in India. After Prime Minister Nehru's death in May 1964, Indira Gandhi became minister of information in the government of Lal Bahadur Shastri (qv), the man who succeeded him. When Shastri died on 11 January 1966, she was elected prime minister by the INC (18 January). She was returned to office in general elections held in 1967 and 1971. During her tenure as prime minister, India was involved in border disputes with Pakistan and with Communist China. At home, crop failures led to food riots and widespread resistance to her programs. There was severe resistance from the many other language groups in India to her adoption of Hindi as the national language. In 1971, Gandhi led India through a successful war with Pakistan over the separation of East Pakistan, later Bangladesh (qv), and West Pakistan (qv). In June 1975, Indira was convicted of two counts of corruption in the 1971 elections. She appealed the verdict, but as she was still prime minister, Gandhi declared a national emergency, arrested hundreds of opposition leaders and forced Parliament to amend the election laws retroactively. Obviously, she was subsequently found innocent of the corruption charges. Gandhi then moved to change the constitution so as to give her much broader powers. She was, however, defeated in a parliamentary election in 1977 and resigned. Gandhi was reelected to Parliament in 1978, but she was soon expelled and jailed. Even though she was under investigation on misconduct charges, Gandhi won a landslide victory that returned her to office in 1980. One of her first moves was to dissolve the assemblies in nine states and place their administration under the central government. In February 1982, talks with opposition leaders and Sikh separatists collapsed after rioting broke out between Hindus and Sikhs in Punjab. She was assassinated by two Sikh bodyguards outside her home on 31 October 1984. Her son, Rajiv (qv), succeeded her as prime minister that same day. Following her murder, widespread rioting broke out in which at least 2,000 Sikhs were killed. Order was restored only after Indians troops entered nine cities, including New Delhi. *Reading:* Francella Butler, *Indira Gandhi* (1987); Dilip Bobb & Ashok Raina, *The Great Betrayal: Assassination of Indira Gandhi* (1985).

Gandhi, Mohandes Karamchand (Mahatma). (b. 2 October 1869, Kathiawar—d. 30 January 1948, New Delhi) Mohandes Gandhi was one of the great leaders of modern times, possibly of all time. At 12 years of age, as was the custom, he was married. He studied law in London and was admitted to the bar in 1891. Gandhi practiced in Bombay and Rajkot in India, but being unsuccessful, he moved to South Africa, where he became the first so-called "coloured" lawyer admitted to the supreme court. In 1894 he formed the Natal Indian Congress to aid the plight of fellow Indians in that country. Still loyal to Great Britain, in 1899, during the Boer War, Gandhi raised an ambulance corps. In 1906 he served the South African government during the Zulu uprising. In that same year Gandhi began his nonviolence campaign by stating he would go to prison before obeying any anti-Asian law. He was soon surrounded by thousands of his countrymen who joined in the peaceful revolution. He was jailed twice during this period. In 1914, however, he again raised an ambulance corps to serve the British cause before returning to India. In 1919 he formed the Indian National Congress

(National (I) Congress) (INC) and began the long campaign for Indian independence. In 1920 he began the noncooperation campaign and urged a boycott of British goods and the court system. He was imprisoned from 1922 until 1924. In 1930 he led thousands of Indians in a 200-mile march to the sea to make their own salt. Some observers called him a master politican; others began to call him Mahatma ("Great Soul,") and saw him as a saint. In 1934 he gave up leadership of the National (I) Congress but he remained its actual leader until his death. During World War II, he demanded immediate Indian independence (1942). He was again imprisoned, this time until 1944. Although a man of great gentleness, Gandhi had an iron determination and nothing could change his convictions. An devout Hindu, he worked tirelessly to mend the ill feelings between Hindus and Moslems. This truly remarkable man was shot and killed by a religious fanatic on 30 January 1948. *Reading:* Leonard E. Fisher, *Gandhi* (1995); Catherine Bush, ed., *Gandhi* (1987); April Carter, *Mahatma Gandhi* (1995).

Gandhi, Rajiv. (b. 20 August 1944, Bombay, India—d. 21 May 1991, Sriperumbudur, Tamil Nadu, India) Rajiv Gandhi was born the eldest of two sons of Feroze and Indira Gandhi (qv). His education included the Welham's School and the Doon School in Dehra Dun and St. Columba School in New Delhi. In Delhi, Rajiv lived with his mother and brother in the official residence of the prime minister, Jawaharlal Nehru (qv), his grandfather. He was then sent to England to study engineering at Cambridge. He failed to finish the program, however, but he did meet and marry (25 February 1968) an Italian girl, Sonia Maino. Thereafter, until May 1981, Rajiv flew for Indian Airlines as a domestic airline pilot. During that period, in mid-1980, his younger brother, Sanjay, was killed in an airplane accident. Sanjay, a politician, had just won a seat in the Parliament (*Lok Sabha*, House of the People). After his brother's death, Rajiv was prevailed upon to stand for election and won Sanjay's vacant seat in a virtual landslide on 15 June 1981. That same month he was appointed to the national executive council of the Youth Congress. In February 1983, Indira Gandhi appointed him secretary of the Congress (I) Party and he became more and more deeply involved in political life. Following the assassination of his mother in October 1984, Rajiv was named prime minister of India. On 12 November, he was unanimously elected president of the Congress Party. On 13 November, he called for new elections, which were held on 24 December 1984. Rajiv was elected in an unprecedented landslide. His leadership proved less than effective, however, and his popularity waned. In 1987, he sent an Indian peacekeeping force to the troubled island of Sri Lanka (Ceylon) (qv), setting off massive problems at home and lowering his esteem around the world. In 1989, the Congress (I) Party lost control of Parliament amid scandals, not all of which focused on Gandhi. On 21 May 1991, while he campaigned for reelection as prime minister, he was killed by an assassin's bomb, probably one planted by members of the Liberation Tigers of Tamil Eelam, a terrorist organization of Sri Lanka. *Reading:* Ved Mehta, *Rajiv Gandhi and Rama's Kingdom* (1995).

"Gang of Four." On 12 October 1976, the newly seated Chinese Communist government of Hua Kuo-feng (qv) ordered the arrest of four prominent citizens, including Jiang Qing (Chiang Ch'ing) (qv), the wife of the late Mao Tse-tung (qv), on charges of plotting a military takeover of the country. Mao had died on 2 September, and Hua had assumed power on 5 October, only five days before the arrest order. The order opened another phase of a power struggle that had begun in late 1975. The other three participants in the "Gang of Four" were Zhang Chunqiao (Chang Ch'un-ch'iao), Wang Hongwen (Wang Hung-wen) and Yao Wenyuan (Yao Wen-yuan). Although all four were known as ultraleftists while Mao was still alive, they were now accused of being "ultrarightists and counterrevolutionaries." In fact, the arrest was the first move in purging the party of pro-Maoist sympathizers in order to consolidate power the new government and to discredit the Cultural Revolution. The group was tried in November 1980, and the guilty sentences were announced in January 1981. Jiang and Zhang Chunqiao, the former mayor of Shanghai, were sentenced to death; the other two were given lesser sentences. Jiang and Zhang were accorded a two-year suspension of sentence to atone for their crimes and confess their treason. In effect, Wang, who was given life imprisonment, and Yao, who received 20 years hard labor, were handed more determinant and severe sentences. *Reading:* David Bonavia, *Verdict in Peking: The Trial of the Gang of Four* (1984).

Gan Island. *See* Maldives Republic.

Gara Marda Pass. *See* Ethiopia.

Garcia, Carlos. Upon the death of President Ramon Magsaysay (qv) in an airplane crash on 17 March 1957, Carlos Garcia, the vice president of the Philippines, became president. Garcia and his Nationalist Party were confirmed in a popular election held on 12 November 1957. He was defeated for reelection, however, on 14 November 1961.

Garcia Meza Tejada, Luis. On 17 July 1980, a military coup led by General Luis Garcia Meza Tejada took control of Bolivia to prevent the seating of the left-wing Hernan Siles Zuaro (qv) who was to be sworn in by the Bolivian Congress on 4 August. Garcia claimed Silas was a communist and set aside the results of the election as a fraud. On 18 July, Garcia heading a new military junta that was to rule the country, declared himself president. There were many arrests of opponents and reports of torture of opposition leaders; universities were closed and judges dismissed. A state of seige was was declared. Pressure from most other South American countries and the United States took the form of swift diplomatic and economic action against the junta. However, several South American countries and some foreign ones (Israel, South Africa and Taiwan) as well recognized Garcia's regime. On 4 August 1981, Garcia could no longer cling to power and, after some negotiation, he resigned. There had been at least five coup attempts against him, the economy was in a shambles, and Bolivia was all but totally isolated from the outside world. A nacent civil war also brewed between a growing rebel force and the government. Garcia was replaced by General Celso Torrelio Villa.

García-Gody, Héctor. On 31 August 1965, following the intervention of an OAS inter-American force to stop the civil war that was raging, Héctor García-Gody was installed as provisional president of the Dominican Republic (took office on 3 September). He remained in office until 1 July 1966, when Joaquín Balaguer (qv) was sworn in as the constitutionally elected president.

Garcia Meza, Luis. On 5 August 1981, Bolivia's president and head of the military junta, General Luis Garcia Meza, was forced to resign in a bloodless military coup. He had withstood a number of other coup attempts after seizing power in July 1980. He was alleged to have had ties with the international drug trade, and his tenure was marked by severe repression. At the moment of his ouster, Bolivia was on the verge of civil war. *See* Bolivia.

Gaza (Ghazzah). The name of an ancient town in Palestine that was located 50 miles southwest of Jerusalem (qv) and 40 miles southwest of Tel Aviv–Jaffa (qv). It was the most important of the five Philistine centers and was captured by Alexander the Great (332 B.C.). For a time the city rivaled Alexandria and Athens as the center of the Hellenistic world. The city is located three miles inland from the Mediterranean and is the most important city in the Gaza Strip (Qita Ghazzah). In more modern times, Gaza was under Turkish rule from 1516 until 1917 and under British rule from 1917 until 1948. A UN General Assembly decision of November 1947 gave the Gaza Strip to the Arabs. When the British Mandate for Palestine was vacated on 15 May 1948, the British withdrew; after some fighting in the Israeli War of Independence, the area was occupied by the Egyptians. The period until 1954 was relatively peaceful in Gaza. In 1955, Israel launched a surprise attack against the Gaza Strip, for which the Egyptians loosed a guerrilla (*fidayun* or *fedayeen*) campaign against Israel that began in April 1956. During the subsequent October 1956 Arab-Israeli War, the Israelis occupied Gaza (2 November). The city was evacuated after the UN inserted an emergency force on 1 March 1957. The Egyptians did, however, take over the administration of the city. In March 1957, the UN mined the demarcation strip between the Arabs and Israelis in the Gaza Strip. The situation stabilized somewhat until 1967 when, in response to threats made by Egypt's Nasser (qv), the UN protective force withdrew (19 May) from the Gaza-Sharm esh-Sheikh (qv) region. By that point the entire Middle East was poised for war. The Six Day Arab-Israeli War began on 5 June 1967. The Israelis quickly took their Gaza Strip objectives (6 June). On 22 November 1967, the UN Security Council adopted Resolution 242, calling for Israeli withdrawal from Jerusalem and the Gaza Strip in return for a lasting peace. Before Israel could react, the Arabs rejected the offer. In February 1969, Arab demonstrations were staged against the Israelis in Gaza. This violence continued into 1970. In March 1980, the UN Security Council voted unanimously to order Israeli settlements in the two territories dismantled. In December 1978, Israel's prime minister Begin (qv) said Israel would abide by the Camp David agreement. Plans for autonomous zones in Gaza and the West Bank would be followed. However, in January 1979, three new Israeli settlements were laid down in the disputed territories. In November 1982, the PLO Central Council meeting in Damascus rejected a U.S.-sponsored proposal that a homeland be established in the two territories. Six years later, on 15 November 1988, the PLO approved the UN resolutions recognizing Israel's right to exist and declared a national Palestinian state. In return, the PLO expected to create a Palestinian homeland in the West Bank (qv) and in the Gaza Strip. Plans for free elections in the territories were developed but never implemented (1989) because of continued terrorist violence on both sides by those opposed to any rapprochement. By October 1993, however, there were signs that a Middle East peace settlement might be close at hand. Israeli occupation of Gaza formally ended on 17 May 1994. About 9,000 Palestinian police took over control of Gaza (and Jericho). Israeli troops remained to protect 140 Jewish settlements, however, which laid the groundwork for future confrontations. Arafat returned to Gaza on 1 July 1994 in the face of an almost total lack of government structure, massive economic problems, and the opposition of several large and vicious Palestinian groups such as Hamas and the Islamic Jihad. A new terrorist campaign began, aimed at disrupting the already blighted peace process. In November, 19 Hamas and Islamic Jihad demonstrators were killed by Palestinian police in Gaza. The Israeli-PLO demands on each other almost were impossible to achieve, given the circumstances. By 1995, terrorist attacks, bombings and shellings prompted the Israelis periodically to close the frontier, which added to the economic burdens in Gaza but also began shifting Arab opinion away from blaming Israel for all regional problems and placing blame at the doorstep of Arab obstructionist groups. *Reading:* Ziad Abu-Amr, *Islamic Fundamentalism in the West Bank and Gaza: Muslim Brotherhood and Islamic Jihad* (1994).

Gdansk. *See* Poland.

Gdynia. *See* Poland.

Gemayle, Amin. (b. 1942 [?]) One week after the assassination (14 September 1982) of his younger brother, president-elect Bashir Gemayle (qv), 40-year-old Amin Gemayle was elected president of Lebanon (21 September 1982). Trained as a lawyer and a member of the Christian (Maronite) Phalangist Party, Gemayle was among his peers classified as a "dove." He had managed to maintain contacts among the Muslim opposition and among the Palestinians during his 12 years in the Lebanese parliament before his election. During Amin's first few days in office, the UN multinational force moved into Beirut, as the occupying Israeli forces began their withdrawal. In mid-July 1983, he visited the United States as conditions were worsening in Lebanon. On 7 September 1983, Gemayle asked President Reagan for assistance in controlling the fighting in Lebanon, especially in the Shouf Mountains. The U.S. had already deployed a naval task force to the vicinity. On 8 September, naval gunfire, first from a frigate and later from the *USS New Jersey,* helped control the ground activity. On 7 February 1984, opposition forces, especially Shi'ite Muslims, demanded Gemayle's ouster, but to no avail. From 1984 to 1988, Gemayle attempted various coalitions to bring peace, but with little success. Gemayle remained in office until 23 September

1988. As the Parliament had not scheduled elections, there was no replacement when he left office. Instead, he was forced to establish a military government under the Christian militia commander, Michel Aoun. *See* Lebanon.

Gemayle, Bashir. (b. 10 November 1947, Bickfawa, near Beirut, Lebanon - d. 14 September 1982, East Beirut) The son of Pierre Gamayle, the founder of the Christian Phalangist Party in Lebanon, In 1980, Bashir led the Maronite wing of the party in 1980 when it captured control of the Christian Phalangist movement by literally destroying the opposition in a two-day gun battle in which at least 80 died. Unlike his older brother Amin (qv), Bashir favored partition in Lebanon and was not above violence to achieve his aims. Bashir also cooperated with Israel when it suited his purposes. Nor apparently was assassination beyond his scope, as he was thought to be instrumental in the death of Tony Franjieh (June 1978), the son of Suleiman Franjieh (qv), former president of Lebanon and archenemy of Bashir through a split in the Maronite community. Bashir's election on 24 August 1982 was precipitated by the retirement of President Elias Sarkis (qv). On 14 September 1982, ten days before he was to assume office, Bashir Gemayle was assassinated when a bomb placed in the Phalangist headquarters in East Beirut detonated.

Geneva. *See* Switzerland.

German Democratic Republic. *See* East Germany and Germany.

Germany. Germany is located in Central Europe and is bordered by Denmark on the north, by Czeckoslovakia and Poland on the east, Austria and Switzerland on the south, and Belgium, France, Netherlands and Luxembourg on the west. The capital city is Berlin. Inhabited since prehistoric times, Germanic tribes indigenous to the region were conquered by Julius Caesar (55–53 B.C.), and Roman movements in the area continued until the ninth century A.D. During the Carolingian period German lands were consolidated into the Frankish empire, and the eastern portion later became the German empire. After the Thirty Years' War (1618–1648), Germany was again divided into a number of duchies and principalities. In the Seven Weeks War (1866), Prussia triumphed over Austria, and Otto von Bismarck formed the North German Confederation. After defeating France in the Franco-Prussian War (1870–1871), a new German Empire was founded, and Wilhelm I was proclaimed kaiser (emperor or caesar). Germany was at its zenith before World War I, but the experience of the lost war left Germany with its empire shattered. The Weimar Republic lasted from 1919 until 1933. During that time the country began a modest economic recovery but it was also torn by political strife as the Nazi party and Adolf Hitler grew in power. Hitler was named chancellor in 1933. When Hindenberg died, Hitler was named president, and the world was set on a collision course for another world war. World War II began with Germany's unprovoked attack on Poland on 1 September 1939. Six years later, Germany was almost totally destroyed, and the course of world history had been changed forever. As an outcome of the war, four-power occupation of Germany began with the USSR administering the area of Saxony, Saxony-Anhalt, Mecklenberg, North East Prussia and Thuringia—or

East Germany (qv) — while the western Allies occupied the western region—or West Germany (qv). The area east of the Oder–Neisser Line was given to Poland — also under Soviet domination. An area of greater Berlin was also created and was administered by the Four Powers *Kommandantura*. In 1948, the USSR withdrew from this arrangement and established its own command in East Berlin. The Soviets then cut off all land resupply of West Berlin, the Allied sectors, and forced the inauguration of the Berlin Airlift (qv), which brought all necessities into the city. The Soviets lifted the blockade in 1949. In 1961, the Berlin Wall was constructed in attempt to staunch the flow of East Germans to the West. The wall remained in existence until 1989. Talks on German reunification began in Ottawa, Canada, in February 1990. In May 1990, Germany was voted full membership in NATO. This decision was approved by the USSR in 1 July 1990. Reunification became official on 3 October. The first all-German elections were held on 2 December 1990. Chancellor Helmut Kohl became the first leader of a reunited Germany. All was not well, however, as the new Germany found itself caught in a downward spiral caused primarily by the need for especially heavy subsidies to the former East German provinces. In 1992, Erich Honecker, the former East German leader who had fled to Moscow, was returned to Berlin to face homicide and corruption charges. The homicide charges stemmed from the "shoot to kill" orders issued to East German border guards. Honecker's trial began in November 1992, but the charges were dropped on 12 January 1993 because of his failing health (terminal liver cancer), and he was allowed to fly to Chile. That year scandal rocked the government of Helmut Kohl, and the economy and politics overshadowed the growing debate over the German constitution and the country's role in NATO. By law, German troops were forbidden to operate outside of German territory, and the growing problem in Bosnia demanded a larger German contribution. Opposition leaders finally gave a grudging acknowledgment, but not without a codicil that they were not approving the extension of German military power. In October 1993, Germany ratified the European Community's Maastricht Treaty. Here again, however, the approval was conditioned on further parliamentary action. There was some economic recovery in 1994 and, on 12 July 1994, the German courts permitted German troops to participate in international peacekeeping and peacemaking operations. *See also* East and West Germany. *Reading:* John Ardagh & Katarina Ardagh, *Germany and the Germans: The United Germany of the Mid-1990s* (1996); Elizabeth Pond, *After the Wall: American Policy toward Germany* (1991); Marc Fisher, *After the Wall: Germany, the Germans and the Burdens of History* (1995).

Gero, Erno (aka Erno Singer). (b. 8 July 1898 Budapest—d. 12 March 1980, Budapest) On 25 October 1956, Erno Gero, a Stalinist communist, was ousted as the secretary of the Hungarian Communist Party in fulfillment of a demand from the Freedom Fighters, who were attempting to rid themselves of the Soviet yoke. Gero had replaced Mátyás Rákosi (qv) as party secretary on 18 July 1956 on orders from Moscow. Dissension in Hungary grew under Gero and finally erupted on 23 October 1956, when a peaceful demonstration for human rights and democracy in Hungary (qv) grew unruly and, at the communist leader's orders, police and army troops fired on the crowds. This was the start of the Hungarian Uprising. Even though out of power at the time, Gero was the person who, asked for Soviet intervention, probably at Moscow's urging.

Geshir (Gesher). *See* Israel.

Ghalib bin Ali. In 1954–1955, Sheikh Ghalib bin Ali, the imam of the tribes of Muscat and Oman, broke a treaty (1920) with the sultan and attempted to establish a separate principality with Saudi Arabian aid. Sultan Saiyid Daid bin Taimur was able to dislodge Ghalib from the capital (Nazwa), but Ghalib was able to gather forces and begin a military campaign against him. The sultan asked for and received British aid, and Ghalib was forced to flee first to Al Jabal al Akhdar and then (1959) to Saudi Arabia.

Ghana. Ghana was formed from the British colony of Gold Coast and a part of the British trusteeship of Togoland. Ghana is bordered on the north by Burkina Faso, on the east by the Togo Republic and on the west by Ivory Coast. The Atlantic Ocean constitutes the southern boundary of Ghana. The capital city is Accra. The central area of the country is covered by an artificial body of water called Lake Volta. The region has been occupied since prehistoric times. A black empire flourished along the Niger River from the fourth until the thirteenth century, but there is no real evidence as to its exact location (probably to the north of Ghana's present boundaries). The area was explored by Portuguese adventurers in 1471. As the principal commodity found there was gold, the name Gold Coast became the region's name until it was changed to Ghana in 1957. Slaves later became another important commodity after the Portuguese hegemony gave way to a broad spectrum of European interest. Permanent military encampments were set up by the British, Dutch and Danes that existed into the mid-eighteenth century. After a major weakening of the native Ashanti tribes, a British colony was declared in 1874. The Ashanti were finally pacified in 1895. Under British rule the colony prospered. The two world wars had little effect on Gold Coast except to mature, especially after World War II, the desire for independence. A nationalist uprising began on 25 February 1948, but it was quickly suppressed by British troops. On 6 March 1957, Ghana became an independent nation, based upon a 1956 UN decision. Republic status within the Commonwealth was conferred in 1960. Also, on 24 December 1960, the presidents of Guinea (qv), Mali (qv) and Ghana signed an agreement signifying the union of the three nations (signed at Conakry). On 7 January 1961, Ghana, Guinea, Mali, Morocco (qv) and the United Arab Republic (UAR) (qv) formed an organization of African states based upon a NATO formula. This became the Charter of Casablanca (qv). In January 1962, Ghana and the other charter nations boycotted a meeting held in Lagos, Nigeria, in which the leaders of 20 African states agreed to form a another organization of African states outside the Charter of Casablanca. On 16 June 1962, a military command was established for the Casablanca states with an Egyptian in command and its headquarters in

Ghana. Unrest broke out in Ghana in 1964, with a major anti-American demonstration on 4 February. Although the government formally apologized to the U.S. on 7 February, it refused to accept responsibility for the demonstration. On 3 December 1965, the government broke relations with Great Britain over the Rhodesian affair. Then, on 24 February 1966, the government of President Kwame Nkrumah (qv) was ousted by a military and police coup led by Lieutenant Colonel Joseph Ankrah (qv). The coup also ejected all Chinese and East German teachers and technicans in the country. Nkrumah was, in fact, in Communist China at the time of the coup. Elections were held in 1969, but they were followed by four more coups and attempted coups, the last two (1979, failed; 1981, successful) led by Flight Lieutenant Jerry Rawlings (qv). In September 1978, the government expelled a number of Soviet and East German diplomatic officials for aiding and abetting unrest among students and unionists in the country. On 1 January 1982, Rawlings was established as head of the ruling Provisional National Defense Council. Former President Hilla Limann was arrested. Unrest during the rest of that year led to a mutiny among troops stationed outside Accra. Troops loyal to Rawlings quelled the uprising. On 2 March 1983, another attempt was made to overthrow Rawlings, but it failed, as did still another attempt on 19 June. In 1992, Rawlings announced a return to civilian rule by January 1993. He also lifted the ban on political parties in May 1992. In a disputed presidential election in November, Rawlings was elected. When the opposition boycotted the legislative elections, Rawling's supporters took almost all (189 of 200) the seats. Rawlings was still in power in 1994, when ethnic fighting broke out in northern Ghana. At least 1,000 were killed and 150,000 forced to flee when two tribal groups clashed over land rights. Fighting ended only when troops were deployed in the area. Rawlings announced that incidents of this type might force Ghana to withdraw its peacekeeping forces in Liberia to bolster its forces at home. Violence of a different kind occurred in 1995, when rioting followed announcement of a 17.5 percent value-added tax (VAT) as a part of the budget. The violence forced the government to back away from the tax plan. In February 1995, the government announced an amnesty for a number of prisoners. At the same time, however, violence broke out once again in the north, this time among coalitions of tribes. Over 200,000 were forced to flee the war zone. *Reading:* Laverie Bennette Berry, *Ghana: A Country Study* (1996); David Apter, *Ghana in Transition* (1973); Jeffery Herbst & Smadar Lavie, *The Politics of Reform in Ghana, 1982–1991* (1992).

al-Ghasmi, Ahmed. On 24 June 1978, North Yemen president Ahmed Al-Ghasmi was assassinated in Beirut, Lebanon. He was there attending a meeting with an envoy of South Yemeni president Salem Ali Rubayyi (qv). Al Ghasmi was killed by a bomb hidden in an attache case carried by the South Yemeni envoy.

Ghavam, Ahmad. Upon the ouster of Mohammed Mossadegh (qv) as premier of Iran, Ahmad Ghavam was installed in that office on 17 July 1952. Five days later, in the wake of bloody rioting, Ghavam was removed and replaced by Mossadegh.

Ghazni. *See* Afghanistan.

Ghaziye. *See* Lebanon.

Ghiorghiu-Dej, (Gheorghe-Dej) Gheorghe. (b. 8 November 1901, Barlad, Romania—d. 19 March 1965, Bucharest) Following World War I Ghiorghiu-Dej became a revoltionary and joined the then-outlawed Romanian Communist Party in 1930. He was arrested for his part in a railwat strike in 1933 and sentenced to 12 years imprisonment. Having escaped from prison in 1944, Ghiorghiu-Dej was the the secretary general of the communist party when the anti-Fascist uprising began on 23 August 1944. He became a minister in the first government and was instrumental in aligning the newly-liberated Romania with the Soviet Union in the continuing war against Germany. He took part in the ouster of the government of Nicolar Radescu in 1945, which cleared the way for the establishment of communist-controlled rule. Ghiorghiu-Dej held several important posts, especially in economic planning, until 1952. Ghiorghiu-Dej then took part in the purge of Romanian communists too closely associated with the Soviet Union and emerged as prime minister. Setting his own course, he led Romania along a nationalist socialist course which was often at odds with Soviet policies. He resigned as prime minister in 1955, but was appointed president of the State Council in 1961. Ghiorghiu-Dej then took an even more independent course and was often at odds with Romania's communist neighbors. In one instance, speaking as the secretary of the Romanian Communist Party. Ghiorghiu-Dej proposed the creation of a neutral buffer zone in the Balkans in a speech before the United Nations on 27 September 1960. He died in 1965.

Ghoddusi, Ayatollah Ali. On 2 November 1980, Iranian Prosecutor General Ayatollah Ali Ghoddusi was killed in a bomb explosion. This attack was tied to the internal tensions in Iran caused by the rule of the Ayatollah Khomeini (qv).

Ghotbzadeh, Sadegh. (b. 1936—d. 15 September 1982, Tehran) On 7 April 1982, former foreign minister Sadegh Ghotbzadeh was arrested and accused of plotting the assassination of the Ayatollah Khomeini. On 15 September, Ghotbzadeh and about 70 others were executed by firing squad for their alleged involvement in the plot. Ghotbzadeh had served as foreign minister from November 1979 until August 1980. Educated in the United States and England, he was a leader of the opposition to the rule of Shah Reza Pahlavi (qv) and a close associate of National Front leader Mohammed Mossadegh (qv). He spent time with the Ayatollah Khomeini during his exile in France and became an ardent supporter of the Ayatollah. Ghotbzadeh was the director of Iranian Radio and Television and was appointed foreign minister after the U.S. hostage crisis began. He resigned because of an impasse in negotiations over the hostages' release. He was arrested briefly in 1980 for criticizing the Islamic Republican Party and retired from public life, where he remained until his last arrest and executio...

Giang River. *See* Vietnam.

Gibraltar. Mount Tarik (*Jabal al-Tarik*) was captured by Tarik ibn Said in 7'1 A.D. and was named in his honor. Gibraltar is a derivative of a Muslim name. In mythology Gibraltar was the *Pillars of Hercules*. To the Romans it was *Mons*

Calpe. The mount guards the western end of the Mediterranean Sea and the strait that separates Gibraltar from Mount Acho on the North African coast separates the Mediterranean from the Atlantic Ocean. Gibraltar has a long history of conflict. It was raided by the Normans in the ninth century and was held by the Moors until taken by the Castilians in 1309. The Moors retook it in 1333 and held it until 1462. Gibraltar was annexed by Spain in 1501 and was considered impregnable for a century before Hapsburg neglect allowed it to deteriorate. The British occupied Gibraltar during the War of Spanish Succession (1701–1713) in 1704–1705. England gained complete control of "The Rock," as it became known in 1711, in a secret agreement with France that nullified Dutch and Spanish claims. In subsequent decades the Spanish and French tried, without success, to recapture Gibraltar. In 1830, it became a crown colony. Gibraltar played a significant role in World War II and was considerably strengthened to meet the needs of modern warfare. In 1954, the visit of Elizabeth II (qv) and her family evoked serious anti-British demonstrations throughout Spain and caused a Spanish blockade of the land route over the isthmus that connects Gibraltar to the Spanish mainland. This blockade continued intermittently until 1964, when the Spaniards closed the frontier, which was accomplished by October 1966. Spain took these actions because of what they felt was an improper British action—the new Gibraltar constitution of August 1964—which they felt abrogated the Peace of Utrecht that ended the War of Spanish Succession in 1713. Subsequent negotiation ameliorated many of the Spanish complaints, but on 5 May 1968, the Spaniards once again closed the border. On 18 December 1968, based on earlier resolutions against colonialism, the United Nations voted to return Gibraltar to Spanish control on 1 October 1969. Other events interceded, however, and, in retaliation for the British publication of a new constitution (effective May 1969) for Gibraltar that followed a 1968 constitutional conference, Spain again imposed a blockade (7 June 1969) along *"La Linea,"* the Spanish-Gibraltan border. Great Britain rejected the the December 1968 UN resolution. On 27 June, Spain cut the Algeciras ferry service between the mainland and Gibraltar. As a further provocation, Spanish warships entered Gibraltan waters on 29 September; on 1 October, all telephone and cable links from the mainland were cut, and Spain set up a blockade of Gibraltar's harbor. In Gibraltar, the populace began an "Integration with Britain Party" that stressed no change without the Gibraltans' consent. The blockade continued until 27 November 1984, when an agreement was reached to hold negotiations on the future of Gibraltar, beginning in February 1985. On 4 February 1985, the border was opened for the first time in 15 years as a precursor to the talks. The talks began the following day; economic ties were reestablished, but air links were not. The airport dispute was settled on 2 December 1987 when joint civilian use was approved, but not without opposition among the Gibraltans. On 6 March 1988, a Special Air Service (SAS) counterterrorist team engaged and killed three Irish Republican Army terrorists on Gibraltar. In 1989, the British reduced their military force strength on Gibraltar, but there was no lessening of the strained relations with Spain. In 1990, Spain claimed that Gibraltar had become a major drug trafficking port and that the banks there were heavily involved in drug money laundering. At the same time, the Gibraltans rejected any notion of integration with Spain. In March 1991, the last British military force departed Gibraltar, leaving only the local militia regiment to secure the enclave. The European Community offered Gibraltar its protection (1991) as a dependency as a move to break the Anglo-Spanish impasse. Gibraltar, for its part, wanted an end to its colonial status (1992) and independence. Meetings on Gibraltar were held between Britain and Spain (March 1993) for the first time in two years. This angered the Gibraltans, as they were not invited to participate in their own future. In June 1995, Spain formally accused Gibraltar of having become a center of the illicit drug trade in Europe and put tighter controls on their border checkpoints. *Reading:* Dennis S. Morris & Robert Haigh, *Britain, Spain and Gibraltar, 1945–90: The Eternal Triangle* (1992).

Giddi (Gidi) Pass, Sinai. *See* Israel.

Gierek, Edward (Edvard). (b. 6 January 1913, Porabka, Bedzin, Russian Poland) Gierek was the son of a Polish miner. After his father's death in an accident, Gierek emigrated to France with his mother. In France he worked as a coal miner and, in 1931, joined the French communist party. He was expelled from France for his party activities and returned to Poland. He was called into military service after he arrived in Poland. He later emigrated to Belgium where he worked in the Limbourg mines. During the German occupation of Belgium he joined the Belgian underground (1943). After the war, he organized the Union of Polish Patriots and became the leader of the Polish section of the Belgian communist party. He returned to Poland in 1948 and picked up his party activities in Katowice province. He took a degree in mining and metallurgy at Cracow in 1951 and was elected a member of the Polish parliament (*Sejm*) in 1952. In March 1954 he was elected to the central committee of the Polish communist party. On 20 December 1970, Wladyslaw Gomulka (qv) and other members of the Politburo of the Polish United Workers' (Communist) Party were forced to resign. Edward Gierek was named as the new party secretary. Gierek had spent 13 years as the first secretary of a Katowice provincial party organization and had been a member of the Politburo since 19 March 1959. Gierek's first move as party secretary was to promise Polish workers a modest pay raise and a revision of the five-year plan (1971–1975). As unrest grew in Poland, Gierek was forced to take a harder stand. On 11 July 1980, for instance, Gierek told Polish workers they would have to pay higher prices for commodities and had to stop demonstrating for higher wages. On 6 September 1980, after a strike had paralyzed the country, Gierek was dismissed as head of the communist party. Keith J. Lepac, *Prelude to Solidarity: Poland and the Politics of the Gierek Regime* (1988).

Gifgafa, Bir. *See* Israel.

Gilan. *See* Iran.

Gilboa, Amos. *See* Israel.

Gio Linh District. *See* Vietnam.

Giscard d'Estaing, Valery. (b. 2 February 1926, Koblenz) Giscard was born into a landowning family and studied at the Lycée Janson-de-Sailly in Paris. His later education was taken at the École Polytechnique and at the École Nationale d'Administration, where he graduated in 1951. He was appointed inspector of finances in 1954 and was elected to the Chamber of Deputies in 1956. In 1959, he served in the Ministry of Economy and Finance, the last nine as its minister. In 1967–1968, he served as the chairman of the finance committee of the National Assembly. A consummate politican, Giscard became one of the most influencial men in France. In May 1974, Giscard succeeded Georges Pompidou (qv), to become the third president of the Fifth Republic. Giscard immediately went about mending some of the political fences that had been trampled by past French policies. He also held the reigns of power with a steady hand, but was criticised for his lifestyle — his whereabouts would often be a mystery, and he did not deal with domestic inflation and unemployment. In August 1975, while on a state visit to Zaire (qv), Giscard announced France's decision to stop supplying arms to the white supremicist government in South Africa. This move was reconfirmed in February 1977, when Giscard visited Mali (qv). Giscard was also able to negotiate an arms deal with Sudan (qv) that culminated in the ouster of all Soviet advisors in that country (May 1977). Giscard remained in office until 21 May 1981, when a socialist government led by François Mitterand was put into power.

Gish. *See* Israel.

Gizenga, Antoine. Antoine Gizenga had been deputy prime minister under Patrice Lumumba (qv) in the Democratic Republic of Congo (see Congo). After Lumumba's arrest by Joseph Mobutu's (qv) forces on 1 December 1960, Gizenga proclaimed himself Lumumba's successor and on 14 December led a procommunist attempt to gain control of the country. Although not totally successful, Gizenga's forces, operating out of Stanleyville, controlled Orientale and Kivu provinces. When an attempt to unify the various factions was put forth in March 1961, it was Gizenga who blocked it because the unification plan's principal aim was to halt communist influence in the country. On 17 April 1961, however, Gizenga acknowledged Mobutu as his commander in chief, thus ending the stalemate and allowing President Joseph Kasavubu (qv) to reorganize the Congolese armed forces. Gizenga was appointed vice premier of the central government. In January 1962, he attempted to take Kasai Province out of the central government. Gizenga was arrested by UN troops, was turned over to the central government on 23 January and was dismissed from the government, this time apparently for good.

Gizikis, Phaidon. On 25 November 1973, the government of Greek president Georgios Papadopoulos (qv) was overthrown by a military coup led by Brigadier General Demetrios Ioannides. Papadopoulos was arrested. Lieutenant General Phaidon Gizikis was installed as president. Gizikis was to have been appointed chief of the armed forces in August 1972, but Papadopoulos, then acting as regent (from 21 March 1972) and prime minister, prevented it. On 22 July 1974 the Greek junta leaders asked Gizikis to call a council of the nation's leading political leaders. At the meeting held the next day, Gizikis informed them that the military was ready to relinquish power. Konstantine Karamanlis (qv) was asked to form a new government as prime minister. On 15 December 1974, Gizikis stepped down as president. On 18 December 1974, Michael Stassinopoulos (qv) became the interim president.

Glubb, Sir John Bagot (Pasha). (b. 16 April 1897, Preston—d. 17 March 1986, Mayfield, Sussex) Born the son of a British general officer, Glubb was educated at Cheltenham and at the Royal Military Academy, Woolwich. He served in the World War I with the British Army's Royal Engineers in France, where he was thrice wounded and awarded the Military Cross. After the war he was posted to Iraq as a lieutenant in the Royal Engineers (although he worked for Royal Air Force intelligence). He learned the Arabic language and customs of the people and resigned (1926) his commission to work in the Middle East. In 1930 he joined the Arab Legion in Transjordan (qv) and trained the Bedouin troops to better control the border strife between Transjordan and Saudi Arabia. Eventually the Arab Legion became the elite force among the Arab armies. In 1939 he assumed command of the legion and spent his time trying to bring the Arab world to the realization that its future lay with the West. He eventually lost his power as Arab nationalists forced King Hussein of Jordan (qv) to dismiss him (2 March 1956). Lieutenant General Glubb Pasha was knighted upon his return to England. Not withstanding his knighthood, he was penniless and went to work as a writer and lecturer. He died at age 89. *Reading:* Sir John Bagot Glubb, *The Story of the Arab Legion* (1976).

Glyfada. *See* Greece.

Gnat. *See* Lebanon.

Goa. Goa is located on the western coast of India. Before its annexation by India in 1961, it was one of three Portuguese enclaves (with Damão and Diu) on the Indian subcontinent. A Hindi city of great antiquity, Goa was part of the Kadamba empire from the second to the fourteenth centuries. In 1312 it was conquered by the Muslims and held until 1367. Goa was established as a city in 1440, and after passing through several Indian dynastic changes it finally fell to the Portuguese in November 1510. The Portuguese put all Muslims to the sword and established a Hindu as governor. In 1809, Goa was occupied by the British after Napoleon invaded Portugal. It returned to Portuguese control after the war and remained as such until 1948, when the newly independent India claimed the territory. On 22 July 1954 Portugese troops drove out bands of Indian nationalists intent upon annexing sections of Goa. On 19 August 1955, diplomatic relations were severed between India and Portugal over the three enclaves. On 18 December 1961, Indian forces entered Goa and the other two enclaves and occupied them. Thereafter, India assumed rights over the territory.

Golan Heights. *See* Israel.

Gold Coast. *See* Ghana.

Gomez, Fernando. On 27 February 1980, terrorists from the leftist M-19 group attacked and seized the embassy of the Dominican Republic in Bogota, Colombia; the attack was timed to coincide with a diplomatic reception. Among the 57 hostages taken in what would become a two-month standoff was Uruguayan ambassador Fernando Gomez. Gomez was able to escape in the early hours of the seige by slipping out a residence window. In retaliation, on 15 April, another band from the M-19 group attacked the Uruguayan embassy in Bogota. The acting ambassador was not there, and the terrorists fled empty handed.

Gómez, Laureano. On 13 June 1953, the goverment of President Laureano Gomez of Colombia was overthrown by a military junta led by Lieutenant General Gustavo Rojas Pinilla (qv). Gómez, the leader of the extremist Conservative Party, had become president in August 1950. One of his first acts had been to remove all members of the opposition Liberal Party from the federal payroll. By 1953 his own party had begun to tire of his authoritarian rule, even though he had been ill since November 1951. On the day he attempted to reassume his office, he was overthrown by military members of his own party. Rojas took his place as head of state.

Gomulka, Wladyslaw. (b. 6 February 1905, Krosno—d. 1 September 1982, Warsaw) As a youth Gomulka worked as a plumber's assistant. At age 16 he organized a socialist youth group, and at age 21 he joined the secret Polish communist party. He was shot and arrested during a demonstration in 1932 and went to prison for two years. Gomulka then went to Moscow, but he returned to Poland in 1936 after spending two years in communist indoctrination programs. He was arrested upon his return, however, and was still in jail (Sieradz) when the Germans invaded Poland in September 1939. He was able to escape and worked his way to Soviet-held territory. After the Germans occupied Lvov, Gomulka went underground and worked with the communist resistance. He went back to Warsaw in 1942 and became a member of the Central Committee of the Polish Workers' Party (PWP). He was elected its secretary general in 1943. When the Soviets occupied eastern Poland in July 1944, Gomulka moved his base of operations behind their lines. On 31 December 1944, he was named deputy premier of the Soviet-backed provisional government and remained in that post until January 1949. He also held the post of minister of recovered territories and his post in the PWP until September 1948. In January 1949, he felt Stalin's wrath and was dismissed from all his posts. In July 1951 he was arrested and remained incarcerated until two years (21 April 1955) after Stalin's death. His release was kept secret until March 1956. In August 1956, he was declared rehabilitated and restored to membership in the party. On 19 October 1956 he was brought into the Politburo. The next day, he apparently faced down Nikita Khrushchev (qv) on the issue of Polish independence. On 21 October he was elected first secretary of the Polish United Workers' Party (PZPR). He remained in power until 20 December 1970, when he and several other members of the Politburo were forced to resign after he ordered troops to open fire on striking workers in Gdansk and Gdynia. He died peacefully in Warsaw at age 72.

Gongola District. *See* Nigeria.

Gonzalez Alvear, Raul. On 1 September 1975, General Raul Gonzalez Alvear led a right-wing coup attempt against the government of Ecuador's president Brigadier General Guillermo Rodriguez Lara (qv). Heavy fighting took place around the palace in Quito. Eighteen were killed and 80 injured in the fighting. Troops loyal to the government caused the coup attempt to fail.

Gonzales, Luis Arturo. On 27 July 1957, Luis Arturo Gonzales was sworn in as provisional president of Guatemala following the assassination of President Castillo Almas (qv) the preceding day.

Gonzalez Márquez, Felipe. (b. 5 March 1942, Seville, Spain) Felipe Gonzalez, the head of the Socialist Workers Party (PSOE), became premier of Spain on 2 December 1982 following an upset in the October elections. Although he started his education as an engineer, he later transferred to law and established a practice in Seville. As a student he joined the socialist movement and eventually became a member of the then outlawed PSOE (1964). He moved to Madrid and later became the secretary general of the party (1974). In 1976 he became vice president of the Socialist International and a close friend of Germany's Willy Brandt (qv). When the PSOE was legalized in 1977, Gonzalez set his sights on the premiership and won the election of 1982 in a sweeping defeat of the opposition. He set three goals for his tenure: getting Spain into the European Community, holding a referendum on Spanish inclusion in NATO and negotiating with Great Britain over the reintegration of Gibraltar into Spain. In 1984, he raised strenuous opposition to the move to bring Spain into NATO and demanded an immediate reduction of US military strength in his country. He remained in office in 1993.

Goodman, Alan Harry. On 11 April 1982, Alan Harry Goodman, a deranged Israeli immigrant soldier, opened fire on Muslim worshipers at the Dome of the Rock in Jerusalem. He killed two and wounded another 20 before he was subdued by police. This incident led to a period of violence in which Muslim mobs rampaged through the city. On 13 April, Goodman was charged with murder.

Goodman, Robert O. On 4 December 1983, following an intensification of of artillery fire on U.S. positions around Beirut Airport in Lebanon, a heavy naval bombardment and air strikes by 28 planes began from U.S. warships stationed off the coast. The attacks were aimed at reducing enemy artillery and antiaircraft emplaced in the Shouf (Shuf) Mountains around Beirut, which had already claimed the lives of eight US servicemen. During the attacks, two US aircraft were shot down by Syrian antiaircraft fire. One US naval aviator, Lieutenant Robert O. Goodman, was captured by the Syrians (the other airman was killed). After a personal appeal by Jesse Jackson to Syria's president Assad (qv), the release of Goodman was arranged; he was freed and returned to US control on 3 January 1984.

Goose Green. *See* Falkland Islands.

Gorbachev, Mikhail. (b. 2 March 1931, Privolnoye, Stavropol District, USSR) Born
the son of a peasant, Gorbachev joined the Komsomol, the Young Communist
League, in 1946. He worked as a tractor driver on a collective farm until he was
sent to Moscow University by the Komsomol (1950). He graduated as a lawyer
and also pursued studies in agriculture. In 1952 he joined the Communist Party
of the Soviet Union (CPSU) and moved rapidly through the ranks of the
Stavropol and provincial party. In 1971 he was elected to the CPSU Central
Committee and, in 1979, became a candidate member of the Politburo. In 1980
he was made a full member of the body. During this period he was befriended
by Mikhail Suslov, the party's ideologue, and by Yuri Andropov (qv), the head
of the KGB. When Andropov succeeded Leonid Brezhnev (qv) as head of the
party, he gave Gorbachev the task of controlling the Soviet Union's agricultural
development. At the same time, Gorbachev became the ideological spokesman
for the party. In 1984, he led a parliamentary delegation to Great Britain,
although he was a relative stranger to the western world. Within a year,
however, he was the leader of the Soviet Union. When Konstantin Chernenko
(qv) died on 10 March 1985, Gorbachev, although not Chernenko's choice to
succeed him, became general secretary of the CPSU (11 March 1985). In the
beginning of his tenure, Gorbachev spent his time insulating his position by
appointing friends and adherents to important posts. Gorbachev became one of
the best known Soviet leaders in the West. He met four times with Ronald
Reagan (qv) and, during a speech at the United Nations, he announced the
withdrawal of one-half million troops from Eastern Europe and introduced a new
Russian word to the Western world — *glasnost,* literally, openness. This, plus
his demand for reform at home (*perestroika*), made all the more visible the
severe economic problems facing the Soviet Union. Gorbachev's decision to
allow the republics to decide their own economic futures probably marked the
beginning of the end of the Soviet system. By 1990, growing nationalism and the
still declining economy made Gorbachev appear a weak leader. Yet, in October
1990, he was awarded the Nobel peace prize for his foreign policy
achievements, especially bringing the Cold War to an end. Thus, Gorbachev
found himself very popular abroad but not so much so at home. In 1991, the
Soviet Union collapsed under its own weight, and with it so did Gorbachev's
rule. In an attempt to save the regime, hard line communists staged an attempted
coup on 19 August 1991. One of the conspirators' moves was to demand
Gorbachev's resignation. He refused, and the failure of the KGB to arrest Boris
Yeltsin, the Russian republic's president and several other top Gorbachev
supporters, collapsed the coup. Gorbachev's attempt at conciliation with the
right caused him an even greater loss of popular support as the vast majority of
the former citizens of the USSR detested the party and what it had done to them.
Gorbachev's rule was over. *Reading:* Frederic J. Fleron et al, eds.,
Contemporary Issues in Soviet Foreign Policy: From Brezhnev to Gorbachev
(1991); Harley D. Balzer, ed., *Five Years That Shook the World: Gorbachev's*

Unfinished Revolution (1991); Vilho Harle & Jyriki Iovonen, eds., *Gorbachev and Europe* (1990).

Gordon, Lincoln. Lincoln Gordon was the U.S. ambassador to Brazil when the government of President Joao Goulart (qv) was overthrown by a military coup on 1 April 1964. Fear of a communist takeover led the United States to reinforce its naval units in the Caribbean. The ruling military junta began an immediate anticommunist purge within the government structure and defused any plans the communists might have had. As a result, Gordon requested that the U.S. naval units be withdrawn as a sign of good faith with the new Brazilian government.

Gorky. *See* USSR.

Gottwald, Klement. On 26 May 1946, Klement Gottwald, the leader of the Communist Party in Czechoslovakia, became premier after his party polled 40 percent of the vote in the national elections. Under Soviet pressure, the government declined the offer of US aid (June 1947). By February 1948, Gottwald had a completely communist cabinet. On 7 June 1948, Edvard Beneš (qv) was forced to resign as president on the pretext of ill health, and Gottwald took his place as the head of state (14 June). Gottwald died in office on 14 March 1953.

Goulart, João. (b. 1 March 1918, São Borja, Brazil—d. 6 December 1976, Corrientes Province, Argentina) Goulart was elected vice president of Brazil in 1955. He ran again for vice president in 1960 and was inaugurated on 31 January 1961. Goulart was on a trip to Singapore when President Jânio Quadros resigned on 25 August 1961. The Brazilian Congress immediately installed the speaker of the chamber of deputies as provisional president. When Goulart returned, he demanded his right, as the constitutional successor, to the presidency. This led the country to the brink of civil war as factions sided with or against Goulart. To avert war, the two sides settled on allowing Goulart to hold office as a figurehead, and a parliamentary form of government was inaugurated on 2 September 1961, with most presidential power being transferred to the prime minister. A national plebiscite was called to confirm the new parliamentary system. With these actions already in place, Goulart had little to do but accept the terms for his holding office, and he was confirmed on 7 September. The national plebiscite held on 6 January 1963 disavowed the parliamentary form of government five to one and full power was restored to Goulart. Still, Goulart could not overcome a divided congress and rampaging inflation. As the political accommodation deteriorated, Goulart moved farther to the far left of the political spectrum. Communist infiltration of the labor unions, for instance, became a major concern of moderates and conservatives alike. Finally, in March 1964, Goulart announced a new agrarian reform program and the nationalization of most oil refineries. On 31 March, the army revolted, and Goulart was out of office the next day. He fled the country for Uruguay on 2 April. He remained there nine years, before moving to Argentina. He died in Corrientes Province, Argentina, on 6 December 1976.

Gowon, Yakubu. On 29 July 1966, the second coup in six months occurred in Nigeria. President Aguyi-Ironsi (qv) was murdered by the opposition Muslim Hausa tribesmen who led the military revolt. A Hausa colonel, Yakubu Gowon was installed as president and began a long reign of terror against the opposition Christian Ibo tribe to the south who had received status during the Aguyi-Ironsi administration. The subsequent civil war that broke out almost destroyed the Ibo people, but it gave Gowon the perfect avenue for his persecution of these people. When, outside aid from a number of countries was offered during the Biafran War (qv), Gowon refused to allow it. The end of the war did not mean the end of the persecution. Then, on 1 October 1974, Gowon announced that he was postponing indefinitely any plans to return to a civilian government. On 29 July 1975, while Gowon was attending a meeting of the Organization of African Union (OAU) in Kampala, Uganda, he was ousted from office by a new military junta headed by Brigadier General Murtala Ramat Mohammed (qv).

Granada. *See* Nicaragua.

Great Bitter Lake (*el Buheirat el Murrat el Kubra*). *See* Israel.

Great Britain. More correctly referred to as the United Kingdom of Great Britain and Northern Ireland, Great Britain is primarily a group of islands off the northwestern coast of Europe. The largest island, containing England and Scotland, lies closest to Europe, while Ireland lies to the west, separated by the Irish and Celtic Seas. About 6000 B.C., the islands were attached to Europe, and the land bridge accounted for the first migrations into the area. The loss of the land bridge did not halt migration, however, and the basic Celtic stock arrived less than 3,000 years ago. Roman occupied, but never competely pacified the British Isles in 43 A.D. and withdrew as the Roman Empire went into decline in 410. Thereafter, waves of Germanic Scandian Jutes, Angles and Saxons arrived who, while fighting their constant internicene wars and beating off Danish attacks, established the basic ingredients of English (Anglo-Saxon) culture. The last great incursion came in the eleventh century, when French-speaking Normans invaded England and subjugated the people, uniting the new dominion with France. As England advanced through the decades, the authority of the king became absolute. The opposition of the nobility forced forced King John to sign the Magna Carta, the great charter of English political and civil liberties (Runnymede, 12 June 1215). England fought the Hundred Years War with France (1338–1453) over dynastic claims in France; England lost. A long civil war followed, the War of the Roses (1455–1485), which culminated in the Tudor dynasty and the establishment of a uniquely English civilization. The economy flourished, and the Church of England was established (1534) outside the realm of the Pope in Rome. Later monarchs established England as a naval and commercial power and expanded the empire both east and west. Again, a bloody civil war was fought (The Second Civil War, 1648–1651) that among other things impelled migration to the New World. For England, the end of the war marked the establishment of the sovereignty of Parliament and a new Bill of Rights (1689). In the eighteenth century, Britain lost its greatest possession,

America, through shortsighted leadership. After a period of readjusting the balance of power, the U.S. and Great Britain became strong allies. In the meantime, however, the English role in the defeat of Napoleon in 1815 gave England great prestige and led to a flowering of the British Empire. By 1901, it could be said with certainty, "The sun never sets on the British Empire." England emerged victorious from the World War I but with disastrous casualties and economic difficulties of major proportions. Ireland (qv), with the exception of Ulster (qv), became independent in 1921. After the fall of France in 1940, England held out singlehandedly for a year and faced a German invasion until Axis miscalculations brought the Soviet Union and the United States into World War II. England suffered much destruction from bombings and missile attacks during this period. The end of the war saw the rise of nationalism and the breakup of the British Empire, yet England remained a strong ally and protected its dwindling empire with great diligence, as in the Falkland Islands (qv) and fought beside the U.S. in Iraq. *See also* individual Commonwealth countries. *Reading:* Mark Phythian, *Arming Iraq: How the US and Britain Secretly Built Saddam's War Machine* (1996); John Darwin, *Britain and Decolonization: The Retreat from Empire in the Post-War World* (1988); S. J. D. Green & R. C. Whiting, eds., *The Boundaries of the State in Modern Britain* (1996); Geoffrey Till, ed., *Britain and NATO's Northern Flank* (1988); Scott Lucas, ed. *Britain and Suez: The Lion's Last Roar* (1996); Ilan Pappe, *Britain and the Arab-Israeli Conflict, 1948–51* (1988); Curtis Keeble, *Britain and the Soviet Union, 1917–89* (1990).

Greater Antilles. *See* Antilles or specific islands.

Grechko, Marshal Andrei Antonovich. (b. 17 October 1903, Golodayevka, Rostov region—d. 26 April 1976, Moscow) Marshal of the Soviet Union (MSU) Andrei A. Grechko began his career during the Russian Civil War. After joining the Red Army as a cavalryman, he was commissioned and rose rapidly through the ranks. As one of General Boris Shaposhnikov's protégés, he graduated from the Frunze Military Academy in 1936 and the General Staff Academy in 1941. He then commanded a cavalry division and, later, a cavalry corps. In April 1942, he was promoted to command of the Twelfth Army. Over the next 18 months he commanded several major formations. In October 1943 he became deputy commander of the First Ukrainian Front. In December of that year he was given command of the First Guards Army, a post he retained until the end of the war. In 1953, he was given command of the forces in East Germany (GSFG) and was promoted to marshal in 1955. In 1957 he was made first deputy minister of defense and, in 1960, took command of Warsaw Pact forces. In April 1967, he returned to Moscow as minister of defense. He was made a full member of the Politburo in 1973. He strongly opposed détente and constantly fought for larger arms appropriations. In February and in May 1973, Grechko visit Cairo for talks that led to increased military aid to Egypt and to the 1973 Arab-Israeli War.

Greece. The history of Greece begins in antiquity. While much of the world lived in barbarism, Greece flourished as the cradle of Western civilization. The classical period of Greece reached its zenith in the fifth century, B.C. Rome expanded over the region in the second and first centuries B.C. By the fourth century A.D., Greece was part of the Byzantine Empire. In 1453, after the Ottoman Turks conquered Constantinople, Greece fell under the Ottoman yoke. Following the war of 1821–1829, Greece regained its independence and became a kingdom. In 1924, Greece changed its form of government to a republic, but it reverted to a monarchy in 1935, with George II on the throne. Italy made aggressive overtures toward Greece in October 1940, but Greece rejected them and held Italy at bay. In 1941, German forces occupied the Greek mainland and culminated their offensive in a major airborne assault against the U.K. and Greek defenders of Crete. The cost of the campaign may have deprived Germany of resources that would have been vital in the campaign against the Soviet Union. In October 1944, the occupying German, Italian and Bulgarian forces withdrew, and Greece found itself facing a communist threat that created further havoc in the country until the communists were defeated by British and Greek royalist forces. During that time a plebiscite restored the monarchy, and George II returned to the throne. Upon his death in April 1947, his brother, Paul I (qv), took the throne. A second communist campaign began in 1947 and lasted until 1949, when the Greeks, with substantial U.S. military aid, defeated the communists. The Dodecanese Islands group, which had been ceded to Greece by Italy as a part of the peace agreement, was annexed in 1948. Greece entered the Council of Europe in 1949. Greece was recommended for membership in NATO in September 1951 (accepted 22 October 1951), and Greek forces were a part of the United Nations Command that fought in Korea (qv) (1950–1953).

A period of stability and economic growth followed under the leadership of Premier Konstantinos Karamanlis (qv), who was elected on 19 February 1956. In that election, women had the opportunity to vote for the first time in modern Greek history. One problem that Karamanlis inherited was that of Cyprus (qv), which was at the time a British colony. Greece's demand for union (*Enosis*) for Cyprus soon led to a confrontation with Turkey, which also held claims to the island. The imperfect solution was independence for Cyprus, which eventually led to fighting. Karamanlis was reelected in 1961, but he resigned on 11 June 1963. Georgios Papandreou (qv) of the Center Union party won a November election, which was confirmed by another on 16 February 1964. One month later Paul I died (6 March 1964), and his son Constantine succeeded to the throne. On 15 July 1965, Constantine dismissed Papandreou because of his left wing intrigues involving the army. A crisis developed, which a number of interim governments could not bring under control. Finally, on 21 April 1967, a military coup seized the government and installed Konstantinos Kollias, a civilian lawyer, as prime minister. The military junta that actually ran the government began a purge of persons opposing the government. On 13 December 1967, Constantine attempted a coup of his own, which failed.

Thereafter, Constantine and his family went into exile in Italy. One of the junta members, Colonel Gregorios Papadopoulos (qv), assumed the premiership, and General Georgios Zoitakis was appointed regent. Papandreou, who had been arrested early in the purge, was released in December 1967, and allowed to leave the country. In November 1969, the government imposed strict censorship rules on the Greek press. On 12 December 1969, Greece withdrew from the Council of Europe before it could be expelled for civil rights violations. The council went on to condemn Greece for human rights violations on 15 April 1970. On 6 February 1972, Greece announced it would allow port facilties on its territory to support the U.S. Sixth Fleet. Twelve days later (17 February) the U.S. resumed military aid to Greece. In January 1973, Greece announced it would no longer accept direct aid but would continue to purchase U.S. military arms. Tensions were building in Greece early in 1973. In February clashes between students and police took place in Athens. On 1 June 1973, the government announced the abolition of the monarchy and the installation of Papadopoulos as president of the new republic. More rioting took place in Athens and Thessaloniki (Salonica)in November. Many were killed or injured in those clashes. Finally, on 25 November, a military coup led by Brigadier General Demetrios Ioannides (qv) ousted Papadopoulos. He was arrested and replaced as president by Lieutenant General Phaidon Gizirkis (qv). On 24 March a Turkish error during a NATO exercise further heightened the tension around the Aegian, and Greece withdrew from the exercise. On 24 July 1974, Karamanlis, after returning from exile, was asked to form a new government. Three days later, on 17 July, Greek and Turkish leaders met to settle the Aegian dispute, but the meeting failed. At this point, the Greek junta collapsed. Then, on 20 July, Turkish forces landed on Cyprus in a move designed to thwart a Greek Cypriot plan to unify the island with Greece. Fighting soon broke out all over the island, especially along the "Green Line" that separated the Greek and Turkish sections of the city of Nicosia. Although the Greek government issued an ultimatum, its relative military weakness became immediately apparent. By 14 August, Turkish forces were on the offensive all over Cyprus and held about 40 percent of the island. The next day, Greece withdrew from NATO, claiming the organization failed to stop the Turkish attack. By the end of the month, Greece was notifying its Western allies that it would begin reassessing the value of foreign bases on its soil. On 8 December, the Greek people voted the return of Constantine and the monarchy. A year later this vote was reversed, but the monarchy was not restored. A right-wing coup was attempted by the military on 24 February 1975, but failed. In April, US military strength in Greece was cut drastically as a result of failed basing-rights negotiations. On 9 August 1976, Greece asked the United Nations to settle the Aegian dispute with Turkey. The dispute continued, however, but an agreement establishing a demarcation line was concluded on 3 October that ended the Aegian crisis. In 1979, the Turks began withdrawing troops from Cyprus to achieve a better atmosphere for impending talks. Thereafter, on 21 August 1980, Greece warned it would close all US bases in the country if it were not readmitted into NATO. Readmission was accomplished on 20 October 1980. In 1981, Andreas Papandreou of the Panhellenic Socialist movement won the premiership. His tenure was marked by substantial changes in the domestic and foreign policies of Greece. Three Greek ships were attacked (*SS Avra,* damaged; SS Antigoni, sunk; SS Iapetus, damaged and abandoned) by Iraqi missiles and jets in the Persian Gulf incident, October–December 1983. Scandal marked the Papandreou administration, and he was defeated in the June 1989 elections. After a year-long period of adjusting party coalitions and a trio of governments, Konstantinos Mitsotakis became prime minister (11 April 1990), ending eight years of socialist rule. In the meantime, terrorists of the November 17 group carried out a series of attacks, including the assassination of a leading politician on 26 September 1989; at least 14 were killed in these attacks. Among Mitsotakis's first actions was an eight-year extension of US basing rights in Greece. Oddly, the collapse of neighboring communist states in the Balkans increased tensions within Greece, especially concerning Yugoslavia and Albania, from which a stream of refugees flooded into the country, further taxing the already depressed economy. Relations with Albania worsened as the number of refugees eventually led to expulsions of illegals in Greece and to border incidents in which a number of Albanians were shot by Greek patrols while attempting to cross the border. A number of Greek descent Albanians were arrested in Albania and charged with espionage and weapons smuggling. Accusations were made that it was Greece's plan to annex southern Albania (Epirus) with its large Greek population. Greece also faced increased tension with Turkey over the western Thracian region with its large Muslim population. The breakup of Yugoslavia and the freeing of its republic of Macedonia led to another problem for Greece, which looked upon its northern region as the true Macedonia. Greece imposed an economic boycott on the Yugoslav Macedonia in 1994 following the UN's acknowledgement of that state in 1993. At the same time, however, in 1990, Greece joined the coalition against Iraq and supplied bases and naval units for that campaign. In 1991, former prime minister Papandreou was tried for bank fraud, but he was acquitted in January 1992. In October 1993, Papandreou was returned to office as prime minister. In 1995, Greek police broke up a right-wing terrorist group called the North Epirus Liberation Front which had been accused of attacking and killing Albanian troops. *See also* Cyprus & Turkey. *Reading:* C. M. Woodhouse, *The Struggle for Greece* (1977); David Close, *The Origins of the Greek Civil War* (1995).

Greek Cypriot Underground Movement (EOKA-B). *See* EOKA-B.

Greenland. The world's largest island, Greenland was probably discovered in the tenth century by Norwegian adventurers led by Gunnbjorn Ulfsson. The discovery was confirmed by Eric the Red in 982. The name "Greenland" apparently was used by Eric to convince others to join in settling the forbidding land, which lies mostly within the Arctic Circle. The first settlement was put down in 986. No real exploration of the island began until 1721. More detailed exploration began in the nineteenth century. In 1814, when the union between Norway and Denmark was dissolved, Denmark retained the rights to Greenland, although the Danes actually possessed only a small part of the island. Full Danish sovereignty was not achieved until 1921. Greenland was made a temporary protectorate of the United States after the German occupation of Denmark in World War II. During the war Allied airbases and communication facilities were placed on the island. On 2 September 1947, the Inter-American Mutual Assistance Treaty was adopted at a conference held in Brazil that made Greenland a part of Hemispheric Defense. On 27 April 1951, Denmark, which had restored full sovereignty over Greenland, and the United States signed a 20-year joint defense accord for the island. Out of that treaty the major air base and early warning base at Thule was established. Life on Greenland remained relatively uneventful until 21 January 1968, when a US B-52 bomber carrying four hydrogen weapons on airborne alert suffered inflight difficulties and attempted a landing at Thule Air Force Base in the northwest part of the island. The aircraft crashed on the ice in Baffin Bay. Only fragments of the aircraft and its weapons load were ever recovered, although a massive search was undertaken. One result of that incident was the loss of power of the pro-American Social Democratic Party in Denmark. *Reading:* Kenneth E. Miller, *Greenland (World Bibliographical Series, Vol. 125)* (1991); Knud J. Rasmussen, *Greenland by the Polar Sea* (1988); Henrik Rink, *Danish Greenland: Its People and Products* (1975).

"Green Line," Lebanon. A demarcation line between the warring factions—generally, Moslems opposing Christian groups—in Beirut, Lebanon. The Green Line generally separated East Christian and West Muslim Beirut and was replete with "border checkpoints" that were manned by whichever faction held the particular section of the demarcation.

"Green March." On 6–7 November 1975, approximately 50,000 Moroccans marched into Spanish Sahara in a peaceful demonstration demanding sovereignty over the territory. Before it ended, at least 300,000 more had joined the march. On 9 November, King Hassan II (qv) of Morocco declared an end to the so-called Green March and ordered his people back home. The march came about as a result of Hassan's promise to liberate Spanish Sahara. On 16 October, he stated he would send his people across the southern frontier armed only with the Koran. This came in the face of an International Court of Justice decision that neither Morocco nor Mauritania had any historic claim to the territory held by Spain. When the marchers crossed the border, Spanish forces in the area withdrew, but they put down a minefield to separate their new positions from the oncoming Moslem Moroccans. After the Moroccans withdrew, the Spanish government announced (14 November) that it would hand over the territory to joint Moroccan–Mauritanean control in February 1976.

Greenpeace, Rainbow Warrior. On 10 July 1985, the Greenpeace flagship, *Rainbow Warrior*, was sunk by two bombs attached to its hull while it rode at its mooring in Auckland Harbor, New Zealand. The ship had been readied to sail into the waters around Mururoa (qv) atoll to protest French above-ground nuclear testing there. One crewman was killed in the explosion. Intelligence sources indicated that five French secret-service agents had been in Auckland at the time of the bombing. France exonerated itself of any part in the attack on 26 August, but the New Zealand government rejected the report the next day. On 20 September, the French minister of defense, Charles Hernu (qv), and the head of France's Foreign Intelligence Service (DGSE), Admiral Pierre Lacoste (qv), were forced to resign in the wake of the investigation that followed. Two days later, on 22 September, the French government was forced to acknowledge that DGSE members were responsible for the sinking. As a counterpoint incident, French commandos seized a sailboat carrying seven Greenpeace members that was allegedly trying to enter the restricted waters around Mururoa. On 22 November, two DGSE officers were tried for manslaughter in a New Zealand court. Both were found guilty and sentenced to ten years' hard labor. One, Alain Marfart, was returned to France for medical treatment in 1987, the same year an international arbitration panel ordered France to pay an $8 million indemnity to Greenpeace. The other French agent, Dominique Prieur, was released on the eve of the French presidential election. *Reading:* John Dyson, *Sink the Rainbow: An Enquiry in the Greenpeace Affair* (1986); Michael King, *Death of the Rainbow Warrior* (1987).

Grenada. Also known as the Isle of Spice, Grenada is the most southerly of the Windward Islands at the eastern end of the Caribbean Sea. The original inhabitants of the island were Carib Indians, when Christopher Columbus sighted Grenada in 1498. Not until 1650 did French traders establish a settlement on the island. For more than a century, the island alternated between French and English occupation. In 1784, the English took the island as a possession. Grenada became a parliamentary state within the British Commonwealth on 7 February 1974, and becoming the smallest independent nation in the Western Hemisphere. The island population was at the moment involved in a general strike. On 13 March 1979, the government of Sir Eric Gairy (qv) was overthrown in a bloodless coup by the New Jewel Movement led by Maurice Bishop (qv). On 12 July, Bishop signed a two-year technical assistance treaty with Cuba as Grenada drifted toward even closer ties with Cuba and the Soviet bloc. On 28 March 1983, the Grenadian government warned that it expected an attack by the United States at any moment. Grenadian forces were put on full alert. On 14 October 1983, a military coup overthrew the government of Prime Minister Bishop, who was put under house arrest. He was later freed by his supporters, but he was shortly rearrested and, on 19 October, executed. General Hudson Austin, as head of the Revolutionary Council, became prime minister. On 25 October, U.S. military forces, with token forces from several Caribbean nations, invaded Grenada (Operation Urgent Fury) quickly overcoming resistance from the Grenadian army and Cuban forces stationed there. Carriacou Island, located approximately 15 miles northeast of Grenada, was seized by U.S. Marines on 2 November 1983. Order was quickly restored on Grenada, and Governor General Sir Paul Scoon established a nonpolitical interim government to rule until an election could be held. In December 1984, the New National Party won the election, and Herbert A. Blaize (qv) became prime minister. The invading forces were withdrawn by June 1985 (the last American combat forces had left on 15 December 1983). The conspirators in the overthrow of the government were later tried in a Grenadian court, found guilty and executed. The new Grenadian government asked the United States on 9 October 1984 to leave forces in Grenada for several years, if necessary, to insure the peace. The last U.S. support forces left the island on 11 June 1985. Blaize was unseated in an inconclusive 1990 election, and Nicholas Brathwaite, who had held the post briefly in the interim government, was made prime minister. In August 1991 the life sentences of the 14 conspirators, including Bernard Coard, in the murder of Maurice Bishop were commuted after a lengthy appeals process. Grenada renewed diplomatic relations with Cuba in 1992. Braithwaite announced he would step down in 1994. This came as a blow to his National Democratic Congress (NDC) Party as it struggled with the serious economic problems that faced the country. In 1995, the NDC lost the elections to the New National Party, which installed Keith Mitchell, a U.S.-trained mathematician, as prime minister. *Reading:* Scott B. MacDonald & Harald M. Sandstrom, *The Caribbean after Grenada: Revolution, Conflict, and Democracy* (1988); John Cotman, *The Gorrion Tree: Cuba and the Grenada Revolution* (1993); Herbert J. Ellison & Jiri Valenta, *Grenada and Soviet/Cuban Policy: Internal Crisis and US Intervention* (1986).

Grivas, George (Georgios Theodoros) (aka *Dighenis*). (b. 23 May 1898, Trikomo, Cyprus—d. 27 January 1974, Limassol, Cyprus) Born a Cypriot, Grivas took Greek citizenship and joined the army, attending Officer Cadets' School in Athens. In 1920–1922, he took part in the invasion of Turkey. He later attended the Greek Staff College and the École Supérieure in Paris. As a major Grivas fought in the Italian invasion of Greece in 1940. He was a lieutenant colonel when Germany conquered Greece in 1941, and after his demobilization, he organized a right-wing resistance group loyal to the royalist cause. After the war he entered politics but failed in two elections (1946, 1950) and returned to Cyprus (1952). In Cyprus, he immediately became involved in the movement to end British rule on the island and helped organize EOKA (qv). Following the departure of the British (1960), trouble began between Greek and Turkish Cypriots. Grivas was appointed commander of the Greek-Cypriot National Guard (June 1964) by Cyprus president Archbishop Makarios (qv). When serious tension continued into 1967, Grivas was recalled to Greece as a means of easing Turkish anxieties. In 1971, Grivas returned secretly to Cyprus and began a campaign against Makarios, who, he claimed, was destroying any chance of *enosis* (union) with Greece in favor of Cypriot independence. Several attempts on Makarios's life were attributed to Grivas's forces in EOKA-B. Grivas also claimed that attempts on his life had been ordered by Makarios. Grivas died in 1974, without fulfilling his dream of joining Cyprus with Greece.

Groesz, Josef. On 28 June 1951, Hungarian Roman Catholic archbishop Joseph Groesz was convicted of conspiracy to overthrow the communist government in Hungary. The same thing had happened in February 1949 to another Hungarian priest, József Cardinal Mindszenty (qv), who had refused to allow the incorporation of the Catholic Church in Hungary into the state. In the first case, Mindszenty was ordered imprisoned for life, and Catholic schools were nationalized. By 1950, only four Catholic orders were still in existence in Hungary as the communists dissolved one after another. Archbishop Groesz was one of the last church leaders to be taken down.

Gromyko, Andrei Andreivich. (b. 5 July (OS)1909, Starye Gromyki, Belorussia—d. 2 July 1989, Moscow) Born of peasant stock, Gromyko was an agriculturalist and economist by training and worked as a member of the Institute of Economics before being assigned to the chief of the American section of the People's Commissariat of Foreign Affairs in 1939. He had joined the Communist Party in 1931. In 1943 he became the Soviet ambassador to Washington. He then had a short assignment at the United Nations and returned to Moscow in 1946, where he became deputy foreign minister. He remained in that post until 1957, with a short tour (1952–1953) as ambassador to Great Britain. In February 1957, he became Soviet foreign minister. In April 1973, he became a member of the Politburo and the first deputy chairman of the Council of Ministers in March 1983. In 1984, he visited the United States and spoke at the United Nations, where he roundly condemned US foreign policy. He also was the first Soviet leader to meet President Ronald Reagan (qv). In October 1984, upon his return to Moscow, he was awarded his eleventh Order of Lenin. Known as a survivor and as a strict adherent to the wishes of the master, Gromyko came through all of the regimes in the Soviet Union from Stalin (qv) to Gorbachev (qv), constantly gaining prestige and influence. In July 1985, he was given the largely ceremonial post of president of the Union of Soviet Socialist Republics. He retired in September 1988 and died quietly in July 1989 at age 80.

Group Areas Bill. On 27 May 1950, the South African government of Prime Minister D. F. Malan implemented the Group Areas Bill, which further segregated the races. This action led to serious rioting among the Black population. *See also* Apartheid.

Grunitzky, Nicholas. When French Togoland became independent within the French Union on 30 August 1956, Nicholas Grunitzky was appointed premier. In subsequent elections held under UN auspices in 1958, Grunitzky's policy of association with France was repudiated in favor of independence and Grunitzky was out of office. He withdrew himself to Dahomey, where he resided until 1963, when he returned to Togo to assume the presidency of an interim government following the assassination of Ghana's Kwame Nkrumah (qv) on 13 January. An attempt to overthrow Grunitzky failed in November 1966. On 13 January 1967, however, Grunitzky's government was overthrown in a bloodless coup led by Lieutenant Colonel Étienne Eyadema, the army chief of staff.

Grytviken. *See* Falkland Islands.

Guadalajara. *See* Mexico.

Guadeloupe. Twin islands in the Leeward group of the French Antilles, the two islands, Basse-Terre to the west and Grande-Terre to the east, are connected by a bridge over the narrow channel (*Rivière Salée*) in the capital city of Point-a-Pitre. The arrangement gives the islands the appearance of a giant butterfly. Columbus discovered Guadaloupe in 1493. The island was inhabited by Carib Indians from the South American mainland who had displaced the indigenous Arawak tribes. Settlement was not attempted until 1635, when the French put down a settlement. In 1674, it became a crown possession and a dependency of Martinique. The British seized the island and held it between 1759 and 1763, and again in 1794. They took Guadaloupe again in 1810 and held it until 1816, when it was returned to French control. In 1848, slavery was abolished in Guadaloupe, and 93,000 slaves were freed. During World War II, Guadaloupe sided with the Free French and, in 1946, became a part of the French Union. The island's history has been generally quiet except for an incident on 14 March 1985, when a bomb exploded in a crowded restaurant in Point-a-Pitre, killing one person and injuring 11 others, four of them Americans. The separatist terrorist organization called the Caribbean Revolutionary Alliance (ARC) was accused of the attack, but no one claimed responsibility. Rioting in Point-a-Pitre occurred in July 1985, when demonstrators sought the release of an Independence Party leader held by the authorities. An ARC leader, Luc Reinette, who had escaped from a Guadaloupe prison in 1985, was captured in July 1987 on St. Vincent. This time, he was flown to France for imprisonment, but he was released under a French general amnesty for Guadaloupe political prisoners in June 1989. In 1988, the Guadaloupe Communist Party announced it would join those other groups demanding independence. Guadaloupean riot police were sent to La Desirade, an offshore island near Grande-Terre, when the mayor, a socialist, was murdered in an ambush there in October 1991. The islands suffered a major disaster following the worst draught in 30 years in 1994.

Guam. The largest island in the Marianas chain, Guam is a U.S. possession in the Pacific Ocean about 3,300 miles west of Hawaii. The capital city is Agana. The island was first discovered by Ferdinand Magellan in 1521, although there is some dispute of these facts. The island was not occupied by Europeans until the Spanish conquered it in the late seventeenth century, albeit with considerable bloodshed. By the end of the seventeenth century, the coming of the Spaniards, war, disease, and typhoons had killed a major portion of the island's indigenous population of Chamorro Indonesian stock. Spain held the island until 1898, when an American warship steamed into the harbor, shelled the Spanish fort and received a surrender. Guam was ceded to the United States in 1899, while the remainder of the Marianas were sold by the Spanish to Germany. Germany, in turn, lost them to Japan after World War I. The Japanese invaded Guam and had occupied the island by 12 December 1941. U.S. army and Marine units retook Guam on 10 August 1944. Some Japanese soldiers held out on the island until the mid-1970s, not knowing the war was over. The island became a major airbase for the bombing of Japan that helped end the war. Throughout the history of American control, the governor of the island was a U.S. naval officer. On 1 August 1950, control of Guam was given over to the Interior Department. Guam is the headquarters of the Trust Territories of the Pacific Islands and is governed under the Organic Act of Guam (1 August 1950). The civilian governor was appointed by the president and confirmed by the Senate. Later, American residents voted for a governor and a 21-member unicameral legislature. The island has also been used in modern times as a Strategic Air Command forward deployment base which was used extensively during the war in Southeast Asia. The island's location also made it an ideal venue for important intergovernmental meetings, as in March 1967, when U.S. President Lyndon Johnson met South Vietnamese leaders there to discuss the prosecution of the Vietnam War. On 23 May 1973, the U.S. granted commonwealth status to the islands of the Marianas. In the late 1970s, an indigenous movement began to change Guam's status. A Commission of Determination was formed in 1984. A draft Commonwealth Act was presented to Congress in 1992. In 1994, Congress passed an act transferring several thousand acres of land formerly held by the US military on the island to local control.

Guantánamo Bay. A bay approximately 40 miles east of city of Santiago de Cuba and about 60 miles west of the southeast end of the island of Cuba, Guantanamo Bay is large and very well sheltered. The bay faces the Windward Passage that links the Atlantic Ocean to the Caribbean Sea. The strategic value of the bay was noted by the Americans during the Spanish-American War and was the scene of a landing during the invasion of Cuba. The U.S. gained rights to the bay as a naval base by a treaty with Cuba signed in 1903. After Fidel Castro (qv) seized control of the Cuban government in the 1960s, there have been periodic demands for U.S. removal. On 1 November 1960, for instance, President Eisenhower responded to such a threat by warning Castro that the U.S. would react to any attempted takeover. In February 1964, Cuba cut the water supply to the base in retaliation for U.S. seizure of Cuban fishing boats operating in restricted waters. The U.S. has on several occasions reinforced the largely U.S. Marine garrison on the base.

Guatemala. Guatemala is a Central American country that has access to both the Atlantic and the Pacific Oceans. It is bordered on the northeast by Belize, on the north and northwest by Mexico, on the southeast by Honduras and on the southwest by El Salvador. The capital is Guatemala City. One thousand years before the arrival of the Spaniards, Guatemala was the home of the Mayan civilization. From 1524 until 1821, it was a Spanish colony. Guatemala then fell briefly under Mexican control (to 1823) and for a short time became a part of the Republic of the United States of Central America (to 1829). It became an independent republic in 1839. War and revolution punctuated its history for the next century. The country was troubled during World War II, although Guatemala joined in declaring war on Japan and the other Axis powers in

December 1941. Since the end of the war and the ouster of dictator Jorge Ubico, the country has passed through a number of phases. A liberal government elected to replace Ubico brought some economic and social relief to the country, but it also led to a rise in communist activity, which was not opposed by the government. A large-scale rebellion was put down in July 1949 by the government of Juan Jose Arévalo (qv). When Arbenz Guzmán (qv) was elected president in March 1951, it was with communist support. In January 1953, he declared the U.S. and Nicaragua were readying to invade the country. A military junta that led an invasion army into Guatemala ousted him (1954) and established a new government under the junta leader Castillo Armas (qv), but Armas was assassinated (26 July 1957) before he could restore order. Next, Ydigoras Fuentes (qv) was elected in March 1958, but he was ousted by the army in March 1963 for allowing the return of unwanted former president Arévalo. In July 1963, Guatemala broke diplomatic relations with Great Britain after London announced it was giving autonomy to British Honduras which, Guatemala claimed. The country wavered back and forth between armed revolt, a threat of Cuban invasion (November 1960), popular unrest and coups and countercoups. In May 1965, however, Guatemala joined in the formation of the OAS Inter-American Peacekeeping Force (qv) to maintain order in the region. On 28 August 1968, the U.S. ambassador in Guatemala, John Gordon Mein (qv), was killed during a kidnap attempt by communist terrorists. Terror continued into the 1970s. On 27 February 1970, for instance, the foreign minister was kidnapped and held for the release of an imprisoned rebel leader, who was released in exchange for the minister. Then, in March, terrorists kidnapped and murdered the German ambassador. Because of these acts and a wave of terrorism around the country, a state of seige was declared that was not lifted until November 1971. In October 1975, British paratroopers were sent to reinforce the garrison in British Honduras after Guatemala threatened to annex that country. Terrorism continued into the 1980s, with right-wing terrorists claiming as many victims as those killed by the other side. By 1982, when army officers seized power, at least 200,000 Guatemalans had fled into Mexico to avoid the bloodshed, terror and unrest. In one bizarre incident in January 1980, the Spanish embassy was burned to the ground after police attempted to free hostages held there by leftist terrorists. Thirty-eight terrorists and all the hostages except the ambassador are killed. The next day, the ambassador, Maximo Cajal y Lopez (qv) was kidnapped from his hospital bed, where he lay recuperating; he was then murdered. Seemingly in retaliation, at least twelve leftist supporters were tortured and murdered in May. In June, police reported that seven right-wing lawyers, professors and politicans were slain. Attacks on army troops and police occurred in August, and the National Palace was bombed by leftists. Attacks on foreigners also increased during the period. In one incident, Army of the Poor terrorists killed an American plantation owner (18 March 1982). Another coup occurred in 1982, when a military group led by General Efrain Rios Montt (qv) toppled the government of Fernando Romeo

Lucas Garcia (qv). The Brazilian embassy was seized by terrorists representing the January 31 Popular Front. In this case the hostages were released unharmed. The country's government was again toppled by a military coup in August 1983, but it was finally returned to civilian control in 1986. Right-wing death squads continued to operate in 1987 despite the government's attempts at regaining political stability. At the same time, left-wing terrorist attacks against military targets continued to expand. An amnesty was declared however for all rebels following talks between the government and rebel leaders in November 1987. On 11 May 1988, a coup attempt failed to overthrow the government. This one was followed by several others during the year. While all failed, they weakened the hand of the government in dealing with the ongoing guerrilla activity. The coup attempts also stepped up death squad activities. Another failed coup took place on 8 May 1989, in an attempt to force key ministers out of the administration. A group of 26 military officers and civilians was subsequently arrested. The year also witnessed a growing terror campaign against candidates for office in the 1990 elections. In addition, death squad activity against journalists, clergy and trade union members increased. If that were not enough, guerrilla activity increased, with action in over half the provinces in the country. Violence continued throughout 1990 with, once again, death squad activity topping the list of sources of the unrest. The elections were finally completed in January 1991 when a runoff put Jorge Serrano Elias in the presidency. In 1992, a UN human rights report condemned the government for a consistent history of human rights violations despite an information campaign by Guatemala aimed at showing that the problem was under control. By 1993 the Serrano government was in deep trouble. On 25 May, Serrano dissolved Congress, instituted censorship and closed the Supreme Court. Twelve days later, on 6 June, he was ousted by a coup composed of just about every group in the country. Ramero de Leon Carpio, a human rights advocate, became president. His choice led to the assassination of his cousin and ally, Jorge Carpio Nicolle; and the new human rights advocate, Jorge Garcia LaGuardia, was threatened with death in an attempt to rattle the de Leon government. Instead, de Leon asked for the resignation of Congress and the Supreme Court to allow constitutional reforms to end the vices of corruption and human rights violations. Although the Supreme Court at first refused the plan, it later approved a referendum for early 1994. The year 1994 proved to be a difficult one for de Leon. There were numerous assassinations and other human rights incidents throughout the year, including the near-fatal beating of an American woman accused by a mob of being involved in a baby-trafficking operation. At the same time the years-long talks with the rebels failed to produce the hoped-for treaty that would have ended the fighting. Presidential elections held in 1995 failed to give a clear majority to either candidate and were rescheduled for 1996. Once again Rios Montt was barred from running for office and, in fact, was indicted on a multitude of charges stemming from his time in office in the 1980s. *Reading:* Jean-Marie Simon, *Guatemala: Eternal Spring, Eternal Tyranny*

(1988); Richardo Falla, *Massacres in the Jungle: Ixcan, Guatemala, 1975–1982* (1994); Jennifer K. Harbury, *Searching for Everardo: A Story of Love, War, and the CIA in Guatemala* (1997).

Guayaquil. *See* Ecuador.

Gueiler Tejada, Lydia. During a period of tension, 15–25 November 1979, more than 250 of Bolivia's top military officials issued a demand for the immediate resignation of President Alberto Natusch Busch (qv). Busch resigned the following day. On 17 November, Lydia Gueiler, the president of the senate, was sworn in as president. She remained in office until 17 July 1980, when another military coup upset the plans for a democratic election.

Guelta Zemmour. *See* Morocco.

Guerrilla Army of the Poor (EGP). Formed in 1975, this leftist insurgent group led a military campaign against the Guatemalan government by attacking army posts around the country. It soon had a large following among the native Quiché Indian population. In 1981, the EPG was thought to be responsible for most of the 127 international terrorist attacks carried out across the country. In one incident, a bomb was detonated at the Chevron Oil Products depot in Guatemala City. About 165,000 gallons of gasoline were destroyed. This attack was thought to be the work of a new organization, the January 31 Popular Front, that had connections with the EPG. On 5 August, that same group bombed the Pan American World Airlines office in downtown Guatemala City. On 18 March 1982, EPG members shot and killed a U.S. citizen, J. Pitts Jarvis, at his plantation at San Christobal, in northern Guatemala. The rebels had raided Jarvis' farm, demanding money and guns, and then dragged Jarvis outside and repeatedly shot him. The terrorists then set fire to the farmhouse and tried to escape, but a passing army helicopter fired on them. There was no report of casualties among the terrorists. On 12 May 1982, 13 members of the January 31 group seized the Brazilian embassy, took hostages and unfurled their flag on the balcony. After the hostages were released, the terrorists were flown to Mexico.

Guevara, Che (Ernesto Guevara de la Serna). (b. 14 June 1928, Rosario, Argentina—d. 8 October 1967, Bolivia) A scholar and athlete in his school days, Guevara studied medicine at the University of Buenos Aires. After graduation he left Argentina to avoid military service in the army of Juan Peron (qv). Guevara embraced socialism during his time in Argentina and witnessed the problems of Latin America firsthand as he travelled throughout the region. In 1954, he was in Guatemala when a U.S.-engineered coup overthrew the government. He then travelled to Mexico, where he met Fidel and Raul Castro (qqv). He went with the Castros to Cuba, where he became involved in the revolution that eventually toppled the Fulgencio Batista (qv) government on that island in 1959. From 1959 until 1965 he held a number of posts in the Castro government. He disappeared in April 1965, but sources claim he visited Latin America, North Vietnam and the Congo, organizing guerrilla warfare. In late 1966, he appeared in Bolivia, where he worked with guerrilla groups. Guevara was captured, along with most of his men, on 8 October 1967 and was executed by Bolivian army captors. He immediately became a hero-martyr to all revolutionaries and gained a stature he never attained in life. His textbook *Guerrilla Warfare* (1961) is considered a classic in the field. *Reading:* Jon Lee Anderson, *Che Guevara: A Revolutionary Life* (1997); Gary Prado Salmon, *The Defeat of Che Guevara: Military Response to the Guerrilla Challenge in Bolivia* (1990).

Guevara Arze, Walter. The 68-year-old Guevara Arze was the president-elect of the Bolivian senate when he became the compromise choice for the presidency (8 August 1979) under the agreement that he would serve only for one year. On 1–4 November he was ousted by a military coup and replaced by Colonel Alberto Natusch Busch (qv).

Guido, José Maria. In March 1962, President Arturo Frondizi (qv) was removed from office by a military coup. On 30 José Maria Guido, former president of the senate, was put into the presidency by the military. Although Guido's 18 month administration was fundamentally a period of civilian rule, it was closely supervised by the military. Guido left office in October 1963, when he was succeeded by Arturo Illia (qv), who won the July elections.

Guillaume, Gunther. (b. 1 February 1927, Berlin) Gunther Guillaume was a member of the Nazi Party in 1944. After the war he worked in East Berlin until he immigrated to the West in 1956. He then joined the Social Democratic Party (SPD) in 1957. He served in the party headquarters from 1964 until 1968. In 1970 he joined the German Chancellery. Guillaume became the personal aide of Willy Brandt (qv), the Chancellor of West Germany, and acted as his liaison with the SPD (1972). On 24 April 1974, Guillaume was uncovered as a East German spy and arrested. The revelation forced the resignation of Brandt (6 May), although he was absolved of any wrongdoing and had probably not been kept informed of the investigation into Guillaume's espionage affairs.

Guinea. More properly called the Republic of Guinea, Guinea is located in West Africa. Shaped like an upside-down crescent, Guinea is bordered by Guinea-Bissau on the west, by Senegal and Mali on the north, by Ivory Coast on the east, by Liberia and Sierra Leone on the south and by the Atlantic Ocean on the southeast. The capital is Conakry. Guinea was a part of the West African empires. There is disputed evidence that the French entered the region in 1364. Portuguese adventurers were there in 1434, and slaving began soon afterwards. Portugal received papal authority for control over the west coast of Africa in the fifteenth century. By the sixteenth century many European expeditions had visited the region. Guinea fell under French control from 1848 until 1849. It remained in the French sphere until 2 October 1958, when President Sekou Toure (qv) proclaimed the nation independent and rejected membership in the French Union. In November of that year, Guinea confederated with Ghana. In May 1959, Guinea took the lead in an attempt to bring about a union of independent Africa. By December of 1960, Ghana and Mali had joined the union. In January of 1961 Guinea joined the UN-sponsored organization of African states known as the Charter of Casablanca (qv). In 1962, Guinea, along with the other Casablanca states, boycotted a meeting held in Lagos, Nigeria, to form a new organization of African states because of the exclusion of Algeria. On 15 November 1965, Guinea severed relations with France over a plot to assassinate President Toure and seize the country. In April 1966, Guinea gave asylum to Kwame Nkrumah (qv) of Ghana. Toure named Nkrumah co-president and threatened to invade Ghana and its ally Ivory Coast. In a military confrontation with Ivory Coast, Toure was forced to back down. Assassination attempts against Toure were thwarted in March and April 1969. A Portuguese-sponsored seaborne invasion of Guinea's capital, Conarkry, took place on 22–24 November 1970. Although the mercenaries made some gains, they were eventually routed by army troops. At least 100 invaders were captured. In December, Toure went before the United Nations to accuse Portugal of massing to invade Guinea. Popular unrest intensified in 1973, when the leader of the African Party for the Independence of Guinea and Cape Verde (PAIGC) (qv), Amilcar Cabral (qv), was assassinated in Conakry (20 January 1973). On 18 September 1973, Senegal broke diplomatic relations with Guinea following incessant verbal attacks by President Toure. Toure died in 1984 of heart problems (27 March). On 3 April, the army seized control of the country. Another coup was attempted in July 1985, but failed against the forces of President Lansana Conté. Conté remained in power in 1992, but his years in office were marred by the restiveness of a populace seeking constitutional government. As people died in pro-democracy demonstrations, fears arose (1993) that the military would step in and stop the violence by creating their own through an armed takeover of government. Nevertheless, Conte won reelection in December 1993, amid charges of vote fraud. More violence erupted out of these charges, but the government remained in power. In June 1994, eight senior military officers were arrested and charged with plotting a coup. Subsequent investigation proved the charges erroneous, and the men were released. Thereafter, Conte acted to remove opposition ministers from government, and police moved to defuse opposition demonstrations before more violence occurred. Things remained relatively quiet in 1995, as opposition parties made and broke alliances preparatory to the expected legislative elections. *Reading:* Adamolekun Ladipo, *Sekou Toure's Guinea: An Experiment in Nation Building* (1976); Amilcar Cabral, *Revolution in Guinea: Selected Texts* (1970); Mustafah Dhada, *Warriors at Work: How Guinea Was Really Set Free* (1993).

Guinea-Bissau. A West African country, Guinea-Bissau is bordered on the north by Senegal, on the east and southeast by Guinea, and on the west by the Atlantic Ocean. The capital is Bissau. There is disputed evidence that the french entered the region in 1364. Portuguese adventurers were there in 1434, and slaving began soon afterwards. Portugal received papal authority for control over the west coast of Africa in the fifteenth century. By the sixteenth century many European expeditions had visited the region, and a flourishing slave trade existed there in the seventeenth and eighteenth centuries. Western colonization did not begin until the nineteenth century. In 1962, a twelve-year rebellion began against the Portuguese government that was led by the African Party for the Independence of Guinea and Cape Verde (PAIGC) (qv). This rebellion culminated in the independence of the colony of Portuguese Guinea and its becoming Guinea-Bissau (27 September 1973). The new independent state was recognized by the United Nations on 2 November 1973. Fighting went on, however, and was did abate until 25 May 1974, when talks opened in London between the Portuguese government and the rebel PAIGC. On 14 November 1980, a socialist-inspired coup led by Premier Joao Bernardo Vieira (qv), overthrew the government of President Luis de Almeida Cabral (qv). The Revolutionary Council put João Bernardo Vieira into the presidency. In January 1981, Cape Verde broke with the PAIGC because of the Revolutionary Council decision to try the Cape Verde born Cabral for murder. The council announced that Cabral would be released. In June 1982, Cape Verde announced it would seek restoration of relations with Guinea-Bissau. Cabral was then released and went into exile in Cuba. In 1991, the Supreme Court moved to halt 17 years of one-party rule in Guinea-Bissau, allowing the Democratic Front, a PAIGC splinter group, and two other opposition parties to continue in existence. Vieira remained in power in 1992, but there were widespread economically motivated army desertions in 1992–1993 and trouble along the border, where suspected rebel bases were shelled by Senegalese forces. After a Vieira denial that Guinea-Bissau harbored rebels, the Senegalese apologized. The murder of a close friend of Virira, Major Robalo de Pina, even though not a coup attempt, led to further government actions in May, demonstrating that the Vieira government assumed the March murder was just that. Eventually the government backed down, and those arrested were released. The scheduled March 1994 multiparty elections were postponed by Vieira, who claimed a lack of funds and voter registration errors. They were held in June, but the results were inconclusive, and a runoff was held in August that returned Vieira and his party to office. The obligatory claims of fraud were shouted by the opposition, but Vieira survived and continued in office in 1995 without serious challenge. *Reading:* Joseph M. McCarthy, *Guinea-Bissau and Cape Verde: A Comprehensive Bibliography* (1977); Rosemary E. Galli, *Guinea-Bissau (World Bibliographical Series, Vol. 121)* (1991). Rosemary E. Galli & Jocelyn Jones, *Guinea-Bissau: Politics, Economics, and Society* (1987); Joshua B. Forrest, *Guinea-Bissau: Power, Conflict, and Renewal in a Western African Nation* (1992).

Gulbahar. *See* Afghanistan.

Guleid, Muhammad Ainanshe. On 5 May 1971, an apparently foiled coup attempt led by Somalia's vice president, General Muhammad Ainanshe Guleid, led to Guleid's arrest and the arrest of two of his associates. They were charged with treason in a plot to assassinate the president, Major General Muhammad Siyad Barrah (qv), and other high officials and to return the socialist country to capitalism. The group was tried and found guilty in May and sentenced to death. The three were publicly executed by firing squad on 3 July 1972.

Gulf Cooperation Council (GCC). An organization of member states: Bahrain, Kuwait, Oman, Qatar, Saudi Arabia and the United Arab Emirates (UAE), the GCC was formed at Mucat, Oman, on 10 March 1981. The first heads of state meeting was held at Abu Dhabi, UAE, on 26 May. The organization's headquarters wwere located in Riyadh, Saudi Arabia. The GCC was set up as a regional economic and defense community. In May 1984, the GCC defense ministers met in Riyadh to coordinate plans against future Iranian attacks on the member states. That meeting was followed by a heads of state meeting at Riyadh on 24 June to codify the defense planning. On 27 November a rapid deployment force was established to defend the region. In November 1986 GCC called for an immediate cease-fire in the Iran-Iraq War (qv). There was also speculation that the GCC was about to set up a maritime protection force by 1987 that would include naval patrol aircraft and submarines. While these efforts were being put forward, there were less than satisfactory results on the economic front. Cooperation was also hindered when Qatar and Bahrain began squabbling over a minor border incident. Further deterioration, brought about mainly by a slump in oil prices, further undermined the GCC in 1987, even through regional security matters remained a high priority. Defense issues dominated the GCC meeting in December 1988, and the question of severing relations with Iran was brought up by at least one nation. Some economic progress was seen in 1989 as the GCC met with the European Community (EC) over the issue of industrial cooperation. As the tides of necessity shifted, the GCC met with Iranian officials in December 1990 to discuss regional security matters over Iraq's threat to the region. After the war in Kuwait (qv), the GCC began to show signs of decay, when Kuwait stated that the only real defense for the region was the West. But, in 1992, after the 1991 Damascus Conference, the GCC was showing some improvement in economic stability as links with the EC were strengthened, although the security aspects of the coalition were still in jeopardy, primarily after Kuwait's claim that only the West could protect Middle Eastern countries. In 1993, the GCC continued its condemnation of Iraq's aggression, but failed to reach a consensus on most other issues dealing with peaceful cooperation. By the end of 1994, the GCC had accomplished the near impossible, its member states having abandoned all but the most fundamental issues in their boycott of Israel. This lifted the fear of Arab economic reaction toward anyone dealing with the Jewish state. *Reading:* Emile A. Nakhleh, *The Gulf Cooperation Council: Policies, Problems and Prospects* (1986); Erik R. Peterson, *The Gulf Cooperation Council: Search for Unity in a Dynamic Region* (1988); Feisal Al Mazidi, *The Future of the Gulf: The Legacy of War and the Challenges of the 1990s* (1994).

Gulf of Aden. The Gulf of Aden is an extension of the Arabian Sea that separates Somalia in the Horn of Africa from Yemen on the Arabian Peninsula. At the same time, it connects the Arabian Sea on the east (and therefore the northern Indian Ocean) with the Red Sea at the *Bab el Mandeb*, the strait that separates

Djibouti from Yemen. On 11 June 1971, it was the scene of a Palestinian attack on an Israeli ship as it transitted the *Bab el Mandeb*. During the 1973 Arab-Israeli War (qv), the strait was blockaded by the Egyptian to prevent supplies reaching Israel through the port of Eilat.

Gulf of Aqaba (*Al 'Aqabah*). Known as the *Sinus Atlanticus* in Roman times, the Gulf of Aqaba is the eastern of the two arms that form the head of the Red Sea, the western arm being the Gulf of Suez (qv). The Sinai forms the west coast of the Gulf of Aqaba, while Saudi Arabia possesses most of the east coast. Jordan has a small holding in the northeast corner: The town of Aqaba is located there, while Israel holds the northwest corner at Eilat. The Strait of Tiran separates the Gulf from the Red Sea itself. The Gulf of Aqaba is sometimes known as the Gulf of Eilat, especially in Israel. In July 1956, Egypt, under the newly empowered Gamal Nasser (qv), sought to blockade the Strait of Tiran so as to block shipping to Israel. When Egyptian troops occupied Sharm el Sheikh following the withdrawal of the UN peacekeeping forces after 17 May 1967, the gulf was again effectively closed to Israeli shipping. On 24 May, Egypt claimed the gulf in the name of the United Arab Republic. With the Israeli recapture of Sharm el Sheikh on 7 June 1967, two days after the beginning of the Six Day War (Arab-Israeli War of 1967), the Israeli port of Eilat was again used as one the main supply routes into Israel. Since that time the Gulf of Aqaba remained nominally free of military confrontation.

Gulf of Eilat. *See* Gulf of Aqaba.

Gulf of Siam. Known also as the Gulf of Thailand, the Gulf of Siam is a large body of water surrounded on three sides by land. To the north and west is Thailand, to the east, Cambodia and Vietnam. The Gulf of Siam connects with the South China Sea to the southeast. In May 1962, the United States sent a naval task force with an 1,800-man Marine battalion landing team (BLT) into the Gulf of Siam in response to repeated cease-fire violations by communist Pathet Lao forces in Laos. In later fighting in Cambodia (1970), access to the gulf became an objective of government troops charged with keeping the route from Phnom Penh, the Cambodian capital, and the seaport of Kampong Saom (Sihanoukville) open. The route was finally cleared by Cambodian and South Vietnamese troops in January 1971. In an action on 24 April 1972, a South Vietnamese naval vessel sank a North Vietnamese trawler loaded with explosives near Pho Quoc island in the gulf. In May 1975, the Gulf of Siam became the scene of another naval drama when a Cambodian naval vessel seized the 10,000-ton American merchant freighter *SS Mayaguez* in international waters, 60 miles off the Cambodian coast. The ship and its crew of 39 were taken to Koh Tang Island, 25 miles southeast of Kampong Som (12 May). Two days later, a U.S. naval task force recaptured the ship in a poorly prepared and executed operation. The crew was not found at that time. On 13 June, Cambodian and Vietnamese naval and land units clashed in an ownership dispute over the Poulo Wai island group about 60 miles off the coast. On 22 June 1980, at least 50 Thai fishermen were killed when a Vietnamese gunboat sank three Thai trawlers in the Gulf of Siam.

Gulf of Sidra (*Khalij Surt*). The Gulf of Sidra is a body of water formed by a large depression in the northern coast of Africa and is a part of the Mediterranean Sea. The gulf occupies the central third of the coastline of Libya, with Benghazi at its westernmost lip. In 19 August 1981, two US Navy F-14 "Tomcat" fighters, operating from the *USS Nimitz* (CVN-68), shot down two Soviet-built Libyan Su-22 "Fitter" fighters with Sidewinder missiles over the gulf as they prepared to attack the Americans. The US aircraft were part of a naval exercise that was taking place provocatively close (60 miles) to the Libyan coast. Colonel Muammar al-Qaddafi (qv) had declared the Gulf of Sidra to be Libyan waters even though generally accepted rules placed most of the gulf within the realm of international waters. Qaddafi called the imposed boundary his "Line of Death" and swore to protect it.

Gulf of Suez. The Gulf of Suez is the left arm of the Red Sea and connects (Strait of Jubal) that body of water with the Mediterranean Sea to the north via the Suez Canal, a series of waterways and lakes, north of the city of Suez (*as Suways*). Egypt forms the western coastline of the gulf, while Sinai lies to the east. The Gulf of Suez has seen warfare throughout the centuries. In recent times it has been the scene of numerous conflicts between Arabs and Israelis. In September 1969, for instance, the Israeli government reported that its fighters had shot down eleven United Arab Republic aircraft over the Gulf of Suez in some of the heaviest Arab-Israeli fighting since the end of the 1967 war. In December 1969, Israeli commandos captured and carted off a Soviet-built radar station in a series of raids on the Egyptian side of the gulf. Small-scale fighting of this kind continued into 1970. On 6 February 1970, for example, Arab frogmen sank an Israeli supply vessel in the harbor of Eilat on the Gulf of Aqaba (Eilat). In retaliation, Israeli jets sank a UAR mine-layer in the Gulf of Suez. Armed clashes continued in and around the gulf over the next several years. In the 1973 Arab-Israeli War, the Gulf of Suez was mined by both sides. After the war, Israel cooperated in sweeping the gulf to remove the mines.

Gulf of Thailand. *See* Gulf of Siam.

Gulf of Tonkin. The Gulf of Tonkin is a large body of water off the coast of North Vietnam. The gulf may be entered from the south from the South China Sea and from the northeast through the *Qiongzhou Haixia*, a channel between the Kwangtung (*Guangdong*) peninsula on the Chinese mainland and the island of Hainan. Hainan forms the eastern shoreline of the Gulf of Tonkin, China the northeastern and northern boundaries, and North Vietnam the western shoreline.The maritime entrance to Hanoi, the North Vietnamese capital, is through the Gulf of Tonkin. Hainan was occupied by Chinese communist forces in May 1950 in one of the last phases of their consolidation of the mainland after the fall of Nationalist China. In July 1964, South Vietnamese naval units, without notifying their American counterparts, carried out a series of attacks against North Vietnamese radar and naval installations along the Gulf of Tonkin coast. Then on 2 August 1964, at least three North Vietnamese navy torpedo boats attacked the destroyer *USS Maddox* off the North Vietnamese coast. With the assistance of aircraft from the American carrier *USS Ticonderoga,* the attack was beaten off. Another similar attack was made on 4 August against the *USS Maddox* and another destroyer, *USS C. Turner Joy.* Two of the attacking motor torpedo boats were sunk in that action. The Americans immediately reinforced their naval presence in the gulf. On 7 August, a Joint Congressional Resolution (signed 11 August [Gulf of Tonkin Resolution , PL 88–4081]) affirmed that the U.S. was prepared to assist any Southeast Asia Treaty Organization (SEATO) member or protocol state requesting defense assistance. By April 1965, dogfights between U.S. and North Vietnamese jets were taking place over the Gulf of Tonkin, and a blockade of North Vietnam's ports was put into place. Naval action in the Gulf continued into 1973. *See* Vietnam.

Gürsel, Jemal. On 26–27 May 1960, Turkish premier Adnan Menderes and his cabinet were ousted from office and arrested in a military coup led by General Jemal Gürsel. The 38-man military junta behind Gürsel was known as the Turkish National Unity Committee. It first action was to schedule free elections. In the interim, the junta leader became provisional head of state.

Gutiérrez, Jaime Abdul. On 17 October 1979, the government of El Salvador's president Carlos Humberto Romero was overthrown by a military coup led by Colonels Jaime Abdul Gutiérrez and Adolfo Arnoldo Majano. Romero was exiled, but political unrest and violence continued throughout the country. After the coup, the junta itself ruled until 13 December 1980, when José Napoleón Duarte was sworn in as president under junta auspices.

Guyana. More properly called the Co-operative Republic of Guyana, the country of Guyana lies on the northeast coast of South America. Guyana is bordered by Venezuela on the west, Suriname on the east, Brazil on the south and the Atlantic Ocean on the north. The capital city is Georgetown. The Guyanan coast was first sighted by Columbus in 1498. Early Spanish attempts at colonization or exploitation were unsuccessful. Dutch settlements were put down along the major rivers by 1616, an accomplishment that led to the founding of the Dutch West India Company in 1621. The English entered the area in 1651, the French in 1674. The slave trade became a major enterprise. Between the eighteenth and early nineteenth centuries areas frequently changed ownership. By 1831, however, the colony of British Guiana was established, although its boundaries are still open to dispute and have been the cause of several major disputes, especially with Venezuela as late as 1960. Gold was discovered in 1879. In 1928, Guiana became a British crown colony. From 1953 until 1966, political tensions pervaded the colony, with communist influence being felt so strongly in October 1953 that the British government suspended the constitution and reinforced the garrison there. From 1961 until 1964, the country was beset by rioting and disorder and, again, British troops were brought in to restore order. In May 1966, the colony became independent and was renamed Guyana. In January 1969, a major uprising began in the Rupununi district that was crushed by army and security forces. The uprising had been supported by Brazilian and Venezuelan factions. That same year, in August, Dutch troops from neighboring

Suriname occupied a disputed region along the border of Guyana. Fighting broke out between the Dutch and Guyanan forces and continued until September, when the Dutch withdrew. In April 1970, an agreement was reached with Suriname that demilitarized the border area along the upper Courantyne River. In June 1970, a ten-year moratorium on the border dispute with Venezuela was arranged between the two governments. In 1978, Guyana joined in the multinational security force designed to gaurantee the security of Belize. In November of 1978, a bizarre incident took place at a largely American settlement established by member of Jim Jones' People's Temple cult (qv). A U.S. congressman was ambushed and killed at Port Kaituma and shortly afterwards the entire cult population of 911 members committed suicide. In 1982, Venezuela reinstated its claim to areas along the common border; the border dispute with Suriname also remained unsettled. Economic problems created havoc in 1983, which in turn led to strikes over the lack of imported food. In December of that year, a group including one American and seven Canadians was arrested on charges of plotting the overthrow of the Burnham government. By 1984 the economic situation had deteriorated further, and talks with the International Monetary Fund (IMF) had broken down. Guyana then turned to Soviet-bloc countries for trade. Then, on 6 August 1985, Burnham died following throat surgery. Desmond Hoyte became president. and Hamilton Green moved up to prime minister. Hoyte and Green began an immediate campaign to improve the very much strained relations with the U.S., although Hoyte announced he would followed Burnham's romance with the socialist bloc. New elections proved Hoyte to be the leader amid the usual charges of fraud claimed by the losers. The economic outlook showed some improvement in 1986, and by 1989 a tentative IMF agreement had been reached. During 1989, however, strikes by bauxite and sugar workers and continual electrical power breakdowns further exacerbated the already tenuous situation. In July 1990, the IMF settled its differences with Guyana and, in a complex plan, approved funding for Guyana. New elections were ordered, this time with Commonwealth observers invited to witness the proceedings. The elections were twice postponed, however, and Hoyte declared a state of emergency on 28 November 1991, further forestalling the referendum. When the vote was finally taken in 1992, the People's Progressive Party (PPP) of Cheddi Jagan (qv) won, with Jagan reelected president after 28 years on the sidelines. Upon taking office it became clear that Jagan had dropped his Marxist-Leninist leanings and moved toward a democratic system of government. Although there were signs of improvement through 1994, a ten-day strike by public works personnel ended only when the government agreed to minimum wage demands, which further destabilized the situation. In 1995, the Jagan government was faced with the problem of addressing the 1980 assassination of the internationally recognized historian and political activist Walter Rodney. Evidence had been accumulated that his death was attributable to the Burnham regime. Jagan directed an international commission to investigate the incident. *Reading:* Dennis Watson

& Christine Craig, eds., *Guyana at the Crossroads* (1992); Raymond Thomas Smith, *British Guiana* (1980); George K. Danns, *Domination and Power in Guyana: A Study of the Police in the Third World Context* (1982); Ralph Premdas, *Ethnic Conflict and Development: The Case of Guyana* (1995); Colin Baber, *Guyana: Politics, Economics and Society: Beyond the Burnham Era* (1986).

Guzmán Fernández, Silvestre Antonio. (b. 12 February 1911, La Vega, Dominican Republic—d. 4 July 1982, Santo Domingo) Born into a socially prominent family, Guzmán spent his early life building a considerable reputation as a businessman. In 1963, he entered politics and joined the Partido Revolucionario Dominicano (PRD), founded by Juan Bosch (qv). In 1966, he and Bosch led the opposition party. Bosch broke with the party in 1973, having embraced socialism. This gave the PRD leadership to Guzmán. Abstaining from the 1973 election, the PRD continued in opposition to the Balaguer (qv) government. In 1978, he Guzmán stood for the presidency, but one day after the election, the army suspended the vote count. International outrage forced the government to declare Guzmán the winner. He was inaugurated on 16 August 1978 in the first peaceful transfer of power in the Dominican Republic in 100 years. During the 1982 elections, Guzmán was to be succeeded by Salvador Jose Blanco. At that time, he discovered that a number of his closest associates had been robbing the national treasury and sending the money abroad. Feeling himself in disgrace, he committed suicide at age 71 on 4 July 1982. His death by shooting was officially ruled an accident so that he could be buried by the Catholic Church.

Gvulot. *See* Israel.

Gwera. *See* Zimbabwe.

Gyani, Perm Singh. An Indian lieutenant general, Gyani took command of the 200-man UN Observer Force sent to Yemen on 27 August 1963. The UN had authorized the force on 1 June 1963 for a two-month tour of duty. When the force was extended on 1 August, the Swedish commander, Major General Karl Von Horn, resigned and was replaced by Gyani.

H

Habash (Habbash), George. (b. 1925, near Haifa, Palestine; also reported as 1926, Lod, Palestine) Born a Greek Orthodox Christian, Habash received his early education in Jerusalem and fought against the Israelis during the War for Independence in 1948. After the war, he became disillusioned with the Arab leadership and moved to Beirut, Lebanon, where he studied medicine. He practiced in Beirut from 1950 until 1956 and then moved his practice to Amman, Jordan. There, however, he spent less and less time at his profession and more and more time in political agitation. He was expelled from Jordan in 1957 as a suspected Syrian intelligence agent. He then lived in Damascus for a time before returning to Lebanon. In 1959 Habash founded the Arab Nationalists Movement (ANM) and set himself up as a Palestinian politican. In 1965, Habash quit his medical practice to devote himself full time to politics. At that time he joined Yasir Arafat (qv) and Naif Hawatmeh (qv) in the formation of a secret Palestinian organization, *al Fatah.* His primary function was recruitment of Arabs for clandestine operations in Israel. After the Arab debacle in the 1967 Arab-Israeli War, Habash and Hawatmeh broke with *Fatah,* and out of the ANM and three other organizations they formed the antiroyalist Popular Front for the Liberation of Palestine (PFLP)(qv), which focused on the development of a Marxist-Leninist ideology for its members. Hawatmeh then broke with Habash in favor of a Maoist ideology. Habash travelled to North Korea and was there during the PFLP highjacking of three airliners to Jordan (6–9 September 1970) and the brief Jordanian civil war (9–27 September 1970). In August 1973, Habash was reportedly on board a Middle East airliner forced down by Israeli jets while on a flight from Beirut to Baghdad. The Israelis blamed Habash for the Athens airport attack on 29 September 1969. The PFLP was relatively inactive after Habash underwent surgery in September 1980. In more recent times, it has been reported that Habash has developed a better working relationship with Yasir Arafat and that Habash is working within the PLO.

Habré, Hissen. (b. 1942, French Equatorial Africa) Born into the Toubou tribe in northern Chad, Habré was educated in France at the Institut d'Études Politiques, graduating in 1971. Upon Habre's return to Chad, then president N'Garta Tombalbaye (qv) entrusted him with the mission of contacting rebellion leader Abba Siddick. After the meeting, Habré joined Siddick and his Chad National Liberation Front (Frolinat). During this period the noted French ethnologist and archaeologist Françoise Claustre was taken prisoner (1974) and held hostage by Frolinat. In October 1976, Goukouni Oueddei (qv), another rebel leader, took power away from Habré and released Claustre in January 1977, after the French government paid a 10 million franc ransom for him. Habré fled to Sudan, where he remained until January 1978, when he again appeared in command of the Armed Forces of the North (FAN). On 29 August 1978, he was appointed premier by President Félix Malloum (qv). In February 1979, fighting broke out in N'Djamena, Chad's capital city, between the Christian forces, Chad National Army (ANT) of Malloum and Habre's FAN troops. The fighting soon spread to the countryside, where it involved Frolinat forces. When four French civilians were killed, the French garrison of 2,000 plus 400 French advisors with ANT were reinforced by French airborne units. Malloum then handed over the instruments of power to the National Police and resigned on 12 February 1979. Habré then resigned as prime minister. A cease-fire was arranged between the ANT and FAN forces. Fresh fighting broke out on 4 March, with 800 casualties reported. On 23 March a new government was formed, with Goukouni Oueddei becoming president. The fighting continued into 1980; peace talks scheduled for March broke down when the sector of the city controlled by forces loyal to Habré were attacked by troops loyal to the new vice-president, Wadal Abdel Kader Kamougue (qv). ANT and FAN forces then engaged in very heavy fighting in the city. On 31 March 1980 a cease-fire was arranged, which remained more or less in effect until December, when Libyan forces entered Chad and attacked FAN forces in and around the capital at the request of President Gourkouni Oueddei. Libyan forces secured the city on 16 December. Habré fled to Cameroon, and an Organization of African Unity cease-fire was put into effect. Oueddei then demanded France withdraw the remainder of its forces in Chad because of their support of Habré and FAN. FAN forces reentered Chad from their safe-haven in Sudan in November 1981 and quickly occupied most of eastern Chad, even though OAU peacekeeping forces had been dispatched to control the situation. By January 1982, FAN controlled two-thirds of the country and entered the capital on 7 June. Then, in a major reversal of roles, Habré took over the nation's leadership. During his tenure he withstood several attempts on his life but did manage to restore relations with Libya. There was sufficient opposition, however, to overthrow his government on 1 December 1990, when forces loyal to General Idriss Deby and his Popular Salvation Movement crossed into Chad from Sudan. On 1 December, Habré fled the capital. Deby's forces entered N'Djamena on 3 December; Deby declared himself president the next day. The whereabouts of Habré were unknown at the time, but it was presumed he had taken refuge in either Sudan or Cameroon.

Habrut. *See* Yemen.

Habyalimana, Juvenal. On 5 July 1973, the government of Rwanda's president, Gregoire Kayibanda (qv) was overthrown in a bloodless coup led by Major General Juvenal Habyalimana, the commander of the National Guard. Habyalimana then took control of the country in the name of the Commission for the Restoration of Peace. The coup came about after Kayibanda attempted to change the constitution so that he could be reelected. The more likely reason was tribal antagonisms toward his high post appointments. Habyalimana was reelected (he ran unopposed) in December 1978 as the country moved slowly up the road to economic and political stability. He won successive terms under the one-party system and remained in power in 1992.

Haddad, Saad. (b. 1938 [?]—d. 14 January 1984, Marj Vyun, Lebanon) Born Greek Orthodox, Haddad joined the Lebanese army and, as a major attended the U.S. Army Infantry School at Fort Benning, Georgia. In 1976, he broke with the Lebanese government and formed a personal 2,500-man militia composed of Palestinian Shi'a Muslims and Maronite Christians in southern Lebanon claiming the southern section of the country under his control as "free Lebanon." At this point, he was dismissed from the Lebanese army (1979). Thereafter he received his supplies and equipment from the Israelis. Haddad's men were accused of the 16 September 1982 massacre of hundreds of Palestinians in two refugee camps (Sabra and Shatila) in West Beirut. Haddad's denial of the charges did not ring true, but blame was never fixed by the Israeli judicial commission set up to investigate the incident (1983), and Haddad was cleared of any responsibility for the atrocity. By the beginning of 1982, Haddad's militia controlled a narrow strip of Lebanon adjacent to the Israeli border. After the June 1982 Israeli incursion into Lebanon, the Israelis gave Haddad control over the entire southern portion of Lebanon. After 1982, Israeli came to realize that Haddad's control over the region under his jurisdiction was tenuous at best and did not constitute the security zone they desired along their northern border. Nonetheless, Israel worked to get Haddad's army integrated into the Lebanese army and given control over the southern Lebanese tier with Haddad in command. Haddad was reinstated in the Lebanese army in January 1984, shortly before his death from cancer.

el Hadj, Mohand ou. On 6–8 October 1963, Colonel Mohand ou el Hadj led a Berber uprising in the Kabylien Mountain region of Algeria. The revolt was put down by troops loyal to President Achmed Ben Bella (qv).

Ha-Galil. *See* Syria.

Hague, The. *See* Netherlands.

Haifa (*Hefa*). *See* Israel.

Haifa Bay (Mifraz Hefa). *See* Haifa.

Haig, Alexander Meigs, Jr. (b. 2 December 1924, Philadelphia) A graduate of the United States Military Academy (1947), Haig earned a master's degree at Georgetown University. He fought in Vietnam as a battalion and brigade commander (1966–1967). Haig served as Henry Kissinger's assistant on the National Security Council and as White House chief of staff for most of the last two years (1973–1974) of the Nixon administration. He was then appointed Supreme Allied Commander, Europe (SACEUR), where he served from 1974 until 1979. An assassination attempt was made on his life at Mons, Belgium, on 25 June 1979. A command-detonated mine, hidden in a culvert, failed to explode under Haig's vehicle but badly damaged a security car following behind. No one was seriously injured. The Red Army Faction's "Commando Andreas Baader" took credit for the attack. In 1981, President Reagan nominated Haig to be secretary of state. He served in that post for two years (1981–1982), a period filled with tension as Haig and Secretary of Defense Caspar Weinberger (qv) sought their relative positions in the White House hierarchy. Haig resigned his post in June 1982.

Haile Selassie (aka Tafari Makonnen). (b. 23 July 1892, near Harar, Ethiopia—d. 27 August 1975, Addis Ababa) Born the youngest son of Prince (*Ras*) Makonnen, a cousin and advisor to Emperor Menelik II, Tafari Makonnen was educated at home by French missionaries. Upon his father's death (1906?), Tafari became the governor of Harar. When Menelik II died in 1916, his oldest daughter, Zauditu, became empress, and Tafari Makonnen was elected regent and became the heir to the throne. In 1923, he brought Ethiopia into the League of Nations, and in 1924, he became the first Ethiopian monarch to visit Europe. In 1928, he assumed the title of king (*Negus*). In 1930, upon the death of the Empress Zauditu, Tafari proclaimed himself emperor. It is at that point he assumed the name Haile Selassie, "Might of the Trinity," based upon the descent, as tradition had it, of the Ethiopian throne from Israel's King Solomon. His best-known appelation was "Lion of Judah." His first task as emperor was to drag Ethiopia out of the Middle Ages. In doing so, however, his progressiveness turned to dictatorship, and before the end of his reign he held all power in his own hands. When Italy invaded Ethiopia in October 1935, the backwardness of his people armed with spears became apparent, and they faired poorly against the fascist Italians. Haile Selassie was forced to flee Ethiopia in April 1936. On 30 June 1936, he addressed the League of Nations, requesting that body's assistance in saving his country. The moribund nature of the League became immediately apparent as he received great sympathy but no support. He returned to Ethiopia only after its liberation by the British in 1941. By that point Haile Selassie had grown more aloof from his people, and his program for reconstruction and rehabilitation of Ethiopia became a seemingly hopeless task. Yet some of his reforms did work against him in the long run. His country was now not entirely ignorant, and students in the universities he built led the way for change. In 1955, Haile Selassie issued a new constitution that gave him total power. An army revolt was suppressed in 1960, but widespread dissatisfaction grew and was aided by an extreme famine in the northern provinces (1973) that claimed 100,000 lives. In 1974, the military backed student demands for change, but the emperor refused to budge. On 12 September 1974, Haile Selassie was deposed in favor of the crown prince (who was himself deposed in March 1975, when a republic was proclaimed). Haile Selassie was confined to an army barracks in Addis Ababa, but before his death he was allowed to return to his palace, where he died under mysterious circumstances on 27 August 1975. *Reading:* Ryszard Kapuscinski, *The Emperor: Downfall of an Autocrat* (1989); Gaitachew Bekele, *The Emperor's Clothes: A Personal Viewpoint on Politics and Administration in the Imperial Ethiopian Government 1941–1974* (1993);

Hainan Island (*Hai-nan tao*). *See* China.

Haiphong. *See* Vietnam.

Haiti. More properly the Republic of Haiti, this nation occupies the western half of the island of Hispaniola in the West Indies. The eastern half of the island is occupied by the Dominican Republic. Hispaniola was discovered in 1492 by Christopher Columbus. At that time the native population were Arawak Indians The Arawak name for the island was Quisqueya or Haiti. By the sixteenth century almost the entire native population had died of disease transmitted by the Europeans or because of their brutality. By the beginning of the seventeenth century, most of the Spanish inhabitants of the western end of Hispaniola had moved to the mainland, and the French moved in to fill the void. In 1664, the French West India Company took control of the western region of the island; Spain ceded this region to France in 1667. At the time of the French Revolution four-fifths of the entire population were slaves. In 1791 a general slave revolt occurred, and by 1801 the entire island was in the hands of Pierre-Dominique Toussant, who proclaimed himself governor-general for life. France's attempt at retaking the island failed, and by 1803 the island was still in again in native hands. Most of the whites who had remained on the island were massacred. France recognized Haiti in 1825, but only after payment of a hugh indemnification. In 1844, the Spanish-speaking population of the eastern end of the island revolted and established the Dominican Republic. Haiti's history over the next half-century was marked by revolts and palace coups. In 1915, the United States intervened and occupied Haiti until 1936. Although there was much Haitian resentment of American interference and several instances of the use of military force to maintain or restore order, this period evinced measureable improvement in the social and political life of the country. In December 1956, Colonel Paul Magliore, who had been elected president, was forced to resign. A period of disorder followed until September 1957, when François Duvalier (qv) was elected president. Almost immediately, Duvalier established a dictatorial regime that was policed by the *Tonton Macoute*, an extralegal secret police force which terrorized the entire population. There were several attempted revolts, but all were smashed. Many foreign governments closed their missions in Haiti because of the threat to their diplomats. In 1964, "Papa Doc," as Duvalier was called, had himself appointed president for life. Duvalier who died in 1971, was succeeded by his son, Jean-Claude ("Baby Doc") (qv), who was unable or unwilling to reverse his father's style of leadership. A drought in 1975–1977 and the effects of Hurricane Allen (1980) raised the level of unrest to a point where Duvalier had to go. In February 1986, Duvalier and his family left Haiti, and a military-civilian council took over the reins of government. In 1987 a new constitution was approved. By December 1990, however, there had been five governments and at least three coups. In

December 1990, Father Jean-Bertrand Aristide was elected president. In January 1991, a Duvalier-inspired coup took place, but was crushed by the army. In the wave of rioting that followed, Aristide was arrested by the military and thrown out of the country. A military junta was then established, which, until December 1993, resisted all international attempts to restore the elected government to that country. The U.S. took the lead in attempting to force out the junta, even though the move was somewhat unpopular. Then, on 31 July, the United Nations called upon its members to move against the Haitian regime. The first move was to close the Haitian-Dominican Republic border to halt smuggling, which was the principal source of revenue for the junta. Past that point, the U.S. found itself standing alone, as no other country was willing to support a military operation. Haiti nevertheless declared a state of siege. Internally, a campaign of assassination continued against all opposition, especially that loyal to Aristide. On 18 September 1994, an unofficial US delegation headed by Jimmy Carter (qv) convinced the junta to step down. Several junta leaders immediately fled the country. The next day, 19 September, U.S. forces began landing in Haiti. While the plan called for U.S. support of the Haitian military in a peacekeeping role, the situation rapidly changed to peacemaking after U.S. officials witnessed the conduct of the Haitian forces in dealing with civilian demonstrators. The U.S. then began direct intervention, quite often needing to use lethal force to stop the outrages. On 24 September, ten Haitian police were killed in one shootout. This heartened the Haitian people to commit equally malicious acts of violence until most of the Haitian police and military forces had fled the cities and towns. Thereafter, only the US military prevented a descent into anarchy. Aristide returned to Haiti on 15 October. His first acts included a move toward reconciliation and the announcement of new elections by December. These were subsequently delayed until March 1995. U.S. troops began withdrawing in January 1995, and UN forces were inserted in their place. This did not mean that the country was pacified, however, even though U.S. commanders indicated that it was "secure." The lack of a police infrastructure led to constant violence, with several killings each day. When expected international funding was slow in reaching Haiti, resentment grew. When the financial situation stabilized, Aristide began the slow process of weakening the military's dominion over the country by forcing senior officers into retirement, with the ultimate goal of abolishing the army altogether. The elections were finally held in June 1995. Aristide's party won a majority of seats in both houses. Aristide then stepped down, on 7 February 1996. The new president, Rene Preval, requested that the UN force remain in-country for an additional six months because the already corrupt new police force could not maintain order. *Reading:* Rayford Logan, *Haiti and the Dominican Republic* (1968); Jean-Bertrand Aristide with Christophe Wargny, *Aristide: An Autobiography* (1993); Alex Dupuy, *Haiti in the New World Order: The Limits of Democratic Revolution* (1997); Frantz Pratt, ed., *Haiti: Guide to the Periodical Literature in English* (1991).

Hal Far. *See* Malta.

Hama (Hamah). *See* Syria.

al-Hamidi, Abdullah Mohammed. Colonel Abdullah Mohammed al-Hamidi was accompanying his cousin, President Ibrahim al-Hamidi of the Yemen Arab Republic (North Yemen), when they were both killed by assassins on 11 October 1977.

al-Hamidi, Ibrahim. On 13 June 1974, a military coup overthrew the government of Yemen's president, Abdul Rahman al-Iryani. A pro-Saudi Arab, Colonel Ibrahim al-Hamidi became head of state and ruled until 11 October 1977, when he was assassinated.

Hammarskjöld, Dag (Hjalmar Agne Carl). (b. 29 July 1905, Jönköping, Sweden—d. 18 September 1961, Ndola, Northern Rhodesia) Born the son of future Swedish prime minister Hjalmar Hammarskjöld, Dag studied law and economics at the universities of Uppsala and Stockholm. In 1933, he joined the faculty in economics at the University of Stockholm. In 1936 he was appointed a permanent undersecretary in the ministry of finance. He also served as the president of the board at the Bank of Sweden. In 1947, he joined the ministry of foreign affairs and, in 1951, became the deputy minister for foreign affairs. He was appointed vice chairman of the Swedish delegation to the United Nations in 1951 and was appointed chairman in 1952. In April 1953 he was elected UN secretary-general and was unanimously reelected to that post in September 1957. He was instrumental in the settlement of the Suez Crisis in 1956–1957 and in the crisis in the Belgium Congo in 1960. He also withstood a 1961 Soviet charge of his complicity in the murder of Patrice Lumumba (qv) and their demand (1960) to reorganize the UN secretariat into a triumvirate in which each representative would hold veto power over all UN decisions. He was on a peace mission to the Congo when he was killed in an airplane crash near Ndola in Northern Rhodesia. Hammarskjöld was posthumously awarded the Nobel peace prize for 1961.

Hanga, Abdullah Kassim. On 12 January 1964, the government of Sultan Mohammed Shamte was overthrown by a leftist-led revolution in Zanzibar. A communist-dominated government headed by Abdullah Kassim Hanga took over two days later, on 14 January. The new government ordered Western diplomats out of the country and slaughtered thousands of Arabs. Hanga later became vice president of the Zanzibar republic after Zanzibar was united with the new state of Tanzania (26 April 1964). In December 1968, Tanzanian president Julius Nyerere (qv) ordered the arrest of Hanga and three others for plotting against the Zanzibar government. Hanga, who had been living in exile in Guinea, had returned to Tanzania on assurances of his safety in 1967. After being arrested, he was held in Tanzania until September 1969 and then flown to Zanzibar, where he was executed.

Hankow. *See* China.

Hanoi. *See* Vietnam.

Harar. *See* Ethiopia.

Harbin. *See* China.

Hariana (Haryana). *See* India.

Harrods Department Store. A fashionable landmark in London, Harrods was the scene of a car bombing on 17 December 1983, when IRA terrorists planted an expolsive device in a car parked behind the department store. The explosion killed five and injured 91 others. Although the Provisional Wing of the IRA claimed credit for the attack, IRA leaders later stated that the attack was unauthorized and that steps had been taken to prevent a recurrence.

Hassan II. (b. 9 July 1929, Rabat) Hassan was born the eldest son of King Mohammed V (qv). He studied law at Bordeaux University in France, where he graduated in 1956. Upon his return to Morocco he was appointed the commander in chief of the Moroccan army (1957) and deputy premier in 1960. Upon the death of Mohammed V in February 1961, Hassan became king. He served as his own prime minister from 1961 to1963 and from 1965 to 1967. On 10–11 July 1971, a right-wing coup was attempted by a group of disgruntled generals, led by General Muhammed Madbouh, who duped a group of army noncommissioned officer cadets at the Ahermoumou training center to attack the royal birthday party at the summer palace at Skhirat. Among the 32 dignitaries killed in the fighting were three Moroccan generals and the Belgian ambassador. When the soldier who confronted Hassan realized who it was he had at gunpoint, he knelt down to kiss the king's hand. This ended the fighting, as the soldiers had been told they were going to protect the king's life. Four generals and a group of junior officers were executed after the investigation of the incident. Hassan then reorganized the army to prevent a reoccurrence of such an event. Even so, other factors at work in his country led to a decline in the prestige of the throne, and Hassan was beset by problems. In August 1972, for instance, he narrowly escaped assassination when his plane was attacked by Moroccan jets as he returned to Rabat from Paris in a coup attempt led by General Muhammed Oufkir, the man Hassan had assigned to investigate the 1971 birthday massacre. Oufkir eventually committed suicide. In 1973, 157 people were tried for treason in a plot to kill Hassan. Sixteen of the plotters were executed. In 1974, his country was at war with Algeria — this was the second such conflict during his reign, over control of the Western Sahara. In January 1984, Hassan faced serious rioting because of rising food and education costs across his country. Later that year, in August, Hassan drew criticism from the West over his treaty of union with Libya. Even so, Hassan was able to use his good offices in the mediation of the ongoing Arab-Israeli conflict. In 1992, Hassan II still ruled Morocco and continued being one of the most astute politicans in North Africa.

Havana. *See* Cuba.

Hawatmeh, Nayef (Naif). In 1965, Hawatmeh, a Greek Orthodox Christian, joined Yasir Arafat (qv) and George Habash (qv) in the formation of a secret Palestinian organization, *al Fatah*. After the Arab debacle in the 1967 Arab-Israeli War, Hawatmeh and Habash broke with *Fatah* and out of the Arab Nationalists Movement and three other organizations formed the antiroyalist Popular Front for the Liberation of Palestine (PFLP) (qv), which focused on the development of a Marxist-Leninist ideology for its members. Hawatmeh then broke with Habash in favor of a Maoist ideology and organized (1969) the

Popular Democratic Front for the Liberation of Palestine (PDFLP) (qv) with three confederates, Yasser Abed Rabbu, Qais Samarral (abu Leila) and Abd-al-Karim Hammed (Abu Adnan). Hawatmeh operated his terrorist organization within Israel and the occupied territories (West Bank and Gaza) but seemed more interested in politics than terrorism. Hawatmeh's group remained active in the early 1990s.

Hawker, Willem. Sergeant Major Willem Hawker of Suriname was placed in prison in 1981 for his part in an abortive coup attempt in March 1981. On 11–12 March 1982, Hawker was released from jail during a right-wing uprising timed to occur during a governmental hiatus. On 12 March, government troops regained control of the situation, captured Hawker and immediately executed him.

Hawkins, Lewis. On 2 June 1973, Lieutenant Colonel Lewis Hawkins, an American military advisor stationed in Iran was shot to death by two assassins believed to be members of a radical left-wing terrorist group.

Hebrew University. On 6 March 1969, an Arab terrorist bomb exploded at Hebrew University in Jerusalem, Israel. No one claimed responsibility, but Israeli security forces, in a typical Hammurabian response, leveled five Arab houses in East Jerusalem.

Hebron (Hevron, Al Khali). *See* Israel.

Hekmatyar, Gulbadin. Gulbadin Hekmatyar was the leader of the Hizbe Islami guerrilla group in Afghanistan in 1980. He reported on 7 March that, contrary to reports, the Soviets had not overrun Kunar province in eastern Afghanistan near the Pakistani border and that it was still in rebel hands. He also reported the Soviets had lost 300 killed and 1,100 wounded in the Kunar operation; he also indicated that his sources indicated that 110,000 Afghans had died since the start of the war.

Helou, Charles. On 24 June 1969, the new president of Lebanon, Charles Helou, ordered all Palestinian guerrilla forces out of the country. This action followed a period of growing tension between the Lebanese government and various Palestinian guerrilla factions that had established themselves in southern and eastern Lebanon. Helou's order was virtually ignored, and by October clashes between Lebanese forces and the Palestinians were a regular occurrence. A cease-fire was arranged on 2 November 1969, but lasted only a short time. Helou left office on 23 September 1970, when the National Assembly decided a new leader was required to try and settle the ever-worsening situation in Lebanon. Helou was replaced by Suleiman Franjieh (qv), the economy minister, as the new president.

Helsinki (*Helsingfors*). *See* Finland.

Helsinki Accords. More properly known as the Final Act (Charter) of the 1975 Conference on Security and Cooperation in Europe (CSCE), the Helsinki Accords, among other things, provided for advance notification any time maneuvers were to be held in Europe involving more than 25,000 troops. This was one of the so-called confidence-building measures that were a part of the agreement signed by thirty-five nations at Helsinki in August 1975. The accords also dealt with the issue of human rights. In 1977, the Soviet Union specifically. violated the terms of the agreement by arresting several members of the human rights monitoring group in the USSR. Among those arrested were Alexander Ginsberg, Yuri Orlov, Anatoly Shcharansky and Vladimir Slepak. In September 1981, the United States accused the Soviet Union of failing to provide advance warning of major maneuvers in the Soviet zone of Germany that could have been mistaken for signs of hostile activity. The CSCE remained in effect into the 1990s.

Heng Samrin. On 7 January 1979, the Communist-backed Kampuchean United Front for National Salvation, reinforced by Vietnamese army units. captured Phnom Penh. The next day, an eight-man revolutionary council was formed under the leadership of Heng Samrin, a former Khmer Rouge (qv) military leader, who had risen to power as a political commissar and division commander under Pol Pot (qv) before defecting to the Vietnamese. The following day, 9 January, the USSR officially recognized the new Soviet- and Vietnamese-backed Heng government. The 45-year-old Heng was immediately faced with a rebel war led from the jungle by Pol Pot. By January 1980, more than 200,000 Vietnamese troops were in Kampuchea, and the West became uneasy over the possibility of an invasion of Thailand. On 13 October 1980, the United Nations voted down a resolution to unseat the Pol Pot delegation, which still held UN credentials, in favor of the Heng Samrim delegation. In July, however, India recognized the puppet government. Heng became the president of the Council of State on 27 June 1981, and secretary-general of the Kampuchean Communist Party on 5 December 1981. He remained in power until October 1991, when the party changed its name to the Cambodian People's Party. At that time Heng was replaced as secretary-general. In November of that year, Prince Sihanouk was named head of state. Heng retained his title as chairman of the Council of State.

Herat. *See* Afghanistan.

Hermosillo. *See* Mexico.

Hernu, Charles. On 20 September 1985, French defense minister Charles Hernu and the director of the French Secret Service, Admiral Pierre Lacoste (qv), were forced to resign in the wake of the revelations of the investigation into the sinking of the Greenpeace flagship *Rainbow Warrior* (qv) as it lay at anchor in New Zealand.

Hinckley, John W., Jr. On 30 March 1981, John W. Hinckley attempted the assassination of President Ronald Reagan (qv) outside the Washington Hilton Hotel in Washington, DC. President Reagan was shot in the chest. White House Press Secretary James Brady was struck in the head by a bullet, and two Washington, DC, police officers was also shot before Hinckley was subdued. Hinckley, the 25-year-old son of a wealthy Evergreen, Colorado, family, used a .22 caliber "Saturday Night Special" in the assassination attempt. Upon his arrest at the scene, it was determined that he was a college dropout with a history of psychiatric problems. His motive in the attack was apparently to impress Jody Foster, a young movie actress. In September following the incident, Hinckley's lawyers indicated they would plead their client innocent by reason of insanity.

He was subsequently acquitted (June 1982) on all thirteen counts arising from the assassination attempt. Although freed of the charges, Hinkley has remained under guarded psychiatric care in a Washington, DC, facility ever since. His acquittal created a storm of protest across the country. *Reading:* Peter W. Low et al., *The Trial of John W. Hinckley, Jr.: A Case Study in the Insanity Defense* (1986).

Hindu Kush Region. *See* Afghanistan.

Hizballah (Hezballah). Hizballah is an Islamic terrorist organization with approximately 3,000 members (1988), of whom about 500 participate in acts of terror. The organization was formed in 1983 and has been known to have its headquarters in West Beirut and in the Bekaa Valley, Lebanon. It seldom takes credit for terrorist acts in its own name but uses one of several code names such as Islamic Jihad, Party of God, Organization of the Oppressed, or Revolutionary Justice Council when claimimg credit for an attack. The Consultative Council (*Shura*) that heads Hizballah reports to Iran and has among its leadership Husayn Musawi, Abbas Musawi and others. A number of Iranian Revolutionary Guards officers are also known to be attached to the group in Lebanon. Shaykh Muhammad Husayn Fadlallah (qv) was the group's spiritual leader until his assassination in 1985. Hizballah espouses the Shi'a Muslim ideology and adheres to a program of militancy that was approved by Iran's Ayatollah Khomeini (qv). Hizballah came into existence through the merger (1982–1983) of Husayn Massawi's Amal (qv) group and the Lebanese branch of the Da'wa (qv) party found usually in Kuwait. Hizballah terrorist operations are closely monitored by the Iranian Revolutionary Guard personnel in the *Shura*. Hizballah concentrates its terrorist efforts in the Middle East and in Europe and has claimed responsibilty for or has been accused of numerous attacks on targets in Lebanon, Kuwait, Paris, Copenhagen and Stockholm. Their most spectacular attack occurred in October 1983, when terrorists drove two trucks carrying explosives into the U.S. Marine and French military barracks in Beirut, killing 241 US and 56 French servicemen. Between 1983 and 1988 alone, Hizballah also kidnapped US diplomat William Buckley (March 1984), Father Lawrence Jenco (January 1985), journalist Terry Anderson (March 1985), American University of Beirut Dean Thomas Sutherland (June 1985), Joseph Cicippio (September 1986), Edward Tracy (October 1986), British Anglican envoy Terry Waite (January 1987), US Marine Lieutenant Colonel Richard Higgins (February 1988), and murdered or kidnapped at least 26 others, including the murder of US Navy SEAL Robert Stethem aboard hijacked TWA flight 847 in June 1985. Most of the American and European hostages were released in 1991. As is characteristic of Middle East affairs, all Hizballah candidates who stood for election in Lebanon in 1992 won their seats. Still, Hizballah remained a terrorist organization and was listed as such by the police and intelligence services of the world. As the Arab-Israeli peace process moved forward, albeit slowly, Syrian-backed Hizballan terrorists continually clashed with the Israelis in southern Lebanon (1994). On 2 June 1994, the Israelis retaliated by bombing a terrorist training base in southern Lebanon, killing an estimated 40 commandos. Hizballah then blew up a Jewish community center in Buenos Aires, killing 96 civilians (18 July). Further attacks also took place in London in July. The Israelis then made control of Hizballah an integral element in any future peace negotiations. *Reading:* Magnus Ranstorp, *Hizb'Allah in Lebanon: The Politics of the Western Hostage Crisis* (1996); Hala Jaber, *Hezbollah: Born with a Vengeance* (1997).

Hoa Hao. A Buddhist religious sect found in Vietnam, Hoa Hao came into existence in 1919 in the village of Hoa Hao in Bassac, southern Vietnam, not far from the Seven Mountains (*That-Son*). The leader of the sect, Huyuh Phy So, received his education from a hermit monk of the Seven Mountains Tra Son Pagoda, who cured him of an apparently incurable disease. On 21 March 1955, the Hoa Hao, along with other militant religious groups, such as the Cao Dai (qv), gave South Vietnamese president, Ngo Dinh Diem (qv) (a Christian), a five-day ultimatum demanding a government reorganization that would have put more members of their sects into influential positions. Diem rejected the demand on 24 March. Heavy fighting broke out on 29 March between government forces and the sects' private armies. The cease-fire was arranged on 30 March but did not hold. On 12 February 1955, the leader of the Hoa Hao, Tran Van Soai, surrendered himself to the government, but the fighting continued. On 3 April, another leader, Ba Cut, was captured by government forces, but, as before, the fighting continued and did so sporadically until the North Vietnamese/Viet Cong insurgency achieved such a level that all efforts had to be focused in that direction.

Hoai An. *See* Vietnam.

Hobeika, Elie. On 9 May 1985, Elie Hobeika replaced Samir Gangea (qv) as the leader of the Lebanese "Christian Forces" (Maronite). On 18 May, Hobeika announced his support of the Syrian intervention in Lebanon. Hobeika later (28 December 1985) took part in a ceremony held in Damascus in which the Christian, Shi'a and Druse militias were disbanded. In 1986, the Damascus accord began to unravel when Hobeika was ousted by his chief of staff, Samir Geagea.

Ho Chi Minh (Nguyen That Thanh). (b. 19 May 1890, Kim-Lien, Indochina—d. 3 September 1969, Hanoi) Ho Chi Minh was first observed as a communist organizer in Indochina in 1923. During the World War II, U.S. personnel of the Office of Strategic Services (OSS) worked with Ho and found him to be an honest nationalist more involved in freeing his country of foreign domination than in the spread of communism. The reports sent back to Washington were largely ignored. At the end of World War II, Ho proclaimed the Democratic Republic of Vietnam, which initiated the French Indochinese War (2 September 1945). Ho soothed French colonial ire over this move by signing a modus vivendi with Paris on 14 September 1946. By March 1947, however, Ho and the French both saw that the attempt at peace had failed. In 1951, Ho ordered (2 April) the Viet Minh to break off main force (frontal) attacks on the French forts and return to guerrilla warfare. In July 1955, Ho was able to sign a $338 million economic aid package with Communist China. In 1956, however, Ho's dream of a unified Vietnam free of foreign domination was interrupted by the partition of the country based upon the Geneva Accords. Ho then turned his attention to the consolidation of power in North Vietnam, but he also began the planning of a war against the south, which began in 1956. In 1964, the North Vietnamese launched their first full-scale offensive into the Republic of (South) Vietnam. In 1966, Ho was again forced to back down, after the North Vietnamese press announced that American prisoners of war would be put on trial as war criminals. United States president Lyndon B. Johnson warned (20 July 1966) of swift and strong U.S. reaction to such a move. Ho backed down three days later stating that "no trials were in view." During the war years, Ho showed little conciliation to American offers to stop the war. Ho's only response was, in essence, "Americans, go home." At the time of his death, Ho still adhered to the principle of victory rather than a negotiated peace. *Reading:* Milton Osbourne, *Ho Chi Minh* (1982); David Halberstam, *Ho* (1986).

Ho Chi Minh City/Saigon. *See* Vietnam.

Ho Chi Minh Trail. Used originally during the French Indochinese War, the system of trails and paths along the Laotian-Vietnamese border was resurveyed after January 1959 by an old man who knew it intimately. In his honor, the trail was called the "Old Man's Trail." It became better known, however, as the Ho Chi Minh Trail. and a large portion of North Vietnamese manpower and supplies entering South Vietnam during the war came over its route. (The bulk of supplies and materiel entered South Vietnam by sea.) The trail was bombed and damaged heavily by Allied bombing raids but was never completely closed and was usually back in service in a matter of hours, thanks to the North Vietnamese 559th Transportation Group, a 50,000-man organization that was charged with keeping the trail open. Other North Vietnamese units occupied areas along the trail and provided security. *Reading:* Richard L. Stevens, *Mission on the Ho Chi Minh Trail: Nature, Myth, and War in Viet Nam* (1995).

Hof, Frederick C. On 17 April 1982, Major Frederick C. Hof, the assistant military attache at the U.S. embassy in Beirut was wounded on the street by an unknown assailant.

Hoi Chanh. A Vietnamese who had been inducted into the Viet Cong and who had surrendered to the South Vietnamese through the *Chieu Hoi*(qv) program was called a *Hoi Chanh*. After a period of retraining and political indoctrination, the *Chieu Hoi* was released back into South Vietnamese society as a *Hoi Chanh*.

Hokkaido Island. *See* Japan.

Hollenben, Ehrenfried von. On 11 June 1970, the West German ambassador to Brazil, Ehrenfried von Hollenben, was kidnapped in Rio de Janeiro by terrorists of the Popular Revolutionary Vanguard while riding in his limousine when the vehicle was blocked by a truck and the kidnapping took place. A ransom for his release was set as the freeing of 40 political prisoners. The political prisoners were flown to Algiers on 16 June, and the ambassador was quickly released.

Holly, Sean M. On 6 March 1970, a U.S. embassy official, Sean M. Holly, was kidnapped in Guatemala City, Guatemala. The Guatemalan government released a number of political prisoners as ransom for the release of Holly and Foreign

Minister Alberto Fuentes Mohr (qv), who was taken in a separate incident. Count Karl von Spreti (qv), the West German ambassador was not so lucky, when he was kidnapped at about the same time, in a third incident. He was murdered (5 April) by the Revolutionary Armed Forces (FAR), who were probably responsible for all the kidnappings.

Holyoake, Sir Keith J. New Zealand Prime Minister Sir Keith J. Holyoake announced on 20 August 1970 that one-half of the New Zealand contingent would be withdrawn from South Vietnam by the end of 1971. The New Zealand contingent was relatively small—about one company (200 men)—at the time of the announcement.

Holy War. *See* Jihad.

Homme, Robert. On 26 March 1984, the U.S. consul in Strasbourg, France, Robert Homme, was shot and wounded by terrorists belonging to the Lebanese Armed Revolutionary Faction (LARF). In claiming credit for the attack, the pro-Palestinian LARF accused Homme of being an agent of the American Central Intelligence Agency.

Honduras. A Central American country located on the Caribbean Sea, Honduras is bordered on the northwest by Guatemala, on the west by El Salvador, and on the south by Nicaragua. Its capital city is Tegucigalpa. The Mayans are known to have inhabited the area in the first millennium, A.D. Columbus visited there in 1502. In 1821, Honduras freed itself from Spain and quit the Federation of Central America on 8 November 1838. In the second half of the nineteenth century, Honduras experienced periods of unrest generally instigated by Guatemala. In the early twentieth century, Nicaragua interfered in Honduran affairs to such an extent that the U.S. intervened in what was to become known as the "Banana Republics." In World War I, Honduras declared war on Germany but did not actively participate in the fighting. After that war, Honduras suffered a long period of unrest until power was taken by General Tiburcio Carías Andino until 1949. His dictatorship was punctuated by several abortive revolutions, as in 1947. In 1941, Honduras declared war on Japan (8 December) and on Germany and Italy (13 December). The war period with its consequent economic distress brought further unrest to the country. Carías was replaced in 1949 by another strongman, Juan Manuel Gálvez, who lasted until 1954, when he was replaced by Julio Lozano Díaz (qv). During his short regime, communist elements fomented strikes led to some government reforms but not enough was accomplished to quiet the national unrest. A bloodless military coup ousted him on 21 October 1956 and installed Colonel Héctor Caraccioli as the head of a military junta. In 1956, Honduras was also faced with a border dispute with Nicaragua that required the intervention of the Organization of American States (OAS) to settle. An election was held in 1957 that installed Ramón Villeda Morales as president. In 1960, Honduras suffered a period of border raids from Nicaragua. Morales was deposed in 1963 by a military coup led by Colonel Osvaldo López Arellano, who then declared himself head of state. López was elected president by a constituent assembly in March 1965. In May 1965, Honduras joined in the formation of the Inter-American Peacekeeping Force.

Open warfare broke out between Honduras and El Salvador over a border dispute in June–July 1969, creating the most serious situation in Central America in the last half-century. In part, the incident began over a soccer game and, in part, over the plight of Salvadoran farmers denied the use of Honduran fields near the undefined border. Salvadoran aircraft had bombed several Honduran cities, and about 10,000 Salvadoran troops were in Honduras when the OAS arranged a truce on 30 July. Talks between the two countries began in Costa Rica in January 1970, but fighting resumed on 17 May. Finally, in June a demilitarized zone was agreed upon, which lessened the chances of conflict. By carrying out two coups, as in December 1972, for example, López remained in office until 22 April 1975, when the army ousted him on charges of bribery. In August 1976, Honduras again reported it had been invaded by El Salvador. Ten days later, another agreement was reached that separated tthe two military forces along the border. In 1978, the government of Colonel Juan Alberto Melgar Castro (qv) was ousted by a bloodless coup led by General Policarpo Paz Garcia (qv), who took over rule of the country. In 1980, the United States announced it would supply military aid to El Salvador as part of a plan to thwart a Marxist takeover of Honduras; the U.S. later furnished $5 million in military aid to Honduras for the same purpose and to prevent that country from becoming a leftist base for raids against the Salvadoran government. In October 1981, Honduras reported Nicaraguan troops had crossed the Coco (Segoria) River into Honduras. Similar incursions were reported in 1982, when Nicaraguan troops entered Honduras and attacked Nicaraguan refugee camps, where more than 200 were killed. On 27 January 1982, nine years of military rule ended in Honduras when Roberto Suazo Cordova was elected president. On 17 September 1982, twelve Salvadoran terrorists siezed the Chamber of Commerce building in San Pedro Sula, taking 107 hostages. They demanded the release of a leftist Salvadoran rebel leader, Alejandro Montenegro, who had been captured by Honduran authorities on 15 September. The seige lasted until 25 September, when the terrorists were escorted out of the country without their demands being met. The United States was forced to admit that Honduras was being used as a military and CIA base against the Sandinista regime in Nicaragua during this period. On 21 March 1983, Nicaragua warned Honduras of war if it did not change its arrangements with the U.S. for basing rights near the Nicaraguan border. In November 1984, the U.S. warned Nicaragua that it would intervene if Nicaragua moved against either Honduras or El Salvador. Finally, in March 1988, the US sent combat troops into Honduras after claiming Nicaraguan troops entered the country in pursuit of Contra rebels seeking refuge in the country. This, in turn, led to resentment of the U.S. presence, especially in light of the abduction of a wealthy Honduran, Juan Ramon Matta Ballesteros, suspected of being a drug lord by U.S. agents even though an extradition treaty between the two countries did not exist. However, a new military assistance treaty with the U.S. was signed that year. Honduras leftist rebels increased their activities in 1989, as a means of emphasizing their objections to the continued U.S. military presence. The inauguration of a new president, Rafael Leonardo

Callejas, in January 1990 caused major reversals in a number of government programs, especially as concerned the national debt, the sum of which made Honduras ineligible for further foreign loans. The end of the Contra war against Nicaragua also reduced US military aid by more than $50 million. An austerity program was implemented, public spending curtailed and the number of public employees reduced. In addition, a massive privatization program was undertaken. In 1991, the next in line for cuts was the military. Congress refused this move, however, which opened a flood of reports about human rights violations in Honduras. There was evidence of atrocities committed by the military and police including murder, rape, intimidation of human rights workers and foreign press representatives and other human rights violations. Although some government action was taken, the root cause, the almost complete autonomy of the army, was not sufficiently addressed. Presidential elections held in 1993 changed the party in power for only the second time in 32 years, but little changed during the incumbency insofar as the power of the military, who appeared to conduct affairs as only they saw fit. In addition, there were charges that children were being exploited in an organized program of kidnapping, murder and the sale of their organs for profit. New charges of human rights violations appeared in 1994 that implicated the United States and Argentina as being aware of the charges, but having done little to change the situation in what was considered a friendly nation. When a law was passed that would have prevented forced conscription into the military, the president was forced to yield temporary authority to continue the practice after threats from the military. In the meantime, the economy of Honduras continued to suffer from government inaction, even though a few attempts were made to introduce austerity measures. A new criminal investigative service was inaugurated in January 1995 to replace what was considered to be one of the principal human rights violators, the secret police (abolished 1994). Israeli police and U.S. FBI instructors were used to train the new force. There were also a number of constitutional initiatives taken in 1995 to take police authority away from the military and put that power in civilian hands. In addition, the Legislative Assembly abolished (1994) compulsory military service and reaffirmed the new law in 1995. As the government of President Reina began to take control, signs for the future looked good. Corruption charges were filed against a number of past and present high-ranking officials and their relatives, and several ministers were forced to resign as a result. *Reading:* Dario A. Eiraque, *Reinterpreting the Banana Republic: Region and State in Honduras, 1870–1972* (1996); Michael Childress, *The Effectiveness of US Training Efforts in Internal Defense and Development: The Cases of El Salvador and Honduras* (1995); Amnesty International, *Honduras: Civilian Authority – Military Power: Human Rights Violations in the 1980s* (1988); David F. Ronfeldt, *US Involvement in Central America: Three Views from Honduras, July 1989* (1989); Donald Shulz & Deborah Shulz, *The United States, Honduras, and the Crisis in Central America* (1994); Thomas P. Anderson, *The War of the Dispossessed: Honduras and El Salvador, 1969* (1982).

Honduras, British. *See* Belize.

Honecker, Erich. (b. 25 August 1912, Neunkirken, Saarland—d. 29 May 1994, Santiago, Chile) Born the son of a communist mine worker, Honecker joined the Communist Youth Movement in 1916. In 1933, at the time of the rise of Nazism, he organized outlawed communist activities in various parts of Germany. In 1935 he was arrested by the Gestapo and sent to prison for ten years. He was released by the Soviet Army as it drove across Germany, and soon after he joined Walter Ulbricht (qv) in setting up the Soviet-controlled East German government. From 1946 until 1955 he was the chairman of the Free German Youth *(Frei Deutsche Jugend)* movement. Also, in 1946, he was elected to the Central Committee of the German Communist Party and helped bring about the union of the communist and socialist parties in East Germany. He also spent two years training in Moscow, where he was undoubtedly prepared to succeed Ulbricht. In 1971, Ulbricht resigned under Soviet pressure, and Erich Honecker replaced him. His first act was to nationalize all remaining private industry in East Germany. Under his tutelage, East Germany became one of the successful nations in East Germany, but the population drain continued as East Germans continued to flee to the West. In 1989, as Soviet puppet states fell like dominoes, Honecker attempted to follow the Soviet line and keep East Germany in the communist camp. On 18 October 1989, however, he was removed from office. He was placed under arrest on 5 December. On 14 March 1991, the ailing Honecker was quietly moved out of a Soviet military hospital near Berlin and transported to Moscow, apparently on Mikail Gorbachev's (qv) orders. On 11 December 1991, after the Soviet authority had disappeared, Honecker was ordered out of Russia. He took refuge in the Chilean embassy in Moscow. He was subsequently returned to stand trial. In 1992, ex-East German border guards standing trial for shooting people attempting to escape from East Germany accused the former East German government and, by inference, its leader, Erich Honecker, of issuing orders to that effect. The court rebuked the defendants stating such orders had no effect on their own conduct. Honecker, himself was still on trial on similar charges at the end of 1992. Specifically, he was charged with 49 counts of manslaughter, 25 counts of attempted manslaughter, and five counts of embezzlement. Honecker, aged 80 and suffering from terminal cancer, was not expected to survive very long under any circumstances. These charges were eventually dropped, and he was allowed to join his family in Chile, where he died in 1994. *Reading:* David Childs, ed., *Honecker's Germany* (1986); Erich Honecker, *From My Life* (1981).

Hong Kong. Hong Kong is a British Crown Colony in the Kwangtung region of southern China. It consists of a series of islands, the Kowloon Peninsula *(Jiulong)* and the New Territories, which are attached to the mainland at the mouth of the Pearl River *(Zhujiang)*. Hong Kong Island was ceded to Great Britain by the Treaty of Nanking in 1842. Kowloon was acquired in 1860, and the New Territories were leased from China for 99 years in 1898. The capital city is Victoria, but is more commonly called Hong Kong. The colony has always been at the center of conflict, as in 1911, when it became a haven for those fleeing the fighting associated with the birth of the Chinese Republic. A boycott of Hong Kong was effected during the 1925–1927 wave of xenophobia that swept China. The arrival of Japanese invaders in Manchuria in the 1930s changed the situation, however, as China sought British friendship. By 1937, refugees by the thousands flooded into Hong Kong from the mainland. The Japanese captured Hong Kong on Christmas Day, 1941. The city was officially liberated on 30 August 1945, but almost immediately another flood of mainland refugees fell upon the city as the Chinese fled before the communists during the civil war (1948–1950). In December 1966, Communist China accused the British of allowing the Americans to use Hong Kong as a base during the Vietnam War. In May 1967, sporadic rioting broke out in Hong Kong and Kowloon following a labor dispute at a factory in the New Territories. Without question the rioting, which was put down by British military action, was the instigated by the communists. On 2 March 1972, the communist Chinese representative at the United Nations claimed Hong Kong and the nearby Portuguese colony at Macao. Tension continued to build and, in January 1979, there were firm intelligence reports that the communists had moved two divisions to assembly areas close to the colony's border with the mainland. The communists kept up the pressure, and warned that China would take back the colony "when conditions were ripe" (30 September 1982). On 20 April 1984, the British government announced it would give up Hong Kong when the lease expired in 1997. A formal agreement to that effect was signed on 19 December 1984. Both parties ratified the agreement in 1985. In 1986, China indicated the precise details of Hong Kong's status as a Special Administrative Region would be forthcoming, indicating at the same time that the Crown Colony should concentrate on economic issues and forget about democratization. Hong Kong's population showed signs of displeasure when China signed agreements with Britain and France (September 1986) that would lead to a nuclear power supply that was reminiscent of the Chernobyl accident. China continued to influence any democratic processes being updated in Hong Kong in 1987. As an example, while laws were abolished that had controlled the press, laws dealing with "malicious" or "false" news were retained, much to Peking's delight. The incarceration of some 8,000 Vietnamese "boat people" refugees in concentration camps in 1987 did almost nothing to impress the Hong Kong populace, who were engrossed in their own affairs. By 1988, the number of Vietnamese refugees had grown to 16,000, some of whom were screened out as having fled economic conditions. By the end of the year another 10,000 Vietnamese had arrived. When the new China-influenced constitution was announced, its vagueness on China's specific rights of interference brought immediate challenges. The Tiananmen Square massacre in Peking in 1989 brought the Hong Kong populace out of its complacency to a realization that China was not disposed to treat lightly threats of the type that appeared to abound in the soon to be "special" region. Several border incidents involving defections and criminal repatriation further exacerbated the already sensitive situation. Also, more than 50 Vietnamese were repatriated to the Hanoi government. A number of other Vietnamese accepted voluntary repatriation to Hanoi control rather than remain in their prison-like camps in Hong Kong. The new Basic Law for Hong Kong was signed in February 1990. Almost entirely orchestrated by Peking, its provisions called for autonomous rule, but with sufficient mainland oversight to worry many citizens. More than 60,000 of the better educated had emigrated to the U.S., Canada and Australia by October 1990. To offset this "brain-drain" Hong Kong's government authorized admission of Chinese mainlanders, with some supposed restrictions, into the Crown Colony. At the same time, the United Kingdom prepared to issue 50,000 addition British passports to Hong Kong citizens (July 1990), giving that number an opportunity to leave, even though the complicated award system was designed to prevent an immediate flight from Hong Kong. In 1991, 65,000 heads of households applied. China also refused (1990) to allow anything resembling a statement of individual rights for Hong Kong to be promulgated. stating that everything was covered in the Basic Law, which had already been determined by Western observers as being vague. Forced repatriation of the Vietnamese refugees began in earnest in November 1991, even though the United States objected to the procedure. In April 1992, Britain assigned a new governor to Hong Kong, Chris Patten. He immediately set about setting up a series of initiatives aimed at securing democratic rights for the Crown Colony after it passed into Chinese hands in 1997, including moving forward with elections that would have broadened the democratic base in the legislative council. Peking blistered the proposals, but Patten proceeded with his plan. When Patten visited Peking in October 1992, he was roundly snubbed by the government. Further vituperation came from Peking when Patten announced he would proceed with a massive airport program that China had already dissapproved. By 1993, relations between Peking and Hong Kong were at best strained. China then threatened to establish its own parallel mechanism for the 1997 takeover. When Hong Kong refused to budge, China backed down enough to allow talks aimed at settling the impasse. Those talks dragged on in the face of Chinese intransigence even after Patten offered a number of concessions. Peking broke off the talks when Hong Kong went ahead with plans for elections. Tensions remained high in 1994, but the election reforms went forward. In reaction, China stepped up its campaign to influence the takeover and indicated that anything accomplished toward democratization that did not suit its purposes after 1997 would be dismantled. Patten announced in October 1994 a willingness to cooperate with China, but at the same time he forbade any official contact with China's Preliminary Working Committee (PWC), which operated in Hong Kong under Peking control. The elections (held in September) gave pro-British groups a near two-to-one majority over those favoring China. Even so, by 1995 it was clear that China would have its way in Hong Kong. In December 1995, for instance, Peking announced that Governor Patten would not be allowed to attend the June 1997 turnover ceremony. China also unilaterally announced a list of 94 individuals who would be a part of the 150-man transition committee. None was a member of any of the pro-British groups. The year 1996 witnessed China already tightening the screws even more securely on Hong Kong. *Reading:* Frank Welsh, *A Borrowed Place: The History of Hong Kong* (1993); Bruce De Mesquita, *Forecasting Political Events: The Future of Hong Kong* (1988); Enbao Wang, *Hong Kong, 1997: The Politics of Transition* (1995).

Hong River (Red River). *See* Vietnam.

Hon Mat. *See* Vietnam.

Hon Ngu. *See* Vietnam.

Hopei Province. *See* China.

Horn, Karl Von. Swedish Major General Karl Von Horn commanded the United Nations Emergency Force that was ordered into the former Belgian Congo on 14 July 1960. He remained with the force until it withdrew August 1964. In June 1963, Von Horn commanded the 200-man UN Observer Force ordered into Yemen for two months. The observer team's stay was extended by the UN on 1 August. On 27 August, Von Horn resigned and was replaced by Indian Lieutenant General Prem Singh Gyani (qv).

Hotel Metropole. On 3 December 1965, the Hotel Metropole located in Saigon, South Vietnam, and used as an American enlisted billet was blown up by Viet Cong sappers. Eight U.S. servicemen were killed. and 172 Americans and Vietnamese were injured in the blast.

"Hot Line." On 5 April 1963, the United States and the Soviet Union were linked together by a direct communications system called the "Hot Line." This action was agreed upon through the United Nations Disarmament Committee (15 March 1963) after the U.S. proposed such a plan. The purpose of the Hot Line was to reduce the possibility of an accident that might lead to war, such as might have occurred during the Cuban Missile Crisis. An additional Hot Line was established between Washington and the West German government in Bonn on 8 August 1969. On 30 June 1976, the French government announced it had opened its own Hot Line with Moscow as a means of preventing accidental war. The original White House-Kremlin Hot Line,and all later versions were kept highly classified, but it was believed the original linkage was by teletype. Later versions became more sophisticated until instantaneous voice communications were achieved.

Hoxha, Enver. (b. 16 October 1908, Gjirokastër, Albania—d. 11 April 1985, Tirana) Hoxha was born in a small town near the Greek border to middle-class Muslim parents. He studied at the French School in Korce and, in 1930, travelled to Montpellier, France, where he attended the university. When his scholarship was discontinued, he went to Paris, where he met French communists and joined the French Communist Party. He then worked with the honorary Albanian consul in Brussels and continued his education in law at Brussels University. He returned to Albania in 1936 and accepted a teaching position at his old school in Korce. At the time of the Italian invasion of Albania, he was fired for refusing to join the Albanian Fascist Party and became a tobacconist in the capital city, Tirana. He organized a communist cell during this period, and on 8 November 1941, he formed the Albanian Party of Labor. In 1943, Hoxha became secretary-general of its central committee. After World War II, Albania was proclaimed a communist republic under Yugoslav protection. Hoxha broke with Yugoslavia in 1948. In 1959, Hoxha affirmed Albania's dedication to Moscow, but in 1961 that allegiance disappeared and almost all contact between the two nations ceased. Thereafter, Albania fell under Chinese communist thrall, which meant increased economic assistance for the tiny Balkan state. This relationship ended in July 1977, when Hoxha criticized the "Three Worlds" concept of Chinese politics. In 1978, China severed relations with the Hoxha government in Tirana. In 1983, Hoxha boasted that his was the only true Marxist-Leninist nation in the world. Hoxha died in April 1985, leaving as his legacy a country both backward and destitute.

Hua Kuo-feng (Hua Goufeng). (b. 1920[?], Shansi Province [?]) When he came to power in Communist China in 1976, little was known of Hua Kuo-feng. Not even his birthplace was accurately reported. He was a minor party functionary, but a staunch supporter of Mao Tse-tung (qv),and was under the chairman's protection. When Mao died in September 1976, Chou En-lai (qv) had died in January, Hua, the minister of public security, became premier. As the head of the Chinese communist government, one of Hua's first acts was to order the arrest of the "Gang of Four" (qv) on 12 October 1976. On 29 June 1981, Chairman Hua was forced to resign in an episode of Chinese politics in which Hua fell because the Party Congress criticized the later phases of the rule of Mao.

Huambo (*Nova Lisboa*) Province. *See* Angola.

Huancavelica District. *See* Peru.

Hua Nghia Province. *See* Vietnam.

Huang Yung-sheng. On 2 December 1968, General Huang Yung-sheng, representing Communist China on an official visit to Tirana, Albania, signed a defense agreement with the government of Enver Hoxha (qv). *See also* Albania.

Hue. *See* Vietnam. *Reading:* Keith W. Nolan, *The Battle of Hue: Tet 1968* (1996); Eric Hammel, *Fire in the Streets: The Battle for Hue, Tet 1968* (1991).

Hukbalahap. The Hukbalahap movement began in earnest in the Philippines after the 1948 inauguration of Elpidio Quirino as president (15 April). The "Huks," as they were known, had actually begun as an underground guerrilla force fighting the Japanese occupation during World War II. After the war, there was sporadic trouble with the communist-oriented Huks as they attacked landowners and committed terrorist acts in the name of reform. In 1947, the government opened a limited military campaign against them. By 1949, the Huks had openly espoused their communist ties - ties that had led earlier to the influence of the Indonesian Marxist, Tan Malaka, and which now caused them to advocate the violent overthrow of the Filipino government. In 1951, the Philippine's secretary of defense, Ramón Magsaysay (qv), opened a major program of military action against the Huks plus a voluntary resettlement program for those who turned themselves in. Much of the overall plan had been worked out by Colonel Edward Lansdale, Magsaysay's American advisor. The communist leader of the Huks, William J. Pomeroy, was captured on 14 March 1952. Most of the Huk guerrilla activity had died out by 1955, but the government did not end the campaign until 1974. Many of the Huks who surrendered were given homesteads on the island of Mindinao.

Huleh Valley. *See* Israel.

Huleiqat. *See* Israel.

Hu-ma. *See* China.

Hungary. An east central European country, Hungary is bounded by the Czech and Slovak Republics on the north, Austria on the west, Croatia on the south and Romania, Slovenia and Moldova on the east. The capital is Budapest. The original inhabitants of the region were Dacians and Pannonians. Romans conquered the region and were in turn replaced by Germanic tribes and then Hunnic tribes. After 453 A.D., Gothic tribes reentered the area. In the sixth century, Lombards and Gepids swept in. The Avars, a new tribe from the east, allied themselves with the Lombards and destroyed the Gepidae, whereupon the Lombards migrated into Italy, leaving the Avars on the land. Charlemagne defeated the Avars between 791 and 797 and established a colony. By the ninth century the Magyars had settled in the region and founded the future Hungarian Empire. The country was attacked by the Ottomans in the fifteenth through the seventeenth centuries. After the defeat and withdrawal of the Turks, following their defeat at the gates of Vienna in 1683, Austria dominated Hungary. In 1867, Hungary gained internal independence, but it was still under Austrian control, with the emperor in Vienna also the king of Hungary. This dual monarchy continued as the Austro-Hungarian Empire until 1918, when the defeat of the Central Powers left Hungary independent but greatly reduced in size. A republic was proclaimed, but a Bolshevik revolt in 1920 directed the Hungarian people to demand a return of the monarchy. Hungary joined the Axis and, with Nazi German approval, regained much of the territory it had lost in the World War I settlement. Soviet troops captured Hungary at the end of World War II, and the settlement once again deprived Hungary of its regained territory. A republic was declared on 1 February 1946, with Zoltán Tildy, an anticommunist, as president and with Ferenc Nagy (qv) as premier (4 February). On 31 May 1947, the Soviets forced Nagy out of office after accusing him of treason. On 12 January 1948, Tildy was forced to resign in favor of a communist sympathizer, Arpad Szakasits (qv). On 26 December 1948, József Cardinal Mindszenty (qv), the Roman Catholic primate in Hungary was arrested by the communist government on charges of treason after refusing to bow to communist demands for control of the church. Cardinal Mindszenty was sentenced to life imprisonment on 8 February 1949. Szakasits was removed as party secretary in 1949 and replaced with Mátyás Rákosi. On 16 June 1949, Laszlo Rajk (qv), the communist foreign minister of Hungary, was arrested for crimes against the state. His arrest marked the beginning of a wholesale purge to rid the system of any anticommunist elements; the purge ended in May 1950. Rajk was given a show trial and hanged on 15 October 1949, while most of his associates were executed or imprisoned. On 28 December of that year, all industry in the country was nationalized. A Catholic archbishop, József Groesz (qv), was convicted of plotting the overthrow of the government on 28 June 1951. The Vatican had already excommunicated all Roman Catholics embracing communism. But the Catholics were not alone; on 21 February 1953, about thirty Jewish communists were purged from the Hungarian party at the direction of Moscow. On 4 July 1953, Mátyás Rákosi was summarily ousted as party secretary on the orders of Nikita Krushchev (qv), and Imre Nagy (qv) was installed as premier in his place. Rákosi's removal was apparently the result of Moscow's attempt to placate Yugoslavia's Marshal Tito (qv), whom Rákosi had offended. The new premier and party secretary was now Erno Gero (qv), a thoroughly pro-Soviet communist. On 14 May 1955, Hungary joined the new Warsaw Pact. On 21–23 October 1956, following months of growing unrest and political turmoil, the threat of a strike among university students quickly developed into a full-scale revolution. A major student demonstration on 23 October in Bem Square turned into a march on Parliament Square, with nearly 100,000 students and workers participating. The demonstrators demanded the return of Imre Nagy and the immediate release of Cardinal Mindszenty, who had been in solitary confinement since 1948. When Nagy was returned—Gero fled the country, and anti-Soviet rioting broke out. When the Hungarian secret police (AVO) were unsuccessful in quelling the disturbance, Soviet occupation troops moved in to suppress it. The revolt spread throughout the country. Large numbers of AVO members and their families fled to Austria to escape the wrath of the newly proclaimed "Freedom Fighters." As Austria accepted all refugees without verification of party affiliations, many communists were able get out, along with the flood of ordinary Hungarians fleeing communist oppression. The Nagy government (27 October) announced a plan for the withdrawal of Soviet occupation forces and the appointment of formerly outlawed members of the Smallholders Party (qv) to the cabinet. The following day the Soviet headquarters in Hungary announced it would begin withdrawing Soviet forces from the country. On 30 October, Soviet troops actually began wiothdrawing from Budapest. That same day, Nagy promised free elections and an end to one-party communist rule. On 2 November, Nagy repudiated the Warsaw Pact and requested that the United Nations move in to control the situation. On 4 November, however, reinforced Soviet forces amounting to sixteen divisions with 2000 tanks, and numbering more than 200,000 men turned back into Hungary to crush the rebellion. Imre Nagy was ousted from office, and János Kádár was installed as premier. Nagy, who had taken refuge in the Yugoslav embassy, and General Pál Maléter, the leader of the Freedom Fighters, were arrested and would be eventually executed (17 June 1958). Now a wholesale flight began from Hungary as tens of thousands escaped to avoid the reimposed Soviet tyranny. Within weeks, more than 200,000 had crossed into Austria, while a general strike in protest of the new regime paralyzed the country (12 December). In May 1958, Moscow announced it was withdrawing one division from Hungary. On 30 November 1959, Kádár announced that Soviet troops would remain indefinitely on Hungarian soil as long as the international situation required them there. In 1963, a broad amnesty freed many anticommunists who had participated in the Hungarian Revolution of 1956. The Hungarian communists also showed their solidarity by allowing African and Asian students in Budapest to attack the U.S. embassy there on 13 February 1965 to protest American involvement in Southeast Asia. Hungarian troops participated in the invasion of Czechoslovakia in 1968. Also, in 1968, the government introduced sweeping economic reforms, which did away with a central planning system. On 9 February 1977, Spain resumed diplomatic relations, broken in 1939, with Budapest. On 7 December 1977, Egypt closed the Hungarian embassy, along with many others, in Cairo in response to the Tripoli Declaration (qv) and ordered all Hungarian diplomats out of the country. In May 1987, demonstrators again took to the streets demanding democracy for Hungary. In 1989, Hungary shifted from a communist to a democratic system of government. In October the communist party was dissolved; the last Soviet troops left Hungary on 19 June 1991. Hungary then found itself in 1992 in a position where its government was more aware of its status than of its obligation to rule. The political situation in the country was both fluid and contentious. Hungary received about 100,000 refugees fleeing the fighting in former Yugoslavia, whom it was not prepared to handle. A new government in 1993, led by Peter Boross, a populist, moved to reconfigure the leadership institutions as a means of replacing the former communist traditions. Many of Boross' proposals were rejected by his government, but one dealing with media control was embraced wholeheartedly. This brought an unfavorable reaction from the populace, who seemed more aware of the ramifications of media control than did the government. Political opposition found itself at such cross-purposes that there was no real voice against the the proposal, even though it controlled, in coalition, a majority of votes. Hungary also suffered from a lack of real support from the West and the specter of a rapid Russian resurgency. The internal political situation took a new turn when Boross's party was defeated by a left coalition in 1994. This, in essence, put the communists back into power in Hungary. Gyula Horn became premier, but soon after taking office in July the new government seemed incapable of any fundamental change. Neighboring countries with strong national identities would have little or nothing to do with the new socialist (communist) government. Horn introduced an austerity program in March 1995, which aimed at gaining economic control of the country and led to great popular dissatisfaction with the new government. Resignations among government officials abounded; suggested replacements, at least in the instance of bringing Sandor Nagy, a trade unionist, into the government, nearly brought the Horn coalition down. Horn retreated before being handed a no-confidence vote, but the damage had already been done. The Horn coalition also failed to gain much ground in the international arena, although it continued to strive for admission into both NATO and the European Union. *Reading:* Agnes Horvath & Arpad Szakolczai, *The Dissolution of Communist Power: The Case of Hungary* (1992); Miklos Mlonar & Arnold Pomerans, *From Bela Kun to Janos Kadar: Seventy Years of Hungarian Communism* (1991); William Bergquist & Berne Weiss, *Freedom!: Narratives of Change in Hungary and Estonia* (1994).

Hungnam. *See* North Korea.

Hunt, Leamon. On 15 February 1984, Leamon Hunt, the American director general of the Multinational Force and Observers in the Sinai, was assassinated by two gunmen while riding in his armored car in Rome. The terrorist attack was claimed by both the Red Brigades and the Lebanese Armed Revolution Nguyen Houng Faction (LARF). Later evidence implicated the Red Brigades in the murder, in which 15 shots were fired into the bulletproof rear window of Hunt's car. One round penetrated the glass, striking Hunt in the head.

Hurley, Patrick Jay. (b. 8 January 1883, Indian Territory (Oklahoma)—d. 30 July 1963, Santa Fe) Hurley began his law practice in 1908. When World War I began, he entered the Army and served in France. In the 1920s, he entered Republican politics and served in Washington during the Hoover administration (1929–1933). During World War II he served as a brigadier general as the personal representative of George C. Marshall (qv) and worked on plans to relieve Bataan. Thereafter he served in a number of diplomatic missions for Franklin D. Roosevelt. He became US ambassador to China in 1944 with the mission of getting China more involved in the war. His principal effort, however, was in trying to reconcile the Koumintang (of Chiang Kai-shek) and communist factions. On 26 November 1945, seeing his mission as a failure, Hurley resigned, claiming a number of State Department officials were sympathetic to the cause of communism and that they had worked to disrupt his mission.

Husain, Arshad. On 28 June 1968, Arshad Husain, the foreign minister of Pakistan, abrogated the ten-year-old mutual assistance pact his government had held with the United States. This occurred three weeks after the announcement (6 June) that Pakistan was withdrawing from the SEATO and CENTO organizations. *See also* Pakistan.

Husain, Zakir. (b. 8 February 1897, Hyderabad, India—d. 3 May 1969, New Delhi) Husain was e.ducated at Aligarh Muslim University, where he became a follower of Mahatma Gandhi (qv). He served as vice chancellor of both the Aligarh Muslim and the Jamia Millia Islamic universities. In 1957 he was appointed governor of Bihar and, in 1962, became vice president of India. He became the Congress Party candidate for president and served in that office from 1967 until his sudden death on 3 May 1969.

Husni al-Za'im. In a bloodless coup, Syrian army chief of staff Husni al-Za'im overthrew the government of Shukri al-Kawatly (qv) on 30 March 1949. His tenure was cut short by another army coup in August.

el-Husseini, Abdel Kader. On 9 April 1948, Abdel Kader el-Husseini, an important Palestinian Arab leader, was killed in a fierce fire-fight near Kastel on the Tel Aviv-Jerusalem road.

Hussein (Husain ibn Talal). (b. 14 November 1935, Amman, Jordan) Hussein was born the son of King Talal of Transjordan, in the direct lineage from the Prophet Mohammed. At age 16, he witnessed the murder of his grandfather, King Abdullah, who was killed by a terrorist of the *Jihad Mukadess*. He received his education in England at Harrow and the Royal Military Academy, Sandhurst, and succeeded to the throne as Hussein I on 2 May 1953, after his father was declared mentally disturbed (schizophrenia) (1952). Hussein's marriage to

Princess Dina Abd-al-Hamid al-Aun was annulled in 1957 when she could not bear him a son and heir. He then married (1961) an Englishwoman, Antoinette Gardiner (Muna Al-Husain), who bore him two sons. In 1965, however, Hussein named his youngest brother, Prince Hasan, as the heir to the throne. Hussein's rule has been punctuated by periods of outside influence. The British were his principal support and benefactors, but he abrogated the treaty with London in 1956. As a prelude, he dismissed the British commander of the Arab Legion, Lieutenant General John Baget Glubb (Glubb Pasha) (qv), on 2 March 1956. He thereafter succumbed to Egyptian influence and to the pressures of his surrounding Arab neighbors, both in their campaigns of destruction against Israel and in their support of the Palestinians. In April 1957, Hussein fought off an attempt to unseat him that was led by his pro-Egyptian military commander. He then dismissed his pro-Egyptian premier, Sulaiman al-Nabulis (qv) (10 April), and began a purge to rid his government and armed forces of Egyptian influence. On 14 February 1958, Hussein announced the merger of Jordan and Iraq under the leadership of Iraq's King Faisal (qv). On 14 July 1958, King Faisal of Iraq was assassinated during a military coup led by General Abdul Karim el-Kassem (qv). Hussein then became king of the Arab Federation. His first act was to ask for US and Turkish aid in the crisis; British troops were the first to arrive (17 July). On 2 August, Hussein dissolved the Arab Federation. Jordan integrated its armed forces and economic policies with Saudi Arabia on 29 August 1962. Hussein was caught in a lie in June 1967, when the Israelis released a tape of an intercepted phone conversation between Hussein and Egypt's president, Gamal Abdul Nasser (qv) in which the two agreed to blame the United States for the war in the Middle East. But, by November 1967, Hussein was ready to recognize Israel if the boundary questions could be settled. Hussein suffered from the Israelis, however, in March 1968, when, after repeated warnings to stop *Fatah* attacks, the Israelis attacked guerrilla training bases near Kerama in the Jordan Valley. After they had destroyed the bases, the Israelis withdrew. Hussein claimed they were driven out after 15 hours of heavy fighting. In another attempt at displaying leadership and Arab unity, Hussein announced, on 17 March 1969, the establishment of the Arab Eastern Command, which comprised the military forces of Iraq, Jordan and Syria. Amid violent anti-American demonstrations in Amman, Hussein was forced to admit that Pakistani troops were in Jordan (16 June 1970). The next day, Washington announced that Jordan had been cut from a planned high-level visit to the Middle East; Hussein retaliated by ordering the U.S. ambassador out of the country. An assassination attempt, probably inspired by the Syrians, failed against Hussein on 9 June 1970. The attack occurred near Amman, where Jordanian forces were battling Palestinian guerrillas. In July, Hussein again made peace with the Palestinians (10 July); on the 26th, he accepted a U.S. peace proposal for the Middle East, only to find himself once again at odds with Iraq and Syria, who rejected it. The Palestinian peace broke down almost immediately, and Jordanian troops engaged in heavy fighting with the Palestinians from 30 August until 10 September, when a third cease-fire was arranged. The interlude that followed was a short one. On 14 September, Palestinian units occupied several towns in northern Jordan. This proved too much for Hussein. The following day he appointed a military government to rule the country and declared martial law (16 July). He then ordered an all-out attack on Palestinian bases in his country. In response to Hussein's drive against the Palestinians, Syria invaded Jordan on 19 September. But, after making significant gains the Syrians were defeated on 23 September. The destruction of the Palestinians then continued until stopped by a Arab-mandated cease-fire which took effect on 27 September. At the same moment, Hussein moderated the martial law edict and returned part of the control of the government to civilian hands. In April 1971, however, the Palestinians once again attacked Hussein demanding he install a government friendly to their cause. Hussein reacted immediately, but before a new battle began, the Palestinians backed down. In April 1972, Hussein announced a plan for a Palestinian state in the West Bank (qv) and Gaza (qv). Israel, the Palestinians and the United Arab Kingdom (qv) immediately rejected the plan; Egypt went so far as to break diplomatic relations with Jordan (7 April). In November 1972, a Libyan plot to assassinate Hussein was foiled. In something of a turnabout, Jordan broke diplomatic relations with Tunisia (17 July 1973), when that country's Habib Bourguiba suggested Hussein abdicate so that Palestine could occupy both banks of the Jordan. As an example of the ever-changing relations in the Middle East, Hussein and Syrian president Assad (qv) announced a combined supreme command to coordinate military and political policy. The US cut off aid to Hussein in March 1979 in an attempt to get Hussein's cooperation on a Middle East peace settlement. Following a meeting in Amman on 11 February 1985, Hussein and Yasser Arafat (qv) issued a joint communique stating they had reached an agreement on a framework for peace talks. On 24 February, through the good offices of Egypt's president Mubarak (qv), the United States was urged to host a Jordanian, Israeli and Palestinian peace conference. The following month, Mubarak and Hussein joined in an attempt to end the Iran-Iraq War (qv). By 1986, Hussein was considered by many to be the key man on the Arab side of the Middle East peace question. "Key" did not necessarily equate with right, however; and by Hussein's actions in closing the Jordanian offices of the PLO's *al-Fatah* (July 1986), he had aligned himself with Israel and against Arab interests. This only tended to intensify the bitterness between Arab and Israeli, with neither side exhibiting much restraint. Hussein's attempts at bringing an end to the Iraq-Irani struggle also brought no end to the conflict. By late November 1987, Hussein's popularity was again on the rise. At an Arab League (qv) summit held in Amman, Hussein was credited with much of the Arab moderation in position vis-a-vis Israel. Earlier in the year, Hussein had condemned the United States in its support of Iran in the ongoing war and vowed that Jordan would never trade in weapons with the United States again. At the same time, after a long period of conflict, Hussein was able to strengthen Jordanian ties with Syria. In   1988   Hussein continued pressure on the Palestinians to accept the secession of the West Bank. In doing so, he gave up his role as the effective spokesman for their cause. Arafat and the PLO stepped in to assume that role. Hussein's goal appeared to have been securing a withdrawal of Israeli forces from the West Bank and the establishment of a Palestinian state. This plan—Hussein had suggested it in 1972—seemed by 1993 to be moving toward a resolution of one of several problems facing the Middle East. It may be that Hussein's plan might have led to the answers to the other questionss as well. Over the same period of the 1990s and the near fruition of the West Bank plan, Hussein found himself, once more, caught in the middle. The Iraqi invasion of Kuwait brought almost universal condemnation of Damascus. Hussein, by deed if not by act, continued to violate United Nations boycotts and sanctions by supplying Iraq with needed materiel over their common border. At any particular moment, Hussein's style of leadership and diplomacy could prove fatal. *Reading:* Robert Satloff, *From Abdullah to Hussein: Jordan in Transition* (1994); Uriel Dann, *King Hussein and the Challenge of Arab Radicalism: Jordan, 1955–1967* (1991); James Lunt, *Hussein of Jordan: Searching for a Just and Lasting Peace* (1989).

Hussein, Saddam At Takriti. (b. 29 April 1937, Takrit, Iraq) Born the son of peasants in northern Iraq, he joined the socialist Baath Party (qv) in 1957. In 1959, he fled to Egypt after he was identified as one of ten who had attempted the murder of Major General Abdul Karim el-Kassem (qv), leader of the 1958 revolution in Iraq. Saddam returned to Iraq after Kassem's execution in 1963 and became a member of the then Council for Revolutionary Command (later the Revolutionary Command Council [RCC]). Saddam took part in the July 1968 coup, which made him vice-chairman of the RCC and deputy to the president in 1969. Saddam also became the dominant figure in the Baath Party during this time. In a January 1977 visit to Moscow, Saddam was able to gain Soviet assurances of increased aid to Iraq. He became president of the republic in 1979 and then secretary general of the Baath Party. Among his first acts as president was to order the executions of 500 Baathists, whom he considered dangerous to his rule. Saddam reestablished his propensity for ruthlessness and aggression when he launched a war against Iran in 1980. (See Iran-Iraq War) There was also strong evidence to suggest Saddam had been carrying out a campaign of genocide against the Kurdish tribesmen in the north of Iraq, using chemical weapons (1988) where necessary. On 2 August 1990, Saddam invaded Kuwait in what became the most universally rejected politicomilitary enterprise of modern times. Although thoroughly defeated and humiliated in the field, Saddam never lost his bluster. Although in 1996 his country still suffered under the weight of the Desert Storm defeat, the continuing UN sanctions and his own cruel and ruthless repression, he managed to continue rattling his sword at the world with relative impunity. Never a soldier, Saddam continues to wear the garb of a military commander, and his uniformed facade peers down from every wall in Baghdad. In Iraq, criticism of his rule is punishable by death. In 1994, Saddam exercised his forces close to the Kuwaiti border in what some saw as a provocation and others viewed as Hussein testing his position. The maneuvers brought an immediate American response, including the dispatch of U.S. combat forces back into Kuwait. When Saddam saw his support from Jordan's Hussein and the PLO back away, he quickly withdrew the troops (11 October 1994). Saddam also imposed Islamic penalties on a number of crimes and on the sale of alcohol, as his country continued to founder under the UN-prescribed economic boycott. By this point, Saddam had assumed the role of prime minister and foreign minister of Iraq. Antigovernment demonstrations in Baghdad were met by government troops and were quickly dispersed. A large force of Turkish troops crossed into Iraq in March 1995, to destroy a Kurdish settlement that spawned cross-border raids into Turkey. The operation was successful and without interference by Iraqi forces, who have also fought the Kurds on occassion. A major uprising began against Saddam on 17 May 1995, when Sunni Muslim tribesmen rebelled following the execution of a Dulaimi general officer accused by Saddam of conspiracy. Thousands were killed or injured in the ensuing battle. On 15 October, Hussein was elected to another seven-year term as president, with an astonishing 99.96 percent of the vote. *Reading:* Miron Rezun, *Saddam Hussein's Gulf Wars: Ambivilant Stakes in the Middle East* (1992); Paul Deegan, *Saddam Hussein (War in the Gulf)* (1991); Elaine Sciolino, *The Outlaw State: Saddam Hussein's Quest for Power and the War in the Gulf* (1991); Jane Claypool, *Saddam Hussein* (1993); Rebecca Steloff, *Saddam Hussein: Absolute Ruler of Iraq* (1995).

Hutu (Bahutu) Tribesmen. One of three major ethnic groups of tribesman occupying the Burundi and Rwanda regions of central Africa, the Hutu (Bahutu) people are the farmers, while the more aristocratic Tutsi (Watutsi) (qv) are the herders and the pigmy Twa people are the nomadic hunters. Since before the establishment of colonial rule in the region in 1907, the Hutu have been restive. In much earlier times, the Twa were indigenous to the Burundi area. The Hutu spilled over out of the Rwanda area and occupied the Twa lands, only to be overrun themselves by the aristocratic Tutsi. After first experiencing German colonial rule, the Hutu lands became Belgian after the World War I. In 1946, the region became a United Nations trust territory. In 1959, a massive uprising of Hutu against the Tutsi aristocracy began in the Rwanda region. Many of the Tutsi fled into Belgian Congo, Uganda and Tanganyika. Rwanda and Burundi became separate and independent countries in 1962. Rwanda was primarily populated with Hutu, the majority of whom are Christian. Episodes of tribal rivalry erupted into conflict in Rwanda, which led to a military coup and a one-party system. In February 1973, for instance, Hutu tribesmen in Rwanda opened a campaign of destruction against the minority Tutsi tribe. Many Tutsi fled Rwanda, but many stayed and fought in a bloody civil war. Burundi, on the other hand, was led by the Tutsi. An unsuccessful military coup took place in Burundi on 19 October 1970, when Hutu tribemen attacked Tutsi officials. Bloody battling continued until almost all of the Hutu leaders were killed. In April 1972, a fierce civil war broke out in which the former king (*Mwami*) was killed on the orders of the president, Michel Micambero (qv). Over 100,000 Tutsi tribesmen were reported killed by Hutu serving in the Burundi army — with support from neighboring Zaire, in two months of butchery. In May 1973, as the conflict between the Hutu and Tutsi continued, Rwandan Hutu crossed into Burundi to support their ethnic kinsmen in the battle against the Tutsi. In June 1973, Burundi troops pursued escaping Hutu guerrillas into Tanzania and Rwanda. In August 1988, in Burundi, battles again broke out between the Hutu and Tutsi peoples; more than 5,000 were killed, and thousands more Hutu fled into Rwanda. To ease the situation in Burundi, a Hutu prime minister was appointed, and most of the country's ministries were given over to Hutu leadership. By late 1989, those Hutu who had fled returned to Burundi. Still, the Tutsi were the educated class, and the Hutu still struggled to catch up.

Hwai Hai. *See* China.

Hyderabad. *See* Pakistan.

I

Ia Drang Valley. *See* Vietnam.

Ibo Tribesmen. *See* Nigeria.

Iceland. The Republic of Iceland is located in the North Atlantic Ocean between Greenland on the west and Norway on the east. The capital is Reykjavik. The island was first visited before the fourth century A.D. Iceland was inhabited in small numbers of Irish settlers sometime before the ninth century. When Norwegian seafarers began moving unto the island in the ninth century, the Irish left the island. From the tenth until thirteenth century, Iceland was an independent republic. In 1262, it was joined with Norway. When Denmark united with Norway after 1380, Iceland was governed from Denmark. Iceland remained in this thrall with minor interludes until 1918, when the island was given its independence from Denmark. In 1937, however, Iceland chose to renew its ties with Denmark. When Denmark was captured by the Nazis in World War I, first British and then American forces occupied the island to prevent its use in the German war effort. On 16 June 1944, the Icelandic parliament (*Althing*) declared the union with Denmark over. (Denmark did not recognize the dissolution until April 1950.) The new island nation joined the UN on 19 November 1946 and joined NATO in 1949. Iceland attended the first meeting of the Council of Europe. In April 1951, in the face of a growing Soviet threat, Iceland asked the U.S. for troops to help defend the island. Troops were sent (7 April), and an agreement for NATO basing rights was put into effect (5 May 1951). Earlier, in 1956, and as a part of the same political processes that Iceland was undergoing, the government on 28 March 1956 asked for the removal of all foreign troops on its soil. The demand was rescinded on 6 December, after diplomatic pressure was applied, especially by the United States. On 10 December 1959, the U.S. withdrew the last of its forces, ending a U.S. military presence that had existed there since 1941. Iceland, however, resumed its demands to be free of the NATO, bases which were considered critical to Europe's defense against the Soviet Union. In May 1952, Iceland had extended its territorial fishing limits to four miles. This matter created a serious problem for British fishing interests and led to more serious diplomatic problems for the two countries. The issue was settled on 27 February 1961, but not for long. On 15 February 1972, the Icelandic government decreed a 50-mile fishing limit and abrogated all former fishing treaties with Great Britain and

West Germany. This action set into motion a series of events that eventually led to the so-called Cod War (qv), which created a rift in NATO and nearly led to armed conflict between Great Britain and Iceland. The matter was defused when an interim agreement was signed with Great Britain on 13 November 1973. In the aftermath, the World Court ruled against Iceland and its 50-mile no-fishing zone. The seating of a new government in 1974 brought an early announcement that Iceland was withdrawing its demands for NATO to leave the island. At the same time, the fishing dispute remained unresolved and was brought into sharp focus when the West German government barred all Icelandic shipping from its ports (2 December 1974) following the seizure of a West German fishing trawler in Icelandic waters — Iceland having rejected the World Court ruling. When Iceland declared its intention on 16 July 1975 to extend its fishing zone to 200 miles, new talks opened between Reykjavik and London (23 October 1975), only to be broken off by Iceland after two days. The Cod War was on again, and the British Royal Navy moved a number of warships into the troubled waters. In retaliation, Iceland began blocking the entrances to NATO bases. On 19 February 1956, Iceland broke diplomatic relations with London. After the settlement of the Cod War, diplomatic relations were restored on 1 June 1976. In 1978, a newly installed communist government failed to close the strategically important NATO air base at Keflavik. In 1984, Iceland joined the other Scandinavian countries in establishing the region as a nuclear-free zone. In 1986, the issue became whaling and was compounded when the U.S. warned Iceland it would employ trade sanctions if the whaling continued. The U.S. also began using American registry vessels to resupply its bases in Iceland, thereby putting a crimp in the local shipping industry. The whaling question continued into 1989, when whaling was stopped. The fishing industry in Iceland also suffered because of a drop in harvesting, most likely caused by decades of overfishing. By 1992, the situation had grown worse, and a severe recession had set in. Also, a demand for the extradition of an alleged Estonian-born war criminal who had immigrated to and become a citizen of Iceland after World War II created a new problem for the the tiny country. Declaring the order illegal, the Icelandic government denied the request. A confrontation with Norway developed in 1993 over fishing rights in a narrow band of international water in the Barents Sea that was claimed by Norway. This problem continued into 1995 with Norway claiming the Icelanders were ruining the delicate equilibrium of the region. Iceland signed an agreement (4 January 1994) allowing a continued U.S. and NATO military presence on the island. At the same time, the decline in the fishing industry devasted the Icelandic economy. The issue of joining the European Union also caused vociferous debate, those opposing it claiming that entering the Union would have serious repercussions on Iceland's membership in the European Economic Community. Some economic recovery was seen in 1995, but many signs of the depression remained. *Reading:* T. K. Derry, *A History of Scandinavia: Norway, Sweden, Finland and Iceland* (1980); Jonathan Porter & Eliot Porter, *Iceland* (1989).

Idris I (Mohammed Idris ei-Senussi). On 3 December 1950, on the eve of Libya's receiving its independence, Mohammed Idris ei-Senussi was proclaimed King Idris I. Idris I ruled Libya until 1 September 1969, when a military coup led by Colonel Muammar al-Qaddafi seized power. The 79-year-old Idris was in Turkey receiving medical treatment when the coup occurred.

Ifni. On 30 June 1969, the Spanish colony of Ifni was ceded to Morocco.

Ileo, Joseph. On 14 September 1960, President Joseph Kasavubu (qv) of the Democratic Congo Republic appointed Joseph Ileo premier after dismissing Patrice Lumumba (qv) from that post. At the height of the civil war raging in the Congo, Ileo asked the UN for peacemaking forces to help quell the disturbances in Katanga province. Ileo was dismissed on 14 September when Joseph Mobutu seized power with UN approval. In the ever-shifting course of events, Kasavubu formed a new, though totally ineffective central government in February 1961 and once again appointed Ileo as premier. He was replaced when another government was formed in April, and Cyrille Adoula (qv) was appointed premier.

Illia, Arturo. In July 1963, a 63-year-old physician, Arturo Illia, was elected president of Argentina on the basis of a popular election as the candidate of the People's Radical Party. He was inaugurated on 12 October to lead a coalition government. His tenure was popular, and for a moment Illia held out the possibility of gaining a national consensus, something not seen in Argentina in many years. The local elections held in early 1966 indicated, however, that the Peronistas still held sufficient strength to cause problems. On 28 June 1966, a bloodless military coup led by Lieutenant General Juan Carlos Onganía (qv) seized power, closed the legislature and banned all political parties.

Illueca, Jorge. On 13 February 1985, Ricárdo de la Espriella stepped down as president of Panama, probably because of pressure from strongman Manuel A. Noriega (qv). Jorge Illueca, the vice president, took his place in the lame-duck administration. On 6 May 1985, the scheduled election was held. After ten days of vote counting, Nicolás Ardito Barletta was elected president. He was inaugurated on 11 October.

Ilobasco. *See* El Salvador.

Ilocos Sur Province. *See* Philippines.

Ilopango Airport. *See* El Salvador.

Inchon. *See* South Korea.

Incirlik. *See* Turkey.

India. Occupying most of the Indian subcontinent in southern Asia, India is bordered by Bhutan, China and Nepal on the north, Myanmar and Bangladesh on the east, the Bay of Bengal on the southeast, the Arabian Sea on the southwest, and Pakistan on the northwest. The capital is New Delhi. Civilization in India has been traced back at least 5,000 years. The first invasion was of Aryan tribes coming from the northwest around 1500 B.C. The mixture of these tribes with the indigenous population created the classical Indian civilization. Buddhism came to India in the third century, B.C., although Hinduism managed to survive in some areas and slowly was restored as the predominant religion. Arab invaders from the west introduced Islam in the eighth century A.D. Northern India was under Turkish control by 1200. The Monguls controlled the lands from about 1526 until 1857. Of the Europeans, the Portuguese first arrived in 1498 and established a number of trading posts under the leadership of Vasco de Gama. In 1609, the British East India Company established a trade in textiles and spices. In time the East India Company controlled most of India, with the British parliament assuming political control of the country. Between 1828 and 1835, the British subdued most of the Rajahs who ruled the various states within India. After the Sepoy Mutiny of 1857–1858, England began a system (the *Raj*) of supporting the local leaders. India's nationalism grew rapidly after World War I, and great leaders such as Mahatma Gandhi (qv) emerged to lead the country toward self-determination. In 1935, Gandhi and organizations such as the Indian National Congress and the Moslem League had forced England to grant a constitution to India under which a bicameral congress was seated. The Moslem League, headed by Mohammed Ali Jinnah (qv), began seeking an independent Moslem state in Pakistan. Following World War II, an All-India Congress rejected a September 1945 proposal of limited autonomy and demanded that Great Britain get out of India immediately. At the same time, the beginning of 1946 introduced a long period of violent clashes between Hindus and Moslems in which thousands died on both sides. On 14 March 1946, Great Britain offered India full independence. As a gesture of friendship, Great Britain named Viscount Montgomery, the commander of the China-Burma-India theater in World War II, as the interim governor-general of India. On 15 August 1947, the Indian Independence Bill took effect. British India was divided into Pakistan and India. India became a self-governing member of the Commonwealth. Since 1945 it had been a member of the United Nations. The partition of India and Pakistan, which had been endorsed by the Muslim League and the All-India Congress, was accompanied by extreme violence, especially in the state of Punjab. Upon gaining independence, Pundit Jawaharlal Nehru (qv) became the first prime minister. Bloodshed continued between the Hindus and Muslims, however, and both India and Pakistan issued a joint statement deploring the situation and moved to stop the conflict. On 28–30 October 1947, heavy fighting began between Indian ground and air units and rebellious Muslims in Kashmir. This clash signalled the beginning of an undeclared war that lasted until December 1949. In December 1947, India handed the problem to the United Nations. Before the end of January 1948, the UN had established a mediation commission to settle the Indian question, especially as it pertained to Kashmir, where fighting between Indian and Pakistani forces was intense. January 1948 also witnessed the assassination of Mahatma Gandhi by a Hindu terrorist. This incident only exacerbated the already dangerous situation, and rioting grew even more deadly. As the innocents on both sides attempted to flee the areas of conflict, more than 12 million Hindu and Muslim refugees crossed the Indo-Pakistani border in a mass transferral of Muslims to Pakistan and Hindus to

India. At the same time, nearly 200,000 had been killed in communal fighting. In August, India ordered the state of Hyderabad to cease its resistance to central Indian rule. When Hyderabad requested UN assistance, Indian forces invaded the reguion (13 September). Capitulation came four days later. The fighting in Kashmir ended on 1 January 1949. On 1 October 1949, the Indian government recognized the newly proclaimed People's Republic of China (Communist China). India became a republic on 25 January 1950. In November, India repudiated the Chinese claims as to the location of the India-Tibet (qv) border and accepted the McMahon Line (qv) as the rightful demarcation between the two countries. By 3 July, the number of Pakistani cease-fire violations in Kashmir forced New Delhi to notify the United Nations. On 25 February 1953, the United States approved a UN-endorsed Indian truce proposal in the Korean conflict (qv). In August the Indian government at first approved, then withdrew support for a plebiscite to settle the long-smoldering Kashmir situation. Kashmir acceded to annexation by India on 20 February 1954. Pakistan vigorously protested the action; India's response was to order U.S. observers out of the state on 1 March. The U.S. then offered military aid to Pakistan to be used in the defense of the nation. Pakistan accepted; India protested. Throughout this period, the Nehru government became more and more aligned with the communist East. On 28 June 1954, India entered into an agreement with Communist China on the future of Indochina. In affairs closer to home, India reached an agreement with Pakistan over the use of the waters from the Indus River (5 August). Two weeks earlier, India had become embroiled in a conflict with Portugal over the status of the three Portuguese enclaves on the India subcontinent (*see* Goa); on 19 August India broke diplomatic relations with Lisbon over the affair. As an offshoot of this activity, France reached agreement with India on 21 October whereby it relinquished control of its four enclaves to New Delhi. Although the French issue was settled without conflict, Portugal still refused to give up its colonies and demanded British support based on a 1937 treaty. On 15 August, Indian demonstrators had poured into Goa and Damao (qv). Rioting followed in which about 150 were killed by police. The Portuguese finally capitulated after Indian troops entered all three enclaves, and the colonies were given over to India. When Chinese troops invaded Tibet and dissolved the government on 28 March 1959, the Dalai Lama sought refuge in India (31 March). The Chinese sealed the India-Tibet border on 23 April. On 31 July the Indian government took over the communist-run state of Kerala and banned the Communist Party there. Border clashes with the Chinese in Tibet occurred in Kashmir in October. In December, Pakistan complained about the Indian partition of Ladakh province, which the Pakistanis claimed as theirs. On 10 June 1960, India claimed Chinese troops had entered India and that heavy fighting had occurred. By February 1961 Chinese troops occupied over 12,000 square miles of Indian territory. Yet, on 14 March, India sent troops to join the UN Emergency Force (UNEF) in the Congo. The border incidents along the Tibetan border continued in May, with more Chinese sorties into India territory. Major fighting broke out in that region in October 1962. After having repudiated the United States for giving aid to Pakistan, the Indian government asked the U.S. for aid on 29 October; additional aid was sought on 19 November. By the end of 1962, following a truce of sorts, Chinese troops began withdrawing from Indian territory. In an attempt to settle the Kashmir situation, India suggested direct negotiations with Pakistan - which it claimed was the cause of the violence. This attempt at peace failed, and the violence in Kashmir continued. The Indian government did release Sheikh Mohammed Abdullah (qv), known as the Lion of Kashmir, from six years imprisonment on 8 April 1964, but gained little from the gesture. (He would again be detained and not be released until January 1968.) Then, on 27 May 1964, Pundit Jawaharlal Nehru died, creating a government crisis. Nehru was replaced by Lal Bahadur Shastri (qv), who inherited the Kashmir problem and all the other ills facing India. In April 1965 large-scale fighting broke out along the Pakistani border in the region known as the Rann of Kutch. The fighting lasted two weeks without result. In September, Indian infantry and tanks crossed into West Pakistan near Lahore. Shastri called the fighting that ensued a "full-fledged war." Pakistan rejected a UN cease fire order on 11 September. Also in September, Chinese forces massed along the Indian border as a threat to continued Indian operations in the Himalayan mountains and sided with Pakistan in its fight with India. India withdrew its outposts along the Tibetan border and reduced the tension in that region. Finally, on 22 September, a UN cease-fire went into effect but fighting did not stop until 27 September. This was followed by the signing of the treaty of Tashkent on 10 January 1966, in which both the Indians and Pakistanis agreed to withdraw from their common border (completed 25 February). Prime Minister Shastri died on 11 January. On 18 January, Indira Gandhi was elected prime minister. In September 1967, skirmishes again broke out along the Sikkim (province)-Tibetan border. On 1 July 1968, India signed the Nuclear Non-Proliferation Treaty. In August, trouble came from a new direction, this time from Burma. The Indian government had to close the border to prevent Naga rebels from crossing into India on their return from China. Internal problems also intruded when pro-Chinese Naxalite extremists began a series of disturbances in Kerala province and elsewhere (November 1968). Rioting also broke out in the state of Andhra Pradesh in January 1969 and in Bombay in February. In the latter incident, Marathi nationalists caused the trouble, which killed 50 people. More rioting took place in September in Ahmedabad. The wave of rioting, often communist-inspired, kept recurring into 1970, usually with loss of life. There were also episodes of fighting, as in September, in the Khasi Hills of Nagaland. Rioting continued in West Bengal and reached a point in November where government troops were ordered to use deadly force against the demonstrators. In April 1970, India closed a deal with the USSR to produce MiG-21 fighters in Indian factories. At the same time, however, India voiced its opposition (November) to the Soviets (and the U.S. and Great Britain) building naval bases in the Indian Ocean. India also accused Pakistan (31 March 1971) of committing genocide in East Pakistan. Pakistan responded by accusing India of supporting the independence forces in East Pakistan in April. When Pakistan opened a military campaign in East Pakistan on 12 April, refugees—some six million people—fled into India. On 9 August 1971, India signed a 20-year friendship treaty with the Soviet Union. At the end of October 1971, following weeks of cross-border shelling by the Pakistanis, Indian troops crossed into East Pakistan. Heavy fighting ensued over the course of the next week. On 27 October, the day the Indian offensive began, New Delhi formally invoked its treaty with the USSR and asked for Soviet aid. Two days later, a Soviet military team arrived to study India's defense requirements. By 22 November, a full-scale invasion of East Pakistan was underway. By 3 December 1971, at least 250,000 Indian troops were engaged in the invasion of East Pakistan and Bengal. That same day, Pakistani aircraft carried out a massive air attack on a number of cities in northern India. The war ended, but not all of the fighting, until on 17 December (see Indo-Pakistani War) when both sides accepted a UN cease-fire order. Again demonstrating the Gandhi government's swing to the left, India established an embassy in Hanoi on 10 January 1972. Still, the social unrest in India continued. On 18 January 1973, Indira Gandhi put the state of Andhra Pradesh under central government control to help curb the separatist rioting. The tiny kingdom of Sikkim was put under India's administrative control after the the king requested that assistance following two weeks of unrest (March–April 1973). In May, the state constabulary mutinied in Uttar Pradesh. This act emphasized the continuing social and economic decline in the country. By January 1974, food price rioting was commonplace, and people were being killed. While these conditions prevailed, the Indian government was carrying out an intensive program to produce nuclear weapons. On 18 May 1974, a nuclear device was detonated in the Rajastan Desert; India now belonged to the nuclear club. Even so, the Indian government was in trouble. Prime Minister Gandhi, faced with election problems and the growing unrest in her country, declared a state of emergency on 26 June 1975 and and ordered the arrests of thousands of opposition leaders throughout the country. Press censorship was imposed, and a number of economic and social reforms, including birth control, were put into place that were roundly resented by the population. In particular, the role of Sanjay Gandhi, who held no government position yet made policy, was widely criticized. In January 1976, Indira suspended constitutional freedom throughout the country. When the opposition formed a coalition (Janata Coalition) against Gandhi, she was defeated in the 1977 elections. On 15 April of that year, India resumed diplomatic relations with Communist China after a 15-year break. In 1978, India gave $50 million in reconstruction funds (25 February) to Vietnam. On 14 January 1980, Indira Gandhi became prime minister for the second time. In the first month of her second administration, India used its nuclear capability to warn the U.S. that further aid to Pakistan would result in an acceleration of its nuclear program. The U.S. responded in February that it would give sophisticated military aid to India if it deferred its nuclear weapons program. In

March 1980, however, India purchased $1.6 billion in military equipment from the Soviet Union; India later bought 40 Mirage 2000 fighters from France (18 October 1982). On 11 October 1982, the Indian House of Parliament was attacked by Sikhs of the Akali Dal (qv) sect. Four were killed and many injured in the incident. The attack was aimed at bringing attention to the fact that 30 Sikhs had died under mysterious circumstances in a Punjab jail. On 14–15 February 1983, serious clashes took place between Muslims and Hindus in Assam during elections. In the several weeks that followed more than 3,000, many of them aliens, were killed. More than 90,000 troops were employed in a futile effort to stop the fighting. Fighting in Punjab state became so bad that the government was forced to assume direct control as a means of restoring order. By November 1983, more than 400 arrests had been made in Punjab. The rioting continued and widened into 1984. Attempts at reaching a settlement that would have given the Sikhs autonomy broke down in February 1984, as the death toll mounted. By April the situation appeared to be out of hand; Sikhs had burned down 40 railway stations. In Amritsar (qv), in Punjab, the High Priest of the Golden Temple was murdered. The protests that followed led to an attack on the temple by Indian troops in which 1,000 Sikhs were killed. This was followed by a mutiny by Sikhs in the Indian army. Many died on both sides in that incident. India then (13 June 1984) accused Pakistan of training the Sikh extremists and declared the state of Punjab in rebellion (23 June 1984). Acts of Sikh terrorism became commonplace as airliners were hijacked and air terminals bombed. Now convinced of Pakistani complicity in the wave of violence in India, New Delhi ordered the border closed on 16 October. On 31 October, Indira Gandhi was assassinated by two of her Sikh bodyguards. Rajiv Gandhi (qv), her son, became prime minister. Widespread rioting followed the assassination, which was probably staged in response to the suppression of the Sikhs in Punjab. In the rioting, thousands of Sikhs were killed and at least 50,000 left homeless. The British deputy commissioner, Percy Norris (qv), was assassinated in Bombay on 27 November 1984 by members of the terrorist Revolutionary Organization of Socialist Moslems. Rajiv Gandhi's tenure lasted until 1989, when he was swept from office amid charges of corruption and incompetence. During the remainder of the 1980s, the Sikh problem continued. Punjab was brought under central government control again in May 1987. Another seige took place at the Golden Temple in Amritsar in May 1988, in which many died. Rajiv Gandhi was assassinated on 21 May 1991 during a campaign to regain the prime ministership. One of the worst waves of violence in India, a country beset by violence, occurred 12–19 March 1993, when the government again announced it was bringing Punjab under central control to relieve the situation. Bombs jolted Bombay and Calcutta, leaving more than 300 dead and 1,200 injured. The rioting was also aggravated by the Hindu destruction of a Muslim mosque (built in 1528) on 6 December 1992, and the situation was further exacerbated by an October 1994 Supreme Court announcement that declined to give an opinion on whether a Hindu temple had even stood at the spot where the razed mosque had been located. India also entered negotiations with China, which culminated in a treaty easing the troop concentrations along the common border and opening it to trade and travel. Indo-Pakistani relations continued to be tense, however, especially after Pakistan announced it had nuclear weapons. The Pakistani problem continued in 1995, as India accused Pakistan of giving aid to rebels in Kashmir and Punjab. India also refused to sign an extension of the Nuclear Non-Proliferation Treaty, as it claimed that only the complete elimination of nuclear stockpiles would suffice. *Reading:* Byron Farwell, *Armies of the Raj: From Mutiny to Independence, 1858–1947* (1991); Arthur S. Lall, *The Emergence of Modern India* (1981); Hermann Kulke & Dietmar Rothermund, *A History of India* (1991); Stanley Wolpert, *India* (1991); S. D. Muni, *India and Nepal: A Changing Relationship* (1992).

Indochina (*Indochine Française*). A region comprising the eastern half of the Indochinese peninsula that today, as before the French occupation, includes the nations of Vietnam, Cambodia and Laos, Indochina was first entered by the French in the seventeenth century with the arrival of French Catholic missionaries. French military forces entered in 1799 to reinstall the dethroned king by force. After three years of campaigning by the French, the king was once again placed on the throne. French influence continued, and in 1867 all of Cochin China (Vietnam) had been annexed by the French. Cambodia had asked for French protection in 1863. The Sino-French Treaty of 1885 ended Chinese suzerainty over the Annam. French protection then moved inland, where the tribes of Laos, nominally under Siamese dominance, were absorbed in the new French condominium (1893). At that point, Indochina consisted of Cochin China, Annam, Tonkin and Laos. By 1899, the French colonies and protectorates had been merged into the Indochinese Union under a French governor general. Nationalist movements began to appear before World War I, although their development differed in the various regions of Indochina. In Tonkin, for instance, land reform was a key element of the nationalist movement. The communists did not become directly involved in Indochinese affairs until 1931, when the local party was founded. During World War II, the French garrison remained in Indochina, although the country was occupied by the Japanese in 1940. With the Vichy government in France losing power in March 1945, the Japanese proclaimed the states of Tonkin, Annam, and Cochin China to be the autonomous state of Vietnam, with Bao Dai (qv) as its emperor. The government of the dissolute Bao Dai collapsed after the end of the war, and the northern region (Tonkin) proclaimed itself the Democratic Republic of Vietnam under the leadership of Nguyen Ai Quoc, better known as Ho Chi Minh (qv). To some extent, this turn of events was the result of France's inability to reoccupy its possession. In the beginning, security in the country was maintained by Chinese and British forces. In some instances, Japanese troops were used by the Allies to keep order in the countryside. British forces withdrew in 1946; Nationalist Chinese forces left a short time later. When the Chinese did

withdraw, the Viet Minh immediately opened a campaign to gain French acceptance of the Democratic Republic of Vietnam. When simple negotiations did not suffice, the Viet Minh began a long guerrilla campaign that eventually led to a series of treaties with each of the states in Indochina that gave each its independence and effectively dissolved the French Union. Thereafter, Indochina ceased to exist as a French possession. *See also* Vietnam, Cambodia and Laos.
Reading: Douglas Allen, *Coming to Terms: Indochina, the United States, and the War* (1991); William Duiker, *The Communist Road to Power in Vietnam* (1996); Steven Hood, *Dragons Entangled: Indochina and the China-Vietnam War* (1992); James Cable, *The Geneva Conference of 1954 on Indochina* (1986); Lea Williams, *Southeast Asia: A History* (1976); Edward Rice-Maximin, *Accommodation and Resistance: The French Left, Indochina and the Cold War, 1944–1954* (1986); Noam Chomsky, *After the Cataclysm: Postwar Indochina and the Construction of Imperial Ideology* (1979); Takashi Shiraishi & Motoo Furuta, eds., *Indochina in the 1940s and 1950s* (1992).

Indonesia. The Republic of Indonesia is located along the Equator in the form of an archipelago running southeast out of Asia. There are some 17,000 islands in the group, which includes Java, Sumatra, Kalimantan (Borneo), and West Irian (western New Guinea). The capital city is Jakarta. Indonesia is known to have been in existence in the first millennium B.C. and the indigenous population was subjected to Hindu and Buddhist influences from India from those early times. Islam entered the region in the fifteenth century A.D., following the trade routes that had already been established by the Portuguese. By the sixteenth century, Islam was the predominant religion. The Dutch replaced the Portuguese as the principal European power in the region in the seventeenth century. The Dutch takeover began in 1750 with the submission of Java. The outer islands were not completely absorbed into the Dutch sphere until the early twentieth century. Japanese forces occupied the islands from 1942 until 1945. Following the liberation and the reestablishment of Dutch colonial rule, nationalist movements began, with such leaders as Achmed Sukarno and Mohammed Hatta proclaiming a republic in 1945–1946. Four years of heavy fighting followed as the Dutch tried to hold back the forces of nationalism. Finally, however, the Netherlands government ceded sovereignty to the republic although the Dutch retained control of West Irian on New Guinea. The final cession was accomplished 27 November 1949, when sovereignty was passed to the United States of Indonesia. On 16 December, Achmed Sukarno was elected president. Even though the Dutch had left, there were sporadic incidents of guerrilla activity throughout 1950. On 17 August 1950, the Republic of Indonesia was proclaimed as a unitary state, replacing the former loose confederation. Almost immediately trouble began. In March 1951, 25,000 government troops had to be ordered to Java to suppress an uprising of *Darul Islam* (qv), a fanatical Muslim group, which had allied itself with a number of communist and other outlaw groups to create havoc on the island. In December 1952, Indonesia decided to participate in the Colombo Plan (qv), but without military commitments. Trouble again broke out in March 1953, when the government attempted implementation of its land reform program. The Netherlands and Indonesia dissolved their union on 10 August 1954, primarily over the unresolved issue of West Irian. Indonesia then expelled all Dutch citizens and began the expropriation of Dutch property (1957); in 1960, Sukarno severed diplomatic relations with The Hague. During the same time, the dispute over Dutch New Guinea (West Irian) was becoming increasingly complex. President Sukarno, with the backing of his Communist Party of Indonesia (PKI), threatened on 28 October 1957 to take West Irian by force, if necessary. When the UN offered to mediate the dispute, Sukarno refused the offer. When voices were raised in opposition, Sukarno dissolved the Constituent Assembly and, in effect, gave power to the PKI. The Indonesians then began a campaign of harassment, leading to an incident in which Dutch forces on New Guinea engaged an Indonesian torpedo boat, which appears to have been the opening shot in a guerrilla campaign on New Guinea. By 26 May 1962, a full-scale war was raging that involved not only Dutch regulars but also Indonesian armed forces supporting the guerrillas. On 29 May, the UN ordered an immediate cease-fire; at the same time, Washington offered to mediate the dispute. The two sides met in Washington on 31 July and were able to agree to put West Irian under UN supervision, with the provision that it would be turned over to Indonesia on 1 May 1963. A United Nations peacekeeping force was established on 21 September and given the mission of supervising an orderly transfer of sovereignty. Having settled that issue, Sukarno turned his attention to the British enclave of Brunei (qv) on Borneo (qv). There, he instigated a rebellion that had to be put down by British troops. Sukarno also voiced objections to the British plan for a Malay federation (13 February 1963). On 18 May, less than three weeks after the West Irian transfer was completed, Sukarno had himself appointed President for Life. On 16 September, the Confederation of Malaysia came into being, and another crisis developed over claims to the territories of North Borneo and Sarawak (qv). Sukarno refused to acknowledge the new confederation and opened a diplomatic and guerrilla campaign to defeat it. By January 1964, another full-scale war was being fought. Great Britain formally warned Indonesia that it would use all the force necessary to uphold its commitments to Malaysia. Indonesia, at the same time, agreed to a U.S. proposal for a cease-fire and the opening of discussions to settle the issue. Later, Thailand agreed to patrol a buffer zone between Indonesian and Malay space (6 February 1964). A week later, Indonesia announced it had infiltrated specially trained Indonesian guerrilla forces into Saba (qv) and Sarawak in Borneo, where they were to operate until an acceptable (to Indonesia) settlement was reached. Following the same tactics that proved successful against the Dutch, Sukarno began an economic and military campaign aimed at disrupting the Malaysian federation. Britain reinforced its garrison in Borneo in 1964, after Indonesia placed an embargo (1963) on all trade with Singapore, another part of the Malaysian federation. When Malaysia was admitted into the United Nations,

Sukarno withdrew Indonesia (21 January 1965). Government-inspired attacks against U.S. interests began in February; by March, the government was expropriating American and other foreign property in Indonesia. In September, communist groups in Indonesia attempted a direct takeover of the country. The army chief of staff and other senior army official were kidnapped by the communists as a part of the plot on 1 September. On 1 October, an abortive communist coup took place that was led by the Central Javanese army and some air force units. The Indonesian Strategic Reserve Force was able to defeat the attempt with a heavy loss of life. Thereafter there began a massive eradication of the PKI, with estimates ranging as high as 400,000 killed in the purge, not all of whom were communists. Many Chinese who had dominated society in Indonesia were among the dead. The massacre continued until December. The losses greatly diminshed Sukarno's hold on the island nation, as many of his supporters had been communists. On 21 February 1966, Sukarno dismissed all of the noncommunist members of his government. By 24 February, massive antigovernment rioting had broken out across the country. On 11 March 1966, the Sukarno regime was overthrown by a military coup led by Lieutenant General Suharto (qv). The PKI was outlawed, and a new purge of communists began. Sukarno was retained in a figurehead role, but not for long. By June 1966, Indonesia and Malaysia had reached an accommodation (ratified 11 August) that restored peace to the region. On 28 September, Indonesia returned to its seat in the United Nations. On 20 February 1967, Achmed Sukarno was forced to relinquish the last of his powers to Suharto. All of this was confirmed by the Consultative Assembly on 27 March 1968, when Suharto was named president and prime minister. The people of West Irian voted overwhelmingly to remain with Indonesia in a vote held on 14 July 1969. With the virtual eradication of the communist party in Indonesia and the ouster of Sukarno, the government began to assert itself in the region. In April 1970, Foreign Minister Adam Malik (qv) announced a meeting of Asian nations to deal with the Cambodian issue. Communist China, North Vietnam and the Soviet Union all opposed the idea, but the conference was held anyway (16–18 May 1970). Among its conclusions were the immediate withdrawal of all foreign troops in Cambodia and the establishment of a new international conference on Indochina. Indonesia also announced its readiness to participate as a member of the proposed UN International Control Commission for Cambodia. Indonesia would later (November 1972) join the International Control and Supervisory Commission overseeing the cease-fire in South Vietnam. Also in 1970, Indonesia began a cooperative program with Malaysia to rid their common border area of troublesome communist-inspired guerrilla bands. A formal agreement to that effect was signed on 6 April 1972 and coordinated anti-guerrilla operations were increased. The relative calm was broken at home in January 1974, when violent demonstrations attended the formal visit of Japanese prime minister Tanaka to Jakarta. The situation became so violent that Indonesian troops opened fire on one group of demonstrators, killing eleven and injuring 137. In September 1975, Indonesia found itself in a conflict over Portuguese Timor and Papua New Guinea. In Timor a civil war raged in which communist-backed forces gained the upper hand. In early December, combined Indonesian land and naval forces attacked into the area and captured the capital city of Dili, driving the rebel forces into the hills. Portugal broke diplomatic relations with Indonesia and took the issue to the UN. In retaliation, the Indonesian government incorporated the the Portuguese enclave of Ocussi Ambeno into Indonesian territory. In July 1976, Indonesia annexed, with Portuguese permission, all of Portuguese Timor. The newly independent state of Papua New Guinea found itself embroiled in its own separatist conflict at home in 1975. Indonesia came to its aid by joining the former Australian colony in denouncing separatism. In 1976, Jakarta became the seat of the secretariat of the newly organized Association of Southeast Asian Nations. The government announced it had released 10,000 political prisoners arrested in 1965, on 20 December 1977. This act, however, brought an immediate reaction from a number of outside sources, such as Amnesty International, who claimed that Indonesia was lying, that no one had been released and that at least 100,000 were being held without due process. Then, on 20 January 1978, Suharto banned four newspapers without explanation. The government's claim to having released more political prisoners in September 1978 also met with derision from Amnesty International. On 28 March 1981, five Indonesian terrorists hijacked a domestic Garuda Airlines flight. Holding 55 hostages, the terrorists demanded the release of 80 political prisoners, the punishment of certain government officials and the expulsion "of all Jewish officials and Israeli militarists" in the country. The hostages were eventually released. The first national elections were held in Indonesia in 1982. Rioting broke out in the port city of Tanjungpriok following the arrest of four Muslims accused of interfering with the police. Many were killed when the rioters attacked a police station (1984). Death squads killed at least 4,000 known criminals between 1983 and 1984. Both the army and the police were suspected, but neither admitted responsibility. Public opinion seemingly favored the action, but the weight of world opinion forced the killers, whoever they were, to curtail their campaign. Also, in 1984, Indonesian relations with its neighboring state of Papua New Guinea became strained as Indonesian troops operating in Irian Jaya moved to deal with rebel activity near the border. A new border agreement (29 October) did little to settle the matter. Forty people were tried for participation in bombing incidents that began in January 1985 (9 were found guilty in May). The attacks continued, however, and many landmarks were destroyed. A series of what were considered show trials was held in 1986, designed to influence the upcoming elections. A number of dissidents and others were convicted of crimes ranging back to the bloody coup of 1965. A diplomatic confrontation developed in April 1986, when an Australian newspaper accused Suharto and others of embezzlement. Indonesia halted military cooperation and imposed visa restrictions in retaliation. The squabble grew more intense when Australia reported a possible Indonesian military plan of attack. Indonesia withdrew Australian landing privileges in September in retaliation. Indonesia also refused entry to two Australian newsmen travelling with President Ronald Reagan's party on an official visit to Jakarta in September. Suharto won his fifth term as president in 1988 amid widespread charges of corruption stemming back a number of years. In 1989 Suharto stated he would suppress any attempts to replace him and his government. Some rioting took place in 1989, mainly over the government's expropriation of land for conservation purposes. Over 30 casualties were reported after troops quelled the uprising in southern Sumatra. That same year, Indonesia and China met in the final round of talks aimed at restoration of diplomatic relations broken in 1965. Relations between the two were restored in August 1990. An incident in northwestern Indonesia culminated in the deaths of between 20 and 100 (some claims showed 200) mourners (12 November 1991) when troops opened fire on an East Timorese group at a funeral. A group of army officers and men were relieved or court-martialed as a result, but most were released in a 1995 Supreme Court ruling that in essence called them "scapegoats." In 1992, Indonesia was confronted by charges of human rights violations by Portugal and the Netherlands. In 1993, the U.S. entered the human rights controversy and halted the sale of jet fighters to Jakarta. Suharto attempted some fence-mending by reducing sentences and lifting travel restrictions on some dissidents, but he did little to assuage the tempest. That same year, Suharto was elected to a sixth five-year term as president, but he made a statement (1994) that he expected to be out of office by 1998. This open the way to increased opposition pressure for social reform. Suharto stopped the unrest in 1994 by suppressing it. Rumors abounded in 1995 that Suharto would seek another term in 1998. *Reading:* Geoffrey Robinson, *The Dark Side of Paradise: Political Violence in Bali* (1995); Matthew Jardine, *East Timor: Genocide in Paradise* (1996); Adam Schwarz, *A Nation in Waiting: Indonesia in the 1990s* (1994).

Indo-Pakistani War. In the 1971 elections held in East and West Pakistan, the People's (*Awami*} League won most of the East Pakistan's seat. This gave the Awami the power needed to reduce centralized control (from West Pakistan) and to gain local autonomy. A legislative standoff followed in which Zulfikar Ali Bhutto (qv), the leader of the West Pakistan's majority party refused to attend the opening of the National Assembly unless guarantees were set that would have blocked most of East Pakistan's expected demands. In part, Bhutto wanted to insure that the Awami leader, Sheikh Mujibur Rahman (qv), would not be elected prime minister. This action only increased the tension between the two parts of Pakistan. On 1 March 1971, President Agha Muhammad Yahya Khan (qv) postponed the opening of the National Assembly. On 6 March, he announced that the assembly would meet on 25 March, but he warned Mujibur that he would use the army to prevent a separation of the two parts of the country. Martial law was installed in East Pakistan, and reports of massacres of civilians were common. Emergency talks were held in Dacca between Yahya

Khan and Mujibur, but to no avail. On 25 March Yahya Khan flew back to West Pakistan. The next day, a clandestine radio station in East Pakistan announced the independence and sovereignty of the "People's Republic of Bangladesh." Before nightfall, a full-scale war was underway. Mujibur and other East Pakistani leaders were arrested and charged with treason, and the Awami League was outlawed. Through the confusion and conflicting claims and counterclaims of the ensuing months, one thing became clear: Millions of Muslim and Hindu refugees had fled into India, a fact that dismayed the Indian government. The Soviet Union sided with India on this point, while most of the other powers viewed the situation as an internal matter. For India, the situation only exacerbated the already tense conditions along its border with West Pakistan, especially in Kashmir. On 21 October, Yahya Khan went to the UN and asked for mediation, claiming India was hindering the return of the refugees into East Pakistan, even though he had granted them all amnesty. India retorted that East Pakistan was unsafe. By 22 November, clashes along the Kashmir border were widespread, with Pakistan claiming India had launched an all-out attack. In the east, there were persistent reports that four columns of Indian troops had moved into the country. By 3 December, at least 250,000 Indian troops were in East Pakistan and Bengal. Also, on 3 December, Pakistani aircraft attacked Indian military bases in Kashmir. The following day, Pakistani ground forces invaded Kashmir and penetrated about 15 kilometers before being stopped by Indian reinforcements. On 5–6 December, a United Nations Security Council cease-fire order was vetoed by the Soviet Union so as to allow India time to gain and consolidate all of its objectives. Pakistan immediately petitioned for action by the UN General Assembly. On 7 December, India forces operating in East Pakistan captured the strategically important city of Jessore, thereby taking control of the western half of the country. By 11 December the capital city of Dacca was under siege. Communist China sided with Pakistan but took no other overt action. By mid-December, the United States had moved additional naval units into the Indian Ocean to offset the Soviet buildup in the waters off East Pakistan. On 14–16 December, the East Pakistani government fled to an International Red Cross safe haven and disavowed any further association with the central government in West Pakistan. On 15 December, the UN General Assembly ordered a cease-fire, but with no enforcement of the order, the fighting continued. That day, Indian troops pushed across the West Pakistan borderin the Hyderabad and Punjab Suba sectors. On 16 December, the 90,000-man Pakistani army in East Pakistan was forced to surrender. This is marked as the time of the end of the fighting. East Pakistan declared its already proclaimed independence as Bangladesh on 17 December. Yahya Khan was forced to resign on 20 December, with Zulfikar Ali Bhutto named as his replacement. The exchange of prisoners would take years to complete. Diplomatic relations between Pakistan and India were not normalized until 25 July 1976. *Reading:* Sumit Ganguly, *The Origins of War in South Asia: Indo-Pakistani Conflicts since 1947* (1994).

Inonu, Ismet. (b.24 September 1884, Smyrna (Izmir), Turkey—d. 25 December 1973) A corps commander in World War I, Ismet Pasha, as he was known, was a close friend of Mustafa Kemal Ataturk, the father of modern Turkey. As General Ismet Pasha he defeated the Greeks in the ill-fated 1921 campaign. Ismet Inonu served as prime minister almost continuously from 1927 until 1937. When Ataturk died in 1938, he was elected president and served in that office until 1950. In 1950, he was defeated by an opposition party that he had helped foster as a part of his belief in two or more parties. He then assumed the leadership of the opposition. In 1961, he again became prime minister in a coalition government in which he was able to withstand army plots in 1962 and 1963. He was defeated in 1965 and gave up the leadership of his Republican People's Party in 1972. He died a year later at age 89.

Inter-American Conference. More properly called the International Conference of American States, the Inter-American Conference, the first hemispheric meeting of all 21 nations, was held on 30 April 1948, in Bogotá, Colombia. At the first meeting, the charter of the new organization was signed, succeeding the Union of American Republics (Pan-American Union). The new organization became known as the the Organization of American States (OAS), with the term Pan-American Union being applied to the administrative structure of the OAS. The history of such conferences goes back to 2 October 1889, when the first meeting of all the states was held. Earlier meetings from 1826 were not truly hemispheric, as none represented all the nations of the hemisphere. The 1889 meeting was held in Washington, DC, at the invitation of Secretary of State Thomas F. Bayard. The meeting was presided over by by the new secretary of state, James G. Blaine. While the prevention of war in the hemisphere was the primary goal of the conference, economics, sanitation and commerce were also on the agenda. *See also* Organization of American States.

Inter-American Defense Board. The Inter-American Defense Board was established on 30 April 1948, at the meeting of the Pan-American Conference that replaced the Pan-American Union with the Organization of American States (OAS). The purpose of the Inter-American Defense Board was to deal defense matters within the hemispheric defense zone established at the 15 August–2 September 1947 Inter-American Conference for the Maintenance of Continental Peace and Security held in Quitandinha, Brazil (Treaty of Reciprocal Assistance, or Rio Pact) (qv). The Inter-American Defense Board is located in Washington, DC.

Inter-American Maintenance of Peace and Security Conference. The International Conference for the Maintenance of Peace and Security was held in Quitandinha, Brazil, from 15 August to 2 September 1947. At the conference the concept that an attack on one American state would be considered an attack on all was adopted, which agreed with Article 51 of the United Nations Charter. A hemisphere defense zone was designated that stretched from Greenland to Argentina and included Bermuda and the Aleutians, but not Hawaii or Iceland. The resulting Treaty of Reciprocal Assistance, also called the Rio Treaty or Rio Pact (qv), was signed at Rio de Janiero.

Inter-American Mutual Assistance Treaty (Treaty of Rio de Janeiro). *See* Rio Treaty and Inter-American Maintenance of Peace and Security Conference.

Inter-American Peacekeeping Force. On 6 May 1965, the Organization of American States agreed to establish an Inter-American Peacekeeping Force (IAPF) made up of contingents from Brazil, Costa Rica, Guatemala, Honduras, Paraguay, the United States and Venezuela. The force was deployed into the Dominican Republic on 23 May 1965, where it began to replace the 20,000-man U.S. force of airborne troops and Marines that had been in country since 30 April. The 8,200-man IAPF began its withdrawal from the Dominican Republic on 28 June 1966 and completed the redeployment in October.

International Atomic Energy Agency (IAEA). In January 1952 the United Nations General Assembly voted to combine the Atomic Energy Commission and the Conventional Armaments Commission into the Disarmament Commission, which was given the mission of preparing proposals for the regulation and limitation of all military weapons and armed forces. This group was also charged with determining a formula for a balanced reduction of these means of war. However, the Soviet Union's entry into the hydrogen bomb arena greatly complicated the commission's work, and little progress was made toward disarmament. On 29 July 1957, following a series of failed initiatives, the UN established the International Atomic Energy Agency to find peaceful uses for nuclear energy. More than 80 nations subscribed to the program, which made nuclear materials, primarily supplied by the United States, available for peaceful applications. The agency was headquartered in Vienna, Austria. The extremely important work of the agency was largely overlooked through the next three decades until 21 February 1985, when the USSR agreed for the first time to allow it to inspect Soviet nuclear facilities. In January 1992, the government of the Democratic People's Republic of Korea (North Korea) signed a treaty with the agency that theoretically opened the country's four nuclear reactors to inspection. In their report, the first overt indications appeared that confirmed North Korea's entrance into the nuclear weapons arena. In one incident, in December 1992, Russian officials prevented the departure of 36 senior nuclear weapons specialists who had been hired by North Korea to help perfect the weapons production industry that had grown around its production of plutonium. To date (February 1994), North Korea has steadfastly refused to allow a detailed inspection of its weapons production facilities. In later times, the IAEA was particularly active in determining the removal or destruction of Iraq's nuclear production capability following the Desert Storm operation.

International Conference on Vietnam. Peace talks to end the fighting in Vietnam (*see* Vietnam) began on 13 May 1968. W. Averell Harriman (qv) represented the U.S.. The North Vietnamese representative was Xuan Thuy (qv),while the Viet Cong (National Liberation Front) sent Nguyen Thi Binh.The South Vietnamese adamantly opposed the meetings, but sent Air Force General Nguyen Cao Ky (qv), the country's vice president, to Paris. At one point, however, on 4 November 1968, President Thieu of South Vietnam announced that his government would boycott the meeting if the Viet Cong were brought to the table. During the first few staff meetings, it became obvious to all concerned that the conference was to be a long one. The principal item on the agenda for those setting up the conference was the size and shape of the table. North Vietnamese intransigence was being orchestrated to play to an American people who had tired of the war and had put U.S. president Lyndon B. Johnson (qv) in an untenable position. On 5 January 1969, the new US president, Richard M. Nixon (qv), replaced Harriman with Henry Cabot Lodge (qv). On 14 January the South Vietnamese government proposed the gradual withdrawal of U.S. forces. Actual peace talks began on 25 November 1969. Ambassador Lodge accused the North Vietnamese of attempting to terrorize the South Vietnamese into accepting their terms by continuing their offensive in the south. On 8 May, the Viet Cong delegate put forth a ten-point plan to end the war. The plan called for an immediate US withdrawal and a coalition government with Viet Cong participation to rule South Vietnam. Over the next months charges and countercharges were leveled by both sides. On 3 November, Nixon indicated that the latest secret US proposals had been rejected and stated that the U.S. would not withdraw but would reduce its forces and that the "Vietnamization" of the war was well underway. Henry Cabot Lodge resigned on 20 November, effective 8 December. Henry Kissinger became the new US chief negotiator. Into 1970, the peace talks remained deadlocked, usually over procedural issues but also over the North's demand for immediate US withdrawal of its forces. To break this impasse, Nixon ordered a renewal of the bombing of North Vietnam. When that occurred, the North Vietnamese and Viet Cong delegates refused to attend any more meetings (6 May 1970). When they did return, the Viet Cong placed an eight-point plan on the table. On 10 December 1970, both sides called for an immediate prisoner exchange, although the North had steadfastly refused to acknowledge that it held any prisoners. Then, on 17 December, the North Vietnamese asked the U.S. for a "reasonable" deadline for the withdrawal of U.S. forces. The North presented a new seven-point plan on 1 July 1971, which included the release of all American prisoners if the U.S. withdrew by the end of 1971. The U.S. publicly rejected the offer on 8 July, but secret negotiations began based on that proposal. Once again, however, the North walked out of the talks to protest the continued bombing of the north on 24 February 1972; an indefinite halt to the peace process was announced by the U.S. and South Vietnam on 4 May 1972. The U.S. also strengthened its naval and air forces in Southeast Asia. On 30 December, Nixon ordered a halt to the bombing of the north, and the peace talks were immediately scheduled to resume (1 January 1973). Citing the progress made in the new round of talks, Nixon ordered an end to all US offensive action above the 17th parallel. On 23 January, Henry Kissinger announced that a cease-fire agreement had been reached that was to go into effect at 8 A.M. Saigon time, on 28 January 1973. All prisoners were to be exchanged. On 26 February 1973, a 16-nation conference on the war in Southeast Asia opened in Paris and, on 2 March, announced a guarantee of the settlement to the war. By that point less than 10,000 U.S. troops remained in country. (All U.S. forces were to be withdrawn by the end of March.) On 19 March, South Vietnam and the Viet Cong opened full-scale discussions on the future of the country. The U.S. war in Southeast Asia was over. The North Vietnamese used the U.S. withdrawal as the prelude for the complete occupation of the Republic of South Vietnam.

International Control and Supervisory Commission (ICC). Following the Geneva Accords that divided Vietnam, the United Nations undertook the supervision of the French and Viet Minh withdrawals to their respective sides of the demarcation line at the 17th parallel. A three-man International Control Commission was established by the UN to supervise the disengagement. The original group was composed of an Indian chairman and Canadian and Polish members who were to supervise, in addition to the separation of the warring parties, the called-for nationwide elections that were to be held in 1956. On 6 April 1956, South Vietnam announced that it would continue to cooperate with the ICC but stipulated that any elections would have to be held under conditions that would be free of North Vietnamese interference. On 30 July 1956, the South Vietnamese government established a liaison mission to assume the functions of the departing French liaison group. On 3 January 1957, the ICC reported that, between December 1955 and August 1956, neither the North Vietnamese nor their southern counterparts had fulfilled their obligations under the 1954 Geneva Armistice Agreement and that both sides were guilty of violating the accords. On 17 April 1958, as Viet Cong terrorism rose in the south, the South Vietnamese government requested that the North Vietnamese liaison mission be withdrawn from its Saigon headquarters. The ICC agreed (17 April 1960) to doubling the size of the US Military Assistance and Advisory Group (USMAAGV), even though the North Vietnamese protested the action. On 10 November 1960, the South Vietnamese government informed the ICC that the October communist attacks in Kontum and Pleiku involving North Vietnamese army (NVA) troops, which had moved into the south through Laos and which were commanded by high-ranking NVA officers, constituted aggression. Then, on 4 April 1961, South Vietnam's President Ngo Dinh Diem appealed to the ICC for a vigorous investigation of the growing communist subversion and terrorism in the south. The U.S. asked (6 May 1962) for an ICC investigation when Pathet Lao (qv) forces captured the village of Nam Tha in northern Laos, to see if there had been a violation of the May 1961 cease-fire agreement (*see* Laos). The ICC reported on 2 June that the North Vietnamese government was actively supporting and supplying the Viet Cong forces operating in the south. The communist Polish member of the ICC refused to sign the report. The South Vietnamese government lodged a formal protest (6 December 1963) with the ICC over the introduction of new Chinese-made weapons into South Vietnam. When US aircraft bombed NVA installations in the demilitarized zone (DMZ) for the first time on 30 July 1966, the ICC announced it would act to keep the DMZ free of military activities by either side. As the situation worsened in the

South Vietnamese countryside, the ICC "temporarily suspended" all fixed and mobile team operations outside the Saigon area. On 7 January 1969, South Vietnam again formally protested to the ICC about continued NVA violations in the DMZ. On 14 October 1969, Cambodia ordered the ICC to remove itself from that nation by 31 December, when the ICC charter expired. South Vietnam continued to protest communist terrorism into 1970. On 22 March 1970, the Lon Nol (qv) government in Cambodia asked Great Britain and the USST to reactivate the ICC to peacefully expel all NVA/VC from the country. This request was seconded by the 11-member Asian conference on Southeast Asia held in Jakarta, Indonesia, on 17 May 1970. On 13 November 1971, South Vietnam lodged yet another protest with the ICC, this time complaining that the NVA was kidnapping children to be taken to North Vietnam for indoctrination and training. On 29 September 1972, the Indian representative at the ICC was withdrawn as the ICC headquarters was moved to Hanoi. The Canadian and Polish delegates remained in Saigon, however, leaving the headquarters without any of its designated members. The United States announced on 15 November 1972 that Canada, Hungary, Indonesia and Poland had agreed to serve on a rejuvenated ICC to supervise any cease-fire in South Vietnam. When the cease-fire went into effect on 28 January 1973, violations of its terms began immediately. On 9 February, the ICC reported that the cease-fire was not working and that there was heavy fighting in several areas. On 29 May 1973, Canada, claiming continuous interference in ICC activities, ordered its 200 personnel home and announced its formal withdrawal on 31 July. Iran was then designated to take its place on the ICC. By that point, however, the value of the ICC in confronting the problems in Vietnam was apparent to all.

International Court of Justice. The first international attempts at judicial settlement through arbitration in modern times may be found in the minutes of the first and second Hague peace conferences held in 1899 and 1907. A Permanent Court of International Justice was formed by the League of Nations (Article 14) in February 1920. Following World War II, the United Nations' replacement of the League also meant the dissolution of the Permanent Court. The United Nations charter provided, however (Article 92), for the establishment of a new court with all UN members ipso facto parties to its jurisdiction (Article 93). The court consists of 15 judges, each from a different country, who are elected by the General Assembly and the Security Council and who serve for nine-year terms. The courts sits in The Hague; its first session was held in April–May 1946. The court hears cases that are submitted to it by the member states and cases on matters specifically provided for in the UN charter and in various treaties. Failure to heed the decision of the court usually means that the offending nation is brought to the attention of the UN Security Council. In 1951, for example, Iran submitted its oil nationalization problem to the court after having repeatedly denied the court's jurisdiction in the matter. In August 1972, Great Britain submitted the Iceland fishing restrictions case (*see* Cod Wars) to the court. Iceland refused to accept the court's ruling which barred the imposition of a 50-

mile no-fishing zone. In June 1973, France refused the court's judgment against further nuclear testing at the French Test Site at Mururoa Atoll (qv), claiming the court had no competence in the matter. In September 1976, the court rejected a Greek request for an injunction against further Turkish oil exploration in the Aegean Sea. The United States declared on 8 April 1984, that it would not be bound by court decisions dealing with Central America. On 9 April, Nicaragua charged the U.S. with illegal military operations against it. The court ruled unanimously against the United States on 10 May in that matter and directed that the U.S. not mine Nicaraguan harbors. In January 1985, the United States declared it would no longer participate in any court proceedings in which it stood accused of aggression by Nicaragua. Since that time, the court has sat in judgment in dozens of other cases affecting the security of the world.

Ioannides, Demetrios. On 25 November 1973, Brigadier General Demetrios Ioannides led the coup that overthrew the government of Greek president George (Georgios) Papadopoulos (qv), who had been in office since 1 June 1973. Papadopoulos was replaced by Lieutenant General Phaidon Gizikis (qv).

Ipoh. *See* Malaysia.

Iquilas. *See* Peru.

Iran. Iran is located in Southwest Asia and is bordered on the north by three former Soviet republics, Armenia, Azerbaijan and Turkmenistan; on the east by Afghanistan and Pakistan and on the west by Iraq and Turkey. On the south, Iran borders on the Gulf of Oman (qv) and the Persian Gulf (qv). The capital is Tehran. The successor of the ancient Persian Empire, Iran's ancestral inhabitants migrated into the region in the second millennium B.C. and were of Indo-European stock. In 538 B.C., Cyrus the Great conquered Babylonia and restored Jerusalem to the Jews. Persia was conquered by Alexander the Great in 333 B.C., only to be taken by the Parthians in the third century B.C. The Parthians were replaced by the Sassanian Persians in 226 A.D. In the seventh century, Islam was introduced in Persia by the Arabs, replacing the Zoroastrian religion, which had existed since before Alexander's conquest. For several centuries the Persian culture flourished. Beginning in the eleventh century, however, Persia was again ruled by foreigners, first the Turks and then the Mongols. In 1502, a native monarchy was established that survived until 1979. In 1941, Shah Reza Khan abdicated in favor of his son, Mohammad Reza Pahlavi (qv), who ruled until the collapse of the monarchy in 1979. During World War II, Iran's strategic importance lay in the fact that its southern coast afforded access to Allied supply ships carrying war goods to the Soviet Union through what was called the Persian Corridor, a route generally protected from German interdiction. Because of this important link in the Allied war effort, Iran was in effect occupied by Allied forces—the northern part of the country being held by Soviet forces. In September 1945, the Allies informed the Shah that they would be out of his country by March 1946. The Soviets, however, refused to leave and in March 1946 were engaged in activities indicating they intended to stay. On 19 March, Iran formally protested to the United Nations. Quick action by the UN and a

U.S. ultimatum of sorts forced the Soviets to begin their withdrawal (April–May 1946). In September, an uprising of rebellious tribesmen broke out in southern Iran that was not settled until October. Another uprising broke out in the province of Fars in the southwest. These incidents established a pattern of resistance against a politically insensitive government that lasted until the fall of the shah in 1979, even though significant economic improvement could be seen and felt throughout the country. In 1947, Iran became a strong ally of the United States. On 6 October a military assistance agreement was signed, and a U.S. advisory mission was established. On 12 September 1951, Prime Minister Mossadegh (qv), a member of the antiforeign Iran Party, issued an ultimatum to Great Britain to evacuate Abadan Island (qv) in the Shatt al-Arab (qv). When England did leave the island, Iranian forces occupied it (27 September 1951). Iran was forced to submit to International Court of Justice rule in December 1951, over the issue of the nationalization of foreign oil holdings, such as the British operations at Abadan. In December 1951, the United States halted all arms shipments to Iran in retaliation for its oil nationalization policies. Not finished with the British, Mossadegh ordered all British consulates in Iran closed on 12 January 1952; the British rejected the order the next day. Mossadegh fell from power on 17 June 1952, but following bloody rioting, he was returned to power with dictatorial authority on 22 July. On 22 October, Iran broke diplomatic relations with Great Britain. In retaliation, the United States informed Iran there would be no further aid until the oil matter was settled with London. In August 1953, the shah tried unsuccessfully to unseat Mossadegh and was forced to flee the country as a result. Later in the month, a CIA-financed coup was able to depose Mossadegh, and the shah returned (22 August 1953). Even so, the political unrest across the country continued, and army troops were often used to restore order. In August 1954, the Anglo-Iranian Oil Company renewed production. Once again the pattern of economic development and political suppression were put back into place by the shah's government. On 12 October 1955, Iran joined the Baghdad Pact (qv) after being warned by the Soviet Union of the consequences of such an act. On 3 March 1959, Iran abrogated a 1921 treaty with the USSR by which Soviet troops were free to enter Iran if the USSR felt threatened by the presence of other foreign troops on Iranian soil. When Iran recognized Israel in July 1960, the Arab League (qv) imposed an economic boycott on Tehran. On 26 January 1965, Prime Minister Hassan Ali Mansour died of an assassin's wounds inflicted on 21 January, in another incident of political unrest in the country. In 1969, a dispute broke out with Iraq over navigation rights in the Shatt al-Arab and over Iranian support of the Kurds. The verbal barrage that followed was often interrupted into open warfare. On 19 April 1969, Iran abrogated the 1937 Navigation of the Shatt al-Arab Treaty, claiming numerous violations by Iraq. Forces began to mass on both sides of their common border. Border incidents continued into September. In 1970, with war with Iraq a distinct possibility, Iran began modernizing its armed forces. The United States received the lion's share of the arms business that accrued from this program. Although the threat of war deminished, Iran again flexed its muscles when it seized the British protectorate of the Great and Lesser Tunb Islands (*Tomb-e-Bozorg and Tomb-e Kuchak*) at the northern end of the Strait of Hormuz (qv). The Iranians also seized the island of Abu Musa, but returned it to the Persian Gulf Emirate of Shanjah, in return for basing rights. Iraq then broke diplomatic relations (30 November) over the incident. In 1973, Iran purchased $2 billion in military supplies from the United States, including 70 F-4 and 111 F-5E fighter aircraft. On 2 June 1973, an American advisor, Lieutenant Colonel Lewis Hawkins, was shot to death by two left-wing assassins in Iran. In July 1973, Iran replaced Canada on the International Control and Supervisory Commission (ICC) in Vietnam. In February 1974, clashes again broke out in the Persian Gulf between Iranian and Iraqi forces. In 1975, the U.S. concluded a $21 billion deal with Iran in which Tehran was to receive nuclear reactors and conventional weapons over a five-year period. In March 1975, Iran reached a border settlement with Iraq by agreeing to stop aiding the Kurds. On 21 May 1975, two more American servicemen were assassinated by Iranian left-wing terrorists from a group known as "Peoples' Strugglers." The same group later assassinated (3 July) a Foreign Service National employee working at the US embassy. Three U.S. civilian employees of Rockwell International were also killed by this group in August 1976. The Iranian government caught ten members of the group and executed nine of them. In May 1976, the Iranian government ordered eight nuclear reactors from France at a cost of $10 billion. In 1976, Iran purchased an additional $10 billion in U.S. military hardware. The U.S. later announced it would sell Iran 160 F-16 fighters. Also, in 1976, Iran dispatched a 3,500 man military force to assist the the Sultan of Oman, Qaboos (*Qabus ibn Da'id*), fight rebellious Dhofari tribesmen. The Iranian force was withdrawn from Oman on 20 January 1977. On 8 June 1977, the new U.S. president took one of the first actions in what would later be perceived as a campaign to topple the shah of Iran. The U.S. announced it would not sell 250 already ordered F-18L advanced fighters to Iran. On 2 March 1978, Iran broke diplomatic relations with East Germany because the East German government allowed an anti-shah Iranian student demonstration in East Berlin. At the same time, however, a new wave of antigovernment demonstrations broke out in Iran. These demonstrations continued and worsened into May of that year. Numbers of demonstrators were killed in clashes with the police and army troops. This only heightened the tension in the country. On 12 August 1978, martial law was declared following the appointment of Jafaar Sharif-Emami (qv) as prime minister. By September at least 1,000 rioters had been killed. On 1 October, the shah declared an amnesty for all those involved in the demonstrations, including the Ayatollah Khomeini (qv), who lived in exile in France. More attacks against Americans followed, as in October, when a bus carrying Bell Helicopter employees was attacked. On 5 November, Sharif-Emami resigned and was replaced by General Gholam Reza Azhari as prime minister. Also in November, Karin Sanjabi (qv), a leader of the political opposition, was arrested. On 19

November, the Soviet Union warned the U.S. against interfering in the Iranian situation. By December, chaos reigned in Iran. On 30 December, Shahpour Bakhtiar (qv), an outspoken critic of the shah, was appointed prime minister to head a new civilian government to replace the military one imposed by the shah a month earlier. Still the unrest continued and grew. On 7 January 1979, Ayatollah Khomeini demanded the shah be captured and tried. The following day, Bakhtiar announced Iran would reevaluate its military contracts, especially a $10 billion one with the U.S. In a last-ditch attempt to stave off what appeared to be inevitable, the Iranian military banned all public gatherings on 26 January. On 1 February, however, Ayatollah Khomeini returned to Iran after 14 years in exile. His first act was to tell the Bakhtiar government to resign, or he would have them arrested.. On 6 February, Iran cancelled $7 billion order for military equipment it was to purchase from the U.S. On 11 February, the Bakhtiar government collapsed, and Khomeini seized power. Two days later, Bakhtiar was arrested. By 21 February, a U.S. naval task force was evacuating foreign nationals through the ports of Bandar Abbas and Char Bahar. On 4 March, Iran broke diplomatic relations with South Africa and refused any more oil shipments to them. Clashes were also reported between Kurds and Khomeini supporters. In March, Iran, Turkey and Pakistan withdrew from the Central Treaty Organization (CENTO). On 1 April, Khomeini declared Iran an Islamic republic. Five days later all foreign contracts were cancelled. Khomeini was attempting to do two things: rid Iran of foreign influence as he began taking his people back into a twelveth-century cultural environment and, at the same time, isolate Iran so that the reign of terror he imposed in clearing away all opposition to his rule would be shielded from outside view. News did leak out, however; and while the world watched, the dynastic change took place. Few intellectuals, except those versed in the Koran, survived the terror. Fewer still were the technicans needed to keep the sophisticated machinery the shah had imported to drag his country out of the very conditions that were again being forced upon it. In addition, the Kurds in the north were causing considerable trouble. By mid-October 1979, whole regions of the northern provinces were in Kurdish hands or were being heavily contested. On 4 November 1979, in a well-orchestrated plan, Iranian "students" attacked and seized the U.S. embassy in Tehran. Sixty-three hostages were taken as the "students" demanded the return of the shah, who was in a New York hospital suffering from cancer, for their release. On 6 November, Khomeini did away with the government of Iran and replaced it with a revolutionary council. As the days wore on in the crisis, some American hostages were released, and the UN Security Council ordered (9 November, 4 December) the intransigent Ayatollah to release the hostages. The reactions of the United States were reflected in the indecision and timidity of the president. All Iranian students in the United States were deported, even those requesting permission to stay. All oil shipments from Iran were suspended, and all Iranian assets in the U.S. were impounded. Some of the hostages were freed by the Iranians, mostly black Americans and women. Several American embassy employees took refuge in the Canadian Embassy and were spirited out of Iran by the Canadians in January 1980. On 5 December 1979, the Soviet Union warned the United States against taking any military action to free the hostages and informed the Iranians of support, albeit unspecified, if the U.S. attacked. At the same time, in northern Iran, opponents of Khomeini fought a number of pitched battles with government forces. On 31 December 1979, the UN Security Council gave Iran one week to release the hostages. Without the threat of Iranian intervention, the USSR invaded Afghanistan (*see* Afghanistan) at the end of 1979. Even so, the Khomeini government condemned the Soviet Union for its attack and promised aid to the Afghans. Soviet troop movements near the Iranian borders were viewed as an attempt to silence Iranian criticism. On 22 March, Carter was briefed on a rescue plan designed to free the hostages. The plan was approved in April. On 7 April, the U.S. formally severed relations with Iran; all Iranian diplomats were ordered to leave the U.S. within 24 hours. On 17 April, a C-130 "Hercules" aircraft penetrated Iran and landed in the Kabir Desert. Intelligence specialists collected soil samples and other data and implanted special electronic devices. The team left without being discovered. On 24 April, an ineptly planned and poorly led rescue attempt was mounted from the U.S. aircraft carrier *USS Nimitz*. Problems encountered during the early phases of the operation allowed a timid American president to abort the mission. Eight US servicemen were killed and a number injured during the first phase of the operation. Meanwhile, in Iran, the Ayatollah was forced to announce (10 June) that internal dissension was creating chaos in the country. On 10 July a military coup attempt was foiled; 36 of the participants were subsequently executed. On 12 September 1980, Khomeini stipulated four conditions for the release of the hostages: the U.S. had to cancel all claims against Iran, return all property belonging to the shah, release all frozen Iranian assets and promise no reprisals. Three days later the speaker of the Majlis, the Iranian parliament, added that the Ayatollah had "forgotten" to mention that the United States had to apologize publicly for all its past interference in Iranian affairs. Renewed fighting was also reported along the Iraqi border. The war that followed, which lasted until 1988 (*see* Iran-Iraq War), created great misery in Iran and greatly depleted their supply of military equipment, yet it somehow also created a resolve among the people. While the war went on, Kurdish attacks in the north complicated matters for Iran. Also of some importance was the demonstration by 5,000 Afghans in front of the Soviet Embassy in Tehran on 27 December, marking the first anniversary of the invasion of Afghanistan (qv). At second demonstration in front of the Afghan Embassy saw a clash with police in which one demonstrator was killed. On 6 January 1981, Iran accepted an Algerian offer to act as guarantor for the release of the American hostages. On 20 January, 52 Americans were released after 444 days of captivity, torture and deprivation. Added to that toll was President Carter's defeat in the US elections against Ronald Reagan (qv). Some analysts place emphasis on the fact that the Iranians probably did not want to face the new Republican president-to-be and timed the release to coincide with the American inauguration. Others claim it was the Republicans who orchestrated the release to insure a Republican victory. The internal political picture in Iran remained murky during the remainder of the year. On 8 March an Iranian judge demanded that President Bani-Sadr (qv) be tried for treason. On 16 March, Khomeini issued an order forbidding all public speeches by political figures. On 1 April, Khomeini began a purge of the judiciary and the Revolutionary Guard. On 10 June, Khomeini dismissed Bani-Sadr as commander in chief of the Iranian armed forces. On 21 June Bani-Sadr was impeached and ordered arrested. A large number of officials were killed on 28 June when a bomb went off at a rally in Tehran. No one claimed responsibility for the attack. By July the executions began that were the climax of Khomeini's purge of opponents. By 5 July, more than 100 had been executed. More bombings took place in August, one of which killed the new Iranian president, the prime minister and three other members of the Supreme Defense Council. The prosecutor general was killed in a bombing on 2 September. On 7 April 1982, former foreign minister Sadegh Ghotbzadeh (qv) was arrested for plotting the assassination of Khomeini. On 24 November 1983, the United States claimed that Iran, with the support of Syria, had planned and executed the 23 October attack on the U.S. embassy in Beirut, Lebanon, that killed 241 US Marines. The Iranian government later (7 October) denied complicity in the attack. During July 1984, Libya secretly mined the Red Sea and allowed *Islamic Jihad* (qv) to take credit for it. On 9 August, Khomeini condemned those responsible for the mining. Such condemnation by Khomeini was often more than moral in nature and involved direct threats on the lives of the perpetrators. In another incident, the U.S. accused Iran of involvement in the hijacking of a Kuwaiti airliner with 166 on board which flew to Tehran on 4 December. Two American diplomats on board were subsequently murdered by the terrorists who demanded the release of Shi'ite prisoners in Kuwait. The hostages were released on 9 December following an attack by an Iranian security forces. The U.S. demand for extradition of the four terrorists was refused. On 8 July 1985, President Ronald Reagan branded Iran, Cuba, Libya, Nicaragua and North Korea as the chief purveyors of terrorism throughout the world. During the remainder of the 1980s unrest continued to manifest itself in the form of bombings, although the number of demonstrations declined. In November 1986, a team of senior U.S. officials visited Iran on a secret mission to exchange arms for Iranian help in freeing Western hostages held in Lebanon. The ensuing weapons deal led to a major, but largely politically motivated, scandal in the U.S. A major political upheaval occurred in Iran when Khomeini ousted his designated successor, Ayatollah Ali Montazeri, and other moderates who would have tempered the Islamic fundamentalist regime Khomeini had set up. In November 1986, U.S. representatives secretly visited Iran to seek help in gaining the release of American hostages being held in Lebanon. This episode eventually led to the Iran-Contra scandal that threatened the administration of U.S. president Ronald Reagan (qv). In an unfortunate incident on 3 July 1988, a U.S. warship shot down an Iranian jet carrying 290 civilian passengers and crew. There was some evidence that the Iranians planned the operation to embarrass the US, but there was never any proof that it was more than a case of mistaken identity. Khomeini's death on 3 July 1989 created a spectacle in Tehran that included millions of mourners and the sight of Khomeini's body being thrown to the ground after his coffin was disturbed by the press of the crowd. Khomeini was replaced by Ayatollah Ali Khamenei as interim president. Before August, Hashemi Rafsanjani (qv) was elected president and Khamenei appointed spiritual leader. Iran was hit by a major earthquake on 21 June 1990 that killed, injured or left homeless nearly one-half million people. The U.S., although it had no diplomatic relations with Iran, offered assistance in the emergency, which was accepted. Iraq's problems with the Kurds in the 1990s has forced over one million Kurdish people to seek refuge in Iran. Iran is also continually accused of fostering international terrorism. Anti-American demonstrations and hard-line Islamic rioting coincided with the American response to the Iraqi invasion of Kuwait, but by 1991 the basis for rioting was enlarged by food-shortages and the strict Islamic social requirements imposed by the government. Also, in August 1991, Iran was accused of complicity in the Bakhtiar assassination in Paris. When the Desert Storm operation had liberated Kuwait, Shi'ite Moslems in Iraq who were still fighting Saddam Hussein sought Iranian help, but it was denied. In 1991, Iran did have some success in negotiating the release of Western hostages held by Shi'ite rebels in Lebanon. More rioting throughout Iran occurred in May 1992 and was followed by summary execution of many of those involved. Iran also began attempts to bring its form of Islamic fundamentalism into the Muslim states that had broken away from the former USSR. This was accomplished through trade agreements, but the fundamentalist issue was just beneath the surface. Iranian jets engaged targets in Iraq that were suspected of being bases for antiregime rebel forces. Iraq shot down one of the jets on 5 April 1992. These attacks continued into 1993. Claims of support of terrorism were leveled against Iran, especially by the U.S., in 1993. Saudi Arabia refused admission to Iranians for the annual vist to Mecca (*Hajj*) because of fear that Iranian fundamentalists would disrupt the event. By 1995, hard-line Islamic fundamentalists had all but isolated the Rafsanjani moderate government and, when coupled with international accusations that Iran was an "outlaw state," weakened chances that Iran could regain a place in the world community at any time in the near future. *Reading:* Fakhreddin Azimi, *Iran: The Crisis of Democracy, 1941–1953* (1989); Shireen T. Hunter, *Iran and the World: Continuity in a Revolutionary Decade* (1990); Farhang Rajaee, ed., *The Iran-Iraq War: The Politics of Aggression* (1993); John L. Esposito, *The Iranian Revolution: Its Global Impact* (1990).

Iran-Iraq War. Also known as the Gulf War, the Iran-Iraq conflict may be said to have begun on 17 September 1980, when Iraq abrogated the Algiers Agreement and claimed the Shatt al-Arab (qv) waterway as Iraqi territory. The actual fighting war began on 22 September, when Iraqi forces entered Kurdistan (qv) and carried out air attacks against at least ten Iranian airfields, including one in Tehran, the Iranian capital city. The oil refinery at Kermanshah was also bombed. Artillery and rocket fire were also reported at Khorramshahr and at Abadan on the Shatt al-Arab. Iran immediate ordered the call-up of several thousand reservists. By October, Iraqi planes attacked Iranian air fields, including the Tehran airport, and Iraqi ground forces moved quickly to occupy Iranian territory, including the important port city of Khorramshahr. Iranian forces recaptured the city and had driven Iraqi forces back across the border by May 1982. Both Iran and Iraq attacked shipping, especially oil tankers in international waters in the Persian Gulf, by 1984. When Saudi Arabian shipping was attacked, Saudi jets shot down two Iranian aircraft on 5 June 1982. Not until May 1988 would Iran agree to a UN cease-fire resolution.

Iraq. Iraq is a Middle East country bordered on the north by Turkey, on the east by Iran, on the south by Kuwait, on the southwest by Saudi Arabia and on the west by Jordan. Iraq has an exit to the Persian Gulf through the Basra corridor. The capital city is Baghdad. The history of the lands of Iraq can be traced to 3,000 B.C., when Sumerian tribes moved into the area from the Iran highlands and northern Anatolia. The resultant Sumer kingdom united with Akkad in around 2350 B.C., under King Sargon of Akkad. In about 2300 B.C., the Amorites assumed control under King Hammurabi, with Babylon as the chief city. After his death, invaders came, first the Hittites and then the Kassites. Out of these invasions came the Assyrian kingdom, which lasted a century, only to be overtaken by more tribal incursions, the last of which, led by the Chaldean King Nebuchadnezzar II, rebuilt Babylon which lasted until the Persian Cyrus the Great conquered the region in 539 B.C. Alexander the Great unseated the Persians in 331 B.C., and established the Seleucid Dynasty which ruled for 175 years. Later Parthian and then Sassanid incursions reestablished Persian rule until 637 A.D., when the first Arab invasion began and conquered Mesopotamia was in the name of Allah. The resultant Muslim Umayyad Dynasty controlled an area greater than Syria and Iraq and lasted until 750, when it was replaced by the Abbasid Dynasty in Iraq. The Abbasids lasted until 1258, during which time Arab religion and culture merged with Persian artistry and civil management to form the basis of a new civilization, one also tempered with Roman and Greek philosophic and scientific works translated into Arabic. Since the twelfth century, Turkish slaves, called Seljuks, had held many of the key administrative and managerial posts in the Abbasid hierarchy. They were actually in control of the government when the Mongol invasion of 1258 captured Baghdad. With that action the Seljuks began their move westward into Byzantium whence, led by the house of Osman, they became the ancestors of the Ottoman Turks. Iraq, at the same time, became a land of small princedoms linked together by incessant warfare. The Ottomans took Baghdad in 1534 and controlled the area of Iraq, along with most of the remainder of the Eastern world, until the World War I. At the end of the nineteenth century, the Young Turk movement created an environment in which non-Turks within the Ottoman Empire were looked upon and treated as second-class citizens. Within Iraq, dissidence grew. When the Turks sided with the Germans in World War I, the Iraqis welcomed British forces sent from India to protect Anglo-Iranian Oil Company interests and the overland route to India. The British were defeated, however, and forced to surrender at Al Kut in April 1916. These activities brought a British officer, T. E. Lawrence into some prominence, but it was later that his real fame grew as Lawrence of Arabia. British reinforcements captured Baghdad in March 1917. In the postwar era, the League of Nations gave Great Britain a mandate to administer Iraq until internal security could be established. As the always-warring tribes fell to squabbling and rebelled against central control, the British installed a Hashemite prince, Amir Faisal ibn Husayn, on the throne as King Faisal I of Iraq (1921). Iraq gained its independence in 1932 and, after the end of World War II, was one of the founders of the United Nations and the Arab League (qv). At almost the same instant (October 1945), Iraq, Eqypt, Syria and Lebanon warned the U.S. that recognition of a Jewish state in Palestine would mean war. In 1946, an uprising broke out in the province of Kurdistan. Iraq signed an alliance with Jordan in April 1947. In April 1948, after heavy fighting broke out between the Palestinians and Jews around the predominantly Arab city of Jaffa in Palestine, Iraq joined other Arab nations by attacking the new Israeli state. Israel declared its independence on 14 May 1948. The Iraqis did well in the early stages of the fighting, capturing the important city of Jenin in the north-central part of Israel. In the end, however, Israel prevailed and the Iraqis withdrew. On 7 November 1950, Iraq declared the Anglo-Iraqi alliance obsolete, and by the end of 1952, anti-British and anti-American sentiment was running high in the country. The situation got so bad that martial law was declared on 23 November 1952. The next day, twelve newspapers were closed, all political parties were abolished and all demonstrations were prohibited. The situation continued for some time before tensions eased. In February 1955, Iraq was instrumental in the organization of the Baghdad Pact (qv) organization, was also called the Middle East Treaty Organization and fashioned after NATO. On 14 February 1958, Iraq united with Jordan to form the Arab Federation under the leadership of King Faisal II (qv) of Iraq. The union was short-lived, however, as a military coup on 14 July 1958 overthrew the monarchy. Young Faisal II and the regent, Crown Prince Amir Abd Al Ilah, were both assassinated, and General Abdul Karim el-Kassem (qv) seized power. The new leftist government in Iraq withdrew from the Baghdad Pact on 24 March 1959 after having proclaimed its alliance with the United Arab Republic (qv). Hussein of Jordan became ruler of the Arab Federation but since Iraq was declared a republic, there was little left to be federated under a king. Unrest once again spread across the land. The government was swift to suppress the uprisings. On 4 April 1959, the Arab League declared the procommunist government of Iraq to be a threat to peace in the Middle East. Not all Middle East states attended the meeting, however, and the rift in the Arab world grew wider. In June 1959, Iraq refused any further aid from the U.S, and turned to the USSR for support. On 1

July 1961, there occurred what may have been the opening gun in a long sequence of events that led to war. On that date, British forces began moving into Kuwait, at that government's request and in accordance with a defensive alliance signed 19 June 1961. The Kuwaiti government made the request after Iraq announced a claim on Kuwait as a province of Iraq. In September, however, Iraq's attention was turned northward, where long-smoldering hostility over the government's refusal to grant the Kurds autonomy erupted into civil war that was to last for the remainder of the decade. On 8 February 1963, an air force-led coup toppled the government of Premier Kassem who was killed in the fighting. A pro-Nasser (qv) junta led by Colonel Abdel Salam Arif took control, with Arif as the de facto ruler. As the new leadership's first order of business, a roundup of communists was begun (16 February) in a move designed to destroy the party in Iraq. Even so, in April, Iraq joined with the United Arab Republic and Syria in forming a new tripartite Arab state. In June, the Iraqi government officially "declared war" on the Kurds. On 18 November, Arif rid himself of his government. In May 1964, Arif and Egypt's Nasser signed a mutual defense treaty that established a joint command in time of war. On 17 September 1965, after the brother of the president, General Abdul Rahman Arif (qv), helped put down a coup attempt, he turned on his brother and had himself installed as president. In December, Iraq agreed to a plan that would have stationed some of its forces in Jordan as a means of bolstering the Jordanian defense against Israeli encroachment. Iraqi troops began to occupy positions inside Jordan in May 1967. On 5 June 1967, the Six-Day War began (*see* Israel). Although Iraq was a part of the UAR-Jordan Defense Pact, its participation was minor. On 17 July 1968, a Baath-led (qv) revolt forced the Arif government out of power. Major General Ahmed Hassan al-Bakr assumed the presidency. At the beginning of 1969, a year-long dispute broke out with Iran. Border clashes punctuated the verbal battle that raged over navigation rights in the Strait of Shatt al-Arab and over Iranian support of the Kurds in their struggle against Iraq. When Iran abrogated the 1937 Navigation Treaty with Iraq, both sides began massing forces along their common border. Hoping to lessen the strain on its armed forces, Iraq offered the Kurds self-determination on 23 May 1969. By September border clashes with Iran had become commonplace. Nothing more happened until 20 January 1970, when a right-wing, Iranian-sponsored coup was foiled in Baghdad. On 11 March, the government announced a plan to grant the Kurds autonomy and a greater voice in the central government. Accepted by the Kurds, the plan ended eight years of fighting. In July, however, Iraq, along with Syria, rejected a U.S. plan to end the hostilities in the Middle East. The UAR and Jordan had already accepted the American initiative. On 21 October, Iraq began withdrawing the troops it had stationed in Jordan in May 1967. On 18 July 1971, Iraq closed its border with Jordan and asked Amman to recall its ambassador in Baghdad. On 29 September, an unsuccessful assassination attempt was made on Mullah Barzani (qv), the leader of the Kurdish Democratic Party. On 30 November, Iran rejected all claims and seized the British protectorate of the Greater and Lesser Tunb Islands (qv) at the northern end of the Straits of Hormuz. The Iranians also seized Abu Musa (qv). Iraq immediately broke diplomatic relations with Great Britain and Iran, the former for allowing the seizure and the latter for carrying out the operation. The Kurdish peace proved short-lived; on 11 January 1972, fighting erupted following Kurdish protests over the expulsion of alleged infiltrators back to Iran. At least 86 people were killed before order was restored. On 14 April, Baghdad radio reported heavy fighting between Iraqi and Iranian forces along the common border. Another coup attempt against the Baathist government took place in February 1973. Seventeen army officers were executed for their part in the coup. On 20 March, Kuwait accused Iraq of attacking its border police post at Sameta, more than two miles inside the Kuwaiti border near the Iraqi Persian Gulf port city of Umn Qasr. The Iraqi troops withdrew by 26 March, upon the arrival of 20,000 Saudia Arabian reinforcements. Both Iran and Jordan also offered forces to secure the Kuwaiti border against further attacks. Another major coup attempt was foiled on 1 July 1973, when vice-president Saddam Takriti (qv) crushed an attempt led by Colonel Nazem Kazzar (qv) against the life of President Bakr. Several senior officials were killed in the fighting. Kazzar and 35 others were executed on 7–8 July 1973. In 1974, the Kurds, once again supported by Iran, began their struggle for independence against Iraq. To halt the fighting, Iraq offered limited autonomy to the Kurds. As the offer fell far short of Kurdish expectations, Kurd forces under the leadership of Mustafa al-Barzani seized a large area of Iraqi Kurdistan along the Turkish border. On 28 March, Iraq granted autonomous rule to the Kurds; however, on 12 April, Iraqi jets attacked Kurdish military positions in the northern part of the country. Then, on 16 December 1974, Iraq accused Iran of shooting down two of its jets operating against the Kurds along the Iranian border. In February, the USSR delivered at least 40 jets fighters to Iraq. On 7 March, Iraq opened an offensive against Kurdish positions in the Mount Serti and Mount Handran areas. An agreement was reached between Iraq and Iran over the border situation on 22 March. For the Kurds this was a mortal blow, as it cut off aid from Iran. Many Kurds were forced to flee to Iran to escape the Iraq onslaught that followed. By 2 May, the fighting had essentially ended. In June 1976, however, trouble appeared on a new front, when Syria accused Iraq of massing troops along its common border. On 1 November, the Iraqis closed their border with Syria and called home their ambassador in Damascus. Before the end of November, a temporary settlement was reached and troops on both sides of the border were withdrawn. In August 1977, Iraq announced it had pledged support to the rebels fighting in Eritrea and in Ogaden. On 5 December 1977, Egypt broke diplomatic relations with Iraq and several other Arab states after the Tripoli Declaration reached in Libya that same day condemned Egypt for being conciliatory toward Israel. Iraq later (2 February 1978) refused to join an Arab conference to plot strategy against Egypt because the group was not radical enough. On 24 October 1978, Syria and Iraq signed the National Charter of Joint Action, which settled the bickering that had gone on over the last several years. The border between the two countries was reopened. In March 1979, Iraq and Syria mediated a cease-fire in the Yemeni war. On 16 July 1979, President Ahmad Hassan al-Bakr resigned his office. He was immediately replaced by by a leading Baathist party member, Saddam Hussein al-Takriti (qv), who began his reign by ordering at least 500 of his would-be opponents executed. When the revolution that overthrew the shah in Iran took place, Iraq supported the new regime. In 1980, however, Iraq abrogated the treaty on navigation rights in the Shatt al-Arab, and the two countries went to war (*see* Iran-Iraq War). A cease-fire was declared in August 1988. Iraq then turned its attention toward Kuwait, and invaded the tiny country in August, after talks had failed to halt what Iraq thought was Kuwait's theft of Iraqi oil and overproduction. After invading Kuwait, Iraq annexed it as a province of Iraq and, at least to some, seemed to threaten Saudi Arabia. The resultant conflict (Operation Desert Shield/Desert Storm) (1991) brought Iraq to its knees but did not go far enough to destroy Saddam's power base. Over the months following the end of the war in Southwest Asia, the Iraqis have thumbed their noses at the United Nations and, indeed, the world. Iraq has launched several campaigns against the Kurds, but with little reaction from other nations. The embargo placed upon Iraq by the United Nations has impacted heavily on the common people (1994), but has seemingly not bothered the Iraqi elite. Iraq's troop movement toward Kuwait in October 1995 drew a swift response from the United States, which dispatched a army brigade to Kuwait with the threat of more force, if necessary. The Iraqi military gambit having failed, the government recognized Kuwait's sovereignty in November. *Reading:* Amatzia Baram, *Culture, History and Ideology in the Formation of Ba'Thist Iraq, 1968-89* (1991); Eliezer Tauber, The Formation of Modern Syria and Iraq (1995); Amatzia Baram & Barry M. Rubin, eds., Iraq's Road to War (1994).

Iraqi Mujahideen Movement. An anti-Iraqi terrorist group operating within the Arab countries. On 3–7 January 1982, the group blew up pipelines carrying crude oil to Mediterranean ports. The attack knocked out the Iraqi pipeline to Tripoli, Lebanon, while the 7 January attack was on the Iraqi pipeline to Turkey.

Iraultza. A Basque terrorist organization formed in 1982 that advocates the establishment of an independent, Marxist nation, *Iraultza* also demands an end to foreign investment in the Basque region and an end to American involvement in Latin American affairs. The group operates primarily in the Basque provinces of Spain. Little is known of its leaders or where it is based. There are probably fewer than 20 members in the organization, but it has committed numerous bombing attacks on American and French business interests in the Basque region. *Iraultza* has carried out more attacks against U.S. business targets in Europe than any other European terrorist group.

Irbid. *See* Jordan.

Ireland (*Eire*). An island in the eastern Atlantic just west of Great Britain, Ireland has as its nearest neighbor Northern Ireland (Ulster), which borders Ireland on the north and shares that part of the island. The capital city is Dublin. The island has been inhabited since at least 6000 B.C. Agriculture was introduced about 3000 B.C., and Bronze Age skills about 2000 B.C.. The Celts came from Europe about 300 B.C. and dominated the indigenous population through their knowledge of ironworking. A highly advanced civilization grew out of these beginnings. Christianity was established by the beginning of the fifth century A.D. Saint Patrick and other missionaries established a number of monasteries, which became centers of learning and remained untouched during the Dark Ages on the continent. During the ninth and tenth centuries, Scandinavian raiders plundered the south and east coasts of Ireland and destroyed many of the monasteries, before their visits turned to trade. The Vikings were defeated at Clontarf, near Dublin, in 1014. Some Scandinavians stayed among the Irish and were absorbed into the culture. England began its conquest of Ireland in 1169, on the pretext of helping a local ruler regain his throne. In 1171, England's Henry II led an expedition that established a number of fiefdoms loyal to the English crown. Many of these lords intermarried with the Irish and became more Irish than English. England's control of Ireland was tenuous at best, and the Irish and many of their English lords were looked upon by the English crown as enemies. In the sixteenth century, Henry VIII of England restored the entire island to English suzereinty, attempting at the same time to suppress the Roman Catholic church, which was strong there. During his reign (1603–1625), King James I began the settlement of English and Scottish Protestants in northern Ireland in the province of Ulster. A Roman Catholic revolt in Ulster in 1641 caused the death of thousands of Protestants. When the revolt spread southward it was put down by Oliver Cromwell (1649–1650). The Roman Catholic king of England, James II (1685–1701), attempted to restore Catholic rights. After he was driven from his throne (1688), he eventually went to Ireland, where the Irish Catholic nobility welcomed him with open arms. In 1690, James and the Irish were defeated at the battle of the Boyne by King William III and his Protestant forces. The Church of England (Anglican) became the official religion for the next 150 years. In 1801, the Act of Union joined Ireland to Great Britain as a part of the United Kingdom. After 1823, agitation for independence spread throughout the Catholic sections of Ireland, but not so much in the six counties of Northern Ireland, especially in the predominantly Protestant county of Ulster, where the Protestants demanded retention of the Act of Union (*see* Northern Ireland). In 1829, the Catholics were given political equality, but this was not enough. Led by Daniel O'Connell, the movement insisted on abrogation of the Act of Union and home rule. In the mid-1800s, the Potato Blight and a general famine caused a massive emigration, primarily to the United States, and a general lessening of the ardor for self-government. Attempts were made to force a Home Rule bill through Parliament in the late 1800s, but all attempts failed. Finally, in 1914, a Home Rule bill was passed that would have set up a separate parliament for all of Ireland. When World War I broke out, the Home Rule bill was suspended. On Easter Monday, 1916, a rebellion (The Rising) broke out in

Dublin, led by the Irish Volunteers and the Citizen Army. British forces were successful in suppressing the uprising. Fourteen Irish leaders were executed, which only raised the furor for independence. The *Sinn Fein*, an Irish revolutionary group, won most of the Irish seats in the English Parliament in the 1918 elections. The group then refused to be seated and set up its own parliament, the *Dail Eireann*, in Dublin. The *Dail* then issued a proclamation of independence, with a government headed by Eamon de Valera. British troops attempted to restore English order, but the Irish Volunteers, now known as the Irish Republican Army (qv) fought back. This led to a period of the Irish fighting the dreaded "Black and Tan," which continued until 1921, when a truce was achieved. This agreement established the southern counties of Ireland as the Irish Free State and a part of the Commonwealth. Civil war followed, in which Irishmen who accepted Commonwealth status fought those who did not. Finally, in 1937, a new constitution went into effect; in 1948, Eire withdrew from the Commonwealth. During World War II there was some evidence that the Irish supported the Germans simply because they were at war with the hated English. On 8 February 1949, Ireland declared it could not join NATO as long as the country was divided. On 18 April the Republic of Ireland was proclaimed. Great Britain affirmed this on 17 May. On 26 January 1950, a treaty of friendship and commerce was signed with the United States. On 14 December 1955, Ireland was admitted into the UN. In March 1964, Irish troops joined the UN peacekeeping force sent to Cyprus. In August 1969, the Irish army was mobilized and sent to the Ulster border after Great Britain refused an offer for a joint UK-Irish peacekeeping force for Northern Ireland. On 5 May 1970, two cabinet ministers were dismissed by Prime Minister John Lynch (qv) for conspiring to ship weapons to Catholic factions in the north. The British began a program of destroying roads across the southern border of Ulster in October 1971, in an attempt to limit arms shipments from Eire. In 1973, the Republic of Ireland acknowledged British dominion in Northern Ireland. The continued fighting in Ulster between the Catholics and Protestants spilled over into Eire on occasion and created strained relations between north and south. This was further exacerbated in 1985, when the British gave Eire a voice in Ulster affairs. The republic has attempted to tighten control of the border with Ulster to prevent arms shipments from reaching the Catholics in the north. British forces on the north side of the border attempted the same thing. As proof of the cross-border operations, the reputed leader, Sean MacStiofain (qv) of the Provisional Wing (PIRA), the terrorist group of the Irish Republican Army (IRA), was captured in Dublin on 19 November 1972. As a further example, the new British ambassador, Christopher T. E. Ewart-Biggs, was killed by an IRA bomb placed under his car at his residence in Dublin on 21 July 1976. Several other embassy personnel were also killed or injured in the blast. A wave of other terrorist acts, mostly claimed by the IRA, followed. To help thwart this outbreak of terrorist violence, the Republic of Ireland declared a a state of emergency on 1 September 1976. On 27 January 1977, however, Ireland refused to sign the

Europeon Convention for the Repression of Terrorism (qv). On 18 March 1978, Prime Minister John Lynch claimed that foreign aid, especially from the United States, helped keep the fighting going in Northern Ireland (qv). On 7 December 1979, Lynch unexpectedly resigned and was replaced by the former minister of health, Charles J. Haughey (qv) of the ruling Fianna Fair party. On 15 January 1980, Irish police carried out an antiterrorist raid that seized more than a ton of explosives and bombs found in an abandoned farmhouse near the town of Dundalk, on the Northern Ireland border. In April 1980, Irish troops serving with the UN peacekeeping force in Lebanon suffered two killed. The two soldiers were killed after being kidnapped, along with two journalists, by armed Lebanese. The murders were in reprisal for the recent deaths of two Arab youths. The journalists were subsequently released. The assassins were reported to be members of the dead youths' family who had declared a blood feud against the Irish. Dublin refused (21 April) to consider withdrawing its troops from the UN peacekeeping force despite criticism about the conduct of its troops and the murders of two of its soldiers. On 17 March 1984, Dominic "Mad Dog" McGlinchey, the chief of staff of the outlawed Irish National Liberation Army (qv), was captured after a 90-minute gun battle with County Clare police. He was immediately extradited to British custody in Northern Ireland to stand trial on murder charges. On 29 September 1984, Irish naval units intercepted and captured a ship carrying IRA members and five tons of arms and ammunition from the United States. The capture ended a two-year undercover operation involving the American FBI and CIA. On 20 February 1985, the Irish government seized $1.6 million said to belong to the outlawed IRA. On 14 October 1987, a group of terrorists, or simply gangsters, led by a former member of the Irish National Liberation Army and the IRA, kidnapped John O'Grady in the mistaken belief that he was his father-in-law, a medical millionaire named Austin Darragh. The motive appeared to be ransom, but the Irish police rescued O'Grady before any deal was struck. In an ensuing comedy of errors, several of the kidnappers, including O'Hare, were allowed to escape. O'Hare was recaptured on 27 November following a gun battle with the police. In 1988, the new Extradition Act of 1987 was tested when captured terrorist Patrick McVeigh was not sent to Northern Ireland because of poor preparation of the charges against him. Patrick Ryan, a Roman Catholic priest accused of terrorism, who was arrested in Brussels, was sent to Ireland. The Irish refused to extradite him because, they said, he could not receive a fair trial in the United Kingdom. Robert Russell was extradited, however, but under unprecedented security safeguards. In January 1988, a British court upheld the convictions of six terrorists accused in a 1974 bombing that killed 21 people in Birmingham. At that point, a British policeman revealed a "shoot-to-kill" policy followed by British police in dealing with suspected terrorists. The British government then announced that it would not prosecute those policemen involved in an alleged 1982 shoot-to-kill incident. In 1990, charges against the Ulster Defense Regiment, a type of police field force, continued to mount. Another attempt to have Father Ryan extradited was refused because, as the Irish director of public prosecutions said, there was insufficient evidence to warrant his release into British custody. Ryan, in the meantime, ran for office on an antiextradition platform. He lost, but showed better in the polls than expected. In 1992, Charles Haughey was forced to resign after 12 years in office as prime minister after charges of wire tapping political opponents were revealed. He was replaced by Albert Reynolds. Reynolds's coalition government collapsed in November 1994, with Reynolds staying on in a caretaker capacity. Part of the collapse was caused by the failure of the government to extradite a Catholic priest to Northern Ireland on charges of child molesting and part by a passports-for-sale disclosure that involved Reynolds's family. It was later proven that the scandal went back to the Haughey administration. John Bruton became prime minister (1995) in the aftermath of the scandal. More charges of child molestation by Roman Catholic priests were leveled in 1995, at least one of which was compounded by a Church attempt to cover up the affair. (*See also* Northern Ireland). *Reading:* F. X. Martin & T. W. Moody, eds., *The Course of Irish History* (1995); Gerry Adams, *Free Ireland: Towards a Lasting Peace* (1994); Edmund Curtis, A History of Ireland (1991).

Irene, Princess of the Netherlands. On 29 October 1983, Princess Irene of the Netherlands took part in a demonstration protesting the deployment of US cruise and Pershing II missiles into Europe. The princess marched with at least 500,000 others in the peace rally held in The Hague.

Irgun Zvai Leumi be Israel **(National Military Organization of Israel [Irgun]).** This terrorist organization began its operations before the partition of Palestine (qv). At first, the Irgun was known as the military wing of the Revisionist Part of Vladimir Jabotinsky, but it soon assumed an identity of its own. The Irgun was founded by David Raziel, who was killed in Iraq in 1943. The future prime minister of Israel, Menachim Begin (qv), then took over the leadership. Many other prominent figures in Israeli politics, the military, and other public positions were members of the Irgun. In the early phases of World War II, the Irgun had fought against the Arabs in response to the February 1940 and November 1940 regulations affecting land transfer and Jewish immigration into Palestine. When the war started the Irgun cooperated with the British; but by 1944 the Irgun had allied itself with the Stern Gang (qv), another Jewish terrorist group, and had conducted a number of attacks on British targets, including the assassination of Lord Moyen, the British minister of state in Cairo, on 6 November 1944. From 1942 until 1947, the Irgun's principal target was the British military government in Palestine. After World War II, these operations were often carried out in cooperation with the Haganah, a secret paramilitary organization. The most prominent early terrorist act of the Irgun was the 22 July 1946 bombing of the King David Hotel in Jerusalem, in which 89 people were killed. On 12 July 1947, two British sergeants were kidnapped by the Irgun in Natanya, Palestine, and held for the ransom of four condemned Irgun members. When the four were executed, the Irgun hung the British soldiers. Thereafter, Irgun often tangled with the Stern Gang over terrorist policies. The Irgun was incorporated into the Israeli Army in 1948.

Irian (West). *See* Indonesia.

Irish Free State. *See* Ireland.

Irish National Liberation Army (INLA). The INLA was born in 1975 when a Marxist terrorist group split away from the Official Irish Republican Army (OIRA). Its leader, Sean (Seamus)Costello, was assassinated (1977) in Dublin by the IRA. The group is headquartered in Dublin and recruits Republic of Ireland citizens for terrorist operations in Northern Ireland. It is now considered to be the military arm of the Irish Republican Socialist Party (IRSP); the IRSP denies the connection, but it reports INLA operations in its newspaper. Attacks by INLA terrorists are often difficult to separate from those of the PIRA because their targets and tactics are similar. The two organizations have been known on occasion to have held joint meetings. In March 1979, the INLA assassinated the leading British Conservative Party member, Airey Neave (qv), in Great Britain. The group was especially active in the 1980s, and its members are considered "wild men" by the other terrorist groups operating in Northern Ireland and in the Republic of Ireland. Their chief source of income appears to be from bank, train and payroll robberies and extortion as they are not favored with outside support. A number of INLA members have been arrested in recent years through the work of informants, limiting their capabilities and operations. Between January and June 1987, at least six people were killed and three injured in internal power struggles within the organization.

Irish Republican Army (IRA). One of the best-known politicoterrorist organizations in the world, the IRA is also one of the oldest, having its roots in the struggle for Irish independence in the nineteenth century, in the Irish Republican Brotherhood. On Easter Monday of 1916, a rebellion (The Rising) broke out in Dublin, led by the Irish Volunteers and the Citizen Army. British forces were successful in suppressing the uprising. The IRA became the military wing of *Sinn Fein* (Ourselves Alone) and fought a protracted struggle against British domination of Ireland from 1918 until 1921 (*see* Ireland). British troops attempted to restore English order, but the Irish Volunteers, now known as the Irish Republican Army fought a vicious urban guerrilla war against them. When the Irish Free State was born, the IRA continued its struggle against presumed or real inequities until 1923–1924, when it was outlawed and forced underground. To this day, however, the IRA still retains a strong backing in the Republic of Ireland and Northern Ireland and around the world, especially in the United States, among Irish Catholics who furnish a large part of its support. Some support was lost, however, when the IRA's Marxist tendancies became known. The Marxist orientation and relatively moderate policies also caused a split in the IRA, and in 1969 the Irish Republican Army Provisional Wing (PIRA) or IRA-Provos came into existence. There is also a provisional wing of *Sinn Fien* to which the PIRA adheres. The IRA then began calling itself the Official Irish Republican Army or OIRA. The goal of the IRA is the unification of the six counties of Northern Ireland with the republic. The goal of the PIRA is to free Northern Ireland in a manner similar to the politicomilitary campaign that brought independence to Algeria (qv). The PIRA works at to keep Ulster in a state of chaos and to force the British to withdraw, leaving the Protestants to become victims of Catholics, that is, PIRA justice. Since the initial repudiation of Marxism by the PIRA, there has been a gradual drift back toward toward such an orientation. The active membership of the PIRA numbers between 300 and 1,000, with about 200–400 hardcore members. Support for the PIRA cause is numbered in the tens of thousands, however. While clashes between the IRA and PIRA have occurred, they are rare, although the two organizations stay away from each other. The PIRA operates primarily in Northern Ireland, but it has headquarters both north and south of the border. The current leadership of the IRA includes Gerry Adams, Sean Garland, Cathal Goulding and Liam Macmillan. The PIRA leadership includes Ruairi O'Bradaigh, David O'Connell, Martin McGuinness and, from 1969 to1974, Sean MacStiofain (qv) as chief of staff. In 1977, police penetration of the PIRA caused the organization to reorganize into cells called Active Service Units (ASU) to improve security and reduce the damage caused by leaks. The primary operational group within the PIRA is called the Northern Command, which delegates authority and missions to local commands or brigades. Generally one person from the brigade is known to one or more members of the ASU, which is how orders are received. Although the same penetration problem that faced the INLA (*see above*), that of informants known as "supergrasses," affected the PIRA, the PIRA showed it was still dangerous in October 1984, when it bombed a hotel in Brighton, England, nearly killing the British prime minister, Margaret Thatcher (qv), and her cabinet. In July 1988, the PIRA bombed the Glamrgan Army Barracks in Duisburg, West Germany, injuring nine British army soldiers and tearing the roof off the building and causing major property damage. It is known the PIRA receives arms and equipment from Libya and has links with other terrorist organizations across Europe. In August 1994, the IRA announced a cessation of hostilities against the British and announced it would seek more conventional means of accomplishing its purpose. *Reading:* Tim Pat Coogan, *The IRA: A History* (1994); Kevin Tollis, *Rebel Hearts: Journeys within the IRA's Soul* (1996); Robert W. White, *Provisional Irish Republicans: An Oral and Interpretive History* (1993); J. Bowyer Bell, The Secret Army: The IRA (1997); J. Bowyer Bell, *IRA Tactics and Targets: An Analysis of Tactical Aspects of the Armed Struggle 1969–1989* (1991).

"Iron Triangle." *See* South Korea or Vietnam.

Irurzun, Hugo Alfredo. On 19 September 1980, Paraguayan police shot and killed Hugo Alfredo Irurzun, a known Argentinian terrorist and the suspected assassin of the former Nicaraguan dictator Anastasio Somoza (qv). The shooting of Irunzun took place in Asunción, two days after Somoza was murdered in the same city.

al-Iryani, Abdul Rahman. On 5 November 1967, the republican government of Abdullah al-Salal (Sallal) (qv) in North Yemen was overthrown by a dissident faction led by Qadi Abdul Rahman al-Iryani. Salal was in Baghdad at the time of his dismissal and was allowed to seek asylum in Egypt. Al-Iryani was a former member of the republican government (as opposed to royalist) and had been under house arrest in Cairo during 1966. The ability of the coup, which placed al-Iryani at the head of a three-man presidency, to succeed was based on the withdrawal of aid from Saudi Arabia and Egypt to both sides in the civil war in Yemen. Al-Iryani was himself overthrown as president of the Yemen Arab Republic in a coup led by a pro-Saudi Arabian Yemenite colonel, Ibrahim al-Hamidi, on 13 June 1974. Iryani was treated with great respect after his departure from office and was allowed to travel to Syria on 18 June.

Isabela Province. *See* Philippines.

Isfahan (Eshfahan). *See* Iran.

Islamic Center in Washington, DC. One of the three locations seized by Hanafi Muslim terrorists on 9 March 1977. Led by Hamaas Abdul Khaalis (aka Ernest McGhee) the group also seized the headquarters of B'nai B'rith, a Jewish national service organization, and the District Building, the seat of government of the District of Columbia. The Islamic Center was taken by a three-man team later in the day after the other two buildings had been seized. The siege ended when Khaalis surrendered to police the next day.

Islamic Conference Organization. Actually the organization of foreign ministers of Islamic countries, the organization formally condemned the Soviet Union for its invasion of Afghanistan in a meeting held in Islamabad, Pakistan, in January 1980.

Islamic Foreign Ministers Conference. *See* Islamic Conference Organization.

Islamic Jihad. A Shi'ite fundamentalist Muslim terrorist organization that serves as the umbrella for several other terrorist organizations, Islamic Jihad (Holy War) was formed in 1982–1983 and gained its first notoriety in the April 1983 bombing attack on the U.S. embassy in Beirut in which 63 were killed and the October 1983 suicide attack on the U.S. Marines stationed at Beirut Airport. The group is credited in some sources with the bombing of the Iraqi embassy in Beirut on 15 December 1981. It may be that the organization began operations somewhat earlier than imagined. In March 1984, Islamic Jihad, also known as Hizballah, took credit for the assassination of William Buckley, the CIA station chief at the U.S. embassy in Beirut. The main support for the Lebanon-based group is Iran, although there is some conjecture that support also comes from Syria. After the Islamic Jihad claimed credit (31 July 1984) for secretly mining the Red Sea in July 1984, the terrorist group was linked with Libya, which was suspected of committing the crime. Islamic Jihad attacked the U.S. embassy annex on 20 September 1984 and killed 14 in a bomb blast that detonated in the lobby of the buiding. The U.S. ambassador was among the 70 people injured in that incident. On 12 April 1985, the group blew up a restaurant near a U.S. air base outside of Madrid. Eighteen were killed and 82 injured, including 15 U.S.

servicemen, in that attack. The Islamic Jihad also claimed credit for an assassination attempt on the life of the emir of Kuwait on 25 May 1985. Six were killed and 12 hurt when a car bomb detonated in a motorcade. The emir escaped injury. Islamic Jihad later bombed a Jewish synagogue and old people's home in Copenhagen on 22 July 1985. Most of Islamic Jihad's attacks have taken place in Europe or the Middle East, usually against targets identified as threats to Iran. The group has been most active in hostage-taking kidnappings of Americans and West Europeans in Lebanon, many of whom were held by the group until 1991. The most active participant groups are Hizballah (Party of God) (qv), Islamic Amal (Islamic Hope) (*See* Amal), Dawa (The Call) (qv), and Jundallah (The Army of God).

Islamic Liberation Organization. A Sunni Muslim terrorist organization, the Islamic Liberation Organization kidnapped four Soviet diplomats in two separate incidents in Beirut on 30 September 1985. All of the hostages were released unharmed. Little is known about this group.

Isle de los Estrados. The name of a ferryboat sunk in Falkland Sound on 10 May 1978. In the heavy fog, the ferry was mistaken on radar for a tanker and was sunk by British naval units blockading the Argentine-held Falkland Islands. *See* Falkland Islands.

Ismail, Ahmed. (b. 1917, Cairo—d. 24 December 1974, London) When United Arab Republic army chief of staff Lieutenant General Abdel Moneim Riadh was killed while observing an Israeli-Egyptian artillery duel along the Suez Canal on 9 March 1969, his replacement was Major General Ahmed Ismail, who was sworn in on 13 March. On 26 October 1972, after General Muhammad Sadek (qv), the Egyptian minister of defense and military commander in chief, resigned over President Anwar Sadat's attempts at reconciliation with the USSR, General Ismail was appointed minister of defense. Ismail attended the meeting between Sadat and Syria's president Hafez Assad (qv) (12 September 1973) where the date of 6 October 1973 was chosen for the joint attack on Israel. On 4 October it was Ismael who was informed by the chief of the Soviet mission in Egypt that the Soviet Union wanted to evacuate their civilians and military dependents before the attack on Israel began. For his part in the war effort, although unsuccessful, Ismail was promoted to the rank of field marshal. He died in London on 24 December 1974.

Ismailia (Ismailiya). *See* Egypt.

Israel. A Middle Eastern state at the center of much of the controversy that has affected the region, Israel is bordered on the north by Lebanon, on the northeast by Syria, on the east by Jordan, on the south by the Gulf of Eilat, on the southwest by the Sinai of Egypt and on the west by the Mediterranean Sea. The capital city is Jerusalem. The lands that are today the State of Israel have their history in the ancient Fertile Crescent, where some of the earliest agricultural and pastoral life was found. Although advanced civilization was known in the third millennium B.C., the Hebrews probably arrived in the second millennium B.C. Judaism developed under the House of David (c.1000 B.C.–597 B.C.). The lands were thereafter conquered by a succession of Babylonians, Persians and Greeks. In the second century B.C. a Jewish state was revived, but it was subsequently conquered by the Romans. Revolts by the Jews were suppressed in 70 A.D. and again in 135 A.D.. After 135 A.D., the lands were renamed Judea Palestine. The Arabs conquered Palestine in 636 A.D., and for the next several centuries Islam and the Arabic language prevailed although Judaism was never completely eradicated. From the eleventh century, various Turkish tribes ruled the region with intervals of Crusader presence (1098–1291). In 1917, the British removed the Ottoman rule and, under the Balfour Declaration, a promise of a Jewish homeland was stated for the land. In 1920, a British Palestine Mandate was acknowledged, and in 1922 the lands east of the River Jordan were detached from Palestine. In the 1930s, Jewish immigration into Ottoman Palestine, which had begun in the late nineteenth century (1878), surged in the first half of twentieth century as European Jews moved to escape the Nazis. At the same time there was an increased immigration of Arabs from Syria and Lebanon. This swelling of the population from two sources had the obvious effect of conflict, and violence occurred in 1920–1921, 1929 and 1936–1939. After World War II, the UN General Assembly voted to partition Palestine into Arab and Jewish states. Serious violence began in 1947. The British Mandate ended in May 1948. Israel was declared an independent state on 14 May 1948. In Tel Aviv, the announcement was made by David Ben-Gurion, the Zionist leader and chairman of the Jewish Agency. The surrounding Arab states rejected the partition, and forces from Egypt, Iraq, Jordan, Lebanon, Saudi Arabia and Syria invaded the new Jewish state. Fighting continued until late 1948. A cease-fire and armistice were arranged in 1949, from which Israel gained more land. Israel held two-thirds of Palestine, twice as much land as had been proposed by the UN. This period of conflict is known as the Israeli War of Independence. No peace treaties were signed, however, and no Arab state gave Israel diplomatic recognition. In 1949, Ben-Gurion was elected the nation's first prime minister and Chaim Weizmann its first president. Israel joined the United Nations in 1949. In 1952, the Arab states demanded Israel withdraw to the original boundaries established by the UN. In 1955, Egypt signed military pacts with Syria and Jordan and blockaded the Straits of Tiran (qv), effectively cutting off Israeli trade with East Africa and the Far East. In April 1956, fighting broke out along the Gaza Strip (qv) where Egyptian-trained *fediyeen* terrorist units engaged the Israelis. In July 1957, Egypt nationalized the Suez Canal (qv) and ignored a UN order for free passage through the canal (October 1957). On 29 October 1957, Israeli troops invaded Sinai, captured the Gaza Strip and were moving toward the Suez Canal when a cease-fire was arranged and the Sinai Campaign ended. The Israelis were replaced by a UN Emergency Force in early 1958. Israel was still refused passage rights through the canal but was granted access to the Gulf of Aqaba (qv). During the remainder of the 1950s and into the 1960s Israel's economy grew. In May 1965, West Germany opened diplomatic relations with Israel. From 1965 until 1967, Arab terrorists launched numerous attacks against Israeli targets, especially those close to the Lebanese, Jordanian and Syrian borders. On 18 May 1967, Egypt ordered the United Nations to remove its forces from positions along the Egyptian-Israeli border. On 5 June 1967, the Six-Day War (qv) began. Israeli immediately bombed a number of Egyptian airbases and almost totally destroyed the Egyptian air force. Iraq, Jordan and Syria suffered the same destruction. Over the next four days, Israeli ground forces took the Golan Heights along the Syrian border, reoccupied the Gaza Strip, captured East Jerusalem and took the West Bank (qv). A UN-sponsored cease-fire went into effect on 11 June 1967. Israel then declared Jerusalem an administratively unified city (28 July). On 22 November 1967, the UN Security Council adopted Resolution 242, which ordered Israel to relinquish control of the occupied territories. The Arab nations rejected the plan before Israel could respond. In October 1973, the Arab nations carried out a surprise attack on Israel in what became known as the Yom Kippur War. The first phase of the attack carried Egyptian forces through the Bar-Lev Line in Sinai near the Suez Canal. The Syrians penetrated deep into the Golan Heights (qv) region. In the initial engagement, the Israelis suffered heavy losses, especially from Soviet-built antiaircraft artillery. Upon recovering from these losses, Israel turned and delivered a crushing defeat to the Arabs. In January 1974, Egypt signed an accord with Israel; Syria did the same in May 1974. A second accord was signed with Egypt in September 1975. Israel withdrew from parts of the southern Sinai and the eastern part of the Golan. The internal ramifications of the war on Israel were far-reaching. The findings of a commission of inquiry into why the country had been surprised led to the resignation of Golda Meir (qv) as prime minister and her Labor Party government in April 1974. In 1977, Menachim Begin and his Likud party were elected, ousting the Labor party, which had held power for years. In July 1976, Israeli commando units carrying out a daring and almost letter-perfect operation attacked Entebbe, Uganda, to free hostages held by Palestinian terrorists. During the 1970s, terrorism by PLO-inspired groups against Israel inside the country and abroad grew. In November 1977, Egypt's president, Anwar Sadat (qv), visited Israel, the first Arab leader to do so. There, he proposed a peace plan before the Knesset (Israeli parliament). A short time later, the Israeli prime minister, Begin, visited Ismailia, Egypt. When the peace talks began to lag, U.S. President Jimmy Carter (qv) stepped in and, in September 1978, began mediating the settlement. At Camp David, Maryland, Sadat and Begin reached an agreement on 26 March 1979 that ended a 30-year state of war between Israel and Egypt. The peace agreement (Camp David Accords) was signed at Washington. Diplomatic relations were established between the two countries, and Israeli ships were allowed passage through the Suez Canal. Israel then began a gradual withdrawal from the Sinai, which was completed in 1982. During the 1970s, however, there was increased activity along the Israeli-Lebanese border. Lebanon, virtually in the hands of the PLO, was the jumping-off place for Palestinian raids into Israel and the haven for their escape. As events developed, Israel found itself facing a better organized

PLO military force, largely trained by Syria and missile attacks from Syrian-introduced and Soviet-built missile launchers. In 1978, the Israelis reacted and attacked into Lebanon. The PLO forces simply withdrew deeper into Lebanese space. By the summer of 1981, the Israelis had had enough. In May, Israeli airstrikes hit both PLO and Syrian missile sites. In June Israeli aircraft penetrated deep into Iraq and destroyed the nuclear reactor site at Daura near Baghdad. The Israelis also attacked numerous Palestinian camps near the border and also in and around Beirut. In 1982, Israeli ground troops attacked into Lebanon with the objective of destroying the PLO power base there. By 14 June, Beirut was surrounded. In August, Israeli forces entered East Beirut and moved to establish an independent Lebanese government there under Lebanese Christian Phalangist control. In the process, two Palestinian refugee camps were occupied. When the Israelis turned control of the camps over to the Phalangists, the Christians proceeded to massacre at least 600 Palestinians and Lebanese. Worldwide outrage followed, aimed as much at the Israelis as at the immediate perpetrators of the crimes. An Israeli-Lebanese agreement was finally reached on 17 May 1983, and the Israelis began an immediate troops withdrawal to the Alawi river based upon a normalization of relations between the two states and joint patrols of the border areas to insure Israeli security. In 1984, Menachim Begin resigned as prime minister and was replaced by Yitzak Shamir. In a close election in July 1984, a national unity government was put in place, with Shimon Peres as prime minister and Shamir as deputy prime minister and foreign minister. In 1986, the two switched offices for the second half of their four year term. The withdrawal of Israeli troops from Lebanon had been completed in June 1985. When PLO attacks continued unabated, Israeli aircraft bombed the PLO headquarters near Tunis, Tunisia, in October 1985. Talks on the West Bank began but were repeatedly stalled; they continued, however, into the 1990s. On 9 December 1987, a Palestinian uprising (*Intefada*) began in the West Bank and Gaza. Many hundreds were killed in the ensuing period, up to March 1994. An agreement on the West Bank was slowly being reached, even over the objectives of both Israeli and Arab extremists, when a crazed Israeli killed 40 worshippers in the mosque at Hebron in February 1994. In 1988, another national unity government was installed, with Shamir as prime minister. After 15 months in office, the coalition crumbled after Shamir refused to accept a plan that would have started Arab-Israeli peace talks. When Peres could not form a new government, Shamir did so and retained the prime minister's office, supported by a number of small religious factions in his new coalition. Terrorist incidents continued throughout the 1980s and into the 1990s that were designed to destabilize the situation for the benefit of the extremists. The terrorist problem was compounded by serious internal economic problems in Israel. The country was faced with difficult choices during 1991. As a result of Iraq's attack on Kuwait and the subsequent Western response, Israel saw itself being left out of Western thinking, especially that of the U.S., on Middle East affairs. Although Israel depended on US support and backing, it found itself watching American support being given to Arab nations, Israel's traditional enemies. Similarly, Iraq's attempts to draw Israel into the war, by carrying out indiscriminate Scud attacks on its cities, were countered by equally strong U.S. proposals that Israel hold back any response to these provocations. In October, however, Israel met formally with Arab states in Madrid, Spain, eventually concluding an agreement whereby Israeli military rule in Gaza and the West Bank was lifted. Russia also resumed diplomatic relations with Israel in 1991. In July 1992 the Shamir (*Likud*) government was replaced with one led by Yitzhak Rabin (Labor). In December, the Rabin government ordered the deportation of 415 Palestinians, setting back the negotiation process, which was still underway. Rabin signed accords with Yasir Arafat's PLO on 13 September 1993 following secret negotiations held in Norway. At the same time Palestinian extremists (*Hizballah*) began a campaign of open warfare, hoping to disrupt the talks. The results caused as many new problems for Israel as the agreement offered solutions. Primary among these was the reaction of West Bank Jewish settlers who refused to leave their homes. The first area affected by the protocol was Gaza-Jericho, and that effort began immediately after signing (13 October 1993). About 10,000 Palestinian political prisoners were also released from Israeli prisons. Assassinations of Israeli pro-Labor leaders followed in the West Bank. On 14 September 1993, Israeli had also signed a peace treaty with Jordan. On 25 February 1994, a deranged Israeli (a U.S.-born doctor dressed in an Israeli army uniform) killed 29 Muslims at worship in Hebron. Although the killer himself died in the attack, the outcry from the event, especially in the Arab world, caused Israel great harm. For one thing, Israel was forced to allow an international observation team to oversee the transition in Hebron. By March, however, the turnover of control in Gaza-Jericho to the PLO was underway, and it was completed by 17 May 1994. By year's end, the peace negotiations with Syria still dragged on. On 3 November 1995, a Jewish extremist shot and killed Prime Minister Yitzhak Rabin amid charges of gross negligence by his security detail. Shimon Peres became the new prime minister and pledged to continue the peace process. The Rabin murder sparked new hope for peace as Syria withdrew some of its objections to concluding a treaty with Israel, but the process went on. When Iranian-backed *Hizballah* terrorists fired on Israeli civilian targets in northern Israel, a US suggestion to Damascus in November brought about a cessation of the incidents. By year's end the search for permanent peace continued, still marred by terrorist incidents. *Reading:* Noam Chomsky, Fateful *Triangle: The United States, Israel and the Palestinians* (1984); Amos Elon, *A Blood-Dimmed Tide: Dispatches from the Middle East* (1997); Ilana Kass & Bard E. O'Neill, *The Deadly Embrace: The Impact of Israeli and Palestinian Rejectionism on the Peace Process* (1996); Geoffrey Wheatcroft, *The Controversy of Zion: Jewish Nationalism, the Jewish State, and the Unresolved Jewish Dilemma* (1996); William Quandt, Camp *David: Peacemaking and Politics* (1986); David A. Charters, *The British Army and Jewish Insurgency in Palestine, 1945–47* (1989); Chaim Herzog, *The Arab-*

Israeli Wars: War and Peace in the Middle East (1984); David K. Shipler, *Arab and Jew: Wounded Spirits in a Promised Land* (1987); Benny Morris, *1948 and After: Israel and the Palestinians* (1991).

Issas. *See* Djibouti.

Istanbul. *See* Turkey.

***Istiqlal* (Independence) Party.** In late World War II (1944), an upsurge of political consciousness in Morocco led to the formation of the *Istiqlal* party, whose major goal was the reestablishment of the sovereignty of that nation. This demand was supported by Sultan Mohammed V (qv), who supported Arab aims and opposed further French domination. The French retaliated by appointing a military governor in Morocco and, in December 1952, by arresting *Istiqlal* leaders. In August 1953, the French enlisted the services of Thami al-Glaoui, a native chieftain, to organize popular opposition to the sultan and *Istiqlal*. The plan succeeded, and the sultan was sent into exile in Madagascar. The French then placed Prince Mulay Arafa on the throne in Morocco, but offered no reform to the people. An armed uprising began in 1955. In late 1955, the French brought Mohammed V to Paris. At this point, al-Glaoui apologized to Mohammed for past mistakes and begged his forgiveness. With this move, the French lost all credibility in Morocco; in November 1955, they approved the Declaration of La Celle Saint Cloud, which acknowledged the independence of Morocco. The final instruments of independence were signed at Fez in March 1956. On 21 October 1958, a civil war began when troops loyal to Mohammed V were attacked by central government forces. The revolt quickly spread to Rif tribemen who opposed the *Istiqlal* rule. Although the fighting between the troops was quickly brought under control, the Rif uprising lasted into 1960. In January 1959, *Istiqlal* split into two groups, adding to what was becoming a much more complicated political system in Morocco.

Italy. Italy, located in the south of Europe, is an elongated, boot-shaped country extending into the Mediterranean. France borders Italy on the west, Austria is its neighbor on the north, and the former Yugoslav state of Slovenia lies along its eastern land border. The Adriatic washes its eastern shore, and the Tyrrenian Sea faces its western and southwestern shores. The capital city is Rome (qv). The Empire of Rome emerged in the fifth century B.C. and conquered both the Etruscans and the Greeks to attain dominance on the Italian peninsula. Until the fifth century A.D. Rome ruled most of the civilized world as it was known at that time. After Emperor Constantine moved his capital to Byzantium in 330 A.D., the western empire went into a decline that ended with the subjection of Rome by Alaric in 410 A.D.. Thereafter, Rome was overrun by waves of barbarians, including Goths, Huns, Lomabards, and Vandals, until its conquest by Charlemagne (against Lombardy) and his coronation as Holy Roman emperor in 800 A.D. Yet the deterioration of Italy continued until Charlemagne allied himself with the papacy. This act helped establish the temporal sovereignty of the Pope over the conquered lands of Lombardy and added another contender in the struggle for power in Italy. With Charlemagne's death (814), the Holy

Roman Empire went into decline until revived by Otto I of Saxony in 962, creating a union between Italy and Germany as they were known at that time. Frederick Barbarossa's attempt to assert power in Italy was met with resistance from a league of Lombard cities. While these matters were being sorted out in the north, Sicily (qv) and southern Italy were, from the ninth century, in the hands of Muslims. By the eleventh century, however, the island of Sicily and the region around Naples were in the hands of the Normans, and the Kingdom of the Two Sicilies and the Kingdom of Naples became factors in the ongoing power struggle. The decline of feudalism attended the growth of city-states. Florence, Venice, Milan and the papacy, among the most powerful, came to dominate the countryside, and the commerce of goods from these fertile lands made for unprecedented wealth in those regions. The papacy's power declined, however, when the Holy See was moved to Avignon, France, between 1305 and 1377. Still, it was the patronage of the papacy and that from such princely families as the Medicis of Florence that brought about the Italian Renaissance, one of the brightest episodes of Europe's release from the Dark Ages. This was a time of growing disharmony among the princes, which led to strife and to blood feuds that lasted decades. Italy soon became a land reigned over by petty despots in their duchys and princedoms separated from each other by the rugged terrain. The people did not think of themselves as Italians, but rather as Venetians or Florentines. This situation allowed outside forces to dominate the region. Spain and France both attempted to control Italy after 1494. By 1544, Spain had defeated France and took control of Sicily, Naples and Milan. The following centuries witnessed a continuation of the struggle for domination through war, marriage and treaty. Only the papacy remained strong enough to withstand these pressures, and the Papal States in central Italy remained relatively untouched. After the Ottoman Turks cut the supply lines to the east, many of the Italian states failed and were taken over by foreign powers that treated the Italians only as revenue-producing pawns. Until 1713, Spain remained the dominant power in Italy. The Treaty of Utrecht signed in that year, which ended the War of Spanish Succession, put the Austrian Hapsburgs in the place of Spain. In 1720, the Spaniards attempted to regain their lost possessions but were unsuccessful in their attack on Sicily. Subsequently, the duke of Savoy became the king of Sardinia, after giving up Sicily; and Don Carlos, the son of Philip V of Spain, became the the king of Naples. By the late eighteenth century, Italy was a land marked by great wealth and abject poverty, where peasants lived in hovels while the rich in Rome, Venice and Naples resided in great pomp and luxury. Crime was rampant in the countryside. As notions of reform swept across Europe, the Italians began to deal with ideas of liberty and freedom. On the eve of the French Revolution secret organizations sprang up in Italy that were bent on agitating for release from absolutism. As Napoleon moved into Italy in the 1790s, Italian partisans supported his operations. Republics grew up in the wake of his conquests; soon it became evident that the Italians had shed their old masters only to get new French ones. With Napoleon's defeat, the old states returned and

Italy fell back into the miasma of a two-class society, with especially brutal treatment at the hands of the Austrians in Lombardy and Venice and the Spanish in Naples and Sicily. This brutality led to the *resorgimento*, a movement aimed at national unity. New secret organizations rose up, and revolts in 1821 and 1831 were crushed by the Austrians with gratuitous brutality. One organization, Young Italy, led by Giuseppe Manzini, demanded that Charles Albert, king of Sardinia-Piedmont, move to liberate Italy. The general European uprisings of 1848 spread to Italy. Charles Albert was defeated at Custozza (25 July 1848), 11 miles from Verona, and Austrian rule was reestablished. In the meantime, Mazzini drove the Pope out of Rome and set up the Kingdom of Rome, which was quickly demolished by the French. In the north, the Austrians forced Charles Albert to abdicate in favor of his son Victor Emmanuel. By 1859, the king's minister, Count Camillo di Cavour, maneuvered Napoleon III into a treaty that eventually led to a confrontation with the Austrians and their defeats at Magenta (4 June 1859) and Solferino (24 June 1859). In 1860, Guiseppe Garibaldi and his red-shirted legion captured Sicily and the rest of the Kingdom of Naples. Garibaldi became the leader of the Italian masses, and Victor Emmanuel II was crowned king of Italy. Venice followed in 1866. This left only the Papal States in central Italy to form a division between north and south, a dividing line protected by the French army. This situation continued until 1870, when the Franco-Prussian War spelled the end of French hegemony in Italy. When the French evacuated Rome, the Italian army was quick to move in, whereupon Pope Pius IX excommunicated the new interlopers and withdrew into the inner core of the papacy, the Vatican, where he and his followers became "voluntary prisoners." Though now free, Italy suffered from massive debt and equally heavy taxation. A rift widened between conservative and socialist elements as the people struggled to adapt to their new government. Conflict followed, in which rioting and disorder marked the close of the nineteenth century. Even so, Italy began to rebuild. A new army and navy were formed, in part to meet the alliance Italy had made with Germany and Austria (Triple Alliance) in 1882. In 1900 King Humbert was assassinated by an anarchist. His son, Victor Emmanuel III (qv), succeeded to the throne. Italy also began a colonial expansion program, gaining two relatively worthless colonies in Eritrea and Italian Somaliland (Somalia) on the east coast of Africa. After the successful 1911–1912 war with Turkey, Italy gained Tripoli on the north coast, facing the Mediterranean. The Triple Alliance was already showing signs of collapse when Austria declared war on Serbia in 1914. Italy used the excuse of treaty violation to declare its neutrality and, in April 1915, signed a secret alliance with England, France and Russia. Italy then withdrew from the pact with Germany and Austria and, on 23 May 1915, declared war on Austria. Although the Italian army was badly mauled during the war, Italy was able to gain a territorial settlement ("Unredeemed Italy") that gave the country land in the Trentino region and in Istria. The postwar period saw Italy slip back into a land of anarchy fomented by the socialists and communists. The Crown appeared powerless to curb the violence that ensued. Ex-servicemen sought vengeance on the troublemakers but were powerless until a new leader, Benito Mussolini, came forward and formed the nucleus of the Fascist Black-Shirt Party. Both rich and poor saw fascism as the means of gaining their ends: the rich, as a bulwark against communism, and the poor, as a means to revive the economy and put food on the table. On 28 October 1922, following a threat to march on Rome, Mussolini was asked to form a new government after the one in power quit. Within three years, Mussolini had captured all power in the country. The king remained on the throne, but as a mere figurehead. All political parties except the Fascist Party were abolished; the Italian parliament closed. Mussolini imposed a complete authoritarian state in which the people were totally subjugated and lost the power to resist. He also dreamed of reestablishing the grandeur of the Roman Empire and raised a large army to support his quest. In 1935, Italian forces invaded Ethiopia (qv) and defeated the weak forces of that country within a year. In October 1936, Mussolini entered into an alliance with Nazi Germany (Rome-Berlin Axis). Italian troops supported Franco (qv) during the Spanish Civil War. In April 1939, Italian troops invaded and occupied Albania (qv). After that, Italy entered into a full military partnership with Germany. When Great Britain and France declared war on Germany on 3 September 1939, however, Italy backed away from the fight, declaring itself a nonbelligerent. After Germany defeated France, Italian troops occupied southeastern France, in what has been called the "stab-in-the-back" invasion (10 June 1940). Italy's military prowess lagged badly. The Greeks fighting in Macedonia mauled the Italian army moving in from Albania and it was again badly defeated by the British in North Africa. The subsequent request for German assistance had far-reaching effects both on the Nazi-Italian alliance and on the German timetable for the invasion of Russia, which had to be postponed. Mussolini, although still full of bluster, was now little more than a German puppet, his soldiers despised by their German comrades. After the Allies invaded Sicily on 3 September 1943, the Italian government collapsed. Mussolini was spirited away to northern Italy by German paratroopers while Italy was reversing its position. On 13 October 1943, Italy declared war on Germany and joined the Allies. Mussolini attempted to form a "Republican Fascist State" in the north, but with little success. When the German defenders in northern Italy surrendered on 29 April 1945, Mussolini was captured; he and his girlfriend and others, were summarily shot by Italian partisans, their bodies later displayed hanging by their heels in a gas station. The end of the war found Italy almost totally destroyed by both German pillaging and Allied bombardment. More United Nations aid was needed in Italy than in any other country. Political turmoil swept the country. Victor Emmanuel III had retained his crown, with Allied help, until 9 May 1946, when he abdicated in favor of his son, Umberto II. On 12 June 1946, however, the Italian people voted for a republican form of government, and a Constituent Assembly was elected to draft a new constitution. Umberto refused to accept the people's will and left the country to avoid the violence that would surely have followed. A peace treaty was signed between the Allies and Italy on 10 February 1947. The terms were especially harsh in view of the fact that Italy had been a "co-belligerent" since 1943. Italy lost the Dodecanese Islands to Greece, Trieste was internationalized, and boundary changes were made along the French and Yugoslav borders. On 14 December 1947, Allied forces withdrew from Italy, but US and British forces remained in Trieste to thwart Yugoslav threats to seize the city. Italy's new constitution went into effect on 1 January 1948. Communist-inspired rioting broke out in Italy following the assassination (14 July 1948) of the communist leader, Palmiro Togliatti (qv). Order was restored only after much bloodshed. Italy was made trustee of Italian Somaliland in 1949 by the United Nations, the same year Italy became a member of the NATO alliance. The question of Trieste was not so simply settled, however, and for a while war seemed a distinct possibility. On 10 September 1951, Yugoslavia's Marshal Tito (qv) held out an olive branch, offering to settle the Trieste situation. By March 1952, unrest in Trieste had led to massive anti-Allied demonstrations against continued occupation. The situation deteriorated even further in 1953 and, late August emergency meetings among political and military leaders took place in the Allied capitals as a Yugoslav takeover of the city appeared imminent. A series of Italo-Yugoslav border clashes occurred 29–31 August, and Yugoslav forces opened fire on Allied patrols as well. (See Trieste.) The situation was finally settled by arbitration. On 5 October 1954, the city was given to Italy, while Yugoslavia got most of the disputed territory east of the Trieste. On 25 March 1957, Rome was the site of the establishment of the European Common Market (qv) and the European Atomic Community (Euratom) (qv). Italy then moved into a period of border disputes (1959) with Austria over the area of Southern Tyrol, given to Italy at Austria's expense at the end of the war. This issue was finally settled through arbitration on 30 November 1969. In July 1960, Italy lost its trusteeship over Somaliland, when the Somali Republic was proclaimed. In January 1963, Italy announced it had reached an agreement with the United States to remove 30 "Jupiter" intercontinental missiles from Italian soil. On 12 March 1968, there was violent student rioting in Rome as Maoist student groups attempts to impose their philosophy. The police were finally able to quell the disturbance. On 14 December 1969, a terrorist bomb explosion in Milan's Bank of Agriculture killed 16 and injured more than 90. After holding left-wing suspects for more than four years, neofascist right-wing terrorists were found to be guilty of the attack. That same day, three more bombs detonated in Rome.In June 1970, serious rioting broke out in one province over the choice of regional capital. This rioting continued sporadically until 14 July 1970 and flaired up again in Reggio Calabria after the new site was chosen. In October, the rioting erupted again when the formal transfer of power was made to Catanzaro, the new capital. Troops were ordered into the region on 16 October to put down the disturbance over the unpopular choice for the capital. The rioting continued, however, until February 1971. On 5 August 1972, Palestinian terrorists blew up the storage facilities at the Trieste terminal of the Trans-Alpine Pipeline. The barracks of the U.S. Marine Security Guard detachment at the American embassy in Rome was badly damaged by a bomb on 5 April 1973. No one was injured. Police arrested five Arab terrorists on 5 September 1973, as they prepared to shoot down an airliner at the Rome airport with Soviet-built SA-7 "Grail" antiaircraft missiles that were also seized. One of the most bizarre terrorist incidents occured on 17 December 1973, when five Palestinian terrorists killed 31 people at Rome's Fiumicino Airport. They then took a number of hostages, including 14 Americans, and threw hand grenades into a Pan Am Boeing 707 readying for takeoff to Beirut. Next, they hijacked a Lufthansa aircraft for Athens, where they demanded the release of a group of PLO terrorists held in Greek jails. The terrorists then flew to Kuwait, where they surrendered. The terrorists were eventually freed. The Trieste incident flaired up again in March 1974, when Italy tried to reannex part of the zone turned over to Yugoslavia in the settlement. Yugoslav troops were moved to the border, and tensions rose. The matter was once again settled by negotiation on 1 October 1975 (effective 10 November 1975), with the existing boundaries once again recognized. Left-wing rioting broke out all over Italy as students, disenchanted with the Italian communist party's recent cooperation with the government, took to the streets on 14 March 1977. On 16 January 1978, the government fell when Premier Giulio Andreotti (qv) rejected a communist demand for more power. Then, on 16 March, 12 Red Brigades (qv) terrorists kidnapped former premier Aldo Moro (qv) in a hail of gunfire that killed five of his bodyguards. Moro's bullet-riddled body was found in the trunk of a car in downtown Rome on 9 May 1978. On 2 August 1980, neofascist terrorists placed a bomb in the waiting room of Bologna's railway station. Its blast killed 76 and injured 200 more. Nine top-level terrorists were later arrested in Great Britain (12 September 1981), and some were charged with the attack. Twenty-three suspects were eventually arrested in several countries. Thirteen people, including members of the Italian secret police, were tried for the attack. In 1990, all those convicted in the attack had their sentences overturned by an appeals court in Bologna. In another bizarre incident, a shuttle plane between Bologna and Palermo fell into the sea near the island of Ustica in late August 1980. All 81 on board were killed. In 1987, when the DC-9 was raised from a depth of 11,500 feet, it was found that it had been shot down by a missile, later (1991) identified as of NATO manufacture. Evidence soon appeared to indicate an Italian Air Force coverup, which later unraveled into an international mystery involving the United States. It was later revealed (1991) that a Soviet-built Libyan fighter went down over southern Italy at about the same time as the DC-9 and that the American CIA had reached the scene before Rome was notified. A number of senior Italian Air Force officers were accused of destroying evidence in the coverup of what is still a mystery. On 12 December 1980, Red Brigades terrorists kidnapped Giovanni D'Urso, director general of the Ministry of Justice, a leader in counterterrorist activities in his country. He was eventually released unharmed after some of the terrorist demands were met.

On 4 April 1981, the reputed leader of one faction of the Red Brigades, Mario Moretti, was arrested in Milan. In 1981, Red Brigades terrorists kidnapped Ciro Cirillo, a construction contract manager, in Naples, where a 1980 earthquake had devastated the city. Three months later he was ransomed for three billion lira. The report of the payment was not released until September 1988, when several political leaders were indicted for conspiracy in making the ransom deal. Italy was also the scene of the Red Brigades' kidnapping of U.S. Brigadier General James L. Dozier in Verona on 17 December 1981. He was eventually freed unharmed by an Italian special police unit on 28 January 1982. Italian troops deployed in Lebanon as part of a UN peacekeeping force came under fire in Beirut on 15–16 March 1983. An Italian court in Turin convicted 12 members of the Red Brigades and sentenced them to life imprisonment on 26 July 1983. Forty-eight others were given lesser sentences, and one was acquitted. American cruise missiles were emplaced on Italian soil in April 1984. On 29 September 1984, Italian police began a wholesale roundup of members of the Mafia. On 23 December 1984, a time bomb exploded aboard a train from Florence to Bologna in a 12-mile long tunnel, killing 29 and injuring 200 others. Although no one took credit for the attack, a right-wing organization was suspected. Professor Enzo Tarantelli (qv), an eminent economist, was assassinated by Red Brigades terrorists at Rome University on 27 March 1985. A bomb injured 12 people at Rome's international airport on 1 July 1985. On 16 September, terrorists threw two Soviet-made F1 grenades into the Cafe de Paris 100 yards from the U.S. embassy in Rome. About 38 tourists were injured. An Abu Nidal (qv) group operating under the cover name " Revolutionary Organization of Socialist Muslims" claimed credit for the attack. Another bomb blew up the British Airways office in Rome on 25 September. An Abu Nidal terrorist was captured near the scene of the attack. On 10 October 1985, U.S. navy F-14 jet fighters forced down an Egyptian airliner carrying the Arab terrorists accused of hijacking the passenger ship *Achille Lauro* (qv). The transport, which had been bound for Tunis, was forced to land at a NATO airbase on Sicily. After a confrontation with American authorities, Italian police took the terrorists into custody, but they allowed Abul Abbas (qv), who had also been on the plane, to go free. Abbas was able to get to Yugoslavia. The bungled affair was blamed on Italian Prime Minister Bettino Craxi (qv). On 27 December 1985, Palestinian terrorists attacked the El-Al check-in counter at Rome's Leonardo da Vinci Airport. Iran and Libya were both linked to the attack, which killed and injured hundreds of people. The attack was said to be in reprisal for an Israeli attack on the PLO headquarters in Tunisia. In February 1986, 474 (later reduced to 452) Mafia bosses were put on trial in Palermo, Sicily, in the largest single crackdown on that organization in Italian history. The evidence for the indictments came largely from two Mafioso members held in the United States. Three hundred thirty-eight were convicted (16 December 1987) with 19 being given life sentences. In March 1986, three alleged Bulgarian accomplices of Mehmet Ali-Agca (qv), the Turkish gunman sentenced for his assassination attempt (May 1981) on Pope John Paul II (qv), were found innocent "for lack of sufficient proof." Libya fired two Soviet-built missiles toward the U.S. Coast Guard navigation station on the Italian island of Lampedusa off the Tunisian coast, in April 1986, in retaliation for the U.S. bombing of Libya (qv). When Libya's Muammar Qaddafi (qv) claimed he had destroyed the island, Italy responded that, if Qadaffi had even hit the island, he now would be dead. In March and August 1991, waves of Albanians attempted to land in Italy following the collapse of the communist government in Albania. Most were sent back to Albania after being rounded up by the police. The year 1992 witnessed widespread charges of government corruption throughout Italy. Two Sicilian magistrates were murdered by the Mafia in a new show of force by that criminal organization in light of the ring closing around the Mafia's real masters. The downfall of corrupt political leaders continued into 1993, at the same time that a number of terrorist bombings rocked Rome, Milan and Florence. On 27 May 1993, the Florence attack on the Uffizi Gallery killed five. No one, left or right, claimed responsibility. In July 1993, Italy was at odds with the United States and the United Nations over UN policy in Somalia, especially over how to deal with the tribal warlords. The revelation of scandal rocked Italy in 1994. The government's new austerity program was greeted by a half-day national strike in October. The prime minister, Silvio Berlusconi, was forced to resign in December 1994; and in 1995, three former prime ministers were caught up in the mushrooming fiscal scandal. One of them, Giulio Andreotti, was put on trial in September on charges of having Mafia connections. Berlusconi was indicted in October. At the same time a large number of judges were under investigation for dereliction of duty. *Reading:* David Ward, *Antifascisms: Cultural Politics in Italy, 1943–46: Benedetto Croce and the Liberals, Carlo Levi and the Actionists* (1996); Martin Clark, *Modern Italy, 1871–1982* (1984); Francesco Guicciardini, *The History of Italy* (1984).

Ituzaingo. *See* Argentina.

Ivanovsky, Yevgeny F. On 2 December 1980, General Yevgeny Ivanovsky, the commander of Group, Soviet Forces, Germany (GSFG) informed the western alliance that the East German-Polish border had been established as a restricted area and closed to outside observers. *See* Poland.

Ivory Coast. The Republic of Ivory Coast lies on the southern coast of West Africa. It is bordered on the north by Burkina Faso, on the east by Ghana and on the west by Guinea and Liberia. To the south is the Atlantic Ocean's Gulf of Guinea. The official capital city is Yamoussourkro, although most of the government's business is conducted in Abidjan. Ivory Coast was first discovered by the Portuguese in the fifteenth century. It soon became an area frequented by traders in ivory and slaves. Two French trading posts were established in the seventeenth century. By 1842, Ivory Coast was a French protectorate. In 1893, Ivory Coast gained French colonial status. Not until 1918 was the northern region of the country brought under control. Native uprisings and yellow fever both took their toll on early French exploration of the the northern border region.

In World War II, Ivory Coast was held by Vichy until 1942. After the war (1946), it became a territory in the French Union. In 1947, the northern districts were separated to form the territory of Upper Volta (qv). On 4 December 1958, Ivory Coast gained its autonomy and became an independent state on 7 August 1960. In March 1966, Ivory Coast was threatened with invasion by neighboring Guinea because Ivory Coast was allied with Ghana. Ivory Coast officially changed its name to Côte d'Ivoire in October 1985. Students and workers protested against the one-man rule of President Felix Houphouet-Boigny in February 1990. In May, Army conscripts mutinied in Adidjan and were soon joined by air force personnel who seized the airport. The French troops stationed near the airport did not interfere. After the government offered concessions, most of the mutineers returned to their barracks. Multiple-party elections were held in October 1990, but Houphouet-Boigny won 85 percent of the vote anyway and was reelected for the seventh time. In August 1991, two journalists were jailed for allegedly insulting the president. More strikes among students and teachers led to attacks by security troops that ended in the wounding of at least 20 people (17 May 1991). There were unconfirmed rumors of a foiled coup attempt in August 1991. More protests occurred in February 1992 because the government failed to chastise the army officers who ordered the attacks on the student demonstrators. Hundreds were arrested, with many being sentenced to two years' imprisonment. The trials were followed by massive demonstrations with more arrests. The president, who had remained in Europe throughout the troubles, returned in June 1992 and ordered most of those sentenced released. Disorder continued into 1993, when the elite Republican Guard mutinied in March. Three thousand students rampaged in April and went on a four-month strike. Tensions were still running high when, on 7 December 1993, Houphouet-Boigny died. He was replaced by Henri Konan Bedie. A border issue with Burkina Faso appeared settled, and the border with Liberia was opened to allow relief supplies to flow into that country before the end of the year. Ivory Coast was able to reduce its staggering debts in 1994 through the forgiveness of $5 billion owed to a French consortium. In the 1995 election held in October, foreigners were prohibited from voting, but the elections were marred by fraud and violence. Bedie was elected president in his own right, but he faced heavy criticism over proposed changes in the electoral system. Along the recently opened Liberian border, rebel attacks on 13 June killed at least 30 people. This led to reprisal attacks against Liberians living in Abidjan. *Reading:* Christian Grootaert et al., *Analyzing Poverty and Policy Reform: The Experience of Cote D'Ivoire* (1996); Jean-Claude Berthelemy & Francois Bourguignon, *Growth and Crisis in Cote D'Ivoire* (1996).

Izmir. *See* Turkey.

J

Jackson, Geoffrey. On 8 January 1971, the British ambassador to Uruguay, Geoffrey Jackson, was kidnapped in Montevideo by Tupamoro (qv) terrorists. The kidnappers demanded the release of 150 political prisoners as his ransom. In response, the Uruguayan government offered a reward of $50,000 for information leading to the ambassador's safe recovery (22 May 1971). On 9 September, Jackson was released unharmed following a 6 September Tupamoro attack on the Punta Carretas maximum security prison, where 111 prisoners were released.

Jadid, Salah. On 28 February 1969, Hafez al-Assad (qv) moved to takeover power in Syria. In doing so, he challenged both the president, Nureddin al-Attassi (qv), and the head of the Baath Party, General Salah Jadid. In a compromise reached in March 1969, Jadid retained his post, as did al-Attassi. Jadid was reelected that year to the Baath National Executive Council. This placed Jadid in direct conflict with Assad over the ascendancy issue. On 13 November 1970, after the Baath Party congress failed to settle the dispute between the military and political wings of the party, Assad placed Jadid under house arrest. On 18 November, Assad seized power.

Jaffa, Palestine. *See* Israel.

Jaffna. *See* Sri Lanka.

Jagan, Cheddi. On 14 June 1964, the royal governor of British Guiana, Sir Richard Luyt, was forced to assume emergency powers after a long period of racial disorder among the East Indian and black population of the colony. In one sense, much of this trouble was caused by the politics of Cheddi Jagan, who led the first elected government in the colony from 1953 until 1966. His People's Progressive Party (PPP) was procommunist and created such havoc that, in October 1953, the British government suspended the constitution and ordered in British troops. The constitution was not restored until 1957. At that time, the PPP split, with Jagan leading the East Indian wing and Forbes Burnham (qv) the African wing , the People's National Congress (PNC). The PPP won the 1957 elections, and did so again in 1961. In 1961, rioting and a long general strike began; British troops were once again called in. When Prime Minister Jagan refused to resign so that a new government could be formed, the royal governor acted. In December 1964, a new election was held using a system of proportional representation. Jagan and the PPP were defeated, and Forbes Burnham and the PNC formed the new government. See also Guyana.

Jakarta. *See* Indonesia.

Jalalabad. *See* Afghanistan.

Jalloud, Abdul Salam. In April 1974, there were reports that Muammar al-Qaddafi (qv) had been relieved of "political, administrative, and traditional duties." It was said at the time that the real power in Libya was in the hands of Prime Minister Major Abdul Salam Jalloud. In July 1972, there had been a major reorganization of the cabinet with many of the positions going to civilians. At that time Qaddafi gave up the office of prime minister and appointed Jalloud to that post. Between 1976 and 1977, Jalloud's office was reassumed by Qaddafi in another of his many reorganizations of the apparatus controlling Libya.

Jamaica. An island in the Caribbean, Jamaica is located approximately 90 miles south of eastern Cuba and 110 miles west of the western tip of Haiti. Kingston is the capital. Jamaica was first visited in 1494 by Columbus. The original inhabitants were Arawak Indians, who died out under the Spanish rule, which lasted until 1655, when the island was taken by the British. Both the Spanish and British imported slaves, and the slave trade flourished there during the eighteenth century. After slavery was abolished in the 1830s, indentured labor was imported from India. When an uprising began in 1865, the British governor, Edward Eyre, put it down with such gratuitous brutality that he was recalled to England and put on trial. In the 1930s, Sir (later) Alexander Bustamante began organizing labor. He and his cousin, Norman W. Manley, eventually founded the two dominant political parties on the island. In February 1956, Jamaica joined with other Caribbean islands in the formation of a federation. Jamaica won its independence from Great Britain on 6 August 1962. In 1974–1976, the socialist government on the island acquired half ownership of the island's bauxite mines and sought to raise the taxes paid by the U.S. and Canada for their mining rights. The socialists were returned to office in 1976. In March 1978, Jamaica joined with Guyana (qv) in the formation of a multinational security force designed to guarantee the territorial integrity of Belize (qv). On 30 May 1980, after rioting broke out in a Kingston slum, Jamaican troops were sent in to restore order. As a result, one person was killed. Beginning in July 1980, roving gangs began killing people at random in Kingston. By 18 July, 70 were dead. A dark-to-dawn curfew was imposed to help stop the killing. On 25 October 1983, Jamaican troops participated in the invasion of Grenada (qv). In January 1985, seven people were killed in demonstrations against a rise in gasoline prices. By 1987, tourism, a major industry, was badly damaged by the increase in street crime against tourists and the murder of reggae singer Peter Tosh. On 12 September 1988, Hurricane Gilbert hit the island, killing 45 people and causing extensive damage. In August 1988, the two leading political parties signed an agreement to avoid violence during the general election scheduled for 10 April 1989. The election was held on 9 February 1989 and put Michael Manley (qv) and the

People's National Party (PNP) in power. In 1992, open warfare erupted between the followers of the PNP and the Jamaica Labor Party (JLP) led by Edward Seaga. During this time, Manley, claiming illness, resigned his office and was replaced by Percival J. Patterson as prime minister (30 March 1992). The fighting started after an imprisoned JLP leader was apparently murdered in jail and the man's son was murdered outside. At least eight people died in the ensuing gun battles, which preceded the swearing in of Patterson. Rioting associated with rising prices and loss of jobs continued until September 1992. Patterson and the PNP were elected in their own right in March 1993, but not without the expected cries of fraud from the JPL. The JPL continued to refuse participation in any elections into 1994, but trouble in the JPL almost forced Seaga to step down as party leader. The political situation continued in 1995, but without violence. *Reading:* Evelyne Stephens & John D. Stephens, *Democratic Socialism in Jamaica: The Political Movement and Social Transformation in Dependent Capitalism* (1986); Darrel Levi, *Michael Manley: The Making of a Leader* (1990); Carl Stone, *Class, State, and Democracy in Jamaica* (1986); Sean Sheehan, *Jamaica* (1994).

Jammu. *See* India.

January 31 Popular Front. On 12 May 1982, thirteen terrorists claiming to be from the January 31 Popular Front seized the Brazilian embassy in Guatemala City. The assailants were armed with two weapons and nine Molotov cocktails. The Brazilian ambassador and eight others were taken hostage. The terrorists demanded a press conference to denounce the military junta that had seized power in March. The next day all the hostages were released unharmed. On 14 May, the terrorists were flown, along with several Brazilian and Guatemalan officials acting as hostages, to Merida, Mexico, where the terrorists were granted political asylum. The January 31 Popular Front was not a well-known group at the time of the incident.

Japan. The islands of Japan form an archipelago at the northwest edge of the Pacific Basin of the east coast of Asia.. Siberia lies to the north. The island of Sakhalin is within a few miles of the northern tip of the northern Japanese island of Hokkaido, and South Korea lies to the west. There are four main islands in the group: Hokkaido, Kyushu, Honshu and Shikoku. The capital city is Tokyo on the island of Honshu. Tradition puts the date of the founding of Japan in 660 B.C., but at least a millennium passed before a unified Japan was evident. Much of Chinese cultural influence may be found in early Japanese development. Buddhism became an important religion after the sixth century A.D. By the end of the twelfth century, a system of military dictators (*shoguns*) ruling feudal domains controlled Japan. This system remained in effect until 1867, when the Emperor Meiji established a firm centralized control (Meiji Restoration). Portuguese and Dutch traders visited the islands as early as the sixteenth century, but the xenophobic Japanese shied away from outside contact and treated foreigners with hostility. In 1854, Commodore Matthew C. Perry opened Japan to foreign commerce in a show of naval power that subdued the Japanese. Japan fought China in 1894–1895, a won the island of Formosa (Taiwan). In

1904–1905, Japan decisively defeated the Russians; St. Petersburg was forced to cede the southern half of Sakhalin in Japan. The U.S.–engineered treaty (Treaty of Portsmouth) that settled the war left Japan feeling betrayed, and distrust of foreigners once again became a fact of life. In 1910, Japan annexed Korea without much outside opposition. After World War I, in which Japan was England's ally, the Japanese occupied a number of important islands in the South Pacific that had been held by Germany. In 1931, Japan occupied Manchuria and established the puppet state of Manchukuo. In 1932, Japan went to war with China. Ultra-right-wing military and civilian groups were defeated in a rebellion in 1936. An undeclared war with China began in July 1937, but while the Japanese army penetrated deeply into the Chinese mainland, the Chinese refused to surrender. In 1940, Japanese troops moved into French Indochina, and Japan joined the Nazi-Italian Axis. The U.S. exerted economic pressure on Japan in an effort to curtail its agression in Asia. When Hideki Tojo became prime minister in October 1941, planning began for war with the United States. On 7 December 1941, not without cause, Japan attacked the United States (Hawaii and the Philippines). The outcome of the war set the stage for much of the history that would be written over the next five decades. The U.S. and the Soviet Union occupied Korea; a generally U.S.–controlled occupation of the Japanese home islands followed. On 3 May 1947, a new constitution was ratified, and the Japanese emperor, always known as the Son of Heaven, was forced to disclaim his divinity. Japan also was forced to renounce war. Tojo and six others were sentenced to death for war crimes on 12 November 1948. When North Korea invaded South Korea in June 1950, U.S. troops stationed in Japan were the first to respond after President Truman decided to intervene. In 1951, when the U.S. and Japan were conducting peace talks, the opposition party in Japan issued a series of demands that included the return of territories in both US and Soviet hands to Japanese control. At the same time, communist-inspired rioting broke out in Tokyo against the use of Japanese territory as a staging area for UN military operations in Korea. For the first time since the war, Japanese military units, although called "security forces," were seen in public on the streets of Tokyo. In February 1952, Japan became indirectly embroiled in the civil war raging between Communists and Nationalists in China. At peace talks between the Nationalists and Japan, the Chinese demanded Japan acknowledge 1937 as the start of the war and recognize all territory in the hands of the Communists as rightfully belonging to the Nationalists. A formal treaty of peace with Japan was signed by China, the US, and 48 other countries on 28 April 1952; the Soviet Union did not sign. In September 1952, the USSR vetoed Japan's entrance into the United Nations. The U.S. and Japan signed a mutual defense treaty on 8 March 1954. In October, Japan announced it had become a member of the Colombo Plan (qv). Burma signed a separate peace treaty with Japan on 5 November 1954. On 19 October 1956, a peace treaty between Japan and the USSR was finally hammered out, but only after the issue of the Kurile Islands (to USSR) was settled. The treaty went into effect on 26 December 1956. In 1957, the U.S. announced it was reducing its troop strength in Japan. On 4 May

1959, the Soviet Union promised "neutrality" for Japan if it ordered all U.S. military bases on its soil closed. Widespread anti-American demonstrations broke out in Japan in mid-June 1960. The Japanese government was forced to ask the United States to postpone a planned visit by President Eisenhower. To protest the expected arrival of the American aircraft carrier *USS Enterprise* at the port of Sasebo on Kyushu, violent demonstrations broke out on 15 January 1968. A leftist student organization (*Zengakuren*) caused the rioting. Fighting again broke out between students and police at Tokyo University on 18–19 January 1969. In April, more general rioting erupted over the issue of the return of Okinawa (qv) to Japanese control. More rioting occurred in celebration of "International Anti-War Day" on 21 October 1969. In November, more rioting occurred when it was announced that Prime Minister Eisako Sato would go to the U.S. to negotiate the return of Okinawa. Over 1,200 were arrested in that disturbance. On 29 September 1971, Japan signed a treaty with Communist China ending the 1937 war. At the same time, however, Japan severed diplomatic relations with Nationalist China. Six months later, on 3 March 1972, the Communist Chinese delegate to the United Nations charged Japan with imperialism and demanded the return of the Senkalu Islands which Japan held and China claimed. On 15 May 1972, the U.S.-Japan Treaty of 17 June 1971 went into effect, and Okinawa was returned to Japanese administrative control. Massive anti-American demonstrations again took place in October 1974, this time protesting the expected visit of U.S. president Gerald Ford (qv). Japan's proximity to the Soviet Union led to the defection of Soviet Air Force Lieutenant Victor I. Belenko on 6 September 1976. Belenko brought with him his supersecret MiG-25 fighter plane. While the Soviets howled, Belenko was granted asylum in the U.S., and U.S. and Japanese intelligence specialists disassembled the aircraft. The plane was given back to the Soviets in packing boxes (12 November). In 1977, relations with the Soviet Union worsened as Japan pressed its claim for the Kurile Islands. In the meantime, the USSR severely restricted Japanese fishing near the islands and later held military exercises in the waters near the island chain (June 1978). On 28 July, Japan warned the Soviet Union against attempting the establishment of a Soviet sphere of influence on the islands near the Japanese home islands. Three years later, in May 1981, the USSR warned Japan not to allow US naval vessels carrying nuclear weapons to land in Japan. Japan rejected the demand. In 1982, Japan initiated a five-year military expansion program. Japan became the stage for a number of terrorist acts in 1985. In one, on New Year's Day 1985, a rocket attack was launched against the U.S. consulate in Kobe. In a second attack, on 23 June, a bomb went off at Narita Airport outside Tokyo as luggage was being transferred from one Air India plane to another. Two workmen were killed in the explosion. On 29 November, railway communications were cut at 16 locations by terrorists of the *Chukaku-Ha* (Nucleus Faction) (qv) terrorist organization. Eleven million people were stranded by the attack. Throughout the postwar period in Japan, however, the most far-reaching development was the country's economic recovery from near destruction in 1945. Freed from the burden of military expenditures, Japan poured its money into industrial production and soon became a leader in the world's commercial inner circle. Instead of military operations, industrial espionage, government corruption—some reaching into the prime minister's office—and, at least as viewed in the United States, unethical foreign trade practices pushed the U.S. and other Western countries into more and more restrictive trade agreements with Japan. At the same time, Japan was suffering an internal economic decline, and the Japanese work ethic was beginning to take its toll. By 1992, the issue of deploying Japanese troops overseas with UN peacekeeping forces became a burning issue. Hotly debated, the matter passed the Diet, and in September 1992 a Japanese contingent was ordered to Cambodia. In addition, an American-educated Japanese, Yasushi Akashi, was named head of the UN mission (UN Transitional Authority, Cambodia, or UNTAC). Still the problem of trade with the United States caused great concern, while relations with Moscow remained unsettled.In particular, the conclusion of a peace treaty was hindered by the issue of control of sections in the Kuriles that both sides claimed. Japan also apologized to Korea for some of its actions in World War II. However, relations with North Korea were not cordial. The new government in 1993 faced numerous political challenges, with various coalitions being made and broken on a regular basis. There were numerous public demonstrations against corruption in government that transcended political parties, but focused most closely on the Liberal-Democrats, who lost power that year. Japanese economic relations with the U.S. also suffered as both sides planned retaliatory schemes to block the perceived trade imbalance caused by unfair trade practices. At the UN, Japan lobbied for a permanent seat on the Security Council. As the turmoil in domestic politics continued into 1994, a new government was installed, the third in a 12-month period. A socialist, Tomiichi Murayama, took office on 29 June. A subsequent breakthough in trade negotiations with the U.S. was hailed as a means of ending the long-standing trade imbalance between the two countries. Also, in 1994, Japan joined in a U.S.-proposed and UN-sponsored move to bring North Korea into compliance with UN nuclear standards, but shied clear of endorsing sanctions against the North Koreans if they refused. Japan's position was based partially on its knowledge of Pyongyang's erratic behavior and partly on the premise that the home islands were probably the first targets of any North Korean retaliation. Murayama again apologized to Korea for Japan's conduct during the World War II. A poison gas attack in Matsumoto in June killed seven and injured 200. In 15 May 1995, another terrorist poison gas attack in the Tokyo subway system killed 12 and injured at least five thousand more. A religious cult (*Aum*) was charged in the incidents after canisters of the gas were found in its headquarters. Several cult members confessed to the first attack and to other crimes as well. The cult was subsequently outlawed. On 9 June 1995, the lower house of the Diet passed a resolution announcing its "deep remorse" for its acts of aggression in World War II. On 29 September, however, three U.S. servicemen were charged in the abduction and rape of an Okinawan child, forcing the United States to issue its own apology to the Japanese people.

Reading: Daikichi Irokawa, *The Age of Hirohito: In Search of Modern Japan* (1995); Michael Schaller, *The American Occupation of Japan: The Origins of the Cold War in Asia* (1987); Mikiso Hane, *Eastern Phoenix: Japan since 1945* (1996).

Japanese Red Army (JRA). The group was founded by Takaya Shiomi, a former Kyoto University student, and was initially composed of disaffected communist student groups. Shiomi was arrested in 1970, thereby leaving the JRA leaderless. The leader of the group was Fusako Shigenobu, who was also known as Marian Fusako Okudaira or as "Miss Yuki." The JRA was reformed in 1971 and was headquartered in Lebanon. Its membership was estimated at no more than 25–30 active terrorists and an overall membership of no more than 70. The JRA operated in Western Europe, the Middle East and Asia and was sponsored by the Popular Front for the Liberation of Palestine (PFLP). It was Marxist-Leninist in its orientation. The JRA was also known as *Nippon Sekigun* and *Nihon Sekigun.* In all, the JRA probably never had more than 100 sympathizers in Japan who gave some financial assistance to the group. The JRA carried out numerous terrorist attacks between 1972 and 1977, most notably the Lod Airport massacre in May 1972, in which three JRA gunmen killed 26 people. This attack was carried out for the PFLP. Although the JRA conducted its own attacks, it usually coordinated its activities with the PFLP. After 1977, the JRA claimed no credit for terrorist attacks, but a number of its members have been linked to other terrorist activities linked to other groups. In 1981 Shigenobu renounced the use of terrorism by the JRA. As late as 1988, however, JRA members have been linked to attacks carried out in the name of the Anti-Imperialist International Brigades (AIIB), which claimed responibility for attacks on US embassies in Jakarta (1986), Rome (1987) and Madrid (1988). Most of JRA's members live in Lebanon. *Reading:* William R. Farrell, *Blood and Rage: The Story of the Japanese Red Army* (1990).

Jaruzelski, Wojciech Witold. (b. 6 July 1923, Kurow, Lublin, Poland) Born the only son of a cavalry officer and, later, estate administrator, Jaruzelski studied at a Catholic college in Bielany, a Warsaw suburb. During World War II, the Jaruzelski family was caught by the invading Red Army, and young Jaruzelski was shipped off to the Soviet Union (Kazakhstan), where he was put to work in a coal mine. In 1943, he joined the Polish (Red) Army and attended the Soviet cadet academy in Ryazan. He fought in the Vistula campaign and at the Magnuszevo bridgehead and then took part in the liberation of Poland. After World War II, Jaruzelski attended the Plish Higher Infantry School and the General Staff Academy. He was promoted to brigadier general in 1956 and became chief of the Central Political Administration in 1960 (served until 1965). In 1962, he was appointed to the post of deputy minister of defense, a post he held until 1968. In 1965, he was appointed chief of the general staff. In March 1968, Jaruzelski became minister of defense. Jaruzelski joined the Polish communist party in 1947. He became a member of the Central Committee in 1964, was elected to the Politburo in 1971 and was reelected in 1975 and 1981. After serious rioting in 1970, the Gomulka (qv) government fell in Poland, and

Edward Gierek (qv) became party secretary. After the formation of the Solidarity movement, Gierek resigned and was replaced by Stanislaw Kania. In 1981, Kania resigned and was replaced by Jaruzelski. Jaruzelski's first act was to ban Solidarity and all other groups not under strict communist control. Although Jaruzelski gave up his post as prime minister (given to Zbigniew Messner), he remained first secretary of the Party and chairman of the Council of State. When the communist bloc began to disintegrate, the communist government (Messner) in Poland resigned and a more conciliatory was one put in its place. Solidarity was restored (5 April 1989) and won the majority of the available seats in a parliamentary election in July 1989. Jarezulski was elected president, even though communist attempts to form a new government failed. A member of Solidarity, Tadeusz Mazowiecki, became the first noncommunist prime minister in over 40 years. Jaruzelski remained in office until 22 December 1990, when he was replaced by his duly elected successor Lech Walesa (qv). Some Polish specialists say that Jaruzelski's place in history is not yet completely visible because it was Jaruzelski, more than anyone else, who held the Polish people to a line, albeit an unpopular one, that probably prevented an invasion of Soviet forces on at least two occasions during his tenure. Reading: Leopold Babedz, ed., *Poland under Jaruzelski: A Comprehensive Sourcebook on Poland during and after Martial Law* (1984); Lynn Berry, *Wojciech Jaruzelski* (1990).

Java. *See* Indonesia.

Jawara, Sir Dawda Kairaba. (b. 16 May 1924, Barajally, The Gambia) Jawara received his early education in Christian schools in Gambia. He later studied veterinary science at Achimoto College in Ghana and veterinary surgery at the University of Glasgow (Scotland). In 1959 he entered politics and helped establish the People's Progressive Party. He was appointed minister of education in 1960–1961 and prime minister in 1962. Britain's Queen Elizabeth II knighted Jawara in 1966 for his leadership in forming the human rights program for the Organization of African Unity. After The Gambia received its independence, he remained in office until 1970, when the new republic was proclaimed. Jawara became its first president. On 30 July 1981, an attempted leftist coup led by socialist Kukli Samba (qv) took place against Jawara's government. Jawara, who was in London at the time, asked for and got Senegalese support. Senegalese troops crossed into Gambia and order was restored, but not without considerable bloodshed. Jawara soon thereafter signed a protocol that would have linked Gambia and Senegal; the plan eventually came to nothing. In 1992, Jawara remained in office and won reelection (29 April) to his fifth term by over 58 percent of the vote, his party winning 25 of the 36 representative seats. He was ousted from office on 22 July 1994 by an army coup led by Lieutenant Yahya Jammeh. Jawara and his family were given safe passage to Senegal aboard a U.S. warship amid rumors that the U.S. had a hand in the coup.

Jayawardene, J(unius) R(ichard). (b. 17 September 1906, Colombo, Ceylon) Born a Christian, and later converted to Buddhism, Jayawardene, the son of a supreme court judge, studied law at the University of Ceylon and established himself as a barrister until 1943. Before that, in 1938, he joined the Ceylon National

Congress, which, in 1946, he helped form into the United National Party (UNP). In 1943, Jayawardene was elected to the State Council, and in 1948 he was appointed minister of finance. In 1950, Jayawardene coauthored the basic documents that were accepted (1951) as the Colombo Plan (qv). He worked at the ministerial level through several UNP administrations; in 1973 he became party leader. In July 1977, he was overwhelmingly elected prime minister of Sri Lanka. During the campaign, Jayawardene moved his party to the left, putting a definite socialist spin on what had been a capitalist party program. Within weeks of his election, Jayawardene was faced with a wave of Sinhalese-Tamil (qv) violence, which left 100 dead and thousands homeless. In 1978, using a plan he had devised and gotten through the legislative process, Jayawardene was elected president. It was not until 1983, however, that he faced his most serious test as president. In mid-1983, the hostility between the Buddhist Sinhalese and Hindu Tamil populations erupted into violent rioting; at least 375 Tamils were killed, although some sources put the number at 2,000. At issue was the Tamil demand for a separate state within some form of loose confederation, if necessary, with Sri Lanka. At about this time, India, with its large Tamil population, injected itself into the affair. Even though Jayawardene had rejected the Tamil demand, he did accept an all-party consensus before proceeding further. This process failed. and by 1987 violence had increased and there was a threat of Indian intervention on the side of the Hindu Tamil minority. When Jayawardene reached an accord with India's Rajiv Gandhi (qv), it was roundly criticized by his own government and by the Buddhist Sinhalese population. On top of all of this, Jayawardene was faced with the terrorist problem posed by a small Sinhalese group dedicated to the his overthrow. The group had been successful in carrying out the murders of several top government officials. Various levels of violence continued throughout the remainder of Jayawardene's tenure. In December 1988, Jayawardene lost to Prime Minister Ranasinghe Premadasa. The inauguration took place on 2 January 1989. However, the violence continued.

Jebel Druze Tribesmen. *See* Syria.

Jebel Libni. *See* Jordan.

Jeddah. *See* Saudi Arabia.

Jedid (Jadid), Salal. On 23 February 1966, the moderate Syrian Baath government of Premier Salal at-Bitar, in office since January, was overthrown by a radical Baathist left-wing coup led by Major General Salal Jedid. Nureddin al-Atassi (qv) was installed as president, and Salal Jedid became assistant secretary-general of the Baath Party.

Jenin (Janin). *See* Israel.

Jerash (Jarash). *See* Jordan.

Jericho (Ariha, Yeriho). *See* Israel.

Jerusalem. *See* Israel.

Jessore. *See* East Pakistan and Pakistan.

Jiang Qing (Chiang Ch'ing). (b. 1914, Zhucheng, Shantung Province) Born the daughter of a carpenter, Jiang Qing studied drama and literature at Qingdao

University. Following graduation, she entered the theater and films in Shanghai. While at the university, she embraced communism and, in 1936, studied Marxist-Leninist theory at the Chinese Communist Party headquarters in Yenan. There she met and later (1939) became the third wife of Mao Tse-tung (Mao Zedong) (qv). At the communist takeover of power in China, she became a member of the Ministry of Culture (1950–1954) and was a leader in the "Cultural Revolution" (1965–1969) that shook the coutry to its foundations. In 1969, Jiang Qing was elected to the the the Politburo, where she remained until Mao's death in 1976. She was arrested as a member of the notorious "Gang of Four" (qv), who were accused of treason in fomenting insurrection. She was expelled from the Communist Party; she tried in 1980 on a number of charges and sentenced to death. The sentence was later suspended.

Jidda. *See* Saudi Arabia.

Jihad. By definition, *Jihad* means a Muslim holy war against infidels or a crusade. To carry out *Jihad* is a duty imposed by Muslim law as a means of spreading Islam. Only religious ideals and purposes are sufficient enough to call for *Jihad*; diplomacy may be applied for other Islamic purposes. There are four levels of *Jihad*: by heart, by tongue, by hand, and by sword. In *Jihad*, the sword is only to be raised against nonbelievers. Both Christians and Jews believe in God; hence, they are not to be treated as nonbelievers. The use of the term *Jihad* appears to be incongruous in the present situation in the Middle East, although scholars differ in their opinions on this point. Non-Muslims who are not nonbelievers are to be offered the opportunity to embrace Islam, to pay a tariff (*jizya*) or to fight on the same footing as other nonbelievers, that is, not in Muslim Arab military units. In the present situation in the Middle East, a call for *Jihad* against Israel was made at a meeting of the Arab League foreign ministers on 25–26 August 1969. On 12 March 1979, the Muslim Liberation Front declared a holy war (*Jihad*) against the Muslim regime of Premier Nur Mohammed Taraki (qv). In October 1980, Muammar Qaddafi called a *Jihad* to "liberate" Mecca, Islam's holiest place, from Saudi Arabia, a strict Muslim country. On 25–28 January 1981, an Islamic summit conference held at Taif, near Mecca, in Saudi Arabia, called for *Jihad* to recover lands taken by Israel. Given the definition of *Jihad*, its present-day use by Muslims seems out of place.

Jiménez, Marcos Pérez. In a November 1948 military coup, the government of Venezuela was overthrown by Lieutenant Colonel Carlos Delgado Chalbaud (qv) and Major Marcos Pérez Jiménez. On 13 November 1950, Carlos Delgado Chalbaud was assassinated under mysterious circumstances. At that point, Pérez Jiménez became the new strongman in Venezuela. A typical dictatorship followed, with rampant disregard for human rights and with an equal drive toward personal enrichment and corruption. An election was held in January 1953, the results of which were so tainted that the National Assembly was forced to name Pérez Jiménez as provisional president. On 31 December 1957 a major revolt started against the policies of the dictator. Pérez Jiménez was able to crush the early rioting, but another military coup, this time led by Admiral Wolfgang Larrazábal (qv), took the country on 23 January 1958. Larrazábal ran the country for a year until an open election gave the presidency to Rómulo Betancourt (qv).

Jinja. *See* Uganda.

Jinnah, Mohammed Ali. On 15 August 1947, the Dominion of Pakistan was proclaimed. Mohammed Ali Jinnah was appointed governor-general. Jinnah's personal integrity and the work of his colleague, Liaqat Ali Khan (qv), are said to be responsible for holding East and West Pakistan together as long as the two were joined. Jinnah died in September 1948. Liaqat Ali Khan became the sole leader of the badly divided country. His assassination in October 1951 ended any hope of keeping the two Pakistans together and caused such a decline in West Pakistan that a military coup was forthcoming. *See* Pakistan.

Jiu Valley. *See* Romania.

Jogjakarta. *See* Indonesia.

Johannesburg. *See* South Africa.

Johannesson, Olafur. The premier of Iceland in 1973, Johannesson headed the government that defied Great Britain during the Cod War (qv), a conflict over Iceland's imposition of a 50-mile fishing limit around the island nation. In retaliation for British warships escorting fishing craft operating in those waters, Johannesson banned (20 May 1974) all British military flights from using the NATO base at Keflavik. In October, Johannesson went to London, where a preliminary agreement was reached that helped defuse the situation. Johannesson became premier on 14 July 1971 as a member of the Liberal Left coalition and left office on 27 August 1974, when the Independence party won a major victory at the polls.

John Paul II. On 13 May 1981, Pope John Paul II, the head of the Roman Catholic Church, was shot by Mehmet Ali Agca, a Turkish terrorist possibly working for Bulgaria, during a ceremony in Saint Peter's Square in Rome. Pope John Paul was invalided until 7 October, when he was able to resume some of his duties. *See* Ali-Agca.

Johnson, Louis A. Appointed secretary of defense by President Truman (qv) in 1949 to replace James V. Forrestal, Lohson, during his one-year tenure, nearly destroyed the military strength of the United States through his "all fat and no meat" budget-cutting policies. After he was replaced as secretary of defense by George C. Marshall, Johnson returned to the practice of law. He died in Washington, DC in 1966 at age 75.

Johnson, Lyndon B. (b. 27 August 1908, Stonewall, Texas—d. 22 January 1973, San Antonio, Texas) Born on a worn-out farm in southwest Texas, Johnson spent his youth hitchhiking around the country doing odd jobs. He later trained to be a teacher at Southwest Texas State Teachers College. He taught at Sam Houston High School in Houston and worked as a volunteer in state politics. In 1932, he was appointed legislative assistant to Congressman Richard Kleberg. In Washington, Johnson was befriended by Sam Rayburn, who later became the Speaker of the House of Representatives. From 1935 until 1937, Johnson served as director of the National Youth Administration and subsequently ran for Congress. Franklin Roosevelt became his sponsor, and Johnson enjoyed the next decade as a Congressman from the 10th District of Texas. He was narrowly elected to the Senate in 1948 and remained there for the next 12 years. He was elected Democratic Whip in 1951. He became the majority leader in 1955. In 1960, he joined the Democratic ticket as the vice-presidential candidate alongside John F. Kennedy (qv). When Kennedy was assassinated in Dallas, Texas, Johnson was sworn in as the 36th president of the United States. He was elected to the office in November 1964, at the head of his own ticket, primarily on the basis of his "Great Society" domestic reform program. The increased U.S. military participation in Southeast Asia soon eroded much of his popular support, and he announced in March 1968 that he would not run for reelection. He returned to Texas to write his memoires and run his ranch in January 1969. He died of a heart attack at age 65. *Reading:* Irving Bernstein, *Guns or Butter: The Presidency of Lyndon Johnson* (1996); Anthony Kaye, *Lyndon B. Johnson* (1988).

Joint Chiefs of Staff (JCS) (U.S.). In 1942, President Roosevelt established a committee of American military staff officers to coordinate the wartime operational strategy of the armed services. Among the first members of the JCS were General George C. Marshall (qv), Admiral Ernest J. King, General Henry "Hap" Arnold, and Admiral William D. Leahy, the president's military assistant, presiding. The JCS was then established as the American component of the Combined Chiefs of Staff, which was a joint U.S.-British staff that prepared and implemented Allied strategy. Before the JCS came into existence a Joint Army-Navy Board already existed that was supposed to limit the service rivalries that often spilled over into the political and budgetary arenas. Neither the Joint Board nor the JCS was able to overcome the problem completely. Joint planning did assist in the successful outcome of World War II. The JCS was not quite so successful in Korea or Vietnam, primarily because of political, that is, White House interference in military operations. The JCS are the princial advisers to the president, the secretary of defense and the National Security Council. After World War II, the JCS received statutory authority and a full-time staff. General Omar N. Bradley became the first chairman of the joint chiefs on 16 August 1949. To date, 13 officers have served in that capacity, with Army General John Shalikashvili replacing Army General Colin L. Powell on 1 October 1993.

Jolo Island. *See* Philippines.

Jonathan, Leabua. On 30 January 1970, Prime Minister Chief Leabua Jonathan overthrew King Moshoeshoe II (qv) of Lesotho. When he seized power, Jonathan also arrested his principal rival, Ntsu Mokhehle, and a number of his supporters. The Labor government in Great Britain immediately cut aid to the country, although Jonathan promised new elections and a new constitution that would have barred communist activity. Moshoeshoe went into exile on 31 March, but he was allowed to return on 4 December 1971 and was restored to his throne, after promising to avoid any interference in parliamentary elections. Jonathan's seizure of power came three days after the first general elections held in Lesotho were found to be tainted by fraud, intimidation and even murder on the part of the communist-controlled opposition led by Mokhehle.

Jones, Herbert. Lieutenant Colonel Herbert Jones, known to his men as "H" and in command of the Second Battalion, Paratroop Regiment, was killed in action (KIA) in front of Darwin Hill along with 16 of his men during twelve hours of fighting on 28 May 1982, near Goose Green, Falkland Islands (qv). The attack on Goose Green and Darwin had been launched at 2 A.M. (0200 hours). Jones was killed at approximately 10:30 A.M. (1030 hours) in an assault on the hill's trench system. The message "Sunray is down" was sent to all units, and the second in command, Major Chris Keeble, took over the battalion and successfully completed the mission. The Argentine defenders lost 234 killed, 120 wounded and 1,400 captured. The excessive casualties were the result of the Argentinian command showing the white flag of surrender and then opening fire on the advancing British troops, killing another officer and two enlisted men.

Jordan. More properly the Hashemite Kingdom of Jordan, this Middle East Arab state encompasses the former British-mandated Transjordan. It is bordered on the north by Syria, on the northeast by Iraq, on the southeast and south by Saudi Arabia and on the west by Israel, from which it is separated by the Jordan River. At its southern tip, where it touches the Gulf of Aqaba (qv), Jordan faces Egypt. The capital is Amman. Jordan was conquered by the Arabs in the seventh century A.D. and by the Ottomans in the sixteenth century. The Turks held the region until the end of World War I. In 1920, the British Mandate for Palestine (now Israel west of the Jordan River) included the lands of Transjordan. The king of Hejaz's son, Abdullah, was installed as emir in 1921. After World War II, an independent kingdom was proclaimed on 22 March 1946. During the 1948 Israeli War of Independence, Transjordanian troops occupied East Jerusalem (qv) and the West Bank region of the Jordan River. On 2 June 1949, the Hasemite Kingdom of Jordan composed of Transjordan and Arab Palestine was proclaimed at Amman. On 24 April 1950, Arab Palestine was incorporated into Jordan amid the protests of most of the Arab League (qv). On 20 July 1951, King Abdullah was assassinated by a follower of the former Mufti of Jerusalem, Haj Amin al-Husaini (qv). The mentally ill Emir Talal (qv) was crowned king on 5 September. Parliament declared Talal unfit to serve on 11 August 1952 and placed the 17-year-old Prince Hussein (Husain ibn Talal) (qv) on the throne. Hussein took the crown on 2 May 1953. Border clashes between Israel and Jordan became commonplace during this period even though a joint Jordan-Israeli armistice commission existed. When the Jordanian cabinet rejected an Anglo-American peace offer, a new cabinet was installed (2 May 1954). On 6 July 1954, a settlement was reported on sharing the waters of the Jordan River by Israel, Syria, Lebanon and Jordan. When Jordan indicated it would join the Baghdad Pact (qv) (19 December 1955), rioting broke out in Amman. A new government, installed in January 1956, stated its opposition to joining the Baghdad Pact. In a turnabout, Hussein dismissed the British commander of the Arab Legion (qv), General John B. Glubb (qv) Pasha, on 2 March 1956 after accusing Glubb of failing to prepare for an Israeli attack. Yet, when the Arab League met a few days later to draw up joint military action plans against Israel, Jordan refused to attend. Jordan disbanded the Arab Legion in May 1956 and merged its troops into the Jordanian army. Meanwhile, border tensions with Israel increased as Nasser's (qv) rise to power in Egypt caused reverberations in Jordan; by August 1956, serious border clashes were taking place on a regular basis. In October, Jordan took its case before the United Nations, where it accused Israel of aggression. On 22 October, an anti-Western, pro-Nasser government was elected based in part on the continued border clashes with Israel. On 29 October, Israel opened a full-scale attack against Egyptian positions in the Sinai. Neither Jordan nor the Arab League participated in the fighting except in a continuation of the border skirmishes. In the spring of 1957, Jordan purged its government and armed forces of pro-Nasser elements. In May, Great Britain terminated its 1948 alliance with Jordan and removed its forces from Jordanian territory (13 July). When the United States offered aid to Jordan, Syria warned Jordan it would retaliate. Jordan responded by accusing Syria of meddling in its affairs. In February 1958, Jordan merged with Iraq as the Arab Federation, with Iraq's King Faisal II (qv) to rule the new state. In the UN, the USSR continually vetoed all attempts to settle the crises in Jordan and Lebanon. When Faisal was assassinated in Iraq on 14 July 1958, Jordan's Hussein assumed the leadership of the Arab Federation and asked the U.S. and Great Britain to send troops. Britain responded with airborne forces (17 July) (withdrawn 29 October). The Arab Federation effectively ceased to exist when Iraq was declared a republic and sided with the United Arab Republic (qv). On 4 April 1959, the Arab League denounced the procommunist government in Iraq. Jordan and several other member states had boycotted the meeting. The premier of Jordan, Hazza al-Mazali, and 11 others were killed in a bomb attack on 29 August. On 29 August 1962, Jordan merged its armed forces with those of Saudi Arabia. In July 1966, Jordan suspended relations with the Palestine Liberation Organization (PLO) (qv). Attacks along the Jordan-Israel border continued; many of the attacks on Israel were carried out by PLO forces. In December 1966, an Arab League plan was put forward in which Saudi and Iraqi forces would be placed in Jordan to help protect against Israeli attacks. The complicated formula worked out for the plan's implementation doomed it from the start. On 14 May 1967, Egypt moved additional forces into the Sinai and announced it was ready to fight. Jordan mobilized, along with most other Arab states. Egypt then attacked into Israeli territory beginning the Arab-Israeli War of 1967. On 5 June, Israeli forces opened a campaign to clear East Jerusalem of Jordanian forces. Within a few days all of Jerusalem and most of the West Bank were in Israeli hands. The next day, 6 June, Israeli intelligence sources released a tape of a telephone conversation in which King Hussein and Nasser decided to blame the United States for the Middle East situation. Many Arab nations, including Egypt, broke relations with the U.S. as a result. King Hussein announced on 6 November that he was ready to recognize Israel if the boundary question could be settled. But the border clashes went on, with both sides blaming the other, but the real culprit, the PLO, escaping much of the wrath. On 21 March 1968, Israel attacked into Jordan, striking the *Fatah* terrorist training center at Kerama. Having completed their mission, the Israelis withdrew in good order, although the Jordanians declared they had been routed. The UN subsequently condemned Israel for the raid (24 March). In January 1969, as part of a trade deal with the Soviet Union, France announced it had placed an embargo on the sale of weapons in the Middle East, including Jordan. On 6 February 1969, PLO leader Yasser Arafat announced he was shifting his headquarters from bases in Syria and the UAR into Jordan. The increased guerrilla activity that resulted brought heavy military reaction from Israel and more attacks into Jordan, this time hitting not only terrorist training camps but Jordanian targets as well, as when they wrecked the East Ghor Canal irrigation project on 23 June. Jordan was now a part of an undeclared war that occupied most of the early 1970s. On 2 August, Syrian forces were reported in Jordan. By February 1970, Jordan was tiring of the PLO. Serious fighting broke out in and around Amman between Jordanian troops and Palestinian commandos after the PLO refused a government order to disarm. Only when other Arab nations threatened intervention did the fighting stop. In April, violent anti-American demonstrations occurred in Amman. The U.S. cancelled a visit by Under Secretary of State Joseph Sisco, and Jordan ordered the U.S. ambassador out of the country. On 23 April, Pakistan acknowledged it had troops in Jordan to help fight the Israelis. In June, renewed fighting between the Jordanian army and the PLO caused heavy casualties on both sides. Once again, the threat of Arab intervention brought about a cease-fire. On 10 June, when the cease-fire went into effect, the U.S. military attache in Amman, Major Robert Perry, was assassinated by Palestinian terrorists. Jordan once again flip-flopped and accepted a US peace proposal, even though all other Arab countries rejected the plan. Through all of this, Israel kept up its reprisal attacks against PLO terrorist bases in Jordan, and the fighting continued between the army and the terrorists. On 1 September, King Hussein narrowly missed death in an assassination attempt. Even though another cease-fire was arranged, the Palestinians continued their attacks within Jordan. On 15 September, King Hussein put a military government in power and moved to rid his lands of the PLO. Heavy fighting followed in which the Syrians invaded Jordan in support of the PLO. Again, an Arab League cease-fire was imposed on 27 September. This did not end the fighting, however, and the rest of 1970 and early 1971 witnessed more clashes. On 4 April 1971, the PLO announced it would adhere to the 1970 peace agreement, and PLO forces began withdrawing from Amman (13 April). Even so, fighting continued, and once again the Jordanian army moved in force to crush further resistance. By 19 July, the PLO and the bulk of the Palestinian refugees had fled into Syria; 2,000 PLO fighters had been captured. On the 18th, the Iraqi government asked Amman to withdraw its ambassador and closed its border with Jordan. The Arab League condemned Jordan on 30 April and pledged support to the PLO. On 12 August, Syria severed diplomatic relations with Jordan because of its crackdown on the PLO. The Jordanian prime minister, Wasfi al-Tal (qv), was assassinated by Palestinian Black September (qv) terrorists while attending an Arab League meeting in Cairo. An attempt on the life of the Jordanian ambassador by Black September terrorists failed in

London on 15 December; another attempt, this time on the Jordanian ambassador in Geneva, also failed (16 December). On 15 March 1972, Jordan announced a plan for a Palestinian state on the West Bank and in Gaza as a part of the United Arab Kingdom. Israel, as expected, rejected the plan, but so did the PLO and several other Arab states, who would be satisfied with nothing less than the destruction of Israel and the restoration of Palestine. Egypt broke diplomatic relations with Jordan over the plan. In early November, a Libyan plan to assassinate King Hussein was foiled. At a meeting of the Arab League on 27–31 January 1973, Jordan agreed to reopen the Jordanian front against Israel after all present bowed to the PLO for more action. On 17 July, Jordan broke diplomatic relations with Tunisia after President Habib Bourguiba demanded the abdication of King Hussein and the establishment of a Palestinian state on both banks of the Jordan. After selecting 6 October as the date for the new invasion of Israel, Egypt restored diplomatic relations with Jordan. In preparation for the forthcoming war, Hussein granted amnesty to 1,500 political prisoners on 18 September. On 6 October 1973, the Yom Kippur War began. The Jordanians participated in the fighting but only to a limited extent. The upshot of that participation was a postwar statement by Israel that it would not give up the West Bank, taken in an earlier war. The Arab League, meeting in Morocco, then put up $2.35 billion to help defend Egypt, Syria and Jordan. On 5 January 1975, Jordan and the PLO pledged mutual constraint in the future. Syria and Jordan formed a joint supreme command to coordinate political and defense matters on 22 August 1975. In November 1978, Amman and the PLO opened their first talks in six years. Jordan, along with 18 other Arab League countries, broke diplomatic relations with Egypt (4 June 1980) after the signing of the Camp David Accords (qv). During the Iran-Iraq War in 1980 Jordan supported Iraq, furnishing food and other supplies to Baghdad. In late November 1980, Jordan voiced concern because Syria had deployed 20,000 troops and 400 tanks along the common border. On 2 December, intelligence reports placed 30,000 Syrian troops on Jordan's border. In February 1981, Jordan withdrew its forces from a joint border post with Syria near the town of Naharayim and called home its ambassador in Damascus for consultations. Amman also abrogated a six-year-old trade and customs agreement with Syria. In November, the government announced it was buying $2 million worth of Soviet-built SA-7 (Grail) shoulder-fired antiaircraft missiles. In January 1982, King Hussein asked for 2,000 volunteers to fight alongside Iraq against the Iranians in a move Hussein called the "arabization" of the war. The first group of volunteers reached the front in March, in what was called the Yarmouk Brigade. On 1 September, U.S. president Ronald Reagan called for self-determination for the Palestinians on the West Bank in association with Jordan. Israel immediately rejected the plan. The PLO said (12 October) it was ready to accept the plan if it would lead to an independent Palestinian state. On 24 March 1984 a bomb was detonated in the parking lot of the Intercontinental Hotel. A second bomb was found and disarmed before it could explode. Two people were injured in the attack. In September, Jordan reestablished diplomatic relations with Egypt. A high-ranking PLO official, Fahd Kawasmeh (qv), was assassinated in Jordan by Black September terrorists. In February 1985, Hussein and PLO leader Arafat announced they had reached an agreement for peace in the Middle East. A plan was unveiled on 27 February for Israeli meetings in Washington with Jordanian and PLO representatives. When the slate of Palestinian attendees representatives was presented in July, Israel rejected it. In September, Jordan signed a multimillion pound arms deal with Great Britain. On 21 October, Israel announced it was ready to end the fighting with Jordan. Jordan announced it had restored diplomatic relations with Syria after a four-year break. Two days later, the US Senate ordered a halt to arms shipments to Jordan, the halt to last until 1 March 1986. In accordance with the 1974 Arab League agreement that the PLO was the sole spokesman for Palestinian interests, Jordan severed its legal and administrative ties with the Israeli held West Bank in 1988. During Operation Desert Shield/Storm in the Persian Gulf in 1990–1991, Jordan actively supported Iraq. On 14 September 1993, Jordan and Israel signed an accord designed to lead to a peace treaty. The following day, 15 September, the U.S. released grant aid money that had been frozen since 1992. The actual Jordan-Israel peace treaty was signed on 26 October 1994. As a part of the treaty King Hussein was declared the keeper of the holy places in Jerusalem, thereby maintaining Muslim control over those places so designated. The settlement of the Israeli problem opened a number of diplomatic avenues to Jordan. In 1995, relations were restored with Saudi Arabia after four years, and friendly relations again occurred with the United States. Jordan also turned its back on Iraq, giving asylum to two of Saddam's sons-in-law and suggesting that anti-Saddam groups, including the Kurds, unite against their common foe. *Reading:* Ilan Pappe, *Britain and the Arab-Israeli Conflict, 1948–51* (1988); Robert Satloff, *From Abdullah to Hussein: Jordan in Transition* (1994); Martin Sicker, *Between Hasemites and Zionists: The Struggle for Palestine, 1908–1988* (1989); Kamal Salibi, *A Modern History of Jordan* (1993).

Jordan River. *See* Israel and Jordan.

Jordan Valley. *See* Jordan.

Joyabaj. *See* Guatemala.

Joyce, William. Known as "Lord Haw Haw" and a German propagandist during World War II, Joyce, a British subject, was hanged for treason in London's Wandsworth Prison on 3 January 1946.

Juan Carlos. *See* Spain.

Jufair. *See* Bahrain.

Jumblatt, Kamal. In March 1976, Kamal Jumblatt, the leader of leftist Druse forces in Lebanon, was prevented from attacking the town of Baabda by the presence of Syrian troops. On 16 March 1977, Jumblatt was assassinated by unknown gunmen. A wave of attacks on Lebanese Christian villages followed his murder.

Juniyah. *See* Lebanon.

Justice Commandos for the Armenian Genocide (JCAG). Also known as the Armenian Revolutionary Army (ARA), the right-wing JCAG was formed in 1975. The size and leadership of the group is unknown, but it is known to support the Basque ETA (qv) and Turkish Kurd groups. The group also has ties to the Dashnaq political party in Armenia. Before the collapse of the Soviet Union, the JCAG was on record as opposing any ties with the Armenian Soviet Socialist Republic of the USSR, but rather favored an independent nation structured on a European social democratic political system. The JCAG was supported by the Armenian community abroad and directed its actions against Turkish officials and facilities worldwide. Its favorite tactic was the use of ambush near automobiles. In 1983, the term JCAG fell from use, and ARA became the favored means of identification.

Juxton-Smith, Andrew T. On 23 March 1967, a military coup led by Lieutenant Colonel Andrew T. Juxton-Smith and Major Charles Smith (qv) successfully overthrew the government of the former British colony of Sierra Leone. On 25 January 1968, Juxton-Smith led a second coup that ousted the military junta of which he had been a part. Juxton-Smith's regime was in turn overthrown by a group of noncommissioned officers on 18 April 1968, in what has become known as the "Sergeants' Coup."

K

Kabir Desert (Desert of Salt). A desert area (*Dasht e Kavir*) located approximately 200 miles southeast of Tehran, Iran. On 24 April 1980 the Kabir Desert played a part in the abortive military operation by the United States to rescue American hostages held in the U.S. embassy in Tehran. Eight U.S. "Sea Stallion" helicopters launched from the *USS Nimitz* in the Gulf of Oman landed at Posht-a-Badam (Desert One) in the first phase of the operation. One hundred eighty men were in the rescue force. Only five of the helicopters were able to complete the flight. As there was no provision made for backup helicopters, President Jimmy Carter, in direct contact with the ground force, aborted the mission. In the preparation for departure, one of the Sea Stallions crashed into a C-130 transport, killing eight Americans. The rest of the force escaped, in one of the most ineptly planned and executed military operations in modern military history.

Kabrikha. *See* Lebanon.

Kabul (Kabol). The capital and largest city in Afghanistan, Kabul is located 180 miles west of Peshawar, Pakistan. The city lies on the Kabul River at a point where the main approaches from the Kyber Pass into Pakistan and India intersect with the passes from the Hindu Kush in the north and Kandahar and Gerdez in the south. Formerly a walled city, Kabul was invaded in 656 by Arabs who took control of it from its Persian-speaking and Parthan populace. Islam was not established there until the sixteenth century, however, until Babur became master in 1504. From 1526 until 1738 it was a provincial capital of the Mongol Empire. In 1747, with the murder of Nadir Shah, Kabul became the a part of the new Afghanistan under Ahmad Shah, the founder of the country, and became its capital in 1773. The British occupied Kabul from 1839 to 1842 and from 1879 to 1880, during the First and Second Afghan Wars. In more modern times, Kabul has been the scene of renewed conflict. On 14 February 1979, Adolph Dubs (qv), the United States ambassador to Afghanistan, was killed in the crossfire of a Soviet-engineered attempt to rescue a group of hostages held in a Kabul hotel. Dubs had been kidnapped from his car by four right-wing Muslim terrorists and was being held in the hotel when the police stormed the building. On 2 August 1979, an Afghan army uprising in Kabul prompted an increase in the Soviet military presence in the city to nearly 4,000 troops. Afghan army units loyal to the government and armed with modern Soviet arms crushed the mutiny. Immediately afterward, Soviet army general I. G. Pavlovski (qv), the USSR's deputy minister of defense and chief of ground forces and the man who commanded the 1968 Soviet invasion of Czechoslovakia, arrived in Kabul for a personal assessment of the situation. On 14–15 September, a coup attempt against the government and Hafizullah Amin (qv) took place. The Soviet ambassador in Kabul was involved, and the coup was supported by 400 Soviet Spetnaz (Commando) troops. The coup failed, and Amin seized power. Amin was murdered on 27 December at the Darulaman Palace outside Kabul. By 28 December, Soviet troops, who had begun a full-scale invasion of Afghanistan, had complete control of Kabul (*see* Afghanistan). By 6 January 1980, fighting had intensified in and around Kabul, and the Soviet forces that had occupied the city were dispersed around its environs. Soviet casualties in and around Kabul began to mount. The city was patrolled by Soviet troops while the new BabrakKarmal (qv) government was executing hundreds, if not thousands, of political opponents in the city and the countryside. On 21 February a general strike paralyzed Kabul. At least 300 were killed in disturbances associated with the strike. On 27 February, the government began making mass arrests in an attempt to stop the strikes. Anti-Soviet rioting led by anti-Marxist students and teachers broke out in Kabul in April 1980. The police opened fire on the demonstrators, and Soviet helicopter gunships attacked Kabul University. More than 200 were killed in the April fighting. Again, in May, thousands of Afghans took to the streets to protest the Soviet invasion and the oppressive government.On 29 June 1980, Afghan troops in a compound just outside Kabul mutinied. At least ten Soviet soldiers were killed and a number of their tanks destroyed in the fighting that followed. On 17 August, nearly 1,200 Afghans were killed when Soviet aircraft attacked a religious celebration of the end of Ramadan on the outskirts of the city. That same day, Afghan *mujahideen* (freedom fighters) attacked an airbase near Kabul and killed 13 Soviet soldiers. Four others were captured; at least 22 Afghan pilots and mechanics were also captured. In September, Soviet troops in Kabul clashed with Afghan army units in the city. Persistent reports in November and December indicated the presence of Vietnamese and Cuban troops landing in Kabul to reinforce the Soviet campaign against Afghan rebels. A rebel attack on a meeting of the ruling People's Democratic Party in Kabul on 15 March 1982 killed five party officials. Rocket attacks on Kabul in April 1982 added a new dimension to the Afghan struggle against the Soviets and the government. These attacks continued sporadically for the next several years. By October 1984, the Soviets were forced to send an additional 70,000 troops to Afghanistan to help quell the fighting in and around Kabul. On 17 January 1987, Soviet forces put on a major show of force in Kabul aimed at reducing the factional fighting going on in the government and to warn the rebels. By January 1987, there were signs of a growing discontent among Soviets living and working in Kabul who knew they were not wanted. In January 1988, fighting continued in and around Kabul with no relief in sight. The rebel blockade around the city created severe food and fuel shortages. On 31 January 1989, the U.S. embassy in Kabul closed, but American personnel could not leave the city because of blizzard conditions. On 2 February 1989, the last Soviet troops in Kabul were airlifted out for Tashkent, using aircraft that had been ferrying food into the city from the USSR. On 3 February, the rebel high command announced it would capture Kabul "in weeks, not months." Kabul was placed under martial law by the Afghan government, now without Soviet backing. Senior Afghan officials began sending their families to India and other cities in anticipation of the rebel takeover. United Nations relief supplies were stopped on 13 February because no one was willing to chance flying into Kabul. On 15 February, the rebels launched an all-out attack on the city. The attack failed to capture the city, but it caused the government to declare a state of emergency. Fighting continued in the outskirts into 1990. By 1993, much of Kabul had been devastated by the fighting. On 17 June Gulbuddin Hekmatyar, one of the seven leaders of the resistance, was sworn in as prime minister in the new government (since 1992) of President Burhanuddin Rabbani. *See* Afghanistan.

Kabylien Mountains. *See* Algeria.

Kádár, János. (b. 26 May 1912, Fiume, Hungary—d. 6 Jul 1989, Budapest) Born János Csermanik, Kádár was abandoned by his father at an early age. With his mother, he moved to Budapest, where he became a mechanic. In 1930, he joined the Union of Young Communists and was twice arrested and jailed for party activities. In 1940, he joined the communist underground in the Hungarian resistance and took the name Kádár as his cover. In 1945, when Mátyás Rákosi (qv) was prime minister, he restored the Communist Party in Hungary. Kádár was elected to the Provisional National Assembly and became a member of the Communist Party's politburo. He held several influential government posts during this period. In 1951, when Stalin carried out his last great purge, Kádár was expelled from the party, arrested (April 1951) and charged with treason and given a four year prison sentence. Upon Josef Stalin's (qv) death (1953), he was released in July 1954, through the intercession of Nikita Khrushchev (qv). In 1956, following the Soviet invasion of Hungary, Kádár was appointed secretary general of the Hungarian Communist Party. A few days later, he was installed as head of a new government of Hungary. Among his first acts was the installation of severe repressive measures to reestablish communist control of the country. This task he did well. Among his other accomplishments was his reception by Pope Paul VI at the Vatican on 9 June 1977, in what has been called "goulash communism," which improved Hungary's external relations. He served in the premiership from 1956 until 1958 and from 1961 to 1965. He remained party secretary from 1956 until 1988, when he was moved to the ceremonial post of party president following a bleak economic forecast. Just before his death, he was removed from the party presidency and from his seat on the Central Committee. *Reading:* William Shawcross, *Crime and Compromise:*

Janos Kadar and the Politics of Hungary since the Revolution (1974); Andrew Felkay, *Hungary and the USSR, 1956–1988: Kadar's Political Leadership* (1989).

Kadesh. *See* Israel.

Kaesong. *See* Korea.

Kagera Salient. *See* Tanzania and Uganda.

Kalakhani, Abdul Majid. On 9 June 1980, The Soviet-supported government of Afghanistan's Babrak Karmal (qv) executed ten supporters and aides of the late president, Hafizullah Amin. Among the number were Amin's brother and nephew. Also executed at the same time was rebel leader Abdul Majid Kalakhani.

Kamalpur, East Pakistan. *See* Bangladesh.

Kamaran Island. *See* Yemen.

Kamougue, Wadal Abdel Kader. Vice President of Chad in 1980, Colonel Kamougue's role was peripheral to those of the main contenders, President Goukouni and Hissen Habré (qv), in the civil war that raged in that country. In March 1980, it was Kamougue who requested, without success, military aid from Libya. Kamouque was named president (in October) of the Transitional Government of National Unity (GUNT) Council of State, following Habré's takeover of the government in June 1982. *See* Chad.

Kampala. *See* Uganda.

Kampuchea. *See* Cambodia.

Kandahar. *See* Afghanistan.

Kania, Stanislaw. (b. 8 March 1927, Wrocanka, Poland) Born the son of a farmer, Kania served in the Polish resistance in World War II and joined the Communist Party in April 1945. After working as a district organizer, he was sent to a party indoctrination school, from which he graduated in 1952. He was made an alternate member of the Central Committee in 1964 and became a full member in 1968. He joined the Politburo in 1975. On 6 September 1980, Edward Gierek (qv) was dismissed as the first secretary of the Polish Communist Party. He was replaced by Stanislaw Kania, who had reported on 5 September that Gierek had suffered a serious heart attack and had been hospitalized. Kania's rise to power came just one week after the Kremlin had voiced its disapproval of Gierek's handling of negotiations with the Solidarity Movement. In 1981, Kania had to face the fact that more than one million members of the Polish Communist Party had deserted into the ranks of Solidarity. On 14 August 1981, Kania met with Leonid Brezhnev (qv) in the Crimea. While Kania argued that Poland needed social order, Brezhnev countered that only communist order mattered. On 5 September, at the first national Solidarity congress held near Gdansk, Kania stated that the party was striving for close cooperation with all social and political movements. On 11 September, the Soviet ambassador in Warsaw warned Kania and Polish president Wojciech Jaruzelski (qv) that the situation in Poland had gone too far and that "counterrevolutionary forces are conducting with impunity" a campaign against the USSR. In an attempt to lessen the threat of Soviet force against Poland, Kania resigned on 18 October. On 13 December, martial law was delared in Poland.

Kano. *See* Nigeria.

Kantara (al-Qantarah). *See* Israel.

Kapwepwe, Simon Mwansa. (b. 12 April 1922, Chinsali, Northern Rhodesia—d. 26 January 1980, Zambia) Born a member of the Bemba tribe, Kapwepwe studied to be a teacher at the Anglican mission school in at Lubwa. He then studied journalism in India from 1951 until 1955. While in India he became a believer in Mohandas Gandhi's ideals. Upon his return to Northern Rhodesia he was arrested for possessing subversive literature. He was again arrested in 1959 and spent a year in prison. When Zambia (qv) became independent (1963), Kapwepwe, then a member of the United National Independence Party (UNIP) (since 1960), was appointed minister of agriculture and foreign minister. In 1967 he was elected vice president. In August 1969, during a political crisis, he resigned his office. Although he subsequently withdrew the resignation, he eventually left office. In August 1971, Kapwepwe resigned his cabinet post as minister of local government and culture to form the new United Progressive Party. By September, the government had arrested 75 key members of the UPP, but Kapwepwe was not touched. In December 1971, a series of by-elections were held for seats in the Zambian National Assembly. Kapwepwe won his place by a narrow margin, but other members of his party were not so lucky. On 4 February 1972, President Kenneth Kaunda (qv) banned the UPP following a period of violence in which it was claimed the UPP attempted to isolate the northern province (Bemba area) of Zambia. Kapwepwe and at least 100 other members of the party were arrested and were not released until the January 1973. Kapwepwe refused to join Kaunda's one-party regime. In March 1974, he won a libel suit against the state-run radio and television service and two newspapers who had accused him of having an army trained to overthrow the government. In 1978, Kapwepwe challenged Kaunda for the presidency, but the UNIP changed the rules to say that only Kaunda could be nominated. Simon Kapwepwe died in 1980.

Kapuuo, Clemens. During the traumatic period that preceded the independence of Namibia, at that time called South West Africa, one facet of the UN-engineered cease-fire between South African forces and the South West Africa People's Organization (SWAPO) was a plan for an election to be held, at South African insistence, without UN oversight. The South African choice for the election was Clemens Kapuuo, the leader of the Democratic Turnhalle Alliance. Kapuuo was assassinated on 27 March 1978.

Kapyong. *See* Korea.

Karachi, Kashmir (Pakistan). *See* Kashmir and Pakistan.

Karamanlis, Konstantinos. (b. 1907, Proti, Turkish Macedonia) Born the first of seven children of a schoolteacher, Karamanlis studied law at the University of Athens, graduating in 1932. In 1935, he entered politics and won a seat in the Greek parliament. In 1950, he joined the party of Field Marshal Alexandros

Papagos, which carried all but 61 of the 300 seats in the November 1952 elections. Karamanlis served as the minister of public works in the Papagos administration. Upon Papagos' death in 1955, King Paul appointed Karamanlis prime minister. By July 1963, he had established an impressive record of service, especially in disengaging Greece from further strife over Cyprus. On 11 July 1963, Karamanlis resigned and went into voluntary exile after King Paul refused his advice on a matter of state. After being recalled by President Phaidon Gizikis (qv), he returned to Athens on 24 July 1974 and was again sworn in as prime minister. Once again he was able to avert war with Turkey over Cyprus. Among his other accomplishments was obtaining Greece's entry into the European Common Market (ECC) (1979). On 5 May 1980, Karamanlis was elected president of Greece by Parliament. He was able to preside over the reintergration of Greece into NATO in October. On 10 March 1985, Karamanlis suddenly resigned the presidency after Prime Minister Andreas Papandreou (qv) reneged on his promise to support Karamanlis's reelection bid for another five-year term. On 5 May 1990, Karamanlis was once again elected president, at age 83. He remained in office until 10 March 1995, when he turned over the largely ceremonial post to Kostis Stefanopoulos. *Reading:* C. W. Woodhouse, *Karamanlis: The Restorer of Greek Democracy* (1982).

Karami, Rashid Abdul Hamid. (b. 30 December 1921, Miriata, Lebanon—d. 1 June 1987, near Beirut) Born the son of the Sunni Muslim Mufti of Tripoli, who later served in Parliament and was prime minister (1945), Karami studied law at Fu'ad University in Cairo. He entered politics in 1951 and was elected a deputy from Tripoli. After serving as the justice minister, Karami joined the opposition and, from August 1953 until July 1955, held several cabinet posts. He became prime minister on 19 September 1955. Karami became a disciple of Egypt's Nasser (qv), opposed the policies of President Camille Chamoun (qv) and resigned his office in March 1956. In 1958, Karami was again named prime minister, a post he held with some interruptions until 24 April 1969, when he was forced to resign in the the bloody aftermath of a pro-Palestinian demonstration. In 1974, Karami began open opposition to the government of President Suleiman Franjieh (qv), who had taken office in 1970. In 1975, Franjieh was forced to appoint Karami prime minister; he now represented the Islamic left. In addition to the top position, Karami also took the offices of minister of defense, finance and information. A civil war followed (*see* Lebanon) in which Karami collaborated with the Palestinian Liberation Organization (PLO) (qv) and with Kamal Jumblatt's (qv) National Movement. Karami's influence began to deteriorate after Elias Sarkis (qv) became president and after Syria entered the intensifying civil war. After leaving office (December 1976), Karami reconciled with Franjieh (1978) and reached a rapproachment with Syria following the Israeli incursion into Beirut. He returned to office in 1983 after President Gemayle (qv) asked him to form a new government. He officially took office on 26 April 1984. He was killed in a helicopter crash on 1 June 1987. Sabotage proved to be the cause of the accident.

Karen (Kayin) Tribe. *See* Burma.

Kariba Dam. *See* Zambia.

Karlskrona. *See* Sweden.

Karmal, Babrak. (b. 1929, near Kabul) In 1961, Karmal graduated from Kabul University. He joined Nur Mohammad Taraki's (qv) *Khalq* party in 1963, when it was formed as the opposition party to the government. When the monarchy was overthrown in July 1973, Karmal broke away from *Khalq* and formed a new organization called *Parcham*, which continued to support the regime of Sardar Mohammed Daud Khan, who had deposed his half-brother, King Zahir Khan (qv). After mid-1975, Daud found he could dispose of *Parcham* support. Soon after, in July 1977, *Khalq* and *Parcham*, under great pressure from Moscow, reunited as the People's Democratic Party (PDP) and, in April 1978, with Soviet help, overthrew Daud. A People's Republic was proclaimed, and Taraki was named president of the Revolutionary Council and prime minister, with Karmal as his deputy. In March 1979, the foreign minister, Hafizullah Amin (qv), became prime minister. Among his first acts was to assign Karmal to the post of ambassador in Czechoslovakia. After the overthrows of Taraki (14–15 September 1979) and Amin (27 December 1979), Karmal was brought back from Prague and appointed president and prime minister of the Soviet-controlled government of Afghanistan. In August, there were reports that Soviet troops had been able to foil a coup attempt against Karmal, and in October, still in the Kremlin's favor, Karmal was feted in Moscow. In December 1980, however, it was reported that three members of his family were killed when they attempted to flee the country. By 1985, the Soviets began to understand their dilemma in Afghanistan, but Karmal, still true to the communist cause, remained in power. On 4 May 1986, Karmal resigned as the general secretary of the communist PDP, ostensibly for reasons of ill-health. Although Karmal was undergoing medical treatment for an undisclosed ailment, it was believed the Soviets had despaired of his leadership and wanted to get better control over the Afghan populace. On 20 November, Karmal resigned the presidency and ostensibly faded into obscurity. On 4 May 1987, however, Karmal was arrested and imprisoned in a Kabul jail. The official Afghan radio report (5 May) was that he had gone to Moscow "at the invitation of the Soviet government," to undergo "medical treatment and to rest."

Karora. *See* Ethiopia.

Karume, Abeid Amani. (b. 1905[?], Belgian Congo—d. 7 April 1972, Zanzibar) Following the anti-Arab revolt of 1964, Sheikh Abeid Amani Karume came to power. Three months later he was able to negotiate an act of union with Tanganyika to form the United Republic of Tanzania. For the next eight years he served as the first vice-president of Tanzania and the chairman of the Zanzibar Revolutionary Council. On 7 April 1972, after he had released about 600 petty criminals from prison in celebration of the eighth anniversary of the revolution, Karume was assassinated by four members of the army, who were all killed in the ensuing gunfight. As two of the assassins were members of the

Umma Party, which had been merged with Karume's Afro-Shirazi Party after the revolution, Abdul Rahman Muhammad Babu, the former leader of Umma, was arrested.

Kasai Province, Independent Congo Republic. *See* Congo.

Kasavubu, Joseph. (b .1917 [?], Tshela, Belgian Congo—d. 24 March 1969, Boma, Congo) After studying for the priesthood, Kasavubu joined the Belgian civil service in 1942. In 1954, he became the president of the *Alliance des Bakongo* (Abako) party, an association of the Bakongo tribe. In 1957, he became mayor of Dendalein, the Leopoldville commune. With the independence of the former Belgian Congo as the Republic of Congo on 30 June 1960, Kasavubu's Abako Party took power when Kasavubu was elected president. The situation in the country rapidly deteriorated, and soon a number of provinces declared their independence. On 5 September 1960, Kasavubu dismissed Patrice Lumumba (qv), after Lumumba, the prime minister, asked the Soviet Union for military assistance in thwarting the Katangan breakaway. The United Nations had committed troops to Congo, but under strict orders to avoid involvement in internal affairs. On 14 September, with UN approval, Colonel Joseph Mobutu (qv) dismissed Kasavubu and seized power. Mobutu and Kasavubu worked out a subsequent arrangement of shared power. By the end of 1960, however, the continuing deterioration saw Congo divided into several parts, each with its own warlord, many of whom refused to obey either Kasavubu or Mobutu. On 9 February 1961, Kasavubu attempted to form a new government, but Lumumba's death dashed any hope of success. Moise Tshombe (qv) of Katanga accused Kasavubu of betraying an agreement reached in March 1961 among several Congolese leaders meeting in Madagascar. Tshombe claimed Kasavubu's willingness to deal with the United Nations was tantamount to treason. Tshombe was subsequently arrested and held for two months before promising to bring Katanga back under central government control. After being released, Tshombe returned to Katanga, where he immediately reneged on his promise. Kasavubu was able to form a new government, however, with Cyrille Adoula (qv) as prime minister. In 1962, Kasavubu watched as UN forces reduced Katangan resistance. Tshombe finally gave up in December and agreed in January 1963 to end Katanga's secession. On 30 September 1963, Kasavubu dissolved the legislature and appointed a constitutional commission to oversee the formation of a new governmental structure. When the commission reported its findings, it recommended less power to the prime minister and the legislature and more to the president (March 1964). In July 1964, Kasavubu asked Tshombe to form a new government. This action further deteriorated Congo's position in Africa by alienating many anti-Tshombe leaders who had supported Kasavubu in the past.In July 1965, Kasavubu rejected one-party rule for Congo and dismissed Tshombe for supporting it (13 October). In November 1965, General Joseph Mobutu dismissed Kasavubu and seized power. Kasavubu died of natural causes at age 52.

Kashmir. The early history of Kashmir is found in Sanskrit records, which, show the history in four parts, up to 1586, when the area was incorporated into the Mongol Empire. Early records recount the history of the region back to the fifth century A.D. The region passed into the hands of the Afghans and remained under their control until 1819. Thereafter, a demarcation is noted in the Sikh conquest of the region and in the rise of the Jammu principality. When the Jammu prince, Gulab Singh extended his control over the remainder of the region, the twin principalities of Jammu and Kashmir came into existence. The Treaty of Lahore (9 March 1846) established Jammu and Kashmir as a part of the British *Raj*, under the leadership of the prince of Jammu. From 1846 until 1947, Jammu and Kashmir formed the largest princely state in India. The Jammu and Kashmir state was bounded on the northwest by Afghanistan, on the north by the Sinkiang-Uigur Autonomous Region of China, on the east by Tibet, on the south by India and on the west by Pakistan. When India and Pakistan were given dominion status in 1947, Jammu and Kashmir were caught between Pakistan and India in a tug-of-war. Jammu is predominantly Hindi and Sikh, while Kashmir is largely Muslim. Pakistan claimed Kashmir because of the Muslim heritage and for economic reasons. On 22 October 1947, Afridi and Mahsud tribesmen from Pakistan invaded Kashmir and captured its capital city of Srinagar. The Maharaja of Kashmir asked for and received Indian military help (27 October) in return for his agreement to union with India (signed 27 October). Fighting continued, however, and, in January 1948, the United Nations stepped in, arranged for a cease-fire (1 January 1949) and set up a plebiscite to determine Kashmir's future (20 August 1953). Both India and Pakistan agreed. In effect the cease-fire divided Kashmir into two zones, the larger of which was in Indian hands. By 1952, India had refused to withdraw its troops, claiming that Pakistan was building its own forces up across the demilitarized zone. Pakistan issued countercharges claiming that India's refusal to withdraw rendered the plebiscite impossible. On 6 February 1954, over the strenuous protests of Pakistan, Kashmir acceded to annexation by India. On 1 March, Premier Jawaharlal Nehru (qv) rejected a U.S. aid offer and demanded that U.S. advisors get out of Kashmir. Later that year, on 4 October, Pakistan issued a white paper on Kashmir and formally requested a UN settlement of the Kashmir situation. On 25 February 1959, Nehru again ordered all Americans in the UN Ceasefire Observer Team out of Kashmir because the U.S. was giving military aid to Pakistan; a similar offer to India had been rejected by Nehru. In October 1959, China invaded northeast Kashmir in the Ladakh area and began construction of a road to link Sinkiang with Tibet. When Indian troops intervened, they were beaten off by the Chinese, who claimed the area as theirs. Sporadic clashes continued between Indian and Chinese forces into late 1962, when the Chinese announced a unilateral cease-fire but made no moves to withdraw from large amount of territory they had conquered. In 1964–1965, border incidents along the demilitarized zone increased until, on 5 August 1965, heavy fighting broke out broke out that lasted until 24 August, when UN forces were able to restore the truce. On 10 January 1966, the Tashkent Agreement was signed. which ended the hostilities and forced both sides back to the demilitarized line. By 1968, the plebiscite still had not been held. On 3 December 1971, Pakistani forces attacked civilian and military targets in Kashmir. This signalled the beginning of the Indo-Pakistani War (*see* Indo-Pakistani War). A settlement was agreed upon on 29 August 1972, which redefined a demarcation separating Kashmir into Pakistani and Indian sectors. In September, however, another border clash was reported in Kashmir. On 7 December 1972, the new demarcation line was formally accepted by both sides, with the treaty being signed on 11 December. In July 1981, another border clash took place that lasted three days with at least 18 killed on both sides. On 13 June 1984, India accused Pakistan of using West Kashmir as a training base for Sikh terrorists employed against India. Internal problems occurred in July, when the governor of Jammu and Kashmir dismissed his chief minister and replaced him with his brother-in-law. Rioting broke out between Hindus and Muslims in Jammu and Kashmir in 1990. In January, the government was dissolved, and a state of virtual martial law was imposed. The vice chancellor of the state university and a business executive were assassinated in April. In May, one of the state's most influential religious leaders, Imam Muhammas Farooq, was murdered. By 1991, the bloody campaign by Muslim extremists established perhaps the worst period of tension since independence. Many Hindus migrated out of the area to avoid the growing Muslim militancy and terrorism, which was aimed at gaining independence for Kashmir or association with Pakistan rather than India. Militancy continued into 1993, with numerous charges of police and military brutality in trying to quell the disturbances. In January, at least 50 people were killed in Sopore. The army surrounded the Hazratbal Mosque in Srinagar in October after it had been occupied by Muslim militants. On 16 November the Muslims laid down their weapons and surrendered. Disorders continued into 1994. *Reading:* Prem Shankar Jha, *Kashmir, 1947: Rival Versions of History* (1996); Sumit Ganguly, *The Crisis in Kashmir: Portents of War, Hopes of Peace* (1997); Victoria Schofield, *Kashmir in the Crossfire* (1996); Mushtaqur Rahman, *Divided Kashmir: Old Problems, New Opportunities for India, Pakistan, and the Kashmiri People* (1995).

el-Kassem (Qasim), Abdul Karim. On 14 July 1958, a military coup led by General Abdul Karim el-Kassem seized control of Iraq. King Faisal II was murdered, and a republic was declared. Most other members of the royal family were also killed in the bloody day of violence. A revolutionary council was established to run the country, and Kassem appointed himself premier. While Jordan looked on in horror, Egypt applauded the coup. The friendship between Iraq and Egypt (and the United Arab Republic) soon soured, however, after Kassem refused to toe the UAR line and when communist influence in Baghdad grew. Kassem quickly resurrected diplomatic relations with the USSR and Communist China. Eventually, communist demands were met with disapproval by Kassem. In July 1959, fighting broke out in Kirkuk, which Kassem blamed on the communists.

In September he ordered the executions of 13 former government officials. Hundreds were arrested following an attempt on Kassem's life in October. Kassem was not seen for the next two months as he "recuperated" from the assassination attempt. On 25 June 1961, Kassem laid claim to Kuwait (qv) immediately after Great Britain had recognized the full independence of that country. Kassem's regime was overthrown on 8 February 1963, by a group of air force–led Baathist officers headed by Colonel Abdel Salam Arif (qv). Kassem and dozens of communists were executed, and Arif became the de facto ruler of the country.

Kastel, Palestine. *See* Israel.

Katakov, Arkady. On 30 September 1985, three Soviet diplomats and a Soviet embassy doctor stationed in West Beirut, Lebanon, were kidnapped in two separate incidents by members of a Sunni-Muslim group calling itself the Islamic Liberation Organization. On 2 October the body of Arkady Katakov was found in West Beirut suburb. The other three hostages were released unharmed on 30 October. The terrorist group claimed they were demanding Syrian intervention to end the fighting in Tripoli. The Soviet response was to evacuate all nonessential personnel stationed in Lebanon.

Katanga Province, ICR. *See* Congo.

Kathmandu. *See* Nepal.

Katowice. *See* Poland.

Katzir, Ephraim. (b. 16 May 1916, Kiev, Russia) Katzir immigrated to Palestine with his parents in 1925. He graduated from Hebrew University in Jerusalem and, from 1941 to 1945, served as an assistant in the university's department of theoretical and macromolecular chemistry. Katzir also served in the Jewish' underground organization known as the Haganah, which he served as scientific advisor. He also accepted a fellowship at Columbia University in New York during that time. In 1949, he was appointed acting head of the department of biophysics at the Weizmann Institute of Science in Rehovot, Israel. He was later appointed the institute's director. In 1966, he was elected to the US National Academy of Sciences for his work on proteins. From 1966 until 1968, he was scientific advisor to the Israeli Ministry of Defense. Never having served in public office before, Katzir became president of Israel on 23 May 1973 upon the retirement of Schneor Zalman Shazar. Golda Meir (qv) was prime minister at the time. On 2 December 1974, Israeli president Ephraim Katzir, announced that Israel had the capability of producing nuclear weapons. He remained in the largely ceremonial post of president of the state of Israel until 28 May 1978, when he was replaced by Yitzak Navon, who was elected without opposition.

Kaumi, Simon. *See* Abaijah, Josephine, for details.

Kaunas. *See* Lithuania.

Kaunda, Kenneth. (b. 28 April 1924, Northern Province, Northern Rhodesia). Born the son of Church of Scotland missionaries, Kaunda trained to be a teacher and, in 1945, joined the anticolonial movement. He helped establish the United National Independence Party (UNIP), which became the ruling party in the country. Zambia received its full independence in October 1964. However, in January of that year full internal self-government was granted to Northern Rhodesia by the British government, and Kenneth Kaunda was elected president. With independence and the country's name change to Zambia, Kaunda remained in office. Trouble in Southern Rhodesia (after independence, Zimbabwe) placed Zambia and Kaunda in great difficulty, and Zambia was given much economic aid by the West. In December 1966, the British government ordered Royal Air units into Zambia at Kaunda's request to help protect the Kariba Dam, which was threatened by Rhodesia. Kaunda was sworn in for a second term as president on 21 December 1968. In August 1969, Kaunda was forced to impose a state of emergency because of growing political unrest, which stemmed from tribal animosities. Part of this problem revolved around the vice president Simon Kapwepwe (qv), who resigned on 25 August, claiming that his Bemba kinsmen were being abused. Kaunda then announced that he was taking personal charge of the United National Independence Party and would rule the country as the UNIP secretary-general. In 1970, he was elected chairman of the Organization of African Unity and, subsequently, chairman of the group of nonaligned nations. On all occasions, he preached his philosophy of nonviolence. In 1971, Kaunda set up a commission to study the charges of tribal bias that were plaguing his government. In February 1972, Kaunda banned the recently founded United Progressive Party formed by Simon Kapwepwe and placed its leaders under close surveillance because of attempts to isolate the Bemba from the remainder of the country. On 26 May 1972, a letter bomb intended for Kaunda seriously maimed a female employee in his office. In January 1973, Kaunda imposed one-party rule once again in Zambia. He also closed the border with Rhodesia and asked the UN for economic aid. He was elected to a third five-year term as president in 1974. In April 1975, Kaunda kicked three black Rhodesian independence groups out of Zambia because of their disruptive influence on his country. In June, he began nationalizing resources following a disastrous drop in copper prices. On 28 January 1976, Kaunda invoked full emergency powers to help control the unrest accompanying the economic crisis facing Zambia. In 1977, amid fears of a Rhodesian invasion, Kaunda focused more on external affairs than on the pressing economic problems at home. In July, however, he dismissed the prime minister, Elijah Mudenda, and replaced him with Mainza Chona. In 1978, Kaunda discovered that, with British assistance, Rhodesia had been receiving oil and other commodities that were under the UN embargo placed on Zambia's neighbor. He was also more convinced that Rhodesia's troubles would eventually spill over into Zambia. His reelection in 1978, although secure—he took 80 percent of the vote—was not won on the same scale as that of 1968. In November 1980, Kaunda was forced to move Zambia to a war footing. Violent demonstrations, were especially aimed at the British high commissioner and the economic situation caused by the problems in Zimbabwe Rhodesia. Rhodesian guerrilla operations launched from Zambia and reprisal raids by Rhodesian troops created a situation that prevented the flow of food, principally maize (corn), into the country. In June 1981, a plot against Kaunda was uncovered that apparently involved South African mercenaries. The economy continued to worsen into 1983; after proposing a new five-year national recovery program, Kaunda was elected to his fifth term in office. In October 1984, Kaunda marked the 20th anniversary of independence and his presidency by releasing 239 people from prison and detention. Protests continued into 1986, when a curfew was imposed in Copperbelt Province to defuse a dangerous situation in which at least 15 people died in some of the worst rioting since independence. In May 1987, Kaunda established new currency restrictions, which, although aimed at stopping the severe economic problems his country faced, ran afoul of the World Bank and the International Monetary Fund, which cut off much of the foreign assistance that had kept Zambia going. The increased rate of inflation that followed caused Kaunda to impose even stronger economic restrictions in February 1988. In October, Kaunda ran unopposed for his sixth term in office. In 1989, he introduced a new five-year plan to halt the spiraling economic decline of his country. Rioting occurred in Lusaka in 1990 after the price of maize doubled. At least 15 people were killed when Kaunda sent in security forces to restore order. Kaunda's rule ended in October 1991, when he and his party were soundly defeated. This ended Kaunda's one-party rule in Zambia, which had existed since 1972. *Reading:* Stephen Chan, *Kaunda and Southern Africa: Image and Reality in Foreign Policy* (1991).

Kawasmeh, Fahd. On 29 December 1984, Fahd Kawasmeh, a senior Palestine Liberation Organization member, was assassinated by two gunmen associated with the "Black September" terrorist organization. The attack was another example of the Abu Nidal (qv) group's attempt to undermine any efforts toward a negotiated Arab-Israeli peace.

Kayibanda, Gregoire. On 5 July 1973, President Gregoire Kayibanda of Rwanda was overthrown in a bloodless coup carried out by the National Guard under General Juvenal Habyalimana (qv). The coup was precipitated by Kayibanda's move to change the constitution to allow him to seek reelection. *See* Rwanda.

Kazzar, Nazem. On 1 July 1973, Colonel Nazem Kazzar, Iraq's director of internal security, led an unsuccessful coup against the regime of strongman Saddam Hussein (qv). The coup plot called for the murder of President Ahmed Hassan al-Bakr (qv). Although Bakr survived, Defense Minister Hammad Shihab was killed and Interior Minister Saadun Ghaidan was injured after they had been taken hostage. Kazzar and 35 of his associates were subsequently executed (7–8 July 1973). Kazzar had held considerable independent power and was probably responsible for much of the violent repression reported in Iraq.

Keflavik. *See* Iceland.

Keita, Modibo. On 19 November 1968, the socialist government of President Modibo Keita of Mali was overthrown by a military coup. A junta calling itself the National Military Liberation Committee took charge of the country. In November 1963, Keita had been instrumental, along with Ethiopia's Emperor

Haile Selassie (qv). in negotiating a cease-fire in the month-old Algerian-Morocco border war.

Kekkonen, Urho Kaleva. (b. 3 September 1900, Pielavesi, Finland—d. 31 August 1986, Helsinki) Kekkonen fought for Finnish independence against the Bolsheviks in 1917. He became a journalist and later studied law at the University of Helsinki. He later took the doctorate and, in 1936, successfully ran for Parliament. He became minister of justice and, in 1937, minister of interior. During the Russo-Finnish War of 1939–1940, he was responsible for the resettlement of nearly 300,000 Karelians dislodged from their homes by the Soviets. After the war, Kekkonen withdrew from politics because of his opposition to the terms of Soviet peace forced on Finland. In 1944 he returned to public life and was a key official in the Finnish war-crimes trials. Between 1950 and 1956, Kekkonen served in a number of governments as prime minister or foreign minister. In 1956, he was elected president, an office he held for the next 25 years. During those crucial years in Finnish history, he managed to keep the Soviet Union at bay for most of his tenure, but he did reach some accommodation with the USSR that included a promise of Finnish neutrality and no foreign troops on Finnish soil. In 1958, however, the Finnish elections upset the Soviets. There was a break in diplomatic relations until the Finnish government resigned and was replaced by one acceptable to the Soviets. In November 1961, Soviet Premier Nikita Khrushchev (qv) forced Kekkonen to get rid of all anti-Soviet influences in the Finnish government. Kekkonen was also a fine athlete who held several national titles in track and field. On 27 October 1981, ill health forced his resignation as president. He died at age 86 in 1986.

Kenitra. *See* Morocco.

Kennedy, John Fitzgerald. (b. 29 May 1917, Brookline, Massachusetts—d. 22 November 1963, Dallas, Texas) Born the son of Joseph P. Kennedy and Rose Fitzgerald, John Kennedy followed his family out of relative middle-class obscurity into political and financial security. John attended Canterbury School (a Roman Catholic boarding school in New Milford, Connecticut) (1930–1931) and then attended the nonsectarian Choate School in Wallingford, Connecticut. In 1935 he entered Princeton, where he lasted less than one year before leaving because of illness. He then entered Harvard, where he majored in government. In 1939, he lived in London, where his father had been posted as US ambassador. He traveled extensively through Europe during this time. Upon his return to Harvard he prepared his senior thesis on the theme "*Why England Slept,*" describing the failure of British policy in the face of rising Nazism. The thesis was published and received wide acclaim. Following graduation in June 1940, Kennedy attended Stanford University's graduate school of business for a few months. He then travelled extensively through South America. In late 1941, he joined the Navy and saw significant action in the Pacific Theater. He was invalided out of service following an action in August 1943 that became the theme of a movie titled "PT-109." After leaving service, Kennedy was undecided on a career until the death of his older brother, Joe, who was killed in action. John Kennedy then assumed his dead brother's destiny—to enter politics. He entered the U.S. House of Representatives in January 1947, and he narrowly defeated Henry Cabot Lodge for the US Senate in November 1952. In September 1953, he married Jacqueline Lee Bouvier. In 1954, Kennedy was hospitalized for aggravation of war injuries. During his convalescence he wrote *Profiles in Courage* (1956), for which he won the 1957 Pulitzer Prize for biography. In 1956, Kennedy ran unsuccessfully for the Democratic vice-presidential nomination as Adlai Stevenson's running mate. (He lost to Estes Kefauver.) In 1960, Kennedy narrowly defeated Richard M. Nixon (qv), to become the 35th president of the United States. In March of his first year in office, Kennedy warned the Soviet Union of the grave consequences of its taking unilateral action in the Congo (*see* Congo). Within a month, he announced that the U.S, would not allow a communist takeover of Laos, and in April 1961 Kennedy announced that the U.S. would take steps to protect the security of the Western Hemisphere. In June 1961, he met with Premier Khrushchev in Vienna. In the face of the rising crisis over West Berlin, Kennedy announced a plan (25 July) to increase U.S. military strength and substantially raise defense spending. On 5 September, he ordered a resumption of atmospheric testing of nuclear weapons. On 25 September 1961, Kennedy announced to the United Nations that South Vietnam was a country "under attack." Two weeks later, he sent General Maxwell D. Taylor (qv) to South Vietnam to evaluate the situation. Based on Taylor's report, Kennedy increased the number of U.S. military advisers in Southeast Asia and began the inexorable process that drew the U.S. into an unpopular war. On 2 September 1962, President Kennedy announced a significant buildup of Soviet military power in Cuba, and on 22 October he announced an air and naval "quarantine" of Cuba following firm evidence that the USSR had introduced offensive weapons into the island nation. This began the event known as the "Cuban Missile Crisis," which forced Khrushchev and the Soviet Union to back down. On 24–26 June 1963, Kennedy told a cheering crowd in West Berlin that an attack on the city would be considered an attack on the United States. At 12:30 P.M. on 22 November 1963, President John F. Kennedy was assassinated in Dallas, Texas. Although Lee Harvey Oswald was arrested for the attack and was himself assassinated by Jack Ruby, many feel the whole story of the assassination is yet to be told. *Reading:* Tom Wicker, *JFK and LBJ: The Influence of Personality upon Politics* (1991); Marta Randall, *John F. Kennedy* (1987); James P. Duffy & Vincent L. Ricci, *The Assassination of John F. Kennedy: A Complete Book of Facts* (1992).

Kennedy, Robert Francis. (b. 20 November 1925, Brookline, Massachusetts—d. 6 June 1968, Los Angeles) Robert Kennedy attended Harvard, graduating in 1948. He took his law degree from the University of Virginia in 1951. From 1951 until 1952, he served in the criminal division of the U.S. Department of Justice. In 1952, he resigned to run John Kennedy's campaign for the U.S. Senate. After service on several senate committee staffs, from 1957 until 1960,

"Bobby" was chief counsel to a select committee on crime in the labor movement. In 1960, he managed his brother's successful campaign for the presidency. John Kennedy appointed him attorney general in 1961. He remained in that post until 1964, when he resigned the Johnson administration to run for the Senate from New York. Even though his residency in New York was, at best, tenuous, he was elected in November 1964. In 1968, firmly entrenched as the leader of the liberal wing of the Democratic Party, Bobby Kennedy announced (March) he would seek the presidency. At 12:16 A.M. on 5 June 1968, Bobby Kennedy was shot three times while attending a function at the Ambassador Hotel in Los Angeles. Kennedy was pronounced dead at 1:44 A.M. on 6 June 1968. Sirhan Bashir Sirhan was arrested at the scene and charged with the murder. He was convicted and sentenced to death, but his death sentence was commuted to life imprisonment in 1972. Many questions still existed about Sirhan's motives in the murder. *Reading:* William W. Turner & J. G. Christian, *The Assassination of Robert F. Kennedy: The Conspiracy and Coverup* (1993); Daniel J. Petrillo & C. Peter Ribley, *Robert F. Kennedy* (1988).

Kent State University. A 21,000-student university in Kent, Ohio, Kent State University was the scene of a disastrous confrontation between students and national guardsmen. At 12.24 P.M., on 4 May 1970, a detachment of guardsmen opened fire on rampaging students, killing four and injuring nine. Subsequent investigations uncovered evidence to support almost any frame of mind. In 1968 and 1969, there had been some disturbances at Kent State that were instigated by the Students for Democratic Society (SDS), a suspected North American terrorist organization. In 1970, however, the campus was relatively calm. On Friday night, 1 May 1970, trouble broke out on campus. Many say the trouble was just boisterousness. Campus activists as well as national antiwar groups claimed it was an expression of outrage over the U.S. invasion of Cambodia ordered by President Richard Nixon (qv). Most students questioned indicated it was "party time," and nothing more. The first night, 1 May, a minor disturbance involving students and others occurred on the other side of Kent. Police overreaction escalated the incident into a real riot. On Saturday, students burned down the ROTC building on campus and prevented firefighters access to the burning building. As the fire was burning, 400 Ohio national guardsmen arrived on the scene. On Sunday, everything was calm, except for a minor disturbance at the front gate of the campus in the evening. On Monday, 4 May, utter confusion reigned on the campus as to who was in charge. The adjutant general of the state, Major General Robert Canterbury, was in civilian clothes and had no idea as to what orders had been issued and to whom. When about 2,000 students gathered, they were in no way hostile, Canterbury ordered them to disperse, which they did not. At 11:59 A.M., 113 armed guardsmen marched onto to the campus, but were led into a cul-de-sac near the football field by theie own leaders. As confusion reigned among the soldiers, the students began taunting them and began throwing rocks. The guardsmen fired tear gas into the crowd, which was tossed back at them. As the soldiers began a withdrawal, some students pursued them. One squad of troops reached a grassy knoll, where they wheeled and opened fire. Firing lasted less than 15 seconds, and only about 60 rounds were fired. The casualties were all at least 265 feet from the troops and were no direct threat to them. The completely inept handling of the situation by the national guard commander and the university administration were the primary cause of the incident. All of the guardsmen were exonerated (8 November 1974); charges against a number of students were eventually dropped. Reports indicate that the Kent State incident led at least 700 other schools to cancel classes and close for the spring term. William A. Gordon, *The Fourth of May: Killings and Coverups at Kent State* (1990); James A. Michener, *Kent State: What Happened and Why* (1971); Joseph Eszterhas, *Thirteen Seconds: Confrontation at Kent State* (1970).

Kenya. A country found in eastern Africa, Kenya is bounded on the north by Sudan, on the northeast by Somalia, on the south by Tanzania, and on the west by Uganda. On the southeast, Kenya borders on the Indian Ocean. The capital city is Nairobi, and the country is divided into seven provinces. From the eighth century, Arab trading colonies existed along the coast that exported slaves and spices to the Arab world. Little was known of the interior until the nineteenth century, when Arab caravans penetrated into the Serengeti region and probably were the first outsiders to view Mount Kilimanjaro (not seen by a European until 1848) and Lake Victoria. German missionary agents were the next to explore the region. Until after 1880, there was no land called Kenya. It was not until the British began colonizing East Africa that boundaries were drawn delineating Kenya much as it appears today. Prior to the English settlement, each tribal region—Masai, Kikuyu, and so on—had their own governmental, social and economic structure. The British imposed a standard administration, economy and religion and transformed the land into a unitary society, or so it seemed. The British colonial office also encouraged English and South African white settlement in the country, which meant a dislocation of native populations as the whites took the best and most fertile lands for themselves. This brought resentment on the part of the black population which had some manifestation before World War I. Although threatened from German East Africa, Kenya, a part of the East African Protectorate, remained relatively unsullied by the war, except for the fact that, as whites enlisted, the agrarian economy faltered. After the war, the economy was on the road to recovery when the Great Depression struck and halted for a time any economic progress. When the economy did begin recovery, political problems began that created even greater obstacles, which were being overcome when war clouds once again gathered over Europe. The beginning witnessed Kenya being once again threatened, this time from Italian Somaliland to the north. The war was spent with relative calm and without too much dislocation. As the country began to recover from the effects of the war, however, the most serious threat ever developed in the 1950s with the Mau Mau (qv) rebellion. Limited primarily to Kikuyu tribal areas, the violence still required the declaration of a state of emergency on 3 October

1952. Those Kikuyu who did not protect the Mau Mau were the most seriously assaulted group in the country, although the killing spread to the white sector as well. The British won a major victory against the Mau Mau in the Aberdare Forest region of central Kenya in June 1953. Again, in the Mount Kenya–Aberdare Forest, in February 1955, 10,000 troops surrounded 4,000 Mau Mau. By November, most of the Mau Mau had been killed or captured. The number of British forces in Kenya was reduced in September 1955, but the state of emergency was not lifted until 1960. Kenya was given its independence within the Commonwealth on 12 December 1963, and Jomo Kenyatta (qv), the convicted Mau Mau leader, was made its prime minister. At the same time, a five-year period of border clashes began with Somalia on Kenya's northeast boundary. In 1964, Kenya, along with Uganda and Tanganyika, asked for and received British military assistance in putting down a series of communist-inspired, antigovernment revolts. In Kenya, the trouble took the form of an army mutiny, supposedly over pay. In 1969, the government undertook a campaign to oust the many Indian merchants living in Kenya. In July 1969, tribal warfare broke out following the assassination of the minister of economic affairs, Tom Mboya (qv). On 30 October 1969, Kenya outlawed the Kenya People's Union, an organization that stood in opposition to Kenyatta's policies. Kenyatta threatened war with Uganda in February 1976, over a series of border incidents over disputed territory. Ugandan president Idi Amin's withdrawal of claims against disputed territory along the Kenyan border (27 February 1976) did not lessen the gravity of the situation, however, and on 16 June 1976 the U.S. announced it would start supplying arms to Kenya to offset the Soviet arming of Somalia and Uganda. In July 1976, Kenya put a tariff in effect on all Ugandan goods and passengers transitting Kenyan territory and later cut off all oil supplies to Uganda. On 18 April 1977, Tanzania "permanently closed" its border with Kenya. The border was not reopened until November 1983. Upon Kenyatta's death on 22 August 1978, Daniel Arap Moi (qv) became acting president. In April 1979, Kenya was forced to close its border with Uganda and to use force to stop the flow of deserting Ugandan soldiers attempting to flee their country in the face of the Tanzanian invasion. In September 1979, Moi met with Somalia's Siyaad Barrah (Siad Barre) (qv) to draw up a treaty of friendship and mutual defense. In February 1980, Kenya agreed to allow U.S. bases on its territory in return for military aid. On 1 August 1982, an air force coup attempt against Moi failed; about 3,000 were arrested in the wake of the revolt. On 25 August, the Kenyan air force was disbanded. In 1985, Kenya began a slow recovery from a major drought that had devastated the country for three years. A series of border clashes took place with Uganda and Tanzania in the late 1980s. Tribal clashes in the western provinces left thousands dead and tens of thousands homeless in 1992. Economic conditions also again began to affect the country. President Moi won reelection in December 1992. The unsubstantiated cries of foul from an inept opposition. The results of fighting in the western highlands throughout most of 1993 had a number of observers convinced that the government was sponsoring Kalenjin tribe raids on Kikuyu villages as a means of driving the Kikuyus off. A number of Kikuyu leaders arrested tended to confirm that notion. Before the end of 1993, IMF donor nations had lifted the boycott on Kenya, hoping to force more democratic ideals on the country. A 1994 investigation into banking irregularities implicated a number of senior banking officials in the embezzlement of $210 million. As the report was kept secret, many believed that high government officials were also involved in the fraud. By 1995, the financial situation had not corrected itself, and the economic pressures were growing. With food shortages due to a severe drought. In addition, tribal restlessness was increased when 2,000 Kikuyus were forcibly relocated out of the Rift Valley. Rioting also broke out in slum areas in Nairobi. The year did not end well for Kenya. *Reading:* Wunyabari O. Maloba, *Mau Mau and Kenya: An Analysis of a Peasant Revolt* (1993); Greet Kershaw, *Mau Mau from Below* (1997); William R. Ochieng̊ & B. A. Ogot, eds., *Decolonization and Independence in Kenya 1940–93* (1995).

Kenyatta, Jomo (Kamau wa Ngengi). (b. c.1894, Ichamevi, Gatundu, Kenya—d. 22 August 1978, Mombasa, Kenya) Kenyatta, born a member of the Kikuyu tribe near Nairobi, was educated in a Church of Scotland missionary school and, for a time, worked for the municipal government as a legal interpreter in Nairobi. In the 1920s he became interested in the movement to recover Kikuyu lands and joined the Kikuyu Central Association (KCA), becoming the group's general secretary in 1928. After a 1929 visit to England, Kenyatta returned to Kenya, only to leave again on an extended sojourne through Europe, including a visit to the USSR. He later studied at the London School of Economics. He did not return to Kenya until 1946 and was elected president of the KCA in 1947. Kenyatta also became the principal of a teacher-training school. He was arrested in October 1952, following the outbreak of Mau Mau (qv) violence. On 8 April 1953, after a trial in which he was identified by a police informer, he was he was sentenced to seven years' imprisonment as the leader of the Mau Mau. In 1960, he was elected president of the Kenya National African Union (KANU) opposition party, a post he accepted in October 1961, after his release from prison in August. In a pre-independence election in May 1963, KANU won power, and Kenyatta was appointed prime minister. The following December he was elected president, assuming the office in 1964. Kenyatta served in that office until his death in 1978. While he was a commanding force in life, his death left a void in African and Kenyan politics that was never satisfactorily filled. *Reading:* Dennis Wepman, *Jomo Kenyatta: President of Kenya* (1985); Veena Malhotra, *Kenya under Kenyatta* (1990).

Keough, Dennis. On 15 April 1984, U.S. diplomat Dennis Keough and U.S. army Lieutenant Colonel Kenneth Crabtree of the US Liaison Office, Namibia, were killed when a time bomb exploded in a service station in Oshakati as they were driving to northern Namibia to monitor the withdrawal of South African army units from Angola. One black civilian was also killed, and four others were injured by the blast. It is uncertain whether Keough and Crabtree were targeted or whether they were in the wrong place at the wrong time. South African authorities blamed the attack on the South West African People's Organization (SWAPO), but SWAPO denied responsibility, even though, if they had planted the bomb, they could not have known the Americans would stop there at that time.

Kerala. *See* India.

Kerama (Karameh). *See* Jordan.

Kerekou, Mathieu. Dahomey (qv) received its independence on 1 August 1960. On 26 October 1972, Major Mathieu Kerekou led the fifth coup against the government since independence. As a result President Justin Timotin Ahomadegbe (qv) was ousted, and Kerekou made himself president and minister of defense. Kerekou remained in power for 18 years, but was defeated in 1991, in the first free elections held in 30 years. He was replaced on 4 April 1991 by former prime minister Nicephore Soglo, but he declined to attend Soglo's inauguration.

Kermanshah. *See* Iran and Iran-Iraq War.

Kerr, Malcolm. On 18 January 1984, two member of a group calling themselves Radical Shia, a part of the terrorist organization known as Islamic Jihad (*Hizballah*), shot to death Malcolm Kerr, the president of American University, in Beirut, Lebanon. Kerr was considered by Islamic Jihad as being a bad influence on the Lebanese students studying at the university.

Kfar Darom. *See* Israel.

Kfar Etzion, Palestine. *See* Israel and Palestine.

Kfar Falous (Falus). *See* Lebanon.

Kfar Shouba. *See* Lebanon.

Kfar Szold, Palestine. *See* Israel and Palestine.

Khaddam, 'Abd al-Halim. On 14 May 1984, Lebanese vice-president 'Abd al-Halim Khaddam met with Shi'ite, Christian Phalangist and Druse representatives in Damascus, Syria, in an attempt to reduce the fighting that was destroying Lebanon. This was one step in a peace procession begun by the new Lebanese government headed by Prime Minister Rashid Karami (qv) and President Amin Gemayle (qv).

Khalid 'ibn Abd al-'Aziz al Saud. (b. 1913, Riyadh, Arabian Peninsula—d. 13 June 1982, Ta'if, Saudi Arabia) Khalid became king and prime minister of Saudi Arabia when he followed his assassinated half-brother, Faisal (qv), to the throne in 1975. He was born the fourth son of Ibn Saud, the founder of the Saudi dynasty, and served as viceroy of Hejaz and minister of interior in the 1930s. In 1964, Khalid became deputy prime minister. He was coopted as crown prince in 1965. Beset by illness after 1970, he seemed unlikely ever to rule. Upon Faisal's death, however, he took the crown and gave a moderate rule to his people. He was especially popular among the Bedouin tribes, among whom he spent much time, leaving affairs of state to Crown Prince Fahd (qv). Fahd assumed the throne on Khalid's death from a heart attack.

Khama, Sir Seretse. (b. 1 July 1921, Bechuanaland—d. 13 July 1980, Gaberone, Botswana) Born the son of a tribal chieftain, Khama went to school in South Africa before going to England to study law at Oxford. His marriage to a white woman in England caused much trouble there and in his homeland. Upon his return home, however, he became a popular figure, even though he was barred from returning to England until he renounced his chieftain rank in his tribe. In 1962, Khama founded the country's Democratic Party and with its help became the nation's first prime minister (1965). He became president of the Republic of Botswana when Bechuanaland gained its complete independence in 1966. He was granted knighthood at that time. Khama ruled successfully and managed to keep both the minority white government in South Africa and the rebel forces operating in Rhodesia from bothering too much the economic growth of his country. His death created a void that was difficult to fill.

Khanh, Nguyen. On 29–30 January 1964, Major General Nguyen Khanh, fearing a French plot to neutralize Vietnam, led a bloodless coup against the government of Duong Van Minh (qv) and established himself as the new leader of the republic. On 8 February 1964, Khanh announced the formation of a new government with himself as premier, Duong Van Minh as nominal head of state and a mixed civilian-military cabinet. On 18 March, Khanh began the task of restoring difficult diplomatic relations with Laos (qv) and ending the border dispute with Cambodia. On 7 August 1964, following an escalation of the war (*see* Vietnam), Khanh declared a state of emergency and took into his own hands the power to impose censorship, military justice, travel restrictions, arrest without appeal, and the death penalty for "speculators, terrorists and saboteurs." Khanh was forced to resign the presidency following demands by students and Buddhists for an end to dictatorial rule. Khanh retained command of the army and joined a triumverate seeking to build a new government. On 29 August, however, Khanh was reported to be suffering from a physical and mental breakdown and was temporarily replaced by Doctor Nguyen Xuan Oanh. On 3 September, the illness miraculously cured, Khanh reappeared "rested and recovered" and resumed control of the government. At that time he announced that he would retain control for two months and then turn the government over to a civilian leader. On 26 September, Khanh offered to make way for a civilian government. A High National Council composed of 17 civilians was inaugurated and given the task of preparing a new constitution for the country. On 27 January 1965, Khanh led another coup and again seized power in Saigon. Claiming that Khanh had become a dictator, a group of senior army officers ousted him from office in a successful coup on 19 February 1965, but Khanh was immediately returned to power by his loyal troops, who recaptured Saigon without firing a shot. A more powerful group of army officers finally ousted Khanh for good on 21 February.

Kharg (Khargu) Island. *See* Iran and Iran-Iraq War.

Khartoum. *See* Libya.

Khartoum. *See* Sudan.

Khasi Hills. *See* India.

al-Khatib, Ahmed. On 18 November 1970, Ahmed al-Khatib, a former schoolteacher, was named president of Syria after defense minister General Hafez al-Assad (qv) had arrested President Nureddin al-Attassi (qv) on 13 November. Al-Assad had himself named premier. Al-Khatib held the largely ceremonial office until 22 February 1971, when he resigned. He was then named speaker of the People's Council while al-Assad became president (14 March). Followers of al-Khatib attempted a coup on 11 June, but it was foiled by troops loyal to al-Assad.

al-Khatim Khalifa, Sirr. On 15 November 1964, President Ibraham Abboud (qv) of Sudan was forced resign his office in the face of mounting unrest in the country. Sirr al-Khatim Khalifa, a civil servant, was installed as prime minister. Abboud was retained for a time as titular president, but this only caused more widespread discontent. Khalifa resigned on 18 February, but he was recalled on 23 February to head a coalition government. He was replaced as prime minister in April following a popular election.

Khe Sanh (KSCB). *See* Vietnam.

Khiem, Tran Thien. As South Vietnamese defense minister, Khiem issued the decree reorganizing the Civil Guard into Regional Forces (RF) (7 May 1964), and the Self-Defense Corps into Popular Forces (PF) (12 May 1964).

Khieu Samphan. On 6 September 1981, an anti-Vietnamese coalition was formed among Cambodia's (Kampuchea) Prince Sihanouk (qv), Son Sann and Khieu Samphan. Samphan was the representative of the Khmer Rouge (qv) who had been sent to Singapore to meet Sihanouk at the behest of China, which was trying to offset the Vietnamese-sponsored government currently in power in Phnom Penh. Samphan had been named head of state of Kampuchea by the assembly from 11 April 1976 (the same day Pol Pot became premier), six days after Prince Sihanouk had resigned, until 7 January 1979, the same day Pol Pot left office and the day that rebel guerrillas supported by Vietnamese forces had captured Phnom Penh. Samphan escaped on a Chinese aircraft, but others in the government were not so lucky. Until September 1981, Sihanouk had steadfastly considered Kampuchea's domination by the Vietnamese as preferable to that of the Khmer Rouge, whom he described as "butchers." Son Sann was a former deputy premier and the leader of the anticommunist Khmer People's National Liberation Front. A combined military council was approved, as was a proposal for a coalition government. The innate suspicions held by the three participants about each other doomed the results of the conference. Later meetings of representatives of the three fell to bickering over who said what and what was agreed upon. *See* Cambodia.

Khmer People's National Liberation Front (KPNLF). An anticommunist group in Kampuchea (Cambodia) in 1984, the KPNLF was led by former premier Son Sann and was a part of a resistance coalition called the Democratic Kampuchea (DK) which operated against Vietnamese occupying forces (*see* Cambodia). The Vietnamese mounted a major offensive against the DK between November 1984 and April 1985, destroying all their major bases in Kampuchea near the Thailand border, including four important KPNLF camps. One of these, at Ampil, was the politicomilitary headquarters of the KPNLF. The Association of Southeast Asian Nations (ASEAN), the KPNLF's chief supporter, continued to give support even though the DK coalition was badly wounded by the loss of its bases. The DK tactics changed to those of guerrilla warfare to mitigate the need for fixed camps. Numerous hit-and-run attacks followed that proved the KPNLF and other noncommunist DK forces could match the Khmer Rouge in guerrilla tactics. Communist China, which had been supplying the Khmer Rouge, now began giving weapons and equipment to the other DK members. Soon, however, the KPNLF and the ANS formed a joint command, ignoring the Khmer Rouge because of its strongarm tactics against their allies. Fighting continued into the late 1980s. In 1989, for instance, the KPNLF and the other rebel forces attacked a number of government strongholds and held most of them until April 1990. In June 1990, the U.S. gave $7 million in aid to the two noncommunist factions and in October, changed the entire aid package, including covert aid so as to give the KPNLF its share. In 1991, heavy fighting continued. On 23 October 1991, however, an agreement was signed by the KPNLF and the other factions, including the Phnom Penh government, that framed a political settlement in Cambodia. A cease-fire had been agreed upon in May. Representatives of the KPNLF then joined the Supreme National Council, and many KPNLF leaders who had been in exile returned home. *See* Cambodia.

Khmer Republic. *See* Cambodia.

Khmer Rouge (KR). A communist insurgent group in Cambodia. The Khmer Rouge name means "Red Khmers" after the predominant people of Cambodia. In 1969, when they first became active as more than local guerrilla bands, Khmer Rouge strength was estimated to be about 3,000. North Vietnamese and Viet Cong leaders reactivated communist cells in Cambodia to supply the Khmer Rouge who began a campaign of attacking Cambodian army units. Prince Sihanouk (qv) warned the Khmer Rouge that their actions were aiding the American cause in Southeast Asia and that the link between the Khmer Rouge and the NVA/VC was well known. As the fighting grew into a full-fledged war in 1970, the ill-trained Cambodian army was being beaten badly. South Vietnamese army units (and eventually US army units) crossed into Cambodia to assist the government forces and to clear the sanctuaries established there by the NVA/VC. After Sihanouk was ousted from office on 18 March 1970, he travelled to Peking where he was warmly received. There, he formed a government-in-exile (5 May) in which a number of Khmer Rouge were placed in important positions. On the night of 21 January 1971, the KR attacked the Phnom Penh airport and, in one action, destroyed the Cambodian air force. By 1972, the KR attacked Cambodian military targets at will and were using tanks supplied by the NVA. In September 1972, an entire Cambodian battalion was destroyed after abandoning its posts on the road between Phnom Penh and Saigon. On 21 March 1972, the KR began a rocket bombardment of the Cambodian capital of

Phnom Penh and by March 1973 had cut virtually all roads into the city. On 4 April, Phnom Penh was under seige. U.S. bombing of KR positions from March until June had little effect on its operations. The seige of Phnom Penh continued into 1974, with casualties reported in the hundreds nearly every day. A U.S. resupply convoy managed to reach Phnom Penh on 23 January 1975 after fighting its way up the Mekong river just before the KR captured the landing area at Neak Luong. Thereafter, the KR mined the river to prevent any more relief convoys from reaching the beleaguered city and sinking a number of the ships in the first convoy as it returned downriver. On the ground, the KR continued tightening the ring around the capital. Aerial resupply into Phnom Penh's Pochentong Airport became increasingly more dangerous and was eventually halted. Between 9 and 13 May 1977, KR forces carried out a number of raids against refugee camps in Thailand. Thailand reacted by putting the country on war alert. On 7 January 1979, the KR, as a part of the Kampuchean National United Front (KNUF) and reinforced with with NVA units, took Phnom Penh. An eight-man council headed by KR military leader Heng Samrin (qv) took control of the country. In 1981, the KR, as a part of the Democratic Kampuchea (DK) movement, opened a campaign to rid the country of the Vietnamese. By January 1982, heavy fighting was reported between the KR and Vietnamese-led Cambodian forces. At the same time, Thailand began supplying war materials to the DK, including the KR. The Vietnamese mounted a major offensive against the DK between November 1984 and April 1985, destroying all their major bases in Kampuchea near the Thailand border. DK tactics changed to that of a more mobile guerrilla warfare to mitigate the need for fixed camps. Communist China, who had been supplying the Khmer Rouge, now began giving weapons and equipment to the other DK members. Soon, however, the other noncommunist elements of the DK formed a joint command, ignoring the Khmer Rouge because of their strongarm tactics against their allies. Fighting continued into the late 1980s. In 1989, for instance, rebel forces attacked a number of government strongholds and held most of them until April 1990. In 1991, heavy fighting continued. On 23 October 1991, however, an agreement was signed by all of the factions, including the KR and the Phnom Penh government, that framed a political settlement in Cambodia. A cease-fire had been agreed upon in May. Representatives of the KR then joined the Supreme National Council. (See Cambodia). When the UN Transitional Authority for Cambodia (UNTAC)–monitored peace process began in January 1992, the Khmer Rouge reacted by refusing to cooperate and stepped up their fighting in northern Cambodia. UN officials were denied access into KR-controlled areas and also refused the previously agreed-to procedures to demobilize at least 705 of their forces. In another face off, the KR kidnapped a group of UN officials in retaliation for an embargo placed on their exports. The KR's campaign of terror against ethnic Vietnamese living in Cambodia continued into 1993 and forced the migration of thousands into the refugee camps of Thailand. In what many perceived as a political maneuver, the KR announced it would integrate its forces into the Cambodian army. The U.S. responded by stating it would cut off all aid to Cambodia if that happened. In the meantime, concerted attacks by government troops in August and December were successful. The restoration of the monarchy in September did much to defuse the KR efforts, and UNTAC was disbanded in November. In July 1994, the KR was declared illegal, even though it had been King Norodom Sihanouk's plan to bring it into a reconciliation government. While setting up talks with the KR, the government launched a major offensive against it. Fighting was heavy in the first quarter of the year, with the KR retaining control of much of northwest Cambodia. In August, the KR proclaimed its own government. Before the end of the year, the Cambodian government indirectly accused Thailand of giving aid to the KR. In early 1995, KR guerrillas murdered an American tourist and her guide at Angkor Wat. Extremely heavy fighting led the government to announce that casualties and defections made the KR no longer a threat. An example of this may be seen in the defection of 1,000 KR troops in the Batambang region in 1996. It also became apparent in 1996 that at least two million Cambodians had died at KR hands during the brief rule in 1975–1979.

Khomeini, Ayatollah Rhuollah Musawi. (b. 17 May 1902 [?], Khomeyn, Iran—d. 3 June 1989, Tehran) Born the son and grandson of Ayatollahs (a term meaning "Gift of God") in the Shi'ite Muslim faith, Khomeini witnessed his father's execution at the order of a landowner. His older brother, Moteza, undertook raising him and seeing to his education in Islamic schools. In 1962, after a career as a writer on philosophic subjects, Khomeini had moved to Qom, which was the center of Shi'ite activity in Iran in the 1920s. He was named Ayatollah in the 1950s and became a leading religious figure. In the early 1960s, he was elevated to Grand Ayatollah. Khomeini was arrested for crimes against the monarchy but was released a short time later. On 4 November 1964, however, he was again arrested for criticizing the shah and was ordered banished from Iran. He first settled in An Najah in Iraq, another Shi'ite holy place, but by 1978 his presence had become a major embarassment to the Damascus government, and he was ordered out of the country. His next stop was France, where he arrived on 6 October 1978. He and a small band of followers set up headquarters near Paris. From there he began his unrelenting campaign to return Iran to Islamic purity. Khomeini called for Islamic revolution in Iran, which brought together Islamic fundamentalists and led to massive unrest. The U.S. abandonment of the shah led to a successful overthrow of the government and the return of Khomeini in triumph on 1 February 1979. Once there he established a clerical hierarchy in government and ordered the execution of thousands of supporters of the shah and anyone who posed a threat to his rule. Under Khomeini's orders, Iranian "students" seized the U.S. embassy in Tehran on 4 November 1979, which led to the threat of war. U.S. president Carter's diliatory response and his ill-advised rescue attempt made the U.S. look foolish. Only when Ronald Reagan became president were the hostages held in Tehran released after 444 days of captivity and torture. Khomeini forced a prolonged war on his people after the Iraqis attacked Iran in 1980. He finally accepted a cease-fire in 1988 after thousands had lost their lives on both sides. Khomeini's last action before his death was to sign a death warrant for Salman Rushdie, the author of *Satanic Verses*, a work Khomeini considered sacrilegious. He died 3 June 1989 and was buried amid some of the most horrendous public demonstrations of grief ever witnessed. At one point, his coffin fell off its carriage, his body being thrown into the street. *Reading:* Matthew Gordon, *Ayatollah Khomeini* (1987); Mohamed Heikal, *Return of the Ayatollah* (1982).

Khorramshahr (Khurramshahr). *See* Iraq-Iran War.

al-Khoury (Khuri), Bisgara (Bishara). In 1943, Bisgara al-Khoury was elected president of Lebanon. As a first move, the president and his new government moved to end French influence by introducing a new constitution. On 11 November 1943, al-Khoury and almost everyone else in the Lebanese government were arrested on orders of the French delegate-general, Jean Helleu. An uprising followed that was settled only by British diplomatic intervention. As a result, the Lebanese government was released from detention and given power to rule for itself. Al-Khoury was deposed and forced to resign in the face of growing unrest and mounting labor strikes on 18 September 1952.

Khrushchev, Nikita Sergeevich. (b. 17 April 1894, Kalinkova, Russia—d. 11 September 1971, Moscow) Khrushchev was born a miner's son in the Kursk region. He worked as a shepherd and, later, in the mines and factories of the Donets region. After the revolution (1917), he enlisted in the Red Guards, and in 1918 he joined the Communist Party. During the Civil War he served the party in political positions. Afterward, he returned to industrial work. In 1922, he entered a three-year program of study at the Donets Industrial Institute. Upon graduation he worked full time with the Ukrainian Communist Party. In 1929 he was selected to study at the Industrial Academy in Moscow. He became a member of the Moscow Committee of the All-Union Communist Party in 1934. and of the Supreme Soviet in 1937. In 1938, Khrushchev became the first secretary of the Ukrainian Communist Party and a candidate member of the All-Union Central Committee. In 1939, he became a full member of the Politburo. At the beginning of World War II Khrushchev was put in charge of the annexation of Poland. Following the Nazi attack on the USSR, he was put in charge of the evacuation of industry from the Ukraine. He also served on a number of military councils and directed partisan operations from behind the German lines and played a role in the defense of Stalingrad. In 1943 he was given the political rank of lieutenant general in the Red Army. After November 1943, he resumed his role of first secretary of the Ukrainian party. In December 1949, he was called to Moscow to become first secretary of the Moscow Region and in October 1952, he was appointed to the Presidium. In September 1953, Khrushchev became first secretary of the Communist Party of the Soviet Union. At the 20th party congress in 1956, Khrushchev delivered a blistering attack on Josef Stalin (qv), which encouraged the subsequent revolts in Poland and Hungary. Khrushchev took on the added duty of chairman of the Council of

Ministers following N. A. Bulganin's (qv) resignation. He was responsible for the deterioration of U.S.–Soviet relations following his denunciation of the U.S. at a meeting with President Eisenhower (qv), after the shooting down of an American U-2 spy plane over the USSR on 1 May 1960. In 1961, Khrushchev authorized the building of the Berlin Wall to stop the flow of the East German labor force to the West. He also authorized the emplacement of Soviet offensive weapons in Cuba in 1962, which led to the "Cuban Missile Crisis." In 1963, the U.S. and the USSR signed a nuclear test ban. On 15 October 1964, Khrushchev allegedly resigned from office because of ill health. Most likely he was deposed for the failure of his domestic policies and because of the distrust of the military leadership. He spent his remaining years in quiet retirement outside Moscow. When a book titled *Khrushchev Remembers* was published in Moscow, Khrushchev issued a statement denying authorship. His death was barely mentioned in the Soviet press, another sign of the disfavor in which he was held. *Reading:* Alexander Dallin, *The Khrushchev and Brezhnev Years* (1992); William J. Tompson, *Khrushchev: A Political Life* (1997); R. I. Medvedev, *Khrushchev: The Years of Power* (1976).

Khushnia (Al Khushniah). *See* Syria.

Khuzestan. *See* Iraq.

Kiansu Province. *See* China.

Kielce. *See* Poland.

Kien Hoa Province. *See* Vietnam.

Kim Dae Jung. (b. 1924, Mokpo, Korea) Born the son of a shipping executive, Kim did not come to public attention until the beginning of the Korean War (1950). He was jailed by the North Koreans and sentenced to death as a "reactionary." Some consider his later release as a sign he collaborated with the enemy. Others claim he escaped and joined the resistance. In 1970, he was elected president of the Korean Democratic Party and stood for the presidency of South Korea in 1973 narrowly losing to Park Chung Hee (qv). Following the election, The Kim campaign vigorously accused the Park government of corruption. Thereafter, Kim was the victim of an assassination attempt. On 8 August 1973, five South Korean CIA agents kidnapped Kim from a Japanese hotel in Tokyo. On 13 August, Kim was located under house arrest in his home in South Korea. Kim had been taken there by speedboat from Japan through a very tightly controlled Korean maritime security system, obviously with government collusion. The Japanese government protested the incident. The South Korean government expressed its regrets on 20 August but did not release Kim. On 15 September, the Japanese released a statement incriminating the South Korean embassy's first secretary in the kidnapping. On 24 August the Japanese government broke off diplomatic talks scheduled for 7–8 September. On 26 October 1973, Kim was released from house arrest, and the South Korean government formally apologized for the incident in December. On 22 May 1980, Kim was again arrested after being accused of plotting the overthrow of the government. He was tried, convicted and sentenced to death. On 17 September, the Japanese government warned Korea's president Chun Doo Hwan that its relations with South Korea would be reexamined if Kim was put to death. After a period of worldwide furor, President Chun commuted the sentence to life imprisonment (a sentence later changed to 20 years). Chun subsequently freed Kim in December 1982 and allowed him to go into exile in the United States. In February 1985, Kim returned to Korea, where he immediately became a leader of the opposition party. In 1987, Kim again lost the election for the presidency, gaining only 25 percent of the vote in what had been a divisive campaign that had split his party. Kim took another setback in 1991, when most city and provincial council seats went to his party's opponents.

Kim Il Sung. (b. 15 April 1912, Pyongyang, Korea—d. 8 July 1994, Pyongyang) Born Kim Song Chu, Kim spent his youth in Manchuria, where he founded the Korean Independence Alliance. He was arrested by the Japanese, who controlled Manchuria, on charges of antigovernment activities. He was jailed for a year. After his release and the start of World War II, he is believed to have gone to Moscow, where he remained until his return to North Korea in 1945 as a captain in the Red Army. He was later decorated by Stalin. By that time Kim had adopted the name of an anti-Japanese resistance hero, Kim Il Sung, to improve his persona as a national leader. In 1946 he was named to head the government of Soviet-occupied North Korea. In September 1948, he proclaimed the Democratic People's Republic of Korea, and in 1949 he consolidated all political activity into the Korean Workers' Party. In 1950, he authorized the invasion of South Korea when his diplomatic efforts toward reunification failed. Radio Pyongyang reported he died in office of a heart attack on 8 July 1994. He was last seen in public in June 1994, when he met with former U.S. president Jimmy Carter (qv) in an attempt to defuse the growing tension over North Korea's refusal to allow inspection of its nuclear facilities. *See* North Korea in Korea. *Reading:* Dae-Sook Suh, *Kim Il Sung: The North Korean Leader* (1995).

Kim Jae Kyu. On 26 October 1979, Kim Jae Kyu, the director of the South Korean Central Intelligence Agency, shot and killed President Park Chung Hee at a dinner party held in a special KCIA restaurant in Seoul, Korea. Five of Park's bodyguards were also killed in the gun battle. Kim was arrested later in the evening at the ROK army headquarters. Kim had apparently been plotting the murder for five months.

King, Martin Luther, Jr. (b. 15 January 1929, Atlanta, Georgia—d. 4 April 1968, Memphis, Tennessee) Martin Luther King, Jr. was born the son of the pastor of the Ebenezer Baptist Church. His mother was a schoolteacher. At age 15 he was enrolled in Morehouse College before completing high school. After graduating (1948), he entered the Crozer Theological Seminary in Chester, Pennsylvania, from which he graduated in 1951. He then entered Boston College, where he received a Ph.D. in theology in 1955. While in Boston he met and married Coretta Scott. In December 1955, King became the head of the Montgomery Improvement Association, which was to lead the boycott against segregation on the city's buses. During the boycott, King's home was bombed. In 1956, the U.S. Supreme Court ordered the desegregation of the buses. In 1957, King won the Spingarn Award from the National Association for the Advancement of Colored People (NAACP). King then became president (1958) of the Southern Christian Leadership Conference (SCLC) and continued his civil rights activities in the South. He visited India in 1959 to study Mahatma Gandhi's nonviolence teachings and, upon his return to the U.S., became the copastor of his father's church in Atlanta. In 1962, he led a "nonviolent army" march in Albany, Georgia. In Birmingham, Alabama, King was arrested in 1963 during a campaign to achieve desegregation of public facilities in that city. In 1964, King was awarded the Nobel peace prize for his civil rights activities. In 1965, he led the movement to register black voters in Selma, Alabama, which erupted into violence. King then led a five-day march in which thousands of black and white sympathizers marched from Selma to Montgomery, the state capital, to protest the denial of the franchise to black citizens. In 1965, King turned his attention to the conditions found in northern cities, where blacks were treated much the same as in the South. He established a headquarters in a slum area of Chicago to protest the city's discrimination in housing and employment. During all of this time and until his death he was under close surveillance by the FBI, which was under the direct orders of J. Edgar Hoover. King also turned his attention to the war in Vietnam, claiming the money spent in the conflict could be better used to fight poverty and discrimination. On 4 April 1967, he called the U.S. the "greatest purveyor of violence in the world" and went on to encourage draft evasion and a merger of the civil rights and antiwar efforts. On 15 August 1967, he called for "massive disobedience" as a means of achieving goals. King also opposed black militants who saw violence as the only means to the end of segregation and discrimination. He helped plan a "Poor People's March" on Washington to take place in 1968. Before that, however, he went to Memphis, Tennessee, to support a strike for higher pay by sanitary workers. While there he was assassinated by James Earl Ray. King's death brought widescale rioting and looting throughout the United States, which took weeks to pacify. King was buried in Atlanta. In 1977, Martin Luther King, Jr. was awarded the Presidential Medal of Freedom. In 1986, the U.S. Congress established a national holiday in his honor.

King Edward Harbor. *See* Falkland Islands.

Kingston. *See* Jamaica.

Kinkuzu. *See* Zaire.

Kinshasa. *See* Zaire.

Kirala (Koirala), B. P. In 1959, B. P. Kirala was named prime minister of the new government of Nepal. Because of government corruption and inefficiency, King Mahendra bir Bikham (qv) dissolved Parliament and ousted Kirala on 15 December 1960. The king then personally assumed the administration of the country.

Kirin. *See* China.

Kirkuk, Iraq. *See* Iran-Iraq War.

Kiryat Shemona. *See* Israel.

Kisangani. *See* Stanleyville.

Kivu Province, Independent Congo Republic. *See* Congo.

Klinghoffer, Leon. During the hijacking of the *Achille Lauro* cruise liner on 7–9 October 1985, Leon Klinghoffer, a crippled American passenger in a wheelchair, was murdered by the terrorists. *See Achille Lauro.*

Kloten Airport, Zurich. *See* Switzerland.

Knox, Clifton. On 23 January 1973, three Haitian terrorists kidnapped the U.S. ambassador to Haiti, Clifton Knox. The U.S. consul general voluntarily went with the ambassador into captivity. Initially, the terrorists demanded the release of 31 political prisoners and a $500,000 ransom. The following day, they reduced their demands to the release of 16 prisoners, a ransom of $70,000 and transportation to Mexico. The Haitian government complied, and the two US diplomats were released unharmed. The terrorists and the released prisoners, accompanied by the Mexican ambassador, were flown to Mexico City, where Mexican authorities promptly seized the ransom money (subsequently returned to Haiti) and refused admission to the group. The group then went to Chile.

Kocaeli Province. *See* Turkey.

el Kodsi (al Kudsi), Nazem. In September 1961, Syrian army officers carried out a coup that ousted the Egyptian administration and forced the country's withdrawal from the United Arab Republic. In the ensuing struggle for power within Syria, a constitutional government was elected with Nazim el Kodsi as president. On 28 March 1962, the Syrian army carried out a bloodless coup that displaced the el Kodsi government. On 13 April, another coup returned el Kodsi to the presidency after he promised to fight for a union of "liberated Arab states." On 8 March 1963, a pro-Egyptian Baathist coup placed a new slate of leaders into power in Syria.

Koh Tang (Kaoh Tang) Island. *See SS Mayaguez.*

Koje Island. On 7 May 1952, a well-organized revolt broke out among the more ardent communist prisoners held at the United Nations prisoner of war compound on Koje Island, located off the southern tip of the Korean peninsula. Many Korean and Chinese prisoners were killed by their fellow prisoners because they appeared cooperative with their captors, and communist flags were raised over the camp. The camp commander, US Army Brigadier General Francis T. Dodd (qv), carelessly allowed himself to be taken prisoner by the prisoners and became the centerpiece of a carefully orchestrated propaganda coup directed from Pyongyang (qv) through a secret radio located in the camp. Order was restored and Dodd freed only after U.S. combat troops, commanded by Brigadier General Haydon Boatner, swept through the camp in June 1952.

Koki Thom. *See* Cambodia.

Kola Peninsula. *See* USSR.

Kolarov, Vassil. In July 1949, Georgi Dimitrov, the premier of Bulgaria under the Fatherland Front government, died. Vassil (Vasil) Kolarov became premier in his place. Kolarov died early in 1950. He was replaced by Vulko Chervenko, the general secretary of the central committee. Chervenko was also the brother-in-law of the late Georgi Dimitrov. Chervenko's ascension to power marked the beginning of a period of purges and an accusation of American meddling in Bulgarian affairs. Diplomatic relations were broken on 21 February 1950.

Kolingba, André. (b. 12 August 1935, Bangui) Kolingba served in the French army before his country received its independence and saw service in Indochina and Cameroon. He was promoted to chief of the armed forces staff only on 30 July 1981. On 1–2 September, the Central African Republic government of David Dacko (qv) was overthrown in a bloodless coup led by General Andre Kolingba. Kolingba, the former chief of the armed force's staff, proclaimed himself head of state. He then suspended the constitution and appointed an all-military government to run the country. Kolingba withstood a coup in 1982. By 1985, however, opposition to his military regime was growing. An opposition government-in-exile had been formed in Paris, but it was not successful in unseating Kolingba. Rather, the vote of the people did that in 22 August 1993, when he was defeated at the polls. He left office on 27 September.

Kolwezi. *See* Zaire.

Komer, Robert. (b.22 February 1922, Chicago) Komer graduated from Harvard Business School in 1947 and joined the Central Intelligence Agency (CIA). He served in the White House during the Kennedy administration as a special assistant for noncommitted nations and as an adviser on disarmament. During the Johnson administration, Komer became one of the chief advocates of the pacification campaign in Vietnam (qv). When the program proved a failure under USAID tutelage in 1967, Johnson ordered Westmoreland (qv) to bring it under his command and sent Komer to Vietnam as Westmoreland's deputy for pacification. The new program, called Civil Operations and Revolutionary Development Support (CORDS), included most social and economic programs across the countryside. The CORDS operations also included Project Pheonix, a program designed to remove the Viet Cong infrastructure and for which, because of its methods, the U.S. received much criticism. After his replacement in Vietnam , Komer became ambassador to Turkey (October 1968), but he resigned under pressure in April 1969. He then became a consultant with the Rand Corporation.

Kompong Cham. *See* Cambodia.

Kompong Som. *See* Cambodia.

Kompong Speu. *See* Cambodia.

Kompong Trabek. *See* Cambodia.

Kompong Trach. *See* Cambodia.

Kong Le. On 9 August 1960, Captain Kong Le led a coup that deposed the pro-Western government of Laos. Tiao Samsonith (qv), the premier, was replaced by Prince Souvanna Phouma. On 16 December 1960, a counter-coup led by

Colonel Phoumi Nosavan (qv) upset the Kong Le regime. Souvanna Phouma fled the country, but Kong Le joined the communist Pathet Lao (qv) guerrilla organization and continued the fight. By May 1964, Kong Le was a general in the neutralist forces, which were defeated by a combined North Vietnamese-Pathet Lao force in the *Plaine des Jarres* region.

Konitsa. *See* Greece.

Kontum. *See* Vietnam and International Control Commission.

Koper. *See* Yugoslavia.

Korea. A peninsula on the northeast coast of Asia, Korea's northern border is bounded on the northwest by China and on the northeast by a narrow border with Russian Siberia. The east coast faces the Sea of Japan, while the west coast is washed by the Yellow Sea. Korean history begins in antiquity, in the third millennium B.C. Legend and fact place the founding of Korea in 2333 B.C. In 1122 B.C., the Chinese wise man Kija led a band of Chinese into northern Korea. In 108 B.C. the Chinese had four colonies there in a province called Lolang. Southern Korea stayed free of Chinese domination and established the Three Kingdoms of Han (Dai Han) (from the Mahan, Chinhan and Pyonhan tribes). This period is usually dated from 57 B.C., when the Silla Empire was formed. For the next 700 years the three kingdoms warred among themselves, against Japan and against the north, which was supported by China. After the seventh century A.D., Korea was associated with the Chinese on several occasions. In 1011, China invaded Korea and burned the capital city. After the Chinese weakened and left, Korea was invaded by the Mongols (1231). In 1274 and 1279, the Mongols attempted invasions of Japan from Korea. The Koreans freed themslves of Mongol domination in 1364. In 1392, a new era (Yi dynasty) took power and remained until 1910, when Japan annexed Korea. From that time until the end of World War II an incessant guerrilla war ensued in which the Koreans fought against Japanese rule. The end of World War II also brought a division of Korea along the 38th parallel, which formed the dividing line between Allied- and Soviet-occupied territories. This division was decided upon at the Potsdam Conference in July 1945.

North Korea. Soviet troops entered northern Korea on 10 August 1945, and the Democratic People's Republic of Korea was proclaimed on 1 May 1948, after North Korea refused to abide by the terms of agreements calling for free elections for all of Korea. Kim Il Sung (qv) became the country's leader and remained in power in 1994. In June 1950, North Korea invaded the south. After three years of war, during which the North Korean army was all but destroyed by the United Nations Command, a tenuous armistice was achieved (*see* Korean War below). In May 1993, North Korea became the first nation to withdraw from the Nuclear Nonproliferation Treaty. In 1994, North Korea refused to allow United Nations inspectors to examine nuclear facilities, and the world supposed North Korea was making nuclear weapons. The United States continued negotiations with North Korea in 1995 to end the stalemate over the nuclear issue and supplied the agreed upon (1994) 50,000 tons of fuel oil to offset the country's inability to produce electricity. The U.S. also promised assistance in North Korean acquisition of two nuclear power plants. Still, North Korea wanted more concessions. An agreement on the issue was reached in December 1995 that led to a U.S. lifting of its trade embargo. Kim Jong Il's role as the successor to Kim Il Sung was still in doubt, however, as he slowly consolidated his power base. By year's end, he was still in control.

South Korea U.S. forces arrived in South Korea on 8 September 1945. In May 1948, the Republic of Korea was proclaimed, with Syngman Rhee (qv) as its first president. South Korea was invaded from the north in June 1950. A three-year war ensued that destroyed much of the country (*see* Korean War below). The subsequent armistice allowed South Korea to rebuild and flourish, but not without periods of intense internal strife. President Syngman Rhee was forced to resign on 26 April 1960, following a time of unrest led by students. An army coup led by General Park Chung Hee (qv) took place on 16 May 1961, which ousted Rhee's successor and established a virtual dictatorship under Park. That regime lasted until 26 October 1979, when Park was assassinated by the head of the Korean Central Intelligence Agency. General Chung Doo Hwan came to power and reestablished much of the police state suppression that was known during Park's time. In 1972, North Korea and South Korea had revised their constitutions, and a North-South Coordinating Committee was established that was to work toward reunification. This effort was disbanded in 1973. Efforts to reopen joint talks were made in 1979 and 1980. In February 1993, the first nonmilitary Korean was elected president. His first project was ridding the administration of corruption. Some of the corruption uncovered implicated U.S. companies in bribery to win contracts for military equipment. Negotiations between North and South Korea broke off in 1994 after the North threatened the destruction of Seoul, the South Korean capital, because of South Korea's continued support of the sanctions against the North because of Pyongyang's adamant refusal to allow inspection of its suspected nuclear weapons production facilities. In March 1994, the U.S. began shipping Patriot anti-missile missile units to Korea and allowed South Korea to buy advanced weapons systems for its defense against northern aggression. The U.S. also began updating its defensive scenarios designed to accomplish the same goal. In June, however, the North and South achieved a breakthrough that aimed at a summit conference, partially as a result of the diplomacy of former U.S. president Jimmy Carter, who visited Pyongyang. Progress was also made in breaking the U.S.–North Korea stalemate over nuclear weapons, but without South Korea's participation. Rioting broke out across South Korea when the populace was forcibly barred from mourning the death of Kim Il Sung and again in August, when students demanded reconciliation with the North. More than 1,000 were arrested in the latter incident. Earlier, in April, security forces attacked a reformist monastery in Seoul that had been the center of a protest against the election of a Buddhist monk as leader of the Buddhist congregation in Korea. Two former presidents were indicted on charges of premediated rebellion in the 1979 military coup.

They were tried in 1995, and one of the pair, Roh Tae Woo, who was president from 1988 to1993, also confessed to charges of corruption, in which he was accused of accepting $650 million in contributions and nearly $400 million more in bribes. South Korea was also rocked in 1994 by the exposure of a large-scale embezzlement operation by city officials in the major seaport of Inchon. When a department store collapsed in Seoul on 29 June 1995, another scandal was heaped on the already enormous pile of corruption charges that led to the highest offices in government and industry. While confronting these internal problems, the issue of rapprochement with North Korea remained an important issue. The death of Kim Il Sung delayed, possibly for years, the expected summit and most other initiatives appeared in limbo, although some economic progress was made. Rioting also occurred in South Korea when a former minister of Japan stated that Korea had "harmoniously" accepted the 1910 Japanese annexation of the country. At year's end, relations between the two countries were, to say the least, strained. The South Koreans contented themselves, however, with the razing of a building in Seoul that had been built as a residence for the Japanese governor-general during the occupation.

Korean War At 0400 (4:00 A.M.) on the night of 24–25 June 1950, North Korean (NK) forces crossed the 38th parallel into Republic of Korea (ROK) territory at 11 points. Elements of at least ten NK divisions took part in the initial invasion. On 25 June, the United Nations Security Council ordered an immediate cease-fire and the withdrawal of the NK forces. That same day, Chiang Kai-shek (qv) offered South Korea the assistance of the Chinese Nationalist Army on Taiwan. On 27 June, U.S. president Harry Truman (qv) directed the U.S. Far East Command in Japan to furnish naval and air support to South Korea. General Douglas MacArthur (qv), Supreme Allied Commander, Far East, recommended acceptance of the Nationalist Chinese offer, but Truman rejected the proposal. That same day, the United Nations voted to aid South Korea and asked for assistance from the member nations of the UN. U.S. ground forces were committed on 30 June, and air strikes were authorized against targets in North Korea. On 2 July, Major General William F. Dean (qv), the commander of the U.S. 24th Infantry Division, was appointed commander of U.S. forces in Korea. On 7 July, the United Nations recommended that all forces in South Korea be placed under one unified command. The next day, General Douglas MacArthur was appointed commander of UN forces. The North Koreans captured Seoul, the South Korean capital, within three days of the invasion and steadily drove the allied forces south into a position that became known as the Pusan Perimeter. Dean was captured at Taejon during the withdrawal on 20 July. On 15 September, U.S. Marine and army forces landed behind the North Koreans at Inchon. At the same moment, the UN forces in the Pusan Perimeter began a drive northward and linked up with the Inchon force at Suwon, on 26 September. At that same time Seoul was recaptured. On 30 September, UN forces reached the 38th parallel. On 1 and 9 October, MacArthur asked for a cessation of hostilities, but in both cases the North

Koreans refused. After the 1 October refusal, MacArthur requested UN permission to continue the attack into North Korea. On 7 October, the UN General Assembly adopted a resolution calling for the unification of Korea and established a commission to pursue the matter. After the 9 October North Korean refusal to surrender, UN forces crossed the border. On 15 October, President Truman met MacArthur on Wake Island to discuss differences between official U.S. policy and statements made by the general. By 30 October, UN forces were approaching the Yalu River, which separated North Korea from Communist China. On 1 November, the North Koreans launched a limited counterattack, but did not or could not follow up on some initial successes. At the same time, the first reports of Chinese "volunteers" began to reach Far East Command headquarters in Tokyo, but MacArthur refused to believe them. For the first time, on 8 November, North Korean fighter planes, flying from Chinese bases across the Yalu, engaged U.S. fighters. On 24 November, UN forces launched an all-out offensive to end the war. The attacks were blunted by large numbers of Chinese troops already across the border in North Korea. On 25–26 November, a Chinese offensive began that did not end until UN forces were pushed south of the 38th parellel. Part of the UN forces were cut off from land withdrawal around the Chosin reservoir and had to be evacuated by sea. Between 5–15 December, more than 100,000 American, ROK and other UN forces were evacuated from the Wonsan-Hungnam perimeters under the heaviest naval gunfire protection since World War II. Meanwhile, new defensive positions were being established in South Korea, and more United Nations forces were arriving; the first Canadian troops arrived on 19 December, to join the Commonwealth Division. On New Year's Day 1951, a Communist Chinese–North Korean offensive began that penetrated UN lines. On 4 January, UN forces evacuated Seoul. Some ROK and U.S. forces had been trapped or overrun during the onslaught, and the U.S. Eighth Army reserve had to be committed to extricate the U.S. 2nd Infantry Division. The front was stabilized on 15 January about 50 miles south of Seoul. On the 17th of January, the United States submitted a resolution to the UN branding the Chinese as aggressors; this motion was passed by the UN on 1 February. In the meantime, Chinese had refused a UN peace plan. On 8 January, an arms embargo was clamped on mainland China. The Labor government in Great Britain balked at the embargo even though it had troops fighting in Korea. A UN offensive south of Seoul, which began on 25 January, was blunted by Chinese forces during the week following 11 February 1951. On 7 March the UN offensive was started up again and recaptured Seoul on 14 March. The next day, President Truman announced MacArthur had full authority to move north of the 38th parallel. By 31 March, the UN had reestablished positions on the 38th parallel. On 10 April, however, MacArthur was relieved of command because of his outspoken criticism of UN/U.S. policy on the war. General Matthew Ridgway assumed command. On 12 April, the UN Command opened a new offensive to protect the strategically important "Iron Triangle" (qv) in Central Korea. A Chinese counteroffensive began on 22 April, but stalled on the 30th, and the Chinese withdrew to break contact. This became a standard tactic of the Chinese for the remainder of the war. This happened again between 14 May and 20 May 1951. A new UN offensive was halted on 31 May when the Soviet Union threatened to intervene. On 29 June, the UN broadcast an offer to meet for peace talks with China and North Korea. On 1 July North Korea agreed to the meeting, and the first preliminary truce discussion took place at Kaesong on 8 July. On 27 September, when the Communists refused a change of venue for the peace talks, the United Nations Command broke off negotiations. Peace talks were resumed on 8 October in a newly chosen demilitarized site at Panmunjom. Formal talks began on 25 October, and on 12 November the UN halted all offensive operations. On 27 November, a provisional cease-fire went into effect, on the proviso that all truce arrangements would be completed within 30 days. When the truce period ended on 27 December, neither side recommended an extension. On 7 May, a revolt broke out in the large UN prisoner of war compound on Koje Island (qv). By 23 June 1952, UN aircraft were engaged in massive bombing attacks against North Korea. On 2 December, after winning the presidential election in the U.S., Dwight D. Eisenhower visited South Korea, where he discovered that finding a solution to the problem would be more difficult than he originally thought. The Chinese again rejected a peace offer on 12 December. On 5 January, the Churchill government in Great Britain announced its firm opposition to expanding the war into mainland China. Churchill expressed himself in believing the main arena of conflict was still Western Europe. On 25 February 1953, the U.S. accepted an Indian peace proposal for Korea and, on 28 March a prisoner exchange was agreed upon. This action also led to a resumption of the peace talks. Operation Little Switch took place in April, when 213 UN sick and wounded were handed over in exchange for 5,800 communist sick and wounded. On 23 April, the UN voted to investigate communist charges that the U.S. was engaging in biological warfare. In May 1953, President Syngman Rhee (qv) unexpectedly announced that he would not be bound by any agreement that kept Korea divided; on 9 June the South Korean government announced it was ready to "march north." On 10 June, Communist forces opened a series of attacks against mostly ROK army positions. On 18 June, Syngman Rhee demanded a resumption of offensive operations in retaliation for the attacks on ROK positions. He repeated his refusal to accept peace terms on 23 June. On 25 June, the communists began a new series of attacks and broke off peace talks. After the fighting once again subsided and the U.S. had exerted pressure on the Rhee government, South Korea announced it was ready to accept an armistice (11 July 1953). On 27 July, the armistice went into effect. At the same time, the 16 nations that had committed forces to the Korean War announced their readiness to resume fighting if the Communists broke the truce. Prisoners were exchanged on 5 August; the exchange was completed on 6 September. Twenty-one Americans, one British, and 225 South Koreans refused to be released from communist control. A mutual defense agreement between the United States and

South Korea was signed on 8 August. United Nations prisoners who refused repatriation became the responsibility of the Neutral Nations Repatriation Commission on 23 September 1953. On 3 December 1953, the UN adopted a U.S.–sponsored resolution expressing grave concern over atrocities committed by the communists. On 23 January 1954, when the UN announced that communist prisoners who refused repatriation were "free men with civilian status," some 14,000 Chinese prisoners were then transfered to Formosa. On 9 February 1954, the United Nations Supervisory Commission investigated a communist violation of the truce. From that time, there have been repeated violation of the truce agreement, some of them quite bloody. *Reading:* Chen Jian, *China's Road to the Korean War: The Making of the Sino-American Confrontation* (1994); Edwin Hoyt, *The Day the Chinese Attacked: Korea, 1950: The Story of the Failure of America's China Policy* (1994); G. L. Simons, *Korea: The Search for Sovereignty* (1995); Bruce Cumings, *Korea's Place in the Sun: A Modern History* (1997); William Stueck, *The Korean War: An International History* (1995); Wayne A. Kirkbride, *North Korea's Undeclared War: 1953–* (1995); Hak-Kyu Sohn, *Authoritarianism and Opposition in South Korea* (1990); Roger Tennant, *A History of Korea* (1996).

Kosovo. *See* Yugoslavia.

Koster, Samuel W. On 16 March 1968, the My Lai massacre occurred within the Tactical Area of Operational Responsibility (TAOR) of the U.S. 23rd (American) Infantry Division, commanded by Major General Samuel W. Koster. Koster was one of thirteen military personnel accused of complicity in an attempt to cover up the massacre. He had been promoted to lieutenant general and was the commandant of the US Military Academy, West Point, when the My Lai revelations came to light. He was forced to resign his commission, but was not formally charged or tried in the affair, nor were any of the other senior officers involved ever charged in the affair. *See* Calley.

Kostov, Traicho. On 25 June 1949, Kostov, the deputy premier of Bulgaria and a member of the executive committee of the Fatherland Front, was arrested along with ten others and charged with treason. He was subsequently tried, found guilty and executed (16 December 1949). Kostov was swept up in the series of arrests that followed the death of Premier Vassil Kolarov (qv). As a part of the general purge following Kolarov's death, the Bulgarian government accused (21 February 1950) the United States of complicity in the treason blamed on Kostov.

Kouandete, Maurice. On 17 December 1967, the government of President Christophe Soglo (qv) of the African nation of Dahomey was overthrown by a coup led by Major Maurice Kouandete. As his first act, he promoted himself to Lieutenant Colonel and then assumed the presidency. In 1968–1969, Kouandete allowed for the establishment of a civilian government led by Émile Derlin Zinsou (qv). In December 1969, however, Zinsou was replaced by Kouandete. A three-man junta ruled the country until elections were held in March 1970. Although the election was eventually annulled, Kouandete was overshadowed by more powerful leaders and faded into obscurity.

Kountché, Seyni. (b. 1 July 1931, Fandou, Niger—d. 10 November 1987, Paris) Kountché was educated in the French army school system and joined the French colonial forces in 1949. Kountché fought in Algiers and Indochina, rising to the rank of sergeant in 1957. After his country became independent in 1960, he transferred to the Niger army. On 15 April 1974, Hamani Diori, the president of Niger, was ousted from office by Lieutenant Colonel Seyni Kountché in a military coup. Kountché had been army chief of staff before the coup. There was little bloodshed, except for Diori's wife, who was killed by a stray gunshot. The new head of state and chairman of the military council inherited a nation bordering on starvation. One of his first moves was to suspend the constitution. In 1984, while Kountché visited France, a coup attempt against his government failed. By 1986, Kountché's policies had become more radical, but his country's economy was making a modest recovery. He died in Paris in 1987.

Kovacs, Bela. The secretary general of the Smallholder's Party in Hungary, Bela Kovacs was arrested on 25 February 1947 for plotting against the Soviet occupation of his country. His arrest marked the beginning of a general purge of non-communist elements from the government. The Smallholder's Party had repudiated Kovacs and a number of other party officials as fascists at the urging of Moscow.

Koza. *See* Okinawa.

Krabi Province. *See* Thailand.

Kracow (Cracow). *See* Poland.

Kratie. *See* Cambodia.

Kreisky, Bruno. (b. 22 January 1911, Vienna —d. 29 July 1990, Vienna) Born the son of a rich manufacturer, Kreisky was educated in the law and political economy and took a doctor of laws degree from the University of Vienna. In college, he joined the Socialist Party. After Austria was annexed by Nazi Germany, he was forced to flee in 1938 in the face of Gestapo persecution because of his Jewish faith and his anti-Nazi beliefs. Having resided in Sweden durinbg the war years he returned after the war to Austria and, in 1956, became a member of Parliament. In 1959, he became deputy chairman of the Austrian Socialist Party. In 1967, he was narrowly elected the party's chairman. Also, from 1959, he was the Austrian foreign minister. On 21 September 1960, he asked the United Nations General Assembly to investigate the status of the German-speaking minority in the Southern Tyrol. This group resided mainly in the Trentino-Alto Adige region of northern Italy. In 1970, when his party won the general elections, he was asked to form the new government and serve as chancellor. On 29 September 1973, Kreisky acceded to the demands of Palestinian terrorists and promised to halt Jewish emigration to Israel through Austria. In the face of a worldwide outcry of protest, he reversed himself within the week (4 October) and resumed Jewish emigration. Kreisky's time in office brought prosperity to Austria, but charges of government corruption and an unfavorable economic climate began to cloud the scene in the early 1980s. On 24 April 1983, Kreisky's party lost its majority in the general elections, and he announced his retirement from active politics, which took effect on 24 May. He remained the honorary party chairman until 1987, however, and died in 1990.

Kroesen, Frederick. On 15 September 1981, a car carrying General Frederick Kroesen, the commanding general of the US Army, Europe (USAREUR), was attacked by terrorists of the group known as the Red Army Faction (qv). Two rocket-assisted antitank (RPG-7) weapons were fired at Kroesen's car; one missed, and the other hit the trunk. The car was severely damaged, but no one was seriously injured, although both Kroesen and his wife suffered from the explosion.

Kuala Lumpur. *See* Malaysia.

Kubitschek, Juscelino. On 11 November 1955, a military junta led by Lieutenant General H. B. D. Teixeira Lott seized power in Brazil. The government overthrow was carried out when it became apparent that the acting president, Carlos Coimbra da Luz (qv), was planning to prevent the assumption of the presidency by the duly elected Juscelino Kubitschek. Kubitschek was sworn in as scheduled on 31 January 1956. Kubitschek's time in office was marked by substantial growth in country's material assets, but it also marked a period of growing inflation and ever-growing international debt. Kubitschek left office in 1961.

Kumhwa. *See* South Korea.

Kunar. *See* Afghanistan.

Kuneitra (Quneitra). *See* Israel.

Kunene Province. *See* Angola.

Kunin-Atiri Area. *See* Lebanon.

Kuntilla. *See* Egypt.

Kurdistan Province. *See* Iraq and Kurds.

Kurds. Ethnically a mystery, the Kurds have inhabited the eastern Taurus and the Zagros mountains region since at least the seventh century A.D. The Kurdish language has an Iranian base but is different from Persian (Farsi), and is itself divided into two rather distinct types. The Kurds were conquered by the Arabs in 636 A.D., and for the next six centuries they created trouble in western Asia. In the twelfth and thirteenth centuries, one of their number, Salah al-din, known in the west as Saladin, fought Richard I (Lionheart) of England and founded a dynasty (Ayyubid) in Egypt and Syria. The Kurds were then subjugated by the Mongols and Turkmens, but again they fought back, this time evolving into a number of minor principalities. Despite an almost continuous effort by both conquerers to bring the Kurds under their control, five principalities survived into the nineteenth century in Turkey and two in Persia before being suppressed. During this long period of resistance, a sense of nationalism developed among the Kurds, which reached a high point followng World War I when, with the defeat of Turkey and because of Woodrow Wilson's Fourteen Points (especially point 12), Kurdish independence appeared assured. The Treaty of Sèvres (August 1920) created the Arab states Iraq, Syria and Hejaz, the nation of Armenia and, to the south of Armenia, the nation of Kurdistan. The resurgence of Turkish militarism under Atatürk blocked the establishment of Kurdistan, however, and while the Treaty of Lausanne confirmed the Arab states, Armenia and Kurdistan were not mentioned. The 1926 Treaty of Ankara effectively destroyed the concept of a Kurdish state by awarding the Mosul Kurd region to Iraq. From 1925, armed risings by the Kurds took place periodically, some of them so successful that Iran, for example, lost control of its northwestern frontier provinces, which in 1946 were declared the Kurdish Republic of Mahabad. These and other short-lived ventures toward Kurdish independence all failed, however, and the Kurds continued to struggle for independence. In September 1981, for instance, Iraq's refusal to grant autonomy to the Kurds led to a civil war that raged for the rest of the decade. In February 1964, Iraq promised to recognize Kurdish national rights, to gain a cease-fire in the revolt led by Mustafa al-Barzani (qv), and offered self-determination to the Kurds in May 1969. Fighting broke out again in January 1972 when Iraq expelled a number of Kurds to Iran. Iraq's granting of limited autonomy on 11 May 1974 fell short of Kurdish expectations and the troubles continued. On 2 May 1975, Kurdish resistance ended in Iraq when it was determined that continuation of the struggle was futile. In February 1979, clashes took place between between the Kurds and Iranian forces under Ayatollah Khomeini (qv). A cease-fire was arranged in March, but fighting erupted again later in the year with the Kurds overrunning the Iranian border town of Paveh northwest of Kermanshah. Fighting continued into the 1980s, with the emphasis in the Kurdish struggle shifting back and forth between Iraq and Iran. The outcome of the Allied operations against Iraq in the Desert Storm operations put the Iraqi part of the Kurdish problem under UN control. Evidence quickly amassed the showed a deliberate Iraqi attempt to destroy the Kurds in the northern part of Iraq. At the same time, Kurdish unrest in Turkey required a large Turkish military commitment to suppress the trouble that existed as late as 1994. In March 1995, some 35,000 heavily armed Turkish troops crossed Iraq's border and carried out a campaign designed to crush the Kurdish Worker's Party (PKK). The operation continued until May without Iraqi interference. A second Turkish raid in force took place in May 1995. Turkey was ostracized by the West for these incursions. Fighting among Kurdish factions also occurred in 1995 in an area protected by Desert Storm Coalition air forces, but outside Iraqi control. *Reading:* Edgar O'Ballance, *The Kurdish Struggle 1920–94* (1996).

Kurile (Kuril) Islands. A chain of islands belonging to Russia that stretches from the southern tip of the Kamchatka Peninsula to the northeast tip of Hokkaido, the Kurile Islands form the eastern delineator of the Sea of Okhotsk and the Pacific Ocean. The islands were Japanese (since 1875) until the Yalta Agreement in 1945 ceded them to the Soviet Union. The World War II peace treaty between the USSR and Japan was not signed (19 October 1956) until the issue of the Kuriles was settled. Talks held in 1975 failed to resolve the long-standing dispute over the islands' ownership. Talks over Japanese fishing rights in the Kuriles failed in April 1977, when Japan refused to acknowledge Soviet ownership. On 2 May 1977, Communist China announced its support of Japan in the Kuriles controversy. Japan protested Soviet military maneuvers in the Kuriles in June 1978, but to no avail. When the Sino-Japanese treaty was signed in 1978, the USSR began reinforcing its military strength in the Kuriles. The breakup of the Soviet Union did little to quiet the situation, and Russia continued the strengthening of its military positions there until December 1991, when the Russian foreign ministry proposed a settlement that would have returned two of the four principal islands in the group to Japanese control in return for aid to the beleaguered Russian economy. This plan fell apart in September 1992. The problem of ownership of the Kurile Islands remained unresolved in 1995.

Kusa, Musa. On 13 June 1980, the British government ordered Musa Kusa, the senior member of the Libyan mission (Libyan People's Bureau) in London, out of the country. His ejection was based upon evidence of his complicity in two murders that had taken place in London, in which Libyans who had refused to return to Libya were assassinated.

Kuseima, Sinai. *See* Israel.

Kuwait (*Al Kuwayt*). An Arab state located at the northwestern angle of the Persian Gulf, Kuwait is bordered on the north and west by Iraq and on the south by Saudi Arabia. The capital city is also called Kuwait. The area was originally occupied by nomadic tribesmen, but in the early eighteenth century, three clans of nomads abandoned the tradition and settled the region. In 1756, the al-Sabah dynasty was formed. To offset Turkish attempts at annexing Kuwait, its rulers entered into a treaty (1899) with Great Britain and thus blocked Turkish-German attempts at terminating the Berlin-Baghdad Railway there. After World War I, Great Britain recognized Kuwaiti sovereignty under British protection. Even so, Kuwait suffered a number of incursions from Wahhabi factions attacking from Najd (today, Saudi Arabia). The Treaty of 'Uqair (1922) finally settled the border between the two states. Kuwait's northern border was settled with Iraq in 1923. In June 1961, however, when the Anglo-Kuwaiti treaty was abrogated by mutual consent, Iraq claimed Kuwait. When the Kuwaiti government appealed to Great Britain for military support, it was promptly sent, and the threatened invasion was cancelled. Kuwait was admitted to the United Nations in May 1963. Kuwait declared war on Israel in 1967, (as did the rest of the Arab world. Kuwait then cut off its oil deliveries to the West. In March 1973, the government accused Iraq of attacking the border police post at Sameta, 2.5 miles inside Kuwaiti space. Iran and Jordan offered additional forces to Kuwait to help secure its borders. In October, Kuwait cut its oil production by 5 percent to force the United States to reevaluate its Middle East policy toward Israel. The Kuwaiti government took over the American and British interests in the Kuwait Oil Company in 1975. On 15 January 1976, Kuwait announced it had agreed to purchase weaponry from the Soviet Union. In 1976 the government resigned after charging that the National Assembly was blocking significant legislation. The emir then dissolved the assembly and suspended parts of the constitution. On 10 February 1980, the government stated it would take part in the liberation of Israeli-held land. In November 1980, Iranian jets attacked Kuwaiti border posts twice in five days. Iranian bombers attacked oil refineries 25 miles below the Iraqi border on 1 October 1981. Kuwait withdrew its ambassador in Tehran four days later. Also in 1981, constitutional government was restored after national elections were held. During 1984, Kuwaiti ships, along with those carrying many other flags, were attacked by Iranian aircraft over the Persian Gulf. In August 1984, Kuwait made another purchase ($325 million) of military equipment from the Soviet Union. Trouble between the elected National Assembly and the ruling government showed itself in 1986. On 31 August, the emir of Kuwait dissolved the last elected body in that country and gave its powers to an appointed minister. In 1987, urban guerrilla warfare increased, as did the tempo of the Iran-Iraq War (qv). Sabotage in the oil fields led to the arrests and execution of a number of Kuwaitis apparently associated with Iranian-sponsored terrorist groups. On 15 April 1987, the government announced national conscription to train all males between 18 and 30 years of age. On 27 August 1988, Kuwait bought 40 F-18 Hornet fighter aircraft from the U.S. at a cost of $1.8 billion. In 1989, Kuwait still felt the full impact of the long Iran-Iraq War and the remaining tensions after its end. Iranian attacks on Kuwaiti coast guard vessels and royal yachts caused great concern. Internally, the Kuwaiti people were petitioning for a restoration of the elected National Assembly. In July 1990 Iraq accused Kuwait of stealing oil from a disputed field on the common border. On 2 August 1990, after talks broke down, Kuwait was invaded by Iraq. Within days the tiny country of slightly more than two million people was completely under Iraqi control and one of the largest concentrations of manpower (Desert Shield) since World War II assembled in Saudi Arabia to thwart further conquest by Saddam Hussein (qv) and to restore Kuwait's independence. In the ensuing battle, albeit only 100 hours in length (Desert Storm) on the ground, the Iraqi army was all but destroyed, but Sadam Hussain survived. Kuwait was restored, but at a terrible price in destruction. The old Al Sabah regime was returned to power with few signs of relaxation of autocratic rule. Defense arrangements were quickly agreed upon in a series of bilateral treaties in 1992; that list included an agreement with Russia signed in October 1992. Border incidents with Iraq continued and included the seizure of British and Swedish workers in the largely undelineated border region. Kuwait aimed much of its diplomacy toward advertising the fact that hundreds of Kuwaitis were still held hostage by Iraq. The concept of reconciliation with Iraq or its allies proved illusive in 1993, and the Kuwaiti government enunciated that position by beginning the fortification of the common border. In February, the UN ordered a battalion of Argentinian troops to Kuwait, which were reinforced by U.S. and British contingents, all aimed at convincing Iraq that the UN meant business. At approximately the same time Kuwait gave diplomatic recognition to an Iraqi group in exile in Iran that constituted the major anti-Saddam force outside that country. Kuwait captured a 14-man group of Iraqi infiltrators on 26 April 1993. In October

1994, more than 50,000 Iraqi troops began assembling near the Kuwaiti border, (*see* Iraq). As this was seen as a provocation, a force of 40,000 US and British forces were deployed to Kuwait. By November, Iraq withdrew its forces and declared Kuwait a sovereign state. Iraq's moves had also backfired, as Kuwaiti factions stopped wrangling and turned to strengthening the nation. Kuwait also tried and convicted 13 Iraqi and Kuwaiti terrorists who had been charged with attempts to kill former U.S. president George Bush. Six were sentenced to death and the rest imprisoned. Ten Jordanians previously condemned for collaboration had their sentences commuted. Kuwait faced the same problems of defense in 1995, and it was becoming apparent that no amount of military arms purchases would improve the country's ability to defend itself without international aid. *Reading:* Boutros Boutros-Ghali, ed., *The United Nations and the Iraq-Kuwait Conflict, 1990–1996* (1996); Frank Clements, *Kuwait* (World Bibliographical Series, Vol. 56) (1985); John Bulloch & Harvey Morris, *Saddam's War: The Origins of the Kuwait Conflict and the International Response* (1991); N. C. Menon, *Mother of Battles: Saddam's Folly* (1992); Richard Hallion, *Storm over Iraq: Air Power and the Gulf War* (1992).

al-Kuwatly, Shukri. On 30 March 1949, al-Kuwatly, the president of Syria since 1943, was ousted from office in a military coup led by Husni al-Za'im (qv). Al-Kuwatly remained out of power until 1955, when he succeeded Hashim al-Atasi (qv). In 1957, three American diplomats were expelled from Syria for allegedly plotting the overthrow of the al-Kuwatly government. On 1 February 1958, al-Kuwatly issued a joint statement with Egypt's Gamal Nasser (qv) proclaiming the establishment of the United Arab Republic. The events following this undertaking soon removed al-Kuwatly from office. *See* Syria and United Arab Republic.

al-Kuzbarti, Mahmoun. On 28–29 September 1961, a military coup led by Mahmoun al-Kuzbarti overthrew the Syrian government following a period of increasing interference from the Egyptian element of the United Arab Republic (qv). Under al-Kuzbarti, Syria withdrew from the UAR and reestablished ties with the Arab League and the United Nations. Al-Kuzbarti was replaced by a constitutional government led by Nazim al-Kudsi.

Kwangju. *See* South Korea.

Ky, Nguyen Cao. (b. 8 September 1930, Son Tay, Vietnam) Ky served in the French colonial forces in the struggle against Vietnamese independence. After the French withdrawal (1954), he joined the South Vietnamese air force. A fervent anti-communist, he was singled out by U.S. advisory personnel as a born leader. When the Ngo Dinh Diem (qv) regime was overthrown in 1963, Ky, who had participated in the coup, was made commander of the air force which he helped build into a coherent fighting machine. Along with army general Nguyen Van Thieu, Ky led the 12 June 1965 coup that ousted the Phan Van Quat (qv) government. As the head of the ruling triumverate and the designated premier, Ky drew a great deal of opposition and resentment because of his bravado and authoritarian way of dealing with problems. After much debate, Ky accepted the role of vice president, under Thieu, in the new government elected in September 1967. This did not suit Ky's style, which began to show in his criticism of Thieu's administration. During the 1971 elections, Ky attempted to oppose Thieu on the ballot, but was forced to withdraw by the military. Thereafter, he returned to duties with the air force. Ky fled Vietnam following the communist takeover in 1975 and now lives quietly in the United States, giving lectures but avoiding the political scene in the American-Vietnamese community.

Kyrenia. *See* Cyprus.

Kyugok. *See* Burma.

Kyushu Island. *See* Japan.

L

Lacoste, Pierre. On 20 September 1985, the head of the French Foreign Intelligence Service, Admiral Pierre Lacoste, was forced to resign along with French Defense Minister Charles Hernu in the wake of the investigation into the sinking of the Greenpeace vessel *Rainbow Warrior* as it lay at anchor in New Zealand.

Ladakh Province. *See* India and Pakistan.

Laghman Province. *See* Afghanistan.

Lagos. *See* Nigeria.

LaGuardia Airport. *See* United States.

Lahad, Antoine. On 4 April 1984, retired general Antoine Lahad was named the new commander of the South Lebanese Army (SLA), one of the two major Christian factions, after the death of its previous leader, the Israeli-supported Saad Haddad. *See* Lebanon.

Lahore. *See* Pakistan.

Laird, Melvin. (b. 1 September 1922, Omaha) Laird graduated from Carleton University and served in World War II. He served in the Wisconsin state legislature from 1946 until 1952, when he won a seat in the U.S. Congress. Laird was made chairman of the Republican platform committee in 1964, where he worked closely with Barry Goldwater in the latter's bid for the presidency and was himself an advocate of a strong military. He was appointed secretary of defense under President Richard Nixon from 1969 until 1973. During his tenure, he was one of the principal advocates of U.S. policy regarding Southeast Asia.

Lake Tiberias. *See* Israel.

Lake Tiga. *See* Afghanistan.

Lalibela. *See* Ethiopia.

La Libertad. *See* El Salvador.

Lamizana, Sangoule. The Mossi-dominated political party in Upper Volta headed by Maurice Yameogo was overthrown by the military, led by Lieutenant Colonel (later General) Sangoule Lamizana, in 1966 after trade-union protests. Under Lamizana (president, 1966–1980), Upper Volta enjoyed more civil liberties than most other African countries. It had a civilian legislature from 1970 to early 1974 and again from 1978 to 1980, when renewed union pressures and

military impatience with squabbling civilian politicians led to a coup. A
politicized officer corps mounted new coups in 1982 and 1983, when Captain
Thomas Sankara and a young, radical officer group seized power and sought to
revolutionize society.

Lam Van Phat. Lam Van Phat, a brigadier general in the South Vietnamese army,
was the leader of a group of young officers who staged a series of abortive coup
attempts against the regime of General Khanh during late 1964 and early 1965.
See Vietnam.

Lang Chi. *See* Vietnam.

Lang Ghia Bridge. *See* Vietnam.

Lang Vei. *See* Vietnam.

Laos. Laos is a small, landlocked country located in the interior of Southeast Asia's
strategic Indochinese Peninsula, bordered by the People's Republic of China to
the north, Vietnam to the east, Kampuchea (Cambodia) to the south and Burma
and Thailand to the west. Until 1353 Laos was part of the Khmer Empire.
Laotian prince Fa Ngum assumed the throne of Muong Swa (Luang Prabang) in
that year and founded the kingdom of Lan Xang. Theravada Buddhism, adopted
from the Khmers, became the state religion. After 1707, dynastic feuds divided
the kingdom, and three competing kingdoms emerged—Vientiane, Luang
Prabang and Champasak. In the nineteenth century, annexation by Thailand was
averted by an appeal for French protection. In 1893, Laos became part of
French Indochina. Laos was occupied by the Japanese during World War II. In
April 1945, King Sisavang Vong of Luang Prabang proclaimed Laotian
independence under Japanese protection. After the defeat of Japan, he accepted
the French reassertion of control, despite the opposition of the Free Lao (Lao
Issara) anti-French revolutionary movement, which formed a government in
exile in Thailand. Laos became a semiautonomous state within the French Union
in 1946. In 1949, under the terms of the Elysee Agreement, France granted
Laos, along with Cambodia and Vietnam, limited independence. In 1953 the
country was granted full independence. By this time, however, the Free Lao
movement, regrouped as the communist-backed Pathet Lao, had established
control of northern Laos. Prolonged civil war ensued, which soon became a
three-way conflict between the Pathet Lao, pro-Western rightists led by Gen.
Phoumi Nosavan and neutralists led by Prince Souvanna Phouma. American
involvement in the country had begun to increase with the designation of Laos
as one of the protocol states under the protection of the South East Asia
Collective Defense Treaty (SEATO), which went into effect in 1955. Although
the Pathet Lao faction was taken into the government in 1957, hostilities
continued through 1961, when a 14-power conference of nations in Geneva
sought to end the Laotian conflict by establishing a neutralist coalition
government under Souvanna Phouma. Terms of the agreement included
cancellation of U.S. advisory assistance to the Laotian armed forces, resulting
in the withdrawal of advisory assistance teams by 1962. Fighting soon broke out
again, however, and Laos became embroiled in the wider conflict of the Vietnam
War. A major factor that drew Laos into the war was the development of the

"Ho Chi Minh Trail" by the North Vietnamese to funnel supplies and men through Laotian border territories into South Vietnam. North Vietnamese occupation of the border areas to ensure security for the Ho Chi Minh Trail and North Vietnamese support for Pathet Lao offensives in the Plaine des Jarres plunged the area into a decade of almost constant warfare. By 1969, U.S. airstrikes intended to interdict traffic on the Ho Chi Minh Trail, along with airstrikes in support of the Laotian army, had become frequent occurrences. In February, 1971 South Vietnamese (ARVN) units with American support launched Operation LAM SON 719, the first of a series of major penetrations into Laos to cut NVA logistics lines on the Ho Chi Minh Trail. By 1973 agreement between the neutralists and the Pathet Lao resulted in a cease-fire and formation of a coalition government. The final coalition government, led by Souvanna Phouma and including his half-brother, the Pathet Lao leader Souphanouvong, was established in April 1974. After the fall of South Vietnam and Cambodia (Kampuchea) to the communists in 1975, the Pathet Lao assumed full control in Laos. In December, Souvanna Phouma's government was terminated, and the monarchy was abolished. About 30,000 former police and government officials were sent to political reeducation centers. After 1975 a flood of refugees, totaling nearly 400,000, including most of the educated, wealthy elite, left the country. In 1977, Laos signed a treaty of peace and friendship with Vietnam and in 1986 signed a border delineation treaty. Vietnam then agreed to provide Laos with aid to develop its infrastructure and to allow duty-free access to port facilities at Da Nang. The Laotian dependence on economic aid and military protection provided by Vietnam and the Soviet bloc was strengthened after Vietnam's invasion of Kampuchea in 1979. The Vietnamese military presence dropped to a few thousand by 1989, and relations with China were normalized. In 1989, as socialism collapsed in Eastern Europe, the Lao leadership sought more economic aid and investment from the West and professed an economic orientation of "state capitalism," dropping the term "Socialist" from its name (1990). The end of the Soviet Union caused Laos monetary problems in 1991. Thereafter, Laos was required to deal with Russia in hard currency. In January 1992, fighting erupted between anticommunist Hmong forces and government troops near Vientiane. This caused an immediate flood of refugees into Thailand. This incident created a furor which engaged Thai troops in repelling rebel incursions and the U.S., which Thailand demanded stop the flow of money from Hmong settlers in the U.S. to the rebels. When the fighting stopped, Thailand and Laos reached an agreement whereby Thailand forcibly repatriated thousands of Laotian refugees back to Laos. On 21 November 1992, President Kaysone Phoumvihan died. He was replaced by another Communist Party member and another veteran of the Pathet Lao campaigns, Nouhak Phoumsavan. Through 1993, Laos continued to expand its diplomatic and economic relations with the outside world. This was especially visible in continued efforts by Laos to aid the U.S. in locating personnel missing in action (MIAs) from the war in Southeast Asia. However, Laotian resistance to accepting back Hmong refugees reduced Laos's future status in many countries. The opening of a bridge between Thailand and Laos in 1994 appeared to signal a Laotian policy shift away from dependence on Vietnam. Still, the communist identity of the government lingered on and showed few signs of disappearing. In 1995, Lao, Cambodia, Thailand and Vietnam reached agreement on controlling the resources of the Mekong River. As China and Burma (Myanmar) did not attend the conference, the agreement was less than wholly operational. *Reading:* Grant Evans & Kelvin Rowley, *Red Brotherhood at War: Vietnam, Cambodia and Laos since 1975* (1990); John Cady, *Thailand, Burma, Laos and Cambodia* (1966); Nelles Verlag, *Cambodia, Laos* (1994); Arthur Dommen, *Laos: Keystone of Indochina* (1985); Roger Warner, *Back Fire: The CIA's Secret War in Laos and Its Link to the War in Vietnam* (1995); Joseph J. Zasloff & Leonard Unger, *Laos: Beyond the Revolution* (1991); Jane Hamilton-Merritt, *Tragic Mountains: The Hmong, the Americans, and the Secret Wars for Laos, 1942–1992* (1993); Timothy N. Castle, *At War in the Shadow of Vietnam: US Military Aid to the Royal Lao Government, 1955–1975* (1993); Martin Stuart-Fox, ed., *Contemporary Laos: Studies in Politics and Society of the Lao People's Democratic Republic* (1983).

La Paz. *See* Bolivia.

La Plata. *See* Argentina.

Laporte, Pierre. On 10 October 1970, the Quebec Minister of Labor, Pierre Laporte, was kidnapped from his home in Montreal. His body was found a week later. Police quickly arrested three French Canadian separatists for the crime.

LaPorte, Roger. On 10 November 1965, Roger LaPorte, a 22-year-old pacifist, burned himself to death in front of the UN building in New York as a protest against the war in Southeast Asia..

Larrazabal, Wolfgang. On 22 January 1958, a military junta led by Admiral Wolfgang Larrazabal overthrew the Venezuelan government of President Marcos Perez Jimenez. The junta assumed power on January 23.

Latakia (*Al Ladhiqiyah*). *See* Syria.

Latrun (*Bab el Wed*). *See* Israel.

Lauca River. *See* Bolivia.

Laval, Pierre. (b. 28 June 1883, Chateldon—d. 15 October 1945, Fresnes) Born the son of a cafe owner, Laval entered the chamber of deputies in 1914 and remained in the French parliament for the next thirty years. In 1931, he was elected premier and served in that capacity and as a minister in several departments until January 1936. The day after France's capitulation to Germany on 22 June 1944, Laval entered the Vichy government of Philippe Petain and led the move for ratification of the treaty with Germany in July 1940. He served as vice premier until December 1940, when he was dismissed. A strong adherent of Hitler's "New Order" in Europe, Laval found himself in an awkward position when he became the new chief of government in France in April 1942 and was forced to negotiate with Germany on terms unfavorable both to France and to Germany. The ambiguity of the Laval policy led to international criticism and much unrest at home. By 1944, France was on the verge of a civil war, notwithstanding the German occupation and the impending Allied invasion. When the Germans retreated from France, they took Laval with them (August 1944). He escaped to Switzerland, then Spain, before returning to France to stand trial for treason. The prosecution at his trial was so inept, and Laval's self-defense so brilliant, that he almost won his freedom, but he was condemned and shot at Fresnes on 15 October 1945, as a traitor to France.

Lavelle, John Daniel. (b. 9 September 1916, Cleveland, Ohio) Lavelle graduated from John Carroll University in 1938 and was commissioned in the U.S. Army Air Corps in 1940. He spent his career in the US air force and rose steadily through the ranks until he directed the super-secret Defense Communications Group. In 1972, Lavelle, then commander of the U.S. Seventh Air Force, the air element of the joint force operating in Vietnam, was relieved (March 1972) and subsequently reduced to three-star rank and retired from the service for ordering the bombing of targets in North Vietnam that had been specifically forbidden by Congress. It later came out that at least 25 such missions had been ordered and that these raids had been covered up by false reports to the Pentagon, which then covered up the coverup. The whole affair became public when Sergeant Lonnie Franks, an intelligence specialist, "blew the whistle" in a letter to Senator Harold Hughes, a member of the Armed Services Committee. Lavelle was returned to the states, where he was summoned before Congress to testify. During his testimony, he implicated General Creighton Abrams, the MACV commander, in the coverup, but further investigation exonerated Abrams. Lavelle did admit (12 June 1972) that he ordered 25 strikes on North Vietnamese targets during a time when delicate negotiations were under way in Paris to end the war. Only later did it become obvious that nothing Lavelle did nor anything that was accomplished through negotiations dissuaded the North Vietnamese from attaining the conquest of the south. *See* Vietnam.

Lavrion. *See* Greece.

League of Nations. The League of Nations came into being as result of popular dissatisfaction with the lack of progress toward peace that followed the end of World War I. Following the January 1919 peace talks held in Paris, a unanimous agreement was reached to form a League of Nations to keep the world at peace. By 1923, the League's structure was essentially complete. Fifty-four members had joined the League by that year, but the United States remained uncommitted to the organization. In that year also, the seeds of the World War II were being sown with the French occupation of Ruhr and the Italian sezure of Corfu. From 1924 until 1931, however, the League, having undergone some reorganization, had managed to keep the general peace. In 1931, Japan opened its military campaign in Manchuria. When by 1933 Japan would not yield to the League, it withdrew from the covenant. Germany also left the League during this period. In 1935 Benito Mussolini invaded Ethiopia. By 1936, the Italian conquest was complete, and the League was unable to recover, although it acted quickly to impose sanctions on Italy,. The establishment of the Axis (Germany, Italy and Japan) in 1936 led many League members to declare themselves no longer bound by the League's covenants. When World War II began in September

1939, the League was all but forgotten. The successful Allies rejected any notions of reviving the League. Six months after the inauguration of the new United Nations Organization (qv) in October 1945, the League met in Geneva for the last time (18–19 April 1946) and voted the organization out of existence and transferred its functions and assets to the UN. It took some time, however, to end all of the League's work. On 27 October 1966, for instance, the UN abrogated a League mandate granting South Africa control over the former German colony of South West Africa. *Reading:* Gary B. Ostrower, *Collective Insecurity: The United States and the League of Nations during the Early Thirties* (1979); Gilbert Murray, *From the League to U.N.* (1987); S. R. Gibbons, *International Co-operation: The League of Nations and UNO* (1992).

Leahardy, Terence. On 4 May 1973, the U.S. consular officer in Guadalajara, Mexico, Terence Leahardy, was kidnapped by members of the *Fuerzas Revolucionarias Armadas Populare* (qv). The terrorists demanded one million pesos ($80,000) for his release. When the ransom was paid, Leahardy was released (7 May) unharmed.

Lebanese Armed Revolutionary Faction (LARF). The Marxist-Leninist LARF is a pro-Palestian, anti-Zionist terrorist organization that came into being in 1979 after the death of Wadi Haddad (qv) and the breakup of the Popular Front for the Liberation of Palestine (qv). The organization was probably founded by George Obraham Abdallah, and its first attacks were against Christian Phalangist targets in 1979–1980. In mid-1980, the LARF moved its operations to Europe. The membership of the LARF is mostly northern Lebanese Christians and not Palestinians. Operating in France, the group established its reputation with the assassinations of a number of US and Israeli diplomats. It is known to have a network of safehouses, arms caches and money reserves stashed throughout Europe and has received financial support from Syria. The group has, on several occasions, cooperated with the French left-wing terrorist group *Action Directe* (qv). Abdallah was captured by the French police in 1984 and the LARF carried out a series of bombings in France that killed 15 and injured 150 in an attempt to gain his release.

Lebanese Revolutionary Guard. On 14 April 1973, twenty members of the little-known Lebanese Revolutionary Guard terrorist organization blew up the U.S.–owned Caltex-Mobil oil facility near Saida. Some damage occurred, but the attack fell short of total success. The group claimed the raid took place as a protest against American support of Israel.

Lebanese Christians. *See* Lebanon.

Lebanon. More properly, the Republic of Lebanon (*al-Jumhouriya al-Lubnaniya*), Lebanon is located at the eastern end of the Mediterranean Sea in the Middle East. Syria borders Lebanon on the north and west, and Israel borders it on the south. The capital city is Beirut. Lebanon was formed from five districts of the former Ottoman Empire and was declared independent on 1 September 1920. It was governed under French mandate, however, until 1941. The French withdrew in 1946 after the end of World War II. Under a national covenant

(1943), Lebanon was governed by a coalition made up of representatives of all the religious groups in the country, with the Christians holding a slight majority. By the 1970s, however, the Muslims had gained the majority and demanded a larger role in the government. Earlier, in May–October 1958, U.S. Marines had intervened to assist the government in suppressing a Syrian-supported Muslim revolt. Southern Lebanon became the scene of Muslim raids into Israel between 1970 and 1975. Also, in 1975–1976, a civil war raged in Lebanon between Christian Phalangist and Maronite militias and leftist Muslims supported by Palestinian factions that cost the lives of an estimated 60,000 people and helped destroy billions of dollars in property. While the Muslims were armed and supported by surrounding Arab countries, the Christians received their support from the Israelis. In 1976, Syria intervened, fighting primarily against the Palestinians, while other Arab League forces tried to impose a cease-fire. More guerrilla attacks into Israel provoked counterattacks into southern Lebanon in March 1978 and again in April 1980. In both offensives, most of southern Lebanon was occupied by the Israelis. In 1981, fighting erupted between Syrian and Christian forces (1 April), which effectively negated the tenuous cease-fire. By the end of April, fighting had also broke out among Muslim groups. In July 1981, Israel began bombing Beirut, causing hundreds of casualties. In a move designed to halt further incursions into Israel and to effectively crush the Palestine Liberation Organization in Lebanon, Israel invaded that country on 6 June 1982. Israeli forces ran into the Syrian army in the Bekaa valley and several pitched battles were fought. By 14 June, the Israelis had surrounded Beirut. The PLO in the city evacuated West Beirut on 21 August after a relentless bombardment by the Israeli air force. The Israelis entered the city after the 14 September assassination of Lebanese president Bashir Gemayle (qv). On 16 September, Christian Phalangist troops entered two refugee camps and massacred hundreds of Palestinian refugees. On 18 April 1983, a terrorist bombing killed 50 people at the U.S. embassy in Beirut. In two suicide bomb attacks, 241 American servicemen and 58 French soldiers were killed in that city on 23 October 1983. More fighting took place between Shi'ite Muslim troops and the PLO in March 1985. In June 1985, Shi'ite Muslims held a group of U.S. hostages for 17 days. Heavy fighting then broke out between Muslim factions in West Beirut and Christians in the eastern part of the city in March–April 1989. Over 200 were killed and 700 injured in the artillery dueling during that period. All through the 1980s, Muslim kidnapping of Western citizens became commonplace. All of the hostages had been released by 1992. Syria and Lebanon signed a treaty on 22 May 1991 that declared Lebanon to be an independent and separate nation. This marked the first such treaty with Syria since Lebanon orginally won its independence. Since that time, Israel has carried a number of raids into southern Lebanon (as in 25–29 July 1993) in reprisal for terrorist guerrilla attacks in Israel. In Lebanon, 1995 was a year of increased political violence. Among the attacks of that year, a church bombing in Junieh on 27 February took over 60 casualties killed or wounded. No group claimed responsibility for that attack, but the Lebanese army was later implicated in its planning. A car bombing in Beirut on 21 December that killed a Hizballah leader was blamed on Israel and led to Hizballah raids on Israeli security zone positions the next day. While there were just four casualties, these attacks added to the total of Israeli soldiers (22) killed in fighting that year. At the same time, Lebanon enacted new laws that added to the list of crimes punishable by death; assassination was one of these new crimes. The UN extended its mandate to maintain an emergency force in Lebanon on 30 January 1995. The situation in southern Lebanon continued to cause conflict with no end in sight. Fighting, while sporadic, was deadly, especially to Lebanese civilians caught in the crossfire. *Reading:* A. B. Gaunson, *The Anglo-French Clash in Lebanon and Syria, 1940-45* (1987); Istvan S. Pogany, *The Arab League and Peacekeeping in Lebanon* (1988); Magnus Ranstorp, *Hizb'Allah in Lebanon: The Politics of the Western Hostage Crisis* (1996); Elias Khoury, *The Kingdom of Strangers* (1996); Itamar Rabinovich, *The War in Lebanon, 1970-1985* (1985); William Harris, *Faces of Lebanon: Sects, Wars, and Global Extensions* (1997).

Leimas. *See* Honduras.

Lemus, Jose Maria. On 26 October 1960, the government of President Jose Maria Lemus of El Salvador was overthrown by a six-man military junta led by Colonel Cesar Yanes Urias. Lemus had won an easy election to office in 1956, given the fact that most opposition parties had been forced to withdraw or were barred from participation in the process. Although he continued one-party rule, Lemus did accomplish some economic goals for his country. The one-party system was his undoing, however, and he was ousted.

Leningrad. *See* Soviet Union (Russia).

Lenin Shipyard. The scene of numerous strikes and unrest during the period of "Solidarity" (qv) in Poland. Located in Gdansk on the Baltic, the Lenin Shipyard employed thousands of Polish workers. On 14 August 1980, for instance, 17,000 workers went on strike. Within days, at least 120,000 workers in northern Poland had joined the strike protesting government suppression of free trade unions. The government announced it would listen to "sensible" demands formulated by "honest" workers. Initial negotiations took place between the government and the Interfactory Strike Committee (IFSC) headed by Lech Walesa (qv). All of the strikers demands were eventually met. *See* Poland and Solidarity.

Lennox Island. *See* Chile.

Leon. *See* Nicaragua.

Leonardi, Eduardo. Seven days after having ousted (16 September 1955) Juan Peron (qv) from his seat of power in Argentina, Major General Eduardo Leonardi was appointed president (23 October). His tenure was short-lived, however, and filled with trouble, as anti-Peronists sought to gain complete control of the government. Leonardi was overthrown in a miltary coup led by Major General Pedro Arumburu (qv).

Leonardo da Vinci International Airport. On 27 December 1985, Palestinian terrorists attacked the El Al (Israeli) check-in counter at Rome's Leonardo da Vinci International Airport. Fifteen people, including three of the terrorists, were killed and 74 injured in the ensuing firefight between the terrorists, who sprayed the area with submachine-gun fire, and airport security police. A simultaneous terrorist attack was launched against the airport in Vienna, Austria, where three people, including one terrorist, were killed and 47 injured. In the combined attacks, five Americans were killed and 20 injured. The PLO splinter-group, Abu Nidal (qv), was accused of the attacks, which investigations showed were supported by Iran and Libya. The attacks were claimed to be part of a reprisal campaign for the destruction of PLO headquarters in Tunisia.

Leopold (King of Belgium). *See* Belgium.

Leopoldville, Belgian Congo. *See* Zaire.

Lescot, Elie. On 11 January 1946, a military junta led by Colonel Paul Magliore overthrew the government of President Elie Lescot of Haiti. The coup occurred after Lescot had had the Congress extend his term of office until 1951. Lescot had been president since 1941 and had supported the war effort against the Axis.

Lesotho. The Kingdom of Lesotho is completely surrounded by the Republic of South Africa. The capital city is Maseru. Lesotho became the British protectorate of Basutoland in 1868.The British had stepped in at the request of King Moshesh to protect the kingdom from the Boers. Lesotho was declared independent on 4 October 1966. South Africa imposed a blockade on Lesotho on 1 January 1986 as a move to curtail rebel activities against the South African government from that tiny kingdom. A military coup overthrew the Lesotho government on 20 January, and the blockade was lifted five days later after the new leadership promised to expel the rebels. King Moshoeshoe II (qv) was sent into exile by the ruling military junta in 1990, and his son, Letsie III, was put on the throne. A civil prime minister was installed in March 1993, ending 23 years of military rule. Street fighting broke out in January 1994, between rival army factions. In April 1994, mutinous soldiers kidnapped four government ministers and murdered the deputy prime minister. The king then dissolved Parliament (17 August 1994) and called for new elections. The crowds that gather to protest these actions were fired upon by army and police forces. Based on the reaction, the government refused to disband. Letsie was finally forced to restore the prime ministry on 14 September, but he refused to abdicate. On 26 January 1995 Moshoeshoe was restored to the throne ,with Letsie, after abdicating the throne, reverting to crown prince. For a while it appeared order had been restored, but in March a group of senior officers was kidnapped by members of the National Security Service, who demanded their own early immediate retirement. The hostages were released two weeks later, but nothing else happened. Moshoeshoe was in killed in an automobile accident on 15 January 1996, and Letsie was restored to the throne on 7 February. A foiled coup attempt followed on 28 February. *Reading:* L. B. B. J. Machobane, *Government and Change in Lesotho, 1800-1966: A Study of Political Institutions* (1990); John Bardill & James H. Cobbe, *Lesotho: Dilemmas of Dependence in Southern Africa* (1985).

Lesser Antilles. *See* Antilles or specific islands.

Letelier, Orlando. On 21 September 1976, Orlando Letelier, a former leftist cabinet minister and the former Chilean ambassador to the United States in the Allende (qv) government (ousted in 1973) and a severe critic of the current Pinochet (qv) government in Chile, was assassinated in a car bombing in Washington, DC. A minor U.S. official, Ronni Moffitt, was also killed. An investigation tied the bombing to members of the Chilean intelligence service (DINA) and a Cuban anti-Castro terrorist group. Letelier's Chilean citizenship had been revoked shortly before the bombing. On 24 June 1978, the U.S. recalled its ambassador to Chile in protest over the Chilean government's failure to properly support the investigation of the assassination, and on 15 May 1979 the U.S. withdrew its ambassador when Chile refused the extradition of three DINA officials, including the organization's director, General Manuel Contreras Sepulveda, on charges they had planned and ordered the murder. Sanctions were imposed on Chile on 30 November 1979 for refusing the extradition. The case is still open; although the criminals involved are known, but at large.

Letourneau, Jean. In April 1952, Jean Letourneau, the French minister of state for the associated states, was named minister-resident of Indochina. Indochina was in the fifth year of the Viet Minh uprising.

Le Van Kim. On 6 January 1964, Le Van Kim and two other South Vietnamese generals, Duong Van Minh (qv) and Tran Van Don (qv), assumed the leadership of the country. On 29–30 January, General Nguyen Khanh (qv) led a bloodless pre-dawn coup and deposed Duong Van Minh and had Le Van Kim and Tran Van Don arrested. They were eventually released.

Levingston, Roberto Marcelo. On 8 June 1970, Argentinian President Juan Carlos Ongania (qv) was forced to resign following a military coup. Brigadier General Roberto Marcelo Levingston then became president. On 22–23 March 1971, however, Levingston's government was overthrown in a bloodless coup led by General Alejandro Agustin Lanusse. Lanusse assumed the presidency on 25 March.

Lhasa. *See* Tibet.

Liaosi Corridor. *See* China.

Liaqat Ali Khan. On 15 October 1951, Pakistan's prime minister, Liaqat Ali Khan, was assassinated. He was murdered by fanatics who wanted a holy war (*Jihad*) with India rather than the policy of moderation espoused by Liaquat. His death ushered in a period of decline for Pakistan that continued until a new revolutionary government came into power in 1958.

"Liberated Arab States." Syrian President Nazim el-Kudsi (qv) used the phrase "liberated Arab states" upon his return to power on 13 April 1962. He had been ousted in March following Syria's withdrawal from the United Arab Republic. His remark referred to those states that had freed themselves from the control of the UAR, then controlled by Nasser (qv).

Liberia. A West African country located on the southwest coast, Liberia is bordered on the northwest by Sierra Leone, on the northeast by Guinea and on the east by Ivory Coast (*Cote d'Ivoire*). The capital city is Monrovia. Liberia was founded in 1822 through the efforts of colonizing societies who settled freed American slaves there. A republic was established on 26 July 1847, under an American-style constitution. The country's politics were dominated by the freedmen until 12 April 1980, when a bloody coup took place, led by Samuel K. Doe (qv). (Another coup attempt had failed on 5 February 1963) During the April 1980 revolt, President William R. Tolbert, Jr. (qv), and 27 other were killed by the members of the Army Redemption Council, led by Doe, which was made up largely of enlisted men from the Liberian armed forces. Doe, who was proclaimed head of state, withstood a coup attempt on 10 August 1981, after which all the perpetrators were put on trial and then executed. In August 1983, Liberia announced it had concluded a military agreement with Israel and had restored diplomatic relations with the Israelis. On 26 July 1984, President Doe lifted a four-year-old ban on political activity in Liberia. Doe survived another coup attempt, during which he narrowly escaped assassination, on 1 April 1985. That attempt was led by the deputy commander of the Palace Guard, Lieutenant Colonel Moses Flanzamaton, who was tried, convicted and executed (7 April). In November 1985, rebel troops attacked the executive mansion with artillery. The rebel leader, Brigadier General Thomas Quiwonkpa, then announced he had overthrown the Doe regime. Doe then announced that he was still in power. Quiwonkpa was subsequently captured and executed. A civil war broke out in Liberia in 1989, when rebel forces sought to oust Doe. The year started with Doe accusing his defense minister, Gray D. Allison, of buying body parts obtained from the murder of a policeman so as to make a potion to be used to get rid of Doe. Allison was tried and sentenced to death. The revolt was announced to have been put down, but by June 1990, the rebels held half the country and were advancing on the capital. On 9 September, Doe was captured, mutilated and executed. Although the fighting subsided, a number of cease-fires failed to keep the rival Krahn (Doe's tribe) and the Gio and Mano tribes from killing each other. By July 1993, a peacekeeping force from several countries restored some order. A new coalition government was established on 16 May 1994. During the fighting, more than half of Liberia's total population of 3 million were refugees. A government reorganization took place in February 1994, but it was hampered by political infighting among the three major factions. Finally, on 16 May, the new government sat for the first time as the UN observer mission watched. At the same time, at least one of the military factions claimed it had been attacked by peacekeeping forces. Finally, on 3 August, a cease fire was arranged. A military coup, led by the former army commander General Charles Julue, occurred on 15 September. The coup attempt failed, and Julue was arrested the next day. A final peace accord was reached by the warring factions in December 1994. Fighting broke out in 1995 over the terms of a new government organization, involving two factions, the National Patriotic Front of Liberia (NPFL) and the Liberian Peace Council (LPC). In one action in April, 62 people were massacred in southern Liberia. While the UN mandate was being extended, Tanzania withdrew its peacekeepers, as that government foresaw no solution to the problem. By year's end, fighting was widespread. *Reading:* Marc Weller, ed., *Regional Peace-Keeping and International*

Enforcement: The Liberian Crisis (1994); Emmanuel Dolo, *Democracy versus Dictatorship: The Quest for Freedon and Justice in Africa's Oldest Republic—Liberia* (1996); J. Gus Liebenow, *Liberia: The Quest for Democracy* (1987); G. E. Saigbe Boley, *Liberia: The Rise and Fall of the First Republic* (1984).

Libya. A country on the northern littoral of Africa, Libya is bordered on the north by the Mediterranean Sea, on the east by Egypt, on the southeast by Chad, on the southwest by Niger, on the west by Algeria and on the northwest by Tunisia. In about 1000 B.C., Garamantes tribesmen captured the important oases along the trade routes running south to the Niger River and controlled the slave and gold routes into sub-Saharan Africa. Greek colonists arrived in the seventh century B.C. and established the important city of Cyrene in the Cyrenaica district. In the sixth century B.C., Phoenicians founded the city-state of Carthage. Romans entered the region later and built a number of important cities there. In 395 A.D., after the division of the Roman Empire, Libya was placed under the control of the Eastern Empire (Byzantium) and remained so until 439, when it was seized by Gothic Vandals. In the sixth century, Byzantine forces reoccupied the region. In 642, Arabs took the cities of Cyrene and Tripolitania and a year later took Fezzan. During this period, the indigenous Libyans, the Berbers, embraced Islam but established their own traditions in the religion and withstood any political pressure from the Islamic centers of Baghdad and Damascus. In the mid-eleventh century, Beni Hilal and Beni Salim tribesmen entered the region and established domination over the Berbers. Under their sway, the Arab language and culture spread throughout Libya. In 1510, the Spaniards came, followed by the Ottoman Turks in 1551. In 1804, Libya fought a brief war with the United States over freedom of the seas (Barbary War). Italy occupied Libya in 1911 after defeating the Ottomans. After World War I, the new Italian dictator Benito Mussolini declared his intention of forming a second Roman Empire there. Italian settlement of the region was extensive. From 1911 until 1932, however, the Libyans fought a guerrilla war against the Italians, especially in the major cities. When the rebel leader Omar Mukhtar was captured and hung in 1932, the rebellion fell apart. During World War II, Libya was the site of major fighting in the North African campaign in which the Germans and Italians were driven out of the country and a British military government established there. The French also entered the scene and governed the region around Fezzan. Following World War II, Libya was the first country to be granted its independence (21 November 1949) by the United Nations. Also, in 1949, a decade-long period of anticolonialism began in Libya. An independent kingdom was established in 1951 under the rule of Mohammed Idris ei-Senussi (Idris I). In 1953, Libya joined the Arab League (qv). In 1954, the U.S. and Libya reached a 20-year agreement on American military basing rights in that country. In April 1959, Libya boycotted the Arab League meeting at which Iraq was branded a procommunist threat. In 1963, Libya became a member of the Organization of African Unity (OAU) after it consolidated the three districts (Cyrenaica, Tripolitania and Fezzan) into one national unit. The following year, on 16 March, Libya voted unanimously to remove U.S. and British military bases from its soil. Libya bought state-of-the-art surface-to-air missiles from Great Britain. Both nations complied in part, but not completely. (The Libyans renewed their demands in October 1969, and both countries were out of Libya by June 1970.) In January 1969, France placed an embargo on all arms shipments to Libya and a group of other Arab nations and to Israel. Libya bought tanks and artillery from Great Britain in April 1969. On 1 September 1969, the monarchy of Idris I was overthrown by a group of army officers calling themselves the Revolutionary Command Council (RCC), who established the Libyan Arab Republic. A 27-year-old colonel, Muammar al-Qaddafi (qv), emerged four and one-half months later (16 January 1970) as the new leader of Libya. Qaddafi was named head of state in 1972. He also commanded the armed forces and was chairman of the RCC. By November 1969, the Libyans were training and housing PLO terrorist groups. Libya joined a short-lived Arab confederation with Syria and the UAR in November 1970 (formally approved as the Federation of Arab Republics (qv) on 17 April 1971). On 19–21 July 1971, Libya, along with Egypt, helped crush a Soviet-inspired coup in Sudan. Later that year, Libya repudiated charges of its complicity in an attempted coup in Chad and then turned around and recognized the rebel movement in that country (18 September). On 26 July, Libyan fighters forced down a British airliner at Bengazi and arrested one of the passengers, who was suspected of being a leader in the failed Sudanese coup. Colonel Babakr an-Nur Osman (qv) was extradited to Sudan and shot. Three days later, Libya condemned Jordan for its treatment of the Palestinians and promised more aid to the PLO. On 20–22 September 1972, a bizarre incident took place wherein five Libyan C-130 transports were forced to land at Khartoum, Sudan. There it was ascertained that they carried 399 combat troops and supplies. They were cleared to fly to Cairo but instead landed at Entebbe in Uganda. Four months later, in January 1973, Libya was training 300 Ugandan soldiers and airmen at its military facilities. Libya then became involved in a Moroccan rebel attack on Morocco, which failed on 2 March. On 21 March, two Libyan fighters shot at, but missed, a USAF C-130 cargo plane flying over the Mediterranean 83 miles off the coast of Libya. In April, Israel accused Libya of transferring Mirage fighters to Egypt even though France had earlier warned Libya against such arrangements. Later, in June, in retaliation for U.S. support of Israel, Libya nationalized a U.S. oil company in that country. On 26 June, two Greek ships hit mines in Tripoli harbor; one ship sank. The Libyans then admitted they had mined the harbor against Israeli coastal raids. In 1973, most political decision-making was controlled by the General People's Committee. But, on 11 July 1973, Qaddafi offered to resign to clear the way for the merger with Egypt which he and Anwar Sadat (qv) had agreed upon on 2 August 1972. Between 18 July and 23 July 1973, about 40,000 Libyans began the "Tripoli to Cairo March" designed by Qaddafi to force the union of Libya with Egypt. Qaddafi had been rebuffed in his drive to get the plan into effect during a visit to Cairo on 29 June–9 July. Egyptian troops stopped the procession at the border on 20 July. That same day,

Qaddafi resigned to "pave the way" for unification. When the marchers returned to Tripoli, Qaddafi withdrew his resignation (23 July). Egypt and Libya agreed to a gradual merging on 8 August and made an announcement to that effect on 30 August. On 19 October 1973, Libya imposed an oil boycott on the U.S. because of its continuing support of Israel during the Arab-Israel War that was raging. Then, on 1 December, Libya closed its embassy in Cairo to show Qaddafi's displeasure at Egypt's poor showing in the war. On 5 April 1974, reports coming out of Libya said that Qaddafi had been relieved of all "political, administrative, and traditional duties" and that the real power was in the hands of Prime Minister Abdul Salam Jalloud (qv). On 12 Sepember 1975, Turkey gave Libya US-built F-5 "Freedom" fighter aircraft as part of a military aid package. Libya arrested and expelled 3,000 Egyptians in response to the 11 March 1975 arrest of 27 Libyans in Egypt, where they were charged with subversion. A Libyan-backed coup attempt against the government of Sudan failed on 2 July 1976. On 19 July, Sudan signed a mutual defense alliance with Egypt, Libya's erstwhile federation partner. Libyan threats toward Egypt caused a mobilization of Egyptian forces along the common border on 19 July. On 2 March 1977, the name of the country was changed to the Socialist People's Libyan Arab Jamahiriya (*al-Jamahiriyah al-Arabiya al-Libya al-Shabiya al-Istirakiya*). The term "*Jamahiriya*" may be equated with "Islamic Socialism." Libya's rich oil supply has enabled the country to increase educational and other social opportunities while building a large modern military force. To this end, Libya bought many weapons from the United States, Great Britain and France over the next decade. In July 1977, France acknowledged it was furnishing aid to Chad in its ongoing border skirmishing with Libya. Similarly, Egypt resorted to air strikes and the use of armor (21 July) in a major battle between Libya and Egypt along their border. Four days later, Egypt declared a unilateral cease-fire, which Libya accepted. After Egypt's president Sadat accepted an invitation to visit Israel, Libya broke diplomatic relations with Cairo (19 November 1977). On 5 December, the leaders of several Arab nations closed a stormy meeting in Tripoli by issuing a declaration condemning Egypt for its conciliatory policy toward Israel. Chad broke diplomatic relations with Libya on 6 January 1978, because of Libya's support of rebels, the Frolinat (qv) operating in Chad. In May, Libya was accused of supporting rebel forces operating in Zaire. On 9 August, Libya established diplomatic relations with Communist China. On 3 October 1978, the Soviet Union announced it was giving Libya a nuclear power complex and research center. Qaddafi threatened war against Tanzania if Tanzania did not halt its invasion of Uganda (*see* Tanzania and Uganda). When Uganda capitulated to the Tanzanians, Ugandan dictator Idi Amin (qv) was expelled and began his exile in Libya. Libya was also required to pay a ransom of $40 million (15 May 1979) to recover its troops captured by the Tanzanians in Uganda. In a surprise move, Libya cut off all financial support to the PLO on 11 December 1979 and ordered the PLO offices in Libya closed (21 December). On 11 April 1980, two Libyan students were arrested in England following the assassination of a Qaddafi political opponent there. Then, on 26 April, Qaddafi ordered all Libyan citizens abroad to come home or face certain "liquidation." Great Britain expelled the head of the Libyan mission in London, Kusa Musa (qv), for his part in supporting Libyan murder squads operating in that country. On 1 September, Qaddafi announced a merger with Syria to better oppose Israel. Syria agreed to the merger after secret negotiations. A previous merger plan had failed in 1973. Saudi Arabia broke diplomatic relations with Libya (28 October) after Qaddafi criticized Saudi relations with the United States and called for a Holy War (*Jihad*) to liberate Mecca. Qaddafi announced that Libya would merge with Chad on 6 January 1981. Sudan accused Libya of blowing up the Embassy of Chad in Khartoum on 25 June 1981 and expelled all Libyan diplomats in the country. Morocco restored diplomatic relations with Libya on 29 July. On 19 August 1981, two U.S. Navy F-14 "Tomcat" fighters armed with Sidewinder missiles, operating from the carrier *USS Nimitz* (CVN-68), shot down two Soviet-built Libyan Su-22 "Fitter" fighter aircraft over the Gulf of Sidra. By October, the Libyan threat against Sudan had grown to the point where the Sudanese parliament was dissolved to make way for emergency rule. On 31 December, Saudi Arabia reestablished diplomatic relations with Libya. Qaddafi was wounded in an assassination attempt by a Libyan army officer on 13 January 1982. On 1 February, Libya claimed its border with Egypt was open for the first time in three years; Egypt denied the statement (2 February). Also, in 1981–1982, there was a decline in oil production in Libya, partially because of a U.S. embargo imposed on 10 March 1982. The U.S. also banned the exportation of any high technology to Libya. New programs in Libya were curtailed, but ongoing ones were maintained. Egypt went on military alert on 16 February 1983, convinced Libya was about to attack Sudan. On 17 March, Chad asked the United Nations to intervene in its long-standing border dispute with Libya. In 1983, Qaddafi promised military support to "revolutionary forces" anywhere in the Arab world. This translated into support of Arab terrorist activities to back Libyan displeasure with U.S. and Egyptian policies toward Israel. One incident in this regard involved four Libyan air transports loaded with weapons that were denied onward passage after landing in Brazil. The four aircraft were eventually allowed to return to Libya. On 17 May 1983, the Libyan charge d'affairs in Upper Volta was expelled for his part in a plot to overthrow the government in that country. Libyan bombed (Soviet-built Tu-22 bomber) an anti-Qaddafi radio station in Omdurman, Sudan, on 16 March 1984. Another assassination attempt on Qaddafi failed when Libyan troops drove off 20 heavily armed men at his compound in Tripoli. All 20 assailants were apparently killed in the fighting. Libya secretly mined the Red Sea and the Gulf of Suez in July 1984. The terrorist group Islamic Jihad claimed the credit, but authorities had proof that Libya had committed the crime. The Egyptian government accused Libya and Iran of involvement in the incident, which damaged 15 ships between 27 July and 11 August. Both Libya and Iran denied the allegations. Allied minesweepers cleared both waters of mines, beginning in August. Libya was deeply involved in the war in Chad (*see* Chad) in 1984. When peace seemed imminent, France withdrew its troops. and Libya claimed it had also. On 30

November 1984, however, about 4,000 Libyan troops remained in Chad. The new government in Sudan restored diplomatic relations with Tripoli on 24 April 1984 and signed a military agreement with Libya on 8 July 1985. A bomb blast in Saddun Square in Tripoli killed 44 Muslims on 20 August 1985. Two days later, in an unrelated incident, Tunisia put its forces on alert on the Libyan border after Tripoli ordered the expulsion of thousands of Tunisian workers. On 4 September, Tunisia cut all trade with Libya and ordered all of its citizens out of the country. On 15 September, heavy fighting broke out in Tripoli among rival Muslim factions. Nearly one-quarter of a million people were forced to flee the city in the wake of the violence. Tunisia broke diplomatic relations with Tripoli on 26 September as a result of the Libyan expulsion of over 30,000 Tunisian workers. On 24 November, Egypt closed its border with Libya after accusing Qaddafi of masterminding the hijacking of one of its airliners on 23 November, in which a number of passengers were killed (*see* Abu Nidal). Egypt relaxed its state of alert on 3 December. After the 27 December terrorist attack on the El Al ticket counter at Rome's Leonardo da Vinci airport, Libya and Iran were linked to the incident. Following this attack and a series of other Libyan-sponsored terrorist attacks in Western Europe, including the murder of an anti-Qaddafi Libyan student in West Germany (6 April 1984), the United States imposed economic sanctions on 7 January 1986, froze Libyan assets in the U.S., and ordered 1,500 Americans, mostly oil workers, out of Libya. U.S. naval vessels steamed into the Gulf of Sidra. Qaddafi responded by establishing a "line of death" across the Bay of Sidra, which violated international rights of free passage on the high seas. Libyan antiaircraft missiles were fired at U.S. warplanes, and the U.S. responded by sinking two Libyan ships and bombing a missile installation in Libya. When Libyan-backed terrorists bombed a West Berlin discotheque frequented by American servicemen, the U.S. retaliated with a bombing attack against targets in Bengazi and Tripoli, including an attack aimed at eliminating Qaddafi. Qaddafi escaped the bombing, but his daughter was killed. In December 1988, the U.S. accused Libya of building a facility to manufacture chemical warfare weapons. That same year, the U.S. allowed five oil companies to resume operations in Libya. The UN imposed limited sanctions against Libya on 15 April 1992, after Qaddafi refused to extradite two of its intelligence agents suspected of carrying out the bombing of PanAm flight 103 over Lockerbie, Scotland, and four others suspected of bombing a plane over Niger. The sanctions were increased as a consequence in December 1993. Libya's isolation continued throughout 1994 and 1995. Even Qaddafi remained quiet, even on the issue of the Middle East peace negotiations. When the issue of the Palestine-Israel peace accords was put forward, however, Qaddafi reacted by beginning the expulsion of Palestinians living in Libya, deporting over 10,000 in the first nine months of 1995. As the UN embargo continued, Libya suffered more and more. *Reading:* Geoff Simons, *Libya: The Struggle for Survival* (1993); BrianDavis, *Qaddafi, Terrorism, and the Origins of the U.S. Attack on Libya* (1990); John Wright, *Libya: A Modern History* (1982); Lillian Harris, *Libya: Qadhafi's Revolution and the Modern State* (1986).

Liegnitz. *See* Poland.

Lima. *See* Peru.

Limann, Hilla. (b. 1934, Gweila, Gold Coast) Born to peasant farmers, Limann gained his education at the London School of Economics and Political Science. He also studied at the Sorbonne in Paris and at the University of London. On 24 September 1979, Hilla Limann was elected president of Ghana as the first civilian president after eight years of military rule. On 31 December 1981, Limann's moderate government was overthrown by former flight lieutenant Jerry Rawlings (qv), who claimed that Limann had not solved the country's economic problems. Limann was arrested on 1 January 1982. Limann thereafter dropped from sight, as Rawlings consolidated his hold over the country.

Linhares, Jose. Following a period of popular unrest in Brazil, President Getulio Vargas (qv) resigned on 25 October 1945, following a fifteen-year dictatorship. He was temporarily replaced by Chief Justice Jose Linhares, who remained in office until 2 December 1945, when General Eurico Gaspar Dutra, the former minister of war and long-time friend of Vargas, was elected president.

Lin Piao (Lin Lu-yung). (b. 1908, Hupeh Province, China—d.12 September 1971[?], Mongolia) Lin Piao graduated from the Whampoa Military Academy and soon found himself in the vanguard of Mao Tse-tung's (qv) communist army. In 1934–1935, he was one of the leaders in the "Long March" from Kiangsi to Yenan that saved the communists from annihilation. After being wounded in 1937 during the Japanese invasion, he spent the next four years in the Soviet Union. In 1946, he worked his way back to China—via the Red Army in Manchuria—and participated in the defeat of the Kuomintang (KMT) army forces, especially in the battle at the Sungari River in January 1947. He was appointed deputy premier of Red China in 1954 and was elected to the Politburo in 1955 and to its Standing Committee in 1958. Also in 1955 he was appointed a marshal of the Peoples' Army. In 1959, Lin Piao succeeded P'eng Teh-hua as minister of national defense, where he began an intensive program of political indoctrination among the troops to ensure their loyalty to Chairman Mao. Over the next six years, he cultivated the position of Mao's "closest comrade-in-arms," and second-in-command of China. In April 1969, he was officially designated Mao's successor and called for preparations for a war against the USSR (14 April). In October of that year he enlarged his preparations for war to include the United States. In 1970, however, he ran afoul of the system by challenging a plan to mechanize agriculture at the expense of the army and thereby injured his position in the party hierarchy. In September 1971, he was accused of engineering a plot to oust Mao and attempted an escape to the Soviet Union (11 September). Enroute through Manchuria, he was killed (12 September) in a plane crash. His death was not officially reported until nearly a year later, on 28 July 1972.

"The Lion of Kashmir." *See* Abdullah, Mohammed.

Lira, Raul. The acting ambassador to Colombia from Uruguay, Raul Lira was away from his embassy when it was attacked by terrorists from the leftist M-19 group on 15 April 1980. Not finding Lira, the terrorists fled empty-handed. M-19 had attempted to kidnap the ambassador, Fernando Gomez, from the Dominican Republican embassy in February, but he had escaped. The attack on Lira was said to be in retaliation for the earlier failure.

Lisbon. *See* Portugal.

Li Tsung-jen. On 21 January 1949, the city of Beijing (Peking) fell to Communist Chinese troops. Chiang Kai-shek resigned as president of China, leaving the vice president, Li Tsung-jen, to attempt a continuation of peace talks with the communists. His efforts proved fruitless.

Little Bitter Lake (*el Buheirat el Murrat el Sughra*). *See* Israel.

Little Rock. On 3 September 1957, Arkansas governor Orval Faubus ordered the Arkansas National Guard into Little Rock to prevent the integration of the city's school system. On 20 September, a federal court order enjoined Faubus from further interference in the federally mandated school desegregation plan. When Faubus failed to heed the court order, the president ordered federal troops into Little Rock to prevent insurrection. The state's National Guard was federalized, thereby taken out of state control, and were ordered to remain in their barracks and not to interfere with the regular army troops entering the city. The incident ended without a clash between the two forces.

Liu Shao-ch'i (*Liu Shaoqi*). (b. 1898 or 1900, Yinshan, Hunan Province, China—d. 31 October 1974 [?], Hunan) Born into a landowning family, Liu was educated at Changsa and Shanghai, where he studied Russian. He then studied in Moscow in 1921–1922. Liu joined the Communist Party in Moscow, and upon his return to China, he became a party organizer in Shanghai. During this period he met Mao Tse-tung (qv) and, as Mao's associate, helped organize the Peasant Red Army. He was the leading organizer of the urban labor force. In 1934, Liu was elected to the Chinese Communist politburo and became the party's leading theorist. In 1943 he became the secretary general of the party and, in 1949, he became its vice chairman. When the communists took over China in 1949, Liu again became secretary general. He became chairman of the People's Republic (Head of State) in April 1959, second only to Mao. Liu advocated a freer market economy and financial incentives to reestablish China's failing economy. During the Cultural Revolution (1966–1969) (*see* China), the Red Guards denounced him as a "bourgeois renegade" and a revisionist. He was deposed and stripped of all party positions in 1967 and banished to Hunan province, where he was placed in detention. His death (c. 31 October 1974) was reported only after several months. In 1980, he was posthumously rehabilitated.

Livingston. *See* Zambia.

Llopis, Rodolfo. On 9 February 1947, Rodolfo Llopis formed an anti-Franco (Francisco Franco [qv]) government-in-exile. By 27 August, the Llopis attempt to overthrow the Spanish dictator had failed, and a new group under the leadership of Alvaro de Albornoz (qv) came forward, but with little or no success.

Loc Ninh. *See* Vietnam.

Lodge, Henry Cabot, Jr. (b. 5 July 1902, Nahant, Massachusetts—d. 27 February 1985, Beverly, Massachusetts) Born into a political family, Lodge graduated cum laude from Harvard in 1924. Eight years later he was elected to the lower house of the Massachusetts legislature and, in 1936, to the U.S. Senate. He left the Senate in 1944 to join the army, but returned to the Senate after the war. He was noted during that period for his work in the development of the Hoover Commission. In 1952, he was defeated by John F. Kennedy (qv). In 1953, he was given a permanent seat on the U.S. delegation to the United Nations. He remained in that office until 1960, when he became Richard Nixon's (qv) running mate in an unsuccessful bid for the vice-presidency. The winner, Kennedy, gave Lodge an ambassadorship to South Vietnam (27 June 1963). He was apparently aware of the plots against President Ngo Dinh Diem (qv) from the beginning. Lodge was later appointed ambassador to West Germany (1968–1969). In 1969, he became the chief U.S. negotiator in the Paris peace talks with the North Vietnamese. From 1970 until 1977, he was special envoy to the Vatican. He died on 27 February 1985.

Logar. *See* Afghanistan.

Lohamut Herut Israel (Lehi). *See* Stern Gang.

Lombardo, Juan Jose. Vice Admiral Juan Jose Lombardo was the commander of the Argentinian forces that invaded the Falkland Islands (qv) on 2 April 1982.

Lomphat. *See* Cambodia (Kampuchea).

London. *See* Great Britain.

Londonderry. *See* Northern Ireland.

Londono y Londono. The foreign minister of Colombia, Londono y Londono was kidnapped by members of the National Liberation Army on 9 July 1970. He was subsequently released on 19 July.

Long An Province. *See* Vietnam.

Long Boret. On 26 December 1973, Long Boret became premier of Cambodia. He had been Cambodia's foreign minister up to that time and had headed his country's UN delegation, which had successfully defended Cambodia's seat in the General Assembly. In 1974, Long Boret was appointed to the High Executive Council, which Lon Nol (qv) had formed after the disintegration of government in his war-torn country. On 16–17 April 1975, Long Boret was forced to surrender his country to the communist Khmer Rouge (qv) and was replaced as premier.

Long Khanh Province. *See* Vietnam.

Longowal, Sant Harchand Singh. (b. 1928, Punjab, India—d. 20 August 1985, Sherpur, Punjab) Longowal joined the Akali Dal (qv) political party in 1944 and adopted the tactics of Mahatma Gandhi (qv) in raising the political consciousness of his people through civil disobedience. He was jailed several times as a result in the 1950s and 1960s. He was elected president of the local Akali-Dal branch in his home area. In 1980, as a compromise candidate, he became president of the party. In 1982, he launched a civil disobedience campaign, which was disrupted by extremists, many of whom were killed in the battle at the Golden Temple. On 20 August 1985, Longowal was assassinated by fellow Sikhs in Punjab, who claimed he had signed an agreement with India's Prime Minister Rajiv Gandhi (qv).

Lon Nol. (b. 13 November 1913, Kampong Leon, Cambodia—d. 17 November 1985, Fullerton, California) Born in Prey Veng province and educated at the Chasseloup High School in Saigon and at the Cambodian Royal Military Academy, Lon Nol entered the French colonial service in 1937. He became a magistrate and later, in 1945, the governor of Kratie province. In 1952, he joined the army and fought the Viet Minh as an area (battalion) commander. He became governor of Battambang province in 1954 and was appointed army chief of staff in 1955. In 1960, Lon Nol became the commander in chief of the armed forces. He was appointed deputy premier in 1963 and became the premier of Cambodia in 1966. In 1967, he resigned after being seriously injured in an automobile accident. He returned to the government in 1968 and was appointed minister of defense. A year later, he again became premier and served for five years in that position. On 15 March 1970, he demanded the immediate departure of all North Vietnamese and Viet Cong forces in Cambodia. When Prince Sihanouk (qv) was overthrown on 18 March, Lon Nol began an unprecedented reign of terror against the estimated 400,000 Vietnamese living in Cambodia. On 19 March, he closed Cambodia's principal seaport, Sihanoukville, to all North Vietnamese shipping. A month later, he announced Cambodia would accept aid from anyone interested in assisting in the fight against communism. On 20 April, he appealed directly to Richard M. Nixon (qv), then president of the United States, for aid. He did, however, complain loudly when a U.S.–South Vietnamese invasion of his country began on 30 April. On 30 June 1970, Lon Nol assumed full wartime powers, as the communist offensive in northern Cambodia had captured four provinces. On 10 February 1971, Lon Nol suffered a stroke and was paralyzed. A government crisis ensued when he announced (20 April) that he was resigning for health reasons. He remained on, however, and on 20 October 1971 declared a state of emergency and announced rule by "ordinance." On 10 March 1972, President Cheng Heng (qv) resigned and turned all his powers over to Lon Nol. Two days later Lon Nol dissolved the government. At least two attempts were made on Lon Nol's life in 1973, and the presidential palace was attacked by Cambodian air force aircraft. On 30 January 1974, Lon Nol declared a six-month state of emergency in the face of heavy fighting between Khmer Rouge (qv) and government forces. With the situation deteriorated to a point of no salvation, Lon Nol fled Cambodia (1 April 1975). He first went to Indonesia, in a move calculated to bring an end to fighting in his homeland. The new military government vowed to fight on, however, and Lon Nol then established his exile in Hawaii. He later moved to California, where he died in 1985.

Lopez, Nicholas Lindley. On 3 March 1963, the military junta that had put him in power unseated the government of Peru's president, General Ricardo Perez Godoy (qv). General Nicholas Lindley Lopez became president. Following the general elections held in June, Lopez stepped down and was replaced by Belaúnde Terry (qv).

López Arellano, Osvaldo. On 30 October 1963, ten days before the scheduled presidential elections in Honduras, the government of President Ramón Villeda Morales (qv) was overthrown by a military coup led by Colonel Osvaldo López Arellano. López declared himself head of state, claiming that Morales had failed to heed the dangers posed by communism. He then dissolved the legislature and cancelled the elections. A subsequent constitutional assembly convened in 1965 was a victory for López, whose candidates won the majority of seats. In March 1965, he was elected president by the assembly. López remained in office until 6 June 1971, when he was replaced by Ramon Ernesto Cruz-Uclés (qv), who won the election held in March. On 3 December 1972, a bloodless coup ousted Cruz. The coup's leader, López, was attending a baseball game in Nicaragua at the time. The next day López, the commander of the armed forces at the moment, announced he would finish the five-year term of Cruz as president. On 22 April 1975, López was himself ousted from office in a bloodless coup.

Lop Nor. On 17 June 1967, Lop Nor became the site of the first hydrogen device detonated in Communist China. Following the blast, the Chinese announced a "no first use" policy. Nuclear tests followed at the Lop Nor site over the next decade, utilizing both atmospheric and subsurface detonations. By September 1977 a total of 22 nuclear detonations had taken place at the site, which is located in eastern Tarim Basin in the Sinkiang Uigur Autonomous Region of China..

Lott, Teixeira H. B. D. On 11 November 1955, a military junta led by Lieutenant General Lott seized power in Brazil. The takeover occurred when it became known that the acting president, Carlos Coimbra da Luz (qv) was seeking a way to prevent the assumption of the presidency by the president-elect Juscelino Kubitschek (qv). Kubitschek was sworn in on schedule on 31 January 1956. *See* Brazil.

Louly, Mohamed Mahmoud Ould. (b. 1 January 1943, Tidjikja, Mauritania) Louly joined the army in 1960 and was trained in French military schools. He held several posts in the Mauritanian general staff and, in 1979, was a member of the Committee for National Salvation. In the Salek government he was the minister of the interior and held several other key posts. When Colonel Mustafa Ould Salek resigned on 3 June 1979, Louly became head of state. On 3 January 1980, Lieutenant Colonel Louly was ousted from office by a military coup. He was replaced by Lieutenant Colonel Mohammed Khouna Ould Haidalla (qv).

Lozano Dias, Julio. From 1954 until 1956, Julio Lozano Dias was dictator of Honduras. During this time he faced communist-backed strikes and other violence. He did, however, manage to improve conditions in his country until a bloodless military coup on 21 October 1956 forced his resignation.

Luanda. *See* Angola.

Luang Prabang. *See* Laos.

Lubango. *See* Angola.

Lublin. *See* Poland.

Lucas Garcia, Fernando Romeo. (b. 4 July 1924, Chamelco, Guatemala) Lucas Garcia graduated from the Polytechnic Institute in 1949 and immediately entered the army. By 1973, he had risen to brigadier general. He also became army chief of staff. For five years, between 1958 and 1963, he also represented Alta Verapaz in the Guatemalan congress. On 23 March 1982, Fernando Lucas Garcia was ousted from office as president of Guatemala by a military coup led by General Efraín Ríos Montt (qv). Montt and his military junta made their move after a 7 March election had been won by the outgoing regime's candidate. Lucas Garcia had been in office since 1 July 1978 after unanimous confirmation by the National Assembly, following an election in which no candidate carried the minimum 50 percent of the popular vote. He was minister of defense at the time of his election.

Lule, Yusefu. On 13 April 1979, Yusefu Lule became the president of Uganda following the expulsion of Idi Amin. After some unexplained government changes, Lule was forced to resign after a no-confidence vote on the Ungandan National Consultative Council. Lule was charged with attempting to establish another dictatorship. He was replaced as president by Godfrey L. Binaisa (qv). *See* Uganda and National Resistance Army.

Lumumba, Patrice. (b. 2 July 1925, Onalua, Belgian Congo—d. 17 [?] December 1961, Katanga) Lumumba never finished school. He did move to Leopoldville (Kinshasa), where he became a postal clerk. There also he became interested in the trade union movement and in the Belgian Liberal Party. He was arrested and convicted of mail fraud and served one year in prison. After his release, he became a salesman, but quickly moved into the nationalist movement. In 1958 he founded the Congolese National Movement. With Congolese independence (30 June 1960), Lumumba was elected prime minister; civil war followed immediately on the heels of independence, and the army was in rebellion. On 14 July, Lumumba asked the United Nations for aid after severe troop mutinies. Katanga (*see* Zaire) and Kasai provinces seceded and attempted to establish independent governments (11 July). Even with the presence of over 20,000 UN troops in Congo, Lumumba was unable to control any of it; on 5 September, President Joseph Kasavubu (qv) dismissed him from office. Lumumba refused the discharge and called his cabinet into session. Thereafter, both he and Kasavubu claimed for months to head the legal government. Lumumba was captured in November, but escaped on 25 November. He was recaptured by Katangan forces and delivered to Mobutu (qv). On 13 February 1961 Katanga announced that Lumumba was killed while trying to escape. It is probable that he was murdered on orders from Moise Tshombe on 17 January. On 14 February the Soviet Union accused UN Secretary Dag Hammarskjöld of complicity in Lumumba's death. *Reading:* Thomas R. Kanza, *The Rise and Fall of Patrice Lumumba: Conflict in the Congo* (1980); Robin McKown, *Lumumba: A Biography* (1969).

Lunar New Year. *See* Tet and Vietnam.

Lusaka. *See* Zambia.

Luvanium University. *See* Congo-Kinshasa.

Luwum, Janani. On 17 February 1977, Ugandan dictator Idi Amin (qv) was reported to have ordered the murders of three opposition leaders, including Anglican archbishop Janani Luwum. Luwum and two former cabinet ministers were in the custody of Amin's notorious State Research Unit at the time of their deaths, after being accused of plotting the overthrow of the government. *See* Uganda.

Luyt, Sir Richard. On 14 June 1964, Sir Richard Luyt, the governor of British Guiana (Guyana), was forced to assume emergency powers when faced with increasingly serious race rioting between Indians and Negroes in the British colony, Much of the blame for the unrest was placed on pro-communist Cheddi Jagan, who refused to resign as prime minister. British troops were ordered into the country to restore order. New and more democratically controlled elections were held in December, and Jagan was forced out of office.

Lynch, John Mary. (b. 15 August 1917, Cork) A close ally of Eamon De Valera, Lynch entered politics as a member of the opposition in 1948. In 1951, he was made parliamentary secretary, a post he held in the Fianna Fail government until 1954. Lynch was minister for the Gaelic-speaking districts of Ireland from March to June of 1957, then minister of education and of industry, commerce and finance. He became prime minister of the Republic of Ireland in November 1966. On 5 May 1970, Lynch sacked two senior cabinet officials for conspiring to ship arms to Roman Catholic factions in Northern Ireland. They were later arrested and tried, along with several others. This action helped defuse some of the divisiveness that was tearing at the heart of the republic. When one of the two conspirators was acquitted (December) and the other had already been released, Lynch was faced with threats of kidnapping. He declared a state of emergency in Ireland. Lynch remained in office until 5 December 1979, during which time he faced a series of political adversities. On 7 December 1979, Charles J. Haughey, one of those accused earlier of running guns to Northern Ireland, was elected prime minister.

M

Ma'alot. *See* Israel.

Macao. The Portuguese colony of Macao (Macau) is an enclave consisting of a peninsula of the Chinese mainland and two small islands (Taipa and Coloane) located on the southern side of the mouth of the Canton River. Macao City is located on the peninsula and is separated from mainland China by a causeway. The colony was first settled by the Portuguese in 1557 and is the oldest European settlement in western Asia. The Portuguese paid an annual tithe to the Chinese for the use of the trading post until 1849, when they declared its independence and closed the Chinese customs house. By that time, Macao had became the chief port for Sino-European trade, but it soon began to lose its importance to the nearby British colony of Hong Kong. Macao was not occupied by the Japanese during World War II, as was Hong Kong, and regained some of its importance as a supplier of goods to southern China. In January 1967, Communist Chinese gunboats entered Macao Harbor in support of Chinese protests over the shooting of communist demonstrators during a December 1966 riot. Communist-inspired violence erupted again in July 1967, following rioting in Hong Kong. The rioting subsided as soon as British troops restored order in Hong Kong. On 1 March 1972, China announced its claim on Macao (and Hong Kong) at the United Nations. Portugal granted the colony broad autonomy in 1976 and made an agreement with China in 1987 to return the colony to China in 1999. Much as with Hong Kong, Macao is to become a "special administrative region." In 1989, the Portuguese issued passports to almost 30 percent of the colony's population. A major bribery scandal rocked the colony in September 1990, when the Portuguese governor was forced to resign and return to Europe after accepting $300,000 in kickbacks from a German firm. In most other ways, Macao followed Hong Kong in the preparations for handing the colony over to the People's Republic. *Reading:* T. Jeff Williams, *Macao* (1988).

MacArthur, Douglas. (b. 26 January 1880, Little Rock, Arkansas—d. 5 April 1964, Washington, DC) Born the son of an army general and Civil War hero, MacArthur entered the United States Military Academy in June 1899 and graduated as an engineering officer with the highest grades achieved in 25 years. His first service was in the Philippines and then in Japan as a military observer. He then served as an aide to President Theodore Roosevelt. After several field assignments he was posted to Washington from 1912 to1913. MacArthur took part in the capture of Vera Cruz, Mexico, in 1914. When World War War I began, MacArthur was a 37-year-old major. He became chief of staff in the 42nd (Rainbow) Division and then, in August 1917, transferred to the infantry, where he was promoted to colonel. In March 1918 he was gassed during an enemy attack on his position. In June 1918, he was promoted to brigadier general. From 1919 until 1922 he was uperintendent of the U.S. Military Academy, West Point. Thereafter, he was again posted to the Philippines, where in 1922 he married Louise Cromwell Brooks. In 1925, Major General MacArthur returned to the U.S. and commanded a corps area for thee years, during which time he served on the courts martial that convicted Brigadier General Billy Mitchell. In 1928 he was placed in charge of the U.S. Olympic Committee (then called the American Olympic Committee). In November 1930 he was appointed chief of staff of the army, where he developed among many a reputation as a "glory hound," a medal hunter, and on occasion, a warmonger and "strident militarist." On President Herbert Hoover's orders, MacArthur directed the removal of "Bonus Marchers" from Anacostia Flat, just outside Washington, in July 1932. He was largely instrumental in the modest modernization of the army that could be accomplished during those austere years. MacArthur was the first officer to be reappointed chief of staff since the post was originated. In 1935, at the request of Manuel Quezon, the president of the Philippine Commonwealth, MacArthur was appointed head of the American military mission. He was appointed field marshal in the Philippine Commonwealth army in 1936. In 1937, he retired from the army, but he was called back in July 1941. Eleven days after Pearl Harbor, he was again appointed general. He directed the defense of the Philippines until March 1942, when he was ordered to Australia to direct the war in the Southwest Pacific Theater. By October 1944, MacArthur's forces had moved up through the islands of the Southwest Pacific and had reentered the Philippines. In December 1944, he was promoted to the newly established rank of general of the army. Following the atomic bombing of Hiroshima and Nagasaki and the surrender of Japan, President Harry Truman (qv) ordered MacArthur to accept the formal surrender (2 September 1945). MacArthur was then designated Supreme Commander Allied Powers and given the mission of establishing the occupation of Japan. On 27 June 1950, the U.S. intervened in the North Korean invasion of South Korea. MacArthur was given command of the United Nations forces sent there and immediately suggested the use of Chinese Nationalist troops to help stop the invasion. President Harry S. Truman (qv) rejected the idea. On 13 September 1950, MacArthur carried off a brilliant amphibious landing at Inchon, which led to a rout of the North Korean army and the pursuit to the Yalu River, where Chinese Communist forces entered the war (November 1950). MacArthur had committed two errors at that time. One was not consolidating the forces in Korea under a single command; the other was not listening to intelligence sources that had predicted the Chinese invasion. For these blunders a terrible price was paid before the UN forces could be reassembled (*see* Korea). MacArthur called the Chinese intervention a "new war." He had met with Truman in October 1950 on Wake Island, where the president attempted to quiet MacArthur's open comments that differed with U.S. policy. When these conflicts in views continued and were reported in the press, Truman relieved MacArthur of command on 11 April 1951 and ordered him back to the states, where he received a hero's welcome. After addressing both houses of Congress, he retired to private life and delivered the Republican keynote address at the 1963 convention. He died in the Walter Reed Army Medical Center in Washington, DC, on 5 April 1964 and was interred in Norfolk, Virginia. *Reading:* Norman Finkelstein, *The Emperor General: A Biography of Douglas MacArthur* (1989); Richard H. Rovere & Arthur Schesinger, Jr., *General MacArthur & President Truman: The Struggle for Control of American Foreign Policy* (1997); Geoffrey Perret, *Old Soldiers Never Die: The Life of Douglas MacArthur* (1996).

Macel (Machel), Samora Moises. (b. 29 September 1933, Xilembena, Gaza, Mozambique—d. 19 October 1986, Nkomati, South Africa) Macel paid his way through grade school by working as a field hand at a Protestant mission. He then trained to be a male nurse at a Catholic mission. In 1961, he met Eduardo Mondlane, who later became the leader of Frelimo. Macel, by this time an avowed Marxist, crossed into Tanzania in 1962 to join the Frelimo guerrilla movement and was sent to Algeria for military training before returning to Mozambique to fight. By 1968 he had become the leader of the Frelimo guerrilla forces. Macel became a member of the Frelimo ruling triumvirate following Mondlane's assassination in 1969. When a provisional government was formed in Mozambique following the Portuguese revolution (*see* Portugal) in April 1974, Macel was a serious contender for the presidency of the new nation (*see* Mozambique). On 25 June 1975, Macel became Mozambique's first president. Macel's tenure was marked by contrasts between his Marxist background and his more fundamental style of leadership that often crossed color lines as well as political ones. Macel was killed in a plane crash near Nkomati, Natal, in South Africa, on 19 October 1986.

Macias Nguema (Nguma), Francisco. (b. 1922, Nsegayong, Rio Muni—d. 29 September 1979, Malabo, Equatorial Guinea) Born a member of the Fang group of the Bantu tribe, Macias assumed the presidency of Equatorial Guinea when the country received its independence from Spain in October 1968. A ruthless dictator, Macias managed to drive off most of the white population following the eviction of the Spanish garrison in 1969. On 5 March of that year, there was an unsuccessful coup attempt against Macias, which was led by the foreign minister, Anastasio N'Dongo, who, along with others, was executed as a result. Following this incident, Macias assumed dictatorial powers and, in 1972, proclaimed himself president for life. In 1973, Macias expelled a UN mission from his country, and in 1976, Nigeria was obliged to evacuate nearly 45,000 of its workers in the country to halt their brutalization. Most of the educated class in Equatorial Guinea were of the Bubi tribe. Macias systematically murdered or exiled most of them. On 3 August 1979, Macias was overthrown in a coup led by Lieutenant Colonel Teodoro Obiang Nguema Mbasogo. Macias was subsequently tried for treason, embezzlement and genocide, found guilty and shot.

Macmillan, (Maurice) Harold. (b. 10 February 1894, London—d. 29 December 1986, Chelwood Gate, West Sussex, England) Born Maurice Harold Macmillan Stockton into a well-established publishing family, Macmillan attended Eton College and Balliol College, Oxford. He fought in World War I and was wounded three times. He became aide-de-camp to the governor-general of Canada in 1919 and married the governor's daughter in 1920. He was elected to Parliament in 1924 as the representative of Stockton-on-Tees and served in that post until 1925, and again from 1931 to1945. He opposed appeasement. During World War II he served as minister to the Allied Headquarters, North Africa, where he became friends with Dwight D. Eisenhower (qv). He also took part in the occupation of Italy and in the British intervention in Greece during the civil war there. He again entered Parliament, but lost his Stockton-on-Tees seat in 1945. He ran again and was seated as the representative of Bromley (Kent) from 1945 to 1964. He served as minister of housing and local government from 1951 to 1954. Thereafter, he served successive terms as minister of defense (1954–1955), foreign secretary (1955) and chancellor of the Exchequer (1955–1957). In January 1957, he was appointed prime minister following the resignation of Anthony Eden (qv). By 1962, his popularity was in decline, and during the next year his cabinet was rocked by scandal. In October 1963, Macmillan fell ill and resigned. He health restored, he helped in the management of the Macmillan publishing empire and wrote his memoirs. During this period he became chancellor of the University of Oxford. He was created earl in 1984 and died two years later. *Reading:* Richard Aldous & Sabine Lee, eds., *Harold MacMillan and Britain's World Role* (1995); John Tyrner, *MacMillan* (1994).

MacStiofain, Sean. (b .February 1928, London) Born John Stephenson, the son of a Protestant law clerk, MacStiofain was educated in a parochial school, where he learned Catholicism. At age 14 he ran away from home and joined a group of Irish emigres in London who worked for Irish unification. In 1950 he married an Irish woman. He then participated in a raid on an armory to steal weapons for the rebels in North Ireland, but he was captured and sentenced to eight years in prison. While incarcerated at Wormwood Scrubbs Prison he changed his name to MacStiofain and studied terrorism under the tutelage of Greek Cypriots also held there. When released from prison he joined the IRA in Ulster and was soon one of the leaders of the Provisional Wing of the Irish Republican Army (PIRA) (1970). He was arrested in Dublin in the Republic of Ireland on 19 November 1972 and sentenced to six months in jail. His inability to carry out a promised hunger strike discredited him among the PIRA, and by 1974 he no longer had a voice in PIRA operations. MacStiofain thereafter went into permanent retirement. *Reading:* Sean MacStiofain, *Revolutionary in Ireland* (1975).

Madagascar. An island slightly smaller than the state of Texas, Madagascar is located off the southeast coast of Africa. It is separated from Mozambique on the mainland by the Madagascar Channel. The island was first settled about 2,000 years ago by Malayan-Indonesian tribesmen.The Arabs established trading posts there in the seventh century A.D. The Portuguese arrived about 1500. The country was unified as a kingdom in the eighteenth century. A French protectorate was established in 1885, and Madagascar became a French colony in 1896. Following World War II Madagascar became a French overseas territory, and in 1958 it became the autonomous Malagasy Republic. In 1960 it was proclaimed an independent republic and was admitted to the United Nations. In April 1971, government forces crushed an uprising in Tulear province in the southern part of the island. On 31 May, a plot to overthrow President Philibert Tsiranana (qv) was foiled. One month later the US ambassador was expelled on charges he interfered in the internal affairs of the country. In May 1972, a number of disturbances brought about the closing of a medical school (13 May). This led to a major clash between students and security forces in which scores of demonstrators were killed. A national state of emergency was declared and a curfew imposed. On 14 May the capital city of Tananarive was burned down and many more people killed. On 18 May 1972, following another week of student violence, a military coup ousted the Tsiranana government and installed one led by General Gabriel Ramanantsoa (qv). Violence continued, however, until 14 December, when a state of siege was declared. The state of siege was lifted on 13 January 1973. In June 1973 an agreement was reached with France whereby 4,000 French troops were to be withdrawn by 1 September and the naval base at Diego Suarez was to be closed in two years. A U.S. space tracking station was also ordered closed. At about this same time, the government obtained Chinese aid. On 5 February 1975, an 11-day government crisis ended with replacement of Ramanantsoa with Colonel Richard Ratsimandrava (qv) as the new head of government. Ratsimandrava was assassinated five days later in the capital city of Tananarive. General Gilles Andriamahazo assumed power at the head of a military junta. A second Malagasy republic was officially proclaimed as the Democratic Republic of Madagascar on 30 December 1975. The next day, an amnesty freed all political prisoners held for crimes committed before 1 January 1975. On 4 January 1976, Admiral Didier Ratsiraka was sworn in as president. Lieutenant Colonel Joel Rakotomalala was appointed prime minister on 10 January. Rakotomalala was killed in a helicopter crash on 30 July, however, and was replaced by Justin Rakotoniaina. By September, however, new violence wracked the country, and in the years following, numerous attempts were made on the president's life. A left-wing group, Power to Underlings, was ordered dissolved by the government as the cause of much of the violence. By 1986, the economic system was so bad that a free market economy was organized. Strikes and violence against the one-party system did not stop Ratsiraka from being elected to a third term in 1989, but did lead to the legalization of opposition parties in 1990. Albert Zafy was elected president in 1993, marking an end to the 17-year Ratsiraka socialist and authoritarian rule. An austerity program was instituted in March 1994, cutting high-level salaries by 10 percent, as one of the plan's initiatives. The economic situation in late 1994 led to antigovernment demonstrations. A hint of scandal led to the dismissal of the leadership of the central bank and the resignation of the finance minister. By the end of 1995, the principal problem facing Madagascar was a bloody conflict between mine owners and conservationists over the environment. *Reading:* Gillian Feeley-Harnik, *A Green Estate: Restoring Independence in Madagascar* (1991).

Madras. *See* India.

Madrid. *See* Spain.

Madura Island. *See* Indonesia.

Maga, Hubert. Maga took office as president of Dahomey (qv) in 1961 and began the process of moving his country toward a one-party political system. On 28 October 1963, a military coup ousted Maga and established a new ruling junta that promptly installed a civilian government. *See* Dahomey.

Magloire, Paul. On 11 January 1946, a military junta overthrew the Haitian government of President Elie Lescot (qv). The coup, led by Colonel Paul Magloire, then installed Dumarsais Estime (qv) as president. On 10 May 1950, Magloire led a second coup, which ousted Estime. Magloire took the presidency for himself, but he was forced to resign on 12 December 1956, when general disorder and violence had reached major proportions throughout Haiti.

Magsaysay, Ramon. (b. 31 August 1907, Zambales Province, Philippines—d. 17 March 1957, Philippines) Born the son of a blacksmith, Magsaysay was educated at the Zambales Academy and the University of the Philippines (1927-1931). He then attended the university's college of engineering (1927–1928) and the Institute of Commerce of Jose Rizal College, from 1928 to 1932. By the beginning of World War II he was a manager of a large private concern. When the U.S. army requisitioned his vehicles, he went with them and participated in the battle on Bataan. He then escaped to the hills (1942) and helped organize the Western Luzon Guerrilla Force, in which he was commissioned a captain in April 1945. The Japanese placed a price of $50,000 on his head. His forces participated in many major guerrilla operations, and on 4 February 1945, he was appointed the military governor of Zambales. He held that post until Filipino civil authority was restored after the war. He was discharged as a major in 1946 and ran for Congress against other candidates from his province he knew to be collaborators. He was elected in April 1946 and was appointed chairman of the House Committee on National Defense. In 1948 he was appointed director of the Veterans' Mission to Washington. He was reelected to the Filipino House in 1949. He was again sent to Washington to get more military aid. In the Philippines he attacked his own Liberal Party (then in power) for not carrying the fight to the Hukbalahap communist insurgents operating on Luzon. Upon the third offer of the post, Magsaysay became the secretary of national defense on 1 September 1950. He immediately moved to clear up the chaotic conditions in the army that rendered it helpless against the Huks, who were rampaging through Luzon. He consulted with military officers known to be plotting a coup and asked for and received 90 days to clear up the situation. They agreed, and Magsaysay began cleaning house, retiring or discharging incompetent leaders, and reorganized the army into counterinsurgent battalions, which were sent into the jungles and hillsides to hunt out and destroy the Huks. In April 1951, he brought the much-despised and feared Philippine Constabulary under the Defense Department and again cleaned house. He himself was constantly in the field checking on his men. In November 1951, Magsaysay's army helped secure a free election. He went so far as to send college student members of the Reserve Officer's Training Corps (ROTC) into the field. The ensuing victory of the Nacionalista Party led to a mass arrest of liberal leaders, who were charged with murder. This group included a province governor, three mayors, and the entire police force of one province. In July 1952, he moved against Muslim Moro rebels who had created major problems on Mindanao. He was elected president of the Philippines on 30 December 1953. Opposition leaders in Congress saw his friendship with the United States as a threat and worked to block most of his programs. His programs won widespread support, however, and the results of by-elections ousted most of his enemies from Congress. Magsaysay was killed in an airplane crash between Cebu city and Manila on 17 March 1957.

Maharashtra. *See* India.

al-Mahdi, Imam al-Hadi. On 27 March 1970, an attempt was made on the life of Sudan's president, Mohammed Gaafar al-Nimeiry (qv), by the followers of Imam al-Hadi al-Mahdi. This attempt was a part of the Ansar movement, the main Muslim sectarian organization in Sudan. When the assassination attempt failed, Nimeiry reacted by moving to suppress the Ansar. In the bloody engagements that followed, al-Mahdi was killed (31 March) and the Ansar defeated.

al-Mahdi, Sadik. On 2 July 1976, the former prime minister of Sudan, Sadik al-Mahdi, orchestrated a coup attempt against President Mohammed Gaafar al-Nimeiry (qv) of Sudan. The coup attempt, which had been backed by Libya, failed. Mahdi, in exile at the time of the attack, was aided by another exile, former finance minister Hussein al-Hindi.

Mahendra, Bir Bikham. On 15 December 1960, King Mahendra Bir Bikham Shah Deva of Nepal led a successful coup against his prime minister, B. P. Kirala (Koirala). To accomplish the coup, the king dissolved the parliament and suspended part of the constitution, assuming many of the administrative duties to himself. He later formed a new council of ministers with himself as chairman.

Mahe Province. *See* India.

Maher, Ali. On 18 January 1952, Ali Maher Pasha was named premier after Egypt's King Farouk (qv) dismissed Mustafa el-Nagas from that post. At the moment, widespread rioting existed in Cairo that caused massive destruction to foreign property and a number of deaths. Ali Maher, after struggling with his appointment, resigned 13 days later, on 1 March. On 24 July, however, Ali Maher was reinstalled as premier by the military junta that had just overthrown King Farouk on 23 July.

Mahgoub, Mohammed Ahmed. On 25 May 1969, Sudan's prime minister, Mohammed Ahmed Mahgoub, was ousted from office by a left-wing socialist military coup led by Colonel Mohammed Gaafar al-Nimeiry (qv). Although the coup was aimed at radical revolutionary reform, Mahgoub's administration was also becoming unpopular because of economic and political mismanagement.

Mai Huu Xuan. Between 29 January and 30 January 1964, Major General Nguyen Khanh led a bloodless pre-dawn coup that deposed Vietnam's Duong Van Minh. The coup was based upon the belief that the government had entered into a plot with the French to neutralize South Vietnam. Mai Huu Xuan was a member of the ousted Military Council and was arrested as a French collaborator. Nguyen Khanh's first act as the head of the new government was to break diplomatic relations with France.

al-Majali, Hazza. The government of Jordan's Hazza al-Majali was forced to resign on 19 December 1955, when rioting broke out in Amman following disclosure of Jordan's intent to join the Baghdad Pact (qv). Majali was killed in a bomb attack on 29 August 1960.

Majano Ramos, Adolfo Arnoldo. One of the two colonels who led a successful military coup against the El Salvador government of Carlos Humberto Romero on 17 October 1979, Majani, along with Jaime Abdul Gutiérrez (qv), became a member of the ruling junta. Just before Jose Napoleon Duarte (qv) was sworn in as president of El Salvador on 13 December 1980, Marjano was removed from power.

Makarios III, Archbishop. (b. 13 August 1913, Pano Panayia, Cyprus—d. 3 August 1977, Nicosia) Born Michael Christodoulos Mouskos, at age 13 Makarios entered a monastery, where he took his church name, Makarios, or "Blessed." He studied both law and theology at the University of Athens and, in 1946, continued his study of theology at Boston University. In 1947, he organized a plebiscite on Cyprus, the results of which showed 96 percent of the populace favoring *Enosis*, union with Greece. That was Makarios's original position. In 1948, he became bishop of Kition and, in 1950, succeeded Makarios II as archbishop of Cyprus, a position that involved both political and spiritual leadership. In this role, Makarios used his power to foster resistance to the British colonial administration of the island. In 1955, a Cypriot guerrilla campaign waged by *EOKA*, led by General Grivas (qv), gained such power that Britain offered a tripartite conference with Greece and Turkey. That displeased the Greek Cypriots. In 1956, the British banished Makarios to the Seychelles (qv), where he was forced to remain one year. He then decided to settle in Athens. In 1957, the United Nations entered the Cyprus question, and the seeds of Cypriot independence were sown. In the meanwhile, Cyprus was suffering from Makarios' absence. Terrorist activities increased against the British, and Greek Cypriots turned against their Turkish Cypriot neighbors. In 1959, the Treaty of Zurich was signed, which made Cyprus an independent "unitary state." Makarios negotiated with the British, thus abandoning his earlier goal of *enosis*. On 14 December 1959, Makarios was elected president, but he did not assume office until 16 August 1960, when the island actually became independent. One part of the treaty forced Makarios to reluctantly accept the provision that Great Britain would retain sovereignty over two military bases on the island, at Akrotiri and Dekhelia. Once the British matter was settled, Makarios then had to face the difficult task of establishing a "liveable" relationship with the Turkish minority of Cyprus. In 1960, the Cypriot constitution tried to provide for both the Greek and the Turkish Cypriot factions of the island's population. Makarios declared that a Turkish Cypriot would be his vice president. Both would be elected for five years, and both would have executive powers. The two of them would appoint the rest of the government. This "liveable" arrangement did not satisfy the two factions, and fighting broke out anew. Makarios and his vice president, Dr. Kücük, disagreed over the integration of the two communities, with Makarios favoring it and the vice president demanding separation. In November 1963, Makarios proposed a constitutional revision that would enforce his view. This engendered more fighting, and the British reinforced their garrisons on the island. During January 1964, both Great Britain and the United States tried to mediate the dispute, but to no avail. Makarios kept increasing his Greek Cypriot forces. On 18 February 1964, Cyprus asked the United Nations to step in and restore peace. UN peacekeepers arrived on 25 March 1964. Fighting continued, however, especially in northern Cyprus. A uneasy truce went into effect, but the UN force had to surround many Turkish villages to keep the peace. In August 1966, the UN had to intervene to prevent a Turkish invasion of Cyprus. This action prompted Makarios to lift some of the restrictions he had imposed on the Turkish Cypriots. On 8 March 1970, an assassination attempt on Makarios failed. In January 1974, General Grivas attempted the overthrow of the Makarios government but failed. After the military took control of Greece, Makarios cooled relations with Athens. When Grivas died in July 1974, the Makarios government knew it had survived another threat to its existence. But a new coup was organized by the Greek National Guard on Cyprus, and on 15 July 1974 Makarios was forced to seek refuge at a British military installation. Nikos Sampson, an old *EOKA* leader and newspaper publisher was named president of Cyprus. Fighting broke out again between the two warring factions in Nicosia. Turkey sent troops, consolidating their positions on a 200-mile area between Nicosia and Kyrenia. The Turks then controlled about 38 percent of the island; the island was de facto divided. Greece asked for an emergency session of the UN Security Council (28 July). As the Turks continued to expand their area of control, the British reinforced their garrison. On 30 July, a cease-fire was signed by Greece and Turkey, but Turkey continued to expand, expelling Greek Cypriots as they moved. On 1 August, the Greek junta fell apart and Greece withdrew its forces from NATO because the organization had failed to stop the Turks. On 7 December 1974, the new Greek government backed the return of Makarios to power to govern the southern, Greek Cypriot part of the island. Makarios tried to work toward a federation of the two parts. This effort went on for three years without success. On 30 May 1976, he rejected a Turkish Cypriot proposal that would have left the island divided. Makarios continued to work toward a settlement until his death in Nicosia on 3 August 1977. *Reading:* P. N.

Vanezis, *Makarios: Pragmatism v. Idealism* (1975); Stanley Mayes, *Markarios* (1981).

Makonnen, Endalkatchew. On 27–28 February 1974, Endalkatchew Makonnen was sworn in as prime minister of Ethiopia. This followed an army mutiny in Asmara, Eritrea, and was one of the reforms attempted by King Haile Selassie (qv) following the resignation of the old government. Makonnen resigned (22 July) after serving only five months in office. He, along with a number of his colleagues, was then arrested by the army. Less than two months later, the imperial rule of Haile Selassie was deposed. *See* Ethiopia.

Malagasy Republic. *See* Madagascar.

Malan, Daniel Francois. (b. 22 May 1874, Riebeeck West, Cape Colony, South Africa—d.7 February 1959, Stellenbosch) Born the son of a farmer, Malan was educated in Cape Colony schools, Victoria College and the University of Utrecht in The Netherlands. In 1905, he became a Dutch Reformed Church minister and was active in the movement to make Afrikaans the official language. After the Boer War he became editor (July 1915) of a Cape Town newspaper and became a close friend and ally of J. B. M. Hertzog, the leader of the Nationalist Party. He chaired the Cape Province congress in 1915. He was elected to Parliament in 1918 and was a member of the delegation that asked for republican independence at Versailles (1919). As a member of Hertzog's cabinets from 1924 to 1933, Malan was responsible for the creation of the laws that created a a South African nationality and that made Afrikaans the nation's official language. In 1934, Malan broke with Hertzog over political differences and became the leader of a new Nationalist Party. He supported Hertzog's attempts at neutrality against Jan Smuts (qv) and was against South Africa's entry into World War II. The end of the war saw the Afrikaaner movement in shambles, but Malan was able to hold his Nationalist Party together and won a narrow majority in the 1948 elections. This led to the first exclusive Afrikaaner government in South Africa. This government set in place the laws of apartheid (qv), although at least one of the laws was declared unconstitutional in 1952. Malan won a wider majority in the 1953 elections, but he retired the following years because of age. He died in 1959.

Malatar, Pal. One of the leaders of the 1956 Hungarian uprising Malatar was executed on 17 June 1958 by the Soviet-controlled Hungarian government, along with Imre Nagy (qv) and two others, for their parts in the uprising. *See* Hungary.

Malawi. A small southeast African country, Malawi is the approximate size of Pennsylvania. The country is located along the western shore of Lake Malawi (Lake Nyasa) and is bordered on the north by Tanzania, on the southeast by Mozambique and on the west by Zambia. The capital is Lilongwe. The area was occupied by Bantu tribesmen in the sixteenth century. Arab slavers appeared in the early nineteenth century, and the region became the British protectorate of Nyasaland in 1891. On 6 July 1964 the country was declared an independent state within the British Commonwealth and named Malawi. On 6 July 1971, Hastings Kazumu Banda (qv) was named president for life. There was guerrilla activity along the Mozambique border in the 1970s. Banda still held power 1993 after 22 years of relatively peaceful rule. He lost office on 21 May 1994, however, in the first multiparty elections held in Malawi. The elections were reported by the UN observer group as being fraught with intimidation, bribery and fraud, but Banda was defeated. The new president, Bakili Muluzi, faced a major famine caused by the drought as his first order of business. Mulizi's government failed to react in 1994, but it was able to come to terms with the issues in 1995 and win International Monetary Fund approval as the year began. Banda and a group of his followers were arrested in January 1995 and charged with murder in the deaths of four former government officials in 1983. More people were later arrested on similar charges, but they were released on technical grounds. Banda's health prevented his presence at his trial. In December, he was acquitted of all charges, but took the opportunity to apologize to the people of Malawi for any suffering they may have endured during his time in office. *Reading:* Alfred John Wills, *An Introduction to the History of Central Africa* (1985); T. David Williams, *Malawi: The Politics of Despair* (1978); Colin Baker, *Seeds of Trouble: Government Policy and Land Rights in Nyasaland, 1946-1964* (1993).

Malaya. *See* Malaysia.

Malay Federation. In 1963, Great Britain proposed a federation that would include Malaya, Singapore (qv), Sarawak, Sabah (qv) and Brunei (qv). All accepted except Brunei. Singapore withdrew in 1965. Malaya (then Malaysia), Sabah and Brunei remain in the Federation of Malaysia.

Malaysia. A country occupying the southern portion of the Malay Peninsula, it is bordered on the north by Thailand; on the east by the South China Sea; on the south and southwest by the Strait of Malacca, which separates it from Indonesia (Sumatra); and on the northwest by the lower reaches of the Andaman Sea. The Republic of Singapore occupies an enclave on its southernmost tip. Portuguese seafaring traders first touched its shores in the early sixteenth century and captured Melaka in 1511. A century later the Dutch had replaced the Portuguese. After the Napoleonic Wars the Anglo-Dutch treaty was signed, which divided the region into spheres of influence, which led to British control of the Malay Peninsula, including present-day Malaysia. A British colonial government was established there in 1867. In 1941, Japan invaded Malaya, which remained under Japanese control until 1945. On 1 February 1948, the Federation of Malaysia was established. That same year, a communist uprising began among the Chinese population, which slowed plans for independence and required significant British military force to quell. In 1957, Malaya gained its independence as a kingdom, with the king elected by a council of hereditary rulers of the individual states every five years. During the process of federation, Prime Minister Abdul Rahman announced that when Singapore and Malaysia merged, Singapore would no longer be used as a SEATO base by the British. Malaysia found itself at war with Indonesia over territorial claims in 1964. Thailand announced its intention to help secure the peace by patrolling the border between the two states. However, Indonesia announced that it would continue the fighting (17 February 1964) in Saba and Sarawak until the situation was settled. Then, on 3 May, President Achmed Sukarno of Indonesia announced his intention to crush Malaysia. On 9 August 1965, Singapore declared itself an independent state in order to reduce tensions created by the ethnic differences between the Chinese of Singapore and the Malays. A peace settlement between Malaysia and Indonesia was announced in Bangkok on 1 June 1966. Fighting ended in July. When Britain decided to withdeaw from the region in September 1967, Australia stepped in with A$20 million in support for Malaysia and Singapore. In September 1968, the Philippines reasserted their claim on Saba province in Borneo. Malaysia immediately broke diplomatic relations with Manila. On 10 February 1969 the first British troops began leaving Malaysia. In April of that year, Malaysian troops joined the Thais in a campaign to rout insurgent forces operating in southern Thailand. On 16 May a state of emergency was declared following four days of clashes between Malay and Chinese factions. At least 196 were reported killed in the fighting. In November 1970, Malay aircraft attacked and bombed rebel bases in Sarawak, East Malaysia, close to the Indonesian border. More guerrilla bases were discovered near Ipoh in north central Malaysia. Fighting also continued in the provinces. In August 1971 Malaysian forces launched an offensive to eliminate the guerrilla threat in Sarawak. In September, Malaysia and Singapore integrated their air defense systems, and in November, Malaysia, along with Australia, New Zealand and Great Britain, joined Singapore in securing the defense of that nation. On 13 March 1972 Malaysia intensified its campaign against the communist guerrillas operating in Sarawak; the initial results were not good for the government forces. On 6 April, Malaysia signed an agreement with Indonesia for more direct cooperation in fighting this communist threat. On 5 February 1973, Australia promised to honor its commitment to Malaysia even though the new Australian Labor government had voted to withdraw all of its combat forces in Southeast Asia. On 31 May 1974, Malaysia's prime minister, Tun Abdul Razak (qv), signed an agreement establishing diplomatic relations with China. The war against the communist rebels continued for years. On 4–8 August 1975, the American and Swedish embassies in Kuala Lampur were captured by Japanese Red Army (JRA) (qv) terrorists, who demanded the release of five JRA members held in Japan. When the release was accomplished, all ten JRA members were flown to Libya. By 1976, Malaysia was also cooperating with Thailand in conducting joint operations against the communists. In 1979, Malaysia faced a crisis of another kind when the deputy prime minister ordered "boat people" escaping from Vietnam to be shot on sight rather than having their boats towed back out to sea. The order was quickly rescinded, but the political damage was already done, not only in Malaysia but around the world. In 1984, the communist rebel problem continued, but the situation was further complicated when the government was faced by a new threat, one from Muslim fundamentalists of the *Partai Islam* (PAS), who wanted an Iranian-style revolution to establish a Islamic government in Malaysia. There was sufficient evidence gathered to assume the PAS had established death squads to assassinate government and ruling party leaders. On 2 December 1989, the government received some relief when the communist rebels agreed to end their 41-year insurgency against Malaysia. Some 1,200 guerrillas were allowed to surrender their arms in Malaysia and Thailand and return to their homes. With one problem over, another cropped up in Sabah in Borneo, where political unrest bordered on more serious problems (1993). Also in 1993, Malaysia supported Muslim concerns in the Middle East and offered to send 1,500 troops to Bosnia-Herzogovina. In 1994, the Malaysian government banned all contracts with Britain following a revelation of the bribery of an official. Even worse was a second revelation of the more than $5 billion in currency exchange fraud since 1992. The year 1995 passed without incident. *Reading:* Robert Jackson, *The Malayan Emergency: The Commonwealth's Wars, 1948-1966* (1991); Anne Munro-Kua, *Authoritarian Populism in Malaysia* (1997); Barbara Watson Andaya, *A History of Malaysia* (1984); James C. Scott, *Weapons of the Weak: Everyday Forms of Peasant Resistance* (1987); Leon Comber, *13 May 1969: A Historical Survey of Sino-Malay Relations* (1983); Peter Dennin & Jeffrey Grey, *Emergency and Confrontation: Australian Military Operations in Malaya and Borneo 1950-66* (1996); E. D. Smith, *Malaya and Borneo* (1986).

Maldives Republic. One of the smallest and most undeveloped countries in the world, the Maldives are a string of nearly 1,200 small coral islands (of which 200 are inhabited) in the Indian Ocean southwest of India. The total land mass in approximately 155 square miles. The capital city is Male. First inhabited in the fifth century A.D. by Buddhists. most likely from Ceylon (today Sri Lanka) and from southern India, Maldives remained Buddhist until the twelfth century, when Islam was embraced. The islands remained a British protectorate until 1965, when they received full independence and became a member of the United Nations. Maldives became a republic in 1968, having abolished the sultanate that had ruled for centuries. On 29 March 1976, Great Britain relinquished its air base on Gan Island to the government. The Maldives were attacked in November 1988 by Tamil (qv) Sri Lankan mercenary terrorists, but they were driven off when Indian troops arrived. Having taken hostages and stolen boats, the terrorists were overtaken by the Indian navy and surrendered. The years 1989 to 1992 were relatively peaceful, with the nation's primary attention being paid to the environmental impact of their geographic situation—nowhere in the tiny country was the land more than six feet above sea level. The elections of 1995 returned President Mauroon Abdul Gayoom to his fifth term in office. By 1995, there were some signs that many citizens of the poor country were becoming restive over the system of no political parties and, therefore, no opposition to the government. *Reading:* C. H. B. Reynolds, *Maldives* (World Bibliographical Series, Vol. 158) (1993); Urmila Phandnis, *Maldives: Winds of Change in an Atoll State* (1985).

Mali. Formerly French Sudan, the Republic of Mali is located in the interior of West Africa. It is bordered on the north by Algeria, on the east by Niger, on the south by Burkina Faso, Guinea and Cote d'Ivoire and on the west by Mauritania and

Senegal. The capital city is Bamako. Mali is known to have been inhabited in late prehistoric times. By 300 A.D. a brisk trade was maintained out of the region across the Sahara with ivory and slaves among the principal trade items. The Mali empire existed from the thirteenth to the sixteenth centuries, with Timbuktu established as a great Islamic center of study and knowledge. The French entered the region in the mid-nineteenth century and conquered the lands as a part of French West Africa (1898). In 1946, French Sudan, as it was called at the time, became an overseas territory of the French Union. On 28 November 1958 it was proclaimed the Sudanese Republic. On 20 June 1960, the Sudanese Republic joined with Senegal to form the Federation of Mali (Federal State of Mali). Because of political differences, Senegal withdrew on 20 August 1960. What was left became the Republic of Mali and joined the United Nations. On 24 December 1960, Guinea, Ghana and Mali signed an agreement that unified the three countries; in January 1961, the agreement was expanded to include Algeria and the United Arab Republic under the Charter of Casablanca (qv). When the Organization of African States (OAS) was formed in January 1962, Mali, along with the other Casablanca states, refused to attend because Algeria had not been invited. In November 1963, Mali was instrumental in bringing an end to the Algeria-Morocco border war that had flaired up. During this period a socialist form of government developed that prevented growth within the country. By 1968, economic conditions had reached a point where a military coup (19 November) led by Moussa Traore (qv) overthrew the socialist government of Modibo Keita (qv). The new ruling junta suspended the constitution, opened trade and halted collectivization. On 7 April 1971, there was an unsuccessful coup attempt against the Traore government. Between 2 January and 5 January 1973, Mali was one of three African states that broke diplomatic relations with Israel in preparation for the forthcoming Arab-Israeli war. A major famine in Mali in 1973–1974 killed about 100,000 people. A new constitution was established in 1974 and led to a one-party system of government. In December 1985, fighting broke out along the Mali–Burkina Faso border that lasted six days before a cease-fire could be arranged. On 26 March 1991, a new military coup, led by Amadou Toumani Toure, replaced the government with one set up with multiple parties and a civilian leadership under Soumana Sacko. Before year's end, Sacko was faced with problems in the north, where Taureg tribesmen continued clashing with the military. Legislatives elections were held without incident in 1992, but the year's biggest event was the disclosure that 5.7 billion in local currency was missing from the treasury. Student rioting broke out in Bamako, the capital, on 5 April 1993, in which one student was killed, 45 injured and numerous public building destroyed. As a result, Younoussi Toure resigned as prime minister. The president then appointed Abdoulaye Sekou Sow as the new prime minister. Former president Moussa Traore and several of his aides were sentenced to death on 12 February on charges of complicity in the deaths of 106 civilians in the March 1991 antigovernment demonstrations. Taureg tribesmen had been merged into the Mali army in February in a move designed to end the fighting in the northern provinces. Bamako was again the site of massive student demonstrations on 2 February 1994. In this case, the ensuing rioting had been orchestrated by a secret rebel group determined to topple the government and destroy foreign support for its operations. Sow resigned the day of the riots, voicing differences with other high-level government officials for his decision. Although the integration of Taureg tribesmen and the repatriation of Taureg refugees who had fled north into Algeria and Mauritania was proceding well, there were still instances of fighting between Tauregs and government forces. By mid-July, at least 18 had died in these skirmishes. Full implementation of a June 1994 peace agreement with the Tauregs began to take hold in 1995, and fighting died down in the north. By July, more dissident Taureg groups had laid down their arms and gathered to discuss a lasting peace. *Reading:* Kim Naylor, *Mali* (1988); Philip Koslow, *Mali: Crossroads of Africa* (1995); Pascal James Imperato, *Mali: A Search for Direction* (1989).

Malik, Adam. (b. 22 July 1917, Pematangsiantar, North Sumatra—d. 5 September 1984, Bandung, Indonesia) Malik's education began at a Dutch-operated primary school and ended at a religious school. At 17 Malik was the chairman of the nationalist Partai Indonesia in his hometown. In 1937 he opened the Antara News Agency; he continued to work there during the Japanese occupation in World War II. At the same time, however, he was involved in the underground movement. After the war he served as the third deputy chairman of the first Indonesian Parliament and as a member of its Daily Executive Board. He then became ambassador to the Soviet Union and Poland in 1959. In 1962, he represented Indonesia at the negotiations that led to the Dutch transfer of West Irian (qv) to Indonesian control. He was appointed minister of commerce in 1963 and foreign minister in 1966. In this latter role he was the architect of Indonesia's nonalignment program and led his country back into the United Nations after former president Sukarno (qv) had severed relations with the world body. It was Malik who announced, on 28 April 1970, that, despite the objections of the USSR, Communist China and North Vietnam, an Asian conference on Cambodia would be held. On 21 September 1971, Malik was elected president of the United Nations General Assembly. He was a proponent of the two China's theory and advocated seating both Communist China and Nationalist China at the UN. He continued to serve as foreign minister until 1977 and then served as vice president of his country from 1978 until 1983. He died in 1984.

Malkya. *See* Israel.

Malloum, Felix. (b. 10 September 1932, Fort Archambault, Chad) Malloum's education came from the French military academies. He served in the French colonial forces in Indochina and in Algeria, rising quickly through the ranks to colonel in 1968. In that year Malloum became chief of the military cabinet in Chad and was appointed chief of the general staff in late 1971. In 1972, he was named chief of the armed forces of Chad. In 1973, however, he was arrested (July) following the government's denunciation of French interference in Chad's internal affairs. Malloum was still in prison when, on 13 April 1975, Brigadier

General Noel Odingar led a military coup against President Francois (N'Garta) Tombalbaye (qv), who was killed. Malloum was then released from prison. He set up a provisional government on 12 May, with Odingar as chief of staff, the post he had held since Malloum's arrest. Malloum was immediately faced with the rebel problem in the north, where the Chad National Liberation Front (Frolinat) was operating with relative impunity. In September 1975, Malloum ordered all French troops out of the country after it was disclosed the French were getting ready to trade arms to the Frolinat in return for French hostages they were holding. Malloum remained in office as president in 1978. On 29 August 1978, Hissen Habré (qv) was appointed prime minister. Malloum was forced to seek refuge in the French compound where the French garrison had reinforced after the deaths of four French civilians (12 February). On 23 March 1979, as a means of ending the constant fighting that beset the country, Malloum and Habré resigned their offices in favor of Frolinat leader Goukouni Oueddei (qv).

Malta. A 124 square mile group of five islands lying about 60 miles south of Sicily, Malta was first settled by Phoencians about 900 B.C. Rome took control of Malta in 218 B.C. In 870 A.D, the Arabs conquered the island, which remained a feudal state into the early sixteenth century. Napoleon captured Malta in 1798 and held it until the British took it in 1800. It became a British colony in 1814. Malta remained under British control through World War II, when it withstood tremendous pounding from the Axis powers. Malta achieved independence within the British Commonwealth on 21 September 1964. The British were authorized to maintain its military bases on the island. On 13 August 1971, however, the Maltese government asked for the removal of the NATO headquarters located on the island. In September, Great Britain announced it had reached an agreement in principle with Malta to retain its bases there. On 29 December, however, Prime Minister Dominic Mintoff issued an ultimatum to the British demanding they leave the island in 72 hours, if an additional $11 million was not paid. The British ordered an immediate withdrawal (8 January 1972). Again, on 15 January, Mintoff ordered the withdrawal of British forces, but he later withdrew the order. By December, the Maltese prime minister had again demanded a 10 percent increase in rent on British installations or all British troops would have to leave by 31 March 1973. A new agreement was reached, but the British announced (6 January 1976) their withdrawal when the current treaty expired in 1979. In August, Malta announced it would become neutral after the British withdrawal. Malta had become a republic in 1974. In January 1977, Malta, along with Ireland, refused to sign the European Convention on Terrorism. On 4 August 1978, Libyan military personnel flew into an abandoned British airbase at Hal Far and began converting it into a helicopter base. NATO and British links with Malta ended on 31 March–1 April 1979. On 13 January 1984, the Craxi (qv) government in Italy reaffirmed its commitment to protect Malta, and, on 29 November, Malta reported it had signed five-year treaty of military cooperation and security with Libya. On 4 December a report issued in the capital city of Valletta stated Libyan troops would begin training the Maltese armed forces. Mintoff left office in December 1984 and was replaced by Carmelo Mifsud Bonnici. Among his first actions were the repair of Malta's relations with Europe and the lifting of trade and travel restrictions with Italy. When a hijacked EgyptAir airliner landed in Malta, Bonnici authorized an Egyptian commando attempt to free the hostages. The inept operation cost the lives of 57 passengers and crew, plus all but one of the terrorists. Two hostages had been killed by the terrorists before the Egyptian rescue mission began. In June, the International Court of Justice ruled in the dispute between Libya and Malta over the sea boundary between the two countries. Political unrest hit Malta in 1986, as the opposition maneuvered for its advantage in the planned 1987 elections. The opposition Nationalist Party won those elections, replacing Bonnici with Eddie Fenech Adami on 12 May. Adami moved to strengthen the economy and get Malta accepted into the European Community (EC) in 1990. However, when the British carrier *HMS Ark Royal* visited Malta in 1988, major disturbances occurred over the presence of nuclear weapons in Maltese waters. Malta maintained its drive toward joining the European Community in 1990, making its application for membership in July. Political criticism from the Labor Party was heaped on the government because of its participation in the war against Iraq in 1991. When two ships loaded with Albanian refugees attempted to land in Malta in August, they were turned back without bloodshed. Adami was returned to office in February 1992 and continued his program of liberalization of all facets of Maltese life and its foreign affairs. When the EC responded to the Maltese application for membership, they did so by proposing discussions to clear a few minor obstacles to approval. When Malta released the one terrorist who survived the EgyptAir hijacking incident in 1985, the United States strongly objected. Malta, however, stated he had been jailed and had served his sentence under their law. On 4 April 1994, Ugo Mifsud Bonnici (not the former prime minister) was sworn in as president. Malta (along with Cyprus) was also informed it would be accepted into the EC in the next expansion. Based on the contiuation of the EC-induction process, Malta moved to open relations with NATO in April 1995. *Reading:* John Richard Thackrah, *Malta* (World Bibliographica Series, Vol. 64) (1986).

Malvinas. *See* Falkland Islands.

Mamelodi Township. *See* South Africa.

Managua. *See* Nicaragua.

Manara (Menara). *See* Israel.

Mancham, James R. President of the Seychelles since their independence in 1975, Mancham was ousted from office by a Soviet supported coup on 5 June 1977. He was in London at the time.

Mancheno, Carlos. On 23 August 1947, the Ibarra (qv) government of Ecuador was overthrown in a military revolt led by Colonel Carlos Mancheno. Eleven days later (3 September) Mancheno was ousted by Carlos Arosemena (qv).

Manchuria. *See* China. *Reading:* Bernard Vincent Olivier, *The Implementation of China's Nationality Policy in the Northeastern Provinces* (1993).

Mandai, Tripura State. *See* India.

Mandalay. *See* Burma.

Mandela, Nelson Rolihlahla. (b. 1918, Transkei) Born into the ruling family of the Tembu tribe, Mandela attended the University College at Fort Hare. While there he became involved in political action and was expelled for starting a student riot. He left Tramskei to avoid a family-arranged marriage and worked for a time as a police officer at the Transvaal mines. He took courses by correspondence, completed his baccalaureate and then studied law at Witwatersrand University. Following graduation he set up a law practice in Tambo. In 1952, he was arrested and sentenced to nine months imprisonment for political activities. He was again arrested in 1956, for high treason, but he was acquitted. In 1962 Mandela was again arrested and held two years before he and seven others were sentenced to life on charges of conspiring to overthrow the government and for organizing the military wing (*Umkonto we Sizwe*) of the African National Congress (ANC) (qv). He was finally freed in 1990 at age 71. He thereafter worked with the white South African government to bring about social and political reform in the country. In 1994 he was elected his country's first black president. Addressing Parliament in February 1995, Mandela stated that South Africa's citizens had to rid themselves of the "culture of entitlement," a comment aimed more directly at the black population than at the white, and that reconciliation of the two races was the primary goal of his administration. *Reading:* Nelson Mandela, *Long Walk to Freedom: The Autobiography of Nelson Mandela* (1994); Rebecca Stefoff & Steven Otfinoski, *Nelson Mandela: A Hero for Democracy* (1994); Steven Otfinoski, *Nelson Mandela: The Fight against Apartheid* (1992).

Mangaldi. *See* India.

Manica Sofala. *See* Mozambique.

Manila. *See* Philippines.

Maniu, Julius (Iuliu). (b. 8 January 1873, Simleu Silvaniei, Transylvania—d. 1953, Sighet Prison, Romania) Born into a peasant family of the Uniat church, Maniu eventually received a degree in law. He became active in the Transylvanian freedom movement (Transylvania was then a part of the Austro-Hungarian Empire) and was elected to the Hungarian parliament in 1906. He served in the Austro-Hungarian army in World War I, fighting on both the Russian and the Italian fronts. In May 1918, he organized a mutiny among the Romanian troops. After the war he went to the Romanian parliament as the leader of the National Party of Transylvania and, in 1926, became the head of the National Peasant Party. In November 1928 he formed a new government and served as prime minister following the first free elections in December of that year. When King Carol II returned to Romania in June 1930, Maniu remained as prime minister until October, when he resigned, claiming Carol had not lived up to his promises. Maniu served again as prime minister from October 1932 until January 1933. In 1937 he aligned himself with the Iron Guard, a fascist movement, but failed to stop the establishment of a dictatorship under its banner. Maniu sided with the Allies during World War II, but he did not directly oppose the Romanian army's role in fighting along side the Germans until they crossed into the Soviet Union. At that point he became a leader of the resistance and actively participated in clandestine meetings with Allied agents in Romania. Maniu also was an active participant in the 23 August 1944 coup d'etat that overthrew the Antonescu government. With the Soviet Union then in control of Romania, Maniu was not bothered until the peace treaty was signed. Then, on 14–15 July 1947, he was arrested along with many of his followers and charged with treason. He was subsequently sentenced to life in solitary confinement. He died in prison in 1953.

Mannar. *See* Sri Lanka.

Mansour, Hassan Ali. On 26 January 1965 Hassan Ali Mansour, the premier of Iran, died of wounds inflicted by an assassin five days earlier.

Manuel Rodriguez Patriotic Front (FPMR). A leftist terrorist organization formed in 1983, the FPMR was estimated to have a membership between 500 and 1,000. The group's headquarters was in Santiago, Chile, and its range of operations was limited to that country. The FPMR was associated with the Chilean Communist Party and was suspected of receiving aid from Cuba and other communist countries. The group took its name from a nineteenth century Chilean executed by the Spaniards. Little was known of its structure or leadership. From March 1984 the group carried out a series of damaging terrorist attacks against urban targets in Chile. A high point in its campaign was the attempted assassination of Chilean president Pinochet (qv) in September 1987. Twelve FPMR terrorists were killed by security agents on 16 June 1987. This led to a new series of attacks in which several policemen were killed and an army officer kidnapped (September 1987) and not released until December.

Manzoor, Mohammed Abdul. On 30 May 1981, President Ziaur Rahman (qv) was assassinated in his sleep during a military uprising in the port city of Chittagong, Bangladesh. Many others were also murdered in the ensuing coup attempt staged by Major General Manzur Ahmed. On 1 June, the government announced the implication of Major General Mohammed Abdul Manzoor and a number of other senior officers in the coup attempt. Manzoor was killed in a gun battle at the time of his arrest. Twelve others were subsequently tried and executed.

Maoist Popular Liberation Army. On 23 August 1984, the Maoist Popular Liberation Army, a leftist terrorist organization in Colombia, signed a truce with the government as a part of a general truce signed with a number of terrorist organizations. The Maoist group was one of the smallest to sign.

Maoist Red Guards. *See* Red Guard.

Mao Tse-Tung (Mao Zedong). (b. 26 December 1893, Shaoshan, Hunan Province, China—d. 9 September 1976, Beijing) Born the son of a peasant and grain merchant, Mao fought in the Chinese Revolution (1911–1912) and later graduated from the First Provincial Normal School in Changsha in 1918. He subsequently became a revolutionary while attending Peking University and joined the communist May 4th Movement. In 1921 he was one of the founders of the Chinese Communist Party. In 1923, after the alliance between the communists and the Kuomintang (KMT)(qv) was formed, Mao became a full-time party revolutionary, stressing the importance of the peasantry in any future revolution. Differences in ideology and as to the question of who was to rule China led to Chiang Kai-shek's (qv) distrust of the communists and he often used the KMT apparatus to victimize them. Mao's first wife was executed by the Nationalists in 1930. In November 1931 the communists organized the Chinese Soviet Republic in Shansi (Jiangxi) province, but the Nationalist army drove them out in 1934. The communists moved northward in what has been described as one of the most arduous and heroic immigrations in history, "The Long March." In 1935 the communists and Nationalists reforged their alliance, this time to fight the Japanese. This alliance remained until 1945. At that point, Mao's communist forces turned on the Nationalists and, by 1949 (*see* China), had driven them out of China. Mao then had to face Josef Stalin (qv), who distrusted everyone, especially a powerful communist leader on his border. Relations between the USSR and Communist China were uneasy from the start. Mao eventually came to see the Soviets as enemies who had betrayed the Marxist-Leninist credo. As leader of China, Mao was hardly seen, except on ceremonial occasions, during the first five years of his rule. This led many to believe that his control was not absolute and that others were able to make decisions not favored by the chairman of the People's Republic of China. Not until 1955 did Mao emerge from his isolation to determine the course of China's future. When his economic and political programs were challenged by the intellectual class, Mao instituted the Great Leap Forward program, which unleased a bloodbath across the country in which the peasantry slaughtered thousands of China's more educated and skillful citizens. This led to an economic disaster that forced Mao to retreat from the Great Leap Forward program and, on the advice of his wife, Jiang Qing (qv), institute in its place the Great Proletarian Cultural Revolution, which led to more mass killings that not only further wrecked the economy but also tore the very fabric of the Chinese Communist party itself. These obvious blunders aside, Mao emerged as a cult figure whose pronouncements of ideology became the standard reading of communist revolutionaries around the world. Upon his death in 1976, a power struggle erupted in China in which many whom Mao had purged arose as the country's new leaders. Even so, the cult of Mao continues to exist. *Reading:* A. Doak Barnett, *China after Mao, with Selected Documents* (1967); Shu Guang Zhang, *Mao's Military Romanticism: China and the Korean War, 1950-1953* (1995); Edgar Snow, *Red Star over China* (1968).

Mapai. *See* Mozambique.

Maputo (Lourenco Marques). *See* Rhodesia.

Marathi Nationalist (*Shiv Sena*) Group. The Marathi are a Hindu group in the state of Maharashtra in India; its ancestry may be traced to 1673 with the founding of the Rajyabhisekasaka era. As with many Hindu groups, the paramilitary *Shiv Sena* took up the fight for independence shortly after India achieved independence. During a period of rioting in 1969, the group was involved in rioting in Bombay in which 50 people were killed.

Marcos, Ferdinand (Ferdnand) Edralin. (b. 11 September 1917, Sarrat, Philippines—d. 28 September 1989, Honolulu) Born the son of a well-to-do politician and landowner, Marcos received a law degree at the University of the Philippines. In 1939 he was tried and convicted of the 1933 murder of one of his father's political opponents. He argued his own appeal before the Philippine Supreme Court and was acquitted (1940). After the outbreak of war Marcos served as an officer in the Philippine army; but he later made exaggerated claims about his role in the Filipino resistance, in which he played little or no part. After the war he became an adviser to President Manuel Roxas (qv) (1946–1947). In 1954, he married Imelda Romanuldez. He was a member of the Philippine House of Representatives from 1949 until 1959 and a senator from 1959 until 1965. He won the presidency in 1965 as the Nationalist Party candidate and was reelected in 1969. His presidency during this period was marked with some economic gain, but major student rioting, such as that which followed the tainted 1969 elections, and urban guerrilla activity punctuated the period. In March 1971, for instance, Muslim insurgency required the employment of government troops to help stabilize the situation. On 21 September 1971 Marcos declared martial law and began jailing opposition leaders, including Benigno Aquino (qv), who spent eight years in jail. Marcos also suspended the writ of habeas corpus and issued a new constitution that increased his personal power to a dictatorship. He also became his own prime minister. In 1983, Marcos was implicated in the assassination of Aquino and was suffering from failing health. In 1986, however, he called for new elections and was surprised when Corazon Aquino, Benigno's widow, stood as the opposition party candidate. After an elections awash with fraud, Marcos was pronounced the winner. A near-rebellion began among the middle class and much of the armed forces. At a point just before a major clash evolved, the U.S. offered Marcos a sanctuary in Hawaii. His arrival in the U.S. was marked with both a further decline in his health and a U.S. indictment on charges of stealing $103 million from the Philippines. An estimate made at that time said he probably had accumulated more than one billion dollars. He was declared too sick to stand trial, however, and died in Honolulu on 28 September 1989. His body was returned to the Philippines for burial in September at Batak in northern Luzon. *Reading:* Gordy Slack, *Ferdinand Marcos* (1988).

Marcos, Imelda (nee Romanuldez). (b. 2 July 1929, Tolosa, Leyte) A former beauty queen who married Ferdinand E. Marcos (qv) in 1954, Imelda Marcos helped her husband win first a seat in the Philippine Senate and then, in 1965, the presidency. She also served as the Philippine's official emissary to China, the Soviet Union and Libya. In 1975, she was appointed the first governor of Metropolitan Manila. She also became the minister of human settlements in 1978. Her goal in the latter office was to stop the threat of "urban revolt." To accomplish this she ordered the relocation of many people and industries. She also sponsored the establishment of the Heart Center for Asia and the National Nutrition Center in Manila. Although she gained a reputation as a patroness of the poor, her own lifestyle excesses became common knowledge. She developed many elitest projects such as the Cultural Center in Manila (1969) and the adjacent Plaza Hotel and other facilities catering to the rich and famous. Between 1981 and1983, she held film extravaganzas in the National Arts Center on the slopes of Mount Makiling. By 1983, these affairs had become so scandalous that she was forced to abandon them. Her lifestyle brought much notoriety. She collected extremely expensive clothes, jewelry, and innumerable pairs of shoes, all at the expense of the people. She was determined to establish a regal line of succession for her three children, but her plans were thwarted when she and her husband were forced into exile in 1986. They were granted asylum in Hawaii, where Ferdinand died of cancer in 1989. Imelda then began working on gaining her return to the Philippines and placing Ferdinand's body "to rest" on Philippine soil. In 1991, she was allowed to return, and on 7 January 1992 she entered the race for the presidency. On 15 May, however, she was forced to concede the election. On 7 September 1993, she was successful in bringing her husband's body, which had been kept in refrigeration in Hawaii, back to the islands. She orchestrated a stopover in Guam on the way back and a major welcoming ceremony in Manila. The government did not try to stop her, as Marcos still had thousands of supporters although he had stolen hundreds of millions from them. On 24 September 1993, Imelda was convicted of defrauding the Philippines of $356 million (along with Ferdinand). She was sentenced to 18–24 years imprisonment but was set free on bail during an appeal. The appeal was successful, and she was exonerated on 23 December 1993. In early 1995, Imelda announced that she and her son, Ferdinand Junior, would run for public office.

Mardoquero Cruz Urban Commandos. The Mardoquero Cruz Urban Commandos were a terrorist group of the Central American Revolutionary Worker's Party (PRTC), a Marxist-Leninist organization formed in 1976 with a membership of several hundred. In 1980, the PRTC joined the *Frente Farabundo Marti de Liberacion National* (FMLN) in the struggle against the El Salvador government and its U.S. advisers. On 19 June 1985, for instance, an attack was carried out on a cafe in the Zona Rosa district in San Salvador by six to ten men. Thirteen were killed, including six Americans (four U.S. Marines and two businessmen). The Mardoquero Cruz Urban Commandos took credit for the attack.

Margaritis, Constantine. On 21 May 1973, a coup attempt led by naval officers, including Vice Admiral Constantine Margaritis, failed. Margaritis, the Greek chief of naval operations, was dismissed. The coup attempted to restore full constitutional rule by seizing ships and occupying an Aegean island. The Papadopoulos (qv) dictator government remained in power.

Mariam, Mengistu Haile, (b. 1938, Ethiopia) Born into the Christian Galla (Oromo) tribe, Mariam was raised in poverty; but for the help of his mother's employer, he would never have been heard from. Mariam grew up with a hatred of the Amhara domination of his country and of the Ethiopian royalty who took no notice of the plight of the people. Because of his lowly status and lack of education he was prevented from realizing his dream of attending the Harar

Military Academy. He did, however, attend the college at Guennete and was commissioned as an ordnance officer. He spent two short training tours in the United States before he joined the so-called soldier's rebellion that overthrew Emperor Haile Selassie (qv) in 1974. Mariam personally led the group that dethroned and humiliated Selassie. On 23 November 1974, Mariam led the force that attempted the arrest of General Aman Andom (qv), who was shot and killed at that time. On 11 February 1977, upon the death of Brigadier General Teferi Benti (qv) (3 February), Mariam emerged as the new chairman of the Provisional Military Administrative Council (*Dirgue*), the ruling junta in Ethiopia. Mariam's orientation was Marxist, and he began to steer the nation in that direction. He broke relations with the US in April 1977 and began receiving Soviet assistance after a visit in May to Moscow, where a number of cooperative treaties were signed. In February 1978, Marian received U.S. assurances that it would not supply weapons to Somalia. In return, Mariam promised not to invade that country. However, in March, Soviet-supplied Ethiopian and Cuban forces clearly defeated the Somalis in fighting in Ogaden province. For most of the 1980s, Mariam had to contend with the uprising in Eritrea. But he was returned to office in a one-party election in 1985. By 1990, however, the rebels had strengthened, and Mariam's position became somewhat more tenuous. On 21 May 1991, Mariam fled the country to Zimbabwe. Addis Ababa was captured, and a new government was imposed on Ethiopia.

Marighela, Carlos. (b. 1908—d. 4 November 1969, Sao Paulo, Brazil) Born the son of an Italian immigrant and a black Brazilian woman, Marighela joined the Brazilian Communist Party in 1928 at the age of 16. In 1967, he broke with the Communist Party and organized an urban terrorist group known as the Action for National Liberation (ALN). For the next two years, Marighela headed this group and used his experiences to write a book called *For the Liberation of Brazil*. He was killed in a right-wing police death squad ambush in Sao Paulo on 4 November 1969.

Markos, (General). *See* Vafiades, Markos.

Marrakech. *See* Morocco.

Marshall, George Catlett. (b. 31 December 1880, Uniontown, Pennsylvania—d. 16 October 1959, Washington, DC) Marshall graduated from Virginia Military Institute in 1901 and entered the Army. His first assignment was in the Philippines, where he served from 1902–1903. He served in France in World War I as a staff officer. After the end of the war, he became the aide to General John J. Pershing (1919–1924) and served with the 15th Infantry in Tientsin, China, from 1924 to 1927. After serving an important tour at the Infantry School at Fort Benning, Georgia, and other stateside assignments, he became chief of staff of the army on 1 September 1939 and remained in that position throughout World War II, giving his wisdom to the president and the war effort. He resigned as chief of staff on 21 November 1945. He was then appointed the special representative of President Harry Truman (qv) to China and given the rank of ambassador. His mission to China failed. He was appointed secretary of state on 21 January 1947. On 5 June 1947, he enunciated the European Recovery

Program (Marshall Plan) (qv), which was enacted into law in April 1948. He resigned on 21 January 1949 and later became the chairman of the American Battle Monuments Commission and president of the American Red Cross. He served as secretary of defense from 21 September 1950 until 12 September 1951. In 1953, he represented the United States at the coronation of Queen Elizabeth II in England. Also in 1953, he was awarded the Nobel peace prize for his work in rehabilitating Europe. He died in Washington on 16 October 1959. *Reading:* Ed Cray, *General of the Army: George C. Marshall, Soldier and Statesman* (1990); Mark Stoler & John Milton Cooper, eds., *George C. Marshall: Soldier-Statesman of the American Century* (1989).

Marshall Islands. The Marshalls are a part of the general series of islands known as Micronesia and are on the eastern rim of that concentration. The Marshalls comprise two chains of atolls known as the Ratak (Sunrise) and Ralik (Sunset) groups. The capital of the present day Republic of the Marshall Islands is Majuro. The Marshalls were first visited in sixteenth century by the Spaniards. The islands were not completely mapped until 1823, however. Spain claimed the islands in 1886, but sold them to the Germans after the Spanish-American War. Japan seized the islands in 1914 and was later given the League of Nations mandate to administer them. The U.S. captured the islands during World War II with particularly heavy fighting on Kwajalein and Eniwetok atolls. The U.S. administered the islands under the UN Trusteeship for the Pacific from 1947. A U.S. nuclear test area was established in the Marshalls (on Bikini and Eniwetok) in 1946, and a number of nuclear tests were conducted there before the sites were closed in 1958. These tests required the displacement of a number of the native population and created major hardships among the islanders. Medical funding and money to clean up Bikini were appropriated by the U.S. Congress only in 1985. On 21 October 1986, the U.S. entered into a free-association compact (until 2001) with the newly recognized Republic of the Marshall Islands, thus ending the U.S. trusteeship. The U.S. was particularly responsible for the defense of the islands, which were otherwise sovereign. Having attended earlier meetings as an observer, the Republic of the Marshall Islands formally joined the South Pacific Forum in 1987. The U.S. also moved, under a $100 million subsidiary agreement, to settle claims arising from the nuclear weapons tests and to make the test sites completely habitable. The republic gained its status as an independent nation on 17 September 1991 by being seated in the United Nations, but was still almost entirely dependent on the United States. The U.S. had a 30-year lease on a missile range on Kwajalein, especially for testing Star Wars projects. By 1992, the new government was making progress in establishing itself, but the source of most of its revenue was still the United States. The Marshall Islands government created a major regional furor in 1994, when it announced the study of a plan (obviously U.S.-suggested) to use Bikini and Eniwetok (which were then thought to be uninhabitable for 10,000 years) as nuclear waste storage sites. These proposals were rejected by the local council for Bikini in 1995. As another money-making scheme, the government moved to establish a passport office in Hong Kong that would sell up to 3,000 passports at more than $30,000 each to Asians wishing to escape the impending Communist Chinese takeover. *Reading:* Jane Dibblin, *Day of Two Suns: US Nuclear Testing and the Pacific Islanders* (1989); Steven Smith, *The Republic of the Marshall Islands: An Emerging Nation* (1986).

Marshall Plan. *See* European Recovery Plan (Program).

Martinique. *See* France.

Marxist-Leninist Armed Propaganda Unit (MLAPU). On 11 May 1979, a group of U.S. servicemen was fired on by gunmen as they waited for a bus in Istanbul, Turkey. One serviceman, a U.S. Navy chief petty officer, was killed, and another man was wounded. The Marxist-Leninist Armed Propaganda Unit (MLAPU) took credit for the attack. This terrorist group also murdered the El Al (Israeli) airport manager and carried out numerous attacks against U.S. and Turkish facilities in that country (1979). In February 1980, Turkish authorities arrested a number of terrorists believed responsible for these attacks.

Masaka. *See* Uganda.

Masan. *See* Korea.

Masaryk, Jan (Garrigue). (b. 14 September 1886, Prague—d. 10 March 1948, Prague) Born the son of Tomas G. Masaryk, young Masaryk travelled to the United States in 1907 but returned to Prague before the outbreak of World War I. He served in the Hungarian army, in which he saw service in Poland. Upon Czechoslovakia's independence he joined the foreign service and, in 1919, was assigned as the charge d'affaires at the embassy in Washington. In 1921, he returned to Prague and became the secretary of then foreign minister Edward Benes (qv). In 1925 he became the Czech minister to London, but resigned following the the September 1938 Munich Agreement. When World War II began, and after the fall of France, Masaryk became the foreign minister of the Czech government-in-exile in London (July 1940). During this time he made repeated broadcasts to the Czech people. making himself a well-known and popular figure in his country. In early 1945, Masaryk accompanied President Benes to Moscow and was later present at the opening ceremonies of the United Nations in San Francisco. He returned to Prague in July 1945 as foreign minister. One of his principal problems was the steadily deteriorating relationship with Moscow. An attempt was made on his life in September 1947. When the Soviets seized the Czech government by coup d'etat on 25 February 1948, Masaryk remained at his post at Benes's request. On 10 March 1948, Masaryk was assassinated by Soviet agents, who threw him from a window of the foreign office. His death was officially reported as a suicide.

Maseru. *See* Lesotho.

Masire, Quett Ketumile Jonny. (b. 23 July 1925, Kenya) Born into the Bangwaketse tribe, Masire was educated as a teacher and later went into journalism. He became politically active, serving on his tribal council and in the executive and legislative branches under the British administration. In 1962, he and Seretse Khama (qv) formed the Botswana Democratic Party and stayed with the party through the period of gaining independence for Botswana in 1966. However, before that time, Masire became deputy prime minister of the British protectorate of Bechuanaland in 1965, when Seretse was appointed prime minister. With independence, he became Seretse's vice president and finance minister. In 1969, Masire's career took a downturn when he was defeated in his home area, and he spent some years rebuilding his political stature. He regained his seat in Parliament in 1974. Upon the death of President Sir Seretse Khama of cancer on 13 July 1980, Masire became president of Botswana. He was knighted by Great Britain in the early 1990s and remained in office in his relatively stable Botswana in 1995. However, in February 1995, Masire faced the most serious challenge in many years when tribal/religious rioting broke out following the ritual murder of a young girl in January. Three men were accused but were set free; the rioting that followed included attacks on government buildings. Opposition party members blamed the administration for the conditions that allowed the affair.

Massamba (Messema)-Debat, Alphonse. On 15 August 1963, following labor riots in Brazzaville, Congo, the government of Youlou Fubert (qv) was overthrown. Alphonse Massamba-Debat, an adherent of Chinese communism, was made president. On 4 September 1968, Massamba-Debat resigned, after a bloody military coup in which Congolese army troops in Brazzaville battled Cuban-trained rebel forces. Upon Massamba-Delat's resignation, another pro-Chinese, officer, Major Marien Ngouabi (qv), became president.

Massu, Jacques. In May 1958 suspicions arose among the French settlers in Algeria that the French government was about to negotiate with the Algerian nationalist rebels. A nationalist uprising had erupted in November 1954. Rioting broke out in Algiers on 13 May 1958. On 15 May, Brigadier General Jacques Massu assumed leadership of the Committee of Public Safety and used the position to seize power in Algeria in what has been called the French Officer Uprising. The chain of events began by this action led directly to Charles de Gaulle's assumption of power in France.

Matabeleland. *See* Zimbabwe.

Matanzas. *See* Cuba.

Matka. *See* Israel.

Matsu Island. A island located northwest of Taiwan close to mainland China. The Nationalist government on Taiwan held the island, and the government of Communist China claimed it, along with Quemoy. The communists shelled the island in the early 1950s in the continuing struggle between the Nationalist and communist governments. In February 1955, communist premier Chou En-lai rejected a UN offer for a cease-fire, but an uneasy truce began on 7 June. On 23 August 1955 the communists began heavy shelling of the Nationalist positions on Matsu. This action was determined to be an attempt to stop the delivery of supplies to the island. On 11 September, U.S. president Eisenhower (qv) declared the U.S. would fight to preserve the status of the island (and Quemoy), but went on to state that negotiation was a better course to follow. That same day, Great Britain announced it would not be bound by the US decision to fight, if necessary, to save the islands from falling into communist hands. On 17 October, Nationalist leader Chiang Kai-shek (qv) announced his determination to maintain control of the islands. On 20 October, the communists resumed heavy shelling. On 23 October, Chiang Kai-shek issued a communique in which he announced that his forces would not attempt to return to the mainland and that his control of the islands might be relaxed to reduce tensions. The situation remained unsettled until 22 January 1962, when the U.S. government again warned Communist China to stay away from the islands. On 24 March, Nationalist gunners shot down a number of communist aircraft over Matsu, which were considered the first step in an invasion. The changing situation saw the U.S. withdraw its advisers on Matsu and Quemoy on 23 June 1976. The islands remained in Nationalist hands in the 1990s, although mainland China still claimed them. *See* Quemoy.

Mau Mau. Literally, the "Hidden Ones," the Mau Mau was primarily a political movement among the Kikuyu tribesmen of Kenya (qv) that based much of its ritual on prophesy and oaths. The Mau Mau practiced a form of terrorism among the population by threats and intimidation that aimed at separating individuals from the populace and bringing them into conformity with Mau Mau customs. The Kikuyu tribe was the largest tribe in Kenya. In 1952, four years of Mau Mau terrorism began, which necessitated the declaration of a state of emergency by the British on 20 October 1952. Additional British troops were immediately ordered into Kenya. The Mau Mau uprising was almost completely a Kikuyu manifestation and was directed primarily against Europeans living in Kenya and their ownership of land. Even so, it was the Kikuyu who refused to support the Mau Mau who suffered the most during the uprising. In April 1953, Jomo Kenyatta (qv) was accused of being the Mau Mau leader and, along with some confederates, was sentenced to seven years' imprisonment. The British conducted a major military campaign to subdue the Mau Mau. The state of emergency did not end until 1960, although the major Mau Mau infrastructure had been destroyed after the battle at Mount Kenya–Aberdare in February 1955. The intervening five years were required to restore order and rehabilitate the land. *Reading:* Wunyabari O. Maloba, *Mau Mau and Kenya: An Analysis of a Peasant Revolt* (1993); Anthony Clayton, *Counter-Insurgency in Kenya: A Study of Military Operations against the Mau Mau, 1952-1960 (1984);* Robert B. Edgerton, Mau: An African Crucible (1989).

Mauritania. A country located on the West Coast of Africa, Mauritania has less name recognition than any other African nation. It is bordered on the northwest and north by the region of Western (Spanish) Sahara (occupied by Morocco), on the northeast by Algeria, on the east and south by Mali, on the southwest by Senegal and on the west by the Atlantic Ocean. The capital is Nouakchott, on the coast. The region was settled by Negroes and Berbers before the eleventh century and was the base from which the Almoravid Berbers captured vast holdings in northwest Africa. In the fifteenth century Arabs conquered the region. In 1442, Portuguese explorers sighted Cape Blanc and six years later founded a fortified settlement at Arquin. Both French and British expeditions explored the coastal areas and up the Senegal River. By the end of the nineteenth century, the French had ended Moorish (Arab) domination; they established Mauritania as a territory of French West Africa in 1920. In 1946, Mauritania became an overseas territory, and in 1957 it fought a successful war against Morocco. On 28 November 1958, Mauritania became independent and voted to become a member of the French Community; it received its full independence on 28 November 1960 as the Islamic Republic of Mauritania. On 1 April 1962 a rebel army, seeking union with Morocco and based in that country, invaded Mauritania but was driven out. Spanish Sahara, a Portuguese possession, was handed over to Morocco and Mauritania for administration on 14 November 1975 and was formally turned over to the two countries in February 1976. On 8 June 1976, Polisario (qv) guerrillas attacked the Mauritanian capital city of Nouakchott. Morocco immediately pledged its support to Mauritania. On 19 December 1977, Polisario attacked a Mauritanian troop position, killing 30 but losing 82 of its own men. The government of Moktar Ould Daddah (qv) was overthrown on 10 July 1978. Lieutenant Colonel Mustafa Ould Salek (qv) took power. At the same time, Polisario called a unilateral cease-fire in its ongoing war against Mauritania. Subsequent peace talks were broken off by the government on 5 December. After resumption of the talks, a peace treaty was signed on 6 August 1979, in which Mauritania renounced all claims on Spanish Sahara. At the same time, Morocco announced it was withdrawing its troops from Mauritania. On 24 October 1979, a token force of 150 French troops landed in Mauritania as a warning to Morocco and the Polisario. The government was again ousted on 4 January 1980, when Lieutenant Colonel Mohamed Mahmoud Ould Louly (qv) left office and was replaced by Lieutenant Colonel Mohammed Khouna Ould Haidallah (qv). Another coup attempt led by two army officer deserters failed to overthrow the government on 16–17 March 1981. The government accused Morocco of complicity in that attempt and severed diplomatic relations. In a turnabout in October 1981, Morocco accused Mauritania of harboring Polisario guerrillas that attacked the Moroccan army garrison at Guelta Zemmour, 25 miles from the common border. President Haidallah, who took power in a coup, lost it the same way in a bloodless takeover on 12 December 1984, while he was at a conference in Burundi. Another lieutenant colonel, Maaouya Ould Sidi Ahmed Taya, proclaimed himself the new leader. There was a failed attempt against his rule in October 1987. Three black officers were executed as a result of the ethnic motivation of the coup attempt. Rioting followed the executions. A school strike followed in April 1988, and charges of government brutality against black prisoners taken after the coup attempt surfaced. In 1991, Taya acted to end 13 years of military rule in Mauritania, most likely brought about by a failing economy due to the isolation of Mauritania after its support of Iraq during the Gulf War. All military and security personnel who were charged with brutality and murder of black prisoners were given amnesty on 29 May 1993, further increasing the tension between the white Moor and black populations. In January 1994, the army arrested several dozen people in connection with a scheme to pass out counterfeit voter registration cards just one week before the elections. Those arrested included members of most of the major political parties in the country.

Voter fraud was immediately charged by the major opposition party when the ruling Democratic and Social Republican Party won a landslide victory. The election stood. In May, a local newspaper was shut down for reasons of "state security." At the same time, plans went ahead to relocate approximately 20,000 Taureg refugees back to Mali (*see* Mali). Sixty Muslim leaders were arrested in October 1994, on charges associated with creating a situation dominated by fear. The government also suspended a number of Islamic organizations' rights to operate. On 21 January 1995, increases in the cost of basic goods brought massive and violent demonstrations that lasted three days. A number of opposition leaders were arrested and charged with inciting the riots. All were subsequently released, but they charged the government with mistreating them while they were incarcerated. *Reading:* Simonetta Calderini et al, *Mauritania* (World Bibliographical Series, Vol. 141) (1992); Virginia McLean Thompson, *The Western Saharans: The Background to Conflict* (1980).

Maximiliano Hernandez Group. A right-wing terrorist organization, the Maximiliano Hernandez Group operated in El Salvador. On 28 November 1980, at least 200 persons in army and police uniforms stormed the Jesuit-run San Jose High School in San Salvador. They dragged away eight leaders of a leftist coalition (and at least 20 other persons) meeting there and murdered at least four of them. The ruling junta denied any part in the affair. *See* El Salvador.

Mayaguez Incident. On 12 May 1975, a Cambodian naval vessel operating in international waters seized the 10,000-ton American freighter *SS Mayaguez* about 60 miles off the Cambodian coast in the Gulf of Siam (Thailand). The ship and its crew were taken to Koh Tang island 25 miles southeast of the Cambodian port city of Kompong Som (Sihanoukville). On 14 May 1975, a U.S. naval task force arrived in the vicinity of Koh Tang island. A U.S. Marine landing party of 250 men with 11 helicopters recaptured the *Mayaguez* after a major firefight with Cambodian troops. The crew was not found. Three Cambodian gunboats were also sunk during the raid. In the meantime, U.S. naval fighter-bombers attacked Cambodia's Ream airbase 200 miles from Koh Tang as a protective measure. Seventeen Cambodian aircraft were destroyed in the attack. The operation was poorly executed, as attested by the loss of 15 U.S. servicemen killed, 50 wounded, and three missing. Twenty-three other Americans were killed in an associated helicopter crash in Thailand. The operation was also a diplomatic failure, as the Cambodian government had already announced the release of the ship and its crew before the attack had begun. The use of bases in Thailand as staging areas for the raid without the permission of the Thai government also brought a diplomatic protest from Bangkok. *Reading:* John Guilmartin & John Keegan, *A Very Short War: The Mayaguez and the Battle of Koh Tang* (1995); Richard G. Head, et al, *Crisis Resolution: Presidential Decision Making in the Mayaguez and Korean Confrontations* (1982); Christopher Jon Lamb, *Belief Systems and Decision Making in the Mayaguez Crisis* (1989).

Mayotte Island. *See* Comoro Islands.

Mazatenanga. *See* Guatemala.

Maze. *See* Northern Ireland.

Mba, Leon. On 17–18 February 1964, the government of President Leon Mba of Gabon was overthrown during an uprising. He was restored to power the next day, however, by French troops flown into the democratic republic to put down the insurrection. *See* Gabon.

Mboya, Thomas "Tom" Joseph. (b. 15 August 1930, Kilima Mbago, Kenya—d. 5 July 1969, Nairobi) Mboya was born into the Luo tribe of Eastern Province and was widely accepted as the successor to Jomo Kenyatta (qv) as president. He joined the Legislative Council in 1957 and then served in the government after Kenya's independence in 1964. He was the secretary general of the Kenya African National Union (KANU) (qv). On 5 July 1969, Mboya, then serving as minister of economic affairs and development, was assassinated. A Luo tribal uprising began the next day following suspicions that the murder was the work of the Kikuyu. On 21 July, a Kikuyu, Nahashon Isaac Njenga Njoroge, was charged with the murder. He was found guilty and executed. The evidence presented at the trial failed to prove a political connection with any group or other individuals.

McDuffie-Tydings Act 1934. On 4 July 1946, the Philippines received their independence from the United States under the terms of the McDuffie-Tydings Act of 1934 (PL 127), which was passed by both houses and signed by the president on 24 March 1934. The bill was ratified by the Philippine legislature on 1 May. The law established a Philippine Commonwealth and provided for independence in 1946.

McGlinchey, Dominic "Mad Dog." On 17 March 1984, the chief of staff of the outlawed Irish National Liberation Army (INLA), Dominic "Mad Dog" McGlinchey, was captured after a 90-minute gun battle with police in County Clare in the Republic of Ireland. He was immediately extradited to Northern Ireland to stand trial on British charges of murder. The INLA was a Marxist splinter group that broke away from the Irish Republican Army (IRA) in 1975. The INLA was considered a group of "wild men" by other terrorist groups.

McGovern-Hatfield Bill. On 1 September 1970, the US Senate rejected the McGovern-Hatfield Bill (an amendment) that would have required the withdrawal of all US military forces from Southeast Asia by the end of 1971.

McMahon Line. *See* India and Tibet.

McNamara, Robert Strange. (b. 9 June 1916, San Francisco) McNamara graduated from Berkeley in 1937 and then attended Harvard, graduating in 1939. He then joined the Harvard faculty. During World War II, he was medically disqualified for service, but worked as a civilian logistician for the Army Air Force. After the war he went to work for the Ford Motor Company as a "whiz kid," a bright, innovative achiever. In 1960, he became the first non–family member to become the president of the Ford Motor Company. One month later, however, he joined the administration of John F. Kennedy (qv) as secretary of defense. There he inherited the enormous task of bringing the military bureaucracy to heel and modernizing the armed forces. He also was one of the innovators of converting the policy of massive retaliation to one of flexible response. In doing all of these things and in his support of U.S. involvement in Southeast Asia, he employed the principal that data that was not quantifiable was of no value. On Vietnam, he instigated a number of reporting systems that allowed for a conspicuous misuse of statistics and he refused to accept information that was not favorable to his defense policies. During the Johnson (qv) administration, McNamara served as its chief spokesman on war aims and worked as Johnson's chief adviser on the conduct of the war, a task for which his training, experience and lack of trust in his military officers left him bereft of competency. After 1966, McNamara began questioning the propriety and wisdom of U.S. involvement in Southeast Asia, perhaps, in part, as he saw reliance on what he considered as sound business practices failing in the arena of military confrontation. Through this, he initiated the preparation of the report that became known as the *Pentagon Papers,* written by a group of his own "whiz kids," who were equally as ignorant of military tactics and strategy as their mentor had been. After 1967, McNamara openly opposed the war, especially the bombing of the North. Discredited, he left the Pentagon in February 1968. His revelation in his book, *In Retrospect: The Tragedy and Lessons of Vietnam (1995)* of the errors he committed in the prosecution of the war reopened the whole issue of U.S. involvement, angered many Americans and, if anything, further discredited McNamara. *Reading:* Paul Hendrickson, *The Living and the Dead: Robert McNamara and Five Lives of a Lost War* (1996).

Medina, Isaias. On 18 October 1945, the government of Venezuela's president Isaias Medina was overthrown in a military coup. Medina had been in office since 1941. A military-civilian junta took over control of the country. Romolo Betancourt (qv) became the chairman of the junta and ruled by decree for the next 28 months.

Medina, Ernest L. *See* Calley.

Meghna River, East Pakistan. *See* Bangladesh.

Mehabad (Mahabad). *See* Iran.

Meimak Heights. *See* Iran.

Mein, John Gordon. On 28 August 1968, the U. S. ambassador to Guatemala, John Gordon Mein, was murdered in an apparent kidnap attempt in Guatemala City. Terrorists of the Rebel Armed Forces (FAR) group carried out the attack. The FAR was among the more active terrorist organizations in Central America during the late 1960s and early 1970s. FAR also kidnapped and murdered the West German ambassador, Count Karl von Spreti (qv), in March–April 1970. The group was finally taken down by specially trained Guatemalan police and U.S. Special Forces in the late 1970s.

Meir, Golda. (b. 3 May 1898, Kiev, Ukraine, Imperial Russia—d. 8 December 1978, Jerusalem) Golda Meir moved to Milwaukee, Wisconsin, in 1906, when her family emigrated from Russia to the United States. There she was educated as a teacher. In 1921, she moved to Palestine with her Russian-born husband, Morris Myerson, also an ardent Zionist (qv). By 1946, Mrs. Myerson (Golda Meir) was the director of the Jewish Agency for Palestine. Upon Israeli independence, she was appointed ambassador to the USSR and later became minister of labor (1949–1956), foreign minister (1956–1966) (at that point she changed her name to Meir) and general secretary of the Labor (*Mapai*) party (until July 1968). She became prime minister (17 March 1969) of Israel upon the death of Levi Eshkol (qv) on 26 February 1969. On 12 March 1970, Meir announced that her country would demand retention of some of the territory seized during the 1967 Arab-Israeli War. On 27 July 1972, Anwar Sadat (qv) of Egypt rejected an offer made by the prime minister for the opening of peace discussions. She won reelection in 1973 against an opposition led by Menachem Begin (qv). That same year she successfully led her country through the 1973 Arab-Israeli (Yom Kippur) War. Immediately after the end of the hostilities, Meir declared Israel would not withdraw to the 22 October cease-fire line. The repercussions of the surprise Arab attack, that opened the war and gained momentary strategic surprise against Israel, forced her resignation on 10 April 1974. She died in December 1978.

Mejia Victores, Oscar Humberto. (b. 1930) On 8 August 1983, the government of Efrain Rios Montt (qv) of .Guatemala was overthrown by a military coup. The ruling junta then appointed Brigadier General Oscar Humberto Mejia Victores as president. Mejia's rule was a tense one, with a high level of violence continuing. Several military coups occurred, and a new alignment of leftist Marxist rebel groups increased the pressure on the government. Mejia promised a return to civilian government, and the elections held in November 1985. Following an inauguration of the new president, Mejia left office on 14 January 1986, but the unrest continued. *See* Guatemala.

Melbourne. *See* Australia.

Melen, Ferit. (b. 1906, Van, Turkey) Melen rose through the financial ranks of government in Turkey to director of revenue in the Ministry of Finance in 1944. In May 1950, he was elected to the Chamber of Deputies. During this period he was noted to be strongly anticommunist. When his party moved too far to the left, he and a group of colleagues formed the Reliance Party, which claimed to carry forward the work of Kemal Ataturk. When Turkish prime minister Nihat Erim (qv) resigned on 17 April 1972, Ferit Melen, then the defense minister, formed a caretaker government, on 22 May 1972. Melen was replaced in office when a new caretaker government was formed.

Melgar Castro, Juan Alberto. On 22 April 1975, Colonel Melgar Castro replaced General Oswaldo Lopez Arelano as president of Honduras following a bloodless coup. Melgar was ousted from his office by another military coup on 8 August 1978. A three-man military junta then took control of the country.

Melilla. *See* Spain.

Meloy, Francis E., Jr. Along with U.S. economic counselor Robert O. Waring, U.S. ambassador Francis E. Meloy and a Lebanese driver, Zuhayr Mughrabi, were detained and then shot and killed as the ambassador's sedan crossed the "Green Line" between East and West Beirut on 16 June 1976. Their vehicle was stopped at a roadblock, which had originally signalled them to pass. The vehicle and its occupants were taken to a nearby headquarters, from which the three men subsequently disappeared. The murderers belonged to the Popular Front for the

Liberation of Palestine (PFLP) (qv). The bodies of the three victims were found in a garbage dump near the beach at Ramlat al-Bayda. The PLO later announced that three Lebanese who confessed to the murders had been arrested. In 1983, Lebanese officials arrested eight other persons alleged to have been involved in the murders; all were connected to the PFLP.

Menderes, Adnan. On 27 May 1960, Turkish prime minister Adnan Memderes and his cabinet were ousted by a military coup led by General Jemal Gürsel (qv). Menderes and the others were arrested. The junta, called the Turkish National Union Committee (National Unity Committee), then began preparations for holding free elections. On 12 September 1961, Menderes and two others were executed for violating the constitution.

Mendez, Aparicio. *See* Uruguay.

Menendez, Mario Benjamin. On 28 September 1951, Menendez led an abortive coup against the government of Juan Peron in Argentina. He survived the aftermath of the coup. On 9 April 1982, as a major general, he was appointed governor of the newly conquered Falkland Islands (*see* Falkland Islands). There he declared martial law and changed the names of Port Stanley and Darwin to Puerto Argentino and Belgrano, respectively. On 14 June 1982, Menendez was forced to asked the for terms of surrender following the overwhelming British success in retaking the islands. Menendez was repatriated to Argentina.

Merida. *See* Mexico.

Merom Golan. *See* Syria.

Mers el-Kebir. *See* Algeria.

Mexico. More properly called the United Mexican States (*Estados Unidos Mexicanos*), Mexico is located in southern North America. It is bordered by the United States on the north, by the Gulf of Mexico on the east, by Belize and Guatemala on the south and by the Pacific Ocean on the west. The capital is Mexico City. Mexico was first inhabited by nomadic tribes that had migrated south across North America. Those that settled in Mexico were the Mayans on the Yucatan Peninsula and the Toltecs. The Aztecs overcame the Toltecs in the 13-14th centuries. The Aztecs founded Tenochititlan on the site of present-day Mexico City in 1328 A.D. Spaniards under Hernando Cortez destroyed the Aztec Empire in three years (1519–1521). The Spaniards ruled Mexico until 1810–1812, when a popular uprising overthrew the foreign rule. One of the leaders of the uprising, General Agustin Iturbide, proclaimed himself emperor, as Agustin I. A republic was proclaimed in 1823. In 1836, one of the northern provinces revolted and proclaimed itself the Republic of Texas. The central government refused to acknowledge the separation, and a series of military clashes took place. In 1846, the United States became involved. The War with Mexico followed, in which Mexico lost all of its territory north of the Rio Grande. In 1864, the French put an Austrian archduke on the throne of Mexico as Maximilian I and supported his crown by force of arms. The French episode ended in 1867, when a popular uprising led by Benito Juarez took control of the country. A dictator, Pofirio Diaz, was president from 1877 to 1880 and 1884 to 1911. His rule led to fighting between opposing groups, which continued until

5 February 1917, when a new constitution was imposed. The dominant party in Mexico since 1929 has been the Revolutionary Party. In 1964, the government announced it would not join in the Organization of American States (OAS) sanctions against Cuba; it was the only state in the Western Hemisphere to maintain diplomatic relations with Havana. Mexico did join in the signing of a 14-nation Treaty on the Denuclearization of Latin America on 14 February 1967. In July 1968, a long period of student unrest developed that centered around the National University in Mexico City. Over 50 students were killed during 18–24 September, when army troops were called in to seize the university. In 1970–1976, the presidency of Luis Echeverria (qv) led the country to the left, but this movement was reversed by succeeding administrations. In 1971, however, Mexico City announced it had uncovered a Soviet plot to train members of a Mexican terrorist organization, *Movimiento de Accion Revolucionaria* (MAR) (qv), in North Korea for the purpose of overthrowing the Mexican government. In the first kidnapping of a government official in modern times, MAR terrorists took Julio Hirschfield, the head of the Mexican Civil Aviation Service, on 27 September 1971. He was released two days later after a $250,000 ransom was paid. On 19 November, the rector of the State University at Guerrero, Dr. Jaime Castrejon Diez, was kidnapped by terrorists. A ransom of $500,000 and the release of nine political prisoners, who were transported to Cuba, gained his release on 1 December. When Haitian terrorists tried to escape to Mexico after kidnapping (23 January 1973) the U.S. ambassador to Haiti, Mexico confiscated their ransom money and sent them to Chile. On 4 May 1973, the U.S. consul in Guadalajara, Terence Leahardy, was kidnapped by members of the *Fuerzas Revolucionarias Armadas Populare* (FRAP). FRAP demanded and got $80,000 and the release of 30 political prisoners before Leahardy was freed (7 May). Then, on 22 March 1974, the U.S. vice-consul in Hermosilla, John S. Patterson, was kidnapped by a group calling themselves the "Peoples' Liberation Army of Mexico." In this case, the Mexican government determined that the kidnappers were actually American criminals. Patterson had already been murdered when the ransom note arrived. On 28 May 1974, an American, Bobbie Joe Keesee, was arrested, and subsequently tried and convicted in San Diego of conspiring to kidnap a diplomat. Another man was also convicted in the kidnapping. In August 1974, the Mexican president's father-in-law was kidnapped and held for $1.6 million and the release of political prisoners. Another man, a possible successor to Echeverria, was also kidnapped. Both men were released without the payment of ransom or the freeing of prisoners. During this period a number of other guerrilla actions and assassinations took place. Mexico restored diplomatic relations with Spain after a 38-year break on 28 March 1977. On 28 January 1985, Mexico joined with five other nations in calling for a ban on nuclear weapons in outer space and an end to the arms race. In the 1990s, pressure was applied by the United States on Mexico for its laxity in controlling the production and distribution of drugs. In 1994, what started as a minor uprising in south central Mexico soon escalated into much larger proportions, and world attention was drawn to the situation.

Military operations against the native rebels in Chiapas Province were still underway as 1994 came to a close. Also, in 1994, Mexico was accused of herding Guatemalan refugees into concentration camp–type settlements near the common border. Debt reduction headed the issues in 1995, along with efforts to settle the lingering effects of the Chiapas rebellion and efforts to curb the drug trade and its associated murderous fallout. *Reading:* Roderic Ai Camp, *Crossing Swords: Politics and Religion in Mexico* (1996); Dan La Botz, *Democracy in Mexico: Peasant Rebellion and Political Reform* (1995); Henry Bamford Parkes, *A History of Mexico* (1972).

Micambero, Michel. On 1 November 1976, Michel Micambero, the president of Burundi (qv), was overthrown by Lieutenant Colonel Jean-Baptiste Bagaza (qv) in an army-led coup. Bagaza was appointed president (10 November). Micambero had taken power after the overthrow of the monarchy on 28 November 1966. He then proclaimed a republic with himself as president. His tenure was marked with internal disturbances, tribal violence and coup attempts. In April 1972, Micambero was implicated in the murder of King Mwami Ntare V, who had been assured safe passage for a return to Burundi. At first Micambero's government announced that Ntare had been killed in fighting near the capital, but later it admitted he had been tried and executed. In the two months of butchery that followed Ntare's death, over 100,000 Tutsi tribesmen were killed by Hutu tribesmen serving in the Burundi army (with the support of Zaire).

Michelin Tire Company. *See* Spain.

Middle Congo. *See* Congo.

Middle East Treaty Organization. *See* Baghdad Pact.

Mifsud Bonici, Carmelo. (b. 17 July 1933, Cospiua, Malta) On 22 December 1984 Dom Mintoff (qv), the prime minister of Malta, resigned and was replaced by Carmelo Mifsud Bonici, who had been the senior deputy prime minister. Mifsud, a lawyer, had served as minister of education since 1983. He remained prime minister until 11 May 1987, when he was replaced by Eddie Fenech Adami. During his tenure, Misfud Bonici continued the policy of cordiality toward communist countries and worked to strengthen ties with Libya, even though that country was known to have sponsored terrorist activities on Malta.

Mikhailovich (Mihallovic), Draja. (b. 27 March 1893, Ivanjica, Serbia—d. 17 July 1946, Belgrade, Yugoslavia) Mikhailovich was educated at the Serbian Military Academy and fought in the Balkan Wars of 1912–1913 and in World War I. On 2 April 1941, when Nazi German forces invaded Yugoslavia, he was chief of staff of a Serbian motorized division. After the Nazi conquest, Mikhailovich organized Chetnik (*Cety*) bands in Serbia. At the same time, a communist-controlled underground organization headed by Josef Broz (Tito) (qv) was operating in Bosnia-Herzogovina and Montenegro. For a time, the two organizations both fought the Germans, but their political goals were different and cooperation against the common enemy faltered. In January 1942, Mikhailovich was appointed minister of war in the Yugoslav government in exile. Soon afterward, "Free Yugoslovia" radio broadcasts emanating from inside the Soviet Union accused him of treason and collaboration with the Germans. This was a lie concocted by Tito's masters in the Kremlin and would have been refuted by US agents serving with his army, if they had been allowed to testify at his trial. This was not to be, however, as the Allies had thrown in with Tito as the more productive Yugoslav leader. In May 1944, King Peter of Yugoslavia abandoned his cause, and as events progressed at the end of the war Mikhailovich was forced into hiding. He was captured on 24 March 1946 and put on trial for treason. On 17 July 1946 he was executed by firing squad amid vociferous protests from the West.

Milan. *See* Italy.

Mindszenty, Jozsef Cardinal. (b. 1892, Csehimindszent, Austria-Hungary—d. 6 May 1975, Vienna) As a priest ordained in 1915, Bishop Mindszenty was imprisoned by the Nazis in the last months of World War II in Europe because he refused to recognize the puppet regime in Hungary. Upon his release, after the Soviet liberation, he was appointed Primate of Hungary and received the "red hat" of a cardinal in the Roman Catholic Church in February 1946. An ardent nationalist and very stubborn man, he publical denounced the communist regime in Hungary and was arrested on 26–27 December 1948, given a staged trial and imprisoned in solitary confinement for life (8 February 1949). In prison he was tortured, both physically and mentally, but never waivered in his convictions. He was freed during the Hungarian uprising on 30 October 1956. Returned to his palace in Buda, he was forced to flee when the Soviet invasion began. He was given asylum in the U.S. embassy (4 November), where he remained until September 1971. In 1963, the Vatican had asked him to leave Hungary under papal protection, but he refused to do so unless the Hungarian government announced his complete innocence of the charges placed against him in 1948. In September 1971, the Pope ordered him to Rome, and Cardinal Mindszenty obeyed. After visiting Rome, he went to Vienna and lived in a religious hostel. Always outspoken, he criticized the Vatican's lenient policies toward the communist regimes in Eastern Europe and was removed as the Primate of Hungary. He died peacefully on 6 May 1975. *Reading:* Jozsef Cardinal Mindszenty, *Memoirs* (1974).

Minh, Duong Van ("Big Minh"). *See* Vietnam.

Minh, Tran Van. *See* Vietnam.

Minh Thanh Base Camp. *See* Vietnam.

"Mini-Tet." In what was listed as a continuation of the 1968 Tet Offensive (*see* Vietnam), the North Vietnamese Army (NVA) and the Viet Cong (VC) launched a series of new attacks on more than 120 towns, military posts and airfields throughout South Vietnam on 5–13 May 1968. As a consequence, 2,500 NVA and VC were killed. Fighting in and around Saigon lasted until 9 May.

Minnesota Mining Company Office (Paris). *See* Youth Action Group.

Mintoff, Dom(inic). (b. 16 August 1916, Kospikwa, Malta) Born the son of a former Royal Navy cook, Mintoff studied engineering at the University of Malta and at Oxford. He worked in England during World War II and returned to Malta after the war to become an architect. Upon his return he joined the Maltese Labor Party. He was elected to the Council of Government in 1945, and he was appointed deputy prime minister for works in 1947. Mintoff first became prime minister of Malta in 1955 and urged Malta's integration into the United Kingdom. When the necessary financial arrangement could not be agreed upon, Mintoff resigned (April 1958) and took up the cause of Maltese independence. He was again named prime minister in June 1971, as the leader of the Maltese Labor Party. His first act was to demand the replacement of the British governor-general and a renegotiation of the Anglo-Maltese defense agreement (1964). He also ordered the removal of the Italian NATO commander at the naval base at Valetta and refused access to any Maltese port to any ship of the U.S. Sixth Fleet. Mintoff demanded an increase to 30 million pounds sterling from the 5 million pounds sterling rent on British bases under the 1964 agreement. After a series of meetings with high ranking British and NATO officials, Mintoff's bad temper prevailed, and NATO announced that its Mediterranean naval headquarters was being transferred to Naples. Meanwhile, Mintoff was courted by Libyan and Soviet officials. On 20 August 1970, the Soviet government announced that henceforth its ships would be repaired in Maltese ports. As to the British issue, Mintoff accepted a rent of 6 million pounds in cash plus 3.5 million pounds in development aid a year after a visit to London. When Mintoff again raised the price, the British announced they would withdraw their forces and bases from Malta. Mintoff immediately began once again courting Muammar Qaddafi (qv). Mintoff found a friend in U.S. president Jimmy Carter, who in 1978 promised to support Malta in gaining other foreign aid. At the same time, however, Mintoff was working with Libya and Algeria in solidifying a number of agreements. In July 1978, British journalists were barred from Malta, and the British broadcasting station was ordered closed. Mintoff resigned his post on 22 December 1984 and turned the government over to Carmelo Mifsud Bonici, the senior deputy prime minister.

Miranda, Rogelio. On 6 October 1970, a military junta led by Bolivian army chief of staff General Rogelio Miranda forced the resignation of President Alfredo Ovando Candia (qv). During the confusion of the next 24 hours, however, the confusion in the capital allowed a left-wing coup led by the recently dismissed commander in chief of the armed forces, General Juan Jose Torres Gonzales (qv), to take over the government and to set himself up as its president. Miranda fled, seeking asylum first in the Paraguayan Embassy and then in the Argentinian Embassy where Ovanda also sought refuge.

Mirza, Iskander. Faced with growing unrest in his country, Pakistan's president Iskander Mirza dismissed his prime minister and abrogated the constitution on 7 October 1958. He then declared martial law and appointed General Mohammed Ayub Khan (qv) to administer it. On 27 October, Mirza resigned as president and appointed Ayub Khan as his successor. *See* Pakistan.

Misgav Am Kibbutz. *See* Israel.

Mishmar HaYardan. *See* Israel.

Mitchell, David. A U.S. Army staff sergeant, David Mitchell, was tried and acquitted of charges growing out of the My Lai massacre. *See* Calley.

Mitla Pass, Egypt. *See* Israel.

Mitrione, Dan(iel) A. On 31 July 1970, US diplomat Dan A. Mitrone and the Brazilian consul were kidnapped in Montevideo, Uruguay, by Tupamaro (qv) terrorists. Mitrione was an American police official and was working as a USAID public safety adviser to the Urguayan government. After the Uruguayan government refused to negotiate for his release, Mitrione's body was found in Montevideo. In 1977, Antonio Mas Mas was tried and convicted for Mitrione's murder and sentenced to 30 years in prison. The counterterrorist operation that followed the murder literally destroyed the Tupamaro group.

Mitterand, Francois Maurice. (b. 26 October 1916, Jarnac, France—d. 8 January 1996, Paris) Born into a middle-class family, Mitterand studied law in Paris and, in 1946, stood for and won a place in the Chamber of Deputies from Nievre. He bcame first secretary of the French Socialist Party in 1971, using his influence to unseat the communists in favor of the socialist movement. He served in the chamber from 1946 to 1958 and from 1962 to 1981 and in the Senate from 1959 to 1962. From 1958 to 1981 he also served as mayor of Chateau-Chinon. Mitterand ran against Charles DeGaulle for the presidency in 1966, and the closeness of the vote forced a runoff, which he lost. He won the presidency in 1981 becoming the first non-rightest (Gaullist) (and the first Socialist) president of France in nearly a quarter-century. One of his first acts was to reestablish a working relationship with NATO, if not full membership. Mitterand has been successively reelected to the French presidency, and his tenure has often seen a union between right and left. He left office in 1995 and died of cancer in 1996.

Mnong Plateau. *See* Vietnam.

Moba. *See* Zaire.

Mobutu, Joseph Desire (Mobutu Sese Seko). (b. 14 October 1930, Lisala, Belgian Congo—d. 7 September 1997, Rabat, Morocco) Mobutu served seven years in the *Force Publique* before being sent for a year's study at a Belgian university, where he majored in social science. Upon his return to Congo he became a journalist and shortly joined with Patrice Lumumba (qv) in the *Mouvement Nationale Congolais.* After independence (*see* Congo), he became defense minister in Lumumba's government and then chief of staff of the army. On 14 September 1960, Mobutu seized power in the Democratic Republic of Congo (qv) and, although President Kasavubu (qv) was allowed to remain in office, Patrice Lumumba was ousted. By 1961, some of the Congo's provinces began to accept Mobutu's leadership, but the situation remained tense. On 24–25 November 1965, Mobutu, now a lieutenant general, led a bloodless coup from which he emerged as the major power figure in Congo. He assumed all of the legislative powers normally held by Parliament on 2 March 1966. Mobutu was able to withstand a coup attempt at the end of May, but the breakaway province situation continued to escalate into 1967, when a civil war erupted that spread into 1969. His rule was ruthless, but he turned his rag-tag army into a modern fighting force. His new party, called the *Mouvement Populaire de la*

Revolution, led the way in the nationalization of many industries in his country, but he was able to maintain friendly relations with the Belgian government. In October 1971, he changed the name of his country to Zaire and caused all personal names to be Africanized, including his own, which became Mobutu Sese Seko Kuku Ngbendu Wa Za Banga. During the next 25 years, his country underwent numerous coup plots and counterplots, rebellions and invasions, but Mobutu remained in power until 1997, when, on 16 May, he was forced to flee in the face of a rebel drive on Kinshasha. *See* Zaire. *Reading:* Crawford Young, *The Rise and Decline of the Zairian State* (1985); Sean Kelly, *America's Tyrant: The CIA and Mobutu of Zaire: How the United States Put Mobutu in Power, Protected Him from His Enemies, Helped Him Become One of the Richest Men in the World, and Lived to Regret It* (1993).

Moch, Jules. On 15 October 1950, Jules Moch, the French socialist defense minister in the government of Rene Pleven, announced that the United States would furnish France $2 billion for a military buildup and that the money would be used specifically to support the French effort in Indochina. Up to that time, Moch had held a ministerial post in every one of the ten governments that had run France since 1946.

"Model Plan." On 11 September 1963, a "Model Plan" was developed to fight Viet Cong insurgency in South Vietnam. Hope was so high for the plan that another plan to reduce U.S. adviser strength in the country by 1,000 men was implemented in November 1963. That same month, General Paul D. Harkins, the U.S. commander in Vietnam, was so optimistic that he claimed victory over the Viet Cong was "just months away and that the reduction of American advisors (could) begin any time now." By 8 April 1964, the situation had deteriorated to such an extent that the U.S. suspended its five-year planning program and scrapped the model plan. On 20 June 1964, Harkins was relieved and replaced by General William Westmoreland.

Moffitt, Ronni Karpen. On 21 September 1976, former leftist socialist Chilean cabinet minister Orlando Letelier (qv) and his associate, Ronni Karpen Moffitt, were assassinated in Washington, DC, when a bomb detonated in Letelier's car. *See* Letelier and Chile.

Mogadishu. *See* Somalia.

Mohammed, Faiz. On 11 September 1980, the minister of frontier affairs for Afghanistan, Faiz Mohammed, and several of his aides were killed by villagers near Lake Tiga. The incident occurred when the minister tried to enlist the support of the village for the Soviet-backed regime in Kabul.

Mohammed, Murtala Ramat. On 29 July 1975, the government of Nigerian president Yakubu Gowon (qv) was ousted from power while Gowon was attending an Organization of African Unity (OAU) meeting in Kampala, Uganda. The ruling provisional military council appointed Brigadier Murtala Ramat Mohammed to be the country's new leader. On 13 February 1976, another military coup, this time led by Lieutenant Colonel Bukar S. Dimka (qv), was attempted but failed. Mohammed was killed during the fighting. Dimka and 29 others were executed on 15 May 1976 for their roles in the murder.

Mohammed (Muhammad) Ayub Khan. (b. 14 May 1907, Hazara, India—d. 19 April 1974, Islamabad, Pakistan) Ayub Khan was educated at the Aligarh Muslim University at Uttar Pradesh, India, and at the Royal Military Academy, Sandhurst. He became an Indian army officer in 1928 and commanded an Indian battalion in the Burma campaign. When India was partitioned in 1947, he joined the Pakistani army and rose quickly through the ranks until he was appointed commander in chief in 1951. In 1954, he served for a brief period as minister of defense. In 1958 he became the chief martial law administrator (7 October) in the administration of President Iskander Mirza (qv) in attempting the suppression of the political turmoil that wracked the country. When Mirza resigned on 27 October 1958 (and was exiled), he appointed Ayub Khan as his successor. Ayub Khan set about reorganizing the political structure of Pakistan and led the way toward an economic recovery of his country. He was reelected president in 1965, having run against strong opposition from the family of Mohammed Ali Jinnah, the founder of Pakistan. Following the Chinese attack on India in 1962 and the subsequent opening of U.S. military aid to India, Ayub Khan moved Pakistan toward a closer relationship with China. He also led his people in the war against India over the Jammu and Kashmir dispute and accepted both the UN cease-fire order and its boundary settlement plan. His failure to get Kashmir for Pakistan and the government's policies of sufferage culminated in considerable violence and unrest, especially among students. In 1968, he announced he would not seek reelection, but this did not relieve the tension. On 26 March 1969 he resigned from office and led the remainder of his life in relative quiet.

Mohammed V (Sidi Mohammed ben Yusuf). (b. 10 August 1909, Fes, Morocco—d. 26 February 1961, Rabat) Upon the death of his father in 1927, Sidi Mohammed was selected by the French to succeed him as Sultan of Morocco. This created some opposition as the 18-year-old was selected over two elder brothers. Within a decade he had proven his worth, considering his office was under close French control. During World War II, Mohammed maintained his support of the French Vichy government but refused to allow Moroccan resistance to the Allied landings that occurred in 1942 or to condone the anti-Jewish programs imposed by the Nazis on Vichy and, in turn, on Morocco. He was impressed by and also impressed the Allied leaders he met and, in 1944, when the *Istiqlal* Party (qv) began the demand for Moroccan independence, Mohammed added his voice to the effort. Thereafter, he tended to ignore France and stressed the relationship of Morocco to the Arab states. This enraged the French, who appointed General Alphonse Juin as resident general with broad powers to maintain French control over their colony. When Juin failed to sway Mohammed, the French officer organized Berber resistance against him (1951), but still failed to sway the sultan. Juin was subsequently replaced by General Augustin Guillaume (1953), who deported Mohammed first to Corsica and then to Madagascar. The French then appointed a true puppet to rule Morocco. This infuriated the Moroccan people, who then saw Mohammed as a redeemer. There followed a major outbreak of terrorism against the French and, finally open warfare, especially in the Rif. By 1955, the French were forced to back down (Declaration of La Celle St. Cloud, November 1955), and Mohammed returned to Morocco in triumph. At this juncture, he became king (1957) and not only ruled but also reigned over his people. On 21 October 1958, forces loyal to Mohammed V were attacked by rebel forces loyal to the left-wing element in the *Istiqlal* Party. On 22 November 1959, Mohammed V demanded the withdrawal of all U.S. forces stationed in Morocco by 1963. The U.S. agreed. The king died suddenly in Rabat on 26 February 1961 and was succeeded by his son, Prince Maulay Hassan (Hassan II) (qv).

Mohr, Alberto Fuentes. On 27 February 1970, Alberto Fuentes Mohr, the foreign minister of Guatemala, was kidnapped in Guatemala City by terrorists of the Rebel Armed Forces (FAR) (qv). He was exchanged the next day (28 February) for an imprisoned rebel leader.

Moi, Daniel Torotich Arap. (b. September 1924, Baringo district, Kenya) Born into a peasant family, Moi received his early education at the American Mission School and at the Government (British) African School at Kapsabet. In 1954 he became a teacher and later a headmaster at a Kenyan school. He entered politics in 1950 and was nominated to the Kenya Legislative Council in 1955. He was elected to the council in 1957 in the first elections that allowed black participation. In 1960, Moi formed a new political organization (Kenya African Democratic Union) after breaking with Jomo Kenyatta's (qv) KANU party. Moi's group included a number of white Kenyan settlers. When Kenya achieved its independence in December 1963, Moi merged his party with Kenyatta's, and following the 1964 elections, Moi became minister of home affairs. Over the years, as Kenyatta aged and his health began to fail, Moi assumed more and more responsibility. Moi was vice-president when Jomo Kenyatta died on 22 August 1978. Moi was sworn in as president in an orderly transfer of power. In September 1979, Moi signed a mutual defense and friendship treaty with neighboring Somalia and became embroiled in the fighting between Uganda and Tanzania. Moi was able to withstand a coup attempt against his government on 1 August 1982. Organized by Kenyan air force personnel, the coup failed when loyal army troops reacted. Some 3,000 people were arrested, including 1,200 from the air force. On 21 August, Moi disbanded the air force, dismissing all its personnel. By 1984, fourteen ex–air force personnel had been tried and convicted, but none had been executed. In addition, Moi, in December 1983, had ordered the release of some 7,000 petty criminals to celebrate the 20th anniversary of Kenyan independence. Moi continued in office into 1989 and was able to demonstrate his authority by forcing the vice president, a member of KANU, to resign. Moi also participated symbolically in the war on ivory poaching by putting the torch to over $3 million in confiscated elephant tusks, for which 2,000 elephants had been killed. On 4 January 1993, Moi was sworn in to serve another five-year term as president. The losers in the first multiparty election in 26 years all cried foul.

Mokhehle, Ntsu. On 30 January 1970, Prime Minister Chief Leabua Jonathan (qv) overthrew King Moshoeshoe II of Lesotho (qv). At the same time, he had his chief parliamentary opponent, the Basutoland Congress Party (BCP) leader, Ntsu Mokhehle, arrested. This all took place three days after the first general elections in Lesotho's history and was Jonathan's attempt to forestall the apparent opposition victory, which the king publicly supported. Ntsu Mokhehle was released from confinement on 8 June 1971. When disorder threatened the country in January 1974, Ntsu Mokhehle fled the country for Zambia. The trouble was brought about by a coup attempt, the aftermath of which was a treason trial in March 1975 in which 15 BCP members were tried for treason. Mokhehle still remained out of the country.

Mollet, Guy. Upon the resignation of the government of Edgar Faure (qv) on 24 January 1956, a new socialist-oriented government was formed in France under Guy Mollet. Mollet remained in office until May 1957, when he was defeated for reelection. Among his achievements was France's signing of the European Economic Community (Common Market) treaty. His tenure also covered a part of the period of crisis in Algeria (*see* Algeria), and that of French participation in the Suez Canal operation in 1956 (*see* Egypt).

Molotov, Vyacheslav Mikhailovich. (b. 9 March 1890, Kukarka, Russia—d. 8 November 1986, near Moscow, USSR) Molotov, whose real name was Scriabin, joined the Bolsheviks at age 16. At that time he assumed the name "Molotov" from the Russian word *molot*, or "hammer" to conceal his real identity. In 1911, he helped found *Pravda*, the Communist Party newspaper. In 1915, he was arrested by Tsarist police and was exiled to Siberia; he escaped, however, in 1916 and fought in the October Revolution of 1917. In 1930, his friend Josef Stalin (qv) appointed Molotov premier. He held that post until 1941, when Stalin took that post for himself because of the war. Molotov also served as foreign minister (commissar of foreign affairs) from 1939 to 1949 and again from 1953 to 1956. During this latter period, Molotov participated in the Geneva Conference (May 1954) that settled the fate of Indochina. In October 1954, Molotov demanded Four Powers (qv) talks on the reunification and neutralization of Germany. This proposal was immediately rejected by the Western Allies. It was Molotov who signed the nonaggression pact with Adolf Hitler in 1939. Molotov also helped found the United Nations in 1945 and headed the Soviet delegation to the UN from 1946 to 1948. After Stalin's death and the rise of Nikita Khrushchev (qv), Molotov firmly opposed the de-Stalinization policies espoused by the new regime. In 1957, Molotov was implicated in a plot to overthrow Khrushchev and was removed (along with Georgi Malenkov, Dmitri Shepilov and Lazar Kaganovich) from the Presidium of the Central Committee and was downgraded to ambassador to Mongolia, where he served until 1960. In 1960–1961, he was the Soviet representative to the International Atomic Energy Agency in Vienna. After 1961, Molotov's whereabouts were unknown, and he was again taken out of the public eye. In 1962, Khrushchev kicked him out of the party. After Khrushchev's demise, he was reinstated into the party by Konstantin Chernenko (qv), in July 1984.

Molucca Islands. *See* Indonesia.

Monash University. *See* Australia.

Mondlane, Eduardo Chivambo. (b. 1920, southern Mozambique—d. 3 February 1969, Dar-es-Salaam, Tanzania) On 3 February 1969, Eduardo Chivambo Mondlane, the leader of the Mozambique Liberation Front (FRELIMO), was assassinated in Dar-es-Salaam, Tanzania, by a bomb blast. Mondlane was considered one of the most wanted men in Portugal. Mondlane held a doctorate in sociology from Northwestern University and had worked for the UN Trusteeship Council before returning to Africa to take up the fight for Mozambique independence.

Mongolia. The lands of Mongolia are found on a vast plateau in central Asia. The region is divided into Inner Mongolia, an autonomous region in the People's Republic of China (*see* China), and Outer Mongolia, today called the Mongolian People's Republic. Outer Mongolia is bordered by Russia on the north and China on the south. It is a land of mountains, lakes and forests. In the southern part of the country lie the northern reaches of the Gobi Desert. Mongolia has served as a place of confrontation between Russia and China throughout recorded history. The capital of Outer Mongolia is Ulan Batar. Mongolia has one of the world's oldest histories. The people of Outer Mongolia are Mongols (90%), while those of Inner Mongolia are generally ethnic Chinese. The population of Outer Mongolia is less than 2.5 million. In the third century B.C., Mongolia became the home of the Huns. Mongolia reached its zenith of power when Genghis Khan and his successors rose out of its lands and conquered China and most of the known world, as far as Poland and Hungary. China was reconquered by the Chinese in 1348, although warfare continued for most of the fourteenth and fifteenth centuries. In 1380, for example, a Chinese raid into Mongolia resulted in the destruction of Karakorum, the ancient capital. For a time, most of Mongolia was a province of China as the old Mongol empire dissolved. The southern and eastern areas of Mongolia became absorbed into the early Manchu hegemony and became part of China after the Manchu subjugation. After the fall of the Manchu dynasty in China, Mongolia declared its independence; but the growing Chinese emigre population and the Chinese army prevented Inner Mongolia, which had generally adopted the Chinese culture, from achieving independence. Outer Mongolia, supported by Tsarist Russia which wanted a buffer state against China, did achieve its independence in this way. That Outer Mongolia was little more than a Russian puppet is undeniable. Following the collapse of Imperial Russia, the Soviets moved in and, in 1921, restored Outer Mongolian autonomy as a Soviet protectorate. A formal alliance was installed between Outer Mongolia and the USSR on 12 March 1936. One year later, on 7 July 1937, Japan invaded China. Following the war, the Mongolian people once again overwhelmingly voted for independence from China and, on 27 February 1946, signed a ten-year treaty of friendship with Moscow. After repeated Chinese raids on Mongolian positions along the border, Mongolian army forces carried out a raid (5–6 June 1947) into Sinkiang province to recover Mongols who had been kidnapped. In May

1972, Mongolia, along with Communist China and the USSR, arranged to give aid to the North Vietnamese during the war in Southeast Asia. With the collapse of communism in 1990, the Mongolian Communist Party relaxed its grip on the country and allowed free elections (July 1990). Still, a former-communist assembly was elected (1990), but a coalition government took power in 1991 and began the process of moving the country toward a market economy. In 1992, Mongolia took another step away from communism and, according to its new constitution, dropped the term "people's republic" from its name, discontinued the use of other Soviet-style symbols and marked the departure of the last Soviet troops from its soil. Another blow came to Mongolian communism when its first presidential election returned the government of President Punsalmaagiyn Ochirbat to office by a landslide vote in 1993. However, as the communist-dominated Mongolian People's Revolutionary Party (MPRP) still controlled the legislative assembly (70 of 76 seats), the political situation was unclear. By 1995, there appeared to be some movement, but the completely dominated assembly acted to block most legislation that would clear the impasse. In the meantime, amid an outflowing of support from the U.S. and others, the more conservative International Monetary Fund and the UN, especially its developmental programs people took a wait-and-see attitude. *Reading:* Mongolian Academy of Sciences, *Information Mongolia: The Comprehensive Reference Source of the People's Republic of Mongolia* (1990); Sechin Jagchid, *Essays in Mongolian Studies* (1988); Harry Harding, *China and Northeast Asia: The Political Dimension* (1988).

Monroe Doctrine. On 2 December 1823, President James Monroe issued a policy statement in his message to congress that enunciated the principle that the Western Hemisphere and Europe were separate and distinct regions and had little to do with each other. George Washington had expressed the same sentiments in his farewell address (19 September 1796), as had Thomas Jefferson in his first inaugural speech. Monroe's reiteration of the basic notion that Europe should refrain from interference in the lives of those living in the Americas was brought on by Russia's establishment of a ban on foreign shipping within 100 miles of its territory in North America—principally Alaska—and the danger of increased European interference in the affairs of Central and South America. The actual threat from Europe was essentially nonexistent, and when one of the European powers did act—as in the British occupation of the Falklands or the French blockade of Mexico in 1838—there was no U.S. reaction. However, when France attempted to impose the principle that the European system of balance of power applied in the western hemisphere, and when France and England dabbled in Mexico, President James Polk restated the doctrine in more decisive terms. Not until the 1850s was the doctrine given congressional sanction and established as a part of U.S. foreign policy. The doctrine was also used on occasion to justify American acts carried out under the rubric of Manifest Destiny. In July 1960, Nikita Khrushchev stated that the Monroe Doctrine had died a "natural death," when questions of Soviet interference in Cuba had arisen. Six days later (14 July 1960), the U.S. State

Department declared the nation would adhere to the Monroe Docrine, stating that the USSR was bent on worldwide expansion. Even later, on 8 November 1984, the U.S. invoked the Monroe Doctrine when it warned the USSR that it would not tolerate the introduction of advanced Soviet-built fighter aircraft into Nicaragua.

Monrovia. *See* Liberia.

Montagnard Tribesmen. The term *Montagnard* is the French word for "highlander" that is applied exclusively to aboriginal tribesmen dwelling in the plateau regions of Vietnam. As such, the name refers to people bounded by the region they occupy and not by cultural or ethnic kinship. Indeed, at least 20 distinct "nationalities" had been determined when the last Western contact was severed in 1975. There never was a Montagnard nation, and each village appears to be independent and led by an elected village elder. There was little conflict between villages, and that which did exist was most often ceremonial. In recent history the Montagnards were often abused by their neighbors; the French specifically identified an individual as Montagnard on his identity card even if that person worked in a city. The South Vietnamese government continued that practice after 1956. As is true of minorities in many other societies, the Montagnard was looked upon as a "second-class citizen." Most Montagnards cooperated with the Allied war effort and U.S. advisers were found in many villages among the people. The Montagnards were superior woodsmen and fought well during the war in Southeast Asia. The Viet Cong and North Vietnamese carried out a deliberate campaign to destroy the Montagnards in areas that the communists wished to occupy without outside observation. The Montagnards, in such circumstances, would simply pack up and move out of harm's way, as their philosophy was to use the land, not to own it.

Montazeri, Ayatollah Hussein Ali. In an act of co-optation, Ayatollah Montazeri was named the future successor of Ayatollah Khomeini (qv) as supreme spiritual leader on 22 November 1985. In 1987, Montazeri's position suffered a setback because of his association with those supporting Mehdi Hashemi, who was executed for corruption. When Khomeini died in 1989, Sayyed Ali Khamenei became the spiritual leader of Iran.

Montenegro, Alejandro. On 17 September 1982, twelve Salvadoran terrorists seized the Chamber of Commerce building in San Pedro Sula, Honduras, taking 107 hostages. They demanded the release of Salvadoran guerrilla leader Alejandro Montenegro, who had been captured by Honduran police on 15 September, and other political prisoners. The siege ended on 25 September without any of their demands being met, and the terrorists were allowed to leave the country for Panama and then Cuba.

Montes, Melida Anaya (aka "Ana Maria"). On 6 April 1983, Melida Anaya Montes, known as "Ana Maria," a leader of El Salvador's rebel alliance, was assassinated in Managua. Montes had apparently been betrayed by a comrade.

Montoneros Group. The Montoneros Group began its existence as an ultra-right-wing Catholic group loyal to the Peron party in Argentina. The group became more left-wing, however, as its terrorist activities increased. By 1973, it was a full-fledged terrorist organization still loyal to the Peronistas, but unsanctioned by that party. After his release from prison (1973), Mario Firmenich became the leader of the Montoneros. The group participated in assassinations, bombings and kidnappings and its membership was counted as approximately 1,000 with hundreds of thousands of supporters. On 26 February 1975, twelve urban guerrillas belonging to the Montoneros group kidnapped the U.S. consul agent in Cordoba, Argentina, John P. Egan (qv), from his home. When the Argentine government refused to negotiate for his release, Egan was murdered, and his body, draped with a Montoneros flag, was left by the side of the road near Cordoba. The right-wing terrorist campaign in Argentina decimated the Montoneros; by the late 1970s, most of the leadership of the group had been caught or killed or had disappeared. The group became almost extinct after 1976, but remnants of the group are still known to operate in consort with the People's Revolutionary Army (ERP) (qv). On 17 September 1980, for instance, the Montoneros assassinated former Nicaraguan president Anastasio Somoza-Debayle (qv) in Asuncion, Paraguay.

Montreal. *See* Canada.

Monzon, Elfego. On 18 June 1954, an anticommunist army led by Colonel Carlos Castillo Armas (qv) invaded Guatemala and ousted the communist-supported government of Jacobo Arbenz Guzman (qv). On 28 June, after Arbenz Guzman had sought sanctuary in the Mexican embassy in Guatemala City, Castillo Armas relinquished power to Colonel Elfego Monzon. Monzon immediately arranged a cease-fire to halt the ongoing fighting and began a roundup of communist leaders. In September, Castillo Armas became president by plebiscite.

Moody Point. *See* Falklands Islands.

Moore, George C. On 1 March 1973, eight Black September (qv) terrorists seized the Saudi embassy in Khartoum, Sudan, during an evening reception. One of those taken hostage was the outgoing U.S. charge d'affaires, George C. Moore. The release of a large group of prisoners held in three countries, including the US, was demanded for their safe return. During the three-day siege, Moore; the US ambassador, Cleo Noel, Jr. (qv); and the Belgian charge d'affaires, Guy Eid (qv), were murdered. Moore had been due to return to the U.S. within days of his capture. The killers surrendered on 4 March and were deported to Egypt and released to the Palestine Liberation Organization (qv) by President Sadat (qv).

Moore, Sara Jane. On 22 September 1975, Sara Jane Moore attempted to assassinate U.S. president Gerald Ford (qv) in San Francisco as he was leaving the St. Francis Hotel. Her aim when she fired was deflected by an alert former U.S. Marine, Oliver Sipple. She was then taken into custody. Moore had been questioned the day before by the Secret Service, which considered her a potential threat. It was later learned that Moore had acted as a police and FBI informant and that she had warned of a protest against the president during his visit. Held on $500,000 bail, she was ordered to undergo psychiatric evaluation after she said she was only testing "the system." She eventually pleaded guilty to charges stemming from the assassination attempt. In January 1976, Moore was sentenced to life in prison.

Morales, Ramón Villeda. Ten days before the scheduled elections, on 3 October 1963, the president of Honduras, Ramon Villeda Morales, was ousted from power by a military coup led by Colonel Osvaldo Lopez Arellano. Morales had been president since 1957, when he was elected as the candidate of the Liberal Party.

Moretti, Mario. On 4 April 1981, the one of the leaders of the outlawed terrorist organization known as the Red Brigades (qv) was captured, along with a number of other Red Brigades members, in connection with the murder of Aldo Moro (qv). Moretti was one of the original leaders of the Red Brigades and had been a left-wing politician in Italy.

Moro, Aldo. (b. 16 September 1916, Maglie, Italy—d. 9 May 1978, Rome [?]) Moro began his career as a lawyer and a professor of law at Bari University in Italy. He entered politics in 1939 and was elected to the Constitutent Assembly in 1946; in 1948 he entered the Chamber of Deputies. He served as minister of justice from 1955 to 1957, as minister of education from 1957 to 1959, and secretary to the chamber from 1959 to1963. Moro became premier of Italy in 1963 and served in that capacity until 1968, when he was appointed foreign minister. In 1974 he served two additional terms as premier. In 1976, Moro left office and became president of the Christian Democrat Party. On 16 March 1978, he was kidnapped in Rome and murdered in or near Rome by 12 terrorists believed to be from the Red Brigades (qv) group. His death was attributed to the government's refusal to negotiate his release in return for 12 Red Brigades members on trial in Turin. His body, riddled with bullets, was discovered on 9 May in the trunk of a car in central Rome. His death set off the most massive police roundup of terrorists in Rome's history.

Morocco (*Al Mamlakah al Maghribiyah*). A country of North Africa, Morocco is bordered on the north by the western Mediterranean, on east and southeast by Algeria, on the south by Western Sahara, and on the west by the Atlantic Ocean. The northernmost tip of Morocco at Tangier forms the southern landfall of the Strait of Gibraltar. The political capital is Rabat. Originally inhabited by Berber tribes, Morocco was subsequently part of the Carthaginian and Roman (first to fifth centuries, A.D.) empires. The Arabs conquered the region in 683 A.D. In the eleventh and twelfth centuries a Berber (Moorish) empire ruled most of North Africa and Spain from Morocco. The western part of Morocco fell under Spanish domination in the nineteenth century; France controlled the rest at the beginning of the twentieth century. Tribal uprisings affected both regions from 1911 until 1933. At one point the British stepped in and issued an ultimatum to Spain that led to the internationalization of Tangier, as London did not want the Spaniards controlling the city directly opposite Gibraltar (1860). A treaty internationalized the city in 1923. This agreement was reestablished by the Allies immediately after World War II. In the early 1900s the Germans also showed an interest in Morocco; during a period of hostilities there between Spain and France (1909–1911), the appearance of a German warship at Agadir created an international crisis. In 1912, the Treaty of Fez granted France a protectorship over its region. In 1944, an organization called *Istiqlal*, or

Independence, arose that demanded the reassertion of the Moroccan monarchy. This helped create a situation of national unrest against the French administration that lasted until 1953, when a French-inspired coup overthrew the rule of Sultan Sidi Mohammed ben Yusuf (Muhammad V) (qv) (14 August 1953), he was deported by the French and replaced by Moulay Mohammed ben Arafa (qv). The French protested this enthronement but without success. In the meantime, however, Berber tribesmen deposed Moulay Mohammed ben Arafa (16 August 1953) and replaced him with Sidi ben Arafa (qv). France accepted this appointment. On 21 January 1954, opposition leaders met and called for the separation of Spanish Morocco and condemned the appointment of the new sultan. France granted Morocco (and Tunisia) more autonomy on 27 August 1954. Violence broke out again in the French colony in August-November 1955. On 27 August 1955, the French government anounced the resignation of the sultan and the governor general, but by 30 August the sultan refused to resign. Finally, on 30 September, Sidi ben Arafa abdicated in favor of Muhammad V, who had been deposed in 1953. Morocco received its independence on 2 March 1956, thus abrogating the Treaty of Fez of 1912, the terms of which returned Tangier to Moroccan control (effective 20 October 1956). France was more than willing to free Morocco, as it had its hands full at the moment in Algeria. Spain recognized Moroccan independence on 7 April 1956 and relinquished its control over Spanish Morocco. On 30 March 1957, Morocco signed a treaty of alliance and friendship with Tunisia. A major revolt in the Spanish enclave of Infi in November 1957 required the use of army troops to quell. Infi was ceded to Morocco in 1969. On 1 October 1958, Morocco joined the Arab League (qv). An army revolt began on 21 October, when forces loyal Mohammed V (now king) were attacked by central government forces. The revolt spread to Rif tribesmen who were dissatified with the *Istiqlal* Party (qv) rule. The Rif uprising lasted until April 1960. On 22 November 1959, U.S. president Dwight Eisenhower (qv) agreed to a demand of King Mohammed for the removal of all U.S. military installations in Morocco by the end of 1963. Withdrawal began in March 1960. Morocco withdrew its troops from the UN peacekeeping force in Congo at the end of 1960. On 7 January 1961, Morocco joined other African states in forming the Organization of African States based on a NATO formula. This became known as the Charter of Casablanca (qv). By August, the last Spanish troops had left Moroccan territory. On 30 September, the French base at Marrakesh was turned over to Moroccan control, thus ending French hegemony in the region. In 1962, Moroccan gave a rebel Mauritanean army the right to stay on its territory. When the army invaded Mauritania (qv), it was driven back. In October 1963, fighting broke out between Moroccan and Algerian forces . Egyptian forces were brought up to reinforce the Algerians. The fighting, quite heavy at times, lasted more than a month. A cease-fire that was arranged through the good offices of Emperor Haile Selassie (qv) of Ethiopia and President Modibo Keita (qv) of Mali went into effect on 20 February 1964. When West Germany recognized Israel in May 1965, Morocco refused to join the ten other Muslim nations that broke diplomatic relations with Bonn. On 30 May 1967, however, Morocco promised aid to the United Arab Republic (UAR) when war against Israel seemed inevitable. Infi, the last Spanish enclave, was ceded to Morocco on 30 June 1969. On 10–11 July 1971, a right-wing army coup against King Hassan II (qv) was suppressed with great bloodshed. A group of disgruntled generals had induced trainees from the Ahermoumou Training Center to attack the guests at the royal birthday party at the seaside palace at Skhirat. A number of dignitaries, including three Moroccan generals and the Belgian ambassador, were among those killed. Four other generals and a number of junior officers were executed in the coup's aftermath. King Hassan II escaped an assassination attempt on 16 August 1972, when Moroccan jets strafed his plane as he returned to Rabat from a visit to France. The leader of the coup, Defense Minister General Muhammad Oufkir, then committed suicide. The country withstood a Libyan-inspired rebel "invasion" on 2 March 1973. Later that year, on 30 August, 157 Moroccans were put on trial accused of plotting the overthrow of the government. Sixteen were executed as a result. Morocco joined other Arab countries in declaring the Palestine Liberation Organization (PLO) to be the only legitimate representative of the Palestinian people on 29 October 1974. On 8 February 1975, Spanish warships were dispatched to the Spanish enclaves of Ceuta and Melilla on the Mediterranean coast after the Moroccan government lay claim to them. In October, the Spanish position toward Morocco stiffened, and the Madrid government announced its intention to intervene directly in the troubles in Spanish Sahara. However, on 14 November 1975, Spain announced it would hand over administration of Spanish Morocco to Morocco and Mauritania. The turnover was completed on 26 February 1976. On 28 January 1976, fighting was reported between Moroccan and Algerian forces near the strategically important town of Amgala. Algerian forces captured the town but later lost it back to Moroccan control. This incident followed by three days (25 January) the shooting down of a U.S.–built Moroccan F-5 fighter by a Soviet-built surface-to-air missile belonging to the Popular Front for the Liberation of Saquia el Hamra and Rio de Oro (Polisario) (qv). A cease-fire was arranged in the Morocco-Algeria dispute on 5 February, but a week later the Egyptian- brokered truce fell apart and more fighting took place. On 8 June 1976, Morocco moved to support Mauritania after Polisario guerrilla forces attacked that country's capital city of Nouakchott. That same month, U.S. military transports carried Moroccan and Senegalese troops into Shaba Province, Zaire. On 16 January 1977, Morocco was accused of allowing the basing and training of the mercenary force that attempted an overthrow of the government in Benin (*see* Benin). In retaliation, Morocco suspended its association with the Organization of African Unity (OAU) on 27 February. In April 1977, about 1,500 Moroccan troops were sent to Zaire after Morocco, along with Communist China, promised to aid the Zaire government in its fight against rebel forces in Shaba Province. French aircraft ferried the troops to Zaire. The Moroccan mission in Zaire was concluded on 22 May. On 30 September 1978, the last U.S. military base, the U.S. Naval Communication Station at Kenitra, was turned over to Morocco. Morocco accepted Nigerian mediation in the ongoing dispute over Spanish (Western) Sahara on 2 October 1978. Polisario attacks continued throughout this period. On 16 December, Algeria accused Morocco of supplying weapons to Algerian rebels. On 15 August 1979, Morocco annexed Western Sahara, the day after Moroccan troops were withdrawn from Mauritania and Mauritania renounced of claims to that region. On 3 September, Egyptian president Anwar Sadat (qv) offered military aid to Morocco in its struggle against Polisario. On 22 October, the U.S. announced the sale of reconnaissance aircraft and helicopter gunships to Morocco. Two days later, France sent a token force of 150 troops to Mauritania as a warning to Morocco and the Polisario. Mauritania broke diplomatic relations with Morocco on 16–17 March 1981, after accusing Rabat of complicity in a failed coup attempt. Moroccan diplomatic relations with Libya were restored on 29 July after a long break. After a major Polisario attack on the Moroccan garrison at Guelta Zemmour, 25 miles from the Mauritanian border, Rabat accused Mauritania of harboring the rebels. A Polisario announcement on 18 April 1982 indicated they would get arms from the Soviet Union if the U.S. continued to supply weapons to Morocco. The United States announced an agreement with Morocco on 27 May that would allow American use of Moroccan air bases in case of a crisis in the Middle East. Morocco signed a "union of states" agreement with Libya on 13 August 1984. On 12 November 1984, Nigeria recognized Polisario in its continuing struggle against Morocco in Western Sahara. A UN-mandated peace between Morocco and the Polisario was finally achieved on 6 September 1991. In the 1990–1991 war against Iraq; popular sentiment favored Iraq; however, some 1,200 troops were sent to Saudi Arabia, but were not employed in the actual Desert Shield/Storm operations. Affairs in Algeria directly affected Morocco in 1992. The assassination of Muhammad Boudafi (*see* Algeria) complicated the settlement of the Western Sahara issue, but the new Algerian leadership did not appear ready to continue support of the Polisario movement. At the UN, Morocco was able to block many initiatives supported by Polisario even though the UN announced it would withdraw its peacekeeping forces by the end of the year, if a settlement could not be reached. While elections held the attention of Morocco in 1993, the Western Sahara issue was still a dominant factor. Relations with Algeria remained strained over the issue, and although negotiations continued, the sticking point of a new census could not be settled. By 1994 the issues involved in the Western Sahara situation were still unresolved. The United Nations Security Council decided on a move to continue negotiations and to complete the registration of voters who would decide the future of the region. All agreed except Polisario, and although the registration proceeded, there was no guarantee that its completion could be expected in the near future, at least until 1996. At the same time Morocco was beset with strained relations with its neighbors. particularly over the Western Sahara issue, and with Islamic fundamentalist activities in the eastern part of Morocco. In the latter region, two Spanish tourists were killed in August, prompting a series of events that culminated in the Algerian decision to close its border with Morocco. The Western Sahara issue continued into 1995, while Morocco underwent economic problems that did not bode well for the future. *Reading:* Will D. Swearingen, *Moroccan Mirages: Agrarian Dreams and Deceptions, 1912-1986* (1987); Henk Driessen, *On the Spanish-Morocco Frontier: A Study in Ritual, Power and Ethnicity* (1992); Stephanie Bernard, *The Franco-Moroccan Conflict, 1943-1956* (1968); Dwight Ling, *Morocco and Tunisia: A Comparative History* (1976).

Moron. *See* Argentina.

Moro National Liberation Front. A Muslim organization, the Moro National Liberation Front sought as its avowed goal the complete independence of the Muslim-inhabited areas of the Philippines. The term "Moro" relates to the nine different Philippine linguistic groups that profess the Sunni branch of Islam. Approximately 91 percent of all Moro Muslims inhabit the island of Mindinao in the southern portion of the country. During the Spanish hegemony, the Moro were able to resist conquest for more than three centuries. A Moro uprising was a part of the Philippine insurrection against the United States in the early 1900s. In the 1960s and 1970s, the Moro National Liberation Front movement gained prominence. President Ferdinand Marcos lumped all insurgency under the communist banner at the time. There were numerous clashes between Philippine army troops and the insurgents in 1973–1974. A plan for amnesty was established, but it was abandoned in April 1973 when less than 250 Muslim rebels turned themselves in. As the fighting grew in intensity, Islamic groups in other countries sought to end the struggle by negotiation. The Marcos government claimed to have established a peace plan that was to lead to a cease-fire on 14 August 1975. The overall plan was to have conceded certain territories to the Moro, but on 11 September 1975 the Moro National Liberation Front repudiated the agreement and vowed to continue fighting until complete autonomy was won. Fighting continued into 1977, when an entire Philippine military team of 34 men was wiped out in an ambush on Jolo Island on 10 October. By 1979, a number of the Moro leaders stated that they no longer sought autonomy but that their goal was independence. Marco continued blaming the Muslims and communists for all the troubles in the land. On 1 June 1984, the Philippine government claimed the Moro conflict was virtually over. The Muslim insurgents signed a truce agreement with the new Philippine government of Corazon Aquino on 5 September 1986.

Morrison, Norman. On 2 November 1965, Norman Morrison, a 31-year-old Quaker, set himself on fire in front of the Pentagon to commit suicide to protest the war in Southeast Asia. Eight days later another self-immolation (Roger LaPorte, a pacifist) took place in front of the United Nations building in New York City.

Moscow. *See* Soviet Union.

Moscow-Vienna Train. On 28 September 1973, two Palestinian terrorists of the *al-Sa'iga* (Thunderbolt) group hijacked the Moscow-Vienna train and took three Jewish passengers and an Austrian customs agent hostage at Vienna's airport. The terrorists demanded that the Schonau Castle Jewish transit point be closed and that Austria restrict Jewish emigrant travel. On 29 September the Austrian government acceded to the terrorist demands and promised to halt Jewish emigration to Israel through Austria and to close the Schonau Castle facility in return for the release of the hostages. The hostages were released, and the terrorists were allowed to leave Austria. International criticism of the government's action forced Chancellor Bruno Kreisky to revoke the decision and to promise to speed Jewish emigrant transit through Austria. Schonau Castle was closed in December, but the Austrians promised to care for Jewish emigrants at another location.

Moshoeshoe II. On 30 January 1970, Prime Minister Chief Leabua Jonathan (qv) overthrew the rule of King Moshoeshoe II of Lesotho. Moshoeshoe went into exile on 31 March, but he returned to Lesotho on 4 December 1970 and reassumed his rule after promising not to interfere in the parliamentary elections.

Moslems. *See* Muslims.

Mossadegh, Mohammed. (b. 1880, Tehran, Iran—d.5 March 1967, Tehran) Mossadegh was born the son of a former minister of finance. Before completing his education he served for a time as the treasurer of Khurasan province. He then studied law in Switzerland, where he received his degree in 1914. Returning to Persia (Iran), he was appointed governor general of Fars but, in February 1921, refused to accept the new government formed under Reza Khan and Sayyid Zia ad-Din. One year later, when a new government was formed, Mossadegh became the minister of finance. Later, in 1922, he became the governor general of Azerbaijan, but he soon resigned after conflicts with the military. In 1923, he became minister of foreign affairs. In 1924, Mossadegh was elected to the Iranian Parliament (*Majlis*) as the deputy for Tehran. He fought the new ruler, Reza Pahlavi (qv), in 1925, and quit the government. In 1944, he was again elected to Parliament and became prominent for his fight against granting the USSR oil concessions in northern Iran. In 1951, he was instrumental in passing the Oil Nationalization Act. He was also appointed prime minister on 30 April 1951 and became embroiled in a dispute with Great Britain (September 1951) which led to the withdrawal of the Anglo-Iranian Oil Company from Iran. When he could not find markets for Iranian oil, Iran bordered on financial ruin. He resigned as prime minister on 17 July 1952, but he was quickly returned to office. Partially in response and partially because of irrational behavior traits that he began to manifest, he attempted to gain dictatorial powers. This strained his credibility with the shah. In August 1953, after the shah had fled the country, Mossadegh was overthrown by a CIA-financed military coup and was tried and sentenced to three years at hard labor. He was subsequently released and went into retirement until his death in 1967.

Mossamedes (Mocamedes). *See* Angola.

Mosul. *See* Iraq.

Mountbatten, Lord Louis. (b. 25 June 1900, Windsor, England—d. 27 August 1979, off the coast of Ireland) Mountbatten was born the great-grandson of Queen Victoria. His father was Prince Louis of Battenburg, who served as First Lord of the British Admiralty in 1914. Francis Albert Victor Nicholas (Louis) Mountbatten joined the navy in 1913. When World War II began he was in command of a British destroyer (*HMS Kelly*) and the 5th Destroyer Flotilla. He took command of the aircraft carrier HMS Illustrious, and, as an acting admiral, became the Supreme Allied Commander, Southeast Asia (China-Burma-India theater). Here, he was successful in the recapture of Burma. He became viceroy and later governor general of India in 1947–1948 and was successful in negotiating the partition of India and Pakistan. From 1950 to 1952 he was Fourth Lord of the Admiralty, and from 1955 to 1959 was First Lord. He was created a viscount in 1946 and an earl in 1947. In 1956 he was appointed admiral of the fleet. On 27 August 1979, his fishing boat was blown up and he was killed, off the coast of Sligo, Ireland, by terrorists of the Provisional Wing of the IRA.

Mt. Grommos. *See* Greece.

Mt. Handran. *See* Iraq.

Mt. Harriet. *See* Falkland Islands.

Mt. Hermon (Hill 2814 - *Jabal esh Sheikh*). *See* Syria.

Mt. Kent. *See* Falkland Islands.

Mt. Kenya. *See* Kenya.

Mt. Lebanon. *See* Lebanon.

Mt. Longdon. *See* Falkland Islands.

Mt. Low. *See* Falkland Islands.

Mt. Serti. *See* Iraq.

Mt. Sinai. *See* Israel.

Mt. Tumbledown. *See* Falkland Islands.

Mt. Two Sisters. *See* Falkland Islands.

Mt. William. *See* Falkland Islands.

Mouvement Populaire pour le Guadeloupe Independente. In early 1985, pro-independence groups on the French Caribbean island of Guadaloupe (qv) carried out a campaign of agitation against French rule, which culminated in a bombing that killed three people, including an American tourist. Several leaders of these opposition groups were arrested. One of those arrested was Luc Reinette, the leader of the Caribbean Revolutionary Alliance. Reinette escaped from jail in June. In July, a week-long general strike and violent street demonstrations were staged. On 25 July, rioting broke out in Pointe-a-Pitre, when the demonstrators demanded the release of of the leader of the banned *Mouvement Populaire pour le Guadaloupe Independente*, Georges Faisans (qv), who was imprisoned in France. The violence subsided on 29 July when Faisans was released pending an appeal of his case.

***Movimiento de Accion Revolucionaria* (MAR).** In 1971, President Luis Echeverria Alvarez of Mexico was beginning to see the results of the reforms he had imposed during his first year in office. Several extremist political groups were not satified, however; and, on 15 March 1971, a plot to overthrow the government by one of these groups, the MAR, was reported to have been uncovered. The leader and ten members of the group were arrested on charges of subversion, and five Soviet diplomats were expelled. The MAR was reported to have been recruited by Moscow and to have been sent to North Korea for

Marxist terrorist training. The MAR began its campaign on 27 September 1971, with the broad-daylight kidnapping of Julio Hirschfield Armada, the head of Mexico's Civil Aviation Service in Mexico City. Hirschfield was released two days later after a ransom of three million pesos (US$250,000) was paid.

Mozambique. About the size of Texas, Mozambique is located in southeastern Africa. It is bordered by Tanzania on the north; by the Indian Ocean's Mozambique Channel (which separates it from Madagascar) on the east; by Malawi, Zambia and Zimbabwe on the west and Swaziland and South Africa on the south. The capital city is Maputo, located at the southern tip of the country. In 1505 the Portuguese established a way station there to service their trade routes with the Orient. Mozambique remained the the seat of the colonial government of Portuguese East Africa until 1897, when its importance began to decline. Portuguese dominance remained, however, into the mid-twentieth century. In 1962, a 12-year rebellion, led primarily by the *Frente de Liberatacao de Mocambique* (Frelimo), began against the Portuguese colonial government. Frelimo forces were, for the large part, based and supplied from Tanzania. On 14 April 1972, in one incident, Tanzanian air defense units shot down a Portuguese reconnaissance plane attempting to locate Frelimo bases along the border. In 1973, there were clear indications that the Soviet Union was supplying arms to Frelimo. On 24 March 1974, Sweden announced it was tripling its aid to the Frelimo guerrillas fighting Portugal. Immediately following a military coup in Portugal on 25 April 1974, the new government ordered the release of hundreds of captured Frelimo rebels held in Mozambique. The Portuguese civil government in Mozambique resigned en masse when it became known (25 July) that the new Portuguese government was about to replace them with a military junta. Frelimo took over administrative control of the country on 20 September 1974 and was able to crush a revolt by rebellious soldiers and police on 18 December of that year. The new Maoist-style government led by Samora Macel (Machel) (qv) was established when Mozambique became independent, after 470 years of Portuguese rule, and immediately began the communization of the country. On 4 February 1975, for instance, even before independence, the right to privately owned property had been abolished. In March 1976, the government closed its border with Rhodesia (Zimbabwe) at the request of the British government to deprive the breakaway Rhodesian government of access to the sea (*see* Rhodesia). A border war followed in which hundreds died. On 8 August 1976, for instance, a Rhodesian raiding party wiped out a guerrilla base inside Mozambique, killing at least 300–600 black rebels. On 16 February 1977, Rhodesia established a military zone along its border with Mozambique to halt further rebel infiltration. In April 1977, U.S. intelligence sources discovered additional evidence that the USSR was supplying arms to Mozambique. Rhodesian forces crossed the Mozambique border on 29–31 May and raided several guerrilla bases in the southern part of the country. On 31 May, they captured the town of Mapai, on the Limpopo river, nearly 100 miles inland from the border. The Rhodesians withdrew on 2 June, leaving 20 dead rebels behind. On 29 June, Mozambique appealed to the United

Nations for protection against further Rhodesian aggression. Rhodesian aircraft attacked 25 ZAPU (Zimbabwe African People's Union) (*see* Zimbabwe) bases in Mozambique on 22–25 September 1978. In September 1979, Rhodesian forces carried out ground attacks against a ZAPU base 50 miles inside Mozambique. By the end of the year, the cease-fire that had been installed broke down once again, and Lord Soames (qv), the British governor of Rhodesia, ordered troops into Mozambique. Mozambique was also beset by internal security problems. On 11 July 1980, the government sent forces to occupy the main rebel camp of the Mozambique National Resistance Movement (Renamo) (qv) . At least 300 rebels were captured in addition to 273 killed. Continued troubles with South Africa found the USSR promising military aid if that country invaded Mozambique (21 February 1981). More internal trouble for Mozambique occurred in January 1983, when rebels blew up the vital Beira-Mutare pipeline that supplied oil to Zimbabwe. As the internal guerrilla fighting and the effects of famine ravaged the country, Zimbabwe reported almost 100,000 refugees had fled across the border by 25 February 1984. On 18 March the government did sign a nonaggression pact, the Treaty of Nkomati (qv) in which each side agreed to stop helping rebels operating against the other side. In May, the South African government agreed to supply Mozambique with military forces to help guard the electric transmission lines of the Cabora Bassa hydroelectric system from Renamo attack. On 3 October 1984, a cease-fire was agreed upon by the government and the MNR. South Africa was asked to monitor the truce. However, the bloodshed was not over; on 6 August 1985, the MNR gunned down 33 people during a funeral procession in Tete province near the Malawi border. On 18 September 1985, the South African foreign minister, Roelof F. Botha, admitted his government was supporting MNR guerrillas in Mozambique in violation of the Nkomati treaty . Throughout the remainder of the 1980s severe drought and continued internal warfare caused severe loss of life. In 1989, however, the Marxist-Leninist philosophy of government was abandoned, and a new constitution was put in place on 30 November 1990. A peace agreement was signed with Renamo on 4 October 1992. However, the peace agreement was proving unworkable in 1993. The UN representative, Aldo Ajello, recommended that multiparty elections scheduled for October be delayed until at least June 1994, because of the destabilizing situation. Both the government and Renamo agreed to this proposal, but this was about as far as agreement between the sides was able to move. The UN reported in May 1993 that Renamo had not yet demobilized its forces and apparently felt no urgency about doing so. At the same time, various minor opposition groups formed a coalition demanding the establishment of an interim government to hold power until the election. This was unacceptable to the government, and the chasm between the sides widened and deepened. By December, however, Renamo did begin the demobilization of its forces following the intervention of the UN secretary general. Mozambique announced general elections for the end of October 1994. Even before the elections, both sides were crying foul. When the election was held, the government candidate, Joaquim Chissano, won, and

Renamo accepted the results. In the meantime work on combining the two armed forces moved ahead, albeit sporadically. Not much was said about the repatriation of refigees during the year. The resolution of that problem was one of the few highlights of 1995. Mozambique's financial stabilization was another, and Renamo's grudging acceptance of a subordinate, but powerful, role in the new government may be seen as a third. In 1995, Mozambique also became the first country not a former British colony to join the Commonwealth of Nations. *Reading:* James Ciment, *Angola and Mozambique: Postcolonial Wars in Southern Africa* (1997); Malun Newitt, *A History of Mozambique* (1995); David Birmingham, *Frontline Nationalism in Angola and Mozambique* (1993).

MR8. On 4 September 1969, the U.S. ambassador to Brazil, C. Burke Elbrick, was kidnapped on the street in Rio de Janeiro by the revolutionary terrorist group "MR8." It demanded the release of 15 political prisoners held in Brazilian jails. The ransom demands were met, and on 7 September, Elbrick was released unharmed.

Mubarak, Muhammad Hosni. (b. 1929, Menoufia Province, Egypt) Born into poverty, Mubarak was able to graduate from the Egyptian Military Academy in 1949 and was commissioned in the air force. He became friends with Anwar as-Sadat (qv) in the early 1950s, when they both were stationed at the El Arish military base. From 1952 until 1961, although outspokenly anticommunist, Mubarak attended several flight schools in the Soviet Union, where he trained as a bomber pilot. He was promoted to general in 1969 and became air force chief of staff. In 1972, he was appointed (by Sadat) as air force commander in chief and deputy minister of war. Mubarak was instrumental in planning the 1973 October attack on Israel and became as a result one of Sadat's closest advisers. In February 1974, Mubarak was appointed air marshal, and in April 1975, he became Sadat's vice president. In 1978, he became the vice president of the ruling National Democratic Party. As Sadat became more involved in the attempted peace process, Mubarak assumed more of the day-to-day operations of the nation. When Sadat was assassinated on 6 October 1981, Mubarak was confirmed as his successor. One of his first major acts of international diplomacy was to inform Israel that Egypt would stand by the Camp David Accords. Internally, Mubarak began a reshuffling of government to rid it of a few corrupt officials. In February 1983, Mubarak became convinced that Libya was about to attack Sudan and asked the U.S. for surveillance aircraft (AWACS) to overwatch the situation. At the same time the U.S. carrier *Nimitz* was ordered into Egyptian waters. In August 1984, Mubarak accused Libya and Iran of mining the Red Sea and the Gulf of Suez. Although both denied the allegations, some 15 ships were damaged before U.S., British, French and Italian minesweeping forces cleared the two areas. In February 1985, Mubarak displayed great statesmanship when he asked the U.S. to host a meeting among Jordanian, Palestinian and Israeli delegates to discuss peace in the Middle East. By 1986, Islamic fundamentalism had gained a foothold in Egypt and was challenging the Mubarak government. Murbarak also faced rising internal dissatisfaction among paramilitary security force conscripts, who rioted near

Giza, destroying local hotels and nightclubs. Mubarak ordered a crackdown on the fundamentalists in April. At the same time, Egypt's economic distress deepened. As Egypt's position in the Arab world strengthened during 1987–1988, Mubarak was able to concentrate on the economic situation and in August requested the Palestine Liberation Organization to moderate its guerrilla campaign. When Iraq invaded Kuwait in 1990, Mubarak first tried diplomacy, then ordered Egyptian forces into the coalition arrayed against Iraq. By 1993, Mubarak again faced rising Islamic fundamentalist activity that all but destroyed the country's tourist trade. This activity, which continued into 1994, brought harsh reaction from the Mubarak government, but this did not overshadow the praise he won for hosting the signing of the accords on the Gaza Strip and Jericho that brightened the Arab-Israeli future.

Mudag Region. *See* Somalia.

el-Mufti, Said. When Jordanian Premier Samir el-Rafai resigned on 21 May 1956, Said el-Mufti was appointed in his place as caretaker. The new premier's first move was to renegotiate the Anglo-Jordanian defense alliance. Five days after his appointment, the Arab Legion was disbanded and absorbed into the regular Jordanian forces. El-Mufti, who tendered his resignation on 30 June 1956, was replaced by an anti-Western, pro-Egyptian government on 22 October.

Mugabe, Robert. (b. 21 February 1924, Kutama, Rhodesia) Born the son of a laborer, Mugabe received a Roman Catholic education and became a teacher. He was politicized by the stern economic measures imposed on the teaching profession and went to South Africa to continue his own education at the University of Hare. From 1956 until 1960 he taught in Ghana. He then returned to Rhodesia and joined Joshua Nkomo's (qv) Zimbabwe African People's Union (ZAPU). He soon broke with Nkomo, however, and helped the Reverend Ndabaningi Sithole (qv) found the Zimbabwe African National Union (ZANU). He was arrested in 1964 and imprisoned until 1974. During his incarceration he studied law and received his degree from the University of London. In 1974 he went into exile in Mozambique and became the political advisor to the military wing of ZANU, which was based there. He then joined Nkomo in the Patriotic Front (ZAPU and ZANU) in the struggle against the government of Rhodesia. He attended the Lancaster House conference in London that brought about the end of the war in Rhodesia. The Patriotic Front then dissolved as ZANU decided to field its own candidates in the elections to be held in Rhodesia. On 18 April 1980, Rhodesia became independent of the British crown and renamed itself Zimbabwe. Mugabe's party won a clear majority in the elections, and he was named prime minister. Mugabe, always thought to be a Marxist, proved his critics wrong by forming a coalition government of both blacks and whites. At the same time, Mugabe also placed Zimbabwe in the nonaligned Third World camp, but looked to the West for economic and other support. On 4 July 1980, Mugabe ordered the South African diplomatic mission in Salisbury closed after it was disclosed that it was being used for recruitment of troops to help destabilize black governments in Africa. Mugabe found himself faced with a major crisis in February 1981 when troops loyal to his Zimbabwe

African National Liberation Army (ZANLA) fought the forces of the Zimbabwe People's Revolutionary Army sworn to Joshua Nkomo (9–17 February). Over 300 people were killed in the fighting. On 17 February 1982, Mugabe dismissed Nkomo from the coalition government after evidence implicating Nkomo in a plot to overthrow the government was disclosed. In February 1984, Mugabe ordered troops into Matabeleland Province where rebels, allegedly trained in South Africa, were setting up base camps among the Ndebele tribe. Political opponents claimed, however, that the military action was against the Ndebele themselves because of the opposition to Mugabe's government. In 1985, Mugabe used his power (ZANU) to emasculate Nkomo's (ZAPU) political campaign through abductions and other terrorist acts. Mugabe's political problems continued into 1987, when the state of emergency that had been put into effect during the Matabele crisis in 1984 was extended. By 1987, the emergency had expanded along the length of the Mozambique border. On 22 September, the Mugabe government had ordered a suspension of all ZAPU activities, which lasted until 22 December, when ZANU and ZAPU were formally united. On 31 December 1987, Mugabe became executive president of Zimbabwe. A socialist government structure was instituted in Zimbabwe, and Mugabe's tenure in the presidency continued into 1995. *See* Zimbabwe.

Mugia Pass, North Vietnam. *See* Vietnam.

Mukden (Shenyang). *See* China.

Munich, West Germany. *See* Germany.

Munsan. *See* Korea.

Muong Soui. *See* Laos.

Murmansk. *See* Soviet Union.

Murunkan. *See* Sri Lanka.

Mururoa Atoll. A French-held atoll in the Pacific Ocean, Mururoa is 750 miles southeast of Tahiti in French Polynesia. Beginning in July 1966, the French began atmospheric testing of nuclear weapons on the atoll. From 2 July until 4 October, when the series terminated, five tests were made. A number of nearby countries protested the tests, but the French ignored them. On 24 August 1968, the French detonated a two-megaton thermonuclear device on the island and ran another similar test on 8 September of that year. By June 1972, the French announcement of another series of tests brought a storm of protest from around the world, but the tests went on. On 22 June 1973, the International Court of Justice issued an injunction sought by Australia and New Zealand forbidding further testing at Mururoa. The French ignored the court order, claiming the court had no jurisdiction in the matter. Thereafter, on 21 July, New Zealand ordered one of its naval frigates into the waters near the atoll. On 5 August, the ship was withdrawn because of resupply difficulties. On 22 July, the French government had announced a continuation of its testing program at Mururoa and detonated the first weapon in the series, a miniaturized warhead for a submarine missile. Four more tests followed before the series ended on 28 August. However, on 29 August a new series began with the detonation of a small-yield bomb. Another test took place on 26 July 1974, followed by another shot on 25

August. On 15 September, the eighth detonation in three months took place. More tests took place in early 1976, and in December an underground test was conducted. Tests of this nature went on into 1985, when a 150-kiloton weapon was detonated on 10 May. On 10 July 1985, French agents sunk the Greenpeace ship *Rainbow Warrior* (qv) in Auckland harbor, New Zealand, as it was being readied to sail to Mururoa to protest any more nuclear tests. In spite of the furor caused by the sinking, France's president Mitterand (qv) announced on 13 September that testing would continue at Mururoa. It was later ascertained that among the tests were neutron weapons. On 24 October, another Greenpeace vessel was seized by French commandos in what the government said were restricted waters near the atoll. Seven Greenpeace members were taken into custody by the French. Also, in August 1985, the island republic of Vanuatu called for a nuclear-free zone in the Pacific. France continued testing in 1986–1987. In 1988, France announced it would begin nuclear testing at an additional site at Fangataufa near Mururoa. France's relations with the countries of Oceania continued to deteriorate as evidence mounted that the continued testing was seriously weakening the atoll and raising the chances of major radiation leaks into the surrounding ocean. Still the testing went on into 1989, despite the growing evidence of a potential ecological disaster.

Musa Sadr Brigade. On 11 September 1984, two Lebanese terrorists of the Shi'ite Musa Sadr Brigade based in Beirut wounded a Libyan diplomatic mission employee in Madrid, Spain. A Libyan exile group, *Al Burkan* (Volcano), also took credit for the attack.

Muscat. *See* Oman.

Museveni, Yoweri Kaguta. (b. 1944, Ntungamo, Uganda) Born of Rwandan refugee parents, Museveni was educated in Uganda and, from 1966 to 1970, attended the University College at Dar es Salaam, Tanzania, where he majored in political science. In Tanzania, he worked with the Mozambique Liberation Front (Frelimo). This would serve Museveni later, as Frelimo won its war and would later provide sanctuary and supplies for Museveni's war. Upon his return to Uganda, he served on Milton Obote's (qv) staff prior to the Obote government's being overthrown by Idi Amin (qv) in 1971 (*see* Uganda). At that time, Museveni fled to Tanzania. There he joined forces with Obote, and the two led an ill-fated invasion of Uganda (1972). The defeat led to a rift between the two leaders, after which Museveni formed the Front for National Salvation. In 1979, the group participated in the overthrow of Amin. Museveni was named minister of defense in the new transitional government, but the next months saw a falling out among the cabinet. Museveni then formed the Uganda Patriotic Movement (UPM) to participate in the 1980 elections. Upon losing the election, Museveni launched a guerrilla campaign against Obote, who had won the election. The formation of the National Resistance Army followed, and a war lasting five years ensued. On 17 December 1985, Museveni signed a pact with General Tito Okello (qv) by which the rebels and the government agreed to share power and combine the two military forces. Kenya's president, Daniel Arap Moi (qv), negotiated the agreement. After his troops marched into the capital, however, Museveni was sworn in as president of a pro-Western government on 29 January 1986. Civil war in Uganda continued, and Museveni found himself arrayed against forces still loyal to Okello and Obote. In November 1987, Museveni withstood an attempt to overthrow led by Alice Lakwena, who claimed to have been ordered to do so by God. Following a border dispute that flared up with Kenya in December, Museveni met with Moi, and the two were able to settle the incident by peaceful terms. In January 1988, following an incident in which a Libyan diplomat was killed by rebels, Museveni called upon all rebel groups to lay down their arms. By February, however, at least 19 had been killed and 47 injured in rebel attacks. By late 1988, the fighting had subsided but not died out. In 1990, Museveni was elected chairman of the Organization of African Unity (OAU) for that year. In 1991, Museveni was accused by Rwanda of engineering an invasion of its territory by Tutsi officers in the Ugandan army. That same year, the level of disturbances in the northern and southwestern provinces intensified. In January 1991, Kenya's Moi accused Museveni of having a direct hand in the Rwandan troubles (*see* Rwanda). Clashes along the Rwanda border intensified into September.

Musko Island. *See* Sweden.

Muslims (Moslems). Those who believe in or adhere to Islam are called Muslims. The popular form of the word is *.Moslem*, but *Muslim* appears favored by scholars. Islam was founded in 611 A.D., when the Prophet Mohammed (Muhammad) declared a revelation from the one true God at Mecca that called upon him to repudiate all pagan idolatry and surrender to the will of *Allah* (God's Will). The teachings of Islam, the body of law, are set forth in the *Koran (Qur'an)* (The Word of God) and incorporate Christian, Judaic and numerous Arabic pagan traditions. Islam calls for submission to *Allah*. The religion has grown and spread throughout the world, especially in Asia and Africa, from those times until today, when it claims more than one billion adherents. The Koran also has a political message in that it details how men should live in a community and how they may wage holy war *(Jihad)*, especially against nonbelievers. Although there are number of sects within Islam that formed as a result of controversy, the two sects of importance today are the *Sunni*, as represented by most Arab states, and the *Shi'ia*, generally represented by Iran. Although Muslim antipathy is aimed at the outside world, especially Israel and the United States, sufficient animosity exists among the various sects that violence has often erupted and continues to erupt among the believers.

Mutesa, Sir Edward Frederick William Walugembe Mutebi Luwangula (Mutesa II - King (36th Kabaka of Buganda) of Uganda). (b. 19 November 1924. Mengo, Kampala, Uganda—d. 21 November 1969, London) Uganda, a former British colony in Africa, was led by the *Kabaka of Buganda*, Edward Mutesa, since 1942. Subsequent to his enthronement he completed his formal education at Cambridge. His early reign was marked by a program of unifying Uganda through popular elections and by his policy of assuring his continuation in power. This latter policy and also his support of the independence movement in his country led to his deportation by the British authorities in 1953. He was allowed to return in 1955 and subsequently took part in the constitutional discussions that led to Ugandan independence 9 October 1962. Mutesa was elected president on 9 October 1963. His open hostility to left-wing and Pan-African movements led to his overthrow by his prime minister, Milton Obote, on 2 March 1966. When Obote's troops occupied the Ugandan capital, Kampala, on 23–24 May 1966, Mutesa escaped to England, where he resided in London until his death in 1969.

Mutshatsha. *See* Zaire.

Mutual and Balanced Force Reduction (MBFR). The question of the use of nuclear weapons in a war between the West and the East was a key issue in the negotiations between NATO and Warsaw Pact agreed upon on 31 January 1973 and begun on 30 October 1973. These talks centered upon the reduction of conventional forces, especially those of the two superpowers, stationed on the European continent, but other considerations were also discussed. The negotiations dragged on with numerous interruptions and very little accomplishment. The MBFR talks were but one occasion of a series of multilateral talks and conferences that centered on arms control. The Strategic Arms Limitation Treaty (SALT) (qv) talks were another. The talks became moot with the collapse of the Soviet Union, but not the issues behind them, which still exist.

Mutual Defense Assistance Act. On 6 October 1949, President Harry S. Truman (qv) signed the Mutual Defense Assistance Act, which made more than one billion dollars available to the members of the newly organized NATO. At least $1.3 billion was expended on the plan. With these funds for arms and services, NATO was able to move forward, but it was not yet capable of fielding a military force, even though the NATO committee had approved an integrated plan. One use of these funds was in support of the French in Indochina in 1954.

Muwanga, Paulo. On 1 August 1985, Paulo Muwanga, a former vice-president in the ousted Obote government of Uganda, was sworn in as prime minister. Three weeks later he was fired and replaced by Abraham Waligo. *See* Uganda.

Muzorewa, Abel Tendekayi. (b. 14 April 1925, Umtali, Rhodesia) Muzorewa was educated in Methodist schools in Rhodesia, and then spent five years (1958–1963) in the Central Methodist College in Fayette, Missouri, and at Scarritt College, Tennessee. Returning to Rhodesia, he worked as a teacher and pastor until, in 1968, he became bishop of the United Methodist Church. During this time, he preached moderation but also insisted on black rule for his country. On 29 May 1979, during the transition to self-rule, Bishop Muzorewa was installed as the first black prime minister of Zimbabwe. The next day, Muzorewa appointed himself minister of defense. Muzorewa remained in office until 7 December, upon which day Zimbabwe reverted for a short time to British colonial status (two days after a cease-fire had been arranged). When Zimbabwe became independent on 17 April 1980, elections were held, but Muzorewa was not returned to office.

Mwambutsa, Mwami (Mwambutsa IV). When Burundi (then called Urundi) was declared independent on 1 July 1962, Mwambutsa IV was established as its ruler. While on a European visit, Mwambutsa was overthrown by his 19-year-old son, Charles Ndizeye (qv). *See* Burundi.

My Lai 4 (Song My), South Vietnam (Codename "Pinkville"). *See* Calley.

N

Nabatiya. *See* Lebanon.

Nablus (*Nabulus or Shekem*). *See* Jordan and Israel.

al-Nabulis, Sulaiman. On 10 April 1957, King Hussein of Jordan dismissed his pro-Egyptian premier, Sulaiman al-Nabulis, as a first step in purging his government of sympathizers of Egypt's Gamal Nasser (qv), who were apparently plotting a coup against the king.

Naftali. *See* Israel.

Nagaland. *See* India.

Nag Hammadi (*Naj' Hammadi*) Hydroelectric Plant. *See* Egypt.

Naguib, Mohammed. (b. 20 February 1901, Khartoum, Sudan—d. 28 August 1984, Cairo [?]) Serving in the army before World War II, Naguib rose to the rank of brigadier by the time of the 1948 war against Israel. Wounded in that conflict, he was promoted to major general in 1951. In 1952, he was elected president of the Egyptian Army Officers Club over the candidate sponsored by King Farouk (qv). During that period he had come into favor with Gamal Nasser (qv) and was asked to be a figurehead leader (under Nasser) in the Free Officers' Movement. In August 1952, Nasser turned over the leadership of the group to Naguib. Naguib resented the implications of this position, and a rift developed between him and Nasser. When the Free Officers' group engineered the overthrow of Farouk (26 July 1952), they made the popular Naguib the president. When the republic was declared in June 1953, a dispute erupted over whether Nasser should be made prime minister, As a compromise, Nasser was appointed deputy prime minister. As president, Naguib wanted to return to constitutional government as quickly as possible, but the revolutionary council had not yet completed its eradication of the opponents still alive from the old regime. In February 1954, Naguib resigned the presidency but was prevailed upon to continue in office. After an assassination attempt against Nasser failed (Naguib probably had no part in it) on 14 November 1954, Nasser grabbed control. Naguib was deprived of his presidency and placed under house arrest until 1970, when he was released by president Anwar Sadat (qv). Thereafter, he faded into obscurity until his death in 1984.

Nagy, Ference. (b. 8 October 1903, Bisse, Hungary—d. 12 June 1979, Fairfax, Virginia) Born the son of Protestant farmers, Nagy began his career in agrarian politics, organizing the Smallholders' Party in the 1920s. In 1930, he became its first secretary general and, from 1939 to 1942, he served in the Hungarian Parliament. In 1944, Nagy was arrested by the Gestapo and jailed. After the war he became the leader of the antifascist coalition and was appointed premier on 4 February 1946. The Soviet-backed Hungarian Communist Party thought he was too conservative and forced him to resign on 31 May 1947. He was then indicted for crimes against the state (1947) when the Soviet Union accused him of treason. He escaped before the trial, however, and fled, first to Austria and then, to the United States. In the U.S., he was chairman of the Captive European Nations Committee in 1961–1962.

Nagy, Imre. (b. 7 June 1896, Kaposvar, Austria-Hungary—d. 17 June 1958, Budapest, Hungary) Born a peasant, Nagy apprenticed as a locksmith. During World War I, he was drafted and then captured by the Russians. He joined the Communist Party and then fought with the Red Army. In 1929 he moved to Moscow, where he remained until 1944 as a member of the Institute of Agrarian Sciences. He returned to Hungary after World War II and, between 1944 and 1948, held several posts in the government. In 1949, he was excluded from the communist government because he refused to abandon his support of peasant welfare. He recanted in public and was reinstated. In 1953–1955, he was appointed premier of Hungary, but his independent streak surfaced again. He was forced from office by his political enemy, Matyas Rakosi (qv), who replaced him as premier. Nagy then became a teacher until 23 October 1956, when anti-Soviet Hungarians persuaded him to lead them as premier once more. Anti-Soviet riots followed his appointment, and the Hungarian uprising began. On 30 October, Nagy promised his people free elections, the withdrawal of Soviet troops and an end to the communist one-party system. On 4 November 1956, Nagy made a dramatic appeal over the radio to the West for aid against the Soviet troops in his country (*see* Hungary). His appeal came too late and found little support. Nagy was then forced to seek asylum in the Yugoslav embassy. The Soviets guaranteed him safe passage to his home, but he was arrested and abducted on 22 November 1956 by Russian troops and deported to Romania. The Romanians returned him to Hungary, where he was tried in secret and executed on 17 June 1958. In July 1989, the Supreme Court of Hungary "rehabilitated" him posthumously. *Reading:* Alajos Dornbach, *The Secret Trial of Imre Nagy* (1994).

Nahariyya. *See* Israel.

el-Nahas Pasha, Mustafa. (b. 15 June 1876, Sammarud, Egypt—d. 23 August 1965, Alexandria, Egypt) Trained as a lawyer, Mustafa el-Nahas was appointed a judge in 1904. After World War I he joined the Wafd Party and, in 1927, became its chairman. In March 1928, he became prime minister of Egypt, but he was dismissed the following June by King Fuad I, who did not want a constitutional government and did not appreciate the British High Commissioner's giving in to certain Wafd Party demands. Nahas was again appointed prime minister in May 1936. Fuad died in May, and Farouk I (qv) became king. Almost immediately there was disagreement between the new king and his prime minister over the limits of power. In August, however, Nahas led the Egyptian delegation to London to sign the Anglo-Egyptian treaty of alliance necessitated by Italy's invasion of Ethiopia, (*see* Ethiopia). Farouk dismissed him in 1937. When World War II broke out, Nahas immediately supported the Allies, but Farouk vaccillated. In February 1942, Nahas was returned to power because of his support of the Allies. In essence, the British ambassador "shoved him down the king's throat." Great Britain issued Farouk an ultimatum, which was backed by military force. The king was given the choice of abdicating or reinstating Nahas as prime minister. In the March 1943 elections, the Wafd Party won a resounding majority. Nevertheless, Farouk once again dismissed Nahas in 1944, after a withdrawal of British support. Following signs of collaboration between the two, Farouk reinstated Nahas as prime minister in January 1950. Nahas, in November 1950, called for abrogation of the 1936 treaty with Great Britain and withdrawal from the Suez Canal and Sudan and supported Farouk as king of Egypt and Sudan. But, as opposition grew among the populace against the Wafd Party and as corruption in the government became more and more apparent, Farouk once again dismissed Nahas on 26 January 1952. This time was the last time.

an-Nahayan, Zaid ibn Sultan (Skeikh Zayed Bin Sultan al-Nahayan [Nuyahan]). (b. 1918 [?]) Raised as a nomad, Nahayan was governor of the eastern province of Abu Dhabi from 1946 until 1966. In 1966, he deposed his brother Sheikh Shakhur ibn Sultan and became emir. He was the principal architect of the federation of the old Trucial States into the United Arab Emirates (UAE) (qv). He became its first president in December 1971. In February 1973 he organized the federal structure of the UAE and brought most of its ministries from Abu Dhabi. He began his second term in office in 1976, making further reforms including integrating the emirates' armed forces. He also raised the budget of each of the UAE's seven members. By taking advantage of the huge oil resources available in the UAE, he increased the standard of living of its citizens both at home and abroad. In 1977, his cabinet tried to reflect a more federalized structure rather than the loosely run former government dependent on the individual emirates. On 19 March 1979, more than 3,000 demonstrated in favor of his plan for doing away with the borders within the UAE and unifying the seven emirates' armed forces. In 1981, Nahayan was reelected president. In 1995, he remains in office despite growing factionalism in each of the emirates and surrounding states.

Nahuga. *See* Saudi Arabia.

Nairobi. *See* Kenya.

Nakfa. *See* Ethiopia.

Nakhal. *See* Jordan.

Naktong River. *See* Korea.

Nambo Regional Committee. In October 1961, the communists established the Central Office of South Vietnam (COSVN) to replace the Nambo Regional Committee, which had directed communist activities and affairs in South Vietnam since the early 1950s. *See* Vietnam.

Namgyal, Chogyal Palden Thonup. In 1963, Crown Prince Palden Thonup Namgyal married New York debutante Hope Cooke. In 1964, he became ruler (*Chogyal*) of Sikkim (qv), but he was not crowned until 4 April 1965, when court astrologers thought the time was auspicious. On 8 April 1973, Namgyal asked for Indian troops following two weeks of antigovernment unrest. In May of that year, he signed an agreement with India that provided for a legislative assembly. In September 1974, Sikkim was absorbed by India when the Indian Parliament made it an associate state. In April 1975, a referendum abolished the monarchy, marking the end of more than 300 years of Namgyal rule and the eclipse of the *Chogyal.*

Namibia. Long known as South West Africa, Namibia is one of the newest nations in Africa. It is located on the southwestern coast and is bordered on the north by Angola, on the east by Botswana, on the south by South Africa, and on the west by the Atlantic Ocean. The capital and largest city is Windhoek. The region was originally occupied by the Khoikon and San people (Hottentots and Bushmen), the Bantu-speaking tribe called Herero and the Ovambo, Kavango and Damara tribal groups. In 1876, Namibia was brought under British colonial rule, but it became a German protectorate in 1884 as a result of the Berlin Conference of 1884–1885. The Germans called the region South West Africa. When German settlers arrived in 1892 and began pushing the natives off the better farmlands, they met violent opposition from the native tribes. The German government then began a campaign of genocide in which the Herero tribe was reduced from about 80,000 to 15,000; at least half of the Nama tribe of 20,000 was wiped out between 1904 and 1906. In 1915, during World War I, Britain ordered South Africa to seize South West Africa. After the war, the League of Nations created a mandate (1920) leaving South West Africa under South African control. A limited legislature was created. After the demise of the League of Nations, South Africa insisted on maintaining the mandate. After World War II, the United Nations created a trusteeship system to supercede the old mandates. South Africa refused to join the new system and continued its insistence on keeping the League's South West Africa mandate, claiming the UN did not have the authority to abrogate the League mandate. In 1946 South Africa tried to annex South West Africa, but the UN rejected its request. In 1966, the UN again voted to end the mandate, this time on the grounds of maladministration. In that same year the Marxist South West Africa People's Organization (SWAPO) (qv), which had been organized in 1957, began a guerrilla war for independence against the South African regime. In 1968, the UN renamed the country Namibia. On 12 August 1969, the UN Security Council ordered South Africa to surrender its mandate by 4 October. South Africa refused. The International Court of Justice ruled in June 1971 that South Africa was in violation of international law with its continued occupation of Namibia. On 18 February

1977, South African forces operating out of Namibia clashed with forces of the Popular Movement for the Liberation of Angola (MPLA) on Angolan territory. On 4 May 1978, South African paratroopers attacked the SWAPO base at Cassinga, Angola. SWAPO agreed to a plan for black majority rule in Namibia on 11–12 July. On 27 July, the UN Security Council backed the Western-brokered plan for Namibian independence (announced 30 August). SWAPO accepted the framework on 10 September. South Africa's counterproposal was rejected by Namibia on 24 October. On 26 October a coalition of black African states asked the UN for economic sanctions against South Africa because of its continued refusal to abide by the UN decision. The Security Council opened debate on the subject on 31 October. On 13 November, the UN directed South Africa to cancel plans for a December election in Namibia or face full economic sanctions. This order was disregarded, and South Africa held government-controlled elections in Namibia on 3 December. The Turnhalle Alliance won 82 percent of the votes cast. Kurt Waldheim (qv), the UN secretary general, asked for a cease-fire in the continuing guerrilla war on 15 March 1979. Finally, on 1 June, the UN General Assembly voted economic sanctions against South Africa in hopes of forcing that government to comply with the law and grant Namibia its independence. By 1981, it had not yet complied; on 6 March 1981 the General Assembly adopted 10 resolutions condemning South Africa and calling once again for mandatory sanctions. During the period of the 1980s, South Africa began to link the destinies of Angola and Namibia. In 1982, the Angolan government (*see* Angola) rejected a plan that would have provided for simultaneous withrawals of Cuban troops from Angola and South African troops from Namibia. In one of its moves to maintain firm control in Namibia, the South African government dissolved the Namibian National Assembly on 18 January 1983. In February, South African troops reportedly killed 96 SWAPO rebels. In February, South Africa renewed its demand that Cuban troops withdraw from Angola before South Africa would consider withdrawing from Namibia and launched an attack on Angola under the pretense of thwarting rebel attacks on Namibia. In early 1984, the UN Security Council condemned South Africa for its attacks on Angola: South Africa began withdrawing its forces from southern Angola. During the withdrawal, two American observers were killed by a bomb in the town of Oshakati in northern Namibia. Although SWAPO was blamed, it denied all knowledge of the incident. Following months of negotiation, the U.S. announced that Angola would reduce its Cuban military strength if South Africa gave up control of Namibia. The South African government finally agreed to think about peace in Namibia dependent on the Angolan situation. The U.S. then began negotiations with Angola and Cuba to implement a policy that would link Namibian independence with Cuban troop withdrawal in Angola. In March 1988, South Africa agreed to join in the talks. Prompted by a military defeat at Cuito Cuanavale, Angola, by the combined forces of Angola, Cuba and SWAPO, South Africa agreed to a formal cease-fire on 8 August 1988. South Africa, Angola and Cuba signed a formal treaty at the UN that granted Namibia independence on 22 December 1988. Cuba agreed to withdraw its forces from Angola by July 1991. A UN Transitional Assistance Group provided a supervisory presence in Nambia beginning on 1 April 1989, and it also began repatriating over 40,000 exiled Namibians. On 6–11 November 1989, elections were held in which SWAPO won 58 percent of the vote; theTurnhalle Alliance won 27 percent. Sam Nujoma was elected the country's first president of a nonracial government and took office on 21 March 1990, the day Namibia became independent. Terrorism occurred in August when a series of bombings led to the revelation of a planned right-wing coup attempt. Namibia decided to stay in the South African Customs Union as a means of helping its serious economic problems. Another move was the decision to retain the use of South African currency for at least two years. While relative calm prevailed in 1991, there was an increase in unemployment due to the narrow commercial capabilities of the country. A severe rise in crime came about as a result. The European Community also was at odds with the Namibian government over the seizure of Spanish fishing boats taking more than their limit in fish. Another two years of calm and some economic progress passed in 1992 and 1993, with Namibia reaching an administrative agreement with South Africa on the Walvis Bay enclave and with Namibia's continuing attempts at solving its financial problems. A number of initiatives were begun in the latter area, including membership in the Preferential Trade Area for East and South Africa. The period was marred, however, by demonstrations against rising taxes and, in July, by intertribal rioting in Katima Mulilo. It took reinforced police units to halt the latter incident. New elections were held in December 1994, which ended in the reelection of Sam Nujoma as president. The South Africa enclave of Walvis Bay was turned over to Namibian sovereignty on 28 February. Namibia's plan was to use the area as a free-trade zone. Namibia also moved against four white police officials for their parts in the 1989 assassination of a SWAPO advocate, Anton Lubowski. The investigation into the case produced evidence involving the South African Civil Cooperative Bureau. *Reading:* David Soggot, *Namibia: The Violent Heritage* (1986); Colin Levs & John S. Saul, *Namibia's Liberation Struggle: The Two-Edged Sword* (1995); John Ya-Otto et al., *Battlefield Namibia* (1982); David Deutschmann, ed., *Changing the History of Africa: Angola and Namibia* (1991).

Nam Tha. *See* Laos.

Nanking. *See* China.

Nan Province. *See* Thailand.

Nanterre. *See* France.

Naples. *See* Italy.

Naqura. *See* Lebanon.

Narkiss, Uzi. *See* Israel.

Nasser, Gamal Abdel. (b. 15 January 1918, Alexandria, Egypt—d. 28 September 1970, Cairo) Although the official Nasserite line was that Nasser was born a peasant (*fellahin*) in Bani Murr, a primitive village in the Upper Nile, which was a home of his ancestors, he was actually born in the Balos section of Alexandria, where his father was the local postmaster. After his birth, his father was transferred to Khatatibah, a very poor delta village, where Nasser attended school. He later moved to Cairo, where he lived with an uncle who was just released from a British prison. The dwelling where he grew up also housed nine Jewish families. In school, Nasser was known as a trouble maker, and he participated in a number of anti-British demonstrations that were aimed at getting the constitution restored. During one of these demonstrations Nasser received a blow to the head that left a permanent scar on his forehead. He associated with a number of political groups, but committed himself to none. He briefly joined the quasi-Fascist Young Egypt group but did not remain long. In 1937, he entered the Royal Military Academy and graduated a second lieutenant. While at the academy, he made friends with Zakoriya Muhyi al-Din, who would later become vice-president of Egypt, and Anwar al-Sadat (qv), who would succeed Nasser as the leader of Egypt. The three were radicalized by the failure of the Wafd Party (qv) to oust the British from Egypt and were further dismayed by the ineffectiveness of the Egyptian government. They formed a secret revolutionary organization known as the Free Officers, with Nasser being the only one who knew the identities of all of its members and how they were organized. When British troops surrounded the Royal Palace on 4 February 1942 and forced King Farouk (qv) to install a Wafd government, Nasser and the Free Officers were incensed. In 1943, Nasser became an instructor at the Military Academy, where he cultivated many of his students and brought many new members to the Free Officers. In 1948–1949, Nasser commanded a battalion in the first Arab-Israeli War (War for Israeli Independence). His unit was surrounded and besieged by the Israelis at Faluja. He and his officers placed the blame for the disaster on the weak and corrupt government. Nasser further decried the the inadequate military planning of the government and the palace's political manipulation of the army and became even further enraged at hearsay that King Farouk's entourage had equipped the army with inferior weapons and equipment. Nasser then set out to recruit new officers who wanted the overthrow of the empire of the king. On 23 July 1952, Nasser and his well-disciplined Free Officers staged an almost perfect bloodless coup. They formed the Revolutionary Council, with General Muhammed Naguib (qv) as its leader. On 26 July 1952, King Farouk was deposed. While Sadat and other members of the Free Officers wanted Farouk executed, Nasser vetoed their plan in favor of exile for the king and his followers. On 9 September 1952, the Revolutionary Council, controlled by Nasser, took over the control of Egypt with great popular support. Nasser remained behind the scenes, but in 1954 he deposed Naguib and named himself prime minister. That same year there was an assassination attempt on Nasser by a fanatic member of the Muslim Brotherhood. This prompted a crackdown on all extremist organizations in the country. In October 1954, Nasser signed a treaty with Great Britain that secured the withdrawal of the British from the Suez Canal by June 1956. In January 1956, Nasser announced a new national constitution that made Egypt a Socialist Arab state with a one-party system and Islam as the official religion. In the June 1956 election Nasser, being the only candidate, won more than 99 percent of the vote.

During this period, Nasser became a very popular figure throughout the Arab world, a symbol of successful independence and resistance to European colonialism. Nasser also signed an arms agreement with Czechoslovakia during that time and increased his support of the Palestinian grievances against Israel. On 23 July 1956 he nationalized the Suez Canal. This precipitated a war in which Israel occupied the Sinai and almost completely annihilated the Egyptian air force. Still, Nasser became a hero with a prestige unequalled in the Arab world. After 1956 he increased his Pan-Arab commitment while avoiding further confrontation with Israel. In 1958, Syria and Egypt formed the ill-fated and short-lived United Arab Republic (UAR) (qv). Syria withdrew in 1961 because of Nasserite meddling in its internal affairs. Egypt continued to call itself the UAR. In May 1967, provoked by Syria, Nasser mobilized and attacked the Straits of Tiran, closing the Gulf of Aqaba to Israeli shipping. Once again Nasser suffered a humiliating defeat at the hands of the Israelis. (*see* Israel, Six-Day War) Nasser then resigned, but massive demonstrations convinced him to remain in office. In 1968, he used aid from the Soviet Union to build the Aswan High Dam, which the U.S. and Great Britain had agreed to finance in the 1950s. Nasser died on 28 September 1970 and was replaced by Anwar Sadat (qv). *Reading:* Kirk J. Beattie, *Egypt During the Nasser Years: Ideology, Politics, and Civil Society* (1994); Faysal Mikdai, *Gamal Abdel Nasser: A Bibliography* (1991).

Nassry, Zia Khan. On 26 January 1980, approximately one month after the Soviet invasion of Afghanistan, one of the rebel *mujihadeen* leaders, Zia Khan Nassry, claimed his forces controlled three provinces in the eastern part of the country. Nassry announced in an interview in Islamabad, Pakistan, that the "Free Islamic Republic" of Afghanistan was the rightful government. The war continued, however, until 1989.

Natal. *See* South Africa.

Natania. *See* Israel.

National Cash Register Company (Damascus and Aleppo). *See* Arab Communist Organization.

National Command for National Liberation (Peronist) (Argentina). The National Command for National Liberation, an Argentine Peronist terrorist organization, claimed credit for the kidnapping and murder of former president Pedro Eugenio Aramburo (qv) during 29 May–1 June 1970.

National Confederation of Labor (CNT). On 27–30 June 1973, parliamentary government was suspended in Uruguay when President Juan Bordaberry (qv) dismissed the congress and established rule by a council of state. A general strike was called by the CNT on 29 June. Bordaberry abolished the communist-dominated CNT the next day. Still factories were taken over, and students boycotted universities. Troops were moved in to secure oil refineries and strikers were arrested, drafted into the army and then ordered to go back to work. The CNT was purged, and its secretary general was arrested.

National European Fascists. On 28 September 1980, terrorists machine-gunned a Jewish synagogue in Paris, France. In was the second such attack in two days. A group calling themselves the National European Fascists attempted to take credit for the attack, but French police discounted the claim. In October, four people were killed in a synagogue bombing in Paris in which many others were injured. The police attributed all of these attacks to a neo-Nazi group or left-wing revolutionaries.

National Front for the Liberation of Angola (FNLA). The later form of the FNLA came into existence in 1975, following the independence of Angola (*see* Angola). Before that time it was one of the three groups that had fought a 14-year war for the liberation of Angola from Portuguese rule. On 5 January 1975, a joint agreement on the rule of Angola was signed by Holden Roberto and the leaders of the Popular Movement for the Liberation of Angola (MPLA), led by Agostinho Neto (qv) and Jonas Savimba of the National Union for the Total Independence of Angola (UNITA) (qv). The agreement broke down in February when fighting erupted between FNLA and MPLA troops in Luanda. Peace was restored in March, and in June it was announced that the three military forces would be combined. A new battle began three days later (24 June), however, between Roberto's forces and those of Agostinho Neto (MPLA). Between 9 July and 11 July, at least 200 were killed on both sides in the fighting. On 7 August, the FNLA withdrew from the agreement. On 2 November a new cease-fire went into effect, and the FNLA and UNITA established a joint military headquarters to coordinate their forces. Two distinct governments were declared, with the communist-supported MPLA taking the capital city of Luanda while the FNLA/UNITA organization set up its capital in Nova Lisboa (Huambo). With this separation, the communist Chinese withdrew their advisers and support from the FNLA. Thereafter (February 1976), the FNLA engaged in a civil war against the Soviet-supported MPLA from bases in neighboring Zaire. On 27 January 1976, the U.S. House of Representatives refused further aid to the FNLA (and UNITA), and the two groups were forced to resort to guerrilla warfare, which actually increased the casualty rates on both sides. In 1977, the FNLA sector in the north of Angola was relatively quiet. In 1978, the FNLA refused to aid the Front for the Liberation of the Enclave of Cabinda (FLEC), an small enclave of Angola bounded by Congo and Zaire, because of fear of the loss of Cabinda's valuable oil deposits. When China appeared ready to deal with the Cuban-backed Angolan (MPLA) government, the FNLA once again became active in the north, where it renewed guerrilla operations. From this point on the FNLA remained in the background as the UNITA forces dominated the scene, until 1994, when an accord was signed with the central government. *See* Angola.

National Front for the Liberation of the South (NLF). *See* Vietnam.
National Guard of Panama. *See* Panama.
National Guard of the United States. *See* United States.
National Home Guard of Lebanon. *See* Lebanon.

Nationalist Afrikander. A South African political organization, on 26 June 1948, the Nationalist Afrikander bloc, with its apartheid platform, won the national elections. Among the party's goals were the reduction of links with Great Britain, the Commonwealth and the United Nations and professed white supremacy by whatever means necessary to advance the power of the Afrikaaner people. *See* South Africa and Apartheid.

Nationalist China. *See* Taiwan.

National Liberation Action (*Acao Liberatora Nacional)* (ALN) (aka National Liberation Alliance). In 1967, after he broke with the communist party, Carlos Marighela (qv) organized an urban terrorist group known as the ALN in Brazil. In Sao Paulo, Brazil, on 4 November 1969, Carlos Marighela was killed in a right-wing police death squad ambush. The activities of the group continued, however; and, on 11 June 1970, it kidnapped West German ambassador Ehrenfried von Hollenben (qv), with a ransom demand for the release of 40 political prisoners. After their release, the ambassador was freed. Additional similar kidnappings were carried out successfully. The organization was subsequently quieted by a massive police crackdown on all terrorist activity in the country.

National Liberation Army (*Ejercito de Liberacion Nacional).* The National Liberation Army (ELN) of Colombia was formed in July 1964. Its area of operation was primarily in the north and northeastern parts of the country, near the Venezuelan border. It later expanded into the central region. The Cuban-supported group was originally led by Manuel Perez Martinez and Nicolas Rodrigues Bautista (aka "Dario"). The organization was pro-Castro, anti–U.S. and Marxist-Leninist in its orientation. It drew its membership (about 1,000) from a variety of Colombians and included students, intellectual, peasants and middle-class workers in its ranks. There were several factions and fronts in the group, including the "Simon Bolivar" faction that opposes the hard-liners in the ELN. The ELN was the one Colombian insurgent group that did not agree to the truce with the government in 1984. The ELN forms a part of the National Guerrilla Coordinator (CNG) and the recently formed Simon Bolivar Guerrilla Coordinator (SBGC). Kidnappings, assassinations, armed robberies, bombings, raids and ambushes have been among the attacks carried out by the ELN. Most recently the ELN has concentrated its efforts on attacking petroleum pipelines and facilities to damage the Colombian economy. In June 1970, ELN terrorists kidnapped the former Colombian foreign minister, but later released him. On 4 October 1973, 50 ELN guerrillas attacked an American-owned gold mine and kidnapped two Americans. A ramsom of 4-million pesos was demanded. When the company attempted to pay the ransom, the Colombian army stepped in and seized the money. The two Americans were rescued at an ELN hideout by Colombian troops on 7 March 1974. In June 1987, the ELN ambushed a Venezuelan National Guard unit on an antinarcotics mission near the Colombian border. Later that year, in November, 19 policemen and four soldiers were killed in separate ambushes laid by the ELN.

National Liberation Front (Frolinat). The Front for the National Liberation of Chad (Frolinat) was organized in 1966 and operated primarily in the northern area of the country from bases around the southern Libyan oasis of al-Kufrah. By 1978, the government of Chad reached a cease-fire agreement with Frolinat and at the same broke diplomatic relations with Libya because of its support of the rebels. *See* Chad.

National Liberation Front (South Yemen). On 26 June 1978, a pro-Soviet coup led by the National Liberation Front overthrew the relatively moderate, yet left-leaning government of President Salem Ali Rubayyi (qv) in the People's Democratic Republic of Yemen (Yemen-Aden). Rubayyi was executed. The coup was probably staged to thwart government moves that would have led to closer ties with Saudi Arabia and other conservative Arab states and because of a mounting power struggle within the government itself.

National Military Liberation Committee (CMLN) (Mali). On 19 November 1968, a military coup overthrew the socialist government of Mali's President Modibo Keita. The junta called itself the National Military Liberation Committee put one of its members, Lieutenant Moussa Traore (qv), into the presidency. There was a coup attempt against the junta on 12 August 1969. After the coup, Traore assumed the position of head of state as well as the presidency.

National Resistance Army (NRA) (Uganda). With the ouster of Idi Amin Dada (qv) from Uganda, the country was largely in the hands of Tanzanian troops (summer 1979). At least 10,000 Tanzanian troops were still in Uganda a year later. Although there was relative calm during this period, political squabbling had begun, and it became known that large numbers of weapons remained in unauthorized hands. A multiplicity of political parties, each with its own agenda usually along tribal lines, had sprung up after Amin's removal. Many of them had their own armies. On 11 May 1980, a military commission took power, ousting President Godfrey L. Binaisa (qv). Milton Obote (qv) was elected president on 11 December 1980. Tanzanian forces began their withdrawal soon after, and a further breakdown in law and order followed. About that time, an underground group calling itself the Uganda Freedom Movement (UFM) established itself and became a campaign of terror against the government. A number of other guerrilla groups also sprang up in various parts of the country. In early 1982, Obote released 200 detainees, among whom were four former members of Parliament, including Yusefu Lule (qv), the chairman of the National Resistance Movement. Guerrilla activity, not all of which was chargeable to the National Resistance Movement, grew in intensity in the northwestern part of the country and around the capital city of Kampala. By 1984, thousands had died of the excesses of both the guerrillas and the Ugandan army forces. In 1985, the main guerrilla force had become identified as the NRA. In the face of a British promise of increased aid to the Ugandan government, the NRA opened a major campaign in the Western Province, thus dashing Obote's hopes for any kind of reconciliation. On 27 July 1985, Obote was overthrown, and General Tito Okello (qv) took power. The NRA was displeased with this as, although they claimed foreknowledge of the coup that ousted Obote, they claimed they had not been a part of the decision to put Okello in power. The NRA threatened to continue its war, and those threats were not lessened when some persons undesirable to the NRA were fired from their government positions. In August 1985, talks began in Kenya between the Ugandan government and the NRA. A peace treaty was signed on 17 December 1985 in Nairobi. Under the treaty's terms, the NRA was to share power with the ruling military council in Uganda. However, when no action had been taken by the Ugandan government to carry out the terms of the treaty, the NRA opened a new offensive in mid-January 1986 and by the end of the month had captured Kampala; the Ugandan government and army were in full flight, with NRA forces in hot pursuit. NRA commander Yoweri Museveni (qv), was sworn in as president on 29 January. A new broad-based government was formed, and in February the NRA was authorized to rule by decree for a period of four years. Museveni was still in power in 1994.

National Resistance Movement (Mozambique). Also known as the Mozambique National Resistance (Renamo), this organization was composed of disenchanted elements of the Mozambique Liberation Front (Frelimo) who, since 1976–1977, undertook rebel activities against the Frelimo government of Samora Macel (qv). The rebellion continued until 1989–1990, when the government eschewed Marxism-Leninism and drafted a new constitution. Although fighting continued for some time, several peace conferences led to a halt in the fighting in late 1991. A final accord was reached on 4 October 1992.

National Revolutionary Movement (MNR) (Bolivia). On 11 April 1952, the Bolivian junta that had ruled the country in one form or another since 1934 was ousted following a three-day revolt led by the National Revolutionary Movement. Pas Estenssoro (qv) was installed as president. The MNR was formed in 1941 and was violently nationalistic. Pas Estenssoro, the exiled MNR leader, had won the election of 1949, but he was not allowed to assume his office until the 1952 Revolution. The MNR remained in power until 1964.

National Revolutionary Movement. *See* Vietnam.

National Security Action Memorandum 288. The U.S. National Security Council issued National Security Memorandun 288 on 17 March 1964. The memorandum accepted Secretary of Defense Robert McNamara's (qv) position calling for "graduated overt military pressure" against North Vietnam.

"National Task Force." *See* Vietnam.

National Union for the Total Independence of Angola (*União Nacional para a Indendência Total de Angola*) (UNITA). Led by Joseph Savimbi, UNITA was one of several rival groups involved in a civil war in Angola. It was founded in 1966 as the third movement in the struggle and was centered around the Ovimbundu tribe, although it also received recruits from the Chokwe and Onambo tribes. UNITA received very little foreign support, although China did provide some aid. Later in the war its anti-Marxist stance brought aid from South Africa and the United States. *See* Angola.

National United Front (Comoro Islands). On 3 August 1975, a pro-French coalition led by four opposition party leaders, under the banner of the National

Liberation Front, overthrew the government of the Comoros (qv) and unseated President Ahmed Abdallah (qv). Abdallah had declared unilateral independence from France on 6 July 1975, which precipitated the crisis. The front put Ali Soilih (qv) in the presidency The front was overthrown on 13 May 1978. The unpopular Soilih was murdered, and a new regime took power. *See* Comoros.

National University. *See* Mexico.

Natusch Busch, Alberto. On 1 November 1979, the government of Walter Guevara Arze was overthown in Bolivia in a military coup led by Colonel Alberto Natusch Busch. The coup took place within hours of the adjournment of the General Assembly of the Organization of American States (OAS) in La Paz. Natusch declared himself president. On 2 November Natusch dissolved Congress, and union leaders called for a general strike, which paralyzed the country. At least 200 demonstrators were killed on 4 November when the military used tanks and airplanes to disperse the crowd. On 15 November, more than 250 senior military officers signed a petition demanding that Natusch step down. The following day, 16 November, Natusch stepped down. On 17 November, Senate President Lydia Gueiler was sworn in as president of Bolivia.

Navigation of Shatt al-Arab (*Arand-Rud*) Treaty (1937). *See* Iran, Iraq and Iran-Iraq War.

Naxalites. *See* India.

Nazareth. *See* Israel.

Ndebele Tribe. *See* Zimbabwe (Matabeleland).

Ndizeye, Charles (King [*Mwan*] Ntare V of Burundi). The 19-year-old Ndizeye overthrew his father, Mwambutsa IV (qv), while the king was absent in Europe. Ndizeye then put himself on the throne as Ntare V, but was in turn overthrown on 28 November 1966 by his prime minister, Captain Michel Micambero (qv), who proclaimed a republic with himself as president. Ndizeye went into exile in West Germany, but returned to Burundi on 30 March 1972. He had been promised safe conduct by Micambero in an arrangement witnessed by Uganda's Idi Amin (21 March). Upon Ndizeye's arrival, he was arrested by the army and charged (31 March) with leading an attempted mercenary invasion. Uganda vehemently denied this allegation (4 April). On 29 April 1972, a bloody civil war began in Burundi, which was termed a "coup attempt" by the government, which also reported that Ndizeye had been killed in the fighting. It was later discovered that Micambero had executed him on 29 April, the night of the attack. At least 100,000 were killed in the tribal warfare that followed.

N'Djamena. *See* Chad.

Ndola, Northern Rhodesia. *See* Zimbabwe.

Neak Luon. *See* Cambodia.

Neave, Airey Middleton. On 30 March 1979, Airey Middleton Neave, the British secretary of state for Northern Ireland, was assassinated by Irish terrorists when a bomb planted in his car exploded in an underground garage at the House of Commons in London. Neave was born in London on 23 January 1916. During World War II he directed the escape network in Europe and was known for his tough stand on terrorism.

Negage. *See* Angola.

Nehru, Pandit (*Pundit*) Jawaharlal. (b. 14 November 1899, Allahabad, India—d. 27 May 1964, New Delhi) Born to a Brahman family, Nehru was one of four children, one of whom, Vijaya Lakshmi Pandit, became the first female president of the United Nations General Assembly. Nehru began his education at home. At age 16, he went to Harrow (1905) in England, where he remained until 1907. He then attended Trinity College, Cambridge, from which he graduated with honors in natural science. He then studied law at Inner Temple, London, and graduated in 1912. After his return to India, he married (1916) and had one daughter, Indira Priyadarshini, who later became prime minister of India, as Indira Gandhi (qv). After practicing law, Nehru joined the Indian National Congress (INC) in 1919, a nationalist organization led by Mohandas K. Gandhi (qv). Nehru rose rapidly through the ranks of the organization and, between 1921 and 1945, was jailed on nine occasions by the British. However, Nehru's philosophy differed from Gandhi's in that he professed a more militant program to gain independence. In 1942, Nehru became the leader of the INC. In 1945, when the British were preparing their withdrawal from India, Nehru was asked to form the interim government. Hi first task was to prevent the partition of India into Muslim and Hindu spheres. In this he failed (*see both* India and Pakistan). On 15 August 1947, after India was declared a dominion in the Commonwealth, Nehru became its first prime minister. When the state of Hyderabad refused to join the new dominion of India, Nehru threatened it with armed attack. He retained his post when India was proclaimed an independent republic in 1950 and until his death in 1964. On 3 July 1951, Nehru filed a formal protest against the Muslim state of Pakistan at the United Nations, charging Pakistan with repeated border violations. Following India's annexation of Kashmir on 6 February 1954, Nehru rejected a U.S. offer of military aid (1March), and, on 28 June 1954, announced an Indo-Chinese (Communist) agreement on the future of Indochina. Then, in June 1955, Nehru concluded a economic and technical assistance agreement with Moscow. On 25 February 1959, Nehru demanded the withdrawal of all American personnel in the UN Ceasefire Observer Team in Kashmir, because of the announced support by the United States of Pakistan, an offer similar to one refused by Nehru. Nehru changed his tune, however, when Chinese forces entered Indian territory. At that point, India was forced to ask the U.S. for military aid. A second request was submitted on 19 November 1962 as the protracted border struggle turned against India. Nehru died in New Delhi on 27 May 1964. *Reading:* Sarvepalli Gopal, *Jawaharlal Nehru: A Biography* (1976); Stanley Walpert, *Nehru: A Tryst with Destiny* (1996); Denis Judd, *Jawaharlal Nehru* (1993).

Nellie. *See* India.

Nepal. A small, landlocked country in the Himalaya mountains, the Kingdom of Nepal is bordered on the north by China and on the south by India. The capital is Kathmandu. Nepal is the state in which Mount Everest is located. The orginal inhabitants of Nepal are lost in antiquity, but later incursions by Mongoloid and Indo-Iranian cultural groups helped establish the current Nepalese people. For centuries, Nepal was divided into tiny principalities, of which the Gurkhas claimed dominance in the last quarter of the eighteenth century. Ruled by a dynastic family, Nepal also had, until 1951, hereditary prime ministers who generally kept the royal family virtual prisoners in their own realm. A palace coup on 7 November 1950 was led by Prime Minister Mohan Shumshere (qv). King Tribhubarra Bir Bikram (qv) was overthrown and fled to the Indian embassy for protection. The deposed king led an unsuccessful attempt to regain the throne on 11–20 November. A revolution, led by members of the Nepali Congress Party, broke out, but terms were reached in early 1951, and the king was eventually asked to again assume the throne. Another unsuccessful revolt, this time communist inspired, took place on 24 January 1952. A period of violence followed until 13 August, when the king assumed dictatorial powers with a succession of ineffectual governments. Indian troops had to be called in in 1953 to help restore order. King Tribhubarra died in 1955 and was succeeded on the throne by his eldest son, Crown Prince Mahendra Bir Birkam Shah Deva (qv). On 24 September, Nepal announced it had signed an agreement with Communist China giving sovereignty over Tibet to China. However, by late June 1960, tension along the border with China had risen, and in December 1960, King Mahendra ousted the prime minister, dissolved parliament and assumed the administration of government to himself. All political parties were banned in January 1961. In March a new civil war broke out that lasted throughout the year. Renewed tension along the Chinese border followed the signing of a treaty that defined the Nepal-Chinese border. In January 1962, a bomb was thrown at the king's car while he was on a tour; he was not injured. In April 1962, Nepal charged India was supporting Nepalese rebels based across the border in India. Polygamy, child marriages and a strict caste system, which had existed for hundreds of years,were abolished in 1963. On 25 June 1969 the Nepalese prime minister announced a cancellation of the government's arms agreement with India, which had been in effect since 1965, and asked that Indian troops stationed in Nepal be removed. India recalled its ambassador in late 1973, after Nepal reacted to an Indian announcement that tiny Sikkim was to be made an Indian department. By 1974, law and order had deteriorated to a dangerous level. Terrorist incidents, including bombings and attacks on outlying police stations, were on the increase. In one incident, in March 1974, a bomb aimed at the king killed two people and injured 37 others. Violence broke out in April–May 1979 over the burning issue of democratic reform. The king announced (24 May) a referendum to determine the country's future. Trouble continued. On 20–21 June 1985, five bombs were set off by terrorists in Kathmandu and Pokhara, including one at the palace. Seven were killed and 24 injured. On 21 June, three more bombs were set off in the border town of Birjungi, killing one person. The communists and others boycotted the 1986 elections, but there was still a heavy turnout, partially due to the 1961 royal proclamation banning political parties. Although numbers of people died in natural and manmade disasters in 1987–1988, the political situation remained calm. In 1989, however, a dispute with India over the terms of trade and a right-to-work agreement caused major problems in Nepal. Gasoline was rationed, food was in short supply and most border-crossing points were closed by the Indians. India accused Nepal of buying weapons from China. At the same time, Nepal was suffering under governmental controls that prohibited democratization. Hundreds of those who demonstrated against those conditions were arrested. Sixty-three demonstrators were killed on 6 April 1990 when troops and police opened fire. This forced King Birenda to loosen the bonds of his people (8 April) when it became obvious that he faced massive demonstrations in retaliation for the killings. A new government was formed that began, for the first time in 30 years, the task of leading the country toward democracy. The government announced the legalization of political parties and held multiparty elections in 1991. The new government also worked to end the impasse with India, and the border was reopened in June 1990. The autocratic rule of the king was ended in June 1991, when a freely elected parliament was seated. While good internally, democracy developed two external problems. One was the realization that Nepal's almost total dependence on India was a drawback, and the other was neighboring Bhutan's accusations that Nepal was exporting its prodemocracy ideas into the last absolute monarchy on earth. Violence attended 1992, when a mob of 2,000, primarily provoked by the communists, took to the streets to protest higher prices and corruption. At least seven died in this April demonstration. As a money-making scheme, Nepal opened more peaks for climbers and increased fees for climbing Mount Everest from $10,000 to $50,000. Communist demonstrations punctuated 1993, as a maneuver to force out the current government. As an excuse, the communists blamed the deaths of two communist leaders who died in a car crash on the government. At least a dozen were killed in the violence that followed. Relative calm settled over the country in 1994, except in the halls of government, where the first democratically chosen prime minister, Girija Prasad Koirala, lost his office in a communist upset following a no-confidence vote. When it was seen in 1995 that the communists could not hold on to power, they attempted an internal coup by having the king dissolve Parliament. After that the Supreme Court nullified the king's order of 13 June. The communists then lost a no-confidence vote and had to give up leadership to the National Congress Party. *Reading:* Michael Hutt, ed., *Nepal in the Nineties: Versions of the Past, Visions of the Future* (1994); Robert Z. Apte, *Three Kingdoms on the Roof of the World: Bhutan, Nepal, and Ladakh* (1990); S. D. Muni, *India and Nepal: A Changing Relationship* (1992).

Netherlands, The. Also known unofficially as Holland, the Netherlands is a constitutional monarchy located in northwestern Europe. It is bordered on the east by Germany, on the south by Belgium, and on the north and west by the North Sea. The capital city is Amsterdam. In the first century B.C., Julius Caesar led a Roman army into the region, where they conquered the local tribes of Frisians and Celts. For the next 250 years the Romans held the land, thereby controlling the several entrances to the Rhine river. After 300 A.D., Roman control of the region was challenged by Germanic tribes moving from the east.

While the Frisians were able to maintain control in the north, Saxon tribes occupied the eastern extent of the region while powerful Frankish tribes occupied the west and south. By 800 A.D. the entire region was under Frankish control and had been converted to Christianity. Charlemagne accepted the Netherlands as a part of his realm. After his death, however, his domain was divided, with The Netherlands becoming a part of Lorraine (Lotheringia) (Treaty of Verdun, 843). In 925, it became a part of the Holy Roman Empire, although the Dutch lands were ruled by local lords. At the same time, the region, including present-day Belgium, became known as the Lowlands (*Nederland*). Viking raiding during the ninth and tenth centuries led to the development of stronger defenses for the emerging cities and more powerful rulers. By the fourteenth century, the region had become an important trading center, with an influential merchant class who often financed the ruling class in their constant internecine struggles. Through this process, important sections developed in the region, such as Flanders and Holland. In the north, the Frisians continued in the old ways and followed only their tribal leaders. While some outside influence was felt from Germany, the major cultural influence came from France. The dukes of Burgundy held power during the fifteenth and early sixteenth centuries. In the mid-sixteenth century, the Holy Roman Empire reasserted its power and, therefore, under Hapsburg control. In 1555, the Holy Roman Emperor, Charles V, gave the rule of both Spain and the Netherlands to Philip II. His oppressive rule over the Lowlands led to a Dutch revolt in the late sixteenth century, which led to the establishment (1648) of the Dutch Republic in the northern provinces. The armies of Revolutionary France conquered the Netherlands in 1795. In 1810, France annexed the country. After Napoleon's defeat in 1815, the present state, known as the Kingdom of Netherlands, came into being. Belgium, which had been a part of this arrangement, seceded in 1830 to seek its own way. Outside meddling by the "Great Powers" led to a war between Belgium and Holland, but the issue of separation was again settled in 1839. Holland was affected by the wave of revolutions of the 1840s, and out of its turmoil a new constitution was promulgated that limited the monarchy and that formed the basis of the present-day constitutional monarchy in the Netherlands. During World War I, Holland remained neutral but suffered extreme hardship from the Allied blockade of the continent. In 1939, with the outbreak of World War II, Holland again declared its neutrality, but it was invaded by Germany in 1940. The city of Rotterdam was almost obliterated in a Germany bombing operation during the invasion. The Dutch in response opened dikes, which flooded large parts of the country and carried out a well-organized resistance during the course of the war. Allied operations to free the country from Nazi domination also caused a great amount of destruction. The country was liberated during the 1944–1945 period. The Netherlands became a charter member of the United Nations in 1945 and in 1948 joined the European Recovery Program. Also in 1948, it joined with Belgium, France, Great Britain and Luxembourg in forming the Brussels Treaty Organization (qv) and was a founder of the European Coal and Steel Community (1952). Holland became part of the North Atlantic Treaty

Organization In 1949, of the European Defense Community (qv) in 1952 and, in 1955, of the London-Paris Accords which joined the Netherlands into the European multinational defense establishment. During this period, the Dutch fought a war against rebel nationalists in its Indonesian colony, which it lost. In 1949 sovereignty of the Dutch East Indies (except for Dutch New Guinea) was transferred to the government of Indonesia. Dutch New Guinea remained under Dutch control until 1962. Other Dutch colonies, such as Suriname (qv) and the Netherlands Antilles became members of the Kingdom of Netherlands in 1954. In the 1960s, the Netherlands passed through a period of instability in government both at home and in its overseas possessions. Dutch Marines had to be dispatched to the Netherlands Antilles in 1969 to assist the local police in riot control. Inflation in the 1970s proved to be a major political problem. The elections held in 1977 caused addition political problems, which were settled after the installation of a new government later that year. In 1980, Princess Beatrix ascended to the throne following the abdication of the venerable Queen Juliana. In the 1990s, the island of Aruba separated from the Netherlands Antilles to become independent in 1996. In 1993, the Dutch government became the first in the world to regulate euthanasia. In May 1994, two ministers were forced to resign following the disclosure of the forced dissolution of a major crime-fighting police operation for purely political reasons having nothing to do with the effectiveness of the police team, which was later brought into question. In 1995, the imminent danger of bursting dikes forced the evacuation of nearly a quarter million people. A UN peacekeeping force of 300 Dutch troops operating in Bosnia in the Srebrenica safe area was disarmed and taken hostage by Serbian troops in July 1995. This raised a furor at home about why lightly armed Dutch troops were sent into a highly contested and hostile area without the proper support. One Dutch soldier was killed during the capture. The hostages were eventually released after NATO threatened severe retaliation. *Reading:* George T. Kurlan, *The Benelux Countries* (1989); Margreit Bruijn Lacy, ed., *The Low Countries: Multidisciplinary Studies* (1990); Robert S. Kirsner, ed., *The Low Countries and Beyond* (1993).

Neto, Antonio Agostinho. (b. 17 September 1922, Bengo, Angola—d. 10 September 1979, Moscow) Neto studied in Portugal and was a poet of some renown, although much of his work infuriated the authorities. He was arrested in 1952 and imprisoned for his connections in the outlawed Portuguese Communist Party. He was again arrested and imprisoned in 1955. In 1958 he graduated as a doctor and returned to Angola (1959), where he was arrested (1960) for his opposition to Portuguese colonial rule. He was held for a time in Cape Verde and then transferred to Lisbon, where he escaped to Morocco. Neto was elected president of the Movement for the Liberation of Angola (MPLA) (*see* Angola) and established his headquarters in Leopoldville, Congo. Although the Soviet Union supported the MPLA, it was not happy with Neto and broke off its support. Soviet support was restored in 1974 following the military coup in Lisbon. Following Portugal's granting independence to Angola in 1975, Neto proclaimed the country to a People's Republic and himself as its president.

Although his tenuous rule was fortified by Soviet and Cuban support, Neto steadfastly refused to turn control of the country over to Soviet hard-liners. However, on 8 October 1976, a Soviet-Angolan treaty of friendship and cooperation was signed. On 27 May 1977, an uprising within the MPLA nearly toppled Neto, but he was able to survive. In 1977, he visited Havana. In September 1979, he was taken to Moscow and was operated on for pancreatic cancer. He died there as a result of the disease on 10 September. Jose Eduardo dos Santos took his place as president of Angola.

Neutral Nations Repatriation Commission. Also known as the Neutral Nations Commission on Repatriation, this organization was charged by the United Nations with the orderly repatriation of prisoners of war on both sides following the signing of the armistice ending the Korean War (27 July 1953). Some 21,809 prisoners—7,582 North Koreans and 14,227 Chinese—refused to be repatriated and chose to stay in South Korea or go to Taiwan.

Nevis. *See* St. Kitts and Nevis.

New Central African Republic. *See* Central African Republic.

New China News Agency (Pinyin Xinhua). The official news organ of the government of the People's Republic of China, the press was founded in 1929 to serve the Chinese Communist Party. The service's headquarters in is Peking, and it maintains offices all over the world, with many of its correspondents actually members of the Foreign Intelligence Department of the Ministry of Internal Affairs.

New Delhi. *See* India.

New Guinea. An island in the western Pacific, New Guinea lies northeast of Australia At its closest point, New Guinea is separated from Australia by the Torres Strait (125 miles). The northeastern coast was first sighted in the early sixteenth century by Portuguese explorers. Spain claimed the island in 1545. German traders established bases in the northwest quadrant of New Guinea in 1870. The British also explored the southeast portion of the island and annexed that region in 1884. Also in 1884, Germany annexed the rest of the island and some of the smaller islands in the vicinity. Great Britain gave control of its section of New Guinea to Australia in 1904–1906, and that region was renamed the Territory of Papau. Australia troops occupied the German portion of New Guinea during World War I and received a League of Nations mandate over it in 1921. This section of the island was at that time called Irian Barat. Australia combined the administration of the two regions into a single entity called Papau new guinea. New Guinea was occupied by the Japanese in World War II and was the scene of heavy fighting. After the war, Australia again administered the territory as a trust of the United Nations. Soon thereafter, however, the Dutch were given control of the northwest region as a part of the Dutch West New Guinea. When Indonesia was declared independent in 1949, it claimed sovereignty over the Dutch possessions and threatened military intervention if the United Nations refused to take up the question (28 October 1957). When the Dutch refused to relinquish control, Indonesia broke diplomatic relations with The Hague (5 December 1957). A plebiscite was held in Irian, which resulted in the western half of the island being given over to Indonesia as the province of Irian Jaya on 1 May 1963 (*see* Indonesia). In December 1973, Papua New Guinea became a self-governing Australian territory and was granted full independence from Great Britain on 16 September 1975. Papau New Guinea opted to remain a member of the British Commonwealth On 31 March 1978, Papau New Guinea, along with Australia, New Zealand and a number of island states, imposed a 200-mile fishing limit around their territories. The new nation suffered from tribal warfare in 1979. About 400 were killed in the fighting, and the government was forced to declare a state of emergency. A no-confidence vote brought the resignation of the prime minister, Michael Somare, on 11 March 1980. He was replaced immediately and peacefully by Sir Julius Chan of the People's Progress Party. Chan was defeated in the 1982 elections and was replaced by his predecessor, Michael Somare. The new government, which was seated in August, inherited the problem of an armed Indonesian border crossing on 2 June, which culminated in the seizure of about 20 Irian Jaya (West New Guinea/Indonesian) refugees, who were taken back to Indonesia. Further problems cropped up in 1983, when Indonesia began a construction project that encroached on Papau New Guinea territory. The situation continued into 1984 when, in March, Indonesian fighters overflew Papuan air space. At the same time, rebel guerrillas of the Free West Papua Movement, who were based on the Papau New Guinea side of the border, stepped up the raiding into Irian Jayan (Indonesian) territory. This led to mass exodus from Irian Jaya, which put a very heavy strain on Papua New Guinea's already strained refugee facilities and the country's ability to render support. Many died of starvation and disease in the camps. October 1984 witnessed a new border protocol that lessened restrictions placed on those Indonesians wishing to return to Irian Jaya. In 1985, domestic unrest replaced confrontation with Indonesia, which displayed the country's inability to effectively police itself. The upshot of the crime wave was twofold: the adoption of new severe laws and the ouster of Somare. A no-confidence vote ended his tenure on 21 November. Paise Wingti assumed office that same month and began to effectively turn the internal situation around and, at the same time, to work toward friendlier relations with Indonesia. In 1987, the general elections kept Wingti in office; crime was still the major internal problem. Parliament gave Wingti a no-confidence vote in July 1988 after Somare had been removed as the head of the party (*Pangu Pati*). Rabbie Namaliu took office on 4 July. Violence broke out that year among striking mine workers over the issue of housing. Secessionist activity rose on Bouganville Island in 1989. In response, Namaliu ordered the military and security forces to use restraint in dealing with the problem, but rebels managed to close much of the island's industry. Finally, a relocation plan and a search-and-seizure order were issued to halt the unrest. The damage caused by the closures began to appear in 1990, when it became necessary to devalue the currency. Rebels of the Bouganville Revolutionary Army (BRA) began a widespread rampage in February 1990 that literally cleared all outsiders off the island. The military was withdrawn in March. In May the BRA declared Bouganville independent. Papuan naval vessels took up a blockade of Bouganville that effectively isolated the island until August, when an interim agreement was reached that ended the standoff. An Australian army officer was assassinated in Port Moresby, bringing about a curfew in several areas. While this alone was an extremely serious matter, the guilty verdict on corruption charges (81 counts) against the deputy prime minister, Ted Diro, created a major constitutional issue when the governor-general refused to dismiss him. Before Queen Elizabeth could act to uphold the law, Diro and Sir Serei Eri resigned. Also, in 1991, a peace accord was signed between the government and the BRA in January but did not immediately end the problem, as the rebels refused to lay down their arms. In April 1992, the chief negotiator of the agreement, Tony Agunu, was murdered. This brought a swift reaction against the rebels in October that ended the rebel dominance on Bouganville. In the meantime, Namaliu was defeated for reelection by one vote, with Wingti being returned to office in his place, and by year's end Namaliu was charged with misappropriation of government funds. Wingti survived a no-confidence vote in September 1993 by clever political maneuvering, but the issue of security still overshadowed his success. He was replaced by Sir Julius Chan in August 1994. By September 1994, the rebels on Bouganville had been decimated but not pacified, but there was no answer to when the mines, the island's major industry, could be reopened. A multinational peacekeeping force enforced a semblance of stability on the island. Fighting continued in 1995 with casualties on both sides. Peace negotiations were broken off in November. (*See also* Indonesia for details of the conflict with the Netherlands and Irian Jaya). *Reading:* Fraiser McConnel, *Papua New Guinea* (World Bibliographical Series, Vol. 90) (1988); Time Life Editors, *New Guinea* (1977); David Alexander, *New Guinea, The Territory and Its People* (1973); Alexander Wanek, *The State and Its Enemies in Papua New Guinea* (1996); Kees Lagerberg, *West Irian and Jakarta Imperialism* (1980).

Ne Win. On 26 September 1958, Burmese Premier U Nu (qv) resigned his office and asked the Army to take control. Army chief of staff General Ne Win assumed the office of prime minister. Following a general election held in February 1960, U Nu again became prime minister (as of April 1960). On 2 March 1962, Ne Win, backed by the army, deposed U Nu and arrested him. Ne Win then proclaimed an anticommunist government under a revolutionary council. Ne Win remained in office until 1974, during which time Burma was renamed the Socialist Republic of the Union of Burma. On 2 March 1974, Ne Win became the country's first president, with U Sein Win appointed prime minister. *See* Burma.

New Jewel Movement (NJM) (Grenada). A left-wing coalition organization that seized power in a bloodless coup on the Caribbean island of Grenada in 1979, the NJM named its leader, Maurice Bishop (qv), prime minister and proclaimed the People's Revolutionary Government (PRG) of Grenada. The new government later deposed and killed Bishop on 19–20 October 1983. The PRG then installed General Hudson Austin (qv) as leader. A U.S. invasion of the island on 25 October 1983 ended the rule of the NJM. *See* Grenada.

New People's Army (NPA). The military wing of the Communist Party of the Philippines (CPP), the NPA was formed in 1969 and was Maoist oriented. The CPP was dedicated to the overthrow of the Philippine government through peasant revolution and protracted guerrilla warfare. Since coming into being, the NPA had grown steadily in strength to about 20,000. In more recent times, however, this number has declined to about 13,000 (1993). Until the fall of 1987, the NPA refrained from targetting Americans, except in an incident in April 1974 near Subic Bay in which three US naval officers were killed. NPA terrorist attacks were usually directed toward Filipino political and military and police leaders and assaults on the Catholic church. On 19 April 1981, for instance, NPA terrorists hurled hand grenades into a Catholic cathedral during Easter services in Davao City, Mindanao. In October 1987, the NPA murdered two American servicemen, an American retiree, and a Filipino bystander. That same year, over 400 Filipinos disappeared and were suspected victims of the NPA. Benito Tiamzon is the suspected (1988) leader of the group. The NPA has remained active and, on 17 January 1992, kidnapped the director of the American Chamber of Commerce, Michael Barnes, in broad daylight in downtown Manila. Barnes was freed after two months, during a police operation in which 14 terrorists were killed. In February 1992, 41 Filipino soldiers were killed in an ambush on the island of Mindanao. After intensive peace negotiations between the government and the insurgents, some signs were seen in 1994 that the NPA was breaking apart, although assassinations and atrocities continued.

Newport Agreement. On 23 August 1948, the roles and missions of the US armed forces were revised in a document called the Newport Agreement. Secretary of Defense James Forrestal and the Joint Chiefs of Staff reached the agreement at Newport, Rhode Island. This meeting followed the one held in March in which the three armed services resolved a number of disputes (Key West Agreement) regarding their respective roles and missions in the national defense.

Newry. *See* Northern Ireland.

New South Wales. *See* Australia.

New Zealand (in Maori, Aotearoa). New Zealand is comprised of two large islands, North Island and South Island, and numerous smaller islands located approximately 1,000 miles southeast of Australia across the Tasmanian Sea. The capital city is Wellington, located at the south end of North Island. From the ninth century, the islands were settled by Maori tribesmen (e.g., Tahiti, c.1350). Having defeated an indigenous people, the Moriori, the Maori withstood most outside interference until the nineteenth century, when English missionaries amd whalers established trading posts and missions, especially on North Island. The islands had been originally discovered by a Dutch explorer, Abel Tasman, in 1642 and were visited by Captain James Cook in 1769. Cook claimed the islands for the British crown at that time, but Great Britain did not acknowledge the claim until 75 years later. In 1839, the New Zealand Company was chartered in England, and immigration began, in the face of Maori opposition. The government finally reached an accord after much bloodshed, in the Treaty of

Waitangi. signed by 50 Maori chieftains and a crown representative. By the treaty, Maori land rights were confirmed, and the Maoris put themselves under British protection. Until 1872 there were violent uprisings over land rights. In 1872, a strong governmental policy protected the Maoris, and peace ensued. In 1907, New Zealand was declared a dominion of the British Empire. In World War I, New Zealand forces fought as a part of the Australian and New Zealand Corps popularly called the ANZAC. Of 124,000 troops furnished, New Zealand lost more than 16,000 killed. In World War II, New Zealand contributed a larger percentage of its manpower than any other nation, with the exception of the British Isles. In that war, New Zealand forces fought in almost all theaters, including the heroic defense of Greece in 1941. New Zealand joined Australia and Great Britain in sending troops into Malaya during the crisis in that country in June 1948. In a plebiscite held on 3 August 1949, the populace voted overwhelmingly to establish a peacetime military service. New Zealand also participated in the Colombo Plan (qv) for Southeast Asia (1950) and in 1951 became a part of the ANZUS defense pact along with Australia and the United States. It also joined the Southeast Asia Treaty Organization (SEATO) (qv) in 1954. New Zealand forces served in Korea (qv) and Cyprus (qv) and in a number of other conflicts during those years. An economic crisis heralded the assumption of power in New Zealand by the Labor Party. The National Party regained power in 1960, and under their leadership New Zealand sent forces to Vietnam to fight in that conflict, the first troops arriving on 21 July 1965. In October 1967, New Zealand, along with Australia, increased its military committment in Vietnam. On 20 August 1970, however, the government announced it would withdraw half its forces in Vietnam by the end of 1971. The entire New Zealand force began withdrawing on 7 November 1971 and completed the withdrawal on 14 December 1972. In November 1971, New Zealand joined in a joint commitment of forces to the defense of Singapore. After 1972, the Labor Party again took power, and in 1973 it established diplomatic relations with Communist China. In June 1973, New Zealand joined Australia in sending warships into French waters around Mururoa (qv) to prevent further nuclear testing on the atoll. The New Zealand warship was withdrawn on 5 August because of resupply problems. In 1975, the National Party returned to leadership, which was again switched to the Labor Party in 1984. Earlier, on 10 September 1977, New Zealand imposed a 200-mile economic exclusion zone around its islands that went into effect on 1 October. That same year, New Zealand banned all nuclear-powered vessels from its ports, which led to strained relations with the United States. In march 1978, the government expanded the exclusion zone to include fishing. New Zealand resumed full diplomatic relations with the Soviet Union on 20 February 1984, and on 31 January 1985 it reaffirmed its commitment to refuse port facilities to nuclear-armed or nuclear-powered ships. On 10 July 1985, the Greenpeace flagship *Rainbow Warrior* was sunk by two bombs attached to its hull by French intelligence agents while it was moored in Auckland Harbor. The ship was being readied to sail into the waters around Mururoa to protest continued French nuclear weapons testing there. One crewman was killed aboard the ship. The French finally admitted to the crime in September 1985. Following a review of New Zealand's actions in banning nuclear warships from its ports, the U.S. abandoned its defense obligations to New Zealand; this led to the dissolution of the ANZUS alliance in 1986. A 1990 election contested primarily along economic lines once again saw a change in government, with the National Party (NP) once again gaining power. The NP held power by the slimmest of majorities following the 1993 elections. The NP's hold on power was strengthened in 1995, when the prime minister's response to French nuclear testing at Mururoa increased his popularity. Violence occurred among the Maori, who demanded compensation and sovereignty over lands confiscated by the British during the white settlement era. One facet of the violence was the torching of the Rangiatea Anglican Church at Otaki by an arsonist. This church was considered the "Maori Cathedral" and the center of their Christian religious faith. As a result of this incident and of the years of conflict with the Maoris, Queen Elizabeth II publicly apologized for the abuses against the Maori in the signing of the Tainui Agreement on 2 November. *Reading:* Gordon L. Steinbrook, *Allies and Mates: An American Soldier with the Australians and New Zealanders in Vietnam 1966-67* (1995); W. Davis McInture, *Background to the ANZUS Pact: Policy-Making, Strategy and Diplomacy, 1945-55* (1995); Malcolm McKinnon, *Independence and Foreign Policy: New Zealand in the World since 1935* (1993).

Ngendandumwe, Pierre. On 15 January 1965, Burundi Prime Minister Pierre Ngenandumwe (a Hutu) was assassinated by a Tutsi gunman in the continuing conflict between the Hutu and Tutsi tribes of Burundi following that country's independence (July 1962). *See* Burundi.

Ngo Dinh Diem. (b. 3 January 1901, Quang Binh Province, Vietnam—d. 2 November 1963, Cho Lon, Saigon, South Vietnam) Born a Roman Catholic into a noble Vietnamese family, Diem was educated at the French school of administration in Hue. He then joined the civil service and served as minister of interior in the Bao Dai (qv) government in the 1930s. He was captured by the communists in 1945, and Ho Chi Minh asked him to join the nationalist cause. Diem rejected the offer and fled the country, living for a time in the United States and in Europe. In 1954, Diem returned to Vietnam to serve as prime minister in the Bao Dai government (7 July 1954) and then to head the U.S.–supported government after he deposed Bao Dai (10 May 1955). (The formal refererendum deposing Bao Dai was completed on 23 October 1955.) He filled many of the top positions in his government with members of his family and began an autocratic rule that was unacceptable to the Buddhist elements in his country. As one of his first acts as president, on 16 July 1955, Diem announced his government would not take part in the Paris Peace Accords unless the signators gauranteed the security of South Vietnam. During his tenure he failed to implement most of his promised reforms and imprisoned or murdered thousands of the majority Buddhist opposition. At the same time, the communist insurgency grew in South Vietnam, which finally led to a withdrawal of U.S. support and a subsequent bloody coup by a number of Vietnamese generals in which Diem and his immediate family were murdered by their captors. *Reading:* Ellen J. Hammer, *A Death in November: America in Vietnam, 1963* (1988).

Ngo Dinh Nhu. The brother and chief advisor of Ngo Dinh Diem.

Ngo Dinh Nhu, Madame. Called the "Dragon Lady," Madame Nhu was the wife of Ngo Dinh Nhu. She was an outspoken critic of the Buddhists and was murdered by her captors along with her husband and brother-in-law. *See* Ngo Dinh Diem.

Ngouabi, Marien. (b. 1938, French Equatorial Africa—d. 18 March 1977, Brazzavile) Ngouabi graduated from the French Military Academy, St. Cyr, in 1962 and became a member of the central committee of the sole political party in Congo, the National Movement for Revolution (NMR). On 4 September 1968, President Alphonse Massamba-Debat (qv) was replaced by Major Ngouabi as leader of the Republic of Congo (Brazzaville) (1January 1969). Ngouabi, a socialist northerner, renamed the country the People's Republic of Congo (31 December 1969). He survived one coup attempt 22 February 1972, which was alleged by his opponents to have been a government-planned trap to expose his opposition. Ngouabi's policies led to even larger southern tribal opposition, and he was assassinated on 18 March 1977. Suspected of complicity in the assassination, Massamba-Debat was arrested and executed on 25 March 1977.

Nguyen Houng. At the height of the sociopolitical upheaval in the Republic of Vietnam that eventually led to the downfall of Ngo Dinh Diem (qv), a 21-year old Buddhist monk, Nguyen Houng, burned himself to death in Phan Thiet. This act set off a chain of immolations in South Vietnam. *See* Vietnam.

Nha Trang. *See* Vietnam.

Niamey. *See* Niger.

Nianio. *See* Senegal.

Niazi, A. A. K. Lieutenant General Niazi commanded approximately 90,000 troops in East Pakistan who were forced to surrender to Indian forces on 16 December 1971. This action ended the fighting in the Indo-Pakistani War. *See* Indo-Pakistani War.

Nicaragua. The Republic of Nicaragua (*Republica de Nicaragua*) is the largest country in Central America. It is bordered on the north by Honduras, on the east by the Caribbean Sea, on the south by Costa Rica, and on the west by the Pacific Ocean. The capital city is Managua. The region was first sighted by Christopher Columbus in 1502, but was not settled until 1522, when Spanish conquistadors landed. A struggle for power existed among the conquistadors until 1531, when the region was placed under the authority of the captain-general of Guatemala. English seamen, notably Sir Franicis Drake and Sir Richard Hawkins, raided the coast frequently. In the eighteenth century, the British, having allied themselves with the black and Indian Miskito people, challenged Spanish authority in the region and from the mid-1700s controlled the Caribbean coastline (called the Mosquito Coast). The Battle of Nicaragua in the late eighteenth century ended

British control of the coast. In the early nineteenth century a movement toward independence from Spain began, and in 1821 Nicaragua declared itself independent. In 1822, Nicaragua became a part of the short-lived Mexican Augustin de Iturbide empire, and in 1823 it joined the United Provinces of Central America. A civil war followed during which the Liberals established Nicaragua as an independent republic (1838). The war continued, however, and in 1855 the Liberals hired a band of mercenaries led by William Walker to lead their forces. After sacking Grenada in 1855, Walker became president of Nicaragua in 1856. When Walker seized the assets of Cornelius Vanderbilt, Vanderbilt began financing the Conservatives, and Walker was forced to flee the country in 1857. A successful Liberal revolt in 1893 brought the Liberals back into power and placed Jose Santos Zelaya in the presidency. He ruled as a dictator until 1909, when he was ousted from office. During a 1912 revolt, the new president, Adolfo Diaz, asked for U.S. military support, and U.S. Marines were sent into the country. When the Byran-Chammoro Treaty was signed in 1916—which would have allowed the U.S. to build a canal across Nicaragua and establish military bases there—serious protests throughout Central America began an anti-American guerrilla campaign in Nicaragua. U.S. Marines remained in Nicaragua until 1925, and soon after their withdrawal rebellion again broke out. U.S. forces were returned into the country in 1926. A U.S.-supervised election was held in 1928, with a Liberal being chosen president. However, other Liberal leaders refused to follow the new president, and another anti-American guerrilla campaign began. In 1933, the U.S. Marines were again withdrawn, leaving Anastasio Somoza in command of the National Guard. Somoza held control in Nicaragua for the next 20 years. During this time, Nicaragua declared war on Germany and Japan on 9 December 1941 and, in June 1945, became a charter member of the United Nations. It joined the Organization of American States in 1951. Somoza was assassinated in 1956 and was succeeded by his son, Luis Somoza (qv). Following his tenure, other Somoza followers held office until 1967, when Anastasio Somoza-Debayle (qv), the older Somoza's youngest son, became president. The new president soon established himself as a dictator, abrogating the constitution in 1971. In the election in February 1972, Somoza's candidates won lopsided victories, at which point Somoza stepped down as president (May 1972) to become the commander of the armed forces and the power behind the three-man junta appointed to run the country. When a major earthquake devastated the capital city of Managua, martial law was declared, and Somoza again assumed dictatorial power. He was formally elected president in 1974. In early 1978 Pedro Joaquin Chammoro, the editor of *La Prensa* and a vociferous opponent of the Somoza regime, was assassinated. Following this incident, the Sandinista National Liberation Front, which had been formed in 1962, plunged the country into a new civil war. By 1979, the countryside was in chaos. The United States urged Somoza to step down in favor of a moderate coalition government in what was seen as a communist attempt to establish a Cuba-like state in Central America. Somoza resigned on 17 July 1979 and went into exile, first in Miami and then in Paraguay, where he was subsequently assassinated (1980). The Sandnistas took control of an economically destitute country and used U.S. aid to restore an equilibrium, but the U.S. soon withdrew its support of the leftest Sandinistas (1981) and began instead to support anti-Sandinista guerrilla (Contra) forces. In 1982, Nicaragua signed an aid agreement with the USSR. In November 1984, the Sandinista presidential candidate, Daniel Ortega Saavedra (qv), won by a large plurality. In October 1985, he declared a state of emergency, which deprived the citizenry of their civil rights. That same year, the U.S. Congress voted down any support to the Contras and none was forthcoming until October 1986. In November 1987, the Iran-Contra affair story broke in the U.S. press which told of arms shipments sent to the Contras while official U.S. aid had been suspended. In March 1988, a temporary truce was signed, and on 25 February 1990, a UN-supervised election was held in which the U.S.–backed National Opposition Union (UNO) defeated the Sandinistas in the National Assembly, thus ousting Daniel Ortega. The new president, Violeta Barrios de Chammora, took office in April 1990. Since that point the economic conditions in Nicaragua have shown marked improvement. In 1991, the president appointed Ortega's brother, Humberto Ortega, to be chief of staff of the army. This angered some Contras, who prepared to reopen the civil war. In 1993, the Contras took 38 hostages in an attempt to force Ortega's resignation. The Sandinistas then retaliated by kidnapping the vice-president and 32 others. All hostages were released in August 1993. In 1994 the president agreed to remove Ortega, but this only further infuriated the Sandinistas. At the same time, however, the National Assembly approved a reorganization that did not provide for a civilian defense minister. This move irritated the opposition because it meant the military council still controlled the country's armed forces. A truce was reached earlier, in February, whereby rebels fighting in the north laid down their arms. Still, there was violence, primarily criminal in nature, in the countryside. In June, the army moved against those armed groups operating in the north. A constitutional crisis occurred in February 1995, when three additional judges (9 became 12) were added to the Supreme Court of Justice by the National Assembly. When the president refused to acknowledge the new additions, a confrontation developed between the presidential and legislative branches of Nicaragua's government. *Reading:* John Brentlinger, *The Best of What We Are: Reflections on the Nicaraguan Revolution* (1995); Glenn Garvin, *Everybody Had His Own Gringo: The CIA and the Contras* (1992); Tomas Borge, *Nicaragua: The Sandinista People's Revolution* (1985); Lawrence Pezzullo & Ralph Pezzullo, *At the Fall of Somoza* (1994); Manzar Foroohar, *The Catholic Church and Social Change in Nicaragua* (1989).

Nicosia. *See* Cyprus.

Niger (*Republique du Niger*). The Republic of Niger is located in northwest central Africa and is landlocked. Niger is bordered on the north west by Algeria, on the upper northeast by Libya, on the east by Chad, on the south by Nigeria, on the southeast by Benin, on the southwest by Burkina Faso and on the lower northwest by Mali. The capital city is Niamey. Niger is known to have been inhabited from Paleolithic times. Saharan farmers moved into the region in the fifth millennium B.C., having drifted south as the Sahara became a desert. The Taureg people established themselves in the region in the eleventh century and established a sultanate there in the fifteenth century. Another people, the Hausa, also entered the region in the fourteenth century and by the eighteenth century had displaced the Tauregs. Another group, the Fulani, overran the Hausa and established the kingdon of Sokoto later in that same period. During the Middle Ages the Niger region lay astride the central caravan routes from North Africa to the Hausa states and the empires of Mali and Songhi. Islam was brought into the region by Muslim missionaries travelling this route. European explorers first entered the region in the eighteenth and nineteenth centuries, and in the latter part of the nineteenth century, France established a sphere of influence there. In 1904, Niger became a part of French West Africa. Fighting erupted during this period that lasted until 1906. In 1916, a new tribal insurrection began but was quickly suppressed. Another rebellion in the northern provinces was quashed in 1932. In 1959, Niger joined the Sahel-Benin Entente (originally called the *Conceil de l'Entente)* along with Dahomey (now Benin), Ivory Coast and Upper Volta (now Burkina Faso). This was primarily an economic pact, but it added to the independence fervor that swept French West Africa. Niger proclaimed its independence on 3 August 1960 (first granted in 1958) and withdrew from the French community. In 1961, however, it signed a bilateral agreement with France that established economic and cultural ties. At that time, Hamani Diori (qv) was elected Niger's first president by the legislature (9 November), and a long period of unrest began. In 1964, government forces crushed a rebellion aimed at Diori's overthrow. In April 1965, there was an attempt on his life. That same year, Diori was reelected president. In January 1973, Niger, along with Congo and Mali, broke diplomatic relations with Israel. In 1974, a military coup overthrew Diori, and Lieutenant Colonel Seyni Kountche (qv) became head of state. In 1980, somewhat overconfident, Kountche released Diori from imprisonment in which he had been held since the coup. An unsuccessful coup attempt was made on Kountche's leadership on 6 October 1983, while he was in France. Upon Kountche's death from a brain tumor in 1987, General Ali Saibou (Seybou), the army chief of staff, and Kountche's cousin became head of state and president. Saibou was reelected in 1989 in a single-party election. In August 1991, the constitution was suspended, but Saibou remained interim president until 1993. In 1993, Niger held its first free elections. The opposition candidate, Mahamane Ousmane, won the presidency. The Tuareg rebellion continued in northern Niger into 1994, but in May peace negotiations between the two sides were attempted in Paris. While the process was advancing, a major battle took place on 28 September. A comprehensive agreement was reached on 9 October 1995 that gave the Tuaregs limited regional autonomy (final signing, 24 April 1995). The government arrested a large number of members of the major opposition party following student violence in March 1995. The issue was a problem of unpaid student grants, which the opposition political party claimed was due to ineffectual government. More demonstrations led to more arrests before the end of the year. Major political infighting in 1995 jeopardized the continuation of the country's move toward democracy. *Reading:* Finn Fuglestad, *A History of Niger, 1850-1960* (1984); Joseph A. Umoren, *Democracy and Ethnic Diversity in Niger* (1996).

Nigeria. More formally the Federal Republic of Nigeria, this country is located in west central Africa. It is bordered on the north by Niger, on the northeast by Lake Chad, on the east by Cameroon, on the south by the Gulf of Guinea and on the west by Benin. The capital city is Abuja. Identifiable people have occupied the region since the fifth century B.C. By the eleventh century A.D., there were migrations of Fulani and Hausa tribes into the northern parts of the region, and the Bornu people in the east who established the kingdom of Kanem. In 1085 A.D., Islam was introduced. The Kanem Empire ended in the late 14th century and shrank to what is present-day Bornu province. The Hausa were several times overrun during this period. By the nineteenth century, nomadic-warrior Fulani rulers dominated a number of Hausa states. The first Europeans, the Portuguese, explored the Nigerian coast in the fifteenth century (1472) and began taking slaves from the Benin region. The British set up a naval force in the area to halt the slaving and also began to trade with the natives. Exploration of the interior came later. Although the British banned slavery in 1807, the practice continued for some time, with most slaves being transported to the Americas. The British annexed Lagos in 1861 and established the British Royal Niger Company in 1879. Nigeria became a British colony in 1886. In 1897 a treaty fixed the boundaries between the British (Nigeria) and French (Niger) regions. In 1914, there was a displacement of the original boundaries, and the region became the Colony and Protectorate of Nigeria. Following World War I, a nationalist movement developed, particularly in the eastern part of the country. No political parties developed, however, until 1944. On 1 October 1960, Nigeria gained its independence within the Commonwealth and joined the United Nations at that time. Nigeria became a republic in October 1963, divided first into 12 states. (By 1991 the number of states had risen to 30.) On 15–16 January 1966, a violent military coup overthrew the government of Prime Minister Sir Abudakar Tafawa Balewa (qv). The prime minister and 50 other senior government officials and politicians were killed. A fight for power among the Muslim Hausa and Christian Ibo military then ensued. General Johnson Aguyi-Ironsi (qv) (Ibo) finally emerged as the victor and established a provisional government. On 29 July of that same year, a second coup took place when the army mutinied. Aguyi-Ironsi was killed by opposition Hausa tribesmen. A Hausa officer, Colonel Yakubu Gowon (qv) (Hausa), took the presidency, and a long reign of terror began against the southern Christian Ibo (*Igbo*) people, which resulted in the killing of thousands of Ibo. The Ibo then fled to the east, where they established (13 May 1967) the independent state of Biafra. On 13 April 1968, the African nation of Tanzania extended diplomatic relations to the breakaway Biafra government. On 24 April, Czechoslovakia suspended arms shipments to Nigeria. Gabon, another African state, recognized Biafra on 8 May, and Zambia did the same thing on 20 May. From 23 May to 31

May, talks to settle the Nigerian crisis were held in Kampala, Uganda. Then, on 6 June, the Netherlands suspended arms shipments to Nigeria, followed by Belgium on 5 July. More peace talks were held in Niamey, Niger, on 20 July. These talks were then moved to Addis Ababa, Ethiopia, on 5 August. On 10 August 1969, the talks had reached a stalemate and were adjourned. By 1969, Nigerian troops had captured much of Biafra, and in 1970 the Biafrans surrendered. Gowon was overthrown on 29 July 1975 by the Hausa general Murtula Ramat Mohammed. He was assassinated on 13 February 1976, and a Supreme Military Council took power, with General Olusegun Obasanjo as leader. Political parties were authorized in 1978, and an election held on 11 August 1979 imposed a new constitution and chose Alhaji Shehu Shagari as president. Shagari was reelected in August 1983. Charges of corruption brought about another coup on 1 October 1983 and brought General Mohammed Buhari to power. Buhari was overthrown in August 1985 by General Ibrahim Babangida, who first promised a return to civilian control by 1992 but then voided the results of a 23 June 1993 election; rioting followed in which many were killed. On 26 August 1993, Babangida resigned in favor of a civilian government, but a military coup overthrew this group on 17 November. In June 1994, Moshood Abiola, the man who had won the 1993 election, declared himself president but was quickly arrested and imprisoned; violence followed. On 6 September 1994, General Sani Abacha, the nation's current leader, declared his regime held "absolute power" in Nigeria. This claim was somewhat proven when Sani Abacha had nine men from the Ogoni ethnic group hanged (10 November 1995) for plotting the murder of four people after a secret trial (31 October). Claiming they were framed, the group went to their deaths protesting their innocence and blaming the president and Nigerian oil interests for their fate. Many countries interrupted diplomatic relations, and the British Commonwealth suspended Nigeria's seat on the council. A possible coup attempt was averted earlier in the year when, in March, 29 officers and civilians were arrested. Many believed that Sani Abacha was simply weeding out his opposition and that no coup had been planned. Entreaties for the release of those arrested fell on deaf ears. Finally, however, the sentences of more than 40 defendants in the case were commuted (1 October) because of international pressure on the government. *Reading:* Roman Loimeire, *Islamic Reform and Political Change in Northern Nigeria* (1997); Herbert Ekwe-Ekwe, *The Biafra War: Nigeria and the Aftermath* (1990); S. Egite Oyovbaire, *Federalism in Nigeria: A Study in the Development of the Nigerian State* (1985); Herbert Ekwe-Ekwe, *Conflict and Intervention in Africa: Nigeria, Angola, Zaire* (1990).

Nile River. *See* Egypt.

al-Nimeiry (Numeiry, Nimeiri), Mohommed Gaafar (*Ja'far Muhammad an-Numayri*). (b. 1 January 1930, Wad Nubawi, Omdurman, Sudan) Born the son of a Muslim postal employee, Nimeiry joined the army and graduated from the Sudanese Military Academy in 1952. Influenced by Gamal Nasser's (qv) revolution of 1952, Nimeiry was involved in several plots to overthrow the

Sudanese government. After graduating from the US Army Command and General Staff College at Fort Leavenworth, Kansas, in 1966, Nimeiry returned to Sudan and, on 25 May 1969, led a successful coup against the government of President Isma'il al-Azhari and Prime Minister Mohammed Ahmed Mahgoub (qv). He then established himself as the prime minister under the Sudanese Revolutionary Command Council (RCC) and followed a socialist economic policy. One of his first acts was to crush the Ansar religious sect, which stood in opposition to his rule, following an unsuccessful coup attempt on 27 March 1970. The leader of the sect, Imam al-Hadi al-Mahdi, was killed as he tried to escape to Ethiopia on 31 March. Nimeiry was temporarily out of power following a successful coup attempt in which control of the country changed hands several times (July 1971), but he was restored, after which he suppressed the communist party in his country. In September 1971, Nimeiry was elected president by an overwhelming majority of voters. He then dissolved the RCC and established the Sudanese Socialist Union (1972). Economic crises continued to hamper his moves to reform his country and brought on a series of coups attempts against his rule, all of which were defeated. When Egypt's Anwar Sadat (qv) moved to establish a rapproachment with Israel, Nimeiry was the first of the few Muslim leaders who supported him. On 6 March 1973, Nimeiry accused *al-Fatah* (qv) of the attack on the Saudi embassy in Khartoum in which a number of diplomats, including two Americans, were killed. Another coup attempt took place on 5 September 1975, when rebellious army personnel seized the radio station in Omdurman. They were later crushed by loyal troops. Another coup attempt, this time backed by Libya and led by former Sudanese prime minister Sadik al-Madhi, failed on 2 July 1976. Nimeiry served as president of the Organization of African Unity (qv) in 1978. On 5 October 1981 he dissolved Parliament as the threat to his country from Libya continued to grow. Intelligence sources told Nimeiry (22 February 1983) that Libya had postponed a planned invasion of Sudan. His attempt to impose Islamic law on his people led to violent unrest in the predominantly Christian southern province. On 29 April 1984, Nimeiry declared a state of emergency and granted special powers to the military. He was overthrown in a military coup led by his defense minister, General 'Abd ar-Rahman Sowar, on 6 April 1985. Nimeiry was visiting the United States at the time.

Niriim. *See* Israel.

Nitzanin. *See* Israel.

Nixon, Richard Milhous. (b. 9 January 1913, Yorba Linda, California—d. 22 April 1994) Born of poor parents, Richard Nixon was graduated from Whittier College (California) in 1934. He then attended law school at Duke University, North Carolina, graduating in 1937. He returned to Whittier where he set up practice and married Thelma (Pat) Nixon in 1940. With the outbreak of World War II, Nixon joined the U.S. Navy, serving in the South Pacific. He left the service at the end of the war as a lieutenant commander. He then entered politics and defeated the incumbent Democrat for a seat in the Congress of the United States. In Congress he gained a wide reputation as a member of the House Un-

American Activities Committee in the investigation of Alger Hiss in the so-called Pumpkin Scandal. In 1950, he ran for the U.S. Senate labelling his opponent, Helen Gahagen, the "Pink Lady." Although he was elected, he was widely critized for his use of the "communist" label without sufficient proof. In 1952, however, he was nominated to be Dwight D. Eisenhower's running mate. The disclosure of questionable sources of campaign funds nearly forced him off the ticket, but his now-famous "Checkers" television speech helped him save his political life. He served as vice president of the United States from 1952 until 1960. In July 1959, he confronted Soviet premier Nikita Khrushchev (qv) in the so-called Kitchen Debate. In 1960, Nixon was chosen as the Republican candidate for president but narrowly lost the election to John F. Kennedy (qv). Returning to California, he was defeated in the race for governor of that state in 1962. He then angrily announced he was leaving political life. In New York City he established a law practice, but continued to speak out on foreign policy issues and to address various Republican functions. In 1968, he was elected president of the United States. In office he left domestic affairs to others and concentrated on international affairs. Along with Henry Kissinger, Nixon crafted the U.S. withdrawal from Vietnam—even so, it took four years and mounting casualties, largely because of North Vietnamese intransigence. He authorized the incursion into Cambodia in 1970 and the bombing of Hanoi and the mining of the harbor at Haiphong (*see* Vietnam) to encourage the North Vietnamese to negotiate. These actions proved unpopular at home, however, and massive demonstrations in protest occurred across the country. Nixon's greatest foreign policy success was in the opening of discussions with Communist China, which culminated in a secret meeting between Kissinger and Chou En-Lai (qv) in July 1971 and in Nixon's visit to China in 1972. Nixon next visited Moscow, where the first steps toward the Strategic Arms Limitation Treaty (SALT) (qv) were taken. This heralded the opening of the period of détente between the two superpowers and the reduction of the threat of nuclear confrontation. Nixon's policies in the Middle East also led to success when, after 1973, the U.S. replaced the USSR as Egypt's friend. In domestic policy Nixon was not quite so successful, which led to, among other things, the recession of 1974. Throughout the period after his reelection in 1972, the specter of Watergate hung over him, and by October 1973 his popularity had plummeted. He was named a coconspirator by a federal grand jury in March 1974, and on 8 August 1974, Nixon resigned the presidency effective 9 August rather than face impeachment proceedings by the U.S. House of Representatives. He was immediately pardoned by his successor, Vice President Gerald Ford (qv). Thereafter, Nixon lived a relatively quiet life until his death on 22 April 1994. *Reading:* Bob Woodward & Carl Bernstein, The Final Days: The Classic, Behind-the-Scenes Account of Richard Nixon's Dramatic Last Days in the White House (1994); Tom Wicker, *One of Us: Richard Nixon and the American Dream* (1995).

Nizzana. *See* Israel.

Nkomati Non-Agression Treaty. *See* Accord of Nkomati.

Nkomo, Joshua Mqabuko Nyongolo. (b. 19 June 1917, Semokwe Reserve, Matabeleland) Born the son of a Karanga tribe cattle-raising teacher and lay preacher, Nkomo took his primary education in Rhodesia before going to South Africa. In South Africa he attended Adams College in Natal and then the Jan Hofmeyer School of Social Work in Johannesburg. In 1945 he became a social worker on the Rhodesian Railway and became the secretary general of the Rhodesian Railways African Employees' Association. Through distance study he earned his Bachelor's degree from the University of South Africa in 1951. He entered politics in 1952 and became involved in a number of illegal nationalist groups, including the African National Congress (ANC). In 1957, he was elected president of the ANC. When the ANC was banned in Rhodesia in 1957, Nkomo fled to England to escape imprisonment. Nkomo returned to Rhodesia in 1960 and organized the National Democratic Party (NDP), which was banned in 1961. He then founded and became the president of the Zimbabwe African People's Union (ZAPU). Because of this, the white Rhodesian government held Nkomo in detention for ten years (April 1964–December 1974) in the remote village of Gonakudwingwa. Upon his release, Nkomo led the guerrilla war that finally won black rule for his nation. Before that, however, he found that his ZANU was eclipsed by the Zimbabwe African National Union (ZANU) led by Robert Mugabe (qv). In 1976, ZAPU and ZANU joined in an uneasy alliance called the Patriotic Front. In 1979–1980, the white minority government in Rhodesia gave way to the black-dominated government of an independent Zimbabwe. When the stronger ZANU swept the parliamentary elections, ethnic fighting broke out after Mugabe, the prime minister, dismissed Nkomo from the cabinet (17 February 1982) upon evidence that Nkomo was involved in plot to overthrow the government. More than 300 deaths were reported in eight days of fighting. In March 1983, Nkomo was forced to flee the country as government forces mopped up residual rebel resistance. He returned from his short exile in England on 15 August 1983. In 1987, Nkomo became vice-president under Mugabe. In 1988, ZAPU and ZANU were formally joined into one party. Nkomo remained in office as vice-president of Zimbabwe in 1995.

Nkrumah, Kwame. (b. September 1909, Nkroful, Gold Coast—d. 27 April 1972, Bucharest, Romania) Born the son of a Roman Catholic goldsmith, Nkrumah was educated in Catholic schools and graduated from Achimota College in 1930. He became a Roman Catholic school teacher, but he was drawn toward politics. He then attended the University of Pennsylvania and Lincoln, where he received master's degrees. During this period he was known to describe himself as "nondenominational Christian and a Marxist socialist." He became the president of the African Students' Organization in the U.S. and Canada. Nkrumah left the U.S. and went to England in May 1945. There, he organized the Fifth Pan-African Congress, which was held in Manchester. In late 1947, Nkrumah was called home to become the secretary general of the United Gold Coast Convention, an organization established to gain independence by constitutional means. After rioting followed a number of meetings at which Nkrumah spoke, he was arrested by the British (February 1948). His detention was brief, and shortly thereafter Nkrumah took the leadership of a splinter group, the Convention Peoples' Party (CPP). In January 1950 he ordered a policy of non-cooperation and non-violent demonstrations against British rule. Because of the crisis, that ensued Nkrumah was again arrested and sentenced to one year in prison. In February 1951, however, he was elected to the Gold Coast parliament and the British released him from jail. In 1952, he became the prime minister of Gold Coast. In March 1957, Gold Coast joined with Togoland to become the independent state of Ghana. Nkrumah became its first prime minister. Even through he adopted an authoritarian style of leadership and arrests without warrant became common for political opponents, his popularity rose. In 1960, when Ghana became a republic, Nkrumah became its president. Although he strove for unity among all Africans, he became out of touch with his own constituency in Ghana, and his once-prosperous nation became impoverished. Following the failure of a number of governmental programs, his rule became one of ever-increasing political repression and drifting toward communism. An attempt was made on his life at Kulugungu in August 1962. This was followed by a series of other assassination attempts, which drove Nkrumah into seclusion and caused a heavy increase in security in the country. Corruption also grew on a grand scale until 24 February 1966, when a military coup overthrew his regime while he was on a state visit to Peking. As Nkumah could not return to Ghana, he sought political asylum in Guinea, where he was named co-president with Sekou Toure (qv) and where he remained until his death. He died of cancer while undergoing medical treatment in Bucharest, Romania, on 27 April 1972. *Reading:* Kwame Arhin, *The Life and Work of Kwame Nkrumah* (1993); Douglas Kellner, *Kwame Nkrumah* (1987).

Noel, Cleo, Jr. On 2 March 1973, Cleo Noel, Jr., the newly appointed U.S. ambassador to Sudan, was murdered in the Saudi embassy in Khartoum, Sudan, during an evening reception. A group of eight Black September terrorists had seized the embassy on 1 March, demanding the release of political prisoners in the U.S., Jordan and West Germany. The U.S. charge d'affaires George C. Moore and the Belgian charge d'affaires Guy Eid were also murdered. The terrorists surrendered on 4 March. After some time, the terrorists were deported to Egypt, where they were released to the Palestine Liberation Organization.

Nokrashy Pasha (Mahmud Fahmi an-Nuqrashi Pasha). In 1937, a split developed in the Wafd Party after King Farouk came of age and assumed the throne of Egypt in his own right. One result of the rift was the expulsion of Nokrashy Pasha and Ahmad Mahir (Maher Pasha), who together formed the Sa'dist Group in opposition to the Wafd. In the December 1938 elections, the Wafd won only 12 seats.

Nolting, Frederick E., Jr. On 27 June 1963, the United States announced that Henry Cabot Lodge would succeed Frederick E. Nolting as the ambassador to the Republic of Vietnam. Nolting had been appointed to the Southeast Asian post by John F. Kennedy (qv) in March 1961. He was a man of excellent reputation but had gained most of his diplomatic experience in Europe, most recently as the chief of the political ection at NATO. He had never been to Asia and had no previous experience with the kind of struggle that was unfolding there. At Nolting's request at the time of his appointment to Vietnam, William Trueheart, a man of much the same background, was appointed Nolting's deputy. Most historians agree that, in his selection of Nolting and Trueheart, Kennedy harvested the fruits of the McCarthy era when almost all of the "China Hands" and Asian experts in the State Department had been irresponsibly branded possible security risks. Few, if any, were later available when Kennedy needed them.

Nomad Guards (Chad). On 1 April 1977, the government of President Felix Malloum of Chad was able to withstand a coup attempt led by mutinous army troops calling themselves the Nomad Guards. Nine of the mutineers were executed on 6 April.

Nong Chan. *See* Kampuchea (Cambodia).

Non Mak Mun. *See* Thailand.

Non-Proliferation Treaty (NPT). Also called the Nuclear Non-Proliferation Treaty, this agreement was signed by Great Britain, the United States, the USSR and 59 other nations on 1 July 1968.. In the treaty the three major signatories agreed not to assist nations not possessing nuclear weapons to procure or produce them. The United States ratified the treaty on 13 March 1969. The treaty went into effect on 5 March 1970. On 27 August 1980, the third periodic review of the treaty took place in Geneva. That group called for a Comprehensive Test Ban Treaty on 21 August.

Norris, Percy. On 27 November 1984, the British Deputy High Commissioner for India, Percy Norris, was assassinated in Bombay by two members of the Revolutionary Organization of Socialist Muslims. Norris was shot to death as he was being driven to work.

North Africa. *See* individual countries.

North America. *See* individual countries.

North Atlantic Council. *See* North Atlantic Treaty Organization (NATO).

North Atlantic Treaty Organization (NATO). NATO was formed after World War II to implement the North Atlantic Treaty signed on 4 April 1949 and was put into force on 24 August 1949. The new organization was to be a military force to offset the threat posed by Soviet military forces in Eastern Europe. The original members of NATO included Belgium, Canada, Denmark, France, Iceland, Italy, Luxembourg, the Netherlands, Norway, Portugal, the United Kingdom and the United States. Greece and Turkey joined in February 1952. West Germany joined in 1955 after the North Atlantic Council approved its membership on 22 October 1954. Spain joined in May 1982. NATO headquarters was established in Brussels, Belgium. France withdrew its forces from NATO control in 1966 but remained a member of the alliance. The alliance came about as a result of the Marshall Plan, which offered economic support to rebuild Western Europe in return for each nation's cooperation in the mutual defense of the European continent. Before NATO existed, Britain, France and the Low Countries had agreed to a mutual defense pact called the Brussels Treaty (March 1948), but it was soon clear that their combined forces were no match against Soviet military power without the aid of the United States. Thus, the North Atlantic Treaty was signed in 1949, in Washington, DC. With the treaty in place, the United States began taking the steps necessary to increase Western military power. To do this, $1 billion was appropriated by the members in military aid to NATO. After the start of the Korean War, the U.S. took additional steps to strengthen the alliance. These included calling Dwight D. Eisenhower out of retirement and assigning him as the Supreme Allied Commander, Europe (SACEUR). That action was confirmed by the North Atlantic Council, NATO's governing body, which is composed of ministerial representatives of the signatories. All NATO commanders to date have been U.S. generals. About $3 billion has been spent in keeping NATO in readiness to fight Soviet aggression. The United States has contributed more than one-third of the total expenditures. With the demise of the Soviet Union and the end of the Cold War, the NATO mission has been under review. One of the outcomes of this review has been the insertion of NATO forces into Bosnia-Herzegovina to enforce the peace. Neither Russia nor its former Soviet satellites have been allowed membership into NATO as of the end of 1995, but a number have applied. *Reading:* Ted Carpenter, *Beyond NATO: Staying Out of Europe's Wars* (1994); John Leech, *Halt! Who Goes There? The Future of NATO in the New Europe* (1991); Philip H. Gordon, ed., *NATO's Transformation: The Changing Shape of the Atlantic Alliance* (1996).

Northern Ireland (Ulster). (For early history, *see* Ireland.) From early times, Irish culture developed somewhat differently in Northern Ireland in the region that was known as Ulster (Celtic, *Ulaid*). By the end of the seventeenth century a large Protestant population inhabited the nine northern counties, while the 23 counties in the south remained predominantly Catholic. The whole of Ireland was joined to Great Britain by the 1801 Act of Union under the name the United Kingdom. By the end of the nineteenth century, however, the issue of Irish Home Rule had taken on major proportions and had been propelled by a number of crises, not the least of which was the Great Famine of the 1840s. Home Rule bills were presented in 1886, 1893 and 1912–1914. World War I caused a postponement of any action on the legislation. Finally, in 1920, the Government of Ireland Act granted six (Antrim, Armagh, Down, Fermanagh, Londonderry and Tyrone) of the nine Ulster counties home rule as one unit, and the 23 southern counties plus three Ulster counties (Cavan, Donegal and Monaghan) were granted a separate home rule option. The northern counties accepted home rule; the southern counties did not and went on to gain independence as the Republic of Ireland (qv). Until 1940, Northern Ireland was governed by the predominantly Protestant majority with paternal guidance from London, and to the suffering of the Irish Catholic minority. At the same time, the Irish Catholic population was shifting as more and more of them gave up rural life for cities such as Belfast, where factory and shipbuilding jobs were to be found. During World War II, when Ireland remained neutral, Northern Irish troops fought alongside their British comrades. Belfast was severely damaged by German bombing. In 1949, when the Republic of Ireland was given its independence, the

British government affirmed Ulster as part of the United Kingdom, to remain so until the Northern Irish parliament decided otherwise. This action, in effect, amounted to a partition of Ireland. Although the new republic agreed to the partition by its silence and its withdrawal from the Commonwealth, it still claimed Ulster as its own. By the 1960s Irish Catholic rights protests brought about violent clashes with the Protestants, and the outlawed Provisional Wing of the Irish Republican Army (IRA) began an intensive terrorist campaign against the Northern Ireland government and Protestants in general. In 1962 the Republic of Ireland government condemned the violence but did little at the time to control the border between the south and north. In 1969, British troops were brought in to maintain order in favor of the status quo ante bellum. In 1972, the British government suspended the Irish constitution and parliament. A 1973 referendum, boycotted by the Catholics, decided for continuing Northern Irish ties with the UK. Violence continued with terrorist acts building into the 1980s, with both sides guilty of gross acts of terrorism. At the same time, however, moderates of both sides were tiring of the bloodshed. Still, the beginning of the 1990s saw British patrols still on the streets of Belfast. Suddenly, however, peace initiatives began to take hold, and on 31 August 1995, the IRA announced a cease-fire, which was followed by Protestant announcements (14 October) promising an end to hostilities. Much is yet to be done to insure the peace will last. *Reading:* John Conroy, *Belfast Diary: War as a Way of Life* (1995);F. X. Martin, ed., *The Course of Irish History* (1995); Edgar O'Ballance, *Terror in Ireland: The Heritage of Hate* (1984); John McGarry & Brendan O'Leary, *Explaining Northern Ireland: Broken Images* (1995); Seamus Dunn, ed., *Facets of the Conflict in Northern Ireland* (1995); Andrew J. Wilson, *Irish America and the Ulster Conflict, 1968-1995* (1995); David George Boyce, *The Irish Question and British Politics, 1868-1996* (1996).

Northern Rhodesia. *See* Zimbabwe.

North Korea. *See* Korea.

North Viet Nam. *See* Vietnam.

North Yemen (San'a). *See* Yemen.

Norway. Officially, the Kingdom of Norway (*Kongeriket Norge*), Norway lies in northern Europe, occupying the northern and western portions of the Scandinavian peninsula. It is bordered on the north by the Barents Sea, on the northeast by Finland and Russia, on the east by Sweden, on the south by the Skagerrak Strait and the North Sea and on the west by the Atlantic Ocean. The capital is Oslo. The first inhabitants migrated to the region in the seventh to sixth millennia B.C. By the end of the first century A.D., the presence of the Norsemen was beginning to be felt in Roman-occupied Gaul, and by the year 600 A.D. numerous contacts had been made. From 800 to 1050, the Viking period characterized the history of Norway as the Norsemen established colonies on Greenland and visited the New World with definite traces of their coming being found in Vinland (Newfoundland). Harald I began the unification of Norway's numerous tribes in the ninth century, and the country was Christianized beginning in the eleventh century. From 1130 until 1240 a series of civil wars were fought over the dynastic condominium. After the ascension of Haakon IV (1217–1273) a period of peace followed. In 1442, the king (Eric of Pomerania , 1389–1442, also king of Sweden 1397–1442) was deposed, and Danes ruled the country until 1814 and the defeat of Napoleon, when it was united with Sweden (Treaty of Kiel). Swedish kings ruled until 1905, when Norway was reestablished as an independent country. Norway remained neutral in World War I, but benefitted economically from its commerce during the conflict. The Great Depression affected Norway more than many of its fellow European nations and saw an unemployment rate as high as 33 percent, yet there was at the same time economic and industrial expansion. When World War II began in 1939, Norway again declared its neutrality, but Nazi troops invaded the country on 9 April 1940, the day after the British announced they had mined Norwegian coastal waters.. When the king and government fled to England, the Norwegian people raised a great resistance against the German conquerers despite a group of disloyal Norwegians led by Vidkun Quisling, who sold out to the Nazis. At war's end the German garrison surrendered with little resistance (8 May 1945) but left behind considerable devastation. Quisling was executed for his collaboration on 24 October 1945. After the war, Norway became a charter member of the United Nations and, in 1949, joined NATO. On 3 March 1947, Norway had rejected a Soviet demand for military basing rights at Spitzbergen. Numerous instances occurred in the postwar period where the Soviets encroached on Norwegian territory. On 6 January 1969, for instance, Norwegian naval units captured three Soviet and two East German "trawlers" operating in a high security area off the Norwegian coast. On 16 November 1977, Norway and the USSR settled the only territorial dispute between NATO and the Warsaw Pact when the two sides decided upon the partition of the Barents Sea. On 16 January 1981, Norway and the United States announced an agreement for prepositioning the heavy equipment for a 10,000-man U.S. Marine brigade on Norwegian territory. Otherwise, from 1945 until 1995, Norway continued on its own path, with numerous shifts in the political climate, but without too much break in the domestic tranquility. *Reading:* Kiel Anne Cohen & Astrid Torad, *Continuity and Change: Aspects of Contemporary Norway* (1993); Thomas K. Derry, *A History of Norway: 1842-1972* (1973); Thomas K. Derry, *A Short History of Norway* (1979).

Nosavan, Phoumi. On 15 December 1959, in the face of renewed fighting against the Pathet Lao (qv), King Savang Vathana (qv) of Laos accepted the resignation of Premier Sananikone and placed the army in control of the country. General Phoumi Nosavan was named to head the right-wing military government. The political situation remained unstable, however, and the Soviet-supported Pathet Lao was successful in staging a rebellion in 1960 that was led by Kong Le (qv), a parachute battalion commander, who was himself a neutralist. In the aftermath, the neutralist Prince Souvanna Phouma (qv) regained power. In September 1960, civil war broke out when Souvanna Phouma attempted to include the Pathet Lao in his government. On 16 December, Phoumi Nosavan's right-wing forces defeated Kong Le, and a new U.S.–supported right-wing government was installed in Laos, with Prince Boum Oum as premier. Souvanna Phouma fled the country. The fighting continued, however, until May 1961, when a cease-fire was signed. A new provisional government was installed under Souvanna Phouma in 1962, but when a split developed in the neutralist camp, the Pathet Lao was asked to support the government. A number of right-wing leaders made several attempts to seize the government over the next few years, including the failed attempt of 31 January 1965 that was led by Phoumi Nosavan. He tried again on 16–30 April 1965, but again failed.

Nouakchott. *See* Mauritania.

Noumazalay, Ambroise. On 22 February 1972, a coup attempt against the government of President Marien Ngouabi (qv) was thwarted in Brazzaville, Congo. Former Premier Ambroise Noumazalay was arrested along with scores of others in what Ngouabi opponents characterized as a government trap to allow a purge of the opposition. On 25 March, Noumazalay and 12 other defendants were sentenced to death; but later that same day, Ngouabi commuted all the sentences to life imprisonment.

Nova Huta. *See* Poland.

Nova Lisboa (Huambo). *See* Angola.

Novosibirsk. *See* Russia.

Novotny, Antonin. (b. 10 December 1904, Letnany, Bohemia, Austria-Hungary—d. 28 January 1975, Prague) Young Novotny was apprenticed as a locksmith and joined the Czech Communist Party in 1921. After the Germans occupied Czechoslovakia in 1938, Novotny was arrested and sent to the concentration camp at Mauthausen, where he remained from 1941–1945. After the war, in 1946, he was elected to the Czech Communist Party's Central Committee, and in February 1948 he played a leading role in the communist takeover of the Czech government. In 1951, he was elected to the Politburo and became first secretary of the Communist Party in 1953. Upon the death of Antonin Zapotocky (13 November 1957), Novotny became president and was reelected to another five-year term in 1964. In the mid-1960s, Czech nationalism and reform movements took their toll on the pro-Moscow leader, and in January 1968 he was replaced as the party leader by Alexander Dubcek (qv). In March of 1968 Novotny was forced to give up the presidency. In May 1971, Novotny was reinstated into the Communist Party in exchange for the new Stalinist government's leniency toward Dubcek. Novotny died in January 1975.

Nsukka. *See* Biafra.

Ntare, Mwami V. *See* Ndizeye.

Nuclear Non-Proliferation Treaty. This treaty was signed simultaneously in Washington, London and Moscow on 1 July 1968. Most of the nations of the world were among its signatories. France, Communist China, Israel, Argentina, Brazil, India, Pakistan, South Africa and Spain refused to sign. The treaty was an agreement whereby the spread of military nuclear technology was to be limited, and no assistance was to be given to nonnuclear nations in getting or making nuclear weapons. On 24 November 1969, the U.S. and Soviet Union again signed, but did not deposit (file), an advanced version of the treaty. On 6

June 1978, the Republic of South Africa stipulated a list of conditions that would have to be met before it would sign. On 5 November of that year the United States cancelled an enriched uranium contract with South Africa because it had refused to sign the treaty.

Nueva Concepcion. *See* El Salvador.

Nueva Island. *See* Chile.

Nui Dat. *See* Vietnam.

Nuremburg. *See* Germany.

Nuristan. *See* Afghanistan.

Nyasaland. *See* Malawi.

O

Oanh, Nguyen Xuan. On 29 August 1964, a civilian Harvard-trained economist, Dr. Nguyen Xuan Oanh, took control of the government of South Vietnam. This action was at the behest of the ruling triumvirate that took over after Lieutenant General Nguyen Khanh (qv) resigned the presidency on 27 August after suffering an apparent physical and nervous breakdown. The new president stated he would head the government for two months. He was replaced by a "rested and recovered" General Khanh on 3 September. Khanh was later replaced by Tran Van Houng (qv), who was in turn ousted by Khanh on 27 January 1965. The next day, Nguyen Xuan Oanh was appointed premier and remained in that post until 16 February.

Oatis, William. On 4 July 1951, William Oatis, an American journalist, was convicted of espionage in Czechoslovakia. On 21 July the U.S. government officially requested that Oatis be released to American custody. When the request was denied, the U.S. initiated diplomatic reprisals.

Obasanjo, Olusegun. (b. 5 March 1937, Abeokuta, Nigeria) Born into the Yoruba tribe, Obasanjo was raised a Baptist; he enlisted in the army in 1958. He trained at the Mons Military Cadet School in England and was commissioned in 1959. He later attended the Indian Staff College and the Royal Military College of Science at Shrivenham and the Royal College of Defense Studies, London, England. He served with the UN command in Congo in 1960 and in the Nigerian civil war in 1969, where he commanded a marine commando unit. After the war he became chief of engineers and also served as minister of works and housing. In 1975, as armed forces chief of staff, he became premier when the government of Yakubu Mohamm Gowon was ousted from power, and Murtala Ramat Mohammed became head of state. On 13 February 1974, a military coup attempt failed in Nigeria. Mohammed was killed in the fighting, however, and Lieutenant General Obasanjo took control of the country (14 February). Obasanjo remained in power until 1 October 1979, when a duly elected new president, Alhaji Shehu Shagari (qv), was installed.

Obiang Nguema Mbasogo, Teodoro. On 3 August 1979, the government of the president of Equatorial Guinea, Francisco Macias Nguema, was deposed in a coup led by his nephew, Lieutenant Colonel Teodoro Obiang Nguema. Obiang headed a Supreme Military Council, to which he added some civilians in 1981. He also declared an amnesty for all political prisoners and reopened all Catholic missions in the country. Obiang also installed a new constitution in 1983. Obiang remained in office in 1994.

Obok. *See* Kampuchea (Cambodia).

Obote, (Apollo) Milton. (b. 28 December 1924, Akoroko, Uganda) Born into a farming family of the Lango tribe, Obote attended Busoga College and Makerere College in Uganda (1948–1949). He was expelled from the latter because of his political activities and did not graduate. He was also denied scholarships to the U.S. and West Germany by the colonial government. In 1950 he went to Kenya and worked as a laborer and salesman. While there he became involved in the independence movement and joined the Kenya African Union. He returned to Uganda in 1957, joined the Uganda National Congress Party (UNCP) and was elected to its ruling council in 1958. In this capacity he criticized British colonial rule. When the UNCP split, Obote led one group to form the Uganda People's Congress (UPC), which united with the Uganda People's Union (UPU). Obote's main concern at that time was the continued existence of the state of Buganda as a separate monarchy under King Mutesa II (qv). In 1961,Obote agreed to Buganda's status as a federal state within Uganda. Obote also formed an alliance with Buganda's Democratic Party in opposition to the royalist *Kabaka Yekka* ("King Alone") party, which eventually allied itself with Obote. Prime Minister Obote assumed full power in Uganda on 22 February 1966. By 1966, however, tensions between Obote and Buganda had reached a perilous level. Obote attacked the royal palace with troops led by Idi Amin Dada (qv). Mutesa was forced to flee to England. Obote then abolished Buganda and centralized power in himself. In 1967, a new constitution codified Obote's centralization of control by eliminating all vestiges of the old federal system. On 19 December 1969, a would-be assassin wounded Obote as he was leaving a rally in Kampala. The following day, a state of emergency was declared. When he proclaimed himself executive president, he signed his own fate, however, as the military rose against him on 25 January 1971, while he was visiting Singapore, and overthrew his government in a coup led by Major General Idi Amin Dada. When Amin was ousted in 1979, Obote returned from exile on 27 May 1980 and won the presidential election held on 14 July 1980. Although he established a multiparty, democratic system in Uganda, his rule was militarized and oppressive to the northern tribes. This and the depredations caused by rebel forces and by his own army caused his ouster on 27 July 1985. Obote fled to Kenya.

October 1 Antifascist Resistance Group (GRAPO) (Spain). Variously, the First of October Anti-Fascist Resistance Group (*Groupa Resistencia Antifascista Primo de Octobre*, hence GRAPO), this terrorist organization was established as the military arm of the outlawed Communist Party of Spain - Reconstituted (PCE-R), which broke away from the recognized Communist Party of Spain (PCE). GRAPO was an urban guerrilla group of fewer than 25 members under the leadership of Manuel Perez Martinez (*Camarada Arenas*). The group was noted for its assassinations, bombings and kidnappings against Spanish citizens and facilities, although it on occasion attacked U.S. interests. Its principal method of attack was the ambush with automatic weapons, and its chief function appeared to be the destabilization of the Spanish government. The group sustained itself through kidnap for ransom, bank robberies and extortion. Although not formally linked with any international terrorist organization, GRAPO supported other groups such as the German Red Army Faction and the Italian Red Brigades. The structure of the group was based on a number of small "cells" to maximize security. Some were unknown to the police, although the Spanish police claimed to have infiltrated the group. GRAPO was founded in 1975 and was decimated by police activity by January 1985. It is known to have rebuilt its organization and to be operating in southern Spain.

October 3 Organization. On 13 October 1980, Armenian terrorists claiming to represent the October 3 Organization bombed the Turkish Airlines office and the Swiss Center in London. At the same time, however, the Armenian Secret Army for the Liberation of Armenia (ASALA) claimed credit for the attack on the Turkish Airlines office. ASALA had bombed that same office in December 1979.

Oder-Neisse Line. The Oder-Neisse Line was the name given to the Polish-German border by the Allied Powers at the end of World War II. This demarcation gave Poland a substantial section of former German territory and was a matter of contention between West Germany and the Soviet Bloc for most of the Cold War period. At the Yalta Conference held in February 1945, the Allied Powers moved the eastern border of Poland to the west, to the approximate location of the Curzon Line, which had been put forth by the British foreign minister in the settlement of the Polish-Soviet dispute (settled 11 July 1920). To make up for the lost Polish territory in the east, the Allied Powers agreed to compensate the Poles by giving them German territory. The exact location of the Oder-Neisse Line remained a matter of contention, however, even though it was described as a line extending southward from Swinoujście (Swinemünde) on the Baltic Sea to the Oder River, passing west of Szczecin, to a point where it joined the Neisse River, then south to the Czech border near Zittau. Although the western Allies argued against this demarcation, no decision was reached at the Yalta Conference. When the Potsdam Conference convened in July 1945, the Soviet Union handed the Allies a fait accompli by having already occupied all of the lands east of the Oder-Neisse Line and by having established Polish control of the former German region. As a result, the demarcation was allowed to stand, and the Poles were authorized to deport Germans living in the region east of the line. The Potsdam Conference ended with the original argument over the line's position unresolved and to be settled at a future date. That occurrence never eventuated. On 6 June 1950, the East German government and Poland, under close Soviet scrutiny, recognized the Oder-Neisse Line as the permanent boundary. West Germany continued to insist, however, that the demarcation was only temporary and would need to be revised at the final peace settlement. In 1970, West Germany did concede the line as the boundary (18 November

1970), as it signed treaties with the USSR (12 August 1970) and Poland (7 December 1970). At the time of German reunification, the line was again confirmed (1990). *Reading:* Phillip A. Buhler, *The Oder-Neisse Line: A Reappraisal under International Law* (1990); Sarah Meiklejohn Terry, *Poland's Place in Europe: General Sikorski and the Origin of the Oder-Neisse Line, 1939-1943* (1983).

Odria, Manuel. On 27–29 October 1948, the goverment of President Jose Bustamante (qv) of Peru was overthrown by a military coup led by General Manuel Odria. Odria was then installed as president. Opponents of Odria, particularly members of the Apra movement, were imprisoned or sent into exile. One of the opposition leaders sought refuge in the Colombian embassy, setting off a bitter dispute between Peru and Colombia. Odria was elected president in 1950. His dictatorial policies led to some economic gains, especially with American capital being fed into the country. In 1956, Odria allowed a new election, in which his candidate ran last and the Apra choice, Fernando Belaunde Terry (qv), won.

Offensive Nuclear Weapons Agreement. *See* Non-Proliferation Treaty (Nuclear Non-Proliferation Treaty).

Ogaden Province. *See* Ethiopia.

Ogaden Region. *See* Somalia.

Ojukwu, Chukwuemeka Odumegwu. (b. 4 November 1933, Nnewi, Nigeria) Born the son of a well-to-do Ibo (*Igbo*) businessman, Ojukwu graduated from Oxford University, England, in 1955. Upon his return to Nigeria, he served two years as a civil servant before joining the army. In January 1966, Ojukwu joined a group of junior officers, many of them of the Ibo tribe, in overthrowing Nigeria's civilian government. Lieutenant Colonel Ojukwu was appointed military governor of the Eastern Region, generally the Ibo homeland in Nigeria. Fearing Ibo domination in the government, officers of the Northern Region (Hausa tribe) and the Western Region (Yorubas tribe) staged a second coup in July 1966, out of which Colonel Yakubu Gowon (qv) eventually became Nigeria's head of state. Ojukwu retained his position in the Eastern Region. In September 1966, Hausa tribesmen carried out a massacre of members of the Ibo tribe, largely civilians. In response to this attack, Ojukwu recommended the establishment of a federation that would allow political autonomy in each region. This recommendation was agreed upon in substance by Gowon in January 1967 but was later repudiated. During March–April 1967, Ojukwu retaliated by cutting off revenues to the central government and isolating the administration of the Eastern Region. By 30 May 1967, however, growing secessionist feeling among the Ibo forced Ojukwu to unilaterally declare the independence of the Eastern Region as the Republic of Biafra. Central government troops invaded Biafra, and a devasting civil war ensued from 1967 until 1970. Ojukwu called for a truce on 1 January 1969 to allow much-needed relief supplies to reach the Ibo civilian population. When this plea was rejected and the Nigerians mounted an offensive designed to crush Ibo resistance once and for all (29 January 1969), Ojukwo ordered a counteroffensive designed to open a supply route to the sea

(February 1969). When success in stopping the Nigerian onslaught waned, Ojukwu signalled his desire for a peace settlement (15 October 1969), which was to be negotiated by the President of Gabon, Albert Bongo (qv). Rather, on 3 December 1969, the Nigerians opened a massive, two-pronged offensive against Biafra. By 2 January 1970, Biafra had been cut into three segments. When Biafra was forced to surrender (15 January 1970), Ojukwu fled to Ivory Coast (*Côte d'Ivoire*) (11 January 1970), where he asked for and received asylum. In 1982, Ojukwu returned to Nigeria, where he unsuccessfuly tried to reenter politics as a member of the National Party of Nigeria in January 1993.

Okello, Tito. (b. 1914, Namukora, Uganda) Okello was born into the Acholi tribe in northern Uganda, where he learned only his tribal language, with a minimum understanding of English. He finished only a primary school education before enlisting in the King's African Rifles regiment in 1940. He served as an enlisted man in Somalia during World War II. He also received additional military training in Kenya, where he was promoted to sergeant. At the end of the war, Okello was transferred to Burma and did not return to Uganda until 1955. Upon the independence of Uganda, Okello was commissioned an officer. He became chief of staff in 1970. When Idi Amin (qv) seized power in Uganda (1971), Okello fled into exile in Tanzania with Milton Obote (qv) and played a major role in the opposition to Amin's rule. In 1979, Okello led the Uganda National Liberation Army (UNLA), which fought alongside Tanzanian forces in ousting Amin from power. Under Obote, Okello was appointed commander of the armed forces. Although Okello was well past retirement age and in ill health, Obote continued him in his duties because of his loyalty and because he represented the north in the fragmented country. This loyalty eventually frayed, and when Obote was overthrown in a military mutiny led by Brigadier Basilio Okello (no relation), Lieutenant General Tito Okello was asked to become head of state as chairman of the nine-man Military Council (26 January 1986). He failed, however, to strengthen his position quickly enough, and rival southern forces of the National Resistance Army (NRA), led by Yoweri Museveni (qv) forced Okello to share power (17 December 1985). Okello was given a purely ceremonial post on 29 January 1986. Okello continued to lead the armed opposition, which committed numerous atrocities during its retreat before Museveni's advancing forces. Okello subsequently fled the country. *See* Uganda.

Okinawa. One of the larger Ryukyu Islands (Nansei Islands), Okinawa lies 400 miles southwest of the Japanese island of Kyushu. It is separated from China on the west by the East China Sea. Naha is the capital city of Okinawa. The island has been inhabited by Japanese and other Southeast Asian people since prehistoric times. Although the Okinawan language is found in the Japanese group, there is little or no compatibility between the two. In antiquity, the Ryukyu Islands formed an independent kingdom. Between the fourteenth and nineteenth centuries, overlordship required the payment of tribute. In 1879, Japan annexed the archipelago, including Okinawa. In World War II, Okinawa was the scene of bitter fighting on 1 April 1945. At the end of the war, the United States held control of Okinawa and kept it under military government until 1951, when a civil administration was established. In 1952, the United States gave Japan residual authority over Okinawa based on the terms of the peace treaty ending World War II. Some of the islands (Amani Group) in the archipelago were turned over to Japan in 1953. A second treaty (1971) stipulated the return of Okinawa in 1972. A part of the treaty allows the stationing of substantial numbers of U.S. troops on the island. In more recent times, U.S. relations with Okinawans have been strained by the suspected rape of a 12-year-old girl by three U.S. servicemen.

Okuchi, Nobuo. On 11 March 1970, the Japanese consul general in Sao Paolo, Brazil, Nobuo Okuchi, was kidnapped by revolutionaries. He was ransomed by the Brazilian government, who released five prisoners who were sent to Mexico City behind a protective screen of children. Okuchi was released four days later.

Olympic Games, Mexico. The Olympic Games in Mexico City were marred by the specter of rioting in October 1968. Disorders began at the National University in Mexico City in July. Between 18 September and 24 September army troops and police fought a bloody battle with students to end the rioting. The students were armed with automatic weapons and Molotov cocktails. More than 50 students were killed, along with the commander of the army forces, General Hernandez Toledo. Ten days later the the XIX Olympiad began.

Olympic Village, Munich. The 1972 Olympic games in Munich, West Germany, were disrupted by terrorist activity. On 5 September, Palestinian Arab terrorists from the Black September (qv) organization broke into the Israeli dormitory and barricaded themselves there, demanding the release of 200 Arab prisoners being held in Israeli jails. The terrorists killed two of the Israeli athletes who resisted and held nine others hostage, as the world watched on television. The terrorists and their hostages were taken to Furstenfeldbruch Airport by helicopter, where they were to be flown out of the country. An ill-conceived and poorly executed assault by West German police resulted in the deaths of five terrorists. But before the hostages could be released, one of the remaining terrorists detonated a grenade in the helicopter and killed all nine of the hostages. A West German police officer was also killed in the firefight. Three more terrorists were subsequently captured. On 8 September, Israeli jets attacked ten Arab guerrilla bases in Syria and Lebanon in retaliation for the massacre. The next day, a major air battle between Israeli and Syrian jets took place, the first such action since 1970. On 29 October, the West German government decided to release the Munich terrorists after another terrorist group hijacked (13 October) a Lufthansa airliner and demanded the release of the Munich Three. On 21 February 1973, Israeli forces attacked Palestinian refugee camps in Lebanon in retaliation. There was some evidence that special death squads were among the Israeli raiding forces, with the mission of killing the leaders of the Munich attack. The leader of the attack, Abu Daoud (qv), a known member of the Palestinian Revolutionary Council, was captured (7 January 1977) by the French, who, on 11 January 1977, refused to extradite him to West Germany and instead set the terrorist free.

Olympio, Sylvanus. On 13 January 1963, a group of noncommissioned officers led a military coup against the government of Togo in the capital city of Lomé. Upon seizing the government, and presumably as a part of the coup, they assassinated President Sylvanus Olympio. Olympio had been Togo's first president after the 1961 elections established the new country's form of government following independence on 27 April 1960. Upon Olympio's death, Nicholas Grunitsky, his rival for power, returned from Dahomey, where he had gone into exile in 1958, to take over control of the country.

Oman. Located on the southeastern coast of the Arabian peninsula, Oman is borderd by Saudi Arabia and the United Arab Emirates on the north, by the Gulf of Oman on the northeast, by the Arabian Sea on the south and Yemen on the west. It is suspected that the region is the site of the legendary land of Magan (c.3000 B.C.). Migrating Arab tribes entered the region in the ninth century B.C. and divided the land between two tribes. The rivalry that ensued between the two lasted into modern times. Oman began converting to Islam in the seventh century A.D. In 751, the inhabitants, now rooted in the Kharijite Muslim sect, elected a religious leader (*imam*) as their spiritual leader. Successive imams ruled until 1154, when a dynasty of kings was put in place by the *Banu Nabhan*. After 1428, however, the imams began reasserting their authority, and from 1624 Nasr ibn Murshid, an imam, was able to end a long period of tribal conflict and take control of the country. Nasr ibn Murshid's successor expelled the Portuguese, who had gained a foothold in the region in 1507. Civil war broke out between the northern and southern tribes once again in the early eighteenth century. The mutual election of another imam in 1744 brought an end to the conflict. During the next hundred years, Oman grew rapidly and soon encompassed considerable territory in East Africa. For a time, Oman's capital was located in Zanzibar. After 1861, through British mediation, Oman returned to its original borders, where rule was in the hands of imam leaders who now called themselves sultans. Tribal warfare continued until 1959, when the last imam, Sheikh Ghalib ibn Ali, was ousted with British help. In October 1955, for example, British troops helped Muscat and Oman forces drive invading Saudi Arabian forces out of the Buraimi Oasis. Full independence came to Oman on 23 July 1970, when Prince Qabus ibn Sa'id (qv) overthrew his father, Sultan Sa'id bin Taimur (qv), and liberalized his country, changing the name of the country from Muscat and Oman to the Sultanate of Oman. The Dhofar uprising by left-wing rebels and aided by Yemen was defeated in 1975 after eight years of fighting (the end of the war was on 11 December 1975). In one action, on 5 May 1972, Omani jets attacked artillery positions in Aden (South Yemen) after the Omani military border post at Habrut had been shelled in support of the Marxist-led Dhofar. Cross-border operations of this sort continued throughout the conflict. The Shah of Iran had supported Oman during much of the struggle. Oman became a member of the Arab League and the United Nations in 1971 and was a founding member in 1981 of the Gulf Cooperative Council (GCC). A military cooperation agreement was signed with the United States on 22 April 1980. In June 1980, Oman refused to join most other Arab League members in breaking relations with Egypt after Cairo signed a peace accord with Israel. The U.S.–Oman defense agreement was implemented in 1981, when the U.S. began upgrading facilities on Masirah Island. In 1987, Omani Red Cross (Red Crescent) facilities were used by the U.S. to repatriate Iranian sailors held after incidents in the Gulf. Omani forces were involved in a border firefight with Yemeni forces on 11 October 1987, after the Yemeni made a relatively deep penetration of Omani space; eight Yemeni soldiers were killed in the action. The matter was settled through arbitration, and on 31 October 1992 a border delineation treaty was signed. In 1990–1991, Oman cooperated with the Western Coalition following the Iraqi invasion of Kuwait by supplying bases for air and special forces units. For several years, Oman had been pressing for a multinational military force under the control of the GCC. However, after Qatar and Kuwait signed bilateral defense agreements with the U.S., the matter cooled. In January 1993, Oman purchased a considerable amount of military hardware from Great Britain and later announced plans to buy French naval vessels. In mid-1994, more than 500 civil servants and business people were arrested in what was later called a conspiracy to overthrow the government. Several death sentences were adjudged in the matter, but the king later commuted all death sentences. In July 1994, Oman accepted more than 9,000 armed refugees from Yemen, who had fled following an abortive attempt to divide north and south Yemen (*see* Yemen). In 1995, Oman concentrated on internal affairs but continued to be a spokesman for Arab-Israeli accord. *Reading:* Joseph A. Kechichian, *Oman and the World: The Emergence of an Independent Foreign Policy* (1996); John C. Wilkinson, *The Imamate Tradition of Oman* (1987); Miriam Joyce, *The Sultanate of Oman: A Twentieth Century History* (1995).

Omani Gulf Airliner. On 23 September 1983, an Omani airliner was blown up in flight near Abu Dubai (qv). All 111 persons on board were killed. The Arab Revolutionary Brigade, an Abu Nidal (qv) group, took credit for the attack and said it was in retaliation for the repression of the PLO in the UAE.

Omdurman. *See* Sudan.

Ongania, Juan Carlos. On 8 June 1970, Argentina's president, Juan Carlos Ongania, was forced to resign after a military coup that gave the leadership to Brigadier General Roberto Marcelo Levingston (qv). Ongania had been president for four years and had been the leader of the revolution proclaimed in 1966. His downfall was laid to a public loss of confidence in his administration, which manifested in labor unrest, and in his lack of resolve during the investigation of the murder of former president Pedro Aramburu (qv).

OPEC. The Organization of Petroleum Exporting Countries or OPEC, is a multinational organization established to coordinate the petroleum policies of its member states and to provide those states with economic and technical assistance and advice. The organization was organized in September 1960 and formally established in January 1961 with five members, including Venezuela. Eight additional members have joined since that date. (Abu Dhabi's membership was transferred to the United Arab Emirates in 1974.) In 1973, OPEC raised the price-per-barrel of oil by 70 percent. This major rise in prices was followed by others, with which the Arab-dominated OPEC sought to punish the West for its support of Israel during the 1973 Arab-Israeli War (Yom Kippur War). By December 1973, prices had been raised an addition 130 percent. At the same time, the Arab producers placed an embargo on oil shipments to the United States and the Netherlands. By 1980, the price of a barrel of crude oil had been raised to ten times the 1973 price of $3.00. After 1980 the influence of OPEC on the world market began to decline as the Western nations began to seek other sources of energy and to exploit oil sources closer to home. These actions forced OPEC by 1982 to reduce oil prices and to cut back production. Internal conflict, such as the Iran-Iraq War (qv), has also lessened the organization's influence. Another organization, the Organization of Arab Petroleum Exporting Countries (OAPEC), which came into being in January 1968, has had an influence on OPEC, as its purpose is to create closer ties among the Arab oil-producing nations thereby excluding all non-Arab countries from its deliberations, and has proven to be more politically oriented. In 1979, for instance, OAPEC suspended Egypt because of its improved relations with Israel. More recently, a pattern of cheating on fellow members has developed (and may have existed from the beginning), in which members produce more oil than their quota and offer special price deals to clients. The Iraqi invasion of Kuwait (August 1990) caused widespread concern and, on the hope of a diplomatic solution, oil prices fell. When the air phase of Desert Storm began and Iraq began blowing up Kuwaiti oil fields, prices rose again. There was also fear that neighboring Saudi Arabian fields would be attacked. The coalition campaign's success soon made it apparent that Iraq was beaten, and prices once again declined. By 1995, OPEC had become fully aware that non-OPEC petroleum production was going to change the way the organization would do its business in the future. *Reading:* Abdelkader Benamara & Sam Ifeagwu, eds., *OPEC Aid and the Challenge of Development* (1987).

"Open Arms" (*Chieu Hoi*) **Program.** This amnesty program was inaugurated by President Ngo Dinh Diem (qv) on 17 April 1963. It was an attempt to induce Viet Cong guerrillas to return to government control. Those that did, called "*Hoi Chanh,*" were given reeducational training and often entered the Republic of Vietnam's armed forces. By 1967, the program was producing 5,000 *Hoi Chanh* per month. Seeing the possible effects of the program on their forces, the North Vietnamese, who were by that time the principal providers of men to the Viet Cong, began a campaign of terror and increased discipline, which cut the number of *Hoi Chanh* to about 500 per month. The US-RVN responded by initiating Operation Pheonix, which was aimed at destroying the VC infrastructure in South Vietnam.

Ophira, Sinai. *See* Israel.

Oporto. *See* Portugal.

Opposition United Front of the Revolutionary Party of Guatemala. *See* Colom Argueta, Manuel.

Ordingar, Noel. On 13 April 1975, President N'Garta Tombalbaye (qv) of Chad was assassinated by a group of mutinous soldiers. Three days later, on 16 April,

Brigadier General Noel Ordingar, who led the mutiny, took control of the country. On 12 May 1975, after Ordingar released him from prison, Brigadier General Felix Malloum (qv) was installed as head of state and premier.

Organia, Juan Carlos. On 28 June 1966, Argentina's president, Arturo Illia, and his government were ousted from power by a military coup. Lieutenant General Juan Carlor Organia was appointed provisional president. Organia remained in office almost four years, until on 8 June 1970 he was quietly removed from office by the chiefs of the armed services. Ten days later, Brigadier General Roberto Marcelo Levingston became the new head of government.

Organization of African States. In January-February 1962, A group of 20 African nations met in Lagos, Nigeria, to seek the establishment of an Organization of African States not associated with the "Casablanca States" (qv) (*see also* Organization of African Unity). A number of states declined the invitation because Algeria had not been invited. The group was formed, however, on 20 February, among the 20 attendees. The group would be short lived and would eventually be absorbed into the OAU.

Organization of African Unity (OAU). The OAU grew out of the pan-African movement that began at the beginning of the twentieth century. In 1900, the First Pan-African Congress was held in London. For the next three decades the promotion of native African solidarity and the abolition of colonial rule were the subject of a series of such conferences. The movement quieted somewhat during the 1930s but resumed its work in the latter days of World War II by founding the Pan-African Federation; the Sixth Pan-African Congress was held in 1945. The demand now was for political independence among the black nations of Africa. As independent states emerged, several new organizations developed. The Casablanca Group was created in January 1961 and, under the leadership of Kwame Nkrumah (qv) of Ghana, argued for political unity as rapidly as possible. The Monrovia Group, formed in May 1961, proposed a more gradual approach. Primarily because of the efforts of Haile Selassie (qv) of Ethiopia, Sir Abubakar Tafawa Balewa (qv), prime minister of Nigeria, and Sekou Toure (qv), the president of Ghana, a meeting of 30 states was prepared at Addis Ababa, Ethiopia, in 1963. On 25 May, the Organization of African Unity was founded. This organization combined the views of the Casablanca and Monrovia groups, and the two groups were subsequently dissolved. One of the OAU's first tasks was to settle the Ethiopia-Somalia border dispute in February 1964, but their efforts were not completely successful until 1 April 1964, when a cease-fire was arranged. At a Cairo meeting held on 21 July 1964, the OAU declared the denuclearization of Africa, a declaration that was not ratified by South Africa, which was not a member of the organization. On 5 December 1965, the OAU threatened to sever relations with Great Britain if the Rhodesian issue was not settled immediately. At least one member nation, Ghana, did break relations with London over the racial policies seen in Rhodesia. By 5 March 1967, the OAU urged the use of force to drive out the white government in Rhodesia. During the civil war in Nigeria, the OAU sponsored peace talks that began in July 1968. These talks extended in 1969 as the Nigerian crisis (*See*

Nigeria) continued to flare. However, the OAU adjourned its heads-of-state meeting in September 1969 having failed to resolve the crisis. In January 1970, the United Nations urged Biafra to accede to OAU negotiations to end the emergency. At an OAU meeting held in Addis Ababa in June 1974, Somalia demanded immediate independence for all Portuguese-held colonies in Africa. The OAU again called for military action against the white government in Rhodesia. During an OAU meeting held in Kampala, Uganda, in July 1975, the government of Nigeria's Yakubu Gowon was overthrown. On 11 February 1976, the OAU recognized the Popular Movement for the Liberation of Angola (MPLA) as that country's rightful government (*see* Angola). After being accused of supporting a coup attempt in Benin, Morocco suspended its association with the OAU (27 February 1977). On 18 July 1978, the OAU approved a Western plan for an all-party conference on the Rhodesia question. The OAU, now with a membership of 50 nations, held a meeting in Nairobi, Kenya, on 28 April 1981. The main point of discussion was the dispatch of a peacekeeping force to Chad. This force, made up of troops from Nigeria, Senegal and Zaire, began its deployment in Chad by 10 November. The OAU had to warn Chad's president, Goukouni Oueddei (qv), on 11 February 1982 that if he continued in his refusal to negotiate with the rebels in his country, the OAU would withdraw its peacekeeping force. The rancor among the various parties involved in the Chad crisis reached such a pitch that the OAU meeting scheduled for Tripoli, Libya, on 25 November 1982 was cancelled before it began. In July 1983, a nine-member OAU committee demanded the immediate withdrawal from Chad of military forces that were not a part of the OAU peacekeeping force. It would appear that this demand was leveled directly at France, which more than once had intervened in Chadian affairs. The OAU also took an interest in the crisis in Western Sahara and adopted a peace plan for that region on 12 June 1983. All was not unity in the group, however, as can be seen in the resignation of Morocco over whether the Saharan Arab Democratic Republic (qv) should be seated as the legitimate representative of Western Sahara (12 November 1984). The OAU has continued and flourished since that point. As of 1995, 53 nations belonged to the OAU. *Reading:* C. O. C. Amate, *Inside the OAU: Pan-Africanism in Practice* (1987); Gino L. Naldi, *Organization of African Unity: An Analysis of Its Role* (1989).

Organization of American States (OAS). Between 1826 and 1889, a number of conferences were held to secure cooperation among the American states and led to the establishment of the International Union of American Republics (1890) (later changed to the Pan-American Union). In 1936, an Inter-American Conference for the Maintainence of Peace was held in Buenos Aires at the request of U.S. President Franklin D. Roosevelt. Subsequent conferences over the next twelve years led to the Ninth Pan-American Conference held in Bogota, Colombia, in April 1948. The OAS was formed at the conclusion of that conference (30 April 1948). The fundamental goals of the OAS are to provide collective security within the hemisphere and to strengthen the peace and security of the Western Hemisphere. Almost all independent states, with the early exception of Canada (joined 1989), belong to the organization (a total of 13) and have adhered to a noncommunist alignment and attendance to the principles set forth in the Monroe Doctrine. The OAS supported the United States when President John F. Kennedy (qv) imposed a quarantine (1962) on Cuba in an effort to remove Soviet offensive weapons from the Western Hemisphere, and when the U.S. intervened in the Dominican Republic (qv) in 1965. In other matters, the OAS established the Alliance for Progress (Treaty of Punta del Este, 1961) and the Inter-American Court of Human Rights in 1979. The OAS charter has been amended several times, with most of the changes aimed at improving economic and social integration among the member states and the eradication of extreme poverty. The last states to join the organization were Belize and Guyana.

Oribe, Berro. *See* Tupamaros.

Oriente Province. *See* Cuba.

Ortega Saavedra, Daniel. (b. 11 November 1945, La Libertad, Nicaragua) Born the son of a member of the peasant army of Cesar Augusto Sandino, Ortega moved to Managua in the mid-1950s. He attended the Central American University there, but left before graduating. In 1963, Ortega joined the Sandinista National Liberation Front (FSLN) and went underground. By 1967, he was in charge of urban resistance again the dictatorial rule of Anastasio Somoza (qv) and his family. He was arrested in late 1967 and spent seven years in prison for bank robbery; he was released (1974) along with a number of other Sandinistas as ransom for several high-ranking followers of Somoza who had been taken hostage. Ortega was sent into exile in Cuba, where he received intensive training in guerrilla warfare. He then returned secretly to Nicaragua and helped restore the unity among the three factions of the FSLN. Ortega's effort were largely responsible for turning the guerrilla campaign into a full-fledged civil war, in which the FSLN came out victorious in 1979. Ortega was made a member of the five-man junta that ruled Nicaragua, and in 1981 he was named leader of the junta. In 1984 he was elected president, but he was defeated in 1990 by Violeta Barrios de Chamorro. In July 1991, Ortega became the secretary general of the FSLN. *Reading:* James Cockcroft & Harold Bloom, *Daniel Ortega* (1991).

Ortuno, Rene Bartientos. *See* Bolivia.

Osan. *See* Korea.

Oshakti. *See* Namibia.

Osirak Nuclear Reactor Facility. *See* Iraq.

Oslo. *See* Norway.

Osman, Aden Abdullah. *See* Somalia.

Osman, Babakr an-Nur. On 26 July 1971, Libyan fighters forced down a British airliner en route from London to Khartoum, Sudan, and arrested Colonel Babakr an-Nur Osman. Osman was accused of being the ringleader in a coup attempt against Sudan's President Nimeiry (qv). Osman was then transported to Khartoum, where he was executed. The coup attempt occurred on 19 July when a group of army officers working with the Sudan Communist Party seized power and arrested Nimeiry. A total of 28 officers and men were shot by the rebels.

Three days later, on 22 July, loyal Sudanese troops, encouraged by Egypt and Libya, regained control of the country and freed Nimeiry. In all, 15 officers and Communist Party leaders were executed by Nimeiry in retaliation.

Osorio, Carlos Arana. *See* Guatemala.

Oswald, Lee Harvey. (b. 18 October 1939, New Orleans—d. 24 November 1963, Dallas) Although much is known about Lee Harvey Oswald, his life is still shrouded in mystery. He was born shortly after his father's death, and his mother, her new husband, and Oswald moved frequently over the next 17 years. A high-school dropout, Oswald joined the U.S. Marines in October 1956, but shortly afterward he began making pro-Soviet and politically radical statements. He was given a hardship discharge on 11 September 1959. On 20 September, he left the United States for the Soviet Union, where he tried unsuccessfully to be granted citizenship. Allowed to live and work in Minsk, Oswald met and married Marina Nikolayevna Prusakova on 30 April 1961. In June 1962, he and his family returned to the United States. In January 1963, Oswald mail-ordered a .38 caliber revolver, and, in March, a rifle with a telescopic sight. On 10 April 1963 in Dallas, Texas, Oswald allegedly attempted to assassinate a retired army general and ultrarightist, Edwin A. Walker. Oswald then left his family in Dallas and travelled to New Orleans, where he set up a "Fair Play for Cuba" operation that consisted primarily of leaflet distribution. At this project, Oswald apparently operated alone. In September 1963, Oswald went to Mexico City where he apparently attempted unsuccessfully to get a visa to visit Cuba and permission to return to the USSR. Daunted in these attempts, Oswald returned to Dallas and secured employment at the Texas School Book Depository. On 22 November 1963, at 12:30 P.M., Lee Harvey Oswald fired three-shots from a sixth-floor window of the depository building, killing John Fitzgerald Kennedy, the president of the United States, and wounding Texas governor John B. Connally. Oswald fled the scene taking a bus and a taxi to his home. He then departed the roominghouse and, one mile away, shot and killed Dallas police officer J. D. Tippit, who had stopped him at 1:15 P.M., as a possible suspect in the assassination. Thirty minutes later, Oswald was captured in a movie theater by police officers responding to a tip. On 23 November, Oswald was arraigned for the murder of the president. On the morning of 24 November, Oswald was being transferred to another facility when he was shot and killed by Jack Ruby (qv), a Dallas nightclub owner, who allegedly killed him in a fit of anguish and rage. The murder took place on national television. The massive investigation that followed failed to tie Oswald to any conspiracy in the assassination, but many doubts still remain. Recent disclosures give the impression that Oswald may have been set up in a CIA/Mafia operation known as "Operation Freedom" that was originally planned by Robert Kennedy (qv) to assassinate Fidel Castro (qv) but was used to kill President Kennedy instead. The actual truth may never become known. *Reading:* Gerald Posner, *Case Closed: Lee Harvey Oswald and the Assassination of JFK* (1994); Mary & Ray La Fontaine, *Oswald Talked: The New Evidence in the JFK Assassination* (1996); Edward Jay Epstein, *Legend: The Secret World of Lee Harvey Oswald* (1978).

Othman, Muhammad Ali. On 30 May 1973, the third member of the three-man North Yemen (San`a) Presidential Council, Muhammad Ali Othman, was assassinated by South Yemeni (Aden) terrorists.

Oudong (Odong). *See* Cambodia.

Oueddei, Goukouni. (b. 1944, Zouar, Chad) Oueddei was born the son of the spiritual leader of the Toubou tribe and was afforded no opportunity for a formal education other than that of a learned devout Muslim. In his early life he managed to survive the 1967 civil war in Chad, but he spent some time in exile in Libya. In November 1976, Oueddei became one of the leaders of the Toubou guerrilla force of the National Liberation Front (Frolinat) (qv) as a replacement for Hissen Habré (qv), who had been his arch rival for power. Oueddei's position was one of using France to protect Chad from the incessant interference offered by Libya, Sudan and Nigeria. Although France was also considered to be an interfering nation, its lack of proximity to Chad made it the most favorable ally in Oueddei's eyes. Throughout this time Oueddei led one of the three major military forces in the on-going armed struggle in Chad. On 23 March 1979, he was appointed president of the new provisional State Council of Chad following the resignations of Habré and Felix Malloum (qv). On 21 August 1979, following the signing of an agreement among all factions, Oueddei was confirmed as president of Chad. At best, his early administration was a tenuous one, as the country's stability constantly threatened to collapse in a return to open warfare. On 10 November 1979, after a period of intense negotiations, an interim transitional government was established with Oueddei as president and with members of all the factions in some position of authority. However, fighting broke out again in March 1980, when the military forces of Oueddei and Habre clashed. French forces evacuated nearly one-half the 900-member foreign population by 24 March, after more than 700 Chadians had been killed in the fighting. On 26 March, when a cease-fire was nearly on paper, a new element arose when troops belonging to Vice-President Wadel Abdel Kadar Kamougue (qv) entered the fighting. A cease-fire was finally arranged on 31 March, with no change in the administration. Fighting erupted again the next day (1 April), however, and lasted for ten days. That time the forces loyal to the foreign minister, Abmat Acyl (qv), joined Oueddei's force against Habré. On 13 December 1980, Soviet-equipped Libyan forces were already in the fight against Habré, although Oueddei supposedly did not request Libyan aid until 16 December. Libyan forces took the capital city of N'Djamena on that day. At that point, Habré fled the country, and a cease-fire was arranged by the OAU. On 28 December, Oueddei asked the French to withdraw the remainder of their forces in Chad after charging they had been supporting Habré. Oueddei's position took a turn for the worse when, on 11 February 1982, the OAU ordered him to begin negotiations with the other factions in Chad or face the loss of the OAU peacekeeping force that had maintained order after the withdrawal of the Libyans. Oueddei was forced to abandon his leadership of Chad on 7 June 1982 and to surrender the country to Hissen Habré. This turn of events was largely due to Libya's refusal of any more support to Oueddei. Oueddei subsequently went into exile in Cameroon. Oueddei resurfaced in June–July, however, when his forces, with heavy Libyan support captured, lost and recaptured (10–12 August 1983) the important northern town of Faya Largeau. At that point, heavy French and Zairean reinforcement arrived to protect the Habré government. In 1984, Oueddei became involved in acrimonious negotiations held by the OAU in an attempt to settle, once and for all, the Chad crisis. Habré had refused to attend because of the status afforded Oueddei. In July 1985, Oueddei attempted to develop an anti-Habré coalition from among the burgeoning number of opposing factions, but to no avail. There were rumors that Oeuddei was being replaced as the opposition leader in mid-1985, but these proved to be wrong. The OAU planned another round of reconciliation talks in 1986, but this time Oueddei refused to attend. At the same time, Oueddei's hold over his faction was eroding, and in November 1986 he was replaced as the group's leader. This move set the entire crazy-quilt of loyalties into motion, with factions and splinters of factions changing sides at will. Oueddei, although not completely out of the picture, remained in Algiers in 1987 and was no longer privy to the affairs of state in Chad.

Ouedraogo, Gerard Kango. On 8 February 1974, a military coup overthrew the government of Premier Gerard Kango Ouedraogo in Upper Volta (Burkina Faso). President Sangoule Lamizana immediately named a new cabinet and appointed himself premier on 11 February. The constitution was then suspended, and the National Assembly was dissolved. Ouedraogo had been premier since 13 February 1971. His ouster marked a point when the military regime of General Lamazana had decided not to fulfill its promise of a return to civil government in Upper Volta. The military had run the country since 1966. *See* Upper Volta.

Ouedraogo, Jean-Baptiste. In November 1980, a coup ousted the government of Burkina Faso (Upper Volta) and installed Colonel Saye Zerbo (qv) as leader. Zerbo's rule was itself overthrown in another coup on 7 November 1982. This coup, led by mutinous army noncommissioned officers, installed Major Juan-Baptiste Ouedraogo as president. Ouedraogo's support soon split into conservative and radical factions, with the radicals seizing power on 4 August 1983. A National Revolutionary Council was set up, with Captain Thomas Sankara (qv) as head of state. President Ouedraogo ousted from office and ordered the arrest of then Premier Sankara and a number of other officers on 17 May after the discovery of a plot to overthrow his government. He also ordered the Libyan charge d'affairs out of the country because of his complicity in the alleged plot.

Oufkir, Muhammad. On 16 August 1972, King Hassan II (qv) of Morocco escaped an assassination attempt when Moroccan jets strafed his plane as he returned to Rabat from a visit to France. The coup leader, defense minister General Muhammad Oufkir, who had also been the minister of interior, supposedly committed suicide the night of the assassination attempt. On 7 November, 11 other officers involved in the plot were given the death sentence, and 32 more were sent to prison.

Ouidah. *See* Dahomey.

Ould Daddah, Moktar. (b. 25 December 1924, Boutilimit, Mauritania, French West Africa) Born into an aristocratic family, Ould Daddah was the first of his countrymen ever to graduate from a university and the first to become a lawyer. He returned from France to Mauritania in the mid-1950s and became a member of the moderate Progressive Mauritanian Union. He was elected to the territorial assembly in 1957. In 1958 he became the president of the Executive Council; in 1959, prime minister; and in 1961 president. He was at that point a member of the new political party, the Mauritanian Regrouping Party, which he helped form in 1958. His initial rule was one of enlightened leadership. In 1964, however, he turned to authoritarian, one-man rule as the secretary general of the Mauritanian People's Party. On 10 July 1978, following a rash and failed attempt to annex Spanish Sahara, Ould Daddah was ousted by a military coup led by Lieutenant Colonel Mustafa Ould Salek. Ould Daddah's ouster brought an end to the guerrilla war that had been going on between Mauritania and Polisario guerrillas seeking independence for Western Sahara.

Ould Haidallah, Mohammed Khouna. On 4 January 1980, the head of state of Mauritania, Lieutenant Mohammed Mahmoud Ould Louly, was ousted from office in a military coup and replaced by Lieutenant Colonel Mohammed Khouna Ould Haidallah. Five years later, on 12 December 1984, while at a Franco-African summit conference in Burundi, President Haidallah's government was overthrown in a bloodless coup led by Lieutenant Colonel Maaouya Ould Sidi Ahmed Taya (qv), who then proclaimed himself president. This was the latest in a series of government turnovers since the imposition of rule by the Military Committee of National Salvation in 1978. When Haidallah returned to Mauritania in December 1984, he was promptly arrested.

Oum Chalouba. *See* Chad.

Oun Cheeang Sun. On 4 January 1956, a communist-controlled government headed by Oun Cheeang Sun was installed in Cambodia. This followed the 2 March 1955 abdication of Norodom Sihanouk (qv) as king; the enthronement of his father, Norodom Suramarit (qv); and Norodom Sihanouk's becoming premier in September 1955, when Cambodia left the French Union (25 September).

Ovamboland. *See* South Africa.

Ovando Candia, Alfredo. Leader of a military coup that overthrew the government of President Luis Adolfo Silas Salinas (qv) of Bolivia, General Ovando appointed himself president on 26 September 1969. He was forced to resign, however, on 6 October 1970, when a right-wing military junta led by the Bolivian army's chief of staff, General Rogelio Miranda (qv), seized power. One day later, a left-wing military coup led by the air force chief of staff, Juan Jose Torres Gonzales (qv), took the presidency.

Owens Falls Hydraulic Station. *See* Uganda.

Owerri. *See* Nigeria.

Pa-ch'a (Goldinski) Island. *See* China.

Pacheco Areco, Jorge. In 1969, Jorge Pacheco Areco became the president of Uruguay, replacing Oscar Diego Gestido. One of his first acts (15 March 1969) was to begin lifting some of the restrictions put into place by the state of emergency imposed in June 1968 (*see* Uruguay). Many of these restrictions were caused by the increasing activities of the Tupamoro (qv) rebels and student violence. On 24 March 1970, Pacheco Areco was forced to reimpose a number of the restrictions. This caused an uproar in within his party and within the general political scene in the country. Also in 1969, Pacheco Areco appointed Juan Maria Bordaberry-Arocena (qv) as minister of agriculture. Bordaberry replaced Pacheco Areco as president on 1 March 1972. Most of his time in office, Pacheco Areco looked to extending his own presidency.

Pacific Ocean. *See* various nations on the Pacific Rim.

Padilla Aranciba, David. On 24 November 1978, Bolivia's president, Juan Pereda Asbun, was ousted from power in a bloodless coup. He was replaced by General David Padilla Aranciba, the army chief of staff, who headed a three-man junta. On 24 November, Padilla promised elections would be held on 1 July 1979, with the winner taking office on August 6. President Walter Guevara Arze (qv) assumed his office on 8 August.

Paghman. *See* Afghanistan.

Pahany State. *See* Malaysia.

Pahlavi, Reza, Shah of Iran (Mohammad Reza Pahlavi Aryamehr). (b. 26 October 1919, Tehran, Iran—d. 27 July 1980, Cairo, Egypt) Pahlavi was born the eldest son of an army officer, Reza Pahlavi, who in 1926 overthrew the Qajar dynasty and proclaimed himself Shah in Shah (King of Kings). Young Reza Pahlavi completed his primary education in Tehran and was then sent to Switzerland to continue his education. Upon his return to Iran in 1936, he entered the army and, after attending the Officer Training College, was commissioned a lieutenant. On 16 September 1941, the elder Pahlavi, a German sympathizer, was forced to abdicate in his son's favor by the Allies. The new shah assumed his throne at a time when large segments of his country were occupied by Soviet and British (later, American) troops. After World War II, the shah adopted a strong pro-Western policy. His relative youth and inexperience worked against him, however, and he could not dominate the Shi'ite religious leaders, the rich landowners and the communist agitators who worked against him. In April 1951, he appointed Mohammad Mossadegh (qv) to be prime minister. Mossadegh, a nationalist, immediately set about to establish his own power base at the expense of the shah. Mossadegh pushed an oil nationalization bill through the *Majlis* (Parliament), which severely strained his relations with Pahlavi. On 11 August 1953, fearing he would be assassinated, the shah fled to Rome, while a military coup carried out an unsuccessful attempt to overthrow Mossadegh. Pahlavi returned to Iran in 1954 and took immediate measures to restore the oil industry. For the next 20 years, oil revenues were used to strengthen the country industrially and militarily until it became a major power in Southwestern Asia. In 1958, Pahlavi divorced Soraya Esfandiari because she had failed to bear him an heir to the throne as had also happened in his first marriage (ended in divorce in 1948). In 1960 he married Farah Diba, who gave him a son in 1960, the Crown Prince Reza. His dynasty seemingly secure, Pahlavi used his time to suppress all opposition, especially that from Muslim conservatives. The oil shortage in 1973 gave the shah more funds to implement his plans to industrialize Iran. The manner in which the new riches were utilized did not sit well with the population, however, who witnessed major outlays of money for weapons while many still lived in poverty and ignorance. The shah sent Iranian forces into Oman in 1976 to assist the government against a Dhofari uprising. In January 1977, he decided to withdraw the forces. In 1978, a revolution broke out, the fires of which were fanned by the Islamic fundamentalists and the communist *Tudeh* (Masses) party. In Tehran, rioters demanded the ouster of the shah (11 May). In June a general strike followed the death of some anti-shah demonstrators in the capital. On 8 September, the shah declared martial law in Tehran and 11 other cities after troops opened fire on demonstrators who had refused to disperse. As many as 1,000 were killed. On 1 October, he declared a general amnesty to all those, including the Ayatollah Khomeini (qv), who were involved in antigovernment activities. On 5 November, a major anti-shah demonstration took place in Tehran. Prime Minister Sharif-Emami (qv) resigned and was replaced by army general Gholam Reza Azhari (qv). On 30 December, Shahpour Bakhtiar, an outspoken critic of the shah, was named prime minister, at the head of a new civilian government. Chaos gripped the country. Rather than use force against his people, he fled the country on 16 January 1979, knowing that remaining would have meant his death at the hands of a mob. His first stop was in Egypt, then Morocco, the Bahamas and Mexico. It was in Mexico he discovered he suffered from cancer. He was then allowed entrance into the United States (where asylum had previously been denied) to undergo treatment for his disease in New York City. On 15 December 1979, he left the U.S. for Panama and remained three months on the island of Contadora. The new Khomieni (qv) revolutionary government in Iran demanded his extradition, but before there was any action, Pahlavi accepted an invitation from Anwar Sadat to move to Egypt (23 March 1980).This Pahlavi did, and remained there until his death. When the U.S.

embassy was seized in Tehran, the Ayatollah Khomieni stated that one of the four conditions for the release of the hostages was the return of the shah's considerable property holdings to Iran (12 September 1980). *Reading:* Marvin Zonis, *Majestic Failure: The Fall of the Shah* (1991); William Shawcross, *The Shah's Last Ride: The Fate of an Ally* (1988); James Cockcroft, *Mohammad Reza Pahlavi* (1988).

Pakistan. More correctly the Islamic Republic of Pakistan, this Southwest Asian country is bordered on the east by India, on the south by the Arabian Sea, on the southwest by Iran, on the northwest by Afghanistan, and on the north by China. The capital city is Islamabad. Pakistan's history, which it shares with India, began with the Indus Valley civilization 5,000 years ago. The lands were invaded by Aryans from the northwest circa 1500 B.C. This conquest established the Hindu religion, which flourished for 2,000 years. In the sixth century B.C., Persia invaded the region. They were followed by the Macedonians under Alexander the Great and by the Sassanids, all of whom left their mark and created cultural differentiations from the people of India. The Arabs invaded the country in 712 A.D. and introduced Islam. From 1526 to 1857, the Mongol Empire ruled the land. From that date until 1947, the lands were part of the British Empire. In 1906, the All-India Muslim League sought political rights for the Muslims under the leadership of Mohammed Ali Jinnah (qv). Muslim agitation in British India grew after World War I. Seeing that the Hindu majority would never permit this, in 1940 Jinnah began the drive for a separate Muslim state in Pakistan. After 14 August 1947 and the departure of the British, Pakistan came into being as a British Commonwealth nation in two regions separated by India (1,000 miles), with Jinnah as the governor-general. An administrative capital was established in Karachi (West Pakistan) and in Dhaka in East Pakistan (later Bangladesh). The departure of the British saw a mass migration of Hindus out of Pakistan into India. This left Pakistan bereft of much of its skilled labor. Religious rioting followed in both parts of the country, and a small war was fought over Kashmir (qv). Kashmir was partitioned between India and Pakistan. Jinnah died in 1948. In 1956, Pakistan adopted its own constitution and became an Islamic republic. In 1958, General Mohammad Ayub Khan (qv) took power in a bloodless revolution. He was elected president in 1960 and reelected in 1965. In 1960, Pakistan and India agreed to share the waters of the Indus River. War broke out again in Kashmir (*see* Kashmir) in 1965, but was ended by the United Nations in a 1966 truce. Ayub Khan resigned his office on 25 March 1969 after a long period of civil unrest, especially in East Pakistan, which demanded its own government. General Agha Mohammad Yahya Khan became the head of state, suspended the constitution, declared martial law and promised reforms. In 1970, Yahya Khan resigned and turned the government over to Zulfikar Ali Bhutto (qv), the deputy prime minister and foreign minister who was elected in December. In 1971, after a brief civil war began in East Pakistan, government troops opened an offensive against the rebels on 25 March. An invasion by India followed, and East Pakistan broke away to become the independent Bangladesh (*see* Bangladesh). India and

Pakistan signed an agreement on 3 July 1972 whereby Pakistani prisoners of war were released and Indian troops withdrawn. Also in 1972, Bhutto withdrew Pakistan from the Commonwealth after some members of the British federation recognized Bangladesh. In 1974, however, Pakistan recognized Bangladesh and in 1989 rejoined the Commonwealth. In July 1977, however, a military coup overthrew Bhutto. On 4 April 1979, he was executed for complicity in a 1974 political murder. His daughter, Benazir Bhutto, returned to Pakistan in 1986, after having lived in Europe. She reestablished her father's Pakistan People's Party, but this led to rioting and violence. She was arrested on 14 August (Independence Day) along with several other opposition leaders. This set off rioting and bloody demonstrations that lasted more than a month. In December, ethnic rioting in Karachi left hundreds dead and injured. The rioting was sparked by an army sweep through a section of the city looking for weapons and drugs. President Mohammed Zia ul-Haq (qv) was killed in a plane crash in August 1988. Benazir Bhutto was elected prime minister in November. She was accused of corruption, however, in 1990, and dismissed. Following the October 1993 elections, she was returned to power. In 1994, Bhutto faced serious economic problems that required major readjustments in the plans for a new Pakistan. Violence erupted in Karachi in August 1994. Several hundred activists were arrested and held without charge. At least 135 lay dead as the violence continued into the fall. Islamic fundamentalists also caused problems in the north with demands for the institution of Islamic law. Trouble in Kashmir also held Pakistan's attention as India attempted to consolidate its hold on the region of Kashmir under its control. India's campaign to suppress the Muslim uprising caused Pakistan to upgrade its arms supply to the rebels, which aided greatly in producing over 8,000 casualties in the fighting. For Pakistan the expenditures translated to very high defense costs, which further affected the overall bleak economic picture. The International Monetary Fund refused to extend any more credit to Pakistan until its fiscal situation improved. One of the discoveries was that only one out of 135 people paid taxes in the country. The Pakistanis did break up a major drug operation in September, in which ten tons of hashish destined for Europe were seized. Pakistan had a horrendous year of violence in 1995, with Karachi being the center of the turmoil. Refugee Muslims from India constituted the major voting block in the area and easily controlled elections, which gave them power over the local Sindh people. The heavy fighting that resulted in the first nine months of the year cost 2,500 lives, including about 150 police and security force personnel. Peace talks foundered, with each side blaming the other for the failure. An Islamic fundamentalist coup planned for October was uncovered and led to the arrest of a large number of senior military officials involved in the plot. The ringleaders admitted they were fed up with the army's continuing support of the Bhutto government. At the time, Benazir Bhutto was able to get a partial relaxation of the American embargo and received some of the $1.4 billion in military arms shipments and a repayment of the balance owed by the U.S. See East and West Pakistan and Bangladesh. *Reading:* Prem Shankar Jha, *Kashmir 1947: Rival Versions of History* (1996);

Sumit Ganguly, *The Origins of War in South Asia: Indo-Pakistani Conflicts since 1947* (1994); J. Henry Korson, ed., *Contemporary Problems of Pakistan* (1993).

Paktia Province. *See* Afghanistan.

Palach, Jan. On 16 January 1969, Jan Palach burned himself to death in protest of the Soviet occupation of his country, Czechoslovakia. Palach's action followed the Soviet invasion of Czechoslovakia, which put an end to the "Prague Spring" (qv). *See* Czechoslovakia.

Palaquina. *See* El Salvador.

Palestine. *See* Israel.

Palestine Liberation Organization (PLO). The PLO came into existence following a proposal by an Arab summit conference held in January 1964 and a Palestinian Congress decision in April that same year. Ahmed Shuqairy was the PLO's first leader. The PLO was a cover for at least five terrorist groups: *al-Fatah* (qv), *al-Saiqah (al-Sa'iga)* (qv), the Popular Front for the Liberation of Palestine (PFLP) (qv), the Popular Front for the Liberation of Palestine–General Command (PFLP-GC) and the Popular Democratic Front for the Liberation of Palestine (PDFLP) (qv). There were also a dozen or more educational and social organizations sheltered by the PLO. Shuqairy's leadership was tainted by the results of the 1967 Arab-Israeli War. By 1969, *al-Fatah*, with its leader, Yasser Arafat (qv), became the dominant force in the PLO. Initially a terrorist organization, the PLO began to shift its orientation toward politics in 1974. This created a rift between the groups in the PLO and a so-called Rejectionist Front appeared, which claimed no allegiance to the organization. Dubbed as the voice of the Palestinian people and endorsed by most Arabs and Palestinians, the PLO was seriously weakened when it was thrown out of Lebanon in 1982. The organization recovered quickly, however, and again assumed its place as the prime negotiator for the settlement of the Palestine Question. In 1988, when Jordan severed its authority for the West Bank, the PLO became responsible for the region, over which only Israeli authority mattered.The PLO was dealt another blow when it became caught up in the Lebanese army move in 1991 to regain control of the country, in accordance with the 1989 Arab League peace agreement. The PLO forces that had returned to Lebanon caused little trouble, however, surrendering their arms without a struggle. That could not be said of the numerous terrorist organizations which are often associated with the PLO, and Israel's reluctance to evacuate its forces in southern Lebanon was tied directly to the clearing of those terrorist-dominated camps. Thus, wrongly or rightly, the PLO was seen as implicated in the Israeli position on Lebanon. By 1992, a series of intervening events had caused a lessening of PLO influence. A number of leadership personnel changes (some would have called the changes "expulsions") restored the PLO's position by December. Some reports indicate that China's establishment of diplomatic relations with Israel in early 1992 was accomplished with the approval of the PLO, which had long nourished a relationship with Peking. Israel and the PLO signed a historic bilateral agreement in Washington on 13 September 1993, whereby Israel made concessions on the control of the occupied territories (Gaza and Jericho) and the PLO recognized the State of Israel. While the deal was good press for Arafat and the PLO, it did little by way of compensation for the several hundred thousand Palestinians dispossessed by the Israelis, nor did it return all of the territory (the remainder of the West Bank) claimed to have been seized by Israel. Another major issue not resolved by the agreement, one which put the PLO at odds with with Islamic religious leaders, was the question of who would control the holy places in Jerusalem. In 1995, Muslim terrorist activities caused Israel to have some second thoughts on the agreement and lessened its resolve on settling outstanding issues. This weakened Arab backing of the PLO in turn. When a deranged Israeli army officer murdered 29 Muslims in Hebron on 25 February 1995, the PLO and several Arab states withdrew from the process. However, by March talks had resumed, and on 17 May, Palestinian police occupied Gaza in the first step of the hoped-for ultimate solution. In July, PLO headquarters relocated into Gaza, and Arafat made a triumphal entrance to begin the process of starting a new government. The PLO and its programs then became a target of radical Islamic terrorist groups. At year's end much had been accomplished, but there was much more that needed to be done. *Reading:* Andrew Gowers & Tony Walker, *Behind the Myth: Yasser Arafat and the Palestinian Revolution* (1992); Jillian Becker, *The PLO: The Rise and Fall of the Palestinian Liberation Organization,* (1984); John Amos, *Palestinian Resistance: Organization of a Nationalist Movement* (1980); Helena Cobban, *The Palestinian Liberation Organization: People, Power and Politics* (1984); Shaul Mishal, *The PLO under Arafat: Between Gun and Olive Branch* (1986).

Palme, Olaf (Sven Olaf Joachim). (b. 30 January 1927, Stockholm—d. 28 February 1986, Stockholm) Born into a wealthy family, Palme attended Kenyon College, Ohio, where he received his baccalaureate in 1948. He then received a law degree from Stockholm University in 1951. Palme became active in the Social Democratic Workers' Party in the 1950s and became personal secretary to the prime minister in 1953. He entered the Swedish Parliament in 1958 and became minister without portfolio in 1963. In 1965, he was appointed minister of communication, and in 1967, he was given the dual post of minister of education and ecclesiastical affairs. Palme became secretary of the Social Democratic Party in 1969. He then began a series of attacks on the United States and freely accepted deserters from the Vietnam War into Sweden, implying that the U.S. was not a "free country." In 1976, Palme's party was ousted after a general election, but Palme continued to espouse his pacifist views. He was appointed president of the Nordic Council in 1979 and chaired the Independent Commission on Disarmament and Security in Geneva. He also acted as mediator in the Iran-Iraq War. Palme was reelected in 1982 and tried to reinstate his socialist policies, with only medium success. He was assassinated on the street in Stockholm by a lone gunman on 28 February 1986. No one ever claimed credit for the murder, but Carl Gustav Chister Petterson, a drug addict, was tried and sentenced to life for the crime in July 1989. The sentence was overturned, however, in October, and his release envoked a series of events dealing with smuggling and security measures against Kurdish resistance groups in Sweden.

Panama. A country of Latin America, Panama is located on the isthmus that connects South America with Central and North America. Panama is bordered by the Caribbean Sea on the north, Colombia on the east, the Pacific Ocean on the south, and Costa Rica on the west. The capital is Panama City. Spanish explorers first set foot on Panamanian soil in 1501, landing near the present site of Portobelo. Columbus visited there in 1502. The lands were put under the Spanish leadership of Diego de Nicuesa in 1508. The region was assigned to the viceroy of Peru in 1718. Panama became the receiving point for the Spanish plunder of the New World. Spanish galleons regularly sailed from Portobelo loaded with treasure. Sir Francis Drake, Sir Henry Morgan and numerous others tried regularly and unsuccessfully to cut the route in the name of England. Following the general uprising against Spain in the New World, Panama declared its independence in 1821 and voluntarily became a part of Colombia. Serious revolts followed, which centered on issues such as the strategic importance of Panama and discontent with Colombian rule. In 1840, Panama held its own destiny, but the following year Colombian authority was reimposed. In 1846, the U.S. received rights of passage across the isthmus, which became the shortest route to the new American territories in the West. A railroad was completed across the isthmus in 1855. That same year Panama was granted home rule by Colombia. Independence was achieved in 1863. Three years later, Colombia reimposed its authority. A repressive rule existed until November 1903, when Colombia, failing to conclude a treaty with the United States, was faced with a Panamanian declaration of independence that was backed by American warships. On 18 November that same year, the United States was given permission to build a canal across the isthmus and control over a strip of land that became known as the Panama Canal Zone. Panama was paid $10 million and $250,000 a year and an American guarantee of independence. America also gave itself the right to intervene in Panama in case of military disorder. From 1907, the U.S. continually intervened in Panamanian affairs, with troops stationed in the Canal Zone. This situation continued after the canal was completed in 1914 and during World War I, when Panama was a co-belligerent. Thereafter, Panama flourished and American interference slackened, but hostility and resentment continued among the people of Panama. Arnulfo Arias (qv) seized power in 1931, but the U.S. did not interfere. Relations improved between the two nations until 1934, when the U.S. devalued the dollar and Panama refused to accept payment in devalued currency for the annual canal payment. In 1939, the 1903 treaty was redrafted. The new version forbade the U.S. from intervening in Panamanian affairs except to protect the canal in time of emergency. In 1941, Arias was ousted from power because of his Axis sympathies. During World War II, Panama's economy boomed from the presence of large numbers of American troops stationed in the country. The withdrawal of these forces was completed in February 1948. Thereafter, Panama's economy faltered, which, when coupled with the enormous birthrate, seriously destabilized the country. In August 1949, following the death of President Florencio Arosemena (25 February), Arnulfo Arias reappeared (24 November 1949) and seized power, but when he dissolved the National Assembly (9 May 1951), Jose Antonio Ramon-Guizado (qv), who had aided Arias back to power, had him deposed. Ramon took power for himself in 1952 and was working toward reform when he was dismissed on 2 January 1955. By 1955, the annual payment for the Canal Zone was $1.3 million. Opponents of the new LaGuardia government agitated for more money, with some groups demanding immediate nationalization of the canal in the manner in which the Egyptians had taken over the Suez Canal in 1956. Anti-American demonstrations raged, with many U.S. buildings and installations in Panama being attacked. Attempts to invade the Canal Zone also took place. Rioting continued for the next decade until 1964, when U.S. troops were employed to quell the disturbances. Panama broke diplomatic relations with the US on 10 January 1964. Relations were resumed on 3 April 1964. In 1967, new treaty terms were arranged. In 1968, Arias returned to power, but less than two weeks later (11 October 1968) he was again deposed by a military junta led by Colonel Omar Torrijos Herrera (qv), who soon abolished all political parties. A military plot to overthrow Torrijos failed on 15 December 1969, and Torrijos returned to power stronger than ever. A new constitution (1972) established an office of president but left all real power in Torrijos's hands. The economy almost immediately began to worsen. As for the canal issue, Torrijos repudiated U.S. revisions to the 1967 treaty (September 1970), but his government returned to the negotiating table in 1971. In March 1973, the U.S. vetoed a UN resolution for the immediate turnover of the canal to Panama, but in January 1974 it signed a "declaration of principles" on the future sovereignty of the canal. In August 1974, Panama resumed relations with Cuba. In October, Panama accepted a group of left-wing terrorists who had held a group of hostages for ransom in the Dominican Republic. By 1977, a new arrangement kept the canal in U.S. hands until 1999 and granted Panama a portion of its revenues. All nations were to have access to the canal, but its defense was left in U.S. hands.The Panamanian Assembly ratified the treaty in October 1977, amid increasing opposition from those who said the treaty did not go far enough. In August 1978, Panama accepted a group of Sandinista terrorists from Nicaragua. Major rioting broke out after it was learned that the deposed Shah of Iran (qv) was residing in Panama (4 January 1980). The Shah moved on to Egypt on 23 March 1980. Torrijos offered to resign in January 1979. Aristides Royo became president on 11 October 1978, but he was forced to resign in July 1982. Torrijos was killed in an airplane crash in western Panama on 1 August 1981. A military junta held power until May 1984, when Nicolas Ardito Barletta was elected president. Barletta lasted until 1985, when he was replaced by Eric Arturo Delvalle. The junta, however, was led by General Manuel Antonio Noriega, who was in complete control of the country. In February 1988, a U.S. grand jury indicted Noriega on drug charges. Heavy political and economic pressure was put on the Panamanian government, but Noriega remained in power. When an opposition candidate, Guillermo Endara, won the general election in Panama, Noriega nullified the election. An unsuccessful coup attempt against Noriega took place in October 1989. Two months later, a force of about 25,000 U.S. troops invaded Panama, installed Endara as president and arrested Noriega. Noriega was flown to the United States, tried and convicted on drug and racketeering charges (April 1992). The U.S. promised Panama $1 billion in reparations. Meanwhile, the Endara administration suffered through a period of economic decline and continued corruption, especially charges of government participation in the drug trade with the concomitant arrest of three senior officials. Many observers noted that crime had increased since the Noriega ouster. There was a period of violence in September 1993. In 1994, a freely elected president, Ernesto Perez Balladares, took office (1 September) in what was described as an almost completely incident-free and open election (May). The first U.S. troops began to leave Panama (and the Canal Zone) in October 1994. Presidents Balladares and Clinton agreed to consult on the issue of an orderly turnover of control of the Canal by year's end. In January 1995, a plot to assassinate Balladares and other officials was uncovered, and at least ten National Police officers were arrested as a result of a plot to restore a military-led government. Panama began a campaign to remove the country from the list of prime gun- and drug-trafficking locations. The initial success was astonishing, but not without friendly casualties. The country also suffered some internal union violence as the government moved to gain better control of the labor sector. Through all of these times, however, everyone watched the calendar for the expected final withdrawal of U.S. forces in 1999 and what might follow. *See* Panama Canal. *Reading:* David Behar, *Invasion: The American Destruction of the Noriega Regime in Panama* (1990); Dennis Donnelly, et al., *Operation Just Cause: The Storming of Panama* (1991); Carlos Guevara Mann, *Panamanian Militarism: A Historical Interpretation* (1996); Graham Greene, *Getting to Know the General: The Story of an Involvement* (1984).

Panama Canal. The acceptance of a short route from the Atlantic to the Pacific Ocean began in the sixteenth century. The concept of a canal across the isthmus of panama was first noted by Cortes, the Spanish conquerer of Mexico. Other routes, especially across Nicaragua, were also discussed in those early times. The present route of the canal was suggested in 1534. After a three century hiatus, when little or nothing was done on the project, the Spaniards again undertook the chartering of a company to build a canal (1819). When the anti-Spanish revolts began in 1821, what little had been accomplished on the project was abandoned. The new Central American republics attempted to revive interest in a canal, especially among the Americans, but the debate that followed brought no action. When gold was discovered in California, interest in a canal once again burgeoned (1848). In 1876, an international company obtained the necessary authority from Colombia, Panama's master at the moment, to begin work. This company failed, however, and was replaced by a French firm headed by the builder of the Suez Canal, Ferdinand de Lesseps. The De Lesseps group went bankrupt in 1889, and thereafter only the U.S. retained a sufficient interest to undertake the project. In 1899, Congress established an Isthmus Canal Commission to study the viability of a canal. Their recommendation was to build one across Nicaragua. When de Lesseps reorganized his failed company in 1902, he offered his services to the U.S. to build the canal across the Panamanian isthmus (at a price of $40 million). The U.S. negotiated an agreement with Colombia, but in the end, the Colombians refused to ratify the treaty. The U.S. then helped instigate a revolt in Panama that separated that country from Colombia. Panama then signed the Hay-Bunau-Varilla Treaty, in which the U.S. guaranteed Panama's independence in return for a ten-mile wide strip across the country—the Panama Canal Zone. This strip was to be held by the U.S. in perpetuity for an initial price of $10 million and $250,000 per year, with the first annual payment to be made in 1913. By 1955, the annual payment had risen to $2 million. A decision was made to construct a canal with locks to take advantage of the best route, rather than a more extensive sea-level canal. Work began under the command of Colonel George W. Goethals of the U.S. Army Corps of Engineers. Construction was completed and the Canal was in operation in 1914. It had been built wide enough to accommodate the largest U.S. warships at the time. Among the other accomplishments that accompanied the prodigious task was the reduction of the disease-infested area where mosquitos bearing both malaria and yellow fever were found. Credit for this effort went to Colonel William C. Gorgas of the U.S. Army Medical Corps. On 1 October 1961, the government of Panama demanded a new treaty for the canal. When U.S. students in the Canal Zone failed to fly the Panamanian flag with the U.S. colors on 10 January 1964, rioting broke out, and Panama broke diplomatic relations with the U.S. Panama's President Chiari (qv) denounced the treaty at that time. Washington first refused, then gave in and agreed to open discussions of the canal treaty. Diplomatic relations were restored on 3 April 1964. On 24 September 1965, President Lyndon B. Johnson (qv) announced that the U.S. would enter into formal negotiations about the canal. By September 1970, Panama had rejected three draft agreements offered by the U.S. Then, on 11 September 1972, Panama refused the annual payment, claiming the Canal Zone was "occupied arbitrarily." On 15 March 1973, the U.S. vetoed a United Nations move that would have meant the immediate turnover of the Canal Zone to Panama. On 7 September 1977, a new treaty replaced the 1903 agreement. The permanent neutrality of the canal was ratified by Congress on 16 March 1978. Under the terms of what were actually two treaties, the Canal Zone was returned to Panamanian sovereignty, and the eventual turnover of control of the canal to Panama was set for the year 2000 (ratified 18 April 1979). Control of the Canal Zone was turned over to Panamanian authority on 2 October 1979. *See also* Panama. *Reading:* G. Harvey Summ & Tom Kelly, *The Good Neighbors: America, Panama, and the 1977 Canal Treaties* (1988); Tim McNeese, *The Panama Canal* (1997); Judith St. George, *The Panama Canal: Gateway to the World* (1991).

Panama City. *See* Panama.

Pan American Conference, 1948. The Ninth Pan American Conference was held in Bogota, Colombia, in 1948. The first conference had been held in Washington, DC, 2 October 1889–19 April 1890. The Bogota meeting, the first held after World War II, was important because of the creation of the Organization of American States (OAS) (qv), which incorporated the older Pan American Union as its secretariat. Subsequent conferences have tackled such subjects as abolishment of colonial rule in the hemisphere.

Panchen Lama. In a line of supposedly reincarnated lamas, each of whom has traditionally headed (as abbot) the Tashilhunpo Monastery near Zhikatse, Tibet, the Panchen Lama has been considered as second only to the Dalai Lama (qv) in spiritual authority within the dominant *Dge-lugs-pa* sect of Tibetan Buddhism. The reincarnation aspect in the choice of the Panchen Lama began in the seventeenth century when the Dalai Lama issued a decree to the effect that the current Panchen Lama would be reborn as a child in a manifestation of the self-birth of Buddha. In 1923, the Panchen Lama was forced to flee to China because his monastery was in arrears in paying its taxes. In February 1938, a Tibetan boy born in Tsinghai, China, was recognized as the new Panchen Lama by the Chinese government, although he was not accepted by the Tibetan religious community. In November 1949, the Panchen Lama made several radio broadcasts urging the communist "liberation" of Tibet. In 1952, he was brought into Tibet to Tashilhunpo Monastery by the Chinese communists and installed as head abbot. Following a revolt against Chinese oppression, the Chinese dissolved the Tibetan government (28 March 1959) and replaced it with a puppet regime headed by Panchen Lama. The Dalai Lama fled to India (31 March), but the Panchen Lama refused to denounce him as a traitor and was subsequently arrested by the Chinese and imprisoned in Peking in 1964. He was not released until the late 1970s and died of a heart attack in his monastery on 28 January 1989.

Pando. *See* Uruguay.

"Panhandle." *See* Vietnam.

Panjshir Valley. *See* Afghanistan.

Panjwin. *See* Iran.

Panmunjom, Korea. A town of the North-South Korean border located southeast of Kaeson, Panmunjom attained significance because the truce agreement ending the Korean War was initialed there. Negotiations for such a truce began following an abrupt turnabout announcement by the Soviet delegate to the United Nations, Yakov A. Malik, on 23 June 1951. The first preliminary truce talk began at Kaesong on 8 July 1951, with top-level talks beginning on 10 July. There were immediate indications of lack of sincerity on the part of the North Koreans and their Chinese allies. The negotiations were broken off on several occasions, usually by the communists. Beginning in September 1951, wrangling began over the meeting site at Kaesong. The UN demanded that the site be moved to a location in "No-Man's Land" between the two front lines to obviate further chance of danger to the security of the UN truce team behind enemy lines. Panmunjom was finally selected, and negotiations began again on 25

October 1951. An armistice was agreed upon there on 27 July 1953 (*see* Korea). Following the end of the conflict, the site was used for truce commission meetings. Panmunjom was also the site selected by the communists for the release on 23 December 1968 of the American captives taken during the *USS Pueblo* incident (qv). On 18 August 1976, North Korean soldiers attacked a work party of U.S. and South Korean soldiers working at Panmunjom. Two U.S. officers were killed in the affray. The truce site at Panmunjom was partitioned on 8 September to prevent more such incidents. A firefight broke out in the truce site on 23 November 1984 that killed three North Korean soldiers and one South Korean soldier. This incident occurred when a Soviet participant in North-South truce talks defected.

Pao Ting. *See* China.

Papadopoulos, George (*Georgios***).** (b. 5 February 1919, Chios, Greece—d. 23 June 1996, Ekali, Greece) When the 1967 elections were about to be held in Greece, there was a clear indication that the Centre Union Party would win. A group of right-wing military officers, led by Colonel Georgios Papadopolous and Brigadier General Styliano Patakos, carried out a successful coup on 21 April 1967 and seized the government. The cause of this revolt was a crisis that arose between King Constantine II (qv) and Prime Minister George Papandreou (qv). Papandreou was subsequently arrested. When a counter-coup failed, Constantine fled into exile (14 December), and Papadopoulos assumed the regency of the country. A period of civil unrest followed. On 1 June 1973, following Papadopoulos's charge of treason against the king, the cabinet abolished the monarchy and proclaimed Greece a republic. On 19 August, Papadopoulos was sworn in as president. On 13 November 1973, violence broke out, which culminated in student riots that had spread all over Greece by 16 November. In Athens, demonstrators were dispersed with much bloodshed. On 25 November, a coup led by Brigadier General Demetrios Ioannides ousted Papadopoulos and placed Lieutenant General Phaidon Gizikis (qv) in the presidency. Papadopoulos was placed under house arrest. He died in 1996.

Papandreou, George (*Georgios***).** (b. 13 February 1888, Kalentzi, Greece—d. 1 November 1968, Athens) Papandreou received his education in law at the University of Athens and in Germany. He was governor of the Aegean Islands district from 1917 until 1920 and then served as minister of education from 1929 until 1933 in the antimonarchist Venizelos government. In 1935, Papandreou broke with the left wing of the Liberal Party and formed the Democratic Socialist Party (DSP). He spent a number of years in exile during the Metaxas dictatorship, but returned to Greece in time to be imprisoned (1942–1944) by the Germans after the occupation. He escaped in 1944 and helped establish and head the government-in-exile from April until October 1944. He then formed a coalition government but resigned in December 1944 when civil war began in Greece. He held several ministerial offices (1946–1952). He later merged his DSP with the Liberal Party to form the Centre Union, a left-center coalition. In 1963, Papandreou was appointed prime minister after a narrow win by his party. He shortly thereafter resigned but he was reelected in 1964, with an absolute majority of power. Once again prime minister, he exercised a series of political and social reforms far wider than anticipated and openly criticized the United States for its excessive meddling in Greek internal affairs. When Papandreou attempted to appoint his son, Andreas, to a ministerial post and clashed with King Constantine (qv), a serious crisis ensued. In July 1965, Constantine dismissed Papandreou. On 21 April 1967, when the Greek military saw that Papandreou and his party were about to be reelected, a military coup took place, and he and his son were arrested. Although released soon afterward, the elder Papandreou died in November 1968.

Papua New Guinea. *See* New Guinea.

Paracel Islands (*Xisha Qundao*) (*Hsisha*). Claimed by China, Taiwan and Vietnam, the Paracel Islands are an archipelago that lies in the north-central part of the South China Sea, approximately 200 miles southeast of Hainan and 250 miles west of the Philippine island of Luzon. The South Vietnamese established three outposts on the islands as a part of their claim to the island group. On 18–20 January 1974, a series of naval and land engagements were fought between South Vietnamese and Communist Chinese forces. The South Vietnamese were driven off the islands as a result. The Chinese claimed "indisputable" rights to the Paracels and other groups of islands in the region, the main reason being the the possibility of large gas and oil deposits around the islands. After the North Vietnamese conquest of the Republic of South Vietnam, the Hanoi government claimed the Paracel and Spratley (qv) islands (6 June 1976).

Paraguay. This land-locked country of South America is bordered on the east by Brazil, on the south and southwest by Argentina and on the northwest and north by Bolivia. The capital city is Asunción. Various Native American tribes of the Guarani dialect were the early inhabits of the region. The country was first visited by Spanish adventurers in 1525, who built a fort (*Nuestra Señora de la Asunción)* on the Paraguay River in 1537. Jesuits began a massive conversion effort there beginning in 1609 and built many missions throughout the region, soon becoming the most powerful force in the region. In 1750, Spain ceded much of Paraguay's territory to Portugal. Thereafter, the Jesuits inspired a revolt among the Guarani and found themselves expelled in 1767. Spain also expelled most of the Jesuits, and the majority of Jesuit missions in the region were closed. When the Viceroy of LaPlata (headquartered in Buenos Aires) was established in 1776, Paraguay, Argentina, Uruguay and Bolivia were included in its territorial control. Paraguay was a backwater during this period. When Argentina claimed its independence in 1810, Paraguay refused to join them, and declared their own independence on 14 May 1811. In 1814 a dictatorship was established under José Francia that lasted until 1840. Always aware of Argentina, Francia maintained a policy of national isolation for his country. His nephew Carlos Antonio López followed Francia's death with his own dictatorship beginning in 1844. His policies reversed the isolationist policy, and Paraguay began a modest growth. Upon López's death in 1862, his son, Francisco Solano López, took power. In 1865, he led his country into a devastating war against Argentina, Brazil and Uruguay. His death in 1870 ended the conflict, but more than half of Paraguay's population had been killed in the fighting, the country was in ruins and the economy in shambles. From 1870 until 1912, the turmoil continued with no presidential officeholder being able to complete one full term. There followed a period of alternating stability and often-violent turbulence. Paraguay remained neutral in World War I and prospered from the relative peace it enjoyed. Between 1929 and 1932 a series of incidents occurred along the undefined border with Bolivia. In 1932, the Chaco War began, which lasted until 1935, when an armistice was arranged. The arbitration that followed gave Paraguay three-quarters of the disputed territory (1938). A new constitution was adopted in 1940 that codified a widespread governmental reorganization. However, that same year, General Higinio Morinigo declared himself dictator and fundamentally disregarded the new constitution. On 7 February 1945, Paraguay declared war on Germany and Japan and subsequently became a charter member of the United Nations. An attempt by the left-wing followers of the former president Colonel Rafael Franco failed on 29 March 1947. Morinigo was deposed, however, in 1948, and a series of presidents came and went in quick order. In 1949, Federico Chávez became another dictator and aligned his country with Juan Peron (qv) of Argentina. Having brought his country through a severe economic crisis, Chávez was reelected in general elections held on 15 February 1953. On 5 May 1954, however, he was overthrown by an army/police coup; a military junta took control of the country. In an election held on 11 July, General Alfredo Stroessner (qv), the army's commander in chief and the only candidate, was elected. On 15 August 1954 the election was confirmed, and Stroessner was sworn in. Leftist attempts to oust Stroessner in 1956 and 1957 both failed, and he was reelected to a second five-year term in 1958. In December 1959, an Argentina-based rebel force invaded Paraguay but was defeated. Within one year, several more such attempts would be made, but all would fail. Paraguay broke diplomatic relations with Castro's Cuba in December 1960 and urged joint action against that country by the Organization of American States (OAS) (qv). Although initially thwarted, Paraguay did join an OAS collective security force, aimed primarily against Cuba, on 6 May 1965. In May 1968, Paraguay became a signatory to the La Plata Basin Pact, which established economic ties with Argentina, Bolivia, Brazil and Uruguay. When Governor Nelson A. Rockefeller was due to vist Paraguay, serious student rioting broke out in the country. The 1970s and early 1980s witnessed a period of relative calm. Declining markets led to a rise in unemployment, however, and economic unrest ensued. On 15 August 1970, an attempt to assassinate President Stroessner failed. Over 100 students were arrested in the aftermath of the attack. A long-standing state of siege was lifted in Ascunción in 1987. Stroessner was reelected to his eighth term in 1988, but he was ousted from power by a military coup on 3 February 1989. He was replaced as president by General Andrés Rodriquez. When the foreign minister stated in July 1990 that the Colorado Party would fight to maintain control of the government, Rodriquez dismissed him. There was growing disarray in within the Colorado Party in 1991, which resulted from their losses in the municipal elections that year. The public displays of acrimony stopped in December, however, when the army put pressure on the Colorados, which enabled them to win support for their candidates for the constituent assembly. When the assembly entered a codicil banning sitting presidents from seeking reelection, Rodriquez backed away, and fears of an army coup became the topic of the day (June 1992). The disruption continued when the Colorados nominated Luis Maria Argana for president in the upcoming May 1993 elections. Cries of vote fraud were heard from the losing segment of the party, and Argana lost the nomination in the process. Juan Carlos Warmosy was the final choice of the Colorados, who won the election and gave him the presidency in August 1993. Once again, however, threats and intimidation by the army appeared to have swayed the voters toward the Colorados. In February 1994, violence erupted when farmers, demanding government subsidies, blocked roads into the capital. Police fired on the demonstrators using rubber bullets. In May, a general strike over falling market prices paralyzed the country. The government reponse was too little and too late. When the opposition-controlled Congress approved a bill banning the military from political activites (28 May 1994), the government and the military filed for a legal remedy. The incident caused the opposition to withdraw from the cooperation that had existed. In January 1995, a human rights report concluded that control was still the key element in the Paraguatan democracy and that any number of crimes committed during the Stroessner dictatorship were still going unpunished. Warmosy forced the retirement of a number of senior officers and reorganized the military with the outcome of strengthening his own position and coopting his successor, thought to be General Lino Ovieda. The law against the military in politics went into effect in 1995. Although the economy remained relatively stagnant, Paraguay joined the Southern Cone Common Market (*Mercosur*) in 1995. *Reading:* Riordan Roett & Richard Sacks, *Paraguay* (1991); David Louis Jones, *Bibliography of Paraguay* (1979).

Park, Chung Hee. (b. 14 November 1917, near Teagu, Korea—d. 26 October 1979, Seoul) Born into peasant circumstances, Park attended Taegu Normal School, where he graduated with honors. He then taught primary school until he was selected to attend the Japanese Military Academy. During World War II, he served as second lieutenant in the Japanese army until the end of the war and the subsequent freeing of Korea. He then attended the U.S.–sponsored military academy and served in the Republic of Korea army (ROKA) in 1946 as a captain. In June 1953, during the Korean War, he was promoted to brigadier general. He was promoted to general in 1961, the same year he took part in a bloodless anticommunist coup (16 May 1961) that took over the government of the Second Republic. The former president, Yun Po Sun (qv), was arrested. On 3 July 1961, Park emerged as the leader of the ruling junta. On 15 October 1963, Park won the election for president of the Third Republic, but only after massive protests forced Park to back down (6 April 1963) from a decision (22 March 1963) to postpone the plebiscite. On 3 June 1964, President Park closed all of the country's universities and declared martial law in the capital city of

Seoul in response to massive student demonstrations against his regime. Student rioting took place again in June 1969, trying to force Park's ouster. He would, however, be reelected two more times to the presidency (1973 and 1978). Park ran a highly controlled administration at home and maintained friendly relations with the United States throughout his tenure. His internal programs, however, led to serious unrest, and on 17 October 1972, he declared martial law, followed on 27 October by the imposition of a new constitution that granted him sweeping powers. On 8 January 1974, after being reelected president, he promulgated two new emergency measures aimed at suppressing dissent. It became a crime, punishable by 15 years' imprisonment, to critcize the government. An unsuccessful attempt on his life took place on 15 August 1974, when a lone gunman of an anti-Park youth group opened fire on the president, killing instead Park's wife. The assailant was arrested. On 30 April 1975, Park informed his people that an attack by North Korea was imminent and put the ROK armed forces on alert. In 1979, Park dismissed the opposition leader of the National Assembly, which caused widespread rioting throughout the country. On 22 October 1979, he declared the industrial regions of Masan and Pusan military areas to help halt the rioting. On 26 October 1979, Park was assassinated by the head of the Korean Central Intelligence Agency (KCIA), Kim Jae Kyu, a long time friend of the president. Five others were also killed in the dinnertime incident at a special KCIA restaurant. Kim was arrested later in the evening at Korean Army headquarters. On 6 December 1979, the new president, Choi Kyu Hah, revoked most of Park's anti-opposition decrees. *Reading:* Michael Keon, *Korean Phoenix: A Nation from Ashes* (1977).

Park Tong Jiu. As South Korean prime minister, in February 1977 Park Tong Jiu declared that his government under the Park Chung Hee (qv) regime, had no intention of asking the U.S. for nuclear weapons to offset the expected withdrawal of U.S. troops.

Parliament Square. *See* Hungary.

"Parrot's Beak." *See* Cambodia.

Parti Populaire Syrien. A right-wing Muslim group in Lebanon, the *Parti Populaire Syrien*, attempted to overthrow the government of President Fuad Shihab on 31 December 1961. The attempt was suppressed by the army, and Shihab remained in office to the end of his term (1964).

Parwan Province. *See* Afghanistan.

Pas (Paz) Estenssoro, Vincent (Victor). In 1950–1951, Pas Estenssoro was in exile from his home country of Bolivia. In the presidential elections of 1951, however, he won the presidency. The president in office, Mamerto Urrliogoitia, turned authority over to a military junta to stop this candidate of the Movement for National Revolution (MNR) from assuming his office. A bloody revolt brought Pas Estenssoro to power. On 8 November 1953, there was an unsuccessful attempt to overthrow his government. He was defeated in the 1956 elections, but he was reelected in 1960. In the 1964 election Pas Estenssoro again won the office (July), but he was removed on 3–4 November by a military coup.

Pastora Gomez, Eden. (b. 22 January 1937, Dario, Nicaragua) Known as "Zero" (*Comandante Cero*), Eden Pastora Gomez led 24 heavily armed Sandinista (qv) rebels disguised as National Guardsmen in an attempt to seize control of the National Palace in Managua, Nicaragua, on 22 August 1978. The attempt failed after two days, when the government refused to meet their demands for the release of 59 political prisoners and for safe conduct and money for the terrorists. Six were killed and more than 1,000 held hostage during the siege. The incident led to a series of uprisings in a number of Nicaraguan cities, all of which were surpressed by government forces. Between 1,500 and 3,000 were killed. After the Somoza (qv) regime was toppled (1979), Pastora Gomez fell out of the Sandinista ranks (5 April 1981) and became a leader of Contra (qv) (properly, *Alianza Revolucionaria Democratica*, or ARDE) forces in the south of the country opposed to Sandinista rule. He was injured in a bomb blast during a news conference inside his headquarters encampment (30 May 1984). Seven were killed, including two newsmen and 27 others injured. He subsequently lost the leadership of his rebel army.

Patakos, Styliano. On 21 April 1967, a right-wing coup led by Colonel George Papadopoulos (qv), Lieutenant General Gregorios Spandidakis and Brigadier General Styliano Patakos overthrew the government of Prime Minister George Papandreou (qv) of Greece. (*see* Greece and Papadoupolos.) Patakos became the minister of interior in the new civil-military government.

Pathankot. *See* India.

Pathan Uprising. *See* India.

Pathet Lao. A leftist-oriented nationalist group in Laos, the Pathet Lao was founded in 1950 and joined the communist Viet Minh in their war against France over rule in Indochina. A legal political wing of the Pathet Lao, the *Neo Lao Hak Xat* (Lao Patriotic Front) was formed in 1956 and participated in several coalition governments over the next decade. In the 1960s and 1970s, the Pathet Lao carried out a guerrilla war against the U.S.–backed Laotian government in Vientiane, gradually winning control of the northern and eastern regions of the country. In May 1975, the Vientiane government fell, and the Pathet Lao emerged as the new leadership of the entire country. *See* Laos.

Patriotic Front. At a conference held in Libreville, Gabon, on 5 July 1977, the leaders of 48 African nations of the Organization of African Unity (OAU) (qv) agreed to support the Patriotic Front in its battle for black power in Rhodesia. The Patriotic Front claimed it alone represented the blacks and that it alone should take control of any interim government following the abolition of white rule in the country. Other black groups contested this assumption. *See* Zimbabwe.

Patterson, John S. On 22 March 1974, the US vice consul in Hermosillo, Mexico, John S. Patterson, was kidnapped by a group calling themselves the "People's Liberation Army of Mexico" (qv). A demand of $500,000 in ransom for his safe return was received on the day of the abduction. The Mexican government came to believe that the kidnapping was actually the work of American criminals. As the ransom was not paid, Patterson's body was found in a creek bed near

Hermosillo on 7 July. In the meantime, an American adventurer, 40-year-old Bobbie Joe Keesee, was arrested in San Diego, California, and charged with conspiracy to kidnap a US diplomat. A second man, Greg Curtis Fielden, was also named in the indictment. Keesee was sentenced to 20 years in prison on the conspiracy charge.

Patutin, Viktor. *See* Afghanistan.

Pauker, Anna (Ana). On 5 November 1947, the Moscow-trained communist Anna Pauker became the minister of foreign affairs of Romania, replacing the noncommunist Jorge Tatarescu. On 29 May 1952, however, as a part of a general purge of the Romanian Communist Party, Pauker, along with a number of others, was removed from the Politburo.

Paul Doumer Bridge. *See* Vietnam.

Paul of Greece. *See* Greece.

Paul VI, Pope. *See* Vatican and Vietnam.

Paveh (Pawe). *See* Iran.

Pavloski, I. G. *See* Afghanistan.

Paz Garcia, Policarpo. On 7–8 August 1978, the Honduran Armed Forces Council removed president Juan Alberto Melgar Castro (qv) from power in a bloodless coup. In his place, the council gave power to General Policarpo Paz Garcia, the chief of the armed forces. The new 46-year-old president was the head of a three-man junta that announced a popular election would be held in 1980. When popular increased unrest was noted, the election was cancelled. This act incurred an increase in unrest in the country and the eventual reinstating of the elections. Garcia held office until 20 July 1980, when governance was taken over by the Constituent Assembly. Garcia remained as provisional president, however, until 27 January 1982, when a duly elected civilian government headed by Roberto Suazo Córdova (qv) was inaugurated.

Peace Corps. The Peace Corps Act of 1961 established an agency of volunteers. The first head of the agency was President John F. Kennedy's (qv) brother-in-law, R. Sargent Shriver. From 1971 to 1982, the Peace Corps was subordinated to another independent agency called ACTION. The principal effort of the Peace Corps was to assist emerging nations in their development by using volunteer professionals and skilled workers to help develop agricultural, educational, health and technology programs through the education and training of local national personnel. Assignments to specific nations was on a need basis, and volunteers were recruited for a two-year period to fill those needs. Volunteers needed their specialty and a working knowledge of the language involved to be eligible. Usually the volunteers lived in the community, however primitive, in which they worked. About 900 signed up in 1961. This number grew to 15,556 working in 52 countries by 1966. After 1989, the program was scaled back by budget cuts, but with the emergence of new Eastern European countries the work of the Peace Corps began to increase. Peace Corps volunteers presently serve in 90 countries. In some instances, the volunteers faced considerable danger, not only from rebel forces attempting to destabilize a nation but also from the governments themselves. On 19 February 1965, for instance,

Venezuelan police mistook Joseph R. Rupley, a Peace Corps volunteer, and his companions to be terrorists and killed him. In another incident, on 7 July 1973, the always unpredictable Ugandan dictator Idi Amin Dada (qv) ordered the detention of 112 Peace Corps volunteers while he determined if they were "mercenaries." The group was released unharmed on 9 July. Funding for Peace Corps activities was reduced in 1989, which reduced the size of the group to a little over 5,000. There have been some budget increases in the 1990s, while volunteers now serve in about 90 countries, including Eastern Europe. *Reading:* Robert Ridinger, *The Peace Corps: An Annotated Bibliography* (1989); Brent K. Ashabranner, *A New Frontier: The Peace Corps in Eastern Europe* (1994).

Peam Reang (Phum Peam Reang). *See* Cambodia.

Pearson, Lester B. (b. 23 April 1897, Newtonbrook, Ontario, Canada—d. 27 December 1972, Ottawa) Pearson was educated at the University of Toronto and Oxford. He joined the Canadian department of external affairs in 1928 and served in both London and Washington. In Washington, he was the Canadian ambassador from 1945 to 1946. He became undersecretary of state for external affairs in 1946, and secretary of state for external affairs in 1948. Pearson was instrumental in the formation of NATO (qv) and was a member of the Canadian delegation to the United Nations from 1948 until 1957. He served as president of the UN General Assembly in 1952–1953. In 1957 he was awarded the Nobel peace prize for his work in forming the international policy that led to the employment of UN emergency forces, especially in the Suez Crisis of 1956. In 1958 he headed the Liberal Party in Canada and became prime minister in 1963. He retired from office in April 1968 and was appointed head of the commission on economic aid of the International Bank for Reconstruction and Development. He died in Ottawa at age 75.

Pebble Island. *See* Falkland Islands.

Pedro Pablo Castillo Front. On 10 September 1985, terrorists of the Pedro Pablo Castillo Front kidnapped the eldest daughter of El Salvador's president Jose Napoleon Duarte (qv), Ines Guadalupe Duarte Duran (qv), and a female companion. The attack was a bloody shootout outside the university in San Salvador. One security guard was killed and another mortally wounded. The two women were held for two months before they were released in a swap for 24 political prisoners.

Peers, William R. Following the disclosure of the My Lai massacre in South Vietnam in March 1968, US Army Lieutenant General William R. Peers was assigned the responsibility for conducting a wide-ranging investigation of the incident. His report was the basis of the government's actions against those believed to have been involved in the incident and the subsequent coverup. *See* My Lai and Calley.

Peking. *See* China.

"Pentagon Papers." In 1967, US Secretary of Defense Robert McNamara (qv) ordered that a history of US involvement in Southeast Asia be prepared. The 47-volume history that resulted (1969) contained more than 3,000 pages of text, and

4,000 additional documents. Among those who worked on the project was Daniel Ellsberg of the Massachusetts Institute of Technology's Center for International Studies. The overall security classification of the study was "Top Secret." The *New York Times* began publishing excerpts of the report on 13 June 1971. The Department of Justice obtained a temporary restraining order preventing the newspaper from publishing more than the first three installments of what was claimed to be papers of extreme importance to national security. Within 15 days the US Supreme Court ruled against the lower court's ban in what was considered to be one of the most important decisions handed down by the court in US history. Ellsberg appeared to be only the "tip of the iceberg," and a massive investigation followed to determine whether any government employees were directly or indirectly involved along with Ellsberg, who claimed to have become disillusioned during the preparation of the report with U.S. policy on Southeast Asia. The *Washington Post* also received a copy of the report through a covert source. When Richard Nixon sought reelection in 1972, he authorized unlawful acts in an attempt to discredit Ellsberg. These efforts were revealed in the subsequent Watergate investigation. *Reading:* David Rudenstine, *The Day the Presses Stopped: A History of the Pentagon Papers Case* (1996); Peter Schrage, *Test of Loyalty: Daniel Ellsberg and the Rituals of Secret Government* (1974).

Pentalateral Agreement. On 23 December 1950, the United States signed the Pentalateral Agreement with France, Vietnam, Laos and Cambodia. By its terms, the United States promised indirect military assistance for use in Indochina. The U.S. Military Assistance Advisory Group (USMAAG) was established, with 128 military personnel under the command of Brigadier General Francis G. Brink. This agreement was overtaken by events in Southeast Asia, and on 1 January 1955 the U.S. began direct assistance to Vietnam, based upon the terms of the original agreement. Lieutenant General John W. "Iron Mike" O'Daniel, the new chief of MAAG Indochina (MAAGI) was assigned the responsibility for assisting South Vietnam in organizing and training its armed forces.

"People's Army." On 17 September 1972, the Ugandan government claimed that it had been invaded in the southwest by a rebel "People's Army," a group that supported former president Milton Obote (qv), reinforced by regular Tanzanian army units (denied by Tanzania). The allegedly combined force met with some initial success, but Ugandan military forces, especially Uganda's Israeli-trained air force, were able to drive the invaders into a swamp near the Tanzania-Uganda border. That Tanzania did not have troops on the ground was finally established, but there was little doubt that Tanzania had knowledge of the preparation for the rebel invasion. This issue was settled through negotiation in October, but the relations between Tanzania's president, Julius Nyerere (qv), and Uganda's Idi Amin Dada (qv) remained strained.

People's Democratic Party, Afghanistan (PDP). *See* Afghanistan.

People's Democratic Republic of Angola. *See* Angola.

People's Democratic Republic of Yemen. *See* South Yemen.

People's Liberation Army (Colombia). *See* Popular Liberation Front (EPL) (Colombia).

"People's Liberation Army of Mexico." A fictitious terrorist organization, the People's Liberation Army of Mexico concocted by at least two Americans as a part of a plot to kidnap a U.S. diplomat for monetary gain. *See* Patterson.

People's Liberation Front (PLF). In early 1971, an armed rebellion broke out in the British parliamentary state of Ceylon. This revolt was aimed at the ruling leftist coalition controlled by Madame Sirimavo Bandaranaike (qv) and was led by the People's Liberation Front, headed by Rohana Wijeweera, who was a graduate of the Patrice Lumumba University in Moscow. Called "Che Guevarists," the PLF was made up of school dropouts, unemployed workers, and young Buddhists displeased with the form of government imposed upon the island since the Bandaranaike Sri Lanka Freedom Party (SLFP) government came to power on 29 May 1970. At that time, the SLFP joined with the Trotskyite Lanka Sama Samaja Party and the Ceylon Communist Party to form a coalition inimical to the PLF. The first attack was against the U.S. embassy in Colombo. On 16 March 1971, a state of emergency had been declared, and on 23 March, the government announced it had uncovered a PLF plot to overthrow the government. The actual rebellion began on 5 April and was well planned. An attempt to assassinate Madame Bandaranaike failed, however, but attacks against police stations and public buildings were more successful. The military was mobilized, but was to be outnumbered by the rebels and short of weapons and ammunition. Appeals abroad brought quick responses from Great Britain, India and the USSR. The PLF, on the other hand, had no discernable outside assistance, although the government did order the closure of the North Korean mission as a safety measure. At least 1,200 died in the ensuing violence, about 60 of them from the government's forces. Some 14,000 were detained. of whom 2,000 were subsequently released. Of the remaining 12,000, 5,000 were tried, while the remainder went to "rehabilitation" camps. The government backed down in some of the areas of contention between the two sides, but did not cave in to the rebels, having won the armed confrontation. An earlier amnesty offer by the government, which expired on 4 March, produced about 4,000 defections from the PLF ranks; and it was believed that only the hard core of the PLF participated in the April uprising.

People's Liberation Movement. *See* Ethiopia and Eritrean Liberation Front.

"People's Park." Located in Berkeley, California, near the University of California campus, the People's Park played a role in the 15 May 1969 rioting that took place there. A so-called counter-institution began on university property and the demonstrators were able to fight off the police in the park. The arrival of National Guard troops forced the rioters out of the park, and order was restored. The park is now a playground.

"People's Prison," Uruguay. In September 1971, 106 Tupamaro (qv) prisoners escaped from Punta Carretas prison. Following the reorganization of Uruguayan security forces, a campaign began against the Tupamaro guerrilla organization. President Bordaberry (qv) had declared a state of "internal war." The police campaign led to the uncovering of numerous rebel arms caches and, on 28 May 1972, to the capture of the notorious "People's Prison" in Montevideo and the release of numerous hostages being held there. Over 2,000 Tupamaros were captured in the roundup, including the leader, Raúl Sendic, who was one of the escapees from Punta Carretas.

People's Resistance Army. On 22 February 1974, terrorists of the so-called Greek People's Resistance Army blew up the Dow Chemical Company plant at Lavrion, 40 miles from Athens. Considerable damage was caused by the four bombs that exploded. Two Greek demolitions men were killed while attempting a fifth bomb discovered at the plant.

People's Revolutionary Army (*Ejercito Revolucionario des Pueblo*) **(ERP).** An urban and rural terrorist organization in Argentina that endangered the government in the mid-1970s. Founded in 1970 by Mario Roberto Santucho Juarez, it was the armed wing of the Trotskyite Workers' Revolutionary Party (PRT) and had the goal of overthrowing the capitalist government of Argentina. The ultimate goal was the "liberation" of all of South America from capitalism. The group's strength was estimated to be 2,000 in 1974, with about 12,000 supporters. The EPR's modus operandi was kidnappings, assassinations and bank robbery. In 1975, the ERP felt strong enough to engage Argentine army units in open combat. In July 1976, Santucho and Jose Urteaga, another ERP leader, were killed in a gun battle with police in Buenos Aires. This seriously weakened the group, but not to the point of extinction. In 1976, a right-wing organization, the Argentine Anti-Communist Alliance (AAA), was formed to combat the ERP with a counterterrorist campaign that was as deadly as the ERP itself. By the late 1970s, the ERP was almost destroyed in the fighting that had taken place. The group is still in existence but constitutes no real threat.

People's Sacrifice Guerrillas. On 28 December 1977, a group calling itself the People's Sacrifice Guerrillas claimed credit for blowing up the Iran-American Society Center in Tehran. This was part of the campaign against the Shah of Iran and his American allies.

People's Strugglers. On 21 May 1975, terrorists belonging to the People's Strugglers assassinated two U.S. air force officers in Tehran. Ten members of the group were captured and tried for the murders. Nine of them were executed on 24 January 1976. The same group had also assassinated an Iranian employed by the U.S. embassy in Tehran on 3 July 1975. On 28 August 1976, three American officials of Rockwell International were assassinated by the same group in Tehran. The rumor at the time was that the People's Strugglers were being supplied by Libya.

People's Temple Cult. Originally founded in San Francisco, this cult was led by James Warren ("Jim") Jones (b. 13 May 1931, Lynn, Indiana). Obsessed by power, Jones, who had been a preacher in Indiana, promised his People's Temple followers a "utopia," which was to be carved out of the jungle with financial support from politicians Jones had served and from the extortion of money and property from among his followers. As investigations into his dealings became more intense in the mid-1970s, Jones moved his followers to

Guyana, where an agricultural commune was established called Jonestown. There, Jones collected everyone's passports and the money they had and extorted more money from the sect through threats of violence. During this same time, he carried out rehearsals for a mass ritual suicide of the entire sect. Back in the United States, the results of the investigations reached the halls of Congress. Representative Leo Ryan of California, along with a group of aides, relatives and reporters, traveled to Guyana on an investigative and sort of rescue mission. Several of the cult members asked Ryan to take them with him. Upon hearing of this, Jones ordered the entire group of visitors assassinated. When only Ryan and a few others were killed, including one cult member, Jones ordered the planned-for mass suicide (18 November 1978). Some obeyed willingly, some were murdered, and some escaped into the surrounding jungle. When Guyanan officials reached the camp, they found 913 bodies, including that of Jim Jones, who killed himself with a gun. Unravelling the affair took years. More than $15 million was eventually recovered from banks around the world. *Reading:* Sue L. Hamilton, *Death of a Cult Family: Jim Jones (Days of Tragedy)* (1989); Marshall Kilduff, *Suicide Cult: The Inside Story of the People's Temple Cult and the Massacre in Guyana* (1978).

Perak Province. *See* Lebanon.

Pereda Asbún, Juan. On 9 July 1978, air force general Juan Pereda Asbún, who had been nominated as the candidate of the ruling junta, was elected president of Bolivia (*see* Bolivia). On 19 July, the National Elections Court voided the election and ordered a new one to be held. President Hugo Banzer-Suarez (qv) announced he would remain in office until 6 August, as had been planned. Pereda then withdrew to Santa Cruz to await the outcome of the situation. A military coup, which resembled a rebellion, took place on 21 July 1978, and Banzer immediately resigned. Pereda then returned to La Paz and assumed the presidency. Banzer then declared himself a candidate for the new election. At the same time (11 August 1978), Pereda lifted the state of seige. On 24 November 1978, Pereda was in turn ousted by a military coup and replaced by General David Padilla Aranciba.

Peres, Shimon (aka Shimon Persky). (b. 16 August 1923, Wolozyn, Poland) In 1934, the Persky family emigrated out of Poland to Palestine. Peres joined the Zionist Haganah movement in 1947, where he was befriended by David Ben-Gurion. After Israel's independence in 1948, Ben-Gurion appointed Peres as the head of the new Israeli navy. Peres was then 25 years of age. He became deputy director general of the Ministry of Defense in 1953 and, the following year, director general. In 1959 Peres was appointed deputy defense minister and was influential in Israel's nuclear development program. He resigned in 1965 to join Ben-Gurion in the founding of the *Rafi* opposition party, which lost its bid to replace the government. In 1967, Peres engineered the merger of *Rafi* with the *Mapai* party and with the leftist *Ahdut Avodah* party. Peres became head of the Labor Party in 1977 and was twice defeated by Menachem Begin (qv) for the office of prime minister. In 1984, he was elected prime minister and, in September 1984, formed a shared-government arrangement with Yitzhak

Shamir of the *Likud* Party. Power-sharing governments continued until 1990, when the *Likud* formed a government without labor support. In 1992, Peres lost the leadership of the Labor Party to Yitzhak Rabin. When labor won the election, Rabin became prime minister and Peres was named foreign minister. When Rabin was assassinated on 4 November 1995, Peres became prime minister.

Perez Godoy, Ricardo. On 18 July 1962, a military coup overthrew the government of Peru's president, Manuel Prado y Ugarteche (qv). A new military junta, led by General Ricardo Perez Godoy, then took power and abrogated most of the constitution's civil rights in the country. A period of unrest followed, which was culminated by another military coup on 3 March 1963, in which Perez Godoy was ousted and replaced by General Nicholas Lindley Lopez (qv). *See* Peru.

Peron, Eva (nee Maria Eva Duarte, "Evita") (b. 1919, Los Toldos, Argentina—d. 26 June 1952, Buenos Aires) An actress by age 15, Eva Peron was a successful radio soap opera star when she met Juan Peron (qv) in 1944. The two were married in 1945, when she became his second wife. Eva became active in politics after Juan's election to president in 1946. By 1949, she was second only to her husband in Argentine popularity and was coleader of the group known as *Descamisados* (shirtless ones), the labor class that was the main support of the Peronist movement. In 1951, the Argentine military blocked her campaign to become vice president. She died in 1952. *Reading:* Nicholas Fraser, *Eva Peron* (1985); Nicholas Fraser & Marysa Navarro, *Evita: The Real Life of Eva Peron* (1996).

Peron, Isabel de (née Maria Estrela Martinez). (b. 1931, La Rioja, Argentina) Isabel Peron worked as a ballet dancer before she met Juan Peron (qv). She became his third wife in 1961 and was elected vice president of Argentina in 1973. Upon Juan Peron's death on 1 July 1974, Isabel became the first woman to head a Western Hemisphere government. Hers was a bloody and turbulent administration. On 6 November 1974, she was forced to declare a state of siege because of the political unrest. In December 1975, right-wing air force officers revolted and seized two air bases near Buenos Aires in an attempt to overthrow her government. On 21 December, the unsuccessful rebellion ended. She was deposed in a bloodless military coup on 24 March 1976. She was convicted of embezzlement, fraud and malfeasance and imprisoned until 1981, when she was allowed to go into exile in Spain.

Peron, Juan Domingo. (b. 8 October 1895, Lobos, .Buenos Aires Province, Argentina—d. 1 July 1974, Buenos Aires) At age 16, Peron entered the *Colegio Militar* (military academy) and graduated in 1913. From 1926 to 1929, he attended the *Escuela Superior de Guerra* (Argentine War College). In 1930 he participated in a successful military uprising against President Hipolito Irigoyen and was appointed private secretary to the minister of war, a post he held from 1930 to 1935. Thereafter he taught at the war college, was military attache to Chile, wrote a number of books on military history and spent time in Italy studying mountain warfare tactics. During this last sojourn he became an admirer of Benito Mussolini. Upon his return to Argentina (1941), Peron became involved in a secret military group that staged a coup in June 1943. Peron was appointed minister of labor in the new government, where he moved to strengthen the regime against leftists and to consolidate his own power base. He soon became vice president and minister of war of Argentina. However, opposition to Peron grew among the armed forces and, on 9 October 1945, he was forced to resign all his posts and was imprisoned. A government crisis ensued that forced Peron's release. Upon his release he married his mistress, Maria Eva Duarte (Eva Peron) (qv), whom he named "Evita." Peron was elected president on 24 February 1946. On 13–14 August 1948, Peron's government was granted extraordinary powers to control growing labor unrest in the country, and after 1950, his support of labor began to wane. On 13 April 1951, Peron ordered the closing of the influential newspaper *La Prensa* because of its editorials against his government. On 28 September 1951, Peron accused the U.S. ambassador of complicity in a failed military uprising against the Peronista government. He thereupon declared martial law. In 1952, Evita Peron died. This event, when added to the growing labor and economic unrest and Peron's excommunication from the Roman Catholic Church by the Pope for interference with the church in Argentina, led to his ouster by the military on 16 September 1955. He went into exile for 18 years, but he was able to maintain many of his labor contacts in Argentina. During his absence, numerous Peronista-inspired incidents of violence took place throughout Argentina, including a massive outbreak of violence on 28 June 1972 that marked the anniversary of his ouster from office. He was nominated for president by the Juristialist Party in July 1972, but indicated he would not leave Spain and return to Argentina for "security reasons" until elected. He was elected president on 13 July 1973, following a period of massive demonstrations. With his new wife, Isabel Peron (qv), who was elected vice president, returned to Argentina from Paraguay. Among his first acts was to establish a strong antiterrorist policy for his country. He died in office on 1 July 1974 and was replaced by his wife, Isabel. *Reading:* Robert D. Crassweller, *Peron and the Enigmas of Argentina* (1988); Laszlo Horvath, *A Half-Century of Peronism, 1943-1993: An International Bibliography* (1993); Joseph A. Page, *Peron: A Biography* (1983).

Perry, Robert. On 10 June 1970, one day after an unsuccessful attempt on the life of King Hussein (qv), the U.S. military attache in Amman, Jordan, Major Robert Perry, was assassinated by Palestinian terrorists.

Peru. A country located along the Pacific coast of South America, Peru is bordered on the east by Bolivia and Brazil, on the south by Chile, on the west by the Pacific Ocean and on the north by Colombia. The capital is Lima. The Inca Empire covered most of Peru (and parts of Bolivia and Ecuador). Before the Incas, the region was controlled by the Andean civilization. Internal warfare weakened the Incas to the point that they were overpowered by the Spaniard Francisco Pizarro, who intended to plunder the land (1532–1533). Lima became the seat of the Spanish viceroy, and Peru remained under Spanish control until 1820–1821. Armies led by Jose de San Martin moving out of Argentina and by Simon Bolivar coming from Colombia drove out the Spaniards (1824) and established a new nation. Peru fought a disastrous war with Chile over nitrate deposits in the Atacama Desert in 1879–1883. Peru's history remained unremarkable until the 1940s, when the political situation became unstable, with military intervention at intervals to restore order. On 27–29 October 1948, the government of president Jose Bustamante (qv) was overthrown and replaced by a military junta led by General Manuel Ordia. Decades of instability followed. In August 1951, fighting broke out along the Peru-Ecuador border over the issue of access to the Amazon River. Peru asked (13 August) for an international investigation of the border dispute. In February 1956, a military uprising at the town of Iqualis was suppressed when support for the rebel cause expected in other districts failed to materialize. On 18 July 1962, a military coup overthrew the government of president Manuel Prado y Ugarteche (qv). The new military government of General Ricardo Perez Godoy immediately suppressed most of the democratic institution in the country. However, on 17 August, the United States restored diplomatic relations with Peru. Godoy was ousted by another military coup on 3 March 1963, and General Nicholas Lindsey Lopez became president. A year-long, Cuban-sponsored revolt created great misery in the Andes region of the country in 1964. On 15 April 1968, the United States cut off all developmental aid to Peru after the Peruvian government had ordered Mirage fighter-bombers from France. A coup led by the army chief of staff, General Juan Velasco Alvarado (qv), overthrew the government of Fernando Belaunde Terry (qv) on 3 October 1968 and installed a military government. Peruvian gunboats opened fire on two American tuna-fishing trawlers on 14 February 1969, when the two vessels were accused of fishing within what Peru claimed were its territorial waters. In retaliation, the U.S. ordered a halt to all arms shipments to Peru. On 23 May, Peru expelled the U.S. military mission. On 3 July 1969, the U.S. government lifted its February 1969 sanctions against Peru. On 1 August 1971, the Peruvian government recognized Communist China. France announced it would cancel its nuclear testing at Mururoa (qv) after the Peruvian government threatened to break diplomatic relations if the tests continued. A state of emergency was declared in the Puno district on 3 July 1972, after a wave of violence by left-wing extremists. On 8 July of that same year, Peru restored diplomatic relations with Cuba. In January 1973, the Peruvian navy seized the American fishing trawler *Apollo*, which it claimed had entered the 200-mile limit established by Peru. The ship was not released until a $100,000 fine was paid. On 9 December 1974, Peru, along with seven other nations, signed the Declaration of Ayacucho (Peru) which, among other things, limited the importation of offensive weapons into Latin America. On 5 February 1975, the Lima police department staged a two-day strike demanding higher wages. Army troops were brought in to maintain order. A national state of emergency was declared as rioting and violence accompanied the strike. At least 100 were killed in the capital city alone. Another national emergency was declared on 2 July 1976 after violence broke out following an increase in food prices. On 1 November 1976, the Peruvian government announced the purchase of 36 Soviet-built Sukhoi (SU-22 "Fitter") jet fighters (delivered 13 March

1980). On 29 August 1977, president Francisco Morales Bermudez (qv) lifted the 14-month state of emergency that had gripped the country. In May 1978, widespread rioting broke out following the announcement of an International Monetary Fund–mandated austerity program. A state of emergency was imposed on 19 April (lifted 9 June). On 6 January 1979, however, martial law was again imposed to halt a threatened 72-hour general strike over economic conditions. More than 120 union officials were arrested on the first day. In 1979, a new constitution was promulgated. Belaunde Terry won the election in 1980. In mid-January 1981, Ecuador invaded Peru and occupied several areas inside the Peruvian border. The Organization of American States (OAS) ordered a cease-fire on 2 February, but it did not hold. On 24 February, the border between the two countries was sealed. Peru and Ecuador agreed to withdraw their troops from the disputed area on 6 March. When the Falklands incident (*see* Falkland Islands) began, Peru sent a number of its Mirage fighters and crews to Argentina (6 April 1982), but they did not see any action in the fighting that lay ahead. The British ambassador's residence was blown up on 27 June by unknown terrorists. On 12 July 1982, Belaunde Terry suspended constitutional guarantees in three southern provinces and ordered special security forces into the area to help quell the violence spread by Shining Path (SP) (*Sendero Luminoso*) (qv) terrorists. Fighting continued into July, when Shining Path terrorists attacked the headquarters of the Popular Action Party in Lima, killing two people and wounding 30 others. The Peruvian Communist Party joined other political groups in denouncing the wave of terrorism. On 26 December 1983, the Shining Path attempted to blow up the Communist Chinese embassy to celebrate the birthday of Mao Tse-tung. This was the third year in which such an incident occurred. On 17 July 1984, Shining Path terrorists attacked high tension towers, the country's main hydroelectric station and a number of other targets in Peru. The Soviet Aeroflot office in Lima was bombed, as were the offices of the Soviet *Novosti* News Agency and the Soviet-Peruvian Cultural Institute at Arequipa. A general strike took place in November 1984. In 1985, Alan Garcia Perez succeeded Belaunde Terry as president. The activities of the Shining Path terrorist group continued to make civilian rule difficult during this period. On 15 May 1985, the U.S. ambassador's residence and a number of other locations were subjected to simultaneous bombings by the Shining Path. By 1989, 15,000 people, including public officials, loyal peasants, foreign aid workers and tourists, had been killed. In 1990, Alberto Fujimori won the presidency with the support of left-wing and rural groups. On 5 April 1992, Fujimori disbanded Congress, fired the federal judges and set up a new government. Fujimori was able to do that with strong military and popular support. On 12 September 1993, Abimael Guzman Reynoso, the Shining Path leader, was arrested and charged with offenses that had led to the deaths of 22,500 people. He was convicted and sentenced to life imprisonment. A determined government campaign against the SP in 1994 further weakened but did not destroy the group. In May 1995, for example, a hotel was bombed outside Lima. Fujimori won a conclusive reelection in the 1995 elections. *Reading:* David Booth & Bernardo Sorj, eds.,

Military Reformism and Social Classes: The Peruvian Experience, 1968-80 (1983); Orin Starn, et al, eds., *The Peru Reader: History, Culture, Politics* (1995).

Pescadores (*Penghu, P'eng-hu Ch'un-Tao*). About 64 small islands approximately 30 miles west of Taiwan in the Taiwan Strait (Penghu Channel), the Pescadores bear the European version of the name that means "fishermen." From about the seventh century A.D., Chinese fishermen frequented the islands and, after 1100 A.D., set up fishing stations there. The Chinese built a fort on Penghu around 1368 and established a civil government there in 1388. That same year, the entire population was transported back to the mainland, and the islands were left to become a pirate's lair. In 1624, the Dutch occupied the islands, and a population of Chinese refugees returned. Taiwan then took over the civil administration of the group. As estern nations attempted the opening of China, Taiwan and the Pescadores took on strategic importance. The French occupied the group in 1884–1885. After the Sino-Japanese War in 1894–1895, they were ceded to Japan. China recovered the islands after World War II. After the Nationalist Chinese occupied Taiwan, the Pescadores became a county (*hsien*) of the new Nationalist government (1950). Several forward military bases were established on the Pescadores in Nationalist China's ongoing dispute with mainland China. In April 1952, Japan renounced any claims on the islands, and on 3 March 1955, the United States recognized Taiwan's control of the Pescadores.

Pescara. *See* Italy.

Peshawar. *See* Pakistan.

Phalangists. *See* Lebanon.

Pham Ngoc Thao. On 19 February 1965, claiming that Nguyen Khanh (qv) had become a dictator, a group of army officers led by Colonel Pham Ngoc Thao carried out a successful coup. As most of the officers involved were Roman Catholics, a Buddhist upheaval followed. But before much could happen, General Nguyen Khanh took back power by force on 20–21 February, only to have to immediately yield power to an even stronger group of officers. There were more government turnovers before year's end. *See* Vietnam.

Pham Van Dong. The premier of North Vietnam since 1955, Pham Van Dong met with Chinese premier Chou En-lai (qv) in Peking to accuse the United States of aggression in South Vietnam (12 June 1961). In April 1965, he met with Soviet premier Alexei Kosygin to outline a four-point program for settlement of the war in Southeast Asia in which withdrawal of all foreign forces was the key element. On 25 April 1977, the longtime Vietnamese premier signed an economic and cultural treaty with France in which France gave a loan to Vietnam of $100 million. In July 1977, he helped bring agreement with Laos on a treaty of military and economic cooperation. He remained premier until 1987, when many of the old colleagues of Ho Chi Minh were discredited and removed following an "election" in April. *See* Vietnam.

Phanomyong, Pridi. On 8 November 1947, the government of Siamese (Thai) prime minister Pridi Phanomyong was overthrown by the military. As a result, the 1932 constitution was restored, but changes were made in the makeup of the National Assembly to allow the king to appoint the upper house. Pridi Phanomyong had been in power since the end of World War II and, after his ouster, was forced to flee the country. *See* Thailand.

Phan Rang Air Base. *See* Vietnam.

Phan Thiet. *See* Vietnam.

Phan Van Quat. Although Nguyen Khanh (qv) held the real power in South Vietnam, a new government was formed by Dr. Phan Van Quat on 16 February 1965. He remained in office only four days before he was ousted by a military coup. In the course of events that followed, he was returned to office, and on 6 May 1965, he received a vote of confidence as a final gesture on the part of the powerful but outgoing Armed Forces Council. On 11 June 1965, he resigned the almost thankless job and returned power to the military, which brought Nguyen Van Thieu (qv) to the forefront. Nguyen Cao Ky (qv) became the new premier on 19 June.

Philippines, The. More formally the Republic of the Philippines, this archipelago lies off the southeast coast of Asia in the Pacific Ocean. It is separated from the mainland by the South China Sea. The nearest land area is Malaysia to the southwest. There are 11 large islands and numerous smaller ones in the group. Manila is the capital city. Chinese traders and some Indian explorers landed in the Philippines in the first millennium A.D., but the visits produced little or no lasting imprint on the islands. Islam was introduced in the fifteenth century, especially in the area around the island of Mindanao. Ferdinand Magellan, a European, discovered the islands in 1521. Spanish colonization began in the late sixteenth century. This movement also brought with it Roman Catholicism. It was also the Spanish who branded the Muslim natives of Mindanao and the Sulu islands as "Moros" and were unable to conquer them. Not until the early 1800s were the Philippines opened to foreign markets, other than those controlled by Spain. The opening of foreign markets played directly into nationalistic hands, however, as the sons of the Spanish landed gentry in the islands went abroad to manage affairs and also to school. Their return produced nationalist sentiment that spread to the Filipino population and led to the uprising in 1898 that was put down with much violence by Spanish troops. At the end of the Spanish American War, the Philippines were ceded to the United States. But the Filipinos, seeing they had simply traded one master for another, rebelled; the insurrection that followed cost many Filipino and American lives and did not end until 1906. By 1935, the Philippines, having been promised eventual independence, were made a commonwealth. The advent of World War II and the brutal Japanese occupation delayed independence until 4 July 1946, when the independent Republic of the Philippines was declared. Manuel Roxas (qv) became the new nation's first president. In 1965, Ferdinand Marcos (qv) was elected president. From 1970, leftist guerrilla activity and terrorism began to rise. On 21 September 1972, Marcos declared martial law, suppressed opposition and began rule by decree. Martial law was not lifted until 1981, but Marcos continued to rule with an iron hand. In 1983, Benigno S. Aquino, Jr., returned to the Philippines after a long exile. He was promptly assassinated in what has been termed a Marcos-directed elimination. The murder, however, became the focal point of massive opposition to Marcos's tyrannical rule, and he was finally forced to resign and flee in 1986, taking with him and his wife Imelda (qv) billions from the Filipino treasury. Aquino's wife, Corazon, became president and remained in office until 20 June 1992, when her freely elected successor, Fidel V. Ramos, was inaugurated. Among Ramos's first acts was to begin the reorganization of the armed forces in coordination with a reassessment of the insurgency threat, which had been waning. At the same time, the Philippine Communist Party was beset by internal strife, and nearly 1,000 rebels had surrendered to authorities by July 1993. Ramos also acted to halt the increasing corruption in the National Police; the entire leadership was dismissed and the police were given a new mission, that of controlling insurgency. The army, which had held that responibility, was then charged with protecting the country from external attack, although the threat was considered a remote one. Ramos also took on the long-standing issue of gaining control over the estimated 562 private armies that dotted the countryside. The body of Ferdinand Marcos was returned to the Phillipines on 7 September and interred three days later. Imelda Marcos was convicted of corruption on 24 September and sentenced to 9–12 years' imprisonment. In March 1994, Ramos issued a general amnesty to the communist National People's Army (NPA). The amnesty also included police and armed forces personnel accused of "overzealousness" in performing their duties. The NPA, already badly sundered, now began battling among themselves over acceptance of the amnesty. The upshot was the assassination of a number of leaders on both sides of the question, and mass arrests, especially in Manila, of other NPA members. The Moro National Liberation Front (MNLF) in Mindinao continued negotiations through which the rebels demanded a separate Islamic state. But while the negotiations were making some progress, a splinter group ignored the cease-fire and continued attacks on military posts and the taking of foreign hostages. While Imelda Marcos' appeal of her 1993 corruption conviction was still being heard, she won a seat in the legislature in 1995. At the same time, $475 million stolen by Ferdinand Marcos was returned to the Philippines by a number of Swiss banks. Fighting on Mindinao increased as several rebel groups not under direct MNLF control stepped up the activities. A confrontation with China seemed likely following the discovery that China had garrisoned Mischief Reef in the Spratly Group (*see* Spratly). *Reading:* Mark R, Thompson, *The Anti-Marcos Struggle: Personalistic Rule and Democratic Transition in the Philippines* (1996); David Timberman, *A Changeless Land: Continuity and Change in Philippine Politics* (1997); John Bresnan, ed., *Crisis in the Philippines: The Marcos Era and Beyond* (1986); Thomas A. Marks, *Maoist Insurgency Since Vietnam* (1995).

Phnom Chat. *See* Cambodia.

Phnom Melai. *See* Cambodia.

Phnom Penh. *See* Cambodia.

Phoenix Program. *See* Phung Hoang Program.

Phong Dinh Province. *See* Vietnam.

Phouc Binh (Song Be). *See* Vietnam.

Phouc Long Province. *See* Vietnam.

Phouc Thanh Province. *See* Vietnam.

Phouc Tuy Province. *See* Vietnam.

Phouc Vinh (Ap Son Thuy or Song Be). *See* Vietnam.

Phu Bai. *See* Vietnam.

Phuc Yen. *See* Vietnam.

Phum Prek Toch. *See* Cambodia.

Phu My. *See* Vietnam.

Phung Hoang (Phoenix) Program. A program used in the war in South Vietnam to eliminate the Viet Cong infrastructure. The program was carried out by CIA-run Provincial Reconnaisance Units (PRU) made up of Vietnamese with American adviser-leaders. In the overall picture, the program was successful, but it suffered so many abuses by those seeking vengeance, or sometimes profit, by accusing someone of treason that the overall value of the program became sullied. In the context of the Phoenix Program, the term "eliminated" often became synonymous with "killed" or "murdered." South Vietnamese president Nguyen Van Thieu made public information on the highly classified program on 1 October 1969. Knowledge of the program caused consternation in the U.S., and it was quietly disbanded.

Phu Quoc Island. *See* Thailand and Vietnam.

Phu Yen Province. *See* Vietnam.

Picado Michalski, Teodoro. On 13–20 December 1948, the Costa Rican government of President Teodoro Picado was overthrown. Picado had been in power since 1944. The ouster came about at the end of Picado's term in office. He was to be replaced by president-elect Otilio Ulate, but the process was interrupted by an uprising led by suspected communist elements wishing to deny Ulate the office. A counterrevolt ensued, and Ulate was finally seated.

Pich Nil Pass (*Col de Pich Nil*). *See* Cambodia.

Picton Island. *See* Chile.

Pine Bluff, Arkansas. On 27 January 1971, in response to unfounded allegations made by U.S. Senator Frank Church (in a 22 January 1971 letter to the White House), that the U.S. was planning to expand its biological warfare (BW) testing at Fort Douglas, Deseret, Utah, President Nixon announced the closing of the BW Development Center at Pine Bluff, Arkansas. The president also announced that all biological agents at that location were to be destroyed. The actual destruction began on 7 July 1971.

Pinkowski, Josef. The premier of Poland, Pinkowski was dismissed on 9 February 1981. General Wojciech Jaruzelski (qv) replaced him. Pinkowski, a hard-line communist, had been premier since 24 August 1980, when he replaced Edward Babiuch, who was felt to be too soft on the striking workers. *See* Poland.

Pinochet (Ugarte), Augusto. (b. 25 November 1915, Valparaiso, Chile) Pinochet
was graduated from the Chilean military academy in 1936 and appointed
commander of the Santiago garrison in 1972. He was appointed commander in
chief of the Chilean armed forces in August 1973. On 11 September, Pinochet
led the military coup he had planned that overthrew the Marxist government of
Salvador Allende (qv). Allende was murdered during the uprising. Pinochet was
appointed chairman of the junta that took control of the country and immediately
moved to crush all opposition to his rule. By 1974, he assumed sole power and
scrapped the plan to rotate the presidency among the junta members. Almost
6,000 were arrested immediately after the coup, and approximately 130,000
were arrested during the first three years. Although Pinochet's regime did work
to improve the economy, his suppressive campaign to obliterate all opposition
to his rule was criticized around the world. On 12 October 1978, Pinochet
announced that he would remain in office another eight years, when a civilian-
military government would assume power. On 11 September 1981, however,
Pinochet extended the ban on political acivity for another eight years. In
December 1982 anti-Pinochet demonstrations led to the arrest of 200 persons.
Violence erupted on 11 May 1983 at a massive anti-government demonstration.
At least two people were killed, and the police began a roundup of suspected
anti-Pinochet citizens. More than 1,000 were arrested. The next day a "Day of
National Protest" was held against the Pinochet regime. Rioting broke out in
Santiago. Between 12 August and 13 August 1983, more than two dozen were
killed and 100 injured in demonstrations against the Pinochet government. In
September 1983, at least ten more people were killed. On 4 September 1984,
a peaceful demonstration against Pinochet turned into a riot when police used
dogs, water cannon and small-arms fire to disperse the otherwise inoffensive
demonstrators. Nine people including a French priest were killed. On 6
November 1984, Pinochet declared a 90-day state of siege following a series of
guerrilla attacks on government installations. An election held in October 1988
resulted in a 55 percent "no" vote for his return to another eight-year term. He
remained in office until a new and free election proclaimed his successor,
Christian Democrat Patricio Aylwin Azocar, on 11 March 1990. Pinochet
retained his post as army commander, however, but the new government opened
an investigation into his regime. Pinochet, in a speech to the officers at the
military academy, denied the authority of the investigation and any wrongdoing
on his part. In May 1992, Pinochet underwent heart surgery, but within a month
he was back at his post to continue his duties until his mandatory retirement in
1997. On 11 September 1993, a memorial was erected to celebrate the Pinochet
takeover from the Marxist Allende government. Rioting followed, in which two
were killed and 100 wounded. Pinochet remained in his position in 1995 and
continued his attacks on those who criticized his former regime. *Reading:* Mary
Ellen Spooner, *Soldiers in a Narrow Land: The Pinochet Regime in Chile*
(1994); Pamela Constable, *A Nation of Enemies: Chile under Pinochet* (1993);
Gerard Arriagada, *Pinochet: The Politics of Power* (1991).

Plaine des Jarres. *See* Laos.

Plain of Reeds. *See* Vietnam.

Plate River. *See* Argentina.

Pleiku City and Province. *See* Vietnam.

Plei Me. *See* Vietnam.

Podgorny, Nikolai Victorovich. (b. 5 February 1903 (OS), Karlovka, Ukraine—d. 12 January 1983) Podgorny was given the largely ceremonial post of head of state of the USSR in 1965. Although he worked to enhance the image of his office, the real power in the Soviet Union rested with the party secretary. On 24 May 1977, when it was obvious that Leonid Brezhnev (qv) desired to hold both titles, and although Podgorny resisted, he found himself removed from office. Secretary General Brezhnev then quickly assumed the title. In June 1977, Podgorny, a communist since 1930, was removed from the chairmanship of the Presidium, but did he maintain his seat as a deputy in the Supreme Soviet. He spent his remaining years out of the limelight.

Point-a-Pitre. *See* Guadeloupe.

Pokhara. *See* Nepal.

Poland. A country in east-central Europe, Poland is bordered on the north by the Baltic Sea, on the east by Lithuania, Belarus and Ukraine, on the south by Slovakia and Czech Republic and on the west by Germany. The capital city is Warsaw. Poland was inhabited during Neolithic times by proto-Slavic tribes, who began migrating to the south and east out of the Vistula basis about 2000 B.C. During the eighth century A.D., a union of a number of tribes formed what became known as the Piast Dynasty in the vicinity of modern-day Poznan. Out of this assembly, Great Poland was established with a founding date of 966. Christianity came to Poland at approximately this same time. Later in the century another tribal union in the south (Little Poland) also swore allegiance to the Piast ruler, Casimir I. After 1386, the Jagiellonian dynasty came to power in Poland and ruled much of Lithuania, Bohemia and Hungary until the early sixteenth century. During this period, the Poles fought off the Germanic Teutonic Knights, the Ottoman Turks and the Grand Duchy of Moscow. Thus, at this early date, Poland's course in history was already carved in stone. After 1572, the rulers of Poland were elected from the royal houses of Europe and later from among the Polish nobility. This system led to a breakdown in the power of the Polish-Lithuanian state, and Poland again began to feel the weight of its powerful neighbors, Moscow and Germany. In the 1650s there was a huge rebellion of Cossacks and Tatars along the southeastern border, which gave Sweden its opportunity to invade Poland (1655). Out of this campaign, Poland was forced to cede much land to Sweden (1660) and to expose its internal weakness, which led to a period of almost continuous warfare among Sweden, Russia and Poland. Internal and religious unrest also appeared because of the poor economic conditions and because Roman Catholicism was opposed by Orthodoxy. In 1772 the first of three partitions of Poland took place, when Russia seized the northeast area to take more than one-quarter of the country. At the same time Austria took the Galician area in the south, and Prussia took the north eastern section. A second partition took place in 1793, when Russia and Prussia added to their territories. The third partition in 1795 accounted for all the rest, and Poland ceased to exist as a political entity. Except in the Austrian section, Poles lost everything as programs of Russification and Germanization sought to eradicate the Polish identity. An independent Poland was restored by the Allies following World War I and the Russian Revolution. Józef Pilsudski became the virtual dictator of Poland between 1926 and 1935. Poland's unfortunate geographical position led to its becoming the first major battleground of World War II when, in 1939, it was invaded by Nazi Germany and by Stalin's Red Army forces. Once again, especially in the German-occupied area, a campaign of eradication began that was aimed at the extermination of the country's large Jewish population. After Hitler attacked the USSR in 1941 and the Red Army had turned the tide, a Soviet column approached Warsaw, but it halted to allow the German army to destroy the core of the Polish Home Army, the principal resistance against the Nazis. When the Soviets completed their occupation of Poland, they ignored the Polish government-in-exile in London and installed a "baggage-train" government made up of Polish communists who had been indoctrinated and trained in the Soviet Union. After the war, Poland's boundaries were shifted, and the country was literally moved to the left, taking German territory in Prussia to the Oder-Neisse Line and giving the USSR considerable territory from eastern Poland. The new communist giovernment made mass arrests of anticommunists, halted all free elections and began collectivizing the country. The Polish United Workers' Party became the only legal (and communist) political entity in the country (1948). Stalin (qv) died in 1953. Three years later a a general strike began in Poland and was suppressed by force. The Polish communist leader Wladyslaw Gomulka (qv), who ruled from 1956 to 1970, attempted to loosen the tight Soviet-style yoke on his country, but in1970, following a new round of strikes, he was replaced by Edward Gierek (qv), who also failed to improve the Polish economy. The visit of the Polish-born Pope, John Paul II (qv), in 1979, brought massive demonstrations of religious fervor, which indirectly taunted the communists. In August 1980, Lech Walesa (qv) led the workers of the Gdansk shipyards out on strike, and the strikes quickly spread throughout the country. Out of this the illegal labor movement Solidarity grew. It became so powerful that it won legal status and other concessions from the Gierek government. Gierek was then replaced by Stanislaw Kania (qv) and then by the defense minister, General Wojciech Jaruzelski (qv). In the face of more Solidarity demands and more strikes, Jaruzelski declared martial law (December 1981). Solidarity was declared illegal, and many of its leaders were arrested. After that, martial law remained in effect for 18 months, after which tight controls were maintained on all aspects of Polish life. Labor unrest reappeared in 1988, and the Jaruzelski government responded by negotiating with Solidarity, even though it remained outlawed. In April 1989, the communist system in Poland began to collapse and for once the fear of a Soviet Czech-style invasion was abated. In June 1989, after free elections, Solidarity and the communists formed a coalition government. The communists also reorganized themselves into a social-democratic party.

Communism was not dead in Poland; it simply changed its name. The economy still needed improvement, and Lech Walesa suffered the same problems faced by any patriot turned politician. He remained in office until 23 December 1995, when he was narrowly defeated in an election won by the former head of the Polish Communist Party. *Reading:* A. Kemp-Welch, *The Birth of Solidarity* (1991); Richard C. Lucas, *Bitter Legacy: Polish-American Relations in the Wake of World War II* (1982); Adam Michnik & David Ost, *The Church and the Left* (1993); Bartomiej Kaminski, *The Collapse of State Socialism: The Case of Poland* (1991).

Pol Pot. (b. 19 May 1928, Kompong Thom, Cambodia) Born into a peasant family, Pol Pot grew up in a Buddhist monastery. For two years he served as a monk. He attended a technical school in Phnom Penh and worked as a carpenter. Pol Pot took part in Ho Chi Minh's (qv) anti-French resistance movement in the 1940s and, by 1946, was a member of the Indochinese Communist Party, Khmer Rouge (qv). In 1949, he went to Paris, where he studied radio electronics and revolution. Spending more time at the latter, he failed his examinations and was denied further scholarship assistance. Pol Pot returned to Phnom Penh in January 1953. From 1954 to 1963, he taught at a private school in Phnom Penh, but he was forced to flee when the police became aware of his communist activities. Until 1975, he worked to build the Khmer Rouge and served as the party secretary in Cambodia and fought a guerrilla war against the central government.. In 1975, the Khmer Rouge overthrew the Sihanouk (qv) government, and Pol Pot became prime minister (1976). During his time in office, it is estimated that two million died because of Khmer Rouge excesses. Pol Pot was overhrown by a Vietnamese invasion in September 1979. Thereafter, he withdrew into the mountainous jungle and led his forces in a protracted struggle against the Vietnamese invaders. In 1985, Pol Pot was stripped of his political and military leadership positions in the Khmer Rouge, but he continued to advise the movement. *Reading:* David P. Chandler, *Brother Number One: A Political Biography of Pol Pot* (1992); Rebecca Steloff, *Pol Pot* (1990).

Pomeroy, William J. On 14 March 1952, William J. Pomeroy, one of the communist political leaders of the rebel Hukbalahap (qv) movement in the Philippines, was captured, along with a number of others, when the secret Huk headquarters in Manila was raided. The entire Huk political leadership was thus arrested in a single night.

Pompidou, Georges. (b. 5 July 1911, Montboudif, France—d. 2 April 1974, Paris) Following in his fa.ther's footsteps, Pompidou graduated from the *École Normale Supérieure* and then became a schoolteacher in Marseilles and Paris. He served in World War II and, in 1944, met Charles de Gaulle (qv) and went to work with him and the provisional French government (1944–1946). He remained with de Gaulle when he resigned the premiership in January 1946. Pompidou then held a number of important governmental posts until 1955, when he joined the Rothchild Bank. Even without any banking background, he rose to become the bank's director general in 1959. When de Gaulle returned to power in June 1958, he made Pompidou his chief assistant, a post he held until January 1959. When de Gaulle became president of the Fifth Republic, Pompidou returned to civilian life. In 1961, however, Pompidou became the chief negotiator in the secret discussions leading to the cease-fire in Algeria. Pompidou was appointed premier of France in April 1962, an office he held—with a discordant break in October 1962—until July 1968. When De Gualle resigned the presidency in April 1969, Pompidou ran for and won the office (15 July 1969). Even though he was in failing health, his sudden death in April 1974 came as a shock.

Pondicherry (*Pondichéry*). On 28 May 1956, France gave up control of its territories on the Indian subcontinent. Pondicherry, along with Mahe, Chandernagore and several other enclaves, was surrendered to Indian control at that time. The town of Pondicherry was the capital of French India before the transfer and was designated the seat of government for the state of Pondicherry by the Republic of India after the takeover. The French had held the region since 1815. The transfer was completed in July 1962.

Popular Democratic Front for the Liberation of Palestine (PDFLP). A splinter group from the Popular Front for the Liberation of Palestine (PFLP), the PDFLP was a terrorist organization that targeted the Israelis and was protected by the Palestine Liberation Organization (PLO). The group's leader, Nayef Hawatmeh (qv), has been tied to both Soviet and Syrian resources. The group was estimated to be no more than 500 strong. On 15 May 1974, three PDFLP terrorists seized an Israeli school in the town of Ma'alot. They demanded the release of 20 Arab terrorists in Israeli prisons. The terrorists were killed by Israeli security troops, but 21 of the 90 hostage children were also killed. One Israeli commando lost his life in the operation. Israeli retaliated the next day with a massive raid on seven guerrilla camps in southern Lebanon. Hawatmeh claimed that the incident and the raid were concocted to disrupt a peace mission by Henry Kissinger. On 13 June 1974, four PDFLP terrorists and three Israeli women were killed in a firefight in an Israeli *kibbutz* in the Huleh Valley. The PDFLP claimed the attack was aimed at protesting a visit by Richard M. Nixon (qv) to the Middle East.

Popular Forces of 25 April (*Forces Populares 25 de Abril*) (FP25). The FP25 was formed in 1980 with the express purpose of achieving the violent overthrow of the Portuguese government and opposition to the U.S. and NATO, especially their presence in Portugal. The name of the group came from the 25 April 1974 incident that overthrew the right-wing regime that had ruled Portugal since 1926. The structure of FP25 is highly cellularized, and the group is extremely careful about outside contacts, even from its own support wing. Most of its targets have been Portuguese government and economic targets and U.S. and NATO interests in the country. There was evidence of some Libyan support of FP25, but no evidence of any linkages with other terrorist organizations in Europe or elsewhere, although FP25 claimed solidarity with such groups. On 25 November 1984, the U.S. embassy in Lisbon was hit by four 60 mm mortar rounds fired by FP25. The were no injuries. On 9 December 1984, FP25 attacked the Iberian headquarters of NATO in Oeiras with grenades, damaging an automobile and several buildings. On 28 January 1985, NATO warships anchored in Lisbon harbor were attacked with mortar fire. None was hit. Beginning in 1984, Portuguese government antiterrorist forces began to whittle away at the FP25 infrastructure, arresting 56 members that year. The group remained active, however, and bombed several tourist resorts in southern Portugal in September 1986.

Popular Front for the Liberation of Oman (PFLO). A communist-controlled organization, the PFLO led Dhofar tribesmen (qv) in the civil war in South Yemen. By December 1975, British forces supporting the Sultan of Oman had forced the PFLO into an isolated area near the Yemeni border.

Popular Front for the Liberation of Palestine (PFLP). The PFLP is one of the oldest Palestinian terrorist organizations and is Marxist-Leninist oriented. It was founded in December 1967, following the Arab defeat in the Arab-Israeli War of 1967. The founder was Dr. George Habash (qv), a graduate of the medical school at American University in Beirut. Initially the group was composed of three smaller organizations: the Palestine Liberation Front, the Returned Heroes and the Youth of Vengeance. The basic aims of the group were inimical to any type of political settlement with Israel. The operational commander of the PFLP was Dr. Waddi Haddad (qv), who led it until his death in 1978. The organization never reached a membership of more than 1,000, but it had a coterie of sympathizers. The group was known to be associated with the Palestine Liberation Organization (PLO); but as a matter of course and to maintain plausible denial for the PLO, the PFLP conducted its operations in its own name. The PFLP was also the first Middle East terrorist organization to conduct operations outside the area, and it was supported by a number of Arab states, principally Libya, South Yemen and Syria. Its last reported headquarters was in South Yemen. The earliest attack confirmed to the PFLP was the hijack of an El Al airliner enroute from Rome to Israel in July 1968. While it attacked a wide variety of targets, its principal ones were Israeli. A splinter organization of the PFLP was the Popular Front for the Liberation of Palestine, General Command (PFLP-GC), which came into being 1968, after Admad Jibril, its leader, became disenchanted with George Habash. This organization was supported almost exclusively by Syria, although Libya helped out and it received arms and materiel directly from the Soviet bloc. Again, the principal targets were Israeli, although the group was very much involved in attacks on American peacekeepers in Beirut in 1982–1983.

Popular Front for the Liberation of Saquia and Rio de Oro (Polisario). A politico-military organization, Polisario was formed to end Moroccan control of what had been the Spanish territory of Western Sahara in northwestern Africa. The makeup of Polisario was largely from nomadic tribes (*Saharawis*) of the region. Originally, Polisario was based in neighboring Mauritania and operated against the Spaniards. When the Spanish withdrew, Morocco and Mauritania partitioned the region of Western Sahara (1976). At that point, Polisario relocated its base of operations to Algeria, and that country supported the rebel bases with military aid. On 8 June 1976, Polisario forces attacked the Mauritanian capital of Nouakchott. In December 1977, Polisario accused France of using its Jaguar fighter-bombers to attack one of the rebel's columns. Polisario attacked a Mauritanian troop position, killing 30, but its losses numbered 82. Then, on 23 December, Polisario released eight French prisoners it had been holding. After the overthrow of the Mauritanian government on 10 June 1978, Polisario decided to call for a unilateral cease-fire in the area. It did, however, keep up its guerrilla campaign against Morocco. After at first breaking off peace talks in December 1978, Mauritania reached an agreement (6 August 1979) with Polisario on Western Sahara, but Morocco immediately annexed the entire region. On 5 September 1979, Egypt offered military assistance to Morocco. France countered by dispatching a token force of 150 troops to Mauritania as a warning to both Morocco and Polisario. Earlier, on 25 January 1976, a U.S.–built Moroccan F-5 fighter was shot down by a Soviet-built ground-to-air missile (suspected of being an SA-6) belonging to Polisario. By that time, Polisario had a well-trained and motorized force of about 15,000 men. Moroccan outposts in Western Sahara were attacked on a regular basis throughout the period. In the late 1980s, Polisario lost some of its Algerian and Libyan support as those two countries looked to their own internal problems. In October 1981, however, Polisario forces attacked the Moroccan garrison at Guelta Zemmour, 25 miles from the Morocco-Mauritania border. Morocco then accused Mauritania of harboring the rebels. On 18 April 1982, Polisario announced it would seek arms from the Soviet Union, if the United States dealt with Morocco. Polisario attacks against Moroccan military targets continued into 1983. In 1984, Mauritania acknowledged the Saharan Arab Democratic Republic (SADR) as the government-in-exile for Western Sahara and the group backed by Polisario. By 1986, Polisario, through its political arm, SADR, had won the recognition of nearly 65 nations, including most of the Organization of African Unity members; Morocco had withdrawn from the OAU in 1984. The principal European states and the U.S. were not among that number, however, and held to Morocco's claim of control over the region. Morocco's control, including six barrier walls, confined the Polisario to areas adjacent to the Mauritanian border. Sporadic fighting continued throughout the year. In 1988, Morocco and Polisario showed signs of ending the struggle when both agreed to a UN-mediated peace plan that provided for an internationally supervised referendum. Fighting broke out again in October 1989, after an informal cease-fire broke down, and the UN referendum had not taken place by 1990. In 1991, however, both sides agreed to the referendum. Polisario's cause was seriously damaged in 1992 by the defection of one of its leaders to Algeria and by defiant Moroccan statements that the UN referendum was a dead issue and that Morocco intended to hold its own elections in Western Sahara. On 17–19 July 1993 meetings were held between Morocco and a much weakened Polisario. These talks failed over the issue of who could vote in the UN referendum. When the UN proposed new recommendations for the referendum in 1994, Polisario expressed strong reservations. However, voter registration began, with a promise that the referendum would take place in 1995. As the dispute dragged on, the referendum for self-determination was put off until 1996.

Popular Liberation Front (EPL) (Colombia). Formed in 1967, this terrorist organization of 600–800 members usually operated in in the Colombian provinces of Antioquia and Cordoba. The group orientation was Maoist, but it was known as the armed wing of the Colombian Communist Party. In the 1970s it was credited with a series of sabotage attacks, kidnappings, bombings and robberies. EPL and other Colombian terrorist organizations such as the National Liberation Army (ELN) (qv) and M-19 comprised the National Guerrilla Coordinator (CNG) structure, but EPL later switched to the Simon Bolivar Guerrilla Coordinator (SBGC) group. On 10 December 1985, approximately 60 armed guerrillas of the EPL attacked the Bechtel Corporation (Occidental Petroleum) construction site in the northern part of Colombia. Two American engineers were kidnapped and held for a $6 million ransom. One of the Americans died in captivity in May 1986; the other was eventually released unharmed. The EPL leader, Jairo Clavo (aka *Ernesto Rodas*), was killed by police in February 1987. The group's other leaders continued to plan and carry out a number of other dramactic terrorist incidents, as in May 1987, when a delegate of the National Voter Registry in Caramelo was kidnapped. Although freed later, the EPL had obtained the official voter list, thereby making any elections in that town impossible.

Popular Liberation Front (FPL) (El Salvador). On 28 November 1979, leftist FPL rebels kidnapped the South African ambassador, Gerdner Dunn, demanding $20 million and the publication of a manifesto for his safe return. He was subsequently murdered sometime in October 1980. His kidnapping and murder and attacks on other diplomats caused a number of nations to close their embassies in El Salvador. The group also took credit for a number of bombings in September 1980. The U.S. embassy in San Salvador was attacked for the third time in three weeks on 25 February 1981, but while there was extensive damage, there were no casualties. *See* El Salvador.

Popular Movement for the Liberation of Angola (MPLA). *See* Angola.

Popular Revolutionary Bloc (PRB) (El Salvador). On 4 May 1979, an antigovernment coalition of peasants, students and labor unions calling themselves the Popular Revolutionary Bloc (PRB) seized the French and Costa Rican embassies and the Cathedral of San Salvador in protest of the economic and political conditions in the country. The one hostage in the Costa Rican embassy managed to escape on 8 May. On 9 May, National Guard troops killed 23 and wounded 38 PRB members and supporters in a confrontation at the cathedral. The PRB then seized the Venezuelan embassy on 11 May. About a dozen more demonstrators were killed when they tried to demonstrate support for the PRB holding the Venezuelan building (22 May). This was followed by a series of other attacks by PRB and other groups which eventually led to the declaration of a state of siege on 24 May.

Popular Revolutionary Vanguard (VPR) (Brazil). Terrorists of the VPR and the National Liberation Alliance kidnapped the West German ambassador, Ehrenfried von Hollenben, in Rio de Janiero on 11 June 1970 and demanded the release of 40 political prisoners for his safe return. The prisoners were released and flown to Algiers on 16 June. Von Hollenben was then released. There were several other diplomatic kidnappings in 1970, but they were not definitely tied to the VPR.

Porkkala Naval Base. *See* Finland.

Port Arthur. *See* China.

Port au Prince. *See* Haiti.

Porter, William. *See* Vietnam.

Port Fuad. *See* Egypt.

Port Harcourt. *See* Nigeria.

Port Said. *See* Egypt.

Port San Carlos. *See* Falkland Islands.

Port Stanley. *See* Falkland Islands.

Port Suez, Sinai. *See* Israel.

Port Tewfik, Sinai. *See* Israel.

Portugal. A small European country found on the Iberian peninsula, Portugal is surrounded by Spain on the north and east and by the Atlantic Ocean on the west and south. The capital city is Lisbon. Inhabited by Neolithic tribes from about the tenth millennium B.C., the Celts occupied the region after 1000 B.C. until they were dislodged by the Romans in the second century B.C.. The land at that time was called Lusitania. The region was Christianized in the third century A.D. Following the collapse of Rome (fifth Century A.D.), Gothic tribes fought over the lands, as did the Muslim Moors who invaded the region in 711. Following the ejection of Muslim rule, Portugal was attached to the kingdoms of Castile and Leon (1095). Several dynastic struggles and continual war against the Moors continued into the thirteenth century. Dynastic struggles went on during the fifteenth century; the Jews were expelled from Portugal in 1497, followed by a general slaughter of those Jews who remained—a number of whom had converted to Christianity—in 1506. In 1580, Portugal was unified with Spain following a Spanish invasion. Portugal suffered from the union in that it became involved in Spain's wars thereafter until 1640, when Portugal rebelled and ejected the Spanish. In the eighteenth century, Portugal found itself commercially subordinated to England. Lisbon was destroyed by an earthquake in 1755. Portugal fought against Napoleon, especially after the French invasion of Portugal in 1807. After Napoleon, Portugal remained under British military government, while the Portuguese royal family remained in Brazil where they had fled to avoid the French. One year after the king returned to Portugal, Brazil declared its independence (1822), and Portugal accepted a liberal constitution. Civil war erupted in 1826 and was not settled until 1834. Civil unrest continued until mid-century. Portugal claimed a large part of Africa after 1880, but was hampered by the British in achieving linkage among its widely separated colonies. The growing colonial empire depleted the treasury, however, and gave rise to republican aspirations to change the form of government. In 1908, King Carlos was assassinated. Two years later a republican uprising drove his son, the reigning monarch, into exile. Portugal fought with the Allies in World War I, but gained little from the adventure. At home, political violence lasted until 1926, when a military junta took control of the government. There followed a quick succession of ineffective governments, which came and went very quickly until Oscar de Fragoso Carmona ascended to power. The economic crisis was almost overwhelming, but the selection of Antonio de Oliveira Salazar (qv) as minister of finance (1928–1940) and as premier (1932–1968) helped stabilize the government. Salazar became the dictator of Portugal, holding his people in abject poverty and with the lowest literacy rate in western Europe. After World War II and into the 1960s, Portugal's overseas possessions began to slip away. In July 1954, for instance, the Portuguese had to use force to eject Indian nationalists from the subcontinent enclave of Goa. India broke diplomatic relations with Portugal over the incident (15 August) and subsequently seized all three Portuguese enclaves (Goa, Damao and Diu) on 18–19 December 1961. Earlier, in December 1954, Portugal envoked a 1937 treaty with Great Britain and asked their aid in defending Portuguese enclaves in India, which was not forthcoming. On 3 January 1962, Salazar lashed out at Great Britain and the United States for not aiding in the protection of the enclaves. In other areas, Great Britain and the United States returned the bases they had held in the Azores to Portuguese control in June 1946. On 6 September 1951, a U.S.-Portugal agreement brought the Azores under NATO control, the treaty was subsequently extended. A military coup attempt against the Salazar regime was thwarted in October 1946. Portugal became involved in bizarre events of the Portuguese liner, *SS Santa Maria*, was hijacked (22 January 1961) with 600 passengers aboard, by followers of a former presidential candidate, Lieutenant General Humberto da Silva Delgado (qv). Portugal requested American and British support in tracking the ship in the Atlantic (27 January). The passengers were subsequently released unharmed. In 1962, a 12-year rebellion began in Portuguese Guinea that culminated in the region's gaining its freedom in 1974 as Guinea-Bissau (qv). That same year, the UN General Assembly ordered Portugal to cease its repressive practices in Angola. Trouble in Angola had escalated after March 1961, when Portugal reinforced its troops there in the face of a native uprising. On 31 July 1963, the UN Security Council moved to embargo Portugal because of Angola. The fighting in Angola spilled over the Congolese border in December 1966, and several Portuguese soldiers were killed. Portugal was also censured by the UN for allowing its war in Angola to spill over into neighboring Zambia. Student rioting began at home (21 February 1970) over a plan to allow conscription for service in Portugal's beleaguered African colonies. The government of Guinea accused Portugal of masterminding a mercenary invasion (22–24 November 1970) that killed over 100 civilians. On 17 December, the UN was asked to investigate the incident. On 8 March 1971, members of the Revolutionary Armed Action (ARA) (qv), an urban guerrilla group, sabotaged a Portuguese military airfield near Lisbon in protest of the government's policies in Africa. On 12 January 1972, a Lisbon warehouse containing French arms for Portuguese troops in Africa was blown up by ARA rebels. Portuguese troops attacked into Senegal on 12 October 1972. The UN Security Council condemned Portugal for the action on 23 October. In January 1973, Portugal reported that rebels operating in Mozambique against their forces were being supplied by the Soviet Union. An attack on the major communications center at Estima, Mozambique, on 1 July 1973, affirmed the use of Soviet weapons. Salazar had suffered a crippling stroke in 1968 and was finally replaced by Marcello José das Neves Alves Caetano (qv) on 16 May 1974, following a March 1974 military uprising against the continued military campaign in Africa. Although the coup failed, it set in motion forces that would bring change to Portugal. Caetano's military support eroded very quickly, and he and President Americo Tomas (qv) were overthrown on 25 April 1974, with a military junta taking control of the country. On 15 May 1974, Antonio de Spinola, the leader of the failed March coup attempt, became the provisional president. One of the first acts of the junta was to ask Great Britain to mediate cease-fire talks in the shooting war going on in Guinea. The former colony won its independence on 27 July 1974. On 9 June 1974, Portugal opened diplomatic relations with the USSR. On 24 July, a Portuguese military junta took control of Angola, but the plan it put forward for independence for the colony was rejected by the rebels. Portugal was more successful in settling the struggle in Mozambique (*see* Mozambique). That colony won its independence on 25 June 1975. Spinola was replaced on 30 September 1974 by a bloodless coup. Another general, Francisco de Costa Gomez, was installed in his place. In October a cease-fire was achieved in Angola as rival parties continued to vie for power. In January 1975, rioting that broke out in Oporto required bringing in airborne troops to quell. Another coup attempt by Spinola supporters was quelled on 11 March 1975. Spinola was forced to flee into exile and was granted asylum in Brazil. On 15 May, Lisbon ordered its troops in Angola (*see* Angola) to suppress the continued factional fighting that was hampering any plans for normalcy. This fighting began to escalate in July with very heavy casualties being reported on both sides of the rival black factions. On 17 July 1975, the fourth coalition government fell and was replaced by the Armed Forces Movement (AFM) military junta. In October of that year, a full alert was ordered when information confirmed rumors of a planned left-wing coup attempt. On 14 November 1975, large mobs attacked government buildings in Lisbon. As the magnitude of the unrest rose, the junta government suspended operations (21 November). In December, after Indonesia invaded the Portuguese colony of Timor, Lisbon broke diplomatic relations with Jakarta (18 December 1975). However, on 17 July 1976, Portugal approved the annexation of Portuguese Timor by Indonesia because of the level of unrest at home. On 7 January 1976, a series of left-wing bombings began, with Oporto and Braga the main targets. The junta was replaced on 23 July 1976 with a socialist government under Mario Soares. The socialist experiment failed, however, and Soares was replaced in July 1978; several other socialist governments also failed. Thereafter

(1982), Portugal was ruled by the right-center Democratic Alliance. In 1983, however, the socialists regained power under Soares. Soares was elected president in 1986 and was reelected in 1991. Protests broke out in June 1994 following the raising of bridge toll prices. Riot police had to be employed to break up the demonstration that followed. The government then temporarily revoked the toll raise, but when it was restored in September, protestors again took to the streets. The situation eventually righted itself. Although the government changed in October 1995, Soares remained in the presidency. *Reading:* Kenneth Maxwell, *The Making of Portuguese Democracy* (1995); Douglas L. Wheeler, *Historical Dictionary of Portugal* (1993).

Posht-a-Badam (Desert 1). *See* Iran.

Pote Sarasin. In 1957, the government of Phibunsongkhram was overthrown in Thailand by a military coup. A caretaker government was installed under Pote Sarasin. On 20 October 1958, Pote was removed in a bloodless coup led by Field Marshal Sarit Thanarat (qv), the man who had put Pote in power.

Potomac Charter. After consultations (in Washington, DC on 20–29 June 1954) with Prime Minister Winston Churchill (qv) and British Foreign Minister Anthony Eden (qv), President Dwight Eisenhower (qv) announced the "Potomac Charter," in which Great Britain promised not to press for Communist China's admission to the United Nations and not to endorse communist victories in Indochina. Both sides agreed to seek alternatives to the defense of Southeast Asia (28 June), if the French peace initiatives were unsuccessful. *See* Indochina and Vietnam.

Poulo Wai (Pulo-Condor) *(Iles de Poulo Condore)* **Islands.** Originally ceded to France by China in 1862, the Poulo Wai islands in the South China Sea 60 miles east of the tip of Vietnam's Ca Mau Peninsula were the scene of a clash between Thai and Vietnamese naval units on 13 June 1975. On 21 August 1978, Vietnam lay formal claim on the islands.

Powers, Francis Gary. (b. 17 August 1929, Jenkins, Kentucky— d.1 August 1977, Encino, California) On 1 May 1960, Francis Gary Powers was captured near Sverdlovsk by Soviet authorities after he was forced to eject from a U.S.–built U-2 reconnaissance aircraft that was on an overflight of the Soviet Union. Powers acknowledged during his interrogation that he worked for the U.S. Central Intelligence Agency and that his mission was an overflight of the USSR with an ultimate destination of the Bodo airbase in Norway. Powers had been based in Peshawar, Pakistan. Powers was tried and convicted of espionage and sentenced to ten years at hard labor. Two years later (10 February 1962), he was released in exchange for a Soviet spy, Rudolf Abel (qv), who had been captured by the FBI. Powers returned to the United States where he wrote an account of his sojourn in a book called *Operation Overflight.* He died in a helicopter crash in 1977 in Los Angeles County, where he worked as a television reporter. *Reading:* Fred J. Cook, *The U-2 Incident, May, 1960: An American Spy Plane Downed over Russia Intensifies the Cold War* (1973).

Poznan. *See* Poland.

Prado y Ugarteche, Manuel. On 18 July 1962, a military coup led by General Richardo Perez Godoy overthrew the government of President Manuel Prado y Ugarteche of Peru. Prado had first been president of Peru from 1939 to 1945. He had been reelected in a runoff vote in 1956. His administration was based on the reinstitution of democracy in Peru and the improvement of the economic lot of the masses. When he was overthrown by the Godoy regime, the new government's first move was to restrict civil liberty. Prado was arrested and imprisoned, the Congress was suspended and the election that had failed to achieve a majority, which had thrown the election to Congress, was overturned. Prado was eventually released from prison and went into exile.

Prague. *See* Czechoslovakia.

"Prague Spring." *See* Czechoslovakia.

Pramoj, Seni. On 6 October 1976, following a number of violent clashes between Thai police and ultra-rightist students belonging to a group called Red Gaur (Red Bull) (qv), a military coup ousted the civilian government of Prime Minister Seni Pramoj. The junta then assumed control of the government of Thailand under the leadership of former defense minister Admiral Sangad Chaloryu. The 70-year-old Seni Pramoj had been prime minister only since 20 April 1976.

Pravda **(Truth).** The official news organ of the Communist Party of the Soviet Union, the newspaper *Pravda* was first published in 1912 in Saint Petersburg as an underground communist newspaper. Vladimir Lenin was a member of its first three-person staff. Although repeatedly suppressed by Imperial Russian police, it continued to be published under different names and finally emerged in Moscow in 1918. The paper continued to be published and was basically the only source of information. There were other papers such as *Izvestia* and *Komsomolskaya Pravda*, but *Pravda* itself set the tone for the "party line" that emerged on its pages. Much of the material used by the official *Tass* news agency abroad was generated at *Pravda*. The paper ceased to exist with the collapse of the Soviet Union.

Pretoria. *See* South Africa.

Prevention of Nuclear War Agreement. On 22 June 1973, President Richard Nixon (qv) and Soviet leader Leonid Brezhnev (qv) signed the Prevention of Nuclear War Agreement in Washington. By its terms, the two sides agreed that if there was the threat of general war, the U.S. and the USSR would "immediately enter into urgent consultations . . . to make every effort to avert this risk."

Principe Island. On 12 June 1975, the West African islands of Principe and Sao Tome received their independence after 500 years of Portuguese rule. The two islands declared themselves the Democratic Republic of Sao Tome and Principe. The first settlers brought to the island after their Portuguese discovery in 1471 were convicts and exiled Jews. The first free election was held in 1991, but a military coup on 16 August 1995 sought to overthrow the government. Angolan intervention restored the equilibrium, however, and the government returned to power. *Reading:* Caroline S. Shaw, *Sao Tome and Principe* (World

Bibliographical Series, Vol. 172) (1995); Tony Hodges & Malyn Newitt, *Sao Tome and Principe: From Plantation Colony to Microstate* (1988); Antonio Carreira, *The People of the Cape Verde Islands: Exploitation and Emigration* (1983).

Prio Socarrus, Carlos. On 10 March 1952, the elected government of Cuba, with Carlos Prio Socarrus as president, was overthrown in a military coup led by General Fulgencio Batista (qv). Prio had been president since 1948. *See* Cuba.

Prisoners of War (POW). *See* particular conflict.

Prome. *See* Burma.

Protestants, Irish. *See* Northern Ireland.

Provisional Revolutionary Government of SVN (PRG). *See* Vietnam.

Pueblo Incident. On 23 January 1968, North Korean motor torpedo boats (MTB) operating in international waters in the Sea of Japan captured the unarmed American intelligence-gathering ship *USS Pueblo*, off the coast of North Korea. The crew of 83 American service personnel were taken into custody and, along with the ship, were taken to the port of Wonsan. Faulty communications, poor contingency planning and lax leadership all have been described as the principal reasons for the lack of American reaction, other than a loud vocal outcry. A later display of American military power failed to dissuade the North Koreans, and the American crew was held in appalling conditions for a total of eleven months before diplomatic negotiations led to their release on 23 December 1968. As a condition of release the U.S. had to acknowledge that the ship was spying and that it would never happen again. The U.S. repudiated the statement even before it was signed. One crew member died during captivity. Numerous investigations failed to fix responsibility, except that of its captain, Commander Lloyd M. Bucher, for giving up the ship. However, no disciplinary action was taken by the Navy. The Republic of South Korea considered the United States weak in the incident, and a heavy strain was placed on U.S.–ROK relations. *Reading:* Frederick Schmacher, *Bridge of No Return: Ordeal of the U.S.S. Pueblo* (1971); Lloyd Bucher, *Bucher: My Story* (1970); Trevor Armbrister, *The Matter of Accountability: The True Story of the Pueblo Affair* (1970).

Puerto Argentino, Argentina. *See* Falkland Islands.

Puerto Deseado, Argentina. *See* Falkland Islands.

Puerto Rico. The island of Puerto Rico was discovered by Christopher Columbus on his second voyage (1493) to the New World. By 1511, the Spaniards had introduced sugar cane and, by 1518, had begun the importation of slaves to cultivate it. In the late sixteenth century, the Spaniards began fortifying the island against frequent Dutch, English and French raids. Spain held the island until the nineteenth century, when the Spainards granted Puerto Rico complete autonomy (1897). The island was ceded to the United States following the Spanish-American War (1898) and was under US military government until 1900. From 1900 to 1917, the island was led by federally appointed officials. In 1917, the Jones Act made all Puerto Ricans U.S. citizens and created an elected legislature. Authority to elect their own governor was not granted until 1948. On 1 November 1950, Puerto Rican nationalists attempted the assassination of the president of the United States. Puerto Rico became a commonwealth in 1952. Puerto Rican terrorists attacked a busload of US naval personnel enroute to a naval communications site. Two naval personnel were killed and ten injured in the attack. On 18 March 1980, nationalist terrorists ambushed a car carrying three Reserve Officer Training Corps (ROTC) instructors on the busy Las Americas Expressway. One of the vehicle's occupants was injured in the attack. Eleven Puerto Rican terrorists of the Armed Forces of National Liberation (FALN) (qv) group were arrested in Evanston, Illinois, and charged with, among other things, 28 bombings. All of them were subsequently convicted. On 6 November 1985, two unidentified terrorists shot and wounded a U.S. Army major on the street in San Juan. A passer-by was also injured. The Organization of Volunteers for the Puerto Rican Revolution claimed credit for the attack. In 1993, citizens living on the island narrowly chose to retain commonwealth status over statehood or independence. *Reading:* Francisco Rivera-Batiz & Carlos Santiago, *Island Paradox: Puerto Rico in the 1990s* (1997); Arturo Moreales Carrion, *Puerto Rico: A Political and Cultural History* (1984); Nancy Morris, *Puerto Rico: Culture, Politics, and Identity* (1995).

Puerto Sandino. *See* Nicaragua.

Pul-i-Charkhi. *See* Afghanistan.

Punjab. *See* India.

Puno. *See* Peru.

Punta Carretas Prison, Montevideo. *See* Tupamaros.

Pusan. *See* South Korea and Korean War.

Puzanov, A. *See* Afghanistan.

Pyonggan. *See* Korea.

Pyongtaek. *See* Korea.

Q

Qabus (Qaboos) bin (ibn) Said (Sa'id). (b. 18 November 1940, Muscat and Oman) Qabus studied at Bury Saint Edmunds school in Suffolk, England. He then attended the Royal Military Academy, Sandhurst. In 1965 he was called home by his father, the Sultan of Oman, and was kept a prisoner for six years. In a palace coup on 23 July 1970, Oman's Sultan Sa'id bin Taimur (qv) was overthrown by his son. Qabus moved immediately to bring his country out of the Dark Ages, but he faced many problems in doing so. These problems included severe labor unrest and trouble with Dhofar (qv) rebels. Qabus received military assistance with the latter from the Shah of Iran (qv). Qabus remained sultan in 1995. *See* Oman.

al-Qaddafi, Muammar. (b. 1942, near Surt, Libya) Qaddafi was born in a tent, the son of a nomadic itinerant farmer. An devout Muslim and ardent nationalist, he graduated from the University of Libya in 1963 and soon afterward began plotting the overthrow of Libya's King Idris II (qv). Qaddafi graduated from the Libyan military academy in 1965 and rose steadily through the ranks while continuing his plotting to overthrow the king. On 1 September 1969, Qaddafi, supported by other army officers, took power through a military coup. He was named commander in chief of the armed forces and chairman of the governing body, the Revolutionary Command Council, at age twenty-seven. By the end of 1970, Qaddafi had ordered all U.S. and British bases off Libyan soil andexpelled thousands of Italian and Jewish citizens and expatriates out of the country. In 1973, he nationalized all foreign-owned petroleum assets in Libya and outlawed all alcohol and gambling according to his strict interpretation of Islamic law. On a number of occasions he tried, but failed, to unify his country with other Arab states. His adamant opposition to any form of rapprochement with Israel led Qaddafi to become the leader of the so-called Rejectionist Front of the Arab world. He has been accused of masterminding several failed coup attempts against Egypt and Sudan and of open intervention in the long-running civil war in Chad (qv). After 1974, Qaddafi became more erratic, and his unpredictable behavior created tensions around the world. His embrace of a populist Islamic socialism called for the nationalization of most sectors of the economy and the promotion of people's government. At the same time, his international strategy was founded on support of terrorist, revolutionary and other organizations such as the Black Panthers and the Nation of Islam in the U.S. and the Irish Republican Army operations in Northern Ireland. He dispatched teams of assassins, many of them Palestinian terrorists, to kill Libyan dissidents living abroad. These activities and other provocations led to an American attack on Libya in April 1986. A number of his family members were killed in the raid, but Qaddafi escaped. Since that time, Qaddafi has either decided to or was forced to temper his remarks and actions, at least in public. This has included his relative silence during the Middle East peace process in 1992–1995. *Reading:* Benjamin Kyle, *Muammar El-Qaddafi* (1987); Martin Sicker, *The Making of a Pariah State: The Adventurist Politics of Muammar Qaddafi* (1987); P. Edward Haley, *Qaddafi and the United States since 1969* (1984); Ronald Bruce St. John, *Qaddafi's World Design: Libyan Foreign Policy, 1969-1987* (1987).

Qantara (Al Quantarrah). *See* Egypt.

Qarabagh. *See* Afghanistan.

al-Qasmi, Khalid bin Mohammed. On 24 January 1972, Sheikh Khalid bin Mohammed al-Qasmi, the ruler of Sharjar, one of the smaller United Arab Emirates, was killed in a coup led by his cousin, Sheikh Saqr bin Mohammed al-Qasmi, who had been deposed as ruler in 1965. Khalid's younger brother, Sheikh Sultan bin Mohammed al-Qasmi, the UAE minister of education, replaced Khalid on the throne.

al-Qasmi, Saqr bin Mohammed. *See* al-Qasmi, Khalid bin Mohammed.

al-Qasmi, Sultan bin Mohammed. *See* al-Qasmi, Khalid bin Mohammed.

Qasr-i-Shirin. *See* Iraq.

Qa'tabah. *See* Yemen.

Qatar (*Dawlat Qatar*). The State of Qatar is bordered on the east and north by the Persian Gulf, on the south by the United Arab Emirates, on the west by Saudi Arabia and on the northwest by Bahrain. The capital city is Doha. The region occupied by Qatar was first reported by Arab explorers in the tenth century. By the eighteenth century the northwestern part of the country was occupied by Arabs migrating from the west and north. In 1783, the Persians, considering the Arabs a threat, invaded Qatar but were defeated by the *Al-Khalifah* tribesmen, who thereafter occupied Bahrain Island, setting up an independent State of Bahrain. A rift eventually developed between the Bahraini and the *Al-Khalifah* in Qatar and in 1867 erupted into full-scale war. The Qataris were routed, with the aid of Abu Dubai, and the capital city of Doha destroyed. The fighting in the region led the British to intervene in 1868; they installed a pro-British government under Muhammad ibn Thani and established a British residency. The Ottoman Empire stationed troops in Qatar soil in 1871, but this too led to fighting, and they were defeated by the Qataris in 1893. After 1918, Turkish influence in the Persian Gulf came to an end. In November 1916, Qatar became a British protectorate. After the discovery of oil in 1940, Qatar modernization moved ahead rapidly. Britain withdrew from Qatar on 3 September 1971. When the Trucial Coast Agreement (qv) was established, which would have had both

Qatar and Bahrain join the United Arab Emirates, both chose to remain independent. Qatar subsequently joined the United Nations and the Arab League. On 22 February 1972, the government of Emir Ahmad bin Ali al-Thani was overthrown in a bloodless coup led by his cousin, Prime Minister Sheikh Khalifa bin Hammad ath-Thani. On 21 October 1973, Qatar joined other Arab nations in refusing to sell oil to the U.S. because of its support of Israel in the Yom Kippur War (qv). After 1978, Qatar, among a number of Persian Gulf states, began receiving arms shipments from France. Emir Khalifa bin Hammad ath-Thani was ousted by his son, Crown Prince Hamad bin Khalifa ath-Thani, on 27 June 1995. *Reading:* Martin Caiger-Smith, *Qatar* (1986).

Qena (Qina) Dam. On 5 November 1968, Israeli commandos attacked the Qena River dam and the Nag Hammadi hydroelectric plant at the confluence of the Nile and Wadi Quen rivers. The river junction at the city of Qena is approximately 70 miles inland from the Red Sea town of Bur Safajah and is nearly 300 miles from the nearest Israeli territory. *See* Egypt.

Qorsel, Jama Ali. On 27 April 1970, the government announced that a military coup attempt led by Major General Jama Ali Qorsel had been put down. Qorsel had been the vice chairman of the ruling Supreme Revolutionary Council and minister of interior. According to the dispatch, Qorsel's plan was to seize the government, provoke a war with Ethiopia and ask for foreign troops. Qorsel was subsequently dismissed from the government and charged with treason.

Quang Duc, Venerable. On 11 June 1963, in a protest against the government of South Vietnamese president Ngo Dinh Deim (qv), a Buddhist monk, Venerable Quang Duc, burned himself to death. Five days later, the Diem government was forced to accede to many of the Buddhist demands, after a statement was made by Madame Nhu (qv) that the best thing for the country was to "barbecue a monk."

Quang Duc Province. *See* Vietnam.

Quang Nam Province. *See* Vietnam.

Quang Ngai Province. *See* Vietnam.

Quang Tin Province. *See* Vietnam.

Quang Tri Province. *See* Vietnam.

Quebec. *See* Canada.

Quemoy Island (*Jinmen Dao*). Located in the Taiwan Strait at the mouth of Amoy Bay, Quemoy Island was once a part of Fukien Province on the Chinese mainland. The island was occupied by Chinese Nationalist troops in 1949, when Chinese Communist forces drove the Nationalists from the mainland (*see* China). On 24 July 1950, the Communists began a heavy bombardment of Quemoy and Matsu (qv) from the mainland in what appeared to be a prelude to an invasion. Based on intelligence that the invasion would begin shortly, the U.S. Seventh Fleet was deployed (3 September 1954) to protect the islands, and a serious diplomatic incident arose. An uneasy truce began on 7 June 1955. On 23 August 1958, the Communists began another heavy bombardment of Quemoy and Matsu, in part as an attempt to starve out the islands' defenders. Four days later, on 27 August, President Eisenhower (qv) declared Quemoy and

Matsu vital to the defense of Formosa (Taiwan) and ordered a U.S. naval carrier task force into the Formosa Strait. By September, U.S. naval units were escorting supply ships to the islands. On 4 September, Secretary of State John Foster Dulles announced that the U.S. would defend the islands and that the U.S. rejected the 12-mile limit established by the mainland, which would have included Quemoy and Matsu in Communist territory. The president reiterated those statements on 11 September and called for negotiations to settle the dispute. Opposition in the Congress forced the administration to declare it had no firm commitment to Taiwan to defend the islands (30 September). On 6 October 1958, the communists declared a one-week cease-fire and called for talks. The U.S. navy stopped convoying supply ships on 8 October with the warning that they would resume again if the shelling was resumed. Nationalist Chinese president Chiang Kai-shek announced his determination to hold the islands on 17 October. On 20 October the Communist shelling resumed. Chiang Kai-shek then announced (23 October) that he might reduce control of the islands to relax tensions. On 19 December 1959, China again shelled Quemoy and overflew the island with military jets. Several of the ommunist aircraft were shot down over the island during the next few weeks. The U.S. periodically thereafter warned Communist China about interfering with the islands. The U.S. withdrew its advisors from the islands on 23 June 1976. The legitimacy of Nationalist control of Quemoy is contested to this day by the Communists. In 1992, Nationalist civilian administration of the island was established. The situation has remained calm into 1995, but the saber-rattling continues between the Nationalists and mainland China. *Reading:* Peter P. C. Cheng, *Truce Negotiations over Korea and Quemoy* (1977).

Quetta. *See* Pakistan.

Quezaltenango. *See* Guatemala.

Quiche. *See* Guatemala.

Quiche Indians of Guatemala. Also called Quiche Maya, these Indians are of the Mayan ethnic group and live in the midwestern highlands of Guatemala. They were an advanced civilization in pre-Columbian times and had a complex class structure. In more recent times they have become predominantly Roman Catholic, although a number of pagan traditions have remained in their their practice of the the faith. On 31 January 1980, 39 Quiche seized the Spanish embassy in Guatemala City and took a number of hostages, including the Spanish ambassador, Maximo Cajal y Lopez. After the Guatemalan police stormed the building, it burned to the ground in a fire caused by a gasoline bomb thrown by the terrorists. Thirty-eight Quiche and all the hostages except the ambassador were killed. The ambassador was rushed to the hospital, from which, the next day, he was kidnapped and murdered. The Quiche used the original attack as a protest against repossession of their land. In the negotiations that followed the seizure, the Spanish ambassador specifically forbade police intervention. Because of this disagreement and the subsequent murder of the ambassador, Spain severed diplomatic relations with Guatemala on 1 February.

Quijada, Hermes. On 1 May 1973, Rear Admiral Hermes Quijada was assassinated by leftist terrorists suspected of belonging to either the People's Revolutionary Army (ERP) (qv) or the Montoneros group, which was known to have cooperated with the ERP in Argentina. *See* Argentina.

Qui Nhon City. *See* Vietnam.

Quintanilla, Roberto. On 1 April 1971, members of the Bolivian terrorist organization *Ejercito Liberacion Nacional* (ELN) assassinated a former Bolivian secret police official, Roberto Quintanilla, in Hamburg, Germany.

Quiryat Shemona. *See* Israel.

Quisling, Vidkun. (b. 18 July 1887, Fyresdal, Norway—d. 24 October 1945, Oslo) Quisling was a former Norwegian army officer who collaborated with the Nazis during the German occupation of Norway in World War II. He was also held responsible for sending nearly 1,000 Norwegian Jews to their deaths in concentration camps. When Norway was liberated (May 1945), Quisling was arrested and tried as a traitor, a word now synonymous with his name. He was executed in Akershus Fortress near Oslo on 24 October 1945.

Quito. *See* Ecuador.

Quiwonka (Quiwonkpa), Thomas. On 12 November 1985, a military coup attempt against the government of Samuel Doe (qv) of Liberia failed. The executive mansion was shelled, the coup leader, Brigadier General Thomas Quiwonka, announced he had overthrown the government. Doe later told his people by radio that he was still in control. Quiwonka, who had helped Doe seize power five years earlier, was tried and executed.

Qum. *See* Iran.

Quneitra (al-Qunaytirah, Kuneitra). *See* Syria, Israel and Arab-Israeli Wars.

R

Rabat. *See* Morocco.

Radio Hanoi. The North Vietnamese government-controlled broadcasting system used extensively to deliver propaganda to South Vietnam during the war.

Rafah (Rafiah). *See* Israel.

Rafid, Golan Heights. *See* Israel; Syria.

Rafsanjani, Hasheimi (Ali Akbar Hashemi Rafsanjani). (b. 1934, Rafsanjan, Kerman Province, Iran) Rafsanjani was born the son of a prosperous farmer who resided in Rafsanjan. His early education was in local religious schools; later he moved to Qom and attended the theological seminary there. In the late 1950s he finished his studies with the rank of *hojatolislam,* the second highest rank among Shi'ite Muslim clergy. In 1958 he became a disciple of Ayatollah Rhuollar Khomeini (qv). Taking up Khomeini's opposition to the Shah of Iran (qv), Rafsanjani remained in Iran when his mentor was exiled in 1962. Raising funds for Khomeini's campaign against modernization in Iran, Rafsanjani was eventually arrested and imprisoned from 1975 to 1978 on charges of dealing with communist terrorists. When Khomeini returned to Iran after the shah's overthrow in 1979, Rafsanjani became one of his chief advisers and helped found the Islamic Republican Party. He also was appointed to the Revolutionary Council and was elected to the *Majlis,* the Iranian parliament. During his nine-year tenure in that body, he was instrumental in the prosecution of the Iran-Iraq War (qv) (1980–1988) and was involved in the cease-fire that ended it (August 1988). Upon Khomeini's death in June 1989, Rafsanjani was elected president of Iran. He was widely criticized among Iranians for his part in the arms-for-hostages deal in the Iran-Contra scandal that touched off a political crisis in the United States. Rafsanjani has also been criticized for his alleged authorizing of the murders of political opponents in Iran and abroad and for dealing with Communist China in the development of nuclear weapons. In 1995, Rafsanjani continued as head of state in Iran.

Ragged Island, Bahamas. On 13 May 1980, five Cuban jets buzzed a small village on Ragged Island. As the Bahamas are within the United States air defense zone, U.S. fighters were scrambled to intercept the intruders, who headed for home as soon as the presence of U.S. aircraft was detected.

Rahman, Abdul (Abdul Rahman Putra Alhaj, *Tunku* **[Prince]).** (b. 8 February 1903, Alor Star, Kedah, Malaya—d. 6 December 1990, Kuala Lumpur, Malaysia) - After completing his normal education in England (1920–1931), Abdul Rahman returned to Malaya, where he entered the civil service. In 1947, he returned to England, where he took a degree at law. Upon his return to Malaya, he was appointed public prosecutor in the Malay Federation Legal Department. He resigned that post in 1951 to enter politics. In 1951, he became the leader of the United Malays National Organization (UMNO), which he was then able to consolidate with the Malayan Chinese Association (1951) and the Malayan Indian Congress (1955). Rahman was elected chief minister by his Alliance Party's lopsided victory in 1955. In January 1956, he led a mission to London to seek independence. The success of his mission was immediate home rule and independence for his country in August 1957 (*see* Malaysia). Rahman then became its first prime minister and foreign minister and continued in that post after the formation of the Malaysian Federation in 1963. Rahman resigned his office in September 1970 following a year of popular unrest over the results of an election in which the Chinese made unexpected gains. Rahman was replaced by Abdul Razak (qv), and he died in Malaysia on 6 December 1990.

Rahman, Mujibur (aka Sheikh Mujib). (b. 17 March 1920, Tungipara, India—d. 15 August 1975, Dacca, Bangladesh) Born the son of middle-class landowners, Mujib was jailed as a teenager for demonstrating for Indian independence from Great Britain. He studied law and political science at the the University of Calcutta and the University of Dacca. He was a cofounder (1949) of the Awami League, which advocated autonomy for East Bengal (later Bangladesh). He was frequently arrested for his political activities in the 1960s. Hugely popular, Mujib became the leader of East Bengal. In 1970, the Awami League won a majority in the Pakistan National Assembly. In East Pakistan rioting in opposition to West Pakistani control broke out, and the government declared martial law (24 March 1971). On 26 March, Mujib declared an independent state. There ensued a civil war, from which emerged the independent Bangladesh (*see* Bangladesh), with Mujib as prime minister, but not before Mujib was put on trial for his life (11 August 1971). He was released from jail on 8 January 1972. In January 1975, Mujib moved to consolidate his power by changing the constitution and having himself declared president. In an army coup d'etat, Mujib and most of his family were murdered on 15 August 1975.

Rahman, Ziaur. (b. 19 January 1936, Shylhet, East Bengal, India—d. 30 May 1981, Chittagong, Bangladesh) Rahman was serving as as an army officer in Bangladesh (formerly East Pakistan) when a military coup overthrew the government of Mujibur Rahman (qv). At that time, Ziaur Rahman was appointed army chief of staff, but, upon the resignation of Abu Sadat Mohammad Sayem for health reasons in April 1977, Ziaur Rahman moved into that position. On 30 May 1981, President Rahman of Bangladesh was assassinated in his sleep during a military uprising in the port city of Chittagong. Many others were also slain in the coup led by Major General Manzur (Manzoor) Ahmed. Vice President Abdus Sattar took over the presidency and quickly restored order in the aftermath of the murder. A state of emergency was declared, followed by a suspension of civil rights. Manzur and eleven others were tried in secret and executed on 23 September.

Rainbow Warrior. *See* Greenpeace.

Raja'i, Mohammad Ali. On 30 August 1981, former Iranian prime minister and the successor as president of Abohassan Bani-Sadr (qv), Mohammad Ali Raja'i, and his prime minister, Mohammad Javad Bahonor (qv), and three other members of the Supreme Defense Council were killed when a bomb went off in Bahonor's office. This attack by the Iranian *mujahedin* followed two months after a bombing that killed 73 people in the headquarters of the ruling Islamic Republican Party (28 June 1981). Raja'i had taken office as president following a landslide election victory on 24 July. Two days after Raja'i's death, the prosecutor general of Iran, Ayatollah Ali Ghoddusi, was killed in another bomb explosion.

Rajasthan Desert. *See* India.

Rajavi, Massoud. Following the seizure of the U.S. embassy in Tehran, Iran (*see* Iran), President Abohassan Bani-Sadr (qv) spoke out in opposition to the incident. He was impeached by Parliament (*Majlis*) and forced to flee the country. Fleeing with him was Massoud Rajavi, the head of the outlawed *Mujahedin-e Khalq* (Fighters for Freedom). Upon arriving in exile in France (29 July 1981), Bani-Sadr and Rajavi formed the National Council of Resistance, which was directed at the overthrow of the Khomeini (qv) government in Iran.

Rajk, Laszlo. On 16 June 1949, following the arrest of Laszlo Rajk, communist Hungary's foreign minister, a wholesale purge began of so-called national wing communists who did not hew to the Moscow line. Rajk was accused of dubious "crimes against the state," was found guilty and executed. Hundreds of others were either imprisoned or executed on equally flimsy charges.

Rakosi, Matyas. (b. 14 March 1892, Ada, Serbia—d. 5 February 1971, Gorky, USSR) Following World War I, Rakosi, who had been held as a prisoner of war in Russia, returned to Hungary a full-fledged communist. He served as a production commissar in the short-lived socialist government of Bela Kun (1919), after which he was forced to flee to Moscow. The Soviets sent him back to Hungary in 1924 to help reorganize the Hungarian Communist Party, but he was arrested in 1925 and, after spending two years in pretrial confinement, was sentenced by a Hungarian court to eight-and-a-half years' imprisonment from the original date of his arrest. Upon the completion of his prison term, he was again arrested and this time was sentenced to life imprisonment (1934). In 1940, he was released and shipped to Moscow, where he remained until 1944, when he returned to Hungary as a part of the so-called baggage-train government that the Soviet army installed over the country. Rakosi was named secretary of the Hungarian Workers (Communist) Party and, by brute force, particularly that supplied by the Hungarian Secret Police (AVO), he soon consolidated all power in his own hands. As a staunch supporter of Josef Stalin, Rakosi ruled Hungary (also taking the title of prime minister in 1952) until July 1953, when he was forced to relinquish the part of prime minister to Imre Nagy (qv). Rakosi remained party secretary, however, and was able to remove the reform-minded Nagy in 1955. At the demand of the Yugoslav dictator, Marshal Tito (qv), Moscow stripped Rakosi of all party leadership in 1956. When the Hungarian Revolution erupted in October 1956, Rakosi was forced to flee again to the USSR, where he died in 1971.

Ramallah. *See* Israel.

Ramanantsoa, Gabriel. On 18 May 1972, following a week of student violence, the government of President Philibert Tsiranana (qv) of the Malagasy Republic handed over control of the government in what has been characterized as a bloodless coup led by General Gabriel Ramanantsoa. A plebiscite held on 8 October of that year confirmed Ramanantsoa as head of government, and on 11 October, Tsiranana, in ill health, formally resigned as president. Ramanantsoa negotiated new agreements with France whereby French troops and bases were removed from Malagasy soil, and all French citizens found themselves listed as aliens. Ramanantsoa then established ties with the Soviet Union and a number of other communist states and withdrew the country from the French market. Joint French-Malagasy ventures were then nationalized by the Malagasy government. Political and civil unrest followed, climaxed on 5 February 1975 by Ramanantsoa's handing over of the government to Colonel Richard Ratsimandrava (qv) in another "bloodless coup."

Ramat. *See* Israel.

Ramla (Ramlee). *See* Israel.

Ramlat al-Bayda. *See* Lebanon.

Ramon-Guizado, Jose A. Panama's president, Jose A. Ramon-Guizado, was dismissed by the National Assembly for his part in the assassination of the former president, Roberto Francisco Chiari (qv), on 2 January 1955. He had served only a few days in office when he was charged with and convicted of conspiracy in the assassination.

Ramtha. *See* Jordan.

Rangoon. *See* Burma.

Rang Rang. *See* Vietnam.

Rann of Kutch. *See* India.

Rao, N. T. Rama. On 17 August 1984, a statewide strike took place in the Indian state of Andhra Pradesh following the dismissal of Chief Minister Rama Rao. Rao, the leader of the Telugu Desam Party, was dismissed as a result of political maneuvering that put his majority in question. When the new chief minister, Bhaskara Rao, could not certify his majority, N. T. Rama Rao was returned to office on 16 September.

Raqqad River. *See* Syria.

Ras al-Khaimah. *See* United Arab Emirates.

Ras Banat. *See* United Arab Republic.

Ras el-Nagb. *See* Egypt.

Ras Muhammad, Sinai. *See* Israel and Egypt.

Ratanakiri Province. *See* Cambodia (Kampuchea).

Ratsimandrava, Richard. When Gabriel Ramanantsoa (qv) stepped down as prime minister of the Malagasy Republic (Madagascar) on 5 February 1975, his former minister of interior, Colonel Richard Ratsimandrava, was handed power. Ratsimandrava quickly assumed the titles of president and prime minister. On 11 February, however, he was assassinted in the capital city of Tananarive.

Rawlings, Jerry J. (b. 22 June 1947, Accra, Ghana) Born the son of a Scottish father and Ghanaian mother, Rawlings was educated at Achimoto College and the Ghanaian military academy (Teshie). He received his commission as a second lieutenant in the Ghanaian air force in 1969 and became an expert pilot during his military career. On 15 May 1979, Flight Lieutenant Rawlings led an abortive coup attempt against the government of Lieutenant General Fred Akuffo (qv). Rawlings was arrested and jailed. On 4 June, however, a second attempt to overthrow Akuffo was successful; Rawlings was released from prison and, shortly afterward, ordered the execution of Akuffo and a number of other former leaders and senior government officials. Rawlings remained in power for 112 days and then turned the government of Ghana over to a civilian, Hilla Limann (qv). Limann's first act was to order the military retirement of Rawlings. After two years in office, Limann was leading the nation, in Rawlings' words, "down to total ruin." Rawlings overthrew the government in a bloody coup on 31 December 1981. A new Provisional National Defense Council was set up to rule, with Rawlings as its leader (1 January 1982). The constitution was suspended; Limann was arrested, along with 200 other politicians. During the next year, Rawlings experimented with several different social and economic programs, all of which failed. During that same year (1983), at least four rebel attempts were made on Rawlings' regime; all of them failed. He thereafter adopted a new conservative approach to the failing economy of Ghana, and the situation began to change for the better. By the 1990s, Ghana showed signs of become a stable and growing, economically viable African state. Rawlings was elected president in a 1992 landslide victory, in the first election held since 1979.

Rawson Prison, Argentina. On 22 (also reported as 16) August 1972, widespread rioting took place throughout Argentina following the killing of 16 of 19 terrorists while they allegedly attempted to escape from Rawson Prison. In the same series of events, Argentina became incensed when Chile refused to extradite ten other guerrillas who had stolen an airplane and escaped. The guerrillas were a part of the left wing Trotskyite People's Revolutionary Army.

Ray, Charles R. On 18 January 1982, Lieutenant Colonel Charles R. Ray, an assistant military attache at the U.S. embassy in Paris, was shot and killed while walking to his car from his home. His lone assailant was reported to be a man of "Middle East appearance" who came up behind Ray and shot him once in the head at point-blank range. The Lebanese Armed Revolutionary Faction (FARL), a Lebanese Christian terrorist group with a Marxist ideology, claimed responsibility for the assassination and threatened more attacks as a result of "American aggression."

Ray, James Earl. On 4 April 1968, James Earl Ray, an escaped prisoner, assassinated Martin Luther King, Jr. (qv), in Memphis, Tennessee. Ray was captured and convicted; in 1996, he was still in prison. King's murder sparked racial rioting that spread throughout the United States and which required more than 55,000 federal and National Guard troops to quell. At least 46 deaths were attributed to the rioting.

Raymond, Jean de. On 29 October 1951, the French High Commissioner in Cambodia, Jean de Raymond, was assassinated. He may have been murdered by Viet Minh (qv) agents operating in Cambodia at that time, or his murder may have been sparked by the activities of local insurgents who were stimulated by Viet Minh or Laotian Khmer Issarak rebels.

Razak, Tun Abdul bin Hussein. (b. 11 March 1922, Pekan, Pahang State, Federated Malay States—d. 14 January 1976, London) Razak joined the civil service in 1950. A lawyer by training, he entered politics in 1955 and was instrumental in gaining independence for his country in 1957 (*see* Malaysia). From 1957 to 1970, Razak served as deputy prime minister and as minister of defense. He also held the additional title of minister of rural development from 1959 to 1969. In 1970, Razak became prime minister, replacing Tunku Abdul Rahman (qv), who relinquished control because of the increasing violence between the Malay and Chinese populations in Malaysia. On 28 June 1971, Razak announced the discovery of several guerrilla bases near Ipoh in the central part of the country. In 1974, Razak established relations with Communist China (31 May 1974) in furtherance of his policy of nonalignment. He died in London on 14 January 1976.

Reagan, Ronald. (b. 6 February 1911, Tampico, Illinois) Born the son of an Irish-American shoe-store owner, Reagan received his education at the conservative denominational Eureka College (1932), where he participated in sports and drama. After graduation he worked at a local radio station as a sports announcer and then migrated to Hollywood, where he became involved as an actor of some reputation in the movie industry. For several years after World War II, with his acting career on the wane, he served as the president of the Screen Actors Guild. In this capacity, he turned away from the Democratic Party and became a staunch Republican, primarily because of his knowledge of communist infiltration of his union. In 1952, he married Nancy Davis, also a staunch conservative. He also worked as a public relations officer with the General Electric Company. In 1966, Reagan won the gubernatorial election in California and had his first experience in dealing with a legislature of the opposition party. He eventually learned the art of compromise and finished his term without further incident. He did, however, learn one other lesson, the use of television to gain popular support for his position on issues. Reagan ran for the Republican presidential nomination in 1968 and 1976. Losing both times to others, he was swept into office in 1980 over the incumbent Jimmy Carter (qv) by a wave of national conservatism, which also gave him a Republican Senate and House. Reagan set his presidential agenda toward a strong national defense and a firm position against the Soviet Union and its various adventures. He also worked to reduce the size of government and to reduce taxes. The national debt rose sharply, however, as his plan to stimulate the economy fell short of its goals, often because of Democratic congressional opposition. Reagan won a second term by a landslide in 1984. Reagan imposed economic sanctions against Nicaragua on 1 May 1984. On 8 July 1985, Reagan designated Cuba, Iran, Libya, Nicaragua and North Korea as the chief purveyors of terrorism in the world and warned then that the U.S. would respond without warning to any terrorist incidents. That same month, he was diagnosed with colon cancer and underwent surgery. Reagan met Soviet General Secretary Mikhail Gorbachev (qv) at the first summit meeting held in six years (Geneva, 19 November 1985), and the two apparently became close friends. Reagan was also able to win the passage of major tax reform legislation in 1986, but his entire administration became engulfed in the politically sensitive Iran-Contra scandal, which hampered most if not all of his programs and produced a political field day for the Democrats. In December 1987, Reagan again met with Gorbachev and concluded the Medium Ballistic Missile (MBM) agreement, which elimated that class of missile from the arsenals of both sides. In May 1988, the two leaders signed similar agreements on intermediate and short-range missiles. When Reagan left office, the cloud of Iran-Contra still hung over him. He was subsequently required to testify in the trial of Oliver North, where he indicated a total lack of knowledge of any of the events surrounding the scandal. He was subsequently diagnosed with Alzheimer's disease.

Ream Airfield. *See Mayaguez* Incident.

Rebel (Revolutionary) Armed Forces (FAR). On 16 January 1968, terrorists, most likely from the Guatemalan Rebel Armed Forces, killed Colonel John D. Webber and Lieutenant Commander Ernest A. Munro and wounded two other American service personnel stationed in Guatemala. On 28 August of that year, the U.S. ambassador to Guatemala, John Gordon Mein (qv), was assassinated in Guatemala City. On 27 February 1970, FAR terrorists kidnapped the country's foreign minister, Alberto Fuentes Mohr. He was exchanged the next day in exchange for an imprisoned rebel leader. The West German ambassador, Count Karl von Spreti (qv), was kidnapped on 31 March 1970. In this case, however, the Guatemalan government refused to release 17 political prisoners as ransom; and even though the West German government tried to intervene, Spreti was murdered (5 April 1970). The FAR proved to be one of the most active terrorist groups in Central America, especially during the 1960s and 1970s. The group's leaders, Yon Sosa, a young army officer, and Turcios Lima, at first led the group. Lima was subsequently killed in a car wreck (1966), and Cesar Montes joined Sosa in the leadership. Although the group claimed 20,000 members, more conservative estimates suggested that there were about several hundred in the group, with a relatively large sympathetic following across the country. The group was finally brought under control by the Guatemalan police, reinforced with US Special Forces.

Recife. *See* Brazil.

Red Army Faction (RAF). This Marxist terrorist group was also known as the Baader-Meinhof Gang (*Baader-Meinhof Gruppe*) (qv). Most of its operations were carried out in West Germany. The RAF was founded in 1968 by members of a breakaway radical faction of the German Socialist Student Alliance. The active membership was about 60, but the group had about 2,000 sympathizers, most from middle-class and professional families. From its earliest times, the RAF supported itself by bank robbery and extortion, but it also carried out attacks on West German, NATO and U.S. targets. The group operated under a collective leadership of at least nine members, six of whom were women. Two RAF (Baader-Meinhof) members took part in the hijacking of a French airliner in June 1976 that led to the Israeli raid on Entebbe (*see* Uganda). In that hostage release operation (3 July 1976) both RAF members were killed. Among their numerous terrorist activities, the RAF attacked NATO commander General Alexander Haig (qv) in June 1979; attacked the U.S. Air Force Europe's headquarters at Ramstein, Germany, in August 1981, injuring 18 Americans and two Germans; and attacked the U.S. Army Europe's commander and his wife with rocket grenades (RPG-7) in September 1981. A number of RAF members allegedly committed suicide (*see* Baader-Meinhof Gang) while in West German prisons. The group continued its terrorist activities and split into several groups. In 1989 the chairman of the West German Bank, *Deutsche Bank* was assassinated by the RAF. After the reunification of Germany it was discovered that the RAF had been supported by, among others, the East German *Stasi* (*Staatsicherheit*), the secret police of the German Democratic Republic. The group still continues to constitute a threat, but it is more vulnerable because of the loss of its East German sanctuary. The Japanese Red Army (qv) was not directly associated with the West German RAF.

Red Brigades (BR). First formed in 1970, the BR (*Brigate Rossi*) had an estimated hard-core membership of approximately 50–75 members. This terrorist group moved its headquarters several times to Rome, Genoa, Milan, Naples and the Tuscany region of central Italy. Its principal area of operations was within Italy. It was classed as one of the most lethal groups in Europe and grew out of the ultraradical section of the Italian labor movement. The BR conducted extensive attacks, including murders, "kneecappings" and kidnapping. The principal target was the so-called Italian establishment. In late 1981, the BR declared war on NATO, and in 1984 it announced its support of Middle East terrorist groups; and some of its members were thought to have trained in Palestinian camps in Lebanon. It later moved to gain solidarity with other West European terrorist organizations, such as the German Red Army Faction (RAF) (qv) and the French group *Action Directe* (AD) (qv), to attack individuals and organizations involved in the Strategic Defense Initiative (SDI) program. The BR operates in a highly compartmentalized structure, which helps its security. In 1978, it was responsible for the kidnapping and murder of former Italian prime minister Aldo Moro (qv). Italian authorities were successful in the late 1970s and early 1980s in bringing to justice a number of BR leaders and in confiscating vast amounts of arms and equipment belonging to the group. The BR kidnapped US Army

Brigadier General James Dozier (qv) in 1981. In 1987, in cooperation with Spanish and French authorities, the Italian government arrested a large group of BR terrorists, including the cell that assassinated Italian Air Force general Lucio Giorgieri in March 1987. After 1984, the BR split into two factions, the Fighting Communist Party (PPC) (also called Militarists) and the Union of Fighting Communists (UCC), or Movementalists. The BR is also suspected of involvement, along with the Lebanese Army Revolutionary Faction, in the 1984 assassination of the American Leamon Hunt (qv). Even though seriously crippled by continual police pressure, the organization remains dangerous. *Reading:* Robert C. Meade & Robert C. Gardner, *Red Brigades: The Story of Italian Terrorism* (1990).

Red Gaur (Red Bull). An ultra-right wing student group, the Red Gaur had clashes with the police in October 1976 that led to the overthrow of the civilian government of Prime Minister Seni Pramoj (qv) and the establishment of a military junta in Thailand (6 October 1976).

Red Guard (*Hongwei Bing*). As a part of the Cultural Revolution in Communist China that ran from 1966 to 1976, groups of militant high school and college students were formed into paramilitary organizations by the Chinese Communist Party (CCP) to help carry forward the programs of Mao Tse-tung (qv). Principal among these was the eradication of political opposition, which was called "revisionist." The Red Guards became a power unto themselves, however, and were soon involved in a wave of unequalled persecution that transcended all classes of Chinese society including members of the Communist Party itself. Estimates of the casualties of the Red Guards' reign of terror run as high as one million, although more conservative estimates place the number at several hundred thousand killed as a result of their activities. The Red Guard caused such chaos that the government was forced to use the Chinese military to quell its rampage. By the 1970s the Red Guard's fervor had been shunted to agrarian activities, which greatly reduced its impact on daily life in China.

Red River. *See* Vietnam.

Red Sea. *See* the countries bordering the Red Sea.

Reggio Calabria. *See* Italy.

Rehovo. *See* Israel.

Remada. *See* Tunisia.

Rene, France-Albert. On 5 June 1977, the coalition government of President James R. Mancham (qv) of Seychelles was overthrown in an apparently Soviet-backed coup. Mancham was in London attending a Commonwealth meeting at the time. Denying any Soviet inspiration in the coup, former Prime Minister France-Albert Rene assumed the presidency. In 1979, Rene revised the constitution. On 25 November 1981, a coup attempt by 50 mercenaries, disguised as rugby players failed to topple the Rene government. In the bizarre incident, 44 of the rebels, who survived the encounter with government troops, hijacked an Indian airliner and flew to Durban, South Africa, where all but five were set free. The Rene government accused South Africa of complicity in the coup attempt. In 1982, Seychelles troops in Victoria mutinied against the Rene government. The rebels captured the radio station but were quickly overwhelmed by loyal troops. A new multiparty constitution was approved in June 1993. Rene remained as president in 1995.

Renner, Karl. (b. 14 December 1870, Unter-Tannowitz, Bohemia, Austria-Hungary–d. 31 December 1950, Doebling, Austria) Born into a peasant family, Renner was educated in law at the University of Vienna and joined the moderate wing of the Austrian Social Democratic Party. He served in the lower house of the Austrian Parliament (*Reichstat*) from 1907 and became the first chancellor of the new Austrian republic after the collapse of the Hapsburg dynasty following World War I. In this office, however, he was unable to prevent the dissection of his country by the Allies. He did sign the Treaty of Saint-Germain (10 September 1919), which prohibited the union of Austria with Germany. Renner's policies included neutralism for Austria and membership in the League of Nations. He served as president of the lower house from 1930 to 1933. In 1938, Renner supported the Nazi annexation of Austria. Upon the occupation of Austria by Soviet troops during World War II, Renner worked with the Soviets in rebuilding the Austrian state and became the first chancellor of the new republic (April 1945). He was unamimously elected president of the republic on 20 December 1945. Renner died of natural causes on 31 December 1950.

Replogle, Thomas. Rear Admiral Thomas Replogle was placed in command (2 October 1979) of a new Joint Task Force headquarters in Key West when President Carter (qv) decided that the U.S. would take additional steps to counter the Soviet military presence in Cuba (1 October). This action followed Soviet press attacks on the United States after U.S.–USSR talks on the issue of Soviet troops present in Cuba (28–29 September). The U.S. had demanded withdrawal of Soviet troops on 22 September.

Republic of Cochin China. On 1 June 1946, the French government proclaimed the autonomous Republic of Cochin China in Saigon, Indochina. Cochin China would later be made a part of the Republic of (South) Vietnam.

Republic of Congo. *See* Congo (Brazzaville).

Republic of Ireland. *See* Ireland.

Republic of Korea. *See* South Korea.

Republic of South Africa. More commonly referred to simply as South Africa, this country occupies the southern fifth of the African continent. It is bordered on the north by Botswana and Zimbabwe, on the northeast by Mozambique and Swaziland, on the southeast and south by the Indian Ocean, on the southwest by the Atlantic Ocean and on the northwest by Namibia. The state has three capitals; the adminstrative capital is in Pretoria, the legislative capital in Cape Town and the judicial capital in Bloemfontein. Pretoria and Cape Town are the seats of government, based on the season. During the Stone Age of the eight millennium B.C., Bushmen (*San*) and Hottentot (*Khoikhoin*) nomadic tribesmen roamed the vast region of South Africa. Over the millennia, the Hottentots settled into a pastoral existence. Beginning in the fifteenth century, A.D., Bantu, Xhosa, Zulu and Sotho tribes migrated into the region; these groups were the first people met by Portuguese explorers in that century. More definitive contact came about in 1652, when a Dutch East India Company trading post was established at Cape Town. Thereafter, Dutch settlers established the Boer tradition that was later called Afrikaner. The Afrikaners developed a unique language (*Africaans*) derive from their native Dutch with an intermingling of San and Khoikhoin. Some intermingling of bloodlines resulted in a group that became known as the "Cape Coloureds." As the Afrikaner population grew, the more adventurous explored the territory north of the Cape. This group took on a seminomadic style and became known as "Trekboers." In the migrations they came into contact with the Xhosa people, a highly cultivated and settled tribe. These contacts became increasingly more complex as cattle raiding became a way of life, and from the late eighteenth century until the late nineteenth century, frontier warfare flared as the two cultures collided. In 1795, the British occupied the Cape Colony; they lost it in 1802 and recaptured it in 1806. Thereafter, the British began a campaign to subdue the Bantu tribes along the ill-defined border between cultures. Many of the Afrikaners became disillusioned with British control and began, in the 1830s, what became known as the "Great Trek," in which the Africaners with all their possessions and slaves moved northward into areas previously unpopulated by Europeans. Crossing the Orange and Vaal rivers they, established two Boer republics, the South African Republic in 1838 and Orange Free State in 1854, both free of British control. The latter republic would later become the Transvaal. After the discovery of diamonds (1867) and gold (1886), the two republics burgeoned economically, and continued to reject British proposals to join the South African confederation. This led to the First Boer War in 1880 and the Second Boer War in 1899. Boer resistance was crushed, and the the British annexed these territories and added them into the Union of South Africa, which came into being under the 31 May 1910 South Africa Act. During World War I, the Union fought on the Allied side and, by 1815, had cleared South West Africa (Namibia) of German control. The League of Nations mandated South West Africa to South African control in 1919. Throughout the remainder of the century, South African politics was centered on the maintenance of control of government by approximately seven million whites over an estimated black population of 72 million. South Africa fought with the Allies in World War II. In October 1945, immediately following the end of the war, the coalition government broke up, leaving the United Party of Jan Smuts (qv) in control of the country. On 21 January 1947, the Smuts government rejected a UN decision to place South West Africa (Namibia) under UN trusteeship and claimed that area as a part of South Africa. In a 20 May 1948 election, the Nationalist Afrikaner bloc won. The new all-white government immediately began the implementation of its policy of "Apartheid" (qv) (June 1949) as a means of definitive racial distinction among whites, blacks and a homogenous group of Indians, Asians and mixed-race people called "Coloureds." The approximately one-dozen black tribal groups were unable to make common cause because of ethnic problems, no mass uprising ensued, which would surely have been one sided. The whites controlled all political power and the resources of the country, while everyone else received the scraps. Rioting took place between Indians and Zulus in Durban on 13 January 1949, leaving over 100 dead. Social unrest continued and spread in the 1950s, and numerous violent confrontations occurred, such as the 30 January 1950 rioting in Johannesburg, which turned South Africa into a police-controlled state. South Africa passed the Group Areas Bill (27 April 1950), which created several Bantu states, known as Bantustans. This act was criticized by black leaders as a means of isolating the black population into separate, but unequal, nations, called "Homelands." The white concept of a homeland proved to be suspiciously similar to a concentration camp in which tribal groups could be held in circumscribed areas, with local governments often as oppressive as that of South Africa itself. On 20 March 1952, the South African Supreme Court found apartheid to be unconstitutional and voided the bill. The government of Prime Minister Daniel F. Malan (qv) circumvented the Supreme Court action by introducing legislation that made Parliament into the highest court in the land (22 April 1952) and passed additional legislation (29 May 1952) limiting the Supreme Court's powers. Apartheid continued, and violence grew apace. On 24 January 1953, Parliament voted Malan virtual dictatorial powers to carry out apartheid. The United Nations condemned South Africa's racial policies on 12 October 1955. A new, even stronger apartheid bill was imposed on 13 January 1956. As an initial phase of the resettlements that were to come, 100,000 nonwhites were ordered out of Johannesburg on 25 August 1956. The United States filed a formal protest with South Africa (21 March 1960) after the massacre of 72 people at Sharpville by the police. An attempt at restoring order came (1960) with the issuance of a state-of-emergency proclamation, invoking rule by proclamation and outlawing the African National Congress (ANC) (qv) and other black political organizations. South Africa received its independence on 31 May 1961 and, as the result of a white-only referendum, became a republic and withdrew from the British Commonwealth. The UN again condemned South Africa because of its racial policies on 13 April 1961. The first homeland, Transkei, was opened in 1963 Transkei gained its independence on 26 October 1976. On 7 August 1963, the UN voted to ban all military aid to the South African government. The UN then warned South Africa about interference with the new states. On 12 June 1964, Nelson Mandela (qv) and seven other black leaders were sentenced to life terms for sabotage and subversion. In 1966, Lesotho (Basutoland) became an independent enclave, as did Botswana (Bechuanaland). That same year, on 6 September, Prime Minister Henrik F. Verwoerd was assassinated. On 27 October 1966, the United Nations abrogated the League of Nations mandate granting South Africa control over South West Africa. South Africa rebuked the announcement, but only for a time. On 12 August 1969, the UN Security Council ordered South Africa to surrender its mandate by 4 October. Even with all of these external condemnations hanging over of South Africa, the French government sold it three submarines in April 1967, and new surface-to-air missiles in May 1969. On 30 January 1970, the UN Security Council condemned South Africa for the third time, in this case over the South West African situation. Also, on 1 July 1968, South Africa, along with France, Israel, Communist China and several other nations, refused to sign the Nuclear Non-Proliferation Treaty (qv). As another means of insuring separation of the white population.from all the rest, in 1969 South Africa announced that only whites could vote or hold office. There was to be an Indian advisory board and a Coloured People's Representative Council, but they were to have little power. The disturbances and concomitant human rights violations grew in a never ending cycle of unrest developing into violence during this period. One of the worst years was 1976, when at least 600, primarily Bantus, were killed during demonstrations. At least 600 white students were arrested on 2 June 1972 after a clash with police in which the students opposed apartheid. The number of dead and missing grew daily. The United States, Great Britain and France vetoed a UN Security Council resolution to expel South Africa from the organization on 31 October 1974, but the General Assembly voted (12 November) to suspend South Africa from all of its activities. In 1975, at the expiration of the Simonstown Agreement (qv), South Africa severed the last of its ties with Great Britain (16 July 1975). France ended its arms dealing with South Africa on 9 August 1975. Under heavy international pressure, South Africa agreed not to intervene in the problems in Rhodesia (14 May 1976) (see Zimbabwe). Beginning in June 1976, the number of clashes increased, with rioting occurring in a number of cities and townships. This rioting continued through September. Once again, however, the U.S., Great Britain and France vetoed a UN resolution imposing sanctions on South Africa (1 October 1976). South Africa announced it was doubling the size of its standing army in 1976. More fighting between South African and Angolan rebel forces was reported on 18 February 1977. On 23 August of that year, South Africa denied French reports that it was about to test a nuclear device. Citing the Riotous Assembly Act as grounds for the arrests, South African police apprehended 1,200 students attending a peaceful commemorative service for Steven Biko (qv) at the University of Hare in Alice. Biko had died of brain injuries suffered while in police custody in Pretoria. The internal investigation into Biko's death later absolved the police of any wrongdoing. Later confessions by police officers involved proved conclusively that Biko had been murdered while in custody. The UN unamimously imposed an arms embargo on South Africa on 4 November 1977. The homeland of Bophuthatswana became independent on 5–6 December 1977, and Venda followed on 13 September 1979. Both homelands remained under South African domination. South Africa broke off UN discussions aimed at finding a solution to the country's racial issues (12 January 1978). On 27 March, King Kapuuo, the South African government's choice to be the leader of South West Africa, was assassinated. On 10 April, the government of Transkei broke diplomatic relations with South Africa. Then, on 12 September 1978, South Africa rejected the UN plan for Namibia that had been agreed upon by all other parties. The South African counterproposal (October 1978) was in turn rejected by all of the other parties. The United States cancelled a rich-uranium contract with South Africa because that government had failed to sign the Nuclear Non-Proliferation Agreement and because South Africa's stipulations to signing the pact had already been rejected. Before the end of 1978, South Africa was also accused of rigging the elections in Namibia in favor of the preferred Turnhalle Alliance Party. On 4 March 1979, Iran broke diplomatic relations with South Africa and placed an embargo on oil shipments to that country. The UN placed an economic embargo on South Africa on 1 June 1979. In one of the earliest signs of change, the South African air force opened its ranks to black aviation cadets on 12 December 1979. Yet, heavy rioting continued into 1980 with such incidents as the police employing tear gas against 3,000 school children peacefully demonstrating against segregated schools in Cape Town on 23 April. Rebel guerrilla activities also increased. Two synthetic petroleum plants and one of South Africa's largest oil refineries were attacked on 3 May by members of the illegal ANC. Three other petroleum storage installations were hit in Johannesburg on 2 June. The government commenced large-scale military operations against Angola and Mozambique in 1980–1981 (South African forces were already in Angola as early as 1975). The Soviet Union warned South Africa that it would use force, if necessary, to support Mozambique, if it were endangered by these operations (21 February 1981). On 6 March 1981, the UN General Assembly adopted a number of resolutions condemning South Africa for its activities in Namibia and called for a mandatory embargo against it; but once again, on 30 April, the U.S., Great Britain and France vetoed the embargo. In February 1982, the U.S. relaxed its trade restrictions on the country. In March 1982, South African troops engaged South West Africa People's Organization (SWAPO) (qv) forces in Angola. On 18 January 1983, South Africa dissolved the Namibian National Assembly and reasserted full control of that country. However, also in 1983, a new constitution went into effect that gave certain rights to the coloureds but which still excluded the blacks. South Africa invaded Angola on 26 December 1983, allegedly to halt thwart rebel attacks aimed at Namibia. It began withdrawing its forces in Angola on 8 January 1984. On 16 February, a U.S.–mediated truce went into effect. On 18 March 1984, a truce was also signed that ended the border struggle with Mozambique. The UN declared apartheid "null and void" on 17 August. On 23 May 1985, the chief of the South African Defense Forces admitted that South African troops were still deployed in Angola and that casualties were still occurring. France tightened the international noose on South Africa by withdrawing its ambassador and imposing economic sanctions on 24 July 1985. Eleven other West European countries also withdrew their ambassadors in August. The South African government admitted it was still aiding guerrilla activity in Mozambique even though the 1984 peace agreement, the Nkomati Treaty (qv), was still in effect. When Bishop Desmond Tutu won the Nobel peace prize in 1986, he used that forum to urge the West to apply sanctions against South Africa to force an end to apartheid. South Africa, having received worldwide condemnation because of its apartheid policies, began a program of conciliation, reducing some of the more heinous programs within the policy of apartheid. In April 1986, for example, the government revoked the racial pass laws that had prohibited free movement in the country and gave blacks an advisory role similar to that offered the Indians and coloureds. That same year, on 19 May, South Africa opened military campaigns against the neighboring states of Botswana, Zaire and Zimbabwe. These operations were designed to destroy the rebel bases of the African National Congress (ANC) (qv) in those nations. On 12 June 1986, a state of emergency was delared in South Africa as civil unrest and rebel activities increased. This decree gave almost unlimited power to the police and miltary in the face of the growing insurrection. In 1990, the government was forced to lift the prohibition on the ANC, and on 11 February of that year, Nelson Mandela was released from prison, where he had been held for 27 years. Later that year, the Separate Amenities Act that legalized segregation was abrogated. In June, the hated Race Registration Law was also repealed. This act often consigned blacks to a homeland without consent. Also, South West Africa, under United Nations supervision, became Namibia and gained its independence in 1990 (*see* Namibia). Work on a nonracial constitution began in 1991, and work was begun on dismantling apartheid. On 17 June 1992, however, a major incident took place in Boipatong Township in which 42 men, women and children were massacred by members of the Inkatha Freedom Party in a case of tribal vengeance. This type of tribal warfare continued throughout the year and did much to delay the transition process. Another cause of continued violence was the 10 April 1993 assassination of the leader of the South African Communist Party, Chris Hani. That incident led to outbreaks in a number of townships. That year, the homelands programs were abolished, and South Africa was divided into nine provinces under a national system. A transition to an interracial government began between the white leadership and representatives of the ANC. The first free elections were held in April 1994 and were swept by the blacks, with Nelson Mandela elected the nation's first black president. *Reading:* Pierre Du Toit, *State Building and Democracy in Southern Africa: Botswana, Zimbabwe, and South Africa* (1995); David Deutschmann, ed., *Changing the History of Africa: Angola and Namibia* (1991); Y. M. Dadoo, *South African Communists Speak, 1915-1980* (1981); Paul Maylam, *A History of the African People of South Africa: From the Early Iron Age to the 1970s* (1986).

Republic of Viet Nam (South Viet Nam). *See* Vietnam.

Restrepo, Carlos Lleras. Restrepo served as president of Colombia from 1966 to 1970 and helped return the country to a program of sound economic development. He was unseated in 1970 by the largely rural National Front's candidate, Misael Pastrana Borrero. Unrest followed the election as urban groups opposed to the National Front took to the streets. As one of his last acts in office, the retiring president imposed a state of siege on the country.

Revolt of the Admirals. On 6 October 1949, the so-called Revolt of the Admirals began in a continuation of the long-standing inter-service battle over shares in the American defense budget. In this instance, the Navy accused the Army and the Air Force of working to destroy naval aviation. Before the rhetoric was finished, rash accusations flew in all directions. An investigation followed into charges leveled during the debate. As a result of that investigation, the Secretary of the Navy ordered that the Chief of Naval Operations Admiral Louis Denfield (qv) be relieved of command. This action effectively ended the "revolt."

Revolutionary Arab Youth Organization. On 28 May 1974, a small bomb went off at the John F. Kennedy Center, a United States Information Service library, in Beirut, Lebanon. The Revolutionary Arab Youth Organization claimed credit for the attack, which injured three.

Revolutionary Armed Action Group (aka Armed Revolutionary Action (ARA) (Portugal). On 8 March 1971, members of the ARA, an urban guerrilla group operating in Portugal, sabotaged a number of military aircraft at a military base near Lisbon in a protest of government policies in Africa. Along with another group, the League of Union and Revolutionary Action (LUAR), ARA was the cause of great concern to the Portuguese government on the eve of NATO meeting to be held in June 1971. Among other acts, the two groups had disrupted communications out of Lisbon and had kidnapped several important people. Portuguese security forces launched a campaign to eradicate the group and, with popular support, in October brought 31 of the terrorists to trial. This action may have slowed down, but did not deter, the ARA, which on 12 January 1972 blew up a Lisbon warehouse containing French arms destined for Portuguese troops operating in Africa. By 1984, the ARA had expanded its operational area and claimed credit for the murder of the Turkish labor attache assigned to Vienna (20 June).

Revolutionary Armed Forces of Colombia (FARC). Also known as the Armed Revolutionary Forces of Colombia, FARC was founded in 1966 as the military wing of the Colombian Communist Party. Its sworn purpose was to overthrow the government and disenfranchise the ruling class. The original leader of this predominantly rural group was Manuel Marulanda Velez, and its strength has been various reported as from 10,000 to 15,000. By the 1970s, FARC had become a kidnap-for-ransom terrorist group and was so successful that it began to sell its services, especially to cocaine producers and exporters, who paid up to 10 percent of their profits for this "protection." By the 1980s FARC had itself entered the drug trade and as a consequence reduced its terrorist activity. A truce was arranged with the Colombian government in 1984 that allowed FARC members greater freedom to operate in the illegal drug industry. FARC did, however, claim, along with the Che Guevarra Faction of the Bolivian National Liberation Army (ELN) (qv), responsibility for the bombing of seven U.S.–owned firms in Medellin on 7 February 1985.

Revolutionary Cells (RZ). An off-shoot of the German Baader-Meinhof Gang (qv), the RZ was organized in 1973 as a single group (cell). By 1976, however, it had cells all over Germany and maintained headquarters in West Berlin and Frankfurt am Mein. The group's original name was Rote Zora. This urban guerrilla, terrorist group supported antifascist, anti-imperialist, anti-Zionist and antimilitary causes. Its main targets have been West German government officials and the U.S. military stationed in Europe. The RZ had possible ties to Palestinian terrorist organizations, the Irish Republican Army (IRA) and other

Western European terrorist groups. The RZ had an autonomous women's contingent called *Rote Zora* (Red Wrath). The group was known to make its own explosives and detonating devices. From June 1976 until November 1987, the RZ carried out more than 200 attacks and campaigns against its targets. Yet, its relatively small size—about 25 members in 1984—saw it dropped from the NATO anti-terrorist list. Among its activities were the attacks on the US V Corps headquarters on 1 June 1976, in which 16 people were injured and on the U.S. Officer's Club at Rhein-Main Air Base, in which 18 were injured and the bombing of the Turkish Consulate in Cologne on 8 February 1984.

Revolutionary Front for the Liberation of East Timor (aka Revolutionary Front for the Independence of East Timor) (Fretilin). A left-wing organization, Fretilin was one of several rival groups in Timor among whom fighting broke out in March 1975 that prevented the referendum to choose independence, annexation by Indonesia or continuation of Portuguese control. By August 1975, Portugal acknowledged that it had lost control of the situation. On 9 September, the communist-supported Fretilin declared it held the entire eastern half of the island. In December, however, Indonesia, acting under the pretext that Timor's citizens had requested its help and after border incidents occurred along the Portuguese-Indonesian demarcation, invaded East Timor, captured the capital city of Dili and set up a provisional government. Frelitin forces retreated into the hills. Portugal broke diplomatic relations with Indonesia. On 13 December 1975, Indonesia formally annexed East Timor.

Revolutionary Government of South Viet Nam. *See* Viet Cong.

Revolutionary Left Movement. On 15 July 1980, four terrorists of the Revolutionary Left Movement assassinated the director of the Chilean Army Intelligence School, Lieutenant Colonel Roger Vergara Campos, and his driver near Santiago. The four assassins escaped.

Revolutionary Organization of Socialist Muslims. On 28 March 1984, a terrorist of the Revolutionary Organization of Socialist Muslims operating in Greece assassinated a British diplomat, Kenneth Whitty, and his Greek driver in Athens. Still focusing on British targets, the group assassinated the British Deputy High Commissioner in India, Percy Norris, in Bombay on 27 November 1984. He was shot to death as he was being driven to work.

Revolutionary Salvadoran Student Movement. At the same time as the February 28 Popular League (qv) was taking over the Spanish embassy in San Salvador (5 February 1980), another group calling itself the Revolutionary Salvadoran Student Movement was seizing the Ministry of Education building in the same city and taking a number of hostages in the process. On 12 February, this latter group attempted to leave the Ministry of Education building, but was engaged by the police. Three of the terrorists were killed. *See* El Salvador.

Revolutionary Vanguard. On 22 November 1974, Peruvian terrorists of a group known as the Revolutionary Vanguard blew up the Sears Roebuck store in Lima. Eleven people were injured in the blast.

Rhee, Syngman. (b. 26 March 1875, Whanghae, (North) Korea—d. 19 July 1965, Honolulu) Rhee, an ardent nationalist, had a traditional Confucian education, followed by Methodist schooling, in which he became a Christian and learned English. In 1896 he helped found the Independence Club, which was dedicated to Korean independence. Government loyalists destroyed the club in 1898 and Rhee was arrested and imprisoned until 1904. Upon his release he journeyed to the United States, where he earned his Ph.D. (1910) at Princeton. He returned to Korea that same year (1910, the year Japan annexed Korea) where he worked for the Young Men's Christian Association (YMCA) and as a high-school principal for two years. In 1912 he returned to the United States feeling that his displeasure with Japanese rule would have further endangered him if he had stayed in Korea. For the next three decades, Rhee was an ardent spokesman for Korean independence. In 1919 he was elected president of the Korean provisional government in exile, a post he held for 20 years. In 1939, Rhee was replaced as president by a younger group of Chinese-based Korean expatriates. Rhee spent the war years in the U.S. and continued his campaign for Korean independence. Immediately after the war, the U.S. returned Rhee to Korea before the arrival of the provisional government to allow him time to gain political strength. In gaining this strength, Rhee was not above using police and strong-arm tactics, possibly including assassination, to become the first president of the newly proclaimed Republic of Korea (1948) (*see* Korea). Rhee was reelected to successive terms in 1952, 1956 and 1960. During this period, Rhee became a virtual dictator, suppressing opposition by driving his opponents into exile or by charging them with treason, which often ended in the execution of his rivals. During the Korean War, Rhee pressed for a reunification of north and south (for instance, 18 June 1953) and refused to cooperate with the United Nations. Following the 1956 elections, widespread student rioting broke out that spurred a violent government reaction in which many died. After Rhee's reelection on 15 March 1960, massive demonstrations broke out accusing the regime of election-rigging. Following an incident when troops and police opened fire on the demonstrators, killing more than 125, Rhee was forced to resign on 27 April, leaving the government in the hands of a caretaker and fleeing into exile in Hawaii. Upon his death in 1965, his body was returned to Korea. Park Chung Hee (qv), the new president, was at the airport for Rhee's return. *Reading:* Robert Oliver, *Syngman Rhee: The Man Behind the Myth* (1973); Q. Y. Kim, *The Fall of Syngman Rhee* (1983).

Rhein-Main Airport. On 19 June 1985, West Germany's Rhein-Main airport was bombed. Four were killed and 60 injured in the attack. At least a half-dozen terrorist organizations claimed credit for the attack.

Rhein-Main US Air Force Base. On 1 December 1976, the Officer's Club building at the Rhein-Main U.S. Air Force Base in West Germany was bombed. The Revolutionary Cells (RZ) (qv) claimed responsibility for the attack that injured 18, including nine Americans. On 7 August 1985, an American serviceman (Edward Pimental) was shot and killed in Wiesbaden, West Germany, by Red Army Faction (qv) terrorists, most likely to get his military identification (ID) card. With the card, terrorists entered the U.S. air base at Rhein-Main and detonated a car bomb on 8 August. Two US service personnel were killed and 20 others injured. The terrorists then sent a communique and the ID card to a news agency.

Rhodesia. *See* Zimbabwe.

Riadh (Riad), Mohammad Abdul (Abdel) Moneim. (b. 22 October 1919, Tanta, Egypt—d. 9 March 1969, Suez Canal Zone) On 30 May 1967, six days before the beginning of the 1967 Arab-Israeli War, Egyptian general Abdul Moneim Riadh took command of the Jordanian Army (general chief of staff of the joint military command of the UAR and Jordan) at the demand of President Nasser of Egypt. Riadh later (June 1967) became the army chief of staff of the United Arab Republic. In July 1967, he headed a military delegation to Moscow. On 9 March 1969, however, Riadh was killed while observing an artillery duel between Egyptian and Israeli forces along the Suez Canal.

Ricardo Franco Front of the Revolutionary Armed Forces of Colombia (*Frente Ricardo Franco*) (RFF). In March 1984, the RFF separated itself from the Revolution Armed Forces of Columbia (FARC) terrorist group and set up its headquarters in Valle del Cauca province near Bogota. The leader of the group was Jose Fedor Alvarez (aka Javier Delgado). The RFF members' disaffection with FARC came after FARC made a truce agreement with the Colombian government, and skirmishes between FARC and RFF forces were not uncommon. RFF began its terrorist activities in May 1984 with the bombing of a Honduran airlines office and another attack on a U.S. diplomatic facility. Thereafter it staged numerous attacks, often on US facilities and personnel. In December 1985, a bloody purge took place within the RFF, which led to the isolation of RFF among the other rebel groups operating in Colombia. Thereafter, RFF fell to banditry rather than political terrorism.

el-Rifai, Samir. On 9 February 1956, Samir el-Rafai, the new premier of Jordan, denounced the Baghdad Pact and stated that Arab unity was the cornerstone of his nation's security. On 21 May 1956, Rifai resigned his office and was replaced by Said el-Mufti, who immediately moved to restore the Anglo-Jordanian defence treaty. *See* Jordan.

Rif (*Riffi*). Berber tribesmen who occupied that region in northeastern Morocco are known as the Rif. There are 19 tribes among the Rif, most of whom speak Arabic, although the Rif language is dominant in many areas. All Rifs are Muslim. A nomadic people, the Rif were autonomous until 1912, when the Treaty of Fez put the Rif territory and that of the neighboring Jibala tribes under Spanish dominion. The Spaniards attempted to pacify the Rif and Jibala tribes but, in the case of the Rifs, suffered a crushing defeat at Melilla. There followed five years of bloody conflict (1919–1926). In 1925 the French entered the stuggle against the Rif, forcing their surrender in 1926. In 1958, Rif tribesmen rose up to join rebel Moroccan troops loyal to King Mohammed V (qv) (*see also* Morocco). The Rif continued this fight until 1960, but they were dealt a series of defeats in 1959 by the *Istiqlal* Party (qv) central government forces. The uprising was finally quelled in April 1960.

Rio de Janeiro. *See* Brazil.

Rios Montt, Efrain. On 22 March 1982, a military coup toppled the government of Guatamala's president Fernando Romeo Lucas Garcia. The junta then asked General Efrain Rios Montt, who apparently had no part in the coup, to take power. Rios Montt assumed the presidency, suspended the constiotution, and banned all political activity in the country. He lifted the state of siege on 21 March 1983, but extended the ban on all political activities, strikes, public assemblies, labor organizations and news about rebel activities. His government was in turn overthrown in another military coup on 8 August 1983.

Rio Treaty. On 16 March 1954, the United States declared that the NATO (qv) and Rio treaties authorized immediate retaliation, if the U.S. or one of its Western or hemispheric allies was attacked. The Rio treaty referred to was accomplished at the Inter-American Conference for the Maintenance of Continental Peace and Security held in Quitandinha, Brazil, 15 August–2 September 1947. The Treaty for Reciprocal Assistance (the "Rio Treaty") was signed in Rio de Janeiro at the close of the conference and stipulated the principle that an attack upon one American state was an attack on all.

Rithisen. *See* Kampuchea/Cambodia.

Riyadh. *See* Saudi Arabia.

Roberts, Hastings. On 3 January 1964, the Angolan "government-in-exile" headed by Hastings Roberts and based in Leopoldville in the Democratic Republic of Congo announced that it had decided to accept aid from Communist China and other communist countries. *See* Zaire.

Rockwell International. On 28 August 1976, three American officials of Rockwell International were assassinated by terrorists in Tehran, Iran. The People's Strugglers group, an anti-Iranian government terrorist group, claimed responsibility for the attack. The group also murdered two American military officers in 1975. On 3 September 1976, Iranian authorities discovered a People's Strugglers cell and reportedly killed one of the assassins in the Rockwell incident.

Rodriguez Lara, Guillermo. On 15 February 1972, the government of President Jose Maria Velasco Ibarra (qv) of Ecuador was overthrown in a military coup. This was the fourth time in five terms as president that Velasco Ibarra had been turned out by the military. Brigadier General Guillermo Rodriguez Lara became president. On 1 September 1973, a right-wing coup attempt, led by General Raul Gonzalez Alvear, was crushed by loyal troops. About 18 were killed and 80 injured in fighting around the government palace in Quito. Rodriquez Lara was replaced following a bloodless coup on 11 January 1976.

Rohan, Michael. On 22 August 1969, Michael Rohan, an Australian Christian, was arrested in Israel and charged with arson in the fire that damaged the Muslim Al Aqsa Mosque in the Old City of Jerusalem (21 August).

Roidoab. *See* Afghanistan.

Rojas Pinilla, Gustavo. On 13 June 1953, the Colombian government of President Laureano Gómez (qv) was overthrown by a military junta led by Lieutenant General Gustavo Rojas Pinilla, the chief of the armed forces. Instead of keeping the promises he made at the time of his elevation as head of state, Rojas imposed his own dictatorship. On 10 May 1957, Rojas was forced to resign in favor of a junta that was to oversee a popular election of a new government. Rojas's resignation came after the Roman Catholic church accused him of authorizing murder in the suppression of student riots against his oppressive regime.

Roldós Aguilera, Jaime. (b. 5 November 1940, Guayaquil, Ecuador—d. 24 May 1981, Andes Mountains) A left-of-center candidate, Roldós became president of Ecuador in a runoff election (29 April 1979) on 10 August 1979, following a period of rule by a military junta. Upon his election he renounced many of his election pledges, and his term in office was stormy. Roldós, his wife and his defense minister were killed in an air crash in the Andes on 24 May 1981.

Rolovic, Vladimir. On 7 April 1971, two Croatian terrorists entered the Yugoslavian embassy in Stockholm on the pretext of applying for passports. They proceeded to shoot the Yugoslav ambassador to Sweden, Vladimir Rolovic, and another Yugoslav. Rolovic, who was shot three times, later died of his wounds.

Romani. *See* Jordan.

Romania. The Republic of Romania is located on the lower Danube River in southeastern Europe, or the Balkans. The Black Sea is on the east, Bulgaria on the south, Hungary and Serbia on the west, Ukraine on the north and Moldova on the northeast. The capital is Bucharest. Romania's name came into existence in 1862, following the 1859 unification of the provinces of Wallachia and Moldavia. Inhabited since prehistoric times by Illyrian people, the area soon became known as Dacia (Dach'). Dacian tribesmen were decisively defeated by the Roman emperor Trajan at Adamclissi in 106 A.D. For almost two centuries, what today is Romania was the Roman province of Dacia. During that period the Romanian language developed from the original native tongue, formalized with Latin. Rome abandoned the province in the third century, and Romania began to develop its tradition of being the crossroads of Europe as succeeding waves of Goths, Slavs and Bulgars crossed and recrossed the land. Transylvania, the northwestern region of Romania was occupied by the Hungarians in the eleventh century. Thereafter known as the Danubian Principalities, Wallachia and Moldavia developed individual identities in thirteenth and fourteen centuries and had just begun their emergence when the Ottoman Turks invaded the lands in the fifteenth century. The Romanians fought bravely and stubbornly and on occasion were successful in defeating the Turks, but never for long. In 1711, the Sublime Porte assigned Phanariot Greeks to govern the region. Their rule lasted until 1821, when a revolt led by Tudor Vladimrescu succeeded in breaking the Phanariot hold even though it did not liberate Romania from Ottoman control. In 1828, Romania was occupied by Russian forces during the Russo-Turkish War of that period. The Romanians quickly learned there was as much to despise about the Russians as about the Turks. In 1848, uprisings began in all three principalities, but all failed. In 1856, the Great Powers of Europe recognized the principalities of Wallachia and Moldavia as autonomous under Ottoman suzerainty. In 1862, the hospodar Alexandru Cuza was recognized as the leader of a now unified Romania. Transylvania was firmly under Austro-

Hungarian control. In 1866, Cuza was replaced by Carol I of Hohenzollern-Sigmaringen, who led his newfound people to their independence during the Russo-Turkish War of 1877–1878. Romanian troops saved Russia from a defeat at Grivitsa (Pleven, Bulgaria) that would have brought more misery to the Romanian homeland. When Russia, in the aftermath of the war, fundamentally occupied Romania and threatened to disarm the Romanian army, Prince Carol stated that the army that fought at Grivitsa could be defeated, but it would not be disarmed. The Congress of Berlin eventually gave Romania its independence. Prince Carol was crowned king and led his country over the next 35 years to begin its industrial development, especially in the production of oil. Romania fought in the Second Balkan War in 1913. Upon Carol I's death in 1914, his nephew Ferdinand became king. Romania's participation in World War I (after 1916) on the Allied side brought Transylvania and two other regions, Banat and Bukovina, under Romanian control as a result of the peace settlement. Thereafter, Romania became active in international affairs and joined the League of Nations and the Little Entente. The latter was a defense agreement among Romania, Czechoslovakia and Yugoslavia to maintain the status quo in the region. After 1938, a royal dictatorship was established in Romania, which lasted until 1940 when King Carol II was overthrown by the Iron Guard, a right-wing fascist group under General Ion Antonescu (qv). At the same time, Romania was forced to cede northern Transylvania to Hungary, southern Dobruja to Bulgaria, and Bukovina and Bessarabia to the Soviet Union. Romania then joined Germany in its invasion of the Soviet Union. Romania's near defeat and the threat of a Soviet invasion forced King Michael and the army to overthrow Antonescu in August 1944. Romania then joined the Allies but, with the help of the Romanian Communist Party, lost Bessarabia again to the Soviet Union. In March 1945, a Soviet-dominated puppet government was installed (19 December 1946). On 17 May 1946, Antonescu had been sentenced to death by a Romanian tribunal. The U.S. Senate ratified the peace treaty with Romania on 5 June 1947. Also, on 30 December 1947, King Michael was forced to abdicate, the monarchy was abolished in the name of a "people's republic" and Communist Party chief Gheorghe Ghiorgiu-Dej (qv) became the country's leader. Industry was nationalized, political opposition suppressed and agriculture collectivized. After 1950, however, Romania began to set its own policy, often at odds with Soviet dictates and desires, and, in 1964, substantially declared its self-determination. On 14 May 1955, Romania did join the Warsaw Pact (qv), and on 12 August 1955, the government announced that Soviet troops would remain in Romania until all Allied forces were withdrawn from Europe; this was reversed, however, on 27 May 1958, when the Soviet Union announced it was ready to withdraw its forces. (Withdrawal completed on 26 July 1958.) Romania had already signed an economic agreement with Communist China, in January 1956. On 27 September 1960, Ghiorghiu-Dej, in a speech before the United Nations, put forward the possibility of a nuclear-free neutral buffer zone between east and west, which was to have included Romania, Hungary, Bulgaria, Albania, Yugoslavia, Greece and Turkey. In 1965 Nicolae Ceaucescu (qv) took control of the country and established a highly nationalistic form of government within the socialist order, but one punctuated with suppression of civil liberties and economic mismanagement. The Soviet Union also forced Romania to tone down its demands for changes in the Warsaw Pact (10 May 1966). However, on 4–6 July 1966, Ceaucescu proposed that both the Warsaw Pact and NATO be abolished and that all troops be withdrawn from all foreign soil everywhere. Romania did not participate in the Czech invasion of 20–21 August 1968, and probably was not even informed of the plan until the movement had begun. Ceaucescu and Yugoslavia's Tito (qv) openly denounced the so-called Brezhnev Doctrine at a meeting on 1–2 February 1969. On 23 June 1969, Romania opened formal diplomatic relations with Communist China. But, on 27 November 1969, Romania openly defied Moscow by refusing to allocate troops to a Warsaw Pact contigency plan to support Arabs in future wars against Israel. Romania again refused to do Moscow's bidding when it balked at the integration of its army into a single Warsaw Pact organization and, at the same time, refused to increase its payment to the Warsaw Pact. Strikes broke out in the coal-mining region of Jiu in October 1981 over the imposition of bread rationing and a general shortage of food. In December 1989, anti-Ceaucescu rioting broke out in Timisoara and quickly spread to other cities, erupting into a revolution. In Bucharest, heavy fighting occurred, especially against the secret police organization (*Securitati*). The upshot of the fight was the overthrow of the regime, the arrest and execution of Ceaucescu and members of his family and the establishment of a new government. Romania, however, still suffers from the excesses of the old regime; in 1995 it was moving forward, albeit slowly. *Reading*: Thomas Carothers, *Assessing Democracy Assistance: The Case of Romania* (1996); Georges Castellan, *A History of the Romanians* (1989); Mark Sanborne, *Romania* (1996).

Rome. *See* Italy. *See also* The Vatican.

Romero, Carlos Humberto. *See* El Salvador.

Romero y Galdamez, Oscar Arnulfo. (b. 15 August 1917, Ciudad Barrios, El Salvador—d. 24 March 1980, San Salvador) Catholic Archbishop Oscar Arnulfo Romero y Galdamez, an outspoken critic of the repression by the dictator of El Salvador, General Carlos Humberto Romero (no relation) (qv), was assassinated while saying Mass. In 1979, he had been nominated for the Nobel peace prize. No one was charged in the murder.

Roopkachorn, Manoon. On 8 September 1985, about 500 soldiers supported by 22 tanks proclaimed that the Revolutionary Party had seized the government in Thailand. After only eight hours, however, the abortive coup was over; five people, including two foreign newsmen, were dead; and the rebel leader, ex-Colonel Manoon Roopkachorn, was negotiating for safe passage out of the country. Roopkachorn had attempted an earlier coup in 1981 and had been cashiered for it. The U.S. refused asylum for him, and he ended up in West Germany.

Rosario. *See* Argentina.

Rosario Chruch. *See* El Salvador.

Rosenberg, Ethel (née Greenglass). (b. 28 September 1915, New York City—d. 19 June 1953, Ossining, New York) The first U.S. female civilian executed for espionage. The collapse of the Soviet Union and the subsequent opening of many of its secret records brought forth evidence the Ethel may have been innocent of all charges brought against her. *See* Rosenberg, Julius.

Rosenberg, Julius. (b. 12 May 1918, New York City—d.19 June 1953, Ossining, New York) Rosenberg was a Communist Party member even before receiving his degree in electrical engineering in 1939. He became an engineer in the U.S. Army Signal Corps in 1940 and, along with his wife Ethel (qv), he began spying for the Soviet Union by turning over to them classified information in his possession. During World War II, Ethel's brother, U.S. army sergeant David Greenglass, was assigned as a machinist to the Manhattan Project at Los Alamos, New Mexico. From this vantage point, Greenglass turned over atomic bomb secrets to the Rosenbergs, which were subsequently transferred to Harry Gold, a courier for Soviet espionage operations in the United States. The Swiss-born Gold's contact was Anatoly A. Yakovlev, the Soviet vice consul in New York City. When the Klaus Fuchs spying affair was exposed in Great Britain, Gold was arrested. The Rosenbergs and Glass were subsequently arrested and charged with espionage. Another member of the ring, Morton Sobell, was able to flee to Mexico, but he was caught and extradited back to the United States where he also stood trial. David Greenglass turned state's evidence and was sentenced to the comparatively light term of 15 years. Gold and Sobell were given 30 years each. The Rosenbergs were brought to trial on 6 March 1951 and were found guilty under the 1917 Espionage Act and sentenced to death. There followed a worldwide demand for clemency, but on 19 June 1953, Julius and Ethel Rosenberg were executed at Sing Sing Prison, Ossining, New York. They were the first two U.S. civilians ever executed for espionage in the United States. *Reading:* Marjorie Garber et al., ed., *Secret Agents: The Rosenberg Case, McCarthyism, and Fifties America* (1995); Joseph Sharlitt, *Fatal Error: The Miscarriage of Justice That Sealed the Rosenbergs' Fate* (1989).

Rota. *See* Spain.

Roxas, Manuel y Acuña. (b. 1 January 1892, Capiz, Philippines—d. 16 April 1948, Clark Field, Philippines) Roxas was educated at the University of the Philippines and entered politics in 1917. He served as governor of Capiz province from 1919 to 1921. In 1922, he became speaker of the Philippine House of Representatives. He held that post until 1934, except for the period when he and Manuel Quezon, the president of the Senate, resigned in protest against a US governor's veto of legislation passed by the Philippine legislature. In 1932, Roxas, along with Sergio Osmena, led the Philippine independence delegation to Washington. In 1938 President Luis Quezon Molina appointed Roxas secretary of finance. When the Philippines were invaded by Japan at the start of World War II, Roxas joined the staff of Douglas MacArthur (qv) and participated in the unsuccessful defense of his country. Roxas joined in the work of the Japanese puppet government of Jose Laurel that followed, but he was cleared of collaboration charges after the war, mostly through the intervention of his friend Douglas MacArthur. He was elected president of the Philippine Commonwealth on 23 April 1946, and when the Philippines achieved their independence, on 4 July 1946, he became its first president. In 1947, his government began a campaign to subdue the communist-inspired Hukbalahap peasant uprising in Central Luzon. Throughout his time in office he advocated strong ties with the United States, although he was often perturbed by U.S. demands placed upon his government.

Rubayyi, Salem Ali. On 22 June 1969, a bloodless coup forced the resignation of the government of President Qahtan al-Shaabi of South Yemen. A leftist-oriented five-man Presidential Council led by Salem Ali Rubayyi took control of the government. On 26 June 1978, a pro-Soviet coup, led by the National Liberation Front, overthrew Rubayyi. He was subsequently captured and executed by a firing squad in Aden. Rubayyi's overthrow came about after he attempted to arrest Abd-al Fattah Ismail, the leader of the United Political Organization, for the assassination of North Yemen president Ahmad al-Ghasmi in Beirut on 24 June. Ismail's Cuban-trained militia was able to move before the arrest and topple the Rubayyi regime.

Ruby, Jack. (b.1911—d.3 January 1967, Dallas) Ruby, a Dallas nightclub owner shot and killed Lee Harvey Oswald, the accused assassin of President John F. Kennedy (qv) in the basement of the Dallas jail in front of millions of TV viewers. Ruby claimed his actions were prompted by anguish and rage over Kennedy's death. Ruby was tried and sentenced to death for the murder on 14 March 1964. His appeals led to a reversal of the conviction, and a new trial was ordered. Ruby died of complications of cancer before he could be retried. The circumstances of Ruby's access to Oswald have never been clearly established, but the Warren Commission claimed that Ruby's crime was not part of any conspiracy. Ruby was later linked to Meyer Lansky, a powerful crime syndicate leader.

Ruhr River. *See* Germany.

Rung Sat. *See* Vietnam.

Rupley, Joseph R. *See* Peace Corps.

Rupununi District. *See* Guyana.

Rusk, (David) Dean. (b. 9 February 1909, Cherokee County, Georgia—d.20 December, Athens, Georgia) Rusk graduated from Davidson College in 1931. A Rhodes scholar, he received his master's degree at St. John's College, Oxford. Rusk then taught political science at Mills College, Oakland, California, from 1934 to 1940. During World War II, Rusk served in the China, Burma, India (CBI) theater on the staff of Lieutenant General Joseph W. Stilwell. After the war, Rusk served both in the War Department as special assistance to the secretary (1946) and in the State Department as director of the Office of Special Political Affairs (1947), director of the Office of United Nations Affairs (1948), first assistant secretary of state for United Nations affairs (1949) and deputy undersecretary of state (1949). In March 1950, he became assistant secretary of state for Far Eastern affairs, which involved him in the conduct of the Korean War. In that capacity, Rush argued against Douglas MacArthur's (qv) plan to expand the war. From 1952 until 1960, Rusk served as the president of the Rockefeller Foundation. With the inauguration of John F. Kennedy (qv) as president, Rush was appointed secretary of state and remained in that office after Kennedy's assassination. In the administration of Lyndon B. Johnson (qv), Rusk became a strong supporter of the Vietnam policy and opposed normalization of relations with Communist China. On 12 May 1964, he formally asked NATO for greater support in the war in Southeast Asia and, in March 1965, fought vigorously against allegations that the U.S. was carrying out "gas warfare" in Vietnam. He retired from office in January 1969 and became a professor of international law at the University of Georgia (1970). He retired in 1984 and died quietly in 1994.

Russia. *See* Union of Soviet Socialist Republics.

Rwanda (Ruanda, *Republique Rwandaise, Republika Y'u Rwanda*). The Republic of Rwanda is a landlocked nation located just below the Equator in east-central Africa. It is bounded on the north by Uganda, on the east by Tanzania, on the south by Burundi and on the west by Zaire and Lake Kivu. The capital city is Kigali. By the fourteenth century, three tribes had occupied Rwanda: the pygmy Twa, the Hutu, and the Tutsi. By the fifteenth century, the Tutsi had established dominance. Several Tutsi kingdoms sprang up, which were absorbed over time, until, by the nineteenth century, most of the region was incorporated into the Rwanda kingdom of Kigeri Rwabugiri. By the twentieth century, the lands of Rwanda were essentially as they are seen today. In 1890, Germany established Rwanda as a part of German East Africa, but their domination was lost during World War I when, in 1916, Belgian forces occupied the country without resistance. The League of Nations established Ruanda-Urundi as a Belgian mandate in 1923. Belgian control was maintained through Tutsi kings, who maintained a dominance over the Hutu and limited their inclusion in the government. Belgium attempted to impose a more democratic environment in Rwanda, but this eventually caused a massive Hutu (Bahutu) uprising that led to civil war (November 1959). The Tutsi king (*mwami*) Kigeri V and thousands of other Tutsi were forced to flee into exile. On 1 July 1962, Rwanda was declared an independent republic with a Hutu leadership. Many thousands of Tutsi again had to flee the country. Beginning in 1963, Tutsi rebel raiding parties, operating from bases in Burundi, began attacking Hutu government installations along the Rwanda-Burundi border. Fighting lasted for four years until 20 March 1967, when a Rwandan-Burundi reconciliation took place. A Hutu uprising began on 15 February 1973, which flamed a new civil war (1 March). A bloodless military coup (5 July 1973), led by Major General Juvenal Habyarlimana (qv), overthrew the government of President Gregoire Kayibanda (qv), promising an end to the tribal conflict. Hutu domination continued, and the Tutsi continued to suffer. A new constitution was introduced in 1981, and an elected legislative body sat for the first time since 1973. A serious drought and declining coffee market worsened Rwanda's economic outlook in the late 1980s. In October 1990, rebel Tutsi forces of the Rwandan Patriotic Front (RPF) invaded Rwanda from Uganda. Negotiations to end the fighting began in 1992, and a peace accord was signed at Arusha, Tanzania, in August 1993. When extremist Hutus refused to share power, the new coalition government was not seated. Then, on 6 April 1994, Rwanda president Habyarlimana and Cyprien Ntaryamira of Burundi were killed when their aircraft was shot down near Kirgali, most likely by members of Habyarlimana's personal guard force, who opposed the unification of the tribes. The next day, the acting prime minister, and a number of other moderate Hutu politicians were murdered. During the months that followed, extremist elements in the military and police killed an estimated half-million civilians, most Tutsis. Hundreds of thousands of civilians were forced to flee into neighboring countries, with at least half of them going into Zaire. French and other troops were inserted to help keep order and to give humanitarian aid. In July 1994, a cease-fire was declared and an RPF victory declared. The French pulled out in August. There were an estimated two million Rwandans in exile. In 1995, a number of relief organization stated they would work to stop all of the aid effort unless justice was meted out to those guilty of genocide. The UN established a criminal tribunal in Tanzania to hear cases of genocide brought before the court. *Reading:* Alain Destezhe, *Rwanda and Genocide in the Twentieth Century* (1996); *Gerard Prunier, The Rwanda Crisis: History of a Genocide* (1995); Fergal Keane, *Season of Blood: A Rwandan Journey* (1996); Catherine Newbury, The *Cohesion of Oppression: Clientship and Ethnicity in Rwanda, 1860-1960* (1993).

Ryan, Jose Maria. On 29 January 1981, Basque terrorists of the Homeland and Liberty (*Euzkadi za Azkatasuna*) (ETA) (qv) separatist group operating in Spain kidnapped Jose Maria Ryan, the chief nuclear engineer at the Lemóniz nuclear power station and, on 6 February, murdered him. This precipitated a general strike throughout Spain protesting his death. The murder followed by one day the three-day visit of King Juan Carlos (qv) to the Basque region of Spain.

Ryan, Leo. *See* People's Temple Cult.

Ryti, Risto. On 21 February 1946, former Finnish president Risto Ryti and a number of other former national leaders were sentenced to prison for their parts in bringing Finland into World War II as an ally of Nazi Germany. The Ryti government had held power from late 1939 until October 1944.

Ryukyu Islands (*Nansei-Shoto, Ryukyu-Shoto*). The group of islands forming this archipelago are better known by their native Ryukyuan name of Okinawa. The group extends from the southernmost point of Kyushu in the Japanese home islands to the northern tip of Taiwan (Formosa). There are about 55 islands in the archipelago, with Okinawa itself being found in the center subgroup. The islands have been occupied since prehistoric times by immigrants from Japan and from the Southeast Asian mainland. Although the languages are unintelligible to each other, Ryukyuan and Japanese are cataloged together. Japanese is spoken as the everyday tongue in the modern Ryukyus. At one time, the archipelago formed a separate kingdom but, from the fourteenth to the nineteenth century, Chinese and Japanese overlordship was common. In 1879, the Ryukyus were annexed by Japan. The United States took control of the islands following World War II and maintained a military government until 1951. In that year, a civil administration was established in Naha, on Okinawa, which was the capital of all the islands. One reason for that change was the rising voices of opposition in Japan, who wanted both the Ryukyus and the Soviet-held Kuriles returned to their control. A U.S. high commissioner appointed the executives of the government until 1966, when the islands' legislature elected the chief executive. In 1968, the chief executive came to be elected by popular vote. The peace treaty ending the war with Japan was signed in 1952. Under its terms, the U.S. recognized Japan's sovereignty over the islands and returned the northern group (*Amani*) in 1953. As a result of negotiations a new agreement was concluded in 1971, and the central (Okinawa) and southern (*Saki Shima*) groups were turned over to Japan in 1972. By that treaty's terms, the U.S. was allowed to maintain almost 90 military installations in the group, along with thousands of U.S. military forces. Resentment of the U.S. presence in the Ryukyus has been growing and was made into an even a larger issue by the September 1995 rape of a Okinawan child by three US servicemen. On 7 March 1996, all three men were convicted, two with sentences of seven years and one with six and one-half years, but feeling still ran high over the incident. *Reading:* Frederick L. Shiels, *America, Okinawa, and Japan: Case Studies for Foreign Policy Theory* (1980).

S

Saang. *See* Cambodia.

Saar Region (Saarland). *See* Germany.

Saba District. *See* Borneo.

Sabah Province, British North Borneo. *See* Borneo.

Sabha, Sinai. *See* Egypt and Israel.

Sabra Camp, Lebanon. On 16 September 1982, a massacre of Palestinians took place in two refugee camps at Sabra and Shatila, near Beirut. At first the Israelis were accused of the atrocity, but it was soon discovered that Lebanese Christian militiamen were actually to blame. In all, over 600 men, women and children were slaughtered in the attacks. In Israel, however, a major scandal erupted over the handling of the entire affair. The two camps, and one at *Burj al-Brajneh*, were attacked by Shi'ite Amal militia on 20 May 1985. The Amal captured the camps on 31 May.

Sabri (Sabry), Ali. On 2 May 1971, President Anwar Sadat (qv) dismissed the vice-president, Ali Sabri, from office. Sabri, a leftist and pro-Soviet, opposed Sadat in many of his programs. Sabry and 90 others were put on trial on 25 August before a special tribunal chosen by Sadat. The trial was postponed when defense lawyers claimed the proceedings were unconstitutional (4 September). On 9 December 1971, the trial ended when Sabri and three others were sentenced to death for treason. However, President Sadat commuted the sentences to life imprisonment.

Sa'dah. *See* Yemen.

el (as) Sadat, Muhammad Anwar. (b. 25 December 1918, Mit Abu al Kom, Nile Delta, Egypt—d. 6 October 1981, Cairo) Sadat graduated from the Royal Military Academy in Cairo in 1938. Thereafter, he joined a dissident group of officers in a secret organization dedicated to freeing Egypt of British rule. He was several times arrested and jailed between 1942 and 1948. While in the dissident organization, Sadat became a close associate of Gamal Abdul Nasser (qv). Following the 1952 revolution (*see* Egypt), Sadat moved through the ranks to become vice president in 1964. After Nasser's death (1970), Sadat was given the presidency by the National Assembly (7 October 1970) and was formally sworn in on 14 October. On 29 December 1970, Sadat ordered a state of war-readiness as Arab guerrillas in Jordan, Lebanon and Syria stepped up terrorist attacks against Israel. As the Suez crisis continued, negotiations between Egypt and Israel over reopening the canal and an Israeli withdrawal from its east bank (since 1967) broke down. On 7 March 1971, Sadat declared that the cease-fire would not be extended. Clashes between Egyptian and Israeli forces on the ground and in the air became more frequent even though negotiators did attempt a peaceful solution. In May, Sadat dismissed Ali Sabri (qv), his vice president. Later that month, Sadat reported his government had foiled a coup attempt. On 28 May 1971, Sadat signed a 15-year Treaty of Friendship and Cooperation with the USSR. Sadat was selected to be the first president of the new Federation of Arab Republics on 4 October 1971. Later that month he paid a three-day state visit to Moscow, and on 1 November he took personal command of Egypt's armed forces and notified his troops that the war with Israel was "at hand." He would later claim (13 January 1972) that the Indo-Pakistani War (qv) had clouded the Arab-Israeli issue. During a May 1972 visit to Moscow, Sadat was promised additional military aid. In July 1972, Sadat expelled some 20,000 Soviet technicans and advisers because of the threat he perceived in their possible value in a pro-Communist coup attempt. On 27 July 1972, Sadat refused an offer of direct peace negotiations with Israel's Golda Meir (qv). In March 1973, Sadat fired his prime minister and assumed the role himself. On 6 October 1973, however, following a November 1972 decision to do so, Sadat launched an attack against Israel that culminated in the defeat of Egypt, even though Egyptians treated it as a victory. (This war followed a secret meeting in Cairo between Sadat and Hafez Assad of Syria on 12 September that fixed the date for the start of hostilities.) (*See* Egypt, Israel and Arab-Israeli Wars.) In January 1975, Sadat complained that the USSR had failed to replace Egyptian arms lost in the 1973 war and on 29 January he announced a $2.2 billion arms deal with France. Thereafter, Sadat worked for peace with Israel. In 1977 he flew to Jerusalem to open negotiations. In November of 1978, Sadat refused to meet with Arab League representatives who were prepared to offer him $50 billion in aid if he would break off peace talks with Israel. He and Israeli Prime Minister Menachem Begin (qv) were jointly awarded the Nobel peace prize (1978) for their endeavors in what became known as the Camp David Accords; on 29 March 1979, Sadat signed the Egyptian-Israeli peace treaty in Washington, DC. This isolated Sadat and Egypt from the rest of the Arab world and generated considerable unrest within Egypt. Sadat did offer military aid to Morocco in its fight against the Popular Front for the Liberation of Saquia el Hamra and Rio de Ore (Polisario) (qv) in September 1979. Some 1,600 dissidents were arrested, mostly Islamic fundamentalists, as a result of the unrest in Egypt (September 1981). On 6 October 1981, Sadat was assassinated while viewing a parade. The five killers, all members of the Egyptian army, were Islamic fundamentalist fanatics; they were executed on 15 April 1982. Muhammad Hosni Mubarak (qv) was sworn in as president of Egypt immediately after the Sadat assassination. *Reading:* Raphael Israeli, *Man of Defiance: A Political Biography of Anwar Sadat* (1985); Arthur Diamond, *The Importance of Anwar Sadat* (1994).

Sadek, Muhammad. On 28 October 1972, General Muhammad Sadek, Egypt's minister of war and commander in chief of the armed forces, resigned in protest of President Anwar Sadat's (qv) attempts at reconciliation with the Soviet Union. Sadek was immediately replaced by General Ahmed Ismail (qv). *See* Egypt.

Sadr, Imam Musa (Moussa). On 19 January 1980, a teenage Lebanese Shi'ite Muslim hijacked a Lebanese airliner over the Mediterranean and demanded to be told the whereabouts of Imam Musa Sadr, who had disappeared in 1978. The incident ended when the hijacker was arrested at the Beirut airport. Musa was the 1975 founder of the Lebanese Shi'ite paramilitary group, Amal. Musa had opposed the PLO and vanished on a visit to Libya (qv). *Reading:* Fouad Ajami, *The Vanishing Imam: Musa al Sadr and the Shia of Lebanon* (1986).

Saf. *See* Afghanistan.

Safad (*Zefat*). *See* Israel.

Safwat, Ismail. An Iraqi general, Ismail Safwat was suspected of being the leader of the Arab Liberation Army (ALA) (qv), which operated out of Syria against Jewish settlements in Palestine in 1948.

Saharan Arab Democratic Republic (SADR). *See* Popular Front for the Liberation of Saquia el Hamra and Rio de Ore (Polisario).

Sahel Subprovince. *See* Ethiopia.

Sa Huynh. *See* Vietnam.

Saida. *See* Lebanon.

Sa'id bin Taimur. On 23 July 1970, Sultan Sa'id bin Taimur of Muscat and Oman was overthrown by his son, Prince Qabus bin Said, in a palace coup at Salalah. The coup was led by the palace guard. Sa'id bin Taimur was slightly injured in the struggle and was flown to Great Britain for treatment. The new leader promised to bring his country out of the medieval repression that had been Sa'id's policy and to modernize the country.

Saigon (Ho Chi Minh City). *See* Vietnam.

Saint Christopher (Kitts) Island. An island group in the Leeward Islands of the Lesser Antilles located in the eastern Caribbean. The capital is Basseterre. First explored by Christopher Columbus in 1493, the islands of St. Christopher, known as Liamuga, and St. Nevis were settled by the British in 1623. British title to the islands was disputed by France until 1713. In the late nineteenth century, the islands belonged to the Leeward Islands Federation from 1871 to 1956 and to the Federation of the West Indies from 1958 until 1962. In 1967, they were granted self-government as an associated state and received their complete independence as members of the British Commonwealth on 19 September 1983, as the Federation of Saint Kitts and Nevis.

Sainte Jean Baptiste Day. On 24 June 1969, what began as a peaceful parade, celebrating St. Jean Baptiste Day, turned into a bloody riot in Montreal, Canada.

Saint Paul's Mission. A site thirty-five miles from Salisbury, Rhodesia, St. Paul's Mission was the site where, on 6 February 1977, seven Catholic missionaries were murdered by black terrorist guerrillas.

al-Saiqah (al-Sai'ga). One of five terrorist groups protected by the Palestine Liberation Organization (PLO) (qv) was al-Saiqah. On 5 August 1975, Israeli forces operating against Lebanon carried out an amphibious and air attack that centered on an assault on a Syrian-operated base used by al-Saiqah guerrillas. At least 16 Arabs were killed in the attack. In another incident, four members of this group, also known as the "Red Eagles of the Palestinian Revolution," seized the Egyptian Embassy in Ankara, Turkey, on 13 July 1979, killing at least two police officers while gaining their entry and two security personnel inside the building. Twenty people were taken hostage, including the ambassador. The terrorists demanded that Egypt renounce its rapprochement with Israel, that two Palestinians held in Turkey be freed, that Turkey break diplomatic relations with Egypt and that Palestine be recognized. The PLO helped during the two days of negotiations that followed in dealing with the terrorists. One hostage was freed, and four others escaped during the siege. In the end, the terrorists released the remainder of their hostages and were arrested. Turkey did grant the PLO permission to open an office with diplomatic status in the capital (27 September 1979), even though there was some information that the entire affair was staged by the PLO itself.

Sakhalin Island. *See* Soviet Union.

Sakharov, Andrei D. On 22 January 1980, the Soviet Presidium stripped physicist Andrei D. Sakharov, the 1975 recipient of the Nobel peace prize, of his Soviet honors and decorations and exiled him to the city of Gorky in retaliation for his outspoken condemnation of the Soviet intervention in Afghanistan. In Gorky, he was given an apartment without a telephone. Sakharov, who was born in 1921, was the father of the Soviet hydrogen bomb and had been a tireless fighter for human rights. He was allowed to return to Moscow in 1986, and he was elected to the Congress of People's Deputies in March 1989. Three days before his death on 14 December 1989, he called for an end to the Communist Party.

Sakiet-Sidi-Youseff. *See* Tunisia.

al-Sakka, Nazmi Mohammed. On 16 March 1983, a lone member of the terrorist group Islamic Jihad (Hizballah) (qv) attacked a US marine patrol in the Ouzai section of Beirut near Beirut Airport. The grenade that wounded five of the Marines was thrown by Nazmi Mohammad al-Sakka. Sakka and a confederate were subsequently arrested. *See* Lebanon and Islamic Jihad.

Salah, Radan. On 13 November 1981, an Organization of African Unity (OAU) peacekeeping force arrived in Chad. Seventy-two hours earlier, Colonel Radan Salah, the Libyan commander of troops in Chad had stated he was convinced that civil war would erupt once his troops were withdrawn and the OAU force attempted to maintain order. The last Libyan forces were withdrawn on 16 November. No civil war ensued.

Salah, Salah. Known to be one of the deputies to Popular Front for the Liberation of Palestine (PFLP) leader Dr. George Habash (qv), Salah Salah was believed to be with Habash when the Iraqi airliner they were thought to be aboard was forced down by Israeli jets while enroute from Beirut to Baghdad on 10 August 1973. Neither Habash nor Salah was on the plane, and both escaped capture.

al-Salal (Sallal), Abdullah. On 27 September 1962, the Free Yemeni Republic (North Yemen) was proclaimed with Colonel Abdullah al-Salal as its leader (31 October). A civil war began between pro- and anticommunist groups. Salal and his republican government were overthrown on 5 November 1967, while Salal was on a visit to Baghdad. A dissident faction led by Rahman al-Iryani led the coup. The new government sought accommodation with the royalists, but the fighting continued.

Salalah. *See* Oman.

Salam, Abdul Arif. On 8 February 1963, an air force–led coup toppled the government of Iraq. President Abdul Karim el-Kassem (qv) was killed. A pro-Nasser (qv) group led by Colonel Abdel Salam Arif took control of the country, and Arif became the de facto leader. As one of his first acts, Arif had the army begin the round-up (16 February) of Iraqi communists based on a decision to eradicate the party. On 26 May 1964, Arif signed an agreement with Egypt's Nasser establishing a joint military command to be activated in time of war (*see* United Arab Republic). After putting down a coup attempt against his brother, President Abdul Arif Salam, on 17 September 1965, General Abdul Rahman Arif (qv) seized the government for himself.

Salam, Saeb. On 25 September 1972, Lebanese prime minister Saeb Salam claimed to have reached an agreement with Palestinian guerrillas based in southern Lebanon to abide by the government's movement restrictions. *See* Lebanon.

Salan, Raoul. As France moved toward civil war in Algeria, a Committee of Public Safety was formed in the French possession on 15 May 1958, under the leadership of General Jacques Massu (qv). With this authority, the committee seized power. Facing the possibility of civil war, French president Rene Coty (qv) appointed Charles de Gaulle (qv) premier of France. On 1 June, de Gaulle announced an offer of self-determination by referendum for Algeria. This was opposed by the French Algerian community. Fighting continued as France attempted to find an accommodation agreeable to everyone. De Gaulle announced, however, that the French army had complete control of Algeria and that General Raoul Salan, the military commander there, would keep communications open with Paris. On 12 December 1958, Salan was relieved as the French representative in Algeria and replaced by Paul Delouvrier (qv). General Maurice Challe was named commander of the French forces in country. Salan was named inspector general of the French armed forces. De Gaulle visited Algeria in March 1960 and again in December of that year, but the unrest continued. On 21–22 April 1961, French army units, led by generals Maurice Challe (qv) and Salan, mutinied and seized control of Algiers. Four days later, however, most of the mutineers, including Challe, were captured by loyal French troops. Algiers was brought back under French control. Salan escaped and became the leader of the Organization of the Secret Army (*Organization de l'Armée Secréte*) (OAS). That group was organized to keep the French government from granting independence to Algeria. After independence was granted, the OAS set up Charles de Gaulle as its chief target, although it also carried out a number of other assassinations and bombings. Its several attempts on de Gaulle failed. After most of the leadership were captured, the OAS stopped its terrorist campaign. On 23 May 1962, Salan was tried in Paris by court martial and sentenced to life imprisonment.

Salang Pass Tunnel. *See* Afghanistan.

Salazar, Antonio de Oliviera. (b. 28 April 1889, Vimiero, Portugal—d. 27 July 1970, Lisbon) Born the son of an estate manager, Antonio Salazar was educated in a seminary before attending the University of Coimbra. Taking a degree in law in 1914, he became a professor of economics. He helped found the Catholic Center Party in 1921 and was subsequently elected to Parliament (*Cortez*). He remained in Parliament for only one session before resigning and returning to the university. Following the army coup that overthrew Portugal's parliamentary government in May 1926, Salazar refused the office of minister of finance, because the junta would not accept his terms. Again offered the office in 1928, this time with guarantees of autonomy, Salazar accepted and, within a relatively short period, reversed the deeply imbedded system of economic chaos traditional in Portugal. Salazar was named prime minister in July 1932. He drafted and pushed through a new constitution that established an authoritarian government (*Estado Novo*) in the country. A period of suppression of opposition began in Portugal. During the period encompassing the Spanish Civil War and World War II (1936–1944), Salazar served as his own minister of war and, until 1947, as minister of foreign affairs. He also recognized the Spanish Nationalist government of Francisco Franco (qv), his friend, in 1938; and he maintained Portuguese neutrality during World War II. In October 1945, he allowed opposition political parties for the first time in his rule, but was easily reelected in the November elections, primarily because most of the opposition boycotted the first general elections in 20 years. In 1949, he allowed Portugal membership in NATO and spent the postwar years modernizing his country. At the same time, however, he steadfastly refused to give up Portugal's African colonies, even though the rest of Europe was rapidly divesting themselves of the onus of colonial rule. On 3 January 1962, he lashed out at the U.S. and Great Britain for not supporting Portugal in the UN after Portuguese colonies on the subcontinent had been invaded by India. In September 1968, Salazar suffered a crippling stroke, which prevented him from accomplishing his duties. In his condition, he was not informed that he had been replaced in government. He died in July 1970.

Saleh, Ibrahim. On 6–8 April 1984, the Palace Republican Guard commanded by Colonel Ibrahim Saleh attempted an overthrow of the Cameroon government of President Paul Biya (qv). A two day battle in the capital city of Yaounde ensued in which more than 70 were reported killed (other estimates place the death toll at 6,000). Saleh and 34 others were tried and sentenced to death on 30 April. The executions were carried out the next day.

Salek, Mustafa Ould. On 10 July 1978, the government of Moktar Ould Daddah was overthrown in Mauritania. Lieutenant Colonel Mustafa Ould Salek took over the leadership. Apparently in response to the change in government, Polisario, which had been carrying on a guerrilla campaign for the independence of West Sahara, decided to call a unilateral cease-fire against Mauritania. On 3 June 1979, Ould Salek resigned his positions as head of state and as the leader of the junta and was replaced.

Salinas, Luis Adolfo Siles. On 27 April 1969, the president of Bolivia, Rene Ortuvo Barrientos Ortuno (qv), was killed in a helicopter crash. Vice-president Luis Adolfo Siles Salinas was immediately sworn in as president. On 26 September 1969, however, Siles and his government were overthrown by a bloodless military coup led by General Alfredo Ovando Candia (qv), who then appointed himself president.

Salisbury. *See* Rhodesia.

Sallustro, Oberdan. On 21 March 1972, the director of the Fiat plant in Argentina, Dr. Oberdan Sallustro, was kidnapped by terrorists of the People's Revolutionary Army (qv) (ERP). Sallustro was later murdered, and his body was discovered on 10 April in a Buenos Aires suburb. The same day that Sallustro's body was found, the commander of the II Army Corps, Major General Juan Carlos Sanchez, was assassinated in the town of Rosario. His death was linked to the Sallustro murder and the ERP was accused of both killings.

Salonica (*Thessaloniki*). *See* Greece.

Salt. *See* Jordan.

Samangan. *See* Afghanistan.

Samaria. *See* Israel.

Samba, Kukli. An attempted coup led by a socialist politican, Kukli Samba, on 30–31 July 1981, against the Gambian government of Sir Dawda Kaibara Jawara, failed. Jawara was in London at the time. Senegalese troops requested by Jawara were successful in restoring order but not without considerable bloodshed. When the rebel force withdrew from the city, it took 135 hostages with it. As an aftermath of this incident, talks between The Gambia and Senegal on forming a confederation were concluded on 17 December. *See* The Gambia and Senegal.

Samchok. *See* Korea (South Korea).

Samdaniya. *See* Syria.

Sameta. *See* Iraq.

Sammu (*Es Samu*). *See* Jordan.

Sam Neua Province. *See* Laos.

Sampson, Nikos. On 15 July 1974, President Makarios (qv) of Cyprus was forced to take refuge at a British military base when a Cypriot National Guard coup attempt, led by Greek Cypriot officers and abetted by the Greek military government, seized power. A Greek Cypriot newpaper publisher and former EOKA rebel leader, Nikos Sampson, was sworn in as the new president of Cyprus. That day fighting broke out between Greek and Turkish Cypriots. On 20 July, a Turkish force was landed at Kyrenia with the avowed purpose of ousting Sampson, after Turkish demands for Makarios's return were rebuffed. On 23 July 1974, Sampson resigned (or was ousted) after the National Guard made his retaining his post impossible. He was then succeeded by Glakos Clerides.

Samsonith, Tiao. On 9 August 1960, the government of Tiao Samsonith was overthrown in Vientiane, Laos. The military coup, led by Captain Cong Le (Kong Le) (qv), then installed Prince Souvanna Phouma (qv) as premier. *See* Laos.

Sam Thong. *See* Laos.

Samuelson, Victor E. On 6 December 1973, the manager of the Esso Oil refinery at Campana, Argentina, Victor E. Samuelson, was kidnapped by the People's Revolutionary Army (ERP) (qv). He was ransomed for $14.2 million on 11 March 1974. The amount of the ransom was said to be enough to equip and maintain 1,500 guerrillas for a year. Earlier that year, on 22 November, John Swint, the American general manager of a Ford Company subsidiary, TRANSAX, was shot to death.

Sanandaj. *See* Iran.

Sananikone, Phoui. In January 1959, Laotian premier Phoui Sananikone began a campaign to wipe out the communist-inspired and -aided, Pathet Lao (qv) insurgency. On 11 February, he abrogated Laotian adherence to the 1954 Geneva Accords and stated that his country would henceforth seek UN support in settling disputes in Laos. On 15 December of that year, however, Phoui Sananikone turned in his resignation to King Savang Vathana (qv), who accepted it and placed the army in control of the country. *See* Laos.

San'a (City). *See* Yemen.

Sanchez, Juan Carlos. On 10 April 1972, Major General Juan Carlos Sanchez, the commander of the II Army Corps, was assassinated in the town of Rosario, Argentina. His murder was linked to the kidnap and murder of Oberdan Sallustro (qv) by the People's Revolutionary Army (ERP) (qv).

Sandinistas (*Frente Sandinista de Liberacion Nacional*) (FSLN). Founded in 1962 (1958?), the group was named for General César Augusto Sandino, a hero of the Nicaraguan resistance to American occupation in 1927–1933, and followed a socialist track in its avowed purpose of overthrowing the government of Anastasio Somoza (qv). From 1962 until 1972, the FSLN spent its time organizing workers, peasants and students and operated out of bases in Costa Rica and Honduras. Attacks on Somoza's National Guard installations brought bloody reprisals in the mid-1970s in which Carlos Fonseca Amador and Silvio Mayorga, two of the group's founders, were killed. In one attack, for instance, on 22 August 1978, 25 Sandinista terrorists seized the national palace in Managua, taking more than 1,000 hostages in the process. Led by the legendary

Eden Pastora (Commander Zero) (qv), the terrorists demanded a general amnesty and $500,000 ransom, both of which demands were met before the terrorists were given safe passage out of the country, eventually landing in Cuba. Other attacks during this period were often aimed at American interests in Nicaragua. Thereafter, because of those deaths and other internal dissension, the group split into three factions. The FSLN was reunited during the rebellion in 1978–1979 under the leadership of Daniel (qv) and Humberto Ortega Saavadra. With a force of about 5,000, the Ortegas opened a full-scale offensive on 20 February 1979 and, by 17 July, defeated the National Guard and ousted Somoza, driving the dictator into exile. The FSLN then established a National Directorate to guide the ruling junta led by Daniel Ortega. As an early move, Humberto Ortega built a 50,000-man army to engage the Honduras-based *Contras,* who were largely supported by the United States. A parallel secret police organization was established to control internal dissent against the regime. Within the government, tensions mounted as some key non-Marxists resigned their offices; this caused the Sandinista movement to swing further to the left, where its only support came from the USSR and Cuba. Although there was some confiscation and some nationalization, the Sandinistas never imposed a Soviet-style system on the country, and many of the smaller property holders were untouched. Some opposition was also tolerated in the political arena, and elections were held on 4 November 1984, in which the Sandinistas won a two-thirds majority of seats in the National Assembly. Daniel Ortega was elected president in a highly criticized election held that same year. In a 1990 election, the Sandinistas were roundly defeated because of the constant turmoil and the weakening economy and turned out of office. Yet, the party still has broad support in the countryside and in the armed forces. *See* Nicaragua. *Reading:* Tomas Borge, *The Patient Impatience: From Boyhood to Guerrilla: A Personal Narrative of Nicaragua's Struggle for Liberation* (1992); Douglas Payne, *The Democratic Mask: The Consolidation of the Sandinista Revolution* (1985); Janusz Bugaiski, *Sandinista Communism and Rural Nicaragua* (1990).

Sanjabi, Karin. On 11 November 1978, Karin Sanjabi, an opposition leader to the government of Shah Mohammad Reza Pahlavi Aryamehr (qv), in Iran was arrested. His arrest coincided with the detention of a number of important people following the declaration of martial law on 5 November.

San Jose. *See* Costa Rica.

San Juan del Norte (Greytown). *See* Nicaragua.

Sankara, Thomas. On 17 May 1983, President Jean-Baptiste Ouedraogo (qv) of Upper Volta ordered the ouster and arrest of a number of senior government officials, including Premier Thomas Sankara. Captain Sankara had held the premiership since 10 January 1983. All were members of People's Salvation Party (CSP), and all were accused of plotting the overthrow of the government. The Libyan charge d'affairs was declared persona non grata and ordered out of the country for what was called his complicity in the plot. However, Sankara was released on 30 May, after the CSP had been dissolved by Ouedraogo. On 4-5

August 1983, Sankara was successful in overthrowing Ouedraogo by the use of elite military parachute units. Sankara then established a National Revolutionary Council, which, on 24 August, named a civilian government to lead the country, with Sankara as head of state. On 28 October, Sankara announced the discovery of an alleged plot to overthrow the government. After his first year in power, Sankara had Upper Volta renamed Burkina Faso (qv). On 27 May 1984, another coup plot was uncovered, which led to the execution of seven of the conspirators. On 19 August 1984, Sankara dissolved the government and formed a new one that excluded Marxist-Leninist elements. On 15 October 1987, Sankara was killed in yet another, and this time successful, coup, led by Captain Blaise Compoare. At least 100 were killed in the fighting that accompanied the coup.

San Louis. *See* Argentina.

San Miguel. *See* El Salvador.

San Pablo. *See* Colombia.

San Pedro Sula. *See* Honduras.

San Salvador. *See* El Salvador.

San Sebastian. *See* Spain.

Santa Ana. *See* El Salvador.

Santa Clara. *See* Cuba.

Santa Cruz. *See* Bolivia.

Santiago. *See* Chile.

Santo Domingo (Ciudad Trujillo). *See* Dominican Republic.

Sanya Dhamasakti. (b. 5 April 1907, Bangkok) On 14 October 1973 in Thailand, the long military dictatorship of Field Marshal Thanom Kittikachorn (qv) was ended by a coup following a long period of civil unrest and violence. Kittikachorn and a group of his followers fled the country (15 October). On 16 October, the king appointed a civilian educator, the rector of Thammasat University, Sanya Dhamasakti, to be the new prime minister. Violence subsided the following day, but not for long. The resurgence of violence caused him to resign on 21 May 1974. There followed several days of great uncertainty in Thailand before the king once again appointed Sanya as prime minister. Sanya was voted out of office on 21 February 1975.

Sao Paulo. *See* Brazil.

Sao Tome Island. *See* Principe Island.

Saravane (Saravan). *See* Laos.

Sarawak. *See* Malaysia.

Sarkis, Elias. On 8 May 1976, after a period of intense political maneuvering, the Lebanese parliament elected Elias Sarkis to replace Suleiman Franjieh (qv). At the time, general fighting raged throughout Lebanon, which to some extent held up the inauguration of the Syrian-backed incumbent until 23 September. During this period, Lebanon had in effect been partitioned along what became known as the "Green Line" (qv) (*see also* Lebanon). Sarkis was instrumental not so much in bringing the fighting to a halt but rather in getting Arab leaders together in a formal summit held on 25–26 October 1976. Then, in early January 1977, Sarkis ordered the Palestine Liberation Organization (PLO) to remove its regular troops from Lebanon by 13 January. The 30,000-man Arab League's peacekeeping force (largely composed of Syrian troops) further ordered that all weapons not already in Lebanese army hands had to be given up by 12 January. Even though the intensity of the fighting diminished, it never really stopped. In 1978, the Israeli invasion damaged the fragile peace Sarkis had helped impose. When the fighting accelerated, Sarkis threatened to resign (6 July), but withdrew his threat on 15 July. In July 1980, Sarkis was forced to accept the resignation of his prime minister, Selim al-Hoss, but the polarization that was taking place in Lebanon made finding a replacement government much more difficult. By 1981, the fighting had increased to the highest level since the 1975–1976 civil war. In mid-1982, Sarkis announced his retirement, and a special election was held to find a new president. Bashir Gemayle (qv), a Christian, was elected, but he was assassinated on 14 September. This murder triggered a renewed Israeli advance in a campaign designed to eradicate the PLO presence in Lebanon. Nine days later, Amin Gemayle (qv), a moderate, was elected president, and Sarkis retired.

Sarobi. *See* Afghanistan.

Sarvari, Asadolla. During a cabinet meeting of the Soviet-backed Babrak Karmal (qv) government in Kabul, Afghanistan on 15 February 1980, a gunfight broke out in which at least one minister was killed and several wounded. Among the wounded was Karmal's deputy, Asadolla Sarvari. Rumors persisted at the time that Karmal was under house arrest. *See* Afghanistan.

Sa'sa' (*Sesa*) (*Saassaa*). *See* Israel.

Sasebo. *See* Japan.

Sassou-Nguesso, Denis. On 5–7 February 1979, the government of President Joachim Yhombi-Opango (qv) of Congo was overthrown in a bloodless coup led by the pro-Soviet former defense minister, Colonel Denis Sassou-Nguesso. On 8 February, the coup leader had himself installed as president and promptly had Yhombi-Opango and his Military Council arrested and imprisoned. A new socialist constitution was adopted, as was a compliant National Assembly. In August, an amnesty was declared for all those who were allegedly involved in the assassination of former president Marien Ngouabi (qv), but a number of political prisoners were still held in custody. On 13 May 1981, Sassou signed a mutual cooperation treaty with the USSR but refused to accept the building of a new Soviet military base in Congo. Relations between Congo and Moscow had deteriorated during this period even though Congo was one of the few states endorsing the Soviet invasion of Afghanistan. The rejection of the new base plan played heavily on the Soviets as Congo was the main transit point for Soviet and Cuban military forces headed for Angola. In 1981–1982, Sassou began courting the French; and in October 1982, President Francois Mitterand paid a state visit to Congo. A delegation of the Soviet Communist Party paid a visit to Sassou in October. In April 1983, Sassou dismissed the minister of information and the

Congolese Labor Party for "ideological inconsistency." Sassou paid a visit to Muammar al-Qaddafi in September 1983, ostensibly to seek a solution to the war in Chad. He was unanimously reelected president in 1984 and proceeded to have the constitution amended to give him virtual sole rule of the country. In August, Sassou replaced his prime minister with a civilian, and in November he announced he had ordered the release of former president Joachim Yhombi-Opango, who had been in prison since 1979. Meanwhile, the economy of Congo was in a downward spiral, but in July 1986 Sassou was elected to chair the Organization of African Unity (OAU). At home in 1986, ten people involved in a 1982 series of bombings were sentenced to death. The economic situation saw some relief when drastic economic moves paved the way for an IMF debt redistribution. In 1989, he was reelected president on a one-party ticket. In 1990, Sassou visited the United States, where he signed an agreement guaranteeing U.S. interests in Congo. In December 1990, the Congo's Congress renounced Social Marxism and adopted a policy that followed social-democratic lines. Political tensions rose in the country, and on 8 January 1991 Sassou was forced to replace his prime minister with General Louis Sylvan Goma. A conference of the various political parties ended on 10 June, with a manifesto included a statement that the conference was an independent body and it replaced Goma as prime minister with Andre Malongo. That same year, Cuban troops left Congolese soil. An internationally supervised election held on 2 August 1992 turned Sassou-Nguesso out of office. *See* Congo.

Sato, Eisaku. (b. 1901) Sato became prime minister of Japan in 1964. That year, Japan hosted the Olympics, and the Japanese people translated that event into a reestablishment of Japan among the community of nations and an expansion of Japan's diplomatic status. Sato, in January 1966, announced a peace mission to Viet Nam, which failed to achieve its goal. On 17 November 1969, Sato traveled to the U.S. to discuss the return of Okinawa. This trip caused major disturbances in Japan, which resulted in the arrest of 1,200 people. One of the issues that caused the rioting was the renegotiation of the U.S.–Japan Mutual Security Treaty, which was looked upon by many leftist Japanese as a sellout to the Americans. Sato renewed the treaty during his Washington visit. He also brought back with him a U.S. promise to return Okinawa and the U.S.–held Ryukyu Islands to Japan by 1972. An agreement to this end was signed on 17 June 1971. On 21 July 1971, Sato told the Diet that he was preparing to visit Peking to restore relations with China but, he added, Japan would support the U.S. in maintaining the presence of Taiwan in the United Nations. China's response was to state it would be happy to receive a "new" Japanese prime minister, but obviously not Sato. In April 1972, Sato was forced to admit his responsibility for irregularities that had been permitted to enter the Okinawa negotiations (the so-called Secret Documents Case) and, on 17 June, Sato resigned the presidency of his party. Sato was replaced as prime minister by Kakuei Tanaka on 5 July 1972.

Sattar, Abdus. On 30 May 1981, President Ziaur Rahman (qv) of Bangladesh was assassinated. Vice President Abdus Sattar became the new president. Sattar's first task was to restore order in the country, which was accomplished by army chief of staff Lieutenant General H. M. Ershad. Sattar also proclaimed a state of emergency and suspended civil rights. Although some progress was made in reestablishing order, but open discussions of a government overthrow were prominent. Sattar was elected president in his own right in November 1981. After that, Sattar became less and less inclined to look to Ershad for advice. The overthrow took place on 24 March 1982, when Ershad led a military coup against Sattar. On 27 March, Abul Fazal Mohammad Ahsanuddin Choudhury became president. The elderly Abdus Sattar was not included in the roundup of government officials that followed. *See* Bangladesh.

Saudi Arabia. A country of South Asia, Saudi Arabia is bounded on the north by Jordan, Iraq and Kuwait, on the southeast by the United Arab Emirates (UAE) and Oman, and on the west by the Red Sea and the Gulf of Aqaba (qv). The capital city is Riyadh. The region is known to be the original home of the Semites, who began migrating into the Mesopotamia and Palestine areas in the fourth millennium B.C. The Minaean kingdom grew up along the Red Sea coast in the first millennium B.C. Alexander the Great laid plans to conquer the region but his death in 323 B.C. prevented that from happening. The Minaeans subsequently left the area in the first century B.C., and were replaced by another tribe, the Nabataeans, who remained in power until the the seventh century A.D. In 630, Muhammad, having been driven out of Mecca (570), returned with his followers and took back Mecca. This act profoundly changed the course of history not only for the region but for mankind, as it was from this beginning that the foundation of Islam was constructed. By the thirteenth century, Muhammad's successors had conquered most of the Middle East and made their presence felt in Africa and· deeper into Asia. After 1269, the Egyptian Mamelukes held sway over Arabia, and they were followed by the Ottoman Empire after the Turkish conquest of Egypt in 1517. The interior of the country was never truly subjugated, however, and during the fifteenth century Muhammad ibn Saud had established near Riyadh the nucleus of the nation that would follow. In the eighteenth century the Wahhabi fundamentalist sect was founded and, with the support of the Saudi army, founded an Arab state at Najd. The Wahhabi took Mecca in 1802, but were ousted and returned to Riyadh ten years later (1812). At that point the Saudis and Wahhabi founded their capital at Riyadh, but, after fighting a series of victorious wars of conquest, the Saudi leaders fell into civil war, which ended in the partition of the country. The Saud family itself fled into exile in Kuwait, where they remained until 1902, when Abdul Aziz ibn Saud attacked and captured Riyadh and, between 1906 and 1925, reconquered most of the Arabian peninsula. Abdul Aziz ibn Saud then declared himself King of Al Hijah. After the completion of the reunification in 1932, he renamed the nation, Saudi Arabia. After oil was discovered, king Saud began the process of bringing his country out of the Middle Ages. Modernization was coupled with opening diplomatic relations with neighboring countries and with the United States and Great Britain. Although supporting the Allied cause during World War II, Saud kept Saudi Arabia out of the war until March 1945, when he declared war on Germany and Japan. He had earlier permitted the building of a U.S. air base at Dhahran. Saudi Arabia joined the United Nations in 1945 and later became a member of the Arab League (qv). Saud opposed the establishment of the Jewish state of Israel but did not give wholehearted support to the Arab League's war against the new country in 1948–1949. In June 1951, the US lease on its air base at Dhahran was extended another five years. In return, Saud received technical aid and weapons under the Mutual Defense Assistance Act. In December 1951, Saud made an agreement with the Arabian-American Oil Company whereby 50 percent of the company's net earnings were paid back to Saudi Arabia. King Abdul Aziz ibn Saud died on 9 November 1953 and was succeeded by his eldest son, Saud. The policy of the new ruler was neutrality and, later, adamant opposition to the Middle East Treaty Organization (*see* Baghdad Pact), which had been formed in February 1955. In October 1955 the Saudi government signed a mutual defense treaty with Egypt. At about that same time, British-led Omani forces retook (26 October) the disputed Buraimi Oasis, which the Saudis had held for three years. A Saudi appeal to the UN went unheeded. In November 1955, Saud gave Syria $10 million for its economy and to build its army. Saudi Arabia took part in the Cairo meeting of the Arab League, 3–11 March 1956, at which a joint military plan for action against Israel was drawn up. A tripartite military alliance of Saudi Arabia, Egypt and Yemen was signed at Jidda on 24 April 1956. The Saudis loaned Egypt $10 million in August 1956, following Cairo's nationalization of the Suez Canal (26 July 1956). Saudi Arabia then severed diplomatic relations with with Great Britain and France following their attack (with the Israelis) on Egypt. At the same time, no oil was loaded on their ships. On 8 February 1957, the U.S. announced it would sell weapons to Saudi Arabia, in return for keeping its rights to the Dhahran air base. In April 1957, Saudi Arabia, in support of Egypt, extended its maritime control to include the Gulf of Aqaba (qv) and indicated that Israeli vessels would be blocked from passage. The Saudi threat was never carried out. In February 1958, the Saudis extended all of their territorial waters to 12 miles. The absolute ruler, King Saud, relinquished much of his power, except for the veto, to a prime minister in March 1958. His brother, Crown Prince Faisal (qv), was appointed to that office, and a cabinet was appointed, largely of family members, by royal decree. Saudi Arabia was one of the founders of OPEC (qv) at the Baghdad conference of 10–14 September 1960. In September 1962, civil war broke out in neighboring Yemen. While Egypt supported the rebels, King Saud threw his support to the royalists, pledging a return of the imam to the throne. Following a series of Saudi attacks on Yemeni rebel positions, Egyptian (UAR) planes bombed a number of Saudi towns (6 November 1962). (On 21 December 1960, Saud had ousted Prince Faisal from his post as prime minister and assumed those duties himself, but once again relinquished that office to Faisal in October 1962.) Saudi Arabia severed diplomatic relations with Egypt and mobilized for war in January 1963. The UN stepped in on 2 March, and the war never came, but in the aftermath, on 28 February 1964, Crown Prince Faisal ousted Saud in a bloodless coup and took the crown for himself (2 November 1964). His half-brother Prince Khalid ibn Abdul (qv) was appointed prime minister. When relations again became strained between the Arabs and Israeli, Faisal sent 20,000 troops to reinforce Jordan's forces (10 December 1966). On 23 May 1967, Saudi forces were put on full alert as the Middle East girded for war. On 6 June 1967, the Saudis cut off oil supplies to the U.S. and Great Britain but did not break diplomatic relations. Following the Arabs' onerous defeat (*see* Arab-Israeli War), the flow of oil out of Saudi Arabia was quietly resumed. Faisal later made huge loans to Egypt to compensate for the loss of revenue from the closed Suez Canal. A plot to assassinate King Faisal was uncovered in June 1969. Saudi Arabia formally recognized the Republic of Yemen (14 April 1970), thereby ending five years of periodic border clashes (*see* Yemen). Incidents along the border continued, however, such as the one on 21 February 1972, when the People's Democratic Republic of Yemen forces repelled an attack by Saudi Arabian–based Yemeni "Army of Deliverance" forces carried out an attack in the Bayhan area. Although Faisal continued to urge Arab unity against Israel—for example, calling (25 August 1969) for an Islamic summit to discuss protection of the Holy Places—he could not be induced to prescribe an anti-Western program. In 1971, along with five other Middle East states, Saudi Arabia signed long-term leases with 17 U.S. and six foreign oil companies. Also, on 15 December 1970, King Faisal reestablished diplomatic relations with Oman after a long period of feuding. The Saudis reinforced their border with Kuwait when that government accused Iraq of attacking a border police station at Sameta on 20 March 1973. In October 1973, Saudi Arabia led the oil embargo against those in the West, primarily the United States (20 October), who supported Israel. Saudi Arabia dispatched a token force and a supply of arms to aid the Arab states during the Arab-Israeli War of 1973. At the end of that war, Saudi Arabia took over control of Aramco, the huge Arab-American oil-producing complex, which greatly increased the Saudi treasury and the rate of modernization in the country. The U.S. sold Saudi Arabia $756 million worth of F-5 fighter aircraft in January 1975. On 22 March 1975, Faisal was assassinated in Riyadh by a nephew, Prince Faisal ibn Musad ibn Abdul Aziz, and was succeeded by Prince as Khalid as the new king. The frail Khalid was not up to the task, and his half-brother, Crown Prince Fahd, became the power behind the throne. In June 1975, Saudi Arabia joined in a call for Israel's ejection from the United Nations. The Saudis purchased an additional $1.2 billion in arms and equipment from the U.S. in February 1976 and, in June of that year, forced North Yemen to sever its links with the USSR. The new Saudi leadership managed to keep OPEC from further raising oil prices. In 1980, Saudi Arabia announced that it had taken full control of Aramco retroactive to 1976. Still, Saudi Arabia suffered from a slowdown in its economy, partially because of huge arms purchases from the West but also because much of the available Saudi money was sent outside the country on financial ventures designed to improve the long-term financial stability of the country. Saudi Arabia did cut off financial aid to Egypt after that government signed a peace treaty with Israel in 1977. Following the Islamic fundamentalist seizure of the Grand Mosque in Mecca, Saudi Arabia began a program to increase its military potential against the Iranian-driven fundamentalists. When the United States announced the sale of several AWACS aircraft to Saudi Arabia, Israel loudly objected to what was viewed as a move that would destabilize the Middle East. When Khalid died in June 1982, Faud was proclaimed king. The Saudi policies toward maintenance of traditional values and modernization remained essentially unchanged. Faud took the Islamic title of "Custodian of the Two Mosques" in 1986 in a move to further isolate Islamic fundamentalist provocation. At least 400 were killed in Mecca 1 July 1987, when Iranian Shi'ite pilgrims clashed with Saudi police. In July 1990, 1,400 were killed there when a freak accident caused a stampede. When Iraq invaded Kuwait in August 1990, Saudi Arabia saw itself threatened by the Iraqis. Saudi Arabia became the marshalling area for more than a half-million U.S. and allied military forces poised to liberate Kuwait. The ensuing Desert Storm operation (1991) freed Kuwait and secured an at least temporary respite for the Saudis. Saudi Arabia also increased its oil output to compensate for the supplies lost from Kuwaiti and Iraqi sources. Somewhat grudgingly, Saudi Arabia put up about $51 billion to pay for the war. Thus, while the border was secure for the moment, the Saudi economy suffered further setbacks. King Fahd's belated attempts at government reforms brought opposition from the ultraconservative religious institutions in the country in 1992. That same year, Saudi Arabia announced their support for Bosnia-Herzogovina in its struggle against Christian Serbian forces. The Saudis also took revenge on neighbors who had supported Iraq in the war. Jordanian fruit was embargoed, supposedly because it was contaminated, and Yemeni-based oil companies were forbidden to explore for oil in a contested border area. Along the Qatar border, the situation became much worse after Saudi forces attacked (30 September) and occupied a Qatari border post, in what the Saudis claimed was their territory. Qatar then abrogated its 1965 border agreement with Saudi Arabia, withdrew from a number of Gulf Cooperation Council (GCC) activities and reopened diplomatic relations with Iraq. The issue seemed settled by diplomacy in December 1992. Also earlier, in September, the new U.S. president, Bill Clinton, held up an arms shipment to the Saudis to insure that the balance of power in the Middle East would not be tipped by the release of 72 F-15 fighters to Saudi Arabia. In 1993, Saudi Arabia adopted a quota system to limit the number of pilgrims from any country who could make their journey (*Hajj*) to Mecca. This was done to preclude a major incident during the event. Iranian pilgrims did manage to stage a minor anti-Israeli, anti-American demonstration (1 June), before the police could break it up. The internal struggle between the government and the religious right continued, with charges and countercharges being politely exchanged. U.S. airstrikes against Iraq in January 1993 flew out of Saudi bases with the king's approval. The most noteworthy event of 1993, was King Fahd's endorsement of the Middle East peace plan. Still, Amnesty International accused Saudi Arabia of multiple human rights violations because of an increased number of public beheadings held since the war's end. In 1994, another Iranian demonstration during the *Hajj* brought death to 270, who were killed in a stampede started when police moved in to halt the Iranians. During the year, the Qatar border squabble continued, with several minor incidents being reported by Qatar. Declining oil prices struck at the heart of Saudi Arabia's economic well-being in 1995, yet enough money was found to purchase a number of U.S.–built Aegis warships at a cost of about $1 billion. A car bomb killed six persons in Riyadh on 13 November. The attack was aimed at U.S. advisers to the Saudi National Guard. By year's end, some prominent Saudis were calling for improved relations with Iraq. *Reading:* Irvine H. Anderson, *Aramco, the United States, and Saudi Arabia: A Study of the Dynamics of Foreign Oil Policy, 1933-1950* (1981); Anthony H. Cordesman, *The Gulf and the Search for Strategic Stability: Saudi Arabia, the Military Balance in the Gulf, and Trends in the Arab-Israeli Military Balance* (1984); Arthur H. Blair, *At War in the Gulf: A Chronology* (1992); Phyllis Bennis & Michel Moushabeck, eds., *Beyond the Storm: A Gulf Crisis Reader* (1997).

Savannaket. *See* Laos.

Schaufelberger, Albert. On 25 May 1983, U.S. navy Lieutenant Commander Albert Schaufelberger, the Deputy Commander, U.S. Military Advisory Group, El Salvador, was shot and killed in his car on a university campus in San Salvador. The Popular Liberation Forces (FLP) wing of the *Frente Farabundo Marti De Liberacion National* was probably responsible for this terrorist attack. In the attack, a Volkswagon microbus carrying three men pulled alongside Schaufelberger's car; one man ran up to the car and fired several shots into the naval officer. All of the terrorists escaped.

Schleyer, Hanns-Martin. On 5 September 1977, Dr. Hanns-Martin Schleyer, the head of the West German Industries Federation, was kidnapped in Cologne by terrorists who demanded the release of Baader-Meinhof (qv) gang members held in prison. Several bodyguards and Schleyer's chauffeur were killed in the firefight that accompanied the kidnapping. On 13–18 October, a Lufthansa 737 airliner enroute to Frankfurt am Main from Palma de Mallorca was highjacked by Palestinian terrorists in retaliation for the West German government's refusal to deal for the release of the imprisoned Baader-Meinhof gang members in return for the release of Schleyer. Upon seizing the aircraft, the hijackers then demanded the release of the same Baader-Meinhof prisoners, a huge sum of money and the release of other terrorists in Turkish jails. In the ensuing travels around the Mediterranean and Middle East, the aircraft's captain is murdered in Aden for his refusal to cooperate. Finally, at Mogadishu, Somalia, West German antiterrorist commandos attacked, the aircraft freeing 86 hostages and killing three and capturing one of the four terrorists. Within hours of the incident, on 18 October, Baader and his two fellow gang members allegedly committed suicide in their West German prison cells. The body of the 62-year-old Schleyer was found in a car near Mulhouse, in northwestern France, on 19 October 1977.

Schneider Chereau, Rene. The Chilean army's commanding general, Rene Schneider, was assassinated by gunfire on 22 October 1970. In retaliation for his death, the government declared a state of emergency (martial law) throughout Chile just before a crucial election. *See* Chile.

Schönau Castle, Austria. On 28 September 1973, Palestinian terrorists boarded the Moscow-Vienna train and took three Jewish passengers and an Austrian customs agent hostage when the train reached Vienna. Among the terrorists demands for the release of the hostages was the Austrian closure of the Schönau Castle transit camp for Jews travelling to Israel. Bruno Kreisky acceded to the demand and, on 29 December, announced that the refugee camp would be closed. Kreisky also promised to halt Jewish emigration to Israel through Austria. Kreisky's decisions brought a storm of protest from around the world. On 4 October, another announcement was made that, in the future, Jews would be transferred through Austria expeditiously.

Schwechat Airport, Austria. On 27 December 1985, Palestinian terrorists armed with automatic weapons and grenades simultaneously attacked the Leonardo da Vinci International Airport in Rome and the Schwechat Airport in Vienna A total of 16 were killed, including a child, and nearly one hundred injured in the attacks. Investigators linked both Iran and Libya to the attacks, which were said to be in reprisal for the Israeli attack that destroyed the PLO headquarters in Tunisia. Further investigation placed the blame for the attacks on the Abu Nidal (*Al-Fatah*) terrorist organization (qv).

Scoon, Sir Paul. *See* Grenada.

Scotland. *See* United Kingdom.

Sea of Galilee. *See* Israel.

Sea of Japan. *See* Japan, China and Korea.

Sebokeng. *See* South Africa.

"Second Tet Offensive." *See* Vietnam.

Selassie, Haile. (b. 23 July 1892, Harer area, Ethiopia—d. 27 August 1975, Addis Ababa) Selassie's real name was Tafari Makonnen, and he was born into the Amhara nobility. His early education consisted of tutoring by French missionaries. As he matured, the emperor Menelik II gave him ever greater and more important governmental posts. He became governor of Sidamo and later, held that same post in his native Harer. His work led to his identification with progressivism in an otherwise feudal society. In 1913, Menelik II died and was replaced by his grandson, Yasu. Yasu, however, was too closely tied to Islam to be a comfort to his subjects and was deposed by Tafari in 1916. Menelik's daughter Zaudita became empress the following year, and Tafari was appointed regent and heir apparent to the throne. Tafari brought Ethiopia into the League of Nations in 1923 and visited most of Europe's major capitals in his quest to learn the progressive ways of the West. In 1928, Tafari became king and, in 1930, upon Zaudita's death, was crowned emperor (2 November), assuming the name Haile Selassie, a salute to the Christian tradition of his country, where his new name meant "Might of the Trinity." He did, however, in 1931, promulgate a new constitution that all but dismantled the country's parliament, which fundamentally ceased to exist by the middle of the decade. Thereafter, Selassie became a power unto himself, but he did work toward the modernization of of his country. In 1935, Mussolini invaded Ethiopia in what some scholars see as the opening salvo in World War II. Although his people fought valiantly, they were overcome by the superior Italian forces. Selassie was forced to flee in May 1936. His appeal to then already moribund League of Nations was ignored (30 June 1936). When World War II started in earnest in 1939, he secured British support and jointly with the British invaded Ethiopia from the Sudan in January 1941, freeing his capital before the end of the year. When Selassie returned to the throne, he discovered his power base had eroded and set about recreating it. In doing so, he once again installed programs of modernization, which were to grow steadily. He once again held total authority as a result. A new constitution promulgated in 1955 gave him power equal to that which he held before the war. Beginning in December 1960, open opposition to his programs began to surface. A battle of some magnitude took place in Addis Ababa between dissident troops and the army in which the loyal forces won. In 1963, Selassie was instrumental in the establishment of the Organization of African Unity (qv). On 26–28 February 1974, another army mutiny erupted in Asmara, following a period of severe drought. The uprising quickly spread to Addis Ababa. The emperor attempted to correct the faults in his rule perceived by the mutineers, but without success. After the government resigned, Selassie was divested of much of his authority (24 June 1974) and became a virtual prisoner in his own palace, while a provisional military government ran the country. The military junta revoked the last of Selassie's powers on 16 August. On 12 September, Selassie was officially deposed, and his son, the 57-year-old Crown Prince Asfa Wossen, was named as his successor. The son, living in Switzerland following a stroke, refused the post, whereupon the junta chose General Aman Michael Andom (qv) as head of state. When Andom was ousted and murdered on 22–23 November 1974, many members of Selassie's family were also killed. The government claimed they had all been tried and "executed." Selassie died in 1975 at the age of 83, supposedly from complications growing out of recent surgery. There were persistent rumors and some evidence to dispute that claim, however, and to allow the suspicion that he was indeed murdered. *Reading:* Ryszard Kapuchinski, *The Emperor: Downfall of an Autocrat,* (1989); Colin Legum, *Ethiopia: The Fall of Haile Selassie's Empire* (1975).

Selich, Andres. On 14 May 1973, Colonel Andres Selich, the former defense minister of Bolivia, was arrested for his part in plotting a right-wing military overthrow of President Hugo Banze-Suarez (qv). Selich had been instrumental in bringing Banzer to power in 1971, but he was subsequently dismissed from his post and began plotting the coup. After his capture, Selich died at the hands of his interrogators.

Semipalatinsk. *See* USSR.

Senard, Jacques. On 13 September 1974, French ambassador Jacques Senard and ten others were taken hostage when Japanese Red Army terrorists seized the French embassy in The Hague, Netherlands. The terrorists demanded the release of another terrorist held in a French prison and $1 million for the release of their hostages. The ransom and a safe conduct were arranged after lengthy negotiations. The terrorists fled to Syria, where they were handed over to PLO control and disappeared. This may have been an operation planned and financed by the terrorist legend Illich Ramirez Sanchez, also known as "Carlos."

Sendic, Raul. *See* Tupamaros.

Senegal. A West African country bordered on the north and northwest by Mauritania, on the east by Mali, on the south by Guinea and Guinea-Bissau and on the west by the Atlantic Ocean. The Gambia is, in turn completely surrounded by Senegal. Senegal's capital is in Dakar. Senegal's population was converted to Islam in the eleventh century, but it was ruled by animist leaders into the eighteenth century. The region was first explored by the Portuguese in 1444–1445. The French established a trading post on the Senegal River in 1648 and founded the city of Sainte-Louis in 1659. The chief exports during those times were gold, ivory and slaves. Between 1693 and 1814, control of Senegal contiually passed between the French and the British. After 1814, however, France became the dominant force in the development of the country. In 1895, Senegal became a part of French West Africa, with Dakar becoming its capital in 1902. Senegal became part of the French colonial system in 1946, with the extension of French citizenship to its inhabitants. It became an autonomous republic under France on 25 November 1958 and entered into a federated status with Mali (French Sudan) on 18 January 1959. When Senegal and Mali received their independence on 20 June 1960, the merger between the two continued for a few months, but then began to break down. On 17 December 1962, an unsuccessful coup attempt occurred against the government of Leopold Sedar Senghor, which was led by the chairman of the Council of Ministers, Mamadou Dia. Senghor then took over the ministerial functions himself. On 12 October 1972, Portuguese military forces using armor attacked the Senegalese military installation at Nianao, on the border with what was then Portuguese Guinea. The UN condemned Portugal for this and other incursions into Senegalese territory (23 October 1972). On 18 September 1973, Senegal broke diplomatic relations with neighboring Guinea following incessant verbal attacks on the country by Guinea's president, Sekou Toure (qv). The Dakar government announced (29 March 1974) that the French military presence in Senegal would be reduced almost in half, and the French base at Dakar would be returned to Senegalese control by April 1975. On 1 January 1981, Abdou Diouf became the new president of Senegal. Having laid the groundwork (14 November 1981) and signed the agreement (17 December 1981), the confederation of Senegal and

The Gambia came into being on 1 February 1982, as the new state of Senegambia. (*See also* Gambia and Senegambia.) In 1983–1984, unrest in several provinces created some problems for Diouf, but these were remedied in part, in 1984, by the dismissal of several cabinet ministers and the resignation of the prime minister. A revolt in one province led to the arrest and imprisonment of 70 people. A multiparty system installed during this time began working well (1985), but the country's economy still suffered from the drought that had plagued all of sub-Saharan Africa. The Senegambian Federation also showed signed of weakness in 1985. In April 1986, Diouf ordered amnesty for eight of the provincial detainees, but left 62 more still incarcerated. The Senegambian process moved forward with the completion of a protocol dealing with the call-up of troops in times of emergency. (*see* The Gambia for a 1981 event) Internal problems related to cabinet shifts, interparty bickering, separatist uprisings and the economy continued to burden the Diouf government. In mid-April 1987, the entire police force in Dakar was fired because they had gone on strike. Several thousand of the police were subsequently rehired. The February 1988 elections resulted in rioting, which led to the declaration of a state of emergency. Although order was restored quickly, tensions remained high. Diouf was forced to acknowledge the need for internal reform in 1989, but rioting continued in several regions of the country. A border incident near the Senegal River on 9 April 1989 erupted into ethnic violence between the Mauritaneans, many of whom had fled to Senegal away from the violence at home, and the Sengalese. The turmoil continued after diplomatic relations with Mauritania were severed in August. Even more important, however, was the dissolution of Senegal's confederation with The Gambia at the end of September 1989, with each side blaming the other for the collapse. In 1991, with Diouf still president, an accord was signed with Mauritania in April ending the border conflict (diplomatic relations restored, April 1992), and a cease-fire was worked out with the separatist factions in Casamance Province. This latter problem erupted again later in 1992, when the rebellion, if anything, intensified. Senegal's other external problems, such as those with The Gambia and with Guinea-Bissau, appeared to be leveling off. With the problems it was having at home, Senegal withdrew its troops from the peacekeeping force that had been sent to Liberia (*see* Liberia) in January 1993. These troops were to be used in providing security during the 21 February elections. Diouf easily won reelection. Several hundred people died in Casamance Province during the early months of 1993 as the rebellion there continued. On 16 February 1994, major violence erupted in which protest rally participants attacked security forces, six of whom were killed before order was restored. Opposition party leaders were arrested on charges of incitement but were later acquitted. Senegal then took the heat of international opinion for its handling of the situation. Senegal suspended its relations with Iran in May 1994, after it was discovered that Iran was subsidizing Islamic fundamentalist activities in Senegal. Diouf remained in office in 1995, as violence continued to build in Casamance Province. *Reading:* Robert Fatton,

The Making of a Liberal Democracy: Senegal's Passive Revolution, 1975-1985 (1987): Lucie Gallistel Colvin, *Historical Dictionary of Senegal* (1981).

Senegambia. *See* Gambia and Senegal.

Seoul. *See* Korea.

Serong, F. P. Serong, an Australian counterguerrilla expert, told the U.S. commander in South Vietnam, General Paul Harkins, in October 1962, that the South Vietnamese army was poorly trained and led, after he had made an extensive examination of the situation. *See* Vietnam.

Sesheke. *See* Zambia.

17 November [Revolutionary] Organization. On 15 November 1983, Captain George Tsantes, the chief of the U.S. Naval Mission in Greece, and his Greek driver were assassinated. Two gunmen on a motor scooter pulled alongside Tsantes's official car at a stoplight on the Athens-Kiffissia highway and fired seven rounds from a .45 caliber automatic into the car. Tsantes was killed instantly and the driver died later in the hospital. The 17 November Revolutionary Organization claimed credit for the attack in retaliation for socialist prime minister Andreas Papandreou's failure to close all U.S. bases in Greece. The group struck again, on 21 February 1985, killing a Greek publisher on an Athens street. Although the terrorists escaped, they left behind pamphlets condemning the socialist government in Greece.

"Seventh Suicide Squad." On 5 August 1973, Arab terrorists armed with submachine guns and grenades opened fire on a group of passengers at the airport in Athens, Greece, killing five—three of whom were Americans—and injuring 55 others. Claiming to be members of the "Seventh Suicide Squad," a hitherto unknown terrorist group, the two surrendered to police after they apparently discovered they had attacked the wrong group, mistaking a group leaving for New York as the target, rather than a Tel Aviv–bound group. The terrorists were sentenced to death, but the Greek courts commuted their sentences to life imprisonment. In May 1974, the two were expelled to Libya, where they were apparently set free.

Seychelles. Formally, the Republic of Seychelles, this is a group of approximately 115 islands in the western Indian Ocean. The larger of the islands are about 1,000 miles east of Kenya in Africa. The islands were uninhabited when first visited in 1609 by an expedition of the British East India Company. They were later explored by the French, between 1742 and 1744. The French annexed the islands in 1756, naming them the *Séchelles*. The British captured the islands in 1810 and gave them their current name after their cession to Great Britain by the Treaty of Paris in 1814. When the English abolished slavery in the 1830s, the economic life of the Seychelles also changed. Cotton farming changed to cinnamon, vanilla and coconut growing, which required less labor. Seychelles received British Crown Colony status in 1903, and an elective legislative government was introduced in 1948. In March 1956, Seychelles became the exile home for Archbishop Makarios (qv) of Cyprus. After issuing statements allegedly calling for a campaign of terror in Cyprus, Makarios was detained by

British authorities, but he was subsequently released In 1970, Seychelles adopted a new constitution and, in 1975, was granted self-government. Independence followed in 1976. In 1975, the new government was headed by James R. Marcham, with France-Albert Rene (qv) as prime minister. Marcham was overthrown on 5 June 1977 in a Soviet-aided coup. Although denying any part in the coup or any ties with the Soviets, Rene assumed the presidency; but, in 1979, he imposed a one-party socialist system on his country. A coup attempt on 25 November 1981 by 50 mercenaries disguised as rugby players failed. When the failure occurred, 44 of the mercenaries hijacked an airplane to Durban, South Africa. Seychelles then accused South Africa of involvement in the plot. In July 1991, South Africa admitted its part in the affair by paying eight million rand in compensation. Changes toward democracy became evident in the 1990s, however, and on 3 December 1991 a multiparty political system was installed. France-Albert Rene won a landslide victory in the 1994 elections and remained in power (1995). *Reading:* George Bennet & Pramila Ramgulam Bennet, *Seychelles* (World Bibliographical Series) (1993); Marcus Franda, *The Seychelles: Unquiet Islands* (1982).

al-Shaabi, Qahtan. As leader of the National Liberation Front (NLF) in Aden (South Yemen), Qahtan Mohammed al-Shaabi led the NLF delegation in the discussions with the British and other organizations that took place in Geneva, Switzerland, on 21–29 November 1967. Upon his return (30 November), Al-Shaabi proclaimed the independence of the newly named People's Republic of Southern Yemen. Al-Shaabi became the new state's first president and pursued a leftist policy. Al-Shaabi made an 11-day visit to the Soviet Union in February 1969 and, upon his return from Moscow, announced that the Soviets were prepared to supply arms and materiel to the country to help it with defense problems. On 5 March, he accused Great Britain of violating South Yemen air space. In June of that year, he visited Damascus, but shortly after his return a bloodless coup forced his resignation on 22 June. A leftist-oriented five-man "Presidential Council," led by Salem Ali Rubayyi (qv), took his place.

Shaba Province. *See* Zaire.

Shadwan Island. *See* Egypt.

Shagari, Alhaji Shehu. (b. May 1925, Yabo, Nigeria) On 31 December 1983, Nigeria's president, Shehu Shagari was ousted from office by a bloodless military coup. Shagari had just been overwhelmingly reelected to a second term. Shagari had taken office on 1 October 1979, following 13 years of military rule in Nigeria.

Shah, G. M. On 2 July 1984, the governor of the state of Jammu and Kashmir dismissed his chief minister, Farooq Abdullah, and replaced him with his own brother-in-law, G. M. Shah. Farooq had lost a majority. Shah was able to secure a majority and won his first vote of confidence on 31 July 1984.

Shahjah. *See* United Arab Emirates; Fujairah.

Shamir, Yitzhak (Yitzhak Jazernicki). *See* Israel and Stern Gang.

Shamte, Mohammed. On 12 January 1964, the Shamte government was overthrown by a leftist-led revolution on the island of Zanzibar. A communist-dominated government led by Abdullah Kassim Hanga (qv) was installed on 14 January.

Shanghai. *See* China.

Shantung Peninsula. *See* China.

Shariat-Madari, Ayatollah Seyed Kazem. On 9 December 1979, rioting broke out in the northwest Iranian city of Tabriz as followers of the Ayatollah Shariat-Madari, one of the Ayatollah Khomeini's (qv) chief opponents and critic of the religious control of politics, fought government troops for control of television and radio stations. Two days later, he warned Khomeini that the mishandling of the revolt in Azerbaijan meant civil war. On 13 December, several hundred thousand marched in Tabriz to support Shariat-Madari. *See* Iran.

Sharif-Emami, Jafaar. Following the Shah of Iran's (qv) appointment of Jafaar Sharif-Emami as prime minister on 12 August 1978, rioting broke out in four cities. Martial law had to be declared. New rioting broke out on 5 November in Tehran, which persuaded Sharif-Emami to resign. He was replaced as prime minister by a military officer, General Gholam Reza Azhari (qv).

Sharjar (Ash-Shariqah). *See* United Arab Emirates; Fujairah.

Sharm esh-Sheikh (Sharm el-Sheikh), Sinai. *See* Israel; Egypt.

Sharon, Ariel. (b. 1929, Palestine) Having an army career that started before Israel's War of 1948, Sharon was noticed by David Ben-Gurion. Sharon then attended Tel Aviv University, where he studied law. He also attended at the British Staff College, Camberly. He commanded the 1953 attack on Jordan and, earlier and subsequently, planned and led (Israeli Special Unit 101) numerous raids into Arab territory. In the 1956 war, Sharon commanded the 202nd Airborne Brigade in the capture of the eastern approach to the Mitla Pass (*see* Israel). In the 1967 war, Sharon was a division commander in the Sinai. He resigned in 1973 to serve in Parliament (*Knesset*) but was recalled during the Yom Kippur War and led Israeli forces across the Suez Canal (qv). Upon return to Parliament, in 1973, he was instrumental in the formation of the Likud Party and was an adviser to Prime Minister Yitzhak Rabin (1975–1977). Thereafter (1977) he became minister of agriculture in the cabinet of Menachem Begin (qv). In August 1981, he was appointed, over some initial opposition from Begin, to be minister of defense, in which post he masterminded the Israeli invasion of Lebanon, where Lebanese Christian militiamen carried out systematic massacres of 600 men, women and children at two Palestinian refugee camps in September 1982 (*see* Lebanon and Sabra Camp). The Israeli purpose had been the removal of the Palestinian Liberation Army (PLO) (qv) from Lebanon, but after the success of the operation, no Arab country would accept the PLO refugees. Sharon then proposed that Israel provide a home for those willing to live in peace. In the storm of criticism engendered by the massacres (and by the PLO resettlement plan), Sharon was accused of negligence and indirect responsibility for the massacres. He subsequently resigned, but he remained in the cabinet as a minister without portfolio.

Sharpburg. *See* South Africa.

Sharples, Sir Richard. On 10 March 1973, the governor of Bermuda, Sir Richard Sharples, was assassinated at Government House in Hamilton. Sharples's aide was also killed in the attack. A state of emergency was declared on 11 March. Sharples's murder followed by six months the assassination of the island's police commissioner. The assailants were not identified, and no one took credit for the attacks. The 63-year-old Sharples had been governor of Bermuda since October 1972.

Shastri, Lal Bahadur. (b. 2 October 1904, Mughalsarai, United Provinces, India—d. 11 January 1966, Tashkent. Soviet Central Asia) Shastri studied at Benares before joining the non-cooperation movement in 1921. He was subsequently jailed for a time, and after his release he studied religion; his learning gained him the title "*Shastri*" (Learned in Scripture). Entering politics, he was jailed several more times, but gained a good reputation in the Congress Party. In 1937 and in 1946, he was elected to the United Provinces legislature. Shastri then moved through a number of increasingly more important posts until he succeeded Pundit Jawaharlal Nehru (qv) as prime minister of India on 9 June 1964. That same month he suffered a heart attack. It was Shastri who managed to bring an end to the Indo-Pakistani War (qv). While in Tashkent, signing an accord with the Pakistanis, he suffered a heart attack and died.

Shatila Camp. *See* Sabra Camp, Lebanon.

Shatt al-Arab River. *See* Iraq, Iran and the Iraq-Iran War.

Shekhem (Nablus, Nabulus). *See* Israel.

Shell Oil Refinery, Nigeria. *See* Biafra.

Shenouda III. *See* Egypt.

Shermarke, Abdi Rashid Ali. (b. 15 October 1919, Somalia—d. 16 October 1969, Las Anod, Somalia) Trained in Somalia and Italy, Shermarke became president of his country in 1966 (inaugurated 1967). On 16 October 1969, he was assassinated at Las Anod, by a national policeman while visiting a drought-stricken part of the country. The murder followed a long period of tension and violence following what was seen as a rigged election held in March, Shermarke was buried on 20 October. The next day, a military coup seized the government. *See* Somalia.

Shihab (*Shehab/Chehab*), Fuad. On 25 October 1958, the last U.S. forces were withdrawn from Lebanon after a new coalition government, led by General Fuad Shihab, took control of the country (*See* Lebanon). An internal crisis, brought about through years of growing tension, erupted into civil war. American forces were inserted there in July 1958, following the revolution in Iraq. By that point, Lebanon was in armed insurrection. The situation began to ease after the election of Shihab, who took office in September 1959. Shihab was in office until 1964, a period punctuated by an attempted coup, led by the *Parti Populare Syrien*, some economic improvement and a calming of tensions. As the Lebanese constitution forbade a standing president from succeeding himself, Shihab, although he had the support of the army, refused to seek reelection.

Shindand Air Base. *See* Afghanistan.

Shining Path (*Sendero Luminoso*) (SL). This Peruvian terrorist organization was
    formed in 1969, under the leadership of Manuel Ruben Guzman, who called
    himself "President Gonzalo, Julio Cesar Mezzich and Carlota Tello Cutti (aka
    "Carla").   Its avowed mission was the overthrow of the constitutional
    government of Peru by the year 2000 and the imposition of a leftist, neo-Maoist,
    ethnic Indian government. This was to be done by attacking U.S. and other
    foreign interests considered "imperialist," to embarrass the government and
    force it to take oppressive measures that would cost it public support. The SL
    began as splinter group that broke away from the Peruvian Communist Party
    (PCP) because the PCP was not radical enough. At most, the SL could claim
    5,000 members, many of them of Quechua Indian ancestry. There was no known
    foreign support for the group, which funded itself through bank robbery and
    extortion and through the imposition of so-called war taxes on the populace. In
    this last regard, the SL went so far as to target illegal drug traffickers as a major
    source of revenue. Twelve- to 15-year-olds are the normal targets for
    recruitment. All cells within the structure of the SL have at least one female
    member. The principal target weapon is assassination, often coupled with
    ritualistic mutilation and the public display of victims. Targets are usually
    civilian employees of government and local political leaders. Bombings of civic
    action project sites and construction equipment is a part of the SL's plan to
    embarrass the government. This objective was partially achieved in July 1982,
    when President Fernando Belaunde Terry (qv) suspended constitutional
    guarantees in three southern provinces and ordered special security forces into
    the area to help quell the violence being spread by the SL. That same month, the
    U.S, embassy was bombed. In May 1983, the state of emergency was extended
    to continue combatting the widespread act of terrorism caused by the SL. On 11
    July, the SL attacked the headquarters of the Popular Action Party in Lima,
    killing two people and injuring 30. At that point the PCP joined in the
    condemnation of theSL. On 17 July 1984, the SL attacked a number of targets,
    one of which was the Soviet Aeroflot airlines office in Lima. The residence of
    the US ambassador and a number of other targets were bombed on 14 May
    1985. In subsequent years, the Soviet embassy was bombed (July 1986), as was
    the Indian embassy (January 1987). A Japanese banker was attacked in March
    1987. By 1989, SL had managed to halt much of the enterprise in the Andean
    region in an attempt to disrupt upcoming elections. In 1991, the SL was facing
    a major competitor in a terrorist organization known as the *Movimento
    Revolucionario Tupac Amaru (MRTA)*, but it continued its attack against its
    standard targets. Leaders of the SL and the MRTA were captured in 1992, but
    the SL's activities did not appear to abate. Guzman apparently offered a peace
    plan after his capture, but it was roundly repudiated by the SL. Many of those
    who had supported the SL earlier began renouncing the organization under a
    government propaganda campaign in 1994. In 1995, the SL continued its
    operations, but in a somewhat more restricted area and in a somewhat subdued

manner. A hotel near Lima was bombed, however, in May 1994. Since 1992, at least 2,000 SL members have been tried and convicted, by judges who were usually hooded to protect them against reprisals. *Reading:* Martin Koppel, *Peru's Shining Path: Anatomy of a Reactionary Sect* (1994); *David Scott Palmer, The Shining Path of Peru* (1994); Debrah Poole & Gerjerdo Renikue, *Peru: Time of Fear* (1992); Simon Strong, *Shining Path: Terror and Revolution in Peru* (1993).

Shishakli, Adib. On the day after he took office (28 November 1951), Maarouf Dawalibi, the pro-Soviet president of Syria, was overthrown. On 2 December 1951, Colonel Adib Shishakli assumed the presidency. By October 1952, Shishakli had systematically abolished all opposition political parties in the country, proclaiming his Arab Liberation Movement (ALM) as the only party. However, Shishkali was forced to resign on 24 February 1953, by an army-led coup. President Hashim al-Atasi (qv), himself a victim of an earlier coup in 1951, was reinstalled as head of state. Shishakli`s ALM was also dismantled.

Shkidchenko, P. T. *See* Afghanistan.

Shomeron Region. *See* Jordan.

Shomron, Dan. On 3–4 July 1976, Brigadier General Dan Shomron led a force of Israeli commands into Entebbe, Uganda, in a spectacularly successful raid to free the hostages being held there in the aftermath of the hijacking of an Air France airliner in Athens. Severe damage was imposed on Ugandan military equipment at the Entebbe airport as a way of punishing Idi Amin (qv) for his part in the affair. All the Arab terrorists involved were killed, 103 hostages were released, and one Israeli soldier, the leader of the ground assault force, died of his wounds.

Shouf (Chouf) Mountains. *See* Lebanon.

Shrar, Majed Abu. *See* Afghanistan.

Shumshere, Maharja Mohan. On 7 November 1950, a palace coup led by premier Mohan Shumshere overthrew King Tribhubarra (Trihuban) Bir Bikram (qv). The king took refuge in the Indian embassy and was subsequently allowed to go to India. Nepal fell into civil disorder, and in the compromise solution, Shumshere, a heritary prime minister of the Rana clan, took outsiders into his cabinet. The king returned in February 1951 as a constitutional monarch, but the government crisis continued. Mohan Shumshere resigned in November as the last Rana prime minister.

Siam. *See* Thailand.

as-Sibai, Yusuf. On 18 April 1978, two Palestinian terrorists assassinated Yusuf as-Sibai, the editor of the influential Egyptian newspaper *Al-Ahram*, in the Hilton hotel in Nicosia. In addition, the terrorists took 30 hostages and then demanded passage to Larnaca Airport. In exchange for transportation to the field, 12 hostages were released. Seven more were released when the terrorists were allowed to board their DC-8 aircraft. After taking off, however, the terrorists were refused landing rights in Algeria, Ethiopia, Greece, Kuwait, Libya, Somalia and Yemen (Aden). The aircraft was then refueled in Djibouti and forced to return to Nicosia the following day. After sitting three hours on the ground at Larnaca, the plane, carrying its crew, the terrorists and 11 hostages, was attacked by a 74-man Egyptian commando force flown in for the operation. In the ensuing firefight, which probably also involved members of the Cypriot National Guard and a 12-man PLO unit operating on behalf of the terrorists, 15 Egyptian commandos were killed. Even though the Egyptian Air Force C-130, that brought the commandos to Cyprus was parked at least one-half mile from the hijacked aircraft, it was destroyed by ground fire during the operation. This led to speculation that Cyprus had been involved in the terrorist attack in the first place. The hostage were subsequently released, and the two terrorists surrendered to the Cyprus police. Three days later, Egypt severed diplomatic relations with Cyprus. On 4 April, the terrorists were sentenced to death, but the sentences were commuted to life imprisonment by the Cyprus government.

Sidi Mohammed ben Arafa. On 14 August 1953, Morocco's Sultan Sidi Mohammed ben Arafa was deposed by a French-inspired coup. Moulay Mohammed ben Arafra (qv) was enthroned in his place. Two days later, following a period of much bloodshed, Sultan Moulay was deposed. On 21 August, Sidi Mohammed ben Arafa was reinstalled as sultan of Morocco. His reappointment was condemned, especially the French part in it, at a meeting of opposition leaders at Tetuan on 21 January 1954. On 27 August 1955, the French announced the resignation of the sultan and of the French governor general in Morocco. This was a part of the compromise reached at Aix-les-Bains to settle the dispute over the separation of French and Spanish Morocco. The sultan abdicated on 30 November. He was replaced by Sultan Sidi Mohammed III (qv), who had been deposed as monarch by the French in 1953.

Sidi Mohammed el-Amin. The Bey of Tunis, Sidi Mohammed el-Amin, was ousted from power on 25 July 1957 by the National Assembly. In his place, Habib Bourguiba (qv) was elected president. *See* Tunisia.

Sidi Mohammed III. On 30 November 1955, Sidi Mohammad III was returned to the throne in Morocco following the abdication of Sidi Mohammad ben Arafa (qv). Sidi Mohammad III had been deposed by the French in 1953. The return of Sidi Mohammad III was the result of the Declaration of La Celle St. Cloud, in which the French capitulated to the rebellion that was growing in Morocco. (*See* Morocco).

Sidky, Aziz. On 17 January 1972, the government of Egypt was reorganized and put on a wartime footing. Aziz Sidky replaced Mahmoud Fawzi as prime minister. On 11 February 1973, the new prime minister imposed a wartime budget on Egypt. On 26 March, however, President Anwar Sadat (qv) removed Aziz Sidky and assumed the prime ministerial role unto himself. *See* Egypt.

Sidon. *See* Lebanon.

Sierra Leone. A West African country, Sierra Leone is bordered on the north and east by Guinea, on the southeast by Liberia, and on the southwest and west by the Atlantic Ocean. The capital city is Freetown. The region was first explored by the Portuguese in 1460 and was named Lion Mountain (*Sierra Leone*) by the explorer Pedro de Cintra. A British colony was established there in 1787 as a haven for repatriated British and American slaves who had been shipwrecked or rescued from enslavement. The Sierra Leone Company, formed under British charter in 1791, administered the region until 1808, when it became a Crown Colony. In 1896, Sierra Leone became a British protectorate. The country held its first constitutional elections in 1924, and a ministerial system was established in 1953. The first chief minister was the leader of the Sierra Leone People's Party, Dr. Sir Milton Margai (1954), who was named prime minister in 1960. Sierra Leone won its independence within the British Commonwealth on 27 April 1961, which culminated a period of anticolonial unrest that began in 1956. A new constitution gave women the vote that same year. A new election reaffirmed Margai as prime minister. The election of Siaka Stevens (qv) of the All-People's Party (APC) as prime minister led to charges of election tampering. A coup followed (8 February 1967), after which the army formed the National Reformation Council. This was followed by a second coup (23 March 1967), which restored civilian rule; on 25 January 1968, another revolt gave power to Andrew Juxton-Smith. What became known as the "Sergeant's Revolt," on 18 April 1968, brought Stevens back to power as prime minister. Violence broke out (21–25 December 1968) but was suppressed by government troops. Opposition to the regime was slowly eliminated. However, on 14 September 1970, a state of siege was declared after two senior ministers resigned in protest of the policies of the Stevens regime. On 5 October 1970, Stevens announced the discovery of an army plot to overthrow his government. This prompted the declaration of a state of emergency. Yet another coup attempt took place on 21 January 1971, when army units revolted, but this one also failed to dislodge Stevens. Within three months, on 23 March 1971, another military coup was attempted. This one failed when Guinean troops were sent into Sierra Leone under the terms of a mutual defense agreement between the two countries. On 19 April 1971, Sierra Leone declared itself a republic and Stevens became president. Stevens was one of the architects of the Economic Community of West African States, which was modeled after the European Community (later European Union) (qv). Stevens's control of the political apparatus of the country was relatively complete when he and his party were reelected unopposed in May 1973. In 1978, Sierra Leone became a one-party state, that party being the APC, and Stevens was sworn in for his seventh term in office. During this period the economy began to sag, and exports could not match the price of imports. Liberia recalled its ambassador from Freetown on 17 November 1985, following an accusation that Sierra Leone was involved in the recent coup attempt against the Doe regime (*See* Liberia). Also, on 27 November 1985, Stevens retired from office and was replaced by Major General Joseph Saidu Momoh (sworn in January 1986), who had been elected in a one-party election on 1 October 1985. In March 1987, an unsuccessful coup attempt was made, and in November of that year, Momoh was forced to impose severe economic restrictions on his country. Rebel opposition arose in the late 1980s. By early 1991 the rebels, with the help of Liberian guerrillas, had captured several towns along the common border. At that point military assistance from Guinea and Nigeria arrived to save the regime. As a result, however, a new constitution was approved that provided for a multiparty system. In April 1992, however, Momoh was removed from office in a coup led by the army and was replaced by Captain Valentine Strasser. Strasser immediately set about suppressing crime, which was so bad it had put Sierra Leone at the bottom of the UN list of the worst countries in the world in which to live. Although Strasser has been roundly praised for reversing in the economic down-spiral, he has also been accused of curtailing freedom of the press, making political opponents disappear and allowing the civil war to continue. In 1994, Strasser was forced to accede to demands for multiparty elections to be held in 1996. A multiparty system was restored on 27 April 1995. Still, the government was unable to bring the rebel situation under control, and fighting was reported within 40 miles of the capital. Strasser was ousted in a military coup led by Brigadier General Julius Maada Bio on 16 January 1996. Strasser fled to Great Britain, while the new government prepared for the promised elections. *Reading:* Alusine Jalloh & David E. Skinner, eds., *Islam and Trade in Sierra Leone* (1997); Joe A. D. Alie, *A New History of Sierra Leone* (1990); George O. Roberts, *The Anguish of Third World Independence: The Sierra Leone Experience* (1982); Eliphas G. Mukonoweshuro, *Colonialism, Class Formation and Underdevelopment in Sierra Leone* (1993).

Sierra Maestra Mountains. *See* Cuba.

Sihanouk, Norodom (Samdech Preah Norodom Sihanouk). (b. 31 October 1922, Phnom Penh, Cambodia) Born into royalty, Sihanouk assumed the throne of Cambodia in 1941, following the death of his grandfather, King Monivong. Sihanouk, with the backing of the Japanese during World War II, attempted to free his country from the French colonial system, but when France reoccupied Cambodia after the war, Sihanouk decided to wait for the eventual ouster of France from Southeast Asia. When this occurred in 1954, Sihanouk won a referendum in February 1955, establishing his People's Socialist Community party (*Sangkum Reastr Niyum*), and then abdicated in favor of his father, Norodom Suramarit. Sihanouk became prime minister and foreign minister and then became the permanent Cambodian representative to the United Nations. When Suramarit died in April 1960, Sihanouk became the head of state. While attempting to steer a neutral course for Cambodia, Sihanouk entered into a secret agreement with the North Vietnamese by which they were given a safe haven in Cambodia during the Vietnam war, in return for a North Vietnamese guarantee of non-support for the communist Khmer Rouge (qv) movement he was facing in Cambodia. At the same time, he refused US assistance by capitalizing on his popularity among the Cambodian population to keep a fragile peace at home. After 15 years of relative calm, Sihanouk was ousted by U.S.–supported General Lon Nol (qv). Sihanouk went to Peking for refuge, but he returned to Cambodia after the 1975 takeover by the Khmer Rouge. Upon his return he was immediately put under house arrest and remained incarcerated until January 1979, when communist Vietnamese forces were rolling over the country. He was sent to the UN to speak for the Khmer Rouge. Instead, after denouncing the Vietnamese invasion, he denounced the Khmer Rouge as well. In 1982, Sihanouk became president of a Cambodian government-in-exile, which was composed of an odd lot of factions. Until 1991, he remained in exile, acting as much as anything else as a mediator in the disputes among the coalition. In 1991, Sihanouk was elected president of Cambodia's Supreme National Council. In September 1993, following a UN-sponsored election (May 1993), Sihanouk was proclaimed king. Sihanouk's first full year (1994) on the throne was spent largely in receiving treatment for cancer in China. Had he been at home, he would have faced considerable upheaval within Cambodia's government, including a failed coup attempt led by a half-brother. *Reading:* Helene Cixous. *The Terrible but Unfinished Story of Norodom Sihanouk, King of Cambodia* (1994); Milton Osbourne, *Sihanouk: Prince of Light, Prince of Darkness* (1994).

Sihanoukville. *See* Cambodia/Kampuchea and Kompong Som.

Sikhs (India). *See* Akali.

Sikkim. A tiny kingdom of Sikkim is actually, today, a state in the Indian Union. It is located mainly in the Himalayan Mountains and is bordered on the north by Tibet, on the east by Bhutan, on the south by India and on the west by Nepal. There is some information about the region from Bhutanese travelers, who entered the region in the fourteenth century and found people of the Lepcha tribe, who were themselves an assimilation of numerous other tribes that had either moved through the region or had been indigenous. The kingdom of Sikkim was established in 1642, and the Namgyal dynasty that ruled from that date remained until 1975. In the early days of the kingdom, Sikkim fought a series of wars against both Bhutan and Nepal. Much of western Sikkim was occupied by the Nepalese as a result. The British forced the return of the land in 1816 because of Sikkim's assistance during the 1814–1816 Anglo-Nepalese War. By 1817, however, Sikkim found itself under British suzerainty and was divested, in 1835, of the major city of Darjiling, which was taken over by the British East India Company. A very low-level insurgency began that culminated in 1849, when Britain annexed the Sikkim lowlands and subsequently defeated the Sikkimese army. The Anglo-Sikkimese Treaty of 1861 made Sikkim a princely protectorate, but with a number of loopholes not common during the heyday of the colonial period. For one thing, as the question of rule was not specified, the Namgyal dynasty continued. The British were given the right to build a road through Sikkim to Tibet, which was probably one of the principal reasons for the treaty in the first place. Another agreement, this one concluded in 1890 between Tibet and Great Britain, acknowledged the Sikkimese border with Tibet. The British then assigned a Foreign Service officer to Sikkim, and he became the power in the country. This situation remained until 1950, when India achieved its independence. Thereafter, it signed a treaty with Sikkim, making it a protectorate of India with access to strategic communications, defense needs and foreign affairs support. During this same period, politics came to Sikkim as separate political parties sprang up. Most of these wanted annexation by India and an end to the extant feudal system. These notions were resisted by the crown, but the terms of the 1950 Indo-Sikkim agreement called for more popular participation in the Sikkimese government and a number of elections to be held between 1952 and 1974 to improve this participation. In the meantime, Communist Chinese incursions developed along the Tibet-Sikkim border (11–14 September 1967). On 8 April 1973, the Sikkimese ruler, Palden Thonup Namgyal, asked India to assume the administration of the country following a two-week period of unrest in the country. In 1974, the Sikkim Congress Party coalition swept the elections. The new government attempted to improve the human condition, but the crown objected and suppressed these moves. In 1975, the Sikkimese population voted to merge with India, which was accomplished on 15 May 1975. *See* India. *Reading:* Tanka B. Subba, *Dynamics of a Hill Society: The Nepalis in Darjeeling and Sikkim Himalayas* (1990); Earl of Ronaldshay, *Lands of the Thunderbolt: Sikkim, Chumbi, and Bhutan* (1987).

Siles Zuaro, Hernan. In July 1980 the Bolivian Congress determined that national elections should be held. By mid-year everything was ready to proceed, but right-wing violence threatened to disrupt the process. When the election was completed (29 June 1980), the left-wing candidate, Hernan Siles Zuaro, was the clear winner, but he did not have the necessary plurality. Congress was to decide the outcome. In the interim, the military led a coup to upset the leftist drive for power. Major General Luis Garcia Meza Tejada was named the leader of the new ruling junta. In new elections held on 5 October 1982, Siles was once again elected president. On 30 June 1984, Siles was kidnapped by a group of 60 police and army officers in an abortive coup attempt. He was released ten hour later after intensive negotiations with the coup leaders. Evidence later showed the coup group was made up of persons involved in the drug trade, and over 100 people were arrested. Siles remained in office until 6 August 1985, when he was defeated in a new election.

Simla. *See* India.

Simonstown Agreement. *See* Anglo-South African Naval Defense Agreement.

Sind. *See* Pakistan.

Sindhi Languages. *See* Pakistan.

Singapore. The Republic of Singapore, which is composed of one major island (Singapore Island) and about 50 lesser islets, is located at the southern tip of the Malay Peninsula. As early as the fourteenth century Singapore was an important trading center in Southeast Asia. It was first recorded as a part of the Sri Vijaya Empire; it then became a part of the kingdom of Majapahit. In the fifteenth century it became a part of the Malacca sultanate. Sir Thomas Stamford Raffles established a British trading post there in 1819, and the site was given to the British East India Company by the Sultan of Jahor in 1824. Singapore became part of the Straits Settlements in 1826, and it soon became one of Britain's most important commercial centers in Asia. During World War I it became the British naval base for east Asia, and a major military fortified installation was constructed there. Unfortunately, the plans were laid to repel an attack from the sea; when the island was attacked from the Malay Peninsula side by the Japanese at the beginning of World War II, the island fell after only a brief, yet heroic, defense. British forces liberated the island on 12 September 1945, when the Japanese garrison finally surrendered. In 1946, Singapore became crown colony; and on 1 January 1957, it became a self-governing state within the British Commonwealth. Independence was achieved on 3 June 1959. On 16 September 1963, Singapore, Malaya and North Borneo were united to form Malaysia. At that time, Malaysia's prime minister, Abdul Rahman (qv), announced (16 October) that after the merger, Singapore could no longer be used as a SEATO base, especially by Great Britain. In July 1964, serious rioting broke out among the Chinese community in a communist-inspired demonstration against Malaysia. On 9 August 1965, Singapore withdrew from the merger with Malaysia to become a sovereign state, still within the Commonwealth. That same year, Singapore became a member of the United Nations. In December 1965, Singapore was proclaimed a republic, with Inche Yusof bin Ishak, who had been head of state since 1959, as its first president. On 18 July 1967, Great Britain announced the complete withdrawal of British forces from both Singapore and Malaysia by the mid-1970s. Australia announced, on 5 October 1967, that it would increase by $A20 million its aid to the two countries. On 1 June 1969, two days of clashes began between Chinese and Malays in Sinapore. Throughout this period, a series of presidents were elected until 1981, when President, Benjamin Henry Sheares died in office. His place was taken by C. V. Devan Nair. When Nair resigned the presidency in 1985, he was replaced by Wee Kim Wee. From 1959 until 1990, however, the real power was held by Prime Minister Lee Kuan Yew, a supporter of U.S. policy in Southeast Asia. In 1971, Singapore entered into a defense alliance with Great Britain, Australia, New Zealand and Malaysia; and Singapore immediately integrated its air defense system with that of Malaysia (2 September 1971). On 13 November 1973, Singapore joined the Arab oil embargo on the United States and Great Britain. On 24 February 1976, Singapore joined the Association of Southeast Asian Nations. Immediately following the end of the war in Southeast Asia, Lee's foreign policy became more friendly to the communist bloc, and diplomatic relations were established with Cambodia in July 1976 and with China in 1990. That same year, Lee resigned after designating his successor, Goh Chok Tong, who was elected in his own right by a landslide in 1991. When the country's first direct elections were held in 1993, Ong Teng Cheong was elected president. The years 1994 and 1995 were spent in enforcing Singapore's tough laws, with the caning of an American, Michael Fay, for malicious mischief, and the execution of a Dutch citizen for drug running. *Reading:* James Francis Warren, *At the Edge of Southeast Asian History: Essays* (1988);

Yaacov Y. I. Vertzberger, *Coastal States, Regional Powers, Superpowers and the Malacca-Singapore Straits* (1984).

Sinhalese. *See* Sri Lanka

Sinkiang Province. *See* China.

Sinkiang Uighr Autonomous Region. *See* China.

Sinn Fein. More correctly *Sinn Fein Pairti na Noibri* (Sinn Fein the Worker's Party) this Irish political party came into existence by a play on words in October 1902, when members of the Society of Gaels (*Cumann na nGaedheal*) adopted a policy of "We Alone" (*Sinn Fein*) in a passive resistance campaign against the British. "The Rising" at Easter 1916 brought Sinn Fein to the fore, as it became a rallying point for opposition to the 1921 settlement with Great Britain (*see* Northern Ireland). One of Sinn Fein's leaders at that time was Eamon De Valera, who led the party to victory in December 1918. In January 1919, Sinn Fein declared itself the parliament of a free Ireland and set up a government in oppposition to the British administration. At that moment Britain was engaged in extended negotiation to create a government. When the Irish Free State was born in 1921, Sinn Fein objected to the agreement and found itself on the outside. In March 1926, De Valera resigned from Sinn Fein and formed a new party called *Fianna Fail*, which brought many Sinn Fein members to its banner. After that, Sinn Fein had little voice in the government of Ireland. The group concentrated on the question of unification and made common cause with the Irish Republican Army (IRA). In December 1969, both Sinn Fein and the IRA split into "official" and "provisional" wings because of major differences about the tactics necessary to accomplish the task of reunification.

Sino-Japanese Treaty. On 12 August 1978, a Sino-Japanese peace treaty was signed. This treaty came about three months after China and Japan had normalized relations for the first time since the end of World War II. In retaliation for the signing of the treaty, the USSR reinforced its garrisons in the Kurile Islands in September.

Sino-Soviet. *See* China and the USSR.

Sipple, Oliver. On 22 September 1975, ex-marine Oliver Sipple grabbed Sara Jane Moore just as she was about to fire at President Gerald Ford (qv) as he was leaving the St. Francis Hotel in San Francisco. The shot was deflected and slightly injured a cab driver among the crowd of about 3,000 waiting for a glimpse of the president.

Sir George Williams University. Rioting broke out on 11 February 1969 at Sir George Williams University in Montreal, Canada. A new school building was set on fire, and student records were destroyed. *See* Canada.

Sirhan, Sirhan Bishara. At slightly past midnight, 5 June 1968, Sirhan Bishara Sirhan assassinated US presidential hopeful Senator Robert F. Kennedy (qv) in a kitchen hallway as he was leaving a party at the Los Angeles Ambassador Hotel. Sirhan, a Jerusalem-born Palestinian of Jordanian ancestry, was subsequently tried and sentenced to death in April 1969. His sentence was later commuted to life imprisonment.

Sisophon District. *See* Thailand.

Sithole, Ndabaningi. (b. 21 July 1920, Matabeleland, Southern Rhodesia) On 12 February 1969, the nationalist leader the Reverend Ndabaningi Sithole was convicted of planning the assassination of Rhodesia's prime minister, Ian D. Smith (qv), and two of his ministers. Sithole, an American-educated Methodist minister and the leader of the Zimbabwe African National Union (ZANU) was sentenced to six year's imprisonment. On 3 December 1974, however, Sithole and Joshua Nkomo (qv) were temporarily released from prison to attend discussions in Lusaka, Zambia, on the future of Rhodesia. When the government began arresting all opposition leaders in March 1975, Sithole was again arrested, this time with charges stemming from the assassination of another ZANU figure, Herbert Chitepo, in Zambia, and plotting the murders of other black leaders. Sithole was tried by a special court and ordered detained as a threat because of his advocacy of violence to overcome white rule in his country. He was shortly released, however, to attend an Organization of African Unity (OAU) (qv) conference in Tanzania and did not immediately return to Rhodesia. He did go back in July 1977, for talks with Prime Minister Smith. By that point, Sithole was leading a dissident wing of ZANU, called the African National Council. ZANU had been taken over by Robert Mugabe (qv), the co-founder, with Sithole, of the group. Sithole, along with other black leaders, was able to reach an agreement with Smith for majority rule in Rhodesia by the end of 1978. That date was later moved back to April 1979. When Bishop Abel Muzorewa won the subsequent election, in April 1979, Sithole and another candidate repudiated the results. In 1983, Sithole was again suspected of engaging in subversive activities against the government, now headed by Prime Minister Mugabe, and was warned not to interfere. In October 1995, Sithole, then a member of the House of Assembly, was arrested in connection with a plot to assassinate President Robert Mugabe. There was sufficient evidence, however, to make it appear that the arrest resulted from Sithole's announced candidacy for the presidency in opposition to Mugabe's one-man rule. *See* Zimbabwe.

Six Day War of 1967. *See* Israel.

Siyaad Barrah (Siad Barre), Muhammad. On 15 October 1969, Somali president Abdi Rashid Ali Shermarke (qv) was assassinated by a national police officer as he toured a drought-stricken part of the country. On the day following Shermarke's funeral (21 October), the army and police carried out a coup in which the prime minister, Muhammad Haji Ibrahim Egal, and his cabinet were arrested and the constitution was abolished. Social reform was promised. Major General Muhammad Siyaad Barrah, the head of the Supreme Revolutionary Council (SRC), took power and declared his country's neutrality, renaming it the Somali Democratic Republic. On 27 April 1970, Siyaad Barrah claimed that a plot had been uncovered, which led to the arrests of members of the SRC and charges of treason. By this move, Siyaad Barrah consolidated his hold on the country. A socialist state was proclaimed on 21 October 1970, and promised elections did not come to pass. Siyaad remained in office until 1987, when he began to relinquish some instruments of power to key subordinates within his party and the government. Although his age had never been revealed, it was believed that he was in his 70s and suffering from injuries incurred in an automobile accident in 1986. By the end of 1990, Siyaad had lost control of much of his country to local warlords and clan groups. On 26–27 January 1991, he fled the capital for his own home area in the southwestern corner of Somalia near the town of Geda. The legacy of economic and social chaos he left behind led directly to the need for Western intervention in Operation Restore Hope in 1993.

Sjarifoeddin, Amir. *See* Indonesia.

Skhirat. *See* Morocco.

Slansky, Rudolf. On 20 November 1952, a major trial began in Czechoslovakia in which a number of individuals, among them former Czech Communist Party secretary and vice-premier Rudolf Slansky and the former foreign minister Vladimir Clementis (qv), pled guilty to charges ranging from treason to espionage and sabotage. Slansky was a Moscow-trained party member. Slansky, Clementis and nine others were condemned to death in the show trial.

Slovakia (Slovak Republic). *See* Czechoslovakia. *Reading:* Carol Skalnik Leff, *The Czech and Slovak Republics: Nation versus State* (1996).

Slovenia. *See* Yugoslavia.

Smith, Charles. On 23 March 1967, a military coup, led by Lieutenant Colonel Andrew T. Juxton-Smith (qv) and Major Charles Smith successfully overthrew the government of Sierra Leone. A military junta was set up and Juxton-Smith was named chairman of the National Reformation Council. *See* Sierra Leone.

Smith, Ian D. (b. 8 April 1919, Selukwe, Rhodesia) Smith was educated in local schools before attending the University of Grahamstown, South Africa. World War II interrupted his education, and he served in the Royal Air Force. During the war, Smith was twice shot down. After the war he completed his education and then successfully ran for the Southern Rhodesian Assembly (1948). When Southern Rhodesia and Nyasaland formed a federation, Smith joined the Federal Party and, in 1958, became the government whip in Parliament. He broke with the Federal Party when a new constitution was drafted that would have given greater freedom to the black Africans. Instead, he formed the Rhodesian Front in 1961, gathering white-supremacist support. In the 1962 elections, Smith's party won a major victory on a platform of independence and white rule. Smith became prime minister of Southern Rhodesia in 1964 following the dissolution of the federation with Nyasaland in 1963. He immediate set about a program of white supremacy by ordering the arrest of a number of black Africans, whom he then had banished as insurrectionists. When serious rioting followed, he used force to suppress it. In July 1964, Smith refused to consider a new constitution that would have given blacks more say in government when the item was brought up at a British Commonwealth prime ministers' conference. After a number of futile meetings with Great Britain, Smith, with the backing of his all-white government, unilaterally declared Southern Rhodesia independent on 11

November 1965. Britain refused to accept this act and moved for sanctions against Southern Rhodesia at the United Nations.Throughout 1966–1968, the British negotiated with Smith, but he adamantly refused the British position of establishing majority rule within ten years. On 12 February 1969, black nationalist leader Ndabaningi Sithole (qv) was convicted of planning Smith's assassination. Smith severed relations with the Commonwealth and, on 2 March 1970, declared Rhodesia a republic. For most of the next decade, Smith was faced by a growing black guerrilla war led by Robert Mugabe (qv) and Joshua Nkomo (qv). Based in Mozambique, the Popular Front rebel forces carried out numerous raids into Rhodesia. Smith retaliated with extreme repressive measures against the black population. These were coupled with a growing economic stagnation brought about primarily by the need to expend large sums to support the embattled white army. A white exodus from Rhodesia then began. On 20 December 1974, Smith announced that a cease-fire had been agreed upon and that all political prisoners would be released as a precondition to setting up a constitutional convention. Finally, in 1977, Smith was forced to open negotiations with moderate black leaders such as Bishop Abel Muzorewa (qv). Discussions with more militant leaders such as Joshua Nkomo were more difficult and were often broken off (19 March 1976), because of demands for an immediate, rather than a gradual transfer of power. On 12 September 1976, Smith announced, following a visit by U.S. secretary of state Henry Kissinger, that he accepted an American proposal for the immediate establishment of a biracial government, with majority (that is, black) rule within two years. Smith continued the fight, however, rejecting a British proposal for an interim government on 24 January 1977. Martial law was declared on 10 September 1978, to strengthen Smith's hand in the ongoing negotiations. The transfer of power to the blacks was also begun in 1978. Smith served as a member of the Transitional Executive Council that supervised the transition to black rule. Smith retained his title of prime minister until May 1979 and then joined the new black majority government of Zimbabwe as minister without portfolio until December 1979. He continued to serve in Parliament until 1987. *See* Zimbabwe.

Smolny Airport. *See* Soviet Union.

Smrkovsky, Josef. On 7 January 1969, the Presidium of the Czechoslovak Communist Party ousted the National Assembly chairman, Josef Smrkovsky. This action was taken as a part of the general housecleaning that followed the Soviet invasion of the country to "restore order." *See* Czechoslovakia.

Smuts, Jan Christian. (b. 24 May 1870, Riebeeck West, Cape Colony—d.1 September 1950, Irene, near Pretoria, South Africa) Born into a Dutch farm family, Smuts was educated at Victoria College, where he majored in science and art. Thereafter, he went to England, where he attended Christ College, Cambridge, where he studied law. He then went to London, where he attended the Inns of Court honors program. After taking top honors in all his schooling, he returned to his native South Africa. Arriving in Capetown in 1895, he became a supporter of Prime Minister Cecil Rhodes. He broke with Rhodes, however, after the raid into Transvaal led by Dr. Sir Leander Starr Johnson in 1895–1896. Johnson, Rhodes's friend, led the operation to spark an uprising in Johannesburg, which failed to materialize. Thereafter, Smuts moved to Johannesburg and, in 1877, married his college sweetheart, Isie Krige. In 1888, he moved to Pretoria and became a state attorney. Smuts participated in the Second Boer War (October 1899–1902) as a part-time soldier, but shortly after the British took Pretoria (5 June 1900), he took up soldiering full time. He became adept at guerrilla warfare and spent much time, now as an independent commander, attacking British supply lines. He eventually struck deep into Cape Colony territory, but the war ended with a British victory. Under heavy guard, Smuts was taken to participate in the drafting of the peace settlement. Unshaken by the turn of events he persisted in his determination for a united South Africa. Upon returning to Pretoria, he reentered politics as a member of Louis Botha's *Het Volk* (the People) party in opposition to the anti-Boer government of Alfred Milner. Through this activity, Smuts made major contributions to the establishment of a responsible government in Transvaal (1906) and to the establishment of the Union of South Africa in 1910. In the former case, Smuts travelled to Great Britain (1905) to argue for Transvaal's autonomy, and during that visit he made a number of important contacts for the future. With the outbreak of World War I, Smuts assisted Botha in suppressing the Boer uprising that followed the Union's declaration of war on Germany. He also helped in the occupation of South West Africa and opened a major campaign for the conquest of East Africa. In March 1917, he traveled again to England, where he so impressed Prime Minister Lloyd George that George appointed him minister for air, in which capacity he helped organize the Royal Air Force, and participated in the Versailles Peace Conference. Smuts is also regarded as one of the architects of the League of Nations. Upon Botha's death in 1919, Smuts became prime minister, but he was defeated five years later and remained the opposition leader until 1933. Upon returning to power under J. B. M. Hertzog, Smuts served unobtrusively until 1939, when he and Hertzog split over South Africa's participation in what was to become the second global conflict. Smuts won a narrow election to be prime minister and brought South Africa into the war on the Allied side in September 1939. Smuts became the de facto leader of the fight to prevent the Germans and Italians from becoming entrenched in North Africa. Although admired by Winston Churchill and other Allied leaders, Smuts and South Africa played a relatively minor part in the outcome of the war. He did represent South Africa at the 1945 chartering conference for the United Nations in San Francisco. Back home, however, Smuts was defeated by the Nationalist Party candidate, D. F. Malan, in 1948. Smuts was then offered and accepted the post of chancellor of Cambridge University. Two years later, Smuts died in his home in Pretoria.

Snyder, Michael. On 6 November 1985, two unidentified assailants shot and wounded U.S. army major Michael Snyder on the street in San Juan, Puerto

Rico. A passer-by was also injured. The separatist Organization of Volunteers for the Puerto Rican Revolution claimed credit for the attack.

Soai, Tran Van. *See* Hoa Hao.

Soames, Lord. *See* Zimbabwe.

Soares de Melo, Henrique. *See* Mozambique.

Sobhuza II. (b. 22 July 1899, Swaziland—d. 21 August 1982, Mbabane, Swaziland) Born the son of King Ngwane V, Sobhuza (*Ngwenyama*) was still an infant when his father died. He assumed the rule under the regency of the queen and was educated both in Swaziland and in Cape Province, South Africa. He became the constitutional ruler of Swaziland on 22 December 1921. Swaziland received its autonomy in 1967. It received its independence in 1968. On 12 April 1973, Sobhuza abrogated the constitution and assumed personal leadership of the country after dissolving the legislature. To accomplish this, Sobhuza had raised and financed a secret army answerable only to him. In 1979, a new parliament (*Libandla*) was established to be an advisory body to the king. He was, as tradition required, buried in a secret grave near the palace. *See* Swaziland.

Socialist Student League. *See* Dutschke, Rudi.

Sofar. *See* Lebanon.

Soglo, Christophe. On 28 October 1963, a military coup overthrew President Hurbert Maga (qv) and his one-party system of government in Dahomey. The coup was led byGeneral Christophe Soglo, who promptly installed a new civilian government, with himself as head of state. A new civilian president and vice-president were installed in January 1964. On 22 December 1965, however, Soglo led another coup to oust the government he had helped put into power two years earlier. Soglo was again installed as president, this time retaining the office. As is the way of such things, Soglo was ousted as president on 17 December 1967 by another military coup headed by Major Maurice Kouandete (qv), who then promoted himself to lieutenant colonel and took the presidency. *See* Dahomey.

Sognefjord. *See* Norway.

Soilih, Ali. On 3 August 1975, a coup led by Ali Soilih overthrew the Ahmed Abdallah (qv) government in the Comoros Islands, less than one month after Abdallah had declared unilateral independence. Soilih himself was overthrown on 13 May 1978 in a foreign coup organized by a French mercenary, Colonel Robert Denard (qv), who immediately restored Ahmed Abdullah to power, with a co-president, Mohammed Ahmed, being installed on 24 May. Soilih was killed in a subsequent attempt to escape house arrest.

al-Solh, Rashid. On 16 May 1975, Rashid al-Solh, who had been in office since 31 October 1974, resigned as prime minister of Lebanon, blaming the continued violence in the country on the Christian Phalangists. He was replaced by Rashid Karami (qv).

Solidarity Movement (*Solidarnoshc*). More properly called the Independent Self-Governing Trade Union Solidarity (*Niezalezny Samarzod Zwiazkov Zawodowych Solidarnoshc*), Solidarity was a Polish trade union that had its origins in another group formed in 1976, the Workers' Defense Committee (KOR), and came into being after a major government attack on striking workers. The intellectuals who started KOR supported the families of jailed workers, provided legal and medical aid and operated an underground network. The KOR published a Charter of Workers' Rights in 1979. When rising food prices fired unrest in 1980, the Lenin Shipyards in Gdansk became the center of agitation for better pay and working conditions. As a major act of defiance, more than 17,000 workers, led by Lech Walesa (qv), barricaded themselves in the shipyard. By August 1980 an Interfactory Strike Committee had been formed in Gdansk to coordinate all strike activity throughout the country. The committee presented the Polish government with a list of demands that were largely taken from the KOR Charter. The government accepted most of these demands, and authorized free unions with the right to strike as a major concession, along with promises of more religious and political freedom. Out of this grew Solidarity, which was founded on 22 September 1980 by delegates of 36 regional unions. Thereafter, KOR disbanded, and most of its members joined Solidarity. Lech Walesa was appointed chairman of the new group. On 14 December 1980, a separate agricultural Solidarity was formed in Warsaw. Almost 10 million, representing most of Poland's workforce, were members of one or the other of these groups by early 1981. Thereafter, Solidarity imposed itself on the communist government of General Wojciech Jaruzelski (qv), demanding more and more freedom and using strikes to emphasize its demands. At the same time, the Polish government was under enormous pressure from the USSR to end Solidarity's activities, including a threat to enter Poland and settle the matter in the typical Soviet way, by force. On 8 December 1981, 100,000 Soviet troops began massing on the Polish border. Beginning in September, the government began cracking down on "law breakers" and all anti-Soviet activities. On 13 December 1981, martial law was declared in an attempt to crush the union. Polish government banned Solidarity as illegal and arrested its leaders. On 1 May 1982, 30,000 demonstrated in Warsaw to demand the release of Walesa. Riot police broke up that demonstration and another one that was staged on 3 May. The government was forced to reimpose a curfew in Warsaw as a result. The parliament (*Sejm*) dissolved Solidarity on 8 October 1982. Instead of disbanding, the group went underground, and a major strike followed in Gdansk on 11 October. On 15 October the government outlawed Solidarity. On 31 August 1983, 10,000 Solidarity supporters clashed with police in Nowa Huta, a town near Cracow, in one of the most serious confrontations. In 1988, another wave of strikes overtook Poland. As a result, the government was forced, in April 1989, to reinstate Solidarity and to authorize free elections for the parliament. Solidarity candidates took 99 of 100 seats in the new Senate, and all 161 contested seats in the lower house (the *Sejm*). A coalition government was the next step, and in August 1989, the first noncommunist premier since the 1940s was elected. Lech Walesa became president of Poland in December 1990. Thereafter, political differences among the membership began to appear, but after the collapse of the Soviet Union, the union's unique role in politics diminished. *Reading:* Robert Eringer, *Strike for Freedom: The Story of Lech Walesa and Polish Solidarity* (1982).

Somalia (*Al-Sumal*). The Democratic Republic of Somalia is a country in northeast Africa (Horn of Africa), bordered on the north by the Gulf of Aden, on the east and southeast by the Indian Ocean, on the southwest by Kenya and on the west by Ethiopia. The nation of Djibouti forms an enclave at the northwest tip of Somalia's border with Ethiopia. The capital city is Mogadishu. The northern and eastern areas of the region were organized as a part of the Kingdom of Puoni (Punt) mentioned in Egyptian sources. As such, the area served as a center of trade with the outside world. Arab Muslim immigrants enterred the region during the seventh to tenth centuries and, along with the Persians, developed a number of trading posts along Somalia's long coastline. After the tenth century, Somali nomads inhabited the northern area, while the southern area was inhabited by the more pastoral Oromo tribes. During this period, Islam was firmly established along the coastal areas. European interest did not begin much before the British occupation of Aden in 1839. In 1884, the protectorate of British Somaliland was established in the north, and by 1905 the southern area had become Italian Somaliland. A Muslim-led insurgency began in the north (British) area by nationalist groups intent on halting further foreign colonization. In Italian Somaliland, on the other hand, foreign settlement was encouraged. In 1936, Italian Somaliland was made a part of the Italian East African Empire. Italian Axis forces invaded British Somaliland in 1940, but a year later British forces reoccupied the colony. A British administration was established over all of Somalia after World War II. In 1950, Italian Somaliland was returned to Italian control as a UN trusteeship. On 1 July 1960, the two areas were recombined as the independent Republic of Somalia. Almost immediately, border clashes along the Somali-Ethiopian border were reported (14 August 1960). An army revolt occurred in December 1961, which was unsuccessful. Beginning in 1963, a five-year series of border clashes began between Somalia and its southern neighbor, Kenya, over disputed territory. On 14 March 1963, Somalia broke diplomatic relations with Great Britain over its siding with Kenya in the on-going border dispute. In February 1964, the OAU stepped into the dispute, moving to replace British forces along the border with an African peacekeeping force and ordering a cease-fire. In the latter, the OAU was initially unsuccessful, but it did manage to arrange a truce on 1 April 1964. In the Declaration of Arusha (Tanzania), Kenya and Somalia agreed to end the border conflict on 28 October 1967. The final peace accord was signed on 31 January 1968. In 1967, the government of Prime Minister Maxamed Xaaji Ibrahim Cigaal was elected, but it was overthrown in a military and police coup (21 October 1969) that had earlier cost the life of President Cabdirashiid Cali Shermarke (qv) (assassinated on 16 October 1969). The coup leader, Major General Maxamed Siyaad Barrah (qv), dissolved the parliament and established a Supreme Revolutionary Council, which renamed the country the Somali

Democratic Republic. The Soviet Union then became Somalia's chief benefactor. There was an unsuccessful coup attempt made on Siyaad's regime on 21 April 1970. Another coup attempt, this time led by the vice-president, Muhammad Ainanshe Guleid (qv), failed on 5 May 1971. This was followed by yet another failed attempt to dislodge Siyaad on 25 May. Somalia called for the independence of all Portuguese colonies in Africa at a 17 June 1974 meeting of the OAU. Somolia signed a treaty of frienship and cooperation with the USSR on 11 July 1974. On 7 January 1976, the USSR delivered two naval vessels outfitted with antiship missiles to Somalia and gave other arms and materiel to Uganda. The U.S. countered by sending arms to Kenya and Zaire on 16 June. In 1977, Somalia invaded Ethopia in a move to occupy the Somali-inhabited Ogaden region. The attempt was unsuccessful, principally because the USSR shifted its support to Ethiopia. Hundreds of thousands of ethnic Somali refugees fled Ogaden and filled refugee camps in Somalia. On 1 May 1977, Somalia announced it was extending naval basing rights to the Soviet Union. Heavy fighting was reported along the Addis Ababa–Djibouti road in July between Ethiopian forces and those belonging to the West Somali Liberation Front (WSLF). In August, the WSLF launched a major offensive against Ethiopian forces in Ogaden province. Tens of thousands were reported to have died in that fighting. Ethiopia then accused the Somali central government of supporting the rebel WSLF. On 1 September, France entered the picture when it cut off its military aid to Somalia until the fighting was stopped. On 5 September, the Arab League told Somalia it would furnish no support until Somalia ceased making war on Ethiopia. Somalia warned the Soviet Union (21 October) that the support it was giving Ethiopia might jeopardize the arrangement it had made with the Somalis. In retaliation for the continued aid received by Ethiopia, Somalia expelled several thousand Soviet and Cuban advisers, broke diplomatic relations with Cuba, and abrogated the 1974 treaty it had with the USSR on 13 November. When West Germany gave Somalia $20 million, Ethiopia expelled the German ambassador in Addis Ababa (22 January 1978). On 11 February 1978, Somalia ordered a general mobilization. In early March, Ethiopian forces, reinforced with Cuban troops and Soviet equipment, dealt Somalia a serious blow in Ogaden. Thereafter, on 9 March, Somalia began withdrawing its regular troops from the region. The withdrawal was completed on 15 March. On 11 September 1979, Kenya and Somalia signed a treaty of friendship and mutual defense and held a meeting of heads of state in Saudi Arabia. The U.S. was granted access to the former Soviet naval facilities in the country on 22 November 1979; this was expanded to a larger agreement on 12 February 1980, wherein the U.S. received major basing concessions in return for U.S. aid. When the Arab League member states voted to break diplomatic relations with Egypt over the signing of the peace accord (see Egypt and Israel), Somalia, along with Oman and Sudan, refused to agree to the action (4 June 1980). Fighting in the Ogaden continued in 1980. On 10 August, a Somali army convoy was ambushed by Ethiopian troops on the Ogaden plateau. At least 1,500

Somalis were killed and nearly 2,000 wounded in the engagement. Internally, Somalia continued to suffer from the age-old ethnic rivalries between the northern and southern parts of the country.That same month, the United States announced it had signed a defense agreement with Somalia that gave the U.S. airbase and naval rights in Mogadishu and Berbera in return for $25 million in aid in 1981, with more aid in later years. The United States made a major arms trade with Somalia in February 1981, in return for naval basing rights at Berbera on the Gulf of Aden. The fighting in Ogaden continued into 1982. On 1 July, for instance, Somalia reported that Soviet-built Ethiopian MiG jets were used in an attack on its positions in the Mugad region of Ogaden and, on 5 July, that Ethiopian troops supported by tanks had actually driven into Somali territory. The situation became grave, and Somalia declared a state of emergency along the Ogaden border. The Ethiopian penetration into Somalia continued into December 1984. On 8 April 1985, Somalia restored diplomatic relations with Libya. Southern guerrillas of the Somali National movement continued sporadic raiding in the north in 1986 and were unknowingly setting the stage for the conditions that would persist into the 1990s. Also, in 1986, the USSR attempted to improve the strained relations that had existed with Somalia since Moscow had sided with Ethiopia in the Ogaden War. Meetings were held with Ethiopia to end that territorial dispute, but no concrete results were achieved by year's end. An auto accident on 23 May 1986 severely injured Siyaad, and rumors spread into 1987 that he would be unable to resume his duties as president. In 1987, the Ethiopian-based Somali Nationalist Movement (SNM) carried out a number of raids against the north, where major unrest was already formenting over the lack of control in the southern-oriented central government. Drought also played a major role that year, and a state of emergency was declared in central Somalia to offset the gross losses in resources and human lives. An SNM-driven civil war erupted in the north in 1987. Beginning in February 1987, a number of trials were conducted against allegedly corrupt senior government officials, who were blamed for the fiscal chaos in the country. Many of them were found guilty and condemned to death. On 3 April 1988, an agreement was reached between Somalia and Ethiopia. Both sides made concessions, not the least of which were promises to cease further support to the rebel group that had been active on both sides of the border. In response, the SNM launched a major offensive that led to a penetration of Somalia that put the U.S.–used port city of Berbera under virtual siege. At least 10,000 were killed in the fighting, several towns were levelled, and 300,000 new refugees were created, who crossed into Ethiopia. Major demonstrations followed in Mogadishu. In an attempt to placate international critics of human rights abuses in 1989, the Somalian government tried an amnesty program but failed to quell the growing rebellion in the country. At the same time, major fighting took place between government forces and the SNM, who claimed, in early 1989, to control most of the country, especially in the predominantly Muslim north. Most foreign aid groups and UN personnel were withdrawn from Somalia after that point. When the Roman Catholic bishop of Mogadishu was assassinated on 9 July, government forces and police went on a rampage. This was followed by Muslim demonstrations in which 450 were killed. There were also reports of mass defections to the rebel cause. By 1990, the government had fundementally lost control of the situation. Replacement of senior officials did not substantially improve the situation. In May 1990, 114 influential politicians signed what became known as the Mogadishu Manifesto Number 1, which called for the resignation of the government. When 45 of these politicians were subsequently arrested in June, the situation went completely out of control. On 6 July, Siyaad Barrah was stoned while making a speech. His personal guard opened fire on the mob, killing 60. When the 45 politicians were tried on 15 July, they were found not guilty and released by the courts. The announcement of a popular referendum on a new constitution came too late to save the regime, and the 85-year-old Siyaad was overthrown on 26 January 1991 by a coalition of tribal-based rebel groups. Thereafter, a warlord mentality gripped the country, with fragmented regional control held by tribal or clan leaders. Civil war followed, was further exacerbated by a severe drought. Rioting took place in Mogadishu and other cities. At least 1.5 million Somalis were threatened by starvation. On 18 May, the north declared itself an independent Somaliland Republic, and some order was restored. The civil war continued, however, and in December 1992 an ill-conceived multinational relief force was ordered into Somalia in Operation Restore Hope, which began with a landing that turned into a media circus. The disarray of the military command structure and the interposition of inept UN civilian representatives led to a fiasco in which an inordinately large number of Allied troops were killed. U.S. forces were all withdrawn by 25 March 1994; most of the other countries involved in the relief effort withdrew at the same time. The expected bloodbath did not eventuate, but neither did the reestablishment of order. The country remained dicvided between the south and the so-called Republic of Somaliland in the north and several other warlord enclaves. The capital, Mogadishu, was still under the control of Muhammad Farah Aydid. Siyaad died in exile in January 1995. At the end of 1995, Somalia had no functional government. *See also* Ethiopia. *Reading:* Colin Darch, *A Soviet View of Africa: An Annotated Bibliography on Ethiopia, Somalia and Djibouti* (1980); Walter Clark & Jeffrey Herbsy, eds., *Learning from Somalia: The Lessons of Armed Humanitarian Intervention* (1997); Jonathan Stevenson, *Losing Mogadishu: Testing U.S. Policy in Somalia* (1995); Terrence Lyons & Ahmed I. Samatar, *Somalia: State Collapse, Multilateral Intervention, and Strategies for Political Reconstruction* (1995); Edward Ricciuti, *Somalia: A Crisis of Famine and War* (1993); Patrick Gilkes, *Conflict in Somalia and Ethiopia* (1994).

Somali Democratic Salvation Front. *See* Somalia.

Somaliland, French. *See* Djibouti.

Somoza-Debayle, Anastasio. (b. 5 December 1925, Leon, Nicaragua—d. 17 September 1980, Asuncion, Paraguay) Somoza-Debayle was the last member of the Somoza family to rule Nicaragua during its 44-year reign. The family rule began with Anastasio Somoza Garcia (1896—1956), who deposed the elected president (1936) and assumed the office of president on 1 January 1937. He held that office until 1947, when he became the power behind the president as commander in chief of the country's armed forces. In 1950, he was "reelected" to the presidency and held that office until he succumbed to wounds suffered in an assassination attempt on 22 September 1956. At that point (29 September), his eldest son, Luis Somoza Debayle, became president, but he refused to run for reelection in 1963. From 1963 until 1967, figurehead presidents held office. Luis Somoza died in 1967. Anastasio Somoza-Debayle, Luis' younger brother, took office and ruled with a firm hand, at the same time stealing the wealth of the nation, in the Somoza tradition, and salting it away in family bank accounts. In 1972, for example, following a severe earthquake (22 December 1972) that devastated the capital city of Managua, killed 6,000 and left 300,000 homeless, the Somoza family diverted much of the international relief funds to their personal use. Somoza left office on 1 May 1972, handing over power to a three-man junta, but he returned to take personal control of the country the day after the earthquake. He was returned to the presidency after a constitutional amendment made it possible for him to serve until 1981.The subsequent Sandinista uprising (beginning in February 1978), plus heavy human rights pressure from abroad, forced him to resign in 17 July 1979 and to flee into exile, where he was assassinated on 17 September 1980. His assailant, Alfredo Irurzun (qv), a known Argentinian terrorist, was shot and killed by Paraguayan police on 19 September. Much of the stolen wealth of the Somoza family was recovered and expropriated by the new leftist Sandinista government. The Nicaraguan people soon found they had simply traded one evil master for another. *Reading:* Claribel Alegria & Darwin Flakoll, *Death of Samoza,* (1996); Knut Walter, *The Regime of Anastasio Somoza, 1936-1956* (1993).

Somoza, Luis. *See* Somoza-Debayle, Anastasio.

Songgram, Luang Pibul. On 8 November 1947, a military coup led by Marshal Luang Pibul Songgram overthrew the government of Prime Minister Prid Phanomyong (qv) of Siam (Thailand). Pibul Songgram had been prime minister from December 1938 until July 1944. This was one of a series of coups d'etat conducted by the military since the end of World War II. In September 1957, Pibul Songgram was forced to flee the country after another successful coup led by Marshal Sarit Thanarat (Srisdi Dhanarajata) (qv).

Son Sann. *See* Khieu Samphan.

Sonsonate. *See* El Salvador.

Son Tay. *See* Vietnam.

Sorbonne University. *See* France.

Soummam Valley. *See* Algeria.

South Africa (Union of South Africa). *See* Republic of South Africa.

South African Defense Force. *See* Republic of South Africa.

South America. *See* individual countries.

South Arabia. *See* Federation of South Arabia.

South Arabian Federation. *See* Federation of South Arabia.

South Arab League. *See* Yemen.

South East Asia. *See* Indochina; Thailand.

South East Asia Treaty Organization (SEATO). This regional defense organization grew out of the Southeast Asia Collective Defense Treaty signed in Manila on 8 September 1954, following demands for regional protection against communist expansion. Some obvious nations were excluded from membership—Vietnam, Cambodia and Laos—because of the terms of the Geneva Accords of 1956, but they were brought under the protective shield of an included protocol. Other nations with nonalignment policies rejected association with the treaty group. No forces were put under SEATO control, the group relying instead on rapid deployment of national forces as needed. National forces did participate periodically in joint exercises. The treaty went into force on 19 February 1955, with Australia, France, New Zealand, Pakistan, the Philippines, Thailand, the United Kingdom and the United States, with SEATO headquarters in Bangkok, Thailand. On 18 February 1956, Prince Sihanouk of Cambodia renounced SEATO support. In October 1961, the growing guerrilla problem in South Vietnam was discussed, but senior U.S. officials announced that the U.S. had no immediate prospects of becoming involved in that situation. Laos refused SEATO support on 22 June 1962 (*see* Laos). Pakistan gradually withdrew from both SEATO and CENTO (qv), beginning on 6 June 1968, and France refused further financial support in 1975. On 24 September 1975, the SEATO Council agreed to disband the organization, but keep the treaty in place. The organization conducted its last joint exercises on 20 February 1976 and formally dissolved on 30 June 1977, after 23 years of association.

South Georgia Island. *See* Falkland Islands.

South Korea. *See* Korea.

South Lebanon Army (Christian). *See* Lebanon.

South Pacific Forum. The South Pacific Forum was organized in 1971 as a forum for the South Pacific chiefs of state to discuss problems and issues facing them in the future as independent and emerging nations. The organization is based at Suva, Fiji, where a permanent bureau (1972) administers to the 14 members, which include Australia, New Zealand, Papua New Guinea and 11 island nations. An offshoot of the forum is the South Pacific Bureau for Economic Cooperation (1973), which works toward improving economic, logistical conditions and tourism among the members. On 31 March 1978, the forum members individually and collectively imposed 200-mile fishing limits on their surrounding waters. The South Pacific Forum members declared the South Pacific a nuclear-free zone on 7 August 1985.

South Viet Nam. *See* Vietnam.

South West Africa. *See* Namibia.

South West Africa People's Organization (SWAPO). This organization was founded on 19 April 1960, for the sole purpose of advocating the immediate independence of the trust territory of South West Africa as the new nation of Namibia (*see* Namibia). The group was founded by Andimba (Herman) Toivo Ja Toiva (qv), who was eventually arrested (1968) and imprisoned with a 20-year sentence in South Africa. Sam Nujoma was its first president. When the UN order to South Africa to evacuate the region was rejected in 1966, SWAPO turned to more violent means of achieving its goal. SWAPO's base was primarily in the northern area of the territory, among the Ovamba people. They also received support from Angola, the territory's northern neighbor, which provided aid and basing to Nujoma and his group. This aid came from the ruling Popular Movement for the Liberation of Angola (PMLA) (*see* Angola), which was itself supported by the Soviet Union and Cuba. The military arm of SWAPO took the name, of People's Liberation Army of Namibia (PLAN). As the conflict continued, South Africa often retaliated by conducting ground and air attacks against suspected SWAPO bases inside Angola. In 1978, the United Nations recognized SWAPO as the legitimate representative of the Namibian people. A cease-fire was arranged, which was signed by both South Africa and SWAPO. Although the UN arrangement called for a withdrawal of South African forces and for UN-supervised free elections, South African political maneuvering and sporadic fighting held up any progress until 22 December 1988. In the meantime, Toivo Ja Toiva was released from South Africa's Robbin's Island prison in 1984. He was then appointed SWAPO's secretary general after he insisted Nujoma remain the group's leader. Nujoma was able to return to Namibia in 1989. On 1 March 1994, the country received its independence, with Sam Nujoma, who had been elected in November 1989, continuing in office as its first president. *Reading:* Morgan Norval, *Death in the Desert: The Namibian Tragedy* (1990); Peter H. Katjavivi, *A History of Resistance in Namibia* (1990); SWAPO, *To be a Nation: The Struggle of the Namibian People* (1981).

South Yemen (Aden). *See* Yemen.

Souvanna Phouma. (b. 10 January 1901, Vientiane, Laos—d. 10 January 1984, Vientiane) Born the nephew of King Sisavangvong of Laos, Souvanna was sent to France for his education. After training as an architectural engineer, he returned to Laos and took up duties at the French Indochinese Public Works Service (1931). Following World War II, Souvanna broke with the king, who had welcomed back French overlordship; with his half-brother, Souphanouvong, Souvanna joined the Free Laos (*Lao Issara*) movement and took part in its breakaway provisional government in Vientiane in 1945–1946. Souvanna was forced to flee when the French reoccupied Laos, and he established his exile in Bangkok. When France granted limited autonomy to Laos in 1949, Souvanna returned and was subsequently elected premier from 1951 to 1954. Out of office two years, he was able to form an awkward coalition and recapture the premiership in 1956. The coalition collapsed in 1958, when civil war broke out, pitting the right and center against the communist Pathet Lao, which was at that time headed by Souphanouvong. Souvanna served again as premier in 1960, following the Kong Le (qv) coup (9 August 1960). On 2 September 1960, the fighting resumed among the three opposing groups. When Kong Le's forces were defeated on 16 December 1960, Souvanna was again forced to flee. Returning in 1961, he asked the U.S. to stop supplying the right-wing forces on the promise he would ask the USSR to stop arming the Pathet Lao. He served again, from 22 June 1962, during another brief respite from the fighting. After his inauguration, he announced that Laos refused any further association with the South Easy asia Treaty Organization (SEATO) (qv). Although Souvanna attempted to remain neutral, he was eventually drawn to seek U.S. aid because of the war in Vietnam. A right-wing coup on 19 April 1964 drove him once again from office. He was returned on 2 May 1964 after acceding to a number of right-wing demands. With the support of the North Vietnamese, the Pathet Lao opened a campaign in May 1964 that led to almost a decade of warfare. Souvanna, upon being reseated, asked the North Vietnamese to stop aiding the Pathet Lao in return for his assurance that Allied bombing in Laos would be halted (20 May 1969). On 25 July 1969, Souvanna accused the North Vietnamese of stationing 60,000 troops on Laotian soil. Although it was true, the Hanoi government vehemently denied the accusation and continued its campaign against Laos. Peace negotiations began in March 1970 (*see* Laos). When the U.S. began its withdrawal, Vientiane and the Pathet Lao concluded a cease-fire in February 1973. On 5 April 1974, a coalition government was formed, with Souvanna continuing as premier. The Pathet Lao campaign started up again, and on 23 May 1975, Souvanna capitulated. Following the establishment of the People's Democratic Republic of Laos that same year, Souvanna became an adviser. He died in 1984.

Soviet or Soviet Union. *See* Union of Soviet Socialist Republics.

Soweto Township. *See* Republic of South Africa.

Spain. The Kingdom of Spain is located on the Iberian Peninsula at the southwestern corner of the European continent. It is bordered on the northeast by Andorra and France, on the east and southeast by the Mediterranean Sea and British Gibraltar, on the southwest by the Gulf of Cadiz (Atlantic Ocean), on the west by Portugal and on the northwest and north by the Bay of Biscay (Atlantic Ocean). The capital city is Madrid. The peninsula has been inhabited since prehistoric times as evidenced by the magnificent cave drawings found in the Cantabrian Mountains in the north. Bronze Age tribes were there in the second millennium B.C., and Celtic incursions from the north began in the ninth and eighth centuries B.C. In the third century B.C., Rome extended its empire into the peninsula, which lasted until the fourth century A.D., when Gothic invaders from the north took the land. A Visigothic kingdom was established. Roman Catholicism was accepted by the seventh century. A Muslim invasion from the south, from Africa, took place in the eighth century. Five hundred years later, the Christian kingdoms of Aragon and Castile had reconquered most of the land, with a union of the two kingdoms occurring in 1479. The last Moorish foothold at Granada was taken in 1492. By 1500, Spain was a colonial power with dominion over most of the known New World. From 1516 until 1700 Spain was ruled by a succession of Hapsburg kings, who managed to keep the country almost continuously at war and who also managed to wreck the exchequer. After 1700, Bourbon kings sat on the throne, the first, Philip V, by his ascension, bringing about the War of Spanish Succession, which lasted from 1701 to 1714. In 1808, Napoleon placed his brother, Joseph, on the Spanish throne. By 1814, however, the defeat of Napoleon at the hands of British and Spanish forces gave the throne back to the Bourbons. After that date, Spain lost most of its colonies in America, culminating in the ignominious defeat of its naval and ground forces in the Spanish American War of 1898 and the subsequent loss of most of its overseas possessions. In 1931, Spain became a republic after election results favoring such a government forced the abdication of Alfonso XIII. The Spanish Civil War that followed in 1936 pitted the German-supported Nationalist forces of Francisco Franco (qv) against the communist-supported Republicans. Franco won the war in 1939 and became the head of state. In March 1946, a number of Western powers appealed to the Spanish people to rid themselves of Franco, but to no avail. Many of these nations then asked, through the UN General Assembly, for breaks in diplomatic relations with Spain (11 December 1946). The principal effect of this was that the UN barred Spain from all UN activities. In February 1947, an anti-Franco government-in-exile was formed under the leadership of Rodolfo Llopis (qv). This "government" failed, but it was replaced by another group led by Alvaro de Albornoz . On 4 August 1949, the U.S. Senate refused to extend Marshall Plan (qv) aid to Spain. A major strike of over a quarter-million workers paralyzed Spain on 23 April 1951. In an attempt to flex its muscles, Spain demanded police authority in the internationalized port of Tangiers directly across the Strait of Gibraltar. The move was successful, and Spain received the control over Tangiers it had demanded on 14 November. Partially in return for its support on Tangiers, the U.S. achieved a ten-year defensive agreement with Spain. On 28 January 1954, carefully orchestrated anti-British demonstrations began over the return of Gibraltar to Spain. The Spaniards then cancelled future British naval unit visits to Spanish ports. The British followed with their own cancellation of such visits (28 April 1954). On 7 April 1956, Spain formally recognized the independence of Morocco, relinquishing all control on 17 April. The last Spanish military base in Morocco was closed on 31 August 1961. (Spain would also pull out of Equatorial Guinea by April 1969.) On 5 May 1968, Spain closed its border with Gibraltar in a unilateral move to tighten the noose around the British stronghold. Maintaining its independent stance, Spain refused to sign the Nuclear Non-Proliferation Treaty in the face of worldwide scorn (1 July 1968). Even so, the UN General Assembly voted on 18 December 1968 to order Great Britain to turn over control of Gibraltar to Spain by 1 October 1969. The British, seemingly ignoring the edict, published a new constitution for Gibraltar in early 1969. Spain, in retaliation, imposed a land blockade (7 June 1969) along the *Lans Linea* frontier with the colony, even suspending the ferry service on 27 June. At about the same time (20 June) the Spanish extended U.S. basing rights an additional 15 months. On 29 September, Spain raised the ante with the British by deliberately anchoring warships inside Gibraltar's waters. Then, on 1 October, Spain severed all telephone and cable connections with the British colony. Also, in 1969, after 30 years of dictatorial rule, Franco coopted Juan Carlos de Borbon y Borbon as his successor. In August 1970, Spain and the U.S. reached a new basing agreement that gave Spain $153 million in military and economic aid, including the leasing of 12 U.S. warships. Rioting broke out during a demonstration in Barcelona on 3 April 1973. Police opened fire on the crowd of 1,500. Strikes and rioting were by this time a relatively common occurrence in an otherwise tranquil country. On 8 June 1973, Franco resigned as premier but kept his title of chief of state. When Franco's age began to impede his leadership, Juan Carlos became head of state on 18 July 1974. Spain was forced to dispatch warships to its enclaves of Ceuta and Melilla when Morocco announced its claim to them on 8 February 1975. In October 1975, the U.S. extended its basing agreement with Spain for five more years. More unrest began in the cities of Spain, when the government announced its intention to intervene in the Spanish Sahara (*see* Polisario). With Franco's death on 20 November 1975, Juan Carlos became king and greatly expanded the democratic privileges of his country. In January 1976, the U.S. and Spain announced a Treaty of Friendship and Cooperation, which extended U.S. basing rights and gave Spain $1.2 billion in military sales credits. In February, Spain gave up its sovereignty over Spanish Sahara to Mauritania and Morocco. Spain resumed diplomatic relations with most of the eastern bloc nations in January–February 1977. These relations had been dormant since the Spanish Civil War. Relations were restored with Mexico after a 38-year hiatus. Interestingly enough, the Spanish Communist Party told the Soviet Union to stay out of Spanish affairs on 26 June 1977 following published criticism of the Spanish party secretary. This was followed by a government refusal to grant the USSR naval basing rights at Algeciras near Gibraltar. By 1977, the Spanish Parliament (*Cortes*) had begun a program of political and economic reform that included the separation of church and state and guarantees of civil liberty. On 2 February 1980, Spain broke diplomatic relations with Guatemala over its handling of a hostage situation at the Spanish embassy in that country; the bungled police operation cost the ambassador his life (he was later murdered in the hospital), and the embassy building went up in flames. A second general strike was called on 16 February 1981, to protest the alleged murder of a Basque prisoner, whom the police were accused of torturing to death. One hundred thousand Spaniards marched in Madrid on 15 November 1981 protesting Spain's entry into NATO (26 November 1981). On 15 January 1982, four of the top military leaders in Spain were relieved on suspicion of being involved in a 1981 plot to overthrow the government. Three army officers would eventually be jailed (15 April 1984) for their parts in planning a government overthrow. The last separation of old and new ways occurred in 1982, when a socialist government was elected. In February of that year, terrorists of the Basque Anti-Capitalist Autonomous Commandos (qv) blew up the Michelin Tire Company warehouse in the Basque (northern) region of Spain. On 2 December 1983, Basque *Iraultza* (qv) terrorists attacked eight U.S. installations in their region, showing their displeasure over U.S. policy in Central America. Another terrorist group, the October First Antifascist Resistance Group (GRAPO) (qv), murdered two policemen (2 January 1984) in retaliation for the death of their leader in a shootout with authorities in Barcelona in December 1983. Also in January, the government placed the military under Spainish civilian authority. On 24 October 1984, the prime minister, Felipe Gonzalez, stated his opposition to full integration into NATO and demanded an immediate reduction in U.S. troop strength in his country. On 27 November 1984, Spain announced an agreement that would lift the 15-year-old blockade of Gibraltar. Negotiations were set for 1985 to settle the future of Gibraltar. Before that, however, Spain voted to remain in NATO, on 16 December 1984. On 4 February 1985, the Spanish-Gibraltar border was reopened. Spain became the site of an Islamic Jihad terrorist attack on 12 April, when a number of U.S. service personnel were among those killed and injured in a restaurant bombing near Madrid. Spain joined the European Economic Community in 1986. Except for separatist Basque and other terrorist activity which had existed for decades, Spain remained relatively calm. *Reading:* Robert P. Clark, *The Basque Insurgents: ETS, 1952-1980* (1990); Stanley G. Payne, *The Franco Regime, 1936-1975* (1987).

Spanish Infi. *See* Morocco; Spain.

Spinola, Antonio Sebastiao Ribiero de. (b. 11 April 1910, Estremoz, Portugal) A cavalry officer, Spinola rose through the ranks to become, as a brigadier general, the governor and commander of forces in Portuguese Guinea (Guinea-Bissau) (qv) from 1968 to 1973. Upon his return to Portugal he was appointed deputy chief of staff of the armed forces. After a period of unrest in which many junior officers were jailed, an order was issued by Premier Marcello Caetano's (qv) government that all senior officers had to swear an oath of allegiance. Spinola and the commander in chief, General Francisco de Costa Gomes, failed to appear. Both were summarily dismissed from their posts but allowed to remain on active duty. This action provoked a military revolt on 16 March 1974, which failed to attract sufficient support to succeed. Twenty of the coup attempt's leaders, all loyal to Spinola, were arrested as a result. Spinola took no part in the subsequent overthrow of the Caetano government by the Armed Forces Movement (AFM) on 25 April 1975, but he was named the provisional president of Portugal on 15 May. His task was complicated by his inability to bring the far-right and far-left factions together. When his attempts at bringing order to the political chaos in Portugal incited the leftists, he was forced to resign on 30 September 1974. Francisco de Costa Gomes was put in his place. A right-wing attempt on 11 March 1975 to restore Spinola to power was thwarted by troops loyal to the government. Spinola fled first to Spain and then to Brazil, where he was granted political asylum. Thereafter, he retired into private life.

Spitzbergen. *See* Norway.

Spratley (Spratly) Islands. A group of small reefs, the Spatley Islands lie in the South China Sea, located midway between the Philippines and Vietnam. The largest island, Itu Aba, covers only 90 acres. The islands are unihabited and are mainly occupied by seabirds and turtles. France controlled the islands from 1933 until 1939. Japan occupied the group during World War II and established a submarine base there. At the close of the war, China put a small garrison on Itu Aba, which was maintained by the Nationalist Chinese after their withdrawal from the mainland to Taiwan. In 1951, Japan renounced all claims to the islands, at which time both Communist China and Vietnam laid claim to them.The Philippines stated its claim to the group in 1955. On 1 February 1974, South Vietnam occupied three of the other islands, including Spratley Island, while Nationalist China continued its occupation of Itu Aba. Communist China, Taiwan and the Philippines all protested the move. The Philippines then occupied seven other islands and built an airstrip on Pagasa. By June 1983, Malaysis had occupied Turumba Layang, making five claimants for the group. All claimants, including mainland China, have troops currently stationed in the group to support their claims. *Reading:* Chi Kin Lo, *China's Policy towards Territorial Disputes: The Case of the South China Sea Islands* (1989); R. Haller-Trost, *The Spratly Islands: A Study on the Limitations of International Law* (1991).

Spreti, Count Karl von. *See* Rebel (Revolutionary) Armed Forces (FAR).

Sri Lanka. Officially the Democratic Socialist Republic of Sri Lanka and formerly known as the island of Ceylon, Sri Lanka lies in the Indian Ocean off the southeastern tip of the Indian subcontinent. The capital city is Colombo. The island was visited as early as the fifth century B.C. by aboriginals from the south and by Indo-Europeans from Khoresm in northern India. The mixture of these two group resulted in the Sinhalese, the principal people of the island. A second group, known as Tamils, probably arrived on the island from Dravidian India sometime before 1200 A.D. Buddhism arrived in the third century B.C. Between 200 B.C. and 1000 A.D. Buddhism spread over the entire island, and Anuradhapura, a major Buddhist trading center on the island, became the seat of a new kingdom. The Sinhalese Anuraradhapura kingdom gave way to a Cola invasion from southern India, which occupied the island from 993 until 1070, when the Sinhalese wrested back power, which they held until 1200 A.D. By 1500, the Sinhalese had settled on the southern half of the island, while the south Indian Tamils had arrived and gravitated to the north, establishing a kingdom there. During this three-century period, the island was invaded by the Indians, Chinese and Malays. In 1505, the Portuguese arrived and were permitted to build a fort. By 1518, trade relations had been established; before 1619, the Portuguese had control of most of the island. After some conniving, the Dutch ousted the Portuguese, and Ceylon was taken over by the Dutch East India Company, an arrangement that lasted until 1796, when the British replaced the Dutch. Ceylon went through an economic boom until a coffee blight destroyed the principal source of income. In the 1880s, tea was proven to be an even more stable crop than coffee, and the Ceylonese economy began to grow again. During the early years of the twentieth century, nationalism began to make its mark in Ceylon. In 1919, the Ceylon National Congress was able to unite the Sinhalese and Tamils, and the British cooperated by adapting the island's constitution to comply with the native desires. In 1948, Ceylon was granted dominion status in the British Empire. Until 1956, the United National Party (UNP) had led the country. In that year they were unseated by the Sri Lanka Freedom Party (SLFP), which favored a predominantly Sinhalese identity. This brought a violent reaction from the Tamils, and by 1965 the UNP had been returned to power. Aiming at the 1970 elections, the SLFP formed a coalition with several Marxist-oriented groups and took back the government in a landslide victory. In 1972, a new constitution was promulgated, and Ceylon declared itself to be the Republic of Sri Lanka. However, in 1977, the UNP was returned to power and immediately set about modifying the constitution to allow a presidential form of government. Its next move was to declare the country to be the Democratic Socialist Republic of Sri Lanka. The racial problems between the Sinhalese and the Tamils continued, however, and grew in violence, while the Tamils demanded their own country, comprising the northern and eastern parts of the island. This situation continued into the 1990s. On 1 May 1993, the president of Sri Lanka, Ranasinghe Premadasa, was assassinated when a bicyclist, suspected of being a terrorist member of the Liberation Tigers of Tamil Eelam, rode into the president's car and exploded a bomb, killing himself and the president. By 1994, over 34,000 had been killed in the fighting in Sri Lanka. The new government lasted until November, when elections placed Sirimavo Bandaranaike in the presidency. The fighting continued against the Tamil rebels with little abatement even though peace talks were supposedly underway. Sri Lanka's largest warship was sunk in one of the actions, with the loss of 22 seaman. At the same time, the government was faced by a growing scandal over the disappearance of about $7 million in treasury funds. The Tamils agreed to a truce in January 1995, and a foreign observer group was put in place to supervise the cease-fire. On 19 April, the Tamils broke the agreement, accusing the government of failure to live up to its terms. Major fighting in April and May severely damaged the Sri Lankan armed forces. A government counteroffensive in July was badly mauled. The Tamils vowed a war of destruction, even though the government offered a regional plan that would have given the Tamil territory considerable autonomy. By year's end the fighting had produced about 300,000 refugees, but there were signs of hope in a Tamil bid to reopen peace negotiations. *Reading:* Stanley J. Tambiah, *Buddhism Betrayed?: Religion, Politics, and Violence in Sri Lanka* (1992); Donald Horowitz, *Coup Theories and Officers' Motives: Sri Lanka in Comparative Perspective* (1980).

Srinagar. *See* India.

Stalin, Josef. (b. 21 December [9 December, Old Style] 1879, Gori, Georgia—d. 5 March 1953, Moscow) Born Iosif Vissarionovich Dzhugashvili, Stalin was the son of a poor shoemaker who, in drunken rages, abused the boy regularly. He attended the church school in Gori, where he learned to speak Russian; Georgian was the only language spoken in his home. After 1894, Dzhugashvili attended the Tiflis (Tbilisi) Theological Seminary, but he spent much of his time engrossed in the prohibited works of Karl Marx and others. He was expelled from the seminary in 1899. This greatly disturbed his mother, who had wanted him to be a priest. In December 1899, he began a brief stint as a clerk at the Tiflis (Tbilisi) Observatory, but in 1900 he joined the illegal political underground. Although never having been a laborer himself, he pushed workers into bloody confrontations with the police, to the annoyance of other underground members who saw him as overly ambitious and bloodthirsty. When the Social Democratic Party (Marxist) (SD) split, Dzhugashvili joined the Bolshevik group, which was, in denial of its name, the smaller of the two main splinters. In the Bolsheviks, Dzhugashvili became an ardent follower of Lenin. Between 1902 and 1913, Dzhugashvili was arrested, imprisoned or exiled seven times as a revolutionary, in each case with a relatively mild sentence. He was able to escape on several occasions, each of which added to the suspicion that he was actually an imperial Russian agent. During that same period, Dzhugashvili attended several SD conferences, all of them held outside Russia, and was involved in a spectacular bank robbery in Tiflis, which was carried out to finance underground operations (25 June 1907). Stalin also married in 1904 and had one child, Jacob (Yakob), whom the father treated with contempt. Between 1904 and 1912, he published a number of articles, which Lenin had ordered produced, on Marxism and edited the first issues of the party organ, *Pravda*; during that same period, he changed his name to Stalin (Steel), probably both as a way of eluding the police and to add to the aura he was building for himself. In 1913, however, Stalin was exiled to Siberia, where he remained until March 1917. When Stalin was freed he went to Petrograd and resumed editorship of *Pravda*. At first he advocated cooperation with the Provisional Government, but he soon changed to a position that held that only armed seizure of the government would suffice. After the October Revolution, when the Bolsheviks did take power, Stalin was in the third position, behind Lenin and his arch rival, Leon Trotsky. Stalin became political commissar during the Civil War (1919–1920) and then served in a number of ministerial posts. In 1922, Stalin became the secretary general of the Communist Party. From this position, Stalin began the series of activities that would eventually give him absolute control of the Soviet Union. In doing so, Stalin ran afoul of Lenin, and Lenin called for Stalin's removal from the Politburo and the party chairmanship. These moves Stalin was able to avoid by guile and by brazen indifference to the ailing Lenin's demands. When Lenin died in January 1924, Stalin orchestrated a new "Third Rome," Byzantine cult-legend around the dead

Lenin, with himself as the "keeper of the flame." Among his first acts, he had the city of Volgograd renamed Stalingrad, and to oust Lenin's designated successor, Trotsky. Stalin then methodically removed all of the other Bolshevik leaders, who in any way threatened his authority. Trotsky was forced into exile in 1929 and was subsequently assassinated in Mexico in 1940. In 1928, Stalin broke with Lenin's five-year plan system and moved into a program of state-controlled industry. The collectivization of farming left 25 million peasants without property and fundamentally reverted to serfdom. When there was resistance to what many peasants saw as the loss of their newly won freedom, Stalin ordered the army and the secret police to suppress it. In this repression, about 10 million peasants were exterminated. The collectivization program also brought famine to the country. Most of the industrial programs also failed through Soviet ineptness and corruption. Executions of managers who failed were all too frequent in Stalin's new order. Beginning in 1934, Stalin opened a new round of purges of those whom he deemed threatening to him. When Sergey Kirov was assassinated, Stalin used this as a cause celebre for the mass extermination of many of the leaders who had helped him to power, their associates and many innocent passers-by. In the military, more than 65 percent of the senior officers were executed or sent into exile. Thought control became a keyword, as an inadvertent utterance or gesture could mean one's end. Before the beginning of World War II, Hitler attempted an alliance against the West. Stalin refused, seeing this as an opportunity to have the Western powers debilitate each other and become easy pickings for the Soviets. In August 1939, the Nazi-Soviet Pact was signed whereby, among other things, the two dictatorships divided Poland in a way reminiscent of the partitions of earlier centuries. Before Hitler's attack on the Soviet Union, Stalin was repeatedly warned. These warning, especially those from Western intelligence sources, were brushed aside. Commanders of front line units along the border were summarily executed or at least relieved of command, if Stalin's specific instructions against taking any defensive measures were disobeyed. When the Germans launched their attack, Stalin went into seclusion and remained hidden for nearly two weeks before moving to regain control of the disastrous situation. His inept military leadership in the beginning turned, during the war years, into a competent understanding of the war, but military commanders and staff officers were often relieved or shot for what Stalin saw as a weakness or other flaw in their performance. When Stalin's son was captured by the Germans, he refused to have him exchanged. Stalin appeared at many of the Allied conferences, where he was judged to be shrewd negotiator who often hoodwinked Roosevelt and Churchill. At war's end, Stalin began his building of a *cordon sanitaire* around the USSR by the enslavement of Eastern Europe into a buffer zone against the West. Marxist-Leninist—actually Stalinist —ideology was reasserted, much to the dismay of the West, which had hoped for some relaxation of authoritarian rule. However, Stalin was becoming more paranoid about his authority, and in January 1953 he began what the West perceived as a new series of purges, when he had a number of Kremlin physicans, most Jewish arrested on charges of murdering a number of senior officials (Doctors' Plot). This purge was ended by Stalin's death, the cause of which has never been completely explained. Subsequent to his death, a program of de-Stalinization began (1956) whereby some, but not all, of his crimes were exposed. *Reading:* Nancy Whitelaw, *Joseph Stalin: From Peasant to Premier* (1992); Steven Otfinoski, *Joseph Stalin: Russia's Last Czar* (1993).

Stanley, Falklands. *See* Port Stanley, Falkland Islands.

Stanleyville. *See* Congo.

"Star Wars." *See* Strategic Defense Initiative.

Stasinopoulis, Michael. During the period of military rule in Greece, following the 1967 coup, the regime held to a resolute course of ignoring civil and political safeguards. In 1969, 21 senior magistrates who were regarded as hostile to the regime were peremptorily dismissed. On 24 June 1969, the administrative tribunal, the Council of the Nation, reversed the dismissal order, declaring it illegal. The military junta then declared the finding of the tribunal void and demanded the resignation of its president, Michael Stasinopoulis. Stasinopoulis refused, and the junta issued a decree (27 June 1969) accepting his "resignation" and naming his successor. Prominent lawyers who had defended the judges were arrested and exiled from Athens.

Statue of Liberty. On 16 February 1965, a joint U.S.–Canada police effort that included the Federal Bureau of Investigation, New York City Police Department and the Royal Canadian Mounted Police broke up a terrorist plot to blow up the Statue of Liberty in New York harbor.

Stern Gang (*Lomane Herut Yisra'el*). An Israeli terrorist organization, the Stern Gang was founded in Palestine by Abraham Stern in 1942, as splinter of the Irgun (qv). Stern was killed in a gunfight with the British in 1942. At that point, Yitzhak Shamir was one of those who took over joint leadership of the group. The size of the Stern Gang was always small, with no more than 200 or 300 active members at any one time, with assassination and bombing used as the principal methods of attack. Eventually, the Stern Gang and Irgun became enemies, but both maintained the singular goal of achieving a Jewish state in Palestine. The Stern Gang assassinated British leaders such as Lord Moyne in Egypt and UN officials such as Count Folke Bernadotte (qv) during his visit to Palestine. When the Israeli army was formed in 1948, the Irgun was incorporated into its ranks. The Stern Gang, however, was ostracized because of its radicalism and ruthlessness, and few of its members were asked to join the army.

Stepinac, Alois (Alojzije) Cardinal. On 18 September 1946, then Archbishop Stepinac was captured and arrested by the forces of Marshal Tito (qv). He was subsequently tried on charges of "forcibly converting Orthodox Serbians to Roman Catholicism" and of collaborating with the Germans. He was sentenced to 16 years at hard labor. In fact, Stepinac had been a wartime leader of Croatian resistance and a member of the Anti-Fascist Council of National Liberation of

Croatia. Therefore, Stepinac constituted a threat to Tito's assumption of total power in a communist Yugoslavia. *Reading:* John Prcela, *Archbishop Stepinac in His Country's Church State Relations Paper* (1990); Stella Alexander, *The Triple Myth: A Life of Archbishop Alojzije Stepinac* (East European Monographs, No. 226 (1987).

Stevens, Siaka. In Sierra Leone, a revolt by a group of noncommissioned officers (called the Sergeant's Coup) led to the overthrow of the government of Andrew Juxton-Smith (qv) on 18 April 1968. Colonel John Bangura (qv), who was in exile at the time, was installed as head of state; Siaka Stevens was appointed prime minister. When violence broke out in November 1968, Stevens imposed a state of siege upon the country that was not lifted until March 1969. Political instability and violence returned in 1970, however; and another state of siege was declared following the discovery in July of a plot to overthrow his government. A number of officials, including Juxton-Smith, were executed as a part of that affair. Stevens's policies led to the resignations in protest of two senior ministers on 14 September 1970. Another plot was discovered on 5 October, and a state of siege was again imposed. One unsuccessful coup attempt by the army did take place on 21 January 1971. This was followed by another unsuccessful attempt to overthrow Stevens on 23 March that was led by the army's commander and to two assassination attempts against Stevens. Stevens was forced to ask for military assistance from Guinea on 26 March under a recent combined arms treaty signed between the two countries, and Guinean troops entered Sierra Leone on 28 March to restore order. There was some speculation that the Guinean troops were already in the country when the request was made. There was also speculation that the revolt might have been triggered by the army's fear of the link with communist-supported Guinea. On 21 April 1971, Stevens became president, after a 19 April declaration of the independence of Sierra Leone. In the 1973 elections, Stevens was returned to office in a one-party election that was accompanied by much violence and bloodshed. Stevens' rule was tightened over the years, and in 1978, a constitutional amendment changed his term to a maximum of 14 years, not including the time he had already held power. Sierra Leone suffered through recurrent bouts of violence and famine, but Stevens held his ground until 28 November 1985, when Major General Joseph Momoh, whom Stevens had designated as his successor, was "duly elected."

Strait of Shatt al-Arab. *See* Iraq; Iraq-Iran War; Iran.

Strait of Tiran. *See* Israel; Arab-Israeli War (1967).

Straits of Hormuz. *See* Iran.

Straits of Taiwan. *See* China.

Strategic Arms Limitation Treaty (SALT). There were two series of SALT meetings. SALT I meetings were held between the U.S. and the USSR after a suggestion by President Lyndon B. Johnson (qv) in 1967. When the Soviet Union agreed (20 January 1969), talks were scheduled. Following a preliminary round, formal meetings began in Helsinki on 17 November 1969. Among the accomplishments of SALT I were the Treaty on Anti-Ballistic Missiles (ABM) and the Interim Agreement and Protocol on Limitation of Strategic Offensive Weapons. Both treaties were signed by the two parties in Moscow on 26 May 1972. The U.S. Senate ratified the ABM Treaty on 3 August 1972. The Interim Agreement was an executive accord and did not require ratification, but it was approved in a joint resolution of Congress. SALT I was a five-year, short-term agreement that imposed a freeze on testing and deployment of Intercontinental Ballistic Missiles (ICBM) and Submarine-Launched Ballistic Missiles (SLBM), and limited each side to the deployment of two ABM sites. This latter item was amended in the revision of 3 July 1974 to allow only one site on each side's territory. Also at the 1974 meetings, a Threshold Test Ban Treaty was added that added a limitation on the size of weapons or devices that could be tested underground to no more than 150 kilotons (KT) of yield. SALT I remained in effect until 3 October 1977, but it was extended in September 1977 until the new rounds of talks were completed. The SALT II series of meetings began in Geneva on 21 November 1972 and was completed when both sides signed in Vienna on 18 June 1979. The new treaty set limits on the number of warheads, Multiple Independently-targetable Reentry Vehicles (MIRV). ICBMs and SLBMs, long-range bombers and the total number of strategic launchers each side could possess at any one time. The treaty was submitted to the Senate for ratification, but it was withdrawn by President Jimmy Carter (qv) in January 1980, after the Soviet invasion of Afghanistan (*see* Afghanistan). Even so, both sides appeared to abide by the SALT II terms until a new round of talks began (*see* START) in 1982. In October 1985, the U.S. accused the Soviet Union of violating SALT II protocols already agreed upon by deploying SS-25 (surface-to-surface) missile launchers. Before START was completed, however, the Intermediate-Range Nuclear Forces (INF) Treaty, which eliminated intermediate- and shorter-range nuclear missile systems from Europe and Asia, was signed in Washington on 8 December 1987. A SALT Standing Consultative Commission had also been established in the SALT treaties and was authorized to use the "Hot Line" (5 July 1985) in carrying out its duties

Strategic Arms Reduction Talks (START). As a continuation of the progress made between the U.S. and the USSR in the SALT negotiations, a new round of talks (START I) was begun on 2 February 1983. These talks were aimed at reducing nuclear weapons, rather than just limiting them, as SALT had accomplished. An agreement was reached and signed in Moscow on 31 July 1991, whereby approximately 30 percent of each side's nuclear arsenal was to be reduced, in three phases over a seven-year period. Senate ratification came on 1 October 1992. Before that date, however, the Soviet Union had collapsed (December 1991), which created a number of problems, as four former Soviet republics now possessed nuclear weapons. Not until February 1994 did the four—Russia, Ukraine, Kazakhstan and Belarus—sort out their differences and ratify the treaty. The treaty then went into force on 5 December 1994. In January 1993, presidents George Bush and Boris Yeltsin (of Russia) signed the START II agreement, which will limit nuclear stockpiles on both sides to approximately one-third their 1993 totals.

Strategic Defense Initative (SDI). Reviewing the threat posed by the Soviet Union to the U.S., President Ronald Reagan proposed the need for an intercontinental ballistic missile (ICBM) defense system in a speech on 23 March 1983. The concept was that land- and air-based weapons systems would be deployed to attack incoming ICBMs before they could inflict damage on the U.S. Dubbed "Star Wars" because much of the system's capability would have to be deployed in space, the SDI was initially approved by Congress in the 1980s. In March 1985, the U.S. invited 17 other nations to join in the project. On 7 September, Canada announced it would not join in the project. The Soviet foreign minister Shevardnadze criticized SDI before the United Nations on 24 September. Great Britain did participate in the project after 6 December. There was great controversy over SDI also in the U.S., with detracters claiming the needed technology was too advanced for immediate employment, that there were too many unanswered questions about effectiveness and that deployment would only heighten the arms race. The collapse of the Soviet Union made much of the debate moot, but it did not lessen the need for the deployment of such a system. There are many former Soviet watchers who claim that the "Star Wars" project helped shorten the life expectancy of the USSR.

Strategic Hamlet Program. *See* Vietnam.

Stroessner, Alfredo. (b. 3 November 1912, Encarnacion, Paraguay) The son of a German immigrant, Stroessner attended the Paraguayan Military College in Asuncion and received his army commission in 1932. He became the commander in chief of the armed forces in 1951. He led a revolt that toppled the government of Federico Chavez. Stroessner took of the leadership of the junta that ruled Paraguay. He later was made president in a one-party election. Thereafter he established a firm dictatorship and was "reelected" president in 1958 without opposition. In a contested election held in 1963, he won by a landslide over the four opposition parties he allowed in his policy of "restricted democracy." An attempt to assassinate Stroessner occurred on 15 August 1970. Over 100 students were arrested for being involved in the plot. Stroessner did make some civic improvements in Paraguay, but he used large sums of money in support of the army, his power base and also his means of maintaining control. Stroessner had the constitution modified to continue the legend of democratic elections and to allow him to remain in power. At the same time, however, any real opposition to his power was dealt with harshly. He was again reelected in 1988, only to be overthrown in a bloody military coup on 3 February 1989. Stroessner was allowed to go into exile.

Strougal, Lubomir. On 28 January 1970, Lubomir Strougal succeeded Oldrich Cernik (qv) as premier of Czechoslovakia. Cernik was expelled from the Czechoslovakian Communist Party at about the same time. Strougal had been minister of interior. This action was a part of a larger issue involving a struggle between Gustav Husak (qv) and hard-liners who feared reform (*see*

Czechoslovakia). Strougal remained in his position until 11 October 1988, when Husak's successor as firstsSecretary of the Czech Communist Party, Milos Jakes, removed him from office because of his popularity, which made him a rival for power.

Student Nonviolent Coordinating Committee (SNCC). A civil rights organization formed in the United States in 1960, SNCC worked against segregation of the races and racial bigotry. The original meeting of the group was held in Raleigh, North Carolina, and was led by Martin Luther King, Jr. (qv). At first the group practiced nonviolence in its demonstrations against racial discrimination, but after a splintering in the mid-1960s, the organization became more militant. SNCC was dissolved in May 1970, at a time when its leader, H. "Rap" Brown (qv), was a fugitive from justice.

Students for a Democratic Society (SDS). An American student activist group, SDS was formed in 1959 as an offshoot of the League for Industrial Democracy (LID).The LID was purported to be a social-democratic educational organization. The SDS held its first meeting in Ann Arbor, Michigan (1960), and elected Robert Alan Haber as its first president. The group's initial involvement was in the civil rights movement. The SDS group charter, called the Port Huron Manifesto, was written (1962) by Haber and Tom Hayden, later to become the husband of Jane Fonda. When U.S. involvement in Southeast Asia began to escalate, the SDS was reoriented on the war effort and the best ways to prevent further involvement. In taking up this task, the SDS became much more militant. The SDS had a hand in many of the campus riots of the mid- to late-1960s. By 1969, the variances in the radical intentions of the group had manifested in its splintering into several factions. Of these, the Weather Underground Organization (WUO)—the Weathermen—was the most violent. It was formed by Mark Rudd and Bernadine Dohrn. At most, the membership of this group numbered about one dozen. The Weathermen are suspected of having participated in about 500 terrorist attacks. A New York City Greenwich Village explosion on 6 March 1970 leveled a building where WUO members were constructing bombs. At least three members of the group were killed in the blast. That incident led to the demise of the group, as some members surrendered to authorities, while others went to ground or joined other terrorist groups. A 1981 Nyack, New York, robbery in which three law enforcement officers were killed was laid at the feet of the WUO, however, and upon the capture of one WUO member, Kathy Boudin, the WUO ceased to exist. As for the SDS, their internal problems and the passage of time left them moribund.

Stung Treng. *See* Cambodia/Kampuchea.

Suazo Córdova, Roberto. Based upon the results of the elections held on 29 November 1981, 54-year-old Roberto Suazo Córdova was inaugurated president of Honduras on 27 January 1982, ending almost ten years of military rule. His party gained an absolute majority in the election. Suazo remained in office until 27 January 1986, when his duly elected successor, Jose Azcona Hoyo, was inaugurated.

Subandrio, Raden. *See* Indonesia.

Subic Bay. *See* The Philippines.

Suchitoto. *See* El Salvador.

Sudan (*as-Sudan*). The Republic of Sudan is the largest country on the African continent and is bordered on the north by Egypt, on the northeast by the Red Sea, on the east by Ethiopia, on the south by Zaire, Uganda and Kenya, on the west by Chad and the Central African Republic and on the northwest by Libya. The capital city is Khartoum. Civilization is known to have existed in the region, especially in the northern section, since around 30,000 B.C. The first societal group were the Nubians who, from the fourth millennium B.C., were intermittently under Egyptian control. At the same time, and from the eleventh millennium B.C., the Negroid Kingdom of Kush held sway over the region and held Egypt from 713 to 671 B.C. Christianity was introduced in the sixth century A.D., and the three principal tribal kingdom, were converted. These Christian kingdoms lived alongside Muslim Egypt until the thirteenth century, when Arab Muslims began emigrating into the region and eventually overcame the Christian kingdoms in the north. By 1500, all of Sudan was Muslim, except for the central area, where the Funj, who were neither Christian nor Muslim, held control. The Sudan was again conquered by Egypt by 1874. When the British attempted to end the slave trade in Sudan, a Muslim uprising led by Muhammad Ahmad (*al-Mahdi*) brought about a siege of Khartoum, which ended in 1885, when General Charles "Chinese" Gordon was beheaded. Mahdists held the Sudan until 1898, when a strong British force commanded by Major General Horatio Kitchener destroyed the Arab army at the bloody Battle of Omdurman (2 September 1898). The British had taken Egypt in 1882 and now held Sudan. Thereafter, the Anglo-Egyptian Sudan was ruled jointly by the British and Egyptians. Sudanese nationalism began to be expressed before World War II. The British informed Egypt on 25 January 1947 that it intended to prepare Sudan for self-government. Amid strong Egyptian opposition, Great Britain began the process of introducing a reform program on 15 July 1948. On 16 November 1950, Egypt demanded a British withdrawal from the Suez Canal (qv) and from Sudan. Then, on 27 December 1951, the Egyptian (*see* Egypt) abrogated the Anglo-Egyptian Defense Treaty of 1936 and the 1899 condominium deal with the Sudan and declared Egypt to be its sole ruler. The British, however, forced negotiations in 1952–1953 that eventually gave Sudan self-rule. Elections held in 1953 indicated the majority favored independence rather than Egyptian rule. In January 1955, a 17-year-long revolt began in southern Sudan, the main cause of which was the racial and religious antagonism between the northern Arab Muslims and the southern black Christians. At the same time, in August 1955, both Great Britain and Egypt withdrew the last of their forces stationed in Sudan. Sudan received its independence on 1 January 1956, at which time a five-man council of state took control of the country. On 19 February 1956, Sudan announced it was joining the Arab League (qv). Efforts toward parliamentary government between 1956 and 1989 often failed, and the country found itself generally under military rule. On 17 November 1958, for instance, the elected government was ousted by the army's commander, Lieutenant General Ibrahim Abboud (qv), who declared himself premier and suspended the constitution. Before the end of the year, three attempts would be made to rid the country of his leadership. Internal strife was compounded by Muslim attempts to impose their beliefs on the Animist and Christian populations in the south. From 1963–1971, guerrilla warfare was prevalent as the Christians fought the northern-oriented, that is, Muslim, central government. On 27 February 1964, for instance, the Sudanese government deported 300 missionaries working in the south on charges they were inciting trouble. Later in that year, in September, Sudan allowed Soviet and UAR supplies to filter through the country to the Democratic Republic of Congo (qv). Abboud was forced to resign on 15 November 1964, in the face of mounting unrest. Sirr al-Khatim, a civil servant (*Khalifa*), was then installed as prime minister. When the UAR claimed the Gulf of Aqaba, Sudan ordered mobilization of its armed forces on 28 May 1967, preparatory to declaring war on Israel on 5 June. Sudan's part in the Arab-Israeli War of 1967 was, if anything, minimal. Sudan concluded military aid agreements with Bulgaria, Yugoslavia and the USSR in February 1968. On 5 May 1969, Yugoslavia announced it had signed an agreement to build a naval base in Sudan. A left-wing military coup, led by Colonel Mohammed Gaafar al-Nimeiry (qv), overthrew the government on 25 May 1969. An attempt to overthrow Nimeiry occurred on 27 March 1970. When the coup failed, its leader, Imam al-Hadi al-Mahdi, tried to escape to Ethiopia but was killed (31 March). In November 1970, Sudan joined Libya and the UAR in attempting the formation of a tripartite confederation. The Sudanese Communist Party (SCP) was ordered dissolved on 11 May 1971. This evoked an uprising on 19–21 July 1971, in which control of the country changed hands several times before loyal Nimeiry forces, with the help of Libya and the UAR, suppressed it. On 1 August, Sudan recalled its ambassador from Moscow in the wake of the SCP-inspired insurrection. The government forces were not so lucky when, in December, Sudanese rebel forces operating near the Ugandan border in the south forced their withdrawal. On 28 February 1972, an agreement was reached with the rebel Anyanya tribe to halt the 17-year conflict. An amnesty and a lifting of the 1955 state of emergency occurred on 19–20 March. Also, in February 1972, the border conflict with Ethiopia was settled. Then, on 27 March 1972, the long struggle between Arab and Christian factions in Sudan ended. On 20 September 1972, Sudanese fighters forced five Libyan C-130 transports loaded with 399 combat troops and their equipment to land at Khartoum. On 21 September, the aircraft were allowed to fly to Cairo, but landed on 22 September in Uganda. On 1 October, following an Egyptian demand to do so, Sudan began withdrawing its troops from the Suez Canal. President Nimeiry banned (6 March 1973) all Palestinian guerrilla activities in Sudan following a Black September terrorist attack (1–4 March 1973) on the Saudi Arabian embassy in Khartoum, which cost the lives of the American ambassador and a Belgian diplomat. (In June 1974, the United States withdrew its ambassador after the Sudanese government released the terrorists to the Egyptians, who turned them over to the PLO.) A period of student and labor unrest forced Nimeiry to declare a state of emergency on 5 September 1973. Another military coup attempt against the Nimeiry regime failed on 5 September 1975. Rebellious troops had seized the radio station in Omdurman but were quickly subdued. Still another coup attempt, this time led by former prime minister Sadik al-Mahdi and backed by Libya, failed on 2 July 1976. When Sudan had negotiated an arms deal with the French, all Soviet advisors were expelled from the country (18 May 1977). Sudan refused to follow most of the other 21 members of the Arab League who broke diplomatic relations with Egypt, after Cairo signed a peace treaty with Israel. Fighting erupted again in the 1980s. On 5 October 1981, Nimeiry dissolved Parliament because of the threat posed by Libya. Yet, in October 1982, Sudan offered troops to Iraq in its war with Iran (*see* Iraq-Iran War). The Libyan threat continued into 1983, when Nimeiry reported (22 February) that intelligence sources indicated that the Libyan invasion timetable had bee delayed another two months. A mutiny took place in May 1983, when troops stationed in the south refused to be deployed north because of tribal differences in that region. The revolt was quickly suppressed. When the fighting broke out in Chad (*see* Chad), Sudan gave permission (3 August 1983) for the two U.S. AWACS aircraft deployed to monitor the war to operate from Sudanese airfields. The aircraft were withdrawn on 23 August. Soviet-built Libyan T-22 bombers attacked Omdurman on 16 March 1984; their apparent target was the anti-Qaddafi radio transmitter located there. In a move to gain greater control over the country, Nimeiry declared another state of emergency on 29 April 1984. Two day later, he established nine military courts to enforce the new restriction imposed by his orders. In a series of encounters with the Sudanese People's Liberation Army in the continuing guerrilla war in the south, Nimeiry forces werre able to kill 165 rebels in June 1984. By March 1985, however, the situation had deteriorated to a point where severe food rioting had broken out in Khartoum. Finally, on 6 April 1985, while Nimeiry was on a state visit to the U.S., his government was overthrown by the military and General 'Abd ar-Rahman Sower (Siwar) el-Dahab (qv) became the nation's new leader. Among its first actions, the new government restored diplomatic relations with Libya (24 April) and signed a military agreement with them for logistical and training support. Democratic elections took place in 1986. On 30 June 1989, a new military central government came to power in a coup that was largely fundamentalist oriented and that refused to accede to any of the wishes of the south. A major civil war followed, exacerbated by a severe drought in the 1980s–1990s that killed thousands. Sudan's support of Iraq during the Persian Gulf War complicated its position with other Arab nations that had condemned that country. In 1992, the UN cut off aid to the south because of the heavy fighting. In 1993, Amnesty International accused Sudan of a genocidal operation against the Nubian tribes in the south. Egypt accused

Sudan of complicity in an attempted assassination of Egyptian President Hosni Mubarak while he visited Ethiopia on 26 June 1995. *See also* Mali for the story of French Sudan. *Reading:* Nicholas Mottern, *Suffering Strong: The Journal of a Westerner in Ethiopia, the Sudan, Eritrea and Chad* (1987).

Suder, Sinai. *See* Israel.

Suez Canal. One of the world's major manmade waterways, the Suez Canal (*Qanat as-Suways*), the canal traverses the Isthmus of Suez through Egypt and delineates the African and Asian continents. The 100-mile-long sea-level canal begins in the north at Port Said on the Mediterranean and runs southward to the Gulf of Suez. The canal utilizes passage through several existing lakes. Built by the French-owned Suez Canal Company headed by Ferdinand de Lesseps, it was completed in 11 years (1869). Egypt closed the canal to Iraeli shipping on 19 May 1950. On 16 November 1950, the Egyptian prime minister, Mustafa el-Nahas Pasha, demanded a British withdrawal from the canal and also from Sudan (*see* Sudan). When the United Nations ordered Egypt to stop interfering with Israeli shipping through the canal, the Egyptian government said it would ignore the order as illegal, branding Israel as a threat to peace in the Middle East. By May 1952, negotiations over the future of the canal had proven fruitless. But, on 19 October 1954, an agreement was signed whereby Britain said it would give up and evacuate the Suez Canal in 20 months. Control of the canal remained in French or British hands until 1956, when Egypt announced it would not renew the Suez Canal Company's concession, and Gamal Abdul Nasser (qv) thereafter nationalized it for Egypt. This led to the Suez Crisis in 1956–1957, which brought British, French and Israeli forces into conflict in the Middle East. Nasser ordered the scuttling of a number of ships to close the canal. A UN emergency force was inserted on 15 November 1956 to keep the peace. Egypt reached a financial agreement with Great Britain over the seizure of the canal on 16 February 1959. Nasser warned of another possible closing on 28 May 1967, before the onset of the Arab-Israeli War (Six Day War). Egypt's near-total defeat in that war required a withdrawal to the west bank of the canal to prevent a deeper penetration into Egyptian territory. The Israelis did use artillery fire across the canal in that war. In the aftermath of the fighting Egypt had to agree to Israeli participation in the discussions about clearing the canal of sunken ships and the other debris of war (January 1968). Later in January, the clearing operation was halted by exchanges of gunfire across the canal. The Egyptian army chief of staff, Lieutenant General Abdul Moneim Riadh (qv), was killed observing one of these frequent artillery duels on 8 March 1969. On 7 July 1969, the UN Secretary General U Thant (qv) informed the Security Council that fighting had resumed on the canal, which eventually brought Soviet air forces into the fight. The fighting quieted somewhat when the Egyptians withdrew their forces from the canal's west bank. By July 1970, a U.S.–brokered cease-fire along the canal went into effect. Both sides, however, were violating the truce agreement before the end of August. Nasser offered to extend the truce agreement in February 1971, if Israel withdrew from the east bank. Israel refused. Then, on 1 April 1971, Nasser offered an extension of the truce, if Israel would only partially withdraw its forces. This demand was repeated on 1 May. On 5 July, Nasser and the USSR again stated the terms of an Israeli withdrawal to get the canal open. Throughout this time the fighting continued around the canal. When the next Arab-Israeli War (Yom Kippur War) began, the Suez was crossed by Israeli forces in division strength (16–18 October 1973). By 22 October, a greatly reinforced Israeli force was within 50 miles of Cairo. When a truce was arranged, work on clearing the canal was begun (8 February 1974), with the reopening of the canal for the first time in eight years, on 5 June 1975. Although there were numerous violations of the truce agreement, shipping once again moved through the canal. Regional tensions continued into 1995, but without too serious an effect on canal operations. *Reading:* Cole C. Kingseed, *Eisenhower and the Suez Crisis of 1956* (1995); Selwyn Troen & Moshe Shemesh, eds., *The Suez-Sinai Crisis, 1956: Retrospective and Reappraisal* (1990).

Suez (*As Suways*) City. *See* Egypt.

Suharto. (b. 8 June 1921, Kemusu Argamulja, Java, Dutch East Indies) As a youth, Suharto enlisted in the Dutch colonial army in Java. After the Japanese occupied his country in 1942, he served in a Japanese-sponsored defense force and became an officer. After the war, Suharto joined the guerrilla movement fighting Dutch colonial rule. By 1950, Lieutenant Colonel Suharto was in the Indonesian army, where he became identified with the majority anticommunist faction opposed to Sukarno's (qv) embracing that ideology. On 1 October 1965, as a lieutenent general in command of the Strategic Army Reserve, the Jakarta garrison, Suharto led his forces against the Sukarno-engineered coup (30 September), which had been designed to give complete control to the communists. Suharto's forces were triumphant, destroying Sukarno's power base and about 400,000 people as well. Suharto took control of the country on 11 March 1966, even though Sukarno still retained some vestiges of power. In March 1967, Suharto was appointed acting president and, on 27 March 1968, was elected to a five-year term in that office. His New Order party sought US help in undoing the economic damage caused by Sukarno's flirtation with communism. Since that time, Suharto's authoritarian government has been reelected on each occasion. An example of that totalitarian form of government may be found in Suharto's closure of four major newspapers in Indonesia on 20 January 1978. Suharto remained in power in 1995; but, after more than a quarter-century in office, Suharto was carefully looking for a replacement.

Sui-fenho. *See* China.

Sukarno (*Soekarno*), Achmed. (b. 6 June 1901, Surabaja, Java, Dutch East Indies—d. 21 June 1970, Jakarta, Indonesia) Born the only son of a schoolteacher, Sukarno was originally named Kusnasosro. As he was a sickly boy, his name was changed as a means of strengthening him, and he became Sukarno. From an early age he was seen as a future leader. He lived for a time with his grandparents, and at the age of 15 he attended the secondary school in

Surabaja, where he resided with a prominent religious and civic patron. There, he was treated as a foster son and was sent to complete his education. At age 20, he married his patron's daughter, Siti Utari. At school he studied languages, especially those of the Indonesian region but also the chief languages of the East and the West. This training, coupled with his embrace of mysticism and his numerous personal contacts with political personages as his patron's protege, prepared him for his future role. In 1927, he received a degree in civil engineering. Sukarno divorced his first wife in 1923 and married another, whom he subsequently divorced in 1943. He then married for the third time and, under Muslim law, married several more women over the following years. Sukarno spent two years (1929–1931) in a Dutch prison because of his nationalistic views. He was later exiled to the islands of Flores and Sumatra from 1933 to 1942. When the Japanese invaded, they appointed Sukarno their chief adviser and procurer of Indonesian labor for their projects. After greeting them with open arms, he demanded that the Japanese give independence to Indonesia. Before the fall of Japan, Sukarno was kidnapped by radical nationalists and, after some not so friendly persuasion, on 17 August 1945, he declared Indonesia independent. Sukarno was captured by the Dutch in December 1948, when his headquarters was taken during a major operation. When the Dutch could not totally wrest back control of their possession, they transferred sovereignty on 27 November 1949. Sukarno moved into the governor general's house in Jakarta. Almost immediately the mystical Sukarno ran into the reality of administering a country, and soon both the political and the economic life of Indonesia were in chaos. Sukarno was successful, however, in securing a national identity for his people. By 1956, Sukarno was establishing for himself a dictatorship without restraint. He abolished opposition parties and abrogated democratic guarantees, putting in their place "Guided Democracy" and "Guided Economy." He established a coterie of minions who were corrupt and self-serving (Cabinet of 100) and drove Indonesia into a state of continuing crises. Sukarno rejected further U.S. aid, which had begun in 1950 and by 4 August 1956 had sunk nearly $1 billion into the country, leaving debts that were now repudiated. He would later do the same thing to the Soviets, who began supplying Indonesian needs in September 1956, after they had also provided nearly US$1 billion. Several uprisings broke out in various provinces, such as in the eastern province of Celebes in March 1957. In October 1957, Sukarno threatened to seize Dutch West New Guinea, if the United Nations did not accede to his demand to take up the question of the ongoing Indonesian crisis. In December 1957, he ordered the closing of all Dutch consular offices in Indonesia and the expulsion of all Dutch citizens. In July 1959, he dissolved the Constituent Assembly, thereby making the Indonesian Communist Party (PKI) that much more powerful. Following the British announcement of its plan for the Malay Federation (*see* Malaysia), Sukarno voiced his opposition. On 18 May 1963, he was named "President for Life." By 1965, inflation was so high that it was "off the scale"; Sukarno then removed Indonesian assets from U.S. banks because of America's support of Malaysia (*see* Malaysia and Indonesia), vowing to destroy Malaysia as a puppet of the imperialists. In fact, in September 1963, he had already begun a guerrilla campaign against his neighboring state. This activity was halted when the U.S. issued what some saw as an ultimatum to Sukarno (23 January 1964). At the same time, Sukarno continued to build his own mystique among his people, who now called him the "Great Leader of the Revolution." On 30 September–1 October 1965, however, a communist-inspired and military-led coup took place in which Sukarno was implicated. A number of senior military anticommunist army officers were kidnapped, tortured and murdered. The apparent purpose of the coup was to establish a more communist-oriented Sukarno government. The attempt failed, however, when the commander of the Jakarta garrison, General Suharto (qv), took over the city and forcibly suppressed the coup. At least 400,000, of whom 100,000 were PKI communists and sympathizers, were killed in the ensuing fighting. At that point, numerous groups, especially young activists, demanded Sukarno's ouster. Antigovernment rioting broke out in a number of regions on 24 February 1966, following Sukarno's dismissal of all anticommunists in his government. On 11 March 1960, Sukarno was forced to turn over power to Lieutenant General Suharto. Sukarno's last vestiges of power were stripped from him on 20 February 1967. After that, Sukarno fell into disgrace and an illusionary world of fantasy. The PKI was outlawed, and a new purge of communists began. Sukarno died of complications from a kidney ailment on 21 June 1970. One-half million attended what had been planned to be a quiet funeral. Sukarno's name was proscribed, and not until the late 1970s was there any attempt at his rehabilitation.

Sulaimaniya. *See* Iraq.

Sumatra. *See* Indonesia.

Summer Institute of Linguistics. On 4 August 1976, a series of bombings took place in Bogota, Colombia, aimed chiefly at US corporations. In one of the attacks, the Summer Institute of Linguistics was bombed, injuring five Americans who had just arrived in the country from Peru.

Sungari River. *See* China.

Sunningdale Agreement. In 1973, the Sunningdale Agreement linked Northern Ireland with the Catholic Irish Republic to the south. On 19 May 1974, a state of emergency had to be declared in the wake of violence precipitated by the 15 May general strike called by Protestant factions who demanded a repeal of the agreement. On 20 May, an additional 500 British troops were deployed to Northern Ireland, to reinforce the 16,000-man garrison already there. Among its other provisions, the agreement called for a "Council of Ireland" to provide for cooperation and consultation between Northern Ireland and the Republic. While the Irish Catholics in Northern Ireland embraced this plan, as did the Republic, the Protestants in the north did not. In 1974, the Fianna Fail party in the Republic brought suit in the High Court to get the agreement declared (January) unconstitutional. Although meetings continued throughout the year, the agreement failed to achieve any concrete results, except an increase in violence.

Suq-el-Gharb. *See* Lebanon.

Surabaya. *See* Indonesia.

Suramarit, Norodom. *See* Sihanouk, Norodom.

Suriname. Suriname is located on the northern coast of South America. It is bordered
on the north by the Atlantic Ocean, on the east by French Guiana, on the south
by Brazil and on the west by Guyana. The capital city is Paramaribo. Historical
evidence indicates the region was first occupied by the Surinen people, who
were displaced by other tribes before the sixteenth century. Columbus sighted
the region in 1498. In 1499, Amerigo Vespucci sailed its coast. A year later
another Spanish explorer, Vicente Pinzon, explored the region. Spanish, Dutch,
French and British settlements all failed in the early seventeenth century,
partially because of native resistance. A British settlement put down in 1651 did
succeed, however, but it was captured by the Dutch in 1667. That same year, the
colony was ceded to the Dutch in trade for the North American settlement at
New York (*Nieuw Amsterdam*). The Dutch, many of whom had been driven out
of Brazil, established a plantation colony using slave labor. When slavery was
abolished in 1863, laborers from China, Java and Madiera were imported to
replace them. Following World War II and the breakup of the colonial systems,
talks began between the Dutch and the Surinamese. The country, along with the
Netherlands Antilles, was granted autonomy by Queen Juliana on 15 December
1954, with the Netherlands supplying most of the needed economic aid. A
socialist party coalition was put in place in 1961. On 19 August 1969, fighting
broke out along the Suriname-Guyana border as Dutch troops stationed in
Suriname occupied disputed territory. The fighting, primarily between Guyanan
military units and Surinamese police lasted until 10 December, when the Dutch
forces finally withdrew. The Dutch retained possession of Suriname until 25
November 1975, when it gained its independence. Later in the 1970s an
economic crisis developed. On 25 February 1980, a group of noncommissioned
officers led by Sergeant Major Daysi (Desi) Bouterse (qv) seized the
government of Prime Minister Henck Arron (qv), to the cheers of most of the
population. A National Military Council was established to run the country with
Hendrick R. Chin A Sen (qv) as prime minister (15 March); he became
president in August 1981. The former president, Johan Ferrier, was arrested. A
proclamation declaring a return to civilian rule in 1982 received Dutch support,
and economic aid was restored. The economy did not improve, however, and
tensions within Suriname began again to rise. In August 1981, Bouterse, as head
of the new Revolutionary Front, took power in a bloodless coup, but most of the
military leadership refused to relinquish command, and tensions once again rose.
In retaliation, the government executed 15 prominent civilians, at which point
the Dutch severed their economic ties with the country. The government
resigned on 4 February 1982; and in the hiatus before a new government was
formed, an uprising among right-wing elements occurred (11 March). Fighting
erupted and did not end until the next day (12 March). Another coup was
attempted on 8 December 1982, but it failed. The military once again took

control. Opposition leaders were rounded up and executed the following day. Martial law was declared on 11 December, and both the U.S. and the Netherlands (17 December) suspended economic aid to the country. In February 1983, a leftist government was formed, but it lasted only one year before the military stepped in again. A rebellion ensued in which a guerrilla force composed of Bush Negroes and calling itself the Surinamese Liberation Army took the lead. The National Army reaction was to massacre numbers of innocent Bush Negroes and to force thousands of others to flee into neighboring French Guiana. Surinameese military leaders then began a series of discussions with the leaders of the political parties that had existed before the coup, and in 1985 a new National Assembly was formed, with a new Cabinet put in place a year later. A new constitution was voted on 30 September 1987. On 25 November 1987, the military were voted out of office. In 1988, Suriname and France opened negotiations with the Surinameese Liberation Army, also called the Jungle Commando (JC), to bring to an end the cross-border fighting that had also affected French Guiana. A July 1989 agreement to allow the safe return of the Bush Negroes and to incorporate the JC into the police force met major opposition in Suriname from the military and from the paramilitary Tucayana Indians. On 24 December 1990, the military again seized power. This time, the OAS (qv), the United States, the Netherlands and France brought pressure to bear, forcing the Surinamese military to hold elections (25 May 1991). The newly elected government's first act was to pass legislation depriving the army of any political power. In 1992, peace was negotiated between the government and the JC and the Tucayana Indians (Amazona) rebels. The Dutch and Americans then resumed economic aid, although intelligence reports indicated growing concern over the flow of illegal drugs through the country and especially targeted the army for suspicion of complicity in the operation. An army mutiny followed the appointment in 1993 of a new commander, General Arthy Gorre, who was devoted to restoring discipline and a sense of purpose to the forces. The National Assembly demanded the resignations of mutinous officers and approved Gorre's appointment. The Netherlands again stopped their financial aid to Suriname after a European Community report stated that the government had not moved to clean up its financial problems. A number of Surinamese officials and top political leaders were forced to resign when evidence of their taking bribes came to light. A senior army officer was arrested on drug-dealing charges on 3 January 1994, but the government was forced to release him for lack of evidence. The Dutch became involved in a major worldwide drug investigation that focused on former Surinamese president Bouterse. At least 81 raids were conducted to gather evidence. An unidentified rebel group captured the all-important Afobaka Dam on 21 March 1994 and held it for four days. They demanded the resignation of the government and better economic and educational conditions. The rebels were finally dislodged by government forces on 25 March. In February 1995, Bouterse declared his candidacy for president in the next election even though he was under suspicion for involvement in the Dutch bribery scandal that had already cost a number of officials their jobs. Bouterse was shunned in May 1995, when he made overtures for a coalition. A fire of suspicious origin on 1 August 1995 destroyed all of Suriname's political and historical records. Jules Wijdenbosch, a Bouterse supporter, was elected president by the National Assembly on 2 September 1996. *Reading:* Rosemarijn Hoefte, *Suriname* (World Bibliographical Series, Vol. 117) (1991); Edward M. Dew, *The Trouble in Suriname, 1975-1993* (1994).

Susangird (Susangerd). *See* Iran.

Suu, Phan Khac. On 27 October 1964, Phan Khac Suu became chief of state of the Republic of Vietnam following the resignation (26 September 1964) of Nguyen Khanh (qv) and his caretaker military government. Following demonstrations in Saigon in mid-January 1965, the government of Phan Khac Suu was overthrown by a military coup on 27 January. Lieutenant General Nguyen Khanh, the man Suu had succeeded, seized power. Phan Khac Suu resigned following the military takeover, but he consented to stay on as caretaker during the transition. *See* Vietnam.

Svay Rieng Province. *See* Cambodia.

Sverdlovsk. *See* USSR.

Swaziland. Formally known as the Kingdom of Swaziland (*Umbuso Westwatini*), this African state is landlocked and bordered by the Republic of South Africa on the north, west and south and by Mozambique on the east. The royal capital is in Lobamba, while the administrative capital is located in Mbabane. Swazi tribesmen migrated into the region from the northeast in the eighteenth century. The Bantu-speaking Swazi conquered the indigenous tribes of the region and established a kingdom there by 1830. They later relinquished the territory north of the Crocodile River to the Ludenburg Republic in 1846. Finding themselves at the hands of the powerful Zulu nation, the Swazi asked for British assistance. By 1888, European settlers had entered the region and had been granted a charter of self-government. In 1890, a joint provisional government was established with Swazi, British and South African participation. In 1893, the Swazi rejected a proposal to be incorporated into South Africa, but they were forced the following year to consent to South African control, but not annexation. After the Boer War, the British established authority over Transvaal (1903); the governor of that South African province was given administrative control of Swaziland and often ordered by proclamation. A high commissioner was assigned to Swaziland, Batsutoland and Bechuanaland in 1906. When the Union of South Africa demanded control of Swaziland in 1949, the British refused. Limited self-rule was granted the Swazi in 1963. On 11 November 1963, following indications of a plan to annex Swaziland, South Africa was warned by the United Nations of the dangers of such aggression. In 1967, Swaziland was made a British protectorate and the following year, on 6 September 1968, was granted full independence. An ageement was reached with South Africa that placed Swaziland in the South African Customs Union.

Internally, all was not well, however; and in 1970 and again in 1977 King Sobhuza II (qv) dismissed Parliament and abolished the constitution, assuming personal control of the country. These institutions were replaced with more compliant people and documents; the new constitution banned political parties as of 13 October 1978. In 1982, King Sobhuza II died, and he was replaced by his son, Prince Makhosetive, who after a regency of four years was crowned King Mswati III (1986). In 1988, Swaziland opposed sanctions against South Africa for its apartheid program and deported any members of the African National Congress found within its borders. Student disturbances occurred in 1991, which forced an indefinite closing of the country's university. In November 1991, Nelson Mandela (qv), just released from prison, visited Swaziland. Human rights organizations began watching Swaziland closely in light of published reports of gross violations. In October 1992, King Mswati dissolved Parliament and abrogated the constitution. Multiparty elections were held for the first time in September 1993. As a result, the prime minister was replaced. That same year, a roundup of opposition leaders suspected of sedition began. By February 1995, violence had grown in the country. On 6 February 1995, the National House of Assembly was burned down, which culminated a string of arson fires all claimed by the Swaziland Youth Congress, which had resorted to terrorism as a result of displeasure with election results. *Reading:* Robert H. Davies et al., *The Kingdom of Swaziland: A Profile* (1986); Alan R. Booth, *Swaziland: Tradition and Change in a Southern African Kingdom* (1983).

Sweden. A country on the Scandinavian peninsula, Sweden is bordered on the north and west by Norway, on the northeast by Finland, on the east by the Gulf of Bothnia and on the south by the Baltic Sea. The capital city is Stockholm. In Roman times, the region was occupied by two warring tribes, the Swedes (*Suiones*) and the Goths (*Gothones*). There was some religious affinity between the two, but everything else was war. In the first half of the ninth century A.D., Frankish missionaries brought Christianity to the region. At that same time, Swedish Vikings began overseas exploration and established a number of colonies in other lands, especially in Eastern Europe and deep into Russia. The Vikings' main purpose was trade and not until the twelfth century did Viking power strengthen to a point where the invasion of Finland was attempted with the concomitant imposition of Christianity on the Finns. During the thirteenth and fourteenth centuries, Sweden became feudal. When the power of the king waned, an aristocracy arose that led to the abdication of Albert I of Mechlenberg and the enthronement of Margaret I, the queen of Denmark and Norway. In 1397, Denmark, Norway and Sweden became a single domain under the queen (Union of Kalmar). A long period of tension, and especially of wars between Denmark and Sweden, followed, culminating in 1520 with an invasion by Danish and Norwegian forces, led by King Christian II to suppress the disorder. Christian proclaimed himself king of Sweden and, by executing most of his opposition, provoked the rebellion of 1521, led by Gustav Vasa. Vasa became king in 1523. The feudal order was circumscribed, the church made subordinate to the state, and Lutheranism established as the state religion. In the seventeenth century, Sweden began a long program of expansion, which did not subside until after its defeat in the Great Northern War of 1700–1721. The results reduced Sweden generally to its orginal boundaries (including Finland), as it lost most of its continental territories. Before the end of the war, Charles XII died (1718), thus ending the male reign of the House of Vasa. The new queen, Ulrika, was forced to accept an end to the absolute monarchy and to install a parliamentary (*Rikstag*) government. This gave power back to the aristocracy until 1771, when Gustav III retook the government for the throne. Following the French Revolution, Gustav III was exposed as a despot and was assassinated in 1792. The new king, Gustav IV Adolph, opposed Napoleon and joined the Third Coalition against him. Then, in 1807, Russia deserted the coalition, joined Napoleon, and invaded Finland (1808). Sweden was forced to capitulate to Russia's terms and to cede Finland and associated Baltic islands to St Petersburg. Sweden was also required to enter into a treaty with Napoleonic France which lefy the selection of a successor to the Swedish throne up to Napoleon. Upon the death of Gustav XIII in 1810, Bonaparte choice was Marshal Jean Baptiste Jules Bernadotte, who served first as crown prince and then on the Swedish throne as Charles XIV John (after 1818). Bernadotte almost immediately withdrew his allegiance to Napoleon and rejoined the coalition (1813–14). In 1814, Denmark was forced to yield Norway to Sweden, a move which was recognized by the Congress of Vienna in 1815. Bernadotte's rule after 1818 was one of tension with the *Rikstag* and equal displeasure with the people because he was a foreigner. He did, however, before the end of his reign in 1844, produce considerable economic gain for Sweden, and his successors were considered Swedes. By 1868, nearly one-half million Swedes had migrated to the United States. In June 1905, the Norwegian parliament dissolved the union with Sweden, a move approved by the Swedish *Rikstag*. At the beginning of World War I, Sweden declared its neutrality and joined Denmark and Norway in announcing a mutual defense agreement to protect Scandinavia. In 1920, Sweden joined the League of Nations. The socialist movement became the leading political body in Sweden and remained so until 1928, when a conservative government was elected. The ensuing worldwide depression brought back the socialists in 1932. The outbreak of World War II saw Sweden again delare its neutrality, which it was able to maintain throughout the war. On 19 November 1946, Sweden became the 54th member of the United Nations, still maintaining its neutral stance. In 1948, it joined the European Recovery Plan (qv) but refused membership in NATO. When it found itself isolated militarily from both East and West, Sweden began a program of what was basically a unilateral defense, in which all its citizens participated. By 1957, however, many Swedes, especially among the military, began to question the conventional wisdom of neutrality and military isolation. One of the suggestions offered at that time was to arm the Swedish forces with nuclear weapons. In

April 1957, the four Scandinavian countries announced the establishment of an institute in Copenhagen to study that issue. In April 1958, the U.S, gave Sweden $350,000 to aid in the construction of a nuclear reactor. In 1959, Sweden became a founder of the European Free Trade Association. In June 1963, a 200-man Swedish UN Observer Force was dispatched to Yemen, in the first of many such Swedish responses to a call from the UN to enforce its mandate. In 1969, Tage Erlander, the long-time prime minister, retired and was replaced by Olaf Palme (qv). In July 1969, Sweden ordered a halt to the exportation of its MFI-9 aircraft which was being used in the war in Biafra (qv). When the war in Vietnam began (1967), Sweden opposed it vociferously. This led to a major strain in relations with the U.S., exacerbated especially by Palme's speeches. A near-severance of diplomatic relations occurred in 1972, and relations remained frigid until 1974. On 7 April 1971, two Croatian terrorists entered the Yugoslav embassy in Stockholm and shot the Yugoslav ambassador and one other Yugoslav diplomat. In counterpoint, Sweden announced that it was tripling its aid to FRELIMO guerrillas fighting the Portuguese in Africa, on 24 March 1974. On 24 April 1975, six West German Red Army (qv) terrorists entered the West German embassy in Stockholm and took 12 hostages, demanding the release of 26 terrorists held in West German prisons. When the Bonn government refused, the embassy's economic attache was murdered. After a mysterious grenade explosion, the captors and their hostages fled the building, where five of the six terrorists were taken by Swedish police (the sixth died of injuries). The terrorists were then extradited to West Germany for punishment. A declining economy led to the loss of the *Rikstag* to a conservative-center coalition in September 1976. The new government resigned over the nuclear power generation issue in 1978 but returned in 1979. In May 1980 a very rare general strike occurred that paralyzed the country for ten days. The government survived a no-confidence vote by one vote in October of that year. In May 1981, a white-collar strike occurred that led eventually to the restoration of the Social Democrats in 1982. During the 1980s, Soviet incursions into Sweden were not uncommon. On 27 October 1981, for example, a Soviet "Whiskey"-class submarine entered a restricted area off the Swedish coast near the naval base at Karlskrona. There the submarine ran aground. It was forced to surface and was finally released amid very loud howling from Moscow, on 6 November. Another submarine incident occured on 1 October 1982, when Stockholm reported a sub in the restricted waters near Musko Island. In November 1984, Sweden joined other Scandinavian states in a discussions about making Scandinavia a nuclear-free zone. Sweden also joined in other nuclear disarmament talks such as the five-continent meeting of small nations held to discuss a ban on nuclear weapons in outer space and an end to the arms race. Even so, Sweden announced the detonation of a nuclear device on 26 April 1985, while denying it was producing nuclear weapons. Following the 1985 elections, Palme continued in office as prime minister until his assassination on 26 February 1986. In 1991, the Social Democrats lost to the moderates, who led a campaign of deregulation. Sweden joined the European Union in May 1994 (accepted January 1995). In September 1994, however, the Social Democrats returned to power. That same month, more than 900 people were killed in the worst ferry accident in history, when a ferryboat traveling between Sweden and Estonia capsized off the Finnish coast. Sweden joined the European Union on 1 January 1995, but ran afoul of the French after protesting renewed French nuclear testing in the Pacific. The sense of a lack of immediate benefit from EU membership caused a voter backlash in the 1995 elections. *Reading:* Franklin D. Scott, *Sweden: A Nation's History* (1989); Klaus Misgeld et al., eds., *Creating Social Democracy: A Century of the Social Democratic Labor Party in Sweden* (1993).

Switzerland. A landlocked Alpine country in Europe, Switzerland is bordered on the west and northwest by France, on the northeast by Germany, on the east by Austria and Liechtenstein and on the south by Italy. The capital city is Bern. From pre-Roman times the region was occupied by Helvetii in the west and the Rhaetian tribes (possibly relatives of the Etruscans) in the east. Julius Caesar captured the region in the first century B.C. and called it Helvetia. Until the fourth century A.D. incursions of Germanic tribes, Helvetia was throughly Romanized. The Germanic Burgundians and Alamanni conquered the region and were, in turn, conquered by the Carolingian Franks in the fifth century A.D. In the ninth century, most of the region came under Swabian (Alemannian) feudal control as a part of the Kingdom of Germany. Part of the region fell under Burgundian control. That Burgundian region was annexed into the Holy Roman Empire in 1033. The petty states in this region later evolved into the Swiss cantonal system. By 1291, several of the cantons around Lake Lucerne allied to protect themselves from further encroachment by the Hapsburgs. However, by 1474, the Hapsburgs gave up their attempts to bring individual parts of Switzerland into their realm and thereafter dealt with the country as a federated dependency. War came in 1499, when the Holy Roman emperor, Maximilian I, attempted to change certain Swiss perogatives. Maximilian was subsequently defeated and was forced to acknowledge Switzerland's virtual independence (Treaty of Basil, 1499). The Swiss federation then began to grow, as new cantons joined. At the same time, the Swiss having proved themselves worthy fighters found a market in supplying mercenaries, as to France in the sixteenth century. As a part of the payment, Switzerland received Italian provinces, which were brought into the Cantonal system. The Swiss then fought the French, but this time they were defeated (1515). Thereafter, the Swiss adopted a neutrality policy but still managed to occupy adjacent areas and bring them into the federation. The Protestant Reformation created pockets of open defiance against the Roman Catholic Church and the Holy Roman Empire. During the ensuing Thirty Years War (1618–1648), Switzerland remained neutral but did get itself declared independent in the Peace of Westphalia (1648). In the 1790s, the French Revolution spread into Switzerland, with France intervening on behalf of the revolution. By 1798, the revolutionaries controlled all of Switzerland and demanded a strong national government for the country. The future emperor

Napoleon unified the country, naming it the Helvetic Republic and imposing a new constitution. The Swiss greatly disapproved of this until 1803, when France withdrew its occupation army. The Swiss then approved a new constitution, and Switzerland's neutrality was affirmed at the Congress of Vienna in 1815. The extent of Switzerland at that time was as it is seen today. Civil war developed during this period between the Catholic and Protestant cantons, with the Catholics being defeated and forced to capitulate to the federal government. New constitutions were imposed in 1848 and in 1874. The League of Nations set up there following World War I, with Switzerland as one of its members. During World War II, Switzerland was known as a center for espionage carried out by both sides and as a haven for refugees from the Nazi onslaught. Switzerland initially refused to join the United Nations, but it did join a number of UN commissions whose roles were not incompatible with Swiss neutrality policies. Switzerland was, for instance, a part of the Neutral Nations Commission that supervised the truce agreement dealing with the war in Korea in 1953 and has contributed in a number of other ways to the accomplishment of UN peace projects. In 1948, Switzerland joined the Organization of European Economic Cooperation and became one of the founders of the European Free Trade Association. On 20–21 July 1954, Switzerland was the site of the signing of the Geneva Accords that dealt with the future of Indochina. Switzerland's neutrality was reaffirmed on 12 December 1956, when the foreign minister stated in effect that Switzerland would fight to maintain its neutral status. To this end, on 11 July 1958, Switzerland decided to equip its forces with nuclear weapons. In 1963, it became a member of the Council for Europe. The headquarters of the International Red Cross was also established in Switzerland in 1963, as were the headquarters of many other organizations who saw Swiss neutrality as a useful tool in their enterprises. On 10 February 1969, Zurich's Kloten Airport was the scene of an Arab terrorist attack on an Israeli El Al airliner. Another terrorist attack occurred at the same location and against El Al one week later, in which a number of people were killed. Rioting broke out in Zurich on 6 September 1980 when 600 youths rampaged following the closure of a youth center because of drug-related problems. On 9 September, the federal president was asked for troops to quell what was now a major riot by 6,000 youths demanding the reopening of the center. On 6 December 1980, six gasoline bombs were thrown into a Zurich army barracks. Although no one was injured, damage from the fire was extensive. On 24 August 1983, the Swiss federal government announced it would buy West German Leopard II tanks instead of the U.S. Abrams tank which the Swiss said was inferior. In 1989 the *Nationalrat* barely defeated a proposal to disband its army. In June 1994, the Swiss rejected a referendum that would have permitted Swiss troops to join UN peacekeeping missions. In September 1994, another referendum was approved that made racial discrimination and denial of the Holocaust illegal. This latter issue also caused the reversal of a World War II senior police officer's conviction for violating an order not to allow any more Jews to cross the border from Germany. An estimated 3,000 Jews were thus saved from Nazi tyranny. The reversal came 23 years after the police officer's death in 1972. *Reading:* Georg Th-Urer, *Free and Swiss: The Story of Switzerland* (1971).

Sykes, Sir Richard. On 22 March 1979, The British ambassador to the Netherlands, Sir Richard Sykes, was assassinated by terrorists from the Provisional Wing of the Irish Republican Army (PIRA). Sykes' valet was also murdered as the two were entering the ambassador's limousine outside his home in the Hague. There was some speculation that the attack might have been carried out by Dutch left-wing sympathizers. Sykes was a specialist on security matters associated with terrorism and had served as ambassador in Dublin. The ambassador's valet died instantly, and Sykes died two hours after arriving at the hospital.

Syria (*Suriyah*). Formally the Syrian Arab Republic, this Middle Eastern (South Asian) country is bordered on north by Turkey, on the east and southeast by Iraq, on south by Jordan, on the southwest by Israel and Lebanon and on the west by the Mediterranean Sea. The capital city is Damascus. Early inhabitants of the region have been traced back to 10000 B.C. The Akkadian culture developed in the third millennium B.C., but it was subsequently destroyed by Amorite nomads before 1800 B.C.. In the sixteenth through fifteenth centuries B.C., both Egyptian and Hurrian incursions attempted to take the land. The Hittites took control of the region in the fourteenth century B.C. and remained there in various configurations until Assyrian domination in the eighth century B.C. The Babylonians overran the Assyrians in the seventh century B.C.; they were replaced by the Persian Achaemenid Empire in 539 B.C. Alexander conquered both Syria and Persia in 333 B.C. From 301 B.C until 164 B.C., Syria was under Seleucid domonation, after which the lands were divided between the Partians and Natabataeans. Rome annexed Syria as a part of Palestine in 64 B.C. and it remained under Roman control until about 300 A.D., when control was passed to Byzantium. Syria remained a Byzantine province until the Arab Muslim invasions of 634. Egypt annexed Syria in 877 and, although Egyptian control was often tenuous, Syria remained a vassal for nearly six centuries. In the thirteenth century, following an uprising, the Mumluks of Egypt reconquered Syria and held it until 1516, when the Ottoman Turks overran it. Syria remained a Turkish vassal into the twentieth century. In World War I, Syria became a battleground where the Turks faced a British force and an Arab army led by the legendary Lawrence of Arabia. After the war, however, Syria became a French protectorate. As early as 1925, nationalist elements formed the People's Party to fight for independence. By 1936, these activities were bearing fruit, but the advent of World War II postponed further action toward independence, and the country spent the war under Vichy French control. The country was eventually occupied by British and Free French forces (1941), and Syria was declared independent. The first elections were held in 1943, but the government of Shukri al-Kuwatly (qv) was overthrown in a bloodless military coup in March 1949. On 20 October 1945, Syria was one of the Arab states that warned the U.S. against the establishment of a Jewish state in Palestine. The last Allied forces still remaining in Syria at war's end were withdrawn by 15 April 1946. On 15 May 1948, Syria joined other Arab nations in their first attack on the new Israeli state (*see* Israel) in an unsuccessful attempt to destroy it. Beginning in January 1949, Syria became a base for terrorist groups operating against Arab enemies, especially Israel. A second coup occurred on 14 August 1949. This time President Husni Za'im (qv) was arrested and executed. The new government of Hashim al-Atasi (qv) was sworn in on 14 December. Syria signed a collective security pact with Egypt, Lebanon, Saudi Arabia and Yemen on 17 June 1950. Border clashes between the Syrians and Israelis occurred in April 1951. A cease-fire restored order on 8 May. On 24 October 1952, having abolished all other political parties, Syrian strongman Adib Shishlaki proclaimed his Arab Liberation Movement the country's sole political organization. In 1953, sporadic fighting began again along the Syria-Israel border. In December of that year, a uprising began among Jebel Druse tribesmen that lasted for three months and was put down by the Syrian army only after heavy fighting. The Syrian government of Adib Shishlaki was overthrown by the military on 24 February 1954. The Arab Liberation Movement was abolished, and former president al-Atasi returned to power. A union, however brief, was formed with Egypt in 1954 (*see* United Arab Republic). A defensive military alliance was formed among Syria, Egypt and Saudi Arabia on 20 October 1955. In response to Israeli attacks along the Syrian border, Syria and Lebanon signed a mutual defense alliance on 13 January 1956. Syria joined in the planning for joint action against Israel in March 1956. On 7 May 1956, Syria warned against further Turkish troop deployments, which had begun 1 May, along the common border. United Nations Emergency Force observation posts were set up along the Syria-Israel border on 16 July 1957. On 13 August 1957, Syria expelled three U.S. diplomats who were allegedly plotting a government overthrow. The Syria warned the U.S. of retaliation if the U.S. shipped arms to Jordan. Another military coup took place on 28–29 October 1961, which at first established a civilian government under a military junta. The new government undid the union with Egypt (29 October). In April 1962, there was an unsuccessful revolt in the ancient city of Aleppo. In September 1963, Parliament was dissolved, and rule thereafter was by decree. A new overthrow took place in which the Baath Party (qv) established a military dictatorship. In April, Egypt announced it had joined Syria and Iraq in forming a new tripartite Arab state. The fighting along the border with Israel continued, with very heavy fighting in August 1963. There was another serious revolt in Hama on 13–15 April 1964. Loyal government troops were able to suppress it, but only after much blood was spilled. Another coup took place on 23 February 1966 in which the government of Premier Salal al Bitar (qv) was overthrown. A radical left-wing group led by Major General Salal Jedid (qv) took power. In 1967, Syria took part in the Arab-Israeli War, losing the Golan Heights (*see* Israel) in the conflict. Even though the war ended in 1967, Israel and Syria continued their armed confrontation unabated through the next two decades. In yet another coup (28 February 1969), defense minister

Lieutenant General General Hafez al-Assad (qv) seized partial power (becoming premier of Syria on 13 November 1970). Jordan's King Hussein (qv) announced the establishment of the Arab Eastern Command comprised of forces from Iraq, Jordan and Syria, on 17 March 1969. One week earlier, on 9 March, the UAR and Syria put their mutual defense agreement into effect. A separate Syrian-Iraqi defense agreement was signed on 30 July. Earlier, on 4 June 1969, Syria recognized the communist government in East Germany and, on 21 October, ordered the border with Lebanon closed as a means of halting Lebanon's growing antiguerrilla campaign. In December of that year, Syria carried out a successful prisoner exchange with Israel, but the ongoing battle between the two continued. On 19 September 1970, Syria sent about 20,000 troops to invade Jordan, in part to halt Jordan's decimation of PLO guerrillas in that country. On 27 November 1970, Syria announced it was joining a new Arab federation along with Libya, Sudan and the UAR. This new organization became effective on 1 September 1971. The arrangement never worked, however, and was soon abandoned. On 12 March 1971, Assad was elected to a seven-year term as president (he had already assumed those powers on 22 February). A joint UAR-Syrian military command structure was established on 16 March 1971. An attempt to overthrow Assad failed on 11 June. In an extension of the Syrian incursion into Jordan, the Jordanian army moved to crush Palestinian resistance by driving the PLO across the border into Syria. In the process, over 2,000 Syrian troops were captured. Syria broke diplomatic relations with Jordan on 12 August 1971, and war appeared imminent, but nothing happened. Syria at this time was receiving military aid from the USSR, and Soviet defense minister Marshal Andrei Grechko (qv) signed a new military aid agreement with Damascus on 14 May 1972. On 12 September 1973, Assad met secretly with Egypt's Anwar Sadat (qv) to set the date (6 October, Yom Kippur) for the planned war against Israel. The Arab loss of the war dug deeply into Syrian resources, but sporadic fighting continued in 1974. A U.S.–brokered disengagement was reached on 31 May 1974, and a UN force was dispatched (5 June) to patrol the agreed-upon buffer zone. By 23 June all Israeli forces had been withdrawn from Syrian territory occupied in the recent war. The Soviet Union supplied Syria with 45 MiG-23 fighters on 18 February 1975. On 21 May 1975, Israel and Syria agreed to a six-month extension of the UN mandate to settle the issue of the Golan Heights. A further extension was arranged in May 1978. Syrian troops in Lebanon clashed with Israeli forces during their own invasion of that country in August 1975. However, amid rumors of a new round of hostilities, Egypt warned Syria on 27 February 1976 that if the Syrians got into a war Egypt would not support them. On 26 March 1976, Syrian troops were observed massing in large numbers along the border with Lebanon. This was sufficient cause for the warring Lebanese faction to arrange a cease-fire (1 April). Syrian troops moved in when the truce disintegrated into some of the bitterest fighting ever witnessed in Lebanon. Athough an Arab League peacekeeping force was authorized in June 1976, to replace some 12,000 Syrian troops in Lebanon, Syrian forces still occupied large portions of Lebanon. Syria and Egypt were able to settle their differences at a meeting held in Saudi Arabia on on 24 June 1976, and both attended another meeting on 17 September to establish a new cease-fire in Lebanon and to form a 30,000-man peacekeeping force. On 10 November, Syrian troops occupied Beirut under the Arab League peacekeeping arrangement. Syria then asked the PLO to cease its operations against Israel and ordered both Christian and Muslim militias to turn in their weapons. From May 1977 to January 1978, intelligence reports indicated the Soviet Union was delivering MiG-21 and 23 fighters, T-62 tanks, and SA-6 ground-to-air missiles to Syria and were promised more aid during Assad's state visit to Moscow on 24 February. Some of the ground-to-air missiles were later deployed with Syrian forces in Lebanon (18 May 1981). Earlier, on 7 February 1978, Syrian forces clashed had with Lebanese army units in East Beirut. Failing to heed a warning to cease skirmishing with Syrian forces in southern Lebanon, Syria attacked Christian positions there on 31 July 1978. A cease-fire was finally arranged on 10 August, but was broken the next day. Syria and Iraq signed a mutual defense pact on 30 January 1979 and declared their intention of creating a unified state. Serious religious rioting broke out in the town of Latakia on 4 September 1979. Some 1,400 troops were required to restore order. In October, the USSR promised Syria additional military aid. The government was required to send 10,000 troops into Aleppo as a show of force when anti-Assad agitation built in that city (15 March 1979). On 1 September 1980, Libya's Muammar Qadaffi announced that, following secret negotiations, Libya and Syria would be merged, to pose a more serious opposition to Israel. A previous attempt at such a merger had failed in 1973. Jordan called its ambassador in Damascus home, abrogated the six-year-old customs agreement with Syria and withdrew its forces from the joint border control point at Naharayim on 10 February 1981, after Syria had accused Jordan of supporting the opposition Muslim Brotherhood in Damascus and began massing troops along the border. Syria also blamed Jordan for supporting Iraq in the Iraq-Iran War (qv). In March 1981, Syria (19 March) refused to extradite a group of terrorists who had hijacked a Pakastani airliner on 9 March. On 21 May 1981, Israel demanded the removal of Soviet-built air defense missiles the Syrians had emplaced along the Lebanon-Israeli border. When the removal was not accomplished, Israeli jets successfully attacked and destroyed most of them on 28 May. Syria extended its territorial waters to 35 nautical miles on 9 September 1981. An act of internal terrorism struck Damascus on 29 November 1981, when Muslim Brotherhood members exploded a car bomb in front of a school building. Ninety people were killed and scores more injured in the blast. On 18 April 1982, Syria, who supported Iran in the Iraq-Iran War, broke diplomatic relations with Iraq. In May 1982, when it heard Israel was moving troops toward the border with Lebanon, Syria reinforced its military units to the north of that border. When the French embassy in Beirut was bombed on 24 May 1982, Syria was accused of the attack by Paris. After the Israeli invasion of Lebanon on 6 June 1982, Israeli and Syrian forces clashed in a number of air and ground engagements. About 25 Syrian fighters were downed in air engagements and at least 17 Syrian missile sites were destroyed. Syria refused to accept Palestinian refugees on 9 July 1982, claiming they had a right to remain in Lebanon until their "legitimate rights" were upheld. On 3 July 1983, Syrian officials ignored a plea from the U.S. secretary of state for a Syrian withdrawal from Lebanon. Syrian joined in a cease-fire in Lebanon on 26 September. Israeli intelligence sources confirmed (18 October) that the USSR had given SS-21 intermediate-range missiles to Syria. On 4 December 1983, Syrian anti-aircraft shot down two U.S. navy fighters over Lebanon. One pilot was killed; the other was captured by the Syrians. He was subsequently released to U.S. custody (3 January 1984). On 5 February 1984, the U.S. formally warned Syria that it would react to any attacks on Lebanese forces by Syria and its controlled militias. Although it welcomed the 2 November 1984 announcement that Israel was withdrawing its forces from Lebanon, Syria refused to guarantee the security of the Lebanon-Israeli border. President Assad personally intervened to secure the release of 39 American hostages who had been aboard a TWA airliner hijacked out of Athens on 14 June 1985; the hostages were released on 30 June. On July 1985, Syria gave 50 Soviet-built T-54 tanks to the Shi'ite Amal militia in Lebanon. Syria held reconciliation talks with Jordan at a meeting in Jidda, Saudi Arabia, on 16 September 1985. In December 1985, Syria moved anti-aircraft missile batteries up to its border with Lebanon to discourage Israeli overflights. Israel complained, but the weapons remained. In 1986, Great Britain broke diplomatic relations with Syria because of its support of international terrorist activities. The European Community also imposed limited sanctions. When Iraq invaded Kuwait in August 1990, Syria condemned the action and sent troops to join the coalition forces of Desert Shield/Desert Storm. In 1991, Syria acceded to U.S. proposals for a settlement of the Middle East question and participated in a number of conferences designed to bring peace between Israel and the Arab world. Although conflict continued, the prospects for peace in the region were good in January 1994. Throughout 1995 Syria was adamant that any peace with Israel would only be discussed as a result of Israel's return of all its occupied territory. Yet there were persistent rumors that the two countries were on the verge of a settlement. When Hizballah guerrillas killed a group of Israeli soldiers in October in southern Lebanon and attacked a South Lebanese Army installation (October 1995), Israel quickly blamed Syria for not controlling the rebels. A peace agreement appeared to be a long way off. *Reading:* Eliezer Tauber, *The Formation of Modern Syria and Iraq* (1995); Patrick Seale, *The Struggle for Syria: A Study of Post-War Arab Politics, 1945-1958* (1987); David Roberts, *The Ba'th and the Creation of Modern Syria* (1987).

Szakasits, Arpad. The continuous tightening of the Soviet overlordship in Central Europe forced the anti-communist Hungarian president, Zoltan Tildy (qv), to resign his office on 12 January 1948. He was replaced by the Soviet-controlled Arpad Szakasits. Although the real power was held by the party secretary and the prime minister, Tildy's resignation ended the Smallholder Party control of the country and witnessed the merger of the Social Democratic Party with the Communist Party and the beginning of the one party Soviet-style political system in Hungary.

Szczecin. *See* Poland.

Szeping. *See* China.

Tabaiev, F. *See* Afghanistan.

Taba Settlement. *See* Israel.

Tabriz. *See* Iran.

Tachen Island. *See* China.

Tadzhik SSR. *See* Union of Soviet Socialist Republics.

Taegu. *See* Korea.

Taejon. *See* Korea.

Tahar ben Ammar. On 7 August 1954, Tunisia received its full internal independence from France's new premier, Pierre Mendes-France. A new Tunisian government was formed under Tahar ben Ammar. He remained in office until Habib Bourguiba (qv) formed a new and completely independent government in November 1955.

Taif. *See* Saudi Arabia.

Taiwan (*T'ai-Wan*). An island 100 miles off the southeast coast of China, Taiwan is surrounded by the East China Sea on the north, the Pacific Ocean on the east, the Bashis Channel on the south, and the Strait of Formosa on the west. The capital is Taipeh. The island was originally inhabited by an aboriginal Malayo-Polynesian people from before the seventh century A.D. when the Chinese first became aware of its existence. Chinese settlement began in the seventeenth century. However, the Portuguese had already visited the island in 1590, naming it *Ilha Formosa*. They did not establish any settlements there, however, and it was not until the seventeenth century that Dutch and Spanish fortified trading settlements were observed. In 1646, the Dutch overran the Spanish settlement and took the island. The Chinese routed the Dutch in 1661 and began in large numbers to settle the island. In 1683, the Manchu Dynasty incorporated Taiwan into Fukien Province. By 1792, the Manchus had settled most of the island and begun a prosperous sugar business with the mainland. In 1865, the capital was designated at Taipeh, and Taiwan became a separate province of China. Following the Sino-Japanese War of 1894–1895, the island was ceded to Japan. The principal export direction thereafter was to the Japanese home islands. Hydroelectric power turned the island toward an industrial economy by the 1930s. Following World War II, Taiwan was ceded back to China (1945). After the Communist takeover of the mainland (July 1949), the Chinese Nationalists fled to Taiwan under the leadership of Chiang Kai-shek (qv). After some disorder among the native population, the Nationalist Chinese government established itself there (1 March 1950) with Chiang Kai-shek as its first president. The United States revealed on 6 January 1951 that it was sending arms and other military supplies to Taiwan, which was formally acknowledged by the secretary of state on 25 April. By the terms of the peace treaty ending World War II, Japan renounced all claims to Taiwan and the Pescadores (qv) and all claims against China. The Soviet Union refused to sign the accord. On 13 August 1954, the Communist Chinese premier, Chou En-lai (qv), called for a drive to force the Nationalists off Taiwan. On 3 September, US naval units took up stations near the Pescadores as Communist China stepped up its shelling of Quemoy Island. In October, the USSR demanded UN condemnation of the U.S. because of its support for Taiwan and demanded a rapid occupation of Taiwan by Communist Chinese forces. Also, on 2 December 1954, Taiwan and the U.S. signed a mutual defense agreement that, among other things, limited Chiang Kai-shek's sphere of military operational authority. During this time, the island and its population flourished. President Dwight Eisenhower (qv) gained strong congressional support for his plan to use US military forces to protect Taiwan and the channel islands on 25 January 1955. A second treaty was signed by the U.S. and the Nationalists to protect the Pescadores (3 March 1955). In August 1958, the Communist Chinese began heavy shelling of Quemoy and Matsu. The U.S. Seventh Fleet began escorting supply vessels to counter the Communist attempt, through the shelling, to starve out the channel islands. On 4 September, Secretary of State John Foster Dulles reiterated that the U.S. would defend Taiwan and its offshore islands (this was again stated by President Eisenhower on 11 September) and rejected the recently imposed 12-mile limit, which would have put the islands in Communist Chinese space. The Nationalists shot down a number of Communist Chinese aircraft in an air-to-air battle on 24 March 1962, as fears of an imminent communist invasion grew. A large military buildup was reported on the Chinese mainland opposite the Pescadores on 10 June 1962, and the U.S. again warned the Communist Chinese that an attack would be met with a U.S. reaction. Also, on 11 September, Great Britain announced it would not be bound by the U.S. position. When France recognized the Communist Chinese (27 January 1964) Nationalist China retaliated on 10 February 1964, by breaking diplomatic relations with Paris. Taiwan was treated as the legitimate government of China by the U.S. and a number of other powers for the next 20 years. The United Nations declared Communist China the official representative of the Chinese people and ousted the Nationalists (25 October 1971). After U.S. president Richard Nixon visited mainland China, numerous countries gave the communists recognition while withdrawing it from Taiwan. Taiwan broke diplomatic relations with Japan when Tokyo signed a peace treaty with Communist China on 29 September 1972. On 1 March 1973, Chiang Kai-shek refused any direct negotiations with Communist China. The Nationalist Chinese laid claim, along with Communist China and the Philippines, to the

Spratley Islands on 1 February 1974. Upon Chiang Kai-shek's death on 4 April 1975, he was succeeded by his son, Chiang Ching-kuo (qv), who started the process of democratizing the island. In April 1976, Taiwan established diplomatic relations with South Africa. The U.S, withdrew its advisers from Quemoy and Matsu on 23 June 1976. On 15 December 1978, it extended recognition to the mainland and withdrew it from Taiwan. The Communist Chinese stopped the incessant shelling of the Pescadores on 31 December 1978. On 10 February 1979, however, President Jimmy Carter (qv) announced the U.S. would continue to protect Taiwan against Communist Chinese aggression. Even so, the last U.S. forces left Taiwan on 26 April 1979, leaving the island's protection up to the U.S. navy. In February 1981, the Communists expelled the Dutch ambassador to Peking after The Hague sold two submarines to the Nationalists. Relations were restored in February 1984, when the Dutch announced they had cut off all further arms shipments to Taiwan. In 1988, Lee Teng-hui became the first native-born president. Among his numerous accomplishments, he opened trade and travel with the mainland. By the 1990s relations between the two Chinas were less strained, but mainland China still looked upon Taiwan as a province. *See also* Communist China and Pescadores. *Reading:* Zhiling Lin & Thomas W. Robinson, *The Chinese and Their Future: Beijing, Taipei, and Hong Kong* (1995); Robert Accinelli, *Crisis and Commitment: United States Policy toward Taiwan, 1950-1955* (1996); John Franklin Copper, *Taiwan: Nation-State or Province?* (1996).

Takev Province. *See* Cambodia.

Takieddin, Halim. On 1 December 1983, Sheikh Halim Takieddin, the president of the Supreme Druze Religious Court, was assassinated by an unknown gunman in West Beirut.

Tal. *See* Israel.

al-Tal, Wasfi. On 2 April 1971, Palestinian guerrillas operating in Jordan announced they were beginning a military campaign to force King Hussein (qv) to dismiss the prime minister, Wasfi al-Tal, and all army commanders hostile to the PLO. Wasfi had been in office only since since 26 September 1970. While the king partly gave in and fired the two army commanders, Wasfi stayed on. On 28 November 1971, however, Wasfi al-Tal was assassinated by Palestinian Black September terrorists while attending an Arab League meeting in Cairo.

Talal, Emir. On 5 September 1951, the mentally ill Emir Talal was crowned king of Jordan. On 11 August 1952, he was judged unfit to serve and was replaced by 17-year-old Crown Prince Hussein (Husain ibn Talal) (qv).

Tamatave. *See* Malagasy.

Tamil. *See* Sri Lanka.

Tam Ky. *See* Vietnam.

Tanaka, Kakuei. (b. 4 May 1918, Kariwa, Japan—d. 16 December 1993, Tokyo) Born the son of a penniless cattle dealer, Tanake left school at 15. He opened a construction business, which flourished during World War II, making him one of the wealthiest men in Japan. He was elected to the lower house of Japan's parliament (*Diet*) in 1947, as a member of the Liberal Democrat Party. He rose rapidly and, in 1957, became minister of communications and postal services. In 1958, he resigned, but in 1962 he was appointed minister of finance. In 1965, Tanaka became the secretary-general of his party. He then served as minister of international trade and industry (1964–1972) in the cabinet of Eisaku Sato (qv) and then, in an upset victory, became prime minister. Among his accomplishments, Tanaka opened a diplomatic dialogue with Communist China and opened relations with that country (29 September 1972). In July 1974, he was unseated following a period of sluggish economic growth in Japan and because of implications that he was corrupt. In July 1976, he was arrested and charged with accepting over $2 million in bribes from the American Lockheed Aircraft Company while he was prime minister. While facing these charges, he still controlled a large segment of his party and was able to influence the future course of Japanese politics. His trial took seven years to complete. He was, however, found guilty (1983) and and sentenced to four years in jail and a ¥ 500 million fine. Two years later, however, while appealing his conviction, he suffered a stroke, that left him with a diminished capacity and he died in 1993.

Tananarive. *See* Malagasy.

Tan Canh. *See* Vietnam.

Tanganyika. *See* Tanzania.

Tangier. *See* Morocco.

Tangi Wardak. *See* Afghanistan.

Tanjungpriok. *See* Indonesia.

Tan Son Nhut Airbase. *See* Vietnam.

Tanzania. More properly the Republic of Tanzania, this central African country is bordered on the north by Uganda and Kenya, on the east by the Indian Ocean, on the south by Malawi and Mozambique and on the west by Zambia, Zaire, Burundi and Rwanda. The capital is presently in the city of Dar es Salaam, but is moving to the new city of Dodoma. During the first millennium B.C., the Cushites, a Caucasoid people from the Ethiopian region, migrated into the northern Tanzanian area and eventually spread throughout the country. From the south, another migration of Bantu people moved into Tanzania from the west during the first millennium A.D. By 1100, people from the region were trading as far away as India, and Arab trading settlements had been established along the Tanzanian coast. The Portuguese appeared in the fifteenth century and eventually took over the coastal trade from the Arabs. The interior of the country, however, remained virtually unspoiled until Arab slave merchants, in the eighteenth century, began penetrating inland to increase their sources of revenue. By 1825, a lucrative ivory market had also been established. By the 1840s, the Arabs had built trading posts on Lake Tanganyika. Germans working as British missionaries discovered Mount Kilimanjaro in the late 1840s. German colonists began to arrive in 1885, and by 1907 they had firm control over the region. British forces occupied Tanganyika during World War I, and a postwar League of Nations mandate gave Great Britain control of the area. Following World War II, Britain relinquished control to a UN trusteeship. Tanganyika became independent on 9 December 1961 and immediately became a member of the United Nations. In 1962, Tanganyika became a republic within the British Commonwealth with Julius Nyerere as its first president. A merger of Tanganyika and Zanzibar on 26 April 1964 formed the state of Tanzania. On 25 January of that year, British forces were dispatched to help suppress communist-inspired antigovernment revolts that had broken out in the country. A new constitution was adopted in 1977 that limited political activity to a one-party sytem (actually, the Tanganyika African National Union and the Zanzibar Afro-Shizari Party, which were joined into the Revolutionary Party on 21 January 1977) and insured Zanzibar's autonomy. In 1967, Nyerere implemented a socialist economic program (*see* Declaration of Arusha), which included the nationalization of some private industries and which by the late 1970s had thoroughly failed amid charges of corruption, inflation and inefficiency. On 8 April 1968, Tanzania recognized the breakaway government of Biafra (*see* Nigeria). Communist China announced on 15 November 1969 that it was building a 1,042-mile-long railroad that would connect Tanzania with Zambia to the west, and on 6 May 1970 the Tanzanian government announced that Communist China was building a naval base at Dar es Salaam. On 7 June 1971, Nigeria broke diplomatic relations with Tanzania because of its continued recognition of Biafra. Uganda's Idi Amin (qv) closed the border with Tanzania on 7 July 1971. This was in response to continued rebel raids on Uganda originating in Tanzania. The next day he ordered any aircraft crossing into Ugandan airspace from Tanzania shot down. On 24–30 August, Ugandan forces attacked Tanzanian positions along the common border. A Tanzanian army base was attacked and destroyed by Ugandan military aircraft on 20 October. The Ugandans claimed the base was used by rebel supporters of former president Milton Obote (qv) (*see* Uganda). When some semblance of order could be restored, Amin reopened the border on 21 November. The chairman of the Zanzibar Revolutionary Council and first vice-president of Tanzania, Sheikh Abeid Amani Karume (qv), was assassinated on 7 April 1972 by members of the army, four of whom were killed in the attack, after he had released 600 petty criminals to celebrate the eighth anniversity of the merger "revolution." Numerous arrests followed, including that of Abdul Rahman Mohammad Bubu (14 April), the head of the *Umma* Party, a group associated with Karume's own Afro-Shirazi Party. On 14 April, Tanzanian gunners shot down a Portuguese aircraft patrolling the common border with Mozambique. An identified aircraft dropped leaflets criticizing the Nyerere government on numerous towns on 31 May 1972. On 17 September, Ugandan rebels supported by Tanzanian regular forces invaded Uganda. Tanzania denied the charges the next day, although they were later confirmed, and leveled its own accusations at Uganda for bombing the border town of Bukoba. The rebel force was quickly routed by Ugandan regulars, and a cease-fire was arranged on 21 September. The neighboring state of Burundi also accused Tanzania of harboring Hutu rebels in the ongoing conflict in that country (10–11 May 1973) (*see* Burundi). On 29 June, Burundian troops crossed into Tanzania and killed ten Hutu rebels in a base camp. In August 1974, the border conflict between Uganda and Tanzania flared up again after Amin accused Tanzania of spying. Both sides reinforced their border positions. In 1976, Tanzania became an outspoken advocate of the overthrow of the white government in Rhodesia (*see* Zimbabwe). Tanzania "permanently" closed its border with Kenya on 18 April 1977, following the breakup of the East African Community and vociferous recriminations on both sides. Between 20 and 31 October 1978, Tanzania claime that Uganda had invaded the country and had pushed some 20 miles into its territory. On 1 November, Uganda announced it had "annexed" about 700 square miles of Tanzania in an area known as the Kagera Salient. Four days later, Amin claimed he was withdrawing its forces, although most other sources contradicted that claim. On 7 November, Tanzania moved nearly 10,000 fresh troops to the annexed territory's border. To that point, the Tanzanian death and injured toll was reported as approximately 10,000. Ugandan attacks continued into December. In a turnaround, in January 1979, Uganda accused and Tanzania confirmed that its troops had driven into Uganda. By 25 February, Tanzanian troops and Ugandan rebels were within 75 miles of Uganda's capital, Kampala. Tanzanian forces were close to Entebbe on 26 March, even through Libyan forces had been introduced in support of Amin. The capital was captured on 11 April. Even through loyal Ugandan troops dressed as Tanzanians had massacred the Ugandan town of Tororo (22 April), Libya announced it would pay a $40 million ransom for the release of Ugandan prisoners held by Tanzania. On 4 June, the war ended with the complete occupation of Uganda. In December, Tanzania announced it had contracted to train the new Ugandan military and police forces. Having settled its six-year dispute with Kenya, Tanzania opened the common border on 17 November 1983. Although President Nyerere resigned on 5 November 1985, and Ali Hassan Mwinyi became president, Nyerere remained the power behind the presidency. One of his first tasks was the breakup of the government's control of the economy and the return to a free enterprise system through such actions as courting the International Monetary Fund (IMF), which Nyerere had always refused to do. When an IMF loan was approved, Nyerere phophesied doom, but the results were positive and clearly visible. In1986, Tanzania was listed among the 25 least developed countries in the world. Tanzania announced in December 198, that it had withdrawn its troops from Mozambique, where they had been helping that country fight right-wing rebels. The question of Zanzibar's autonomy within the Tanzanian federation began to show some signs of strain in 1989. The Zanzibar population seemed convinced that the merger did more harm than good. In February 1991, attention was given to the abrogation of the one-party system and to reexamining the Arush Declaration as means of improving the overall state of affairs in Tanzania. While the commission meetings were underway, Great Britain offered Tanzania a loan of £2 million contingent on an outcome that would improve government. On 21 August 1991, 23,000 prisoners that Mwinyi had ordered released were pardoned. As another step in the direction of improving conditions, the East Africa Economic Community (Tanzania, Kenya and Uganda) was restored on 15 February 1992. When Zanzibar joined an Islamic organization (January 1993), members of mainland Tanzania's legislature became understandably upset. Assurances from Zanzibar that the move was economic and not political appeared to settle the matter. A number of Muslim teachers were fired in April 1993 when the government discovered they were teaching Islamic fundamentalist rebellion. The genocidal situation in Rwanda (*see* Rwanda) in May 1995 forced Tanzania to order the border closed. Before that could happen, at least 250,000 Rwandans had already entered the country. On 23 November 1995, Mwinyi left office and was replaced by another Revolutionary Party member, Benjamin W. Mkapa. *Reading:* Severine M. Rugumamu, *Lethal Aid: The Illusion of Socialism and Self-Reliance in Tanzania* (1997); Colin Legum & Geoffrey Mmari, eds. *Mwalimu: The Influence of Nyerere* (1995).

Ta Phraya District. *See* Thailand.

Taraki, Nur Mohammed. *See* Afghanistan.

Tarantelli, Enzo (Enzio). On 27 March 1985, Rome University Professor Enzo Tarantelli was assassinated by members of the Red Brigades (qv) terrorist group. Tarantelli had been a noted economist and labor union official.

Tarshia. *See* Israel.

Tartus. *See* Syria.

Tasa. *See* Jordan.

Tassigny, De Lattre de. *See* Vietnam (Indochina).

Tatarescu, Jorge. On 5 November 1947, the noncommunist Jorge Tatarescu was removed as minister of foreign affairs of Romania and replaced by the communist Anna Pauker (qv). Tatarescu's ouster came about as a by-product of Romania's show trial of National Peasant Party leaders. Tatarescu was the only noncommunist to be given a post following the 19 November 1946 elections, before the National Peasants Party was declared illegal.

Tatum, Kampuchea. *See* Cambodia.

Taya, Maaouya Ould Sidi Ahmed. On 12 December 1984, the government of President Mohammed Khouna Ould Haidallah (qv) of Mauritania was overthrown in a bloodless military coup. Haidallah was at a Franco-African conference in Burundi at the time of the overthrow. Lieutenant Colonel Maaouya Ould Sidi Ahmed Taya proclaimed himself president. Taya, who had been defense minister and premier from 1981 until 8 March 1964, was replaced in both posts by Haidallah. Taya then went back to his job as army chief of staff, until the coup. Taya had Haidallah arrested when the former president returned to Mauritania. Taya remained in power in 1995, having won several elections in his own right.

Taylor, Maxwell D. *See* Vietnam.

Taylor-Rostow Report. *See* Vietnam.

Tay Ninh City and Province. *See* Vietnam.

Tchepone (Xenon). *See* Laos.

Teal Inlet. *See* Falkland Islands.

Tehran. *See* Iran.

Tejero Molina, Antonio. On 23 February 1981, a right-wing coup led by the Spanish Civil Guard failed. The Civil Guard, led by Lieutenant Colonel Antonio Tejero Molina, had stormed into a session of the Spanish parliament (*Cortes*) and took the cabinet and about 350 lower house legislators hostage. He then announced that the country was "now in the hands of competent military authority." The unnamed authority was to arrive shortly to begin the process. The government immediately reacted by declaring a state of emergency, and troops were ordered into their barracks. The king persuaded those commanders who had deployed their troops to return to their garrisons. By midday of 24 February, the attempt to seize the government had obviouly failed. After some negotiation, Tejero and his followers surrendered and were taken into custody. As a result of the incident, the deputy chief of staff of the army, General Alfonso Armada Comyn, thought to be the "competent military authority," and Lieutenant General Milans del Bosch, the commander of the Valencia military district, were relieved.

Tel al-Zaatar. *See* Lebanon.

Tel Aviv. *See* Israel.

Temple Mount. *See* Israel.

Teng Hsiao-ping. *See* Deng Xiaoping.

Terceira. *See* Portugal.

Termez. *See* Afghanistan.

Tet. *See* Vietnam.

Tete Province. *See* Mozambique.

Tet Offensive. *See* Vietnam.

Tetuan. *See* Morocco.

Thach Han River. *See* Vietnam.

Thailand (*Sayam/Prathet Thai/Muang Thai*). A country located on the Indochinese Peninsula of Southeast Asia, the Kingdom of Thailand is bordered on the northeast by Laos, on the southeast by Cambodia and the Gulf of Thailand, on the south by Malaysia, on the southwest by the Andaman Sea and on the northwest by Burma (Myanmar). The capital is Bangkok (*Krung Thep*). The earliest known habitation of the region is dated from the eighteenth millennium B.C., but it was not until the tenth century A.D. that Tai-speaking tribes began to migrate southward out of China. By the mid-thirteenth century, two kingdoms had emerged: the Sukhothai (c.1220) and the somewhat older Khmer. In 1350, the Sukhothai was succeeded by the kingdom of Ayutthaya. By the fifteenth century, the Ayutthaya kingdom held most of the region, although it was often challenged by the Burmese and, in 1569, succeeded in defeating Ayutthaya. After a 15-year rule the Burmese retired only to return again in 1767, this time ending the Ayutthayan dynasty. In 1782, the Chakri clan came to power under the leadership of Rama I (Chao Phraya Chakri). One of his deeds was to move the capital to Bangkok. During the reign of Rama III (1824–1851), there was a period of expansion during which the empire occupied part of the Malay Peninsula, Laos and Cambodia. In 1856, the empire was named Siam. Siam was obliged, however, during the nineteenth century, to make concessions to one or another European country. Cambodia, for example, was given to France in 1967.

France later received the rights to Laos from Siam. During World War I, the now somewhat westernized Siamese joined the Allied cause. The absolute monarchy was abolished in 1932, and in 1939 Siam's name was officially changed to Thailand. The Thais became forced allies of Japan during World War II, after the Japanese occupied the country in 1941. After the end of World War II, Thailand was faced with major fighting involving its border forces and communist forces operating in Malaysia. A state of emergency was declared in the southern provinces. On 29 June 1951, a naval uprising began that took three days to suppress. Another military uprising erupted on 29 November, which was also suppressed, but not until concessions were made by the government. The First Indochinese War caused problems for Thailand along its border with Cambodia. One such incident occurred on 26–30 May 1946, when Thai and French Indochinese forces fought a pitched battle along the Mekong River. Later, as more such incidents occurred, on 29 May 1954 the government asked the UN for assistance in halting French aggression and in preventing the spread of the fighting into Thai territory. The request asked for UN observers to supervise the border. On 18 June, the Soviet Union vetoed the proposal. Thailand was admitted to the Colombo Plan (qv) on 5 October. The year-old government of Premier Pote Sarasin was overthrown in a bloodless coup on 20 October 1958. A military government led by Field Marshal Sarit Thanarat (qv) was established to lead the country. In November, another two months of border clashes began between Thai and Cambodian forces. In March 1961, Thailand was faced with another problem; large numbers of Nationalist Chinese troops, who had fled southward into northern Thailand, Laos and Burma to avoid the communist advance, had become restive and were causing problems in all three regions. The Nationalist Chinese government mounted an operation to evacuate them to Taiwan. When Pathet Lao forces began making major gains in Laos, in violation of the May 1961 cease-fire (*see* Laos), the United States dispatched an 1,800-man U.S. Marine Battalion Landing Team (BLT) into the Gulf of Siam (12 May 1962). At the same time, thousands of fleeing Royal Laotian troops were streaming into Thailand. On 19 May, thousands of U.S. army and marine ground troops were sent into Thailand to forestall any threats posed along the Thai border. These U.S. forces were withdrawn in increments during July–November. In 1964, a decade of communist terrorism began along the Cambodian border, and numerous clashes between Thai border police and army units and Cambodian forces occurred (*see* Cambodia). On 9 March 1967, the United States announced it was using bases in Thailand to carry out its bombing campaign against North Vietnam. The Thai government gave permission to the U.S. to move B-52 bombers into Thailand on 22 March 1967. The first B-52s arrived on 10 April and were stationed at U Tapao airbase. This airbase remainded in operation until the end of the war and was on several occasions, such as 10 January 1972, attacked by guerrilla forces, causing much damage. Internal communist activity, which had been growing since 1964, required the Thai government to declare martial law in twelve provinces on 1 December 1967. During this same period additional Thai troops were being sent into South

Vietnam (about 7,400) to take part in the campaign against the north. The first Thai forces had been sent into Vietnam on 21 September 1967. By February 1969, this number would be 11,250 troops deployed. In return, the U.S. furnished Hawk anti-aircraft missiles to the Thai government. On 26 July 1968, the government reported a major communist raid against one of its installations. On 1 April 1969, a joint Thai-Malayian operation began to clear communist rebels out of their common border area. As a follow-on, in November 1969, a joint command with cross-border operating authority (7 March 1970) was established to combat the insurgent problem along the border. The U.S. announced it was opening talks with Thailand to reduce the number of U.S. troops stationed in that country (22 August 1969). At that time, 48,000 U.S. troops were in Thailand. The resultant reduction plan (30 September) called for the withdrawal of at least 6,000 Americans within the next ten months. About 4,200 had been withdrawn by February 1970. On 22 March 1970, the Thai government announced it had at least two battalions of troops operating in Laos as "volunteers." Thailand renewed its often strained or broken diplomatic relations with Cambodia on 28 May 1970 (as would occur several more times over the next two decades), but rejected a Cambodian request to station Thai military forces in that country. It did offer to supply large-scale military assistance and to help train troops of Cambodia ancestry (2 June). Another request to deploy Thai forces in northern Cambodia to block communist penetration was rejected on 23 July. On 7 September 1970, a joint U.S.–Thai statement announced the withdrawal of an additional 9,800 U.S. troops from Thailand and the withdrawal of 12,000 Thai troops from Vietnam. In November, the Thai government announced all of its troops would be out of Vietnam by 1972. On 17 November 1971, a bloodless coup took place that overthrew the government. Prime Minister Thanom Kittikachorn seized full power, abrogated the constitution and declared martial law throughout the country. On 10 January 1973, the Thai government announced that the U.S. could maintain its bases in Thailand after the cease-fire in Vietnam. The U.S. Marines' 11-year commitment in Southeast Asia ended on 1 September 1973, when about 100 F-4 fighters and other aircraft and 3,500 marines departed Thailand for home. On 1 January 1974, 35,000 American troops still remained in Thailand. The military dictatorship of Thanom Kittikachorn was ended on 14–16 October 1973, by a coup that followed a long period of unrest and violence. On 15 October, the former dictator and a group of his followers fled the country. The next day, the king appointed a civilian educator, Sanya Dhamasakti (Thammasak) (qv), to head the new government. In March, a joint statement announced the withdrawal of another 10,000 American troops. Even through relations with the U.S. had been excellent, the government lodged a formal protest when the operation to free the USS Mayaguez (qv) was launched from Thai bases without its consent. Thailand, following the course of many other countries, recognized Communist China on 1 July 1975. At the same time, it severed relations with Nationalist China on Taiwan. Into late 1975, the border clashes with Cambodia continued. Thailand joined the the Association of

Southeast Asian Nations in February 1976. In a carefully worded message, the Thais ordered the United States to withdraw all its forces from Thailand on 20 March 1976. One exception was the 270 American advisers to the Royal Thai armed forces. (The withdrawal was completed on 20 July 1976.) Throughout the entire period of the war in Vietnam, Thailand and Malaysia continued their border campaign against communist rebels operating along the common border. Pursuit across the border was still a part of the joint operation, but, as on 6 June 1976, a too-deep penetration often brought a swift rebuke. In this case, Thailand asked that Malaysian forces who had penetrated Thailand be withdrawn immediately. Rebel activity also continued in other areas of Thailand. On 8 July 1976, an army post in the central area was attacked by insurgents. In something of a surprise, Thailand established diplomatic relations with the communist government in Vietnam on 6 August 1976. By October 1976, the internal situation in Thailand had once again deteriorated. On 6 October, following a number of violent clashes between police and ultrarightist students belonging to a group known as Red Gaur (Red Bull), the military stepped in and overthrew the government in a bloody coup. The defense minister, Admiral Sangad Chaloryu took power. Another military coup against the junta failed on 26 March 1977. The view was turned outward again, however, on 9–13 May, when three separate pitched battles were fought between Thai border police and Khmer Rouge (qv) forces on the Cambodian border. A war alert was ordered for the entire country. On 21 July, a major battle was fought near the town of Aranyaprathet in which the Thais employed armor and air support to gain control of the area. Thirteen Thais were killed in the action, while Cambodian losses were reported as being nearly 50 killed. Another military coup overthrew the government on 20 October 1977, and a new junta was installed. When intelligence reports indicated a major Vietnamese buildup along the Laos-Cambodia (Kampuchea) border (1 December 1978), Thailand alerted its forces to be prepared against the expected Vietnamese move into Cambodia (10 December). In the face of this growing threat, the United States sold $99.8 million in F-5E/F fighter aircraft to Thailand on 5 March 1979. By January 1980, U.S. concerns were focused on some 50,000 Vietnamese and Khmer Rouge troops deployed along the Thai border. The concern was that they would attack into Thailand to disperse the thousands of Cambodians in refugee camps, which no doubt the communists saw as a threat of their own. Indeed, in one incident on 19 March, 45 refugees were killed in a fight among rival factions of the noncommunist Cambodian National Liberation Movement within one of the camps. This sort of fighting broke out in the next few days in a number of border camps. In the camp at Sisphon, Thai army units were ordered in fight after Vietnamese artillery in Cambodia began shelling the camp to add to the general confusion. In this particular incident (21 October), at least 100 were killed. Another battle took place on 26 June 1980, but this time the Thais were witness to the engagement, which took place in Cambodia between Vietnamese and Cambodian rebel units. This fighting continued into February 1982 and quite often involved incursions into Thailand with Vietnamese troops usually chasing

Khmer Rouge units. Also on 26 June 1980, some 8,000 Vietnamese troops were observed digging in along the Thai border. It was assumed that was done to prevent the forces of Pol Pot (qv), which were known to have already crossed into Thailand, from returning to Cambodia. Also, approximately 2,000 Vietnamese troops that had crossed into Thailand, were suspected of having been withdrawn over the last two days. The U.S. reacted to these incidents by carrying out a massive airlift of military equipment to Thailand on 5 July to assist in maintaining the integrity of the border. Still the fighting continued in the border refugee camps between rival Cambodian factions. Many were killed and wounded in these battles. A series of communist terrorist incidents occurred during the second half of 1980, which were capped off by an explosion at the main military ammunition depot in Bangkok. A large number were killed and hundreds injured in the blast. On 7 February 1981, Thai air and naval forces, using $2 million in U.S. aid, began a campaign to rid the Gulf of Thailand (Siam) of pirates who had been preying on Vietnamese refugees ("Boat People") attempting an escape from communist Vietnam. The next day, Thailand closed its border with Laos, as skirmishing along that border increased. In the latter part of 1982, Thailand inaugurated an amnesty program that, by December, had induced nearly 1,000 Thai rebels to surrender. By January 1983, that number had almost doubled. When the Vietnamese launched an offensive against Cambodian villages near the Thai border on 31 March 1983, nearly 25,000 refugees fled into Thailand. Then, on 4 April, Royal Thai air force jets attacked Vietnamese troops who had crossed into Thailand. By December 1983, after some 5,000 rebels had accepted the offer of amnesty, the Thai communist rebel threat in the north was effectively terminated. When 40 Vietnamese troops were captured inside Thai territory on 29 March 1984, the government lodged a formal protest, but to little avail. About 35,000 more Cambodian refugees flooded into Thailand after the Vietnamese opened another major offensive in April 1984. The border incursions continued as Vietnamese troops continued operations against Cambodian rebels near the border. In retaliation, the Thais reinforced their positions (November 1984). By the end of the year, nearly 60,000 additional refugees had arrived at the Thai refugee centers. More border clashes occurred in March 1985. Another military coup was attempted in September 1985, but this one failed. On 4 August 1988, Chatichai Choonhavan became prime minister following an election. But, on 23 February 1991, the military again took control of the government. The constitution was abolished, the cabinet dismissed, Chatichai arrested and a military National Peacekeeping Council installed. Chatichai was allowed to leave the country two weeks later. In 1992, a crackdown on demonstrations led to the deaths of more than 50 people. In August 1993, 35 government schools in predominantly Muslim areas in the southern provinces were burned by Malay terrorists as a part of a campaign to destabilize the government. There were also attacks on government forces and random shootings at trains and buses. Red faces abounded when a member of the opposition party, Thai Nation, was identified by the American DEA as involved in a major drug-smuggling operation. To even up the game, the government was accused of "misplacing" $20 million in recovered (in Bangkok) jewelry (weighing almost 200 pounds) stolen from a Saudi prince by a Thai servant. The police chief and about six others were arrested in the theft from the police evidence room as the first step in an ever-widening investigation of theft, negligence and murder. General elections were held on 2 July 1995, and a new prime minister, Banharn Silparcha, was installed. In October the U.S. cut military aid to Thailand after allegations that Thai police officers were involved in a July 1995 coup attempt in Cambodia. *Reading:* Nicholas Tapp, *Sovereignty and Rebellion: The White Hmong of Northern Thailand* (1990); David K. Wyatt, *Thailand: A Short History* (1986); M. L Jumsai, *History of Thailand and Cambodia* (1970); Robert M. Blackburn, *Mercenaries and Lyndon Johnson's "More Flags": The Hiring of Korean, Filipino and Thai Soldiers in the Vietnam War* (1994); Jeffrey Glasser, *The Secret Vietnam War: The United States Air Force in Thailand, 1951-1975* (1996); David Elliott, *Thailand: Origins of Military Rule* (1978); David Van Praagh & Stephen L. Solarz, *Thailand's Struggle for Democracy: The Life and Times of M. R. Seni Pramoi* (1996).

Thamad. *See* Egypt.

Thanarat, Sarit. *See* Thailand.

Thanh Hoa (Dragon's Jaw) Bridge. *See* Vietnam.

Thanh My. *See* Vietnam.

al-Thani, Emir Ahmad bin Ali. During its first year of independence, Qatar's ruler, Emir Ahmad bin Ali al-Thani, was overthrown in a bloodless coup while he was away hunting on 22 February 1972. His cousin, the leader of the coup, the deputy ruler and prime minister, Sheikh Khalifa bin Hammas ath Thani, assumed the rule and immediately gave all civil servants a 20 percent pay raise, and cut the royal family's budget. *See* Qatar.

ath-Thani, Sheikh Khalifa bin Hammad. After assuming the rule and the prime ministership following the February 1972 bloodless coup (*see* al-Thani). In 1989, ath-Thani reorganized the government, bringing many new and younger officials up from the ranks, even though the ruling clan still retained much of the power. Ath-Thani remainded in power generally unscathed until 27 June 1995, when a bloodless palace coup replaced him with his son, Sheikh Hamad ibn Khalifa ath-Thani, as emir. *See* Qatar.

Thanin, Kraivichien. *See* Thailand.

Thanom, Kittikachorn. *See* Thailand.

Thatcher, Margaret. (b. 13 October 1925, Grantham, Lincolnshire, England) Born Margaret Hilda Roberts, Thatcher studied at Oxford's Somerville College, where she took her master's degree in chemistry. Working for a time as a research chemist, she went on to marry Denis Thatcher and then to study for the bar, specializing in tax law (1954). She stood for Parliament in 1950 but failed to win a seat. In 1959, she did win and went to the House of Commons as the representative of Finchley, a north London suburb. From 1961 until 1964 she served as joint parliamentary secretary to the Ministry of Pensions and National

Insurance. She became the Conservative leader of Commons in 1975. In 1979, she became prime minister as a right-wing conservative. Thatcher was instrumental in the final phases of the orderly turnover of power to the new Zimbabwe government (1980) (*see* Zimbabwe) and, in 1982, in the recapture of the Falkland Islands (qv). This gave her a landslide victory in the election of 1983. She was again reelected in 1987, but at that point the majority was relatively slim. Known as the "Iron Lady" or "Iron Pants," she ruled with an iron hand and accomplished much during her tenure. Not the least of these accomplishments was her strong commitment to NATO and to Britain's independent nuclear policy. She did, however, favor retention of Northern Ireland, which led to an IRA Provisional Wing assassination attempt against her at the Conservative Party Conference held at the Grand Hotel, Brighton, on 12 October 1984. Four were killed and some 30 others injured in the blast. She did, however, cause a split in her party over issues concerning the European Common Market, and resigned on 14 November 1990. At that time she was made Baroness Thatcher of Kesteven (her husband was awarded a baronetcy) and awarded the Order of Merit (7 December). Thereafter, she continued in Parliament in "the back benches." Her's was the longest tenure of a prime minister since 1827.

Tha Vieng. *See* Laos.

Thich Tinh Khiet. *See* Vietnam.

Thieu, Nguyen Van. (b. 5 April 1923) Born the son of a small landowner, Thieu joined the communist-oriented Viet Minh in 1945, but later he switched and aided the French against them. In 1954, he became the commandant of the new Vietnamese Military Academy, and after the Paris Accords that partitioned Vietnam in 1956, he joined the southern government of Ngo Dinh Diem (qv). Thieu (then a major general) was instrumental in Diem's overhrow in 1963, and on 14 June 1965 he was a member of the military junta that took power and became chief of state, with Nguyen Cao Ky (qv) as premier. Thereafter he met several times with Lyndon B. Johnson (qv) to plan U.S. involvement in the war against North Vietnam. Following the promulgation of a new constitution, Thieu (then a lieutenant general) was elected president in 1967 and was reelected without opposition in 1971. Following the 1968 Tet offensive (*see* Vietnam), Thieu's government declared martial law (31 January), and ordered a partial mobilization and a reserve callup (9–10 February). On 4 November 1968, Thieu's government announced it would boycott the upcoming Paris peace negotiations, if the Viet Cong (qv) were invited. When Thieu offered to negotiate directly with North Vietnam on 25 March 1969, Hanoi rejected the request. In May 1969, Thieu was able to rally six political groups into what became known as the National Social Democrat Front to support his government. Following an announcement (8 June 1969) that the U.S. would withdraw 25,000 troops by 31 August, Thieu ordered a new Accelerated Pacification Plan to bring increased security to the countryside. When Thieu offered (11 July 1969) a six-point peace proposal to the North, this time supported by the U.S., Hanoi again rejected the plan. As the U.S. withdrawal continued, Thieu announced on 27 September 1969 that the U.S. withdrawal would not succeed because South Vietnam had neither the ambition nor the will to fight the war singlehandedly. (On 9 January 1970, Thieu would state that a U.S. withdrawal was "impossible and impractical.") Thieu disclosed the existence of the previously secret Phoenix Program (*Phung Hoang*), in which communist sympathizers in the south were being "eliminated," on 1 October 1969. In November 1969, he repudiated the American-coined word "Vietnamization" and proposed that "*Ba Tu*" (Three Selves) be used in its place. On 8 May 1970, as another incident that was part of the growing controversy with the United States, Thieu announced that his country would not be bound by the 30 June deadline established by the U.S. Congress for the withdrawal of forces from Cambodia (*see* Cambodia). He also rejected any thought of a coalition government that included the North Vietnamese (21 July). Thieu reiterated this objection again in October. In January 1972, he did accede to a secret plan that would require his resignation, if the North renounced violence to obtain its goals. Obviously, nothing came of that proposal. On 10 May 1972, Thieu again imposed martial law on South Vietnam and established a curfew in Saigon to help halt the enemy encroachment. He was given the power to rule by decree on 27 June of that year. Then, on 5 August, he imposed censorship on what had been a relatively free press in the country. Thieu's government found the peace terms worked out by Secretary of State Henry Kissinger in Paris unacceptable on 24 October 1972. Thieu's ability to maintain himself in power was due, however, largely to the support of two American presidents, even though his government, albeit perhaps necessarily, was seen as authoritarian. President Thieu only reluctantly joined in the peace talks that ended the war in Vietnam and allowed for the American withdrawal from his country. Still, after the withdrawal in 1973, Thieu showed some gains in his consolidation of power. When the communist North Vietnamese invaded the South in 1975 and Thieu realized that there would be no US direct support, he planned to defend Saigon and withdrew troops, especially the airborne division, from the more distant provinces to accomplish that objective, Communist pressure was such, however, that the withdrawal turned into a rout and the communists were able to surround the city. After several days, it became apparent that Thieu was the principal impediment to negotiating a truce that would save the city from total destruction. Thieu resigned on 21 April 1975, in a speech in which he roundly denounced the United States. The government was left to the keeping of Tran Van Houng (qv), and Thieu fled the country, first to Taiwan and then to England, where he took up residence.

Thimbu (*Tashi-Chho Dzang*). *See* Bhutan.

Thirty-eighth Parallel, Korea. *See* Korea.

Tho, Le Duc. The chief North Vietnamese negotiator at the Paris peace talks for which he shared the Nobel Peace Prize with Henry Kissinger in 1973, Tho remained active in government affairs until 1987, when many of the old colleagues of Ho Chi Minh were discredited and removed following "election" in April, when he was removed from the Politburo. *See* Vietnam.

Tho, Nguyen Ngoc. When Ngo Dinh Diem was removed from office in the military coup of 1–2 November 1963 and subsequently murdered, Vice President Nguyen Ngoc Tho was named head of the provisional government of the Republic of Vietnam. At the same time, the ruling military junta suspended the constitution and dissolved the National Assembly. Tho lasted in office until 6 January 1964, when the military took direct control of the country.

Thompson, John R. On 18 June 1973, the president of the Firestone Rubber Company subsidiary in Buenos Aires, John R. Thompson, was kidnapped by terrorists of the People's Revolutionary Army (qv). Thompson was released unharmed on 6 July, after a substantial ransom was paid.

Thompson, Robert Glenn. On 1 January 1965, Robert Glenn Thompson of Bay Shore, New York, was arrested on charges of being a spy in the pay of the Soviet Union during and after his service in the U.S. air force. Thompson was tried for his crimes and, on 13 May 1965, found guilty and sentenced to 30 years in a federal prison.

Thompson, Sir Robert K. G. *See* Vietnam.

Thrace. *See* Greece.

Thua Thien Province. *See* Vietnam.

Thule Air Force Base, Greenland. On 21 January 1968, a U.S. B-52 bomber carrying four hydrogen weapons on airborne alert suffered difficulties and attempted an emergency landing at the U.S. airbase at Thule, Greenland. The aircraft crashed on the ice in Baffin Bay. Thereafter, a frantic search took place, which produced little more than fragments. Because of this incident, the Social Democratic Party of Denmark, Greenland's owner, lost its bid for reelection. *See* Denmark.

Tiberias, (Teverya), Palestine. *See* Israel.

Tibesti Desert. *See* Chad.

Tibet (*Hsi-tsang Tzu-chih-chü*). Today the Tibet Autonomous Region of China, the almost mythical country of Tibet is bordered by the Chinese province of Tsinghai on the northeast, Szechwan on the east, Yunnan on the southeast, Nepal, Bhutan and Burma (Myanmar) on the south, Jammu and Kashmir (disputed by India) on the west, and the Sinkiang Uighur autonomous region on the northwest. The capital is Lhasa. The origin of the Tibetans is obscure, but there is evidence that, as the Chinese pushed the *Hsung Nu* tribes away from their borders in the first millennium B.C., some *Yue Chi* tribes moved into the region to avoid clashing with the more powerful *Hsung Nu*. By the seventh century A.D., Buddhism had been introduced into the region. Buddhism brought enlightenment and a long-time struggle against the prevalent shamanistic religion. Lamaism eventually became the principal religion about the same time that a powerful lamaist hierarchy developed that controlled almost all aspects of life in the country. By the tenth century, however, signs of trouble began to appear, and the kingdom split into a series of petty principalities. The Mongols under Ghengis Khan conquered the country in 1206, and it became a part of his empire. In 1270, power was given to the Lamaist hierarchy to run the internal affairs of the country. China took control of Tibet in the seventeenth century, but by the nineteenth century most of China's power in the region had dissipated. When the British attempted to move into the region from India, they failed, primarily because Britain allowed and supported the Nepalese invasion of Tibet in 1790. In 1904, Britain simply invaded the country, having seen that China had lost nearly all of its control and because of a perceived threat to the region from Imperial Russia. An Anglo-Chinese convention on Tibet was signed in 1906, which gave China sovereignty over Tibet in return for a huge indemnity paid by the Chinese. An Anglo-Russian treaty was signed in 1907 in which both sides pledged to leave Tibet alone. When the Chinese revolution overthrew the Manchu Dynasty in 1912, Tibet enjoyed a relatively peaceful and independent time. The Tibetans expelled all Chinese troops, officials and most other Chinese in 1913. A boundaries convention was signed by the Chinese, British and Tibetans in 1914. The agreement also granted China sovereignty over Inner Tibet, that area contiguous with China, and gave the rest of Tibet virtual independence. This treaty was subsequently repudiated by China. By September 1918, a war had erupted between Tibet and China, which ended in a truce brokered by the British. Tibetan relations with China thereafter remained strained and were not helped when the Panchen Lama (qv) urged a communist liberation of Tibet in a radio broadcast from Peking. China announced it planned to intervene both politically and militarily in Tibet, on 1 January 1950. On 7 October 1950, Communist Chinese troops invaded Tibet. As a means of offsetting this bad omen, the 15-year-old fourteenth Dalai Lama (qv) was vested with complete authority to oversee the country. That did not necessarily impress the Chinese, however, and they forced the Tibetans to capitulate in November, although widespread fighting continued as the Tibetans resorted to guerrilla warfare. Unrest would continue for decades. An appeal to the United Nations for a peaceful solution was to no avail. In 1950, however, Tibet was able to salvage the power of the Dalai Lama to control internal affairs, while all external and military affairs were given to the Chinese (5 March 1951). The Chinese also required the return of the Panchen Lama, who was still favorably disposed toward the communists. The Panchen Lama returned in April 1952. Among other improvements accomplished by the Chinese was the construction of a main military highway (Chungking to Lhasa) across Tibet and several lesser highways designed not for improving the Tibetan condition, but rather to reinforce strategic Chinese considerations. At the same time (1953), a purge of anticommunists in Tibet began. The following year, to add to Tibet's troubles, the Indian government recognized China's sovereignty over Tibet. India also withdrew most of its forces from the Tibetan border. The Chinese also moved to suppress (1954) the guerrilla activity that had been growing over the last six months. There was much blood spilled in the repression. The Dalai Lama was then elected a vice president of the Chinese-controlled National People's Congress. India, in April 1956, relinquished control over the Tibetan telephone, telegraph and postal system, which had been established under the British *Raj*. Also in 1956, the Dalai Lama was named chairman and the Panchen Lama named vice chairman of a committee to draft a new constitution. That same year, however, rumors began to spread out of India and Nepal of uprisings and guerrilla activity against the Chinese in Tibet. In September 1956, Nepal recognized China's rights in Tibet. By the second half of 1958, rebellion was widespread in Tibet, mostly against Chinese attempts to communize the country. Even after China revoked its instructions, the revolt continued and, by 13 March 1959, the uprising had spread to Lhasa itself. The expected reaction from the Chinese was not long in coming. The revolt was crushed with gratuitous brutality, the Dalai Lama was forced to flee to India (actually, spirited out by the British on 31 March) after his government was dissolved by the Chinese and the Panchen Lama was installed as China's puppet (28 March). The Dalai Lama arrived in India on 3 April, and asked for and received the protection of the Indian government. On 28 August, India announced that Chinese troops operating in Tibet had violated the Indian border (*see* India). On 21 October 1959, the UN General Assembly passed a resolution deploring China's civil rights violations in response to the Dalai Lama's 9 September request for such action, an action that obviously had no effect on the situation. A second such resolution was passed on 9 March 1961. In the meantime, tens of thousands of Tibetans had fled, mostly into India, and some into Bhutan and the other tiny kingdoms in the Himalayan mountains. Heavy fighting between the Chinese and the Tibetan populace broke out again in June 1960. The Chinese reported they had fired on Nepalese troops who had strayed into Tibetan territory on 28 June 1960. The Panchen Lama was removed from office by the Chinese in 1964 (*see* Panchen Lama). The Chinese made Tibet into an autonomous region in 1965. Therafter, Tibet was subjected to the one of the greatest mind-control endeavors in modern times as the transformation to Chinese socialism moved into high gear. In September 1967, India reported border clashes with Chinese troops along the Tibetan-Sikkim border. The border incidents continued into 1971, when the Chinese filed an official protest over Indian incursions into Tibetan territory. In 1978, the Panchen Lama was restored to the position of head of state. Back in office, the Panchen Lama appealed to the Dalai Lama to return to Tibet, knowing he was the only one who could bring order to the country. The Dalai Lama wisely declined. In 1980, the Chinese admitted they had mishandled the situation in Tibet, but they did little more than announce future reforms. Violent anti-Chinese rioting broke out in October 1987 and again in May 1993. By August 1993, Chinese representatives were holding talks on neutral ground with the representatives of the Dalai Lama. *See* China. *Reading:* Petra K. Kelly et al., eds., *The Anguish of Tibet* (1991); David Snellgrove & Hugh Richardson, *A Cultural History of Tibet* (1995); John F. Avedon, *In Exile from the Land of Snows: The Dalai Lama and Tibet since the Chinese Conquest* (1994).

Ticuantepe. *See* Nicaragua.

Tien Phouc. *See* Vietnam.

Tientsin. *See* China.

Tikrit. *See* Iraq.

Tildy, Zoltan. On 4 November 1945, the first postwar elections were held in Hungary. Soviet forces occupied Hungary at that time, but the Communist Party polled only 17 percent. Zoltan Tildy, a member of the majority anticommunist Smallholders Party, was elected prime minister of the the coalition government, which included communists, insisted upon by the Soviet occupation. On 1 February 1946, however, the country declared itself a republic, and Zoltan Tildy was elected president, with Imre Nagy (qv) as prime minister. On 12 January 1948, as the communists continued their typical consolidation of power, Tildy was forced to resign as president and was replaced by the communist-controlled Arpad Szakasits (qv).

Times of Viet Nam. *See* Vietnam.

Timor. *See* Indonesia.

Tinsulanond, Prem. *See* Thailand.

Tipia. *See* Honduras.

Tirana. *See* Albania.

Tiran Strait. *See* Egypt.

Tiso, Josef. On 16 March 1947, the former president of Slovakia, Josef Tiso, was tried and executed for wartime crimes against his people. Although Slovakia had been occupied by the Germans, the Nazis had allowed Slovakia to achieve an unprecedented level of prosperity. When the Benes government was reestablished in Czechoslovakia, retribution was quickly administered.

Tito (Josip Broz). (b. 7 May 1892, Kumrovec, Croatia, Austria-Hungary—d. 4 May 1980, Ljubljana, Yugoslavia) Josip Broz was born the seventh child to a poor peasant family living on the border between Croatia and Slovenia. He became a locksmith's apprentice at age 13 in the town of Sisak and later went to work as a metalworker in Trieste, Bohemia and Germany. During this period he also became a member of trade union and the Social Democratic Party of Croatia. He fought in the Croatian infantry against Serbia in World War I. He was, however, arrested on charges of spreading subversive material and put in jail. The charges were later dropped (January 1915) and he rejoined his regiment to fight on the Carpathian Front. There he was decorated for bravery. He was later transferred to the Bukhovia Front, where he was wounded and captured by the Russians. He remained in Russia until 1920, when he returned to Croatia, bringing a Russian wife (divorced 1934) with him, and went to work in a steel mill in Bjelovar. During this period he joined the Communist Party of Yugoslavia (CPY), for which activity he was again jailed in 1923, but he was subsequently released. He was arrested again for his party activities at the shipyards at Kraljevica and received a short probationary sentence. Moving up through the party ranks, he was appointed deputy of the Politburo of the CPY in 1928, but on 4 August he was again arrested and sentenced to five years. Upon his release in 1934, he became a member of the Central Committee of the CPY and travelled extensively through Europe on party business. At that point, Broz used several aliases to obscure his movements and identity. One of these was "Tito." Tito returned to Moscow in 1935 and worked in the Balkan office of the Communist International (Comintern). In August 1936, he became the organizing secretary of the CPY. Tito survived the Stalinist purge of 1937 and later in the year was appointed secretary general of the executive committee of the Comintern itself. Tito then returned to Yugoslavia to undertake the task of rebuilding the purge-decimated CPY. One of his first assignments was to recruit a 1,000-man Yugoslav force to fight in the Spanish Civil War. This force would later became the nucleus of Tito's Partisan Army in World War II. By 1940, he had accomplished the rebuilding of the CPY, and, at a secret conference held in Zagreb, he was chosen secretary-general of the CPY and its 36,000 members, including those of the Young Communists League (Komsomol). When Germany invaded Yugoslavia on 6 April 1941, the resistance was carried out by others. Not until Germany invaded the Soviet Union on 22 June 1941 did Tito react, issuing a proclamation for a general uprising. By late 1941, half of Yugoslavia had been liberated, with Montenegro and Serbia in Chetnik (Yugoslav Army of the Fatherland) hands. The remainder was in the hands of Tito's Partisans. When, counter to Moscow's instructions, a revolutionary administration was established in the liberated areas, the rift between Tito and the leader of the Chetniks, Dragoljub "Draza" Mihajlovic, deepened. The Germans opened a costly campaign to re-pacify Yugoslavia in November 1941. To accomplish this they had to withdraw troops from the Russian and Greek fronts, something that even the overwhelmingly powerful German army could ill-afford to do. The German offensive against Tito's Partisans in western Serbia was not without heavy losses on both sides. In the engagement Tito was almost captured. By 1943, Tito's forces had grown to a point where Hitler sent two more area offensives against him. Although surrounded by about 15 Axis divisions, Tito's forces were able to break out of the encirclement, carrying with them 4,000 wounded comrades. Partisan casualties were over 6,000 in one of the areas, including Tito himself being wounded. By September 1943, Tito commanded more than a quarter-million Partisans. Again, without advice from Moscow or informing the other Allies, Tito convened a Partisan's Parliament (Anti-Fascist Council of the National Liberation Front), which, among other things, made Tito a Marshal of Yugoslavia and declared Yugoslavia to be a federal community of equal states. Tito's Partisan army was granted Allied status at the Tehran Conference (28–30 November 1943). This afforded Tito military aid and advice, especially from the British and Americans. In May 1944, Hitler's forces carried out a surprise parachute and armored attack against Tito's headquarters in Bosnia, but he once again eluded the trap. At about this same time, the Allies (in particular, Churchill and Stalin) decided that Tito's quasi-government should receive equal standing with the already established Yugoslav government-in-exile in London. Tito diplomatically rejected this scheme, however, in meetings with the two leaders in August and September 1944. When the war in Europe ended on 9 May 1945, German troops in Yugoslavia were ordered to continue the fight. Fighting continued until 15 May, when the German command and its Yugoslav allies surrendered. Tito's war continued, however, and he found himself facing the Western Allies when he attempted the capture of Trieste. His forces also shot down two U.S. transports over Slovenia in 1946, which did little to help the situation, nor did the establishment of a communist government in Yugoslavia (11 November 1945). Tito also did not win too many Western friends when his forces captured Draza Mihajlovic, the Chetnik leader, tried him and executed him (17 July 1946). Tito had specifically refused to allow American OSS officers who had served with Mihajlovic to journey to Yugoslavia to testify on the general's behalf. When the chances of a Western Allied reaction were at its highest, Stalin ejected Tito's CPY from the Cominform (28 June 1948), fundamentally leaving Tito to fend for himself. In retaliation, the CPY purged all Cominform members from its group and later (1 June 1953) removed all political commissars from the Yugoslav army. Thereafter Moscow worked to destroy Tito's independent Yugoslavia through an economic blockade and military provocations. All that happened was that the Yugoslav people rallied behind Tito as never before. In September 1951, Tito moved to resolve all outstanding problems with Italy, which would have included the question of Trieste, but which was not settled until later. In July 1952, following several overtures to do so, Tito rejected the idea of alliances but did state a willingness to cooperate with such countries as Austria, Greece and Turkey. Following Stalin's death on 5 March 1953, the Soviets changed their tactics and became solicitous of Tito. Tito, however, had been elected the first president of Yugoslavia on 13 January 1953 and kept his own course, revamping his country in what were definitely non-Soviet ways, for instance, giving more autonomy to the five republics. Soon after the death of Stalin, Tito announced (31 March) that Great Britain had become Yugoslavia's protector, based on his agreement that Yugoslavia would fight aggression from any source. In October 1953, Tito threatened to send military forces into Trieste, if the Italians made any move to do so. However, on 1 November, he agree to meet the West on the Trieste issue. On 5 December, Tito announced he was withdrawing his forces from around Triest, and the Italians agreed to do the same. His policy of Yugoslav nonalignment took him into the world of nonaligned states such as India and Egypt, which denounced colonialism in all its forms and condemned South Africa for its apartheid policies. He did enter into the Balkan Alliance with Greece and Turkey, which stated that an attack on one of the members by Bulgaria would be considered an attack on all three (22 December 1953). On 2 June 1955, following a meeting with Nikita Khrushchev, the two leaders called for a ban on nuclear weapons, a European collective security treaty and the admission of Communist China into the United Nations. On 15 October 1956, the U.S. announced it would continue economic aid to Yugoslavia, but it refused to give Tito any military assistance. Tito made an inflammatory speech against the USSR at a CPY conference held on 11 November 1956, which deepened the already dangerous rift between the two countries. However, in what was viewed as a conciliatory gesture to the Soviet Union by Tito, Yugoslavia recognized East Germany on 7 October 1957. He loudly criticized the 20–21 August 1968 Soviet invasion of Czechoslovakia (Tito had visited Prague on 9 August 1968, and had received a hero's welcome), and proposed the development of a regionally oriented partisan army to be trained to fight an aggressor, obviously in this case the Soviet Union, should it attack Yugoslavia. Following a meeting with Romania's Nicolae Ceaucescu (qv) on 1–2 February 1969, the two leaders roundly denounced the Soviet "Brezhnev Doctrine" (*see* Soviet Union). On 21 September 1970, he instituted a collective presidency for the country (adopted in September 1974), which was implemented upon Tito's death in 1980. Before that time, however, Tito was faced with internal problems when an outbreak of violence occurred in Croatia on 22 December 1971. He warned at that time that he would use the army against further appearances of "internal enemies." By August 1977, the Soviet Union had bowed to Tito's demand for self-determination and had stated as much in a joint communique issued on 19 August. Tito died after a long illness in a Ljubljana hospital on 4 May 1980. *Reading:* Sabrina Petra Ramet, *Balkan Babel: The Disintegration of Yugoslavia from the Death of Tito to Ethnic War* (1996); Ruth Schiffman, *Josip Broz Tito* (1987); Stevan K. Pavlowitch, *Tito: Yugoslavia's Great Dictator: A Reassessment* (1992); Richard West, *Tito and the Rise and Fall of Yugoslavia* (1996).

Tlatelolco Treaty. *See* Treaty on the Denuclearization of Latin America.

Tobago. *See* Trinidad and Tobago.

Tobruk. *See* Libya.

Togliatti, Palmiro. (b. 26 March 1893, Genoa—d. 21 August 1964, Yalta, Ukrainian SSR) Born the son of a middle-class family, Togliatti studied law in Turin before World War I and served during the war as an officer. He was wounded, after which he returned to Turin as an instructor. In 1919, Togliatti helped found the left-wing publication *L'Ordine nuovo* (New Order), which rapidly became the organ of the Italian Communist Party, recently having broken away (1921) from the larger Socialist Party. He became editor of *Il Comunista* in 1922, and in 1924 he was elected to the Central Committee of the Italian Communist Party. In 1926, while at a Comintern meeting in Moscow, Italy's fascist dictator, Benito Mussolini (qv) banned the Communist Party. All its members, obviously excepting Togliatti, were rounded up and jailed. Togliatti thereafter remained in exile, working for the Italian communist cause from abroad. In 1935, Togliatti, operating under cover of an alias—Ercoli—became a member of Comintern. During World War II, he broadcast anti-Fascist propaganda into Italy, and after the war he returned there to work in the government of Marshal Badoglio (1944) and later to serve as vice premier in the De Gasperi government (1945). He was able to influence the 1948 election to the point that a large number of communist deputies were seated. On 14 July 1948, a young fascist shot and mortally wounded Togliatti. There was an immediate reaction in which thousands of workers went on strike throughout Italy in protest (14–15 July). To these protests, Togliatti violently objected and claimed a peaceful road to socialism was the only course to take. Order was restored only after much blood was spilled by the police and military. Togliatti was taken to Yalta for treatment but died of his wounds on 21 August 1964. *Reading:* Joan Barth Urban, *Moscow and the Italian Communist Party: From Togliatti to Berlinguer* (1986).

Togoland. Properly the Republic of Togo (*Republique Togolaise*), the west African country of Togoland is bordered by Burkina Faso (Upper Volta) on the north, Benin on the east, the Atlantic Ocean's Gulf of Guinea on the south and Ghana on the west. The capital city is Lome. First inhabited by Voltaic people in the north and Kwa tribesmen in the southwest, Togoland was later flooded with approximately 120 tribes of Ewa moving out of Nigeria beginning in the fourteenth century A.D. After the seventeenth century Ane tribesmen from Ghana also immigrated into the region. After the eighteenth century Denmark controlled the region for the slave trade. In 1847, German missionaries moved into the region, and by 1884 most of the coastal tribes had accepted German protection. The German protectorate increased in size up to 1899. During World War I, British and French forces occupied Togo, and in 1922 they were issued mandates by the League of Nations to continue their protection of the region. Western Togo, under British care, became closely associated with Gold Coast, while eastern Togo, under the French, gained greater contact with what were then Dahomey (Benin) and French West Africa. Following World War II, both Britain and France placed their Togo protectorates under UN trusteeship. Gold Coast, in accordance with a 1956 decision, received its independence, as Ghana, on 6 March 1957, and absorbed British Togoland into its structure, while French Togoland became an autonomous state within the French Union. French Togoland received its independence as Togo on 27 April 1960, but continued to maintain its relationship with France. It joined the Organization of African Unity (OAU) in 1963. That same year, on 13 January 1963, a military coup led by a group of noncommissioned officers seized the government, killing President Sylvanus Olympio (qv) in the process. Togo's relations with neighboring Ghana were strained until the downfall of Ghana's Kwame Nkrumah (qv). Internally, a number of assassinations and coups eventually led to the coup in which Lieutenant Colonel Etienne (Gnassingbe) Eyadema (qv) (13–14 April 1967) overthrew the government of President Nicholas Grunitzky (qv). In 1979, Eyadema issued a new constitution, won the one-man election with 99.9 percent of the vote and proclaimed the Third Togo Republic (13 January 1980). Eyadema was instrumental in gaining a truce (8 April 1980) in the war in Chad (it started up again almost immediately), and he continued to try to gain peace through the rest of the year. Opposition groups outside Togo announced numerous human rights violations in that country in 1981, but these were largely ignored, especially in France. That same year, after visiting France and meeting with President Mitterand, Eyadema visited China and North Korea. Ghana closed its common border with Togo in 1982 to forestall the movement of forbidden goods, the sale of which had been helping Togo's sagging economy. Hundreds of thousands of Ghanaians were allowed into Togo after being expelled from Nigeria. Their passage through Togo was troubled by the closed border with Ghana. Ghana reopened the border on several occasions throughout 1983 to facilitate the the movement of these refugees. Before Eyadema was to visit Paris in June 1985, French authorities effectively muzzled Togolese opposition groups by refusing permits for press conferences. In August in Togo, a series of bombings in Lome led to a number of arrests. Amnesty International filed complaints about how these prisoners were treated. More bombings took place in December 1985. A violent and bloody military coup attempt took place on 23–24 September 1986. Togo claimed the troops had crossed into the country from Ghana and had been trained in Ghana and Burkina Faso. This prompted once again the closure of the border with Ghana, and France answered a request for aid by deploying French paratroops in the country. A total of 13 were executed (14 more imprisoned) following the abortive coup. Eyadema won the one-man race for another seven-year term as president in December. In May 1987, Togo established a human rights commission to investigate the mountain of allegations filed by Amnesty International about its conduct of affairs. Togo recognized Israel in 1987. Student rioting erupted in October 1990 following the arrest and imprisonment of two opposition leaders. Although there had been signs of some progress toward democracy in the country, these were superficial, and the situation in Togo was exacerbated by continuously falling commodity prices. In April 1991 there was a period of violent protest after the discovery of the bodies of 27 people allegedly killed by security forces. To defuse the situation, Eyadema authorized the establishment of a multiparty system, but the rioting continued. When France backed away from sending forces into Togo, Eyadema called a national conference that, as its first act, suspended the constitution and then declared itself to be the government. This provoked a strike of government workers and the military who sought to unseat the conference. Troops attempted to break up the conference in August 1991, but they were met by thousands of civilians who shielded the conferees. A prime minister was then elected, and plans were laid for a multiparty election in 1992. Before disbanding, the conference stripped Eyadema of most of his power but left him in the presidency. Troops loyal to Eyadema captured the prime minister, Joseph Kokou Koffigoh, on 3 December. He and Eyadema then met and were able to settle upon the formation of a provisional government, but as the military now seemed in control, there was no certainty for the future. One of the opposition candidates, Gilchrist Olympio, was wounded and 10 others were killed by assassins in May 1992. This led to massive demonstrations, which demanded Eyadema's immediate resignation. Another opposition leader was mortally wounded on 23 July. This led to an even larger demonstration that closed down the capital; civil war seemed only moments away. Loyal troops captured the radio station and destroyed most of the voter registrations in an obvious attempt to halt the elections. In October, loyal troops occupied the National Assembly building to stop further activities. Taking hostages, the group demanded and got concessions that allowed Eyadema to continue operating. Renewed antigovernment rioting broke out in January 1993. When the police opened fire on the demonstrators, 22 were killed. This led to a mass exodus to Ghana and Benin of some 25,000 attempting to escape the growing unrest. Rebel activity at an army base cost the lives of at least 40 people in January 1994. Gnassingbe Eyadema remained the president in 1995. *See also* Ghana. *Reading:* A. A. Curkeet, *Togo: Portrait of a West African Francophone*

Republic in the 1980s (1993); European Communities Staff, *Country Profile: Togo 1991* (1991); Maxine McCarthy, *Togo* (1996); Amnesty International, *Togo: Impunity for Killings by the Military* (1993).

Toivo Ja Toivo, Andimba (Herman). (b. 22 August 1924, Ovamboland, South West Africa) Born in an Ovambo tribal village, Toivo Ja Toivo was educated by the Anglicans. He later became a railroad police officer and then joined the South African army, serving in North Africa during World War II. After the war, he went to work in Cape Town, where he helped form an Ovambo worker's support group (1950). This group was to become the nucleus of the South West Africa People's Organization (SWAPO). He was caught trying to smuggle evidence on social conditions in South Africa to the United Nations and was arrested. After banishment to Ovamboland, he worked with SWAPO until South African police discovered a SWAPO guerrilla training camp at Ongulumbashe, whereupon he was again arrested and, after two years incarceration without trial, charged and tried for treason. After receiving a 20-year sentence at Robbens Island prison facility, Toivo continued his opposition to South African policies by refusing any of the kind of treatment usually afforded political prisoners, but instead used his time to improve his rudimentary education. After serving 16 years, Toivo was released (March 1984). He even fought his release saying he did not want freedom until all other Namibian political prisoners were released. He was, however, forcibly removed from prison. Upon his return to SWAPO, he refused to accept the leadership and insisted that Sam Nujoma, who was younger and had run SWAPO in his absence remain the leader. Toivo was instead elected secretary-general. *See* Namibia.

Tokyo. *See* Japan.

Tolbert, William R., Jr. (b. 13 May 1913, Bensonville, Liberia—d. 12 April 1980, Monrovia, Liberia) Tolbert served as president of Liberia from 1971 until 1980, during which time he attempted to overcome the corrupt practices of his predecessors, especially William Tubman. While his efforts were partially successful, he made a serious mistake by ordering the arrest in March 1980 of opposition leaders who had planned a general strike. This led to a military coup on 12 April, led by Samuel Doe (qv). Tolbert was murdered immediately, and most of his family and associates were executed shortly afterward.

Toledo, Hernandez. *See* Mexico.

Tomas, Americo. *See* Portugal.

Tombalbaye, Francois. Tombalbaye became the African Republic of Chad's first president upon its independence on 11 August 1960. In 1963, he found himself faced with a conspiracy among Muslim elements and solved the problem by dissolving the National Assembly, arresting a number of his ministers and declaring a state of emergency. After that point, Chad became a one-party country. Tombalbaye was "reelected" to his second seven-year term as president on 15 June 1969. Tombalbaye asked France to restore order in Chad on 11 August 1969. He was also, by this time, Chad's premier. There was a coup attempt against him in August 1970, which was suppressed. Tombalbaye then accused Libya of instigating the trouble, although the country was already in trouble from within caused by a number of disaffected elements. As Tombalbaye's position became more and more tenuous, arrests rates increased, with large numbers of ministers and former ministers being jailed. Special courts were set up to try political prisoners. In August 1973, one of Tombalbaye's chief opponents, Outel Bono, was assassinated in Paris. Evidence pointing to a Chadian plot in the murder was vehemently denied. Tombalbaye then accused French president Pompidou (September) of planning unrequested French intervention in Chad. In the past he had often requested such aid. Also, in 1973, Tombalbaye gave up his Christian name, François, and adopted his African name, N'Garta. Tombalbaye's ire against France rose in 1974, when Paris refused to extradite his political opponents, who held French citizenship and had fled to France. On 13 April 1975, Tombalbaye was overthrown in a bloody coup. In the fighting that ensued when the presidential palace was stormed, Tombalbaye was killed. A military junta took power three days later. *See*Chad.

Tonga. The Kingdom of Tonga (also known as the Friendly Islands) is a constitutional monarchy located in the southwestern Pacific Ocean, 1,600 miles east northeast of Sidney, Australia, and 600 miles east of Fiji. There are three major groups of islands and several separate ones in the kingdom. The capital is Nuku'alofa on Tongatapu Island. The native inhabitants of the group are of the general Austronesian culture, possibly having arrived more than 3,000 years ago from the west. In the thirteenth century, Tongan power reached as far as the Hawaiian Islands, 3,200 miles to the northeast. The first European visitors were the Dutch, who arrived in 1616. Abel Tasman made a number of visits to the group in 1643. Not until 1773 and the arrival of Captain James Cook, the British explorer, were the islands named "Friendly." In 1826, a Methodist mission was established that eventually converted most of the main islands away from their pagan religions. A ruling dynasty under Tu'i Tonga, that had been established in the tenth century A.D., lasted into the 19th century. In 1845, a series of civil wars placed the Tupou family on the throne. When King George Tupou I died in 1893, he was succeeded by his grandson King George Tupou II, who set about gaining British aid for his kingdom. In 1900, a British consular office was set up in the capital to handle Tonga's foreign affairs; but in a 1905 codicil to the treaty, the British received veto power over Tongan external decisions, which essentially made Tonga a British protectorate. When George Tupou II died in 1918, he was replaced on the throne by his daughter, Salote Tupou III. In turn, in 1965, she was replaced by her son, who continued (1996) to rule as Taufa'ahau IV. The British protectorate was abolished on 4 June 1970, when Tonga received its independence within the British Commonwealth. The Soviet Union attempted to get the right to build a fishing station in Tonga in return for building the Tongans an airfield in May 1976. This created something of a situation for Tonga, as it felt the strain of its relations with New Zealand, which was attempting to halt a flow of migrant workers, most of whom came from Tonga. In 1978, Tonga and its South Pacific Forum neighbors declared a 200-mile economic zone around their individual islands (groups). Tonga continued its refusal of Soviet requests to be allowed to build a fishing station on Tonga.

In 1979, Tonga established diplomatic relations with Libya and received a $A3 million loan from its new friend. At the same time, world attention came to focus upon how the Pacific islands' larger neighbors exploited the available labor without proper recompense. Diplomatic relations with Israel were confirmed in 1981. A 1982 typhoon devastated Tonga and threw the islands' already weak economy into chaos. Tongans working abroad were forced to increase their remittances to the homeland in 1984. More damage was was done to the economy when two cyclones did great damage in January 1985. A scandal erupted in 1988 over the misuse of funds by some government officials. This brought a police reaction warning people about being respectful to the king. Part of the scandal involved the sale of passports to non-Tongans in return for sizeable payments. Critics claimed large portions of the money received were never reported. In 1995, Tonga rejected a Japanese request to build a whaling station and added its voice to the condemnation of France for resuming nuclear testing in the Pacific. *Reading:* Stephanie Lawson, *Tradition versus Democracy in the South Pacific: Fiji, Tonga and Western Samoa* (1996).

Ton That Dinh. *See* Vietnam.

Toriello, Guillermo. *See* Guatemala.

Torngren, Ralph. *See* Finland.

Tororo. *See* Uganda.

Torrelio Villa, Celso. On 18 July 1982, the government of President Celso Torrelio Villa of Bolivia resigned under extreme pressure from the military. General Torrelio had taken office on 4 September 1981, when a military junta elected one of its members, Torrelio, to be president. Most of Torrelio's plans for democratizing Bolivia during his administration had been thwarted by the military. Another military man, Brigadier General Guido Vildoso Calderon, held office as head of state until 10 October, when the newly restored Congress elected Hernan Siles Zuaro (qv) president.

Torres Gonzales, Juan Jose. (b. 5 March 1921, Cochabamba, Bolivia) Torres attended the Autonomous National University before joining the Bolivian army in 1941. He joined the conservative Socialist Falange Party in his youth, but with age he moved more to the left in his nationalist views. Beginning on 6 October 1970, President Alfredo Ovando Candia (qv) was forced to resign during a bloodless coup led by a rightist military junta under the chief of staff, General Rogelio Miranda (qv). Within 24 hours, a left-wing coup led by the recently dismissed armed forces commander in chief, Torres, ousted the right-wingers and took the government. Both Ovando and Miranda were given refuge in the Argentine embassy. Among Torres's first acts in office was the recognition of Cuba and a call on the OAS to look at "real problems." On 11 January 1971, Torres reported he had crushed a right-wing coup d'etat attempt by the army. There was another coup attempt on 22 June 1971, which was met by a declaration of a state of emergency. A third attempt proved more successful, however, and an uprising against the Torres regime, which began on 18 August 1971, led to his overthrow on 21 August by a right-wing junta led by Colonel Hugo Banzer-Suarez (qv), who was allegedly supported by the U.S. CIA.

Torrijos Herrera, Omar. (b. 13 February 1929, Santiago, Panama—d. 31 July 1981, western Panama) In 1968, Brigadier General Omar Torrijos Herrera led the National Guard in a coup against President Arnulfo Arias Madrid (qv). Torrijos thereafter became the the the de facto head and strongman of the Panamanian government for the next 13 years. From 1972 until 1978, when he declined to run for reelection, he served as the country's chief of state. For the remainder of his time, he ran Panama with an iron hand. Torrijos was known to associate with Cuba's Fidel Castro (qv) and had the support of left-wing elements in Panama. Colonel Muammar Qaddafi (qv) was another associate, but Torrijos could never be identified as a leftist. In December 1979, he allowed the former Shah of Iran, Reza Pahlavi (qv), the use of the island of Contadora, and he also used his good offices to gain the release of Isabel Perón (qv) from house arrest and her exile to Spain. On 31 July 1981, Torrijos was killed in an military airplane crash in western Panama.

Tortuga Island. *See* Haiti.

Toukan, Shmed. *See* Jordan.

Toungoo. *See* Burma.

Toure, Ahmed Sekou. (b. 9 January 1922, Faranah, Guinea—d. 26 March 1984, Cleveland, Ohio) Toure was born the son of indigent Muslim parents, but he claimed in later years that he was descended from a Guinean patriot who had fought against French domination in the nineteenth century. At age 14 and in his first scholastic year, he was expelled from a French technical school in Conakry for fomenting food rioting (1936). In the ensuing decade he held a number of jobs, but he developed an interest in the labor movement and helped organize the first successful strike of 76 days in the history of French West Africa. He became the secretary-general of the Post and Telegraph Workers' Union in 1945 and then helped found the Federation of Workers' Union of Guinea as a part of the World Federation of Trade Unions. He later became its vice president. When the *Rassemblement Democratique Africain* (RDA) was formed in Ivory Coast in 1946, Toure decided to enter politics. Although he was elected to the French National assembly in 1951, he was refused his seat. This happened again in 1954, when for the second time he won the election but was refused his seat. In 1955, however, after winning the mayorial race for Conakry by a huge margin, he was given his seat in the National Assembly (1956). In 1957, he became the vice president of the Executive Council of Guinea. Toure then led the campaign for Guinean independence, which came about on 1 October 1958. Toure was then elected the country's first president and immediately rejected membership in the French Union. This brought about a French reaction in which the French recalled all of their advisory personnel and removed all of the transportable equipment they had in Guinea. Fundamentally, Toure had no recourse but to deal with the communist bloc, although he did ask for help from the West. Also, in November 1958, Toure, working with Ghana's Kwame Nkrumah (qv), sought to unify the two countries. The plan never worked, however, but when Nkrumah was overthrown in 1966 , Toure offered him asylum and on 10 March made him co-president of Guinea. Earlier, on 15 November 1965, Guinea had severed diplomatic relations with France after the discovery of a French-instigated plot to assassinate Toure and overthrow his government. Another unsuccessful coup attempt occurred on 10 March 1969, which was followed by yet another attempt on 21 March. In the latter case, two cabinet ministers were arrested for having been involved in the plot. Following an unsuccessful invasion from Portuguese Guinea (*see* Guinea-Bissau) on 22–24 November 1970, Toure began a purge of his government and imposed severe political restrictions on the country. On 19 December 1971, Toure asked the United Nations to investigate evidence of Portuguese complicity in the thwarted invasion. He thereafter ruled Guinea unopposed. His incessant rantings against Senegal, however, caused that country to break diplomatic relations with Guinea on 18 September 1973. Toure led an unsuccessful Islamic peace mission to end the Iraq-Iran War in March 1981. When both sides rejected the attempt, the mission returned home. He failed again as a peace negotiator after the Islamic Conference Organization had sent him to end the Gulf War in October 1982. Toure was slated to become the chairman of the Organization of African Unity in May 1984, but he died in a U.S. hospital where he had been flown following a heart attack.

Trabzon. *See* Turkey.

Tran Van Don. *See* Vietnam.

Tran Van Houng. On 30 October 1964, Tran Van Houng, the mayor of Saigon, became the Republic of Vietnam's prime minister. On 27 January 1965, Lieutenant General Nguyen Khanh (qv) seized power, ousting the Tran Van Houng government. When the government of Major General Nguyen Van Thieu (qv) was seated on 12 June 1965, Tran Van Houng once again became premier. On 19 July 1969, Thieu announced a major governmental reorganization. Part of this was aimed at getting stronger people in positions of influence in the government. One of those singled out for removal was Houng, who had already received a vote of no confidence from the National Assembly on 16 June, having been charged with being too soft on corruption and ignoring Vietnam's faltering economy. Houng was replaced as premier on 23 August 1969. *See* Vietnam.

Trang Bahn. *See* Vietnam.

Tranninh Plateau. *See* Laos.

Trans-Arabian Pipeline. *See* Saudia Arabia.

Transjordan. *See* Jordan.

Transkei. Transkei is one of the "homelands" designated for the Bantu Xhosa people by the apartheid policies of South Africa (*see* Republic of South Africa). It became the first such homeland under the South African government's Promotion of Bantu Self-Government Act of 1959. In 1963, Transkei established a Legislative Assembly, whose action still had to be approved by South Africa. When Transkei received its independence in 1973, all blacks with any language ties to the Xhosa lost their South African citizenship and were given Transkei citizenship. The Organization of African Unity immediately asked that the nations of the world refuse recognition to Transkei on the grounds that such acceptance would in effect approve apartheid. This view was supported by the United Nations, and most countries withheld recognition (26

October 1976).The United States, however, abstained from voting for the resolution. Transkei began to show its independence when, on 22 January 1978, it ordered all South African military advisers out of the country and, on 10 April, broke diplomatic relations with South Africa. One month later, on 10 May, Transkei abrogated the nonagression pact it had with the South African government. When the South African authorities offered Nelson Mandela (qv) his freedom from prison in March 1984, he refused because it would have meant his isolation in Transkei. Throughout this period, Transkei became more and more aligned with the African National Congress, Mandela's party. In December 1992, there was a mutiny of sorts in Transkei when some 3,000 soldiers held a group of their senior officers trying to resolve a pay dispute. The matter was settled without bloodshed. In June 1993, an eight-day sit-in staged by a group of teachers who were demanding the resignation of the minister of education ended when riot police stormed the ministry building. In March-April 1994, Transkei and the other nominally independent homeland states of Bophuthatswana, Ciskei and Venda were reincorporated into the newly free black-dominated Republic of South Africa. *Reading:* Roger Southall, *South Africa's Transkei* (1983).

Transvaal. *See* Republic of South Africa.

Traore, Moussa. On 19 November 1968, a military coup overthrew the socialist government of Mali. President Modibo Keita (qv) was ousted by a junta calling itself the National Military Liberation Committee. Keita was arrested and awaited a trial for his alleged crimes. One of the leaders of the junta, Lieutenant Moussa Traore, was proclaimed president on 9 December. On 12 August 1969, a coup attempt by friends of Keita failed to reclaim the government. Traore thereafter cleaned out his government, including the head of the junta, Captain Yoro Diakite. Another failed coup attempt occurred on 7 April 1971. Traore remained in power in 1984 and once again reorganized his government following a long period of negotiations with Burkina Faso over an old border dispute. In 1989, Troare, having promoted himself to general, was appointed the chairman of the Organization of African Unity (OAU). Troare was forced to allow political opposition in April 1990, and before the end of the year, he was faced with calls for a multiparty system in government. On 26 March 1991, a military coup overthrew Traore after a period of violent demonstrations, which claimed he lives of several hundred people. The news of the coup's success was greeted by great celebration. Traore and a number of his associates were arrested.Traore's trial began in November 1992. He was found guilty of complicity in the deaths of 106 people in March 1991 and sentenced to death on 12 February 1993. An appeal was denied by Mali's high court, and all were executed.

Treaty of Fez. The 1912 treaty that bound Morocco as a French protectorate is known as the Treaty of Fez. The agreement was dissolved by mutual consent on 2 March 1956.

Treaty of Rio de Janeiro. More properly called the Inter-American Mutual Assistance Treaty, this agreement established an American defense zone stretching from Greenland to Antarctica. The treaty was initialed in Rio de Janeiro on 2 September 1947.

Treaty of Tashkent. A treaty signed by India and Pakistan on 10 January 1966, the Treaty of Tashkent required both sides to withdraw their forces from the frontier areas along their mutual border to prevent the possibility of future confrontations. The agreed-upon withdrawals were completed by 25 February, but this did not constrain the two sides from later border conflict. *See* Indo-Pakistani War.

Treaty of Tlatelolco. *See* Treaty on the Denuclearization of Latin America.

Treaty on the Denuclearization of Latin America. At a meeting held in Mexico City on 14 February 1967, the representatives of 14 Latin American countries signed a treaty denuclearizing Latin America. Known as the Treaty of Tlatelolco, the treaty went into effect on 25 April 1969, when the Barbados parliament approved it. The United Nations General Assembly had already approved the treaty on 5 December 1967. The United States endorsed the treaty on 12 May 1971, and the Soviet Union signed the treaty on 25 April 1978.

Tribhubarra (Tribhuban) Bir Bikram. On 7 November 1950, King Tribhubarra Bir Bikram of Nepal was overthrown in a coup led by the prime minister, Mohan Shumshere (qv). The deposed king led an unsuccessful counter-coup on 11–20 November. Tribhubarra took refuge in the Indian embassy. A revolt took place in early 1951, which ended in Mohan acceding to demands and forming a new cabinet with opposition participation. Tribhubarra then returned to Katmandu as the constitutional monarch. Mohan resigned in November. Tribhubarra died in 1955, and he was succeeded as king by his eldest son, Mahenda Bir Bikram Shah Deva.

Trieste. *See* Italy and Yugoslavia.

Trinidad and Tobago. Located off the northeastern shore of Venezuela, Trinidad and Tobago is constituted by two adjunct islands at the lower end of the chain of islands stretching southward from Puerto Rico and inclusive of those groups thought of as the "Islands of the Caribbean" or the West Indies. In the fifteenth century, when Columbus explored the two islands (1498), he discovered Trinidad to be inhabited by Arawak Indians, while the smaller island of Tobago was inhabited by the more warlike Carib Indians. Spain claimed the islands at that time and held them in a neglected state until 1797, when the British occupied Trinidad. African slaves were imported for labor, as most of the native Arawak Indians had been worked to death by the Spaniards. The British occupied Tobago in 1721, but lost it to the French in 1781. Tobago went back to British control in 1802. With the abolition of slavery in 1834–1848, paid levies of Indian immigrants were brought in to replace the African slaves that had gotten the sugar trade running. Trinidad and Tobago were made into one administrative district in 1889. Partial self-government was allowed in 1925, and the colony received its autonomy in 1945, limited self-government in 1956 and independence on 31 August 1962. Also on 26 February 1956, Trinidad and

Tobago joined most of the other Caribbean states in reaching a preliminary agreement on the formation of a Caribbean Federation. Four days of rioting between blacks and East Indians began on Trinidad on 21 April 1970. British and U.S. naval units began arriving offshore the next day. At that moment, about one-quarter of the local army mutinied (about 200 men). Without the insertion of outside forces, the uprising was put down by loyal troops on 24 April. The islands declared themselves to be a republic within the British Commonwealth in 1976. During the next decade, Trinidad and Tobago used their relative wealth to aid other Caribbean countries, primarily by supplying petroleum at a low price to stimulate sagging economies. Tobago was given considerable autonomy over its own affairs, and a careful watch was maintained over the political situation in neighboring Grenada (qv). Although Trinidad and Tobago remained the wealthiest state in the Caribbean, 1983 witnessed the beginning of a down-swing caused by falling oil prices. The country's position *vis-à-vis* the majority of other Caribbean states also went down, after the government sided with Grenada following the invasion (*see* Grenada). An austerity plan was put into effect in 1984, to help the economy recover. A major political shift occurred in 1986, when the long-ruling People's Nation Movement (PNM) was soundly defeated by a coalition of four parties calling themseves the National Alliance for Reconstruction (NAR). The new government immediately put an even more stringent austerity program into effect to try to halt what was called a "catastrophic economic situation" inherited from the PNM. In 1987, a number of judges and police officers were suspended on charges of participation in drug running. Demonstrations occurred in September 1988, following a failure to pay government workers on time because of the now-chaotic economic situation. On 27 July 1990, about 150 Muslim extremists occupied the parliament building, taking some 50 hostages in the process, including the prime minister. They also blew up the police headquarters in Port of Spain. After a six-day siege, the attempted coup was deemed a failure, and the Muslims surrendered. The economic situation in Trinidad was blamed for the uprising. At least 30 people died in the incident. The ensuing wrangle over trying 114 of the rebels would go on until 1992, when they were released on a technicality based on an amnesty granted by the president to avoid bloodshed. (In 1994, the "technicality" was set aside, but the rebels were not rearrested.) In December 1991, the PNM returned to power but was met over the next several years by a rapidly rising crime rate and a lessening of popular support for its programs. The reimposition of the death penalty also engendered a worldwide protest. Crime, especially organized crime, dominated the country in 1995. As drug-trafficking became a major problem, the incorruptible paid the price by being targeted for assassination. *Reading:* Mahin Gosine, *East Indian and Black Power in the Caribbean: The Case of Trinidad* (1987).

Tripoli. *See* Lebanon; Libya.

Tripoli Declaration. At the close (5 December 1977) of a stormy four-day meeting held in Tripoli, Libya, the leaders of Algeria, Iraq, Libya, Yemen (Aden) and Syria signed a declaration condemning Egypt for its conciliatory policy toward

Israel. In retaliation for the issuance of the declaration, on that same day, Egypt's President Anwar Sadat (qv) broke diplomatic relations with all of the signatories and ordered 270 of their diplomats out of the country. Sadat closed a number of Soviet consular and cultural offices at the same time.

"Tripoli to Cairo March." *See* Libya.

Trujillo Molina, Rafael Leonidas. (b. 24 October 1891, San Cristobal, Dominican Republic—d. 30 May 1961, Ciudad Trujillo, Dominican Republic) -Trujillo's career started in 1918, when he joined the army, which was then being trained by U.S. marines who were on occupation duty. He was commissioned in the National Police in 1919 and rose rapidly through the ranks, becoming a general in 1927. In 1930, he led a revolt against President Horacio Vasquez and took power for himself. Although he was an able administrator, Trujillo's methods were both repressive and ruthless, often using the expedient of murder to rid himself of opposition. Corruption also flourished under his rule, and the rich only got richer. In the later years of his regime, opposition began to grow both internally and externally. He also most dangerously began to lose the unstinting support of the army that had been his main tool of control. When a small Cuban-sponsored invasion force landed on the island on 23 June 1959, for instance, it was quickly ejected by the army. Although he was officially president for only 18 years (1930–1938, 1942–1952), his regime stayed in power 31 years, until he was assassinated by machine gun fire as he drove toward his San Cristobal home on 30 May 1961. Most of those involved in the assassination plot were subsequently captured and executed. By November 1961, many of Trujillo's followers had already fled the country. Those who remained, however, feared for their lives in the face of a rumored coup. U.S. warships patrolled near to the Dominican Republic. *Reading:* Howard J. Wiarda, *Dictatorship and Development: The Methods of Control in Trujillo's Dominican Republic* (1968); Jesus Galindez-Suarez, *The Era of Trujillo, Dominican Dictator* (1973).

Truman, Harry S. (b. 8 May 1884, Lamar, Missouri—d. 26 December 1972, Kansas City, Missouri) Born the son of a farmer, he attended school in Independence, where he persevered despite poor eyesight and graduated high school in 1901. For five years he worked as a bank clerk, before taking over operation of his grandmother's farm in Independence. Doing this period he joined the National Guard, and in World War I he served with distinction in France as an artillery captain. He married Elizabeth (Bess) Wallace in 1918 and became a haberdasher in Kansas City. When the business failed, he worked to pay off his debts and entered politics under the tutelage of the Democratic machine boss, Thomas Pendergast. He was elected a county judge in 1922, but in 1924, he was defeated by an anti-Pendergast–Ku Klux Klan coalition. He then went to work as an automobile club salesman and attended the Kansas City Law School at night for two years. Entering banking, Truman enjoyed some success and although he had a crooked partner, and he opened the Community Savings and Loan Association in Independence. In 1926, he was elected the presiding judge of the Jackson county court—again with Pendergast's help—where he became known as an honest judge. This did not please the Pendergast machine, which ran everything in Jackson County. Truman, who wanted to be governor, was refused the nomination. In 1934, Truman was Pendergast's fourth choice for the U.S. Senate. The Pendergast cloud hung over Truman after he was elected, but his hard work in Washington, especially in the area of transportation, helped redeem him. Truman won again in 1940, even though Pendergast was then in prison and his machine in total disarray. Truman then undertook an investigation into the defense posture of the United States, exposing extensive graft and waste in government procurement. This brought Truman to Franklin Roosevelt's (qv) specific attention, although Roosevelt had already recognized his talent. Truman's friend, Robert E. Hannigan, by then, and with Truman's help, the Democratic national chairman, convinced Roosevelt to have Truman replace Henry Wallace as vice president on the 1944 ticket. When Roosevelt won, Truman was catapulted to a position where, 82 days after inauguration, upon the death (12 April 1945) of President Roosevelt, he became the 33rd president of the United States. He stated at the time that there must be "a million people" better qualified for the job. During those 82 days, Truman had seen Roosevelt only three times, was completely unaware of the Manhattan Project that was developing of the atomic bomb and almost completely ignorant of the international structure that was prosecuting the war. After he became president, it was Truman who completed the preparations for the conference in San Francisco that chartered the United Nations, helped orchestrate the surrender of Germany, and gave the order to bomb Hiroshima and Nagasaki that helped end the war against Japan. In December 1945, Truman sent General of the Army George C. Marshall to China as his personal representative to seek peace in that country. After a short period of tranquility with Congress, Truman ran afoul of that body when he presented his Economic Bill of Rights, which in effect, meant that control of the Congress was passed to the Republicans in 1946. In the 1948 elections, Trumans chances of winning on his own were rated as next to nil. He confounded everyone with a clear victory over Thomas Dewey in November. In 1949, Truman proposed the "Fair Deal," which failed miserably in Congress. Truman, however, did much better in foreign affairs and was among the first leaders to identify the Soviet Union as the real opponent in the battle for peace. He called for a restriction on Soviet aggression through a policy of "containment." In the ensuing months he established the Truman Doctrine, which gave aid to Greece and Turkey (12 March 1947), helped push the $17 billion Marshall Plan (31 March 1948), which allowed for the economic recovery of a free Europe, and helped in the design and implementation of NATO (1949). Truman also extended the containment policy to include China when that country became a communist menace. His executive orders dissolved the Office of Strategic Services and established the Central Intelligence Agency. He was also responsible for the start of the Berlin Airlift when Soviet authorities attempted to starve Berlin into submission in 1948. Truman also installed the Point Four Program that brought aid to emerging nations and issued the orders to build the hydrogen bomb, after the USSR had entered the nuclear race

(September 1949). In 1950, following the invasion of South Korea, Truman pushed the United Nations (27 June 1950) into action whereby North Korea and Communist China were forced to pay an exorbitant toll for what became a Phyrric victory. In January 1951, the president assured the nation that there would be no bombing of China without a declaration of war by the Congress. Of singular importance during this period was Truman's removal of General of the Army Douglas MacArthur, a national hero, who overstepped his role as a military commander. For this proper act and the disclosure of improper conduct by several administration figures, Truman was again vilified, but he endured and was eventually vindicated. He left office in January 1953 and spent his remaining years as a private, but very popular, figure. He died in 1972. Historians now consider him among the nation's ten greatest presidents. *Reading:* Harry S. Truman, *The Autobiography of Harry S. Truman* (1980); Nancy Skarmeas, ed., *Great Americans: Harry S. Truman* (1996).

Trucial States. *See* Oman; United Arab Emirates.

Tsakane. *See* Republic of South Africa.

Tsantes, George. On 15 November 1983, the chief of the U.S. naval mission assigned to the U.S. Joint Military Assistance Group in Greece (JUSMAGG), Captain George Tsantes, and his Greek driver were assassinated while driving in downtown Athens. The 17 November Revolutionary Organization claimed credit for the attack. In a message given to the Greek press, the terrorist group denounced JUSMAGG and other U.S. government military and intelligence facilities in Greece and criticized the socialist prime minister, Andreas Papandreou, for having failed to have all U.S. installations in Greece closed.

Tshombe, Moise-Kapenda. (b. 10 November 1919, Musumba, Belgian Congo—d. 29 June 1969, Algiers) Tshombe was born the son of a wealthy businessman, and later inherited the family businesses. When these enterprises began to fail, he entered politics and from 1951 to 1953 served on the Katanga Provincial Council. In 1959 he became the president of the *Conferation des Associations Tribales du Kantanga* (Conakat), the political organization of Tshombe's Lunda tribe, a group also supported by powerful Belgian mining interests. As the leader of Conakat, Tshombe did not fare well in the discussions of Congo's independence. Nor did Joseph Kasavubu (qv), another leader who believed in a loose confederation. The winner of these discussions was Patrice Lumumba (qv), who believed in a strong central government. While Conakat did rather poorly in ensuing national elections, they did very well in the Katanga province elections for the Provisional Assembly. When an army mutiny occurred, Tshombe used his Conakat power to declare Katanga's independence. After Lumumba was ousted by President Kasavubu in September 1960, Tshombe sought to end the Katangan independence through negotiation. When Swedish UN forces attempted to fly into Katanga on 12 August 1960, Tshombe at first refused to allow them to land, but finally acquiesced. The negotiations with Kasavubu failed, possibly over Lumumba's murder (13 February 1961), in which Tshombe was almost certainly implicated. When Tshombe discovered that another UN force was headed for Katanga, he ordered (21 February 1961) a mobilization of the province. Tshombe also failed in his efforts to gain diplomatic recognition of Katanga, and after withdrawing the Katangan delegation he was arrested and charged with treason on 24 April 1961. He was released on 22 June 1961, after promising to adhere to the confederation negotiations. However, on 28 July, he announced he would fight, if necessary, to keep Katanga independent. On 21 August 1961, UN forces captured Katanga's radio station in hopes of compelling Tshombe to stop the use of white mercenaries in the conflict. Tshombe complied. When UN forces attempted to disarm the Katangans, after the Kasavubu government had received assurance of UN support, fighting once again broke out. The UN secretary general, Dag Hammerskjöld (qv), was killed in an air crash going to negotiate with Tshombe on 18 September. On 29 December 1962, Tshombe once again violated the UN truce agreement, and United Nations forces opened an offensive against Katanga in January 1963. Tshombe was forced to flee to Spain after announcing (15 January) the end of Katanga's independence.. He returned to Congo at Kasavubu's invitation on 10 July 1964, however, to assume the premiership and to help end a Chinese Communist–inspired rebellion in Kivu province in eastern Congo. Kasavubu dismissed him on 13 October 1965, on charges that he used white mercenaries to subdue the rebellion and also on rumors that Tshombe intended his overthrow. Thereafter, Tshombe returned to Spain. In 1967, amid rumors that he intended to return to Congo, Tshombe was kidnapped and spirited to Algieria, where the government refused his extradition to Congo to answer charges of treason. Tshombe was tried in absentia on 13 March 1967, found guilty and sentenced to death. Tshombe remained under house arrest in Algeria until his death from a heart attack on 29 June 1969.

Tsiranana, Philibert. On 14 October 1958, Malagasy was declared an autonomous republic within the French Community, and Philibert Tsiranana was elected its first president. Malagasy received its complete independence in June 1960. Tsiranana chaired an inaugural session of the *Union Africain et Malgache* in March 1961, in which 12 African states participated. He won a second seven-year term as president in March 1965. Everything remained relatively quiet for Tsiranana until 1970, when he suffered a long bout of illness following a stroke in January that kept him away from his desk in a Paris hospital until May. At the same time, a new government was formed that was dominated by Tsiranana's Social Democratic Party, although opposition was evident from Madagascar, where strong separatist feelings abounded. Also, on 20 November 1970, Malagasy reached a number of agreements with the white government in South Africa, which though monetarily profitable for Malagasy incensed many because of South Africa's policies toward its own black population. Violence broke out in January 1971, when a bomb exploded at a minister's home. The University of Tanarive was closed in March following disturbances. The president appealed for order after an outbreak of violence that killed 30 in south Madagascar in April. On 31 May, Tsiranana announced the discovery of a plot to overthrow the government. Violence continued into 1972, and after a week of student violence Tsiranana's government was overhrown in a bloodless coup carried out by

General Gabriel Ramanantsoa (qv) on 18 May 1972. Tsiranana was allowed to stay in office until 8 October, when, stripped of his last powers, he was forced into retirement. *See* Madagascar.

Tsitsihar. *See* China.

Tucuman. *See* Argentina.

Tulear Province. *See* Malagasy.

Tunb (Tamb) Islands, Greater and Lesser (*Tomb-e-Bozorg and Tomb-e-Kuchak*). On 30 November 1971, having rejected the territorial claims of the tiny sheikhdom of Ras al-Khaimah, Iranian forces seized the Tamb Island at the mouth of the Persian Gulf at the north end of the Strait of Hormuz. The island of Abu Musa was also seized, but it was returned to the sheikhdom of Shahjah after basing rights on the island were granted to Iran.

Tunguyan, Mohammad Jawad Baqir. *See* Iraq-Iran War.

Tunis. *See* Tunisia.

Tunisia. The Republic of Tunisia lies along the North African littoral of the Mediterranean Sea. It is bordered on the southeast by Libya, on the southwest and west by Algeria. The remainder of its border is washed by the Mediterranean. The capital is at Tunis. From the twelfth century B.C., the Phoenicians held a number of trading posts along the Tunisian coast. The city of Carthage was built on the present site of Tunis in the eighth century B.C., and by the sixth century B.C. the Carthaginians ruled most of the region that today is Tunisia. In 146 B.C. the Romans absorbed the Carthaginian Empire as a part of its provinces following the Punic Wars. The Muslims came in the mid-seventh century A.D., and between that time and the nineteenth century a constant stream of conquerers, including the Spaniards and the Ottoman Empire (1574), held the region. Following the decline in the power of the Sublime Porte, Britain, France and Italy vied for the region. However, in a deal made in 1881, France became the protector of Tunisia, while Great Britain settled for the island of Cyprus. Although Tunisia had been relatively autonomous during the latter years of the nineteenth century, the imposition of French will soon became apparent. Tunisia did support France in World War I, but it also began demanding a larger voice in its own destiny, with equal participation in government as one of its chief goals at that moment. In the 1930s, a new leader appeared on the scene, Habib Bourguiba (qv), the head of the Neo-Destour party, which counted among its allies the French Popular Front government. The Neo-Destour party was dissolved during World War II, but it revived at war's end to continue the struggle for independence. On 14 January 1952, Tunisia appealed to the United Nations for a hearing on its demands for autonomy. When the request was denied, widespread anti-French rioting followed throughout the country. On 15 May 1952, the Bey of Tunis, bowing to heavy French pressure, removed the pro-independence members from the government and appealed for calm. A French call for greater self-reliance within the French Union was rejected by the separatists on 23 July. The Bey was again forced by the French (20 December 1952) to issue a series of decrees dealing with government reform, all of which complied with French "guidance." On 7 August

1954, Tunisia was given full internal independence, and a government was formed under Tahar ben Ammar. France's National Assembly then voted greater autonomy for both Tunisia and Morocco on 27 August. But, in December 1954, France voiced grave concerns on the issue of giving any of its North African territories, including Tunisia, complete independence. Negotiations leading to complete autonomy began between the Tunisian government and the Bourguiba faction and France in May 1955, and complete autonomy was achieved on 1 September, with Habib Bourguiba elected president. Complete independence came on 20 March 1956. A republic was declared at that time under the Destourian Socialist Party (PSD). The PSD later changed its name to the Democratic Constitutional Party. Tunisia signed a treaty of alliance with Morocco on 30 March 1957. On 25 July, the Bey of Tunis was ousted by the National Constituent Assembly. Bourguiba then asked (12 September) the U.S. for military aid following clashes (9 September) with French and Algerian forces along the common border. Both the U.S. and Great Britain responded with offers of help (14 November). In February 1958, five months of sporadic warfare began when French planes bombed the village of Sakiet-Sidi-Youseff, killing 73 people. The French claimed the raid was retaliatory as the town had been used as a base for rebels operating in Algeria. On 17 June, France announced it was withdrawing all French forces in Tunisia, except those at one major base at Bizerte. Tunisia joined the Arab League (qv) on 1 October 1958. However, when the league moved to declare the procommunist government of Iraq a threat to peace, Tunisia and several other states boycotted the meeting. Tunisian forces took part in the UN Emergency Force operations in Congo beginning in July 1960. On 19–20 June 1961, Tunisia forces laid siege to the French bastion at Bizerte. The investment was broken, however, upon the arrival of French reinforcements. The French garrison was withdrawn and the post relinquished to the Tunisians on 18 September 1961. Evacuation of all French forces, except for several air bases, was completed in June 1962. Tunisia recognized Communist China on 10 January 1964. In April 1965, Tunisia announced an indeterminate boycott of the Arab League because of its criticism of Bourguiba's plan for Arab peace with Israel; and when League members severed relations with West Germany for its recognition of Israel, Tunisia refused to go along. Then, on 3 October 1966, Tunisia broke diplomatic relations with the United Arab Republic. Tunisia indefinitely postponed a proposed merger with Libya, three days after Muammar Qadaffi (qv) made the announcement. Bourguiba fired his foreign minister for his part in making the arrangements. On 26 January 1978, Bourguiba declared a state of emergency in Tunisia following a nation-wide strike that spawned the worst violence in decades. Tunisia put its military forces on alert after indications that the situation in Chad were worsening. Bourguiba was force to declare another state of emergency on 3 January 1984, because of rioting over higher food prices. The restriction was lifted three days later. On 22 August 1985, Tunisia ordered an alert along its border with Libya after the Libyan government expelled thousands of Tunisian workers. Then, on 2 September, Tunisia cut all trade with Libya and ordered all Libyan citizens out of the country. Diplomatic relations with Libya were broken on 26 September when at least 30,000 Tunisians had been expelled. As Tunisia moved forward in its internal development, it began to experience more widespread unrest until Bourguiba was declared mentally unfit to govern and removed from office (7 November 1987). Officials of the Bourguiba era were removed from office, and early elections were announced in a move designed to remove all remnants of his rule. A new government under General Zine al-Abidine Ben Ali began a program of Muslim fundamentalism. In 1988, Tunisia reestablished diplomatic relations with Egypt and began improving its position *vis-à-vis* Libya. In mid-1989, a general amnesty was declared, and over 5,000 political prisoners were released. The order excluded those who had been charged with fraud. Islamic fundamentalist pressure to force the resignation of the education minister failed. President Ben Ali went on record as opposing U.S. intervention in the Iraq-Kuwait situation. This forced the departure of the foreign minister, who differed with the president's view. Ben Ali also objected to the pro-American initiative presented the Arab League in August 1990. As a result of Ben Ali's condemnation of the United Nations campaign against Iraq, the U.S. cancelled its 1991 military aid package to Tunisia and slashed its economic aid package as well. At the same time, Kuwait cut off all financial aid to Tunisia. The transfer of the Arab League headquarters from Tunis to Cairo (in October 1990) was another indication of the isolation of Tunisia at a time the country was in a rather serious financial predicament. The unstable situation also engendered increased Islamic fundamentalist activity, which provoked a series of violent incidents. In one case, a watchman at a leading party headquarters was killed. Three fundamentalists were arrested and executed as a result, and a number of others were later arrested on charges of treason. In 1992, Amesty International released a scathing report stating Tunisia was holding over 8,000 political prisoners. It was also later proven that Tunisia harassed civil rights workers and instituted laws limiting human rights progress. Ironically, after siding with Iraq during the Gulf War, in 1992 Tunisia refused Iraqi requests for the release of frozen funds and airliners it held. In 1993, Tunisia joined other Arab countries in planning to inhibit the spread of Islamic fundamentalism. That same year, discussions with the PLO were aimed at a continuation of the presence of the Palestinian organization, which had maintained its offices there since being expelled from Lebanon in 1982–1983. The year 1994 witnessed renewed attacks on Tunisia's human rights records. This time the reports focused on the repression of Islamic fundamentalists. Civil rights issues were also raised over government interference in the electoral process. Tunisia signed a transitional agreement on 17 July 1995 that would allow it to enter the European Union within 12 years, provided certain economic goals are achieved. Ben Ali remained in power in 1995, through the use of force when necessary. *Reading:* Clement M. Henry, *The Mediterranean Debt Crescent: Money and Power in Algeria, Egypt, Morocco, Tunisia, and Turkey* (1996); Mira Zussman, *Development and Disenchantment in Rural Tunisia: The Bourguiba Years* (1992); Norma Salem, *Habib Bourguiba, Islam and the Creation of Tunisia* (1984).

Tupamaros. A Uruguayan terrorist organization, the Tupamaros group is more properly called the Movement of National Liberation (*Movimiento de Liberacion Nacional*) (MLN). Founded in 1963 by Raul Sendic (qv) as a Marxist rural guerrilla group, the name Tupamaros comes from Tupac Amaru, an Inca chieftain executed by the Spaniards in 1748. In October 1969, a Tupamaros column captured the town of Pando but was quickly ejected by government forces. The group quickly shifted its operations to an urban environment in Montevideo. MLN reached its zenith in the 1970s. On 31 July 1970, it carried out its most famous attack by kidnapping U.S. diplomat Dan A. Mitrone, along with the Brazilian consul, off a Montevideo street. Mitrione's body was found in Montevideo after the Uruguayan government refused to negotiate with the terrorists for his release. On 8 January 1971, the MLN kidnapped the British ambassador, Geoffrey Jackson, in Montevideo and demanded the release of 150 political prisoners for his release. The new government killed or imprisoned most of the Tupamaros leadership of the approximately 3,000 members of MLN in its heydey. The MLN released the Brazilian diplomat who had been kidnapped with Mitrione on 21 February 1971, after a ransom of $500,000 was paid. On 10 March, the Tupamaros kidnapped Uruguay's attorney general to question him about the upcoming trials of a group of MLN leaders who were currently in jail. In this case, the man was released unharmed on 23 March. Also released unharmed was an Argentinian industrialist kidnapped on 14 July 1971, but only after an exorbitant ransom was paid. On 30 July, the MLN broke into a Montevideo prison and released 38 women prisoners. On 6 September, they broke into the Punta Carretas maximum security prison and released 111 inmates. Thereafter, on 9 September, the British ambassador, who was kidnapped in January, was released unharmed. After a truce had been signed, the MLN broke it by blowing up the golf course at Punta Carretas on 22 December. Proving Punta Carretas not the maximum security facility it was claimed to be, 16 Tupamaros prisoners held there were able to escape on 12 April 1972. On 14 April, four people were murdered by Tupamaros terrorists. Eight MLN members were also killed in the incident, and the Uruguayan government "declared war" on the terrorist organization. As a part of that campaign, seven people were killed when Montevideo police opened fire on a communist club in the city. In a police raid on 28 May 1972, the infamous Tupamaros "People's Prison" in Montevideo was found and destroyed. Raul Sendic was wounded and captured on 1 September. The kidnappings and murders commited by MLN over these months led to the overthrow of the government and the establishment of a military dictatorship in Uruguay. On 10 January 1973, the military handed a list of 19 demands to the government. President Juan Maria Bordaberry was forced to yield considerable power to a military junta in a move designed to end Tupamaros operations. Thereafter, the military conducted the internal war campaign against the MLN. *Reading:* Carlos Wilson, *Tupamaros: The Unmentionable* (1974); Arturo C. Porzecanski, *Uruguay's Tupamaros: The Urban Guerrilla* (1974).

Turbuison, Piter. On 25 October 1980, government forces in El Salvador opened a major campaign against rebels operating in a remote mountainous area near the Honduran border. At least 150 rebels were killed as the government forces swept through several guerrilla training camps. They also captured a Swedish journalist, Piter Turbuison, who was held for questioning.

Turin. *See* Italy.

Turkey. The Republic of Turkey is bordered on the east by Georgia, Armenia and Iran, on the south by Iraq, Syria and the Mediterranean Sea, on the west by the Aegean Sea and Greece, on the northwest by Bulgaria, and on the north by the Black Sea. European Turkey (Thrace) is separated from Asian Turkey (Anatolia) by the Dardinelles, the Sea of Mamara and the Bosphorus. The capital city is Ankara. Original habitation of Anatolia is dated from the eighth millennium B.C. Indo-European Hittites occupied Anatolia around 1900 B.C., but the empire collapsed about 1200 B.C. Anatolia was then divided between the Phrygians and Lydians in the west and the Armenian Uratu kingdom in the west. By the sixth century B.C., Persia ruled, only to be displaced by the Greco-Hellens and, in the first century B.C., by Rome. Rome remained into the Christian era, when the emperor in the East, Constantine, declared Constantinople to be the capital of Byzantium, the Second Romam Empire. By the eleventh century, Turkic nomads, called Seljuk or Oguz, began to drift westward and soon held most of Anatolia. One of their leaders, a Kayi tribesman named Osman, founded the Ottoman Empire. The first move was to advance against the vestigal Byzantine Empire, which equated to taking Constantinople. After a campaign to take the Byzantine provinces in western Anatolia, the Ottomans captured Constantinople in 1453. Until 1683, when they were forced to withdraw from a beseiged Vienna, the Ottoman Empire held sway over much of eastern Europe, especially in the Balkans, as far east as the Euphrates River, and in much of the Middle East, including Syria, Lebanon, Iraq, Jordan, Palestine, Saudi Arabia and Yemen, most of the Aegean Isles and in northern Africa. The fortunes of the Ottomans began to decline in the sixteenth century. Austria had cleared Hungary of Turkish control by 1718, and Russia seized and annexed the Crimea in 1783. By the nineteenth century, the Balkans and Egypt had also been freed. The Young Turks Revolt (1908) attempted a revitalization of Turkey but fomented an insurrection instead. On 13 April 1909 a military revolt in Constantinople took place but was put down by troops from Macedonia. The sultan was deposed on 26 April 1909 and replaced by an even more inept one. Turkey's alignment with the German and Austro-Hungarian side served little purpose in the war. Unrest grew as the twentieth century began and culminated in a Turkish attempt to wipe out the Armenian population in a genocidal massacre before and during World War I. As a loser in that conflict, Turkey lost its Arab holdings and its territories in the east (Treaty of Sevres, 20 June 1920). There followed a civil war in which the Allies intervened to protect the Armenians and to keep the supply lines open to the White Russians. A provisional government was established in Ankara under Mustafa Kemal (Ataturk), which ended in the establishment of a republic on 29 October 1923 and a war with Greece (1921–1923) that culminated in the present territorial configuration of Turkey based on the Lausanne Conference (1923). Ataturk modernized his country, reduced the influence of Islam and secularized Turkish society. After Ataturk's death in 1938, a parliamentary system of government prevailed although there were several periods of upheaval and military rule. Turkey remained neutral during World War II, joined the United Nations in 1945, and turned to the West for support after the war. Military and economic aid was received from the United States under the Truman Plan (March 1947), and Turkey joined in the fight in Korea as a part of the United Nations Command forces (1950). Turkey joined NATO in 1952, and that same year seven years of guerrilla warfare began between Greek and Turkish nationals on Cyprus. In January 1953, the Turks joined other area nations in talks about beginning a Balkan defense alliance. Yugoslavia, Greece and Turkey reached an agreement in principle on the term of the alliance on 22 December. If any one of the three wwere attacked by or through Bulgaria, it would be considered an attack on all three. Pakistan signed a five-year mutual defense pact with Turkey on 2 April 1954. On 24 February 1955, Turkey joined the new Baghdad Pact (Middle East Treaty Organization [METO]) along with Great Britain (5 April), Iraq, Pakistan (23 September) and Iran (12 October). Following a rash of anti-Turkish rioting in Greece, anti-Greek rioting broke out in Turkey over the issue of Cyprus in September 1955. In an effort to settle the Cyprus issue, Britain offered a plan on 2 July 1956, which was rejected by Turkey. By March 1957, the Balkan Alliance question had yet to be agreed upon even though the principles had been put forth in 1953. Now the main stumbling bloc was the dispute over Cyprus between Greece and Turkey. Also, in early May 1957, Turkey again deployed troops along the Syrian border. On 7 May, the Syrians warned against further deployments. The U.S. accelerated arms shipments to Turkey on 5 September in an attempt to match Soviet aid to Syria. On 14 July 1958, upon assuming the leadership of the Arab Federation, King Hussein of Jordan asked the U.S. and Turkey for military aid. Great Britain had already sent troops into Jordan (qv). Great Britain was able to announce an agreement between Greece and Turkey dealing with the independence of Cyprus on 19 February 1959. The agreement did not hold, however, and more conflict was to come, even though Cyprus was declared independent on 16 August 1960 (*see* Cyprus). Turkey, along with Iran and Pakistan, signed bilateral defense agreements with the United States on 5 March 1959. On 19 August, the Baghdad Pact became the Central Treaty Organization (CENTO). Turkey immediately joined; some of the other Baghdad Pact members did not. Turkey agreed to allow the United States deployment of Intermediate-Range Ballistic Missiles (IRBM) on Turkish soil on 10 October. On 28 April 1960, a month of student unrest began in Turkey. The matter worsened when military academy cadets joined the demonstrations. Martial law was declared on 21 May, and the rioting was suppressed by the army with a heavy loss of life. The military then proceded to oust the government of Adnan Menderes (qv) on 27 May, in a coup led by General Jemal Gursel (qv). A military junta called the Turkish National

Union Committee took power and prepared to hold free elections. On 12 September, Menderes was executed for having violated the constitution. A mutiny broke out at the Turkish Military Academy on 27 February 1962, but it was put down without bloodshed. Another mutiny took place at the academy on 20 May 1963; this time the suppression was somewhat more vigorous, and some lives were lost. Turkey, as a member of NATO, joined in discussions on the development of an integrated nuclear naval force in early October. Turkey's position on Cyprus was left in a shambles when Cyprus president Makarios (qv) abrogated the 1959–1960 treaties of guarantee among Great Britain, Greece, and Turkey in 1964. Heavy fighting among the Greek and Turkish Cypriots ensued. Then, on 11 June, Greece rejected talks with Turkey to solve the problem. As the fighting continued on Cyprus, the chance of war between the two grew. On 7–9 August 1964, Turkish Air Force jets attacked Greek Cypriot positions on the western part of the island. War was averted only by the imposition of a UN-mandated cease-fire (9 August). Turkey remained on a near-war footing, however, until January 1968, when it began demobilizing some of the forces that had been alerted for the impending conflict. Also, on 16 January, a major riot broke out in Istanbul that involved more than 20,000 people who were protesting the visit of U.S. Sixth Fleet naval units. The left-wing riot cost one man his life, but the U.S. navy cancelled a visit to Izmir as a result of the violence. Anti-American rioting sprang up again in March 1970. These demonstrations were organized by the Federation of Revolutionary Youth at a number of universities and were supported by militant union workers from the small Confederation of Reformist Workers Union. By June, Turkey was once again under martial law, which lasted until 1 July. Violence continued, however, through 1971, mostly due to the efforts of the Turkish People's Liberation Army (TPLA) (aka Turkish People's Liberation Party/Front TPLP/F [qv]). Prime Minister Suleyman Demirel (qv) was forced to resign his post (12 March) because of a military takeover threat. On 26 April martial law was imposed by the newly installed government of Nihat Erim (qv). On 17 May, the TPLA kidnapped an Israeli diplomat, Ephraim Elrom (qv) and murdered him. This incident began a manhunt of unprecedented proportions, that somewhat inhibited but did not stop the TPLA. Many TPLA members were shot "resisting arrest" during this period. Turkey recognized Communist China in August. In a bizarre incident in November 1971, a group of imprisoned terrorists were released and after a lengthy investigation of the incident dismissed 68 army officers and enlisted personnel. A large number of other Turks were arrested and charged with conspiracy in the affair. The TPLA continued its reign of terror for the next decade. In April 1972, Erim resigned under heavy political pressure and the always present fear of a military takeover. A caretaker government took over the country. When Turkish attack aircraft participating in a NATO exercise penetrated Greek airspace on 28 March 1974, the Greeks immediately withdrew from the exercise and filed a formal protest. Then, on 7 April, both Greece and Turkey put their forces on alert due to a growing dispute over oil rights in the Aegean Sea. Negotiations held in June to settle the dispute failed. To add to the tension caused by this incident, Turkish forces landed on Cyprus on 20 July 1974, with the intent of preventing a Greek Cypriot seizure of the entire army. The Greeks then mobilized, but it was quickly apparent that their military strength as compared to the Turks was poor. Still, Greece sent troops into Cyprus and reinforced its common border with Turkey in Macedonia. On 22 July, both sides accepted a UN cease-fire order, but the fighting on Cyprus continued. As an untoward part of this action, Turkish fighters sank the Turkish training destroyer *Kocatepe* on 24 July, killing 80 sailors. Forty-two were rescued by an Israeli maritime training vessel. The Cypriot government charged Turkey with repeated truce violations on 31 July. In actuality, although the truce was in effect, Turkish forces on Cyprus continued to expand their operational area throughout August and expelled over 20,000 Greek Cypriots from these areas. Because of the continued threat of war over Cyprus and Turkish recalcitrance at the Geneva peace talks, Greece withdrew from NATO on 15 August. On 16 August, however, Turkey declared a unilateral cease-fire and announced that it had completed its operations on Cyprus, which were aimed at establishing a clear demarcation between Greek and Turkish areas of the island. On 14 September, shortly after taking office, U.S. president Gerald Ford (qv) vetoed a military appropriation for Turkey as a means of forcing the Turks to reevaluate their negotiating strategy on Cyprus. The Turks retaliated by withdrawing from the peace talks on 5 February 1975 and, on 25 July, ordered all U.S. bases in Turkey closed within 24 hours. In September, Turkey gave U.S.–built F-5 "Freedom" fighter aircraft to Libya as a part of an arms deal. Seeing the handwriting on the wall, the U.S. Congress voted to lift the embargo on Turkey on 17 September. Even so, the Geneva peace talks ended in failure on 20 June 1975. On 29 July 1976, the government ordered a military alert as a result of a Greek threat to use military force to protect the Aegean from Turkish penetration. Then, on 15 August, the Turks offered to renew negotiations on the Aegean crisis and ended its military alert (22 August). The crisis continued, however, when the Turks sent an oceanographic research ship into the Aegean on an oil exploration mission. The Greeks immediately put their Aegean naval forces on alert. By 3 October, however, a peaceful solution had been found wherein a demarcation line was established between Turkish and Greek areas of the Aegean. Turkey signed a treaty of friendship with the USSR on 29 December 1975. A huge May Day (1977) rally in Istanbul was disrupted by gunfire from leftist terrorists hiding on nearby rooftops. Thirty were killed and more than 200 injured. On 5 May of that same year, a U.S. congressional committee blocked the sale of F-4 fighters to Turkey as had been proposed by President Carter (qv). Carter asked Congress to lift the 1975 arms embargo on Turkey on 6 April 1978. Congress acted to do so on 1 August 1978. In September 1978, a $2.5 billion International Security Act agreement was signed with Turkey. This led to Turkey allowing the reopening (9 October 1978) of four important intelligence collection stations that had been closed since 1975. Also, on 19 April 1978, the government on Cyprus rejected a Turkish plan to end the lingering Cyprus problem as "inadequate." The United Nations voted to oust Turkey from Cyprus on 9 November. Widespread rioting began in southeastern Turkey between Sunni and Shi'ite Muslim factions on 26 December 1978. Martial law had to be declared in 13 districts to prevent any more than the 100 lives already lost. Although the U.S. and Turkey began negotiations on a new defensive alliance in January 1979, the Turkish government refused to allow U.S. marines stationed at the NATO base at Adana to participate in the evacuation of Americans stranded in Iran (see Iran). As trouble continued in the southeastern districts, the martial law edict was extended two months on 25 February 1979; it was extended again in April. Turkey, Iran and Pakistan all withdrew from CENTO on 15 March. As a continuance of their long campaign against Turkey and the West, the TPLA shot two U.S, servicemen in Izmir. One was killed, the other seriously wounded. The Turks eventually caught the assailants (1981). The TPLA struck again on 14 December 1979, this time killing four Americans in Istanbul. In an effort to improve the climate for the pending summit negotiations on Cyprus, Turkey began withdrawing some of its troops deployed on the island on 1 May 1979. In another move to placate the Soviets, Turkey refused to allow the U.S. to launch SALT verification flights from Turkey or to overfly Turkey on such flights (24 July). By the terms of a new agreement with NATO (January 1980), Turkey authorized the use of 24 bases on its soil. The government of Turkey was overthrown in a bloodless military coup on 12 September 1980. This coup came about in part as a result of the government's inability to check the reign of violence that had plagued the country, even under martial law. The chief of the general staff, General Kenan Evran (qv), became head of state, parliament was dissolved and the constitution suspended. Trouble did not end, however, as the Kurds (qv) blew up an important petroleum pipeline on 28 September 1980. In a continuation of its hard-line policies, the military junta confiscated the assets and abolished all political parties in the country on 16 October 1981. Another pipeline was blown up on 7 January 1982, this time an Iraqi one, by a group known as the Iraqi Mujahedeen Movement (qv). The government signed a treaty with the U.S, on 29 November 1982 that allowed the U.S. use of a number of Turkish airfields. The Council of Europe suspended (27 January 1983) Turkish voting rights until democracy was restored in the country.The rights of most political parties was restored on 24 April. Terrorism continued in Turkey, however, as on 16 June 1983, when members of the Armenian Secret Army for the Liberation of Armenia (ASALA) (qv) indiscriminately opened fire on a crowd in an Istanbul bazaar. Two were killed and 23 injured in that attack. On 10 November 1983, the Turkish National Security Council tightened censorship controls throughout the country. On 5 December, however, the military junta was dissolved and a civilian, Turgut Özal, was decisively elected prime minister. In January 1984, Turkey again reduced the number of troops it had stationed on Cyprus. As progress toward democracy was still moving slowly, the U.S. cut $85 million from the military aid package for Turkey on 9 May 1984. When Greece approved the transfer of forces stationed on the strategically important island of Lemnos in the northern Aegean to NATO control, Turkey accused

Greece (18 November 1984) of using NATO as an instrument of power in the ongoing Greco-Turkish squabble. Greece, in turn, announced that it was shifting forces from its border with Bulgaria to the one facing Turkey. Greece also announced (8 January 1985) that its new defense policy emphasized that Turkey, rather than the Soviet bloc, was the primary threat against its security. When Bulgaria imposed Bulgarian names on its citizens of Turkish origin, Turkey suspended diplomatic relations and withdrew its ambassador (14 February 1985). During these years the state of martial law was gradually lifted, and the economy once again began to flourish. Özal was reelected on 29 November 1987 as a result. The problem of terrorism remained, however, but was beginning to focus again primarily on the Kurdish problem in southeastern Turkey. Even though both Syria and Iran had become friendly toward Turkey, anti-Turkish attacks still appeared to originate from one or the other of these two neighbors. Özal became president of Turkey in November 1989. That same year the Turks opened a broad-scale military operation against the Kurds in what the Turks said was Turkey and the Kurds claimed was a part of the almost mystical Kurdistan. The dispute over Bulgarian mistreatment of Turks living in that country also continued into the 1990s. The former problem was exacerbated by the displacement of Kurds away from the battle area during the Desert Storm operation in 1991. Many of the Kurds began moving into Turkish territory that was still, to the Kurds, Kurdistan, which created great military and political operational and logistical problems for the Turks. In November 1991, Suleyman Demirel, who was ousted in 1980 by the military, again assumed the position of prime minister. When President Özal died on 17 April 1993, a caretaker took his place until 16 May 1993, when Demirel was again made president.. The new prime minister at that time was Tansu Ciller, the first woman to hold that post in history. The year was, however, more closely associated with the terror campaign of the separatists of the Kurdish Worker's Party (PKK). The Kurds kept up a steady campaign, punctuated in March and Arpil by a truce, that carried out ambushes and assaults on military and civilian targets. The Turks retaliated in kind in the southeast region. By November a number of Kurdish guerrillas had been captured, and 15 were sentenced to death. There were also confrontations between the PKK and Islamic fundamentalist factions. The Kurds continued their attacks into 1994. In response, Turkey carried out a massive military campaign against guerrilla bases in northern Iraq. On 8 December, eight radical Kurdish members of Parliament who had been arrested in March were sentenced to 15 years each at hard labor for advocating Kurdish rights. (Four were released in 1995, along with a number of other Kurdish supporters.) Part of the reaction to this and other human rights violations was the U.S. decision to withhold a part of the annual aid package. The U.S. also demanded some progress in settling the Cyprus dispute with Greece. *Reading:* Mehmet Ali Birand, *Shirts of Steel: An Anatomy of the Turkish Armed Forces* (1991); Christos P. Ioannides, *In Turkey's Image: The Transformation of Occupied Cyprus into a Turkish Province* (1991); Richard Knolles, *Turkish History* (1997).

Turkish National Union Committee. *See* Turkey.

Turkish People's Liberation Party/Front (TPLP/F). This Marxist-Maoist terrorist organization, also known as the Turkish People's Liberation Army (TPLA) was formed in the early 1970s, with the avowed purpose of bringing down the government of Turkey. Led by Mahir Cayan and Deniz Gezmis, the TPLA carried out assassinations, bombings, kidnappings and other act of terrorism in the 1970s. Both leaders were killed by Turkish security forces in the early 1970s. On 17 May 1971, the TPLA kidnapped the Israeli consul general, Ephraim Elrom, in Instanbul, demanding the release of political prisoners for his release. His murdered body was discovered on 23 May in an Istanbul apartment less than a quarter-mile from the building housing the Israeli Consulate. Two university student members of TPLA were captured and sentenced to death in December 1971.The Acilciler Faction of TPLA attacked the residence of the U.S. consul in Istanbul using automatic weapons and a pipe bomb. The attack, on 29 March 1977, caused considerable damage, but no injuries. Several suspects were taken into custody. One U.S. serviceman was killed and another seriously injured in Izmir when TPLA terrorists attacked them as they walked down the street on 12 April 1979. In 1981, four people were arrested and charged with the crime. Four more Americans were killed by TPLA terrorists as they returned from work at a NATO base in Istanbul on 14 December 1979. The military coup on 12 September 1980 curtailed most TPLA activity, and most of the 300 TPLA members have been arrested, killed or executed, or have gone to ground. *See* Turkey.

Turkmen Soviet Socialist Republic. *See* Union of Soviet Socialist Republics.

Turko-Syrian Crisis. A short-lived crisis that began when the United States announced plans on 5 September 1957, to increase arms shipments to a group of countries, including Turkey. On 11 September, the USSR complained that Turkey was concentrating troops on the Syrian border. This was followed on 13 September with a Soviet warning to Turkey to stop preparations for an attack on Turkey. Then, on 19 September, Secretary of State John Foster Dulles (qv) accused the Soviet Union of building up Syrian strength for an attack on Turkey. President Nasser (qv) of Egypt announced at the United Nations meeting on 3 October 1957 that his country supported Syria in the growing confrontation with Turkey. Syria accused Turkey of aggression on 10 October, which was added to by Nikita Khrushchev (qv) when he attempted to incite European labor unions against alleged U.S. and Turkish aggression in the Middle East (12 October). On 14 October, Egyptian troops were moved into Syria. That same day, the U.S. informed the USSR that an attack on Turkey would bring a swift military response. The Syrian government then, on 16 October, asked the United Nations to investigate the border dispute with Turkey, while declaring a state of emergency in fear of an immenent Turkish attack. On 20 October, Saudi Arabia offered to mediate the crisis, but Syria immediately rejected the offer. By 31 October, when the Arab League offered its backing to Syria, the tempest in a teapot had already died down.

Turnhalle Alliance. *See* Namibia; Republic of South Africa.

"Turn in your Draft Card Day." A number of anti-Vietnam War groups called 14 November 1968, "Turn in Your Draft Card Day," on which all Americans of draft age were to turn in their draft registration cards and defy the government to draft them for what was considered an illegal and immoral conflict in Southeast Asia. A few did attempt to turn in their cards, but not many.

Tutsi (Batutsi/Watusi) Tribe. *See* Rwanda.

Tuyen Duc Province. *See* Vietnam.

12th of January Liberation Movement. On 27 September 1974, terrorists of the leftist 12th of January Liberation (Freedom) Movement carried out a number of coordinated attacks in the Dominican Republic. In one, they captured the director of the local United States Information Service (USIS) at the Venezuelan consulate in Santo Domingo. In all, seven hostages were taken. The terrorists demanded $1 million in ransom and the release of 38 political prisoners and safe passage out of the country. At first the government refused to deal with the terrorists, but on 9 October the seven hostages, including the USIS officer, were released unharmed. After some negotiation, the terrorists were allowed to fly to Panama, the only ransom demand that was fulfilled.

Tyre (Sour). *See* Lebanon.

Tyrol Area. *See* Austria; Italy.

U

U Aung San. On 19 July 1947, the Anti-Fascist People's Freedom League leader, General U Aung San, and a number of members of the newly established provisional government of Burma were assassinated in Rangoon. The assassins were members of the opposition party of U Saw (qv) and were caught, tried and executed (8 May 1948) for their crime. *See* Myanmar/Burma.

Uganda. The Republic of Uganda (*Jamhuri ya Uganda*) is a landlocked country of eastern Africa. It is bordered on the north by Sudan, on the east by Kenya, on the southeast by Lake Victoria, on the southwest by Rwanda and Tanzania and on the west by Zaire. The capital city is Kampala. The region was originally inhabited by Bantu tribes. By the eighteenth century, Nilo-Hamitic tribes had made inroads in northern Uganda, them moving southward over the next century. A brisk Arab slave and ivory trade operated there in the early to middle nineteenth century. By 1862, the Buganda kingdom of eastern Uganda was visited by Captains John Hanning Speke and James Augustus Grant—Speke (with Sir Richard Francis Burton) had discovered Lake Victoria and the source of the Nile (1858)—who arrived at the lodge of Mtesa (Mutesa) I, Kabaka (king) of Buganda, on 19 February 1862, near present day Kampala. Mtesa allowed British missionaries to preach in Buganda in 1877. His son, Mwanga, upon his assumption of the throne in 1884 began a persecution of Christians and Arabs with the intent of ridding himself of all of them. The Arabs turned the tide and threw out the Christians and Mwanga, seizing the entire kingdom. This was a short-lived Arab victory, however, as the Christians helped put Mtesa back on the throne. A treaty of German protection of Buganda (1889) was abrogated by the Anglo-German treaty of 1890, which put the Uganda region within the British sphere. The Imperial British East African Company took over administration of the region and signed a treaties of protection with Mwanga and the two western kingdoms of Toro and Ankole, thereby assuming control over all of Uganda. Uganda was declared a British protectorate in 1894. During World War I there was some fighting on the southwestern border, but Uganda was not ever in danger of invasion from German Africa as were other areas. Uganda also survived World War II fundamentally unscathed, although Ugandans served with the British overseas forces. The political realities of the postwar era struck Uganda, however, when rioting broke out in Kampala in 1945. As was true for most of Africa, anticolonial unrest began in 1949. Uganda received its independence in 1962, with Milton Obote (qv) as prime minister. On 9 October 1963, Uganda was declared a republic and (Sir Edward) Mutesa II (qv), the Kabaka of Buganda, became its first president. That same year Uganda became a member of the United Nations and the British Commonwealth. Uganda asked for British military assistance in January 1964, to help fight a wave of communist-inspired antigovernment revolts. British forces began to arrive on 25 January. Anti–U.S. rioting broke out in Uganda when it was learned the Americans were supporting the government of Moise Tshombe (qv) in Congo. During 22 February–2 March 1966, however, Obote deposed Mtesa, and proclaimed himself president. Mutesa still the ruler of Buganda province, fled to Kampala and ordered all Ugandan military forces out of his province. On 23–24 April, however, Ugandan federal troops had overrun Kampala, forcing Mutesa to flee to England. In 1967, Obote imposed a new constitution. A would-be assassin wounded Obote as he was leaving a rally in Kampala on 19 December 1969. A state of emergency was declared the following day. While visiting Singapore, the recovered Obote was overthrown in a military coup led by Idi Amin Dada (qv) on 25 January 1971. The new leader then began an immediate campaign to eliminate all opposition to his rule. On 7 July, Amin ordered the border to Tanzania closed to help stop the rebel activity that was emanating from that country. A coup attempt against the Amin government by troops of the northeast garrison failed on 11 July 1971, but news of the attempt was suppressed until mid-October. Ugandan troops began cross-border operations against Tanzania in August 1971, to forestall further incursions of Ugandan rebels from bases there. Claiming that pro-Obote rebels were operating from a Tanzanian army base near the border, Ugandan jets attacked and destroyed it on 20 October. A truce of sorts was thereafter arranged, and Amin reopened the border with Tanzania on 21 November. Fighting also broke out (15 December 1971) along the Sudanese border, although in this case it was between Sudanese regulars and rebels operating from Ugandan bases against Sudan. Amin accused the Israelis of attempting to subvert his regime in March 1972 and refused to renew the military aid pact he had with them. Then, on 4 August 1972, he ordered all noncitizens of Asian descent out of Uganda within 90 days. Foreign journalists began to be arrested in September, after reports the rebel "People's Army" forces supported by Tanzanian regulars had invaded Uganda (17 September). The action, later confirmed, was inconclusive, and Ugandan forces were able to drive out the invaders. On 7 July 1973, Amin had 112 Peace Corps volunteers detained on charges of being "mercenaries." They were released unharmed two day later. In a bizarre incident on 29 October 1973, Amin ordered the U.S. Marine Security Guard at the U.S. embassy in Kampala removed on charges they were carrying out "subversive activities." On 24 March 1974, an abortive military uprising took place, which was not put down by loyal troops until after six hours of bitter fighting. Two days later, Amin began the systematic execution of all officers involved. Amin moved reinforcement to the Tanzanian border on 1 August, after accusing Tanzania of spying. Uganda did withdraw its claim to disputed territory along the common border with Kenya in February 1976, possibly to reduce the number of directions from which threats to the Amin regime could emanate. An attempt on Amin's life failed on 10 June 1976, just 14 days before he had himself proclaimed "president-for-life." In early July 1976, Uganda became the focal point of the Palestinian hijacking of an Air France liner out of Athens, which was flown to Entebbe Airfield near Kampala. On 3–4 July 1976, Israeli commandos carried out a superbly planned and executed raid that led to the release of a number of Jewish and other passengers held at the airfield. Later evaluation of the incident shows without doubt that Idi Amin was directly involved in the affair. Heavy military losses were also incurred by the already debt-ridden Ugandan government. This manifested itself on 8 July, when Kenya ordered the Ugandans to pay, in Kenyan currency, for all Ugandan goods and passengers transiting Kenya because of the monetary debt already owed. Amin then began a bloodbath (11 July) against Kenyans residing in Uganda; those who could fled back to Kenya. On 16 July, Kenyan truck drivers and railway personnel refused to cross into Uganda. Then, on 25 July, Kenya cut off the flow of oil to Uganda, and Idi Amin threatened war. On 30 July, however, Amin agreed to negotiate the problem. Persistent rumors came out of Uganda in February 1977 that Amin had had three opposition leaders, one of them the Anglican archbishop of Uganda, murdered by his secret police, the infamous State Research Unit. In September, Amin banned most Christian church activities, claiming they were subversive. On 12 October 1978, Ugandan radio claimed Tanzanian forces had invaded Uganda. Tanzania replied that the reports were "complete lies." In 27 October 1978, in fact, Amin had invaded Tanzania, annexing about 700 square miles of territory in the Kager Salient (1 November). Then, on 4 November, Amin announced he was withdrawing his forces, but foreign intelligence reported the fighting was continuing. Tanzanian casualties at this point were estimated at about 10,000 killed or wounded. The Tanzanians quickly regrouped and carried the invasion back into Uganda (27 November). On 25 February 1979, Uganda admitted its forces were facing disaster and asked friendly countries for immediate assistance. The only friend that responded was Libya, and Libyan troops began arriving early in March. Even so, Tanzanian troops pushed into Entebbe on 26 March and captured Kampala on 11 April 1979. On 13 April, Idi Amin was expelled from Uganda, thereby ridding the country of his cruel and vicious rule. Amin fled first to Iraq and then to Libya. Even after his departure, however, troops loyal to Amin carried out a number of atrocities while dressed as Tanzanians in an attempt to provoke a pro-Amin uprising against the invaders. On 15 May 1979, Libya paid Tanzania $40 million for the return of Libyan prisoners of war taken during the fighting in Uganda. By 4 June the fighting was over, and the country was under total Tanzanian and Ugandan rebel control. On 5 August, the provisional government of President Godfrey L. Binaisa (qv) offered a substantial reward for the capture and return of Idi Amin. One year after the end of the fighting, at least 10,000 Tanzanian forces still remained in Uganda. In April 1980, they began to withdraw. Provisional governments ruled Uganda until 1980, when Obote was returned to power. On 12 May, troops took over the radio station and central post office in Kampala as military resistance grew against the Binaisa government. Binaisa went to Entebbe and remained under Tanzanian protection. A six-man military commission then took control of the presidency (13 May 1980). On 14 July, Milton Obote was sworn in as president. In April 1981, antigovernment rioting broke out in Kampala after the Uganda Freedom Movement (UFM) carried out a terrorist bomb attack. In response, Tanzania sent an additional 10,000 troops back into Uganda to maintain the tatus quo. Most of these troops were withdrawn by June 1981. UFM activity intensified in 1982; on 23 February the main army barracks in Kampala was attacked in a battle that lasted eight hours. By April, nearly 10,000 had been arrested on charges stemming from the UFM attacks. When the U.S. accused Uganda of committing mass atrocities, Obote's government suspended its military ties with America. On 16 November 1984, about 200 North Korean troops arrived in Uganda to assist in the campaign against the UFM. Still, the UFM bombings and other attacks continued into the new year. On 27 July 1985, Obote was again deposed by the military, who were shortly deposed themselves by a rebel force of the National Resistance Movement (Army) under the leadership of Yoweri Museveni (qv). Museveni signed an accord with the government on 17 December 1985 whereby the two sides would share power. On 26 January 1986, Museveni was sworn in as president and as minister of war. The new government experienced its own problems in 1987, when revolt broke out in northern Uganda, where tribesmen of Milton Obote and Tito Okello (qv), another opposition leader, abided. Regardless of what the government succeeded in doing or failed to do, the fighting continued. Many were murdered in Kampala and around the country. Other groups grew stronger and coalesced against the Museveni government. Cross-border artillery and other shooting incidents involving Kenya also began in late 1987, but they were soon settled. Rebel activity from a growing number of groups continued into 1988, even though Museveni had asked for a cessation of the fighting. In 1989, parliamentary elections were held, but action on a new constitution was postponed. Although a number of elections were contested, the opposition's opportunity to reach the people was denied because all political groups were still banned in Uganda. By the end of 1990, Uganda was again in serious economic trouble. It was also disclosed after the release of 336 prisoners from the 1986 fighting that more than 600 remained imprisoned. Trouble occurred in the north and in the southwest in 1991. When it was discovered that Rwanda rebels were carrying out operations from bases in Uganda, Kenya protested in January 1991 that the Ugandan government had full knowledge of and had abetted the rebel action. Kenya then accused Uganda of helping send young Kenyans to Libya for guerrilla training preparatory to causing trouble in Kenya. Uganda met with Tanzanian and Kenyan representatives in February 1992, in hopes of revitalizing the moribund East African Community. Also, by August 1992 Uganda had settled its dispute with Rwanda. In 1993, Uganda in cooperation with the International Monetary Fund seemed on the road to economic recovery. Uganda still had a one-party political system, but promised the election of a constituent assemby in 1994, even though President Museveni still objected to the multiparty concept. The elections were held on 28 March 1994, and the results were attested by independent observers. The manner in which the election was held proved favorable to Museveni in that he controlled sufficient appointments to the assembly to maintain personal control of the situation. Museveni remained in power in 1995, even through his country still remained one of the poorest in the world. *Reading:* Kenneth Ingham, *Obote: A Political Biography* (1994); Thomas P. Ofcansky, *Uganda: Tarnished Pearl of Africa* (1996); Phares Mutibwa, *Uganda since Independence: A Story of Unfulfilled Hopes* (1992).

Ugheli. *See* Nigeria.

Uitenhage. *See* Republic of South Africa.

Ulbricht, Walter. (b. 30 June 1893, Leipzig, Germany—d. 1 August 1973, East Berlin) Ulbricht apprenticed as a cabinetmaker and joined the Social Democratic Party (SPD) in pre-World War I Germany. During the war he served on the Russian front with the German army, from which he twice deserted. After the war he joined the German Communist Party (KPD) and was elected to its central committee in 1923. He was elected to the federal lower house (*Reichstag*) in 1928 and was KPD chairman in Berlin from 1929. He was forced to flee when Adolf Hitler came to power in 1933, and for five years he served the Comintern and the KPD at various posts in Paris, Moscow and Spain, during the Spanish Civil War (1936–1939). Ulbricht returned to Moscow and remained there during World War II, spending his time proselytizing German prisoners of war to communism. He returned to Germany in the Soviet "baggage train" in April 1945 and helped rebuild the KPD in East Germany. He was also in charge of administering the the Soviet-occupied zone. Ulbricht played a key role in the amalgamation of the KPD and the SPD into the Socialist Unity Party in 1946. When the German Democratic Republic was declared on 11 October 1949 (*see* Germany), he was appointed deputy prime minister in addition to the post as SED secretary general in 1950. He became chairman of the East German Council of State in 1960 and thereafter carried out a program of liquidation of all opposition. His power became so great that he was able to block the de-Stalinization process in East Germany. Ulbricht throughout remained absolutely opposed to any rapprochement with the West, especially West Germany. This stance led to his forced retirement as secretary general of the SED in May 1971, a move obviously sanctioned by Moscow. But his past service was such that he was allowed to retain his post as chairman of the Council of State until his death. *Reading:* Gregory W. Sanford, *From Hitler to Ulbricht: The Communist Reconstruction of East Germany* (1983).

Ulster. *See* Northern Ireland.

Um-Aish. *See* Kuwait.

Umberto II. *See* Italy.

Umn Qasr. *See* Iraq.

Umuahia, Biafra. *See* Nigeria.

Unified Popular Action Front. On 29 January 1980, leftist rebels of the Unified Popular Action Front seized a church in Ilobasco, El Salvador, in retaliation for the killing of 22 demonstrators at a large leftist rally on 23 January. A group of civilians representing other views opened fire on the crowd. Army troops stormed the church, killing three of the terrorists. This incident was but one of many in 1980 in which right-wing "death squads" precipitated the deaths of innocent civilians as El Salvador experienced the first stages of civil war. Some 4,000 died in the first half of the year.

Union of Central African States. On 4 February 1968, the Union of Central African States (UEAC) was created. Three nations initialed the charter: Chad, Congo-Kinshasa and the Central African Republic. The formal signing of the charter took place on 2 April. On 13 December 1968, President Bokassa (qv) of the Central African Republic pulled his country out of the agreement to rejoin instead the Central African Customs and Economic Union. This created much antagonism, especially from Congo-Kinshasa, especially since Congo-Brazzaville was a member of the latter group and, at the moment, at odds with Congo-Kinshasa. UEAC never accomplished its goals.

Union of South Africa. *See* Republic of South Africa.

Union of Soviet Socialist Republics (USSR). *See* Introduction.

United Arab Emirates (UAE) (*Dawlat al-Imarat al-'Arabiyah al-Muttahidah***).** Seven unified emirates on the eastern coast of the Arabian Peninsula comprise the UAE. Excavations at Bahrain and Kuwait attest to those areas' importance as trading and commercial centers of the Persian Gulf. The UAE is bounded on the north by the Gulf of Oman, on the northeast and southeast by Oman, on the east by the Gulf of Oman, on the south and southwest by Saudi Arabia and on the northwest by Qatar. The capital city is Abu Dhabi, although each emirate has a chief town. Almost 90 percent of of the UAE is the emirate of Abu Dhabi; the other five original members are Dubai, 'Ajman, Ash-Shariqah, Umm al-Qaywayn and Al-Fujayrah. Ra's-Khaymaj, the seventh state, joined later. The region has been occupied since Sumerian times (c. 3000 B.C.), and was known even then as a rich trading and commerce complex. Conversion to Islam occurred during the time of the Phophet Muhammad but required reinforcement to maintain the Muslim beliefs from non-Sunni sects, especially those from Iran (Shi'ite), across the gulf. Many succumbed to Shi'ism, however, and converted. By the early sixteenth century, Portuguese explorers had visited the region and carried on some enterprise there. The British East India Company arrived in the late seventeenth century and established some commercial ties, but they were never allowed to settle and were subjected to piracy on a regular basis. The British attacked the coastal towns in 1819–1820 and forced concessions (1820) which caused a reduction in piracy and increased trade. The Treaty of Maritime Peace in Perpetuity (1853) gave the area the name "Trucial States" and included Qatar and Bahrein. The 1892 Treaty of Exclusive Agreements with the Rulers of the Trucual States gave Great Britain protector status over the region. British India administered the states until 1947, when with the independence of India, the British Foreign Office took administrative control. The Trucial States were unique in that Great Britain never established any of the "standard" colonial appendages to them and they each maintained complete control in all things except foreign policy. A Trucial States Council was established in 1960 in which each state was represented. On 18 July 1971, following the general withdrawal of Great Britain from the Persian Gulf, the Trucial States combined, first into the Federation of Arab Emirates and then, on 2 December 1971, into the United of Arab Emirates (UAE), but Bahrain and Qatar chose separate independence. Trucial Oman joined as Dubai. Ra's al-Khaymah, after at first refusing, joined a year later on 10 February 1972. By that point, the UAE had already joined the Arab League and the United Nations. Before that, however, on 24 January 1972, Sheikh Khalid bin Mohammed al-Qasmi (qv), the ruler of Sharjah ('Ajman, Ash-Shariqah), was killed in a coup led by his cousin, Sheikh Saqr bin Mohammed al-Qasmi (qv), who had been deposed as ruler in 1965. Khalid's younger brother, Sheikh Sultan bin Mohammed al-Qasmi (qv), became the new ruler of Sharjah. In June 1972, tribal warfare broke out between Sharjah and Fujairah. Only about 20 people were killed in the border conflict, which was settled by the UAE's leader, Sheikh Zaid ibn Sultan an-Nahayan (qv), after intervention by a UAE military force. After March 1978, France began supplying arms to the UAE. Mass demonstrations in favor of Sheikh Zaid's plan to do away with borders inside the UAE and combine the armed forces took place on 19 March 1979. When the UAE suppressed PLO activities in the country, the Arab Revolutionary Brigades, an Abu Nidal (qv) offshoot, retaliated by blowing up an Omani airliner over the emirates, killing 111 people (23 September 1983). On 15 November 1985, the UAE opened diplomatic relations with the Soviet Union. Sheikh Zaid was reelected federal president in 1986, and the articles of federation for the UAE were extended an additional five years. In 1986, at the height of the Iraq-Iran War (qv), the UAE once again opened a dialogue with the PLO. The UAE also suffered considerable loss of income as a side effect of the nearby fighting. Another coup was attempted in Sharjah in June 1987, when the ruler's older brother, Sheikh Abdel-Aziz, threatened him. A news report (17 June) about a successful takeover was somewhat exaggerated, but Abdel-Aziz was named crown prince and deputy ruler on 23 June. The UAE began to recover from the effects of the Iraq-Iran War in 1988 and were wooed by the Iranians. Poland and East Germany also courted the UAE as a means of obtaining hard-to-get petroleum. In 1989, the UAE purchased over $170 million in British arms. Dubai's ruler, Sheikh Rashid ibn Daid al-Maktum, who had been incapacitated by a stroke in 1981, died on 7 October 1990. Rashid had also been vice president of the UAE. He was replaced in Dubai by his eldest son, who had in effect ruled since the onset of his father's illness. A third coup took place in Sharjah on 4 February 1990. This time, Sheikh Sultan rid himself of his elder brother, Abdel-Aziz, who had been crown prince and deputy ruler since 1987. The UAE became involved in the scandal following the collapse of the Bank of Credit and Commerce International (BCCI) in July 1991. This fiasco, in which Abu Dhabi had been a major shareholder, strained the UAE's reputation with the international banking industry, especially the Bank of England. A number of Abu Dhabi financial executives associated with the BCCI were arrested as the UAE went about rebuilding the BCCI. The UAE also gave unstinting support to the coalition against Iraq during the Desert Storm operation, including the billeting of American and French forces and the use of naval facilities. UAE troops fought alongside other coalition forces in the liberation of Kuwait and suffered at least six casualties. The UAE also underwrote more than $3 billion of the cost of the war. The UAE position toward Iran soured in 1992, after Iran refused to negotiate the fate of the Tunb Islands and Abu Musa, which were seized by Iran during the Iraq-Iran War. One theory was that Iran feared the UAE would turn the islands over to U.S. control if it released them. When the UAE announced it would submit the question to international arbitration, Iran rejoined the negotiations (May 1993). On 13 October 1993, 13 BCCI officials went on trial after Abu Dhabi filed a $9 billion lawsuit against the group for forgery and bank fraud. The bank's founder, who was tried in absentia, was sentenced (1994) to eight years in prison, once he was apprehended. By 1994, the islands issue had not yet been settled with Iran, and in December the UAE referred the case to the International Court of Justice. In July 1995, the UAE signed a defense agreement with the United States. This may account for Iran's continued obstinacy over releasing the Tunb Islands and Abu Musa. *Reading:* Abdullah Omram Taryam, *The Establishment of the United Arab Emirates, 1950-1985* (1987); Frauke Heard-Bey, *From Trucial States to United Arab Emirates* (1981); Rosemarie Said Zahlan, *The Origins of the United Arab Emirates: A Political and Social History of the Trucial States* (1978); Malcolm C. Peck, *The United Arab Emirates: A Venture in Unity* (1986).

United Arab Republic (UAR). The UAR was proclaimed on 1 February 1958 by Egypt's Gamal Abdul Nasser (qv) and Syria's Shukri al-Kuwatly (qv) and was later approved by the two countries in national referenda. The UAR faced its first challenge on 6 June 1958, when Lebanon accused it of aggression in the United Nations. The UN then moved observer teams into Lebanon (11 June) to investigate the allegations. On 15–19 July, Lebanon claimed the UAR was provoking civil war in its country. In December 1960, the UAR, along with Yugoslavia and Ceylon, pulled its forces out of the UN peacekeeping force from their almost impossible mission in Congo. On 7 January 1961, the UAR joined Ghana, Guinea, Mali and Morocco in creating an organization of African states under what became known as the Charter of Casablanca (qv). The UAR existed for just over three years, until 28 September 1961, when a military coup overthrew the government of Syria and the new government abrogated the union. Nasser had been prepared to send Egyptian troops into Syria to help curb the violence that preceded the takeover, but events moved too swiftly for the Egyptian reaction. The UAR broke diplomatic relations with Yemen on 26 December 1961, after it had decided to throw its support behind the rebels operating in North Yemen. Egypt retained the name UAR until 2 September 1971, when the Arab Republic of Egypt was declared. *See* Egypt and Syria, especially Egypt, for the period after September 1961. *Reading:* Donald N. Wilber, ed., *United Arab Republic - Egypt* (1969); John Allan Carpenter, *Egypt (United Arab Republic)* (1972).

United Front for the Liberation of Zimbabwe (FROLIZI). On 1 October 1971, the two principal black politicomilitary organizations opposing white rule in Rhodesia, the Zimbabwe African People's Union (ZAPU), and the Zimbabwe African National Union (ZANU), combined into the United Front for the Liberation of Zimbabwe (FROLIZI). This move came about almost two months before the white government of Rhodesia and Great Britain announced an accord that would have ended Rhodesia's isolation but would have done little to give equality to its black citizens. On 21 December 1972, FROLIZI rebels attacked a white-owned farm in the first terrorist attack since 1966. *See* Zimbabwe.

United Kingdom, *See* Great Britain.

United Nations. Originally, the term "United Nations" was used to describe the Allies during late-World War II. As the second international organization of the twentieth century, it was formed out of a universal desire to maintain peace and equilibrium in the world. The United Nations Conference on International Organization met at San Francisco from 25 April to 26 June 1945. The first such organization, the League of Nations (qv), was formed at the end of World War I and was moribund by the time Hitler ascended to power in Germany in 1933. At the San Francisco meeting, the Charter of the United Nations was signed by 50 nations on 26 June. Poland was the 51st nation to sign (15 October 1945) and was considered one of the charter members of the new organization. The charter came into effect on 24 October, upon ratification by the five permanent members of the Security Council—the United States, United Kingdom, France, China and the USSR (until 1991, then Russia) and a majority of the original signatories. The role of the League of Nations was assumed by the UN, and many of the League's agencies were absorbed into its new framework. The League was formally disbanded in 1946. The Security Council originally had five permanent members and six nonpermanent seats that were rotated periodically among the member nations on a group or regional basis. The number of nonpermanent seats was increased to ten in 1965, because of the increased number of national memberships in the organization. Each permanent member can exercise a veto, which effectively prohibits the execution of any Security Council decision. The USSR and the U.S. exercised their veto prerogatives on a regular basis. Another important instrument of the UN is the International Court of Justice (also known as the World Court). This body is located in The Hague and exercises judicial control, although its decisions have often been ignored by offending nations, who simply claim the court has no jurisdiction. A number of other programs and agencies within the UN structure have played roles in the resolution of conflict and in the public good. The UN peacekeeping forces are part of a program designed to keep or impose peace. Not always successful in this area, the UN has suffered criticism because of a lack of structure that has often (as in Somalia) been mismanaged by civilian representatives without the necessary military acumen and by forces bound by national rules. The primary tool available to the UN for maintaining peace is a General Assembly resolution suspending the offending nation. Yugoslavia, for example, was suspended in 1992 for violations stemming from the fighting in Bosnia-Herzogovina. By the 1990s, more than 175 nations were members of the United Nations. *See* individual nations for their interaction with the UN.

United Popular Front. On 16 January 1979, the Mexican Embassy, the offices of the Organization of American States and those of the Red Cross in El Salvador were seized by about 30 terrorist members of the United Popular Front. More than 120 hostages were taken for ransom by the terrorists who, among other things, demanded the release of political prisoners. The siege lasted 48 hours, at which point the terrorists gave up most of their demands but were allowed safe passage to Mexico. *See* El Salvador.

United Progressive Party. In Zambian elections held in December 1971, Simon Kapwepwe of the United Progressive Party (UPP) won a seat in the National Assembly. A long period of violence then followed, much of which was instigated by the African National Congress. None of the other UPP candidates won. However, on 4 February 1972, President Kenneth Kaunda (qv) banned the UPP and arrested its leaders, including Kapwepwe, on charges of treason stemming from a UPP effort to isolate the northern province. Kaunda then moved to install a one-party system in his country. *See* Zambia.

United States of America. *See* Introduction.

United States of the Congo. *See* Zaire.

Universal Declaration of Human Rights. On 9–10 December 1948, the United Nations General Assembly adopted the Universal Declaration of Human Rights drafted by the Commission on Human Rights. Although also mentioned in the 1945 UN charter document, the issue of human rights was never clarified to a point where the member nations were bound to adherence, as the "domestic jurisdiction" clause in the charter and the variety of social conditions within the membership left the subject too vague for application. In 1948, the Commission on Human Rights began a draft of a covenant that would have been binding, but this was subsumed into a document that included economic and cultural conditions as well and that was submitted to the General Assembly in 1954. In 1964, nothing had been accomplished. In 1965, however, an international convention went out for signature. Even if it were approved, the United Nations would have little recourse in cases brought before the body under its terms. *See* United Nations, Apartheid, South Africa, Romania and Hungary, for examples.

University of Caracas. *See* Venezuela.

University of Fort Hare. *See* Republic of South Africa.

University of Pristina. *See* Yugoslavia.

U Nu. (b. 25 May 1907, Wakema, Burma—d. 14 February 1995, Rangoon) Born Thakin Nu, U Nu attended the University of Rangoon (Yangôn), receiving his degree in 1929. After serving as headmaster of the National High School in Pantanaw, he returned to the university to study law (1934). There, he entered student politics and became president of the Student Union. He and a colleague, U Aung San (qv), were expelled in 1936 because of these political activities. The expulsion led to student rioting that was notable not so much for its intensity as for its being the first confrontation between a new generation of Burmese and British authority. The rioting catapulted U Nu into national prominence as a leader of Burmese nationalism. In 1937, he joined the We-Burmans Association and, in 1940, was imprisoned by the British for his independence activities. When the Japanese invaded Burma, he was released. In 1943, U Nu joined the Ba Maw government as foreign minister, where he learned much about the Japanese invaders. In July 1947, after U Aung San was assassinated, U Nu became the nominal leader of the Anti-Fascist People's Freedom League and the new head of government for Burma. Upon independence in January 1948, he became the nation's first prime minister, serving almost continuously in that office for the next ten years. The period 1948–1958 in Burmese history was one of communist infiltration an ethnic violence (*see* Myanmar/Burma). On 26 September 1958, U Nu requested an army takeover and resigned. A military government sympathetic to the communists and headed by General Ne Win (qv) took over the leadership of the country. In February 1960, when a parliament government was restored, U Nu was again elected prime minister. On 2 March 1962, however, a military coup led by Ne Win toppled the government, and U Nu was imprisoned. Upon his release seven years later (1969), U Nu left Myanmar (Burma) and established a resistance movement to fight the Ne Win regime. When the resistance movement failed, U Nu settled in India, but upon Ne Win's invitation (1980), he returned to Myanmar, where he became a Buddhist monk. He died peacefully in 1995.

Uongbi. *See* Vietnam.

Upper Volta. *See* Burkina Faso.

Urcuyo Malianos, Francisco. When President Anastasio Somoza (qv) fled the country on 17 July 1979, to avoid possible capture by the Sandinistas (qv), the government of Nicaragua continued with Francisco Urcuyo Malianos as head of state. Urcuyo's first act was to announce his refusal to deal with the Sandinistas. His second act in office was to flee the country on 19 July. At that point the Sandinistas took control of the government.

Urgun. *See* Afghanistan.

Urias, Cesar Yanes. On 26 October 1960, President Jose Maria Lemus (qv) was overthrown in a coup led by Colonel Cesar Yanes Urias. A six-man junta then took control of the country and, three months later, held democratic elections.

Urriolagoita, Mamerto. On 16 May 1951, a military junta led by General Hugo Ballivan (qv) forced the resignation of President Mamerto Urriolagoita. Urriolagoita had been in office since 1949, when as vice-president he had replaced Enrique Hertzog, who was incapacitated by illness. When the elections of 1951 placed Victor Pas Estenssoro (qv) in office, the junta moved to take power and void the election.

Urrutia, Bolivar. On 11 October 1968, a military coup d'etat led by the Panamanian National Guard ousted the recently seated government of President Arnulfo Arias (qv). A military junta then elected Colonel Jose Pinilla as the provisional president and Colonel Bolivar Urrutia as the country's power behind the throne. Before the end of 1969, however, both had been replaced by Colonel Omar Torrijos (qv), who became the power in Panama.

Uruguay (*República Oriental del Uruguay*). A country of southeastern South America, the Oriental Republic of Uruguay is bordered on the north and northeast by Brazil, on the southeast by the Atlantic Ocean, on the south by Argentina, although separated by the great estuary of the Rio de la Plata, and on the west by Argentina. The capital city is Montevideo. Uruguay was originally inhabited by tribes belonging to the Charruas culture, who were largely wiped out by the eighteenth century. Spanish explorers arrived in 1516 and explored the mouth of the Rio de la Plata, but not until 1680, when the Portuguese were operating from their colony in Barazil, a settlement put down at *Colonia del Sacramento* on the Plata. In 1726, the Spaniards established their own settlement at Montevideo, driving off the Portuguese in the process. In 1776, the Uruguaryan area was incorporated into the Rio de la Plata Viceroyalty. Uruguay fought and lost a five-year battle for independence in 1816, and was occupied by a joint Spanish-Brazilian force until 1828, when, after three years of struggle, the country received its independence. From 1839 to 1859 an inconclusive civil war was fought; and from 1865 to 1870 Uruguay fought a war with Paraguay, mainly because of Argentine and Brazilian meddling. Thereafter, Uruguay came under military rule until 1903, when a Colorado (Red) Party candidate, Jose Batlle y Odroñoz, was elected president. Batlle y Ordoñoz held power until 1929, during which time Uruguay established a stable political and economic base. A period of dictatorship carried the country through World War II, and in 1951 a new constitution was adopted. In 1958, a Nationalist (White) Party government was established, which almost immediately brought about an economic crisis in the country that led to an eruption of leftist rebel activity. Principal among the terrorist threats facing Uruguay during this period was that posed by the leftist Tupamaro (qv) rebel activity, which began in earnest in 1967. A state of emergency was declared in June 1968, which remained in place until 15 March 1969, when President Jorge Pacheco Areco (qv) began lifting some of the restrictions imposed. A rise in unrest, especially among students, forced the government to reassert the state of siege on 24 June 1969. Tupamaro activity continued to grow and become more violent as the year progressed. On 8 October 1969, for instance, Tupamaro guerrillas captured the town of Pando.

The army had to use force to eject them. From that point, Tupamaro activity grew and began to include the kidnapping and murder of diplomats and high goverment officials and bombings. The Tupamaros had turned urban and become the major threat to Uruguay's security. Prisons were not safe, as the Tupamaros opened them seemingly at will. A truce was arranged, but the Tupamaros broke it on 22 December 1971 by blowing up a golf course. The situation became so bad that, on 15 April 1972, a "state of war" was declared against the rebel group. The "war" ended on 11 July, after the Tupamaros had been decimated, but not destroyed. The head of the Tupamaros was captured on 1 September 1972. Even so, the chaos caused by the "war" led to the presentation of 19 demands by the military on 10 February 1973, led to a right-wing military coup on 14 February 1973 and reversed the trend but also imposed a period of civil rights and other abuses, quite often common to military governments. On 27–30 June, for example, parliamentary government was suspended, the Congress dismissed and a ruling Council of State imposed. This led to a general strike on 29 June, which led President Bordaberry to abolish the National Confederation of Labor the next day. On 1 July, the military occupied Montevideo. On 13 February 1974, the leading rebel groups in Uruguay, Argentina, Bolivia and Chile announced a coalition of "revolutionary coordination" to continue their fight. Finally, on 12 June 1976, Bordaberry was removed from office in a bloodless military coup. Alberto Demicheli (qv) was appointed provision president, and remained in power until an election on 1 September moved Aparicio Mendez (qv) into the presidential office. The military still held firm control, however. In February 1977, the Uruguayan government rejected all U.S. military aid after being criticized for its human rights violations. By late 1983, the populace was becoming more and more restive over the military leadership of the government. On 25 September, at least 25,000 marched in Montevideo against the military. A much larger demonstration took place on 27 November, when 300,000 took to the streets demanding a return to democracy. On 18 January 1984, a general strike, the first in over ten years, paralyzed Uruguay. Opposition White (*Blanco*) Party leaders were rounded up on 16 June 1984, in what appeared to be a conspiracy between Uruguay and Argentina. The Argentine ferry carrying the *Blanco* leader, Wilson Ferreira (qv), and his party was captured in Uruguayan waters, after the ferry "strayed" into Uruguayan space. That fact that Ferreira was on his way to Montevideo for a meeting seemed not important. A new civilian government was installed in 1985, which ended most of these abuses of power and brought the country back onto the road toward democracy. Even so, all was not calm in Uruguay. Opposition unions continued to strike, but there was movement toward national consensus. The years 1987–1989 passed uneventfully, although there were charges of police abuse of power. Elections in 1989 cut the Colorado majority and gave considerable power to the National White Party, including the presidency. Numerous strikes hit the country in 1991, aimed at higher wages to offset the increased cost of the necessities of life. Strikes continued into 1992 as the inflationary spiral continued to rise. At about this point, the International Monetary Fund (IMF) reminded Uruguay about its promised fiscal reforms, which had not yet achieved their goals but which had to be made to work. While 1993 proved to be another year of political squabbling that largely caused the problem of inflation, the major crisis of the year was caused by the bizarre circumstances surrounding the kidnapping of a Chilean secret agent by a joint Argentine, Chilean and Uruguayan military team. He was sequestered in Uruguay, whence he escaped, and after turning himself in to the police, he was given back to the military. He again escaped to Italy, but as he was thought dead at the hands of the Uruguayan military, his case created an internal furor in Uruguay and a near confrontation between the military and the civilian government. Elections held in 1994 once again witnessed a change in government back to the center-right Colorados. President Julio Maria Sanguinetti took his office on 1 March 1995 and immediately imposed a severe austerity program to return the country to normalcy. *Reading:* Saul Sosnowski & Louise B. Popkin, eds., *Repression, Exile, and Democracy: Uruguayan Culture* (1992); Philip Bates Taylor, *Government and Politics of Uruguay* (1984); Luis E. Gonzalez, *Political Structures and Democracy in Uruguay* (1992); Martin Weinstein, *Uruguay: The Politics of Failure* (1975); Edy Kaufman, *Uruguay in Transition: From Civilian to Military Rule* (1979); Servico Paz Y Justica Uruguay, *Uruguay Nunca Mas: Human Rights Violations, 1972-1985* (1992); William C. Davis, *Warnings from the South: Democracy versus Dictatorship in Uruguay, Argentina, and Chile* (1995).

U Saw. (b. 1900, Tharrawaddy, Burma—d. 8 May 1948, Rangoon) U Saw never received a formal education, but he held a license to practice some types of law in Burma and as such was involved in the defense of the leader of a peasant revolt in 1930–1932. Thereafter, U Saw called himself Galon U Saw, where "Galon" stood for the name of the peasant rebel army. U Saw later became a member of the Burmese legislative council and a newspaper editor. He visited Japan in 1935 and was geatly impressed by the authoritarian Japanese system. In 1938, he founded the Patriot (*Myochit*) Party and organized a new Galon army, which was modeled after his concept of Nazi *Sturmtruppen*. In 1939, U Saw was instrumental in the overthrow of Prime Minister Ba Maw and himself became prime minister in 1940–1942. After failing to receive dominion status for Burma in London in 1941, U Saw travelled to Lisbon, where he met in secret with Japanese representatives in an effort to strike a deal on Burma. He was arrested by the British in Haifa on his trip home and imprisoned in Uganda until war's end. In 1945, upon returning to Burma, he reactivated the Patriot Party and became the chief opposition to U Aung San's (qv) Anti-Fascist People's Freedom Party. U Saw accompanied U Aung San to London, but he refused to participate in the signing of Burma's independence agreement with Prime Minister Clement Attlee (qv), wanting a more favorable deal than he thought had been struck by U Aung San. U Saw's party was thoroughly defeated in the April 1947 elections in Burma. On 19 July 1947, U Saw ordered the assassination of U Aung San and his new cabinet. For his crimes, U Saw was tried, convicted and executed. *See* Myanmar/Burma.

Ushusia. *See* Argentina.

Ussuri River. *See* China; Manchuria.

Usulutan. *See* El Salvador.

U Tapao Airbase. *See* Thailand.

U Thant. (b. 22 January 1909, Pantanaw, Burma—d. 25 November 1974, New York City) Born into moderate means in Burma (Myanmar) U Thant attended the University of Rangoon (*Yangôn*) and the Rangoon Arts and Sciences University. He did not finish the latter because of the death of his father, but he did have the opportunity to meet Thakin Nu (later U NU [qv]) there and became friends with him. During World War II, U Thant was active against the Japanese occupation of his country, and after the war he was recruited into government service by U Nu and U Aung San (qv). In 1947, U Thant became press secretary and then director of broadcasting in 1948. When U Nu became prime minister, U Thant was elevated to secretary for the minister of information. From 1952 until 1953, he served as a Burmese delegate to the UN and became Burma's permanent delegate in 1957. He was elected vice-president of the UN General Assembly in 1959. He was a compromise choice for acting secretary-general of the UN following the death of Dag Hammarskjöld (qv) (1961). During his acting tenure, U Thant proposed that a UN inspection team be sent to Cuba to monitor the Soviet missile sites there that had created the Cuban Missile Crisis (*see* Cuba). He was elected the third permanent secretary-general of the United Nations on 2 December 1962. That same month, he urged the United States to immediately stop bombing North Vietnam. Over his own personal objections, he was reelected to that post for an additional five years on 2 December 1966. U Thant was found to be critical of both the East and the West in the Cold War. For example, he criticized North Vietnam when it rejected his "stand still" proposal to end the war in South East Asia (28 March 1967). He was forced to back down by Egypt's Nasser (qv) on 18 May 1967, after Nasser demanded the UN emergency force leave the Sinai. Although U Thant had no other legal options, he was criticized for withdrawing the force. The 1967 Arab-Israeli War followed. U Thant worked on tirelessly, attempting to end the war in Southeast Asia. In February 1968, he said that if the U.S. would stop its bombing of the north, North Vietnam would open "meaningful" negotiations to end the struggle. Throughout his time in office he worked to end fighting wherever it occurred, especially in the Middle East. In September 1967, he recommended that Communist China be included in future arms talks, even though China was not a UN member. At the end of his tenure, he retired (1971) and remained in New York, where he underwent treatment for cancer, to which he succumbed in November 1974. His death did not end his saga, however, as, after his body was returned to Rangoon for burial, it was stolen by university students on 5 December 1974 and interred in a mausoleum at the Arts and Sciences University. Found there by the police, the body was forcibly recovered and reburied privately on 11 December, in a concrete tomb. This whole affair created disorder in Rangoon that required the ruling junta (*see* Myanmar) to declare martial law. Several people were killed in the accompanying rioting.

Uttar Pradesh. *See* India.

V

Vafiades, Markos. (b. 28 January 1906, Asia Minor—d. 22 February 1992, Athens, Greece) Born in what is present-day Turkey, Vafiades worked as a laborer in Istanbul before having to flee the country in 1923. After settling in Greece, he became the founder of the Greek Communist Party. In May 1946, the Greek Civil War began when communist rebels, led by Vafiades, seized control of key border installations in northern Greece. The Greek communists were aided by Soviet-controlled Albania, Bulgaria and, at that time, Yugoslavia. The war would last until October 1949. On 24 December 1947, Vafiades, who called himself "General Marcos," proclaimed the First Provisional Democratic Government of Free Greece, which encompassed most of the northern mountains of Macedonia. By that point some 20,000 rebel insurgents were under his command. When Yugoslavia defected from the Soviet bloc to steer its own course, the Yugoslav border was closed to Vafiades and his rebels, and the Greek Civil War collapsed. Vafiades fled the region, settling in the Soviet Union. Running afoul of Stalin, he was purged from the party in 1950 but was later rehabilitated (1956). In 1964, however, he was again purged for five years. Restored in 1969, he returned to Greece, where he received an amnesty (1983) and was eventually elected (1989) to the parliament as a Panhellenic Socialist. *See* Greece.

Vakis, Christos. On 27 July 1973, Cyprus's minister of justice, Christos Vakis, was kidnapped by followers of General Georgios (George) Grivas (qv), the leader of the movement aimed at uniting Cyprus under Greece. This incident stunned Cyprus as it illustrated the strength of the Greek rebel forces. Vakis was released unharmed in August amid rumors that Grivas's next target was the assassination of Bishop Makarios. Grivas vehemently denied the charge.

Valencia. *See* Spain.

***Valhalla* Incident.** On 17 October 1984, U.S. customs officers seized the 82-foot fishing trawler *Valhalla*, which was claimed to be smuggling weapons from the United States to the Irish Republican Army (IRA). This was the second such confiscation within 30 days. Irish naval units had intercepted and captured another ship carrying IRA members and five tons of arms on 29 September.

That capture and the later taking of the *Valhalla* was a part of a two-year undercover operation involving the FBI, the CIA and Irish and British intelligence organizations. Evidence taken off the first ship indicated that the New York Irish Aid Committee had contracted for the weapons purchases. This led to an international hunt for the second ship, which was soon identified as *Valhalla*.

Valverde Barbery, Carlos. A former minister of health in Bolivia, Valverde led a right-wing coup attempt against the government of Hugo Banzer-Suarez (qv) on 20 August 1973. The coup failed. Valverde was allowed to escape to Paraguay.

Vance, Cyrus Robert. (b. 27 March 1917, Clarksburg, West Virginia) Vance received his undergraduate education from Yale University, graduating in 1939. He went back to Yale for a degree in law which he received in 1942. He served four years in the U.S. Navy during World War II, after which he joined a New York law firm. Vance became the general counsel of the Department of Defense in 1960 and was appointed secretary of the army in 1962. President Lyndon Johnson (qv) appointed him deputy secretary of defense in 1963. After his resignation in 1967, he became an outspoken critic of U.S. policy in Southeast Asia and used his influence in an attempt to dissuade the administration from continuing its bombing of North Vietnam. Johnson appointed Vance as deputy chief delegate to the Paris peace talks on Vietnam in 1968. He returned to private practice in 1969. President Carter (qv) appointed Vance secretary of state in 1977, where he became a proponent of quiet diplomacy, working on the problems of detente and SALT. He also had a major role in the Camp David Accords that at least lightened the horizon in the Middle East. He was involved in the negotiations dealing with the U.S. diplomatic hostages being held in Iran, but resigned in protest of not having been consulted about the Carter-managed fiasco of the failed rescue attempt. Thereafter he returned to private practice, this time for good.

Vandor, Augusto. On 30 June 1969, a limited state of siege was imposed on Argentina following the assassination of Augusto Vandor, the head of the Metal Workers Union. The 49-year-old Vandor was shot and killed by unidentified assassins during the violence surrounding the visit of Nelson Rockefeller to Argentina. Vandor had refused to support a general strike call issued by labor factions that opposed the Organia (qv) government. *See* Argentina.

Van Tuong. *See* Vietnam.

Vanuniya. *See* Sri Lanka.

Vargas, Getulio. On 25 October 1945, Brazil's president, Getulio Vargas, was forced to resign after a 15-year dictatorship. He was temporarily replaced by Chief Justice Jose Linhares (qv). On 3 October 1950, Vargas was reelected president. He was forced to resign again on 8 August 1954, following widespread disorder throughout the country. Vice President Joao Cafe Filho was installed in his place. On 24 August 1954, Vargas apparently committed suicide.

Vathana, Savang. *See* Laos.

Vatican, The. Officially the State of Vatican City (*Stato della Citta del Vaticano*), the Vatican is the seat (Holy See) of the Roman Catholic Church. It is located in

Rome, Italy, on the west bank of the Tiber River. The Pope becomes the chief executive of the state upon election and has an administrative, legislative and judicial staff for separate from the staff of the Holy See for its operation. Most of the city is closed to the public. On 11 February 1929, the fascist government of Italy signed the Lateran Treaty (Treaty of Conciliation), which gave the Vatican sovereignty over its territory, which has existed in one form or another since the fourth century. Although the Vatican state held itself aloof from World War II, it harbored a large number of people, Christians and Jews, who were escaping the fascist tyranny. The Vatican's role in world affairs, especially in conflict and resolution, has often been shrouded in secrecy, which is not to say it has been without impact. The intercession of the Pope carries great weight in many nations, especially those such as Poland with a large Catholic population. On 1 July 1949, for example, a decree was announced that excommunicated all Roman Catholics adhering to communism. The Tito government in Yugoslavia broke diplomatic relations with the Vatican because the Vatican refused to intercede on the part of Yugoslavia in the struggle it was having in making the Catholic Church toe the communist mark in that country. The moral pressure available to the Pope is tremendous, but it works only when the sides in an argument are willing to listen and when the Holy Father's good offices do not contravene fairly defined parameters. The Pope's pleas to end the war in Southeast Asia failed, for example, because neither side was willing to listen. These failures might lead to the assumption that the Vatican's role in world affairs is diminishing. That is probably not the case. In January 1979, for instance, the Pope was able to mediate the Beagle Channel Crisis that threatened war in South America, supporting a treaty that was negotiated on 23 January 1984 and signed 29 November 1984. The realities of the secular world were brought home to the Vatican when Pope John Paul II was shot during a ceremony in Saint Peter's Square on 13 May 1981. Upon his recovery, His Holiness sought out his would-be assassin and forgave him. Because of the principle of the separation of church and state, the United States had severed diplomatic relations with the Vatican in 1867. Not until 10 January 1984 were these relations restored. At that time, a pro-nuncio was assigned to Washington and an American envoy to the Vatican. Israel established diplomatic relations with the Vatican on 30 December 1993.

Velasco Alvarado, Juan. (b. 16 June 1910, Piura, Peru—d. 24 December 1977, Lima) General Juan Velasco Alvarado, the Peruvian army commander in chief, led a bloodless coup against the government of President Fernando Belaúnde Terry (qv) on 3 October 1968. During his tenure, Peru often defied the United States by seizing without compensation a number of U.S. oil company holdings and by capturing U.S. fishing vessels operating within a nonrecognized 200-mile coastal fishing limit. Valasco also demanded the lifting of Organization of American States (OAS) sanctions against Cuba and sought Latin American independence from the United States. On 29 August 1975, Velasco and Premier Vasco dos Santos Goncalves were ousted from office in a bloodless military coup. The reason for the coup was stated as the fact that both individuals were leftist. Valasco was ill at the time of the coup. He died two years later in December 1977. *See* Peru.

Velasco Ibarra, Jóse María. (b. 19 March 1893, Quito, Ecuador—d. 30 March 1979, Quito) Born into wealth, Velasco was educated in Peru and France. After a period of service in various public offices, he was elected president of Ecuador in 1934. When parts of his economic program proved to be communistic in design—the division of large estates—by the Peruvian Congress, Velasco retaliated by establishing a dictatorship with the attendant arrest of opposition leaders and press censorship. An army-led coup ousted him in 1935, after only 11 months in office. Velasco was forced into exile in Colombia, where he remained until 1944. He returned to Ecuador that year to be president again under a multiparty coalition that had defeated Carlos Arroyo, who had resigned under pressure. With Velasco as president, the economy again declined, and his repressive measures to maintain control alienated him further from his people. He was once again overthrown and forced into exile on 23 August 1947, this time to Argentina. He returned to Ecuador in 1952 and reclaimed to the presidency, for once serving his full four-year term in office. He was reelected in 1960, but he was forced to resign by a coup on 6 November 1961. He returned to the presidency in 1968, and on 22 June 1970, following major rioting in Quito and Guayaquil, he declared a military-backed dictatorship. However, the military deposed him on 15 February 1972, and he was again ordered into exile, this time returning to Argentina. He returned to Ecuador shortly before his death in March 1979.

Venezuela. More formally the Republic of Venezuela, this South American country is at the northern extremity of South America. Venezuela is bordered on the north by the Caribbean Sea, on the northeast by the Atlantic Ocean, on the east by Guyana, on the south by Brazil and on the west by Colombia. The capital city is Caracas. The original inhabitants were relatively disparate tribes from the Andes, Amazon and Caribbean cultures of 2000 B.C. These tribesmen developed a unique pre-Columbian culture, having been left alone until the sixteenth century A.D., even though Columbus did explore the coast in 1498. Spanish explorers at the beginning of the 1500s called the region "Little Venice" because the natives lived over water in stilted houses. For three hundred years Venezuela lived under Spanish rule. The labor force was Indian untilthat population was killed off, and then black slaves and indentures were utilized. The Spanish whites of native birth, called Creoles, were the middle managers and overseers on the extensive, often Church-owned, agricultural estates of the country. It was two of these creoles, Francisco de Miranda and Simon Bolivar, who led the independence movement that, over the period 1810–1821, brought about Venezuela's freedom from Spanish rule. Venezuela then joined Colombia and Ecuador in forming the republic of Grand Colombia. Venezuela broke with the trinational plan in 1830 and declared itself an independent republic. After 1830 and until 1958, Venezuela was ruled most of the time by military dictators. Among these, the regime of Juan Gomez, who ruled from 1909 until 1935, is most interesting, as it is during that period that petroleum production began in the country with a concomitant improvement of the economy and the standard of living following the exploitation of Venezuela's oil resources. The real boom came in the 1940s and 1950s, as Venezuela became the leading oil exporter in the world. Venezuela also used its wealth to help other Latin American countries during this period. On 13 May 1950, the Communist Party was outlawed in Venezuela. On 27 November 1950, the ruling military junta appointed Suarez Flammerich (qv) president. The outlawed communists, with the help of other groups, carried out an uprising in Caracas on 13 October 1951. Government troops had to be employed to quell the revolt. On 9 January 1954, Marcos Pérez Jimenéz (qv) was appointed president by the National Assembly after charges that the November 1953 elections had been rigged. Pérez Jimenéz faced an insurrection against his policies on 31 December 1957 and was overthrown after a struggle lasting until 23 January 1958. He was replaced by another military junta that ruled amid several coup attempts until an elected democratic government (13 February 1959) began, with its president, Romulo Betancourt (qv), being the first man to complete an elected term in office. Betancourt had served as provisional president under the military junta from 22 October 1945 until 24 November 1948, when he was overthrown on by a military group headed by Carlos Delgado Chalbaud (qv). A long period of communist-inspired insurgency began in 1960. That same year, on 24 June, an attempt was made on Betancourt's life. The five-nation investigation team set up by the OAS determined that the Dominican Republic had instigated the assassination attempt. A military uprising began in Venezuela in late June 1961, but it was quickly suppressed. Another such uprising occurred on 4 May 1962, but it too was thwarted by troops loyal to the government. Yet another attempt occurred on 4 June, but it too failed. In November 1963, a series of raids were conducted in which government forces broke up a Castro-inspired and Cuban supported plot to overhrow the government. The OAS subsequently voted (26 July) diplomatic and economic sanctions against Cuba. When the OAS established an Inter-American Peacekeeping Force on 6 May 1965, Venezuela contributed a military contingent. Between 1964 and 1984, five new presidents served in a series of successful administrations. Trouble began in the disputed border area between Venezuela and Guyana in early January 1969. The uprising had been backed by Venezuelan and Brazilian factions but was quickly suppressed by Guyanan military and security forces. On 19 March 1970, Venezuela announced it was integrating its defense system with that of Colombia. Venezuela announced it had reached a 12-year moratorium on its border dispute with Guyana. When the government closed the University of Caracas on 22 April 1971, a wave of student violence erupted on other campuses around the country. A cache of arms was discovered in a search of the Caracas campus in June 1971. Venezuela restored diplomatic relations with Cuba on 30 December 1974. On 17 September 1978, Nicaragua accused Venezuela of carrying out air strikes against Nicaraguan positions in support of rebel forces attacking from Costa Rica. Venezuela, one of the founders of the Organization of Petroleum Exporting Countries (OPEC), nationalized the oil industry (with compensation) on 1 January 1976. When oil revenues dropped sharply in the 1980s–1990s, Venezuela suffered a severe cash crisis and looked to diversify away from its dependence on oil as its major resource. There was a military coup attempt on 4 February 1992, followed by another one in November. Then, in May 1993, President Carlos Andres Perez was suspended from office on charges of misappropriating government funds. On 5 December 1993, Rafael Caldera Rodriguez was elected president. On 27 June 1994, he suspended a number of civil and constitutional rights because of violence engendered by a severe economic downturn in the country. Most rights were restored by 6 July 1995. *Reading:* John A. Peeler, *Latin American Democracies: Colombia, Costa Rica, Venezuela* (1986); Judith Ewell, *Venezuela: A Century of Change* (1984); Louis W. Goodman et al., *Lessons of the Venezuelan Experience* (1995).

Ver, Fabian C. General Fabian C. Ver was the Philippine armed forces chief of staff when he headed the conspiracy to assassinate Benigno Aquino (qv) upon his return to Manila on 21 August 1983. An independent commission, established under heavy international pressure by President Ferdinand Marcos (qv), on 23 October 1984 found Ver and 25 others responsible for the plot to kill Aquino. The commission did not go so far as to implicate Marcos in the plot, but very little transpired in those days in the Philippines without his knowledge. Charges were filed against the 26 on 23 January 1985. Ver and the other conspirators were acquitted of all charges in the murder by a three-judge Marcos-appointed panel In 1985. Immediately after the trial, Ver, who had been suspended from duty during the investigation, was reinstated in his former rank and duties.

Versailles Palace. *See* France.

Verwoerd, Henrik Frensch. On 6 September 1966, Henrik F. Verwoerd, the prime minister of South Africa, was assassinated. The murderer was a parliamentary messenger, named Dimetrios Tsafendas, who Verwoerd as he sat in the chamber awaiting the start of the day's business. There had been another attempt on Verwoerd's life on 9 April 1960. One week after Verwoerd's murder, Balthazar J. Vorster (qv) was named to replace him. Verwoerd had been prime minister since 2 September 1958. *See* Republic of South Africa.

Victor Emmanuel III. *See* Italy.

Victoria. *See* Seychelles.

Videla, Jorge Raphael. (b. 2 August 1925, Argentina) Videla became chief of staff of the Argentine Army in 1973 and was elevated to commander in chief by Isabel Peron (qv) in 1975. He used the latter office to reorganize the military structure and rid the services of Peronistas. Also, in 1975, he opened a military campaign to rid the country of its most dangerous and annoying rebel threat, the People's Revolutionary Army (qv) (*Ejercito Revolucionario des Pueblo*) (ERP). The military campaign was a great success, and when Isabel Peron was ousted on 24 March 1976, Lieutenant General Videla was offered and accepted the title of head of state as the leader of the ruling military junta. One of Videla's first acts was to suspend Congress, establishing in its place a nine-man military commission to make law. Videla also closed the courts and banned political parties and labor unions. Most civil service positions were then filled with military personnel. Anyone remotely suspected of leftist sympathies was arrested, with several thousand "disappearing" in the process. Videla narrowly escaped assassination in Buenos Aires on 2 October 1976. He was appointed president on 3 May 1978. Although some of his economic initiatives were successful, his repression of human rights isolated Argentina on the international scene. The use of the military and death squads to enforce rule by edict led to his eventual arrest after he retired from office in 1981. He was charged with murder on 22 April 1985 and sentenced to life in prison (9 December 1985). *See* Argentina.

Vieira, Joao Bernardo. On 14 November 1980, a socialist-inspired coup, led by Premier Joao Bernardo Vieira, overthrew the government of President Luis de Almeida Cabral of Guinea-Bissau. Vieira made the move to offset a new, two-day-old constitution that would have stripped the premiership of much of its power. He became the president of the Council of the Revolution. This racially and tribally invoked coup resulted in Cabral's indictment for murder and other crimes. Vieira claimed that over 500 political prisoners had been murdered during the Cabral rule. By 1983, Vieira was able to restore friendly relations with Cape Verde (*see* Guinea-Bissau and Cape Verde), which had been damaged following the 1980 coup. An attempted coup in 1985 failed, but its consequences cost Guinea-Bissau's attorney general his job, when it became evident he had supported the coup attempt. On 21 March 1994, Vieira postponed promised multiparty elections, claiming the government was without the necessary financial resources to properly enroll and poll the voters. The elections were finally held in July 1994, and as an outcome, Vieira remained in office in 1995, although the several opposition parties claimed foul play.

Vienna. *See* Austria.

Vientiane. *See* Laos.

Viet Cong (VC) (*Viet Nam Cong San*). As the Vietnamese Communist Party in the Republic (South Vietnam), the VC took up the struggle against the government of Ngo Dinh Diem (qv) after he took office 1954. Up to that time, the struggle against the central government had been carried out primarily by the Buddhist Cao Dai (qv) and Hoa Hao (qv) religious groups. These two sects were joined after 1954, by the southern branch of the Viet Minh (qv), which was a communist oriented- and -supported group better known for having fought the French colonial government in Indochina. The VC came into prominence (1960) as the military arm of the National Liberation Front (NLF), which was itself subservient to the North Vietnamese government in Hanoi. In the beginning, most VC recruits were found in South Vietnam and were trained and equipped and fought in their home areas, thus becoming a part of the daily life of the area. Attrition through casualties and a tightening of VC discipline brought a decline in available manpower in the south, and many members of the VC after 1967–1968 were in fact North Vietnamese Army (NVA) regulars. Another source of attrition of the VC was the *Chieu Hoi* Program, which accepted VC defectors—*Hoi Chanh*—back into South Vietnamese society. The program worked well but could not break the VC. Central control of the VC was carried out through a headquarters called the Central Office of South Viet Nam (COSVN), which was actually a link with Hanoi but served to coordinate some of the larger VC activities in the south. Many times, for safety's sake, COSVN was located in the sanctuary of Cambodia. In 1969, the NLF began the practice of establishing provisional revolutionary governments (PRG) in VC-controlled areas. The principal VC purpose was the overthrow of the government of the Republic of Viet Nam and the reunification of the country under the government of North Vietnam. VC tactics varied, but they usually could be categorized as raiding, ambushes, terrorism, sabotage and proselyting. While some of these involved contact with Allied or South Vietnamese military forces, the VC was most vicious in its attacks on South Vietnamese villages, where taxes were collected, recruits for VC service dragooned and communist indoctrination performed. Villages which balked at the almost always extravagant demands of the VC were made to suffer such indignities as have all the children in the village beheaded or the public execution of schoolteachers or village leaders. Rape, loot and pillage were the standard tools of terrorism among the VC. After the end of hostilities in 1975, the NVA quickly disarmed the VC guerrilla bands, knowing they constituted a threat. The PRG was given control of the areas under VC control, but regardless of the window-dressing, the real control was in the hands of the Vietnamese Communist Party and the North Vietnamese government in Hanoi. *Reading:* K. Bowra & K. Conboy, *The NVA and Viet Cong* (1992).

Viet Minh (VM) (*Viet Nam Doc Lap Dong Minh Hoi*). Known as the League for the Independence of Viet Nam, the VM was organized in China by Ho Chi Minh (qv) in May 1941. Supposedly begun as an Indochinese revolutionary organization, the VM was in reality a Chinese-sponsored nationalist coalition of anti-French and anti-Japanese groups, some of which were ommunist. During World War II the VM carried out some intelligence-gathering activities and conducted some minor guerrilla raids against the Japanese. Most of these latter activities began in 1943 under the leadership of Vo Nguyen Giap and were carried out in the northern provinces of Vietnam. Upon the surrender of Japan at the end of the war, the VM occupied Hanoi and declared the independence of the Democratic Republic of Vietnam (2 September 1945). After an initial promise of recognition by the French, a change occurred in which France decided to maintain its Indochinese colony after months of fruitless negotiation, and on 23 November 1946 it shelled the port city of Haiphong, killing at least 6,000 Vietnamese. This marked the beginning of the First Indochinese War. VM forces opened a series of attacks against the French in a number of areas throughout the country on 19 December 1945. The French "watchtower" mentality gave the VM the countryside while the French concentrated their forces in the urban areas. In January 1946, the VM forces encircled the South Vietnamese city of Hue and besieged the city into February, when French reinforcements arrived. By October 1950, the French had suffered a series of disastrous setbacks, but they continued the fight to retain their colony. French operations against the VM were stepped up in January 1953, but by April, VM forces, along with Laotian Pathet Lao (qv) forces, had opened a campaign in Laos in the region known as the Plaine des Jarres. By 23 December 1953, Vietnam had been fundamentally cut in half near the 17th parallel, with the VM holding the territory to the north. By March 1954, French forces still operating in the north were surrounded in a strategically and tactically unsound position in a large bowl-shaped valley at Dien Bien Phu. Dominated on all sides by higher elevations held by the Viet Minh, the French garrison was doomed. The fort fell on 7 May 1954, and that loss ended French influence in Asia. The VM took formal control of North Vietnam and the capital city of Hanoi on 11 October 1954. Coincidental with the end of World War II, a new organization, the *Lien Viet* (Vietnamese National Popular Front) came into existence, which superseded the VM. By 1951, most of the VM's leadership had been absorbed into the *Lao Dong* (Vietnamese Worker's Party), which later became the Vietnamese Communist Party (VCP). The VCP remains the single party of Vietnam—initially only in the north—to this day. Viet Minh military forces, materially supported by the Communist Chinese, defeated the French in the First Indochinese War and then turned their attention toward the beginning of the Second Indochinese War, better known in Western circles as the Vietnam War. Some VM moved south into the Republic of Vietnam and joined the Viet Cong (qv), which waged a guerrilla war against the southern Republic of Vietnam and its American ally. Although the Viet Minh ceased to exist as an entity at the end of World War II, the popular use of the name continued into the 1960s. Many of the VM leadership still remained involved in governing the reunited Vietnam after the fall of the South in 1975.

Vietnam. Today known officially as the Socialist Republic of Viet Nam (*Cong Hoa Xa Hoi Chu Nghia Viet Nam*), the country occupies the eastern coast of the Indochinese Peninsula in Southeast Asia. Vietnam is bordered on the north by China, on the east by the Gulf of Tonkin, on the south by the South China Sea, on the southwest by Cambodia and on the northwest by Lao. The capital city is Hanoi. The region was inhabited in the distant past by a group of people who, by the second century B.C. had established a unique culture within the kingdom of Nam Viet. This kingdom was later annexed into the Chinese kingdom of Funan. By the first century A.D., Funan controlled most of the region of Vietnam to the Mekong Delta in the south. The Funanese kingdom disappeared in the sixth century, and, by the end of the tenth century, Chinese control had all but disappeared throughout the country. By the thirteenth century, the region suffered a series of attacks by the Mongols, which were all thrown back. In 1407, however, China reconquered the region, only to be ousted again in 1428. A dynastic rule was then established by Emperor Le, who conquered almost all of Vietnam. By the 1750s, however, Vietnam was again divided into two distinct parts, which remained in existence until 1802, when they were reunited by Nguyen Ahn, who later ruled as Emperor Gia Long. The French conquered all of Indochina (including Vietnam, Laos and Cambodia) by the late nineteenth century and established the region as first a colony, from 1883 to 1939, and then a possession, from 1939 until 1945. Largely communist Viet Minh (qv) forces opened a campaign against the French to seize Vietnam in 1945 and forced a French withdrawal by 1954. Thereafter, an agreement was signed in Geneva (21 July 1954) that divided the country into North and South Vietnam and caused the start of the Second Indochinese War. The United States then became deeply involved in the affairs of the Republic of (South) Vietnam. American influence in Vietnam actually began with a brief encounter in 1873, when President U.S. Grant promised military aid to Emperor Tu Duc to help prevent French encroachment in Indochina. Political conditions in the United States prevented any aid from being furnished. At the end of World War II, America again became involved in Southeast Asian affairs when President Harry Truman (qv), espousing Roosevelt's previous annoyance with France, openly opposed French policies in Vietnam. Truman's adamancy on the issue led to a refusal even to allow U.S.–built propellers used on British aircraft to be shipped to the French in Vietnam. However, in 1948, when the US policy of containment came into being, the policy was altered and a threat conceived to be communist-inspired, even if purely nationalistic in nature, had to be opposed. Thus, the Viet Minh became the enemy, and the U.S. moved to support the French. By 1954 and the siege at Dien Bien Phu, the United States even toyed with the notion of reinforcing the French with U.S. ground and air forces. President Eisenhower (qv) quickly vetoed any such plans, although the supply of military equipment, increased geometrically. When France withdrew from Southeast Asia, the U.S. stepped into the void. By 1965, U.S. ground troops were actively engaged in the fight against the Viet Cong and their North Vietnamese Army comrades. On the political front, neither the Government of (South) Vietnam (GVN) nor the U.S. had signed the Geneva Peace Accords (1954), but the U.S. continued military and economic aid to the GVN. The Emperor Bao Dai (qv) was deposed in a referendum held on 23 October 1955, at which time Vietnam declared itself a republic, with Ngo Dinh Diem (qv) elected president in what was clearly a fraudulent election. Diem then announced that the Geneva-directed countrywide elections would not be held because the people of North Vietnam "were not free." Most scholars accept this pronouncement as the beginning of the Vietnam War or the Second Indochinese War, even though fighting had gone on before this date. Diem's government was faced with two problems: It could not defeat the communists, and it faced growing unrest among the Buddhist population in South Vietnam. The Buddhists mounted an antigovernment campaign, with a number of Buddhists publicly burning themselves to death as a symbol of the resistance. Many Buddhists were arrested as Diem correctly charged them with infiltration and agitation by the communists. However, there was a level of major disagreement between the generally Christian government of Ngo Dinh Diem and the Buddhista that defied Western logic. It was also true that, good or bad, Diem's was the only nationally recognizable name in South Vietnam. Regardless of that fact, his government was overthrown in a military coup on 1 November 1963, and Diem and his brother, Ngo Dinh Nhu (qv), were murdered. That the U.S. knew of the coup in advance and did nothing to stop it has been determined beyond doubt, and subsequent revelations revealed that the United States had indicated before hand that it was ready to deal with a successor government. Diem was replaced by Brigadier General Duong Van "Big" Minh (qv), who led a procession of ten different governments in South Vietnam over the next 18 months, none of which was capable of stopping the communist activity or bringing order to the political chaos in the the south or of halting the infiltration from the north. The last group, a military council headed by generals Nguyen Van Thieu (qv) and Nguyen Cao Ky (qv), was able to restore some semblance of order after 1965. Thieu became president by elections held in September 1967. Thieu and Ky maintained an uneasy relationship thereafter, but the country had a semblance of order, even if it was largely superficial. Both the political and military administrations were riddled with corruption and were infiltrated at many levels by communist sympathizers. Most specifically, however, even the new government could not stop the Viet Cong or their North Vietnamese counterparts. Morale in the national military army (ARVN) was at best poor, and local militias could not handle the VC/NVA. There were, of course, exceptions. Some ARVN units fought extremely well, as did some of the militia units. To stop the VC/NVA, however, took a larger and larger commitment of U.S. and Allied ground troops until, by 1968–1969, over one-half million Allied forces, mostly American, were engaged in a war not for victory, but to maintain the status quo. Earlier, in August 1964, the war had begun to escalate when North Vietnamese torpedo boats attacked two U.S. naval destroyers in the Gulf of Tonkin. This evoked the Tonkin Gulf Resolution (7 August 1964), which authorized U.S. troop deployment to South Vietnam and opened the way for the United States and its few allies to carry the brunt of the war against the North Vietnamese Army while the South Vietnamese usually operated against the VC. The effect of this major deployment was rising casualty figures in the U.S. and a concomitant disillusionment on the part of the American people about what the U.S. purpose was in Southeast Asia. In 1967–1968, North Vietnamese General Vo Nguyen Giap (qv) planned and executed a masterful stroke of strategic surprise in the Tet Offensive, which coincided with the Lunar New Year celebrations that generally brought everything else to a halt in South Vietnam. At least 100 urban targets, including Saigon, were attacked in force by VC/NVA troops. What Giap had hoped would be a decisive victory turned into a logistical nightmare for the North, however, as at least 85,000 VC/NVA became casualties before the Tet Offensive ended. The psychological effect of the campaign was devastating, however, and deepened American pessimism over the purpose of the war. When the U.S. announced on 31 March 1968, a halt to the bombing of North Vietnam, the North Vietnamese responded by announcing a willingness to negotiate. At the same time, the North used the occasion to rebuild their defenses and to reinforce their shattered forces in the South. By November 1968, the U.S. had halted all aerial activity over North Vietnam, but the negotiations in Paris proved fruitless. (Several months were wasted on determining the shape of the table to be used for the talks.) Meanwhile, the DRV—North Vietnam—had continued its growth as a communist state with ties to both the USSR and Mainland China. The conditions in the North were at best harsh in the beginning with the elimination of thousands of landlord-class citizens and the collectivization of agriculture. However, the communism of Ho Chi Minh was nationalistic, in the form of Tito's Yugoslavia, and even managed to sustain an industrial base throughout the heavy U.S. bombing. The tactics used by North Vietnam in the war in the South was an adaptation of Mao Tse-tung's (qv) "people's war" in which guerrilla warfare was stressed except where a main-force engagement was advantageous. As the war proceeded, even as the negotiations dragged on, the North continued its type of war while the South and its allies fought a war of attrition, taking horrendous casualties among the NVA/VC, without ever being able to deal a crippling blow that would have ended the fighting. At the same time, political objectives often thwarted commanders iin the field in the prosecution of the war. The upshot of all of that occurred, from Tet to the faltering Paris negotiations, was President Johnson's determination that the war needed to be "Vietnamized," that is, the Theiu government had to be forced to accept responsibility for its own destiny and its own defense. While the North fought and talked, the South simply continued on its path of letting the United States carry the burden of the main force war. Over the years, attempts at stiffening South Vietnamese resolve, such as the Strategic Hamlet Program and the Accelerated Pacification Plan, worked well but failed because of South Vietnamese lethargy and the government's failure to rally the people. When the U.S. began its withdrawal from Vietnam, a process that lasted several years and ended in 1973, the South Vietnamese were forced to take up the main force war. That they failed became evident in 1975, when many ARVN units simply disappeared. Others fought and fought well, but the North Vietnamese, having signed the Paris Peace Accords (13 January 1973), simply swept through the South, conquering that country, on 30 April 1975, when Thieu's replacement, Duong Van Minh, surrendered. Vietnam was formally reunified on 2 July 1976, with Hanoi quickly assuming leadership and absorbing the communist elements that had operated in the south, the PRG and the NLF. Saigon was renamed Ho Chi Minh City, and "reeducation" camps were established throughout the South where some 10,000 internees remained for "instruction" in 1986. One of the worst fears after the fall of South Vietnam never eventuated; there was no wide-spread bloodbath imposed on the South's educators, politicians and those Vietnamese who had dealt with the Americans, as had been expected. At the same time, the new government of Vietnam found itself economically destitute and with very few contacts outside of the communist world. In 1977, two things of importance happened: Vietnam invaded Cambodia to depose the despotic Pol Pot (qv), who had already murdered about 1.5 million people in that country in what would become a military operation lasting until 1980, and, after 3 July 1978, China cut off economic aid, partially in retaliation for abuses to ethnic Chinese residents of Vietnam. Then, on 17 February 1979 China attacked Vietnam with substantial military forces, an attack which Hanoi called "major aggression." This Chinese invasion became more ominous on 22 February, when the Soviets began moving naval forces into the South China Sea. At that same juncture, the USSR began a major airlift of military equipment and other material into Vietnam. China began withdrawing its troops from Vietnam on 5 March 1979, claiming it had met all of its military objectives. The animosity that arose between the Vietnamese and the Chinese following the 1975 communist takeover led to a mass exodus of southern Vietnamese, especially those of Chinese background, who left the country by whatever means available. More than 50,000 may have died in the attempt to escape. By that juncture, Vietnamese reliance on the USSR had become almost total. With the collapse of the Soviet Union in 1991, Vietnam was forced to turn its attention toward gaining recognition in the West. The United States held back, mainly because of Vietnamese intransigence in settling the fate of thousands of Americans still declared "missing in action" (MIA) and because of Vietnam's attack on Cambodia. After the Vietnamese reluctantly began cooperating on the MIA issue, the United States lifted (3 February 1994) the trade embargo that had been in effect since 1964 against North Vietnam and had been extended to the entire country after 1975. Diplomatic relations between the United States and Vietnam were reestablished on 11 July 1995, by President Clinton. *Reading:* Patrick J. Hearnden, *The Tragedy of Vietnam* (1995); William Appleman Williams et al., *America in Vietnam: A Documentary History (*1989); Ilya V. Gaiduk, *The Soviet Union and the Vietnam War* (1996); George Herring, *America's Longest War: The United States and Vietnam, 1950-1975* (1996); Gabriel Kolko, *Anatomy of a War: Vietnam, the United States, and Modern Historical Experience* (1994); Lloyd C. Gardner, *Approaching Vietnam: From World War II through Dienbienphu, 1941-1954* (1989); Ngo Vinh Long, *Before the Revolution: The Vietnamese under the French* (1991); Steven Hurst, *The Carter Administration and Vietnam* (1996); H. R. McMaster, *Dereliction of Duty: Lyndon Johnson, Robert McNamara, the Joint Chiefs of Staff, and the Lies That Led to Vietnam* (1997); Steven J. Hood, *Dragons Entangled: Indochina and the China-Vietnam War* (1992); Gontran De Poncins, *From a Chinese City: In the Heart of Peacetime Vietnam* (1991); Timothy Lomperis, *From People's War to People's Rule: Insurgency, Intervention, and the Lessons of Vietnam* (1996); Robert S. McNamara, *In Retrospect: The Tragedy and Lessons of Vietnam* (1996).

Villa Quesada. *See* Costa Rica.

Villarole (Villaroel), Gualberto. On 17–21 July 1946, a popular revolution erupted in Bolivia, led by students, working-class citizens and the military. The government of President Gualberto Villarole was ousted from power. Villarole was killed in the ensuing fighting. In fact, he was lynched from a lamppost outside the presidential palace. Villarole had himself been brought to power by a military coup in December 1943.

Villasmil, Garcia. *See* Venezuela.

Vinh. *See* Vietnam.

Vin Linh. *See* Vietnam.

Vinogradov, Vladimir. *See* Egypt.

Viola, Roberto Eduardo. On 11 December 1981, a three-man military junta ousted the Argentine government of President Roberto Eduardo Viola and put Lieutenant General Leopoldo Galtieri (qv) in his place. General Viola had taken office on 29 March 1981, at the completion of the term of Lieutenant General Jorge Raphael Videla (qv). Viola's ouster came about because the military did not agree with his plans to liberalize the country.

Vlore. *See* Albania.

Vo Nguyen Giap. *See* Viet Minh; Vietnam.

Vorster, Balthazar Johannes (John). (b. 13 December 1915, Jamestown, Cape Province, South Africa—d. 10 September 1983, Cape Town) Born into a large and wealthy sheep-raising family, Vorster studied at the University of Stellenbosch before becoming a clerk in the court system of Cape Province (1938). He then practiced law, before the start of World War II. During the war he joined an anti-British organization (*Ossewa Brandwag*) that praised the Germans. For this he was arrested on charges of subversion in 1942 and spent 14 months in jail. Unbelievably, he was allowed to reopen his law practice when he was released. He was not, however, favored by the National Party and, although interested in politics, was denied access to party politics after the war. Only in 1953 was he successful in winning a seat in the South African Parliament. In that capacity he worked to get Hendrik F. Verwoerd (qv) elected prime minister in 1958. In turn, Verwoerd appointed Vorster deputy minister of education, arts and sciences, and social welfare (October 1958). After the Sharpeville incident (*see* Republic of South Africa) in March 1960, Vorster was appointed minister of justice, police and prisons. In this capacity he assiduously enforced apartheid (qv). When Verwoerd was assassinated on 6 September 1966, Vorster was the natural choice of the National Party to succeed him (13 September). In fact, his handling of the apartheid policy was less extreme than was expected, and he worked with black leaders in neighboring countries such as Namibia and Rhodesia, after their loss of their colonial masters. He also sent South African forces into Angola to halt the Soviet and Cuban-backed Popular Movement for the Liberation of Angola (MPLA). On 28 September 1978, Vorster resigned, stating health reasons, but was shortly elected president. In November 1978, he became embroiled in a major scandal involving misappropriation of government funds and government abuses. He was charged with misprision of a felony in that he knew of the situation but failed to act, and he was forced to resign the presidency on 4 June 1979.

Vung Tau (Cap-Sainte Jacques). *See* Vietnam.

W

Wadi Qena River. *See* Egypt.

Wakhan Corridor. *See* Afghanistan.

Waldheim, Kurt. (b. 21 December 1918, St. Andrea-Worden, Austria) Waldheim was educated in Austria and attended the Vienna Consular Academy. In World War II, he served in the Austrian army under Nazi control. He received a doctor of laws degree from Vienna University in 1944. He then served in the Austrian embassy in Paris and then in the Austrian Foreign Ministry from 1951 until 1954. Waldheim was then appointed Austria's first ambassador to Canada. In 1964, he became his country's permanent representative to the UN. In 1968, he was appointed the Austrian minister of foreign affairs. On 21 December 1971 he became the fourth secretary-general of the United Nations, succeeding U Thant (qv) of Burma. At the same time, Waldheim was defeated for the presidency of his own country (April 1972). He welcomed the seating of Red China in the UN and, on 24 July 1972, publicly criticized the U.S. for its bombing campaign against North Vietnam. In July 1978, he urged Lebanon to deploy troops along the Lebanon-Israeli border to assist the United Nations Emergency Force sent there to keep the peace. In 1979, he worked for a cease-fire in Namibia. In 1982, after serving two terms as secretary-general, he left the United Nations. He was elected president of Austria in 1986, but suspicions about his wartime role in the liquidation of Jews, as charged by the World Jewish Congress, reached a level in 1988 such that an international commission was convened to study his activities. Although the commission could find no direct evidence linking him to any atrocities, it did conclude that he was completely knowledgeable about the Holocaust and other atrocities of the Nazi forces, especially in the Balkans. After Waldheim refused to step down as president, he was shunned by most of the world's leaders and was declared an undesirable alien by the U.S., which effectively barred him from entry. During this period,Chancellor Franz Vranitsky carried out most of the affairs of state. Waldheim remained in office until 8 July 1992, when he was defeated for reelection. *Reading:* Richard Mitten, *The Politics of Antisemitic Prejudice: The Waldheim Phenomenon in Austria* (1992); Jack Saltman, Kurt Waldheim: A Case to Answer? (1990).

Walesa, Lech. (b. 29 September 1943, Popowo, Poland) Born the son of a carpenter, Walesa finished technical high school and in 1967 began working as an electrician at the Gdansk shipyard. By 1970 (*see* Poland) he was involved in the free trade union movement, but was fired from his job for being an agitator. He was again dismissed from his job in an electrical plant for demonstrating against the working conditions there. By 1980, Walesa had risen to the leadership of Solidarity (qv), an independent trade union that operated without sanction from the communist government in Poland. A number of strikes followed that showed the government the meaning of Solidarity. On 31 August 1980, Walesa signed for the unions the Gdansk Agreement, with the government conceding the right of workers to organize. However, in 1981 the Polish crisis increased as more workers joined Walesa's Solidarity movement. When the government imposed martial law in December 1981, Walesa and the other Solidarity leaders urged a nationwide strike, which did not materialize. Numbers of workers were killed by police and army troops in scattered disorders. Walesa was arrested and held in detention outside Warsaw for almost one year before his release. Solidarity was outlawed. On 1 May 1982, more than 30,000 demonstrated in Warsaw for the release of Walesa. Police restored order on 3 May, and a curfew was established in the city. Walesa was released from detention on 11 November. In 1985, Walesa, now the leader of a largely underground organization, was accused of slander when he criticized the results of a general election that was claimed by the government. By 1988 Walesa was seen as more of a politician than a union spokesman and received much criticism from members of his own Solidarity movement, especially the younger ones. As a result of long discussions in February–April 1989, Solidarity was relegalized. Free general elections were held in the second half of 1990 that put Walesa in the presidency of Poland. He remained in office until 23 December 1995, when he was replaced by Aleksander Kwasniewski, a former communist, following a runoff election that gave Walesa less than 49 percent of the vote. *Reading:* Lech Walesa, *The Struggle and the Triumph: An Autobiography* (1992); Caroline Lazo, *Lech Walesa* (1993).

Waring, Robert O. Along with U.S. ambassador Francis E. Meloy and a Lebanese driver, U.S. economic counselor Robert O. Waring was detained and then shot and killed as the ambassador's sedan crossed the "Green Line" between east and west Beirut on 16 June 1976. The murderers belonged to the Popular Front for the Liberation of Palestine (PFLP) (qv). The bodies of the three victims were found in a garbage dump near the beach at Ramlat al-Bayda.

Warsaw. *See* Poland.

Warsaw Pact. More properly called the Warsaw Treaty Organization, the Warsaw Pact was the unified military command established by the Warsaw Treaty signed on 14 May 1955. The treaty was a 20-year mutual defense agreement signed by the USSR and Albania, Bulgaria, Czechoslovakia, East Germany, Hungary, Poland and Romania. Yugoslavia refused to sign the agreement. The first commander was Marshal of the Soviet Union Ivan S. Konev. The pact came into existence soon after Nikita Khrushchev (qv) and Nikolai A. Bulganin (qv) assumed power in the Soviet Union and was meant to bring the satellite nations in the Soviet sphere into greater compliance with the edicts of the Kremlin and to serve as a counter to the North Atlantic Treaty Organization's (NATO) inclusive of West Germany. The charter stated also that the Warsaw Pact would lapse immediately upon the signing of an East-West collective security agreement, a political move designed to enhance the Soviet bargaining position. In July 1955, the Soviet Union proposed the abolition of both NATO and the Warsaw Pact in favor of a Euuropean collective security agreement that would include the United States. As might have been expected, Soviet officers filled all sensitive positions in the Warsaw Pact and held multilateral status in its forces. In October 1956, following the rehabilitation of Wladyslaw Gomulka (qv) and his reinstatement in the Central Committee of the Polish Communist Party, the then commander in chief of the Warsaw Pact, Marshal of the Soviet Union Konstantine K. Rokossovsky, ordered a troop buildup around Warsaw to insure compliance with the Soviet directives on the future of Polish politics. On 2 November 1956, In Hungary, at the height of the revolution going on in that country, Premier Imre Nagy (qv) repudiated the Warsaw Pact and asked NATO to control the situation. The Hungarian Revolution was put down by a massive Soviet invasion. On 28 May 1958, the Kremlin announced a withdrawal of Soviet forces from Romania and a reduction in the national forces of the countries in the Warsaw Pact. In May 1966, Romania suggested the Warsaw Pact be modified. Instead, the country received a visit from Leonid Brezhnev (qv) and was forced to tone down its talk about independent policy making. The Romanians did not give up, however, and at the Warsaw Pact meeting held 4–6 July 1966 suggested the dissolution of both NATO and the Warsaw Pact and the withdrawal of all foreign troops from every country in Europe. In July 1968, Czech prime minister Alexander Dubcek (qv) demanded a revision in the Warsaw Pact to prevent its use for political purposes. On 20–21 August 1968, more than 200,000 Warsaw Pact troops invaded Czechoslovakia, ending what was called the "Prague Spring." Eventually, 650,000 Soviet troops were in that country. With the reinstitution of Soviet control in Czechoslovakia, the government of prime minister Oldrich Cernik (qv) announced it would increase the Czech contribution to the Warsaw Pact. Also in 1981, Albania, whose presence in the Warsaw Pact was more symbolic than substantial, withdrew from the organization. On 17 March 1969, a joint command was formed in the Warsaw Pact, further tightening Soviet control over the organization. On 25 May 1969, Romania's Nicolae Ceaucescu (qv) once again called for the dismantling of the Warsaw Pact and NATO. In November 1969, all Warsaw Pact members except Romania pledged support for the Arabs in their current crisis with Israel. On 27 May 1970, the NATO Council of Ministers invited the Warsaw Pact to join in a mutual balanced-force reduction (MBFR) in Central Europe. Acting as a rubber stamp for the already concluded Soviet–West German nonagression treaty signed on 12 August 1970, the Warsaw Pact officially endorsed the agreement on 21 August. On 3 March 1971, the Warsaw Pact decided to increase military forces committed to the organization toward meeting the "unceasing strengthening of the aggressive NATO bloc." On 26 January 1972, however, the Warsaw Pact called for a troop and arms reduction. In November, NATO reciprocated by inviting four Warsaw Pact members to discuss such a plan. Arrangements for the meeting took place on 31 January 1973 and discussed the MBFR, and the actual discussions began in Vienna on 14 May. Over the next several years proposals and counter-proposals were made without result. On 9 December 1976, NATO formally rejected a Warsaw Pact proposal for a mutual no-first-use of nuclear weapons, but it did endorse a freeze on membership in the two organizations. In November 1977, the only territorial dispute between NATO and the Warsaw Pact was settled when Norway and the Soviet Union agreed upon a division of the Barents Sea. Still the MBFR discussions continued, with new initiatives being presented and rejected on a regular basis by both sides. On 25 November 1978, Romania announced it would no longer permit integration of its forces into the Warsaw Pact and that it would not increase its payment to the pact as had been demanded. At a meeting held in Warsaw on 1 May 1980, pact members gathered to coordinate the organization's position on the Soviet war in Afghanistan and their position on Iran. When tensions rose in Poland in 1980, a pact meeting in Moscow closed without the expected condemnation of the Poles and without the threat of the use of force to restore "order." Only Poland's declaration of martial law in 1981, however, saved Poland from an invasion of Warsaw Pact forces. In 1983, the MBFR talks were still going on, with little or nothing having been accomplished in the last decade of negotiations, save for respites caused by several suspensions that had been forced upon the conferences by one side or the other. In January 1984, the USSR suggested the talks be expanded to discuss chemical weapons abolition in Europe. Later in the year (May) the Warsaw Pact suggested a nonaggression pact to rule out the use of force to settle disputes. On 27 September 1984, the 34th round of MBFR talks began. Little was accomplished throughout the remainder of the decade. The reform policies put into effect by Mikail Gorbachev in the USSR instigated the breakup of the Soviet bloc beginning in 1989. Soviet forces began to be withdrawn from many of the pact nations. East Germany formally left the Warsaw Pact in 1990, after it ceased to exist as a nation. NATO and the Warsaw Pact declared in November 1990 that they were "no longer adversaries," and the Cold War ended. The Warsaw Pact was disbanded on 1 July 1991. *Reading:* George Brunner, ed., *Before Reforms: Human Rights in the Warsaw Pact States, 1971-1988* (1991); Andrew Michta, *East Central Europe after the Warsaw Pact: Security Dilemmas in the 1990s* (1992); Michael Sadykiewicz, *Organizing for Coalition Warfare: The Role of the East European Warsaw Pact Forces in Soviet Military Planning* (1988).

Watts. A predominantly black section of Los Angeles, California, Watts was the scene of a major racial disturbance that began on 12 August 1965. Some 15,000 police and National Guardsmen were required to restore order. The racial disturbance was one of the most serious incidents ever experienced in the United States up to that time. The rioting lasted for several days with hundreds of rioters looting stores and setting builings on fire. Police and firemen were being shot at when the governor ordered in the National Guard. Order was restored and a curfew put into effect. Some 4,000 perpetrators were arrested; 35 people were killed and at least 600 injured during the riot. Damage was estimated at more than $40 million dollars. The investigation (McCone Commission) that followed the incident did little to rectify any of the reasons for the outbreak.

Watusi. *See* Tutsi and Rwanda.

al-Wazzan, Shafiq. On 6–7 February 1984 heavy fighting broke out in Beirut between the Lebanese army and Druse and Shi'ite Muslim militias. The army was routed, and the militia took control of most of the city. Several reports indicated that many members of the army deserted and joined the militias during the fighting. As a result, the Lebanese prime minister, Shafiq al-Wazzan, and most of his cabinet were forced to resign.

Weh Syen, Thomas. On 10 August 1981, a coup attempt against the Samuel E. Doe (qv) regime in Liberia was crushed by loyal military forces. The plotters were rounded up, tried and executed (14 August). Among those executed were five members of the Liberian People's Redemption Council, including Thomas Weh Syen, the deputy head of state.

Weinberger, Caspar W. "Cap." (b. 18 August 1917, San Francisco) Weinberger attended Harvard University, where he graduated magna cum laude. He then took his degree in law at Harvard. In service in the U.S. army from 1941 until 1945, he went from private to captain. After the war he served as a law clerk in the U.S. Court of Appeals, and then in a law firm until 1969. He was a member of the California legislature from 1952 to 1958. Weinberger served as finance director of California under then governor Ronald Reagan (qv) from 1968 to 1969. He then moved to Washington, where he became the chairman of the Federal Trade Commission (1970) before becoming deputy, then director, of the Office of Management and Budget (1970–1973) in the Richard Nixon (qv) administration and, later, as the secretary of health, education and welfare (1973–1975) under both Nixon and Gerald R. Ford (qv). During this service, he became known as "Cap the Knife" because of his budget cutting. After Reagan's election to the presidency in 1980, Weinberger became secretary of defense. During his tenure, Weinberger carried on a running feud with Alexander Haig (qv), the secretary of state in the Reagan administration, over a number of issues concerning foreign policy and military readiness. It was an open secret that Weinberger had desired the appointment to the State Department rather than the equally important assignment at Defense. On 22 November 1983, Weinberger made the announcement that Iran, with the assistance and approval of Syria, had planned and executed the 23 October 1983 attack on the U.S. embassy in Beirut that killed 241 Americans. In March 1985, it was Weinberger who issued the invitation to 17 nations to join in the Strategic Defense Initiative "Star Wars" program. On 5 November 1987, Weinberger announced that he would step down as secretary of defense once a successor was named. Upon the appointment of Frank C. Carlucci as the new secretary, Weinberger retired to private life to spend more time with his ailing wife. After his retirement to private life, Weinberger held a number of positions, including that of editor of *Forbes* magazine.

Weizmann, Chaim.   (b. 27 November 1874, Motol, Russian Poland—d. 9 November 1952, Rehovot, Israel) Weizmann's early years were spent in Poland, where he was raised according to Jewish tradition. He studied in Germany and Switzerland and, in 1904, became a teacher of biochemistry at the University of Geneva. He continued his education at the University of Manchester, England. His work in organic chemistry soon gave him a worldwide reputation, but it would be his interest in Zionism (qv) that would give him a place in history. During World War I, Weizmann became the leader of the Zionist movement in England, while also using his scientific skills to aid the war effort. In 1917, Weizmann was largely responsible for the issuance of the Balfour Declaration in which the British government affirmed support for the establishment of a Jewish homeland in Palestine. From 1920, Weizmann was the president of the World Zionist Organization and, from 1929, chairman of the Jewish Agency for Palestine. Weizmann fell out of grace for a short period (1931–1935) because of his stand supporting the ability to work with the British government on the Palestine question, but the rise of Nazi Germany and its obvious threat to Judaism quickly put Weizmann back in office. Thereafter, he became the chief spokesman for the settlement of the Palestine question both in England and worldwide. Weizmann ended his career fighting both the British government for its Palestine policies and the Jewish organizations themselves because of their increasing recourse to violence. He resigned his offices in 1946 and returned to the scientific world, working at the Institute of Science in Rehovot in Palestine. When Israel won its independence in 1948, Weizmann was elected to the largely ceremonial post of president, first of the provisional government and then (1949) of the republic. Failing health kept him out of public view in his last years, and he died peacefully on 9 November 1952 at Rehovot' where the Institute of Science is now the world-famous Weizmann Institute. *Reading:* Jehuda Reinharz, *Chaim Weizmann: The Making of a Statesman* (1993); Barnet Litvinoff, comp., *The Essential Chaim Weizmann: The Man, the Statesman, the Scientist* (1983).

Welch, Richard. On 23 December 1975, Richard Welch, the special assistant to the U.S. ambassador in Athens, Greece, was assassinated by three unidentified gunmen in front of his home. Welch was the CIA chief of station at the embassy, a position often identified to the host government.

Wellington. *See* New Zealand.

West Azerbaijan Province. *See* Iran.

West Bank. A portion of old Palestine west of the river Jordan, the West Bank was taken by the Kingdom of Jordan during the 1948 Israeli War of Independence. It was capture by the Israelis during the 1967 Arab-Israeli War. It contains part of the city of Jerusalem (East Jerusalem), the cities of Hebron and Nablus and the region of the hills of Judaea and Samaria. The West Bank held obvious strategic importance to Israel, and it also was considered the Palestinian homeland by the Palestinian Liberation Organization (PLO). From 1967 until

1993, the West Bank was a source of constant upheaval and military clashes between the Israelis and Palestinians. On 13 September 1993, Israel and the PLO signed the Declaration of Principles, which included the 1994 withdrawal of Israeli security forces from the West Bank and the establishment of Palestinian control over the region. *See* Israel.

West Bengal. A state in the Republic of India, West Bengal is bordered on the north and northwest by the Indian state of Bihar, on the east by Bangladesh, on the south by the Bay of Bengal and on the west by the Indian state of Orissa. West Bengal came into existence when India won its independence in 1947. It had formerly been the western one-third of the British province of Bengal, which became East Pakistan (later Bangladesh). At first, West Bengal consisted of two parts because the boundary was based on the religious preferences of the area's population. This was corrected in 1956, with the addition of 3,100 square miles of the province of Bihar to West Bengal. In March 1970, the chief minister of West Bengal resigned in protest over the tactics of violence practiced by the Marxist Communist Party in India. That same month, West Bengal was the scene of a Marxist-inspired strike that led to rioting. In November, security forces were given authority to use deadly force to suppress the procommunist Naxalite violence in the state. *See* India.

West Berlin. *See* Berlin.

Western Alliance. The concept of a Western Alliance came into being after World War II, when the former Allies against Germany and Japan polarized into the East-West confrontation. The original western Allies, the United States, Great Britain, France and a number of smaller countries arrayed themselves against what was viewed as the common enemy, the Soviet Union. In 1949, the concept of a Western Alliance was codified in the establishment of the North Atlantic Treaty Organization (NATO). With the dissolution of the threat in the early 1990s, NATO began changing its emphasis to political action and the rapid deployment of forces tailored to meet local crises in accordance with the Charter of the United Nations. *See* NATO.

Western Deep Levels Gold Mine. Near Carletonville, South Africa, the Western Deep Levels Gold Mine was the site of a 12 September 1973 confrontation between black miners and South African police in which 11 demonstrators were shot and killed. The original cause of the demonstration was wages. *See* South Africa.

Western European Union. Formed in 1955, the Western European Union (WEU) sought to replaced the European Defense Community (EDC) (qv) in implementing the policies of NATO. The problems that had faced the EDC continued into the WEU, especially the problem of rearming Germany, a plan that France and others vehemently opposed. In fact, the WEU came into existence for that very purpose after the U.S. had pressed for four years to get a German contribution to NATO. In its initial form the WEU included the six EDC countries, plus Great Britain. Germany was allowed to participate only after a Franco-German agreement was reached by which French control of the Saarland would be given over to the WEU. The plan was rejected by the voters, however, in October 1955. The WEU continued to operate, and in June of 1984 cancelled a thirty-year-old prohibition on West German production of long range missiles and strategic bombers. Spain and Portugal were admitted to membership in the WEU in 1989, but not without acrimony over their arms control and nuclear policies. In 1991, the nine-nation WEU coordinated European support of the campaign against Iraq. Because of the failure of Europe to provide more than token support in the Kuwait crisis—Germany was constitutionally prohibited from joining the coalition—Germany and France recommended that the WEU become a European defense organization under the control of the European Community. Discussions continued, however, over how such a force would fit into the NATO structure. In the ongoing crisis in Bosnia, the WEU provend its inability to function effectively on its own. By 1993, however, the WEU was able to form a full European Army Corps of 50,000 French, German, Spanish, British and Belgian troops (Eurocorps) as the forerunner of a full army answerable to the EC. Troops and equipment that had been allocated to NATO were used to fill the organization. *Reading:* A. Bloed & Ramses A. Wessel, eds., *The Changing Functions of the Western European Union: Introduction and Basic Documents* (1994); Charles Jeffery, ed., *The Regional Dimension of the European Union: Towards a Third Level in Europe* (1997).

West Falkland Island. *See* Falkland Islands.

West Germany. The Federal Republic of Germany was codified by the vote of the 11 states (*Lander*) that comprised the area of old Germany occupied by the western Allies, on 23 May 1949. The question of Berlin was left unresolved (*see* Berlin). The first elections were held in West Germany on 14 August 1949. Konrad Adenauer (qv) was elected chancellor. One month later, on 19 September, the United States, Great Britain and France gauranteed the security of the new German republic. Three days later, on 21 September, the occupation authority of the Allied military government ended and was replaced by an Allied high commission. On 24 November, the Allied high commission allowed Germany some rights toward maintaining a minimal military force, rebuilding a merchant fleet, and participating in the Council of Europe (qv). West Germany became a recipient of Marshall Plan (qv) aid on 21 December. The situation improved to the point that Germany was able to end rationing on 16 January 1950. On 19 September 1950, the U.S., along with the other Western powers, warned the Soviet Union that an attack on West Germany or Berlin would be considered as an attack upon itself. The communique went on to state that West Germany would be allowed to strengthen itself both politically and economically. A West German foreign office was established on 6 March 1951, and on 24 September 1951 the three Western powers informed Chancellor Adenauer that the occupation statute would be abrogated and the Allied High Commission abolished if Germany took part in the defense of Europe. After lengthy negotiations, the internal independence of West Germany was approved by the U.S., Great Britain and France on 26 May 1952. On 10 September 1952, West Germany agreed to pay Israel $820 million in reparations. Two incidents occurred on 10 and 12 March that nearly brought war. In the first, a U.S. fighter aircraft was shot down over West Germany by Soviet fighters. Two days later a British bomber was also shot down. While nothing much came of those incidents, Soviet recognition of East German sovereignty on 25 March 1954 was timed to coincide with the West German announcement that it would rearm under a just passed constitutional amendment (26 March) that allowed West German participation in the European Defense Community (EDC) (qv). On 23 October 1954, the occupation of West Germany was officially ended, and arrangements were made for the stationing of foreign troops on German soil in the Status of Forces Agreement (SOFA). On 15 January 1955, the USSR recognized West German sovereignty. In May, West Germany joined the newly formed Western European Union and, on 9 May, West Germany joined NATO —four days after the ratification of the peace treaty that officially ended World War II, at least in the West. The West German government passed a bill providing for a 6,000 man cadre to raise a half-million man army on 22 July 1955, and compulsory military service was introduced on 20 July 1956. After years of uncertainty, the Saar region was returned to German control on 27 October. (The return was accepted by West Germany in January 1957.) Before the plan was implemented, however, many of the area's citizens, who had earlier voted for French rule, carried out a period of often violent dissent. In November 1956, Germany became the center of considerable military activity as U.S. forces stationed there were put on alert for commitment in either Hungary or Egypt (*see* Egypt or Hungary for details). On 1 July 1957, the first three West German (*Bundeswehr*) divisions were turned over to NATO. Nine more divisions would eventually be incorporated into NATO ground forces. The question of reunification of the two Germanys was raised on 25 July 1957, when the United States, France and West Germany signed the Berlin Declaration. West Germany announced the decision to arm its forces with nuclear weapons (28 March 1957) and at the same time refused a Soviet proposal on reunification. On 30 November 1961, the USSR informed Finland that West Germany posed a threat and demanded consultations on implementation of the 1948 Finno-Soviet Mutual Defense Pact. In a further weakening of Soviet–West German relations, West Germany announced on 8 August 1962 that it would break off relations with any country supporting the recently issued Soviet peace plan. A treaty of reconciliation was signed by Konrad Adenauer and France's Charles de Gaulle (qv) on 22 January 1963. When West Germany prepared to sell $80 million dollars' worth of surplus U.S.–made military hardware to Israel in January 1965, the protests from a number of Arab countries forced a curtailment of the plan before it was completed (10 February). After accusing Egyptian president Gamal Nasser of meddling in German affairs by inviting East German president Walter Ulbricht (qv) to Cairo, the Bonn government cut off all economic aid to Egypt (24 February 1965). When West Germany recognized Israel in May 1965, ten member countries of the Arab League severed diplomatic relations with the Bonn government. On 1 January 1968, Great Britain began withdrawal of 5,000 troops from its forces stationed in West

Germany. This move was made for economic reasons and was based on a 2 May 1967 agreement with the US and West German governments. At about the same time, France began withdrawing 5,000 troops from West Germany as a part of the French pullout from NATO. On 31 January, Yugoslavia reopened diplomatic relations with West Germany for the first time since World War II. On 11 March 1969, an Ethiopian airliner was blown up at Frankfurt Airport by terrorists representing the Arab Liberation Front for Eritrea (qv). A "Hot Line" (qv) was established between Washington and Bonn on 8 August 1969. On 22 January 1970, Chancellor Willy Brandt (qv) announced his government was ready to open talks to settle the issue of the two Germanys. On 27 July, the USSR began renouncing its force agreement with West Germany. East Germany offered to negotiate a Berlin (qv) access treaty with West Germany if all Allied forces left the city (8 November). On 18 November, West Germany initialed an agreement that normalized relations with and accepted the "Oder-Neisse" Line as the western boundary of Poland. East Germany was not consulted in the decision even though it is East Germany that borders on Poland. The formal agreement was signed on 7 December. By its terms 40,000 square miles of German territory was thus given to Poland. On 15 February 1972, Iceland abrogated a fishing treaty with West Germany when it extended its national fishing limit from 12 to 50 miles. An incident took place on 28 June 1973, when an Icelandic gunboat fired on a West German trawler that was said to have been fishing inside the 50-mile limit. Germany banned all Icelandic ships from its ports after another trawler was seized in December 1974. Although a number of terrorist attacks took place in West Germany over the years, none was more dramatic than the 5 September 1972 incident in which Palestinian terrorists from the Black September (qv) organization broke into and barricaded themselves in the Israeli dormitory during the Olympic games in Munich. The terrorists demanded the release of 200 Arabs held in Israeli jails. Two Israeli Olympic team members were already killed, and nine were held hostage. Later, the terrorists and their hostages were flown by helicopter to Furstenfeldbruck airport outside Munich. A bungled West German rescue attempt led to the deaths of all nine hostages and five of the terrorists. A West German police officer was also killed, and three of the terrorists captured alive. These three killers were released by the West German government on 29 October to gain the freedom of hostages held on a Lufthansa airliner hijacked by Black September. In December 1972, East and West Germany signed a treaty that effectively recognized East German sovereignty. Diplomatic missions were exchanged in March 1974. In December 1973, West German also resumed diplomatic relations with Czechoslovakia for the first time since the 1938 Munich Agreement. Relations were normalized on 10 July 1974. In May 1974, a major scandal rocked West Germany. Willy Brandt was forced to resign as chancellor when it was discovered his aide, Gunther Guillaume (qv), was an East German spy. In October 1976, 10,000 French troops were withdrawn from West German territory in what Paris called a major reorganization of its armed forces. In 1978, 12 more regiments were withdrawn, leaving about 53,000 French troops on

German soil. On 28 April 1976, the terrorist leader Andreas Baader (qv) and two of his associates were sentenced to life imprisonment. The German ambassador to Ethiopia was expelled on 22 January 1978, when Bonn announced that $20 million in credit had been given to Somalia. On 1 March 1978, West Germany sold about $500 million in warships to Iran. In June, West Germany attended an emergency meeting of the Western powers in Paris to discuss the invasion of Zaire (qv); however, agreement was reached on the composition of a pan-African force to handle the situation. Amid a great clamor, Chancellor Helmut Schmidt reaffirmed, on 21 June 1981, the West German decision to allow U.S. nuclear weapons on German territory. In April 1983, more than 500,000 demonstrated in West Germany against nuclear weapons not only on German territory but anywhere in Europe as well. On 22 October 1983, more than two million demonstrated for the same cause throughout Western Europe. Demonstrations against missile deployments also took place in West Germany in April 1984. On 27 June 1984, the Western European Union (qv) cancelled a 30-year prohibition on West German production of long-range missiles and strategic bombers. On 10 July, the USSR warned West Germany of the grave consequences of beginning such programs. On 19 June 1985, a major terrorist incident took place when Rhein-Main Airport was bombed. Four were killed and 60 injured in the attack, for which at least four different terrorist groups attempted to take credit. Yet, on 24 November, when a car bomb exploded near a U.S. military shopping center in Frankfurt and 36 were injured, no one claimed credit for the attack. In the next five years, terrorism continued to spread across West Germany. In 1986, for instance, West Germany expelled a number of Syrian diplomats accused of supplying explosives, via their legation in East Berlin, used in a 29 March bombing in West Berlin. After the communist empire toppled in 1989, East and West Germany were reunified. The actual unification took place on 3 October 1990. Soon after, Germany reiterated the Polish border decision it had made earlier. Also, on 12 September 1990, during the "Four plus Two" negotiations, a decision was reached that ended the postwar occupation of two Germanys by the Four Powers on 1 October 1990. Germany also signed a commitment never again to become a threat to world peace. Germany stayed within the NATO structure and agreed to pay the USSR $7.5 billion to withdraw its troops from German soil. Germany did not participate in the war against Iraq in 1991 because of its constitutional prohibition on German troops fighting abroad. Germany also decided to cut its armed forces from 600,000 to 370,000 troops. *See* Germany for the period after reunification. *Reading:* George Crews McGhee, *At the Creation of a New Germany: From Adenauer to Brandt: An Ambassador's Account* (1989); Stephen Szabo, *The Changing Politics of Germany* (1990); Eva Kolinsky, ed., *The Federal Republic of Germany: The End of an Era* (1991); Hanna Behrend, ed., *German Unification: The Destruction of an Economy* (1995); Sean Dolan, *West Germany: On the Road to Reunification* (1991).

Westmoreland, William C. (b. 26 March 1914, Spartanburg, South Carolina) Born the son of a textile factory manager, Westmoreland attended the Citadel before entering West Point. Upon graduation in 1936, he was commissioned in the artillery. He fought in North Africa and Sicily and took part in the Normandy invasion of Europe. During the Korean War he commanded a regimental combat team. In 1958 he took command of the 101st Airborne Division, and in 1960 he was appointed superintendent of the United States Military Academy. In January 1964, Westmoreland became the deputy to General Paul D. Harkins, who commanded the advisory effort in South Vietnam. In June 1964, Westmoreland took command of the U.S. effort in Vietnam and helped enlarge the U.S. role from one of advice to one of direct combat involvement. In assuming his role, Westmoreland did not heed the advice of generals Maxwell D. Taylor (qv) or James M. Gavin, who recommended a strategy of defending coastal enclaves; rather, he ordered US combat forces into the countryside to find and destroy the enemy. As casualties mounted, Westmoreland's "search and destroy" tactics came under more and more criticism with some senior military officers and many politicians accusing him of squandering men and treasure in an unwinnable war. In April 1967, he was brought home to address Congress, where he received a warm reception. In November 1967, Westmoreland stated that the "end" was beginning "to come into view." When the Tet Offensive struck in January 1968, Westmoreland characterized it as a "desperate act by a demoralized enemy." After Tet, Westmoreland requested an additional 200,000 troops to add to the half-million already in Southeast Asia. The rising dissatisfaction with the war in the U.S. and the report of a bipartisan commission assembled to review the conduct of the war pressed President Lyndon B. Johnson (qv) to turn down the request. In March 1968, Westmoreland was replaced by General Creighton Abrams, and he returned to the U.S. to become the chairman of the Joint Chiefs of Staff. Westmoreland retired from the army in June 1972. He was defeated in a race for the Republican nomination for governor of South Carolina in July 1974. Over the years, Westmoreland bitterly criticized the Johnson administration's handling of the war, especially the effect Robert S. McNamara (qv) had on the war effort while secretary of defense.

West Pakistan. *See* Pakistan.

West Somali Liberation Front (WSLF). One of the groups which operated in the Eritrean region of Ethiopia in the late 1970s, the WSLF forces attacked Ethiopian positions in Ogaden province (*see* Ethiopia) in August 1977 in a final offensive to drive out the Ethiopians. Somalian troops supported the operation but probably had their own objectives. The initial fight with the WSLF took place near the town of Dire Dawe on the Djibouti (qv)–Addis Ababa road on 17 July 1977. By 29 September, the WSLF had captured the Gara Marda Pass in northern Ogaden.

Wheeler, Earle Gilmore. (b. 13 January 1908, Washington, DC—d. 18 December 1975, Frederick, Maryland) An Army officer who saw some combat service in World War II, Wheeler was known best for his administrative capabilities and his grasp of the realities of politicomilitary requirements. A protégé of General

Maxwell D. Taylor (qv), Wheeler became the staff director of the Joint Chiefs of Staff in 1960. During the elections held that year, Wheeler briefed presidential candidate John F. Kennedy (qv) on the military situation. Upon his election, Kennedy appointed Wheeler chief of staff of the army (October 1962). As Army Chief of Staff, Wheeler impressed the secretary of defense, Robert McNamara (qv), by his defense of the nuclear test ban treaty in 1963. President Lyndon B. Johnson (qv) made Wheeler the chairman of the Joint Chiefs of Staff in July 1964. Wheeler favored a more extensive commitment of U.S. troops during the Vietnam War telling Johnson that no fewer than 850,000 troops were required to achieve victory. He further stated that the bombing of North Vietnam was not preventing the North Vietnamese buildup in the south.

Wheelus Air Base, Libya. On 1 September 1969, a military coup overthrew the king of Libya. The new government, led by Muammar al-Qaddafi (qv), immediately announced the closing of all American and British bases in the country upon the expiration of the agreements covering their use. One of the most important of these was the U.S. Air Force base at Wheelus Field. The U.S. announced it would withdraw from Wheelus on 23 December 1969. The last U.S. forces left the base on 11 June 1971.

Whitlam, Gough. Gough Whitlam became prime minister of Australia on 5 December 1972. One of his first acts after his Australian Labor Party government was seated was to order an end to the draft and to promise a withdrawal of Australian troops from South Vietnam. Whitlam's government lost control of Parliament on 11 November 1975, and he was replaced in office by a conservative.

Whitty, Kenneth. On 28 March 1984, a terrorist of the Revolutionary Organization of Socialist Muslims assassinated Kenneth Whitty, a British diplomat serving as deputy representative of the British Consul, and his Greek driver. The attack took place in central Athens in broad daylight. No arrests were made in the incident.

Wiesbaden. *See* Germany.

Williams, Samuel T. *See* Vietnam.

Wilson, Charles E. (b. 18 July 1890, Minerva, Ohio—d. 26 September 1961, Norwood, Louisiana) Born the son of a high school principal, Wilson moved with his family to Mineral City in 1894 and to Pittsburgh in 1904. He graduated from the Carnegie Institute of Technology with a degree in electrical engineering in 1909. Throughout this period, Wilson openly supported the presidential candidacy of Eugene Debs, an avowed socialist. This association effectively closed most doors to Wilson's career as an engineer and forced him into the less lucrative field of patternmaking. He then became business agent for the patternmaker's union local. In 1910, he went to work as an engineer at Westinghouse. In 1912, he designed the first electric automobile starter built by Westinghouse. He married Jessie Ann Curtis in 1912. In 1916, he became head of all Westinghouse automobile electrical products. During World War I, Wilson designed electrical equipment for the military. He went to work for a General Motors subsidiary after the war, and by 1926 he was the general manager and then president of Delco-Remy. In 1928 he became vice-president of GM. He was appointed executive vice-president in 1939 and president in 1941. In 1943, he collapsed under the strain of GM's war work schedule and suffered circulatory problems and headaches the rest of his life. In 1952, President Eisenhower nominated Wilson to be secretary of defense, but his confirmation hearings went badly when he refused to divest his holdings of $2.5 million in GM stock. He was confirmed, however, only after he agreed to sell the stock. After the Korean War, Wilson slashed the defense budget to the bone and made few friends in the military with his policy of reducing conventional forces in favor of nuclear deterrence. He forced the Joint Chiefs of Staff to support him publicly on this issue, but he was reversed by the president when he ordered the military in the Pentagon to work in civilian clothes. He also ran afoul of organized labor when he publicly criticized unemployed workers in Toledo, Ohio. After he left the Defense Department in 1957, he continued his criticism of the military, taking particular aim at Lieutenant General James A. Gavin, whom he accused of poor planning in the nuclear defense of the U.S. against the vastly superior, but actually mythical, missile strength of the USSR. After his federal service, Wilson became the chairman of the Michigan advisory committee to the U.S. Commission on Civil Rights.

Windhoek. *See* Namibia.

Wireless Ridge. *See* Falkland Islands.

Wiriyamu. *See* Mozambique.

Wollongong. *See* Australia.

Wonju. *See* Korea.

Wonsan Harbor. *See* Korea.

Woo, Brian. On 15 August 1980, an American diplomat, Brian Woo, was wounded by Salvadoran troops during three days of heavy fighting with leftist rebel forces in the streets of San Salvador.

Woodward, John. Rear Admiral John "Sandy" Woodward commanded the main British naval task force during the Falkland Islands campaign of 1982. *See* Falkland Islands.

Workers' Defense Force. In March 1984, the government of Colombia signed a cease-fire agreement with the Colombian Revolutionary Armed Forces (FARC), the Marxist-Leninist peasant rebel force that was considered the most coherent of all of the rebel groups and one of the two major dangerous groups in that country. On 23 August of that year, two other smaller leftist guerrilla groups, the Maoist Popular Liberation Army and the Workers' Defense Force, signed similar truce agreements. The other major terrorist group, M-19 (*Movimiento 19 Abril*), signed at the same time, but under different circumstances, and really did not cease operations until 1989.

World Court. *See* International Court of Justice; United Nations.

World Cup Soccer. An annual sporting event noted for the deaths, fights and stampedes that have attended a number of the matches. The World Cup Soccer matches held in Honduras (qv) in June 1969 are especially noted, as the anti-Salvadoran rioting that broke out on 15 June 1969 led to an invasion of

Honduras by El Salvador in mid-July. El Salvador was, at the moment, in the process of severing diplomatic (26 June) relations with Honduras because of its expulsion of 11,000 Salvadoran settlers from Honduran territory under a 1962 Agrarian Reform Law. The results of the playoffs in the World Soccer competition, which was won by El Salvador, only inflamed the situation. By August, troops from the Organization of American States (OAS) had restored order and secured the withdrawal of the invading troops.

SS World Knight. On 9 October 1984, the supertanker *SS World Knight* was attacked by Iraqi aircraft off Kharg Island during the Iran-Iraq War. Seven crewmen were killed and eight injured. The ship was able to complete its voyage.

Wossen, Asfa. On 14 December 1960, Imperial troops seized the Ethiopian capital city of Addis Ababa and proclaimed Crown Prince Asfa Wossen as king. Enperor Haile Selassie (qv) was on a state visit to Brazil at the time. Regular army troops crushed the uprising and restored order. Asfa Wossen, who had been held captive by the mutineers, was freed. Many of mutinous troops were taken into custody. Selassie returned to Ethiopia immediately and resumed his throne. On 12 September 1974, Haile Selassie was deposed in a bloodless coup. The 57-year-old Asfa Wossen was named his successor by the army, but he refused to return to Addis Ababa from Geneva, Switzerland, where he had lived since having a stroke in 1972. The ruling junta named army general Aman Michael Andom (qv) to head the government.

Wroclaw. *See* Poland.

Wuhan. *See* China.

Wyszynski, Stefan Cardinal. (b. 3 August 1901, Zuzela, Russian Poland—d. 28 May 1981, Warsaw) Wyszynski was born the son of a village schoolteacher and church organist. Wyszynski attended schools in Warsaw and Lomza before entering the seminary at Wloclawek. Wyszynski was ordained a priest on 3 August 1924 and assumed his first duties as vicar of the basilica at Wloclawek. He also served as editor of two Catholic journals before attending the Catholic University in Lublin, where he received a doctorate in sociology and canon law (1939). He also studied abroad in Belgium, France and Italy. It was during this period that he became known as the "labor priest" because of his dedication to the working class. He was widely acknowledged as the champion of labor and wrote several books on labor subjects. When the Nazis invaded Poland in September 1939, Wyszynski was a professor of sociology at the Higher Seminary of Wloclawek. He was also the director of the Catholic Workers University, which he had founded in 1935. After the Nazi occupation began, Wyszynski joined the Polish resistance and worked against the Nazis in Lublin and Warsaw. By the end of the war, about 40 percent of all clergymen in Poland had been imprisoned, and many were martyred for their refusal to acknowledge their Nazi masters or because they served in the underground. On 12 May 1946, he was consecrated Bishop of Lublin and continued for a time as the rector of the Catholic University. In 1948, he became the Archbishop of Gniezno and Warsaw and the Primate of Poland. This was at the same time that the Polish

Communist Party took control of the country. From that moment, Archbishop Wyszynski's role was as protector of the Catholic faith against the communist government of Poland. Although the Church and the communist government achieved a modus vivendi in 1950 that allowed the co-existence of Catholicism and communism in Poland, the government maintained a steady stream of criticism against Wyszynski. When Pope Pius XII nominated Wyszynski to become Cardinal (November 1952), the Polish priest informed Rome that his departure to attend the Consistory scheduled for January 1953 might be used as an excuse for the communists to deny him the right of return. He was arrested in September 1953 for refusing to denounce one of his bishops and was sentenced, after a three-year incarceration without charges, to 12 years in prison. His internment was in a monastery, where, with his duties suspended by the state, he remained three years before the intercession of Wladyslaw Gomulka (qv) obtained his release. He visited the Vatican in May 1957, at which time he received his symbols of princehood in the Church. The relationship between Wyszynski and Gomulka, although they seldom met with each other directly, has been credited with preventing a Soviet invasion of Poland in response to anti-communist demonstrations. In return for his support of Gomulka, Wyszynski secured many accommodations for the Church. In later years, Cardinal Wyszynski provided both encouragement and his influence in the development of the Solidarity (qv) movement and of Lech Walesa (qv). He died of natural causes in Warsaw on 28 May 1981. He was 80 years old. *Reading:* Andrzei Micewski, *Cardinal Wyszynski: A Biography* (1986); Stefan Wyszynski, *A Freedom Within: The Prison Notes of Stefan Cardinal Wyszynski* (1984).

Xa Loi Pagoda. One of the Buddhist pagodas occupied by Army of Vietnam (ARVN) troops during a crackdown on dissident elements in Saigon was the Xa Loi Pagoda. The police and army troops arrested a number of Buddhist priests during the operation which was ordered by Ngo Dinh Diem (qv), Vietnam's president.

Xieng Dat. *See* Laos.

Xieng Khoaung. *See* Laos.

Xuan, Nguyen Van. On 5 June 1948, the State of Vietnam was established by the Baie d'Along (Ha Long Bay) Agreement. The agreement was signed by Bao Dai (qv), by the French high commissioner for Indochina, Emile Bollaert and by General Nguyen Van Xuan. Bao Dai was designated chief of state within the French Union.

Xuan Loc (Xa Xuan Loc). *See* Vietnam.

Xuan Thuy. On 6 November 1969, the North Vietnamese delegate to the Paris peace talks on Vietnam criticized U.S. president Richard M. Nixon (qv) for disclosing information on the secret peace talks. Ironically, North Vietnam had already rejected the accords that had been reached.

Y

Yad Mordechai. *See* Israel.

Yahya Khan, Agha Mohammed. (b. 4 February 1917, Chakwal, Peshawar, British India—d. 9 August 1980, Rawalpindi, Pakistan) Yahya Khan was born on the northwest frontier into the Kizilbash clan and was a descendent of an elite military family dating back to the times of Nadir Khan of the eighteenth century. He attended Punjab University and the Indian Military Academy. During World War II he fought in the Middle East and Italy. After the 1947 partition of India and Pakistan, he helped organize the Pakistani Staff College and became a brigadier in 1951 at age 34. At age 49, he was a lieutenant general. He played a leading role in the 1958 coup that brought Ayub Khan (qv) to power. He became commander in chief of the Pakistani armed forces in 1966. To forestall further unrest in country, Ayub Khan resigned the presidency on 25 March 1969. At that point, the government was placed in the hands of Yahya Khan. His first act was to declare martial law. National elections were then set for 5 October 1970. On 1 January 1970, he lifted political restrictions to allow for free discussions before the election. The continuing unstable conditions in Pakistan in 1970 and one of the worst natural disasters in history—the cyclone and tidal wave in East Pakistan that left more than 200,000 dead—caused the elections to be postponed until 7 December 1970. Yahya Khan resigned the presidency on 20 December 1971, at which time Zulfikar Ali Bhutto took office. Yahya Khan's loss of power could be blamed on the disastrous war with India (*see* Indo-Pakistani War) and the loss of East Pakistan (*see* Bangladesh). Yahya Khan was forced to reinstitute martial law on 24 March 1971. On 8 January 1972, three weeks after he had resigned, Yahya Khan was arrested and remained in house detention for the next five years. After his release, he lived quietly until his death in 1980.

Yakovievich, Vasily. On 23 November 1984, a Soviet citizen, Vasily Yakovievich, working with the North Koreans, defected to South Korea. A firefight between North and South Korean forces developed along the Demilitarized Zone (DMZ) at Panmunjom in which three North Koreans and one South Korean were killed. Following the incident, North Korea broke off trade talks with the South Korean government.

Yalta Agreement. On 4 February 1945, the wartime Allied leaders, Roosevelt (U.S.), Churchill (UK) and Stalin (USSR) met in the Crimean seaside resort at Yalta. The conference (codename, Argonaut) dealt with problems such as Poland, the final defeat of Germany, the fate of southeastern Europe, and the Soviet Union's future role in the defeat of Japan. Regarding Germany, the policy of unconditional surrender was reaffirmed, and the methods for controlling the country following the surrender were worked out. The demarcation between Germany and Poland was established along the Oder-Neisse Line. The fate of the smaller countries was also decided, as much by their actual occupation by liberating forces as by agreement. Arrangements were also made for a Soviet attack on Japan three months after the fall of Germany. The conference concluded on 8 February with a banquet at which Josef Stalin stated that the most difficult task would be to maintain the alliance after the war ended.

Yalu River. *See* Korea.

Yameogo, Maurice. On 5 August 1960, Maurice Yameogo became the first president of the newly independent Republic of Upper Volta. In 3 January 1966, internal disturbances prompted a military coup led by Lieutenant Colonel Sangoule Lamizana (qv), which forced Yameogo to resign. Lamizana then became head of state.

Yaounde. *See* Cameroon.

Yarmouk Brigade. On 28 January 1982, King Hussein of Jordan called upon the youth of his nation to fight alongside Iraq against Iran (*see* Iraq-Iran War) in an "arabization" of that conflict. A volunteer organization called the Yarmouk Brigade was formed to enter the fight.

Yarmuk Valley, Golan Heights. *See* Israel.

Yemen (*al Yaman*). A country located on the southern edge of the Arabian peninsula, Yemen is bordered on the north by Saudi Arabia, on the east by Oman, on the south by the Gulf of Aden and on the west by the Red Sea. In the southwest corner, it is separated from Djibouti (qv) by the Strait of Mandeb (*Bab el Mandeb*). Yemen's territory was once part of the biblical kingdom of Sheba (*Sara*) and predates the Christian era. In 632 A.D., Yemen was united along with all of Arabia under the Caliph Abu Bakr. The next ten centuries approximate the types and focus of development observed in all Muslim nations. In 1618, the English, with a firman (license) from the Sublime Porte, opened a trading center at Mocha (*al Mukha*) on the Red Sea coast. The British occupied southern Yemen (Aden) in 1839, stopping an Egyptian advance into the region. The Turks returned to northern Yemen (San'a), however, in 1849. An Anglo-Turkish agreement signed in 1914 established a border between north and south Yemen with the south under British protection, while the north remained generally under Ottoman rule until 1918. After the war the frontier between north and south raised many problems. In 1934, an agreement was reached that codified the status quo of the frontier for 40 years. Intermittent clashes took place along the frontier in 1954. The leader of the north (San'a) signed a tripartite military alliance with Saudi Arabia and Egypt on 24 April 1956 (Jidda Pact) and, in 1958, federated with the United Arab Republic (the federation was called the United Arab States). These arrangements were dissolved in 1961. San'a also claimed South Yemen (Aden). When the treaty was broken, a long period of Egyptian-supported subversion began in San'a. The San'a leader, Ahmed (qv) (Imam Seif al-Islam Ahmad), who took power in 1948, died in 1962 and was replaced by his son, Crown Prince Mohammed al-Badr (qv). Nine days later (27 September), a revolution began in which imam Mohammed was killed in the shelling of his palace. A trusted aide, who had led the revolt, Abdullah al-Sallal, took power and proclaimed the Yemen Arab Republic (YAR). It soon became apparent that Egyptian influence was behind the coup and the construction of the new Yemeni government. Communist states flocked to recognize the YAR, and later the U.S. joined in granting recogition. Royalist forces that reached the mountains joined with the local tribesmen, and civil war ensued. On 28 March 1964, in retaliation for an attack on Saudi Arabian positions in South Yemen, British aircraft attacked and destroyed a North Yemeni fortification. By 1965, a procommunist government had been installed in North Yemen. Over 60,000 Egyptian troops were reported in the country. On 24 August 1965, a cease-fire was arranged between all of the warring factions. This was the third such arrangement in two years. During June 1967, Egypt began withdrawing substantial numbers of its troops deployed in North Yemen. On 24 August 1967, Egypt and Saudi Arabia agreed to stop the fighting in Yemen. Also, in 1967, South Yemen, formed out of Aden and the protectorate, won its independence from Great Britain. Meanwhile, back in North Yemen, a bloodless coup took place on 5 November 1967. Peace talks, which began on 12 January 1968, broke down on 19 January. Fighting continued in North Yemen between republican and royalist forces. On 6 September 1969, republican forces captured the last royalist stronghold at Sa'dah. In November 1969, a series of border clashes occurred near the Al Wadeiah oasis on the North Yemen–Saudi Arabian border. In December, Saudi Arabia resumed its military support to the royalist forces in North Yemen. On 13–14 January 1970, republican forces attacked the Saudi border town of Nahuga. Saudi forces immediately retaliated by attacking a rebel-held border post. A peace treaty was signed in North Yemen in April 1970. North and South Yemen signed a peace agreement that also pledged reunification within one year on 28 October 1972. Also in 1972 the South Yemen, the only Marxist government in the Arab world, took the name People's Democratic Republic of Yemen and continued its conflict with neighboring Oman, while North Yemen turned toward Saudi Arabia and the West for support. On 13 June 1974, a military coup took place in North Yemen that placed Colonel Ibrahim al-Hamidi (qv) in power. He was assassinated in 1977. In 1979, South Yemen signed a 20-year friendship treaty with the USSR that allowed Soviet troops to be stationed on its territory. Since 1967, more than 300,000 South Yemenites had fled into North Yemen. Numerous border clashes between north and south occurred during the period before an Arab League-sponsored agreement aiming toward unification was signed by the two countries on 29 March 1979. The concept of unification was thereafter discussed, even though South Yemen continued support of North

Yemeni rebels (1982) and sporadic fighting continued, along the common border between North Yemen and rebel forces. In 1984, South Yemen recognized Oman for the first time in 20 years and began the task of reestablishing its relations with Great Britain, its former colonial master. North Yemen's border with Saudi Arabia became the site of a border clash when Yemeni border forces attempted to set up two customs checkpoints on what Saudi Arabia claimed as its territory. A very violent coup (estimated casualties as high as 10,000) overthrew the government of South Yemen's president, Ali Nasir Muhammad Husani, on 24 January 1986. Muhammad fled to Egypt, and a new Yemen Socialist Party government was put in place. Although an amnesty was declared for Muhammad's followers, South Yemen's action during the year indicated rather strong measures, including forcing down a Djibouti airliner to find the more prominent among the passengers. In the worst clash since 1975, South Yemen and Omani forces fought a pitched battle along their common border on 11 October 1987. Eight Yemeni troops were killed, and only diplomatic intervention helped prevent a full-scale confrontation. In December of that year, former president Muhammad Husani was tried in absentia and sentenced to death. South Yemen restored diplomatic relations with Egypt in 1988. The two countries formally united on 21 May 1990. When Iraq invaded Kuwait in August 1990, Yemen's stand was pro-Iraqi, and it voted against the UN order for Iraq to withdraw. Already in 1991, the effects of Yemen's position on Iraq began to be felt economically and in other ways. For instance, nearly one million Yemenis were forced to leave Saudi Arabia with an approximate loss of about $7 billion in wages. The U.S. cut more than $20 million in aid. Only the PLO showed support for Yemen during this period. A period of internal violence followed (1992), which forced Yemen to postpone scheduled elections. Bombings and other attacks on leading politicians began in April 1992 by terrorists assumed to be backed by northern extremist groups. When Yemen accused Saudi Arabia of involvement in the affair, the Saudis revoked over three-quarters of a million Yemeni work permits and cut all aid and assistance to Yemen. Thirteen were killed in the ensuing rioting in Yemen (December 1992). Yemen did, however, reach a border demarcation agreement with Oman in October. The situation became even more weird when the Yemeni vice president indicated (August 1993) that he was informed in the U.S. of a threat on his life if he attended certain meetings in San'a. The prime minister supported him and demanded better security and a removal of the conditions causing the violence. By that point, nearly 150 Yemeni Socialist Party (YSP) members had been murdered. By 5 May 1994, a civil war had broken out between the north and the south. On 21 May, the YSP with support from the Sons of Yemen League declared a secessionist state. Heavy fighting continued. The UN denounced the north (1 June), while the south was supplied with sophisticated ex-Soviet fighters by Moldava. By mid-July, the north had all but won the war and a reconciliation plan was adopted to restore the country. While YSP members were being replaced in government, their replacements were largely Islamic fundamentalists with a different agenda. By 1995, the armed forces of north and south had been integrated without undue incident as the country moved slowly toward complete integration. However, clashes along the Saudi Arabian border occurred throughout 1995 despite the signing of an agreement between the two countries that should have obviated such incidents. Yemen also experienced difficulties with Eritrea over alleged encroachment on Red Sea islands claimed by Yemen. *Reading:* Paul Dresch, *Tribes, Government, and History in Yemen* (1994); Joseph Kostiner, *The Struggle for South Yemen* (1984); Ali Abdel Rahman Rahmy, *The Egyptian Policy in the Arab World: Intervention in Yemen, 1962-1967* (1983).

Yenan. *See* China.

Yen Vien Railroad Yards, North Vietnam. *See* Vietnam.

Yepishev, A. A. Yepishev was the director of the Main Political Directorate of the Soviet Ministry of Defense when he visited Afghanistan in April 1979. Among his other functions during that visit, he was charged with assessing the politicomilitary situation prior to a Soviet response to an Afghan government request for Soviet military assistance in stabilizing the deteriorating situation in that country. *See* Afghanistan.

Yhombi-Opango, Joachim. (b. 1940, Owanda, northern Congo) On 18 March 1977, Congo president Marien Ngouabi (qv) was assassinated. A bloody repression of political opponents followed until 4 April 1977, when Colonel Joachim Yhombi-Opanga, a close friend of the slain Ngouabi, took over as head of state of the Congo People's Republic. Yhombi-Opanga had been a noncommissioned officer in the French army and had been sent to France's military academy, Sainte-Cyr. In 1962 he returned to Congo and became an aide to the president, Alphonse Massamba-Debat (qv). After Massamba's overthrow, Yhombi-Opanga became chief of staff (1969) and inspector general of the army (1973). He was appointed secretary-general of the Council of State in 1974 and acting minister of defense in 1975. He was in that post when elevated to the nation's leadership. On 7 February 1979, Yhombi-Opango was overthrown in a bloodless coup led by the pro-Soviet former minister of defense, Colonel Denis Sassou-Nguesso (qv). On 1 April 1979, Yhombi-Opango was tried for treason and imprisoned. He was granted amnesty in August 1979.

Yoffe, Avraham. *See* Israel.

Yola City. *See* Nigeria.

Yom Kippur War. *See* Arab-Israel Wars.

York Harbor. *See* Falkland Islands.

Youlou Fubert. Youlou Fubert, a priest, became the first president of the Republic of Congo in November 1958. He remained president when the nation gained its independence from the French Community in 1960. On 15 August 1963, he was ousted from office after labor rioting broke out in Brazzaville (*see* Congo). Youlou was imprisoned and replaced in the presidency by a pro-Chinese communist, Alphonse Massamba-Debat (qv). On 7 February 1964, a number of Youlou's supporters broke him out of prison. His escape was followed by widespread rioting in Brazzaville.

Youth Action Group. On 15 December 1974, an extreme right-wing terrorist group calling itself the Youth Action Group, detonated bombs outside the TWA offices and the Coca-Cola Company offices in Paris, France. They also attacked the Minnesota Mining Company offices in Paris. The three attacks were claimed to be in protest of a Franco-American summit meeting being held in Martinique. No one was hurt in the blasts.

Yueh Ya-pao District. *See* China.

Yugoslavia. A country located on the Balkan Peninsula in southeastern Europe, Yugoslavia is today (1994) bordered on the north by Hungary, on the east by Romania and Bulgaria, on the south by Albania and Greek Macedonia and on the west by Bosnia-Herzogovina and Croatia. Yugoslavia is, in its present configuration, composed of the provinces of Serbia and Montenegro. The capital city is Belgrade. After the collapse of the Austro-Hungarian Empire following World War I, the provinces of Bosnia, Croatia, Dalmatia, Herzogovina, independent Montenegro, Serbia, Slovenia and Voyvodina were formed into the Kingdom of the Serbs, Croats and Slovenes. The name was later changed to Yugoslavia. During World War II, the German invasion of Yugoslavia prompted a massive resistance that generally followed the lines of two insurgent armies, one led by Draja Mikhailovich (qv) and the other led by the communist Josef Broz, known as Marshal Tito (qv). Tito also had British support during the war. When the Germans were driven out of Yugoslavia in 1945, Tito's forces controlled most of the country. Mikhailovich was captured (24 March), tried, and executed on 17 July 1946 by Tito. In May 1946, Tito began assisting the Greek communist insurgents in that country. Yugoslavia proclaimed itself an independent federated republic on 29 November 1945 and adopted a Soviet-style constitution on 31 January 1946. Tito became the head of state. Almost immediately, Tito rejected the Soviet Union's—that is, Josef Stalin's (qv)—practice of meddling in the affairs of its satellites. On 18 September 1946, the wartime Croatian leader, Alois Cardinal Stepinac (qv), was captured by Tito forces and sentenced to 16 years in prison. Yugoslavia sought aid from the West and supported Czechoslovakia before the Soviet invasion of that country in 1968 (*see* Czechoslovakia). In August 1947, Yugoslav troops threatened the city of Trieste, Italy. U.S. occupation forces deployed to repel them, and a near-war incident was averted. Tensions in the region did not, however, subside. Tito supported the Soviet Union in its 1947 demands regarding a peace settlement with Austria. That issue was not settled until 1950. In March 1948, however, the USSR withdrew its military and technical missions from Yugoslavia. On 28 June, the COMINFORM expelled Yugoslavia for practices contradictory to Marxist-Leninist teachings. On 27 November 1948, the United States condemned Yugoslavia (along with Albania and Bulgaria) for its part in supporting the communist side in the Greek civil war. In September 1951, Tito offered to settle all outstanding problems with Italy. On 17 December 1952, Yugoslavia broke diplomatic relations with the Vatican when the Pope refused to intervene in the struggle between the Catholic church and the Tito government. In January 1953, talks began in Belgrade on the formation of a

Balkan Alliance (qv). An agreement in principle was reached among Yugoslavia, Turkey and Greece on 22 December 1953 and reaffirmed by Yugoslavia on 16 April 1954. Great Britain announced its determination to protect Yugoslavia as long as that country would fight any aggression (31 March 1953). In another affront to the Soviet Union, Tito removed political commissars from his armed forces. Two weeks later, Moscow asked for a resumption of full diplomatic relations with Yugoslavia. On 6 October of that year, the U.S. and Great Britain announced a plan to divide Trieste between Italy, which agreed to the plan, and Yugoslavia. Tito denounced the plan and the city remained under Italian control upon the withdrawal of the occupation forces. Five days later, Tito threatened to use force to stop the Italians from occupying the eastern part (Zone "A") of Trieste. The next day, 12 October, Tito asked for a conference on the situation, while the USSR demanded UN intervention. A joint meeting was held on 1 November, and, on 5 December, both Yugoslavia and Italy announced they would withdraw their troops near the city. A Yugoslav-Italian treaty was signed on 5 October 1954 in which Italy got Trieste while Yugoslavia received the eastern part of the Trieste enclave. Yugoslavia reinstated diplomatic relations with Albania on 22 December 1953. In June 1955, Nikita Khrushchev (qv) traveled to Belgrade for a conciliation meeting with Tito. Following the meeting, the two leaders called for a ban on nuclear weapons, a European collective security treaty and the admission of Communist China to the UN. In return, Khrushchev gave Tito a nuclear reactor (3 January 1956). In October 1956, the U.S. declared it would continue sending economic aid to Tito but ruled out any military assistance. Yugoslav relations with the USSR worsened near year's end as a result of an inflammatory speech made by Tito at a party congress meeting. On 19 February 1957, Khrushchev announced there would be no further economic aid to Yugoslavia, but the USSR rescinded the order on 29 July. On 7 October, Tito recognized East Germany, probably as a conciliatory gesture. In September 1960, Yugoslavia became part of a scheme to install a neutral buffer in the Balkans between East and West. In September 1961, Yugoslavia hosted a conference of 25 nonaligned nations that hoped to ask the superpowers to halt the arms race and to avert war. On 31 January 1968, Yugoslavia opened diplomatic relations with West Germany. Student demonstrations in Yugoslavia in June 1968 were forcibly suppressed by the police. On 2 February, a joint Yugoslav-Romanian communique denounced the "Brezhnev Doctrine." An agreement was reached with Sudan in May 1969 to build a naval base in that country. In September 1976, however, Yugoslavia turned down a Soviet request for basing rights on the Adriatic coast. In October 1978, however, western intelligence sources showed evidence that Yugoslavia was servicing Soviet submarines. In August 1977, the Kremlim and Tito issued a joint communique reasserting Yugoslavia's right to choose its own course. In a conference of nonaligned nations held in Belgrade in July 1978, Tito openly criticized Cuba's entry into the Angolan struggle as a Soviet ploy. Reversing its policy against military sales to Yugoslavia, the U.S. sold it 400 jet engines in September 1978. From the beginning of Tito's regime, unrest grew in the various provinces, and separatist movements sprang up in the Federated Republic of Croatia. Tito clamped down on this by ordering the arrest of the movement's leaders and by changing the republic's government (14 January 1972) to one more compliant with Belgrade's orders. A fear of a Czech-style Soviet invasion led to a tightening of political and intellectual controls throughout the country. Part of this situation grew out of Tito's 1965 decision to decentralize control as an economic stimulus to enable better competition with the West. After Tito's death on 4 May 1980, the presidency of Yugoslavia and the chairmanship of the Communist Party became rotating positions held by the heads of individual republics, a plan Tito had announced in September 1970. Rioting broke out at the University of Pristina over the cost of living in March 1981. The predominantly Albanian region of Kosovo was put under a state of emergency order after a month of student unrest in April 1981. Eleven were killed and 57 injured during the episode. In May 1981 the University of Pristina was closed after new ethnically-motivated disorders broke out. On 22 January 1990, a Communist Party congress announced that it no longer subscribed to its constitutionally guaranteed right of leading the country and asked parliament to amend the law to allow political pluralism and a multiparty system. Croatia (qv) and Slovenia declared their independence from Yugoslavia on 25 June 1991. This action brought about an immediate state of civil war in which the Croats began battling ethnic Serbs residing in Croatia. The Serb rebels were supplied arms and other supplies from predominantly Serbian Yugoslavia. Croat forces also engaged Yugoslav military forces along the border in August 1991. On 15 October 1991, Bosnia-Herzogovina declared its sovereignty and, on 29 February 1992, its independence. The referendum that accomplished this act was hotly contested by the predominantly Christian ethnic Serbs in Bosnia-Herzogovina, and civil war broke out, which was again initally endorsed and fostered by Yugoslavia. Yugoslav forces entered the fighting against the largely Muslim ethnic Bosnian population. United Nations sanctions against Yugoslavia forced it to change its policies. A UN peacekeeping force was sent to Bosnia to help restore order, but the centuries-old ethnic and religious hatreds insured a continuation of the struggle, including the Serbian plan of "ethnic cleansing." The UN was seemingly incapable of coping with the situation, and NATO forces were introduced into Bosnia in 1995 to keep the peace. A fragile peace agreement was reached in December 1995. The presence of NATO forces, which are strong enough and willing to fight, has helped maintain at least the semblance of order, although the Serbs still refuse full cooperation. Yugoslavia's president, Slobodan Milosevic, has been accused by world opinion of abetting the crisis in Bosnia. While Milosevic has made some attempts to bring Bosnian Serb leaders into compliance with UN and NATO orders, he has been relatively unsuccessful. His ever-strengthening control in Yugoslavia has seen to it that little of these difficulties is transmitted to the people. The people of Yugoslavia suffered in the meantime from UN sanctions, and in 1995 Yugoslavia was still treated as an outcast nation. In 1995, Yugoslavia continued its military support of Serb rebels, operating under such banners as the "Serb Republic of Krajina" in Slavonia and Croatia. At the same time, however, the results of negotiations in which Milosevic played an important role (Balkan Accords, Paris, 14 December 1995) have aided in the lifting of some sanctions, but did not settle the very complex and often acrimonious relations among the former Yugoslav states. *Reading:* Sabrina Petra Ramet, *Balkan Babel: The Disintegration of Yugoslavia from the Death of Tito to Ethnic War* (1996); Susan L. Woodward, *Balkan Tragedy: Chaos and Dissolution after the Cold War* (1995); Martyn C. Rady, *The Breakup of Yugoslavia* (1994); Lenard J. Cohen, *Broken Bonds: Yugoslavia's Disintegration and Balkan Politics in Transition* (1995); Jeffrey B. Symynkywicz, *Civil War in Yugoslavia* (1997).

Yu-min. *See* China.

Yunis. *See* Israel.

Yun Po Sun. On 16 May 1962, an anticommunist military coup forced the resignation of the South Korean government of President Yun Po Sun. The coup leaders then installed General Park Chung Hee in his place. Yun Po Sun was subsequently defeated in a general election held for the presidency in an October 1963 election.

Zahedi, Fazollah. On 4 March 1951, Mohammed Mossadegh (qv) became prime minister of Iran. By 1953, his policies had lost him most of the support that had originally put him in power. After April 1953, an open power struggle developed between Mossadegh and General Fazollah Zahedi, a former minister of interior. In August, the shah issued an edict appointing Zahedi prime minister. An attempt to arrest Mossadegh failed, and he was able to rally sufficient support that civil war appeared imminent. The shah fled to Rome, and Zahedi went into hiding (15 August). Four days later, however, the army overthrew Mossadegh, and Zahedi was installed as prime minister. Zahedi remained in office leading a Western-oriented government until 1955, when he was replaced by Husain 'Ala. Zahedi's government had been returned to office by a huge majority in the elections held on 20 February 1954.

Zahir Khan, Mohammed. Zahir Khan became king of Afghanistan in 1933. On 17 July 1973, a coup led by the king's brother-in-law, Lieutenant General Prince Mohammad Daud Khan (qv), overthrew the monarchy. Zahir Khan was in Italy undergoing medical treatment at the time and elected to remain there after Afghanistan was declared a republic. *See* Afghanistan.

Zahle (Zahlah). *See* Lebanon.

al-Za'im, Husni. On 30 March 1949, a bloody military coup led by the army chief of staff, Husni Za'im, overthrew the government of Syrian President Shukri al-Kuwatly (qv). Za'im was installed as president. On 14 August 1949, Za'im was overthrown in another coup, this time led by Sami al-Hinnawi. Za'im was arrested and executed. Hashim al-Atasi (qv) became president at that time.

Zaire. The Republic of Zaire is located in central Africa. It is bordered on the northwest by the Central African Republic, on the northeast by Sudan, on the east by Uganda, Rwanda, Burundi and Tanzania, on the southeast and south by Zambia, on the southwest by Angola and on the west by Congo. Zaire is drained by the mighty Congo River, which remains inside the Zambian border until it empties into the Atlantic Ocean. In the period before European expansion into the region, the lands that are today Zaire were organized in several major kingdoms—Kongo, Luba, Lunda, Lele, Kuba and Bola—the last three being little more than vast tribal areas. In the last half of the nineteenth century, King

Leopold II of Belgium acquired the Congo basin in his own name as a part of the Treaty of Berlin (1885) and proclaimed himself the sovereign of the Independent State of Congo. Funds put forth by the Belgian government for the exploitation of the region led to the Belgian annexation of Congo in 1908. This new land took the name of Belgian Congo. From that time until 1950, when two universities were opened, the Belgian administration kept the Congolese people in near-total ignorance. The first half of the twentieth century was a time of great change in Zaire, but was not a time of the awakening of a national ideology. Administrative districts established by the Belgians created an ethic and a regional atmosphere. In the Kongo region of the first African political parties, *Alliance des Ba-Kongo* (ABAKO) came into existence, led by Joseph Kasavubu (qv). In 1958, this organization had grown into the *Mouvement Nationale Congolais* (MNC), which worked for independence under Kasavubu. On 28 November 1958, the Republic of Congo was proclaimed an independent republic within the French Union. The rapid growth of the independence movement led to much political and civil unrest; independence was achieved on 30 June 1960, with Kasavubu as president and Patrice Lumumba (qv) as prime minister. The new country assumed the name Democratic Congo Republic. Unfortunately, the stage was set for an outbreak of violence that led to a bloody civil war. Within weeks of independence, the UN was asked for military aid (14 July) following army mutinies and separatist-inspired unrest. Two regions, Katanga and Kasai, had broken away from the central government on 11 July. On 12 August a UN force of Swedish troops led by UN Secretary General Dag Hammerskjold arrived in Katanga province. The arrival of the 250-man detachment created a crisis. The breakaway Katangan government's leader, Moishe Tshombe (qv), at first refused their landing request, but finally relented. On 24 August, Lumumba ordered central government troops into Kasai province to put down the revolt there. Then, on 5 September, President Kasavubu removed Lumumba from office. Lumumba refused the order and called the cabinet into session. On 11 September, UN forces intervened to block Lumumba's attempt to seize the radio station in Leopoldville. The next day, Congolese army troops arrested Lumumba, but within 24 hours both houses of Parliament voted Lumumba extraordinary powers. On 14 September, a coup led by army chief of staff Colonel Joseph Mobutu (qv) took over the government. Kasavubu remained the president, but Lumumba was finally ousted from office and arrested. Two days later, on 16 September, Kasavubu ordered Soviet and Czech diplomatic missions out of the country for their part in supporting Patrice Lumumba. In October major clashes were reported between UN and Congolese troops as the Congo army rampaged and pillaged the countryside. At the UN, a decision was reached on 22 November to seat the Kasavubu delegation, rather than one of those representing splinter elements of the country. On 25 November, Lumumba escaped his house arrest, but he was later recaptured by troops loyal to the central government. Then, on 14 December, procommunist troops attempted to seize national control. Led by Lumumba colleague Antoine Gizenga, the rebellious group expanded its power base to large areas of the country. In 1961 Kasavubu was returned to power. Lumumba was assassinated in Katanga province on 13 February (although he may have been killed as early as 17 January), and Moise Tshombe was almost certainly responsible for his murder. When the UN ordered the use of force to quell the disturbances (21 February), Tshombe ordered a mobilization in Katanga province. On 22 February the central government also protested the UN decision as a violation of Congolese sovereignty. Two days later, however, the prime minister asked for UN military action to quell the revolt. Then, on 28 February, the warring factions agreed to cooperate against communist "tyranny" and UN "tutelage." In March 1961, Gizenga at Stanleyville blocked an attempt to gain a confederation among the several warring factions. On 17 April, Gizenga announced his support of Mobutu as his "commander in chief." This action allowed Kasavubu to consolidate the government and, with UN aid, to reorganize the armed forces. When Tshombe withdrew the Katangan delegation from a meeting on 24 April, he was arrested and charged with treason. When the meeting was concluded, a decision to form a federal republic of 20 states was announced (31 May 1961). Tshombe was ordered from custody on 26 April, if he agreed to cooperate with this plan; his release finally came about on 22 June 1961. After his release, however, the Katangan parliament decided to boycott the National Parliament, which was to meet in Leopoldville (4 July). On 1 August 1961, the National Parliament met and appointed Cyrille Adoula (qv) prime minister. Three weeks later, UN forces operating in Katanga captured the radio station as a move to compel Tshombe to end the use of white mercenary troops in his private war against the central government. Tshombe eventually complied. On 13 September, the UN assured Kasavubu that the central government was the only legitimate authority in the country. Thereafter, however, when UN forces attempted to disarm the Katangans, heavy fighting broke out and the UN forces were nearly defeated. Five days later, on 18 September, Dag Hammerskjold was killed in an air crash near Ndola, in Northern Rhodesia. On 20 September, a cease-fire was arranged, which lasted until November, when fighting once again broke out in Katanga province. Thirteen Italian UN troops were killed during a Congo army mutiny in the eastern region of the country. United Nations forces captured Elizabethville in Katanga on 18 December. Another cease-fire was arranged on 21 December. In January 1962, the vice premier of the central government, Antoine Gizenga, attempted to force the breakaway of Kasai province. Central government troops captured Stanleyville, and Gizenga was dismissed. On 15 February, the Katangan Assembly voted to reunite the province with the central government. A relative calm set in until 20 October, when fighting again broke out in Katanga. This situation continued into December, when Tshombe once again defied the UN and violated the truce agreement. At that point, UN forces opened an offensive action into Katanga province. By 15 January 1963, Tshombe, fearing capture by the advancing UN forces, ended Katanga's independence and fled the country. Communist influence began to grow during this period. An Angolan "government in exile" was set up in Leopoldville that acted as a conduit for Chinese Communist aid to

Angola, but it also gave more communists the opportunity to exploit the Democratic Republic of Congo. In June 1964, fighting broke out between government forces and communist-backed rebels; by this time the country was near chaos. The last UN forces left the Congo on 30 June; almost immediately the rebellion flared up again throughout the country. On 10 July, Tshombe returned and was appointed premier. He was able to stop the fighting in Kivu province where the Chinese Communist–backed *Comite National de Liberation* was active. Congolese forces captured the Kivu province town of Albertville on 30 August. However, on 13 October 1965, President Kasavubu dismissed Tshombe. On 24–25 November 1965, Mobutu led a coup that ousted the Kasavubu government. Mobutu declared himself head of state, but inherited little more than a nearly bankrupt country. On 1 March 1966 he assumed all legislative powers from the parliament. His own government was challenged by an unsuccessful coup attempt on 23–24 May. Mobutu was able to consolidate his power and established a strong central government with a new constitution in which all citizens over 18 automatically became members of the one authorized party. Moise Tshombe, who had again fled the country, was tried in absentia on 13 March 1967 and sentenced to death. In June, Katanga, again supported by white mercenaries, rose against the central government. By July, most of the rebelling foreign mercenaries had been driven out of the country into Rwanda, but the fighting was not yet over, as Katangan rebels and white mercenaries captured the Kivu capital on 9 August. By the beginning of May 1968, order had been restored, and those mercenaries who had been captured or interned were turned over to the International Red Cross. The country was renamed Zaire on 27 October 1971. In 1972, Mobutu changed his name to Mobutu Sese Seko so as to have it sound "more African." Mobutu moved to nationalize all foreign-owned agricultural enterprises in Zaire in November 1973 and followed by announcing that all foreign-owned mining interests would be required to present the government with 50 percent of their holdings. This created major problems for many corporations, along with governmental concerns about the safety of their foreign nationals in Zaire. Many had already been robbed of their belongings by corrupt local police officials, and there were numerous problems in the financially encumbered country in paying compensation for losses. In June 1975, Zaire expelled the US ambassador because of his alleged complicity in an assassination attempt on Mobutu's life. Seven officers were executed as a result of the coup attempt and 26 imprisoned. The outcome of the Angolan War (1976) put Zaire into even more trouble as Mobutu was forced to recognize the opposing winners, the Popular Movement for the Liberation of Angola, against his brother-in-law's (Holden Roberto) National Front for the Liberation of Angola (qv). Katangan rebels, who had fled to Angola in 1963, invaded Zaire on 8 March 1977. Mobutu immediately accused the USSR and Angola of engineering the invasion and stated Cuban troops were in the invasion force. Cuban diplomats were then ordered out of Zaire, and Mobutu asked the U.S. for additional aid. When the U.S. response was considered too small, Mobutu's appeal to France brought Moroccan troops into Zaire to help dislodge the rebel invaders (May 1977). Paramount in the episode were the perceived weakness of Zaire's armed forces and the exacerbation of already very complex political and economic tides throughout Africa. Another plan for an armed revolt against Mobutu was broken up in March 1978. This time over 100 were arrested, with many of the alleged conspirators being executed after summary trials. When Katangan rebels again crossed the Zaire border in May 1978, French troops were inserted to restore order and stop the atrocities being committed by the rebels. Belgium soon sent in troops, while the U.S. supplied military equipment. Once again, Zairean troops proved totally ineffective against the invaders. When the rebels withdrew back into Angola, the foreign troops left Zaire. The main result of the incident was a further deepening of Zaire's economic chaos and additional complication of the political situation. Fear of another rebel invasion in June caused African francophone nations to form an emergency security force, which was inserted into Zaire with U.S. air force help. Beginning in 1979, Zaire's orientation began to shift more toward the Soviet Union. Mobutu was also faced that year with the threat of widespread violence stemming from unemployment and inflation. Beginning in 1979 and also in 1980, Mobutu's government was charged with corruption. Mobutu was able to convince the U.S. that the situation was improving, and in August 1979 the African peacekeeping force was withdrawn. In December, a coup was foiled and a number of Zairian officers executed. The International Monetary Fund cut off money to Zaire in January 1980 when the deficit for 1979 was announced. At the same time Amnesty International cited at least 1,000 human rights violations in the country. Rioting and strikes rounded out the year. By 1981 some economic stability began to be seen. Mobutu threatened to sever diplomatic relations with Belgium if Belgium did not stop aiding Zairian rebels. Belgium took steps to accomplish this, but without much success. The issues of IMF support and corrupt mismanagement arose again in 1981. At that point, Mobutu renounced all U.S. aid. Trials against opposition leaders were held to break the backs of those opposed to Moubutu's rule. A border incident with Zambia occurred in February 1982, when Zairian troops were accused of hijacking a grain shipment in Zambian territory. Some shots were fired, and thousands of Zambians fled the area. The border was closed (2 March) by Zaire, and tensions remained high despite negotiations to settle the matter. In a tit-for-tat situation, a number of Arab states broke relations with Zaire after the government announced its decision to reopen diplomacy with Israel in May 1982. In July 1983, Zaire sent troops into Chad to support the Hissan Habré's (qv) government. This action was roundly condemned by the OAU, but it gained favor in the U.S. In 1984, Mobutu ran as the sole candidate and won his third seven year term as president. Opposition groups began a series of bombings in March 1984. Belgium immediately announced its disapproval of Zairian opposition groups operating out of Brussels. French troops had to aid Zairian forces in putting down an uprising in Shaba province in November, but fighting continued into 1985. A mutiny in the Zairian army was the apparent cause of the conflict. The Zaire government denied that charge and claimed the fighting was caused by rebel forces based in Tanzania, a charge Tanzania denied. Mass expulsions of each other's citizens, which began in 1984, continued to strain Zaire-Zambia relations. Congolese National Movement rebels claimed to have attacked a number of towns in eastern Zaire in July 1987. A subsequent meeting of more than a dozen opposition groups in Switzerland in September 1987 concluded with the formation of a government-in-exile devoted to the overthrow of Mobutu. That same year, U.S. forces held maneuvers in Shaba province with the ambivalent consent of Kinshasa. When Belgium announced it would reschedule Zaire's debt (November 1988), an outcry arose from critics who claimed such a move only put more money in Mobutu's pockets. Eventually, all of Mobutu's assets in Belgium were seized, but when Mobutu threatened diplomatic retaliation, the order was lifted. In April 1990, Mobutu lifted the ban on opposition parties and allowed for a transition government to rule until elections could be held. This was but one move designed by Mobutu to defuse the growing international condemnation (1991) of his rule. The now more united opposition organized strong resistance to Mobutu's announcement of a constitutional convention, set up under his rules, in April 1991. Demonstrations against the convention fostered clashes between demonstrators and police in a number of locations. In September, the U.S. halted all aid to Zaire because of continued human rights violations. Foreign nationals contiued to leave Zaire, but Mobutu continued to refuse to yield any power. Troops put down a mutiny and a takeover of the radio station in January 1992, following a demand for Mobutu's resignation. On 16 February, troops opened fire on a peaceful demonstration, killing and injuring a number of participants. More pressure on the government came in the form of a UN Human Rights Commission report charging the Mobutu regime with the deaths of between 12 and 14 students at Lubumbashi University in a May 1990 incident. (Amnesty International had set the death toll at 100, while Kinshasa said one had died) In April 1992, the Constitutional Convention declared its sovereignty and established a transitional government with Mobutu as its head. As Mobutu attempted to maintain his power in 1993, strikes caused major disruptions In 1994, Zaire was the recipient of thousands of refugees fleeing the civil war in Rwanda, which only worsened the already chaotic situation. The refugee situation continued into 1995. Forcible repatriation began in August. The days of Mobutu's virtual dictatorship began to dwindle in number. *Reading:* Alan James, *Britain and the Congo Crisis, 1960-63* (1996); Crawford Young, *The Rise and Fall of the Zairian State* (1985); Sean Kelly, *America's Tyrant: The CIA and Mobutu of Zaire: How the United States Put Mobutu in Power, Protected Him from His Enemies, Helped Hime to Become One of the Richest Men in the World, and Lived to Regret It* (1993); Eric S. Packham, *Freedom and Anarchy* (1996).

Zaldivar. *See* Batista.

Zalmanson, Vulf. On 30 October 1970, a Soviet airliner was hijacked at Smolny airport in the USSR and diverted to Turkey. On 5–7 January 1971, a military court in Leningrad sentenced Vulf Zalmanson to ten years' imprisonment for his part in the affair. The Turkish government had refused to hand over the two actual hijackers.

Zambia. Zambia is a country of south-central Africa bordered by Zaire on the north, Tanzania on the northeast, Mozambique and Zimbabwe on the south and Angola on the west. About 75 miles of Zambian border in the southwest corner of the country along the Zambesi river abuts a narrow finger of land belonging to Namibia. The earliest known settlers of the region were Tonga tribesmen who drifted into the area about 1000 A.D. In the 1890s, Cecil Rhodes and the British South Africa Company claimed the lands between the Portuguese colony of Angola and Mozambique for Great Britain. The territory was later divided into Nyasaland (*see* Malawi) and Northern and Southern Rhodesia (*see* Zimbabwe). From 1889 until 1924, the country was administered by the South Africa Company. In 1924 a British governor was introduced and, subsequently, a legislature. Northern Rhodesia gained its independence as a republic in the British Commonwealth on 24 October 1964. After the white population of Rhodesia claimed its independence in 1965, a period of strained relations developed between Zambia and its southern neighbor. Zambia allowed black Rhodesian rebels sanctuary on its territory. On 18 July 1969, however, Zambia asked the United Nations to assist in stopping Portuguese raids into Zambia. These raids were an attempt on the part of the Portuguese to destroy rebel bases in Zambia. The UN censured Portugal for those incursions (28 July 1969). Internal problems also beset Zambia during that period. President Kenneth Kaunda (qv) was forced to declare a state of emergency in the face of growing political unrest stemming from tribal rivalries. Trouble with Portugal sprang up again in 1971, when Kaunda accused the Portuguese of imposing an economic blockade on his country in reprisal for rebel raids across the border with Mozambique. In 1972, the government began a crackdown on dissident groups and banned the United Progressive Party after a long period of violence. More than 100 of the UPP were arrested, including its leader, Simon Kapepwe (qv). On 25 February 1972, Kaunda took additional steps to turn Zambia into a one party country. In 1973, Zambia responded to a Rhodesian claim that its border was open by stating it was not. The years 1973 through 1976 were important as Zambia became a meeting ground for various factions fighting independence struggles in neighboring nations. On 25 March 1976, for example, Rhodesian rebel leader Joshua Nkomo (qv) met with the presidents of Botswana, Mozambique, Tanzania and Zambia to endorse a full-scale guerrilla war against the white Rhodesian government of Ian Smith (qv). In June 1978, the Western powers gave Zambia $1 billion in aid to insure a noncommunist state in that country. On 18 October 1978, Rhodesian aircraft attacked guerrilla bases inside Zambia, 12 days after the border between the two countries was opened after years of political and economic boycott. Before the end of the month, Great Britain had shipped air defense weapons to Zambia. Rhodesian aircraft attacked a rebel base near Livingston on 23 February 1979, and on 10 April they attacked a rebel base near Lusaka. Rhodesian ground attacks across the Zambia in November caused heavy casualties on both sides. On 23 February 1979,

Zimbabwe jets again attacked taregets near Stanleyville and then attacked again on near Lusaka (Nkomo's headquarters) on 10 April. In November, Zimbabwe cut off all supplies of maize (corn) to Zambia in an effort to force the Zambians to stop giving refuge to Rhodesian guerrillas. Zambia refused to yield to this intimidation. Three bridges were destroyed on 18 November when Rhodesian forces cut the principal roads leading to the Rhodesian (Zimbabwe) border. The bombings and raids continued until Great Britain exercised authority and arranged a cease-fire among all parties. In September 1981, South African troops entered Zambia and attacked military and civilian targets at the town of Sesheke, north of the area known as the Caprivi Strip. Not until 1984, when South African troops agreed to leave Angola, was the threat of further South African incursions lifted. In the mid-1980s Zambia was hit by a severe drought, which did not abate until 1986. The results were a further worsening of the economic picture for the country. By 1990, the foreign debt of Zambia exceeded $7.2 billion, and inflation rose to 122.5 percent. Rioting broke out in June over the price of maize, which had been doubled by the government. Security forces quelled the disturbances, but not without loss of life. The Kaunda one-man rule was threatened by a coup, but the attempt to overthrow the government failed. Kaunda was defeated in the general election held in October 1991. This ended one-party rule, which had existed in Zambia since 1972. The new president, Frederick Chiluba, inherited a country faced with monumental economic problems. In 1993, Chiluba was forced to envoke a state of emergency in early March to block an attempted takeover of the government by opposition leaders. Four senior ministers were dismissed in the aftermath of the incident. The opposition had criticized the government for corruption and drug dealing, and this criticism was also voiced by international financial circles, who warned Zambia (1994) to clean up its drug-trafficking activities or lose its funding. Chiluba remained in office, in 1995. *Reading:* Robert Rotberg, *Rise of Nationalism in Central Africa: The Making of Malawi and Zambia, 1873-1964* (1965); Jan Pettman, *Zambia: Security and Conflict, 1964-1973* (1974); Munyonzwe Hamalengwa, *Class Struggles in Zambia, 1889-1989 & the Fall of Kenneth Kaunda, 1990-1991* (1992).

Zamboango dal Sur. *See* Philippines.

Zanzibar. *See* Dar-es-Salaam; Tanzania.

Zapotocky, Antonin. Zapotocky became premier of Czechoslovakia when a new communist constitution was put into effect in June 1948 and Klement Gottwald (qv) became president. When Gottwald died, Zapotocky was named to replace him (21 March 1953). His rule was marked by serious rioting over currency reform and little else. He died in office on 13 November 1957.

Zarqa (Az Zarqu). *See* Jordan.

Zegharta. *See* Lebanon.

Zemach. *See* Israel.

Zengakuren. On 15 January 1968, violent clashes with police took place in the port city of Sasebo, Japan. The trouble began when a left-wing Japanese student organization called *Zengakuren* protested the expected visit of the aircraft carrier *USS Enterprise*. By mid-1969, student disorders had spread throughout Japan; almost 6,000 were arrested by police in the last six months of 1969. *See* Japan.

Zerbo, Saye. On 25 November 1980, Colonel Saye Zerbo led a bloodless and successful coup that ousted the Upper Volta government of Major General Sangoule Lamizana. The coup culminated a period of strikes by teachers, who were supported by a number of opposition groups. On 7 November 1982, as he was preparing for an official visit to France, Saye Zerbo was removed from office by a group of junior officers and noncommissioned officers. An army doctor, Major Jean-Baptiste Ouedraogo, became head of state.

Zhou Enlai (Chou En-lai). (b. 1898, Huaian, Kiangsu Province, China—d. 8 January 1976) Born the son of a well to do Mandarin, Zhou completed his university education in Japan (1917–1919). Upon his return to China and already a communist, he worked with his friend Mao Tse-Tung (qv) who sent him to Paris for further study. In France he became a communist organizer and met the Vietnamese Ho Chi Minh (qv). Zhou returned to China in 1924 where, at age 26, Mao appointed him a political officer at the Whampao Academy, where he met Chiang Kai-shek (qv). In 1927, Zhou was elected to the politburo of the Chinese Communist Party. In 1928, Zhou went to Moscow; by 1931, back in China, he was working with the communist underground in Shanghai. In 1934 he became the political commissar of the Chinese Red Army and participated the the Long March to Shensi as the communists retreated from the forces of Chiang Kai-shek. During World War II, Zhou served as commissar of foreign affairs in the Yen-an (Yenen) government and supported Chiang Kai-shek in the war against Japan. He accompanied Mao to the meetings in Chungking with Chiang Kai-shek (1945) and to the failed meeting with George C. Marshall (1946) that was aimed at establishing a cooperative government between the Communist and Nationalist Chinese. When the People's Republic of China was proclaimed on 1 October 1949, Zhou became its premier, a post he held until his death in 1976. During his tenure he headed the Chinese delegation at the Sino-Soviet meeting (14 February 1950) that established a 30-year military alliance with Moscow. In June 1954, Zhou met with France's Premier Mendes-France in Berne, Switzerland, and arranged a political settlement on Indochina that accompanied the military settlement arranged at Geneva. In July 1954, Zhou called for the removal of the Nationalist Chinese government from Taiwan (Formosa). In April 1955, Zhou addressed the 29-nation Afro-Asian Bandung Conference (qv) in Indonesia and disavowed any desire for war with the United States. Thereafter, until 1964, he travelled the world; in June 1961, while visiting Hanoi, he accused the U.S. of aggression and intervention in the internal affairs of South Vietnam. That same year (October), Zhou exposed the Sino-Soviet rift by walking out of the Soviet Party Congress in Moscow. In 1965, Zhou demanded the establishment of a new United Nations free of "the manipulation of United States imperialism." During the Great Proletarian Cultural Revolution in China Zhou counselled moderation, an advocacy not followed by those who slaughtered thousands on noncommunist and communist

Chinese. In 1972, Chou arranged the historic meeting between Mao Tse-Tung and U.S. president Richard M. Nixon (qv) aimed at ending the decades of hostility in Sino–US relations. Zhou's death in 1976 sparked rioting between conservative and liberal elements of the communist Chinese world. *Reading:* Han Suyin, *Eldest Son: Zhou Enlai and the Making of Modern China, 1898-1976* (1995); Ronald C. Keith, *The Diplomacy of Zhou Enlai* (1990).

Zia-ul-Haq, Mohammed. (b. 1924, Jullundur, Punjab, India—d. 17 August 1988, near Bahawalpur, Pakistan) Zia graduated from the Royal Indian Military Academy in 1945 and served in postwar tours of duty in Burma, Malaya and Indonesia. In 1964, then Lieutenant Colonel Zia became an instructor at the Command and Staff College, Quetta, Pakistan. From 1966 to 1968, he commanded a cavalry regiment and in 1968 was promoted to colonel. For the next four years, he held successively more important command assignments and was promoted to major general in 1972. In that year he was president of the courts martial that tried a number of Pakistani officers charged with plotting the overthrow of the Bhutto (qv) government. From 1972 until 1975, Zia attended various senior military schools in the United States and Great Britain. He was promoted to lieutenant general in 1975. In 1976, he was appointed chief of staff of the army. When the army took charge in Pakistan (qv), Zia remained as chief of staff and also became the administrator of martial law in the country. As a devout Muslim, he made his pilgramage to Mecca in 1976. On 5 July 1977, Zia seized power in Pakistan, ousting his patron, Prime Minister Zulfikar Ali Bhutto. His first act was to promise national elections in three months, but he did not make the promise good. On 16 September 1978, Zia became president. In April 1979, he signed the death warrant for Bhutto's execution. Massive demonstrations followed Bhutto's death. On 17 October 1979, Zia cancelled the upcoming general elections and instituted censorship throughout Pakistan. He also banned all opposition political parties. Zia played an important role in the fighting in neighboring Afghanistan (qv), as his country was a major base and sanctuary for Afghan *mujahideen* rebels. In February 1981, Zia had scores of political opponents arrested for demanding an end to the martial law edict put out when he seized power. A major clash took place in Karachi between pro- and anti-Zia demonstrators on 14 August 1983. At least 50,000 people were involved in the fighting. On 30 December 1985, he lifted the martial law order that had been in effect periodically since he took office. Incidents of violence continued into 1986. On 17 August 1988, Zia, along with several senior Pakistani military officers and the U.S. ambassador, Arnold Raphel, were among the 30 people killed when the U.S.–built C-130 transport plane in which they were flying exploded in mid-air, shortly after taking off from Bahawalpur. There was considerable discussion over whether the cause of the crash was mechanical trouble or sabotage.

Zimbabwe. The Republic of Zimbabwe is located in south-central Africa. It is bordered on the north by Zambia, on the east by Mozambique, on the south by South Africa and on the west by Botswana. The capital city is Harare. The ruins of Great Zimbabwe, the capital of the Monomotapa Empire, which ruled the land from the fifth until the fifteenth centuries, are located about 110 miles south of the present capital. The first European excursions of note into the area occurred in 1890, when Cecil Rhodes marched north out of South Africa in search of minerals known to exist in the region. The first station of the British South Africa Company was established near Harare at Fort Salisbury. Treaties made with the local chieftain, Lobengula, gained extensive mineral holdings south of the Limpopo River. The land to the north of the Limpopo, he claimed for Great Britain, parcelling it out to the white members of his exploration party. Tribal uprisings broke out in 1893 and 1896, but white settlers continued to increase in number; a railway coming up from the south soon helped pacify the region. The region was granted independence as Southern Rhodesia within the British Commonwealth in 1923. In 1931, however, the Land Apportionment Act put most of the political power in the hands of the white minority in Rhodesia. In October 1953, Northern Rhodesia (Zambia) was joined with Southern Rhodesia and Nyasaland (today Malawi) as the Federation of Rhodesia and Nyasaland. Nationalist groups in Nyasaland and North Rhodesia (Zambia) vigorously opposed this confederation and forced its dissolution in 1963. In 1964, Northern Rhodesia was granted its independence as Zambia, and Nyasaland became an independent Malawi. At the same time, Southern Rhodesia, still under white control and still within the British Commonwealth, was refused independence (11 April 1960). Two nationalist groups emerged: Joshua Nkomo's (qv) Zimbabwe African People's Union (ZAPU) and Robert Mugabe's (qv) Zimbabwe African National Union (ZANU). Both groups were soon forced to flee and seek refuge and safe-havens in neighboring countries from which they waged a seven-year guerrilla war for independence and majority (i.e., black) rule. On 11 November 1965, Rhodesia's white prime minister, Ian Smith (qv), issued a Unilateral Declaration of Independence (UDI) separating his country from the Commonwealth. On 5 December 1965, the Organization of African Unity (OAU) threatened to break relations with Great Britain unless a solution could be found to the racist policies of the Rhodesian government. When London asked the United Nations for assistance, it was rebuked, but it went ahead with its own sanctions against Rhodesia. The United States joined its British ally in sanctioning Rhodesia on 18 April 1966. In March 1967, the OAU urged the use of force to eliminate the white Rhodesian government, but little serious thought was expended on that plan. On 9 May 1968, however, the United Nations ordered a trade embargo against the all-white government for failing to negotiate in good faith with Great Britain. Additional UN sanctions were imposed on 29 May. In August, the Rhodesian government carried out a number of antiguerrilla operations around the country. It was at this point that ZAPU and ZANU established their bases of ooperation outside the country. By the end of the year, however, the Smith government still refused to budge. Then, on 7 November 1968, the UN authorized Great Britain to use force to end the situation. In February 1969, the Rhodesian government announced the conviction of black nationalist leader Ndabaningi Sithole on charges of plotting the assassination of Ian Smith. Then, on 24 June, Britain severed all ties with Salisbury. This was followed by a 21 November UN order directing Britain to use force against Rhodesia. On 2 March 1970, Rhodesia put its new independence constitution into effect, breaking its last ties with England and putting into law rules that effectively prevented full black representation through income tax requirements. On 17 March, the U.S. exercised its first Security Council veto and blocked the condemnation of Great Britain for refusing to use force in the Rhodesian situation. The next day, 18 March, the UN condemned Rhodesia. The year 1971 saw the emphasis on Rhodesia shift to a long period of black insurgency. After being forced to move into neighboring countries for sanctuary, both ZAPU and ZANU carried out a long series of raids in a successful campaign to topple the government in Southern Rhodesia. In October 1971, ZANU and ZAPU joined forces to form the United Front for the Liberation of Zimbabwe (FROZILI). By December 1972, FROZILI attacks on white-owned farms were reported for the first time since 1966. On 9 January 1973, Rhodesia closed its border with Zambia after two South African police on duty on the border were killed by an antipersonnel mine (8 January). On 17 May, the Rhodesian government implemented a program of forcibly removing natives from "restricted areas" and confiscating or destroying anything thought usable by the rebels. In December 1974, a cease-fire was announced in the guerrilla war and a release of political prisoners was carried out as a prelude to a constitutional convention. But, on 4 March 1975, the government once again began arresting opposition leaders. By March 1978, more than 6,000 military personnel and civilians had been killed in the fighting. After much negotiation and several failed attempts, an "internal" agreement was reached that brought the principal rebel groups and Ian Smith into an accord to hold national elections. Elections were held on 21 April 1979, in which Bishop Abel T. Muzorewa's (qv) United African National Council won by a slim majority. At the same time, Britain began normalizing its relations with the new black government in Salisbury. Muzorewa was appointed prime minister on 29 May, the first black man to hold that office. He immediately appointed himself minister of defense. A formal cease-fire was achieved with the rebels on 5 December 1979, but the fighting continued until a formal announcement of Rhodesia's independence was made on 18 April 1980. On 25 August 1980, Zimbabwe was admitted into the United Nations. Fighting continued in Zimbabwe, however, and a major clash took place between army troops and forces loyal to President Mugabe and to Prime Minister Joshua Nkomo from 9 February to 17 February 1981. Then, on 21 February, Zimbabwe established diplomatic relations with the Soviet Union. By November, the clashes in Zimbabwe had slackened, and the merger of the rebel forces with the army was completed. Popular elections based on majority rule were held, and Robert Mugabe's party won by a landslide. In February 1982, an enormous cache of weapons was uncovered in Matabeleland, enough to outfit a 5,000 man force. On 17 February, Prime Minister Mugabe dismissed Nkomo after evidence was uncovered linking the minister to a plot to overthrow the coalition government. On the night of 25 August, twelve military aircraft were destroyed at the Grewa Airbase, where a number of white and black employees were later arrested and charged with sabotage. Acts of sabotage continued; on 5 January 1983, for example, the Beira-Mutare pipeline was blown up in Mozambique, effectively cutting off Zimbabwe's supply of oil. As the violence continued to build, at least 100,000 refugees fled across the Zimbabwe-Mozambique border by late February 1984. The violence continued into 1985 as Nkomo tried to make his case before the public. In 1987, Mugabe and Nkomo united their parties under the name Zimbabwe African National Union Patriotic Front (ZANU-PF). Mugabe was reelected in March 1990, but voter turnout was low. Some analysts saw this as a sign that Mugabe's role was coming to an end. Mugabe was still in power in 1995 and was facing increased pressure from the World Bank and the IMF to improve the Zimbabwean economy. *Reading:* Ngwabi Bhebe, *Soldiers in Zimbabwe's Liberation War* (1996); Carol Thompson, *Challenge to Imperialism: The Frontline States in the Liberation of Zimbabwe* (1986); W. H. Morris-Jones, *From Rhodesia to Zimbabwe: Behind and Beyond Lancaster House* (1980); Bruce Hoffman et al., *Lessons for Counterinsurgencies: The Rhodesian Experience* (Rand-3998-A) (1991).

Zimmermann, Ernst. On 1 February 1985, two terrorists of the Red Army Faction (qv) invaded the Munich home of German industrialist Ernst Zimmermann. After being tortured, he was shot in the head dying, 12 hours later. The Red Army Faction claimed credit for the attack in the name of Commando Patrick O'Hara, a member of the Irish National Liberation Army, who died on a hunger strike in 1981.

Zinsou, Emile Derlin. On 12 July 1969, Dahomey president Emile Derlin Zinsou thwarted a coup attempt against his civilian rule by having the conspirators, who included the former president Lieutenant Colonel Alphonse Alley (qv) arrested. On 10 December 1969, Lieutenant Colonel Maurice Kouandete (qv) was successful in ousting Zinsou, after which he proclaimed himself president. Zinsou remained outside the political world until 16 January 1977, when a mercenary force trained in Morocco was airlanded at Catonou Airport in Benin (to which Dahomey's name was changed in 1975) with the intent of ousting the Kerekou government. When the unsuccessful attack was put down, evidence developed that indicated the mercenaries were probably in the pay of ousted president Emile Zinsou and others.

Zionism. Zionism holds a strong political and religious significance for the world's Jewish population and to many others as well. Beginning in the sixteenth, and into the mid-eighteenth century, there were periodic attempts by a number of Jews—some of whom were regarded as prophets—to encourage resettlement in Palestine. As the Age of Enlightenment developed in Europe, many Jews saw the opportunity for assimilation in their local communities and gave up the notion of "going home." Home, to them, was where they lived and worked, and the thought of Palestine became less important. This idea of assimilation was anathema to Zionists and also to some Christian fundamentalists, who viewed the restoration of Israel as a sign of the coming end of the world. In some cases the Zionist movement became more aggressive, but in most regions of the world it maintained a quiet presence. This changed in the late nineteenth century, however, when persecution of the Jews was rampant in Russia, Poland and Eastern Europe. Modern political Zionism rose up under the leadership of Theodor Herzl, an Austrian journalist. His writings spoke of a modern, secular Israel, neutral in religion, and living in cooperation with its Arab neighbors (*Altneuland*, 1902). Herzl convened the first Zionist Congress in Basel, Switzerland, in 1897. The first Zionist center was established in Vienna, although Austrian persecution of Jews was on the rise. Herzl died in 1904, and the center was moved to Germany. It was German and Austrian Jews who led the movement, but the largest membership was in Russia. As earlier, not all Jews embraced Zionism, and even among those who did, divergent opinions on the desired form of the Jewish state—a strictly orthodox or a modern secular state—were rampant. Even so, many Jews moved to Palestine and were relatively well integrated into the land. World War I halted most of the settlement in Palestine. Also, in Europe, the center of the Zionist movement shifted from Germany to Great Britain, where leadership shifted from German to Russian in the person of Chaim Weizmann. Weizmann was able to get the British foreign secretary, Lord Balfour, to write a letter, dated 2 November 1917, in which he declared Britain's determination to see a Jewish homeland. Although the Balfour Declaration fell short of what the Zionists wanted—giving Palestine to the Jews—it did appease most Jewish/Zionist desires. The Allied powers approved the declaration, which was accepted as British policy and incorporated into League of Nations policy as a British mandate over Palestine. By 1925, the Jewish population in Palestine was about 110,000; in 1935, it was 300,000, with 100,000 living in Tel Aviv alone. World War II saw another resurgence of Zionism and an increase in emigration, even though it was almost impossible to travel. The revelations of the Holocaust softened many views toward Zionism. During the war, the center of the movement appeared in the United States. A 1942 conference in New York now demanded the founding of a Jewish state inclusive of all of Palestine and the right of unlimited immigration. On 29 November 1947, the United Nations proposed a partition that satisfied no one and led to war in Palestine. Although the State of Israel was proclaimed in 1948, Zionism continued to champion its cause around the world. In some instances, the agitation produced unwanted results for the Jewish cause. On 10 November 1975, for instance, the UN General Assembly adopted, amid much acrimony, a resolution calling Zionism a form of racism.

Zubair. *See* Iraq.

Zulu Tribe. *See* South Africa.

Zurich. *See* Switzerland.

INDEX

This index includes most of the major names, places, events and concepts of importance to the reader. Page numbers are presented in three forms: Those referring to an item or article are presented in **bold** type, those referring to a book are presented in *italic* type, and those referring to persons, locales, events and concepts are presented in normal type.

About the Author

JOHN E. JESSUP is a retired Colonel in the U.S. Army and a retired university educational director. He spent his last five years on active duty as Chief, Histories Division, U.S. Army Center of Military History, and from 1992 to 1995 he was Academic Dean of American Military University. He is the author of a number of books on military history and world affairs and has lectured and taught both in the United States and abroad on international security issues and military history.

ISBN 0-313-28112-2

9 780313 281129

HARDCOVER BAR CODE